CW00393777

A-Z *of*
POWER
METAL

GARRY SHARPE-YOUNG

www.rockdetector.com

This edition published in Great Britain
in 2003 by Cherry Red Books Ltd.,
Unit 17, 1st Floor, Elysium Gate West,
126–128 New King's Road,
London SW6 4LZ

Copyright © 2003, Garry Sharpe-Young.

All rights reserved. No part of this book
may be reproduced or transmitted in any
form or by any means, electronic or
mechanical, including photocopying,
recording or any information storage
and retrieval system, without
permission in writing from the publisher.

This book is sold subject to the
condition that it shall not, by way of
trade or otherwise, be lent, re-sold,
hired out or otherwise circulated
without the publisher's prior consent
in any form of binding or cover other
than that in which it is published
and without a similar condition
including this condition being
imposed on the subsequent purchaser.

Typeset by Sarah Reed.
Printed and bound in Great Britain by
Biddles Ltd., Guildford and King's Lynn.
Cover Design by Jim Phelan at Wolf Graphics Tel: 020 8299 2342

ISBN 1-901447-13-8

Introduction

Power Metal

Power Metal is Heavy Metal taken to the absolute, surgically precise, limit. When the major Metal institutions staked their claim they engendered a whole legion of followers in their wake. These up and coming acts were not simply content to match the volume levels of their forefathers though. Riffs evolved into complex, labyrinthine proportions, vocals scorched a path to higher altitudes and, yes, they even managed to crank out some more volume as part of the formula.

Power Metal vocalists are, almost without exception, masters of their craft. Second best won't suffice in this game. Whether it's Udo Dirkschneider squealing like a stuck warthog, Eric Adams' Mount Olympus toppling roars or the squall of Rob Halford's stentorian, planet busting shockwaves, Power Metal frontmen excel or die. Are those Heinkels on the horizon or is Bruce Bruce just clearing the phlegm from his pipes?

The acceleration of aggression afforded by the Thrash Metal movement helped boost the rise of Power Metal. As the first wave of Thrash waned a ready audience of Metal fans lay waiting for something just as heavy but with sophistication. The British guard such as Iron Maiden and Judas Priest had opened the door, now a whole flood of American Metal flooded through – Attacker, Jag Panzer, Iced Earth, Savatage and Queensryche. In Europe bands rooted in Thrash matured at an alarming rate with Helloween, Gamma Ray, Blind Guardian, Running Wild and Grave Digger establishing lengthy careers. In latter years Power Metal itself has branched off on its own evolutionary trail spawning Symphonic Metal and Progressive Metal. A recent upsurge in the fortunes of bands such as Sonata Artica from Finland, Angra from Brazil and Rhapsody from Italy and illustrated just how global the reach of Power Metal has become. Cult acts from the 80s have been reforming at an alarming rate in order to cope with demand.

Traditionally, Power Metal has been rooted in Great Britain and the USA, borne out of a desire to breed a tougher, more technically advanced successor to '70s Heavy Metal. Pinpointing the inception of this genre one has to understand the impact of Judas Priest's early 1978 opus 'Stained Class'. Whilst lacking in production technique this record moulded sci-fi themes, identifiable 'Metal' riffing, the landmark speed intro of 'Exciter' and the bombastic epic 'Beyond The Realms Of Death' into one groundbreaking release. They had of course explored these themes with 'Sad Wings Of Destiny' and 'Sin After Sin' but it was 'Stained Class' that pushed the whole thing over the edge. Evolution had taken a left turn, Glenn Tipton and KK Downing had taken the Wishbone Ash twin guitar theory beyond all accepted safeguards and Rob Halford was delivering vocal notes that were so stratospheric they were in danger of crippling overhead satellites.

Oddly, the band tamed a little musically for their next outing 'Killing Machine' but at the same time introduced the last missing piece of the puzzle - leather and studs. Power Metal had arrived in both form and function. The NWoBHM was subsequently triggered, Armored Saint strapped on their codpieces, David DeFeis raised his sword, Thor, er... blew up hot water bottles and the world quaked in fear. The equation then took on a life of its own - Thrash, Speed, Death and Black Metal. Just when analysts hail the next extreme they find another, deeper abyss to stare into...

With NWoBHM in full bloom Germany was not too far behind and exploded its spores like an alien fungus across Europe with alarming rapidity. This window of opportunity, a veritable mullet n' tasch revolution, gave free rein for acts such as Accept, Helloween, Grave Digger, Steeler, ad infinitum. While all this was going on Manowar put body building, baby oil and Heavy Metal on the same map. In recent times it is Scandinavia, the Mediterranean countries and South America that provided the breeding grounds.

Power Metal has diverted into new avenues of excess. Onto what was once considered 'Melodic Rock' a new branch, has been grafted exemplified by excessive speed guitar ability and, what can only be described as "Pomptastic" (isn't that a Derek Oliver copyright?) keyboards. The Swedish guitar protégé Yngwie Malmsteen took his obsession with Deep Purple, Hendrix and the Classical masters, transferred it to the electric guitar and became God - at least in Japan. The Finnish maestros Stratovarious took up the mantle and the Italian act Rhapsody (somehow) brought the perm, ruffled shirts and gold medallions back into fashion. What ensued was a deluge of bands and albums so fixated on dragons that one had to wonder if Ronnie James Dio had been genetically engineering the Latin gene pool.

On the other side of the Atlantic North America had twisted off into Progressive Metal. This adjunct, personified by major artists such as Dream Theater and Fates Warning, retained the riffs and the sheer muscle but imbued the music with cerebral, lyrical challenges straight out of '70s Prog. Songs began to stretch out into half hour marathons of frenzied Hammond organ workouts and mind boggling time changes. Metal became a maze of confusion and intricacy.

With so much emphasis placed on the hedonism of Classical, Baroque and Renaissance institutions Opera was next on the cards. Arjen Anthony Lucasson, in creating Ayreon, triggered a plethora of imitators and pioneered the concept of Metal Opera, guest lists that sound like Metal roll calls and (gulp!) the re-birth of the concept album. Queensryche's 'Operation Mindcrime', a pivotal moment in Power Metal history and without question one of the top five albums of the genre, played a large part in this phenomenon too. Savatage, once a meat n' two veg Heavy Metal band, found both redemption and a valuable second lease of life with grandiose, almost Broadway like extravaganzas. What Lucasson did though to make Aryeon unique was to invite half the population of Holland to sing on his record.

Avantasia, Nostradamus, Genius, et al all followed in his wake.

Paradoxically the land that spawned the two, undoubtedly greatest Power Metal institutions in Judas Priest and Iron Maiden, went into a 'talent famine' and has suffered from a dearth of activity in the last decade. Priest and Maiden still reign although both have suffered at their own hand, both circumstances involving the departure of an irreplaceable lead vocalist. Iron Maiden has enjoyed the good times better than their Brummie counterparts simply by sticking to their guns until the exit of Bruce Dickinson. Two below par records sans the air raid siren and the Londoners swallowed their pride and jumped straight back on the rails. Judas Priest, on the other hand, has confused fans with persistent attempts at commerciality and chasing the tails of lesser 'modern' artists.

Power Metal will morph, mutate and manifest itself into unexpected realms. But, as sure as Joey De Maio eats four fatted calves for breakfast, sits on a throne constructed of gold Manowar albums and will teach his offspring the art of bowmanship and swordcraft before the age of three, Power Metal is here to stay.

ABOUT ROCKDETECTOR

www.rockdetector.com is the world's largest Rock devoted website. These pages are taken directly from the website. As I write it hosts information, including unique biographies and full global discographies, on over 15,000 bands. When you pick up this book tomorrow it will have even more.

We're on a mission at Rockdetector to document Rock music of all genres, persuasions and nationalities, old and new and of every persuasion.

We try to do this in a non-biased, non-opinionated manner. It matters to us that we get our facts straight and aid the promotion of all Rock artists.

We thrive on information. If you have any fact, album cover, band history or discography detail we're presently missing then contribute. If we've got anything wrong – tell us.

We are also actively looking for dedicated Rock fans with specialist knowledge of genres or territories to contribute. If you're the man who knows all the ins and outs on the Bangladeshi Emocore scene then we need to hear from you. Seriously – we're looking for quality writers.

Where do we get our information from? We're often asked this. Fortunately 15 years of journalism has helped. Very often facts are gleaned from face to face interviews with bands. Day to day stuff we get from record companies from all over the world, bands and fans.

We include ALL submissions. There is only one criteria – the band has to Rock. That covers everything in our scheme of things from AOR, Prog Rock, Classic Rock right through to Nu-Metal, Rap Metal and onto Death & Black Metal. We want it all.

Here's the address for submissions:

Musicdetector Websites Ltd.
P.O. Box 3138,
New Plymouth,
Taranaki,
New Zealand

For inclusion on the site we need one of each product format, a full biography and a high quality photo. Information regarding linking to your URLs is also of benefit to you.

If you want a record reviewing we need two copies as we send these out for review.

Here's our e-mail address: info@rockdetector.com

Bands / Labels: DON'T send us an e-mail asking for us to look at your website. We simply don't have time. Be proactive and send the stuff in. Then we'll contact you.

THANKS:

Grace-Anne, Kerr, Krystan, Kjaric of course. Marco Barbieri at Century Media, Olly Hahn and the SPV team, Peter Klapproth at CMM, Benjamin Niebla II at Desert Rock Promotions, Lars Ratz at Monster Productions, Michael Langbein, Mat Sinner and Markus Wosgein at Nuclear Blast, Andy Pyke, Andy Southwell, Dave Martin, Roland Hyams at Work Hard PR, Johnny Stoj of Pegazus, Scott Waldrop of Twisted Tower Dire, Paul Nelson & Joe Comeau of Liege Lord, Lance King of Balance Of Power, Gerhard Simanke at Universal, Matt Sampson and Nico Wobben.

The Cherry Red people - Iain, Tim, Adam, Jim, Sarah and Karl for proofreading.

The Efinity people - Kevin Best & Grant Pui.

A doff of the cap & felicitations to Jayne Andrews, Al Atkins, Chris Bradley, Steve Burton, Gloria Butler, John Cadden, Dave Corke, Jess Cox, Andy Dawson, Bob Daisley, Dig at Earache, Bernard Doe, KK Downing, Andy Faulkner, Steve Grimmett, Rob Halford, Hammy & Lisa at Peaceville, Harry Harrison, Lea Hart, Ian Hill, David & Irene Howells, Lemmy, Simon & Diana Meadows, Phil Mogg, Horst Odermatt & Armin Schafer, Stuart Ongley & the SGO team, Gemma & Martin Peyerl, Wayne 'Spearchucker' Renshaw, Dave Reynolds, Uli Jon Roth, Greg Russell, Rik Sandford, Helen & Eddie Shaw, Glenn Tipton, Pete Way, Martin Walkyier & Stevie Young.

Major thanks to all the musicians, bands, labels & promotion companies that have aided this & other books in the Rockdetector series.

If your band is not included blame your useless promotion department / useless bass player.

ABRAXAS (GERMANY)
Line-Up: Chris Klauke (vocals), Oliver Minder (guitar), Stephan Rohner (guitar), Jan Muller (bass), Andreas Hittlinger (keyboards), Heiko Burst (drums)

A 'True Metal' band formed in 1985 by bassist Jan Muller and drummer Heiko Burst, ABRAXAS completed their line-up by adding guitarist Oliver Minder and vocalist Joachim Hittlinger and their initial gigs included supports to KRUIZ, SINNER, U.D.O. and ZED YAGO.

ABRAXAS debuted with the 'Vampire' demo, following this with an EP in 1989 entitled 'Shattered By A Terrible Prediction'. Shortly after the band augmented their sound with the recruitment of second guitarist Stephan Rohner and keyboard player Andreas Hittlinger.

Joachim Hittlinger departed in 1990 to be supplanted by ex-MANIA vocalist Chris Klauke. This revised line-up debuted with a further demo, 'Gate To Eden', followed by the 'Signs' tape.

ABRAXAS' debut, the 1993 album 'The Liaison', would be issued in Japan by the Teichiku label. Later releases include 1997's 'Tomorrow's World' on the Milecrest Music label and 2001's 'Prophecies'.

Albums:
THE LIAISON, Teichiku TECX-25584 (1993)
Cry Of The Nature / Dream Dealer / Crusaders Prayer / Gates Of Eden / Dreamers Island / Explorers / Tomorrow's World / Place Without Mirrors / The Liaison / Euphoria / Signs
TOMORROW'S WORLD, Limb Music Productions LMP 9802-002 (1998)
Gates To Eden / Explorers / Tomorrow's World / Dreamers Island / Crusaders Prayer / Dream Dealer / Cry Of The Nature / Signs / Euphoria / Place Without Mirrors / The Liaison / Stolen Memories / Faded Photographs / Into The Light

ABSTRACTA (ITALY)

ABSTRACTA vocalist Titta Tani, previously with GLORYHUNTER, would later go on to join EMPTY TREMOR, Progressive Metal band DGM and DAEMONIA.

Albums:
TRIP, Elevate ER02006 (1998)
T.R.I.P. / Aenigma / Distant / The Disoriented Oriental / Red Sunsets On Earth / Tears Of God

ACACIA (ITALY)
Line-Up: Franco Scardina (vocals), Martino Lo Cascio (guitar), Davide Licciardello (guitar), Mario Tarsilla (bass), Mimmo Lo Prete (keyboards / drums)

A band in the Progressive Metal mould, after releasing a demo Italian outfit ACACIA got a deal with Underground Symphony Records.

Albums:
DEEPER SECRETS, Underground Symphony USCD008 (1995)
Sibran's Words / I Don't Believe / Behind The Lies / The Day Begins To Droop / Palermo / Funerals Of State / Why / Nothing New / Tears Of Life

ACCEPT (GERMANY)
Line-Up: Udo Dirkschneider (vocals), Wolf Hoffman (guitar), Jorg Fischer (guitar), Peter Baltes (bass), Stefan Kaufmann (drums)

ACCEPT is a Solingen based ultra Heavy Metal band dating from a creation by diminutive, close cropped front man Udo Dirkschneider in 1971 that has, in its time, produced some absolute classic albums of the genre. ACCEPT is unarguably recognised as one of the leading names in the history of German Hard Rock.

ACCEPT's initial line-up comprised the aforementioned Dirkschneider, guitarists Michael Wagener and Jan Komet along with drummer Birke Hoe. The band was originally titled BAND X, becoming ACCEPT in 1971. Later additions would be bassist Dieter Rubach and drummer Frank Friedrich. However, during 1975 Komet made his exit, later to form BAD STEVE.

ACCEPT really began to take shape with the addition of teenage axe slinger Wolf Hoffmann, from the Wuppertal based BAAL, second guitarist Gerhard Wahl and ex-PYTHAGORAS bassist Peter Baltes in 1976. Wagener's part in the story was far from over though as he would quickly go on to become a renowned Heavy Metal producer. ACCEPT's head start into the Rock world came courtesy of winning third place in a Dusseldorf band competition. The prize was a recording deal, which resulted in the debut album.

The band would settle on second guitarist Jörg Fischer and drummer Stefan Kaufmann during 1978. Both Fischer and Kaufmann had previously played in FRENZY and the strangely titled FATHERS OF INTENTION. The band's earliest albums, whilst hinting at glories to come, tended to be of a distinctly poppier and anthemic nature than the style of

Rock the band would become synonymous with. It was with the third album, 'Breaker', where ACCEPT got the breaks and soon gained notoriety for the lyrics to the track 'Son Of A Bitch' which had to be re-recorded, not so much for radio play but more to please the censors!

By the release of 'Breaker' Dirkschneider had developed his vocals into an unmistakable ear piercing siren wail complemented by the gruffest of smoker's coughs which soon became an ACCEPT trademark alongside the distinctive lead playing of Hoffmann.

Despite being only known to a small handful of import buyers, ACCEPT self-financed a 1981 British support tour to JUDAS PRIEST which instantly won the critics over despite almost complete lack of record company promotion. So much so that in most venues the band were billed as 'ATTACK'! And the tour also had other costs, personality clashes leading to the departure of Fischer on the tour's completion.

During this period of transition ACCEPT recorded what is widely acknowledged to be one of the most outrageously over the top Heavy Metal albums ever. Blessed with crushing guitars, Dirkschneider's banshee wail and overtly classical influences, fourth album 'Restless And Wild' stylistically set the foundations for the rest of their career.

'Restless And Wild' gained widespread underground kudos thanks to the generation of thousands of pre-release bootleg cassettes traded between fans months upfront of the official launch. Upon its release Hoffman soon found a replacement for Fischer playing in a local band and thus one Herman Frank joined in time for a world tour, with the record gaining an official release in Britain through Heavy Metal Records sporting a brand new sleeve.

Problems between the band and Udo Dirkschneider resulted in ACCEPT covertly auditioning possible replacements. ACCEPT auditioned STEELER vocalist Karl Holthaus upon producer Dieter Dierks' recommendation, but eventually settled their differences with Dirkschneider without the media getting wind of the original problem.

In spite of their star rapidly ascending ACCEPT were already suffering tensions within the band that would plague their career. According to unsubstantiated reports in 1983 Dirkschneider was briefly replaced by Englishman Mark Kelser. Dirkschneider apparently soon re-joined the ranks and Kelser travelled home to create CARRERA.

With their profile growing on a worldwide basis, ACCEPT split with their German label Brain and were signed to Epic Records. The resulting album 'Balls To The Wall', whilst building on the success of the band, did raise questions due to the sometimes bizarre lyrical content of cuts such as 'London Leatherboys' and the perceived gay macho sleeve photo. Still, the rumour mongering failed to prevent ACCEPT from further success and the band toured constantly, including American tours with MÖTLEY CRÜE, KISS and OZZY OSBOURNE, as well as putting in a highly creditable performance at the 1984 'Monsters Of Rock' festival at Donington Park in the Britain.

With the touring completed the band was to swiftly part company with Hermann Frank who would pursue playing roles in HAZZARD, SINNER, VICTORY and MOON' DOC. With the latter outfit Hermann released one album prior to joining ECHOPARK with former ZENO vocalist Michael Flechzig and former ELOY bassist Klaus-Peter Matziol.

'Balls To The Wall's successor, 'Metal Heart' (produced by long-time SCORPIONS mentor Dieter Dierks) continued the trend of experimentation whilst still retaining the band's trademark heaviness, even segueing Tchaikovsky and Beethoven's 'Für Elise' into the title track. 'Metal Heart' continued the upward trend in ACCEPT's popularity, resulting in their first tour of Japan which was later commemorated with the release of a live album, 'Kaizoku - Ban' (which, translated, means 'Bootleg'), recorded in Japan and issued in 1986. ACCEPT quickly released a brand new studio album, 'Russian Roulette', the same year.

The record was to enter the German national charts at number 10. ACCEPT again undertook a mammoth world tour including British dates with opening act DOKKEN and a German tour with UFO as support. ACCEPT's show routine during these dates including the band goose-stepping on stage for their encores! Dirkschneider in particular cut a unique figure decked out in military fatigues with a sidearm truncheon. However, much to fan's dismay Dirkschneider announced his displeasure at his belief in ACCEPT's more recent commercial leanings and left the band to form U.D.O.

In a bizarre twist U.D.O.'s debut album featured a repertoire built up of entirely ACCEPT songs deemed too heavy for 'Russian Roulette's successor! The first U.D.O. album proved a success, notching up sales of 60,000 in Germany alone.

At this juncture ACCEPT went into a period of flux, announcing a new vocalist in the form of ex-BABY TUCKOO front man Rob Armitage. However, as fans and press wondered how Armitage's much smoother vocal style could possibly fit in within the confines of ACCEPT's material his departure was announced prior to anything being recorded.

Eventually the band settled on Minneapolis native and ex-DARE FORCE singer David Reece and released 'Eat The Heat' in 1989. ACCEPT toured America in alliance with W.A.S.P. but found achieving album sales without Dirkschneider tough going. Surprisingly, Jörg Fisher also returned to the fold only to leave shortly afterwards! The guitarist was to later be found in BILLIONAIRE BOYS CLUB and then CONGRESS.

Another American, Jim Stacey filled in the guitar parts for the 'Eat The Heat' record, although the subsequent tour was a disaster, with Baltes and Reece coming to blows and Kaufmann, afflicted with a muscular disease, being replaced on the road by FIFTH ANGEL's Ken Mary. It was inevitable that news would emerge that ACCEPT had called it a day in the wake of such incidents.

Whilst Wolf Hoffman retired from music to practice photography, Peter Baltes surfaced alongside both former EUROPE guitarist JOHN NORUM and ex-DOKKEN vocalist DON DOKKEN's solo project, whilst Stefan Kaufmann renewed his interest in production, including handling the desk on two U.D.O. albums 'Mean Machine' and 'Faceless World'. David Reece meanwhile put together the infinitely more commercial BANGALORE CHOIR which released only one album before the singer returned to action with the heavier SIRCLE OF SILENCE.

ACCEPT, however, maintained their hardcore fan following throughout this period which, as well as blighting Dirkschneider's solo career, provided a constant demand for more records. Thus, in 1990, Kaufmann produced tapes of ACCEPT's 1985 Japanese dates in a thundering live album 'Staying A Life'. Sales proved beyond doubt the unflagging worldwide interest in the band and in 1993 the various members succumbed to pressure and reformed. Kaufmann during the interim turned up as drummer for Thrash act TOXIN but would return to ACCEPT.

The subsequent album 'Objection Overruled' witnessed a return to straight down the line Metal. ACCEPT's world tour to promote its release saw the band playing in such far flung territories as America, Japan, South America, Russia, Bulgaria and naturally Western Europe. The band was to have added ex-VENGEANCE guitarist Arjen Lucassen for live work but despite press announcements this liaison never transpired.

Buoyed by their successful return, the band chose to record yet another studio album, 'Death Row', but it lost the band some momentum as fans deemed the band to have bowed to pressure from the Grunge explosion and slightly softened their approach.

Interestingly, the British Rock scene had become so deflated in general around the time of 'Death Row's launch that this album did not get officially released in Britain.

However, a 1996 album, 'Predator', recorded in New York, saw ACCEPT back to their full Metal glory. Drums on this album were handled by DAMN YANKEE's Michael Cartellone and, in a radical change for latter day fans; Peter Baltes took over lead vocals for a number of tracks. (In fact Baltes had previously taken on vocal duties for a brace of tracks on ACCEPT's debut album).

In the wake of the 'Predator' tour confusion reigned as to the band's status as ACCEPT seemingly was put on ice. Dirkschneider, never one to rest on his laurels, was quick to issue a further solo album 'Solid' in 1997.

With ACCEPT's profile at their highest since the glory days of the mid '80s, Norwegian Black Metal exponents DIMMU BORGIR paid homage by including a rip roaring version of 'Metal Heart' on their 1998 mini-album 'Godless Savage Garden'.

The band's third live album found a release in 1997 as ACCEPT stifled the rumours and announced that they were still very much a going concern. Udo issued a further U.D.O. album 'Holy' on his new label Nuclear Blast, the label preceding this with an epic ACCEPT tribute album that included homages from HAMMERFALL, AXXIS, GRAVEDIGGER, PRIMAL FEAR, SINNER & SODOM amongst others. HAMMERFALL's track 'Head Over Heels' featured a vocal duet with Herr Dirkschneider.

During 2000 Schwarzmann would add another port of call to his list of bands by joining VOICE.

The overwhelming success of the debut tribute affair prompted Nuclear Blast to issue a second volume during 2001. Along such acts as THERION, ROUGH SILK, WITCHERY, RAISE HELL, AGENT STEEL and DARKANE all paying homage the album novelly saw the U.D.O. band covering 'X.T.C.', a track culled from the only Udo Dirkschneider-less ACCEPT album, 1989's 'Eat The Heat'.

Ongoing demand for ACCEPT product would be met in July of 2002 with the DVD release 'Metal Blast From The Past'. The release compiled previously unreleased tracks, a rare Japan bonus track 'Rich And Famous' alongside demo takes of five 'Breaker' album cuts. Video material included a live gig from Osaka, a documentary of the group's debut Japanese tour as well as footage from ACCEPT's show in Sofia, Bulgaria in 1983.

Singles/EPs:
I'm A Rebel / No Time To Lose, Logo

GO389 (1980)
Balls To The Wall / Losing More Than You've Ever Had, Portrait A 4311 (1984)
Restless And Wild / Fast As A Shark, Heavy Metal Worldwide (1984)
Midnight Mover / Balls To The Wall / London Leatherboys / Wrong Is Right, Portrait A 6130 (1985)
London Leatherboys (Live) / Wrong Is Right / Metal Heart / Midnight Mover, Portrait 12 3P 646 (1985) (Japanese release)
Monsterman, RCA (1986)
Balls To The Wall (Live), Crash (1986) (Free 7" from Crash Magazine split with DIO)
Generation Clash (Long Version) / Generation Clash, RCA (1989) (USA promotion 12")
Generation Clash / D-Train / I Can't Believe It, RCA (1989) (12" single)
Generation Clash / D-Train / I Can't Believe It, RCA PD 42814 (1989)
All Or Nothing / Rich And Famous / Sick, Dirty And Mean, RCA 74321 14123-2 (1993)
Hard Attack / Run Through The Night / Crossroads, RCA 74321 37291 2 (1996)
Rich And Famous / Breaker / Writing On The Wall, Drakkar (2002)

Albums:
ACCEPT, Brain 006 188 (1979)
Lady Lou / Tired Of Me / Seawinds / Take Him In My Heart / Sounds Of War / Free Me Now / Glad To Be Alone / That's Rock n' Roll / Helldriver / Street Fighter
I'M A REBEL, Refektor 0060.273(1980)
I'm A Rebel / Save Us / No Time To Lose / Thunder And Lightning / China Lady / I Wanna Be No Hero / The King / Do It
ACCEPT, Brain 0060.389 (1980) (The same album as 'I'm A Rebel' with different title and cover)
I'm A Rebel / Save Us / No Time To Lose / Thunder And Lightning / China Lady / I Wanna Be No Hero / The King / Do It
BREAKER, Brain 0060 390 (1981)
Starlight / Breaker / Run If You Can / Can't Stand The Night / Son Of A Bitch / Burning / Feelings / Midnight Highway / Breaking Up Again / Down And Out
RESTLESS AND WILD, Brain 0060.513 (1982) **27 SWEDEN, 98 UK**
Fast As A Shark / Restless And Wild / Ahead Of The Pack / Shake Your Heads / Neon Nights / Get Ready / Demons Night / Flash Rockin' Man / Don't Go Stealing My Heart Away / Princess Of The Dawn
BALLS TO THE WALL, Lark INL 3563 (1984) **10 SWEDEN**
Balls To The Wall / London Leatherboys / Turn Me On / Head Over Heels / Losing More Than You've Ever Had / Love Child / Fight It Back / Guardian Of The Night /

Losers And Winners / Winter Dreams
METAL HEART, Portrait PRT 26358 (1985) **4 SWEDEN, 50 UK, 94 USA**
Metal Heart / Midnight Mover / Up To The Limit / Wrong Is Right / Screaming For A Love Bite / Too High To Get It Right / Dogs On Leads / Teach Us To Survive / Living For Tonite / Bound To Fail
HUNGRY YEARS, Metronome (1986)
Fast As A Shark / Burning / Son Of A Bitch / Princess Of The Dawn / I'm A Rebel / Breaker / Restless And Wild / The King / Midnight Highway
KAIZOKU-BAN (LIVE IN JAPAN), Portrait PRT 5916 (1986) **91 UK**
Metal Heart / Screaming For A Love Bite / Up To The Limit / Head Over Heels / Love Child / Living For Tonite
RUSSIAN ROULETTE, Portrait PRT 26893 (1986) **9 SWEDEN, 80 UK**
TV War / Monsterman / Russian Roulette / It's Hard To Find A Way / Aiming High / Heaven Is Hell / Another Second To Be / Man Enough To Fight / Stand Tight
BEST OF ACCEPT, Brain (1987)
Burning / Restless And Wild / Son Of A Bitch / Breaker / Do It / I'm A Rebel / China Lady / No Time To Lose / Princess Of The Dawn / Lady Lou
METAL MASTERS, Razor RAZ CD11 (1988)
Lady You / Tired Of Me / Seawinds / Sounds Of War / Free Me Now / Glad To Be Alone / That's Rock n' Roll / Helldriver / I'm A Rebel / Save Us / No Time To Lose / Thunder And Lightning / China Lady / The King / Do It
EAT THE HEAT, Epic 465229 2 (1989) **26 SWEDEN**
XTC / Prisoner / Love Sensation / Chain Reaction / D-Train / Generation Clash / Turn The Wheel / Mistreated / Stand 4 What U R / Hellhammer / Break The Ice
STAYING A LIFE (LIVE), Epic EK 46944 (1990)
Metal Heart / Breaker / Screaming For A Love Bite / Up To The Limit / Living For Tonight / Princess Of The Dawn / Guitar Solo Wolf / Restless And Wild / Son Of A Bitch / London Leatherboys / Love Child / Flash Rockin' Man / Dogs On Leads / Fast As A Shark / Balls To The Wall
THE COLLECTION, Castle CCSCD 311 (1991)
Lady Lou / I'm A Rebel / Thunder And Lightning / Breaker / Burning / Son Of A Bitch / Fast As A Shark / Restless And Wild / Princess Of The Dawn / The King / Balls To The Wall / London Leather Boys / Love Child / Metal Heart / Up To The Limit / Screaming For A Love Bite / Monsterman / TV War
OBJECTION OVERRULED, RCA 74321 12466 2 (1993) **21 SWEDEN**

Objection Overruled / I Don't Wanna Be Like You / Protectors Of Terror / Slaves To Metal / All Or Nothing / Bulletproof / Amamos La Vida / Sick, Dirty And Mean / Donation / Just By My Own / This One's For You
DEATHROW, RCA 74321 23016-2 (1994)
Death Row / Sodom And Gomorra / The Beast Inside / Dead On! / Guns 'R' Us / Like A Loaded Gun / What Else / Stone Evil / Bad Habits Die Hard / Prejudice / Bad Religion / Generation Clash II / Writing On The Wall / Drifting Apart / Pomp And Circumstance
RESTLESS (THE BEST), Brain (1994)
Restless And Wild / I'm A Rebel / Save Us / Son Of A Bitch / Fast As A Shark / Thunder And Lightning / China Lady / I Wanna Be No Hero / The King / Get Ready / Ahead Of The Pack / No Time To Lose / Burning / Feelings / Midnight Highway / Breaking Up Again / Flash Rockin' Man / Neon Nights
STEEL GLOVE, Castle Collectors CCS CD 422 (1995)
Fast As A Shark / I'm A Rebel / Restless And Wild / Lady Lou / The King / Starlight / China Lady / Save Us / Down And Out / No Time To Lose / I Wanna Be No Hero / Free Me Now / Do It / Can't Stand The Night / Breaker / Son Of A Bitch / Hell Driver / Burning / Thunder And Lightning
ACCEPT NO SUBSTITUTES, Sony Special Products (1995)

Too High To Get It Right / Russian Roulette / Princess Of The Dawn / Metal Heart / Fast As A Shark / Turn Me On / Shake Your Heads / Demon's Night / London Leatherboys / Balls To The Wall
PREDATOR, RCA 74321 33570-2 (1996)
Hard Attack / Crossroads / Scream / Diggin' In The Dirt / Lay It Down / It Ain't Over Yet / Predator / Crucified / Take Out The Crime / Don't Give A Damn / Run Through The Night / Primitive
ALL AREAS - WORLDWIDE - LIVE, G.U.N. Records GUN 150 (1997)
Starlight / London Leatherboys / I Don't Wanna Be Like You / Breaker / Slaves To Metal / Princess Of The Dawn / Restless And Wild / Son Of A Bitch / This One's For You / Bulletproof / Too High To Get It Right / Metal Heart / Fast As A Shark / Balls To The Wall / What Else / Sodom And Gomorra / The Beast Inside / Stone Evil / Death Row
HOT AND SLOW, BMG (2000)
Mistreated / Drifting Apart / All Or Nothing / Amamos La Vida / Just By My Own / Generation Clash / It's Hard To Find A Way / Walking In The Shadow / Guardian Of The Night / Winter Dreams / Run Through The Night / Hard Attack / Generation Clash II / Writing On The Wall / Living For Tonite / Pomp And Circumstance
FINAL CHAPTER, Sanctuary SANCD030

ADAGIO

(2001)
Starlight / London Leatherboys / I Don't Wanna Be Like You / Breaker / Slaves To Metal / Princess Of The Dawn / Restless & Wild / Son Of A Bitch / This One's For You / Bulletproof / Too High To Get It Right / Metal Heart / Fast As A Shark / Balls To The Wall / What Else / Sodom & Gomorra / The Beast Inside / Bad Habits Die Hard / Stone Evil / Death Row

ADAGIO (FRANCE)
Line-Up: David Readman (vocals), Stephan Forte (guitars / keyboards), Dirk Bruinenberg (drums), Richard Anderson (keyboards)

ADAGIO is the Progressive Power Metal vision of French speed guitarist Stephan Forte. The 'Sanctus Ignis' record, a brew of lengthy symphonic neo-classical works and traditional melodic Metal, saw Forte in alliance with PINK CREAM 69 vocalist David Readman, ELEGY drummer Dirk Bruinenberg, MAJESTIC keyboard player Richard Anderson and bassist Franck Hermany.
The whole affair, which novelly saw the inclusion of a totally instrumental take on LED ZEPPELIN's classic 'Immigrant Song', was ably produced by Dennis Ward of PINK CREAM 69.

Albums:
SANCTUS IGNIS, Limb Music Productions (2001)
Second Sight / The Inner Road / In Nomine… / The Stringless Violin / Seven Lands Of Sin / Order Of Enlil / Sanctus Ignis / Panem Et Circenses / Immigrant Song / Niflheim (demo)

ADRAMELCH (ITALY)
Line-Up: Vittorio Ballerio (vocals), Gianluca A. Corona (guitar), Sandro Fremiot (guitar), Franco Avalli (bass), Luca Moratti (drums)

ADRAMELCH had developed a good name for themselves on the Underground Metal scene thanks to the 'Irae Melanox' album, a record that displayed strong melodies and intelligent song-writing. Although the group in some ways pioneered the Prog Metal genre in Europe the group split up soon after it emerged.
Some ex-ADRAMELCH members are still playing the Milanese Rock playing in trad Rock bands. Vocalist Vittorio Ballerio and guitarist Gianluca Corona reformed ADRAMELCH in early 2000.

Albums:
IRAE MELANOX, Metal Master MET104 (1988)
Fearful Visions / Zephirus / Irae Melanox / Lamento / Decay (Saver Comes) / Was Called Empire / Eyes Of Alabaster / Dreams Of A Jester

AEMERALD (ITALY)
Line-Up: Davide Baduena (vocals), Andrea Floris (guitar), Francesca Poma (guitar), Andrea Brunazzo (bass), Marco Raviolo (keyboards), Raffaello Allemanini (drums)

Power Metal band AEMERALD date to 1998, founded by lead vocalist Sid Terry and guitar player Andrea Floris. The group line-up was fluid until the introduction of a stable rhythm section comprising Andrea Brunazzo on the bass and Raffaello Allemanini on the drum kit. Shortly after guitarist Francesco Poma and Marco Raviolo on keyboards completed the band. As such, AEMERALD put in their inaugural live baptism of fire supporting DRAKKAR at the Millennium Club in Turin during January of 1999.
The band gigged extensively and also worked up material for a five track demo session 'The Storytellers' convened in Spring of that year. Taking their cue from the burgeoning Italian symphonic Power Metal movement 'The Storytellers' displayed the expected baroque and classical influences but with an added embellishment of Folk to set the band apart from the pack. A further promotion disc entitled 'Magical Wonder' was delivered in the summer of 2000, mixed by DRAKKAR guitarist Dario Beretta. Although this effort reaped praise amongst the European Metal media, AEMERALD suffered a severe setback as Sid Terry was sacked.
AEMERALD signed up Davide Baduena as their new lead vocalist in June of 2001. Shortly after a deal was struck with the Elevate label for a debut album 'Shadows Of A Past Life'.

Albums:
SHADOWS OF A PAST LIFE, Elevate (2002)

AFTERSHOK (Pittsburgh, PA, USA)
Line-Up: Vic Hex (vocals), George Mihalovich (guitar), Nick Griska (bass), George B. (drums)

Heavy Metal band founded in 1996 by former SHOK PARIS and BANGER singer Vic Hex. Bass player Nick Griska is ex-NIGHTSTALKER, BANGER and SHOCKWAVE. The band debuted live on October 29th 2000 guesting for TENSION at the Attic venue in Barnesville, Ohio. Later gigs included a landmark show with BREAKER at the Cleveland Odeon Club at which a sampler CD, featuring recordings of 'War Machine' and 'Armed And Dangerous', were distributed to fans.

AFTERSHOK have latterly supported LIZZY BORDEN, DORO, BRITNY FOX, YNGWIE MALMSTEEN, NEVERMORE and SAVATAGE. A self-financed album was geared up for release in late 2001.

AFTERWORLD (FINLAND)

Line-Up: Mika Kuokkanen (vocals), Petri Saasko (guitar), Ville Koskela (guitar), Marko Salo (bass), Jani Outinen (drums)

Melodic Power Metal unit dating to 1993. Drummer Jani Outinen was previously operating as lead vocalist for NORTIA. AFTERWORLD's second album 'Connecting Animals' proudly sported a cover version of ABBA's 'Money Money Money'.

<u>Albums:</u>
DARK SIDE OF MIND, T&T TT 0044-2 (1999)
Dark Side Of Mind / To The Afterworld / Lost In The Dark / Never Ending Sleep / Sixteen Innocent Children / Power To Kill / The End Becomes / The Silence Of The End / Virtual Angel / Touch Of Hate / The Final Winter / Prison Without Walls / Are We Alone
CONNECTING ANIMALS, T&T TT 0047-2 (2000)
Second Chance / Promises / Tell Me Why? / Behind Your Eyes / Money Money Money / The World Of Hypocrates / The World Of Hypocrates Part II / The Seventh Year / Ending Our Days / Nothing To Lose / Let It Go / After The Dark

AGENT STEEL (Los Angeles, CA, USA)

Line-Up: Bruce Hall (vocals), Juan Garcia (guitar), Bernie Versailles (guitar), Karlos Medina (bass), Rigo Amezcua (drums)

Created by ex-SCEPTRE and ABATTOIR front man John Cyriis AGENT STEEL soon forged a reputation for surgically precise intense Metal honed by Cyriis' distinct high altitude vocal range. AGENT STEEL's reputation in the Metal world is also undoubtedly enhanced by the band's Sci-Fi apocalyptic lyrical stance.

The roots of AGENT STEEL lay in the SCEPTRE track 'Taken By Force' contributed to the Metal Blade Record compilation album 'Metal Massacre IV'. The guitarist for SCEPTRE, the Brazilian born John Camps, would capitalise on this exposure with a further three track demo. Renaming himself

'John Syriis'- later 'Cyriis' - he auditioned for the position of lead vocalist with ABATTOIR. After demonstrating an impressive multi-octave range, he secured the position easily. However, within six months Cyriis was ousted and along with drummer Chuck Profus engineered a new proposition billed as SANCTUARY. This band, rounded out by guitarists Sill Simmons and Mark Marshall with bassist George Robb soon evolved into AGENT STEEL. This inaugural line-up cut the '144,000 Gone' demo in 1984.

AGENT STEEL had a complete switch of guitarists when Marshall and Simmons were ejected. Marshall would later make his mark with SAVAGE GRACE.

John Gott briefly occupied the six string position before ex-ABATTOIR man Juan Garcia and Kurt "Kiltelt" Colfelt were inducted as permanent members for the groundbreaking 'Skeptics Apocalypse' album. This album would make an immediate impact globally. The leading Thrash Metal journal of the time, Britain's 'Metal Forces' magazine, would see editor Bernard Doe citing 'Skeptics Apocalypse' as one of his favourite albums of the year whilst readers voted Cyriis fourth best Metal vocalist.

The band made their first live appearance opening for SLAYER in September 1984 at the Los Angeles Country Club. A brace of headliners later and AGENT STEEL were invited to open dates for British metallers RAVEN. Colfelt would bow out, later gaining recognition with HOLY TERROR, and in his stead would come the teen protégé of Bernie 'Versailles' Versye. Robb too made his exit in favour of bassist Michael Zaputil.

With Thrash Metal riding high AGENT STEEL put in a notable show at the infamous Dutch 'Aardschok Dag' festival and toured Europe as support to OVERKILL and ANTHRAX during May of 1986. The band released a highly praised EP the same year titled 'Mad Locust Rising' which featured an extreme cover version of JUDAS PRIEST's 'The Ripper'. The band's media profile would be raised during this period with stories that Cyriis, convinced that a Mayan end times theory was set to signal the end of the world, started to sign his autograph as "2011"- the supposed date of the impending apocalypse. The 'Unstoppable Force' album, produced by Dan Johnson, only served to heighten the band's reputation although critics did note a mellowing of Cyriis' vocal delivery. AGENT STEEL were by now the subject of numerous major label inquiries and in November of 1986 reports leaked out that Capitol Records were showing a serious desire to sign the band. AGENT STEEL showcased successfully for the label but as negotiations dragged on the proposed deal withered.

Garcia quit to form EVIL DEAD with his ex-ABATTOIR colleague bassist Mel Sanchez. Garcia, alongside future TESTAMENT and SLAYER drummer John Dette, would also found the Spanish language Metal band TERROR cutting the Mexican release album 'Hijos De Los Cometas'.

Cyriis and Profus, now relocated to Florida, conducted a European tour by drafting in hired hands. Guitarists JAMES MURPHY and Jay Weslord figuring among their number. Another musician to be included in the AGENT STEEL ranks would be ex-PURGATORY bassist Richard Bateman, added to NASTY SAVAGE in 1989. A decade later Bateman founded AFTER DEATH with ex-MORBID ANGEL / NOCTURNUS / INCUBUS man Mike Browning. (Bateman would later tragically be killed in a car accident).

This variant of AGENT STEEL put in a London Hammersmith Odeon gig supported by NUCLEAR ASSAULT and ONSLAUGHT.

In December 1987 members of AGENT STEEL were arrested in Arizona on charges of aggravated assault on a youth. The bizarre allegations centred upon a 17 year old male (actually a band roadie) the band had allegedly tied to a bed whilst they subsequently urinated on him and exploded firecrackers on his chest. Charges were dropped, but the group folded shortly after following another strange incident in which Cyriis allegedly tried to force band members to get AGENT STEEL tattoos. Whether the rumours of forced tattooing are true or not are unclear but the fact remains that many of Cyriis' former associates sport AGENT STEEL tattoos!

In 1988 AGENT STEEL officially disbanded. Whilst Cyriis and Profus joined PONTIUS PROPHET, guitarist JAMES MURPHY later joined HALLOWS EVE, DEATH, OBITUARY and CANCER. He would also figure in the ever fluid TESTAMENT line-up, record with Danes KONKHRA and release solo product.

Cyriis would declare his intention to retire in 1988. Profus would put his efforts into a new venture billed as MALFEITOR in union with ex-PONTIUS PROPHET guitarist Michael Hill. Intriguingly it was soon revealed that MALFEITOR's vocalist 'Max Kobol' was in truth none other than John Cyriis.

Cyriis / Kobol would next be spotted as front man for Tampa, Florida band LEMEGETON appearing on their 'Evil Against Evil' demo. Cyriis re-emerged in 1990 fronting New York's BLACK REIGN.

AGENT STEEL reformed in 1999 prompted by an offer to perform at the annual German 'Wacken Open Air' festival. German label Century Media would aid their cause by re-issuing their entire back catalogue.

AGENT STEEL's re-formation line-up now comprised ex-SYBIL singer Bruce Hall, guitarists Juan Garcia and Bernie Versailles, erstwhile EVIL DEAD bassist Karl Medina and drummer Chuck Profus. Versailles also contributed the ENGINE project album assembled by ARMOURED SAINT's Joey Vera and FATES WARNING's Ray Alder.

The band cut another JUDAS PRIEST track 'Beyond The Realms Of Death' for the Dwell Records tribute album 'Hell Bent For Metal'. This track would also be included as a bonus track on American release versions, on the Metal Blade label, of the band's uncompromisingly intense comeback album 'Omega Conspiracy'.

The band toured Germany in early 2000 on a package bill with RIOT, ANVIL and DOMINE. Cyriis, apparently now going under the title of 'Havlock', resurfaced again in 2000 with a fresh act titled OUTER GATEWAYS.

AGENT STEEL would re-title themselves ORDER OF THE ILLUMINATI for new recording projects in 2001. As such the band laid down a cover of BLACK SABBATH's 'Hole In The Sky' for donation to a tribute album.

The same year would witness the retirement of Profus with Rigo Amezcua taking over the drum stool for the band's appearance at the 'Kalamazoo Metal' festival. Versailles would also find time to act as producer for Death Metal band SADISTIC INTENT.

As 2002 dawned it appeared that the relationship between Cyriis and the ongoing band had defrosted somewhat with a possibility that the next studio album may emerge under the AGENT STEEL banner after all. In March the band performed the second annual 'Hellfest' event in Whittier, California ranked alongside fellow vets EXODUS.

Albums:

SKEPTICS APOCALYPSE, Roadrunner RR 9759 (1985)
Calling / Taken By Force / Bleed For The Godz / 144,000 Gone / Back To Reign / Agents Of Steel / Evil Eye / Children Of The Sun / Guilty As Charged

MAD LOCUST RISING, Music For Nations KUT124 (1986)
The Swarm Is Upon Us / Mad Locust Rising / The Ripper / Let It Be Done / The Day At Guyana

THE UNSTOPPABLE FORCE, Music For Nations MFN 66 (1987)
Unstoppable Force / Never Surrender / Indestructive / Chosen To Stay / Still Searchin' / Rager / The Day At Guyana / Nothing Left / Traveller

8

OMEGA CONSPIRACY, Candlelight (1999)
Destroy The Hush / Illuminati Is Machine /
Fighting Backwards / New Godz / Know Your
Master / Infinity / Awaken the Swarm / Into
The Nowhere / Bleed Forever / It's Not What
You Think

AGE OF REBELLION (GERMANY)
Line-Up: Andreas Leyer (vocals / guitar), Dirk
Mies (guitar), Peter Viergutz (bass), Christian
Müller (keyboards), Bastian Winkels (drums)

Albums:
IKARUS DREAM, Around The Music
DSRCD027 (1997)
Why Am I? / Mind In Memories / Hungry /
Forgotten Hero / Ikarus Dream / On Their
Own / Welcome To Reality / All These Years /
Holy War / Emotional Rain
DIVIDING HORIZONS, Treasure Hunt (1999)
Awakening / Of Jesters And Fools /
December Dawn / Praying For Silence /
Dividing Horizons / Angel / When There Is
Demand / Tears Of Destiny / Now And
Forever

AGONY (COLOMBIA)
Line-Up: Cesar Botero (vocals), Andres
Jaramillo (guitar), Carlos Alberto Marin
(guitar), Carlos Reyes (bass), Alfonso Pinzon
(drums)

Bogata based Power Metal act AGONY was
formed in 1992. A 1994 demo preceded the
1995 album 'Live All The Time'. Bass player
Carlos Reyes would be usurped by Hans
Vollert following the 1996 'Millennium' album.
Vollert is also involved with the Industrial DJ
PE-YE project.

Albums:
MILLENIUM, (1996)
Snake Land / Forever Decay / Die Alone /
Guerrillas / Slaves Of Fear / Millennium /
Fear Of God / The Blessing / Falling Again /
Walls Of Black / The Last Power

AHRKANA (ITALY)
Line-Up: Halley (vocals), Alessio (guitar),
Franz (guitar), Lele (bass), Gianluca (drums)

Milan Metallers borne as DARK ELF in 1998
comprising singer Andrea, guitarists Andrea
and Alessio, bassist Lele, having switched
instruments from guitar and last being a
member of UNDERBREAD, with drummer
Gianluca. Guitarist Alessio had come from the
Death Metal scene having operated as a
member of THUNDERHEADS and
MASSACRO. The next year Franz usurped
Andrea on guitar as the group evolved into

PROPHECY. Lead vocalist Halley, joining the
band as replacement to Andrea in March of
2000, cited previous experience with his own
HALLEY as well as TUNKASHILA, SWEET
AGGRESSION and DARK QUEEN.
PROPHECY adopted the revised title of
AHRKANA in mid 2001.

Singles/EPs:
Long Life To Dark Elf / The Immortal / We'll
Reborn / Stormmaster, (2002)
('Stormmmaster' EP)

AIRBORN (ITALY)
Line-Up: Alessio Perardi (vocals / guitar),
Roberto Cappuchio (guitar), Alberto Leschi
(bass), Tony Serra (drums)

Turin Power Metal act formulated in 1995 by
vocalist / guitarist Alessio Perardi. Apparently
the man's conversion to Heavy Metal (he had
previously been treading the boards as part of
a DIRE STRAITS cover band) came when a
friend gave him a GAMMA RAY album to
listen to in 1994. Duly bowled over Perardi set
about constructing his own Metal group,
pulling in former AMPLIFY bassist Alberto
Leschi as the first recruit.
Signing to the German Remedy label
AIRBORN pulled in IRON SAVIOR's Piet
Sielck to produce the 'Against The World'
album.

Albums:
AGAINST THE WORLD, Remedy (2002)
Infernal Machine (Intro) / Against The World /
Born To Fly / The Hero / Projectile / Cry Now
/ New Hope / Wings / Return To The Sky /
No More Kings / Freedom To The World /
Sky City / Infernal Machine Two (Outro)

AKASHIC (BRAZIL)
Line-Up: Rafael Gubert (vocals), Marcos De
Ros (guitar), Fábio Alves (bass), Éder
Bergozza (keyboards), Maurício Meinert
(drums)

Progressive Metal act created in 1998 and
centred upon guitarist Marcos De Ros of the
well known DE ROS power trio. DE ROS, also
including AKASHIC bassist Fábio Alves,
released three albums in 1994's 'Ad Dei
Glorium', 1997's 'Universe' and the 1999
offering 'Masterpieces'.
AKASHIC undertook extensive touring in
Southern Europe before recording of their
'Timeless Realm' debut.

Albums:
TIMELESS REALM, (2000)
Heaven's Call / For Freedom / Voices And

Signs / Who Am I? / Fire Of Temptation / Dove / Memories / Salvation / Gates Of Fimament / Veiled Secrets

AKILLES (SWEDEN)
Line-Up: Magnus Styrén (vocals), David Asp (guitar), Lotta Olderberg (guitar), Niemi (bass), Robin Thuresson (drums)

AKILLES date back to 1989, a band centred upon ex-TITAN bassist Andreas Niemi and featuring Peter Wold on drums. The formative version of AKILLES performed Punk Rock but with Niemi's influence steered into a Hard Rock direction. A single, 'Passaway' was issued on the Active label with the band being credited as vocalist Stefan, guitarists Thomas and Jarkko, Andreas Niemi on bass and drummer Janne. This group fractured but by 1999 Niemi had been asked to help forge a fresh band with Wold on guitar, drummer Peter Jürgensen and CRIKEY singer Magnus Styrén. This new band gigged initially billing themselves as NASTY, performing a set comprising cover versions of artists such as JUDAS PRIEST, IRON MAIDEN and DIO, but then Jürgensen made his exit. Another temporary name of DEMIGOD was put into use as the group sought a new drummer.
The group issued a debut demo in April of 2000 and subsequently resurrected the name AKILLES, spending time thereafter on the hunt for a suitable drummer. Uffe Stanislaus of the SPEEDFREAKS rehearsed with the band but it was to be Robin Thuresson, of HIGHLANDER, HOPE N' GLORY and FORBIDDEN DREAMS repute, who secured the position. Shortly after recording an April 2001 two track demo both Johnny Johansson and Peter Wold left the band. AKILLES would react swiftly, trying out Peter Tjernström of FATA MORGANA and David Asp from ANCIENT DREAMS to fill the vacancies. However, although Asp was duly inducted the second guitarist position would go to Lotta Olderberg of SATYRIA. Before the year was out vocalist Magnus Styrén had decamped. In January of 2002 FORBIDDEN DREAMS guitarist Michael Fuhrman would rehearse with the band.
Andreas Niemi also performs with FATA MORGANA.

Singles/EPs:
Passaway / Taste Of Blood, Active Music HEJ S-039 (1991)

ALKEMYST (FRANCE)
Line-Up: Roberto Messina (vocals), Severin Bonneville (guitar), Arnaud Menard (guitar), Denis Mellion (bass), Arnaud Gorbaty (drums)

Progressive Metal act ALKEMYST would draft Roberto Messina, previously with Italians SECRET SPHERE, for their inaugural 2001 album 'Meeting In The Mist'.

Albums:
A MEETING IN THE MIST, (2003)
Fiat Lux / Still Alive / It's Time / Up To Heaven's Gate / Hold On To Your Dreams / A Meeting In The Mist / Passage / Empty Skies / Nameless Son

ALLEGIENCE (AUSTRALIA)
Line-Up: Conrad Higson (vocals), Tony Campo (guitar), Jason Stone (guitar), Dave Harrison (bass), Glenn Butcher (drums)

Aggressive Perth Metal band created in 1990. ALLEGIENCE, featuring ex-INFA RED and INQUISITION bassist Dave Harrison, originally saw John Mihos behind the microphone but when he quit drummer Conrad Higson took over lead vocals and his drum stool was occupied by Glenn Butcher. ALLEGIENCE built up an enviable live reputation in Australia backed with a succession of demos 'Make The Pledge', 'Torn Between Two Worlds' and 'Studio Live'. ALLEGIENCE also contributed the cut 'Morally Justified' to the Roadrunner 1993 compilation 'Redrum'.
ALLEGIENCE caught the eye of former JUDAS PRIEST vocalist Rob Halford who duly signed them to his E.M.A.S. Management organisation. This union resulted in a deal with major label Polygram and ALLEGIENCE bowed in proper with the 1994 'Destitution' album.
ALLEGIENCE supported KREATOR, FEAR FACTORY, Rob Halford's FIGHT and MORBID ANGEL in support of the record.
Although a second album 'Skinman' received excellent reviews ALLEGIENCE found themselves label-less soon after. A live album 'Time To React' marked their end of passage. Harrison founded BLACK STEEL.

Albums:
DESTITUTION, Polygram (1994)
Intro / Chaos Dies / One Step Beyond / Hate Frenzy / Torn Between Two Worlds / Destitution / Morally Justified / Pack Of Lies / Dealt The Cruel Hands / Downward Spiral / Twisted Minds / Tranquillity
TIME TO REACT - LIVE, Polygram (1995)
Chaos Dies / Pity / Trapped Behind A Shadow / Hate Frenzy / Time To React / Taken By Force / Torn Between Two Worlds / One Step Beyond / Downward Spiral

SKINMAN, Polygram (1996)
Ripped To Shreds / Face Reality / Give Yourself / Scorn / Time To React / Trapped Behind A Shadow / Wasted Life / Taken By Force / Pity / Hands Of Fate

ALSION (GERMANY)
Line-Up: Sven Kolbow (vocals), Ingo Kolb (guitar), Florian Eisele (guitar), Michael Brazda (bass), Roland Klein (drums)

A fantasy flavoured Metal act. ALSION include erstwhile FIRESTORM, BENEFACTOR and EVOLUTION MACABRE guitarist Ingo Kolb. Florian Eisele on second guitar also cites credits with FIRESTORM.
ALSION would issue a self-financed, self-released eponymous mini-album in January of 2000. The following year would bring turbulent times for the band with keyboard player Umberto Federico decamping in March. ALSION persevered without keyboards and released a second album 'A Kingdom Beyond' in April. However, during September bassist Emanuel Tippet made his exit to be swiftly superseded by Michael Brazda. A further blow came with the departure of Eisele in November.

Albums:
ALSION, Alsion (2000)
Welcome To Alsion / Lawhammer / On The Top / Fiery Dragon / This Is A Story… / Made Of Fire
A KINGDOM BEYOND, Alsion (2001)
Welcome To Alsion / Way To Eternity / Fiery Dragon / Made Of Fire / This Is A Story … / Lawhammer / Set The Sails! / Santa Maria / Kings Of Alsion / Show Me Your Heaven / Legends Of The Dragon

ALTA DENSIDAD (CHILE)
Line-Up: Carlos Flores (vocals), Gabriel Hernandez (guitar), Franco Zapata (bass), Mauricio Eyzaguirre (keyboards), Christian Vallejos (drums)

Chilean Power Metal band ALTA DENSIDAD was forged in 1997, issuing the 'Almas Jovenes' demo the following year.

Albums:
PRINCESS AURA, (2001)
Intro / Rebelión / Día "D" / Cruel Poder / Esclavos del Aguila / La Muerte del Aguila / Irrealidad / Almas Jóvenes / Apocalipsis / Aura / Princesa Aura / Coronación / Sueños de Dos

ALTARIA (FINLAND)
Line-Up: Jouni Nikula (vocals), Jani Liimatainen (guitar), Marko Pukkila (bass), Tony Smedjebacka (drums)

The rhythm section of bassist Marko Pukkila and drummer Tony Smedjebacka, previously members of Christian Hard Rock act BLINDSIDE, would forge a fresh project during 2000 billed as ALTARIA. Joining them in this new venture would be singer Johan Mattjus, previously having made a name for himself with STORMWING, and SONATA ARTICA guitarist Jani Liimatainen.
ALTARIA debuted with a November 2001 promotional EP 'Sleeping Visions'. During early 2002 ALTARIA enlisted new vocalist Jouni Nikula, also singer with REQUIEM and UNITAR. ALTARIA were projecting the release of the album 'Foundation' for early 2003 issue. For live dates the band inducted NIGHTWISH guitarist Emppu Vuorinen as stand in second guitarist.
ALTARIA would feature on the second volume of tributes to guitarist JASON BECKER, donating their rendition of 'Stranger' from CACOPHONY's 'Go Off!' album.

Singles/EPs:
Fire And Ice / Innocent / Kingdom Of The Night, (2001) ('Sleeping Visions' EP)

ALTURA (Charlotte, NC, USA)
Line-Up: Rain Irving (vocals), Franklin Ervin (guitar), Jeremy Osbourne (bass), Jason Lingle (keyboards), Chad Gibson (drums)

Albums:
MERCY, Magna Carta MA-9014-2 (1996)
Mercy / The Calling / One Dimension / The Continuum / One By One / Alternate Lines / Alone / Horizons Fade

AMARAN (SWEDEN)
Line-Up: Johanna De Pierre (vocals), Kari Kainulainen (guitar), Ronnie Backlund (guitar), Mikael Andersson (bass), Robin Bergh (drums)

Female fronted Stockholm based Metal act that employ trad Heavy Metal styles combined with the aggression of Death Metal. The band was formulated by guitarists Kari Kainulainen and Ronnie Backlund, shortly after adding bass player Mikael Andersson and singer Johanna De Pierre. The title of AMARAN was decided upon in January of 2001, a debut demo session arriving in April. AMARAN would complete their line-up with the inclusion of Robin Bergh on drums.
The French Listenable label picked up the band for an inaugural album, 'A World Depraved', released in 2002.

Albums:
A WORLD DEPRAVED, Listenable
POSH036CD (2002)
Faith Healer / Rusty Warhorse / Void /
Daffodil / Lullaby / Imperfect / Little Victory /
Karma In Flesh / Received A Kiss / Ode

AMBERMOON (ITALY)
Line-Up: Umberto Mordenti (vocals), Paolo
Offredo (guitar), Andrea Carraro (guitar),
Davide Betelli (bass), Roberto Ragazzo
(drums)

Power Metal act AMBERMOON began life
during 1995 entitled DARK AVENGER,
issuing the 'Epitaph Of Credulous' demo
under that title. The band comprised lead
singer Marco 'Moz' Moranzoni, guitarists
Paolo Offredo and Andrea Carraro, bassist
Davide Betelli and ARKHE drummer Viviano
Crimella.
A switch of titles to AMBERMOON led to a
recording deal with the Underground
Symphony label for debut album 'Facing The
Storm'. For this outing the band were now
fronted by Umberto Mordenti, with drums
supplied by Roberto Ragazzo.

Albums:
FACING THE STORM, Underground
Symphony USCD041 (2000)
King George's Madness / Facing The Storm
/ Turbins Of The Sea / The Everlasting /
Shadow Master

AMETHYST (SWEDEN)
Line-Up: Oskar Lindholm (vocals), Johannes
Forsberg (guitar), Kristian Lindstrom (guitar),
David Lindegren (bass), Michael Kallin
(keyboards), Daniel Tiger (drums)

Örnsköldsvik based Progressive Metal band,
operating in their formative stages under the
bizarre handle EVIL SNIGELS. With the
addition of drummer Daniel Tiger the band
evolved into MYSTERY. At this juncture the
band added lead vocalist Joakim Åström and
keyboard player Jonas Håkansson. A demo
recording was embarked upon but studio
equipment failure curtailed this project.
Shortly after David Lindegren joined the band
on bass, replacing previous incumbent
Tomas.
The band then underwent a radical shift in
line-up with both Åström and Håkansson
bidding farewell. Inducting a new singer in the
form of Oskar Lindholm the group used the
opportunity to make another title change,
becoming AMETHYST. The 2000 four track
EP 'Reaching Skies' was a self-financed
affair.

Singles/EPs:
Unmasked Vision / Reaching Skies /
Winternight / Beyond The Horizon, (2000)
('Reaching Skies' EP)

AMON (RUSSIA)
Line-Up: Oleg Zhilyakov (vocals), Genadiy
Katurin (guitar), Vladimir Nazarov (guitar),
Yuriy Lauless (bass), Oleg Zagryazkin
(drums)

Albums:
THE TALE OF DARK DREAMS, (1997)

ANACRUSIS (St. Charles, MO, USA)
Line-Up: Ken Nardi (vocals / guitar), Kevin
Heidbreder (guitar), John Emery (bass),
Mike Owen (drums)

Highly rated ANACRUSIS date from 1984 and
are based in St. Louis, Missouri. At first
ANACRUSIS made a sharp impression on
the Thrash scene with their technically
precise delivery. Front man Ken Nardi had
previously operated with HEAVEN'S FLAME.
ANACRUSIS debuted with the 1987
'Annihilation Complete' demo. A track was
featured on the Metal Forces magazine
compilation 'Demolition' in 1988.
The band would record the inaugural
'Suffering Hour' album, self-financing it to the
tune of $1200. The European Axis label,
headed by 'Metal Forces' magazine editor
Bernard Doe, would be quick to snap the
band up.
1989's 'Reason' would be issued on the
Active imprint, actually an evolution of the
Axis concern. However, an American issue
licensed to Metal Blade witnessed completely
different artwork. Touring in the States found
ANACRUSIS as openers to DIRTY ROTTEN
IMBECILES.
Drummer Mike Owen was superseded by
Chad Smith as the band signed to the Metal
Blade concern on a global basis for the 'Manic
Impressions' outing. Promotion included a 38
date American tour in the Autumn of 1991
third on the bill to GALACTIC COWBOYS and
OVERKILL. The group would then secure
further supports stepping up to larger venues
with MEGADETH.
The fourth and final ANACRUSIS effort,
1993's 'Screams And Whispers', would herald
another change on the drum stool with Paul
Miles taking on duties. By this stage the band
had shed the greater degree of their Thrash
tradition and were operating in ambitious
Progressive Metal territory.

Albums:
SUFFERING HOUR, Axis LP4 (1988)

Present Tense / Imprisoned / ROT / Butcher's Block / A World To Gain / Frigid Bitch / Fighting Evil / Twisted Cross / Annihilation Complete / Disembowelled
REASON, Active ATV9 (1989)
Stop Me / Terrified / Not Forgotten / Wrong / Silent Crime / Misshapen Intent / Afraid To Feel / Child Inside / Vital / Quick To Doubt / Killing My Mind / Injustice
MANIC IMPRESSIONS, Metal Blade ZORRO23 (1990)
Paint A Picture / I Love The World / Something Real / Dream Again / Explained Away / Still Black / What You Became / Our Reunion / Idle Hours / Far Too Long
SCREAMS AND WHISPERS, Metal Blade ZORRO59 (1991)
Sound The Alarm / Sense Of Will / Too Many Prophets / Release / Division / Tools Of Separation / Grateful / A Screaming Breath / My Soul's Affliction / Driven / Brotherhood? / Release

ANARION (AUSTRALIA)
Line-Up: Riccardo Mecchi (vocals / guitar), Steve Stergiadis (guitar), Erf (bass), Luke Burnham (drums)

Melbourne Power Metal band ANARION is known internationally as being the post PEGAZUS port of call for vocalist Danny Cecati. The group first assembled in 1999 with guitarist Riccardo Mecchi handling lead vocals, the inaugural line-up comprising second guitarist Michael Vrljic, bassist Simon D'Alfonso with drummer Luke Burnham swelling the ranks in October of that year.
In January of 2000 Cecati suggested a union. Having rehearsed previously with the PEGAZUS front man Mecchi agreed to concentrate his energies on guitar. With Cecati now enrolled it would be only a short time before he was fired from his position in PEGAZUS. In June both Vrljic and D'Alfonso bailed out. Steve Stergiadis filled the vacant second guitar position in November and the four string position was subsequently occupied by Chris Binding. A further switch had another erstwhile member of THE EMBER TIDE, the Iranian born Erf, as the next bassist in line.
Although Cecati left for Progressive Metal act EYEFEAR, necessitating Mecchi resuming his prior responsibilities as lead vocalist, ANARION recorded a self-financed debut album 'The Journey Begins' for December 2001 release. The band toured Australia as support to EDGUY in May of 2002.

Albums:
THE JOURNEY BEGINS, (2001)

Space-Time / My Own / The Battle Of Old / Kingdom Of Stone / Earth Reborn / Life Of Descent / Hidden Mind / Principles Of Uncertainty / The Journey Begins...

ANCIENT WYRM (ITALY)
Line-Up: Danilo Cagliari (vocals / guitar), Massimo Cozza (guitar), Davide Palombo (bass), Mirko Dani (keyboards), Pietro Terzano (drums)

ANCIENT WYRM made their first impressions on the Italian Rock scene under the guise of the symphonic, Black orientated BLACK SWAN, releasing two commendable demo sessions; 1998's 'Immortal' and 'Lord Of My Dreams' in 2000. The self-financed 2002 album 'A New Life' included an ambitious cover version of MANOWAR's 'Black Wind, Fire And Steel'. A second offering, 'The Metal Opera', was set for December release.

Singles/EPs:
Carpe Diem / Destiny / Heroes / Kronos / Lord Of Time, (2002) ('Lord Of Time' EP)

Albums:
A NEW LIFE, (2002)
A New Life (Intro) / Heaven's Flames / Lord Of My Dreams (1996-2002) / Lost / Don't Go Away / Gethsemani / Black Wind, Fire And Steel / It Can't Rain All The Time / The End (Outro)

ANDROMEDA (SWEDEN)
Line-Up: Lawrence Mackrory (vocals), Johan Reinholdz (guitar),

ANDROMEDA is a multi faceted Metal vehicle for Swedish guitar hero in the making Johan Reinholdsz. Andromeda. The band unites intense unrelenting Metal juxtaposed with tranquil mood swings.
ANDROMEDA would sign to Swedish label War Music in 1999. This union brought Reinholdz in contact with erstwhile DARKANE vocalist Lawrence Mackrory for the Daniel Bergstrand produced debut 'Extension Of The Wish'. The record would be re-promoted in America through a licensing deal with the German Century Media label in May of 2001.

Albums:
EXTENSION OF THE WISH, War Music (2001)
The Words Unspoken / Crescendo Of Thoughts / In The Deepest Of Waters / Chameleon Carnival / Star Shooter Supreme / Extension Of The Wish / Arch Angel

ANESTHESIA (GERMANY)

Line-Up: Schraubäh (vocals), Hendrik Schött (guitar), Andreas Mier (guitar), Jan Rubach (bass), Thomas Nack (drums)

ANESTHESIA was convened in 1996 by the former GAMMA RAY rhythm section of bassist Jan Rubach and drummer Thomas Nack. The drummer had also earlier been operating a side project TWORK in league with ex-KINGDOM COME guitarist Heiko Radke. The drummer would later reunite with GAMMA RAY mainman Kai Hansen in his IRON SAVIOR project band, appearing on the 'Interlude' album.

Albums:

THE STATE OF BEING UNABLE TO FEEL PAIN, Semaphore 37936-422 (1997)
Welcome To The Church Of The Numb / My Age / Cancer / Triptychon / Winter / Heroes Of Research / Emperor Time / ILOI / The Prophet Song / Caligula's Dance / Atrocious Silence / Egomania / Habits

ANGEL DUST (GERMANY)

Line-Up: Dirk Thurisch (vocals), Bernd Aufermann (guitar), Frank Banx (bass), Steven Banx (keyboards), Dirk Assmuth (drums)

Dortmund's ANGEL DUST has proven to be stoic Thrash flag bearers since their inception in 1984. The band has made no less than three reunion attempts, each more successful than the last. Enduring numerous line-up changes ANGEL DUST have stuck to their guns watching musical trends come and go. With the close of the millennium ANGEL DUST are still reaching out to an ever appreciative and growing international fan base.

ANGELDUST, founded by bass player Frank Banx and drummer Dirk Assmuth, created ripples outside of Germany with their uncompromising Speed Metal debut album 'Into The Dark Past'. The record would sell over 30,000 copies in Germany alone. However, the band were never totally capable of promoting the product other than a few European gigs as guitarists Andreas Lohrum and Romme Keymer were committed to their homeland's military service.

ANGEL DUST folded in November 1989, only to be resurrected by Coe, Banx and Assmuth with two new guitarists Vinni Lynn and Stefan K. Nauer. The ensuing 'To Dust You Will Decay' album was produced by the highly regarded veteran Kit Woolven.

Vocalist S.L. Coe later joined SCANNERS and REACTOR. He was later to issue a creditable solo album in 2000 titled 'Metal'.

ANGEL DUST
Photo : Volker Beushausen

Banx joined Speed Metal band CROWS in 1991 alongside the future SODOM duo of guitarist Bernd Kost and drummer Bobby Schottkowski together with SCANNER's Leczek Szpigiel. The CROWS issued the Century Media album 'The Dying Race' but folded in 1993.

1998 saw the re-formation of ANGEL DUST with the 'Border Of Reality' album for new label Century Media. Joining Banx was his sibling Steven on keyboards, vocalist / guitarist Dirk Thurisch and guitarist Bernd Aufermann.

ANGEL DUST toured Europe in the Spring of 1998 on a package bill with OVERKILL, NOCTURNAL RITES and NEVERMORE. A later jaunt found the band sharing European stages with JAGPANZER and the comeback was completed with appearances at the 'Wacken Open Air' and 'Rock Hard' festivals.

The 'Bleed' album, produced by Siggi Bemm and crafted in less than three weeks, would spread word of ANGEL DUST's resurrection globally. American variants of the album would come complete with differing artwork and no less than three bonus tracks.

ANGEL DUST, marking their growing maturity, issued the 2000 album 'Enlighten The Darkness'. Touring in September to promote the release had the band as part of a package billing in Europe alongside STEEL PROPHET, LEFAY and STORMHAMMER. The following month founder member Dirk Assmuth announced his departure as the band inducted former HOUSE OF SPIRITS man Michael Sticken for live work.

In November ANGEL DUST retired to the recording studio to commit to tape tracks for tribute albums, namely 'Believe' by SAVATAGE and URIAH HEEP's seminal 'Easy Livin'. Thurisch would also find time to guest on the GB ARTS album 'The Lake'.

Aufermann would find his services requested by DEMONS & WIZARDS for live work but turned this offer down. In June of 2001, as the guitarist busied himself with a solo side project dubbed THE SHINING, he would find himself ejected from the band. Ironically his quick fire replacement would be none other than DEMONS & WIZARDS touring guitarist Ritchie Wilkinson. Assmuth would also be welcomed back into the fold as ANGEL DUST got to grips with their debut American shows billed alongside NEVERMORE, OPETH and GOD FORBID.

ANGEL DUST would perform at the 2001 'ProgPower' festival utilising drummer Nick Seelinger of Colorado act SILENCER as stand in. The 2002 album 'Of Human Bondage' would surprisingly include a cover of the SEAL tune 'Killer'.

Albums:
INTO THE DARK PAST, Disaster 10004 (1987)
Into The Dark Past / I'll Come Back / Legions Of Destruction / Gambler / Fighters Return / Atomic Roar / Victims Of Madness / Marching For Revenge
TO DUST YOU WILL DECAY, Disaster 10008 (1988)
Third Challenge / Mr. Inferno / Wings Of An Angel / Into The Dark Past (Chapter II) / The King / To Dust You Will Decay / Stranger / The Duel / Hold On
BORDER OF REALITY, Century Media CD 77220-2 (1998)
Border Of Reality / No More Faith / Nightmare / Centuries / When I Die / Where The Wind Blows / Spotlight Kid / Behind The Mirror / Coming Home
BLEED, Century Media (1999)
Bleed / Black Rain / Never / Follow Me (Part I) / Follow Me (Part II) / Addicted To Serenity / Surrender / Sanity / Liquid Angel
ENLIGHTEN THE DARKNESS, Century Media (2000)
Let Me Live / The One You Are / Enjoy! / Fly Away / Come Into Resistance / Beneath The Silence / Still I'm Bleeding / I Need You / First In Line / Cross of Hatred / Oceans Of Tomorrow
OF HUMAN BONDAGE, Century Media (2002)
The Human Bondage / Inhuman / Unreal Soul / Disbeliever / Last Forever / Unite / Got This Evil / The Cultman / Freedom Awaits / Killer

ANGELWITCH (UK)

Line-Up: Kevin Heybourne (vocals / guitar), Kevin Riddles (bass), Dave Dufort (drums)

A band that generated a cult following among the Metalheads of the American West coast based upon the occult overtones and marked speed and heaviness of their original album recorded with drummer Dave Hogg. Latterly the band has found appreciation amongst the Doom crowd for the acknowledged Sabbathian sounds delivered on their debut album. ANGELWITCH were founded in 1977 by guitarist Kevin Heybourne. Originally titled LUCIFER Heybourne switched to ANGELWITCH when he heard of another LUCIFER doing the rounds. The band went through numerous line-ups before the classic power trio.

The band's official debut on record was the cut 'Baphomet' on the now legendary 'Metal For Muthas' compilation in early 1980. ANGELWITCH also submitted a track 'Extermination Day' to the 1980 BBC compilation album 'Metal Explosion'. Sadly, Hogg was found to be suffering from leukaemia necessitating Ex-E.F. BAND drummer Dave Dufort stepping in as replacement after the album release.

Dufort actually has a lengthy history in rock n' roll being a prior member of 1965's THE VOICE, THE SCENERY and PAPER BLITZ ISSUE. All of these mid '60s acts featured latter day SAVOY BROWN, DOG SOLDIER and CHICKENSHACK guitarist MILLER ANDERSON. Dufort then moved on to EAST OF EDEN in the late '60s (he appears on the 1969 album 'Mercator Projected'), as well as being a member of KEVIN AYERS band.

At the height of their popularity ANGELWITCH ranked alongside IRON MAIDEN and SAXON at the forefront of the NWoBHM. The band's success was relatively short lived though, as gigs became few and far between. British shows were limited to London Marquee appearances and one off events, whilst the only date abroad was at the East German Erfurt Festival.

At one point Polydor were due to release a live album culled from a 1982 show, but this never surfaced. The original band split after the debut with Riddles and Dufort going on to form TYTAN. Riddles was last spotted in a covers band with ex-ONSLAUGHT and TORINO and HIGHWIRE vocalist Tony O'Hora.

The beginning of 1982 saw Heybourne flirting briefly with DEEP MACHINE before persevering by playing the odd club gig as ANGELWITCH featuring DEEP MACHINE members, namely bassist Gerry Cunningham and drummer Micky Bruce.

ANGELWITCH became Heyborne's full time act once more in early 1982 as Cunningham and Bruce were enticed away from DEEP MACHINE along with vocalist Roger Marsden. The line-up was merely a brief tenure, however as Heybourne eventually ended up in BLIND FURY.

Marsden joined Swedish band E.F. BAND then in 1984 forged a union with another ex-ANGELWITCH and E.F. BAND man drummer Dave Dufort to create NEVADDA FOXX.

ANGELWITCH surfaced again in 1985 with Heybourne and Gordelier splitting from BLIND FURY and enrolling original drummer Dave Hogg together with vocalist Dave Tattum. With this incarnation of the band they laid down the quite commercial edged 'Screamin And Bleedin' album. Hogg left the band once more after its release and was replaced by former DEXYS MIDNIGHT RUNNERS drummer Spencer Hollman. Gigs were still few and far between.

Third album 'Frontal Assault' saw ANGELWITCH return to their former heaviness but Tattum left upon its completion to join NIGHTWING leaving Heybourne to assume vocal duties.

In 1989 the band added a second guitarist Grant Dennison. A short tour of Holland followed with support act SATAN, but Heybourne eventually relocated to America where nostalgia for early ANGELWITCH reaped the reward of a live set of 'classics'. The band recorded a demo with EXODUS drummer Tom Hunting and Lee Altus of HEATHEN but failed to secure a new deal.

Although ANGELWITCH failed to live up to the legend that was created around the band early on the band remained an influence with groups that arrived on the scene in later years with both ONSLAUGHT and TROUBLE covering the ANGELWITCH classic 'Confused'.

Interest was renewed in the late '90s by the release of a live album on High Vaultage Records. ANGELWITCH themselves were far from dormant issuing a CD compilation of various demos including the 1987 'Psychopathic' tapes and 1999's set 'Twist Of The Knife'. The resulting album 'Resurrection' was only available via the internet.

ANGELWITCH were back in 2000 for live gigs and a projected new album. Alongside Heybourne the fresh look band comprised guitarist Keith Herzberg, bass player Richie Wicks - a former lead vocalist of SONS OF EDEN and VIOLENTLY FUNKY, and drummer Scott Higham. The band bounced back in quite spectacular style with a performance at the prestigious 'Wacken' Metal festival in Germany before setting to work on fresh studio material.

The list of bands to have covered 'Confused' increased in 2001 as Americans SIX FEET UNDER cut a grindingly heavy take for their latest album. In August of 2001 it was announced that Higham had decamped to join the highly regarded SHADOWKEEP. Ace Finchum, a former member of Glam band TIGERTAILZ, took his place.

In November the ANGELWITCH ranks splintered further with Weeks opting to resume his former role as a lead singer and opting to join fellow NWoBHM resurrectees TYGERS OF PAN TANG. Statements issued by band members in January of 2002 would confirm the fact that ANGELWITCH had folded once again, Wicks resuming action with SONS OF EDEN. However, in August a surprise official statement confirmed that Kevin Heybourne, Keith Herzberg, Richie Wicks and Scott Higham had resolved their differences and were back in action yet again.

Singles/EPs:
Sweet Danger / Flight Nineteen, EMI 5064 (1980) **75 UK**
Sweet Danger / Flight Nineteen / Hades

16

Paradise, EMI 12 EMI 5064 (1980) (12"
single)
Angelwitch / Gorgon, Bronze BRO 108
(1980)
Loser / Suffer / Dr Phibes, Bronze BRO 121
(1981)
Goodbye / Reawakening, Killerwatt KIL
3001(1985)

Albums:
ANGELWITCH, Bronze BRON532 (1981)
Angelwitch / Atlantis / White Witch / Confused
/ Sorcerers / Gorgon / Sweet Danger / Free
Man / Angel Of Death / Devil's Tower
SCREAMIN' AND BLEEDIN', Killerwatt
KILP4001 (1985)
Who's To Blame / Child Of The Night / Evil
Games / Afraid Of The Dark / Screamin' And
Bleedin' / Reawakening / Waltz The Night /
Goodbye / Fatal Kiss / UXB
FRONTAL ASSAULT, Killerwatt Records
(1986)
Frontal Assault / Dreamworld / Rendezvous
With The Blade / Religion (Born Again) /
Straight From Hell / She Don't Lie / Take To
The Wing / Something Wrong / Undergods
DOCTOR PHIBES, Rawpower RAWLP025
(1986)
Angelwitch / Atlantis / White Witch /
Confused / Sorceress / Loser / Dr. Phibes /

Gorgon / Sweet Danger / Free Man / Angel
Of Death / Devil's Tower / Suffer
LIVE, Metal Blade ZORRO 1 (1990)
Angel Of Death / Sweet Danger / Confused /
Sorceress / Gorgon / Baphomet /
Extermination Day / Atlantis / Flight 19 /
Angel Witch / White Witch
'82 REVISITED (LIVE), High Vaultage HV-
1005 (1996)
Gorgon / Nowhere To Run / They Wouldn't
Dare / Sorceress / Evil Games / White Witch /
Angel Of Death / Angel Witch / Evil Games
(Studio Version) / They Wouldn't Dare (Studio
Version) / Nowhere To Run (Studio Version)
RESURRECTION, Angelwitch (1998)
Psychopathic I / Time To Die / Violence /
Silent But Deadly / Twist Of The Knife /
Psychopathic II / Slowly Sever / Worm /
Scrape The Well / Inertia

ANGRA (BRAZIL)
Line-Up: Andre Matos (vocals), Kiko Loureiro
(guitar), Rafael Bittencourt (guitar), Luis
Mariutti (bass), Ricardo Confessori (drums)

ANGRA rank alongside SEPULTURA as
Brazil's biggest Hard Rock export., fronted for
many years, by erstwhile VIPER vocalist
Andre Matos, ANGRA boast complex
Progressive Rock within a definite hard hitting

ANGRA

Metal framework. Titled after an ancient fire goddess, the band was convened during 1991 and saw Matos joined by the ex-SPITFIRE duo of guitarist Rafael Bittencourt and drummer Marco Antunes, former FIREBOX bassist Luis Marutti and second guitar player Kiko Loureiro. This unit debuted with the grandiose 'Reaching Horizons' demo. The 'Angels Cry' album, which boasted an adventurous cover version of KATE BUSH's 'Wuthering Heights', was recorded at GAMMA RAY guitarist Kai Hansen's studios in Hamburg, Germany. Both GAMMA RAY guitarists Kai Hansen and Dirk Schlächter contribute solos, as does HEAVEN'S GATE's Sascha Paeth. Studio drums are by SIEGES EVEN man Alex Holzwarth. Shortly after recording Antunes would make way for new drummer Ricardo Confessori.

The album, issued in Brazil during 1993, proved a runaway success and in Japan alone succeeded in shifting over 100,000 copies. Videos for 'Time' and 'Carry On' would remain on heavy Brazilian MTV rotation for many months. ANGRA would dominate the polls of the leading Brazilian 'Rock Brigade' magazine scooping awards for 'Best new band', 'Best album', 'Best singer', 'Best album cover' and 'Best keyboard player'. In Japan a special EP was issued comprising remixed versions of 'Evil Warning', 'Angels Cry', 'Carry On' and 'Wuthering Heights'. 'Angels Cry' would be licensed to Europe through Dream Circle, and C.N.R. in France, the following year reaping yet further praise.

ANGRA formed part of the package billing for the inaugural Brazilian 'Monsters Of Rock' festivals, sharing the stage with KISS, BLACK SABBATH and SLAYER. Touring Brazil proved equally successful for the band, selling out the enormous Sao Paulo Aeroanta venue for two consecutive nights in the process. By May of 1995 ANGRA hit the road in Europe.

The 1996 'Holy Land' album, an ambitious concept involving choirs and orchestration once more produced by Sascha Paeth and Charlie Bauerfiend, saw increased sales on mainland Europe and in Brazil. The Japanese Victor release included a bonus track 'Queen Of The Night'. The mini-album of the same year 'Freedom Call' included a cover version of JUDAS PRIEST's 'Painkiller'. 'Holy Live', recorded in Paris, sustaining the momentum into 1997.

1998's 'Fireworks' was produced by Chris Tsangerides. A lengthy world tour opened up with Brazilian headline shows before the band's debut Japanese shows then an appearance at the Buenos Aires 'Monsters Of Rock' festival. 2000 bowed in with European shows with Italian act TIME MACHINE as support then co-headliners with STRATOVARIUS. At their Milan gig Lucretia Records, ANGRA's Italian distributor gave out 1,000 free CDs with two tracks by ANGRA and two from TIME MACHINE. 1998 also witnessed the issue of 'The Holy Box', a lavish limited edition box set released by Lucretia Records and including exclusive acoustic tracks.

ANGRA split in two during mid 2000 with Matos, Mariutti and Confessori all bailing out. Matos reportedly began work on a solo project VIRGO in Germany. Later announcements had the entire trio working together under a new band name of SHAMAN. Loureiro took time out to produce the debut album from countrymen THOTEN.

As 2001 dawned it emerged that Loureiro and Bittencourt were endeavouring to persevere as ANGRA drafting former SYMBOLS vocalist Eduardo Falaschi and drummer Aquiles Priester, the latter being from the PAUL DIANNO band. A latter recruit was keyboard player Gunther Werno who has previous credits with Norwegian act CONCEPTION. Meantime, former ANGRA bassist Felipe Andreolli would join KARMA in 2001. ANGRA's resurrection opus 'Rebirth' won over fans in consummate style and by February of 2002 the album had shifted over 100,000 copies. European headline dates commenced in Nancy, France on the 26th February. A mini-album, 'Hunters And Prey', arrived in May of 2002 including acoustic takes plus a cover version of 'Mama' originally by GENESIS. Live dates found ANGRA in Japan during June with appearances at the 'Rock Machine' festival in Spain, the famed 'Wacken Open Air' event in Germany and the Atlanta, Georgia 'ProgPower' festival. The band would also lay claim to the honour of being the very first South American Rock band to play Taiwan, playing a show in Taipei on June 14th.

Kiko Loureiro would guest session on the 2002 BLEZQI ZATSAZ album 'The Tide Turns', paradoxically the project band of SHAMAN keyboard player Fabio Riberio.

ANGRA had their version of 'Kashmir' included on the Locomotive Music LED ZEPPELIN tribute album 'The Metal Zeppelin — The Music Remains The Same'.

Singles/EPs:
Freedom Call / Queen Of The Night (Remix) / Reaching Horizons / Stand Away (Orchestral Version) / Painkiller (remix) / Deep Blue (Edit), Rising Sun 35885-3 (1996)
Angels Cry (Live) / Chega De Saudade (Live) / Never Understand (Live), (1999) (Japanese release)
Evil Warning ('94 version) / Angels Cry ('94

version) / Carry On ('94 version) / Wuthering Heights (Edit) / Time (Demo version), Rising Sun (2001)

Albums:
ANGELS CRY, Rising Sun 35897 (1993)
Unfinished Allegro / Carry On / Time / Angels Cry / Stand Away / Never Understand / Wuthering Heights / Streets Of Tomorrow / Evil Warning / Lasting Child - a) The Parting Words, b) Renaissance
HOLY LAND, Rising Sun 34601-422 (1996)
Crossing / Nothing To Say / Silence And Distance / Carolina IV / Holy Land / The Shaman / Make Believe / Z:I:T:O / Deep Blue / Lullaby For Lucifer
FIREWORKS, SPV 085-18482 CD (1998) **41 FRANCE**
Of Reality / Petrified Eyes / Lisbon / Metal Icarus / Paradise / Mystery Machine / Fireworks / Extreme Dream / Gentle Change / Speed
REBIRTH, SPV, (2001) **74 FRANCE**
In Excelsis / Nova Era / Millennium Sun / Acid Rain / Heroes Of Sand / Unholy Wars (Part 1 - Imperial Crown) / Unholy Wars (Part 2 - Forgiven Return) / Rebirth / Judgement Day / Running Alone / Visions Prelude
HUNTERS AND PREY, (2002)
Live And Learn / Bleeding Heart / Hunters And Prey / Eyes Of Christ / Rebirth (Acoustic version) / Heroes Of Sand (Acoustic version) / Mama / Hunters And Prey (Portuguese version)

ANGUS (HOLLAND)
Line-Up: Edgar Lois (vocals), Bert Foxx Ettema (guitar), Mike Schults (bass), William Lawson (drums)

Amsterdam thundering Metal band ANGUS, named after an affection for both the famous AC/DC guitarist and a hardy breed of Scottish cattle, came together in the Spring of 1983. The first foursome to brandish the ANGUS title comprised vocalist Edgar Lois, guitarist Ed Sprey, bass player Gerard Carol and drummer William Lawson. With various members having been classically trained the sound on their 1984 demo tape stood them apart from the plethora of other Euro Metal acts.
ANGUS debuted with two tracks 'Aliens' and 'Lonesome Fighter' included on the 1985 Power Tower compilation 'The Heavy Touch', sharing vinyl with acts such as REVENGE, WIZZARD, VULTURE, SCARFACE and LOST GRAVITY. The line up for these sessions comprised vocalist Edgar Lois, guitarists Bert Foxx Ettema and Jack Winder, bass player Gerard Carol and drummer

William Lawson.
ANGUS' debut album 'Track Of Doom' surfaced on the Megaton label during 1986. By this time the band was down to a quartet with the departure of Winder. 'Track Of Doom' fared well, even charting in Poland and seeing a North American license through the Restless label. However, Gerard Carol was forced out of the band due to medical problems. The group, now including Mike Shults on bass and with all four unafraid to sport women's lingerie in press photos, would spoof MADONNA the following year with the 'Papa Don't Freak' 12" single.
For the 1987 John Tilly produced album 'Warriors Of The World' ANGUS employed Andre Versluys to handle bass guitar in the studio whilst Mike Shults took over for live work. Although ANGUS was certainly in the ascendant Lawson quit in 1988 and the band promptly folded.
In 2001 ANGUS had the track 'When Giants Collide' included on the compilation album 'Heavy Metal Maniacs'. Also featured on this record would be the HEAVY METAL MANIACS band with two compositions 'Little Bitch' and 'Hungry For Power'. This band actually included ANGUS drummer William Lawson alongside EMERALD vocalist Bert Kivits, HAMMERHAWK guitarist Paul van Rijswijk, VORTEX guitarist Martjo Brongers and GODDESS OF DESIRE bass player Harm Noort.
The US specialist Metal label Sentinel Steel re-issued both 'Track Of Doom' and 'Warrior Of The World' as a two-in-one release. Interest in ANGUS was further piqued with the Steelhunter label's collection of rarities 'Metal Warriors'.
ANGUS are once more a going concern with Lawson and Foxx recruiting former HURRICANE and DEVIL'S ROPE vocalist Jay Cee in April of 2001.

Singles/EPs:
Papa Don't Freak (Long version) / Papa Don't Freak (Single version) / Papa Don't Freak (Guitar dub version), Megaton 1219 (1987) (12" single)

Albums:
TRACK OF DOOM, Megaton 0017 (1986)
The Centaur / When Giants Collide / Track Of Doom / Heavyweight Warrior / Finally Out / The Gates, / Dragon Chase / Lost Control
WARRIOR OF THE WORLD, Megaton 0020LP (1987)
Warrior Of The World / Moving Fast / Leather And Lace / Money Satisfies / Black Despair / 2086 / Freedom Fighter / I'm A Fool With Love / If God's In Heaven (Why Is There Hell

19

On Earth)
TRACK OF DOOM / WARRIOR OF THE WORLD, Sentinel Steel (2001)
The Centaur / When Giants Collide / Track Of Doom / Heavyweight Warrior / Finally Out / The Gates / Dragon Chase / Lost Control / Warrior Of The World / Moving Fast / Leather And Lace / Money Satisfies / Black Despair / 2086 / Freedom Fighter / If God's In Heaven (Why Is There Hell On Earth?)
METAL WARRIORS, Steelhunter SHR-002 (2002)
Ruthless Men / Keep On Shouting / Aliens / 2086 / Lonesome Fighter / When Giants Collide / Virgin Girl / Leading You Back / Night Fight

ANKHARA (SPAIN)
Line-Up: Pacho Brea (vocals), Antonio Pino (guitar), Cecilio Sanchez (guitar), Sergio Martinez (bass), Jesus Alcalde (drums)

ANKHARA are a Spanish Power Progressive Metal band founded in 1995. ANKHARA garnered national media coverage appearing on their first tour throughout Spain with the 'Duro Con El 98' festival. Following this run of dates the band toured throughout Spain again, this time as support to SAXON.
Their debut album ´Dueño Del Tiempo´ was released in 1999. In February 2001 sophomore effort 'Ankhara II' arrived.

Albums:
DUENO DEL TIEMPO, Locomotive Music (1999)
3:40 / Demasiado Tarde / Un Paso Mas / Frio Infierno / Un Paso Mas / No Mires Atras / Mente Atormentada / Junto Al Viento / En Mis Manos / Aqui Estoy / Nunca Mueras Por Un Sueño
ANKHARA II, Locomotive Music (2001)
Jamás / Mundo De Odio / Entre Tinieblas / Océanos De Lágrimas / No Digas Nunca / Buscando Mi Camino / Quema Tu Miedo / Junto A Mi / Una Vez Más / Tu Sangriento Pasado / Ankhara

ANNIHILATOR (CANADA)
Line-Up: Joe Comeau (vocals), Jeff Waters (guitar), Curran Murphy (guitar), David Scott (bass), Randy Black (drums)

Vancouver based straight down the line Heavy Metal band first coming to attention with their opening 1984 'Psycho Metal Kids' tape. Guitarist and band mentor Jeff Waters is known for infusing his band with a creative edge personified by his inventive riffing style. Prior to founding ANNIHILATOR guitarist Jeff Waters had been a member of TROJAN HAMMER. Featuring a line-up of Waters, vocalist John Perinbam, bass player Kevin Jung and drummer Mike Lane TROJAN HAMMER only managed two gigs, at the Churchill Arms. Waters and Perinbam also assembled a recording project, along with drummer Mike Farmer, dubbed THE JEFF WATERS PROJECT prior to assembling the first ANNIHILATOR line-up.
At this stage ANNIHILATOR was basically a duo of vocalist / guitarist Jeff Waters and bassist David Scott. In 1985 the band demoed once more resulting in 'Welcome To Your Death' which saw John Bates on vocals and Richard Death on drums. This line-up soon folded and a further demo 'Phantasmogoria' with Paul Malek on drums landed the band a deal with Roadrunner Records.
ANNIHILATOR's traditional approach to Metal gave them prominence toward the end of the Thrash boom and their debut 1989 album 'Alice In Hell' won them many converts. The band's main personalities were the peroxide maned hard drinking ex-D.O.A. bassist RANDY RAMPAGE and songwriter Waters. D.O.A. had been a renowned act, which also provided the launch platform for BLACK FLAG and DANZIG drummer Chuck Biscuits. Pre ANNIHILATOR Rampage had also issued a solo album.
Although guitarist Anthony Greenham, bassist Wayne Darley and former ASSAULT drummer Ray Hartmann are credited on the debut ANNIHILATOR album they did not take part in recording as Waters himself laid down all the instrumentation. Previous to the album a rhythm guitarist Casey Toews joined ANNIHILATOR but was out within days.
Despite rapid progress, ructions within the band found Rampage out much to fans chagrin. Second guitarist Anthony Greenham also made way for Dave Scott Davis for 1990's 'Never Neverland'. PANTHER singer Coburn Pharr took the vocal position, as ANNIHILATOR seemed poised on the edge of becoming a major act. Meantime, drummer Paul Malek would opt out too, creating IVORY KNIGHT alongside former Waters compatriot singer John Perinbam, for the demo 'Voices In Your Nightmare'.
Waters still had his eye on potential recognition outside of the band though as he auditioned for MEGADETH in 1990. According to Dave Mustaine Waters came close to securing the position but it was not to be.
ANNIHILATOR grabbed the much sought after support slot to JUDAS PRIEST's 'Painkiller' British tour. Further line-up changes slowed progress with 1993's 'Set The World On Fire' seeing another singer in

Aaron Randall (Pharr now fronting OMEN) and Neil Goldberg supplanting Davis. The single from the album featured a reworking of JUDAS PRIEST's 'Hell Bent For Leather'.

Mike Mangini occupied the drum stool during this period of flux before he bailed out to join EXTREME in time for their 1994 Castle Donington festival appearance. Further line-up shuffles continued and ANNIHILATOR in 1994, now minus their deal with Roadrunner, had Waters with a reunited Davis, bassist Cam Dixon and drummer Randy Black.

By 1996 ANNIHILATOR had effectively trimmed down to a duo of Waters and Black. Contributing musicians to the 'Refresh The Demon' album included guitarist Davis and bassist Lou Bujdoso.

Waters took time out from his main act to guest on rather more mellow outings including POKERFACE's 1996 album 'Life's A Gamble' and the following year's self-titled effort from THE DISTANCE.

By the 1997 effort, the suitably titled 'Remains', ANNIHILATOR had become Waters solo project. Contributing musicians included guitarist John Bates.

1999 had the band bowing to fan pressure and reinstating Rampage for the much lauded 'Criteria For A Black Widow' album. Randall meantime had founded SPEEED with SEVEN WITCHES / FROSTBITE guitarist Jack Frost for their 1999 album 'Powertrip Pigs'.

Ex-LIEGE LORD and OVERKILL man Joe Comeau joined the band in 2000. Comeau would divert himself in late 2000 for a one-off reunion with his erstwhile LIEGE LORD guitar partner Paul Nelson to cut a version of 'Too Scared To Run' for a URIAH HEEP tribute album.

February of 2001 found ANNIHILATOR on a headlining tour of Germany supported by a strong billing of NEVERMORE, SOILWORK and RAWHEAD REXX. Drummer Ray Hartman would bow out in favour of a returning Randy Black. The returning drummer had also been busying himself with an ambitious German based conceptual project band entitled REBELLION. Fronted by erstwhile XIRON and BLACK DESTINY vocalist Michael Seifert REBELLION had been established by ex-GRAVE DIGGER men guitarist Uwe Lulis and bassist Tommi Göttlich, Black as drummer and with WARHEAD's Bjorn Eilen on second guitar. This unit issued the Shakespeare inspired 'A Tragedy In Steel' debut in March of 2002.

Throughout the latter half of 2001 ANNIHILATOR would be in preparation for a new studio album provisionally billed 'Waking The Fury' and slated for a March 2002 release through SPV/Steamhammer. The European version came complete with a bonus live recording of 'Shallow Grave' whilst Japanese variants added a live 'Refresh The Demon', recorded in Rumania.

During November guitarist Curran Murphy of AGGRESSION CORE and NEVERMORE joined the ranks. However, bassist David Scott would be forced out of the band due to injury. ANNIHILATOR announced European tour dates for April / May 2002, commencing in Vienna, Austria, backed up with strong support from SEVEN WITCHES and DEBASE.

In an odd twist of events Waters would end up joining the veteran epic Power Metal band SAVATAGE for their summer European 2002 dates. Al Pitrelli, SAVATAGE's regular and then only recently re-inducted six stringer, was unable to make the tour due to prior commitments.

Singles/EPs:
Stonewall / W.T.Y.D. (Live) / Word Salad (Live), Roadrunner RR 24256 (1991)
Set The World On Fire / Hell Bent For Leather, Roadrunner RR 23856 (1993)
I'll Show You My Gun, Mokum (1994)

Albums:
ALICE IN HELL, Roadrunner (1989)
Crystal Ann / W.T.Y.D. / Burns Like Buzzsaw Blade / Schizos (Are Never Alone) (Parts I & II) / Human Incesticide / Alison Hell / Wicked Mystic / Word Salad / Ligeia
NEVER NEVERLAND, Roadrunner RR 93742 (1990) **48 UK**
The Fun Palace / Road To Ruin / Sixes And Sevens / Stonewall / Never, Neverland / Imperilled Eyes / Kraf Dinner / Phantasmagoria / Reduced To Ash / I Am In Command
SET THE WORLD ON FIRE, Roadrunner RR 92002 (1993)
Set The World On Fire / No Zone / Bats In The Belfry / Snake In The Grass / Phoenix Rising / Knight Jumps Queen / Sounds Good To Me / The Edge / Don't Bother Me / Brain Dance
BAG OF TRICKS, Roadrunner RR 8997-2 (1994)
Alison Hell / Phantasmagoria / Back To The Crypt / Gallery / Human Insecticide / Fun Palace / WTYD/ Word Salad / Live Wire / Knight Jumps Queen / Fantastic Things / Bats In The Belfry / Evil Appetite / Gallery '86 / Alison Hell '86 / Phantasmagoria '86
KING OF THE HILL, Music For Nations MFN171 (1994)
Box / King Of The Hill / Hell Is A War / Bliss / Second To None / Annihilator / 21 / In The Blood / Fiasco (Slate) / Fiasco / Catch The Wind / Speed / Bad Child
REFRESH THE DEMON, Music For Nations

MFNCD 197 (1996)
Refresh The Demon / Syn. Kill 1/ Awaken / The Pastor Of Disaster / A Man Called Nothing / Ultraparanoia / City Of Ice / Anything For Money / Hunger / Voices And Victims / Innocent Eyes
IN COMMAND LIVE 1989, Roadrunner RR 8852-2 (1996)
W.T.Y.D. / Wicked Mystic / Ligeia / Alison Hell / Word Salad / W.T.Y.D. / The Fun Palace / Never, Neverland / I Am In Command / Stonewall / Road To Ruin / Sixes And Sevens / Alison Hell / Live Wire
REMAINS, Music For Nations CDMFN 228 (1997)
Murder / Sexecution / No Love / Never / Human Remains / Dead Wrong / Wind / Tricks And Traps / I Want / Reaction / Bastiage
CRITERIA FOR A BLACK WIDOW, Roadrunner RR 8640 (1999)
Bloodbath / Back To The Palace / Punctured / Criteria For A Black Widow / Schitzo / Nothing Left / Loving The Sinner / Double Dare / Sonic / Mending
CARNIVAL DIABLO, Roadrunner (2000)
Time Bomb / Battered / The Perfect Virus / Carnival Diablo / Shallow Grave / Denied / The Rush / Insomniac / Liquid Oval / Epic Of War / Hunter Killer / Chicken And Corn
WAKING THE FURY, Roadrunner (2002)
My Precious Lunatic Asylum / Nothing To Me / Ritual / Striker / The Blackest Day / Cold Blooded / Torn / Fire Power / Ultra-Motion / Prime-Time Killing
DOUBLE LIVE ANNIHILATION, (2003)
Murder / Ultra Motion / The Box / Denied / The Blackest Day / King Of The Kill / Torn / Lunatic Asylum / Set The World On Fire / I Am In Command / Refresh The Demon / Syn. Kill 1 / Never, Neverland / Striker / Bliss / Phantasmagoria / Crystal Ann / Alison Hell / Shallow Grave

ANNON VIN (GERMANY)
Line-Up: Erik Grösch (vocals / guitar), Tom Brenneis (vocals / bass), Uwe Ruppel (vocals /drums)

Formed in 1989, ProgMetal act ANNON VIN comprise three vocalists. The trio mix their voices with some extremely complex instrumentation and released their debut, self-produced EP in 1993.
1996 saw the arrival of the band's debut album, 'A New Gate', produced by Ralph Hubert and including an unexpected cover of the STYX track 'Mr. Roboto'. ANNON VIN supported RAGE and STRATOVARIOUS in Offenbach later the same year.

Albums:
A NEW GATE, Zardoz IRDCD 995.202 (1996)
White, Red - Not Rotten Yet / Today's Heroes / Remind The Differences / One Word / Somewhere In Life: i) Reality, ii) Wishes, iii) Love / A Spark, A Drop And The Universe / Higher Spheres / Invisible Scars / Mr. Roboto

ANTARES (POLAND)
Line-Up: Jaroslaw Drag (vocals), Roman Wrobel (guitar), Aleksander Gawrylarz (guitar), Rafal Majchrowski (bass), Marcin Magiera (drums)

Wroclaw Heavy Metal formation put together in July of 1999 by guitarist / vocalist Roman Wrobel and drummer Marcin Magiera, shortly after adding bass player Rafal Majchrowski. During these formative stages ANTARES went through a succession of temporary lead vocalists. The group cut a demo in October of 2000 as the trio of Wrobel, Majchrowski and Magiera. A further tape, 'Whip Of Life', followed in November.
In March of 2001 lead vocalist Jaroslaw Drag joined up and in April second guitarist Krzysztof Radomski. However, this latest member would decamp before the summer was out. Nevertheless, ANTARES still managed to record an EP 'Run Away' in September, promoting this product with support gigs to ACID DRINKERS and TURBO in the December.
ANTARES added guitarist Aleksander Gawrylarz in February of 2002.

Singles/EPs:
Private Angel / Whip Of Life / Shutting The Door / Hard Like Stone / Run Away, (2001) ('Run Away' EP)

ANTITHESIS (Cleveland, OH, USA)
Line-Up: Ty Cook (vocals), Sean Perry (guitar), Tom Guignette (guitar), Jim Lewis (bass), Paul Kostyack (drums)

Cleveland Christian Heavy Metal act of some repute dating back to 1997. Although far from shy in delivering technically inclined, thundering Progressive Heavy Metal, ANTITHESIS steer clear of any war mongering, hatred, the occult or negativity in their lyrics. Guitarists Sean Perry and Paul Konjicija convened the band, the remaining members being recruited through musician want ads in a local free newspaper. By October of the same year, St. Louis native bass player Jim Lewis had joined. Vocalist Ty Cook was the next onboard, ANTITHESIS being rounded off with the addition of drummer Paul Kostyack in February of 1998. Later that year the band entered the recording studio to self-finance their debut eponymous album. The record would be issued through the Danish Intromental Management concern during February of 1999 with a print run of 1000 copies which soon sold out. However, in April Konjicija decamped, ANTITHESIS drafting Tom Guignette as substitute. With their new guitarist in place the band quite remarkably re-recorded the entire album, gave the record an entirely new packaging and re-marketed it in November of the same year.

Guignette left the band in October 1999, his replacement being none other than former member Paul Konjicija.

Albums:
ANTITHESIS, Voice Of Wonder (1999)
Netherworld / Breeding The Beast / Limbo / Sword Of Mouth / The Web / Secret Fires / Plastic / The Curse / Descend
DYING FOR LIFE, Massacre (2001)
Consequence / Soul Of Ice / Times Of Trial / Deceiver Within / Distanced / Mad Poet / Politicide / Dying For Life / Netherworld / Secret Fires

ANVIL (CANADA)

Line-up: Lips (vocals / guitar), Dave Allison (guitar), Ian Dickson (bass), Robb Reiner (drums)

Originally known as LIPS upon their formation in 1978, the first ANVIL album was originally issued under the LIPS handle. ('Lips' is the stage name of front man Steve Kudlow). The debut album was in fact intended to be purely demo material but as an enterprising unit and eager to recoup their recording costs the band issued 1,000 vinyl copies on their own Splash label.

Still as LIPS the outfit's initiative came to the attention of Attic records who quickly re-released the album although now under the band name of ANVIL due to protestations from disco act LIPPS INC.

An uncompromising slab of heaviness, 'Hard And Heavy' was the first in line not only to demonstrate the band's adherence to full on metal but also to their obsession with sex. Tracks such as 'Bondage' and 'School Love' being prime examples. Onstage Lips would cultivate press coverage too by performing lead guitar solos with the aid of a vibrator!

ANVIL made their first foray onto the live scene in Canada with a bunch of club shows leading to the nation-wide support to GIRLSCHOOL. Mainman Lips did take time out though to produce a demo for KRAKEN.

1982's 'Metal On Metal' boasted the unique honour of having the track 'Mothra' being recorded by Lips using a vibrator on his guitar rather than the more usual plectrum. The follow up 'Forged In Fire', an equally heavyweight offering, increased the band's stature worldwide.

ANVIL went into the studio in 1985 to cut demos with producer Ric Browde. A strange choice for ANVIL as Browde's credits include lighter acts such as POISON. Songs recorded were 'Rockin', 'Mad Dog', World's Apart' and 'Straight Between The Eyes'.

Allison, after recording the 'Pound For Pound' album, quit in 1989 prompting a period of inactivity for the band. They bounced back signed to the Belgian label Mausoleum and Canadian label Maximum for the 1992 'Worth The Weight' album with new guitarist Sebastian Marino in tow. Following the album release ANVIL pulled in bassist Mike Duncan. Guitarist Sebastian Marino made himself busy with RAMROD cutting two demos in 1994 prior to teaming up with cult New York Speed Metal merchants OVERKILL for their 1997 effort 'From The Underground And Below'. Marino had also found time to produce the 1996 album by DEVESTATOR.

With Germany's fascination in the late '90s for early '80s cult metal acts ANVIL made a return to the touring circuit undertaking dates with FLOTSAM AND JETSAM and fellow Canucks EXCITER. The band rounded off 1998 by performing at the long established 'Wacken Open Air' festival in Germany.

ANVIL at this juncture in their career included the lynchpin of Lips, original drummer Rob Reiner and new faces guitarist Ivan Hurd and bassist Glenn Five (real name Gyorffy).

Meantime English Metal crew BENEDICTION had covered 'Forged In Fire' for their 1992 album 'Dark Is The Season'. TUNGSTEN also paid tribute to the same song on their 1996 album '183.85'.

ANVIL toured Germany in early 2000 sharing a package bill with RIOT, AGENT STEEL and DOMINE.

German Massacre label variants of the 2001 album 'Plenty Of Power' differed to Canadian distributed CDs in having the final exclusive track as 'Dirty Dorothy'. The Hypnotic Canadian imprint replaced this song with 'Left Behind'.

Marino and his colleagues in the RAMROD rhythm section took to the stage at the German 'Wacken Open Air' festival the same year as part of a reunion line-up of LIEGE LORD.

ANVIL would be scheduling a new album, 'Still Going Strong', for release through Massacre Records in June of 2002. The band headlined the Montreal 'Powerpack' festival on November 8th, topping a bill over Powerpack, HANKER, HEAVEN'S CRY and SOULFORGE.

Singles/EPs:
School Love / Paint It Black, Polydor (1981) (Japanese Release)
Steamin' / Tease Me, Please Me / Jackhammer / Stop Me, Noir MET 12 001 (1982)
Make It Up To You / Metal On Metal, Noir MET12 002 (1983)

Albums:
HARD AND HEAVY, Attic LAT 1100 (1981)
School Love / AC/DC / At The Apartment / I Want You Both (With Me) / Bedroom Game / Ooh Baby / Paint It Black / Oh Jane / Hot Child / Bondage
METAL ON METAL, Attic LAT 1130 (1982)
Metal On Metal / Mothra / Stop Me / March Of The Crabs / Jackhammer / Heat Sink / Tag Team / Scenery / Tease Me, Please Me / 666
FORGED IN FIRE, Attic LAT 1170 (1983)
Forged In Fire / Shadow Zone / Free As The Wind / Never Deceive Me / Butter Bust Jerky / Future Wars / Hard Times – Fast Ladies / Make It Up To You / Motormount / Winged Assassins
BACKWAXED, Roadrunner RR 9776 (1985)
Pussy Poison / Back Waxed / Steamin' / You're A Liar / Fryin' Cryin' / Metal On Metal / Butter Bust Jerky / Scenery / Jackhammer / School Love
STRENGTH OF STEEL, Roadrunner RR 9618 (1987)
Strength Of Steel / Concrete Jungle / 9-2-5 / I Dreamed It Was The End Of The World / Flight Of The Bumble Beast / Cut Loose / Mad Dog / Straight Between The Eyes / Wild Eyes / Kiss Of Death / Paper General
POUND FOR POUND, Metal Blade 73336 (1988)
Blood On The Ice / Corporate Preacher / Toe Jam / Safe Sex / Where Does All The Money Go? / Brain Burn / Senile King / Machine King / Fire In The Night / Cramps
PAST AND PRESENT LIVE, Roadracer RO 94532 (1989)
Concrete Jungle / Toe Jam / Motornaut / Forged In Fire / Blood On The Ice / March Of The Crabs / Jack Hammer / Metal On Metal / Winged Assassins / 666 / Mothra
WORTH THE WEIGHT, Mausoleum 904 004-2 (1991)
Infanticide / On The Way To Hell / Bushpig / Embalmer / Pow Wow / Sins Of The Flesh / AZ 85 / Sadness / Love Me When I'm Dead
PLUGGED IN PERMANENT, Massacre (1996)

Racial Hostility / Doctor Kevorkian / Smokin' Green / Destined For Doom / Killer Hill / Face Pull / I'm Trying To Sleep Five Knuckle Shuffle / Truth Or Consequence / Guilty
ABSOLUTELY NO ALTERNATIVE, Massacre MASCD0134 (1997)
Old School / Green Jesus / Show Me Your Tits / No One To Follow / Hair Pie / Rubber Neck / Piss Test / Red Light / Black Or White / Hero By Death
SPEED OF SOUND, Massacre MAS C00173 (1998)
Speed Of Sound / Blood In The Playground / Deadbeat Dad / Man Over Board / No Evil / Bullshit / Mattress Mambo / Secret Agent / Life To Lead / Park That Truck
CLASSIX SHAPE VOL. 10, Massacre MAS SH0204 (1999)
Blood On The Ice / Doctor Kevorkian / Old School / Speed Of Sound / Metal On Metal (Live)
ANTHOLOGY OF ANVIL, Hypnotic (2000)
Metal On Metal / Smokin' Green / Winged Assassins / Free As The Wind / Old School / Bushpig / Blood On The Ice / March Of The Crabs / Jackhammer / Speed Of Sound / 666 / Stolen / Paper General / Forged In Fire (Live) / School Love / Motormount / Doctor Kevorkian / Mothra
PLENTY OF POWER, Hypnotic HYP 1079 (2001)
Plenty Of Power / Groove Science / Ball Of Fire / The Creep / Computer Drone / Beat The Law Pro Wrestling / Siren Of The Sea / Disgruntled / Real Metal / Left Behind

ANVIL CHORUS
(San Francisco, CA, USA)
Line-Up: Aaron Zimpel (vocals), Thaen Rassmussen (guitar), Douglas Piercy (guitar), Bill Skinner (bass), Gere Fennelly (keyboards), Joe Bennett (drums)

Formed from the ashes of the Progressive Rock band LEVIATHAN and other Bay Area groups, assorted members of the defunct San Franciscan bands began jamming with another local act HEAD ON. The story has it that HEAD ON's manager was impressed enough to offer the guys a support slot to HEAD ON in 1982.
Adopting the name ANVIL CHORUS, the new group not only played the HEAD ON show but also opened up for MÖTLEY CRÜE's earliest forays into Northern California. Other ANVIL CHORUS gigs had METALLICA as the opening act. Early rehearsals were held with Rassmussen, Piercy bassist Grant Williams, drummer Michael Hegos and vocalist Tim Montana.
By early 1982 ANVIL CHORUS comprised ex-LEVIATHAN vocalist Aaron Zimpel,

guitarists Thaen Rasmussen (ex-VY-KING) and Doug Piercy (ex-COBRA and DELTA), bassist Bill Skinner and drummer Ken Farragen (both previously with LEVIATHAN). The latter was eventually replaced by Joe Bennett, Farragen seemingly having ideas to become a policeman. Gere Fennelly, Rasmussen's girlfriend and a member of BLEU FOOD, was brought in on keyboards.

There were strong links between ANVIL CHORUS and the Seattle Metal band METAL CHURCH, Aaron Zimple (a.k.a. Aaron Whymer) having played drums on some early demos. Both bands would also play the old LEVIATHAN track 'Red Skies' in their live sets.

METAL CHURCH mainman Kurdt Vanderhoof had once been in the San Franciscan Punk band THE LEWD and had formed METAL CHURCH with ex-LEVIATHAN guitarist Rick Condran, Aaron Whymer and bassist Steve Haat. For the group's first demo the act was titled ANVIL CHORUS - THE CHURCH OF METAL. When this early incarnation of METAL CHURCH folded Whymer took the name ANVIL CHORUS. The links between the two acts remained though as ANVIL CHORUS paid homage with their track 'Bow To The Church Of Metal'.

Despite strong sales of the ANVIL CHORUS single 'Blondes In Black', especially in Europe as an import, ANVIL CHORUS never released further product and drifted into a more keyboard orientated direction. Although Warner Brothers expressed some form of interest in the band, the Bay Area band faded into oblivion.

Fennelly and Zimpel quit in 1985. Piercy, having produced demos for LEGACY (later to be re-titled TESTAMENT) and EXODUS wished to pursue harder material and joined CONTROL. After CONTROL's second guitarist Dino Carvosia bailed out Rasmussen joined the ranks of CONTROL too in a line-up comprising the two ex-ANVIL CHORUS guitarists with vocalist Ed Bull, bassist Michael Thinger and drummer Eric Rasmussen (no relation). When the latter departed another ANVIL CHORUS refugee Joe Bennett joined.

Doug Piercy would appear with HEATHEN. For HEATHEN's second album the band re-cut the ANVIL CHORUS track 'Guitarmony' with a guesting Rasmussen. Percy quit HEATHEN in 1991 for ANGELWITCH and the German based THE COMPANY. Gere Fennelli toured with RED KROSS circa the band's 'PhaseShifter' tour.

ANVIL CHORUS reformed for a one-off San Francisco gig in 1987 opening for EXODUS and MEGADETH at the Kabuki venue. Rasmussen founded an ANVIL CHORUS II in

the '90s with ex-RELEASE man Steve Kilgore, bassist Ryan Connor and the now jailed Dan Brian. His later work included Pop act PORCELAIN.

Rasmussen and Piercy formed part of the HEATHEN re-formation in 2000.

Singles/EPs:
Blondes In Black / Once Again, Leviathan (1982)

ARACHNES (ITALY)
Line-Up: Enzo Caruso (vocals), Franco Caruso (guitar), Paulo Casalini (bass), Graziano Rampazzo (drums)

ARACHNES

Power Metal band centred upon the sibling talents of vocalist Enzo Caruso and guitar player Franco Caruso. ARACHNES, previous to their 1997 debut album for Lucretia Records 'The Goddess Temple', operated under the name of FIREHOUSE releasing the album 'Labyrinth'. For their first album 'The Goddess Temple' the ARACHNES rhythm section would consist of bassist Paulo Casalini and drummer Stefano Caironi. The band would switch to the Underground Symphony label for the 2000 mini-album 'Metamorphosis' which saw Graziano Rampazzo on drums.

Changing labels again, this time to Scarlet Records, a third album 'Parallel Worlds' witnessed the induction of new members bass player Max Clementi and drummer Jaco. ARACHNES would also re-issue a re-mastered version of 'The Goddess Temple'. This revised version came complete with an extra track - cover of IRON MAIDEN's 'Flash Of The Blade'.

The third ARACHNES album, 2002's 'Apocalypse', would witness the utilisation of full choirs and harpsichord to add colour to the band sound.

25

Singles/EPs:
Arachne / Lady Death / Open Your Eyes /
First Of All (Acoustic version), Underground
Symphony USCD037 (2000)
('Metamorphosis' EP)

Albums:
THE GODDESS TEMPLE, Lucretia (1997)
Black Rain / The King / Shut The Door / The
Four Elements: Fire / The Four Elements:
Earth / The Four Elements: Air / The Four
Elements: Water / First Of All / Against My
Heart / Sometime / With My Freedom /
Coloured Worlds / The Barber Of Seville
PARALLEL WORLDS, Scarlet (2001)
Arachne / Narrow Road / Lobotomy /
Loveless / Suite In A Minor: Vivace / Suite In
A Minor: Moderato / Suite In A Minor: Adagio
/ Running Now / Tears / War / Danger Of
Death / Sheet Steel / Parallel Worlds
APOCALYPSE, Scarlet (2002)
The Concept Of Time And Space / Decisive
Battle / Apocalypse / Prayer (Part I) / Prayer
(Part II) / My Destiny / A New Breathing /
Decisive Battle (Reprise) / Tango / The Rain
Song / Forever / The Blade Of My Brain /
The Dreamer / The Power Of God / Realm
Of Spirits

ARCANE (Arlington, TX, USA)
Line-Up: Oscar Barbour (vocals), Doug
Judah (guitar), Byron Hawk (guitar), Kurt
Joye (bass), Kelly Sanford (drums)

Progressive Thrash Metal band ARCANE,
founded in 1987, debuted with the 1989
'Mirror Deception' demo. Drummer Kelly
Sanford was previously a member of BANG
GANG.

Albums:
DESTINATION UNKNOWN, (1991)
Recurrent Inception / Enshrouded Crypt /
Infernal Domicile / Ancient Internecine /
Life's Illusion / Impasse Of Humanity / Mirror
Of Deception / Agaememnon

ARCHETYPE (Brecksville, OH, USA)
Line-Up: Greg Wagner (guitar), Chris Matyus
(guitar), Jamie Still (bass), Keith Zeigler
(drums)

Ohio's ARCHETYPE was founded by guitarist
Chris Matyus, recipient of a degree in
Classical Music from the University of Akron,
during 1997 in union with bassist Jamie Still
and drummer Keith Zeigler.
As an instrumental trio ARCHETYPE set
about gigging and recording a four song
promotional EP 'Archetype'. This release
scored a recording contract with the Danish

Intromental Management and, adding lead
vocalist Greg Wagner, the band cut the 1999
'Hands Of Time' EP. The following year the
'Dawning' album was issued but, dissatisfied
with the album's production, ARCHETYPE re-
recorded the majority of it. 'The Dawning' was
finally completed in December of 2001.

Singles/EPs:
Hands Of Time EP, Intromental IMP003
(1998)

Albums:
DAWNING, CDM Productions CDM0001
(2002)
Final Day / Hands Of Time / Dawning /
Dissension's Wake / Inside Your Dreams /
Premonitions / Visionary / Arisen / The
Mind's Eye / Year's Ago

ARCHONTES (RUSSIA)
Line-Up: Andrey Fedorenko (vocals /
keyboards), Gene Savostianov (guitar),
Sergey Shvora (bass), Alexey Biekov
(drums)

A Russian Power Metal band led by vocalist
and keyboard player Andrey Fedorenko.
ARCHONTES has had a complex history
since its inception in 1993. The band's original
line-up cited Fedorenko, guitarists Eugene
Savostianov and Alexander Rekonvald,
bassist Grigory Kozlov and drummer Vladimir
Latinsev. The following year Sergey
Rassokhin replaced Latinsev.
1995 would signal yet more line-up changes
with both Rassokhin and Kozlov out of the
picture. ARCHONTES would welcome
onboard a new rhythm section of bassist
Sergey Zakharov and drummer Dennis
Karpukhin. The band fractured yet again in
1996. Karpukhin and Rekonvald excited with
guitar player Roman Zorkaltzev and drummer
Alexey Bykov taking their positions. The group
also pulled in keyboard player Vasily Dubov.
The debut ARCHONTES album 'Saga Of
Eternity' emerged through the MetalAgen
label in 1997, the follow up 'The World Where
Shadows Come To Life' arriving some two
years later but securing some degree of
Western distribution.
In August of 2001, guitarist Zakhov Karpikov
and drummer Sergey Belyavsky would bid
farewell. The band drafted two erstwhile
LEGION members Vyacheslav Molchanov
and Dmitrey Krivenkov respectively to plug
the gap.

Albums:
SAGA OF ETERNITY, Metal Agen (1997)

Epigraph / Under Bloody Sun / The Crown Of Spring / Children's Crusade / ...In The Dark / Quest For Glory And Might / Saga Of Eternity / The Glory Anthem / Don't Say Farewell, Say Goodbye / Death's Not The End

THE WORLD WHERE SHADOWS COME TO LIFE, Valiant VMP001 (1999)
The Opening Incantation / The World Where Shadows Come To Life / Runaway From Dark / Whisper Of Time / Fear Is The Conscience Of Villains / Mother Russia / The Rules Of Real Life / Victory Or Death

ARIA (RUSSIA)
Line-Up: Valery Kipilov (vocals), Sergey Mavrin (guitar), Vladimir Holstinin (guitar), Vitaly Dubinin (bass), Maxim Udalov (drums)

Russian Heavy Metal combo ARIA have released numerous albums, many of which have sold over a million copies. ARIA date to their formation in 1984 by guitarist Vladimir Holstinin, previously with ALPHA. Another erstwhile ALPHA member bassist Alik Granovsky joined him and in 1985 vocalist Valery Kipelov was recruited.

ARIA's first recordings, the 'Megalomania' ('Mania Welichia') cassette, was laid down with the aid of drummer Lvov and keyboard player Kirill Pokrovsky. For live work ARIA pulled in second guitarist Andrey Bolshakov as Lvov became a full time member.

In 1986 ARIA, now with a strong fan base dubbed "Arians", performed at the Russian 'Rock Panorama '86' festival. The state Record label Melodia issued a double live album featuring bands from the event but pointedly missed out ARIA. Live shows by the band were attracting hardened fans and also protesters making ARIA a constant thorn in the side of the authorities. ARIA's logo was even banned making it difficult to advertise live shows.

ARIA knuckled down to business with their second tape album 'Whom Are You With' which featured a fresh line-up. ARIA had split down the middle with those band members wishing to go more in a Thrash direction leaving. Joining Holstinin and Kipilov in the new look ARIA were guitarist Sergey Mavrin, bass player Vitaly Dubinin and drummer Maxim Udalov.

Such was the band's popularity Melodia Records picked up the band for their next release. The band delivered their album titled 'Serving Evil Force' but were horrified to find that Melodia had re-titled it without consulting them 'Hero Of A Speedway'. Not only had the record company changed the title but had ruined the sound quality. ARIA dubbed the album 'Hero Of Asphalt' ('Geroj Asfalta').

Nevertheless, despite the problems the album sold over a million copies.

the winter of 1988 ARIA played their first dates in the West with shows in Germany. Udalov quit after a tour of Bulgaria and in came Alexander Manyakin on drums for the 'Play With Fire' album. However, Dubinin and Mavrin left to join a German band.

ARIA regrouped with ex-GALACTICA and KRASNAYA PLOSHAD guitarist Dimitry Gorbatikov and bassist Alexes Bulkin. By August of 1990 Dubinin and Mavrin returned to the fold.

'Blood For Blood' was issued on Syntez Records then ARIA signed a lengthy contract with Moraz Records who promptly reissued the first two cassettes onto vinyl.

Just when they had secured a new deal and were setting to work on a fresh album Kipilov quit to join MASTER. Seeing no future for ARIA without the vocalist Mavrin also walked out. Guitarist Sergey Teretvev, who had been recording his own solo album in the same studio took Mavrin's place. The album was finished as Kipolov returned and 'Night Is Shorter Than Day' finally saw a release in 1995.

A double live album followed before band members set about projects outside of ARIA. Dubinin and Holstinin created AVARIA whilst Kipilov and former guitarist Mavrin formed DARK AGE.

ARIA returned with 1998's 'Generator Of Evil'.

Singles/EPs:
The Time Has Come / Easy Angel / Hero Of Asphalt '99 / Easy Angel (Karoake version), Moraz (1999) ('A Tribute To Harley Davidson' EP)

Albums:
MANIA WELICHIA, (1985) (Cassette release)
This Is Doom / Torero / Volunteer / Tusks Of Black Rock / Megolomania / Life For Free / Dreams / America Is Behind
S KEM TY, (1986) (Cassette release)
Will And Reason / Stand Up, Subdue Your Fear / Metal Is Being Made Here / Whom Are You With? / Without You / Memory About... / Icarus / Games Not For Us
HERO OF A SPEEDWAY, Melodia (1987)
Serving Evil Powers / Hero Of A Speedway / Dead Zone / Almost 1000 / Rose Street / Ballad Of Old Wars
PLAYING WITH FIRE, Melodia (1989)
What Have You Done To Your Dreams? / We'll Rock The World / Slave Of Fear / Temptation / Playing With Fire / The War Goes On / Power Up!
KROW SA KROW, Syntez (1991)

Farewell Norfolk! / Zombie / Antichrist / If You Don't Want - Don't Believe Me / Blood For Blood / Demons / All, That Have Been / Follow Me
MEGOLOMANIA, Moroz (1994)
This Is Doom / Torero / Volunteer / Tusks Of Black Rock / Megolomania / Life For Free / Dreams / America Is Behind
NOCHJ KOROCHE DNJA, Moraz (1995)
Slavery Of Illusions / Paranoia / Angels Dust / Go Away And Don't Return / Road King / Take My Heart / Beast / Spirit Of War / Night Is Shorter Than Day
MADE IN RUSSIA - LIVE, Moraz (1996)
Slavery Of Illusions / Paranoia / Let's Rock This World / Road King / Angel's Dust / Go away And Don't Return / Antichrist / Take My Heart / Follow Me / Night Is Shorter Than Day / Farewell Norfolk! / Volunteer / Spirit Of war / Torero / Fight Is Going On / All, What Have Been / Hero Of Asphalt / Rose Street / Kick Some Ass
RUSSIAN ROCK LEGENDS, Moroz (1997)
Volunteer / Torero / Will And Reason / Give Me A Hand / Hero Of Asphalt / Rose Street / Fight Is Goin On / Play With Fire / Farewell Norfolk! / Antichrist / Blood For Blood / Take My Heart / Road King
GENERATOR OF EVIL, Moraz (1998)
Behold! / Dirt / Deserter / Torture With Silence / Run For The Sun / Deseption / Hermit / Sunset / Diabolic Heart / Closed Circle
2000 AND ONE NIGHT (LIVE), Moraz (2000)
Rose Street / Lost Paradise / Without You / Dirt / All, What Have Been / Take My Heart / Go Away And Don't Return / Who Are You / Torture With Silence / Temptation / Dreams / Sunset

ARISE (SWEDEN)
Line-Up: Erik Ljungvist (vocals / guitar), L.G. Jonasson (guitar), Patrick Skoglow (bass), Daniel Bugno (drums)

ARISE, founded in Alingsas during 1994 and titled in honour of the SEPULTURA album of the same name, blend traditional Swedish style Death Metal with retro Thrash influences. The group was assembled by a triumvirate of erstwhile HOLOCAUST members guitarist Erik Ljungqvist, bassist Patrick Skoglow and drummer Daniel Bugno. Second guitars were on hand from L.G. Jonasson, an ex-member of FUTURE DEVELOPMENT.
Initially the band was fronted by vocalist Jorgen Sjolander who was in turn replaced by Bjorn Andvik. When Andvik decamped Ljungvist took over the lead vocal role as ARISE switched from playing covers to writing original material. They then proceeded to

issue a rush of demos including 'Hell's Retribution', 'Resurrection' and 1999's 'Statues'.
ARISE cut an April 2000 session 'Abducted Intelligence' with KING DIAMOND man Andy LaRocque at the production helm. This last tape duly secured a deal with the Finnish Spinefarm label.
ARISE would also contribute a version of 'Communication Breakdown' to the Dwell Records LED ZEPPELIN Death Metal tribute album 'Dead Zeppelin'. Japanese issues of the debut album 'A Godly Work Of Art' include an extra track, namely a cover of METALLICA's 'Motorbreath'.

Albums:
THE GODLY WORK OF ART, Spinefarm (2001)
A Godly Work Of Art / Generations For Sale / Within / Delusion Of Life / Haterush / Cellbound / Wounds / Abducted Intelligence / ...And The Truth Is Lies

ARK (NORWAY / USA)
Line-Up: Jorn Lande (vocals), Tøre Ostby (guitar), Randy Coven (bass), Mats Olausson (keyboards), John Macaluso (drums)

Project band assembled by THE SNAKES / MUNDUS IMPERIUM singer JORN LANDE, erstwhile CONCEPTION guitarist Tøre Ostby and drummer John Macaluso of TNT, POWERMAD and RIOT. Although conceived during 1990 the band members various other commitments meant ARK would only get to issue their eponymous debut in 1999.
2000's 'Burn The Sun' album is produced by former VICTORY guitarist Tommy Newton. For this effort ARK drafted bassist Randy Coven, a veteran of American Metal bands HOLY MOTHER and BURNING STARR together with keyboard player Mats Olausson. Both Olausson and Coven rank as ex-YNGWIE MALMSTEEN band members.
Lande and Macaluso too joined YNGWIE MALMSTEEN in November 2000 for a brief if eventful tenure. Both would abruptly decamp Malmsteen's band in the midst of American tour dates.

Albums:
ARK, Inside Out Music IOMCD082 (1999)
Burning Down / Where The Winds Blow / The Hunchback Of Notre Dame / Singers At The Worlds Dawn / Mother Love / Center Avenue / Can't Let Go
BURN THE SUN, Inside Out Music IOMCD075 (2000)
Heal The Waters / Torn / Burn The Sun /

Resurrection / Absolute Zero / Just A Little / Walking Hour / Noose / Feed The Fire / I Believe / Missing You / Silent Is The Rain

ARKANGEL (VENEZUALA)
Line-Up: Paul Gillman (vocals), Giancarlo Picozzi (guitar), Freddy Marshall (guitar), Breno Díaz (bass), Mickey Tedeschi (keyboards), Giorgio Picozzi (drums)

One of the foremost of Venezuelan Metal bands. ARKANGEL's history traces back through the 1977 act POWER AGE, a band unit comprising Paul Gillman on lead vocals, Freddy Marshall on guitar the Picozzi brothers Giancarlo and Giorgio on guitar and drums respectively and bass player Rogelio Gutiérrez.

For the debut eponymous album, recorded in just three days, ARKANGEL's line-up was made up of the Picozzis, Gillman, Marshall and bassist Breno Díaz, the latter having been introduced just before the name switch from POWER AGE to ARKANGEL. The 1982 follow up 'Rock Nacional' combined new studio recordings with live tracks. The third album 'Represion Latinoamericana' saw the addition of keyboard player Mickey Tedeschi. ARKANGEL lost the services of Gillman but with Giancarlo Picozzi taking over the lead vocal role committed two tracks 'Parte Di Mi' and 'Conmigo Estarás' to the 1987 'La Respuesta' compilation album.

ARKANGEL returned in 1992 for with a four track EP 'No Mas Apariencias'. Alongside the familiar Picozzi siblings, Marshall and Díaz for this outing would be singer Sergio Marín and keyboard player Klaus Kikas. Then supplanting Marín with former CRONOS man José Gregorio Spíndola ARKANGEL issued a six track cassette 'Inmortal' the same year.

After a lengthy hiatus ARKANGEL made a return in 2000 with the album 'Angel De La Muerte'. The band at this point had Joad Manuel Jiménez out front with Felipe Arcuri new on bass. ARKANGEL, bringing Robert Puccia in on keyboards, supported BARON ROJO on their visit to the country in November of 2001.

Singles/EPs:
Nunca te detengas / No Mas Apariencias / Pasajero Como El Viento / No Puedes Reprocharme, (1992) ('No Mas apariencias' EP)

Albums:
ARKANGEL, (1981)
Vagon De La Muerte / Libertad / Loco Por El Rock & Roll / Barón Rojo / Nada Es Eterno / Hombre Robot / Un Niño Nace / Asesino /

Héroes Caídos / Arkangel
ROCK NACIONAL, (1982)
El Rey Dinero / Calles Violentas (De La Granciudad) / Viajes Sin Regreso / Castillo Sobre Le Mar / La Procesión De Satanás / Rock Nacional (Live) / Libertad (Live) / El Rockero (Live) / Zombie (Live)
REPRESION LATINOAMERICANA, (1983)
Desempleado / Represión Latinoamericana / Juicio Final / Los Gusanos Del Poder / Ni Plata Ni Religión / Destrucción Natural / Todo Costó Sacrificios / Tu Eres El Amor
INMORTAL, (1992) (Cassette release)
Paremos La Guerra / El Último Chance De Elvis / La Gran Carrera / Inmortal / Capitán Mandarria / Rock & Roll No Morirá
ARKANGEL, (1994)
Vagon De La Muerte / Libertad / Loco Por El Rock & Roll / Barón Rojo / Nada Es Eterno / Hombre Robot / Un Niño Nace / Asesino / Héroes Caídos / Destrucción Natural / Juicio Final / Los Gusanos Del Poder / Tú Eres El Amor / Desempleado / Represión Latinoamericana / Ni Plata, Ni Religión / Arkangel
EL ANGEL DE LA MUERTE, (2000)
Intro / Luces Y Espadas / Justicia Y Poder / La Farsa Y La Máscara / Motín En Occidente / Hacia La Eternidad / Madre Tierra / Dios Perdona Yo No / Derrota final / Paper Life / Damas De La Noche / El Angel De La Muerte / Al Irse / Gabriel / Inmortal (New version) / Despierta America

ARKHE (ITALY)
Line-Up: Pino Tozzi (vocals), Gianluca Ferro (guitar), Michelle Buzzetti (bass), Lorenzo Milani (keyboards), Claudio Riotti (drums)

Albums:
ARKHE, Underground Symphony US CD-022 (1997)
Chains / Wings Of My Freedom / Birth Of Your Soul / The Grey Falcon / The Dark Light (The Other Lights) / Unison / Silence And Fear / Le Voyant De Salon

ARMORED SAINT (USA)
Line-Up: John Bush (vocals), Dave Pritchard (guitar), Phil E. Sandoval (guitar), Joey Vera (bass), Gonzo (drums)

Officially formed in the summer of 1982, ARMORED SAINT immediately attracted attention for the quality of a five track demo tape and the headbanging nature of the quintet's live show. The band was initially founded in 1981, yet only fully completed in mid 1982. The individuals concerned had all played in other bands, but none had recorded with anybody previously. Bassist JOEY VERA had played with MÖTLEY CRÜE's Tommy Lee and then OZZY OSBOURNE guitarist JAKE E. LEE during his formative years, however.

Joey Vera (then a guitarist) and vocalist John Bush first got together in their El Sereno school band RHAPSODY. A covers band including songs by the likes of FOREIGNER and DEEP PURPLE in their act. RHAPSODY also included guitarist David Avila, bassist Channing, keyboard player Mark Patton and drummer Martin Zuniga.

Vera and Bush stuck together to create their next school band ROYAL DECREE in an alliance with drummer Gonzo and guitarist Phil E. Sandoval. Vera was now on bass after Bush initially made an attempt but got bored with the instrument. Upon ROYAL DECREE's demise Bush and Vera hooked up with SAPPHIRE but shortly after Bush was ousted by vocalist Brad Parker. The band underwent numerous line-up changes but toward the end of the band's career Vera found himself playing alongside Tommy Lee.

Vera joined ex-DOKKEN guitarist Greg Leon in his GREG LEON INVASION following Lee's departure to MÖTLEY CRÜE. During this time Gonzo, Sandoval and Vera were jamming in a garage, latter day MX MACHINE / MOTOFURY man Diego Negrate having a brief stint on bass. This unnamed unit pulled

John Bush in on vocals although were quite happy to inform the front man the only reason he got to join was because he owned an impressive PA system. This line-up began to formulate early ARMORED SAINT material as well as covering IRON MAIDEN tunes. One song that didn't make it to any official release was subtly titled 'You Suck My Anal Dry'.

Vera continued his bass duties with the GREG LEON INVASION whilst the mysterious Mike took his role in the garage band. In April of 1982 Vera officially joined the newly titled ARMORED SAINT.

As legend has it, ARMORED SAINT's demo tape was paid for from compensation arising from injuries sustained by Joey Vera in an automobile accident whilst a passenger in a car driven by Tommy Lee.

ARMORED SAINT's first recorded appearance came with a contribution to Metal Blade's 'Metal Massacre II' album. The group offered 'Lesson Well Learned'.

Naturally, Metal Blade then stepped in with a deal for an EP, resulting in the 3 track 12" single issued the following year. The record included 'Lesson Well Learned' with 'False Alarm' and 'On The Way'.

Chrysalis stepped in to snap the group up, placing them in the studio with producer Michael James Jackson (fresh from his work

ARMORED SAINT

on KISS' 'Creatures Of The Night' album) to deliver the 'March Of The Saint' record. Most fans agree that whilst the material couldn't be faulted, the production left a good deal to be desired, not capturing the intensity of the group at all.

'March Of The Saint' was released in 1984, the band touring America opening up for METALLICA soon afterwards, the two bands now sharing management.

The group's second album, 'Delirious Nomad' surfaced a year later. Produced by Max Norman, the record found ARMORED SAINT a quartet following the exit of guitarist Dave Sandoval during recording.

A third album, 'Raising Fear', was recorded with Chrysalis before the two parties split after its release in 1987. For touring with KING DIAMOND in America during 1988 ARMORED SAINT drafted former ODIN guitarist Jeff Duncan as the band also parted company with Q-Prime Management.

The 1988 live album, recorded at Cleveland's Agorra Ballroom in October 1987, provided the band with a useful stopgap product and included a brand new studio recording featuring Phil Sandoval 'No Reason To Live'.

As ARMORED SAINT floundered Duncan quit, having his position taken by Alan Barlam. Duncan put together BIRD OF PREY with his brother and ex-ODIN colleague Shawn on drums, vocalist Kyle Michaels (later of MASI and GEEZER BUTLER BAND) and Paul Puljiz (later of KILLING KULTURE). Vera meantime joined LIZZY BORDEN for their 1989 album 'Master Of Disguise'.

ARMORED SAINT guitarist Dave Pritchard died from Leukaemia in February 1990. His life was celebrated in the video 'A Trip Thru' Red Times'.

The 'Symbol Of Salvation' comeback album was graced with Pritchard's guitar parts on the track 'Tainted Past'.

Having resisted overtures from the likes of METALLICA in the past, John Bush decided to take up an offer from ANTHRAX to become the New York outfit's new vocalist in the wake of Joey Belladonna's departure in 1992. With Bush gone ARMORED SAINT ceased to exist.

Following the band's split Joey Vera released a solo album, 'A Thousand Faces', through Metal Blade. He then joined FATES WARNING and was involved in the recording of new band colleague Mark Zonder's side project CHROMA KEY in 1998.

ARMORED SAINT with the Sandoval brothers, Vera, Bush and Duncan had the opportunity to reform during 1999 as Bush's career with ANTHRAX appeared on the wane. The comeback album 'Revelation' garnered heady praise from the European Metal press and proved to be a return to former glories. Duncan also issued his solo project band DC4's first outing the same year. In 2001 a highly collectable compilation 'Nod To The Old School' was issued featuring a glut of early demo tracks, three new songs, covers of JUDAS PRIEST's 'Never Satisfied' and ROBIN TROWER's 'Day Of The Eagle' and live cuts. Also included were the tracks from the bands very first EP.

In March of 2002 Joey Vera, still maintaining his posts in both ARMORED SAINT and FATES WARNING, would team up with SAVATAGE guitarist Jack Frost's side endeavour SEVEN WITCHES for European touring. The bassist would also handle production chores for ENGINE's 'Superholic' album.

The other ARMORED SAINT personnel maintained their sense of industry too, Jeff Duncan readying a Joey Vera produced DC4 album release for Europe and Gonzo busying himself with his MONSTER G venture in alliance with Phil Sandoval.

Singles/EPs:
Lesson Well Learned / False Alarm / On The Way, Metal Blade MBR 1009 (1983)
Can U Deliver, Chrysalis (1984)
Take A Turn, Chrysalis (1984)
Long Before I Die, Chrysalis (1985)
Over The Edge, Chrysalis (1985)
Isolation, Chrysalis (1987)

Albums:
MARCH OF THE SAINT, Chrysalis CHR 1479 (1984)
March Of The Saint / Can U Deliver / Mad House / Take A Turn / Seducer / Mutiny On The World / Glory Hunter / Stricken By Fate / Envy / False Alarm
DELIRIOUS NOMAD, Chrysalis CHR 1516 (1985)
Long Before I Die / Nervous Man / Over The Edge / The Laugh / Conqueror / For The Sake / Aftermath / In The Hole / You're Never Alone / Released
RAISING FEAR, Chrysalis CHR 1610 (1987)
Raising Fear / Saturday Night Special / Out On A Limb / Isolation / Chemical Euphoria / Frozen Will - Legacy / Human Vulture / Book Of Blood / Terror / Underdogs / Crisis Of Life
SAINTS WILL CONQUER - LIVE, Metal Blade ZORRO 28 (1988)
Raising Fear / Nervous Man / Book Of Blood / Can U Deliver / Mad House / No Reason To Live
SYMBOL OF SALVATION, Metal Blade ZORRO20 (1991)
Reign Of Fire / Dropping Like Flies / Last Train Home / Tribal Dance / The Truth Always Hurts

/ Half Drawn Bridge / Another Day / Symbol Of Salvation / Hanging Judge / Warzone / Burning Question / Tainted Past / Spineless
REVELATION, Metal Blade 3984-14288-2 (2000)
Pay Dirt / The Pillar / After Me, The Flood / Tension / Creepy Feelings / Damaged / Den Of Thieves / Control Issues / No Me Digas / Deep Rooted Anger / What's Your Pleasure / Upon My Departure
NOD TO THE OLD SCHOOL, Metal Blade (2001)
Real Swagger / Unstable / March Of The Saint / Day Of The Eagle / Never Satisfied / Tainted Past / After Me The Flood (Live) / Creepy Feelings (Live) / Lesson Well Learned / False Alarm / On The Way / Stricken By Fate / Reign Of Fire (Demo) / Betty 79,15 People (Demo) / Get Lost (Demo) / Nothing Between The Ears (Demo) / Pirates (Demo) / Medieval Nightmare (Demo)

ARTCH (NORWAY)

Line-Up: Erikur Hauksson (vocals), Cato Olsen (guitar), Geir Nilsson (guitar), Bernt A. Jansen (bass), Jorn Jamisson (drums)

Sarpsborg quintet Power Metal band with an Icelandic vocalist, ARTCH formed in 1982 by guitarist Cato Olsen and bassist Bernt A Jansen. The group underwent numerous line-up changes before drummer Jorn Jamisson and second guitarist Geir Nilsson joined in 1984 from OXYGEN.
The band's original vocalist, Espen Hoss, was tragically killed in a motorbike accident, so Erikur Hauksson (who later adopted the pseudonym Eric Hawk), who had previously been a contestant for Iceland's Eurovision song entry, was poached from Icelandic Metal band DRYSILL. The self-financed debut 'Another Return', issued by the enterprising Active label formed by 'Metal Forces' publishers Bernard Doe and Dave Constable, was met with rave reviews from the world's Metal press.
In 1991, the year second album 'For The Sake Of Mankind' appeared on Brian Slagel's Metal Blade label, ARTCH performed at the Icelandic 'Breaking The Ice' festival alongside THUNDER, THE QUIREBOYS and BULLETBOYS.
Hawk contributes guest vocals to the debut GARDENIAN album 'Soulburner' issued in 1999.

Albums:
ANOTHER RETURN, Active ACTLP 5 (1988)
Conversio Prelude / Another Return To Church Hill / Power To The Man / Loaded /

Where I Go / Metal Life / The Promised Land / Shoot To Kill / Living In The Past / Reincarnation
FOR THE SAKE OF MANKIND, Metal Blade 92 6526 (1991)
When Angels Cry / Appologia / Burn Down The Bridges / Paradox / To Whom It May Concern / Titanic / Confrontation / Turn The Tables / To Be Or Not To Be / Batteries Not Included / Razamanaz

ARTENSION (USA)

Line-Up: John West (vocals), George Bellas (guitar), Barry Sparks (bass), Vitalij Kuprij (keyboards), Mike Terrana (drums)

A solo project from ex-BADLANDS and MICHAEL LEE FIRKINS BAND vocalist John West that would provide a hotbed a Rock talent for some seasoned players. The first two albums saw West joined by guitarist Roger Staffelbach, Bassist Barry Sparks, keyboard player Vitalij Kuprij and former ZILLION, BEAU NASTY and YNGWIE MALMSTEEN drummer Mike Terrana. AGENT STEEL, DEATH and TESTAMENT guitarist JAMES MURPHY also lends a hand in the studio.
Sparks went on to join YNGWIE MALMSTEEN's band. Terrana joined METALIUM then German Metal crew RAGE.
ARTENSION would be joined by bassist Kevin Chown. Latter day ARTENSION guitarist George Bellas released a solo album of his own, 'Turn Of The Millennium' through Roadrunner in 1997 and played on ex-UFO duo Phil Mogg and PETE WAY's MOGG/WAY project.
2000's 'Machine' album had West joined by drummer Shane Galaas, bassist John Onder and guitarist Roger Staffelbach. Vitalij featured on YNGWIE MALMSTEEN vocalist MARK BOALS solo album 'Ring Of Fire'. Bellas would later join Boals' live band RING OF FIRE.
The industrious Chown would journey on to MAGNETUDE 9, EDWINDARE and LIFE, DEATH & GIANTS as well as undertaking light hearted live work with THE BLUES ROCKERS and THE LOUNGE LIZARDS.
ARTENSION regrouped in 2001 for a comeback album on the Italian Frontiers label billed as 'Sacred Pathway'. The group convened for these sessions comprised the familiar line-up of John West, Roger Staffelbach, Kevin Chown, Vitalij Kuprij and Mike Terrana.

Albums:
INTO THE EYE OF THE STORM, Roadrunner (1996)

World Of Illusion / Into The Eye Of The Storm / Smoke And Fire / The Wind And The Rain / Lost Memory / The Key / Song Of The Desert / Red's Recovery / Let It Ride / I Don't Care
PHOENIX RISING, Shrapnel (1997)
Area 51 / Through The Gate / Valley Of The Kings / Blood Brother / Into The Blue / Phoenix Rising / Forbidden Love / The City Is Lost / Goin' Home / I Really Don't Care
MACHINE, Shrapnel 1139 (2000)
Machine / The Way / Madness Calling / Mother Earth / Wings Of War / Evolution In Reverse / Time Goes Slowly By / The Loser Never Wins / I See Through Your Eyes
SACRED PATHWAYS, Frontiers (2002)
Voyage To Nasca / Your Victory / Running Out Of Time / Sacred Pathways / Silent Temple / The Emperor / Nightmare / The Killing / The Calm Before The Storm / March To Ruin / Flower Of The Orient / Nightmare (Radio Edit)

ARTHEMIS (ITALY)

Line-Up: Alessio Garavello (vocals), Andrea Martongelli (guitar), Matteo Ballottari (guitar), Matteo Galbier (bass), Alessio Turrini (drums)

The beginning of Power Speed Metal act ARTHEMIS trace back to 1994 when the band debuted on the Italian club circuit as a covers act. Endeavouring to pursue an original sound the band set about fusing neo-Classical European styles with the aggression of American of Speed Metal. After numerous line-up shuffles the group stabilised somewhat in 1998, comprising lead guitarists Andrea Martongelli and Matteo Ballottari, bassist Matteo Galbier and drummer Alessio Turrini. At this stage the vocal position alternated between Andrea Martongelli and Alberto Caria.
During 1999 ARTHEMIS laid down their debut album 'Church Of The Holy Ghost', featuring the vocals of Caria. The album was issued in December of 1999, at the same time ARTHEMIS inducting a new lead singer Alessio Garavello.
In March of 2000 ARTHEMIS signed contracts with the Underground Symphony label to re-issue 'Church Of The Holy Ghost'. The album would sell so fast that the label put the band back in the studio to record an extra track, a version of the STRATOVARIUS tune 'Shattered', to add as a bonus for a subsequent digi pack version.
Drummer Alessio Turrini left the band in the summer of 2002, ARTHEMIS duly enrolling a former member Paulo Perazzani as replacement.
ARTHEMIS members vocalist Alessio Garavello and guitarist Andrea Martongelli both also hold down positions in the British based Symphonic Metal band POWER

QUEST.

Albums:
CHURCH OF THE HOLY GHOST, (1999)
War Act I: Darkness, Act II : The Prophecy, Act III: Sounds Of Victory / Tyrant's Time / Time To React / Tomorrow's World / Claws Of The Devil / The Storm / Twilight In The Dark / Church Of The Holy Ghost
THE DAMNED SHIP, Underground Symphony USCD057 (2001)
Quest For Immortality / Voice Of The God / Sun's Temple / Starchild / The Wait / The Night Of The Vampire / Earthquake / Noble Sword / The Damned Ship

ASHES TO ASHES (NORWAY)

Line-Up: Kenneth Brastad (vocals), Michael Stenberg (guitars), Björn Luna (bass), Kristian Johansen (drums)

Exceptionally heavy Progressive Doom Metal band. ASHES TO ASHES was forged in 1992 by guitarist Michael Stenberg, bass player Björn Luna and drummer Kristian Johansen. Two demo tapes, 'Between The Devil And The Deep Blue Sea' and 'Temples Of Ice', set the scene for their debut 1998 album 'Shapes Of Spirits'. ASHES TO ASHES signed to Dutch label DVS Records for the 2001 outing 'Cardinal VII'.

Albums:
CARDINAL VII, DVS DVS006 (2001)
New World Obscure / Embraced In Black / Among Mortals / Truth On Scaffold / Iben / Dualism / Sic Transit Gloria Mundi / Ravenous Unleashed / Behind Closed Eyes / Cardinal VII / Iben II

ASKA (Dallas, TX, USA)

Line-Up: George Call (vocals), Darren Knapp (guitar), Daryl Norton (guitar), Keith Knight (bass), Danny White (drums)

ASKA has the unique distinction of having no less than eight world tours under their belts, recruited by the US military to provide on base entertainment. As such the group has gigged in such far flung places as Saudi Arabia, Iceland, Bosnia, Korea, Guam and Croatia.
Fresh out of school the first ASKA line-up witnessed a union of guitarist Darren Knapp, vocalist George Call and his brother Damon Call on drums, the latter an erstwhile PEGASUS member.
Following the third album 'Nine Tongues' ASKA pulled in new drummer Jason Sweatt although his tenure would be brief.
The band gained the honours of supporting

JUDAS PRIEST in their hometown during 2001. The fourth album 'Avenger' was delivered through the Steelheart label, the band also donating a cover version of IRON MAIDEN's 'Flight Of Icarus' to a tribute album issued by the same concern. Without a permanent drummer ASKA took on shows in February utilising the temporary services of HAMMER WITCH man Terry Simms and ex-ARTESIA sticksman Pat Murphy. The band's former drummer Damon Call would also help out as did Gerald Salgaldo of ALICE & HAMMER. Promotion in the early half of 2002 included support gigs to LIZZY BORDEN and SAXON. ASKA introduced new drummer Danny White in mid 2002.

Albums:
ASKA, EMA (1994)
Could You Do This To Me / Delta Force / Don't Walk Away / Destruction / Fooled Again / Take Action / Zonlan / He She You And I / If I Could Change Things / Vices / T.A. II / Number Five
IMMORTAL, EMA (1995)
Immortal / Vigilante / Feel Me, Touch Me / Jane's Going Away / You Suck / Before You Came / How Long '94 / Dream In Color / Don't Know Much About Love / Major Mistake / As Far As I'm Concerned / Can't Break Free
NINE TONGUES, EMA (1997)
The Stalker / Leprosy / The Question / Little Sister / Blood Of The Wolf / Killashandra / Captain Crunch / Liquid Courage / Nightmare / The Dream
AVENGER, Steelheart STH-021 (2002)
Crown Of Thorns / Leather / Escape: Victorious / Angels Of War / Prelude To Darkness / Eternal Night / Imperial Rome / Against The Gods / Lethal Injection / Valkyries / Warriors Return

ASSAILANT (SWEDEN)
Line-Up: Marcus Karlsson (vocals / guitar), Hampus Mörk (bass), Albin Johansson (keyboards), Anders Wier (drums)

ASSAILANT was initially formed a loose collective in 2000 with the sole intention of performing YNGWIE MALMSTEEN cover versions. This proto- line-up comprised a quintet of vocalist Marcus Karlsson, guitarist Mattias Moberg, bass guitarist Hampus Mörk, ex-INNOCENT VOICES keyboard player Albin Johansson and drummer Joel Dittmer. Both Karlsson and Mörk had previously been a members of MYXAMATOSIS and MORIA. A switch was made to composing original material but losing Moberg necessitated Karlsson taking on guitar responsibilities. Anders Wier, also an active member of

NOBILITY, subsequently usurped Dittmer.

Singles/EPs:
The New Dawn / Enter Into Infinity / Hills Have Eyes, (2001) ('Enter Into Infinity' EP)
Samhain / Before The Storm / Ringbearer, (2002) ('Samhain' EP)

Albums:
UNDEAD, Metal Fortress (2002)
Undead / Assailant / Samhain / Before The Storm / The Ringbearer / Serenity / A Tyrant Breed / Love Sank Wounded / Day And Dream / Enigma / A Hope Forlorn

ATHENA (ITALY)
Line-Up: Alessio Mosti (vocals / guitar), Simone Pellegrini (guitar), Alessio Sabella (bass), Gabriele Guidi (keyboards), Matteo Amoroso (drums)

A Progressive Hard Rock act. ATHENA was joined by former LABYRINTH vocalist Joe Terry who supplanted Alessio Mosti after the album release. Terry fronts the hugely successful symphonic Metal band RHAPSODY under his real name of Fabio Leone. For the 2001 'Twilight Of Days' album ATHENA would be fronted by lead vocalist Francesco Neretti and have added an additional guitar player Graziano Poggetti.

Albums:
INSIDE THE MOON, Pick Up PK 1907 (1995)
Part I: Elements: Prelude To A Dream / Forests Of Sound / Wind Of Illusion / Desert / Waterfalls / Part II: Unlocked Dreams: Memories / Crystal Eyes / Inside The Moon / Unlocked Dreams
A NEW RELIGION?, Rising Sun 007299 2 RS (1998)
In The Beginning / A New Religion? / Soul Sailor / Apocalypse / Every Word I Whisper / Dead Man Walkin' / My Silence / Secret Vision / The Keeper / Twisted Feel / Not Too Far
TWILIGHT OF DAYS, Noise (2001)
Twilight Of Days / Till The End / The Way To Heaven's Gates / Hymn / Your Fear / Falling Ghosts / The Highest Tide / Touch My Heart / Lord Of Evil / Take My Life Away / End Of A Life / Making The History

ATLAIN (GERMANY)
Line-Up: Peter Müller (vocals), Andreas Buttner (guitar), Jorg Pryztarski (guitar), Andre Chapelier (bass), Christoph Efthimiades (drums)

German Power Metal outfit ATLAIN featured amongst a host of new, young German Metal bands that were being snapped up by

European independent labels in the Teutonic Metal boom of the early to mid '80s.
ATLAIN's drummer Christoph Efthimiades was to join RAGE in 1988.

Albums:
GUARDIANS OF ETERNITY, Earthshaker ES 4015 (1985)
Waste / Guardians Of Eternity / Break Down Your Neck / Brainstorm / Out On The Streets / Fast Attack / Space & Time / Demon's Feast / Break That Wall
LIVING IN THE DARK, Mausoleum (1985)
Hallowed By The Priest / Living In The Dark / Sinner / Dig It / Satanica / Sphinx / Thousand Nights In Hell / Hold Back The Night / Evil Forces

ATTACK (GERMANY)

Line-Up: Ricky van Helden (vocals / bass), Peter Oko (guitar), Thorsten Kohne (guitar), (bass), Zacki Tsoukas (drums)

Formed in 1984 and based around vocalist / bassist Ricky van Helden. ATTACK has released a string of Power Metal albums in their time.
The line-up for 1984's 'Danger In The Air' debut comprised van Helden, guitarist Andy Kammer and keyboard player TROS.
For the sophomore 'Return Of Evil', the band had undergone a considerably drastic change, with only Van Helden remaining. New members were guitarists Andy Niewidok and Jörg Franz and drummer Thomas Ewermann. The 1989 album 'Destinies Of War', also witnessed major changes. ATTACK actually split but reformed with a brand new line-up. Alongside van Helden were new guitarists Gerd Sossnierz and Chreddy Piepert and drummer Athanasios Taoukas.
With this line-up still intact the group recorded 'The Secret Place' album as recently as 1995.

Singles/EPs:
Mouse In A Maze, Good Time (1984)

Albums:
DANGER IN THE AIR, Pro-Sound (1984)
Danger In The Air / The Dragon From The Hill / Sunday Morning / Lonesome Rock n' Roller / Stoneway No. 3 / The Parade / The Trees / When The Dragon Flies
RETURN OF THE EVIL, Pro-Sound (1985)
Warriors In Pain / No Mercy / Hateful And Damned / Indian Lady / Dirty Mary / The End / Missing You / Hard Times
BEASTKILLER, Sonic Polygram (1986)
DESTINIES OF WAR, ZYX Mikulski (1989)
Wonderland / Back To Attack / You're Not Free / Live Or Die / Blind Man / The Battle's

Lost / Death Rider / The Last Surviving Man / Destiny Of War
SEVEN YEARS IN THE PAST, JVC Victor (1992)
In The Gloom / Seven Years In The Past / The Fighter / On The Run /Eternal War / Never Die / Battledrums / Hades Of Steel / Indian Lady / The Seventh Year Of The Past
REVITALISE, Iceland Tin Can Discs (1994)
The Wish To Die / Return Of The Warrior / In The Gloom / Eternal War / The Fighter / On The Run / Wonderland / Death Rider / Heroes Die Young / Dirty Mary / Danger In The Air / The Time Before / Way Out From Hell / Live Or Die / Warriors In Pain
THE SECRET PLACE, Tin Can Discs TIN41942 (1995)
Light In The Dark / I Know / Forgotten Dreams / The Prophecy / Walk Alone / Mortal Energy / Tsoukata / The Warrior / Heroes Die Young / Warp Speed, Now!

ATTACKER (Hoboken, NJ, USA)

Line-Up; Bob Mitchell (vocals), Pat Marinelli (guitar), Jim Mooney (guitar), Lou Ciarlo (bass), Michael Sabatini (drums)

Founded by guitarist Pat Marinelli and drummer Mike Sabatini under the handle of WARLOC at the beginning of 1983, the line-up was swiftly completed by Bob Mitchell (real name Bob Nunez) on vocals, John Joseph on bass and Jim Mooney on guitar.
Mitchell earned a good deal of praise for his performances on the group's first demo tape, a three track affair consisting of '(Call On) The Attacker', 'Slayer's Blade' and 'Disciple'. This tape was recorded shortly before a name change to ATTACKER due to the emergence of the debut album from the Doro Pesch fronted WARLOCK on import from Germany. Mitchell was often compared favourably to major name vocalists with the twin pronged guitar attack of Mooney and Marinelli likened to better known European counterparts.
Joseph was replaced by ex-HADES bassist Lou Ciarlo during the recording of debut album 'Battle At Helm's Deep' for Metal Blade Records, who had picked up on the underground buzz developing on the New Jersey-ites. Ciarlo re-recorded all Joseph's bass tracks prior to the release of the album. As coincidence would have it, Joseph went on to replace Ciarlo in HADES!
A mixing problem delayed the album's release further and the band's original choice for the album cover was rejected by Metal Blade for a less than satisfactory affair.
There was some interest from Dan Johnson's PAR Records label around the time ATTACKER were making plans to record their second album, a more aggressive affair all

35

round.

Vocalist John Leone and guitarist Tom D'Amico (replacing Mooney) were recruited for the album that aptly wound up being titled 'Second Coming' (the original, tentative title was 'The Deadly Blessing', however)

The choice of Leone was an inspired one as the new man had a similar style to Mitchell, so the switch was incredibly smooth.

The album was produced by Alex Perialis and RAVEN drummer Rob Hunter and eventually emerged through the newly formed Mercenary label in 1988. Prior to the album's release the label had included the track 'Emanon' on the 'L'Amour Rocks' compilation album in 1987.

In late 1988 Sabatini and Ciarlo quit to form JERSEY DOGS with Lou Ciarlo taking over a front man's role. An EP 'Don't Worry, Get Angry' was issued the following year. Mitchell formed SLEEPY HOLLOW and NIGHTHUNTER.

The specialist label Sentinel Steel reissued both albums in the late '90s, which invigorated renewed interest in ATTACKER in Europe. Mitchell, who had been operating side project ALCHEMY X, created a new version of ATTACKER comprising Rolando Marcias, John Armstrong, Tommy Ackel and erstwhile DARK VENGEANCE and KEVORKIAN HOUSECALL guitarist Rob Oriani to put in a live show at the 2000 'Powermad' festival. This version of ATTACKER put in a total of three live performances all told.

Matters became extremely confusing though when in August 2000 Sabatini, Marinelli and Ciarlo, together with ex-JERSEY DOGS and SLEEPY HOLLOW guitarist Mike Benetatos, also reformed ATTACKER! (Sadly Mooney had recently passed away).

Unable to use the name ATTACKER Mitchell and Oriani assembled a new unit entitled VYNDYKATOR. Other members included guitarist William G. Peria of PSYCHODRAMA and KEVORKIAN HOUSECALL, bassist Steven Ratchen from ALCHEMY X, TRINITY, DOMINION and THE FRIGID EARTH and drummer Mark Mari. The latter having credits with SNEAK ATTACK, DOG EAT DOG and THE FRIGID EARTH. This new band would score a deal with King Fowley's Battle Zone Records for a projected 2001 album release.

Albums:
BATTLE AT HELMS DEEP, Metal Blade (1986)
The Hermit / The Wrath Of Nevermore / Disciple / Downfall / Slayer's Blade / Battle At Helms Deep / Kick Your Face / Dance Of The Crazies / (Call On) The Attacker
THE SECOND COMING, Mercenary (1988)
Lords Of Thunder / Desecration / Zero Hour /

Revelations Of Evil / The Madness / Captives Of Babylon / Octagon / Emanon

AT VANCE (GERMANY)
Line-Up: Oliver Hartmann (vocals), Olaf Lenk (guitar), König Rainald (guitar), Jochen Schnur (bass), Uli Müller (keyboards), Jurgen Lucas (drums)

Power Metal act formerly known as CENTERS. The band includes in its ranks guitarist Olaf Lenk, previously a member of both ZED YAGO and VELVET VIPER. Other personnel number four former members of SPIDER in vocalist Oliver Hartmann (who also lists credits with HEAT and MERLIN), keyboard player Uli Müller (also ex-ESCAPE and BREAKPOINT), bass player Jochen Schnur and drummer Jurgen Lucas. Second guitarist König Rainald is ex-CONFRONT.

AT VANCE's debut 1999 album 'No Escape' would ambitiously not only tackle a Vivaldi piece 'Summer' but also an attempt at ABBA's 'Money, Money, Money'. The Japanese version of the album would give listeners there the chance to hear two more covers in SURVIVOR's 'Eye Of The Tiger' and TEARS FOR FEARS 'Shout'.

The band would get to grips once more with ABBA on their second outing 'Heart Of Steel' by taking on 'S.O.S.'

Oliver Hartmann contributed to EDGUY man Tobias Sammet's ambitious AVANTASIA eponymous project album of 2000.

Japanese versions of the 2001 album 'Dragonchaser', issued on the JVC Victor label, boasted an additional track 'Winner Takes It All'. AT VANCE would switch labels from the Shark concern to AFM Records in mid 2001.

AT VANCE formed part of a package billing with RHAPSODY and ANGEL DUST for European dates during April of 2002. The accompanying album, the Sascha Paeth produced 'Only Human', included the by now expected cover version in RAINBOW's hit 'I Surrender'. Japanese versions on the Avalon Marquee label added a bonus track in 'Heroes Of Honor'.

Hartmann, Schnur and Lucas also operate side project band HANZ DAMF.

Albums:
NO ESCAPE, Shark 199901 (1999)
Flying High / No Escape / No Speak / Die In Your Arms / All For One, One For All / Money, Money, Money / Four Seasons - Summer / Lost In Your Love / Power & Glory / Seven Seas
HEART OF STEEL, Shark 200003 (2000)
Prelude / Soldier Of Time / The Brave And

The Strong / Heart Of Steel / S.O.S. / King Of Your Dreams / Princess Of The Night / Goodbye / Why Do You Cry? / Don't You Believe A Stranger / Chopin - Etude No. 4
DRAGONCHASER, Shark (2001)
Dragonchaser / Ages Of Glory / Crucified / Beethoven, 5th Sinfoni / Heaven Can Wait / My Bleeding Heart / Two Kings / Too Late / Aces Death / Bandinerie
ONLY HUMAN, AFM 506382-2 (2002)
The Time Has Come / Only Human / Take My Pain / Fly To The Rainbow / Hold Your Fire / Four Seasons - Spring / Take Me Away / Time / Solfeggietto / Sing This Song / Witches Dance / Wings To Fly / I Surrender

AVALANCH (SPAIN)
Line-Up: Víctor García (vocals), Alberto Rionda (guitar), Roberto García (guitar), Francisco Fidalgo (bass), Iván Blanco (keyboards), Alberto Ardines (drums)

Spanish Heavy Metal band founded during 1991. AVALANCH's 1993 album 'Ready To The Glory' was crafted by a line-up of vocalist Juan Lozano, guitarists Juan Ángel Alaez and Javier de Castro, bassist Charly García and drummer Alberto Ardines. Keyboard contributions would come courtesy of Fernando Mon. The band line-up fluxed again in 1995 with Mon out of the picture and Javierín coming in on guitar. The following year Roberto García took Javierín's position. The 1997 AVALANCH album 'La Llama Eterna' would see the band having undergone a radical line up change with only Ardines and Lozano surviving. New members would comprise guitar players Alberto Rionda and Roberto García with Francisco Fidalgo on bass. This album would see an English lyric version, 'Eternal Flame', released by the Underground Symphony label. For 1999's ' El Llanto De Un Heroe' Víctor García took over the role as singer. The same year AVALANCH contributed their version of IRON MAIDEN's 'Run To The Hills' to the Locomotive Music tribute compilation 'Transylvania 666'.
The band would later induct keyboard player Iván Blanco who appeared for the first time on the live offering 'Dias De Gloria'. The album included a cover version of QUEEN's 'Save Me', also issued as a radio single and included on the tribute album 'Attack Of The Dragons'. AVALANCH would also cover JUDAS PRIEST's 'Hell Patrol' in 2000 for the Zero Records collection 'Metal Gods'.
March of 2002 brought yet another shift in personnel for AVALANCH with the induction of Ramón Lage of the PACOJONES BAND on lead vocals and former DESTILERIA drummer Marco Álvarez. The introduction of this last recruit now meant the band was

operating with none of the original members. Erstwhile AVALANCH members vocalist Víctor García, guitarist Fernando Mon and drummer Alberto Ardines would unite with guitarist Pablo García from RELATIVE SILENCE and DARNA bass player Alvaro Jardón to found WARCRY for an eponymous album.

Albums:
READY TO THE GLORY, Vodu (1993)
Intro / Misery / Ready To The Glory / Red Night / Vencers / Excalibur / Strangers In The Night / Treat Them Fine / The Wink Of The Moon
LA LLAMA ETERNA, (1997)
La Llama Eterna / El Mundo Perdido / El Despertar / Vicio Letal / Esclavo De La Ira / Avalon, La Morada Del Rey Arturo / Excalibur / Sigue Asi / Rainbow Warrior / Juego Cruel / La Taberna / Avalanch / El Cierre De La Taberna
ETERNAL FLAME, Underground Symphony USCD028 (1998)
Eternal Flame / Lost World / Awake / Slave Of The Anger / Avalon, The King´s Abode / Excalibur / Falling / Rainbow Warrior / Cruel Game / The Tavern / Avalanch / Closing Of The Tavern
EL LLANTU DE UN HEROE, Zero (1999)
Intro / Torquemada / Por Mi Libertad / Pelayo / Vientos Del Sur / Polvo, Sudor Y Sangre / Cid / Días De Gloria...? / No Pidas Que Crea En Ti / Cambaral / Aquí Estaré / Llanto De Un Héroe
DIAS DE GLORIA, Zero (2000)
Intro / Torquemada / Por Mi Libertad / El Despertar / Vicio Letal / Vientos Del Sur / Pelayo / I Want Out / Epilogo / Save Me
EN ANGEL CAIDO, Flames (2001)
Intro / Alma En Pena / Tierra De Nadie / Antojo De Un Dios / Xana / Las Ruinas Del Edén / El Angel Caído / Corazón Negro / Levántate Y Anda / El Septimo Dia

AVALON (GERMANY)
Line-Up: Many Stürner (vocals), Sebastian Eder (guitar), Petra Hasselkuss (bass), Jens Kucklkorn (keyboards), Peter 'Ringo' Kei (drums)

Heavy Rockers founded in 1992 out of Munich, AVALON came on the scene with the 'More Than Words' mini-album. AVALON toured America and Canada on the back of their full-length SPV debut 'Why Now' debut returning to Europe to open for SAVATAGE, GOTTHARD and SINNER.
AVALON's third album, 'Mystic Places', was produced by the esteemed Charlie Bauerfeind.

37

AVALON toured as guest to URIAH HEEP to promote the album although drummer Peter Kei had to be replaced mid tour because of spinal problems. His substitute was Ronny Dehn.

Prior to recording the 'Vision Eden' record vocalist Marty Stumer quit, the singer having throat problems. AVALON pulled in ex-COURT JESTER man the Sri Lankan born Chity Somapala, the resulting 'Eurasia' album being imbued with far Eastern influences. AVALON also increased their international membership for this album by drafting French drummer Jacques Voutay.

Somapala would divert off to found a side outing entitled THE SILHOUETTE in early 2001 in collusion with guitarist Lou St. Paul from American Metal band WINTER'S BANE.

Albums:
MORE THAN WORDS, Omega (1994)
Why Now ? / Rhythm Of My Heart / Foreplay / Just Try ! / True Metal / Never / More Than Words Can Say / Follow Me / Ever And Ever / One Night
WHY NOW, SPV 84-24302 CD (1995)
Why Now / Rhythm Of My Heart / Never / True Metal / Follow Me / Foreplay / Just Try / More Than Words Can Say / Ever And Ever / One Night
MYSTIC PLACES, Semaphore 37745CD (1997)
Places / I'm Falling / Passion For Glory / Crystal Ball / Through The Eye Of The End / Prisoner In My Mind / Two Mental / Time Of The Universe / Wasted Time / Burning Down The House / Isolation / Blind Dance
VISION EDEN, Omega (1998)
Are In Between Us / Children Of War / Lord Of Dignity / Fate Of Centuries / Age Of Salvation / Dancing With The Devil / The Road To Eden / Far Away / Gene Genius / Solitune
EURASIA, Omega (2000)
Aurora / Burning Souls / Temujin / Black Hole Wisdom / Eternal Flame / Save The Holy Land / The Last Call / Eurasia / The Stranger / The Painting / Kyrie / Semaruma

AVANISH (GERMANY / SWITZERLAND)
Line-Up: Joerg Graeter (vocals), Juergen Polarczyk (guitars), Tino Rothe (guitars), Mitch Koontz (bass), Alex Diehl (keyboards), Peter Steinbach (drums)

A Swiss / German collaboration. Power Metal band AVANISH issued their 'Gods Of Destiny' album through Ebola Records. AVANISH lost the services of bass player Mitch Koontz during 2002.
Albums:
GODS OF DESTINY, (2000)

Intro / Gods Of Destiny / Gods Of Destiny / Sign In The Sky / Dragon's Paradise / Help Yourself / Blood Of Love / Devil Beside / Change / Father's Eyes / Guardian Angel / Ten Years / When The Rain Begins To Fall

TOBIAS SAMMET of AVANTASIA

AVANTASIA (GERMANY)
Mammoth assemblage of Metal talent brought together by EDGUY's Tobias Sammet. Included were members of EDGUY guitarist Jens Ludwig, RHAPSODY drummer Alex Holzwarth, GAMMA RAY,'s Kai Hansen and Henjo Richter and HELLOWEEN's Marcus Großkopf.

Vocals were on hand from VIRGIN STEELE's David De Feis, AT VANCE's Oliver Hartmann, STRATOVARIUS' Timo Tolkki, ex-ANGRA man Andre Matos, former IMPELLITERRI and AXEL RUDI PELL singer ROB ROCK and Sharon Den Adel of WITHIN TEMPTATION. The album would prove an instant success shifting enough copies to even crack the national German album charts. It would be swiftly licensed to Century Media Records for an American release in July.

The second AVANTASIA album of 2002 would once again benefit from a huge wealth of outside talent. Including would be former HELLOWEEN singer MICHAEL KISKE, GAMMA RAY's Kai Hansen, VIRGIN STEELE front man David DeFeis, HELLOWEEN's Marcus Großkopf, KISS drummer Eric Singer, STRATOVARIUS man Timo Tolkki, MAGNUM's Bob Catley and Andre Matos of

38

SHAMAN. The album would break into the top twenty on the national German album charts.

Albums:
AVANTASIA - THE METAL OPERA, AFM 0046722 (2000) **36 FINLAND, 35 GERMANY, 48 SWEDEN**
Prelude / Reach Out For The Light / Serpents In Paradise / Malleus Melleficarum / Breaking Away / Farewell / The Glory Of Rome / In Nomine Patris / Avantasia / A New Dimension / Inside / Sign Of The Cross / The Tower
THE METAL OPERA PART II, AFM (2002) **17 GERMANY**
The Seven Angels / No Return / The Looking Glass / In Quest For / The Final Sacrifice / Neverland / Anywhere / Chalice Of Agony / Memory / Into The Unknown

AVENGER (GERMANY)
Line-Up: Peter Wagner (vocals / bass), Guiness (guitar), Jörg Michael (drums)

AVENGER later adopted the name RAGE to avoid confusion with the British act of the same name. Under their new guise RAGE, led by Peter 'Peavey' Wagner, would go on to become one of Germany's premier Metal acts and are still a powerful force to this day.
Drummer Jörg Michael would post RAGE find himself in great demand appearing with MEKONG DELTA, LAOS, HEADHUNTER, SCHWARZ ARBEIT, GRAVE DIGGER, STRATOVARIUS, AXEL RUDI PELL and RUNNING WILD.

Singles/EPs:
Depraved To Black / Down To The Bone / Prayers Of Steel (Live) / Faster Than Hell (Live), Wishbone WBLP 4 (1985) ('Depraved To Black' EP)

Albums:
PRAYERS OF STEEL, Wishbone WB 1412 (1984)
Battlefield / Southcross Union / Prayers Of Steel / Halloween / Faster Than Hell / Adoration / Rise Of The Creature / Sword Made Of Steel / Blood Lust / Assorted By Satan

AVENGER (UK)
Line-Up: Ian Swift (vocals), Lez Cheetham (guitar), Mick Moore (bass), Gary Young (drums)

The first incarnation of AVENGER evolved when ex-BLITZKRIEG vocalist Brian Ross teamed up with former AXE VICTIM bassist Mick Moore, drummer Gary Young and guitarist Steve Bird in September 1982. The band contributed the track 'Hot And Heavy Express' to the Neat 'One Take No Dubs' EP. Shortly after Bird left due to hearing problems (!) to be replaced by John Brownless.
This line-up recorded the 'Too Wild To Tame' single before Brownless was sacked and in came Cheetham. Ross left to fill the vacant slot as SATAN's vocalist when Ian Swift left and, in a bizarre turn of events, Swift joined AVENGER.
In 1985 AVENGER toured Europe with an additional guitarist Ginger, a former member of IPANEMA KATZ. However, after a handful of shows Ginger was allegedly sacked for taking too long in the dressing room applying make up! Ginger journeyed through ZIG ZAG, THE QUIREBOYS, THE THROBS and THE WILDHEARTS.
AVENGER contributed promo footage for three tracks 'Under The Hammer', 'Run For Your Life' and 'Revenge Attack' to the Neat video compilation 'Metal City' in 1985.
American guitarist GREG REITER replaced Lez Cheetham prior to recording 'Killer Elite'. Cheetham would later figure in the VENOM history.
Reiter's pedigree pre-AVENGER included stints with HOT ICE, TELEPATH, PSYCHOPATH (at one time fronted by a pre-CINDERELLA Tom Kiefer) and METALWOLF. Young was superseded by another American Darren Kurland.
The band toured the East coast of America, including dates opening for LIEGE LORD, but disintegrated midway through the dates. Towards the end there were plans to add an American vocalist.
Whilst Swift joined another Newcastle Upon Tyne Thrash act ATOMKRAFT Reiter founded GHOST DANCE with ex-PSYCHOPATH man Billy Gram and PRETTY POISON drummer Bobby Corea. By 1990 Reiter had joined Dutch Rockers HIGHWAY CHILE for the 'High Noon' album. Later work had Reiter as part of the Glammed up BITCH BOY alongside ex-PLASMATICS and WENDY O WILLIAMS drummer T.C. Tolliver. The guitarist would cut a solo album 'Fireflies' in 1996.
AVENGER were set to reform in 1995 with a line-up of Moore, Reiter and ex-RAVEN drummer Joe Hasselvander but this liaison never materialised.
Moore spent most of the nineties in a legal battle with Neat Records in a dispute over royalty statements and payments allegedly winning an out of court cash settlement and the reversion of his rights to the AVENGER back catalogue in 1997. To date these recordings have still not been reissued.

Singles:
One Take No Dubs EP, Neat 25 (1982)
Too Wild To Tame / On The Rocks, Neat 31

(1983)

BLOOD SPORTS, Neat 1018 (1984)
Death Race 2000 / Warfare / You'll Never Take Me Alive / Rough Ride / Victims Of Force / N.O.T.J. / On The Rocks / Enforcer / Matriarch
KILLER ELITE, Neat 1026 (1985)
Revenge Attack / Run For Your Life / Brand Of Torture / Steel On Steel / Right To Rock / Hard Times / Under The Hammer / Face To The Ground / Dangerous Games / Yesterday's Hero / M.M. 85 / Sawmill

AXE LA CHAPELLE (GERMANY)
Line-Up: Harry Kreiger (vocals), Ulli Wollgarten (guitar), Volker Marx (guitar), Uwe Wessel (bass), Uli Kusch (drums)

A Power Metal act with a Progressive touch from Aachen, AXE LA CHAPPELLE came together in 1987. Three demos were issued prior to the debut album. The band's debut album, which includes former GAMMA RAY and HOLY MOSES drummer Uli Kusch and ex-HELICON guitarist Volker Marx, features GAMMA RAY vocalist Ralf Scheepers on backing vocals.
Uli Kusch later enjoyed prominence with HELLOWEEN and is latterly with MASTERPLAN.

Albums:
GRAB WHAT YOU CAN, Major CC029/049-2 (1993)
XYZ / National Fools / Life In Cockaigne / Never Know What Fun Is / Addiction / What You Get Is What You Take / Eye Of The World / Your Game / My Way / New Ideals / Ambiguity

AXEHAMMER (USA)
Line-Up: Bill Ramp (vocals), Jerry Watt (guitar), Kit Carlson (bass), Joe Aghassi (drums)

A straight ahead Metal band, Los Angeles' AXEHAMMER recorded an album's worth of material in late 1986 / early 1987 with an undisclosed and allegedly, well-known producer. A major deal looked as if it was a mere formality, but the whole thing fell apart and the tapes remained unreleased. The specialist independent label Sentinel Steel caught wind and wound up releasing five of the band's songs from the sessions together with three tracks from AXE HAMMER's 1984 demo tape.
AXEHAMMER had previously only appeared on the New Renaissance compilation album 'Satan's Revenge' with the track 'Axehammer'

in the mid '80s.
The group had originally been formed in 1982 by guitarist Jerry Watt and bassist Kit Carlsen with the intention of putting together a European style Metal band. Recruiting drummer Mark Sky, the trio added a singer and cut a three song tape before parting company with him and eventually hooking up with Bill Ramp and second guitarist Jim Bratton. The track recorded for 'Satan's Revenge' (a compilation seemingly originally titled 'Metal Magic') featured Sky on drums, but not Bratton.
The drummer was to depart the group after the compilation appeared and this led to a brief period of inactivity as Watt and Carlsen decided to put the group on hold for around six months before reforming with Ramp and new skinsman Joe Aghassi. A decision was then taken to self-finance the recording of the aforementioned album in late 1986.
Needless to say, despite the appearance of the 'Lord Of The Realm' package in early 1998 AXEHAMMER split up long ago.

Albums:
LORD OF THE REALM, Sentinel Steel (1998)
Princess / Lord Of The Realm / Sands Of Time / Break Down The Walls / Axehammer / Wings Of Fire / Sword And Shield / Axehammer

AXENSTAR (SWEDEN)
Line-Up: Magnus Eriksson (vocals), Peppe Johansson (guitar), Thomas Eriksson (guitar), J. Magnus Ek (bass), Pontus Jansson (drums)

The roots of Metal band AXENSTAR date back to the 1998 covers band POWERAGE, founded by guitarist Peter 'Peppe' Johansson and bass player J. Magnus Ek. POWERAGE was fronted by vocalist Mr. Eddie with Magnus Söderman of LOST SOULS on lead guitar and Johan Burman of CHEMICAL CO-OPERATION on the drums. In this guise the band contributed their rendition of IRON MAIDEN's 'Hallowed Be Thy Name' to the 'Maiden Scandinavia' tribute album.
During 1999 Magnus Eriksson took over the lead vocal role, Thomas Eriksson took the lead guitar position and Pontus Jansson became the band's new drummer. With this revised formation the group began composing original material and cut the demo CD 'In The Beginning' during 2000. Two further songs, 'Confess Thy Sins' and 'Seventh Labyrinth', were committed to tape early the following year and by March the name switch to AXENSTAR had taken place.

A third promotion session, simply billed as 'Promo 2001', was cut in August.

AXENSTAR signed to the Spanish Arise label in 2002 for the debut album 'Perpetual Twilight'. The band also featured on the Arise HELLOWEEN tribute offering 'The Keepers Of Jericho Part II' with their take on 'Twilight Of The Gods'. Thomas Eriksson would also act as session guitarist for FRETERNIAS on their 2002 album.

AXXIS (GERMANY)

Line-Up: Bernhard Weiss (vocals), Walter Pietsch (guitar), Markus Gfeller (bass), Harry Oellers (keyboards), Richard Michaelski (drums)

Enjoying a reasonable amount of exposure in their time, German Melodic Metal outfit AXXIS' first demo tape, released in 1988, was titled 'Tears Of The Trees' and featured the initial line-up of AXXIS featured vocalist Bernhard Weiss, guitarist Walter Pietsch, bassist Werner Kleinhans and drummer Richard Michaelski. On first submission of this demo EMI rejected the band but upon a second push AXXIS were duly signed.

The first AXXIS album, February 1989's 'Kingdom Of The Night', gave the band one of the most successful debuts in German Rock history with exceptional sales in excess of 100,000 copies. Recognition of this feat was afforded by the Multimedia organisation, presenting AXXIS with an award for the 'Best Selling Debut by a German Rock Band'. Touring to promote the album in September of 1989 included guest slots to BLACK SABBATH.

The group added keyboard player Harry Oellers for the second album, released in August of 1990 and simply billed as 'II', and upon its release set off on a European headline tour. A live album, 'Access All Areas' issued in May 1991, cemented their reputation. 1993 continued the upward trend for AXXIS as their 'The Big Thrill' album, their first to be recorded in America and produced by Joey Balin, broke open new markets, necessitating increased live work including Japan. This territory would also witness the release of an exclusive album 'Profile', promoted by an acoustic tour by Weiss and Pietsch. AXXIS would do the European rounds once again with Russian band GORKY PARK as support.

The 1995 album 'Matters Of Survival' was produced by Keith Olsen, noted for his work with WHITESNAKE. The band still commanded popularity as evidenced by their appearance at the Rock Am Ring Festival in front of 30,000 people.

The 1997 effort 'Voodoo Vibes' was, working

alongside engineer Thomas Kemper, a self-produced work laid down in just 18 days at the legendary Dierks studios. Naturally, AXXIS found themselves on the road in Germany to promote its release in May of that year. A later bout of touring had AXXIS co-headlining alongside U.D.O. However, in January of 1998 guitarist Walter Pietsch opted to depart.

AXXIS, touting the 'Back To The Kingdom' album, made a welcome return in March 2000 on the independent Massacre label. Touring to promote the release found the band on the road with label mates PINK CREAM 69. The September 2001 'Eyes Of Darkness' album, which included a cover version of the APHRODITE'S CHILD track 'The Four Horsemen', would witness a band line-up of Weiss, Oellers, Michalski, guitarist Guido Wehmeyer and bass player Kuno Niemeyer.

AXXIS forged an alliance with KAMELOT for a lengthy run of European tour dates commencing on the January 16th 2002 at the Planet B in Korbach, Germany. AXXIS headlined on the German dates before switching to opening act for shows in the rest of Europe. The band had their version of 'Good Times, Bad Times' included on the Locomotive Music LED ZEPPELIN tribute album 'The Metal Zeppelin - The Music Remains The Same'.

Singles/EPs:
Living In A World / Young Souls, Electrola 147422-2 (1989) (7" Picture Disc)
Fire And Ice, Electrola 147437-2 (1989)
Kingdom Of The Night / Living In A World / Never Say Never / Tears Of The Trees, EMI P 518 821 (1989) (Promotion release)
Kingdom Of The Night / Young Souls / Kings Made Of Steel, Parlophone CDR 6225 (1989)
Hold You, Harvest (1990)
Touch The Rainbow, Harvest (1990)
Another Day (Special Acoustic Version) / Touch The Rainbow (Special Acoustic Version) / C'Est La Vie (Special Acoustic Version) / Another Day (Album Version), Spin 7243 8 6217424 (1995)
Sarajevo (Original version) / C'Est La Vie (Acoustic Tango version) / Fire And Ice (Acoustic version) / Sarajevo (Radio edit), (1998)

Albums:
KINGDOM OF THE NIGHT, Electrola CDP 564 7 91829 2 (1989)
Living In A World / Kingdom Of The Night / Never Say Never / Fire And Ice / Young Souls / For A Song / Love Is Like An Ocean / Tears Of The Trees / Just One Night / Kings

Made Of Steel / Living In A World (Extended Version)

AXXIS II, Harvest 951401 (1991)
The World Is Looking In Their Eyes / Save Me / Touch The Rainbow / Hold You / Ships Are Sailing / Little Look Back / Face To Face / Get Down / Gimme Back The Paradise / Hold You (Acoustic)

ACCESS ALL AREAS - LIVE, Harvest 797950-2 (1991)
Kingdom Of The Night / Trash In Tibet / Little Look Back / Touch The Rainbow / Face To Face / Tears Of The Trees / Ships Are Sailing / Living In A World / Save Me / Fire And Ice / Back To The Wall

THE BIG THRILL, Electrola 0777 7 81377-2-6 (1993)
Better World - Livin' In The Dark / Against A Brick Wall / Stay Don't Leave Me / Little War / No Advice / Love Doesn't Know Any Distance / Heaven's Seventh Train / Brother Moon / Waterdrop / The Wolf / Road To Never Neverland

MATTERS OF SURVIVAL, EMI Electrola (1995)
Ecstasy / Idolater / C'Est La Vie / On My Own / Just A Story / All My Life / Freedom Comes / Another Day / Fan The Flames / Watch Out / Hide Away / Back My Bones

VOODOO VIBES, EMI Electrola (1997)
Helena / Voodoo Vibes / Fly Away / Sarajevo / Desert Song / A Little Mercy / World Of Mystery / Alright / Love And Pain / A Life For A Life / Spider / The Show Is Over

BACK TO THE KINGDOM, Massacre MASSCD0238 (2000) **59 GERMANY**
Shadowman / Like A Sphinx / Flashback Radio / Heaven In Black / Only God Knows… / Sea Of Love / White Lights / Why Not?! / My Little Princess / Without You / Ice On Fire / Nana, Hey, Hey, Kiss Him Goodbye / Be A King

COLLECTION OF POWER, Massacre (2000)
Shadowman (Live) / Flashback Radio (Live) / Little War (Live) / Kings Made Of Steel (Live) / Julia (Acoustic version) / Heaven In Black (Acoustic version) / Moonlight (Demo) / AXXIS Screensaver No.1

EYES OF DARKNESS, Massacre (2001) **83 GERMANY**
Eyes Of Darkness (Chapter I) / Wonderland / The Four Horsemen / Brand New World / When The Sun Goes Down / Keep Flying / Battlefield Of Life / One Million Faces / At The Crack Of Dawn / Angel / Larger Than Life / Lost In Love

AYREON (HOLLAND)
Line-Up: Robert Soeterboek (vocals), Edward Reekers (vocals), Okkie Huysdens (vocals), Arjen Anthony Lucassen (guitar), Cleem Determeyer (keyboards), Rene Merkelbach (keyboards)

A Rock opera concept solo project by ex-BODINE and VENGEANCE guitarist / keyboard player Arjen Anthony Lucasson. AYREON would make a sizeable impact upon the Rock world and inspire a plethora of imitators internationally. The grandly titled 'The Final Experiment - A Rock Opera' album, a tale of a 6th century minstrel, features many guests including KINGDOM COME vocalist Lenny Wolf, VAN EE's Robert Soeterboek, KAYAK singer Edward Reekers, ELEGY's IAN PARRY and GOREFEST vocalist Jan-Chis De Koeijer. Lucasson's old comrades in arms Jay van Feggelen of BODINE and Leon Goewie of VENGEANCE would also be in force.

On the musical side drums would be held down by Ernst van Ee of VAN EE and HELLOISE whilst bass was delegated to Q65 man Peter Vink and Jan Bijlsma. FINCH's Cleem Determeijer provided the elaborate keyboard work.

The single, 'Sail Away To Avalon' finds GOLDEN EARRING's Barry Hay on lead vocals and flute. The 'Actual Fantasy' album was issued as a CD-ROM in the Netherlands, which included video footage for 'Strangers From Within'.

Oddly, despite the mammoth worldwide success of 'The Final Experiment' AYREON would temper the grandiosity down for 1996's follow up 'Actual Fantasy', this record, with both Soeterboek and Reekers in evidence once again, coming across as a straight forward accessible Hard Rock album.

'Into The Electric Castle', over 100 minutes of music lavished across a two CD set, would break the band internationally. The guest list was even more edifying than the debut. For this outing individual voices portrayed story line characters with Sharon van Edel of WITHIN TEMPTATION as 'Indian', FISH suitably cast as 'The Highlander', Anneke van Giersbergen of THE GATHERING as 'Egyptian', Jay van Feggelen as 'Barbarian', THRESHOLD's Damian Wilson as 'Knight' and Edwin Balogh of TAMAS as 'Roman'. The whole affair was held together by the esteemed patronage of ROGER DALTREY of THE WHO as the main 'Voice'. GOREFEST and LANA LANE man Ed Warby took on percussive duties throughout with Robby Valentine of VALENTINE, Ton Scherpenzeel of KAYAK and Clive Nolan of PENDRAGON demonstrating their skills on piano and keyboards. 'Into The Electric Castle' had a huge impact on the international Rock scene, which was soon awash with imitators.

42

Whilst the sprawling 'Into The Electric Castle' set had made it onto a double CD package the follow up 'Universal Migrator' was spread over two packages billed as 'The Dream Sequencer' and 'Flight Of The Migrator'.

'The Dream Sequencer' hosted the mellower side of AYREON. Donating their talents for this outing would be Johan Edlund of TIAMAT, Floor Jansen of AFTER FOREVER, LANA LANE, Jacqueline Govaert of KREZIP, Neal Morse of SPOCK'S BEARD and THRESHOLD's Damian Wilson. Rob Snijders of CELESTIAL SEASON manned the drum kit.

The latter sequence 'Flight Of The Migrator' would prove to be AYREON's most heavyweight offering to date. It pulled in such guests as PRIMAL FEAR's Ralph Scheepers, HELLOWEEN frontman ANDI DERIS, ELEGY's IAN PARRY, TIMO KOTIPELTO of STRATOVARIUS, Russell Allen of SYMPHONY X and RHAPSODY, VISION DIVINE and LABYRINTH vocalist Fabio Lione. Most notable of all though was the undoubted coup of attaining IRON MAIDEN's BRUCE DICKINSON.

Lucassen found time amidst all this activity to make a guest appearance on ERIK NORLANDER's 2000 album 'Into The Sunset'.

Such was the success of the AYREON project that an album collection of demos and alternate takes arrived in early 2001 dubbed 'Ayreonauts Only'.

Lucassen would divert his energies briefly onto another ambitious venture entitled AMBEON releasing the 'Fate Of A Dreamer' album in 2001. Lucassen announced the formation of a new Sci-Fi themed project STAR ONE in late 2001, a confederation of name musicians which included Dan Swanö of EDGE OF SANITY and NIGHTINGALE, Damian Wilson of THRESHOLD, Russell Allen from SYMPHONY X and countryman Floor Jansen of Doom merchants AFTER FOREVER.

Lucassen would form part of LANA LANE's touring band for 2002.

Albums:
THE FINAL EXPERIMENT - A ROCK OPERA, Trancemission TM001 (1995)
Prolgue: A - The Time Telepathy Experiment B - Overture, C - Ayreon's Quest / Act I 'The Dawning': The Awareness, A - The Premonition, B - Dreamtime (Words Become A Song), C - The Awakening; Eyes Of Time, A - Eyes Of Time, B-Brainwaves; The Banishment, A - A New Dawn, B - Gathering, C - The Accusation, D - The Banishment, E - Oblivion / Act II 'King Arthur's Court': Ye Courtyard Minstrel Boy,

Sail Away To Avalon, Nautre's Dance / Act III 'Visual Echoes': Computer Reign (Game Over), Waracle, Listen To The Waves, Magic Ride / Act IV 'Merlin's Will And Ayreon's Fate': Merlin's Will, The Charm Of The Seer. Swan Song, Ayreon's Fate - A - Ayreon's Fate, B - Merlin's Prophecy, C - Epilogue
ACTUAL FANTASY, Trancemission TM008 (1997)
Actual Fantasy / Abbey Of Synn / The Stranger From Within / Computer Eyes / Beyond The Last Horizon / Farside Of The World / Back On Planet Earth / Forevermore
INTO THE ELECTRIC CASTLE, JVC Victor VICP-60478~9 (1998)
Welcome To The New Dimension / Isis And Osiris / Amazing Flight / Time Beyond Time / The Decision Tree (We're Alive) / Tunnel Of Light / Across The Rainbow Bridge / The Garden Of Emotions / Valley Of The Queens / The Castle Hall / Tower Of Hope / Cosmic Fusion / The Mirror Maze / Evil Devolution / The Two Gates / "Forever" Of The Stars / Another Time, Another Space
UNIVERSAL MIGRATOR PART 1: THE DREAM SEQUENCER, Trancemission TM019 (2000)
The Dream Sequencer / My House On Mars / 2084 / One Small Step / The Shooting Company Of Captain Frans B. Cocq / Dragon On The Sea / Temple Of The Cat / Carried By The Wind / And The Druids Turn To Stone / The First Man On Earth / The Dream Sequencer Reprise
UNIVERSAL MIGRATOR PART 2: FLIGHT OF THE MIGRATOR, Trancemission (2000)
Chaos / Dawn Of A Million Souls / Journey On The Waves Of Time / To The Quasar / Into The Black Hole / Through The Wormhole / Out Of The White Hole / To The Solar System / The New Migrator
FOR AERONAUTS ONLY, Trancemission (2001)
Into The Blackhole / Out Of The White Hole / Through The Wormhole / Carpe Diem (1992 Home Demo) / Temple Of The Cat (Acoustic version) / Original Hippie's Amazing Trip (Medley) / Beyond The Last Horizon (2000 Version) / The Charm Of The Seer (1994 Home Demo) / Cold Metal (AMBEON)

AZRAEL (JAPAN)
Line-Up: Akira 'Akiller' Ishihara (vocals), Shigeru Shirao (guitar), Kentaro Sasagawa (guitar), Takehiko Yasuda (bass), Takuya Kita-Taku (keyboards), Yutaka Sagawa (drums)

Singles/EPs:
King Of The Steely Nation / Lethal Lover, PureRockJapan (1999)

RUN FOR THE NIGHT, Azra 9727 (1997)
Prologue / Soldiers Of The Pain / Magic In Your Eyes / Judgement Day / Run For The Night / Never Say Never / Going For Glory / Riding Through The Midnight / Miracle / Broken Dream / Calling You / Closing Insanity / Waiting For You
KING OF THE STEELY NATION, Highways TKCU-77041 (2000)
Knight In The Night / Behind The Mask / Beyond The Wall / King Of The Steely Nation / Hold On To The Young Love / Shadowdancer / Burning Down / Lethal Lover / Break The Ice / Taking Your Heart / Close To The Soul

AZRAEL (SPAIN)

Line-Up: Manuel (vocals), Enrique (guitar), Mario (guitar), Salas (bass), Miguel (keyboards), Maolo (drums)

Assembled in 1991, the Granada Power Metal band AZRAEL officially bowed in with the 1996 album 'Nada por Nadie'. Follow up 'Futuro' arrived in 1998. Both these early albums mixed Spanish and English lyrics.
During 1999 AZRAEL gained the honours of supporting MERCYFUL FATE on their Spanish tour. The same year the band cut a rendition of 'The Evil That Men Do' for and IRON MAIDEN tribute album 'Transilvania 666'.
AZRAEL signed with Locomotive Music in 2000 for the 'Mafia' opus, sung entirely in Spanish. Fourth workout 'Dimension IV' saw a 2001 release.

Albums:
NADA POR NADIE, (1996)
Azrael / Satan Time / Noticia Final / Prisoner / Mundo Sin Ley / The Blade / No Lo Quisieron Ver / Nada Por Nadie / Poer Que Animales / El Hechizo De Galadriel
FUTURO, AMB AMB001 (1998)
Intro: Traición / Entra La Spada Y La Pared / Inevitable Fin / Run On The Wind / Desilusión / Seventh Heaven / Nostradamus / Innocence / La Sombra
MAFIA, Locomotive Music LM042 (2000)
Vuela / Tarde Ya / Mafia / Volver A Nacer / Jehová / No Muerto / Alas De Cristal / Saca La Cabeza / Atrapado / Vendiste Tu Propia Vida / El Inexpugnable Ocaso Del Laberinto De La Razón
DIMENSION VI, Locomotive Music LM071 (2001)
En El Umbral / Sacrifico / Nada Que Temer / Sentencia / Mujer De Hielo / La Luz De Ishtar / La Noche Cae / Incierta Realidad / Tres Y El Apocalipsis / En La Otra Dimension

AZEROTH (ARGENTINA)

Line-Up: Diego Valdez (vocals), Juan Manuel Villagra (guitar), Oscar Castro (guitar), Fernando Ricciardulli (bass), Maria Eugenia Ricciardulli (drums)

Melodic Heavy Metal band AZEROTH, from the Argentinean province of Bs, was assembled in 1995 by the sibling Ricciardulli rhythm section of bassist Fernando and drummer Maria Eugenia along with guitarist Juan Manuel Villagra. The following year second guitarist Julio César Marcus was added and in 1997 singer Luis Alberto Luna. With this line-up AZEROTH undertook their first gigs in Beunos Aires.
The 2001 'Azeroth' album, recorded earlier in 1999, benefited from a final mix conducted by Charlie Bauerfeind. Lead vocal duties would be shared between Christian Bertoncelli of HORCAS and Adrián Barilari of RATA BLANCA.
The band would also figure on the RATA BLANCA tribute album of the same year 'La Leyenda Continua' donating the track 'Rompe El Hichizo'. The group line-up for this recording comprised former DHAK and BIZARRO vocalist Diego Valdez, guitarists Juan Manuel Villagra and Pablo Gamarra, bassist Fernando Ricciardulli, keyboard player Gustavo Jawanske and drummer María Eugenia Ricciardulli.
The band scored a notable support to NIGHTWISH and BARON ROJO at the 'Metal Rock Festival VI' in 2000, AZEROTH having two tracks 'La Salida' and 'Campana Al Deseirto' featured on the subsequent NEMS 'Festival Power Progressivo' compilation album. Further high profile gigs in 2001 had AZEROTH acting as opening act to SHAMAN and HELLOWEEN.

Albums:
AZEROTH, NEMS (2001)
El Dominio / En Agonía / La Salida / Esclavo Del Tiempo / Campaña Al Desierto / En La Frontera De Toda Razón / El Fin / Historias De Hoy / El Ocaso De Los Reyes

AZTEC JADE (New York, NY, USA)

Line-Up: Leon Ozug (vocals), Matt Howenstein (guitar), Bryan Kowalski (guitar), Tim Becker (keyboards), Rick Miller (drums)

Albany's AZTEC JADE started life as a covers band entitled SIDEWINDER delivering renditions of QUEENSRYCHE and DREAM THEATER tracks in the New York clubs. Adding vocalist Leon Ozug in 1994 the band ventured into penning original material, which first surfaced on the 1995 release 'Modern

Prophet'.

The 2000 album 'Paradise Lost' is a combination of the two earlier works with additional tracks. AZTEC JADE would donate covers to Adrenaline Record's tribute albums in homage to DREAM THEATER and QUEEN before signing to the Steelheart label for the 2002 album 'Concrete Eden'

Albums:

MODERN PROPHET, CMG (1995)

FRAME OF MIND, CMG (1998)
The Calling / To Believe / Mad Not Crazy / Desperate Land / Nosferatu / Atlantis / Regatta Fugue II / Stained / Gates Of Babylon / Requiem

PARADISE LOST, Rising Sun (2000)
Regatta Fugue Part I / The Calling / To Believe / Mad Not Crazy / Desperate Land / Nosferatu / Atlantis / Regatta Fugue Part II / Stained / Gates Of Babylon / Requiem / Modern Prophet / Dirty Secrets / Soul Inside Of Me / The Creator / Indian Summer / Odyssey

CONCRETE EDEN, Steelheart STH0202 (2002)
Concrete Eden / The Machine / Black October / Someone Not Me / Manifestation / Victory Procession / Visions / Revelations / The Final Hour / Issues / End Of Days

BACKSLASH (GERMANY)
Line-Up: Heike Grebita (vocals),
Holger Michel (guitar), Frank
Exner (guitar), Wolfgang
Scheler (bass), Jens Koehn
(drums)

Female fronted Melodic Heavy Metal. Forged
in 1995, BACKSLASH's first outing was a
single track 'Free' included on a local
Bamberg compilation album. During 1998 the
group set about recording their first album,
being joined by bassist Wolfgang Scheler in
the midst of these sessions to complete the
line-up.

Albums:
INTENTION, TTS (1999)
Sandman / Free / Hidden In My Arms /
Intention / Scream / Take My Hand / Shadows
/ Stole My Heart / Help Me / Don't Go
INSANITY, Point Music (2001)
Make Me Walk / Turn The Page Of Time /
Insanity / Lies / Angel From Hell / God
Knows / Perfect Game / Wild / Whispers In
The Garden Of Eden / Live Your Life / Fly
Away
PRINCESS OF DISHARMONY, (2002)
Wake Me / Princess Of Disharmony / The
Angels Leave The Sky / Pain / Summer In
Your Hair / Hit Me / Waiting Till The End /
Give Me A Sign / River Of Darkness / Licht
der Nacht / Rising Like A Shadow

BAD LIZARD (BELGIUM)
Line-Up: Eddy (vocals), Frank (guitar), Erwin
(guitar), Lou (bass), Patrick (drums)

Singles/EPs:
Killer On The Loose, Antler (1983)
Hot Girl / Mistake, Antler (1984)

Albums:
POWER OF DESTRUCTION, Antler (1986)
Black Hole / Out Of The City / Come Back /
Destroy The World / Deeds Of Darkness /
Power Of Destruction / Breaking Through /
Optical Illusion / Far Away From Home / No
Peace After War

BAD STEVE (GERMANY)
Line-Up: Phillip Magoo (vocals), Jan Komet
(guitar), Accu Becher (guitar), Rubi Rubach
(bass), Fritz Friedrich (drums)

Formed by ex-ACCEPT musicians guitarist
Jan Komet and drummer Fritz Friedrich. The
duo engaged ex-SIN CITY vocalist Phil
Magoo and former KANAAN guitarist Achu
Becher to the cause alongside bassist Rubi
Rubach.

BAD STEVE toured Germany in 1984 as
support to ACCEPT and, after the group split,
Rubarch briefly reunited with ACCEPT
vocalist Udo Dirkschneider in his U.D.O.
project band.

Albums:
KILLING THE NIGHT, Mausoleum (1985)
Bad Steve Is Coming / Light Up My Soul /
Killing The Night / Running To You / Inside
Looking Out / Across The Rainbow / Living
On The Frontline / Leather Girl /
Nightbreaker

BALANCE OF POWER (UK)
Line-Up: Lance King (vocals), Pete Southern
(guitar), Bill Yates (guitar) Ivan Gunn
(keyboards), Tony Ritchie (bass), Lionel
Hicks (drums)

Formed by one-time HEAVEN AND EARTH
guitarist Bill Yates and keyboard player Ivan
Gunn, the duo forged an alliance with ex-KID
WICKED men singer Tony Ritchie and
drummer Lionel Hicks. A second guitarist was
found in Paul Curtis, previously of LADY
LUCK - a band that had also once involved
Ritchie and Hicks. Bassist Chris Dale, ex-
ATOM SEED, THE MACHINE and BRUCE
DICKINSON band, was the last to join
although Gunn would be dismissed prior to
recording.
In 1997 the band would draft a new face out
front in the form of American Lance King. The
singer had previously operated with
FREELANCE and GEMINI, issuing two
albums with the latter act - a 1990
eponymous debut followed by 1992's 'Out For
Blood'. King's next port of call was THE
KINGS MACHINE and the resultant album 'A
State Of Mind'.
Whilst a brand new album was expected in
the early half of 1998, both Ritchie and Hicks
found time to add their touch as guest
musicians on the third VAN DAMNE album
'Renaissance'. Meantime Pete Southern had
supplanted Curtis. The BALANCE OF
POWER album 'Book Of Secrets', securing
releases in Japan through Pony Canyon and
Europe via Germany's Point Music, would
solidify the band's initial promise.
BALANCE OF POWER, minus Gunn, toured
Europe in 1999. Keyboards were in the
temporary hands of Leon Lawson of
PRAYING MANTIS.
Ritchie created UNITED STATES OF MIND
the same year. For the UNITED STATES OF
MIND album 'Silver Step Child' BALANCE OF
POWER men guitarist Pete Southern and
drummer Lionel Kicks contributed. 2000
found BALANCE OF POWER, now signed to

Germany's Massacre label, stepping up a gear for a full blown European tour in alliance with AXXIS and PINK CREAM 69.

Dale created SACK TRICK for the 2000 multi guest album 'Penguins On The Moon'. The bassist would eventually part ways with BALANCE OF POWER in the summer of 2001, his replacement in the four string position being none other than original band vocalist Tony Ritchie. This line-up issued the 'Perfect Balance' record.

Meanwhile, Lance King would also be found deputising for LIFEFORCE and, in partnership with VANIZE guitarist ROLF MUNKES, donating a track to a JASON BECKER tribute album. The King / Munkes alliance would be solidified with the star studded EMPIRE project album the same year.

A planned BALANCE OF POWER 2001 tour of America would end up being scrapped, the band only putting in the one gig at the 2nd annual Atlanta 'Progpower' festival. Bonus tracks on the Japanese version of the 'Perfect Balance' album, 'The Other Side Of Paradise' and 'The Time Of Our Lives', would be revealed as being archive UNITED STATES OF MIND material with newly added vocals from Lance King. This album found BALANCE OF POWER's global reach stretching further with 'Perfect Balance' being issued in North America by the Nightmare label, in Europe through Massacre, in Brazil, Irond Records in Russia by Frontline and by Avalon Marquee in Japan. Many of these releases were clad in differing cover art.

King would add session vocals to the 2002 DEFYANCE album entitled 'Transitional Forms'.

Albums:

WHEN THE WORLD FALLS DOWN, Anthem (1997)
Against The Odds / Overnight Sensation / Can't Close The Book / Hide Your Heart / Balance Of Power / Don't Wait Until Tomorrow / Something For Your Head / When Love Is On Your Side / The Real Thing (Carry On Dreaming) / These Are The Days / Summers Over

BOOK OF SECRETS, Point Music (1998)
Desert Of Lost Souls / Walking On Top Of The World / Book Of Secrets / When Heaven Calls Your Name / It's Not Over / Do You Dream Of Angels / Seven Days Into Nevermore / Miracles And Dreams / Stranger Days (To Come)

TEN MORE TALES... OF GRAND ILLUSION, Massacre MASSCD0229 (1999)
Day Breaker / Prisoner Of Pride / Savage Tears / Under The Spell / Blind Man / About

BALANCE OF POWER

To Burn / Under Innocence Wing / Sins Of The World / The Darker Side / Ten More Tales Of Grand Illusion

PERFECT BALANCE, Massacre (2001)
Higher Than The Sun / Shelter Me / Fire Dance / One Voice / The Pleasure Room / Killer Of The Cure / House Of Cain / Hard Life / Searching For The Truth

BAL SAGOTH (UK)

Line-Up: Byron A. Roberts (vocals), Chris Maudling (guitar), Mark Greenwell (bass), Jonny Maudling (keyboards), Dave Mackintosh (drums)

A Dark, Black neo-Pagan "Battle" Metal band out of Yorkshire with a predilection for lengthy song titles. BAL SAGOTH was formulated as an idea by vocalist Byron Roberts as early as 1989 but it would not be until July of 1993 that the Maudling siblings guitarist Christopher and drummer Jonny involvement took the concept into a band format. Further draftees in September of the same year, bassist Jason Porter and keyboard player Vincent Crabtree brought BAL SAGOTH up to full strength and by the close of the year an inaugural demo had been cut.

The band duly signed a three album deal with the Cacophonous label but delays held back the issue of the tantalising debut album 'A Black Moon Broods Over Lemuris' until May of 1995. During this timeframe Crabtree departed and was duly replaced by Leon Forrest. BAL SAGOTH was scheduled to put in their first live performances supporting CRADLE OF FILTH but Roberts sustained an injury whilst stage diving at a CANNIBAL CORPSE concert which scotched these plans.

It would be April of 1995 that BAL SAGOTH finally embarked on the live trail with a gig at the Dublin Castle in London. Upon the album's eventual release support dates to Portuguese Gothic Black Metal act MOONSPELL were put in during July upfront of a tour of the UK and Ireland with label mates PRIMORDIAL and SIGH in September. However, BAL SAGOTH would pull out of these shows due to disagreements with the promoter. The band's stature was already ascendant in mainland Europe though and BAL SAGOTH headlined the Belgian 'Ragnarok' festival in November.

The following month bassist Jason Porter was ousted by the recruitment of Alastair McLatchy. The band toured Europe for the first time on a package billing with DARK FUNERAL and ANCIENT in February of 1997. BAL SAGOTH supported EMPEROR at the London Astoria and SINISTER in Belgium before completing a second round of

European shows in alliance with EMPEROR and NOCTURNAL BREED in October of the same year.

As 1998 broke Forrest announced his exit for a career in the police. Jonny Maudling manoeuvred over to keyboards to plug the gap and Dave Mackintosh took the drum stool. During the summer MacLatchy broke ranks too and Mark Greenwell took over on bass.

Jonny Maudling found himself on loan to MY DYING BRIDE for European touring during 1999. The band signed to Nuclear Blast during 1999 for 'The Power Cosmic' album.

BAL SAGOTH supported arch Black Metal Swedes MARDUK at the London Dome in December of 2001.

Albums:

A BLACK MOON BROODS OVER LEMURIA, Cacophonous NIHIL 4CD (1995)
Hatheg Kla / Dreaming Of Atlantean Spires / Spellcraft And Moonfire (Beyond The Citadel Of Frosts) / A Black Moons Broods Over Lemuria / Enthroned In The Temple Of The Serpent Kings / Shadows 'neath The Black Pyramid / Witch-Storm / The Ravening / Into The Silent Chambers Of The Sapphirean Throne (Sagas From The Untedelivian Scrolls) / Valley Of Silent Paths

STARFIRE BURNING OVER THE ICE VEILED THRONE OF ULTIMA THULE, Cacophonous NIHIL 18 CD (1996)
Black Dragons Soar Above The Mountain Of Shadows (Epilogue) / To Dethrone The Witch-Queen Of Mytos K'unn (The Legend Of The Battle Of Blackhelm Vale) / As The Vortex Illumines The Crystalline Walls Of Kor-Avul-Thaa / Starfire Burning Upon The Ice - Veiled Throne Of Ultima Thule / Journey To The Isle Of Sists (Over The Moonless Depths Of Night-Dark Seas) / The Splendour Of A Thousand Swords Gleaming Beneath The Blazon Of The Hyperborean Empire / Ad Lo, When The Imperium Marches Against Gul-Kothoth, Then Dark Sorceries Shall Enshroud The Citadel Of The Obsidian Crown / Summoning The Guardians Of The Astral Gate / In The Raven-Hunted Forests Of Darkenhold, Where Shadows Reign And The Hues Of Sunlight Never Dance / At The Altar Of The Dreaming Gods (Epilogue)

BATTLE MAGIC, Cacophonous NIHIL (1998)
Battle Magic / Naked Steel (The Warrior's Saga) / A Tale From The Deep Woods / Return To The Praesidium Of Ys / Crystal Shards / The Dark Liege Of Chaos Is Unleashed At The Ensorcelled Shrine Of A'Zura-Kai (The Splendour Of A Thousand Swords Gleaming Beneath The Blazon Of The Hyperborean Empire Part II) / When

Rides The Scion Of The Storms / Blood Slakes The Sand At The Circus Maximus / Thwarted By The Dark (Blade Of The Vampyre Hunter) / And Atlantis Falls
THE POWER COSMIC, Nuclear Blast NB 421-2 (1999)
The Awakening Of The Stars / The Voyagers Beneath The Mare Imbrium / The Empyreal Lexicon / Of Carnage And A Gathering Of Wolves / Callisto Rising / The Scourge Of The Fourth Celestial Host / Behold, The Armies Of War Descend Screaming From The Heavens! / The Thirteen Cryptical Prophecies Of Mu
ATLANTIS ASCENDANT, Nuclear Blast NB 584-2 (2001)
The Epsilon Exordium / Atlantis Ascendant / Draconis Albionensis / Star-Maps Of The Ancient Cosmographers / The Ghost Of Angkor Wat / The Splendour Of A Thousand Swords Gleaming Beneath The Blazon Of The Hyperborean Empire (Part III) / The Dreamer In Catacombs Of Ur / In Search Of The Lost Cities Of Antarctica / The Chronicle Of Shadows / Six Keys To The Onyx Pyramid

BATTLE BRATT (New York, NY, USA)
Line-Up: Anthony 'Odessa' Bourray (vocals), Michael R. Mostert (guitar), Robert Dexter (bass), Matt C. Aghetti (drums)

BATTLE BRATT issued a solitary album. Produced by David De Feis of VIRGIN STEELE the album is now a highly collectable item.

Albums:
BATTLE BRAT, U.S. Metal US15 (1988)
Winds Of Change / Cruizin' For Action / Don't Fight The Power / You're The One / Back To Love / Heat Of The Night / Rock n' Roll Sin / Lost Without Love / Can't Let Your Love Go

BATTLORN (TURKEY)
Line-Up: Yasam Hancilar (vocals), Serkan Ozay (guitar), Yalim Alatli (bass), Koray Alarsan (keyboards), Onur Senturk (drums)

BATTLORN would lose bassist Sevan Amyroglou to KNIGHT ERRANT before recording of the self-financed EP 'Long Way From The Dark' during 2001.

Singles/EPs:
Minotaur / Harper's Song / Deepest Cut / One Ring, (2002) ('Long Way From The Dark' EP)

BATTLEFIELD (GERMANY)
Line-Up: Connie Ernst (vocals), Arthur Schilling (guitar), Frank Nitti (guitar), Patrick Renner (bass), Gerd Haußmann (drums)

BATTLEFIELD, a Power Metal quintet, was formed in 1987 by guitarists Arthur Schilling and Frank Nitti. The duo was joined by drummer Gerd Haußmann before adding bassist Andres Rückle and female vocalist Conny Ernst.
Following the bankruptcy of BATTLEFIELD's record label T.R.C. the band released a demo tape in 1990 aptly entitled 'Time To Rethink'. Ernst would join an early line-up of IVANHOE. Vocalist Tanja Ivenz was fronting the band by the second album in a revised BATTLEFIELD line-up that also saw new faces in bassist Patrick Renner and drummer Stephan Fiedler.
The group played with the likes of PSYCHOTIC WALTZ, LIFE ARTIST and GYPSY KISS.

Singles/EPs:
We Come To Fight / Nuclear Death / Knock On Your Door / Grave Of The Unknown / Possessed Preacher, TRC 011 (1988) ('We Come To Fight' EP)

Albums:
STILL AND EVER AGAIN, Rising Sun IRS 972 223 (1991)
Experienced To Die / Still And Ever Again / Battlefield Of Misery / Red Rag / A Leap In The Dark / Experienced To Kill / Suction Of Eternity / If Our Earth Could Cry / Garden Of Stones
SPIRIT OF TIME, Rising Sun SPV 084-62162(1993)
Walls In Deformation / Heat In November / Living Skin / Through The Moment Of Changes / 7th Sky / There Ain't No Sorrow / Geradine / Spirit Of Time / Oh Moon

BATTLEROAR (GREECE)
Line-Up: Vagelis Krouskas (vocals), Kostas Tzortzis (guitar), Manolis Karazeris (guitar), Christos Remoundos (bass), Nick Papadopoulos (drums)

BATTLEROAR, founded in September of 2000, are an industrious renaissance act musically rooted in the American mid '80s Metal scene. The band have had the good fortune of supporting two of their musical inspirations, BROCAS HELM and OMEN, on their Greek tours of 2001 and March 2002 respectively. BATTLEROAR bowed in with an eponymous self-financed 'live in the studio' EP during November of 2001. A 7" single

'Dragonship' arrived in March of the following year.

Singles/EPs:
Swordbrothers / Almuric / Battleroar / Morituri Te Salutant / Dragonship, (2001) ('Battleroar' EP)
Dragonship / Swordbrothers, (2002)

BATTLEZONE (UK)

Line-Up: Paul Dianno (vocals), Graham Bath (guitar), John Wiggins (guitar), Pete West (bass), Steve Hopgood (drums)

BATTLEZONE was the title of renowned former IRON MAIDEN vocalist PAUL DIANNO's first band to come to the attention of the public following the break up of DIANNO and found Paul very definitely back into Metal territory. Dianno had previously formed STRIKE whilst in America with drummer Bob Falck and guitarist John Hurley, but the project eventually wound up as BATTLEZONE upon the vocalist's return to Britain.

The band's initial line-up comprised Dianno, guitarists Hurley and Darren Aldridge, bassist Laurence Kessler from Swiss act EMPIRE and former WOLF, CONQUEST and AUNT MAY Adam Parsons on drums. The latter had gone under the stage name A.D. Dynamite whilst in AUNT MAY. However, Parsons left shortly after to form the London based Glam troupe BELLADONNA and Falck reappeared on the scene in time to record the band's first album.

1986 also saw the enrolment of former DEEP MACHINE, LONEWOLF and TOKYO BLADE guitarist John Wiggins.

BATTLEZONE performed a club tour of America in 1987 to promote the debut 'Fighting Back', but musical differences within the group led to the departure of John Hurley and Bob Falck. Following the tour's completion their places were taken by PERSIAN RISK members Graham Bath and Steve Hopgood respectively. Hopgood had during the early '80s been a member of SHY and CHINATOWN.

Following the break up of BATTLEZONE, Dianno and Hopgood formed Power Metal band KILLERS releasing four albums. Hurley would later join LO GIRLS. 1990 also found Dianno fronting PRAYING MANTIS for a tour of Japan and the subsequent 'Live At Last' album.

Wiggins joined a reformed TOKYO BLADE in 1995. Dianno also kept his hand in during and after KILLERS by issuing a succession of solo albums.

By 1998 Dianno had resurrected the name

BATTLEZONE. Joining him were Wiggins and fellow ex-TOKYO BLADE members bassist Colin Riggs and drummer Marc Angel. The latter had also been a member of BERLIN and CHINATOWN. Second guitars were supplied by Paulo Turin. This line-up cut the 'Feel My Pain' album.

The band toured Brazil in the same year playing a three-week tour to sell out audiences up to 6,000 fans a night. BATTLEZONE were brought back down to earth upon their return home when they put in a gig at the Walthamstow Royal Standard!

Dianno has since gone solo again recording with Brazilian musicians for a new DIANNO album, the highly praised 'Nomad'.

Albums:
FIGHTING BACK, Rawpower RAWLP 020 (1986)
(Forever) Fighting Back / Welcome To The Battlezone / Warchild / In The Darkness / The Lord God Gave Us Caine / Running Blind / Too Much To Heart / Voice On The Radio / Welfare Warriors / Feel The Rock
CHILDREN OF MADNESS, Powerstation LC 9067 (1987)
Rip It Up / I Don't Wanna Know / Nuclear Breakdown / Torch Of Hate / Whispered Rage / Children Of Madness / Metal Tears / It's Love / Overloaded / The Promise
WARCHILD - THE BEST OF BATTLEZONE, Powerstation (1988)
(Forever) Fighting Back / Welcome To The Battlezone / Warchild / The Land God Gave To Caine / Too Much To Heart / Voice On The Radio / Rising Star / Rip It Up / I Don't Wanna Know / Nuclear Breakdown / Torch Of Hate / Whispered Rage / Children Of Madness / Metal Tears / It's Love / Overloaded / The Promise / To The Limit
FEEL MY PAIN, Zoom Club ZCR CD10 (1998)
Feel My Pain / C.O.M. '98 / Victim / The Forgotten Ones / Push / Snake Eyes / Smack / The Black / Fear Part 1

BEFORE EDEN (BRAZIL)

Line-Up: Jaison Peixer (vocals), Alessandro Kotlinsky (guitar), Marcos R. Cardoso (bass), Juliano Scharf (keyboards), Júlio César K. Kuhlewein (drums)

Progressive Power Metal out of Blumenau, Santa Catarina. BEFORE EDEN came into being during 1998 as a totally instrumental unit of guitarist Alessandro Kotlinsky, bass player Marcos R. Cardoso, keyboard player Juliano Scharf and drummer Júlio César K. Kuhlewein. Although on the search for a singer, the first series of live performances

PAUL DIANNO of BATTLEZONE
Photo : Nico Wobben

were undertaken entirely instrumentally.

The departure of Kuhlewein set the fledgling band back but in 1999 vocalist Jaison Peixer was to sign up. Some time after Kuhlewein resumed his post.

Marlon Silva, previously with PERPETUAL DREAMS, became BEFORE EDEN's new front man in July 2002.

Albums:

BEFORE EDEN, (2001)
Prelude / Fallen Angel / Elemental Master / Space Labyrinth / Between Love And Glory (Part 1) / Between Love And Glory (Part 2) / Before Eden

BEHOLDER (ITALY)

Line-Up: Patrick Wire (vocals), Leanan Sidhe (vocals), Matt Treasure (guitar), Markus Mayer (guitar), Andy McKein (bass), Mark Vikar (keyboards), Thyus Onil (drums)

Power Metal BEHOLDER employs both male and female lead vocalists in Patrick Wire and Leanan Sidhe. BEHOLDER made their entrance with a 1999 demo 'A Dream Of Eternal Majesty'. A promotional CD 'Between Death And Glory', produced by Marco Cecconi of POWER SYMPHONY and featuring new drummer Mike Sachs, was to follow. With interest from various labels now piqued BEHOLDER, adding another member in second guitarist Markus Mayer, cut a further three track demo, 'Between Death And Glory II', which secured a deal with the Dragonheart label.

Prior to recording of the album 'The Legend Begins' Andy McKein stepped in as the band's new bass player, supplanting previous incumbent Andy Newman. SECRET SPHERE guitarist Aldo Lonobile also lent his talents in a guest capacity. There were yet more changes to come in January of 2001 with both keyboard player Peter Ryan and drummer Mike Sachs leaving. Bringing the band back up to strength would be Mark 'Njordhr' Vikar on keyboards and drummer Thyus Onil.

Promoting the debut BEHOLDER performed at the prestigious JUDAS PRIEST headlined 'Gods Of Metal' festival in Italy during 2001.

Matt Treasure is an erstwhile member of Black Metal band MYSTICAL FULLMOON. Besides their BEHOLDER duties Markus plays with Thrash band UNSCARRED. Keyboard player Njordhr is a member of POWER SYMPHONY.

Albums:

THE LEGEND BEGINS, Dragonheart (2002)
Enter The Realm / The Ring Of Freedom / Ivory Tower / Call For Revenge / Blood And Pain / The Ancient Prophecy - The Journey / The Ancient Prophecy - The Oath / The Fallen Kingdom / Until Darkness Falls / Chains Of Fate

BETO VASQUEZ INFINITY
(ARGENTINA)

Line-Up: David Lazar (vocals), Diego Leone (vocals), Ailin Alybel (vocals), Javier Bagalá (guitar), Gonzalo Iglesias (guitar), Pablo Soler (guitar), Beto Vasquez (bass), Lilah Bertolini (flute), Danilo Moschen (keyboards), Marcelo Ponce (drums)

An adventurous Progressive / Symphonic Metal extravaganza convened by erstwhile NEPAL bassist Beto Vasquez. For the eponymous debut 2001 album Vasquez was able to assemble a whole array of international talent to fulfil his musical vision. For initial live work in South America Vasquez compiled an Argentinean band numbering former NEPAL colleagues drummer Marcelo Ponce and guitar player Javier Bagalá, HUMANIMAL guitarist Pablo Soler, SHANGRI LA singer Max Ditamo, flautist Lilah Bertolini, keyboard player Danilo Moschen and guitarist Gonzalo Iglesias. With this line-up the group opened for NIGHTWISH in Buenos Aires during 2000, followed later the same year with a guest slot to LABYRINTH and VISION DIVINE. Unashamed to show their influences BETO VASQUEZ INFINITY would perform live cover versions of PINK FLOYD's 'High Hopes' and RHAPSODY's 'Land Of Immortals'.

In January of 2001 Ditamo returned to his former act SHANGRI LA. Vasquez drafted no less than three singers en masse as replacements in David Lazar, Diego Leone and Ailin Alybel. Donating their talents to recording the album would be STRATOVARIUS drummer Jorg Michael, RHAPSODY vocalist Fabio Leone, Candice Night of BLACKMORE'S NIGHT, Tarja Turunen of NIGHTWISH and Sabine Edelsbacher from EDENBRIDGE.

Latterly BETO VASQUEZ INFINITY has recorded a version of JUDAS PRIEST's 'Freewheel Burning' for inclusion on a tribute album.

Singles/EPs:

The Battle Of Valmourt (Vocal duet version) / Promises Under The Rain / (Multimedia track), NEMS NEMS267 (2001)

Albums:

BETO VASQUEZ INFINITY, NEMS NEMS268 (2001)

Until Dawn (Angels Of Light) / Wizard / The Battle Of The Past / Sadness In The Night / Voyagers Of Time - Through Times Part I / Voyagers Of Time - Through Times Part II / Voyagers Of Time - Golden Hair / Voyagers Of Time - Infinity Space / Voyagers Of Time - Through Times Part III / The Laws Of The Future / Promises Under The Rain

BEYOND REALITY (Hampton, CT, USA)
Line-Up: Martin O'Brien (vocals), Anthony Ciarleglio (guitar), Chris Isreal (guitar), Duke Gunn (bass), Mike Meneo (drums)

A combination of pure Power Metal and conceptual Progressive Rock, BEYOND REALITY started life as RED ALERT as long ago as 1988. The band switched to their current moniker and have undergone a number of line-up changes as time has progressed.
The band's third album, 'Lost Shade Of Light' features new guitarist Jeff Vaccino.

Albums:
BEYOND REALITY, (1993)
BALANCE OF CONTRAST, (1995)
LOST SHADES OF LIGHT, BR CDD01 (1996)
It Was A Dark And Stormy Night... / Wolves Of Winter / Losing Faith / America / If I / The Voices In My Head / Childhood Soldier / My Obsession / I'll Always Be There / Hunting The Demon / Before The Dawn / Beyond Reality / Last Goodbyes / A Return To Reality / Scarred / It Was A Dark And Stormy Night...

BITCH (Los Angeles, CA, USA)
Line-Up: Betsy (vocals), Dave Carruth (guitar), Mark Anthony Webb (bass), Robbie Settles (drums)

S&M fanatic Betsy Weiss was previously fronting Los Angeles Ska band THE BOX BOYS before discovering the delights of Heavy Metal and carving out a niche in American Metal history for herself as front woman with the notorious BITCH
The original line-up of the band featured Betsy, guitarist David Carruth, bassist Richard Zusman and drummer Robby Settles. This incarnation recorded the first BITCH demo, from which they contributed the semi-classic 'Live For The Whip' for the first 'Metal Massacre' compilation album issued by Metal Blade in 1982, signing a deal with the label soon afterwards.
Prior to the recording of the band's 'Damnation Alley' mini-album, Zusman was replaced by former MOLTEN LEATHER

bassist Mark Anthony Webb. MOLTEN LEATHER had been a featured act on the second 'Metal Massacre' volume released in late '82.
'Riding In Thunder', a track to be featured on BITCH's first full-blown album, 'Be My Slave', was one of the tracks chosen for inclusion on 1983's 'Metal Massacre III'.
In late 1983 bassist Mark Webb departed, his position being filled by Ron Cordy, previously with fellow Los Angeles act OVERKILL.
In order to pursue a more commercial direction BITCH changed their name in favour of their lead vocalist's, recording a self-titled album under the BETSY handle for Metal Blade in 1988.
A BITCH odds n' sods album was issued by Metal Blade in 1989 featuring a selection of unreleased and remixed tracks, including 'Walls Of Love' from the then forthcoming BET-Z project.

Singles/EPs:
I'm In Love, Mystic (1983) (Split 7" with HELLION)

Albums:
DAMNATION ALLEY, Metal Blade (1982)
He's Gone / Never Come Home / Saturdays / Damnation Alley / Live For The Whip
BE MY SLAVE, Metal Blade (1983)
Right From The Start / Be My Slave / Leatherbound / Riding In Thunder / Save You From The World / Live For The Whip / Heavy Metal Breakdown / Gimme A Kiss / In Heat / Make It Real (Make It Rock) / World War III
THE BITCH IS BACK, Metal Blade (1987)
Do You Want To Rock / Hot & Heavy / Me And The Boys / Storm Raging Up / The Bitch Is Back / Head Banger / Fist To Face / Turns Me On / Skull Crusher
A ROSE BY ANY OTHER NAME, Metal Blade (1989)
Walls Of Love / Throw Me In / Sunset Strut / Skullcrusher / Crashthepartysmashthecake / Make It Real

BLACK ABYSS (GERMANY)
Line-Up: Olliver Hornung (vocals), Stefan Roder (guitar), Markus Weiser (guitar), Bernd Gerosa (bass), Andreas Heidemann (drums)

'80s style Heavy Metal act out of Southern Germany. Founded in 1990 BLACK ABYSS first came to notice with the 1992 Falk Gruber produced demo tape 'For Eternity'. The group self-financed 1998's 'Why' album before signing to the Bossy Ogress label.
The July 2001 BLACK ABYSS album 'Land Of Darkness' would include a cover version of

53

IRON MAIDEN's 'The Trooper', the track featuring a guesting Sven D'Anna of WIZARD on vocals. BRAINSTORM's Marcus Jürgens also guests on these sessions.

BLACK ABYSS, despite losing the services of bassist Bernd Gerosa in May, was projecting a third album for 2002 release entitled 'Angels Wear Black'.

Albums:
WHY, Black Abyss (1998)
Black Abyss / Never / Day By Day / Revolution / Why / One And Only / Key Of Hope / Sleep / Father / Use The Day
LAND OF DARKNESS, Bossy Ogress (2000)
Eye Of The Storm / Black Mirror / Chainbreaker / Burning Bridges / Frozen Tears / Hunted Forever / The Trooper / The Missing Link / Betrayer / Land Of Darkness

BLACK FATE (GREECE)
Line-Up: Stelios Papakostas (vocals), Elias Tsintzilonis (guitar), Albertos Oikonomou (bass), Maravgakis Giorgos (keyboards), Nikos Tsint

BLACK FATE was first convened as covers act METAL INVADERS during 1990. By 1992 this band's line-up cited vocalist / bassist Heracles Fanarakis, guitar player Elias Tsintzilonis and drummer Nikos Tsintzilonis, issuing a demo that year entitled 'Blackfate'. By 1994 Giannis Theologis on bass and Maravgakis Giorgos had been enrolled on keyboard, Fanarakis now solely devoted to lead vocals. Under this revised formation a second promotion session, 'A Piece Of Dream', was recorded. However, with various members fulfilling their military national service added to the departure of Fanarakis from the fold, 1995 signalled a period of unproductivity.

The band made a return in 1999 just as the Mediterranean Power Metal book was cresting. As BLACK FATE the band were now fronted by Stelios Papakostas, actually an earlier METAL INVADERS member. Signing to the Greek Secret Port label BLACK FATE delivered their 'Uncover' debut, recorded between September and November 1999 at the RockSound studio at Thessaloniki, in 2002.

Albums:
UNCOVER, Secret Port (2002)
Intro / No Mask / Exile Of Dreams / Why? / Queen Of The Night / Part Of The Act / Bleeding / Mindscape / Out Of This Place / Desperate

BLACK JESTER (ITALY)
Line-Up: Alex D'Este (vocals), Paolo Viani (guitar), Gil Teso (bass), Nick Angel (keyboards), Alberto Masiero (drums)

Neo Classical styled Progressive Metal that delivered three albums of high calibre. The debut 1993 'Diary Of A Blind Angel' featured keyboard player Nico Ordorico who possibly adopted the stage name Nick Angel for their next effort 'Welcome To The Moonlight Circus'. Sometime following the epic conceptual third outing 'The Divine Comedy' in 1998, which saw Rocco Prete handling keyboards, the band folded.

BLACK JESTER guitarist Paolo Viani and drummer Alberto Masiero would both later figure in MOONLIGHT CIRCUS. The guitarist also figures in the Progressive Metal band MAEVE OF CONNACHT. By the summer of 2002 Viani was announced as having joined the recently reformed cult American Power Metal band WARLORD.

Albums:
DIARY OF A BLIND ANGEL, Music Is Intelligence WMMS 021 (1993)
Night Voices / The Tower And The Minstrel / Diary Of A Blind Angel / Time Theater / King Of Eternity / Mother Moon / Black Jester Opera
WELCOME TO THE MOONLIGHT CIRCUS, Music Is Intelligence WMMS 037 (1994)
The Labyrinth / Mirrors Song / The Wayfarer / Glance Towards The Sky / Consciousness Hymn / Symphonies Of Immortal Winds / Welcome To The Moonlight Circus
THE DIVINE COMEDY, Elevate ER01001 (1997)
Inferno: Enigma Overture / Inferno: Towards The Black Theatre / Inferno: Behind That Gate / Inferno: On The Neon Crucifixes' Road / Inferno: The Abyss / Inferno: Another Childhood's Stake / Inferno: Falling In The Nightwhirl / Inferno: Room After Room / Inferno: Requiem For An Endless Jigsaw / Inferno: The Final Stage / Purgatorio: The Angel And The Fisherman / Purgatorio: Harbour Of Sinners / Purgatorio: The Detaching March / Purgatorio: Tears Of Dew / Paradiso: One More Time / Paradiso: Towards The Light / Paradiso: Sailin' On The Rainbow's Wave / Paradiso: The Flying Ship / Paradiso: Lost In The Open Skies / Paradiso: The Divine Parade / Paradiso: Epilogue For A White Rose

BLACK MAJESTY (AUSTRALIA)
Line-Up: John Cavaliere (vocals), Steve Janevski (guitar), Hanny Mohamed (guitar), Joe Fata (bass), Pavel Konvalinka (drums)

BLACK MAJESTY evolved from two acts in succession - KYMERA and ARKAYA. Featuring vocalist John Gio, CYCLONE TRACY guitarist Steve Janevski and AMETHYST drummer Vestra ARKAYA, for a brief spell, also had erstwhile PEGAZUS front man Danny Cecati as their lead vocalist. Corey Betts, also bassist with PEGAZUS, would also serve a term with ARKAYA.

The ties between PEGAZUS and ARKAYA were strengthened when it was learned that ARKAYA guitarist Hanny Mohamed had taken the bass position vacancy in PEGAZUS, coincidentally just as Betts short-lived tenure with ARKAYA had come to an end. Mohamed would maintain a foot in both camps.

The mid 2002 line-up of ARKAYA would announce a name switch to BLACK MAJESTY and the recording of a projected debut album 'Sands Of Time'. A promotional three track EP emerged beforehand which featured former PEGAZUS singer Danny Cecati duetting with vocalist John Cavaliere on the track 'Guardian'. The band at this stage comprised Cavaliere, guitarists Steve Janevski and Hanny Mohamed, bass player Joe Fata and former KRYPTOR drummer Pavel Konvalinka.

Singles/EPs:
Fall Of The Reich / Guardian / Beyond Reality, (2002) ('Sands Of Time' EP)

BLACK STEEL (AUSTRALIA)
Line-Up: Matt Williams (vocals), Jamie Page (guitar), Andrew DiStefano (guitar), Dave Harrison (bass), Damien Petrelli (drums)

Perth based Power Metal band that has gained the honours of opening for international heavyweights such as DEEP PURPLE and JUDAS PRIEST. The band was founded by a trio of musicians that had already made a sizeable mark on the Australian Metal scene in ALLEGIENCE bassist Dave Harrison, ex-BLACK ALICE and TRILOGY guitarist Jamie Page and drummer Damien Petrelli of Progressive act SYZYGY.

BLACK STEEL debuted with the self-financed 2000 four track EP 'Battle Call'. Recorded in a mere two days Petrelli had only just joined the band prior to recording, managing to squeeze in just two rehearsals before the recording sessions. 'Battle Call' was originally intended as a promotional cassette but positive reaction led to this release being upgraded to a CD format EP.

In 2001 BLACK STEEL reaped the rewards for their efforts, radio play of 'Battle Call' being significant enough for the band to be invited to guest on the DEEP PURPLE tour of Australia.

The full-length 'Destructor' album, produced by Adam Keene, followed the same year. BLACK STEEL subsequently supported JUDAS PRIEST in early 2002.

Singles/EPs:
Battle Call / We Are One / The Power / Heart Of A Lion, (2000) ('Battle Call' EP)

Albums:
DESTRUCTOR, Black Steel BLST2001 (2001)
Breaking The Chains / Time Marches On / Destructor / Hell's Gates / Bonded By Steel / Rise Up / Vengeance Of The Damned / Hail Of Fire / Too Wild To Tame / Forever (The Sands Of Time)

BLACK SYMPHONY (USA)
Line-Up: Ric Plamondon (vocals), Rick Plester (guitar), Rev Jones (bass), Martin Burstrom (keyboards), Pete Holmes (drums)

A technically minded Progressive Power Metal band. Although BLACK SYMPHONY's history had been turbulent the debut release 'Believe' afforded the band a bona fide success story, shifting over 50,000 copies world-wide. BLACK SYMPHONY was the brainchild of Canadian guitarist Rick Plester, the 1993 incarnation of the band being fronted by none other than ex-RIOT man RHETT FORRESTER. The rhythm section was made up of erstwhile RELISH bassist R.J. Killenger and drummer Tim Waterson. Just six months after making his exit from BLACK SYMPHONY Forrester would be shot dead.

The group underwent numerous line-up shuffles prior to laying down the 'Believe' album in 1996. BLACK SYMPHONY's line-up for this release comprised Plester, singer Mike Pierce, bassist Robbie Bennett, keyboard player Robert Vasicek and drummer Jeff Martin. The latter of course known for his work with SURGICAL STEEL, BADLANDS and RACER X. Bennett's place was taken a week after recording by former FORTE man Rev Jones.

The album, although it emerged in 1996 through the Nuela label, was not sanctioned by the band. Officially the record would be issued by the German Rising Sun label in April 1998. Touring in Europe witnessed festival performances at the renowned Dutch 'Dynamo' festival and southern Germany's 'Bang Your Head' event. BLACK SYMPHONY would also act as official support to DIO. A major influx of sales would come the band's way due to their music being played as part of a national TV hockey event with an estimated

70 million viewers having watched in total. Martin would later join veteran British Rockers UFO and Plester assembled an all new look band. Jones maintained his position but in would come ex-MENACE and SKITZOTIK singer Ric Plamondon, keyboard player Mike Burstrom and former BLACK N' BLUE drummer Pete Holmes.

A limited run first edition of the February 2002 album 'Tears Of Blood' came complete with a bonus CD of four cover songs comprising 'Behind Blue Eyes' by THE WHO, 'Smoke On The Water' by DEEP PURPLE, 'Zero The Hero' by BLACK SABBATH and QUEENSRYCHE's 'Deliverance'.

Jones found himself also ensconced in the MICHAEL SCHENKER GROUP for the German guitar guru's 2001 opus 'Be Aware Of Scorpions'.

BLACK SYMPHONY would spend the Spring of 2002 recording the Rick Plester produced third album 'Trust'.

Albums:
BLACK SYMPHONY, Rising Sun (1998)
The Poor - The Edge / End Of Your Life / Breathe / Are You Cryin? / The Wind / Never / Listen / Period Of Morning / The Black Symphony
TEARS OF BLOOD, (2002)
Tears Of Blood / It Remains A Mystery / Take Me Down / I Am Hate / Death / Burned / Over And Over / Tears Of Blood (Part II) / Forgive Me / Left In Confusion / Into The Dark / The Black Symphony (Part II)

BLACK TEARS (GERMANY)
Line-Up: Mathias Staub (vocals), Peter Kohler (guitar), Frank Kühn (guitar), Uwe Köhler (guitar/bass), Björn Greinert (drums)

A quite successful German Metal band, although the band's sales were strictly confined to the domestic market.

Albums:
CHILD OF THE STONE, Steamhammer (1984)
Black Tears / Crown Of The Damned / Perfect Demon / Silver Woman / Child Of The Storm / Rockin' To The Top / Dialog Between The Evil And The Good / Only Memories
THE SLAVE, Steamhammer (1985)
March Without Fear / The Wikings / The Slave / This Feeling Called Love / Watch Out / Mad Killer / Gloomy Fate / Shoot Down And Run / For Those About To Die / On Stage

BLADERUNNER (UK)
Line-Up: Steve Mackay (vocals), Gary Jones (guitar), Mark Wilde (guitar), Mick Cooper (bass), Greg Ellis (drums).

GARY JONES of BLADERUNNER
Photo : Joe Bangay

Humberside Heavy Metal band. Guitarist Gary Jones is ex-SAVAGE ROSE. Jones formed PHANTASM with former ANGELWITCH and TYTAN drummer Dave Dufort, drafting in Wilde for a short stint. Jones later joined covers band TROOPER with ex-PHANTASM vocalist Carol Hendrix.

Singles/EPs:
Back Street Lady / Too Far, Too Late, Ebony EBON 26 (1985)

Albums:
HUNTED, Ebony (1984)
Too Far, Too Late / Run From The Night / Back Street Lady / The Stealer / Hunted / I've Got To Rock / Dogs Of War / Back On The Street / Looking From The Outside
WARRIORS OF ROCK, Ebony EBON 35 (1986)
Eyes Of The Beholder / Warriors Of Rock / Snow Queen / Wings Of Fear / Lionheart / She's Ready / Where Eagles Dare / The Verdict

BLAZE (UK)
Line-Up: Blaze Bayley (vocals) John Slater (guitar), Steve Ray (guitar), Rob Naylor

(bass), Jeff Singer (drums)

Metal act fronted by ex-WOLFSBANE and IRON MAIDEN vocalist Blaze Bayley. Guitarist John Slater is a former member of both STORMWATCH and MINDFEED. Heavily criticised during his tenure and ultimately ousted from a then flagging IRON MAIDEN, Bayley surprised many with the undoubted quality of his 'Silicon Messiah' comeback effort.

Sophomore outing 'Tenth Dimension' would be produced by former SABBAT guitarist Andy Sneap. BLAZE toured Germany in February 2001 supporting HELLOWEEN and would put in a creditable performance at the Derby 'Bloodstock' festival in the UK later that year. BLAZE would be announced as support band to the SAVATAGE / VICIOUS RUMORS package 2002 European tour. Further shows would see an appearance at the Italian 'Gods Of Metal' event upfront of June dates in Europe as opener to OVERKILL. However, the band's June 16th support gig to OVERKILL at the Biebob venue in Vosselaar, Belgium was cancelled after drummer Jeff Singer's brother was taken seriously ill. The band resumed the tour in London, pulling in ex-WAYSTED and present day DORO and BRITNY FOX drummer Johnny Dee to fulfil interim dates. Jeff Singer made a return in order to complete the tour.

The band had their version of 'Dazed And Confused' included on the Locomotive Music LED ZEPPELIN tribute album 'The Metal Zeppelin - The Music Remains The Same'. A first for the act came in November, GRAVE DIGGER's first gig in Moscow at the 4,500 capacity Luzhniki Small Sport Hall co-headlining with German act GRAVE DIGGER.

Albums:

SILICON MESSIAH, Sanctuary (2000)
Ghost In The Machine / Evolution / Silicon Messiah / Born As A Stranger / The Hunger / The Brave / Identity / Reach For The Horizon / The Launch / Stare At The Sun / The Day I Fell To Earth
TENTH DIMENSION, SPV 088-7263020 (2001)
Forgotten Future / Kill And Destroy / End Dream / The Tenth Dimension / Nothing Will Stop Me / Leap Of Faith / The Truth Revealed / Meant To Be / Land Of The Blind / Stealing Time / Speed Of Light / Stranger To The Light

BLIND FURY (UK)
Line-Up: Lou Taylor (vocals), Steve Ramsey (guitar), Russ Tippins (guitar), Graeme

BLAZE
Photo : Nico Wobben

English (bass), Sean Taylor (drums)

BLIND FURY arose from the ashes of Newcastle Metallers SATAN catering for the band's new found, mellower direction with new vocalist Lou Taylor (who had replaced Brian Ross). BLIND FURY, had been the moniker of one of Taylor's previous outfits.

SATAN fans did not appreciate the change in direction though, and, after one album for Roadrunner, the band promptly reverted back to SATAN, ousting Taylor in the process. Following a brief tenure with PERSIAN RISK the singer later formed TOUR DE FORCE in 1988 alongside guitarists Fred Avesque, previously with TROY and DRIVESHAFT, and Andy Warnock, bassist Mike Antoine and drummer Gary Burfort. TOUR DE FORCE, however, never recorded. Taylor has long since become one of London's leading Rock club DJs.

Back in Newcastle, Steve Ramsey and Graeme English formed the successful Folk Metal band SKYCLAD after the demise of SATAN.

Albums:
OUT OF REACH, Roadrunner (1985)
Do It Loud / Out Of Reach / Evil Eyes / Contact Rock n' Roll / Living On The Edge / Dynamo (There Is A Place...) / Back Inside / Dance Of The Crimson Lady (Part One)

BLIND GUARDIAN (GERMANY)
Line-Up: Hansi Kürsch (bass / vocals), Marcus Siepen (guitar), André Olbrich (guitar), Thomas Stauch (drums)

BLIND GUARDIAN, probably more so than any other German act, epitomise the very essence of 'Teutonic Metal'. Despite being an extremely powerful Heavy Metal band and gaining massive success in their native Germany, the reputation of BLIND GUARDIAN unfortunately means little in the English speaking countries.

Antecedent to their more familiar guise the group had operated as LUCIFER'S HERITAGE, releasing a demo under that name in 1986. The then self-managed group evolved into BLIND GUARDIAN and signed to No Remorse Records for the release of the 'Battalions Of Fear' album in 1988. The opening track from that record, 'Majesty', remains a live favourite to this day.

Produced by Kalle Trapp at Karo Studios in Münster 'Battalions Of Fear' served the group well, selling 10,000 copies and found the group supporting it on tour with GRINDER. The sophomore album, 'Follow The Blind', also produced by Trapp, saw the group experimenting with orchestral passages and a strange choice of a cover song in the form of the BEACH BOYS' 'Barbara Ann' (!), although the record also included a cover of NWoBHM act DEMON's 'Don't Break The Circle'. Kai Hansen, latterly of GAMMA RAY fame guests on vocals and guitar parts on the tracks 'Hall Of The King' and 'Valhalla'.

'Follow The Blind' not only improved the group's standing in their native Germany but also led to heavy interest in Japan and enabled them to negotiate a Japanese deal. Oddly, despite the success of the records BLIND GUARDIAN's live appearances were rather sporadic. Instead the band remained content at improving their musical prowess in the studio, evolving from a Speed Metal outfit to one that combined many different Metallic styles and arrangements as well as lyrics often inspired by the works of Stephen King or J.R.R. Tolkien.

1990's 'Tales From The Twilight World' was the first album to highlight the improved standards and promptly sold over 30,000 copies in Germany and was also a big hit in Japan. The album found Kalle Trapp still producing and featured another guest showing from Kai Hansen.

In 1991 the band finally toured again, in this instance with ICED EARTH. They also appeared at the 'Rock Hard' festival the same year. By this time BLIND GUARDIAN had plans to produce their own demo material and work began on the building of the group's own studio. They also split from No Remorse and signed to Virgin Records.

1992's 'Somewhere Far Beyond' (once more featuring the work of Trapp and Hansen!) was a conceptual album and witnessed further experimentation with bagpipes making a debut showing on a BLIND GUARDIAN record! The CD version featured the addition of a cover of QUEEN's 'Spread Your Wings' and SATAN's 'Trial By Fire'. The album sold 130,000 copies and enabled BLIND GUARDIAN to tour once more with ICED EARTH and another showing at the 'Rock Hard' festival.

In 1993 BLIND GUARDIAN visited Japan for the first time, recording the 'Tokyo Tale' live album whilst there. The group were reported to have played to an average of 2,500 people at each gig and sold 175,000 DMs worth of merchandising!

Upon their return to Germany the quartet set to work on a new album and wound up working at Sweet Silence in Denmark with producer Flemming Rasmussen. 'Imaginations From The Other Side' took eight months to complete and saw PRETTY MAIDS' Ronnie Atkins guesting on backing vocals.

The album would, upon release, sell more than 220,000 copies worldwide and open up markets in southern Europe, South Korea and Thailand.

At this point the group engaged MANOWAR manager Tom Miller to handle their affairs as they toured Germany in 1995, with NEVERMORE opening, and travelled to Japan and Thailand, playing Bangkok in front of 7,100 people. The band rounded off the year headlining the 'Christmas Metal Meeting' over SAXON, YNGWIE MALMSTEEN, RAGE, SKYCLAD and LOVE/HATE.

The release of 'The Forgotten Tales' album was more or less a 'Best Of…' package that contained such delights as covers of the '50s chestnut 'Mr Sandman', the BEACHBOYS' 'Surfin' USA', URIAH HEEP's 'The Wizard' and MIKE OLDFIELD's 'To France'. Other highlights included an orchestral version of 'Theatre Of Pain' and a live rendition of 'The Bard Song - In The Forest' which the crowd sings rather than the band! This latter track is said to have been included to illustrate the strong bond that has grown between BLIND GUARDIAN and their fan following from the release of the debut.

BLIND GUARDIAN honoured British Metal institution JUDAS PRIEST by including their version of 'Beyond The Realms Of Death' on the Century Media JUDAS PRIEST tribute albums 'Legends Of Metal'.

The quartet headlined the 1996 'Bang Your Head' festival in Southern Germany on a bill including GLENMORE, TOKYO BLADE and SAVAGE before starting work on a new album.

The 1998 album 'Nightfall In Middle Earth' was a Rock first being recorded on a massive120 channel mixing desk. Once again Tolkein themes abounded.

For touring the band drafted former SIEGES EVEN bassist Oliver Holzwarth.

Kürsch allied himself with guitarist Jon Schaffer from American Metal band ICED EARTH in 1999 to create the hugely popular DEMONS & WIZARDS. The resulting self-titled album, sounding not too dissimilar to BLIND GUARDIAN, scored a number one record in Greece.

Holzwarth would also accompany Kürsch and Schaffer on tour with DEMONS & WIZARDS. BLIND GUARDIAN announced a return to action in December of 2001 with the epic 14 minute single 'And There Was Silence'. The CD single, the first ever released on the Century Media label, also included the rare outtake 'Harvest of Sorrow' recorded during the 'Nightfall In Middle-Earth' sessions. The accompanying album 'A Night At The Opera' would reap an impressive tally of European chart placing going top five in Germany and

BLIND GUARDIAN
Photo : Nico Wobben

grabbing the no. 1 position in Greece for two weeks. The band would also be announced as headliners of the 2002 'Bloodstock' festival, BLIND GUARDIAN's debut UK appearance, as well as putting in their first North American appearance scheduled for the 'ProgPower' USA festival in Atlanta, Georgia during November. Although South American dates were also organised, scheduled shows in Argentina would be pulled due to the county's financial crisis.

The band's status in Europe was such that they ambitiously revealed plans for a full blown 'Blind Guardian' festival in Coburg, Germany during mid 2003. A supporting cast numbering artists such as A.O.K., BRAINSTORM, FREEDOM CALL, GRAVE DIGGER, MAGO DE OZ, METALIUM, RAGE, STORMHAMMER, TANKARD and WHITE SKULL would quickly be confirmed. The group planned to perform two completely different sets over two nights made up of tracks requested from their fans through their website.

With regular drummer Thomas Stauch suffering from a tendon infection BLIND GUARDIAN pulled in the services of RHAPSODY drummer Alex Holzwarth for Brazilian dates.

Singles/EPs:
Banish From Sanctuary, No Remorse (1989)
Lost In The Twilight Hall / Traveller In Time / Lord Of The Rings / Goodbye My Friend, No Remorse 663502 (1990) ('Tales From The Twilight World' EP - Promotion release)
A Past And Future Secret / Imaginations From The Other Side / The Wizard / A Past And Present Secret (Orchestra Mix), Virgin 892744-2 (1995)
Mr. Sandman / Bright Eyes (Edit Version) / Hallelujah, Imaginations From The Other Side (Demo Version) / The Script For My Requiem (Demo Version), Virgin 892960-2 (1996)
Mirror, Mirror / And The Story Ends (Live) / Imaginations From The Other Side (Live) / Beyond The Realms Of Death, Virgin 7243 8 949202-6 (1998)
And Then There Was Silence / Harvest Of Sorrow / Born In A Mourning Hall (Video), JVC Victor VICP-61576 (2001) (Japanese release)

Albums:
BATTALIONS OF FEAR, No Remorse NRR 1001 (1988)
Majesty / Guardian Of The Blind / Trial By Archon / Wizard's Crown / Run For The Night / The Martyr / Battalions Of Fear / By

The Gate Of Moria / Gandalf's Rebirth
FOLLOW THE BLIND, No Remorse NRR 1006 (1989)
Inquisition / Banish From Sanctuary / Damned For All Time / Follow The Blind / Hall Of The King / Fast To Madness / Beyond The Ice / Valhalla / Barbara Ann / Don't Break The Circle
TALES FROM THE TWILIGHT WORLD, No Remorse NRR01014 (1990)
Traveller In Time / Welcome To Dying / Weird Dreams / Lord Of The Rings / Goodbye My Friend / Lost In The Twilight Hall / Tommyknockers / Altair 4 / The Last Candle / Run For The Night (Live)
SOMEWHERE FAR BEYOND, Virgin 263 066 (1991)
Time What Is Time / Journey Through The Dark / Black Chamber / Theatre Of Pain / The Quest For Tanelorn / Ashes To Ashes / The Bard's Song - In The Forest / The Bard's Song - The Hobbit / The Piper's Calling / Somewhere Far Beyond / Spread Your Wings / Trial By Fire / Theatre Of Pain (Classic version)
TOKYO TALES LIVE, Virgin 77562-1 (1993)
Inquisition / Banish From Sanctuary / Journey Through The Dark / Traveller In Time / The Quest For Tanelorn / Goodbye My Friend / Time What Is Time / Majesty / Valhalla / Welcome To Dying / Lost In The Twilight Hall / Barbara Ann
IMAGINATIONS FROM THE OTHER SIDE, Virgin 840337-2 (1995)
Imaginations From The Other Side / I'm Alive / A Past And Future Secret / The Script For My Requiem / Mordred's Song / Born In A Mourning Hall / Bright Eyes / Another Holy War / And The Story Ends
THE FORGOTTEN TALES, Virgin 841626-1 (1996)
Mr. Sandman / Surfin' USA / Bright Eyes / Lord Of The Rings / The Wizzard / Spread Your Wings / Mordred's Song / Black Chamber / The Bard's Song (Live) / Barbara Ann / Long Tall Sally / A Past And Future Secret / To France / Theatre Of Pain
NIGHTFALL IN MIDDLE EARTH, Virgin 724 384589929 (1998) **7 GERMANY, 44 SWEDEN**
War Of The Wrath / Into The Storm / Lammoth / Nightfall / The Minstrel / The Curse Of Feanor / Captured / Blood Tears / Mirror, Mirror / Face The Truth / Noldor (Dead Winter Reigns) / Battle Of Sudden Flame / Time Stands Still (At The Iron Hill) / The Dark Elf / Thorn / The Eldar / Nom The Wise / When Sorrow Sang / Out Of The Water / The Steadfast / A Dark Passage / Final Chapter (Thus Ends...)
A NIGHT AT THE OPERA, JVC Victor VICP-61739 (2002) **17 AUSTRIA, 67 FRANCE, 5**

GERMANY, 1 GREECE, 11 ITALY, 8 SPAIN, 10 SWEDEN
Precious Jerusalem / Battlefield / Under The Ice / Sadly Sings Destiny / The Maiden And The Minstrel Knight / Wait For An Answer / The Soulforged / Age Of False Innocence / Punishment Divine / ...And Then There Was Silence

BLITZKRIEG (UK)
Line-Up: Brian Ross (vocals), Jim Sirotto (guitars), Ian Jones (guitars), Steve English (bass), Steve Abbey (drums).

BLITZKRIEG are perhaps most noted for METALLICA's rendition of their theme song 'Blitzkrieg', featured on the B side of the Bay Area monsters 'Creeping Death' single.

Despite this notoriety and a strong cult following BLITZKRIEG releases have been few and far between, although this hasn't been for the lack of trying.

Vocalist Brian Ross is the guiding force behind the band and has a colourful career including auditions with TYGERS OF PAN TANG, requests to join SAMSON and E.F. BAND and forming, albeit very briefly, a band with noted former WHITESNAKE guitarist BERNIE MARSDEN.

BLITZKRIEG formed in October 1980 in Leicester, the line-up listed above being the original. Brian Ross answered an advert placed by SPLIT IMAGE comprisingJim Sirotto, Ian Jones, Steve English and Steve Abbey looking to replace their previous vocalist, Sarah.

Ross had previous form with KASHMIR (an act that featured WHITESNAKE's David Coverdale's cousin Kev Stevens on drums) and ANVIL. Upon Ross joining SPLIT IMAGE Jez Gilman suggested the new name of BLITZKRIEG, although various paying club gigs were still for a while performed under the old moniker.

The band's first product was a three track demo cassette, which led to a single for the Newcastle based Neat Records entitled 'Buried Alive'. The same year BLITZKRIEG also contributed the track 'Inferno' to the Neat 'Leadweight' compilation.

In February 1981 the band underwent a line-up change adding ex-ELECTRIC SAVAGE guitarist John Antcliffe and bassist Mick Moore.

The latter had previously played in the Leicester outfit AXE VICTIM with Ian Jones and Moore tells the tale that the legendary 'Blitzkrieg' (the B-side of the 'Buried Alive' single) had originally been conceived by AXE VICTIM under the title 'Bitch'. Jones had taken the nucleus of the song to BLITZKRIEG with him, the riffs of which had been a lame

attempt to duplicate those of Dutch outfit FOCUS' legendary 'Hocus Pocus'!

With a revised line-up BLITZKRIEG gained welcome press coverage by featuring in the very first issue of 'Kerrang!' and went on to record a show supporting TRUST in Newcastle for an officially released tape entitled 'Blitzed Alive'. However, the band spilt in December 1981 with Moore and Ross eventually forming AVENGER and Antcliffe joining CHROME MOLLY. Ross was to subsequently perform vocal duties with SATAN for a tour of Holland and wound up leaving AVENGER for the ranks of SATAN.

Ross kept in touch with Mick Moore and, along with Jim Sirotto, teamed up again as BLITZKRIEG to record the album 'Blitzkrieg - A Time Of Changes' with Sean Taylor of SATAN on drums and TYGERS OF PAN TANG guitarist Mick Proctor. At this point, Ross was also managing and singing for LONEWOLF.

The band, almost a pet project by this stage, underwent further reshuffling in June 1986 leaving Ross as the sole surviving member with Proctor teaming up with SPEAR OF DESTINY. BLITZKRIEG was reassembled with guitarists J.D. Binnie of MANDORA repute and Chris Beard, bassist Darren Parnaby and drummer Sean Wilkinson. This incarnation recorded a four track demo in 1987, but the band split once more at the close of 1987 with Wilkinson, Parnaby, Binnie and Beard staying together in a Glam Metal act called LIBERTY.

Ross, after a rethink, started afresh in the summer of 1988. The singer gathered around him guitarists Glenn S. Howes and Steve Robertson, bassist Robbie Robertson and drummer Kyle Gibson, yet the only recorded product was a two track demo before BLITZKRIEG once more succumbed to another drastic line-up shuffle.

By August of 1989 only Ross and Howes remained from the most recent band, augmented with new guitarist Tony J. Liddle - previously a member of SARATOGA, PREDATOR and VIOLET ERUPTION, bassist Glen Carey and former AVENGER drummer Gary Young. A video, 'At The Kazbah', was released and the long awaited second album '10 Years Of Blitzkrieg' on the Roadrunner label.

Inevitably there were to be more departures. In early 1991 Carey, Young and Howes quit to form HURRICANE. Ross turned to his old comrade Mick Moore together with ex-SATAN drummer Sean Taylor and guitarist Paul Nesbitt, although Moore had left within a year, BLITZKRIEG trimming down to a quartet of Ross, Liddle, Taylor and former WHEELBARROWS FROM HELL bassist

Dave Anderson. This line-up recorded the album 'Unholy Trinity' in 1992. However, it was not to be released until the close of 1995.

BLITZKRIEG undertook a short tour of Greece in early 1996 with yet more new members - bassist Steven Ireland and drummer Paul 'Sid' White. Liddle would decamp in January of 1997 for TENDAHUX - recording an as yet unreleased album, but further gigging found BLITZKRIEG on tour in their strongest market; Germany, during the winter of '97. Ireland was unable to fulfil these dates and a stand in bassist Gavin Gray the same year the band recorded a Japanese language version of the track 'Blitzkrieg', the original version of which will forever remain the group's legacy.

During 1998 BLITZKRIEG were working on new material for Neat Metal Records although predictably the band line-up had evolved once more. Joining Ross were a returning Howes on guitar, fellow guitarist Martin Richardson and drummer Mark Hancock. This line-up put in a rare appearance at the 'Wacken Open Air' festival in Germany.

Early 1999 found BLITZKRIEG back in action performing their first American show in New Jersey sharing a billing with SWEET SAVAGE and RAVEN.

As 2002 drew in Ross announced not only the planning of a projected album to be titled 'Absolute Power' for the Metal Nations label but yet another completely revised BLITZKRIEG line-up. Tony Liddle made a return to be joined by second guitarist Paul Nesbitt, bassist Andy Galloway and erstwhile WHATEVER and DISPOSABLE HEROES drummer Phil Brewis. With this line-up BLITZKRIEG performed at the 'Motala Metal' festival in Sweden and would be confirmed for appearances at the 'Metal Meltdown' in Asbury Park, New Jersey and Germany's annual 'Wacken Open Air'.

Singles/EPs:
Buried Alive / Blitzkrieg, Neat NEAT 10 (1980)

Albums:
BLITZKRIEG - A TIME OF CHANGES, Neat 1023 (1985)
Ragnarok / Blitzkrieg / Pull The Trigger / Armageddon / Take A Look Around / Hell To Pay / Vikings / A Time Of Changes / Saviour
TEN YEARS OF BLITZKRIEG, Roadrunner RO9302 (1991)
Blitzkrieg / Buried Alive / Night Howl / The Sentinel / Nocturnal Vision
UNHOLY TRINITY, Neat Metal NM002 (1995)
Hair Trigger / Struck By Lightning / Taking Care Of Business / Field Of Dreams / Take A

Look Around / After Dark / Crazy For You / Zip / Unholy Trinity / Calming The Savage Beast / The Wraith / Easy Way Out / All Hallows Eve / Countess Bathory / Jealous Love / House Of Pleasure / Return Of The Zip
TEN, Neat Metal NM 012 (1996)
Cavo D'Oro / Fighting All The Way To The Top / Buried Alive / The Sentinel / The Power Of The King / Night Howl / I'm Not Insane / Court In The Act / Blitzkrieg '96 / Nocturnal Vision
THE MISTS OF AVALON, Neat Metal NM032 (1998)
The Legend / Tranquil State / I Am The Doctor (Who Are You?) / Deceiver / Princess For The World / The Mighty 'A' / Smell Of Roses / Love's Too Late / Anasazi / Yesterdays (Hope For The Future) / Another Interview? / Vicious Rumours / I Was Having A Great Time And Stayed Longer Than I Should, So When I Got To The Railway Station The Train Had Gone!
ABSOLUTE POWER, Metal Nations (2002)

BLITZKRIEG (USA)
Line-Up: Don Ross (vocals), Eric Von Theumer (guitar), Jeff Johnson (guitar), Neil Moore (bass), Jeff Wills (drums)

As coincidences go, American Metal outfit BLITZKRIEG found themselves involved in one of the strangest.
Not content with sharing their band name with the infamous Newcastle based NWoBHM BLITZKRIEG group, the Americans also boasted a singer with the surname of Ross and a bassist called Moore, the same names as their British counterparts!
BLITZKRIEG's album was produced by KEEL's front man Ron Keel.

Albums:
READY FOR ACTION, Talen / Greenworld GWD 90521 (1985)
Winner Takes All / Ready For Action / Young Forever / First Strike / Let Me Know / Misbeliever

BLODEN-WEDD (CHILE)
Line-Up: Dan Elbelman (vocals / guitar), Patota Atxondo (guitar), Ricardo Palma (bass), Max Acuña (drums)

A South American Power Metal band, unusually taking the Celtic title of BLODEN-WEDD – 'Gods Of The Sunrise'- dating back to June of 1993. The band had been founded by vocalist / guitarist Dan Ebelman and drummer Carlos Silva, both previously members of BLACK BART and ASPID.
BLODEN-WEDD's opening demo, billed as

'Demo 1: The Kid Warrior', was recorded in November of 1995. The band comprised Dan Ebelman, ex-BLACKSMITH lead guitarist Patota Atxondo and Carlos Silva. Ricardo Palma of CYRANO would handle bass during these recordings on a session basis. Subsequently Silva departed with Max Acuña of DILEMMA being drafted in his stead. For a period Acuña opted out to join the ranks of SLAVERY and 'Snow' Espinoza of BEWITCHED took over the drummer's role. However, Acuña would trade places with Espinoza in SLAVERY to make a return for the 1998 'Time Goes On' album released by the Picoroco label.

A second album, 'Raging Planet', saw F. Bull of PROHIBIT coming in as the new bass player. Gigs to support this release included support slots to visiting artists such as RHAPSODY and CHILDREN OF BODOM. The group switched bassists yet again though with Pedro Aragon making his debut onstage in March of 2002.

Albums:
TIME GOES ON, Picoroco (1998)
The Travel Begins (Intro) / Learning From A Beast / P.O.R.K.S. / Mohicans / Skyland / Happy Time / Bloden-Wedd / Times Go On
RAGING PLANET, (2001)
Intro / Raging Planet / As The Rain & The Rainbow / Lord Of The Final Sin / Liberty / Skyland II / Winter Son / Angels From Future / By My Side

BOANERGES (ARGENTINA)
Line-Up: Gabriela Sepúlveda (vocals), Hernan Fortuna (guitar), Gustavo Rodriguez (guitar), Marcelo Rodriguez (bass), Alberto Sabbatini (drums)

Female fronted Brazilian Christian Power Metal act assembled in 1990. Founder guitarist Eduardo Subic would subsequently be replaced by Hernan Fortuna for a three track demo issued in 1993. The band title BOANERGES translates as 'Children of thunder', taken from Mark 3.17.

BOANERGES underwent a series of line-up changes in 1999 with the departure of Fortuna, his place taken by Adrián Velázquez, and the recruitment of Aldo Tamashiro. This later recruit provides a touch of uniqueness to the band who now employs two drummers.

Albums:
SENALES ANTES DE FIN, Boanerges (1998)
Boanerges / Give Yourself Another Chance / Fulfilled Prophecy / Wake Up From Lies / Fools Without A Reason / The Final Time /

Nothing At All / Psalm 96 / Sovereign Power

BOULDER (Cleveland, OH, USA)
Line-Up: Jamie Walters (vocals), Terence Hanchin (guitar), Mark Gibbs (guitar), Patrick Munn (drums)

BOULDER, whose hackneyed logo is made up of two crossed flying V's, operate in the surreal Stoner infused world of Southern sludge style desert Rock and cliché '80s Heavy Metal, giving cause for justifiable comparisons to both KYUSS and JUDAS PRIEST! Indeed, singer Jamie Walters has been known to arrive onstage in full leather gear, including ass-less chaps astride a moped as his BOULDER band mates crank out 'Hell Bent For Leather'!

BOULDER's brand of avant-garde Metal humour was first felt in 1992 when ex-PROCREATION members Walters and Gibbs united with former Hardcore exponents Munn and Hanchin from BLATANT DISREGARD.

BOULDER opened with a limited edition single 'Sac' only pressed up in 100 copies. Their 1994 demo 'Jailbreak' set the scene for what was to follow opening up with the less than subtle 'Kick The Pregnant'.

A shared 1995 single saw the band doubling up with DIMBULB. That same year the 7" 'Fist' EP would contain cover versions of BLACK SABBATH's 'Trashed' and VENOM's 'In League With Satan'. Another limited run single 'Pilzner's Bible' split with SLOTH gave the collectors something else to hunt down, again only seeing 100 copies pressed. The 1997 cover of BLACK DEATH's 'Screams Of The Iron Messiah' took BOULDER to new levels of audacity being a split 7" with no less than THIN LIZZY! The cover artwork depicting Phil Lynnot with a speech bubble stating "I gave full permission for this record". Again, another limited run of 300 only.

The 2000 'Ripping Christ' album, graced with an album cover depicting Jesus crucified upside down on a stack of Marshall amps, is a compilation of all the previous demos and singles.

Singles/EPs:
Sac / Dirt Cheap, Boulder (1993) (7" single)
Kick The Pregnant / Ming The Mercyless / Shifty, Lost And Found (1994) (7" single)
Anchored Down /, Alley Sweeper AS015 (1995) (7" split single with DIMBULB. 500 copies)
The Eternal Quest For Edward B. Yatsko / In League With Satan / T.G.W. / Trashed, Flexovit FLX002 (1995) ('Fist' 7" EP)
Pilzner's Bible /, (1996) (7" split single with SLOTH. 100 copies)

Screams Of The Iron Messiah, (1997) (7" split single with THIN LIZZY (!) 300 copies)

Albums:
555, Flexovit FLX007 (1997)
DLR Is King / Mayhem Gook / Love Honkey / 555 / Rage With The Dead / Full Throttle
THE RAGE OF IT ALL, River On Fire ROF003 (1999)
D U Lay / The Dealer / Disrespector / Workin' For Nobody / Make And Take / Total Business / Random Hellholes / Blow Up The Fire / Who Care, Baby?
RAVAGE AND SAVAGE, Tee Pee (2000)
The Invasion / Rev It Up / Funeral Day / Southern Salvation / Heavens Ice / Ravage And Savage / Two Track Mind / Sin Goals / Fall From Graves
RIPPING CHRIST, Outlaw Recordings (2000)
DLR Is King / Mayhem Gook / Love Honkey / 555 / Rage With The Dead / Full Throttle / Sinners Gross Beerd / Amigbro / The Power Of 1,000 Satanic Black Moons / Anchored Down / Kick The Pregnant / Ming The Mercyless / Shifty / Kill The Captain / The Eternal Quest For Edward B. Yatsko / In League With Satan / T.G.W. / Trashed / Pilzner's Bible / We Like No Hero
REAPED IN HALF ACT I & ACT II, Tee Pee (2002)
Krank It Up / Live Or Dead / Ripped In Half / Ripe And Innocent / Arrect Me / Should've Seen Blood / Yellow Fever / Back For The Show

BRAINFEVER (GERMANY)
Line-Up: Horst Neumann (vocals), Marco Böttcher (guitar), Heinz Schreiber (bass), Eric Hirschhäuser (drums)

A German outfit that sprang up during a period of significant activity on the European Metal scene in the early '80s, the quartet debuted with the self-financed 'Capture The Night' single in 1983 and were snapped up by Mausoleum.

The Belgian based label released BRAINFEVER's self-titled debut in 1984 and the group continued until 1988 when Horst Neumann and Eric Hirschhäuser left the band before the recording of the 'You' single. Marc Simon and Michael Jacobs came in on vocals and drums respectively and this line-up would later play shows with fellow German outfit GLENMORE.

Wollo Reddig is known to have contributed keyboards in the studio for the band.

Singles/EPs:
Capture The Night / Vargary, (1983) (7" single)
Capture The Night / Brainfever, Mausoleum (1984)
You / Dangerous Lies / Shots Break The Silence / Hoist Up The Sails, Steamhammer 75595 (1988)

Albums:
BRAINFEVER, Mausoleum SKULL 8362 (1984)
Into The Sky / Hangman / Danger Of The Night / Thunder And Lightning / Dirty Streets / Brainfever / Capture The Night / Midnight Train / Tool For The Show / Suicide
FACE TO FACE, Bellaphon (1986)
Black Jack / Face To Face / Savoir / Look Out / Memories Of Tomorrow / Sweettalker / Devil's Eyes / Master Of Evil / Caught By The Fire

BRAINSTORM (GERMANY)
Line-Up: Andy B. Franck (vocals), Torsten Ihlenfeld (guitar), Milan Loncaric (guitar), Andreas Mailänder (bass), Dieter Bernert (drums)

Heavyweight Metal band BRAINSTORM, centred upon guitarists Torsten Ihlenfeld and Milan Loncaric on guitar and drummer Dieter Bernet, date back to 1989, the group issuing their debut demo, 'Hand Of Doom', the following year. The band cut their teeth on the live circuit guesting for artists such as EXCITER, RAGE and STORMWITCH. Bass player Andreas Mailänder teamed up with BRAINSTORM in April of 1991.

A second cassette, entitled 'Heart Of Hate', quickly followed and the good reviews garnered gave vent to a third tape, 'The Fifth Reason' with new front man Marcus Jürgens. It would be BRAINSTORM's fourth demo, recorded in 1996, that would have them elevated to 'Newcomer of the month' status according to 'Rock Hard' magazine and in turn led to a deal with Bossy Ogress Records. The band's 'Hungry' debut album included guest vocals by ex-GAMMA RAY singer Ralph Scheepers and BRAINSTORM toured Germany as support to MORGANA LEFAY and SOLITUDE AETURNUS to push the record after its release in 1997. A further round of dates saw the band on a European package billing with SKYCLAD and MARAYA. BRAINSTORM were by now paving their way into the German Metal major league with second album 'Unholy'. The record would witness a rare musical departure for the band with the closing track being a cover of the old Rock n' Roll number 'Wooly Bully'. Limited edition variants came packaged in a metal box sleeve. The Japanese release also boasted an extra track 'Up From The Ashes'. Despite progress BRAINSTORM found themselves in the unenviable situation of being without a singer just after the album release. Matters were solved when Henne Basse signed on in time for tour operations with ICED EARTH, SENTENCED and WICKED ANGEL.

To open 1999 the band toured Italy in alliance with LABYRINTH. However, upon their return Basse decamped to join the METALIUM project band. BRAINSTORM regrouped quickly enlisting Dirk Barron for a 'Wacken Open Air' festival performance but would eventually decide on Andy B. Franck of SYMPHORCE.

BRAINSTORM switched to the Metal Blade label for their third effort 'Ambiguity'. BRAINSTORM would also donate their version of 'Savage' to the HELLOWEEN tribute album 'Keepers Of Jericho'. Promoting 'Ambiguity' BRAINSTORM toured as support to ARMORED SAINT, JACOB'S DREAM and KING DIAMOND in Europe during 2000. Drummer Dieter Bernert would found the project band TAROT'S MYST.

Upfront of recording the group's fourth album, 'Metus Mortis' produced by Achim Köhler, BRAINSTORM would put in high profile shows at both the 'Bang Your Head' and 'Wacken Open Air' festivals. The 'Metus Mortis' album arrived in 2001, Japanese editions replete with an extra three tracks. Reaction from the media to the album was enthusiastic to say the least, the highly influential German magazine 'Rock Hard' granting it the 'Album of the month' honours. The band would tour Spain alongside GRAVE DIGGER in January of 2002 but projected German gigs for March would be cancelled as both Franck and GRAVE DIGGER guitarist Manni Schmidt was incapacitated with a virus the guitarist had caught whilst on the Iberian continent.

Singles/EPs:
Overkill / Hölle / Frieden / Sodom, Wishbone 1012 (1994) ('Overkill' EP)

Albums:
HUNGRY, Bossy Ogress BO 001 (1997)
Nails In My Hands / King Of Fools / Innocent Until Caught / The Other Side / Tomorrow Never Comes / Liar's Edge / Tell Tale Heart / Welcome To The Darkside / Bring You Down / Deep Down into Passion / Mr. Know It All
UNHOLY, Bossy Ogress 007366-2 (1998)
MCMXCVIII / Holy War / Here Comes The Pain / Voices / The Healer / Don't Stop Believing / Heart Of Hate / Rebellion / For The Love Of Money / Love Is A Lie / Into The

ANDREAS B. FRANCK of BRAINSTORM
Photo : Nico Wobben

Fire / Dog Days Coming Down / Wooly Bully
AMBIGUITY, Metal Blade 14330 (2000)
Crush Depth / Tear Down The Walls /
Beyond My Destiny / Arena / Coming Closer
/ Darkest Silence / Maharaja Palace / Far
Away / Demonsion / Lost Unseen /
Perception Of Life
METUS MORTIS, Metal Blade (2001)
Metus Mortis / Blind Suffering / Shadowland
/ Checkmate / Hollow Hideaway / Weakness
Sows Its Seed / Into The Never / Under
Lights / Cycles / Behind / Meet Me In The
Dark / Strength Of Will

BREAKER (GERMANY)

Line-Up: Eberhard Weyel (vocals / guitar),
Bertram Kölsch (guitar), Thorsten Feisel
(bass), Volker Borchert (drums)

Albums:
DEAD RIDER, Bacillus (1985)
Run For Your Life / Born To Rock / Dead
Rider / Shout Out Loud / Cold Hearted
Woman / Rapist Killer / Street Fighter /
Lucifer's Dream / Out Of Control / Together
We Are Strong

BREAKER (USA)

Line-Up: Jim Hamer (vocals), Don Depew
(guitar), Michael Klein (guitar), Ian Shipley
(bass), Mark Klein (drums)

Metal band BREAKER, named after and
heavily influenced by ACCEPT's third ball
busting album, were founded as a quintet of
vocalist Jim Hamar, guitarists Michael Klein &
Don Depew, bassist Ian Shipley and drummer
Mark Klein in late 1982.
After the self-financed single release the
band also benefited from two tracks 'Ten
Seconds In' and 'Walking The Wire' appearing
on the 'Cleveland Metal' compilation album.
BREAKER's exposure was capitalised on by
their refusal to play gigs requiring cover tunes
and headline shows allied to supports to
RAIL, GIRLSCHOOL, NAZARETH,
METALLICA and LITA FORD.
Hamar was asked to leave in August of 1984
midway through recording a proposed album
but the band, unable to find a suitable
replacement, resigned to fate and persuaded
Hamar to rejoin. Hamar retained a side
project act dubbed THE DANCE.
During 1986 Shipley quit to get married and
was replaced by ex-BRAT bassist John
Urban.
BREAKER re-formed in 2000. At live shows
the band gave away free compilation CDs
which included other acts on the bill and
BREAKER's version of the SCORPIONS
song 'Pictured Life'. The band would draft

erstwhile WRETCH guitarist Nick Giannakos
for Autumn shows and announce the
donation of their take on - naturally - 'Breaker'
to an ACCEPT tribute record.
During January of 2002, in the midst of
recording a fresh album 'I Destroy', Hamar
walked out - for the third time in the band's
career. As luck would have it Jeff Shirilla, of
Doom merchants ABDULLAH, was able to
step in to complete the recordings at short
notice.

BRIDE ADORNED (FINLAND)

Line-Up: Tuomas Nieminen (vocals), Mikko
Mustonen (guitar), Panu Kiskola (guitar),
Jukka Hoffren (bass), Tapio Kuosma
(keyboards), Ville Mannila (drums)

Albums:
THE GREY EMINENCE, (2000)
Otherworldly / Ivory Towers Fall / Bridewell /
The Grey Eminence

BROCAS HELM

(San Francisco, CA, USA)
Line-Up: Bobbie B. Wright (vocals / guitar),
Tom Behney (guitar), Jim Schumacher
(bass), Jack Hays (drums)

First heard of with the Maiden influenced
jousting of their 1984 debut 'Into Battle',
strongly inspired by English medieval
imagery.
BROCAS HELM released a demo in 1987
titled 'Black Death' which carried the tracks
'Fly High', 'Satan's Prophets', 'Hell's Whip'
and 'Prepare For Battle', eventually releasing
the tracks as a full-blown album two years
later.
Quite sensationally BROCAS HELM would
reform in 2000 issuing the limited edition red
vinyl 'Blood Machine' 7" single. The band
toured the Heavy Metal stronghold of Greece
in the Autumn supported by domestic Metal
bands DREAM WEAVER, RAGING STORM
and BATTLEROAR.

Albums:
INTO BATTLE, First Strike (1984)
Metallic Fury / Into Battle / Here To Rock /
Beneath A Haunted Moon/ Warriors Of The
Dark/ Preludious / Ravenwreck / Dark Rider /
Night Siege / Into The Ithilstone
BLACK DEATH, Gargoyle NO 13-8801
(1989)
Black Death Overture / Black Death /
Prepare For Battle / Hell's Whips/ Satan's
Prophets/ Fly High/ Prophet's Scream / The
Chemist / Fall Of The Curtain

BREAKER
Photo : Nico Wobben

BURNING IN HELL (BRAZIL)
Line-Up: Leandro Moreira (vocals), Roberto Alquati (guitar), Geraldo Alquati (guitar), Gabriel Dória (bass), Marcelo Moreira (drums)

Caxias Do Sol Power Metal act in the Euro style. BURNING IN HELL was convened during 1995. The band, comprising vocalist / guitarist Leandro Moreira, guitarist Emanuel Pieruccini, bassist Alessandro Moreira and drummer Marcelo Moreira, prepared for their first live performance in the November but just up front of the gig Pieruccini quit unexpectedly. Paulo Schroeber hastily filled the position on a temporary basis but the gig was destined not to be as sickness forced a cancellation.
Pieruccini made a return some two months later and in August of 1996 the group travelled to Porte Alegre to record the opening five track demo 'Under My Dominate'.
Live action followed to promote the demo but before long Alessandro Moreira announced his exit. Leandro Moreira deputised on bass to maintain momentum and Christian Rigon filled the newly made guitar vacancy. Rigon's stay lasted just five months though. BURNING IN HELL drafted Tiago Gregoletto to substitute on bass and, for a while, had Rodrigo Couto of LETHAL handling lead vocals. However, the second demo, entitled 'World Of Illusion' and recorded in late 1998 / early 1999, saw Leandro Moreira back with the microphone for some tracks. With both Couto and Gregoletto making their exit the band relied upon the stand in services of ANESTHESIA bassist Luciano Zanotto. The 'World Of Illusion' tapes were re-worked to feature Moreira as vocalist on all the songs and subsequently re-issued. BURNING IN HELL suffered a major tragedy when Pieruccini committed suicide.
The band opted to persevere but completely re-shuffled the line-up. Leandro Moreira took on responsibilities as singer whilst guitars were delegated to new comers Roberto Alquati and Geraldo Alquati Aita. Bass was now in the hands of Gabriel 'Skywalker' Dória with Marcelo Moreira maintaining his position on drums.
In April of 2000 the 'World Of Illusion' tracks were issued on CD format as a shared album release in alliance with Japanese act AIMING HIGH on the Metal Crusade label. The band would also strike a deal with the Brazilian Encore label for a full length album release. Gigs saw BURNING IN HELL opening for a visiting HAMMERFALL.

Albums:
WORLD OF ILLUSION, Metal Crusade (2000) (Split album with AIMING HIGH)
World Of Illusion / Brave Warriors / Revelation Knights / Holy Wars In The Sky / Judgement Day

BURNING POINT (FINLAND)
Line-Up: Pete Ahoren (vocals / guitar), Jukka Kyrö (guitar), Toni Kansanoja (bass), Jari Kaiponen (drums)

A Power Metal band that started out life proudly displaying their Doom styled influences under the banner of PLANET CARAVAN. As a duo of vocalist / guitarist Pete Ahoren and guitarist Jukka Kyrö PLANET CARAVAN cut a demo which elicited strong response. With the addition of rhythm section bassist Toni Kansanoja and drummer Jari Kaiponen the group evolved into BURNING POINT. The band's debut album, 'Salvation By Fire' released by the German Limb Music Productions, would benefit from keyboard contributions courtesy of ETERNAL TEARS OF SORROW's Pasi Hiltula.

Albums:
SALVATION BY FIRE, Limb Music Productions LMP 0109-035CD (2001)
The Burning Point / Under The Dying Sun / Lake Of Fire / Fall Of Thy Kingdom / Higher / Black Star / Stealer Of Light / The One / Signs Of Danger / Salvation By Fire

BYRD (Seattle, WA, USA)
Line-Up: Michael Flatters (vocals), James Byrd (guitar), Brian Hutchison (bass / drums)

Noted Rock guitarist JAMES BYRD, an ex-member of the esteemed FIFTH ANGEL and having previously issued product under the JAMES BYRD'S ATLANTIS RISING handle, reverted to simply BYRD for the 2002 'Anthem' release issued by the Finnish Lion Music label. The album sees Byrd in collaboration with vocalist Michael Flatters, citing credits with HEIR APPARENT and TAKARA, and bassist / drummer Brian Hutchison. Flatters had previously appeared on the JAMES BYRD album 'Flying Beyond The 9'.

Albums:
ANTHEM, Lion Music LMC2218-2 (2002)
Anthem - Dealt By Darkness / Omen / Messages From Home / Home Day / All I Want / Killing Machine / Thank You / The Price Of War / Only Love

JAMES BYRD (Seattle, WA, USA)

Solo outings from JAMES BYRD, left handed guitarist extraordinaire known for his work with the fabled Seattle Metal band FIFTH ANGEL and his JAMES BYRD'S ATLANTIS RISING projects. A JAMES BYRD solo album 'Octoglomerate' surfaced in 1993 recorded with bassist Joey Blair Mudarri and Jeff Robinette on drums. The follow up, '1995's 'Son Of Man' utilising a fresh rhythm section of fretless bassist Bill Roman and drummer Chase Culp, would bear the rarest of endorsements from the guitar genius YNGWIE MALMSTEEN who penned sleeve notes highly praising the guitarist.

Byrd would work once again with drummer Chase Culp and also with erstwhile LYNCH MOB singer Robert Mason for the 1996 effort 'The Apocalypse Chime', the album including a cover version of JIMI HENDRIX's 'Dolly Dagger'. That same year the guitarist founded his own Byrd Guitar Company. The JAMES BYRD'S ATLANTIS RISING album 'Crimes Of Virtuosity' was delivered for the Japanese JVC Victor label in 1997.

The 2001 JAMES BYRD offering 'Flying Beyond The 9' would see lead vocal contributions from Michael James Flatters. Originally Byrd had requested the services of former HEIR APPARENT vocalist Steve Benito but prior commitments prevented this union. Instead, Benito suggested Flatters for the position. Ironically, after completing his tasks on 'Flying Beyond The 9', Flatters would make his mark fronting HEIR APPARENT for a one off 'Wacken Open Air' festival gig as well as recording with TAKARA.

JAMES BYRD's 2002 album release 'Anthem' was issued under the revised project title of simply BYRD.

Outside of his musical career Byrd has made a name for himself in the most unlikely of subjects. A college major in Physical Anthropology, the guitarist spent two years on a Federally funded archaeological excavation of an ancient Indian burial ground. Whilst there, he captured a strange rodent believed to have been extinct for ten thousand years. The university subsequently re-instated the animal as a viable species. The diversity of his talents does not end there; Byrd holds not only a degree in internal combustion engine theory and practice but also the equivalent of a European Master's degree in traditional Italian metal-shaping and fabrication.

Albums:
OCTOGLOMERATE, Shrapnel (1993)
Heavy Water / Sunburst / Octoglomerate / War Hero / Yoshimi's Mourning / Time Alone / Morning World Blues / Dances With Knives / Why Have You Forsaken Me
SON OF MAN, Shrapnel (1995)
In The Beginning / Adam / The World Requiem / Ezekiel - Son Of Man / Yeshua - Adonai Elohim / Out Of The Temple / The Teacher - Beatitude / Golgotha - The Right Hand Of Power / In My Father's House
THE APOCALYPSE CHIME, Shrapnel (1996)
Bosnia / "One" / Visigoth / Cold Paradise / Death (Is) / Dolly Dagger / I've Got A Line On You / Lighting The Sky / The Long Road
FLYING BEYOND THE 9 – SYMPHONIC METAL FOR THE NEW AGE, Lion Music LMC 210-2 (2001)
Flying Beyond the 9 / Dark Heart / W.T.O. (We Took Over) / Nevermore / Everything To Me / Unity (While You Were Sleeping) / Paradise Tonight / All of Me (An Allegory) / Avianti Suite Op.1, Nº63

JAMES BYRD'S ATLANTIS RISING
(Seattle, WA, (USA)
Line-Up: Freddy Krumins (vocals), James Byrd (guitar), Evan Shelley (bass), Scott Hunt (drums)

JAMES BYRD'S ATLANTIS RISING is the band project of ex-FIFTH ANGEL guitarist JAMES BYRD and former TKO and Q5 bassist Evan Shelley. The 'James Byrd's Atlantis Rising' album, recorded in 1990 with Shelley, vocalist Freddy Krumins and Byrd's erstwhile FIFTH ANGEL compatriot Ken Mary on drums, suffered at the hands of a legal battle between distributors which saw the work shelved for nearly a year. Byrd released a string of laudatory solo works with 'Octoglomerate' surfacing in 1993, 1995's 'Son Of Man' and the 1996 effort 'The Apocalypse Chime'. That same year the guitarist founded his own Byrd Guitar Company.

The ATLANTIS RISING album 'Crimes Of Virtuosity' (that included a cover of ANDREW LLOYD WEBBER's 'Heaven On Their Minds' from the 'Jesus Christ Superstar' musical) was released in Japan through the JVC Victor label in 1998 although much to Byrd's chagrin. The guitarist had not been pleased with the finished mix and offered to re-mix the entire record out of his own pocket. Unable to wait JVC Victor released the album anyway. The Mascot Records version, licensed in Europe, features the intended mix. Having never gained North American distribution for the record Byrd released 'Crimes Of Virtuosity' through MP3.com during 2000, this third version substituting 'Heaven On Their Minds' for the unreleased 'Symphony for Electric Guitar and Orchestra - First Movement'.

The recording line-up for 'Crimes Of Virtuosity' featured the line-up of vocalist Torry Kendall, bassist Randy Mathieson and drummer Chase Culp. Mathieson's day job is as an engineer for a recording company based in the North West that has seen him work with many major name acts. Culp, meantime, has often been called upon as a session drummer.

JAMES BYRD's 2002 album release 'Anthem' was issued under the revised project title of simply BYRD.

Albums:
JAMES BYRD'S ATLANTIS RISING, (1990)
Into The Light / Let It Out / After The Fire / Fallen Warrior / Angel Of Mercy / Driven By Desire / Eye Of The Storm / Remember Love / Bay Of Rainbows / Fly To The Sun
CRIMES OF VIRTUOSITY, (1998)
Prelude In Sea / Metatron / Heaven On Their Minds / In My Darkest Hour / The Hunted Heretic (When I Was Young) / Jane / Get Free / Storm King / Goodbye My Love / Going Home

CACOPHONY (USA)

Line-Up: Peter Marrino (vocals), Marty Friedman (guitar), Jason Becker (guitar), Jimmy O'Shea (bass), Atma Anur (drums)

CACOPHONY arrived with perfect timing in the mid '80s heightened interest in speed guitarists.

Antecedent to this formation guitarist MARTY FRIEDMAN had paid his dues with HAWAII and VIXEN and forging an alliance with another six string whizz kid JASON BECKER founded CACOPHONY with erstwhile LE MANS singer Peter Marrino. The resulting album 'Speed Metal Symphony' sparked considerable interest; enough for both guitarists to capitalise on it with solo outings. Friedman launched 'Dragon's Kiss' whilst Becker's 'Perpetual Burn' was released simultaneously.

Drummer Atma Anur departed prior to the second CACOPHONY album 'Go Off!' and was superseded by former LE MANS skinbasher Kenny Stavropoulos. However, Deen Castronovo, most recognised for his work with WILD DOGS, HARDLINE, OZZY OSBOURNE and JOURNEY in fact supplies drums on the album. Stavropoulos later joined STARSHIP.

Friedman was later to enjoy global recognition as part of MEGADETH and for his subsequent solo workouts. Becker has also made a name for himself with a string of authoritative solo albums and an appearance in DAVID LEE ROTH's band.

Albums:
SPEED METAL SYMPHONY, Roadrunner 349577 (1987)
Savage / Where My Fortune Lies / The Ninja / Concerto / Burn The Ground / Desert Island / Speed Metal Symphony
GO OFF!, Roadrunner RR 94991(1988)
X-Ray Eyes / E.S.P. / Stranger / Go Off! / Black Cat / Sword Of The Warrior / Floating World / Images

CAGE (San Diego, CA, USA)

Line-Up: Sean Peck (vocals), Dave Garcia (guitar), Anthony Wayne McGinnis (guitar), Mike Giordano (bass), Mike Nielsen (drums)

Much vaunted San Diego Power Metal act CAGE has carved out a valuable niche in the European market. The band was bravely forged as a no frills Metal unit by a union of ex-CRUSHER and NOMAD personnel in 1992 in the full teeth of the Grunge wave. CAGE recorded a projected first album in 1994 but this release was shelved. The 'Unveiled' album, issued by Omega Records, would see CAGE with a line-up of vocalist Sean Peck, guitarists Dave Garcia and Eric Horton, bassist Mike Giordano and drummer Damian Arletto. CAGE honed their reputation further, acting as guests to acts such as DIO, IRON MAIDEN, JUDAS PRIEST and DOKKEN.

During 1999, and unbeknown to the band, a German Metal journalist named Jurgen Tschmaler entered CAGE into an unsigned band contest for the prestigious 'Rock Hard' magazine. The first prize was to perform at the 'Dynamo Open Air' festival in Holland. CAGE not only won the contest, voted by for by Rock fans and beating over 600 other acts, but also won by a huge majority. CAGE, who also saw their 'Shoot To Kill' song featured as the lead cut on a 'Rock Hard' cover mount CD, duly performed at the Dynamo event with drummer Mike Nielsen newly on board, headlined that year by METALLICA.

With interest riding high in Europe CAGE secured appearances at the legendary 'Wacken Open Air' Metal festival in Germany followed up by a showing at the Swiss 'Metal Dayz' event. The 'Astrology' album, released on Los Angeles World War III Records, would be re-issued in September to back up the dates.

Anthony Wayne McGinnis would take the place of Eric Horton on guitar. CAGE signed to the German Massacre label for a July 2002 release 'Darker Than Black', produced by Joe Floyd of WARRIOR fame.

Albums:
UNVEILED, Cage CDX-336647 (1998)
Shoot To Kill / Modern Darkness / I Live / Buried In The Box / Devil Inside / Dancing Around The Fire / Release Me / Unveiled / The Iron Priest / Nomad / Influence / E.B.S. / Disaster / Sudden Death / Asta La Vista
ASTROLOGY, Omega 99090-1 (2000)
Astrology / Final Solution / Psychotically Deranged / The Edge / Echelon / Root Of All Evil / The Trigger Effect / Souls And Flesh / Fountain Of Youth / Broken Dreams / Vandalize / Victim Of Society / The Astrologicon

CALVARIA (MEXICO)

Line-Up: Mario Montaño (vocals), Juan Pablo Agudelo (guitar) Oswaldo Blanco (guitar), Laszlo Kalloi (bass) Vicente Gazano (keyboards), Juan Pablo Ramírez (drums)

Not to be confused with the Polish Death Metal act of the same title. Mexico City's CALVARIA, dating to 1998, operate strictly in the Speed Power Metal zone and have built

SEAN PECK of CAGE
Photo : Nico Wobben

up a solid reputation supporting visiting artists such as ANGRA, RHAPSODY, GAMMA RAY, SHAMAN and RATA BLANCA.

Albums:
CALVARIA, Argenta (2001)
El Rostro De La Muerte / Alas Al Viento / Destructor / Metalia / Requiem / El Heroe / Ultimo Viaje / Salvame / Sigues Aqui / Naufrago Del Tiempo / Valle De Soledad

CAPRICORN (GERMANY)
Line-Up: Adrian Ergün (vocals / bass), David (guitar), Stefan Arnold (drums)

Previously known as GRINDER, this German outfit formed as CAPRICORN in 1991. Following the debut album CAPRICORN supported GRAVEDIGGER on a German tour.
Front man Adrian Ergün guested on the 1996 album from CRASH MUSEUM.
Ergün would create NEMESIS for an eponymous 1997 album in collusion with guitarist Axel Katzmann and Arnulf Tunn of TANKARD.

Albums:
CAPRICORN, Shark SHARK 030 (1993)
Mob In The Hood / One Shot From Murder / Burn / Light Up Your Mind / Lonely Is The World / Mr. Voorhees / Bomb Eden / Shotdown Downtown / The Harder They Fall / Long Way Home / Exceeding The Limits Of Pain
INFERNO, (1995)
Iced Age / Claws Of The Mad / The Wire Fence / Dead Can Walk / Moonstruck / Iron Biter / Gun For Hire / A Call For Defiance / You Can't Stop Rock n' Roll / Camp Blood / Inferno

CARISMA (DENMARK)
Line-Up: Kare Amelung (vocals / bass), Jan Black (guitar), Jon Froda (keyboards), Jesper Arvidson (drums)

Albums:
1825, Carisma HGDSRRR 3 (1996)
Marriage Of Convenience / Wind Dreams / Heed My Call / Closing Rhyme / Tears In My Eyes / Lean On / Killing Tribe / Nothing Left (But Saying Goodbye) / Twisted Minds / Hate Is Homeless Love / Epilogue

CARPEDIEM (GERMANY)
Line-Up: Rainer Hennings, (vocals), Arnt Bünz (guitar), Michael Beyer (guitar), Marion Elm (bass), Martin Reinsch (keyboards), Robert Stöhr (drums)

Albums:
THE PARALYZED YEARS, (2000)
XXX / Paralyzed / Northwinds / Waive The Wisdom / I Try To Fly

CASTLE WELL (GERMANY)
Line-Up: Christoph Niksch (vocals / keyboards), Frank Schrange (guitar), Chris Klomann (bass), Thomas Niksch (drums)

Trad Metal act dating back to 1985, then going under the name of BLOODY MARY. The group switched to CASTLE WELL in 1988 and quite miraculously have maintained the same line-up for over a decade.

Albums:
HELPLESS, (2001)
Win Or Lose / He Comes Alive / Helpless / Eye Of The Storm / Attila / At Dawn / Life Is A Long Hard Fight / Go To Hell / 2020 / Time Couldn't Heal / Hymn

CATHARSIS (RUSSIA)
Line-Up: Oleg Zhilyakov (vocals), Anthony Arikh (guitar), Igor Polyakov (guitar), Vadim Bystrov (bass), Julia Egorova (keyboards), Vladimir Moochnov (drums)

Albums:
DEA, Irond 00-19 (2001)
Igni Et Ferro / A Trip Into Elysium / My Love, The Phiery / Etude A-Moll For Piano Opus 1 / Pro Memoria / Silent Tears / ... Into Oblivion

CATHARSIS (USA)
Line-Up: Scott Fox (vocals / guitar), Pete Cleary (bass), Mike Nielsen (drums)

A Progressive Metal band that left a legacy of a solitary, highly regarded album for the Danish Nordic Metal label. Drummer Mike Nielsen later joined NEW YORK BLADE then Power Metal act CAGE.
'Pathways To Wholeness' is regarded as a lost classic.

Albums:
PATHWAYS TO WHOLENESS, Nordic Metal NMCD0295 (1995)
The Premise / Here And Now / Shadows / Reign Of Dissonance / Behind The Mask / The Truth? / Black Box / Pathways To Wholeness / Casting Stones / Burn The Page / Fire / Seasons Of Madness

CAULDRON BORN (Atlanta, GA, USA)
Line-Up: Zane Matthews (vocals), Howie Bentley (guitar), Shawn Kascak (bass), Bill Parsons (drums)

Atlanta based Epic Power Metal band. The group rose out of the Norcross HOWIE BENTLEY BAND, founded by guitarist Howie Bentley after his relocation from Kentucky. Early recordings with vocalist Christian Schulze, entitled 'Beyond The Shade Gates', led to the formation of CAULDRON BORN in late 1994, Bentley and Schulze being joined by bassist Shawn Kascak and drummer Bill Parsons. A demo session billed as 'Swords, Sorcery And Science' garnered a deal with the Italian Underground Symphony label.

Schulze made his exit prior to recording of the inaugural 1997 album 'Born Of The Cauldron', Danny White taking the lead vocal mantle. With response strong in Europe Underground Symphony combined the two formative demos and released them compiled as the 1998 'Gods Of Metal' album. CAULDRON BORN meantime enlisted the studio services of singer David Louden for the third album 'And Rome Shall Fall'. With Louden only ever committing to studio work the search was on for a vocalist to fulfil live obligations. Erstwhile ABWHORE bass player Zane Matthews was duly inducted in late 2001.

Albums:

BORN OF THE CAULDRON, Underground Symphony USCD018 (1997)
Crusader / The Sword's Lament / Synchronicity At Midnight - A Baying Of Hounds / Imprisoned With The Pharaohs / The Final Incantation - In The Dreaming City / In Fate's Eye A King / Born Of The Cauldron / Unholy Sanctuary

GODS OF METAL, Underground Symphony USCD031 (1998)
Calling From The Crystal Tower / In Fate's Eye A King / Crusader / The Final Incantation - In The Dreaming City / Dreaming With The Incubus / Wicker Man / Unleashing Wrath / On Broken Wings Of Sorrow

AND ROME SHALL FALL, Underground Symphony USCD059CD (2001)
By This Axe I Rule / ...And Rome Shall Fall / Finder Of The Black Stone / Blood Bath In The Arena / Dragon Throne / Clontarf / Storming The Castle / People Of The Dark Circle

CENTAUR (GERMANY)

Line-Up: Stefan Keßel (vocals), Stefan Lohmann (guitar), Michael Böing (bass), Christoph Weiß (keyboards), Guido Gallus (drums)

Melodic keyboard driven Metal debuted with the Peter Stabenow produced 'Mob Rules The World' album. CENTAUR's line-up for the 1993 Ralf Hubert produced 'Power World' album comprised lead vocalist Rainer Kuppers, twin guitarists Stefan Lohmann and Michael Böing, bass player Markus Lenzen, keyboard player Christoph Weib and Reiner Schultzer on drums.

By the time of 1996's '...Perception...' outing Stefan Keßel was fronting the band with Guido Gallus on drums, both being former HEAVENWARD members. In addition CENTAUR had adopted a single guitar stance with Böing shifting to bass.

Albums:

MOB RULES THE WORLD, Virgin (1990)
Just A Man / Mob Rules The World / Looking For Someone / Got To Believe In Love / Dreamin' / No More Excuses / Centaur / Take Me This Way / Right In Time

POWER WORLD, Liga CD BB 202/2000 (1993)
Part Of Me / In This World / Heartache / Insane / Trick By Trick / Centaur Part II / Black Rain / No More Rules / Break It / Got To Believe In Love / Right In Time

IBERIAN KILLERS - LIVE IN SPAIN, Liga CC 383 3000 (1995)
Insane / World Times / Centaur / Trick By Trick / Heartache / Black Rain / Live In This World / Looking For Someone / Mob Rules The World / Wild Sister

...PERCEPTION..., Zardoz 9611 R IRS CD 995.201 (1996)
Times Out / The Beholder / The Legionnair / Introspection / Signs / Your Tool / New Beginning / Awake / Another Beginning / Children Of The Revolution

GOD COMPLEX, Bossy Ogress CD 007377 2 B.O. (1998)
Sonnenkind / Game Of Life / The Price Of Money / Echo Of An Empty Shell / The Seed / Land Of Gold / An Ode To A Memory / Ultimate Answer / To Be Or Not To Be / Axiom

CENTURION (ITALY)

Line-Up: Germano Quintaba (vocals), Fabio Monti (guitar), Luciano Monti (guitar), Massimiliano Ricci (bass), Sebastiano Massetti (drums)

Founded in 1992 CENTURION, as the name implies, employed both Roman empire imagery and lyrical content for their distinctive brand of Heavy Metal. The group were initially entitled SCALA MERCALLI and then with a name change to SHARPENED RAZOR debuted with a 1996 demo entitled 'Hellbringer'. A subsequent demo 'Mors Tua Vita Mea' secured them a deal with the Scarlet label. However, despite drawing commendable reviews for their opening 'Arise Of The Empire' album they would shed their rhythm section of bassist Manuele Maricotti and drummer Marco Bracciotti, this outgoing pair prioritising their main act DELIVERANCE. Massimiliano Ricci on bass and Sebastiano Massetti on drums swiftly filled the vacancies.

CENTURION covered JUDAS PRIEST's 'Riding On The Wind' on their 2000 'Hyper Martyium' album.

CENTURION drummer Sebastiano Massetti was replaced by Emanuele Beccacece in October 2001 for the 'Non Plus Ultra' album.

Albums:
ARISE OF THE EMPIRE, Scarlet SC 006-2 (1999)
Centurion / Steel Breath / Guns Are Screaming / Metal Gladiator / Snow Covers Imperial Alps / Bloodstreets / Mors Tua Vita Mea / Razor Blade / Ragin' Power
HYPER MARTYRUM, Scarlet SC 023-2 (2000)
Arise Of The Empire / Deflagration Of Violence / Hyper Martyrium / Talis Pater / Katerpillar / Monolithic Triumphator / Into The Arena / Stormfront Vanguard / Call Of The Blood / Riding On The Wind
NON PLUS ULTRA, Scarlet SC 052-2 (2002)
Maximum Golgotha / M.A.S. / Non Plus Ultra / Panzer March / The Crucifier / Megalometal / Roma Caput Mundi / Ius Primae Noctis / Soap Opera / Neanderthal

CETI (POLAND)
Line-Up: Grzegorz Kupczyk (vocals / guitar), Andrzej _ysów (guitar), Maciej Przybylski (bass), Maria Wietrzykowska (keyboards), Jacek Jab_o_ski (drums)

A ProgMetal act led by Grzegorz Kupczyk of TURBO and NON IRON fame. The band CETI, named after the NASA search for alien life 'Communication with Extraterrestrial Intelligence', was formulated during 1989. Initially the band comprised Kupczyk handling both lead vocals and bass guitar, Andrzej _ysów on guitar, keyboard player Maria 'Marihuana' Wietrzykowska and drummer Jacek Jab_o_ski. Subsequently Maciej Przybylski took the bass role. CETI's first album 'Czarna Roza' ('The Black Rose') fared well gaining national TV exposure.

The 1992 album 'Lamiastrata' saw Marcin 'Mucek' Krystek take over the drum stool. This line-up also cut the live album 'Extasy '93'. However, during recording of 1994's 'Rasizm' conflict erupted within the band and the following year ex-MONASTERY and UZURPATOR guitarist Przemys_aw

Burzy_ski, former DIGNITY and CARRION bass player Bartek Urbaniak usurped their predecessors.

Kupczyk issued a solo record, on which Wietrzykowska guested, and in 2000 performed a major concert bringing together past band mates of TURBO, NON IRON and CETI. The next CETI offering 'Demony Czasu' ('Demons Of Time') was recorded for Metal Mind Productions and found the band pursuing a much more modern path.

Singles/EPs:
Rasizm / Epitafium / Piosenka / Epitafium II, (1995) ('Maxi Promotion' EP)

Albums:
CZARNA ROZA, Arston (1989)
Bieg Strace_ców / CETI'a / Samotna Tancerka / Ogie_ i _zy / Sztylet / Brama T_czy / Prawo Pi__ci / Na Progu Serca / _ciana P_aczu / Like An Eagle / Holidays In Agrigento / B_azen
LAMIASTRATA, Izabelin Studio (1992)
Intro / Harley's Soul / Lamiastrata / Burning Fantasy / Kap_ani K_amstwa / Z_o Jest Wsz_dzie / Kamikadze'45 / Satan's Cavalary Part III / Sztuczne Oddychanie / Hot Body & Hair / Piosenka / Greensleves
EXTASY '93, (1993)
Intro Welcome / Bieg Strace_ców / Harley's Soul / Burning Fantasy / Lamiastrata / Kap_ani K_amstwa / Prawo Pi__ci / Sztuczne Oddychanie / Ogie_ i _zy / Fire Angels / Satan's Cavalery Part III / Kamikadze '45
RASIZM, Lazer Sound (1994)
Rasizm / Quo Vadis? / Epitafium / Media – Tor / Visions / Krótki Utwór O Zabijaniu / Mi_o__, Nienawi__, Smier_ / Somewhere Over The Rainbow / Wojna / Po__danie / Faraon
DEMONY CZASU, Metal Mind Productions (2000)
XIV - Nie Pytaj / Sati (Hakhim - Al Farikka) / Przemijanie / Ciemno__ / Atlantyda - Historia Zaginionej Oceanii / Kometa Halley'a / Demony Czasu / Krzycz_c Na Wiatr / _ycie I Kres / Pearl Harbor / Feniks / A.K.I.A. / Feniks (Video)
PROLOG, Oskar Productions 1014 (2002)
Falcon's Flight / I Know / Lot Sokola / In The Name Of Law

CHAINSAW (GERMANY)
Line-Up: Frank Von Schmidt (vocals), Burkhardt Rautenberg (guitar), Andreas Klimowitsch (guitar), Gerd Gutsche (bass), Arndt Kermer (drums)

Deutsche Heavy Metaller!! When the German

quintet sent out promo copies of their 'Hell's Burnin' Up' album the group ensured a miniature 'Action Man' size chainsaw was included in the package daubed with the band's logo!

Albums:

HELL'S BURNIN' UP, Bonebreaker BONE 2 (1986)
Hell's Burnin' Up / Dungeon / Last Fortress / Cut Loose / Rage And Revenge / Midnight Hunter / Born To Kill / He Knows You Are Alone / Ageless Force

CHASTAIN (USA)
Line-Up: Leather Leone (vocals), David T. Chastain (guitar), Mike Skimmerhorn (bass), Ken Mary (drums)

An incredibly prolific guitarist hailing from Cincinnati, DAVID T. CHASTAIN was regularly releasing albums with two band projects CJSS and CHASTAIN as well as the odd solo album in the late '80s. Chastain played in mostly original Hard Rock bands during his career, including a Progressive Rock mob called TARGET. Atlanta born Chastain - who claimed never to have had a guitar lesson in his life - joined a commercial venture known as SPIKE. This led to the recording of an album entitled 'The Price Of Pleasure' plus three 45s and a couple of appearances on local radio station promo albums. SPIKE made quite a name for themselves on the local circuit supporting the likes of BLUE OYSTER CULT, HELIX and KROKUS.
SPIKE switched vocalists and became CJSS. Interestingly, two tracks - 'The Gates Of Eternity' and 'Living In Exile', that were originally SPIKE songs appear on CJSS' debut.
Mike Varney of Shrapnel Records picked up on Chastain after the guitarist had sent some of his material to Varney in the hope of a mention in his popular column in 'Guitar Player' magazine. Varney wasn't impressed with SPIKE but liked the material Chastain was working on as a side project and decided to sign the guitarist to Shrapnel and form a band. Chastain and SPIKE and C.J.S.S. bassist Mike Skimmerhorn found themselves working with erstwhile RUDE GIRL vocalist Leather Leone.
The drummer on the debut CHASTAIN album 'Mystery Of Illusion' released in 1985 was Fred Coury, who left to deputise for an injured Randy Castillo in OZZY OSBOURNE's band then went on to make his name with CINDERELLA. The CHASTAIN drum stool was taken over by former FIFTH ANGEL and TKO man Ken Mary for the 'Ruler Of The

Wasteland' album.
The original CHASTAIN line-up did, however, play seven or eight shows together, two being showcase events for major labels - including EMI's Manhatten subsidiary.
Leather's old band RUDE GIRL released a two track 12" under the new name of MALIBU BARBI in 1987 featuring Leather on vocals.
1997's comeback release 'In Dementia' featured the fine vocal talents of Kate French, with the CHASTAIN line-up completed by former DAMIEN bassist Kevin Kekes and ex-TROUBLE and STYGIAN drummer Dennis Lesh.
CHASTAIN were put on temporary hold during 1998 due to Kate French's pregnancy. Chastain himself busied himself with yet another band project SAINT SAVAGE in the interim.
By 2001 CHASTAIN was back on track with Chastain and French joined by a fresh rhythm section of bassist Dave Starr and drummer Larry Howe, both previously with VICIOUS RUMORS. The high profile Swedish Metal band HAMMERFALL would lend CHASTAIN added exposure by covering 'Angel Of Mercy' on their 2002 album.

Albums:
MYSTERY OF ILLUSION, Roadrunner RR 9742 (1985)
Black Knight / When The Battle's Over / Mystery Of Illusion / I've Seen Tomorrow / Endlessly / I Fear No Evil / Night Of The Gods / We Shall Overcome / The Winds Of Change
RULER OF THE WASTELAND, Roadrunner RR 9689 (1986)
Ruler Of The Wasteland / One Day To Live / The King Has The Power / Fighting To Stay Alive / Angel Of Mercy / There Will Be Justice / The Battle Of Nevermore / Living In A Dreamworld / Children Of Eden
THE 7TH OF NEVER, Leviathan Black Dragon BD 025 (1987)
We Must Carry On / Paradise / It's Too Late For Yesterday / 827 / The Wicked Are Restless / The 7th Of Never / Take Me Back In Time / Feel His Magic / Forevermore
VOICE OF THE CULT, Roadrunner RR9548 (1988)
The Voice Of The Cult / Live Hard / Chains Of Love / Share Yourself With Me / Fortune Teller / Child Of Evermore / Soldiers Of The Flame / Evil For Evil / Take Me Home
FOR THOSE WHO DARE, Roadrunner RR9398 (1990)
The Mountain Whispers / For Those Who Dare / Please Set Us Free / I Am The Rain / Night Of Anger / Barracuda / Light In The Dark / Secrets Of The Damned / Not Much Breathing / Once Before

SICK SOCIETY, Leviathan (1995)
I Know The Darkness / Sick Society / Violence In Blame / Those Were The Daze / Destructive Ground / To The Edge / The Price Of War / Every Emotion / The Vampire / Sugarcaine / Love And Hate / Angel Falls
IN DEMENTIA, Massacre MAS PCO122 (1997)
Human Sacrifice / Blackening / Seven / Sick Puppy / Tongue / In Dementia / House Of Stone / Conformity / Desperately

DAVID T. CHASTAIN (Atlanta, GA, USA)

CHASTAIN and CJSS driving force guitarist David T. Chastain was originally from Atlanta, Georgia but wound up making a name for himself in Cincinnati, Ohio where he would also indulge himself in a series of solo records. Other musicians making an appearance include CHASTAIN drummer Ken Mary, bassist David Harbour and for the 'Elegant Seduction' album, drummer Rick Porter.
1994's 'Next Planet Please' saw the retention of Harbour with fresh drummer Mike Haid.
Chastain teamed up with ARCH RIVAL's Michael Harris in 1999 for a new project ZANISTER. A further project band SOUTHERN GENTLEMEN with CHASTAIN's rhythm section of bassist Kelly Kekes and drummer Dennis Lesh issued the 2000 album 'Exotic Dancer Blues'.

Albums:
INSTRUMENTAL VARIATIONS, Black Dragon BD 029 (1988)
Now Or Never / Capriccio In E Minor / 18th Century Inamorata / Wild And Truly Diminished / Horizons / Spontaneous Combustion / It Doesn't Have To Be / Project 107: Code 3X / The Oracle Within
WITHIN THE HEAT, Leviathan (1989)
Excursions Into Reality / Dangerzone F 107 / The Visionary / The Return Of The Six / Nightmares / Within The Heat / Zfunknc / It's Still In Your Eyes / In Your Face / Pantheon / Desert Nights
ELEGANT SEDUCTION, Leviathan (1991)
Schizophrenia / Elegant Seduction / Trapped In The Void / 7 Hills Groove / Pompous Rompous / Blitzkrieg / Menage A Trois / Fortunate Happenstance / No Repeat Discourse/ Images / Positional Strategy
MOVEMENTS THRU TIME, Killerwatt KCLCD 1002 (1992)
Thunder And Lightning / 827 / Fortunate And Happenstance / Citizen Of Hell / Blitzkrieg / The Oracle Within / New York Rush / We Must Carry On / Cappricco / In E Minor / No Man's Land / 7 Hills Groove / Now Or Never

/ Trapped In The Wind / Zoned In Danger / The Bargain
NEXT PLANET PLEASE, Bulletproof VEST 9 (1994)
Project Transformation / Next Planet Please / Realisation / Fusion Delusion / Forever Searching / Sophisticated Debauchery / Dunk The Funk / Blame It On Rio / Homage To An Unknown Hero / Watching Time Go By
ACOUSTIC VISIONS, Guitar Nine 199812(1998)
Set / Pyramid Of The Sun / Appassionata Minore / Cadenza In A Harmonic Minor / Inner Journeys / Dirge For Yesterday / Evening With Juilliard / Lifetime / Time And Time Again / S.T.C. / Escape From Thera
D-DAZE: A NEW DAY, Diginet CD 8983951179-79272 (2001)
Agony Of Life / Come On Home / I Know About You / Say Your Prayers / A New Day / Land Of Greed / First Sight Of Light / Never Too Much / Nothing But A Sin / The Bottom Line / Return To Hades / Hunger Kills
INSTATREASURE, Diginet CD 8983951179-81598 (2001)
Illusions Of Eternity / A Girl On Every Planet / Room With A Blue View / Out Of Body / Eminent Confrontation / Father Time / Guitar Symphonica In G Minor / First Sight Of Light / Never Too Much / Day Of Judgement / The Bottom Line / Return To Hades
RIFFOLOGY: WICKED RIFFS, Diginet CD 8983951179-83144 (2001)
Into The Edge Of Sanity / Crash And Burn / Freedom / I Feel Your Passion / It's Nevermore / House Of Blood / Final Line / We Still Believe / Feel The Rain / In The Light Of The Day / Kings / We Kill No More
ROCK SOLID GUITAR, Leviathan 20012-2 (2001)
Burning Passions / Sounds Cool To Me / Dancing With The Devil's Mistress / Never Too Much / Getting A Little Crazy / In Memoriam / Riding In Style / Keeper Of Tomorrow / Hats Off To Angus And Malcolm

CHATEAU (GERMANY)
Line-Up: Jioti Parcharidis (vocals), Henni Franzbecker (guitar), Eddie Stumm (bass), Burkhard Becker (keyboards), Kalli Wilken (drums)

Hildesheim Progressive edged Metal band dating to 1996. Kalli Wilken originally manned the drum stool. Keyboard player Burkhard Becker was previously a member of WILLOW. Singer Jioti Parcharidis previously fronted Hannover act HYDROTOXIN.
Following the highly praised 1998 EP 'Starlight Ecstasy' the Greek born Laki Zaios took over on drums. However, by the following year Andreas Tegeler of POVERTY'S NO

CRIME would become the latest percussionist.

Subsequent changes saw Tegeler returning to his priority act and CHATEAU losing the skills of Parcharidis. New recruits would be vocalist Frank Liener and drummer Gerd Peter Mumme, the latter a veteran of DEFORMED, KING CARRION and ACT OF FATE. The band would soon lose Liener though and BIRD OF PREY's Eric Weise was next in line as CHATEAU singer.

Mumme also operates with EBULATION.

Singles/EPs:
Starlight Ecstasy EP, Sicus Rock 101-2 (1998)

CHATEAUX (UK)

Line-Up: Krys Mason (vocals / bass), Tim Broughton (guitar), Chris Dadson (drums)

Cheltenham Heavy Metal band CHATEAUX had formed originally under the title of STEALER, but switched titles to CHATEAUX with their first vinyl appearance, a track on the 1982 Ebony Records compilation 'Metal Maniaxe'.

The group was promptly signed by Ebony to an album deal and the first release (preceded by the 'Young Blood' single) was recorded with original vocalist and bassist Alec Houston, whilst Andre Baylis contributed drums. The record also featured lead vocals by GRIM REAPER's Steve Grimmet.

Both Baylis and Houston were to quit after 'Chained And Desperate's release and were replaced by ex-CONFESSOR vocalist / bassist Krys Mason and former SAM THUNDER and ARAGORN drummer Chris Dadson, although Mason was to leave in 1986.

Singles/EPs:
Young Blood / Fight To The Last, Ebony EBON 9 (1982)

Albums:
CHAINED AND DESPERATE, Ebony EBON13 (1983)
Chained And Desperate / Spirit Of The Chateaux / Burn Out At Dawn / The Dark Surrendered / Straight To The Heart / Baton Rouge / Son Of Seattle / Shine On Freedom
FIREPOWER, Ebony EBON 18 (1984)
Rock n' Roll Thunder / Roller Coaster / Eyes Of Stone / Hero / Run In The Night / Street Angel / V8 Crash
HIGHLY STRUNG, Ebony EBON 31 (1985)
Highly Strung / Turn It On / Hot Touch At Midnight / Phalanx / Chase The Sun / Through The Fire / First Strike / One Too

Many / Midnight Star

CHIAROSCURO (Seattle, WA, USA)

Line-Up: Ian Dorsch (vocals / keyboards), Richard Chambliss (guitar), Cliff Chambliss (bass), Aaron Ellsworth (drums)

Challenging Progressive Metal out of Seattle. Titled after a famous Italian classical painting technique the idea for CHIAROSCURO was apparently formulated by various members whilst waiting in line to see a DREAM THEATER concert. Frontman Ian Dorsch was previously a member of SUB ROSA.

During October of 2000 CHIAROSCURO would lose drummer Aaron Ellsworth to MINE! A replacement would be found in Julian MacDonough. However, after laying down recordings for a three track demo MacDonough left in May of 2001. He would be replaced by Jason Northover of STARSEED.

Albums:
BRILLIANT POOLS OF DARKNESS, Chiaroscuro CBP04 (1999)
Broken Everything / Crucifixion / No Need / Bloody Hell / Caliban's Dance / Waiting / Winter Girls / Luminescence / Divinity / Children's Crusade

CHILDREN OF BODOM (FINLAND)

Line-Up: Alex Laiho (vocals / guitar), Ale Kuoppala (guitar), Henkka Seppäiä (bass), Janne Wirman Pimeys (keyboards), Jaska Raatikainen (drums)

A powerful, modern Metal act from the town of Espoo, named after Finland's infamous Lake Bodom, the scene of a horrific, unsolved attack in 1960 that left three teenagers dead. Founder member and vocalist Alex Laiho made his name as part of THY SERPENT maintaining CHILDREN OF BODOM, created in 1993 with drummer Jaska Raatikainen, as a going concern. Initially the group had gone under the title of INEARTHED, issuing a brace of melodic Death Metal demos 'Ubiquitos Absence Of Remission' and 'Shining' with keyboard player J..Pirisjoki onboard under that title. As INEARTHED the group scored a label deal in Belgium but a better offer from the highly respected Finnish Spinefarm concern convinced the band their way. At this stage the band, now with Janne Wirman Pimeys on keyboards, switched title to CHILDREN OF BODOM recording the 'Something Wild' debut.

The album was issued in Finland in November of 1997 and picked up for European license by the German Nuclear

Blast corporation shortly after. The group recorded an additional track, 'Children Of Bodom', which, when released as a single alongside tracks from CRYHAVOC and WIZZARD, scored the unprecedented achievement of hitting the no. 1 spot on the charts. The band supported DIMMU BORGIR on their 1997 Finnish dates and in February of the following year hooked up with HYPOCRISY, COVENANT and BENEDICTION for mainland European gigs. For these shows a friend of the band, Erna, substituted for Wirman Pimeys who could not get time out of schooling. With album sales on a sharp rise CHILDREN OF BODOM were back out on the road in Europe during September, performing as part of another package bill with DISMEMBER, AGATHODAIMON, RAISE HELL and NIGHT IN GALES. Once again Wirman Pimeys had to sit it out and Kimberley Goss of AVERNUS, DIMMU BORGIR and THERION repute filled in.

CHILDREN OF BODOM scored a further national number 1 single with 'Downfall' in early 1999. The single also contained a cover version of STONE's 'No Commands'. The 'Hatebreeder' album would also witness the band's presence in the national German album charts for the first time peaking at no. 75. Touring began with inaugural dates in Japan during the summer followed by a familiar Nuclear Blast package European venture allied with IN FLAMES, DARK TRANQUILITY and ARCH ENEMY. This time Janne Wirman Pimeys was in place behind the keyboards. In band down time Wirman, under the title of WARMAN, cut a solo album in 2000 titled 'Unknown Soldier'.

The B side to CHILDREN OF BODOM's 2000 single 'Hate Me' features a cover version of W.A.S.P.'s 'Hellion'. The ensuing album 'Follow The Reaper' found the Japanese version with an extra bonus track, a version of OZZY OSBOURNE's 'Shot In The Dark'.

As a precursor of what was to come the band's 'Hate Me' single of October 2000 swiftly reaped Platinum sales status in Finland by selling over 10,000 copies. Raatikainen deputised for SINERGY toward the close of the year before CHILDREN OF BODOM supported PRIMAL FEAR for a German tour in February 2001. Their current 'Follow The Reaper' album quickly shifted over 50,000 copies in Europe, attaining a no. 46 placing in the German national charts and reaching the top five in Finland. In October the band featured on the Spinefarm compilation 'Metal Rocks' with an exclusive cover version of IRON MAIDEN's 'Aces High'. Jaska Raatikainen, along with TAROT and SINERGY bassist Marco Hietala and TAROT

CHILDREN OF BODOM
Photo : Toni Härkönen

keyboard player Janne Tolsa would also convene a 2001 endeavour dubbed VIRTUOCITY. Raatikainen would also find time to session on the EVEMASTER EP 'Wither'.

CHILDREN OF BODOM broke their silence in mid 2002 unveiling plans for an August single comprising a new track 'You're Better Off Dead' coupled with a cover version of THE RAMONES 'Somebody Put Something In My Drink'.

Singles/EPs:
Children Of Bodom, Spinefarm (1997) (Split single with CRYHAVOC and WIZZARD) **1 FINLAND**
Downfall / No Commands, Spinefarm (1999) **1 FINLAND**
Hate Me / Hellion, Spinefarm SPI 98CD (2000)
You're Better Off Dead / Somebody Put Something In My Drink, Spinefarm (2002)

Albums:
SOMETHING WILD, Nuclear Blast NB 308-2 (1998)
Deadnight Warrior / In The Shadows / Red Light In My Eyes (Part I) / Red Light In My Eyes (Part II) / Lake Bodom / The Nail / Touch Like Angel Of Death
TOKYO WARHEARTS LIVE, Nuclear Blast (1999)
Intro / Silent Night, Bodom Night / Lake Bodom / Bed Of Razors / War Of Razors / Deadnight Warrior / Hatebreeder / Touch The Angel Of Death / Downfall / Towards Dead End
HATEBREEDER, Nuclear Blast (1999) **75 GERMANY**
Warheart / Silent Night, Bodom Night / Hatebreeder / Bed Of Razors / Towards Dead End / Black Widow / Wrath Within / Children Of Bodom / Down Fall
FOLLOW THE REAPER, Nuclear Blast (2000) **36 AUSTRIA, 3 FINLAND, 88 FRANCE, 46 GERMANY, 85 ITALY**
Follow The Reaper / Bodom After Midnight / Children Of Decadence / Every Time I Die / Mask Of Sanity / Taste Of My Scythe / Hate Me / Northern Comfort / Kissing The Shadows / Hellion

CHINCHILLA (GERMANY)
Line-Up: Michael Marquardt (vocals), Udo Gerstenmayer (guitar), Jürgen Wursche (guitar), Ralf Faber (bass), Achim Krieg (drums)

Southern German outfit with a reputation for gigging hard proving Germans do in fact possess an ironic sense of humour when it comes to choosing names for Heavy Metal bands! CHINCHILLA actually folded after the 'No Mercy Tonight' album but re-emerged with a fresh line-up for 1994's 'Who Is Who' mini-album. New recruits were erstwhile LETTER X and BROTHERS IN ARMS vocalist Martin Obermeier, bassist Mike Kühner and drummer Michael Vetter.

CHINCHILLA have undergone further line-up ructions welcoming in bassist Marc Peters and drummer Steffan Theurer. Peters had previously been in BROTHERS IN ARMS, the act that also comprised ex-JEALOUS HEART and RAW drummer Chris Grenzer, former HALL OF FAME guitarist Alan Le Baron as well as Obermeier.

By 1996 CHINCHILLA had added a keyboard player Marc Steck. The 'Horrorscope' album, released in Europe by Point Music in 1999 and featuring new vocalist Thomas Laasch, was originally issued a full two years earlier in Japan by Virgin.

In January of 2000 the band played its first European tour as a support for VANDEN PLAS. The band would also put in appearances at the German 'Bang Your Head' festival and the Swiss 'Biker Union 2000' events.

This run of dates increased the band's profile enough to land a deal with Metal Blade Records. A third album, 'Madness' once more produced by Achim Köhler, arrived in March of 2001. CHINCHILLA's line-up at this juncture comprised Thomas Laasch on vocals, Udo Gerstenmeyer on guitar, Marc Peters on bass, keyboard player Marc Steck and drummer Steffen Theurer.

CHINCHILLA would form part of a touring package alongside TAD MOROSE and veteran British act DEMON for dates throughout February and March 2002. Later shows in October found the band packaged with POWERGOD and VALLEY'S EVE.

Albums:
NO MERCY TONIGHT, Big Fun Momo MMR 00114 (1990)
King Of Hell (And The Lady Love) / No Mercy / Dyin' In The Dark / Tears / Danger / Love Bites Tonight
WHO IS WHO, Skywalk SKW 86015 (1994)
Heaven Or Hell / How The Children Dance / Metal Of Honor / Reborn Of God / Who Is Who
HORRORSCOPE, Limb Music Productions LMP 10079 (1998)
Hill Of Secret / Heaven Or Hell / King For A Day / How The Children Dance / Reborn Of God / Who Is Who / Horrorscope / The Cross / She's So Evil / Crack In The Mirror / Lies Of Tomorrow / Help
MADNESS, Metal Blade 14351 (2000)

Intro / Fight / Freedom / Queen Of The Rain / Broken Heart / I Stole Your Love / Madness / Living On My Own / Where The Brave Belong / Tears / Dark And Light / Anymore
THE LAST MILLENIUM, Metal Blade (2002)
The Last Millenium / War Machine / Demons We Call / Nightrain Of Death / Father Forgive Me / After The War / Victims Of The Night / The Boys Are Back In Town / They Are Liars / The Highest Price

CHROMING ROSE (GERMANY)
Line-Up: Gerd Salewski (vocals), S.C. Wuller (guitar), Harry Steiner (bass), Tino Mende (drums)

CHROMING ROSE are steeped in Germanic Metal traditions. The original line-up, forged in 1985, brought together vocalist 'Wotan', guitarist Matze Mende, bassist Harry Steiner and drummer Tino Mende.
In 1987 'Wotan' was superseded by 'Orä' and the group stabilised for a couple of years before adding second guitarist S.C. Wuller in 1989 and ditched 'Orä' in favour of Gerd Salwski.
In 1990 guitarist Matze Mende was the next casualty, departing after the release of the debut album 'Louis The XIV' for EMI, and his position was taken by Rikki Rieger.
The band toured as support to PINK CREAM 69 and U.D.O. during 1990 and opened for SAXON's German tour the following year. 1991 also saw the emergence of sophomore effort 'Garden Of Eden' which, like the debut, was produced by Tommy Hansen.
Both 'Garden of Eden' and 'Louis the XIV' are produced by Tommy Hansen. 'Pressure' is produced by Flemming Rasmussen.
In 1992 the band undertook its first headline tour of Japan prior to a double headliner of Germany with Swedes TREAT. A 1993 German headline tour saw Brazilians VIPER supporting.
In 1994 the group unleashed the live album 'Artworks Live Now', debuting new vocalist Tom Reiners and a new label in Miez. 1996 gave birth to CHROMING ROSE's second album for Miez in 'New World'

Singles/EPs:
Louis XIV / Shoot The Fox, EMI CDP 566-7 93774-2 (1990)
Hell In My Eyes, EMI (1991)
Garden Of Eden, EMI (1991) (Promotion release)

Albums:
LOUIS THE XIV, EMI CDP 566-7 93774 2 (1990)
Power And Glory / Pharaoh / 10,000 Miles /

Right To Me / Louis XIV / Gods Of Noise / You And I / Jodle Dodle / Angel / Shoot The Fox
GARDEN OF EDEN, EMI CDP 564-7 96125 2(1991)
Heroes Of The Modern World / Hell In My Eyes / Integration / Time Will Never Change / Babylon / Garden Of Eden / Music Is The Gate / Top Fuel / Don't Turn Your Head / Heavy Birthday
PRESSURE, EMI CDP 564-0777 7 80377 2 9 (1992)
Under Pressure / Never Ending Nights / Metamorphic Dreamer / Skyline Of The World / They Will Always Find A Reason / The Snake / They Want More / You Can't Lie Anymore / Price Of My Life / Temple Of Shelter
ARTWORKS LIVE NOW, Miez 9501 (1994)
Heroes / Right To Die / Music Is A Gate / Louis XIV / Under Pressure / The Snake / Metamorphic Dreamer / Shoot The Fox / Power And Glory / Alert / New World / Gotta Give Me More / Far From Nowhere
NEW WORLD, Miez 9601 (1996)
Help Me / GGM / 40 Nights, 40 Days / Groove Me / I Died A Little / Far From Nowhere / Alert / When The World Cries / Spread Your Epitaph / Voodoochild / New World
INSIGHT, Miez MIEZ 9901-2 (1999)
Love / Wherever / Stay / Pain / I Know Your Name / I Feel You / I Lied For You / Planet 7 / Tell Me / Hypocrisy / Wherever (Private version)

CIRITH UNGOL (Ventura, CA, USA)
Line-Up: Tim Baker (vocals), Jerry Fogle (guitar), Greg Lindstrom (guitar), Michael Flint (bass), Robert Garven (drums)

With a name inspired by Tolkien's Kirith Ungol (the lair in which the spider Shelob made an attempt to destroy Baggins in 'Lord Of The Rings') and a semi-legendary logo featuring two praying, kneeling skeletons.
Ventura, California's CIRITH UNGOL, based around former TITANIC duo of guitarist Jerry Fogle and drummer Robert Garven, mixed up a bundle of varying influences and gained a loyal, cult following in a career that had first been established as early as 1972. The original incarnation of the band was fronted for many years by vocalist Neal Beattie. The group would, however, not record an album until 1981's 'Frost And Fire' on their own Liquid Flames label.
Although CIRITH UNGOL's debut album 'Frost And Fire' sported an amazing piece of cover artwork, the actual contents of the record disappointed many critics. It even featured a track, an instrumental track entitled

'Maybe That's Why' that, through an error, lyrics for appeared in the album packaging! In spite of bad reviews though, particularly in the UK, CIRITH UNGOL sold substantial numbers of albums.

Following the album's release, CIRITH UNGOL parted company with second guitarist Greg Lindstrom and, amazingly, many proclaimed the band's ensuing contribution to the first 'Metal Massacre' compilation album ('Death Of The Sun') as rather listenable!

Metal Blade picked up the band for a further album, the highly rated 'King Of The Dead' emerging during 1984 (on Roadrunner in Europe) and this record would not only show a vast improvement in the standard of song-writing and musicianship. It would push the Californian mob further into the hearts of the true believers, gaining a host of new admirers along the way.

The group also began to become inspired the work of novelist Michael Moorcock lyrically, a fact that gained more prominence on 1986's 'One Foot In Hell' album. The band would bow out in 1991 with the Ron Goudie produced 'Paradise Lost' album. The group personnel had shifted yet again seeing Garven and Baker now working alongside guitarist Jim Barraza and bassist Vernon Green.

Bearing in mind the almost universal derision heaped upon their early albums the band began to attain a cult status in mainland Europe during the '90s. Italian act DOOMSWORD would cover the CRITH UNGOL track 'Nadsokar'. CIRITH UNGOL's legacy took a bizarre twist in 1995 when a live single was issued, financed by none other than DECEASED's King Fowley. Their appeal spread with the September 2001 retrospective 'Servants Of Chaos', a double CD compiling unreleased studio material, rehearsal and live tapes.

Singles/EPs:
I'm Alive (Live) / Atom Smasher (Live), Old Metal (1995)

Albums:
FROST AND FIRE, Liquid Flames HM 13666 (1981)
Frost And Fire / I'm Alive / A Little Fire / What Does It Take / Edge Of A Knife / Better Off Dead / Maybe That's Why
KING OF THE DEAD, Roadrunner RR 9832 (1984)
Atom Smasher / Black Machine / Master Of The Pit / King Of The Dead / Death Of The Sun / Finger Of Scorn / Toccatta In D / Cirith Ungol
ONE FOOT IN HELL, Roadrunner RR9681 (1986)
Blood And Iron / Chaos Descends / The Fire / Nadsokar / 100 M.P.H. / War Eternal / Doomed Planet / One Foot In Hell
PARADISE LOST, Restless 7-72510-2 (1991)
Join The Legion / The Troll / Fire / Heaven Help Us / Before The Lash / Go It Alone / Chaos Rising / Fallen Idols / Paradise Lost
SERVANTS OF CHAOS, Metal Blade (2001)
Hype Performance / Last Laugh / Frost And Fire (Early version) / Eyes / Better Off Dead (Alternate version) / 100 MPH (Alternate version) / I'm Alive (Alternate version) / Bite Of The Worm / The Twitch / Maybe That's Why (original version) / Ill Met In Lankhmar / Return To Lankhmar / Darkness Weaves / Witchdance / Feeding The Ants / Obsidian / Death Of The Sun (Remix) / Fire (Alternate version) / Fallen Idols (Alternate version) / Chaos Rising (Rehearsal) / Fallen Idols (rehearsal) / Paradise Lost (Rehearsal) / Join The Legion (Rehearsal) / Before The Lash (Rehearsal) / Atom Smasher (Live) / Master Of The Pit (Live) / King Of The Dead (Live) / Last Laugh (Live) / Cirith Ungol (Live) / Secret Agent Man / Ferrari 308QV On Dyno At 8000 RPM

CITIES (New York, NY, USA)
Line-Up: Ron Angell (vocals), Steve Mironovich (guitar), Sal 'Mayne' Italioano (bass), John Angell (drums)

New York Power Metal act CITIES were, at one time, considered to be perhaps the best unsigned band on the American East Coast, supporting many well known acts in the local clubs such as JOE PERRY PROJECT, MANOWAR, ANVIL, RIOT and METALLICA.

Several excellent demos eventually led to a deal with British label Metal Masters, who issued a six track mini-album, 'Annihilation Absolute', in 1985. Shortly before the record was released CITIES parted company with drummer Scott DuBoys. The band would be plagued by problems with this position for much of their career, never quite coming to terms with the loss of A.J. Pero to TWISTED SISTER in 1982. Ironically, Pero had not long been in the CITIES ranks before he accepted the TWISTED SISTER gig, the drummer having auditioned for the slot just prior to joining CITIES!

Signing to Metal Blade for America, the band took the unusual step of re-recording the entire album with A.J. Pero guesting. The second version of 'Annihilation Absolute' also featured three new tracks and a revamped cover with a likeness of Pero replacing the unidentified drumming tank commander on the original!

Pero later rejoined CITIES on a permanent basis and was replaced in TWISTED SISTER by ex-GOOD RATS and THE LADDER drummer Joe Franco.

Albums:
CITIES, Metal Masters METAL P M108 (1985)
In The Still Of The Night / Innocent Victim / Not Alone In The Dark / Burn Forever / Fight For Your Life / Stop The Race
ANNIHILATION ABSOLUTE, Metal Blade 72176 (1986)
Stop The Race / Fight For Your Life / Burn Forever / Not Alone In The Dark / Cruel Sea / In The Still Of The Night / Innocent Victim / Shades Of Black / Deceiver

CJSS (Cincinnati, OH, USA)
Line-Up: Russell Jinkens (vocals), David T. Chastain (guitar), Mike Skimmerhorn (bass), Les Sharp (drums)

A Cincinnati based band led by workaholic guitarist DAVID T. CHASTIAN, CJSS released a brace of convincing hard rock albums in between the guitarists other on-going band project, the female fronted CHASTAIN's releases. The debut effort included a worthy version of LED ZEPPELIN's 'Communication Breakdown'.
CJSS basically evolved from the Cincinnati outfit SPIKE, a commercially inclined Metal band who featured Chastain, bassist Mike Skimmerhorn (who shared duties between CJSS and CHASTAIN) and drummer Les Sharp. Vocalist Russell Jinkins was the new man recruited from PRIZONER to CJSS when the band shed its SPIKE skin.
Chastain's guitar skills came to the attention of Shrapnel Records boss Mike Varney - who was just as well known for his enthusiastic column in 'Guitar Player' magazine. Varney didn't go for the SPIKE material but was impressed by David's other songs. Varney immediately decided to piece a band around Chastain, which is how the guitar player found himself in the unusual situation of recording with two bands at the same time, Varney having hooked him up with vocalist Leather for CHASTAIN.
Whilst Varney wasn't particularly interested in CJSS the French label Black Dragon were, so the albums that had been released on Leviathan in America were issued in Europe through Black Dragon.
CJSS cut two albums, 'World Gone Mad' and 'Praise The Loud' respectively, before Chastain announced the disbanding of the group in April 1989 due to the guitarist wishing to concentrate on CHASTAIN and his solo work.
Bassist Mike Skimmerhorn teamed up with Chastain and drummer Mike Haid to record an album under the name of CINCINATTI IMPROVISATIONAL GROUP in 1996.

Albums:
WORLD GONE MAD, Leviathan (1986)
Hell On Earth / No Man's Land / Communication Breakdown / World Gone Mad / Run To Another Day / The Gates Of Eternity / Destiny / Welcome To Damnation / Purgatory - Living In Exile
PRAISE THE LOUD, Leviathan (1986)
Out Of Control / Land Of The Free / Don't Play With Fire / Praise The Loud / Citizen Of Hell / Danger / Metal Forever / Thunder And Lightning / The Bargain
RETROSPECT, Black Dragon (1990)
Hell On Earth / No Man's Land / Run To Another Day / World Gone Mad / Citizen Of Hell / Praise The Loud / Don't Play With Fire / Welcome To Damnation / The Gates Of Eternity / The Bargain
KINGS OF THE WORLD, Pavement Music PVMT 32352 (2000)
King Of The World / The Final Frontier / The Executioner's Song / Wild In The Streets / Thief Of Hearts / I4I / The Fall Of Babylon / All Is Fire / Locomotive Breath / The End Of The Rainbow / Cries Of the Dawn
SANDS OF TIME, Diginet CD 609996297299-101520 (2001)
Bloodlust / Sand Of Time / Fight For Your Life / Movement QP827 / I'm Alive / Forever Young / Tell Me You're Near / Kick Some Ass / Need Of Dreams / Knock Down The Door / Annemoragan
EMBRYONIC ANIMATION, Diginet CD 8983951179-91953 (2001)
Ready For Action / Too Hot For Love / Welcome To Damnation / On the Hunt / Caught You Red Handed / No Man's Land / Ready For War / Hell On Earth / Les Sharp's Drum Solo / Lady Your Mine / The More You Get / World Gone Mad

CLOCKWORK (USA)
Line-Up: Douglas Gillin (vocals / keyboards / flute), M. Thomas Gammarino (guitar), Chris Pignatelli (guitar / keyboards), Chris Pignone (bass), Anthony Sciamanna (drums)

Complex Prog Metal. Joel Altman would handle bass for the self-financed 'Search' EP. He would be supplanted by Chris Pignone for the full length 'Surface Tension' album in 1999.

Singles/EPs:
Search EP, (1997)

Albums:
SURFACE TENSION, Sensory SR3003 (1999)
Secrets Of Centuries / One Wing / East Of Knowing / If These Walls Could Talk / The Guardin' Of Eden / The Convolution Box / Smile Under Sad Eyes / Design Of Enlightenment

C.O.E. (GERMANY)
Line-Up: S.L. Coe (vocals), Wusel (guitar), Tom (guitar), Udo (bass), Markus (drums)

C.O.E. is the band venture of respected vocalist S.L. Coe, a man who has more than made a lasting impression on the Euro Metal scene with his vocals on albums SCANNER's 'Terminal Earth', REACTOR's 'Farewell To Reality' and ANGEL DUST's 'To Dust You Will Decay'. As a producer Coe's influence looms large, having manned the helm for artists such as SACROSANCT, TORCHURE, BLOOD, DR. DEATH, PANACEA, RAWSIDE, MORBID JESTER and DISHARMONIC ORCHESTRA among many others.
The 'Metal' album boasted a host of guest lead guitar breaks from the likes of ULAN BATOR's Andreas Meiswinkel, GALLOW'S POLE man Zokk Milosh, BONNEVILLE's Bernd Seibel and former SCANNER colleague John Smith.

Albums:
METAL, Shark 2000-04 (2000)
Iron Sword / Warrior Don't Be Afraid / Open The Gate / Stargate / The Die Is Cast / The Tale Of Baba Yaga / Burning The Witches / Have A Drink On Me / Fate Keeper / Slavian Symphony / Paradise City / Holiday In Hell

CONCEPTION (NORWAY)
Line-Up: Roy S. Kahn (vocals), Tøre Ostby (guitar), Hans C. Gjestvang (keyboards), Ingar Amlien (bass), Arve Heimdal (drums)

One of the finest, yet overlooked, Norwegian acts. CONCEPTION boasted the enormous guitar talents of Tøre Ostby and the distinctive vocals of Roy S. Kahn. Over a series of albums that found the group evolving from Death styled Speed Metal through to luxuriant Progressive Metal CONCEPTION peaked with the quite awesome 'Flow' album. It was delivered too late to save the band's career though. CONCEPTION bass player Ingar Amlien was previously in late '70s act ROCQUEFIRE alongside future TNT guitarist Ronnie Le Tekrö.
CONCEPTION's debut self-financed album, produced by VICTORY guitarist Tommy Newton, was re-released in 1993 by Noise Records.
CONCEPTION also featured on the Noise live video of 1993, 'The Power Of Metal', alongside RAGE and GAMMA RAY. CONCEPTION utilised the services of keyboard player Hans C. Gjestvang for a brief period.
The band supported SKYCLAD on their '94 British tour and also put in some dates with TROUBLE and THRESHOLD.
The group's fourth album, 'Flow', found the band in receipt of rave reviews throughout Europe, although the critical acclaim, unsurprisingly, stopped at the front door of the major British Rock press.
CONCEPTION duly folded with vocalist Roy Kahn joining American Metal band KAMELOT. Guitarist Tøre Ostby and bassist Ingar Amlien founded A.R.K. with VAGABOND, THE SNAKES and MUNDUS IMPERIUM singer JORN LANDE and TNT and YNGWIE MALMSTEEN drummer John Macaluso.
Amlien forged a Black Metal project CREST OF DARKNESS releasing three albums to date. The 1999 CREST OF DARKNESS release 'The Ogress' sees both Kahn and Heimdal contributing.

Singles/EPs:
Roll The Fire / Silent Crying, Noise N0218-3 (1994)

Albums:
THE LAST SUNSET, Conception CSFCD 9101 (1991)
Prevision / Building A Force / War Of Hate / Bowed Down With Sorrow / Fairy's Dance / Another World / Elegy / The Last Sunset / Live To Survive / Among The Gods
PARALLEL MINDS, Noise N0218 (1994)
Water Confines / Roll The Fire / And I Close My Eyes / Silent Crying / Parallel Minds / Silver Shine / My Decision / The Promiser / Wolf's Lair / Soliloquy
IN YOUR MULTITUDE, Noise N0229-2 (1995)
Under A Mourning Star / Missionary Man / Retrospect / Guilt / Sanctuary / A Million Gods / Some Wounds / Carnal Compression / Solar Serpent / In Your Multitude
FLOW, Noise N 0274-2 (1997)
Gethsemane / Angel (Come Walk With Me) / A Virtual Lovestory / Flow / Cry / Reach Out / Tell Me When I'm Gone / Hold On / Cardinal Sin / Would It Be The Same

CONCERTO MOON (JAPAN)
Line-Up: Tako Ozaki (vocals), Nosifumi Shima (guitar), Kosaku Mitani (bass), Toshiyuki Koike (keyboards), Ishiro Nagai

(drums)

Japanese '80s style Symphonic Rock specialists. CONCERTO MOON guitar wizard Norifumi Shima also plies his trade with DOUBLE DEALER, a collaborative project in alliance with SABER TIGER vocalist Takenori Shimoyama.

By 2002 the CONCERTO MOON line-up read vocalist Takashi Inoue, guitarist Nosifumi Shima, bass player Kosaku Mitani, keyboard player Toshiyuki Koike and drummer Junichu Satou.

Singles/EPs:
Time To Die / King Of Judas / Waltz For Masquerade / Run To The Sky / Alone In Paradise
VPCC-81290, (1999)

Albums:
FRAGMENTS OF THE MOON, VPCC-81284 (1998)
Alone In Paradise / Run To The Sky / Cry For Freedom / Holy Child / Hold On / Midwinter Night / Over The Century / Take You To The Moon / The Last Betting (Live) / One And Only (Live) / Into The Fire (Live)
FROM FATHER TO SON, VPCC-81276 (1998)
Dream Chaser / Surrender / Moonlight / After The Rain / Inside Story / One And Only / From Father To Son / Somewhere In Time / The Last Betting / Into The Fire / Change My Heart
RAIN FOREST, VPCC-81291 (1999)
Prologue / Time To Die / Lonely Last Journey / Fight To The Death / Half Way To The Sun / Rain Forest / Unstill Night / Live On The Memory / Victim Of Desire / Pictures Of An Old Man, Break It Down
THE END OF THE BEGINNING: LIVE 1999 AND MORE, VPCC-81317-8 (1999)
Time To Die / Fight To The Death / King Of The Judas / Lonely Last Journey / Victim Of Desire / Alone In Paradise / From Father To Son / Take You To The Moon / Surrender / Unstill Night / When The Moon Cries / Norman Island / When The Moon Cries (Off vocal version)
GATE OF TRIUMPH, (2001)
Waiting For The Coming Strikes / To Die For / Over And Over / Gate Of Triumph / Tears Of The Prayers / Ambitions And Lies / To Always Be Myself / Suffering / Everlasting Nightmare / Alone In The Paradise '01 / Take You To The Moon '01
DESTRUCTION AND CONSTRUCTION, VPCC-81407 (2002)
Unstill Night / King Of The Judas / Lonely Last Journey / Dream Chaser / Holy Child /

Half Way To The Sun / From Father To Son / Fight To The Death / Change My Heart / Out Of Deep Freeze / Angels In Black / Second War In Heaven

CONVICT (USA)

CONVICT were actually a totally fictitious band purposely made in the studio. Vocalist Gord Kirchin, previously with MAINSTREAM and FIST, cut the lead vocals anonymously. Kirchin was better known as his other pseudonym the shock Thrash Metal singer PILEDRIVER.
CONVICT's guitars were supplied by Conrad Taylor.
Kirchin later created DOGS WITH JOBS and SOFA Q.

Albums:
GO AHEAD MAKE MY DAY, Conra CL1002 (1985)
Evil Eyes / Manic Obsession / Edge Of The Sword / Bloodsucker / Bite The Hands That Feeds You / Metal Warriors / When Your Dreams Are Over / Don't Turn Away

D.C. COOPER (USA)

Solo outing from Pennsylvania born ROYAL HUNT vocalist. Cooper's distinctive vocal style had done much to further the career of the Danish melodic Metal act and it came as a surprise to many fans when he left the fold. Pre-ROYAL HUNT Cooper had been one of the finalists in auditions for the position of vocalist with JUDAS PRIEST. His 1999 solo album, produced by PINK CREAM 69 bassist Dennis Ward, would witness a studio band line-up of CONCEPTION guitarist Tore Ostby, PINK CREAM 69 drummer Kosta Zafiriou and VANDEN PLAS keyboard player Guenter Werno. Cooper repaid the services to PINK CREAM 69 by contributing to their album 'Electrified'. Promoting the album in Japan, where it was released in December 1998 by the JVC Victor label, Cooper performed a batch of acoustic shows in union with PINK CREAM 69 guitarist Alfred Koffler.
Shortly after the album was released Cooper was fired from ROYAL HUNT.
In 2000 Cooper would form an alliance with SINNER and THE SYGNET guitarist Alex Beyroth to create SILENT FORCE.

Albums:
D.C. COOPER, Bottom Row Productions (1999)
Dream / Easy Living / The Angel Comes / Until The End / Within Yourself / Three Generations / Chained / Freedom / Take Me

In / Forgive Me / Whisper / The Union

CORSARIO (ARGENTINA)
Line-Up: Martín Ceballos (vocals), Juan C. Repetto (guitar), Pablo Yunis (bass), Francisco Repetto (keyboards), Ignacio Barletta (drums)

Melodic Metal outfit convened in 2001. CORSARIO went through a number of vocalists, including 'Curly' and 'Rocky' before settling on Martín Ceballos in 2002.

Singles/EPs:
Guerrero Inmortal EP, (2002)

CRIMSON GLORY (Sarasota, FL, USA)
Line-Up: Midnight (vocals), Jon Drenning guitar), Ben Jackson (guitar), Geoff Lords (bass), Dana Burnell (drums)

Sarasota, Florida based CRIMSON GLORY first came to attention with their image of each band member's identity hidden behind silver face masks. Although technically proficient the media soon decided CRIMSON GLORY's brand of epic Metal, and in particular MIDNIGHT's distinctly Geoff Tate tainted vocals, were a bit too close to their better known Seattle counterparts for comfort. Fortunately as time passed successive releases shed this stigma.

The group originally had first used the name BEOWULF upon their formation in 1981. The group's founding line-up incorporated the trio of Jon Drenning, Ben Jackson and Dana Burnell. Bassist Jeff Lords was added a while later and the vocal talents of Midnight were recruited two years later in 1983. It's a little known fact that the group did not play a full scale live show until five years after their original formation.

CRIMSON GLORY debuted in 1986 on the PAR label. The group's self-titled first album was subsequently licensed to Roadrunner for European consumption and, upon promoting the first album, the band put in a solitary British show opening for ANTHRAX and METAL CHURCH at London's Hammersmith Odeon.

Following 'Transcendence', for which the band's mask's had now become 'half-masks' revealing more of their features, CRIMSON GLORY were racked by line up problems with both guitarist Ben Jackson and drummer Dana Burnell leaving the fold. Jackson joined PARISH and recorded an album entitled 'Envision'. Dana Burnell made a guest appearance.

The 'Strange And Beautiful' album saw the band ditching the facial disguises altogether and debuted new drummer Robi Jakhotia.

Midnight quit the group after getting married and wishing to spend more time with his new bride and left before an upcoming tour. David Van Landing, who had previously worked with TONY MACALPINE was recruited for the shows. Further dates in Japan were booked yet subsequently cancelled as the group broke up, Van Landing hooking up with the MICHAEL SCHENKER GROUP. Meantime Swedish Metal band MORGANA LEFAY covered 'Lost Reflections' on their 1995 'Past, Present, Future' album.

Drenning, Lords and Jakhotia formed the Arizona based EROTIC LIQUID CULTURE during 1996 and released an album of Funk Metal through a Japanese label.

The trio were soon back in the ranks of the CRIMSON GLORY mothership by the following year in a revised line-up that featured Drenning, Lords, Jakhotia, guitarist Billy Martinez and new vocalist Wade Black, previously with LUCIAN BLAQUE, to record a new album entitled 'Astronomica'. After many delays the album was greeted with almost universal appreciation especially in Europe.

MIDNIGHT, meanwhile, was approached by the Swedish group ZOIC to record with them but the group's finances were too tight so the deal fell through. However, the singer did unite with ATHEIST guitarist Rand Burkey to work on new material until the pair fell out publicly.

Black decamped to SEVEN WITCHES in 2000. As 2001 dawned it emerged that Black, Ben Jackson and Jesse Martillo had founded a new Progressive Rock act SECTOR 9.

Jackson would also develop THE BEN JACKSON GROUP announcing a roll call of Jackson on vocals and guitar, guitarist Mark Borgmeyer, bass player Danny Binz and drummer Rich Tabor. Recordings for a debut album entitled 'Here I Come' would see guitarist John Bajas guesting and CRIMSON GLORY colleagues vocalist Wade Black and bassist Jeff Lords contributing.

MIDNIGHT's album 'M' arrived in December 2001. Former singer Wade Black broke away from SEVEN WITCHES in mid 2002 and enlisted the services of the former NOCTURNUS pairing of guitarist Mike Davis and bassist/vocalist Emo Mowery for a fresh side band project billed as TIWANAKU.

Singles/EPs:
Dream Dancer / Lost Reflection. Roadrunner RR 2467-1 (1988)
Dream Dancer / Lost Reflection, Apollyon MP10-1 (1988) (Japanese release)
Lady Of Winter, Roadrunner (1988)
Lonely (Remix) / In Dark Places / Dream Dancer, Roadrunner 24482 (1989)

Albums:
CRIMSON GLORY, PAR (1986)
Valhalla / Dragon Lady / Heart Of Steel /
Azrael / Mayday / Queen Of The
Masquerade / Angels Of War / Lost
Reflection
TRANSENDENCE, Roadrunner RR95082
(1989)
Lady Of Winter / Red Sharks / Painted Skies
/ Masque Of The Red Death / Where
Dragons Rule / Lonely / Burning Bridges /
Eternal World / Transcendence
STRANGE AND BEAUTIFUL, Roadrunner
RR 9508-2 (1991)
Strange And Beautiful / Promised Land /
Love And Dreams / The Chant / Dance On
Fire / Song For Angels / In The Mood / Star
Chamber / Deep Inside Your Heart / Make
You Love Me / Far Away
ASTRONOMICA, Spitfire 5043-2 (1999)
March To Glory / War Of The Worlds / New
World Machine / Astronomica / Edge Of
Forever / Touch The Sun / Lucifer's Hammer
/ The Other Side Of Midnight / Cyber-Christ /
Cydonia

CRISES (GERMANY)
Line-Up: Russel Gray (vocals), Ondrej
Hurbanic (guitar), Pavel Hurcik (bass), Marko
Brenzinger (keyboards), Thomas Abts
(drums)

CRISES underwent a line-up change
between recording of the independent 1995
EP and signing to Angular Records for 1998's
'Broken Glass' album. Out went bassist
Harald Zimmermann and keyboard player
Richard Metzler and in came Pavel Hurcik
and Marko Brenzinger respectively.

Singles/EPs:
Choices / Tears Fall / Heroes / Wait Longer /
One Sided, (1995) ('Crises' EP

Albums:
BROKEN GLASS, Angular SPV085-10032
(1998)
Save Me / The Blame / Am I Awake / Crises
- Descent Into Paradise / The Only One / In
My Sleep / Last Candle / Drops Of Rain

CROSSFIRE (BELGIUM)
Line-Up: Peter De Wint (vocals), Marc van
Caelenberge (guitar), Rudy Van De Sjipe
(guitar), Patrick van Londerzele (bass), Chris
De Brauwer (drums)

One of the first signings to the Mausoleum
label, CROSSFIRE released two albums that
were much lauded in the underground Metal
press.

The band started out in 1980 as a Punk outfit
entitled THE ONION DOLLS, with De Wint
handling drums as well as lead vocals.
The band contributed two tracks to the Dutch
'Aardschock' magazine compilation album
'Metal Clogs' on the Rave-On label, although
original CROSSFIRE guitarist Ner Neerinckx
left the band and was subsequently jailed for
the murder of a policeman (possibly
documented in the lyrics of 'Killing A Cop' on
CROSSFIRE's first album 'See You In
Hell'?!?)
Enjoying strong album sales throughout
Europe the group supported the likes of
ACCEPT and IRON MAIDEN in their time and
also played their first English dates in 1985,
playing two dates in London; the first at the
Wellington in Shepherd's Bush promoted by
Shades Records.
Following the demise of the act De Wint and
De Brauwer formed Melodic Rockers
MYSTERY in 1989.

Albums:
SEE YOU IN HELL, Mausoleum SKULL
8314 (1983)
Demon Of Evil / Killing A Cop / Magnificent
Night / Danger On Earth / Fly High / Lover's
Game / Starchild / See You In Hell
SECOND ATTACK, Mausoleum SKULL
(1985)
Second Attack / Feeling Down / Highway
Driver / Atomic War / Master Of Evil /
Scream And Shout / Running For Love
SHARPSHOOTER, Mausoleum SKULL
(1986)
Break Out / Killer Queen / Metal Knifes /
Motorcycles (Live) / Crossfire (Live) / Sound
Of War
LIVE ATTACK, Bellaphon (1987)
Second Attack / Starchild / Killer Queen /
Master Of Evil / Scream And Shout / Sound
Of War / Fly High / Highway Driver / Feeling
Down

CRUSH (GREECE)
Line-Up: P. Constantinides (vocals), P.
Rodostogiou (guitar), J. Vrettakes (bass),
C.Voyiajzogioy (drums)

Albums:
KINGDOM OF THE KINGS, Crush 550
(1993)
Beyond The Gates... / March Of The Deads /
The Gloriest Night / Kingdom Of The Kings /
Run To The Highway / Unborn / Flag Of Hate
/ Princess Of Hell / Ballad Of Sorrow

CRYONIC TEMPLE (SWEDEN)
Line-Up: Johan Johansson (vocals), Leif
Collin (guitar), Esa Ahonen (guitar), Jan J.

Cederlund (bass), Janne Söderlund (keyboards), Sebastian Olsson (drums)

The Metal band CRYONIC TEMPLE was created in late 1996 by a fusion of erstwhile personnel from IRON MAIDEN covers band TROOPER and Progressive Rock unit LEX CREDO. Upon their initial formation CRYONIC TEMPLE cited a line-up comprising Johan Johansson on lead vocals and rhythm guitar, lead guitarist Esa Ahonen, bassist Mika Nyyssölä, keyboard player Andreas Cromnow and Mikael Eriksson on the drums. Although the band displayed admitted Progressive leaning initially the new union would steadily develop much harder edged material.

During 1997 Eriksson made his exit and the group took on board friend David Kangasniemi as a fill in measure until the introduction of their new full time drummer Kim Lundh, this line-up cutting the four track demo session 'Seasons In Hell'. Three of these tracks garnered the band further exposure with their inclusion on a compilation album entitled 'Nerve'. The songs provoked the interest of DISMEMBER drummer Fred Estby whom offered to act as producer for a second tape billed as 'Before The End'.

In the Autumn of 1998 second guitarist Leif Collin was inducted into the fold. CRYONIC TEMPLE received a contract from a Belgian based label but would turn the offer down. The following year Cromnow bailed out, the band soon finding a substitute in Janne Söderlund. 2000 would witness the issue of a third demo, a five track affair called 'Warsong'. However, that same year both Nyyssölä and Lundh decamped. CRYONIC TEMPLE's new rhythm section comprised Jan J. Cederlund on bass and drummer Sebastian Olsson. Unfortunately Olsson was not able to take up his new found position immediately, ensconced in percussive studies in Piteå in the far north of Sweden. In the interim Lasse Bäcke took command of the drum kit. With these changes taking effect the group signed to the Italian Underground Symphony label, debuting with the January 2002 album 'Chapter 1'.

Albums:
CHAPTER 1, Underground Symphony (2002)
Heavy Metal Never Dies / Metal Brothers / Warsong / Gatekeeper / Rivers Of Pain / King Of Transilvania / Steel Against Steel / Mighty Warrior / Over And Over

CRYPTIC VISIONS (Chicago, IL, USA)
Line-Up: Joe Lawson (vocals), Jeff Bagherpour (guitar), James Link (guitar), Scott Trubich (bass), Michele O'Day (keyboards), Donny Mizanin (drums)

CRYPTIC VISIONS is rooted in two underground Metal acts TYRANT'S REIGN and PHOENIX RISING mentored by guitarist Jeff Bagherpour. The six stringer assembled PHOENIX RISING by drawing in vocalist Russell Barron, younger brother of WINTERKILL's Randy Barron, and his erstwhile TYRANT'S REIGN colleague bassist Phil Fouch. After having added keyboard player Michele O'Day for PHOENIX RISING's 'Up From The Ashes' demo the group soon discovered other Rock acts employing the same title and duly switched to CRYPTIC VISIONS.

An eponymous, self-financed album arrived in 1999 although the band dispensed with the services of drummer Brad Burger upon release, pulling in new recruit Donny Mizanin. Unfortunately the following year both the band's lead vocalist Russell Barron and bassist Phil Fouch drifted off to other acts. CRYPTIC VISIONS was subsequently re-built by pulling in singer Joe Lawson, bassist Scott Trubich and second guitarist James Link.

Albums:
CRYPTIC VISIONS, (1999)
Phoenix Rising / Cemetery Man / Street Anger / Eternal Dreams / The Devil Showed Me / Rushed / The Band Plays On / Blood In The Sand / Can't Stop The Pain / Die For Me / Battles End

CRYSTAL BALL (SWITZERLAND)
Line-Up: Mark Sweeney (vocals), Scott Leach (guitar), Tom Graber (guitar / keyboards), Danny Schallibaum (bass), Marcel Sardella (drums)

Melodic Metal CRYSTAL BALL originated as a covers band during 1995. The band received exposure in Germany in 1997 when their track 'Stand By Me', produced by KINGDOM COME and CHINA guitarist Angi Schilliro, was broadcast on a national TV talk show. This success led to CRYSTAL BALL scoring another song, 'Eye To Eye' produced by erstwhile VICTORY guitarist Tommy Newton, for use as the theme music for Swiss international boxer Stefan Angehrn in early 1998.

CRYSTAL BALL's debut album 'In The Beginning', with production on hand once more from Newton, arrived later that year. The album would be picked up for a Japanese release by Zero Corporation Records for issue in February 1999. This version of the record included an extra bonus track 'Silence

CRYSTAL BALL Photo: Hugo Räber

Of The Night'. With Zero Corporation's demise the record was re-issued in Japan by Toshiba EMI in September and a European imprint came courtesy of Germany's Point Music. CRYSTALL BALL opened for KROKUS on their Autumn 1999 Swiss tour.

The band's second outing 'Hard Impact', once more handled in the studio by Newton, would be promoted on the European mainland by support gigs to PRETTY MAIDS in February of 2001. Japanese versions of the album, released on Pony Canyon Records, included an extra track in 'Goodbye Hero'.

CRYSTAL BALL would act as guests to DORO and then U.D.O. on their November 2002 tour of mainland Europe.

Albums:

IN THE BEGINNING, Point Music 20325 (1999)
Twilight Zone / Magic / Fire Still Burns / Me And You / Lay Down The Law / Shake Me / Leave Me Alone / Take Me Down / Promised Land / A Million Tear

HARD IMPACT, Point Music (2000)
Reincarnation / Soul Mate / Won't Bite / FM / Own Way / Queen Of The Night / Crystal Ball / Never Surrender / Shine On / Step By Step / Passion / Stare At The Sun

VIRTUAL EMPIRE, Nuclear Blast NB 329-2 (2002)
3rd Dimension / Hands Of God / Savage Mind / Am I Free / Virtual Empire / Night And Day / Dance With The Devil / Night Is Over / Blind Side / Talk In Circles / Private Visitor / Find Your Ground / Look In My Eyes

CRYSTAL CASTLE (CANADA)
Line-Up: Phillipe Harvey (vocals), Jerome Berube (guitar), Jimmy Pouliot (guitar), Regis Grosset (bass), Francis Marmen (drums)

Rimouski Power – Thrash act forged in the late '90s by guitarists Jimmy Pouliot of ZAM FIRE and FAUNE X and Éric Lechasseur. The band was rounded out with the induction of ZAM FIRE vocalist Phillipe Harvey and bassist Regis Grosset, the latter a veteran of ZAM FIRE, CONSPIRACY and DRAGONLORD. Aiding the band during this period would also be STATES OF MIND drummer Michel Gagnon. During these formative stages CRYSTAL CASTLE operated on the club scene as a covers act.

By April of 2000 CRYSTAL CASTLE had located a permanent drummer in Francis Marmen, a man citing credits with GORELUST, DRAGONLORD and IMMORTELLYS. However, at the same

89

juncture Pouliot decamped and ABSOLUTE GRIEF guitarist Simon Laliberté was duly enrolled. A series of live gigs ensued after which Laliberté returned to his priority act. Further ructions hit the band as Lechasseur opted out in order to pursue a solo venture in May of 2000.

Former six stringer Jimmy Pouliot was asked to re-join and second guitarist Jerome Berube soon followed to make up the numbers. With a newly stabilised line-up CRYSTAL CASTLE decided to concentrate on original material and released their debut album 'October Hymns' in December of 2001.

Albums:
OCTOBER HYMNS, (2001)
Crystal Heart Of Season / October Hymn / Heavy Metal / Lady Of Spring Spell / The Willow's Cry / Devil's Blessing / The Dark Storm Is Back / The Silent Voice Of Insanity (The Apotheosis)

CRYSTAL EYES (SWEDEN)
Line-Up: Mikael Dahl (vocals / guitar), Jonathon Nyberg (guitar), Claes Wikander (bass), Kujtim Gashi (drums)

Power Metal band CRYSTAL EYES would release a consistent run of impressively packaged demo cassettes upfront of their 1999 commercial debut 'World Of Black And Silver'. The band was put together during 1992 by ex-PAINTED SKIES vocalist/guitarist Mikael Dahl and guitarist Niclas Karlsson. The duo rounded off the line-up with bass player Christian Gunnarsson and a drum machine. In 1993 the band brought in a real drummer Martin Tilander to commit to tape a debut demo, 'Crystal Eyes', released in 1994. Also becoming involved was lyricist Andreas Götesson.

In early 1995 the band splintered with Tilander and Karlsson pursuing another project FIERCE CONVICTION. Karlsson would later wind up as a member of Power Metal band ZONATA. Meantime CRYSTAL EYES regathered its strength by enrolling guitarist Jukka Kaupaamaa, bassist Kim Koivo and ex-DAMNATORY drummer Kujtim Gashi. The stability would not endure though as Koivo made his exit just prior to recording of a follow up demo, 1996's 'The Shadowed Path'. He would be replaced by Marco Nicolaidis.

January of 1997 would witness the drafting of SUNRISE bass player Claes Wikander, and in March a third promotional tape 'The Final Sign' was recorded. Line-up ructions continued though as in October Kaupaamaa's position was taken by Jonathan Nyberg.

CRYSTAL EYES would issue yet another demo, 'The Dragon's Lair', during the Spring of 1998. Media praise attracted the attention of the Crazy Life label who inked a deal with the band for their inaugural 'World Of Black And Silver' album. Recording took place in Germany during November with the album being shipped to stores in April of 1999.

A second album, In Silence They March', followed in 2000. In January of that year CRYSTAL EYES put in a bout of touring on a package billing with LEFAY and EVERGREY. Stefan Svantesson of FRETERNIA would supplant Gashi, the former drummer being regrettably forced out due to an illness in his family. By June of 2002 Svantesson had cut his ties with FRETERNIA in order to concentrate his efforts on CRYSTAL EYES and their new album provisionally entitled 'Vengeance Descending'. By coincidence, an ex-CRYSTAL EYES drummer, Martin Tilander, would fill Svantesson's vacancy in FRETERNIA.

Dahl and former member Niclas Karlsson also operate a JUDAS PRIEST tribute band.

Albums:
WORLD OF BLACK AND SILVER, Crazy Life Music (1999)
Interstellar World / Gods Of The World / Winds Of The Free / Power Behind The Throne / The Dragon's Liar / Eyes Of The Forest Gloom / Rage Of The Sea / Victims Of The Frozen Hate / Extreme Paranoia / Glory Ride / World Of Black And Silver
IN SILENCE THEY MARCH, Shark SHARK 200010 (2000)
Time Flight / Cursed And Damned / Sons Of Odin / The Grim Reaper's Fate / The Undead King / In Silence They March / Adrian Blackwood / Witch Hunter / The Rising / Knights Of Prey / Somewhere Over The Sun / Winternight

CRYSTAL SHARK (GERMANY)
Line-Up: Didi Schulz (vocals), Wolle Tewes (guitar), Jurgen Pastuch (guitar), Carsten Meyer (bass), Marlon Erdmann (drums)

Hamburg's twin guitar Metal band CRYSTAL SHARK evolved out of a former act UNDERFIRE during the Autumn of 1998. From their inception CRYSTAL SHARK opted to plough along a deliberate '80s style Metal path. Singer Didi Schulz has a tradition with SYSTEMS FAIL, ADVICE and an ACCEPT covers band RESTLESS & WILD. Bassist Carsten Meyer was previously operating as a guitar player in PENTAGRAM before switching to bass for stints in NO DENY and MIDAS prior to CRYSTAL SHARK.

The debut album 'Galley Of Pain' was recorded in February of 1999 with follow up 'Downfall Of Eden', with new drummer Marlon Erdmann of XANDRIL, laid down in December of 2000. CRYSTAL SHARK also contributed their version of 'Born To Raise Hell' to a 2001 MOTORHEAD tribute album.

The band signed to the Black Arrow label in 2002, performing at the prestigious 'Wacken Open Air' festival that same year.

Albums:
GALLEY OF PAIN, (1999)
Face The Fear / Galley Of Pain / Destination Unknown / No Time For Romance / Sinful Mile
DOWNFALL OF EDEN, (2001)
Born Dead / Maelstrom Of Hate / Warchild / Princess Of Starlight / Down By Law / Downfall Of Eden / Shout / Flame Of Life / Steelbound / Time After Time

CULPRIT (Seattle, WA, USA)
Line-Up: Jeff L'Heureaux (vocals), John DeVol (guitar), Kjartan Kristoffersen (guitar), Scott Earl (bass), Bud Burrill (drums)

An exceedingly British influenced Seattle Metal band showing huge chunks of British influences in their raw, aggressive style.

During early 1979 North Seattle natives guitarist John DeVol, bassist Scott Earl and drummer Bud Burrill created ORPHEUS playing parties and local 'Battle of the bands' contests. Meantime AMETHYST, from the east of the city and including guitarist Kjartan Kristoffersen and vocalist Jeff L'Heureaux in their ranks were playing their favourite cover versions.

The two bands came into contact with AMETHYST supporting ORPHEUS at Mr. Bills club resulting in the headliner making a play for L'Heureaux's services. The singer was willing to join on the condition his colleague Kristoffersen was part of the deal and CULPRIT was borne.

The band signed to Shrapnel Records after gigs in California with WILD DOGS and CINEMA before appearing on one of the label's series of 'U.S. Metal' compilations with the slightly Progressively tinged 'Players' and followed it up with the Mike Varney produced 'Guilty As Charged' album.

The band frequently gigged in their native Seattle, in particular the Metal stronghold of Bellevue but would split when Kristoffersen and Earl joined local legends TKO in 1984. However, although the duo appeared on the cover of the 'In Your Face', the album was recorded long before the band were signed by Combat Records in the States (the album was

released by Music For Nations in Europe) and the erstwhile CULPRIT pair had come on board.

Jeff L'Heureux would later turn up fronting another Seattle band, MISTRUST. The group appeared on the 'Pacific Metal Project' compilation before recording the 'Spin The World' album. John DeVol meantime re-emerged in 1987 with DEVOL, a group boasting a line-up of vocalist Terry Tandeski, bassist Dennis Quintella and drummer Jeff McCormack.

Following the TKO stint, Kristoffersen and Earl formed the Glam outfit BANG GANG, having relocated to Los Angeles in the late '80s. Earl would form SHAKE THE FAITH in 1992 although was ousted by the recording of their solitary album.

Albums:
GUILTY AS CHARGED, Shrapnel 1008 (1983)
Guilty As Charged / Ice In The Back / Steel To Blood / I Am / Ambush / Tears Of Repentance / Same To You / Fight Back / Players

CUSTARD (GERMANY)
Line-Up: Guido Brieke (vocals), Dirk Wierezorck (guitar / keyboards), Karsten Knüppel (guitar), Michael Marquardt (bass), Christian Klapper (drums)

In spite of the somewhat bizarre name CUSTARD, far from being an English pudding sauce, are in fact a raging Heavy Metal band. Apparently the band, founded in 1987, were duped into the title of CUSTARD unaware of the culinary meaning! CUSTARD first made their presence felt in the European Metal landscape with the five track 1997 demo 'Signum Inferre'. At this stage CUSTARD numbered Michael Marquardt on lead vocals and bass guitar, lead guitarists Karsten Knüppel and Sven Horsini, Dirk Wierczorek on keyboards and drummer Christian Klapper.

Following this with a 1998 mini-album 'God Of Storm' the band replaced Horsini with Dirk Wierczorek on guitar.

The band appeared at the 1998 Wacken festival. CUSTARD added new vocalist Guido Brieke for December 2000's 'For My King' album.

Albums:
GOD OF STORM, Custard (1998)
God Of Storm / Rest In Peace / Blessed By The Light / Trees Of Hope
KINGDOMS OF YOUR LIFE, Belphigor 10049 (1999)
Remember The Storm / Imprisoned /

Promised Land / Kingdoms Of Your Life / Denials / Failed Mission / Fading Memories / The Sea / Barricades
FOR MY KING, Bossy Ogress CD 5 3021 20 561 (2000)
Rise / Up To The Sky / I Know You / Charon's Call / Signs / Freedom For All / Deliver Me / Master Of The Dice / Trees Of Hope / Ambrosia / For My King

CUTTY SARK (GERMANY)
Line-Up: Conny Schmitt (vocals), Uwe Cossmann (guitar), Helge Meier (bass), Michael Schmitt (drums)

Bonn based Heavy Metal band CUTTY SARK originated as far back as 1976. Bassist Helge Meier was the only remaining founder member by the time the group recorded debut product.
With the Schmitt brothers (Michael on drums and Conny on vocals) teamed up with the band in 1979. Guitarist Uwe Cossmann joined in 1981. After gigging hard in their native Germany, the band self-financed a four track mini-album, 'Hard Rock Power', produced by Gert Rautenbach and were then picked up by Mausoleum following strong press support throughout Europe.

Singles/EPs:
Hard Rock Power / Fire And Ice / The Dice / Attack, Bernie TEST 128330 (1983)

Albums:
DIE TONIGHT, Mausoleum SKULL 8339 (1984)
Stupid Lies / Die Tonight / Vultures In The Air / Go For Death / Hands Up / October Holidays / Down And Out / Burning To Ashes
HEROES, Mausoleum SKULL8375 (1985)
Firebird / Heroes / Do Come True / Smell A Rat / Sold To Kill / Love The World Away / Invitation To Dance / Let's Go

CYDONIA (ITALY)
Line-Up: Dan Keying (vocals), Steve Sguario (guitar), Trevor O'Neal (bass), Lee Crow (keyboards), Mat Stancioiu (drums)

Italian Power Metal band CYDONIA emerged in 2001 touting a conceptual Sci-Fi album based on a mythological history of the planet Mars. Indeed, the band is titled after a Mars region. CYDONIA vocalist Dan Keying had previously come to attention in 1997 replacing Fabio Leone as front man for LABYRINTH.
Keying, alongside LABYRINTH drummer Mat Stancioiu, guitarist Steve Sguario, bassist Trevor O'Neal and keyboard player Lee Crow, founded CYDONIA during 1999.

Albums:
CYDONIA, Metal Blade CD 085-103172 (2001)
The King / Legend In Time / Land Of Life / Great Soul Of Steel / Last Prayers / Confused Future / Masters Of Stars / Slave To Dream / Eternal Night

CYDONIAN (GERMANY)
Line-Up: Mike Gerold (vocals), Tony Berger (guitar), Markus Grutzner (bass), Erik Damkohler (keyboards), Karl Furhrmann (drums)

Bavarian Progressive Metal act CYDONIAN was conceived by the former NIGHTINGALE duo of vocalist Mike Gerold and guitarist Tony Berger in January of 1999.
Gerold broke ranks in April of 2001.

Albums:
ESTRANGED, (2001)
Tranceformation / Distance / Exit 2 Eden / Dutch Mountains / Present Moment / General Next To God / Mice ELF / Freedom Of Speech / Black Sun / Waiting For A Star

DALI'S DILEMMA
(San Jose, CA, USA)
Line-Up: Matthew Bradley
(vocals), Patrick Reyes (guitar),
Steve Reyes (bass), Matt
Guillory (keyboards), Jeremy
Colson (drums)

San Jose Progressive Hard Rock band
DALI'S DILEMMA released an astonishingly
mature debut album in May of 1999 on the
Magna Carta label. Keyboard player Matt
Guillory is an established veteran on the
scene having played with ENCHANT
previously. Guillory has also sessioned on
albums by MOGG/WAY, GEORGE BELLAS,
MULLMUZZLER, EXPLORERS CLUB,
JAMES MURPHY, ZERO HOUR and JOHN
WEST.

Albums:
MANIFESTO FOR FUTURISM, Magna
Carta MA-9024-2 (1999)
Within A Stare / Miracles In Yesteryear /
Despite The Waves / Whispers / Ashen Days
/ Andromeda Sunrise / This Time Around /
Hills Of Memory / Can't You See / Living In
Fear

DAMAGE (BRAZIL)
Line-Up: Antonio Moraes (vocals), Fabiano
Freitas (guitar), Luciano Schirmer (guitar),
Mini Bagestan (bass), Cezar Nogueira
(drums)

Five teenagers assembled DAMAGE during
1993. Initially a covers band it would take the
band until 1997 to record their first three track
demo tape. DAMAGE's line-up for this
recording stood at lead vocalist Antonio
Moraes, guitarists Eduardo Barreto and
Fabiano Freitas, bassist Ricardo Bello and
drummer Cezar Nogueira.
DAMAGE signed to the Megahard label in
1999, this union bearing fruit with the 2001
album 'Hopes And Fears'. By this stage the
band had replaced Barreto with Luciano
Schirmer and Bello with Mini Bagestan. By
September Preto Cardosa had taken
Bagestan's place in the bass role. The band's
live set would still be peppered with covers by
acts such as STRATOVARIUS, METALLICA,
IRON MAIDEN and ANGRA.
Leandro Schirmer would be inducted on the
drum stool in February of 2002 as the band
prepared a fresh demo recording billed as
'Faith'.

Albums:
HOPES AND FEARS, Megahard (2001)
Awakening / Turn Back / Distant Skies /
Memories Running / Hopes And Fears /
Dream Of Life / Sacred Song / A Place To
Belong / Seventh And Last / Until The End

DAMASCUS STEEL (USA)
Line-Up: Terry Brown (vocals), Ron Stear
(guitar), Joe Komenda (bass), David Adkins
(drums)

Albums:
CRY OF THE SWORDS, Hidden Metal Gems
HMG003 (2000)
The Big Ride / Make Up Your Mind / Still I
Wonder / Soul Excavation / Thrill Of The
Chase / Tunnel Vision / Place In Time / Say
That You Love Me / Running On The Edge /
Oasis

DAMN THE MACHINE (USA)
Line-Up: Dave Clemmons (vocals / guitar),
Chris Poland (guitar), David Randi (bass),
Mark Poland (drums)

Political edged Progressive Metal featuring
former MEGADETH guitarist CHRIS
POLAND. The 1993 album was lent heady
praise but the band called it a day after this
effort. A now highly sought after promotion
single 'Silence' included exclusive cover
versions of ALVIN LEE's 'I'D Love To Change
The World' and KING CRIMSON's 'Cat Food'.
Clemmons would decamp and, pulling in
singer John Skipp, the band faltered on as
MUMBO'S BRAIN before disbanding.
Dave Clemmons later turned up in JUD whilst
Poland reverted back to solo outings plus the
OHM endeavour with brother Mark.

Singles/EPs:
Silence / I'd Love To Change The World / Cat
Food, A&M (1993) (USA promotion release)

Albums:
DAMN THE MACHINE, A&M 314540103 2
(1993)
The Mission / Fall Of Order / Corporate
Reign / Honor / Lonesome God / On With
The Dream / Patriot / I Will / Silence /
Russians / Countryside / Humans

DARK AVENGER (BRAZIL)
Line-Up: Mario Linhares (vocals), Leonel
Valdez (guitar), Osiris di Castro (guitar),
Gustavo Vieira (bass), Rafael Galvão
(keyboards), Kayo John (drums)

Taking their title from a MANOWAR song
DARK AVENGER could only ever be True
Metal. The band was rooted in the Brasilia
based band ATENA, a Portuguese language
Rock n' Roll act centred upon the trio of front

man Mario Linhares, guitarist Leonel Valdez and bassist Wagner Marcello. This formation adopted a Heavy Metal style with the adoption of the new name RAT WHITE, soon evolving into DARK AVENGER. Now singing in English and strictly Power Metal in their approach the band delivered the goods in the form of a February 1994 demo tape 'Choose Your Side - Heavy Or Hell'.

For the debut eponymous DARK AVENGER album of 1995 the band line-up stood at lead vocalist Mário Linhares, guitarists Leonel Valdez and Osiris di Castro, bass player Gustavo Vieira, keyboard player Rafael Galvão and drummer Luciano Toledo.

The album would be repackaged in new sleeve artwork, remastered and have the addition of a bonus new track 'Morgana' for a 1998 European re-release through the Italian Scarlet label. The new track featured the new drummer Kayo John.

DARK AVENGER underwent a complete overhaul of personnel following the 2001 album 'Tales Of Avalon – The Terror' with only Mario Linhares surviving. At first Julio Cesar usurped di Castro on guitar but then Marcelo Barbosa ousted the long standing Valdeze and Fabio Hejera became the new bassist.

The singer subsequently built up a brand new band comprising guitar players Hugo Santiago and Marcus Valls, bassist Michel Brasil, keyboard player Thomas Galuf and drummer Rafael Dantas, the latter a veteran of MORBID WHISPER, LAST RITES, AMALGAMA and RAZORBLADE. Brasil had previously plied his trade with AMALGAMA, GLAMDRING and MENTAL ASYLUM.

DARK AVENGER would contribute (naturally) the track 'Dark Avenger' to a MANOWAR tribute album 'Revenge' issued by the Northwind label in 2002.

Albums:
DARK AVENGER, Zen (1995) (Brazilian release)
Armageddon / Die Mermaid! / Who Dares To Care / Give A Chance / Green Blood / Rebellion / Dark Avenger / Half Dead Eyes / Madelayne / Ghost Divinity / Call Of Fight
DARK AVENGER, Scarlet (1995)
Armageddon / Die Mermaid! / Who Dares To Care / Give A Chance / Green Blood / Rebellion / Dark Avenger / Half Dead Eyes / Madelayne / Ghost Divinity / Call Of Fight / Morgana
TALES OF AVALON – THE TERROR, Megahard (2001)
The Terror / Tales Of Avalon / Golden Eagles / Heroes Of Kells / Crown Of Thorns / Wicked Choices - Part I / Clas Myrddin / As The Rain / De Profundis / Caladvwch / The White Of Your Skin / Crownless Queen /

Morgana / The Lament

DARKFIRE (ITALY)

Singles/EPs:
Fear / Skyriders, (2001)

DARK HORIZON (ITALY)
Line-Up: Roberto Quassalo (vocals), Danielle Mandelli (guitar), Tiziano Ruggeri (guitar), Andrea Galli (bass), Alessandro Battini (keyboards), Luca Capelli (drums)

A Symphonic Metal band based out of Piacenza. DARK HORIZON was the brainchild of guitarist Danielle Mandelli and keyboard player Alessandro Battini, first formulated in September of 1996. Shortly after the band was brought up to full compliment with the addition of vocalist Pietro Gandalfi and the rhythm section of bassist Claudio Gallini and Luca Capelli. This line-up cut the opening demo 'Legend In Opera' issued in 1998.

DARK HORIZON underwent a line-up shift upfront of a follow up 1999 demo. New on vocals would be Luigi Maione with bassist Andrea Galli and drummer Marco Polledri also coming in as fresh blood.

During 2000 DARK HORIZON submitted two tracks to compilation albums, namely WARLORD's 'Aliens' and MANOWAR's 'Heart Of Steel'.

The band, now fronted by Roberto Quassalo, signed to the Northwind's subsidiary Steelborn Records for recording of a debut November 2001 album 'Son Of Gods'. Tiziano Ruggeri had been recruited as a second guitarist and Luca Capelli had returned to the drum stool.

Albums:
SON OF GODS, Northwind (2001)
My Dark Lord / Wizard / Son Of Gods / Light Of The New Age / Power Of The Rune / Crimson Sky / Neverending Battle / Wind Of Tomorrow

DARKLIN REACH (Chicago, IL, USA)
Line-Up: Alan Pangelinan (vocals / guitar), Ed Chapa (bass), Tony DiVozzo (drums)

High intensity Metal band DARKLIN REACH included former AMULANCE drummer Tony 'T-Bone' DiVozzo in the ranks. The solitary DARKLIN REACH album was produced by the esteemed SAVATAGE duo of Jon Oliva and Steve Wacholz.

DARKLIN REACH folded during September 2001 with DiVozzo going on to join BLACK CUNTRY ROCK.

WHERE EVIL DWELLS, Corpse 005CD (1992)

DARK MOOR (SPAIN)
Line-Up: Eliza C. Martin (vocals), Enrik Garcia (guitar), Alberto Maroto (guitar), Anan Kaddouri (bass), Roberto P.C. (keyboards), Jorge Saez (drums)

DARK MOOR

Madrid act DARK MOOR, fronted by erstwhile SABATAN vocalist Eliza Candelas Martin and founded in 1994, debuted with the 'Shadowland' album. DARK MOOR would donate their version of 'Halloween' to the HELLOWEEN tribute album 'Keepers Of Jericho'. Outside of Spain this cover version drew attention to the band with ex-HELLOWEEN man Kai Hansen citing it as his favourite on the record. The track had been recorded during the sessions for the Luigi Stafanini produced 'The Hall Of Olden Dreams' album. DARK MOOR would land the valuable support slot to DEMONS & WIZARDS Spanish tour dates that year too.
A mini-album, 'The Fall Of Melnibore' limited to 1500 copies for the Spanish market, would arrive in May of 2001. Comprising new material, the HELLOWEEN cover plus 'Wood Song' being an exclusive bonus from the Korean licensed version of 'The Hall Of Olden Dreams' and 'The Fall Of Melnibore' from the Japanese variant.
DARK MOOR's fourth opus, 'The Gates Of Oblivion', would see CYDONIA vocalist Dan Keying acting as session guest. This release saw DARK MOOR expanding their international audience, being their first record

licensed into North America. Keyboard player Roberto Pea de Camus made his exit in June of 2002 just upfront of the band's appearance at the 'Rock Machina' festival. Izabel took over keyboards for this event.

Albums:
THE HALL OF OLDEN DREAMS, Arise (2000)
Ceremony / Somewhere In Dreams / Maid Of Orleans / Bells Of Notre Dame / Silver Lake / Mortal Sin / The Sound Of The Blade / Beyond The Fire / Quest For The Eternal Fame / Hand In Hand / The Fall Of Meniboe
SHADOWLAND, Bossy Ogress BO19CD (2000)
Shadowland / Walhalla / Dragon Into The Fire / Calling On The Wind / Magic Land / Flying / Time Is The Avenger / Born In The Dark / The King's Sword / The Call
THE FALL OF MELNIBORE, (2001)
The Fall Of Melnibore / Silver Lake / Wood Song / Halloween / Cuentos De Ayer Y De Hoy
THE GATES OF OBLIVION, JVC Victor VICP-61796 (2002)
In The Heart Of Stone / A New World / The Gates Of Oblivion / Nevermore / Starmaker (Elbereth) / Mist In The Twilight / By The Strange Path Of Destiny / The Night Of The Ages / Your Symphony / The Citadel Of The Light / A Truth For Me / Dies Irae (Amadeus)

DEADLINE (ITALY)
Line-Up: Rob D.F. (vocals), Jerry Citarella (guitar), Emidio Tonello (bass), Steve Addis (drums)

DEADLINE are a technical Power Metal act. Although first assembled in 1991 the band was wrought by numerous line-up shuffles before finding some stability in order to record the February 1996 demo simply billed as 'Deadline'. 1997 brought further roster fluxes including the addition of drummer Stefano. A 2 track promotion tape 'Dreamland' elicited favourable media response and prompted a further effort, 'Violated Child' delivered in 1998. In August of the same year DEADLINE signed to the Underground Symphony label for their debut album 'Dressed To Kill', engineered by LABYRINTH drummer Frank Andiver.
DEADLINE issued a six track promo in 2001 which featured a cover version of MANOWAR's 'Hail To England'. Bassist Emidio Tonello left in April and was swiftly replaced by Luca Semprini.

Albums:
DRESSED TO KILL, Underground

Symphony USCD043 (2000)
The Seventh Gate Of Destiny (Intro) / Now Is Your Time / Fallin' Angel / The Flight Of A Free Man / Lost Memories / Violated Child / Instinct Of War / Fire In The Eyes / Dreamland / Dressed To Kill / Run To Hyperspace

DEATH OR GLORY (ITALY)
Line-Up: Fabio Vyper (vocals), Lex (guitar), Marco Kriminal (bass), Danny Hell (keyboards), Nik (drums)

Metal act founded as a JUDAS PRIEST covers band AFTER MIDNIGHT during 1998. The band was forged by erstwhile personnel from acts such as SIN, DARK WYLDERNESS and FUORIMODA. By the time of their inclusion on a compilation album with the track 'Consecrated Steel' and an opening 2000 demo 'Thundersblade' the band had switched title to DEATH OR GLORY.

Albums:
IN THE MIDDLE OF A STORM, Steelborn (2002)
In The Middle Of The Storm / Consecrated Steel / Fight For Glory / Dawn Of Victory / Metal Crown / Ghost Knight / Lost In Nowhere / Revenge / Frightening Dreams / Screams O' Fear / Symphony Of Fire / March Of The Titans

DEATHROW (GERMANY)
Line-Up: Milo (vocals / bass), Sven Flugge (guitar), Thomas Priebe (guitar), Markus Hahn (drums)

Dusseldorf Thrash band DEATHROW was created when guitarist Sven Flugge and drummer Markus Hahn split from Bremen's HÖLLENHUNDE in 1983. Relocating to Dusseldorf, the duo teamed up with vocalist / bassist Milo and second guitarist Priebe via advertisements in music magazines and formed SAMHAIN. However, an American act also existed of that name, so upon signing to Noise Records they changed monikers to DEATHROW.
The quartet's debut album was originally titled 'Riders Of Doom', but the album was repackaged with a different title ('Satan's Gift') after objections from the American market. DEATHROW toured Europe in 1986 with VOIVOD and POSSESSED.
DEATHROW's second album, 'Raging Steel', was another praiseworthy effort, but the band did little touring to back up its release. Priebe left in late 1988 forcing the recruitment of former END AMEN and MEKONG DELTA man Uwe Osterlehner in time to play dates in

Italy with CORONOR and record the third album 'Deception Ignored'.
Although firmly in the Thrash camp DEATHROW injected their Metal with some pre-Prog Metal complexities.

Singles/EPs:
Towers In Darkness / Somewhere In This Night / We Can Change, Metal Machine (1991)

Albums:
RIDERS OF DOOM, Noise N 0044 (1986)
Winds Of Death / Satan's Gift / Riders Of Doom / Hell's Ascent / Spider Attack / Slaughtered / Violent Omen / Dark Tales / Samhain
RAGING STEEL, Noise N 0081 (1987)
The Dawn / Raging Steel / Scattered By The Wind / Dragon's Blood / The Thing Within / Pledge To Die / Mortal Dread / The Undead Cry / Beyond The Night
DECEPTION IGNORED, Noise NUK 128 (1989)
Events In Concealment / The Deathwish / Triocton / N.L.Y.H. / Watching The World / Narcotic / Machinery / Bureaucrazy
LIFE BEYOND, West Virginia 084-57222 (1992)
Life Beyond / Behind Closed Eyes / Towers In Darkness / Hidden Truth / Harlequins Mask / Homosapiens Superior / Suicide Arena / Deathrow / Reflected Mind / The Remembrance

DECEASED (VA, USA)
Line-Up: King Fowley (vocals), Mark Adams (guitar), Mike Smith (guitar), Lez Snyder (bass)

DECEASED band leader King Fowley also owns Old Metal Records, a label specialising in re-releasing '80s Metal underground classics. DECEASED were founded in the mid '80s and opened up proceedings with the inaugural 1987 demo session 'Evil Side Of Religion'. Pre-DECEASED vocalist and drummer Kingsly 'King' Fowley had paid his dues with school band SLACK TYDE and the 1982 unit MESSENGER.
As DECEASED, Fowley, with guitarists Doug Souther and Mark Adams, played their debut gig in April 1986 performing a set of covers such as SODOM, BATHORY, SLAYER and MOTÖRHEAD at a friend's house. Progress was swift and soon DECEASED were becoming a draw on the local club circuit.
However, tragedy would strike the band in March of 1988 when bass player Rob Sterzel, along with two friends of the band, was killed in a hit and run incident. Stopping his car to

change a flat tyre the three friends were mown down by a van driver. Needless to say the media had a field day when it was revealed Rob's band was titled DECEASED.

Following this huge setback the 1989 set 'One Night In The Cemetery' ensued. Two further cassettes ensued with 'Birth By Radiation' and 1990's 'Nuclear Exorcist' before DECEASED hooked up with Death Metal specialists Relapse Records for the debut album 'Luck Of The Corpse'. Frictions within the band though led to DECEASED recording the live 'Gutwrench' single minus Souther. Shortly after recording Souther quit with Mike Smith taking his place.

The 1995 release 'Death Metal From The Grave' comprises early demo material with live cuts and a cover version of VENOM's 'Die Hard'.

Simon Effemey produced DECEASED's 2000 album 'Supernatural Addiction'. The band's live album includes a cover version of KROKUS's 'Headhunter'.

DECEASED also cut various other covers for tribute albums and laid down in quick succession their takes on SODOM's 'Witching Hour', AUTOPSY's 'Charred Remains' and KREATOR's 'Tormentor'.

The 2002 album 'Zombie Hymns' would virtually be a textbook of King Fowley's Heavy Metal upbringing pulling together a collection of cover versions. Honoured acts included SLAYER with 'Chemical Warfare' and 'Die By The Sword" VENOM's 'Black Metal' and 'Die Hard', IRON MAIDEN's 'Wrathchild' and '2 Minutes To Midnight' and the MERCYFUL FATE pairing of 'Nuns Have No Fun' and 'Doomed By The Living Dead'. Also included would be the METAL CHURCH anthem 'Metal Church', SAXON's 'Fire In The Sky', IMPETIGO's 'Dis Organ Ised', VOIVOD's 'Blower', EXCITER's 'Violence And Force' and OZZY OSBOURNE's 'S.A.T.O.' amongst others. The solitary non-traditional Metal offering would be a rendition of THE DOORS 'Not To Touch The Earth'.

Fowley also operates the Trad Metal act OCTOBER 31 as well as DOOMSTONE.

Albums:

LUCK OF THE CORPSE, Relapse (199-)
Fading Survival / The Cemetery's Full / Experimenting With Failure / Futuristic Doom / Haunted Cerebellum / Decrepit Coma / Shrieks From The Hearse / Psychedelic Warriors / / Feasting On Skulls / Birth By Radiation / Gutwrench

THE THIRTEEN FRIGHTENED SOULS, Relapse (1994)
The 13 Frightened Souls / Robotic Village / Voivod / Planet Graveyard / Nuclear Exorcist

DEATH METAL FROM THE GRAVE, (1995)
Immune To Burial / Worship The Coffin / Birth By Radiation / Vomiting Blood / Virus / Deformed Tomorrows / Nuclear Exorcist / Shrieks From The Hearse / A Trip To The Morgue / After The Bloodshed / Sick Thrash / Futuristic Doom (Live) / Fading Survival (Live) / Haunted Cerebellum (Live) / Robotic Village (Live) / Die Hard

THE BLUEPRINTS FOR MADNESS, (1995)
Morbid Shape In Black / The Triangle / Island Of The Unknown / The Blueprints For Madness / The Creek Of The Dead / Mind Vampires / Into The Bizarre / Alternate Dimensions / Midnight / Negative Darkness /A Reproduction Of Tragedy

FEARLESS UNDEAD MACHINES, Relapse RR 6957 (1997)
The Silent Creature / Contamination / Fearless Undead Machines / From The Ground They Came / Night Of The Deceased / Graphic Repulsion / Mysterious Research / Beyond Science / Unhuman Drama / The Psychic / Destiny

SUPERNATURAL ADDICTION, Relapse (2000)
The Premonition / Dark Chilling Heartbeat / A Very Familiar Stranger / Frozen Screams / The Doll With The Hideous Spirit / The Hanging Soldier / Chambers Of The Waiting Blind / Elly's Dementia

UP THE TOMBSTONES - LIVE 2000, Thrash Corner (2000)
The Silent Creature / The Premonition / The 13 Frightened Souls / Robotic Village / The Triangle / Dark Chilling Heartbeat / Fearless Undead Machines / The Psychic / Headhunter / Sick Thrash

BEHIND THE MOURNER'S VEIL, (2001)
It's Alive / The Mausoleum / Zombie Attack / Reaganomics / New Age Of Total Warfare / Deathrider / Victims Of The Masterplan (I-V)

ZOMBIE HYMNS, Crook'D (2002)
Black Metal / Violence And Force / Witching Metal / 2 Minutes To Midnight / S.A.T.O. / Blower / Doomed By The Living Dead / Dis Organ Ised / Die By The Sword / Not To Touch The Earth / Metal Church / Wrathchild / Bombs Of Death / Fire In The Sky / Nuns Have No Fun / Headhunter (Live) / Stay Clean / Die Hard / Tormentor / Chemical Warfare

DEFENDING THE FAITH (GERMANY)
Line-Up: Jürgen G. Allert (vocals), Robert Balci (guitar), Roberto D'Amico (bass)

Power Metal trio incorporated in January of 1998 by the duo of bassist Roberto D'Amico and guitarist Robert Balci, both having been members of Heidenheimer based SCREAMING. Balci had also enjoyed terms with Death Metal band DEATH IN ACTION as a drummer and the cult act STORMWITCH. Initially the band was fronted by singer Eberhard Paduch and with this line-up the group issued the 2000 album 'Defender'.

In January of 2000 D'Amico loaned himself out to ETERNAL DARKNESS, guesting on their album 'Out Of Control'. He would also perform live with ETERNAL DARKNESS but by September had resolved to make DEFENDING THE FAITH his priority act. With Paduch bailing out DEFENDING THE FAITH pulled in a new front man in Jürgen G. Allert, previously having been employed in the ranks of NIGHTWOLF, MINDCRIME and LYONS as a bass player.

DEFENDING THE FAITH would spend August of 2002 locked in the studio recording their second album 'Radical Change'.

Albums:
DEFENDER, (2000)

DEFYANCE (Knoxville, IA, USA)
Line-Up: Lance King (vocals), Marcus Peterson (guitar), Brent Scott (guitar), Aaron Bell (bass), Doug Beary (drums)

Iowa Progressive Metal. For the 1996 'Amaranthine' album DEFYANCE incorporated vocalist Brian Harrington, guitarist Marcus Peterson, bass player J.J. Wagner and drummer Doug Beary. The band line-up evolved to include singer Scott Andreus and bassist Rob McGrath for 1999's 'Time Lost' opus.

The 2002 DEFYANCE album would see Lance King of BALANCE OF POWER acting as guest lead vocalist. Bass came courtesy of DEGREE ABSOLUTE's Aaron Bell. Beary also performs with DEGREE ABSOLUTE, appearing on their eponymous 2002 album.

Albums:
VOICES WITHIN, (1995)
I Burn For You / To Your Heart / Devil's Daughter / Goodbye / Second Death
AMARANTHINE, (1996)
Without Your Love / Wings Of Angels / Coming Home / Seize The Day / Invention 4 In D Minor / Freedom Forever / Your Love Lies / Voices Within / Where Are You Now / Running Free
TIME LOST, (1999)
Turn To Yesterday / Shadows In My Mind / West Horizon / Between The Lies / From The Sky / Unturned Stone / The Game / My Nightmares / Break The Silence
TRANSITIONAL FORMS, Nightmare (2002)
Tied To A Wheel / Passing Of The Night / A Force To Face My Fears / A Notion / Connected / Fire Of Ancients / Just Beyond

My Sight / Silent Tears / Never Fade Away

DEMONS & WIZARDS
(USA / GERMANY)
Line-Up: Hansi Kürsch (vocals / bass), Jon Schaffer (guitar), Ritchie Wilkinson (guitar), Oliver Holzwarth (bass), Richard Christy (drums)

Metal act forged between BLIND GUARDIAN mentor Hansi Kürsch and ICED EARTH's Jon Schaffer. The debut album scored a huge success charting in Germany and even reaching number 1 in the Greek national charts. The Japanese version of the album saw two bonus tracks with an alternate version of 'The Whistler' and a rendition of CREAM's 'White Room'.

For touring on the European festival circuit DEMONS & WIZARDS drafted ex-SIEGES EVEN bassist Oliver Holzwarth, guitarist Ritchie Wilkinson and the noted CONTROL DENIED / DEATH drummer Richard Christy. Holzwarth later reunited with some of his ex-SIEGES EVEN colleagues to create LOOKING GLASS SELF. In 2001 Wilkinson would join ANGEL DUST for their American tour dates. Christy would feature on the 2001 ICED EARTH album 'Horror Show'.

Albums:
DEMONS & WIZARDS, JVC Victor VICP-60984 (2000) **35 SWEDEN**
Rites Of Passage / Heaven's Denies / Poor Man's Crusade / Fiddler On The Green / Blood On My Hands / Path Of Glory / Winter Of Souls / The Whistler / Tear Down The Wall / Gallows Pole / My Last Sunrise / Chant / White Room / The Whistler (Alternate version)

DESDEMONA (ITALY)
Line-Up: Andrea Marchisio (vocals), Christian Rosso (guitar), Alessandro Musso (bass), Foca Torchia (keyboards), Maurizio Anello (drums)

Symphonic Metal act DESDEMONA was created in 1997 and made their entrance with the 'Soul Foreclosures' demo the following year. However, a subsequent split in the ranks would witness the departure of vocalist Giuseppe Careddu and the rhythm section of bass player Marco Scagliola and drummer Roberto Risso. For recording of the debut album 'Lady Of The Lore' issued by the Northwind label, the band drafted vocalist Andrea Marchisio, bass player Alessandro Musso and drummer Maurizio Anello. Marchisio also doubles duties acting as singer for HIGHLORD.

DEMONS & WIZARDS
Photo : Nico Wobben

Albums:
LADY OF THE LORE, Northwind (2001)
Black Lady / Shadows Of My Life / Event
Horizon / Lancelot / Othello's Crying /
Neptune The Mystic / If I Were Fire /
Changing Skin

DESTILLERY (GERMANY)
Line-Up: Florian Reimann (vocals), Daniel
Hartelt (guitar), Roland Smigerski (guitar),
Mark Brüdigam (bass), Lars Janosch
(drums)

An ultra heavy act founded in 1993
DESTILLERY are based in Marl, Germany.
Added guitarist Daniel Hartelt in 1994 before
enrolling erstwhile CRYPTIC VISION singer
Florian Reimann. January of 1997 saw ex-
CRESTFALLEN guitarist Roland Smigerski
inducted into the ranks.
The band bowed in with the 1997 mini-album
'Interior Fire' issued as a private pressing. The
full length album 'Immortal Sun' released in
January 1999 on the Iron Glory label would
follow this up.
'Behind The Mask' followed with 'Ferrum',
produced by Achim Köhler, arriving in
January 2002.

Albums:
INTERIOR FIRE, (1997)
Hope Is A Frame / Interior Fire / Soul To
Soul / The Beginning Of… / Warland
IMMORTAL SUN, Iron Glory IG003 (1999)
Deluge Of Spite / Magical Man / The View /
Memorial Of Eternity / Downhearted /
Timerunner / Heavy Metal / Intentions /
Hope Is A Frame
BEHIND THE MASK, Iron Glory (2000)
Masquerade / Cage Of Time / Eraser /
Legend Or A Lie / Decades Of Execution /
Traitor / Second Face / Pride Of The
Mourner / Inflamed / Behind The Mask

DESTINY (SWEDEN)
Line-Up: Kristoffer Göbel (vocals), Niclas
Granath (guitar), Jan Ekberg (guitar), Stefan
Björnshög (bass), Birger Löfman (drums)

Original incarnations of Swedish troupe
DESTINY date back to 1980, but it was not
until 1984 that their debut album 'Beyond All
Sense' was released. A straight forward
Heavy Metal band, DESTINY leaned heavily
on '70s influences rather than the Thrash that
dominated the scene at the time. 'Beyond All
Sense' would be recorded with a DESTINY
line-up of vocalist Håkan Ring, guitarists John
Proden and Magnus Osterman, bassist
Stefan Björnshög and drummer Peter
Lundgren.

Amongst their non-recording achievements
DESTINY toured Scandinavia supporting
MANNINYA BLADE between the first two
albums.
In 1987 the band demoed six tracks, having
recruited new members in guitarists Floyd
Constantin, formerly with KING DIAMOND,
and Jörgen Petersson in addition to new
vocalist Zenny Hansson. This tape led to a
deal with German label US Metal Records
and began recording the follow up 'Atomic
Winter' in 1988, which emerged with a cover
painting courtesy of Derek Riggs, famed for
his work with IRON MAIDEN. Despite global
praise from the Rock media being heaped
upon 'Atomic Winter', and in particular
Hansson's vocals, the album suffered from
poor distribution and failed to give the band's
career the impetus they needed.
Both Konstantin and Peterson departed after
the album release, necessitating the
recruitment of guitarists Knut Hassel and
Gunner Kindberg, the latter having actually
been with the band in its formative years.
DESTINY's third album, 'Nothing Left To
Fear', was recorded as a trio with former
drummer Peter Lundgren contributing. A
permanent drummer was found later in Stefan
Svantesson. Overall the album proved a
darker affair than its predecessors but still
maintained the heaviness. Valuable TV
exposure would be gained from a promotional
video shot for the track 'The Evil Trinity'.
However, in a major blow, Zenny Hansson
then left the fold. Daniel Heyman, later of
LOST HORIZON replaced him for a short
period.
DESTINY regrouped in the late '90s. The
band numbered a returning Zenny Hansson
on vocals, Knut Hassel on guitars, Stefan
Björnshög on bass and drummer Björn
Öhrfeldt, the latter on loan from PAGAN.
Former member Gunnar Kindberg would later
rejoin as live guitarist. This incarnation of the
band, now with Håkan Svantesson taking
control of the drum kit, recorded a fourth
album titled 'The Undiscovered Country',
although Zenny Hansson has changed his
surname to Gram and now fronts
TREASURELAND.
During 1999 DESTINY contributed their
version of 'Into The Nightmare' for a DEMON
tribute album 'Day Of The Demon' as well as
'Anguish And Fear' for the YNGWIE
MALMSTEEN homage 'A Guitar Odyssey'.
The line-up for these sessions had Gram,
Kindberg and Björnshög joined by ex-
ACHERON and PAGAN guitarist Anders
Fagerstrand and drummer Tomas Fredén, the
latter a member of Danish act BEYOND
TWILIGHT.
Ex-DESTINY members Lundgren and Hassel

are now in 7TH PLANET. The 2002 version of DESTINY, celebrating the band's twentieth anniversary, witnessed a complete overhaul in the band line-up, now comprising vocalist Kristoffer Göbel, guitarists Janne Ekberg and Niclas Granath, bass player Stefan Björnshög and ex-BISCAYA man Birger Löfman on drums. An album, provisionally entitled 'Future Of The Past', was being scheduled for release the same year.

Albums:
BEYOND ALL SENSE, Musik Bolaget (1985)
Intro - Destiny / Rest In Peace / Spellbreaker / Hang Them High / Sirens In The Dark / Kill The Witch / Lost To Heaven / More Evil Than Evil / Power By Birth / Sacrilege
ATOMIC WINTER, U.S. Metal US (1989)
Bermuda / Who Am I? / Spellbreaker / Beware / Religion / The Extreme Unction / Dark Heroes / Living Dead / Atomic Winter
NOTHING LEFT TO FEAR, Active ATV18 (1991)
Nothing Left To Fear / Medieval Rendezvous / The Evil Trinity / Sirens In The Dark / Sheer Death / F.O.S. / Beyond All Sense / No Reservation / The Raven / Rest In Peace / Du Gamla Du Fria
THE UNDISCOVERED COUNTRY, Gothenburg Noiseworks (1998)
Devil In The Dark / Balance Of Terror / A Taste Of Armageddon / Wink Of An Eye / Dagger Of The Mind / By Any Other Way / Tomorrow Is Yesterday / The Undiscovered Country
FUTURE OF THE PAST, (2002)
Holy Man / Sabotage / In The Shadow Of The Rainbow / Magic Forest / Angels / Flying Dutchman / On The Outside / Ghost Train / Future Of The Past

DESTINY DREAMING (GERMANY)
Line-Up: Sascha Kratzer (vocals), Danny Fundinger (guitar), Andreas Essig (guitar), Sascha D'Agnano (bass), Marco Muller (drums)

Karlsruhe Progressive Metal band DESTINY DREAMING first came to attention with a 1994 demo 'Horizons'.

Albums:
WATER BREAKS THE STONE, Bossy Ogress 0073552 (1998)
Seeker / Delightful Tears / In Morpheus' Arms / Dimensions Forlorn / Quicksands / The Hands Divide / Within A Shadow

DESTINY'S END (USA)
Line-Up: James Rivera (vocals), Dan Delucie (guitar), Eric Halpern (guitar), Nardo Andi (bass), Brian Craig (drums)

DESTINY'S END saw the return to action of noted HELSTAR singer James Rivera. Joining him were former members of SHADOW INSANE and NEW EDEN drummer Brian Craig and bassist Nardo Andi alongside erstwhile NEW EDEN, SECRET WISDOM and CRAB NEBULA guitarist Dan Delucie. Making up the full complement would be guitarist Perry Grayson, a former member of OBSCURE - an act which also included PROTOTYPE personnel Mike Brew and Kragen Lum alongside one time NEW EDEN singer Mike Grant.
DESTINY'S END would sign up with Metal Blade records cutting their opening shot 'Breathe Deep The Dark' with producer Bill Metoyer.
By 2000 the Rivera was also fronting side outfit RIVERA PROJECT. Despite DESTINY'S END being announced as performing at the German 'Bang Your Head' festival in May of 2000 Grayson decamped to concentrate on literary work and forge a Progressive Thrash act RELENTLESS. Eric Halpern of Houston's Z LOT Z and tribute act MINDCRIME swiftly took his place. At 'Bang Your Head' Rivera was even granted the honour of performing onstage with the SCORPIONS for a rendition of 'He's A Woman, She's A Man'. Rivera would find himself invited back to the 'Bang Your Head' 2001 festival with a HELSTAR reunion concert.
The band would record their second effort, the Vivaldi infused conceptual 'Transition', working with producer Joe Floyd of WARRIOR. Mastering was handled by Ty Tabor of KINGS X. However, the end results were not initially as expected and the whole record would be delayed for a remix in November by Achim Kohler. 'Transition' would eventually arrive in early 2001.
DESTINY'S END would also contribute their take on 'Dressed In White' to a KING DIAMOND tribute album on Necropolis Records. It would be reported in August of 2001 that Rivera had joined FLOTSAM & JETSAM after their longstanding vocalist Eric A.K. departed.
Drummer Brian Craig would join Jack Frost's SEVEN WITCHES project band in November 2001. The same month would witness a return to action of former DESTINY'S END man Perry M. Grayson together with vocalist Mike Brew ('Mike Bear') with their new act ARTISAN. Joining the duo for this new venture would be RAPTURE guitarist Ana Greco and drummer Matt Conley. In July of 2002 ex-frontman Rivera teamed up with SEVEN WITCHES, debuting with the band at

the 'Classic Metal Fest II' in Cleveland, Ohio.

Albums:
BREATHE DEEP THE DARK, Metal Blade
14178 (1998)
Rebirth / Breath Deep The Dark / To Be
Immortal / Idle City / The Fortress
Unvanquishable / Sinister Deity / Unsolved
World / Under Destruction's Thumb /
Clutching at Straws / Where Do We Go? /
The Obscure
TRANSITION, Metal Blade 14340 (2001)
Transition / The Watcher / A Passing Phase /
The Suffering / From Dust To Life / Storm
Clouds / First You Dream, Then You Die / The
Legend / A Choice Of Graves / Vanished

DESTRUCTION (GERMANY)

Line-Up: Marcel 'Schmier' Schirmer (bass /
vocals), Michael Siffringer (guitar), Harold
Wilkens (guitar), Thomas Senmann (drums)

Formed in 1983 under their original title of
KNIGHT OF DEMON this German Speed
Metal band went on to win much acclaim and
healthy album sales. The band made their
recording debut when they recorded the
'Bestial Invasion' demo which featured the
track 'Mad Butcher', which was to become so
popular that it would feature as the leading
title track on a 1987 issued EP.
The 'Eternal Devastation' album was
produced by Manfred Neurer. The 'Mad
Butcher' EP released in 1987 features a cover
version of the PLASMATICS 'The Damned'.
This release was the first with additional
guitarist Harold Wilkens and new drummer
Oliver Kaiser after Thomas Senmann quit the
music business to become a policeman.
DESTRUCTION scored notable sales with
the 'Mad Butcher' EP and with renewed fire
opened for MOTÖRHEAD on their 1987
European tour including their first British
show at the Brixton Academy. They kept up
the momentum with their first shows in
America including dates opening for SLAYER.
'Release From Agony', produced by Kalle
Trapp, enabled DESTRUCTION to break into
the worldwide market. DESTRUCTION
returned to Britain once more in 1989
supporting CELTIC FROST, promoting their
live album 'Live Without Sense' which was
recorded at shows in Austria, Spain and
Portugal.
In 1990 the band fired Schmier claiming his
studio performances were below par. Schmier
began negotiations with PAGANINI but ended
up fronting a totally new outfit
HEADHUNTER. Schmier's place was filled by
former POLTERGEIST vocalist Andre and the
resulting album 'Cracked Brain' provided fans

with more of the same gut wrenching fare
only let down by an appalling cover of THE
KNACK's 'My Sharonna'.
In early 1991 ex-ARTILLERY vocalist
Flemming Ronsdorf joined DESTRUCTION
but lasted barely two weeks.
Schmier and Siffringer resolved their
differences in 1999 and DESTRUCTION put
in some triumphant return performances at
European festivals. Sure enough the band,
with new drummer Sven, signed to Nuclear
Blast for the 2000 Peter Tägtgren produced
album 'All Hell Breaks Loose'. As a bridge
between the DESTRUCTION history of yore
and the band's renewed position, the classic
'Mad Butcher' track from the 1984 'Sentence
Of Death' EP, a firm fan favourite, was
answered with a new cut entitled 'The Butcher
Strikes Back'.
Sales were strong and the album attained a
number 67 position on the national German
album charts. A brief warm-up tour led to
European festivals performances.
DESTRUCTION would then hit the road as
part of the 'Nuclear Blast Festival' road show
packaged alongside HYPOCRISY,
KATAKLYSM, CREMATORY and RAISE
HELL. The partnership with Canadians
KATAKLYSM was re-forged with American
dates, which saw DYING FETUS as openers.
During April 2001 the group once again
entered Abyss Studios with Peter Tägtgren to
record the follow up 'The Antichrist'. The
album ran into a whole slew of production
problems when finished copies were found to
have the track order compiled incorrectly,
sleeves printed in red instead of full colour
and mysterious sound drop outs on the
"hidden" bonus track 'Curse The Gods'. These
initial mis-pressings would soon be snapped
up by eager collectors. The problems did not
end there though as the album would also be
seized by Swiss customs officials but later
released.
DESTRUCTION parted ways with drummer
Sven Vormann during October, replacing him
with Berliner Marc Reign, a veteran of ORTH
and GUNJAH, in time for a nostalgic Thrash
Metal mammoth tour of Germany with
compatriots SODOM and KREATOR
commencing 26th December in Ludwigsburg
and running through into the new year.
The band's successful live alliance with
KREATOR would be furthered abroad as the
pairing revealed tour plans for dates in Brazil,
Chile, Peru, Colombia and Venezuela
throughout August and September. The
Thrash union would then hit North America
with CEPHALIC CARNAGE and DECEMBER
in tow. DESTRUCTION would also be
confirmed as headliners at the anti racism
benefit gig 'The Mosh Club Open Air' in

Kolmberg. The band also cut a rendition of 'Whiplash' for a Nuclear Blast METALLICA tribute collection.

Meantime a fresh act with DESTRUCTION connections would be unveiled with the arrival of a three track demo by the strangely titled Thrashers JESUS CHRYSLER SUPERSKUNK. This band including in its ranks former DESTRUCTION members guitarist Michael 'Ano' Piranio and drummer Sven Vormann working alongside vocalist Thomas Rosenmerkel, DRYROT guitarist Micheal Gerstlauer and NECROMONICON bass player Bernhard 'Erna' Matt.

DESTRUCTION's new studio album projected for a 2002 release was announced as having the first 10,000 copies coming complete with a bonus CD compilation of up and coming Thrash acts.

Singles/EPs:
Mad Butcher / The Damned / Reject Emotions / The Last Judgement, Steamhammer SPV 601 897 (1987)
Decisions / I Kill Children / Things Of No importance / Smile, UAM 0447 (1994) ('Destruction' EP)

Albums:
SENTENCE OF DEATH, Steamhammer SPV NR60-1838 (1984)
Intro / Total Disaster / Black Mass / Mad Butcher / Satan's Vengeance / Devil's Soldiers
INFERNAL OVERKILL, Steamhammer SPV 081806 (1985)
Invincible Force / Death Trap / The Ritual / Tormentor / Bestial Invasion / Thrash Attack / Antichrist / Black Death
ETERNAL DEVASTATION, Steamhammer SPV 08-1885 (1986)
Curse The Gods / Confound Games / Life Without Sense / United By Hatred / Eternal Ban / Upcoming Devastation / Confused Mind
RELEASE FROM AGONY, Steamhammer SPV 087503 (1988)
Beyond Eternity / Release From Agony / Dissatisfied Existence / Sign Of Fear / Unconscious Ruins / Incriminated / Our Oppression / Survive To Die
LIVE WITHOUT SENSE (LIVE), Noise NUK126 (1989)
Curse The Gods / Unconscious Ruins / Invincible Force / Dissatisfied Existence / Reject Emotions / Eternal Ban / Mad Butcher / Pink Panther / Life Without Sense / In The Mood / Release From Agony / Bestial Invasion
CRACKED BRAIN, Noise NUK 136 (1990)
Cracked Brain / Frustrated / SED / Time

Must End / My Sharrona / Rippin' You Off Blind / Die A Day Before You're Born / No Need To Justify / When Your Mind Was Free
BEST OF, Steamhammer SPV 084-76482 CD (1992)
Intro / Total Desaster / Mad Butcher / Devil's Soldiers / Invincible Force / Death Trap / The Ritual / Tormentor / Black Death / Beyond Eternity / Release From Agony / Sign Of Fear / Incriminated / Our Oppression / Survive To Die / Confound Games / United By Hatred / Upcoming Devastation / Confused Mind / Curse The Gods / Unconscious Ruins / Thrash Attack / Reject Emotions / Mad Butcher / Pink Panther - Life Without Sense / In The Mood - Relapse From Agony / Bestial Invasion
ALL HELL BREAKS LOOSE, Nuclear Blast (2000) **67 GERMANY**
Intro / The Final Curtain / Machinery Of Lies / Tears Of Blood / Devastation Of Your Soul / The Butcher Strikes Back / World Domination Of Pain / X-treme Measures / All Hell Breaks Loose / Total Desaster 2000 / Visual Prostitution / Kingdom Of Damnation
THE ANTICHRIST, Nuclear Blast NB0632 (2001)
Days Of Confusion / Thrash Till Death / Nailed To The Cross / Dictators Of Cruelty / Bullets From Hell / Strangulated Pride / Meet Your Destiny / Creations Of The Underworld / Godfather Of Slander / Let Your Mind Rot / The Heretic / Curse The Gods

DESTRUCTOR (USA)
Line-Up: Dave Overkill (vocals / guitar), Pat Rabid (guitar), Dave Holocaust (bass), Matt Flammable (drums)

Albums:
MAXIMUM DESTRUCTION, Auburn (1986)
Prelude In Sledge-Minor Opus 7 1st Movement / Maximum Destruction / Destructor / Take Command / Instrumental / Pounding Evil / Overdose / Iron Curtain / Hot Wet Leather / Bondage

DESYRE (GERMANY)

Albums:
HANDS OF FATE, (2002)
Open The Gates / Hands Of Fate / After All / God Forgive Me / What Is Reality / Peace In Your Mind / Network Overload / Believe In You

DEUCE (Laurel, MD, USA)
Line-Up: Tom Gattis (vocals / guitar), Timmy Meadows (guitar), Chris Hall (bass), Billy Giddings (drums)

103

Formed in 1978 by guitarist Tom Gattis, the Baltimore heavyweights first line-up featured vocalist Eddie Day (hired because he was a sound-a-like for CHEAP TRICK's Robin Zander and quickly dispensed with!) guitarist MARTY FRIEDMAN, bassist Steve Leter and drummer Chris Tinto. The latter duo were soon replaced by Chris Hall and Billy Giddings respectively. Gattis took over vocal chores after Day's departure.

Friedman quit for the sunnier climate of Hawaii and eventual fame as a member of MEGADETH via Hawaii acts VIXEN and HAWAII. His replacement, Timmy Meadows, joined the fold in 1980.

Meadows was the brother of ANGEL's Punky Meadows and had been a member of the ANGEL roadcrew in the '70s.

DEUCE released a self-financed single in 1981, quickly earning themselves comparisons with British Metal acts by merging viciously precise twin guitar work with raw NWoBHM like aggression.

In 1982 Hall left the group and DEUCE were thus joined by Mike Francis, a former compatriot of Meadows' on the ANGEL roadcrew. This line-up completely revamped a demo tape recorded after the single and both feature the DEUCE rendition of the Marty Friedman penned 'Angels In The Dust'

The band changed their name to TENSION prior to recording their proposed debut album. However, a Duluth, Georgia based record label titled O.P.M. Records released an album full of DEUCE demo material with the blessing of the band, despite having the appearance of a bootleg.

The first four tracks and tracks six to nine were recorded between 1978 and 1979 whilst tracks five and ten were cut between 1979 and 1980 with Timmy Meadows on guitar.

Gattis was last seen as a member of Heavy Metal band WARDOG touting the 'Scorched Earth' album. Post WARDOG Gattis announced the formation of a new band entitled AFTERBURN, a reunion with erstwhile TENSION colleague Tim O'Connor on bass, Bulgarian master guitarist Peter Petev and erstwhile VYPER and PRIZONER drummer Michael Scott. The title of this new venture would later be switched to BALLISTIC.

Singles/EPs:
I'm Saved / Bad Boys, (1981)

Albums:
DEUCE, OPM Records OPMR 1000 (1999)
Barnburner / Angels From The Dust / 72 Hours / One Nation Underground / Bad Boys / Atomic Age / Telemann's 3rd / Love's

Massive Suicide / Lords Of The Universe / I'm Saved

DGM (ITALY)
Line-Up: Luciano Regoli (vocals), Diego Reali (guitar), Marco Marchiori (bass), Maurizio Pariotti (keyboards), Fabio Constantino (drums)

A Progressive Power Metal band created in 1994 as an instrumental trio of former ICEFIRE and DAYZE keyboard player Maurizio Pariottia, ex-RANDOM speed guitarist Diego Reali and drummer Gianfranco Tassella. The following year DGM added bass player Marco Marchiori and pulled in vocalist Luciano Regoli of SAMADHY and RITRATTO DI DORIAN GRAY for a self-financed mini-album 'Random Access Zone'. The full length 'Change Direction' followed in November of 1997.

During late 1998 Tassella opted out and DGM drafted Daniele Conte to act as session drummer for the 1999 'Wings Of Time' album. Shortly after recording Fabio Constantino, previously with CARNAL RAPTOR, took the drum role on a more permanent basis.

In April of 2000 Marchiori made his exit, DGM pulling in former RIVER OF CHANGE man Andrea Arcangeli as replacement. DGM then added new vocalist Titta Tani, a veteran of such acts as YTSE JAMMERS, MINDSCAPE, GLORYHUNTER, ABSTRACTA and EMPTY TREMOR for the 2002 offering 'Dreamland', generally regarded as the group's best offering to date. Japanese variants of the album included a cover version of YNGWIE MALMSTEEN's 'You Don't Remember (I'll Never Forget)' as an exclusive bonus track. Tani also operates with DAEMONIA.

Albums:
RANDOM ACCESS ZONE, (1996)
Hard Rain / Run / Data Error / Melpomenia
CHANGE DIRECTION, Elevate ERO2003 (1999)
Brainstorming / In My Heart / The Last Memory / Lonely Hearts / Anthem / Do What You Want / Change Direction / Flyin' Fantasy
WINGS OF TIME, Elevate ERO3008 (2000)
Guiding Light / I'll Dream Of You / Mirrors Of The Night / Deep Inside / The Other Side / Waiting For The Sunrise / A Drop Of Shadow / Nightmare
DREAMLAND, Elevate ERO5019 (2002)
Dreamland / Eternity / Lost In Time / The Rain Falls In The Desert / Reason To Live / Ego's Battle / Lie! / Sweet Surrender / Feeling Forever

BRUCE DICKINSON (UK)

Noted Heavy Metal vocalist Bruce Dickinson was dubbed the "air raid siren" whilst a member of IRON MAIDEN, a role he performed extremely successfully over ten years before quitting for a reasonably successful solo career. Singing is only one of a number of talents possessed by the man who has ranked as one of the top ten fencers in Britain as well as taking up the role of a novelist, penning two satirical works based upon the 'Lord Iffy Boatrace' character.

Previous to IRON MAIDEN Dickinson was known as 'Bruce Bruce' whilst fronting IRON MAIDEN's NWoBHM compatriots SAMSON and joined IRON MAIDEN in 1981 after recording a trio of albums with his former act. Dickinson first made a foray into solodom whilst still a member of IRON MAIDEN, recording 'Tattooed Millionaire' in 1990 and subsequently touring in support of it purely for the fun of doing so.

The follow up proved a torturous affair to deliver. Initially recorded with ex-JAGGED EDGE musicians guitarist Myke Gray, bassist Andy Robbins and former VAMP drummer Dick Flizcar with production handled by Chris Tsangarides. These tapes were never used. Gray, Robbins and Flizcar went on shortly thereafter to form the successful SKIN.

Further recording sessions ensued with noted producer Keith Olsen. Utilised in the studio were top rated session guitarist Tim Pierce and former SCARLET members bassist Martin Connolly and drummer Andy Bierne, the latter a veteran of GRAND PRIX.

Dickinson had by now announced his split from IRON MAIDEN. Drafting in a completely new set of musicians in the form of Los Angeles act TRIBE OF GYPSIES, the resulting 'Balls To Picasso' album was finally laid to rest and found the man travelling down a more experimental, though not unproductive, road.

In July 1994 Dickinson announced his touring band was to consist of former ATOM SEED bassist Chris Dale, ex-MIDNIGHT BLUE and GUN guitarist Alex Dickson and Italian drummer Alex Elena. This new band toured in Britain with the unsigned MAITREYA as support and throughout Europe with support from SKIN and THE ALMIGHTY. The European trek included the performance of a gig for NATO forces in war torn Sarajevo during December 1994 which involved a hazardous journey to the city hidden in a truck after military officialdom declined to guarantee the band's safety.

Oddly, despite the relative success of his ventures, Dickinson lost his deal with EMI shortly before the close of the year, but soon found a new home at Rawpower Records and toured Europe in early 1995 sharing the bill with HELLOWEEN with a band billed as 'Skunkworks'.

The 'Skunkworks' album found Dickinson in an experimental mood in keeping with the times but this effort was found severely wanting by many of his long-term fans. Dale departed to join BALANCE OF POWER and later create SACK TRICK. Dickson joined Pop Star ROBBIE WILLIAMS band.

Eschewing a further foray into the world of the Alternative, Dickinson went back to his roots in more ways than one with his ensuing 1997 album 'Accident Of Birth'. Not only did the album contain unashamed traditional Heavy Metal but it was also graced with cover artwork by Derek Riggs, the artist who made such an impact with his sleeves for IRON MAIDEN.

The connection did not end there however as Dickinson was reunited with erstwhile IRON MAIDEN colleague guitarist Adrian Smith. Dickinson also collaborated on song-writing with ex-DRIVER man Roy Z.

The shift in direction was endorsed as Dickinson's album pulled in exemplary reviews and tour dates succeeded in pulling in capacity audiences. A further album 'The Chemical Wedding', based upon the philosophies of William Blake, struck an even heavier chord and exemplary reviews.

With IRON MAIDEN under pressure from fans to sever the relationship with Blaze Bayley it came as no great surprise in early 1999 that Dickinson and Smith were reunited into the IRON MAIDEN camp.

In the midst of recording the IRON MAIDEN 'Brave New World' album Dickinson and solo band cohort Roy Z also took time out to aid ex-JUDAS PRIEST vocalist Rob Halford with his HALFORD album project. Dickinson would appear on the subsequent 'Resurrection' opus and on the 'Live Insurrection' too. Rumours also circulated about a possible collaboration between Halford, Dickinson and QUEENSRYCHE vocalist Geoff Tate billed as THE THREE TREMORS!

A 'Best Of Bruce Dickinson' compilation arrived in September of 2001. Alongside existing tracks the album numbered two new songs 'Silver Wings' and 'Broken' as well as original Dickinson versions of the adopted IRON MAIDEN numbers 'The Wicker Man' and 'Bring Your Daughter To The Slaughter'. Initial limited edition variants included a bonus CD of an extra 70 minutes plus of rare material.

Although IRON MAIDEN had witnessed a massive upsurge in support and were set to maintain the momentum into 2002 with their live album recorded in Rio De Janeiro, Dickinson would make space for further outside work the same year, announcing a solo appearances at the 'Wacken Open Air' festival in Germany, the 'Sweden Rock' festival, 'Graspop Metal' in Belgium and the 'Tuska Metal' event in Finland. Dickinson's live band for these gigs comprised the former 'Skunkworks' team of bassist Chris Dale, guitarist Al Dickson and drummer Robin Guy, now all members of spoof Rockers SACK TRICK. Dickinson would guest on SACK TRICK's 2002 opus 'Sheep In KISS make up', an album entirely composed of KISS cover versions.

Singles/EPs
Tattooed Millionaire / Ballad Of Mutt / Winds Of Change, EMI EM 138 (1990) **18 UK**
Tattooed Millionaire / Ballad Of Mutt, EMI EM 138 (1990) (7" single)
Tattooed Millionaire (Remix) / Interview, EMI (1990) (USA Promotion)
All The Young Dudes / Darkness Be My Friend, EMI EM142 (1990) **23 UK**
All The Young Dudes / Darkness Be My Friend / Sin City, EMI 12EM142 (1990) (12" single)
All The Young Dudes, EMI (1990) (USA Promotion)
Dive! Dive! Dive! / Riding With The Angels (Live), EMI EM151 (1990) **45 UK**
Dive! Dive! Dive! / Riding With The Angels (Live) / Sin City / Black Knight, EMI 12EM151 (1990) (12" single)
Born In '58 / Tattooed Millionaire (Live), EMI EM 185 (1991)
Born In '58 / Tattooed Millionaire (Live) / Son Of A Gun (Live), EMI CDEM 185 (1991) (CD single)
Tears Of The Dragon / Fire Child, EMI EM 322 (1994) 28 UK
Tears Of The Dragon / Elvis Has Left The Building, EMI EMPD 322 (1994) (7" picture disc)
Tears Of The Dragon / Fire Child / Breeding House / No Way Out... To Be Continued, EMI CDEMS 322 (1994) (CD single)
Tears Of The Dragon / Fire Child / Winds Of Change / Spirit Of Joy, EMI CDEM 322 (1994) (CD single)
Shoot All The Clowns / Over And Out, EMI EM 341 (1994) 37 UK
Shoot All The Clowns / Tibet / Tears Of The Dragon: The First Bit.., EMI CDEMS 341 (1994) (CD single)
Shoot All the Clowns / Cadillac Gas Mask / No Way Out - Continued, EMI CDEM 341 (1994) (CD single)
Shoot All The Clowns / Laughing In The Hiding Bush (Live) / The Post Alternative

Seattle Fallout (Live), EMI EM341 (1994) (12" single) **37 UK**
Back From The Edge / I'm In a Band With An Italian Drummer, Rawpower RAW 1012 (1996) **68 UK**
Back From The Edge / Rescue Day / God's Not Coming Back / Armchair Hero, Rawpower RAWX 1013 (1996)
Back From The Edge / R101 / Re-Entry / Americans Are Behind, Rawpower RAWX 1012 (1996)
Accident Of Birth / Ghost Of Cain / Accident Of Birth (Demo version), Rawpower RAWX1042 (1997) (CD single) **54 UK**
Accident Of Birth / Star Children (Demo) / Taking The Queen (Demo), Rawpower RAWX 1045 (1997) (CD single)
Man Of Sorrows (Radio edit - single chorus) / Man Of Sorrows (Radio edit - double chorus) / Man Of Sorrows (Spanish version) / Man Of Sorrows (Spanish edit - single chorus) / Man Of Sorrows (Orchestral version), Rawpower RAWP1046 (1997) (Promotion release)

Albums:
TATTOOED MILLIONAIRE, EMI CDP 79 4 273 2 (1990) **33 SWEDEN, 14 UK**
Son Of A Gun / Tattooed Millionaire / Born In '58 / Hell On Wheels / Gypsy Road / Dive! Dive! Dive! / All The Young Dudes / Lickin' The Gun / Zulu Lulu / No Lies
BALLS TO PICASSO, EMI 7243 8 2968 2 1 (1994) **21 UK**
Cyclops / Hell No / Gods Of War / 1000 Points Of Light / Laughing In The Hiding Bush / Change Of Heart / Fire / Sacred Cowboy / Tears Of A Dragon / Shoot All The Clowns
ALIVE IN STUDIO A (LIVE), Rawpower RAWDC 102 Disc 1 (1995)
Cyclops / Shoot All The Clowns / Son Of A Gun / Tears Of A Dragon / 1,000 Points Of Light / Sacred Cowboys / Tattooed Millionaire / Born In '58 / Fire / Change Of Heart / Hell No / Laughing In The Hiding Bush
A LIVE AT THE MARQUEE CLUB (LIVE), Rawpower RAWDD 102 Disc 2 (1995) (Limited edition CD, free with 'Alive In Studio A' Album)
Cyclops / 1.000 Points Of Light / Born In '58 / Gods Of War / Change Of Heart / Laughing In The Hiding Bush / Hell No / Tears Of The Dragon / Shoot All The Clowns / Sacred Cowboys / Son Of A Gun
SKUNKWORKS, Rawpower PD 106 (1996) **41 UK**
Space Race / Back From The Edge / Inertia / Faith / Solar Confinement / Dreamstate / I Will Not Accept The Truth / Inside The Machine / Fast Garden / Meltdown / Octavia / Innerspace / Strange Death

ACCIDENT OF BIRTH, Rawpower PD 124 (1997) **46 SWEDEN, 53 UK**
The Freak / Toltec 7 Arrival / Star Children / Taking The Queen / Darkside Of Aquarius / Road To Hell / Man Of Sorrows / Accident Of Birth / Magician / Welcome To The Pit / Omega / Arc Of Space
THE CHEMICAL WEDDING, Air Raid AIRCD1 (1998) **31 SWEDEN**
King In Crimson / Chemical Wedding / The Tower / Killing Floor / Book Of Thel / Gates Of Urizen / Jerusalem / Trumpets Of Jericho / Machine Men / The Alchemist
SCREAM FOR ME BRAZIL - LIVE, Air Raid AIR CD4 (1999)
Trumpets Of Jericho / King In Crimson / Chemical Wedding / Gates Of Urizen / Killing Floor / Book Of Thel / Tears Of The Dragon / Laughing In The Hiding Bush / Accident Of Birth / The Tower / Dark Side Of Aquarius / The Road To Hell
THE BEST OF BRUCE DICKINSON, Metal Is (2001) **6 FINLAND, 72 GERMANY, 42 SWEDEN**
Broken / Tattooed Millionaire / Laughing In The Hiding Bush (Live) / Tears Of The Dragon / The Tower / Born In '58 / Accident Of Birth / Silver Wings / Darkside Of Aquarius / Chemical Wedding / Back From The Edge / Road To Hell / Book Of Thel (Live) / Bring Your Daughter To The Slaughter (original version) / Darkness Be My Friend / Wicker Man (original version) / Real World / Acoustic Song / Real World / No Way Out… Continued / Midnight Jam / Man Of Sorrows / Ballad Of Mutt / Re-Entry / I'm In A Band With An Italian Drummer / Jerusalem (Live) / Dracula

DIGITAL RUIN (Providence, RI, USA)
Line-Up: Matt Pacheco (vocals), Joe Sawyer (guitar), Dave Souza (guitar), Michael Keegan (bass), Tim Hart (drums)

Rhode Island Progressively inclined Metal band DIGITAL RUIN was forged during 1988 by the rhythm section of bassist Michael Keegan and drummer Tim Hart. A successive series of line-up changes included the addition of guitarist Joe Sawyer in late 1989. By 1992 the band had stabilised with the induction of singer Matt Pacheco and second guitarist Dave Souza.
The band gained national exposure by being picked as guests for the final leg of DREAM THEATER's 'Wake' tour. During 1995 the group entered the recording studio intending to cut an EP but finally emerged brandishing a full blown album, the Sci-Fi themed 'Listen'. However, shortly after the release of 'Listen' longstanding member Joe Sawyer made his exit. DIGITAL RUIN signed to the German

Progressive Rock label Inside Out Music for the 2000 sophomore opus 'Dwelling In The Out'.

Albums:
LISTEN, Siegen SR0008 (1998)
January 27, 2019 / Of The Hand / Becoming / Pieces Of Me / In The Mirror / The Message / Their Secrets / 3:20 AM / Escape / Within / Listen / It's Only Me / Revelation
DWELLING IN THE OUT, Inside Out Music IOMCD042 (2000)
Living For Yesterday / Darkest Day / Dwelling In The Out / The Forgotten / Adrift / Night Falls Forever / Machine Cage / Letting Go / The Agony Column / Along The Way

DIO (USA)
Line-Up: Ronnie James Dio (vocals), Doug Aldrich (guitar), Jimmy Bain (bass), Scott Warren (keyboards), Simon Wright (drums)

Ronnie James Dio is a man blessed of a quite awesome vocal talent and as such as remained at the very pinnacle of esteem bestowed upon him by the Rock community for two decades and counting. Dio has fronted some of the biggest names in the business most notably BLACK SABBATH and RAINBOW with many citing both bands as enjoying renaissance periods whilst Dio was at the helm.
Dio has always imbued his projects with unfettered medieval romanticism with familiar, some might say overly familiar, imagery such as dragons and rainbows. This trademark lyrical content has been delivered with a majestic vocal range and tone that has made Dio one of the true Rock greats.
Born Ronald Padova the first acts to feel the DIO touch were school outfits such as THE VEGAS KINGS in 1957, RONNIE & THE RUMBLERS and RONNIE & THE RED CAPS. The latter act released a 7" single 'Lover' / 'Conquest' in 1958. The sixties had Dio fronting RONNIE DIO & THE PROPHETS, a band in which he not only sang but played piano, bass and trumpet. THE PROPHETS were to release a string of singles and one album 'Dio at Dominos' on Lawn Records in 1963. In 1967 a fresh project, THE ELECTRIC ELVES (latterly ELF) was forged with Dio's cousin and guitarist David 'Rock' Feinstein.
With ELF Dio began to break into the big league supporting DEEP PURPLE and issuing consistently better albums. Dio's relationship with DEEP PURPLE guitarist RITCHIE BLACKMORE eventually resulted in Dio's all conquering stint with RAINBOW, before an equally lucrative if fraught sojourn

with the mighty BLACK SABBATH. This relationship fostered the titanic albums 'Heaven and Hell' and 'Mob Rules', both records indelibly stamped with Dio's quite staggering vision and succeeding in not only breathing new life into BLACK SABBATH but placing them firmly in renaissance. The BLACK SABBATH tenure was, however to disintegrate in a vicious public airing of grievances and vilification's.

Assembling his new solo vehicle DIO in October of 1982 the singer, keeping his partnership with ex-BLACK SABBATH drummer Vinnie Appice intact, pulled in hotshot Irish ex-SWEET SAVAGE guitarist Vivian Campbell and veteran ex-WILD HORSES and RAINBOW bassist Jimmy Bain. Keyboards were supplied by ex-MAGIC and ROUGH CUTT member Claude Schnell. In his previous outfit Schnell had adopted the stage name of Claude Steel but reverted to his birth name for DIO.

Dio's inaugural post BLACK SABBATH outing the glorious 'Holy Diver' album was a sharp statement of intent and an album of such magnitude it succeeded in carrying many BLACK SABBATH fans along with the new project. Indeed, 'Holy Diver' would be seen by many as more of an example as to the natural evolution of BLACK SABBATH had Dio stayed the course than BLACK SABBATH's own follow up 'Born Again'. As well as delivering an album of world class DIO also aided their cause enormously with an electrifying performance at the annual Donington 'Monster Of Rock' festival.

These shows, illustrating a pattern throughout DIO's career, paid equal homage to Dio's liaisons with BLACK SABBATH and RAINBOW as well as fresher material. These dates also gave an indication of future extravagances with a stage set of mountains based on the album cover.

'The Last In Line' witnessed new heady peaks in Dio's song-writing ability. The world tour found the band backed by an Egyptian theme echoing the album artwork.

During 1984 Dio also added backing vocals to the Australian act HEAVEN's 'Where Angels Fear To Tread' album although for contractual reasons the man was credited simply as "Evil Eyes".

Although 1985's 'Sacred Heart' gave DIO another hit album it was generally recognised that the songs were not up to the standard of its predecessors. A further successful tour ensued, complete with an 18 foot mechanical dragon and a pair of duelling knights, but all was not well within the confines of the band. Obviously disgruntled with an ongoing internal power struggle between himself and Dio the Irish guitarist quit in May of 1986 to form a new act TRINITY with bassist Davy Watson and drummer Pat Waller. He would not be out of the limelight long though and was to enjoy high profile stints in WHITESNAKE and later DEF LEPPARD.

Craig Goldy, an associate of DIO's from his time in the Wendy Dio managed ROUGH CUTT, was recruited from DRIVER. Since leaving ROUGH CUTT the guitarist had been involved with GIUFFRIA's successful first album and subsequent tour.

Locked into a gruelling seemingly endless touring situation the band put forward the idea for a full blown DIO live album to keep the momentum flowing. DIO's American record company Warner Bros. rejected the plan flat and so a compromise was reached in the stopgap mini-album 'Intermission' featuring mainly live tracks bolstered by one new studio cut 'Time To Burn'.

With Goldy's recruitment DIO seemingly appeared to be losing ground and creatively treading water.

'Dream Evil' heralded Schnell's admission as a full time band member, the keyboard player appearing onstage for the first time rather than in the wings. Touring commenced with a showing at a Los Angeles 'Children Of The night' charity event before a special guest appearance at the 'Monsters Of Rock' festival second on the bill to BON JOVI reminding one and all that DIO was very much still a force to be reckoned with. The lavish stage production for the headline dates had the singer battling with not only a dragon but a huge mechanical spider. The tour was not without incident though as, whilst travelling in Europe, the band's bus was involved in a multi vehicle pile up.

DIO also achieved a rare honour of performing in China along with YNGWIE MALMSTEEN for 'Shanghai Aid'.

After the world tour DIO effectively splintered. During July of 1988 Bain stepped into the breach to aid CINDERELLA for their tour when Eric Brittingham had to attend to his new born baby.

Bain and Appice would then forge a new muscular Metal act WWIII for one over the top album fronted by Mandy Lion with guitars from Tracy G.

Following his CRAIG GOLDY'S RITUAL project album Goldy would found HARD LUCK in 1992 with ex-ALIEN, FOUR HORSEMEN and BONE ANGEL singer Frank Starr, guitarist Tim Propearcy, ex –KILLERWATT, STEVE JONES and BONE ANGEL bassist Terry Nails and drummer Mark Bistany.

July 1989 was to provide the announcement that Dio had found his replacement for Goldie in the form of the fresh faced 17 year old

British guitarist Rowan Robertson. Dio had deferred for quite some time on Robertson, then a member of his own act SHOOT THE MOON, due to his tender years but eventually announced his recruitment.

Longstanding ally Appice departed just weeks before recording of a new album and in his stead came former TYTAN and AC/DC drummer Simon Wright. The same year DIO added New York based former HOTSHOT bassist Teddy Cook and former YNGWIE MALMSTEEN colleague keyboard player Jens Johansson, the latter drafted after the parting of ways with Claude Schnell. DIO debuted his new look band at the small Oliver's Pub in New York in July 1989.

Supporting the 'Lock Up The Wolves' album DIO gained the valuable guest spot on METALLICA's European tour on a bill that also included WARRIOR SOUL and BONHAM prior to British headline shows with openers TROUBLE. In August of 1990 the vocalist's erstwhile BLACK SABBATH cohort bassist Geezer Butler appeared as guest onstage in Minneapolis. It was a portent of what was to come.

1991 saw Dio succumbing to the temptation of a BLACK SABBATH reunion as Johansson found fresh employment with noted Finns STRATOVARIUS. During Dio's BLACK SABBATH interlude Wright joined UFO. Robertson formed the short-lived FREEDOM with LYNCH MOB vocalist Oni Logan and TRIANGLE drummer Jimmy Paxson. The guitarist would later be found with his own act VIOLET'S DEMISE before joining V.A.S.T. for their 'Music For The People' album. Teddy Cook joined CHINA RAIN before enlistment into the ranks of GREAT WHITE in 1992, VIRGIN STEELE, RONDINELLI and THE SIGN.

The resulting BLACK SABBATH album 'Dehumaniser' was a patchy affair with few songs making the grade achieved by the illustrious early eighties predecessors but the subsequent tour had both Dio and BLACK SABBATH back on track. Predictably it was to end on a sour note. BLACK SABBATH's management agreed to a brace of shows as guests to OZZY OSBOURNE. Playing second fiddle to Osbourne was anathema to Dio who promptly announced he would not undertake the shows. Dio remained steadfast in his refusal to perform the shows and the resulting stalemate forced his departure once more. SABBATH went ahead with the shows using the guest talents of former JUDAS PRIEST vocalist Rob Halford.

The vocalist had soon re-founded DIO with Appice and Bain in November of 1992. The errant bassist was soon forced out again though. Unfounded rumours also suggested the singer was part of a project titled VIENNA involving guitarist STEVE VAI and veteran drummer COZY POWELL. If true, the act never materialised.

The 1993 album 'Strange Highways' found DOKKEN man Jeff Pilson on bass and Appice's ex-WWIII colleague guitarist Tracy G (real name Grijalva) in the fold. The Japanese version of the album featured an exclusive cut 'God Hates Heavy Metal'.

Pilson had to opt out of touring as the reformed DOKKEN were getting into gear and Larry Dennison took the bass slot. However, with DOKKEN's fortunes as tumultuous as ever Pilson returned in November of 1994. Bassist Jerry Best, previously with LION and FREAK OF NATURE, joined DIO in August of 1995 for a little over a month but Pilson resumed the role.

For the 1996 DIO album 'Angry Machines' Dio utilised the on loan talents of Jeff Pilson guitarist Tracy G once more. Employed on keyboards was ex-KEEL man Scott Warren. (The album track 'Stay Out Of My Mind' would later resurface on Pilson's WAR AND PEACE 2001 album 'The Light At The End Of The World').

DIO, with Larry Dennison taking over on bass again, set about a mammoth world tour to revive the band's fortunes touring in America and Europe co-headlining with MOTÖRHEAD prior to American headliners with support from MY DYING BRIDE. Following these dates Warren hooked up with WARRANT for their American tour and would later session Pop Rockers BERLIN as an aside to DIO.

Appice and G undertook negotiations with the UFO pairing of vocalist Phil Mogg and bassist PETE WAY to create a new version of UFO. Contractually the new act could not be titled UFO minus guitarist Michael Schenker so the legalities put paid to this venture.

DIO's 1997-98 tour promoting the double live album 'Dio's Inferno' hit problems with Appice soon being forced out through ill health, the drummer contracting pneumonia. KINGDOM COME and SCORPIONS drummer James Kottak took over the reins until Appice resumed fitness. Pilson also made a return for the South American leg of the tour after which Dennison was back in position.

Late 1998 found DIO opening for MOTÖRHEAD in Scandinavia backing up the release of a double live album. Unable to make these date due to prior commitments Dennison did not appear and in October the veteran ex-OZZY OSBOURNE, URIAH HEEP, RAINBOW and MOTHERS ARMY man Bob Daisley filled the gap. Vinnie Appice also left the fold to rejoin BLACK SABBATH then create his own HUNGER FARM and previous incumbent Simon Wright was re-enlisted.

During 1999 Craig Goldy made a return to the band in time for appearances at European festivals. DIO was then linked to speculations regarding a classic RAINBOW reunion apparently involving guitarist RITCHIE BLACKMORE, drummer COZY POWELL and Jimmy Bain. Despite Dio himself stating he would not be averse to such a move any such moves were crushed with the death of Powell in a car crash.

The millennium was rounded off nicely for Ronnie with the release of an album 'Holy Dio', a worthy collection of name acts offering tribute including YNGWIE MALMSTEEN, HAMMERFALL, STRATOVARIUS, etc.

2000 found DIO full steam ahead with the 'Magica' album, a Sci-Fi conceptual record that had many critics announcing a return to former glories. The album climaxed with an 18 minute spoken narration by Ronnie. Both Bain and Wright returned to their former positions. DIO went back out onto the road on a strong double billing in Europe with DEEP PURPLE, these shows providing an opportunity to witness Dio with the headline acts' bassist ROGER GLOVER performing a track from their 'Butterfly Ball' album.

Joining the band for these dates was former L.A. GUNS and BEAUTIFUL CREATURES bassist Chuck Garrick. The new four stringer's stay was fleeting and he was soon back in Los Angeles with KILLOWATT.

In 2001 DIO veterans Tracy G and Larry Dennison would re-emerge with his new project DRIVEN. This new unit, which released their debut in September, would see the involvement of vocalist Tim Saxton and pedigree drummer Mike Terrana of RAGE, YNGWIE MALMSTEEN and ARTENSION amongst others.

DIO, with Bain reinstated, joined forces with YNGWIE MALMSTEEN and DORO for a November American tour prior to a guest slot in May opening for ALICE COOPER in the UK. European shows, billed as the 'Monsters Of The Millennium' festivals, saw RATT included on the billing. Dates in South Africa would also be projected although with Goldy unable to make these shows former guitarist Rowan Robertson, currently a member of Pop Rock band AM RADIO, deputised for rehearsals. The gigs, planned for October, would be shelved after the September 11th terrorist attacks. Robertson got back to work on his VIOLETS DEMISE project, a union with erstwhile LYNCH MOB frontman Oni Logan.

As 2002 broke it emerged that erstwhile LION, BAD MOON RISING and HOUSE OF LORDS guitarist DOUG ALDRICH had taken Goldy's place in time for recording of a fresh studio album 'Killing The Dragon'. The record debuted at no. 199 on the Billboard album charts as DIO geared up for a high profile run of American arena dates packaged with SCORPIONS and DEEP PURPLE.

A lavish Bill Schacht directed video for the single 'Push' would include appearances from the unlikely TENACIOUS D duo of Jack Black and Kyle Gass. TENACIOUS D had already signalled their respect for the band with the inclusion of the track 'Dio' on their current album. The video concept, in which a multitude of special effects would be employed, involved TENACIOUS D jamming BLACK SABBATH's 'Heaven And Hell' as an intro. With interest in DIO at a renewed high, Spitfire Records re-issued the 'Killing The Dragon' album in September. This revised version contained two tracks 'Fever Dreams' and 'Rainbow In The Dark', both recorded live at the Ahoy in Rotterdam, Holland on the DIO / DEEP PURPLE Concerto tour and featuring guesting members of DEEP PURPLE.

DIO set out for a further round of North American headline dates throughout the winter supported by rising Swedish Metal revivalists HAMMERFALL and the esteemed KINGS X.

Holy Diver / Evil Eyes, Vertigo DIO 1 (1983) (7" single) **72 UK**

Holy Diver / Evil Eyes / Don't Talk To Strangers, Mercury DIO 1-12 (1983) (12" single)

Rainbow In The Dark / Stand Up And Shout (Live), Vertigo DIO 2 (1983) (7" single) **46 UK**

Rainbow In The Dark / Stand Up And Shout (Live) / Straight Through The Heart (Live), Mercury DIO 2-12 (1983) (12" single)

Rainbow In The Dark / Holy Diver / Evil Eyes / Stand Up And Shout (Live) / Straight Through The Heart (Live), Mercury 15PP41 (1983) (Japanese release)

Rainbow In The Dark / Gypsy, Warner Bros. 29527 (1983) (USA release)

We Rock / Holy Diver (Live), Vertigo DIO 3 (1984) (7" single) **42 UK**

We Rock / Holy Diver (Live) / Rainbow In The Dark (Live), Vertigo DIO 3-12 (1984) (12" single)

We Rock / Breathless, Mercury (1984) (USA promotion)

Mystery / Eat Your Heart Out (Live), Vertigo DIO 4 (1984) **34 UK**

Mystery / Eat Your Heart Out (Live) / Don't Talk To Strangers (Live), Vertigo DIO 4-12 (1984) (12" single)

Mystery / We Rock/ Eat Your Heart Out (Live) / Don't Talk To Strangers (Live), Vertigo 15PP45 (1984) (Japanese release)

Mystery / We Speed At Night, Warner Bros. 29183 (1984) (USA release)

Rock n' Roll Children / We Rock (Live), Vertigo DIO 5 (1985) (7" single)

Rock n' Roll Children / Sacred Heart / We Rock (Live) / The Last In Line (Live), Vertigo DIO 5-12 (1985) (12" single)

Rock n' Roll Children / We Rock (Live) / The Last In Line (Live), Vertigo DIOW 5-12 (1985) (White vinyl 12" single)

Hungry For Heaven / Holy Diver (Live), Vertigo DIO 6 (1985) (7" single) **72 UK**

Hungry For Heaven / Holy Diver (Live) / Rainbow In The Dark (Live), Vertigo DIO 6-12 (1985) (12' single)

Hungry For Heaven / Holy Diver (Live) / Rainbow In The Dark (Live), Vertigo DIOW 6-12 (1985) (White vinyl 12" single)

We Rock (Live) / Holy Diver (Live) / Like The Beat Of A Heart (Live), Warner Bros. (1985) (USA promotion)

King Of Rock n' Roll / Sacred Heart, Vertigo (1985)

Hide In The Rainbow / Hungry For Heaven / Shame On The Night / Egypt (The Chains Are On), Vertigo DIO 712 (1986) **56 UK**

Stand Up And Shout, Crash (1986) (Free split flexi with ACCEPT for 'Crash' magazine)

Night People / Sunset Superman, Vertigo (1987) (Promotion)

I Could Have Been A Dreamer / Night People, Vertigo DIO 8 (1987) (7" single) **69 UK**

I Could Have Been A Dreamer / Night People / Sunset Superman, Vertigo DIO 8-12 (1987) (12" single)

I Could Have Been A Dreamer / Overlove, Warner Bros. (1987) (USA release)

All The Fools Sailed Away / Overlove, Vertigo (1987)

When A Woman Cries (LP version) / When A Woman Cries (Edit), Mercury (1987) (USA promotion)

Hey Angel / Walk On Water, Vertigo DIO 9 (1990) (7" single)

Hey Angel / Walk On Water / Rock n' Roll Children / Mystery, Vertigo DIO 9-12 (1990) (12" single)

Hey Angel / Walk On Water / We Rock / Why Are They Watching Me, Vertigo DIOP 9-12 (1990) (12' picture disc single)

Hey Angel / Walk On Water / Rock n' Roll Children / We Rock, Vertigo DIOCD 9 (1990) (CD single)

Albums:

HOLY DIVER, Vertigo VERS 5 (1983) **18 SWEDEN, 13 UK, 56 USA**
Stand Up And Shout / Holy Diver / Gypsy / Caught In The Middle / Don't Talk To Strangers / Straight Through The Heart / Invisible / Rainbow In The Dark / Shame On

The Night

LAST IN LINE, Vertigo VERL 16 (1984) **6 SWEDEN, 4 UK, 23 USA**
We Rock / The Last In Line / Breathless / I Speed At Night / One Night In The City / Evil Eyes / Mystery / Eat Your Heart Out / Egypt (The Chains Are On)

SACRED HEART, Vertigo 834 848-2 (1985) **6 SWEDEN, 4 UK, 29 USA**
King Of Rock n' Roll / Sacred Heart / Another Lie / Rock n' Roll Children / Hungry For Heaven / Like The Beat Of A Heart / Just Another Day / Fallen Angels / Shoot Shoot

INTERMISSION, Vertigo VERB 40 (1986) **22 UK, 70 USA**
King Of Rock n' Roll (Live) / Rainbow In The Dark (Live) / Sacred Heart (Live) / Time To Burn / Rock n' Roll Children (Live) (incl. Long Live Rock n' Roll / Man On The Silver Mountain / We Rock)

DREAM EVIL, Vertigo 832 530-2 (1987) **4 SWEDEN, 8 UK, 43 USA**
Night People / Dream Evil / Sunset Superman / All The Fools Sailed Away / Naked In The Rain / Overlove / I Could Have Been A Dreamer / Faces In The Window / When A Woman Cries

LOCK UP THE WOLVES, Vertigo 846 033-2 (1990) **23 SWEDEN, 28 UK, 61 USA**
Wild One / Hey Angel / Between Two Hearts / Night Music / Lock Up The Wolves / Evil On Queen Street / Walk On Water / Born On The Sun / Twisted / My Eyes

DIAMONDS - THE BEST OF DIO, Vertigo 512206-2 (1992)
Holy Diver / Rainbow In The Dark / Don't Talk To Strangers / We Rock / The Last In Line / Rock n' Roll Children / Sacred Heart / Hungry For Heaven / Hide In The Rainbow / Dream Evil / Wild One / Lock Up The Wolves

STRANGE HIGHWAYS, Vertigo 518486-2 (1993)
Jesus, Mary And The Holy Ghost / Fire Head / Strange Highways / Hollywood Black / Evilution / Pain / One Foot In The Grave / Give Her The Gun / Blood From A Stone / Here's To You / Bring Down The Rain

ANGRY MACHINES, SPV Steamhammer 085-18292 CD (1996)
Institutional Man / Don't Tell The Kids / Black / Hunter Of The Heart / Stay Out Of My Mind / Big Sister / Double Monday / Golden Rules / Dying In America / This Is Your Life

ANTHOLOGY, Connoisseur Collection VSOPCD245 (1997)

DIO'S INFERNO - LAST IN LIVE, SPV Steamhammer 085-18842 (1998)
Intro / Jesus, Mary And The Holy Ghost / Straight Through The Heart / Don't Talk To Strangers / Holy Diver/ Drum Solo / Heaven And Hell / Double Monday / Stand Up And Shout / Hunter Of The Heart / Mistreated /

Guitar Solo / The Last In Line / Rainbow In The Dark / Mob Rules / Man On The Silver Mountain / Long Live Rock n' Roll / We Rock

MAGICA, Spitfire15020 (2000)

40 GERMANY, 52 SWEDEN

Discovery / Magica Theme / Lord Of The Last Day / Fever Dreams / Turn To Stone / Feed My Head / Ebeil / Challis / As Long As It's Not Love / Losing My Insanity / Otherworld / Magica / Lord Of The Last Day / Magica Story

KILLING THE DRAGON, SPV (2002)

30 GERMANY, 24 SWEDEN, 199 USA

Killing The Dragon / Along Came A Spider / Scream / Better In The Dark / Rock And Roll / Push / Guilty / Throwaway Children / Before The Fall / Cold Feet

DIONYSUS (GERMANY / SWEDEN)

Line-Up: Olaf Hayer (vocals), Johnny Öhlin (guitar), Magnus Noberg (bass), Kaspar Dahlqvist (keyboards), Ronny Milianowicz (drums)

A German / Swedish symphonic styled Metal collaboration with a rich tradition of talent. DIONYSUS was created in 1999 after drummer Ronny Milianowicz made his exit from SINERGY just having completed a Japanese tour that year. Milianowicz also boasts stints with FALCON, R.A.M.P. and SATURNINE. The man also figured on HAMMERFALL's 'Legacy Of Kings' album as a backing vocalist and has been endeavouring to forge a Rock Opera venture with HAMMERFALL's Joacim Cans.

DIONYSUS lead vocalist Olaf Hayer has a tradition stretching back through bands such as CHRYZTYNE, TREASURE SEEKER and LORD BYRON. Hayer also made his mark lending vocals to LUCA TURILLI's solo works. Keyboard player Kaspar Dahlqvist cites credits with TREASURELAND, STORMWIND and SAHARA. Guitarist Johnny Öhlin and bassist Magnus 'Nobby' Noberg operate as active members of NATION.

DIONYSUS distributed a demo entitled 'Paradise Land', soon landing a deal with the German AFM label. The debut album, at first dubbed 'Sign Of Truth' but later switched to 'Bringer Of Salvation', was produced by Tobias Sammet of EDGUY and AVANTASIA fame.

Albums:

BRINGER OF SALVATION, AFM (2002)

DISARM GOLIATH (UK)

Line-Up: Steve Surch (vocals / bass), Ben Oakley (guitar), Karl Wade (drums)

DIONYSUS

Wolverhampton Power trio bucked the trends by sticking to tried and trusted Heavy Metal formula for their 1999 self-financed mini-album 'No Moon, No Power'. It would appear the album saw a re-release in 2001 newly titled 'Only The Devil Can Stop Us'.

Albums:
NO MOON, NO POWER, (1999)
No Moon, No Power / Armed To The Teeth / Candle To The Devil / Serpents Illusion / Snake In The Grass / Arm The Gods / By Hook Or By Crook / Look On The Darkside / Pleased To Eat You / Evil Has A New Name

DIVIDING HORIZONS (GERMANY)
Line-Up: Matthias Pfaff (vocals), Steffen Krüchten (guitar), Dietmar Kalmann (bass), Jörg Enke (keyboards), Mike Fuenter (drums)

Albums:
SEIZURE, (1994)
Alone / Second Sunrise / Domination / Remembrance / Soul Trap / Deep Within A Sigh / Always & Forever

DIVINE REGALE (Dover, NH, USA)
Line-Up: Dwight Hill (vocals), Daniel Elliott (guitar), Gary Leighton (guitar), Frank Couture (bass), Jason Keazer (keyboards), Chris Anderson (drums)

Christian Progressive Metal act debuted with the 'Horizons' mini-album. The band line-up for this outing comprised lead vocalist Dwight Hill, guitarists Daniel Elliott and Gary Leighton, bass player Shawn Marcotte, keyboard player Jason Keazer and drummer Chris Anderson.

Securing a deal with the Metal Blade label, and swapping Marcotte on bass for Frank Couture, the band issued the commendable 'Ocean Mind' album, supporting by North American touring as support to FATES WARNING. In February of 1999 DIVINE REGALE parted ways with vocalist Dwight Hill.

Albums:
HORIZONS, Whin Chin Chin Productions (1994)
Dawn / Horizon / Underworld / Missing / Fear The Storm
OCEAN MIND, Metal Blade 1984-1-4132-2 (1997)
Ocean Mind / Change? / Shadowed Words Forgotten / No Part Of This / Leaves / Horizon / Cry To Heaven / Underworld / Forever Changing Winds

THE DOGMA (ITALY)

Albums:
SYMPHONIES OF LOVE AND HATE, (2002)
Dark Winter / The Return / Paradise / Shades Of The Night / Breaking My Heart / The Last Drop Of Blood / The Bringer Of The Light

DOMINE (ITALY)
Line-Up: Morby (vocals), Enrico Pauli (guitar), Riccardo Paoli (bass), Riccardo Lacono (keyboards), Stefano Bonini (drums)

Florence based DOMINE proudly form part of the European retro trad Metal movement. The band bowed in with an eponymous four track demo with a band unit comprising vocalist Stefano Mazzella, guitar players Enrico Paoli and Agostino Carpo, bassist Riccardo Paoli and drummer Carlo "Funa" Funaioli. This line-up remained stable for the follow up demo sessions, 1989's 'Champion Eternal' and the 1991 cassette 'Bearer Of The Sword'. However, with a promotional tape issued in 1994 DOMINE had switched frontmen to Simone Gazzola and second guitarist Carpo had left the ranks.

Drummer Mimmo Palmiotta, formerly with the cult band DEATH SS, was enrolled for the 1997 debut album 'Champion Eternal'. DOMINE once again found themselves with a new vocalist as Morby stepped into the role. Palmiotta appeared on the ambitiously sprawling 'Dragonlord' sophomore outing but would be superseded by Stefano Bonini. The record, which included an ambitious seven part suite entitled 'The Battle For The Great Silver Sword', found a ready market in Europe and would be taken up for license in the United States by Metal Blade Records. Japanese versions of the album would come with an exclusive track, a version of QUEENSRYCHE's 'Queen Of The Reich'.

DOMINE toured Germany in early 2000 as opening act on the RIOT / ANVIL / AGENT STEEL package tour. The band would also prove industrious on the festival circuit throughout the summer with appearances at the 'Metal Gladiators 2000' event alongside GAMMA RAY and FREEDOM CALL and the 'Powermad' festival headlined by RUNNING WILD and GRAVE DIGGER.

A new album 'Stormbringer Ruler' emerged in October 2001. Japanese copies added an exclusive track, a version of the RAINBOW classic 'Stargazer'.

Albums:
CHAMPION ETERNAL, Dragonheart CHAOS 001CD (1997)
Hymn / The Mass Of Chaos / The Chronicles

Of The Black Sword - Part 1: Doomed Lord Dreaming, Part 2: Stormbringer (The Black Sword) / The Freedom Flight / Army Of The Dead (A Suite In 5 Parts) - Part 1: The Vision And The promise, Part 2: Promise Denied, Part 3: Prophecy Fulfilled, Part 4: Army Of The Dead, Part 5: Doomed City / The Proclamation / Dark Emperor / Rising From The Flames / The Midnight Meat Train / The Eternal Champion (A Suite In 7 Parts) - Part 1: Prologue, Part 2: Screaming The Battlecry, Part 3: Blow By Blow (Into The Flight), Part 4: Death Of The Champion, Part 5: Heroes In Tears, Part 6: Destiny Revealed, Part 7: Epilogue

DRAGONHEART (TALES OF THE NOBLE STEEL), Dragonheart CHAOS 007 (1999)
Anthem (A Declaration Of War) / Thunderstorm / Last Of The Dragonlords (Lord Elric's Imperial March) / Blood Brothers' Fight / Defenders / Mars, The Bringer Of War / Dragonlord (The Grand Master Of The Mightiest Beasts) / Uriel, The Flame Of God / The Ship Of The Lost Souls / The Battle For The Great Silver Sword (A Suite In VII Parts, Opera III) - i) Overture - The Dawn Of Steel / The Battle For The Great Silver Sword - ii) The Pipes Of War / The Battle For The Great Silver Sword- iii) The Sacrifice Chant / The Battle For The Great Silver Sword - iv) War / The Battle For The Great Silver Sword - v) Sword Fight / The Battle For The Great Silver Sword - vi) The Sword Is Broken / The Battle For The Great Silver Sword - vii) Finale - The Sunset Of Steel

STORMBRINGER RULER – THE LEGEND OF THE POWER SUPREME, Dragonheart (2001)
The Legend Of The Power Supreme (Intro) / The Hurricane Master / Horn Of Fate - (The Chronicles Of The Black Sword – The End Of An Era Part 2) / The Ride Of The Valkyries / True Leader Of Men / The Bearer Of The Black Sword (The Chronicles Of The Black Sword – The End Of An Era Part 1) / The Fall Of The Spiral Tower / For Evermore (The Chronicles Of The Black Sword – The End Of An Era Part 3) / Dawn Of A New Day – A Celtic Requiem (The Chronicles Of The Black Sword – The End Of An Era Part 4)

DOMINUS PRAELLI (BRAZIL)
Line-Up: Ricardo Pigatto (vocals), Silvio Rocha (guitar), Evandro Romero (guitar), Rene Warrior (bass), Rafael Guilhen (drums)

Heavy Metal band DOMINUS PRAELII was forged during 2000 by guitarist Silvio Rocha and Rafael Guilhen on drums, both former colleagues in acts such as PREDATOR, MURDER and PSICODEATH. They would

later be joined by ex-PEACEFUL TOMB bassist Rene Warrior, the band being completed by vocalist Ricardo Pigatto and guitarist Evandro Romero. A demo, 'The First Battle', preceded the band's signature with Megahard Records for the debut album 'Holding The Flag Of War'.

Albums:
HOLDING THE FLAG OF WAR, Megahard (2001)
Hard Deadly Wheels / Scent Of Death / Khan´s Warriors / Khan´s Legacy / Cold Winds / Knight Of The Silver Moon / Saga Of Killing Riders / Hall Of Power / Waves Of War

DONOR (HOLLAND)
Line-Up: Ard van Bers (vocals), Bart Vreken (guitar), Jelle Bakker (guitar), Cees van Petten (bass), Toni van Petten (drums)

DONOR, who deal in technical Progressive Metal with high ranging vocals, first featured on the compilation album 'Metal In Rocks Volume Two' in 1989 and then released a demo tape entitled 'Inexplicable Knowledge' before signing to Mausoleum and touring stints with NAPALM DEATH and ARTILLERY. The debut self-produced album 'Triangle Of The Lost' embodied demo material plus newly recorded songs. Gigs followed with PSYCHOTIC WALTZ before vocalist Ard van Bers quit. For 1994's 'Release' the band were fronted by Richard Dijkman.
DONOR guitarist Jelle Bakker went on to enjoy a diverse career with the highly rated FROZEN SUN before joining high profile Gothic act WITHIN TEMPTATION. By late 2002 Bakker was touting a Hip Hop Crossover act CHEN MO.

Albums:
TRIANGLE OF THE LOST, Mausoleum 904007-2 (1993)
Relatives Of The Dreamtime / Cimmerian Darkness / Triumph Fires / When The Valkyries Ride / Triangle Of The Lost / The Pendulum / An Invasion Somewhere / Siren Voices / They Rode By Night / In The Hours Of Tragedy
RELEASE, Mausoleum 904025-2 (1994)
Portrayal / Prejudice Judge / Void / Hidden Truth / Blind / Whispering Waves / Swallowed / Release / Crossing Fields / Blessed By Sorrow

DOOMSWORD (ITALY)
Line-Up: Nightcomer (vocals), Deathmaster (vocals / guitar), Guardian Angel (guitar), Dark Omen (bass), Wrath Lord (drums)

A deliberately retro '80s style Doom Power Metal band conceived as a side project of AGARTHI's Deathmaster during 1997. Previous to AGARTHI Deathmaster had been involved with Progressive Rock outfit ARKHE and WARHAMMER. Initially conceived as a medieval based venture billed as 1014 A.D. Deathmaster, together with ex-WARHAMMER colleague guitarist / drummer Guardian Angel, would soon steer their operations into classically inspired majestic Metal and re-dubbed their union DOOMSWORD.

A 5 track demo 'Sacred Metal' was cut utilising bassist Soldier of Fortune. However, when AGARTHI split Deathmaster was free to pursue DOOMSWORD as a full time occupation and enrolled ex-AGARTHI bassist Dark Omen into the fold. DOOMSWORD would be completed with the addition of vocalist Nightcomer, a member of Prog Rock act MADRIGAL.

Session lead guitar solos for a number of tracks on the 'Doomsword' debut came courtesy of Gianluca Ferro of ARKHE. Other contributing guitarists included Alex Festa and Paco Trotta. The album included a cover version CIRITH UNGOL's 'Nadsokar'.

Following the album release both Guardian Angel and Nightcomer decamped, the latter in order to concentrate on his Progressive band FURY AND GRACE. The band replaced Guardian Angel with (naturally) Guardian Angel II and Deathmaster took over the lead vocal role.

Later in 1999 DOOMSWORD would record a rendition of WARLORD's 'Lucifer's Hammer' for a tribute album.

The DOOMSWORD line-up for the June 2002 album 'Resound The Horn' stood at vocalist Deathmaster, guitarists Guardian Angel II and The Forger, bassist Dark Omen and ANCIENT drummer Grom. DOOMSWORD members also operate in FIURACH. This relationship was tightened in September as Wrath Lord of FIURACH joined DOOMSWORD on the drum stool.

Albums:
DOOMSWORD, Underground Symphony USCD033 (1999)
Sacred Metal / Warbringers / Helms Deep / One Eyed God / Return To Imrryr / Nadsokar / Swords Of Doom / On The March
RESOUND THE HORN, Dragonheart (2002)
Shores Of Vinland / Onward To Battle / The DoomSword / MCXIX / The Early Days Of Finn MacCool / Resound The Horn: Odin's Hail /

DOUBLE DIAMOND (BELGIUM)
Line-Up: Filip Lemmens (vocals), Erwin Suetens (guitar), Tom van Steenbergen (guitar), Marc Vinckier (bass), Jack Franken (drums)

Belgian Heavy Metal band DOUBLE DIAMOND marked their arrival with a three track 1990 demo tape 'Reflections'. A follow up promotional session, the five track 'Behind Your Eyes', was offered up in 1992. The 'Live In Turnhout' album amply displayed the band's influences as alongside original compositions DOUBLE DIAMOND blasted through renditions of JUDAS PRIEST's 'Victim Of Changes', IRON MAIDEN's 'Number Of The Beast', BLACK SABBATH's 'Paranoid' as well as an AC/DC medley. DOUBLE DIAMOND had the good fortune to have their 'In Danger' album produced by former SCORPIONS drummer Rudy Lenners. The band supported HAMMERFALL on their dates through the Low Countries during 1998 and subsequently opened for both OVERKILL and ANNIHILATOR. The group also co-headlined dates with Brazilian Speed Metal band STEEL WARRIORS in 2001.

The band shared a split 12" single 'Conquer With Steel' with AFTER ALL in February of 2002. With the entire stock selling out in less than a week the EP would be re-pressed in picture disc format.

Singles/EPs:
Conquer With Steel / Metal Rules, Steelhunter (2002) (Split 12" single with AFTER ALL)

Albums:
LIVE IN TURNHOUT, (1996)
The Law Of The Runes / Victim Of Changes / White Dead (Insanity) / Something Out There / Another Sleepless Night / Operation Desert Storm / The Number Of The Beast / Let The Rider Decide / AC/DC medley / Paranoid
IN DANGER, (1997)
Operation Desert Storm / Anubis / Crime Of Passion / The Law Of The Runes / Another Sleepless Night / In Danger / White Dead (Insanity) / Shadow Of The World / Something's Out There / Let The Rider Decide / Regrets

DRACONIAN (GERMANY)
Line-Up: Mathias Edelmann (vocals), Frank Fuchs (guitar), Volker Zimmermann (guitar), Markus Pachner (bass), Frank Schneider (drums)

Metal band DRACONIAN came into being

during mid 1995. The group was founded upon the trio of guitarist Frank Fuchs, bassist Markus Pachner and drummer Frank Schneider, being augmented by second guitarist Jens Lachner in the Autumn of 1996 and singer Markus Rapp some two years later. A four track promotional CD 'Awakening Of The Dragon' was recorded in 1999. By 2001 DRACONIAN was brandishing a revised line-up that saw Mathias Edelmann in command of vocals and Volker Zimmermann on guitar.

Singles/EPs:
Shadows / Far Away / This Could Be Love / Celebrated Killer, (2000) ('Awakening Of The Dragon' EP)

DRACONIAN (SPAIN)
Line-Up: Guillermo D. Prados (vocals / bass), Francisco J. Ruiz (guitar), Antonio Cano (guitar), Antonio Cano Gonzales (keyboards), José Antonio Ferrer (drums)

Singer Guillermo D. Prados has a tradition fronting acts such as TWILIGHT, RANGERS and WASTELAND. Guitarist Antonio Cano was previously with ASIRIA and LEGACY whilst second guitarist Francisco J. Ruiz was with Death Metal band AGONIZE. Drummer José Antonio Ferrer occupied the same position with ROCKANGULAR. The band's keyboard player Antonio Cano Gonzales has held down roles in OSCURO, DUCATI and SILENCIO.

Albums:
TO OUTLIVE THE WAR, (2001)
Intro - To Outlive The War / Dracon Metal / Siren's Song / Don't Give Up / Words & Memories / Out Of Control / Indecision / The Eyes Of The Rain / I'll Never Leave You / Sequences / Forever I'll Be Free / The Mandate Of Heaven

DRAGONFORCE (UK)
Line-Up: Z.P. Theart (vocals), Herman Li (guitar), Sam Totman (guitar), Steve Scott (bass), Steve Williams (keyboards)

London based Power Metal band for much of their early career known as DRAGONHEART. The band became operational during 1999 but upfront of signing to the Sanctuary label the band switched to DRAGONFORCE due to the plethora of acts brandishing similar titles.
For the band's first rehearsals in October of 1999 DRAGONHEART employed a cast of Z.P. Theart on vocals, guitarists Herman 'Shred' Li and Sam Totman, both members of

uprooted New Zealand Black Metal act DEMONIAC, New Zealand born bass player Steve Scott and Matej Setinc of DEMONIAC on the drums. With Setinc's departure Peter Hunt briefly occupied the drum stool and the group also enrolled former DOG DAY SUNRISE keyboard player Steve Williams.
A demo entitled 'Valley Of The Damned' surfaced in June of 2000. These recordings would have the distinction of being produced by Karl Groom of THRESHOLD with Clive Nolan of PENDRAGON repute adding keyboard touches. DRAGONHEART bassist Steve Scott would join competitors SHADOWKEEP during 2000. Diccon Harper, previously a member of PHOENIX filled the vacancy that November. The band, brandishing an all new line-up, Williams having made his exit, supported both HALFORD and STRATOVARIUS in December of 2001. For these shows Vadim came in as the new keyboard player for the HALFORD gigs with just two days notice. Meantime Steve Williams forged the Symphonic Metal act POWER QUEST, pulling in not only former DRAGONFORCE bassist Steve Scott but also drawing into the fold Sam Totman, the guitarist maintaining a foot in both camps, and personnel from Italian Metal band ARTHEMIS.
Harper decamped in March of 2002. The recent DRAGONFORCE line-up comprised vocalist Z.P. Theart, guitarists Herman Li and Sam Totman, keyboard player Vadim and drummer Didier.

Albums:
VALLEY OF THE DAMNED, Sanctuary (2003)

DRAGON HAMMER (ITALY)
Line-Up: Max Aguzzi (vocals /guitar), Gae Amodio (bass), Alex Valdambrini (keyboards) Raf Condemi (drums)

The band issued a self financed album in 1999 entitled 'Age Of Glory', the group at this point being a trio of vocalist / guitarist Max Aguzzi, bassist Gae Amodio and drummer Marino Deyana. The DRAGON HAMMER line-up for the recording of the 2001 album 'Blood Of The Dragon' stood at Max Aguzzi, Gae Amodio, keyboard player Alex Valdambrini and drummer Milko Morelli.
DRAGON HAMMER, having enrolled new drummer Raf Condemi, signed to Scarlet Records for a projected 2003 album.

Albums:
AGE OF GLORY, (1999)
THE BLOOD OF THE DRAGON, Legend

Music (2001)
Legend / It's War / Dragon Hammer / Age Of Glory / Scream / You Kill (Fortuna In Battaglia) / Black Sword / Fire / Blood In The Sky / In Your Eyes

DRAGON HEART (BRAZIL)
Line-Up: Eduardo Marques (vocals / guitar), Marco Caporasso (guitar), Maurício Taborda (bass), Marcelo Caporasso (drums)

Curitiba based Euro style Heavy Metal act DRAGONHEART came together in 1997, rooted in a prior Metal band titled BRUJAH. The group's initial formation counted Eduardo Marques on vocals and guitar, guitarist Marco Caporasso, bassist Mauricio Taborda and Marcelo Caporasso on drums.
The band debuted by issuing the opening EP 'Gods Of Ice' by 1999. An album entitled 'Underdark' surfaced on the Megahard label during 2000. DRAGONHEART promoted this release by support slots to visiting international artists such as VISION DIVINE, LABYRINTH and NIGHTWISH.
The 2002 album 'Throne Of The Alliance' included a cover version of GRAVE DIGGER's 'Rebellion (The Clans Are Marching...)'.
At the close of August Eduardo Marques unexpectedly left the band.

Albums:
UNDERDARK, Megahard (2000)
Intro / Arcadia Gates / Battlefield Requiem / Dynasty And Destiny / Tied In Time / Night Corsaries / Sir Lockdunam / Underdark / New Millennium / Mists Of Avalon / Gods Of Ice
THRONE OF THE ALLIANCE, (2002)
The Beginning... / Throne Of The Alliance / The Blacksmith / Ghost Galleon / Facing The Mountain / Mountain Of The Rising Storm / Mystical Forest / Into The Hall / Hall Of Dead Knights / Betrayal In The Coast Of Raven / ...And The Dark Valley Burns / Sunrise In The Akronis Sky / Rebellion (The Clans Are Marching...)

DRAGONLAND (SWEDEN)
Line-Up: Tomas Heidgert (vocals), Nicklas Magnusson (guitar), Olle Mörck (guitar), Christer Pedersen (bass), Elias Holmlid (keyboards), Jesse Lindskog (drums)

DRAGONLAND include former PROPHANITY and NIGHTSHADE guitarist Nicklas Magnusson and KING DIAMOND touring keyboardist Elias Holmlid in the ranks. DRAGONLAND's debut album 'The Battle Of The Ivory Plains' was clad in fantasy cover art

executed by SUPREME MAJESTY guitarist Chrille Andersson. In August of 2002 former NOSTRADAMUS drummer Jesse Lindskog was inducted into the line-up.

Albums:
THE BATTLE OF THE IVORY PLAINS, Black Lotus BLRCD 025 (1997)
Dragondawn / Storming Across Heaven / A Last Farewell / Ride For Glory / The Orcish March / The Battle Of The Ivory Plains / Graveheart / Rondo A La Turca / A Secret Unveiled / Worlds End / Dragondusk
HOLY WAR, Black Lotus (2002)
Hundred Years Have Passed / Majesty Of The Mithrill Mountains / Through Elven Woods And Dwarven Mines / Holy War / Calm Before The Storm / The Return To The Ivory Plains / Forever Walking Alone / Blazing Hate / A Thousand Points Of Light / One With All

DRAGON LORD (SPAIN)
Line-Up: Samuel Martiartu (vocals), Miguel Gortari (guitar), Xabi Baron (guitar), Jorge Arca (bass), Gorka Elso (keyboards), Nagore (drums)

Pamplona Power Metal. DRAGONLORD vocalist Samuel Martiartu previously fronted BRAM STOKER whilst the trio of guitarists Xabi Baron, Miguel Gortari and bass player Jorge Arca are all erstwhile EXCALIBUR personnel. Arca also has experience with WALKIRIA and Baron with both EVOLA and KRATEN.

Albums:
DIVE, Goimusic (2002)
Overture / Kamikaze (I'll Go To Die) / Dive / Power Of The Chain / No Time To Cry / Requiem / Home Of Fight / Excalibur / I Will Fight / Battle Of Drums / So Deep / Finale / So Far Away (Demo) / Victims Of War (Demo)

DRAGONLORD (USA)
Line-Up: Eric Peterson (vocals / guitar), Steve Smyth (guitar), Steve DiGeorgio (bass), Lyle Livingston (keyboards), Jon Allen (drums)

DRAGONLORD, originally billed as DRAGONHEART, was a post millennium high profile union of some of America's most respected Metal performers. The band was assembled as a side endeavour to the players priority acts by TESTAMENT guitarist Eric Peterson. With Peterson unexpectedly taking on the lead vocal role, with commendable results, DRAGONLORD included VICIOUS

RUMOURS and TESTAMENT guitarist Steve Smyth, SADUS drummer Jon Allen, keyboard player Lyle Livinston and bassist Steve DiGeorgio of SADUS, DISINCARNATE, ICED EARTH and DEATH. The band bowed in with the 'Rapture' album issued through Spitfire Records.

During March of 2002 DiGeorgio was replaced by TESTAMENT man Derrick Ramirez. Steve Smyth would temporarily hook up with the esteemed Seattle Metal crew NEVERMORE for summer European shows and US 'Vans Warped' dates. DRAGONLORD, following a batch of gigs supporting INCANTATION, would put in showings at major European festivals in August such as Germany's 'Wacken Open Air', Belgium's 'Eurorock' and the Swiss 'Z7 Metal Days' events.

Albums:
RAPTURE, Spitfire (2002)
Vals De La Muerte / Unholyvoid / Tradition And Fire / Born To Darkness / Judgement Failed / Wolfhunt / Spirits In The Mist / Rapture

DRAGONSLAYER (SPAIN)

Line-Up: Sergio Bermúdez (vocals), Jordi Foraster (guitar), Xavier Esteve (guitar), Ferran Cardona (bass), Raül Cabedo (drums)

Barcelona band DRAGONSLAYER's first album 'Noches De Tormenta' closed with a cover version of the ANGELES DEL INFIERNO track 'Maldita Sea Tu Nombre'.

Albums:
NOCHES DE TORMENTA, (2001)
El Encuentro (Intro) / Ave Fénix / La Dama Del Lago / La Leyenda / La Tierra Del Olvido / Lluvia Eterna / Dragonslayer / Mares De Hiel / Ni Angel Ni Juez / Maldito Sea Tu Nombre

DRAKKAR (ITALY)

Line-Up: Davide Dell'Orto (vocals), Dario Beretta (guitar), Daniele Persoglio (bass), Corrado Solarino (keyboards), Christian Fiorani (drums)

Viking inspired Milan Heavy Metal band founded in 1995 and releasing their suitably titled 'Sailing Alive' demo the following year. A second tape, 'We Sail At Dawn', arrived in 1997. Signing to the Dragonheart label DRAKKAR cut the opening 'Quest For Glory' album with a line-up of vocalist Luca Capellari, guitarist Dario Beretta, bass player Alex Forgione and drummer Christian Fiorani.

Keyboards would be on hand from CROWN OF AUTUMN's Emanuele Rastelli.

In June of 1998 DRAKKAR were chosen as the opening act for the 'Monsters Of Rock' festival in Turin, sharing the stage with HAMMERFALL, SAXON, PRIMAL FEAR, DREAM THEATER and DEEP PURPLE. However, shortly after line-up shuffles witnessed Forgione's place being taken by Alex Ferraris and the introduction of keyboard player Eleanora Ceretti. The group would also support the SCORPIONS in May of 1999.

DRAKKAR's second album 'Gemini', issued in March 2000, would see a guesting ROLAND GRAPOW of HELLOWEEN adding lead solos to the track 'Voices In The Wind'. Once more though DRAKKAR underwent personnel difficulties as both Ferraris and Capellari bowed out. New man on bass would be former HOLY GATES player Daniele Persoglio. EXILE's Davide Dell'Orto would take the mantle as lead vocalist just days later. The ructions had yet to cease though and the keyboard position too changed hands, the new incumbent being Corrado Solarino. The revised DRAKKAR soon had a third album on the shelves, April 2002's 'Razorblade God'. Included would be a cover version of MAGNUM's 'Kingdom Of Madness'.

DRAKKER guitarist Dario Beretta would guest as a session lead player for MESMERIZE, contributing their version of 'Die Young' for a Dio era BLACK SABBATH collection issued by the American Midwest label. DRAKKAR drummer Christian Fiorani would act as session player on the 2002 'Witchunter Tales' album for Doom merchants THUNDERSTORM.

Albums:
QUEST FOR GLORY, Dragonheart CHAOS 003CD (1998)
Welcome On Board (Intro) / Coming From The Past / Dragonheart / Follow The Prophet / Under The Armor / The Walls Of Olathoe / Wings Of Fire / Morella / Quest For Glory (Valhalla) / Raising The Banners / Towards Home (Outro)
GEMINI, Dragonheart CHAOS 009CD (2000)
Beginning (Intro) / Eridan Falls / Pure Of Heart / Soldiers Of Death / The Climb / The Voice Of The Wind / Dragonship / The Secret / Until The End / Death Of Slayn / The Price Of Victory
RAZORBLADE GOD, Dragonheart (2002)
Razorblade God / Man And Machine / To The Future / Inferno / The Matrix / Galadriel's Song / Lo Shan Shen Long Pa (Great Dragon Rising From The Mountain Of Lo) / The Next Generation / Witches' Dance /

Kingdom Of Madness

DREAM CHILD (FRANCE)
Line-Up: Gérard Fois (vocals), Dominique Leurquin (guitar), Sylvain Cochet (bass), Alain Blanc (drums)

DREAM CHILD are a Progressively inclined Melodic Rock outfit, created in the early '90s and hailing from Annecy, France. Their first foray into the public arena would be delivered by the June 1992 demo session 'First Visions'. This tape prompted a deal from the French NSR label in 1994 and DREAM CHILD's debut commercial release, the 'Torn Between Two Worlds' album, arrived in September 1996.
A second album 'Reaching The Golden Gates' emerged in 1998, licensed to Metal Blade Records for American release early the following year.
During mid 2002 Gérard Fois, uniting with guitarist Christophe Offredi, bass player Nicolas Jeanpierre and drummer Arnaud Gorbaty founded a fresh Power act entitled ETERNAL FLIGHT.

Albums:
TORN BETWEEN TWO WORLDS, NSR Productions (1997)
Waves Of Chaos / Train Of Fools / You Shall Lie In Hell / Same Old Song / Eternal Flight / Torn Between Two Worlds / Reign Is Crumbling / Join Us / Heavy Dance Of Chaos / Roll The Dice / No More Darkness / Create A New World
REACHING THE GOLDEN GATE, Metal Blade 14195 (1999)
To Our Dreams / Bells Of Nemesis / The Search / Acalmy / Alchemy / Fly Again / Kadesh Battle / Crystal Lady / Shade On Your Sun / Answer

DREAM DEVOID (GREECE)
Line-Up: Dimitris Zalahoris (vocals), Liberis Tsabras (guitar), Panos Argyriou (bass), Panos Milonas (keyboards), Fotis Giannakopoulos (drums)

DREAM DEVOID is an Athens based Power Metal act unafraid to use sheer speed to ram their point home. The group was conceived in July of 1993 by bass player Panos Argyriou and guitarist Liberis Tsabras.
The band would have a fluid line-up until January of 1997 when guitarist Akis Triantafillou and vocalist Dimitris Zalahoris were enrolled. Drummer Kostas Agouras, on loan from DISHARMONY, would session for the band on their opening 'Nebulous' demo of May 1997. DREAM DEVOID would also have

the track 'Consequent Sin' included on the Metal Invader magazine compilation 'Warzone II'.
In 1998 Fotis Giannakopoulos was inducted on the drum stool and Panagiotis Mylonas assumed keyboard duties. With this line-up DREAM DEVOID laid down their debut album 'Aeons Of Forget Fullness' for the Steel Gallery label.
Post recording Zalohoris disembarked but guitarist Vasilis Krilakis was drafted. DREAM DEVOID maintained a low profile during much of 2001 in main due to Tsabras' national service army service.

Albums:
AEONS OF FORGET FULLNESS, Steel Gallery SGR CD004 (2001)
...In The Sky / Dreams In Void / Dreamweaver / A Song To Whisper / Leaves Of Sorrow / Aeons Of Forget Fullness / Not A Cloud... / Consequent Sins / Nebulous / Internal Battle

DREAM EVIL (SWEDEN)
Line-Up: Niklas Isfeldt (vocals), Fredrik Nordstrom (guitar), Gus G. (guitar), Peter Stafors (bass), Snowy Shaw (drums)

A 2002 Swedish Metal combo, DREAM EVIL - debuting with the 'Dragonslayer' album, would be able to boast a rare pedigree of talent. Fronted by Niklas Isfeldt the group witnessed a union of guitarist Fredrik Nordstrom, MYSTIC PROPHECY and FIREWIND guitarist Gus G., bassist Peter Stalfors and drummer Snowy Shaw. The latter is of course a veteran of the Scandinavian Metal scene noted for his work with MERCYFUL FATE, KING DIAMOND, MEMENTO MORI and NOTRE DAME.
Isfeldt, Nordstrom and Stalfors all have strong HAMMERFALL connections. Isfeldt having acted as studio backing vocalist, Nordstrom as HAMMERFALL's producer and Stalfors as song writer.
Gus G. would lay down several lead guitar solos on the 2003 OLD MAN'S CHILD album 'In Defiance Of Existence'.

Albums:
DRAGONSLAYER, Century Media 8022-2 (2002)
Chasing The Dragon / Save Us / Dragonheart / Losing You / Hail To The King / Heavy Metal In The Night / The Prophecy / H.M.J. / In Flames You Burn / Kingdom Of The Damned / The 7th Day / The Chosen Ones / Losing You (Instrumental) / Outro

119

DREAMLORE (USA)

A solo technical Metal venture of one David Christy.

Albums:
CONFINED TO DESTINY, Purple Moon PMI 701 (1992)
Creature Of Obedience / Chasing Tomorrow / Original Sin / September Wind / One Dark Night / Beyond The Dream / From Afar I See / It's A Strange Life / Without Reason / World Of Madness / Confined To Destiny

DREAMSCAPE (GERMANY)
Line-Up: Hubi Meisel (vocals), Wolfgang Kerinnis (guitar), Stefan Gabner (guitar), Benno Schmidtler (bass), Jan Vacik (keyboards)

Munich Progressive Metal band founded in 1986. Following the release of their debut album 'Trance Like State' vocalist Tobi Zoltan quit and was superseded by Hubi Meisel. DREAMSCAPE's 1999 album 'Very' includes a cover of ULTRAVOX's 'Dancing With Tears In My Eyes'. The band toured Germany in December 1998 as support to AXEL RUDI PELL.
In later years HUBI MEISEL would act as

guest frontman for the Italian act MAEVE OF CONNACHT, appearing on their 2001 album 'Imaginary Tales'. The man would also issue a solo album entitled 'Cut'.

Albums:
TRANCE LIKE STATE, Rising Sun 35894 (1997)
Spirits / Fateful Silence / Streets / Changes / One And A Million / Face Your Fears / Loneliness / Decisions / Final Thoughts / It's Not The End / Don't Take Care / Center Of Time / The Wall
VERY, Rising Sun (1999)
When Shadows Are Gone / Lost Faith / Thorn In My Mind / Reborn / A Voice Inside / Winter Dreams / Fearing The Daylight / I Leave The Past Behind / Alone - Panterei Part I / She's Flying - Panterei Part II / A New Beginning - Panterei Part III / Dancing With Tears In My Eyes

DREAMTALE (FINLAND)
Line-Up: Tomi Viiltola (vocals), Rami Keränen (guitar), Esa Orjatsalo (guitar), Pasi Ristolainen (bass), Turkka Vuorinen (keyboards), Petteri Rosenbom (drums)

Having been formulated during 1999 DREAMTALE would offer up their first demo

'Shadow Of The Frozen Sun' in Autumn of that year. The group went through a variety of players until settling on a stabilised line-up in time for a debut live showing as opening act for SINERGY in July of 2000. DREAMTALE's line-up at this stage counted former HARDWARE man Rami Keränen on vocals and guitar, second guitarist Esa Orjatsalo, bass player Alois Weimer, SYMBIOSIS keyboard player Turkka Vuorinen and Petteri Rosenbom on drums. A second tape, 'Refuge From Reality', scored well in a national talent contest leading to TV exposure and pulled in commendable reviews from the Finnish Metal press.

DREAMTALE signed to·the Spinefarm label, working with producer Pasi Ristolainen for their inaugural 2002 album 'Beyond Reality'. However, vocalist Rami Keränen suffered throat problems in April and decided to concentrate solely on guitar. Just upfront of the album release bassist Alois Weimer opted out but the band's producer Pasi Ristolainen soon plugged the gap. The multi talented Ristolainen has a wealth of experience as guitarist for DEAD CITY KLOWNS and as drummer for both YLIANNOSTUS and the bizarrely titled ROBUST DUCK. That same month DREAMTALE welcomed onboard new lead singer Tomi Viitola, a man with credits in acts such as SANTHYR and ALLIANCE.

Albums:
BEYOND REALITY, Spinefarm SPI 151CD (2002)
The Dawn / Memories Of Time / Fallen Star / Heart's Desire / Where The Rainbow Ends / Time Of Fatherhood / Dreamland / Call Of The Wild / Dancing In The Twilight / Refuge From Reality / Silent Path / Farewell

DREAM THEATER (USA)
Line-Up: James LaBrie (vocals), John Petrucci (guitar), John Myung (bass), Derek Sherinian (keyboards), Mike Portnoy (drums)

Without doubt the most important Progressive Rock act to have emerged in recent years. DREAM THEATER have combined heady acclaim within the genre matched by hard album sales and status. Previously known as MAJESTY, John Myung and John Petrucci were childhood friends who met Mike Portnoy at the famous Berkeley School Of Music in Boston. Kevin Moore was engaged on keyboards, having known Petrucci from elementary school, once the trio had settled back home in Long Island.

Having initially worked with vocalist Chris Collins, the fledgling band soon replaced him with Charlie Dominici and recorded a four track demo that despite its poorly produced frame sold out rather quickly, before the band was forced to change its name due to MAJESTY already being owned by another party. The new moniker of DREAM THEATER was adopted after a suggestion from Mike Portnoy's father who had recently seen a movie in a cinema of that name.

Releasing a new selection of better produced demos, DREAM THEATER were offered a deal by the MCA affiliated Mechanic Records label and, once signed, the group found themselves working with producer Terry Date on what would become the 'When Dream And Day Unite'. The record was reportedly completed with a three and a half week deadline hanging over their heads. Producer Terry Brown was drafted in to remix two of the album's tracks (namely 'After Life' and 'State Of Confusion')

Wanting to be released from Mechanic Records who, the band claimed, offered no promotion for the first album, DREAM THEATER eventually had to buy themselves out of their contract.

Searching for a replacement for Charlie Dominici in 1989 DREAM THEATER had begun to tentatively work with another singer when they received a tape from Canadian James LaBrie, who was about to sign a solo deal with Aquarius Records. LaBrie (who had previously had tenures with WINTER ROSE and CONEY HATCH) was invited down to New York to try out for the group and, after one jam session, the Canadian had got the job.

Having been virtually guaranteed a deal with Atco if they found the right singer, DREAM THEATER signed to the label in 1991 and entered Beartracks studios in Suffern, New York in October of that year to record their second album, 'Images And Words', which was produced by David Prater.

Moore quit, resurfacing in 1998 with the melancholic CHROMA KEY, and was replaced temporarily for live work with Jordan Rudess of SPEEDWAY BOULEVARD before eventually being replaced by ex-KISS associate Derek Sherinian for a full tour. Rudess joined famed Jazz Rockers DIXIE DREGS. The 'Change Of Seasons' mini-album in 1996 followed prior to work on writing with the group for the first time on a brand new studio album.

The album, 1997's 'Fallen Into Infinity', produced by Kevin Shirley, featured a guest vocal appearance from KINGS X man Doug Pinnick on the track 'Lines In The Sand' and a surprisingly impressive co-write with Desmond Child on 'You Not Me'.

DREAM THEATER toured America the same year alongside DIXIE DREGS which was later to bear fruit with musical liaisons between the two sets of musicians. Portnoy and Petrucci were both involved in the side project group LIQUID TENSION EXPERIMENT alongside respected sessioneers Tony Levin (PETER GABRIEL / KING CRIMSON) and Jordan Rudess once again. LIQUID TENSION EXPERIMENT released a self-titled album through Magna Carta in early 1998.

By 1999 Sherinan was out of the band and in came his logical successor Jordan Rudess for 1999's 'Metropolis Part 2: Scenes From A Memory' album. The album continues the theme of 'Metropolis Part 1' recorded on the 'Images And Words' album.

Side projects continued unabated though with Rudess pairing off with his ex-DIXIE DREGS drumming colleague Rod Morgenstein for the RUDESS/MORGENSTEIN project album and his inclusion on the classical 'Steinway To Heaven' album alongside his predecessor Sherinan and YES maestro RICK WAKEMAN. Myung would not be left out either as he reunited with erstwhile band mate DEREK SHERINAN in an unlikely alliance with, yet again, Rod Morgenstein and KINGS X frontman TY TABOR to forge the PLATYPUS project.

A further union of Prog Rock stars came in 2000 when Portnoy allied himself with MARILLION bassist Pete Trewavas, SPOCK'S BEARD's Neal Morse and THE FLOWERKINGS Roine Stolt to create SMPT releasing the 'Transatlantic' album on Rising Sun.

Sherinan meantime teamed up with guitar virtuoso TONY MACALPINE for their PLANET X project record 'Universe'.

In September of 2001 a triple CD emerged titled 'Live Scenes From New York' comprising the band's entire show recorded at the Roseland Ballroom in New York on August 30th 2000. However, in a surreal example of bad timing bearing in mind the September 11th terrorist attacks on America the record, due to a ghastly coincidence of the highest order, was pulled from the retail shelves the day of its release - September 11th. The sleeve artwork unbelievably depicted New York, including the Statue of Liberty and - most presciently of all - the World Trade Centre, in flames. Needless to say the artwork was hastily revised.

In more encouraging news the DREAM THEATER Brazilian Fan Club announced the assembly of a tribute album featuring artists such as SIGMA 5, EVORA, LAST RITES, OPERACT, LONGJAM and ABSTTRAKT.

The DREAM THEATER 2002 album 'Six Degrees Of Inner Turbulence' would number only six songs, albeit one of those would be the marathon 40 minute title track. The band added a rather novel twist to their touring activities in 2002. When booked for a two night consecutive venue run the band would perform the entirety of METALLICA's 'Masters Of Puppets' album live. Needless to say, fans who had not been made aware of DREAM THEATER's intentions, would be somewhat mystified. It would seem DREAM THEATER would spend much of the year on the road, also being announced as part of an Autumn package billing for U.S. dates in alliance with KINGS X and JOE SATRIANI.

Portnoy would be revealed as the mentor behind a new Prog Rock 'supergroup' in May, having assembled an impressive line-up numbering erstwhile DREAM THEATER and presently CHROMA KEY keyboard player Kevin Moore. Also involved would be FATES WARNING guitarist Jim Matheos, ex-CYNIC and current GORDIAN KNOT bassist Sean Malone with the whole affair fronted by PAIN OF SALVATION vocalist Daniel Gildenlöw. Before long Gildenlöw was out of the frame and the band project was being billed as set OSI (Orchestra Of Strategic Influence).

DREAM THEATER announced European tour dates, performing two sets with an intermission and no support act, for October.

Singles/EPs:
Status Seeker / Afterlife, Mechanic CD 45 17783 (1989) (USA promotion)
Lie, East West A 5835 (1994)

Albums:
WHEN DAY AND DREAM UNITE, Mechanic MCAC 42259 (1989)
A Fortune In Lies / Status Seeker / The Ytse Jam / The Killing Hand / Light Fuse And Get Away / Afterlife / The Ones Who Help Set The Sun / Only A Matter Of Time
IMAGES AND WORDS, Atco 792148-2 (1992) 61 USA
Pull Me Under / Another Day / Take The Time / Surrounded / Metropolis Part 1: The Miracle And The Sleeper / Under A Glass Moon / Wait For Sleep / Learning To Live
LIVE AT THE MARQUEE, Atlantic 756792286-2 (1993)
Metropolis / Fortune In Lies / Bombay Vindaloo / Surrounded / Another Hand / The Killing Hand / Pull Me Under
AWAKE, Atlantic 7567 90126-2 (1994)
65 UK, 32 USA
6.00 / Caught In The Web / Innocence Faded / Erotomania / Voices / The Silent Man / The Mirror / Lie / Lifting Shadows Off A Dream / Scarred / Space-Dye Vest
A CHANGE OF SEASONS, East West 7559 61830-2 (1996) **58 USA**

A Change Of Seasons / Funeral For A Friend - Love Lies Bleeding / Perfect Strangers / The Rover - Achilles Last Stand - The Song Remains The Same / The Big Medley

FALLEN INTO INFINITY, East West 7559-62060-2 (1997) **14 SWEDEN, 52 USA**
New Millennium / You Not Me / Peruvian Skies / Hollow Years / Burning My Soul / Hells Kitchen / Lines In The Sand / Take Away My Pain / Just Let Me Breathe / Anna Lee / Trial Of Tears: I) It's Raining, II) Deep In Heaven, III) The Wasteland

ONCE IN A LIVETIME, Elektra 62308 (1998)
A Change Of Seasons I / A Change Of Seasons II / Puppies On Acid / Just Let Me Breathe / Voices / Take The Time / Keyboard solo / Lines In The Sand / Scarred / A Change of Seasons IV / Ytse Jam 12. Drum solo / Trial Of Tears / Hollow Years / Take Away My Pain / Caught In A Web / Lie / Peruvian Skies / Guitar solo / Pull Me Under / Metropolis / A Change Of Seasons VII

METROPOLIS PART TWO: SCENES FROM A MEMORY, Elektra 62448 (1999) **40 FRANCE**
Act I: Scene One: Regression / Act I: Scene Two: I. Overture 1928 / Act I: Scene Two: II. Strange Deja Vu / Act I: Scene Three: I. Through My Words / Act I: Scene Three: II. Fatal Tragedy / Act I: Scene Four: Beyond This Life / Act I: Scene Five: Through Her Eyes / Act II: Scene Six: Home / Act I I: Scene Seven: I. The Dance Of Eternity / Act II: Scene Seven: II. One Last Time / Act II: Scene Eight: The Spirit Carries On / Act II: Scene Nine: Finally Free

LIVE SCENES FROM NY, East West (2001) **117 FRANCE**
Regression / Overture 1928 / Strange Deja Vu / Through My Words / Fatal Tragedy / Beyond This Life / John & Theresa solo / Through Her Eyes / Home / The Dance Of Eternity / One Last Time / The Spirit Carries On / Finally Free / Metropolis Pt. 1 / The Mirror / Just Let Me Breathe / Acid Rain / Caught In A New Millennium / Another Day / Jordan Rudess' keyboard solo / A Mind Beside Itself / Learning To Live / A Change Of Seasons

SIX DEGREES OF INNER TURBULENCE, Elektra 62742 (2002) **35 BELGIUM, 2 FINLAND, 17 FRANCE, 12 SWEDEN, 46 USA**
The Glass Prison / Blind Faith / Misunderstood / The Great Debate / Disappear / Six Degrees Of Inner Turbulence

DREAM WEAVER (GREECE)
Line-Up: Jim Marcou (vocals / guitar),
George Zacharoglou (guitar), Michael Kypreos (bass), John Basimakopoulos (drums)

Doomladen Power Metal act created in May of 1990 by guitarist George Zacharoglou and vocalist / guitarist Jim Marcou, former members of INFECTION. The duo would issue the 'Infection' demo tape the following year. DREAM WEAVER would be solidified in mid 1992 with the enlistment of bassist Michael Kypreos and drummer John Basimakopoulos.
In May of 1995 DREAM WEAVER recorded the 5 track 'Dream Within A Dream' demo session. Due to members obligations with national service it would be a full five years before DREAM WEAVER would issue their opening gambit 'Fantasy Revealed' through the Secret Port label in January 2001. Following these recordings DREAM WEAVER switched bassists, bringing in Takis Fytos. The band would support the resurrected American Heavy Metal band BROCAS HELM on their Autumn Greek shows. A 7" single, 'Soulsearching', arrived in early 2002.

Singles/EPs:
Soulsearching / Voice To Run The Miles, Eat Metal Music (2002)

Albums:
FANTASY REVEALED, Secret Port (2001)
Destiny Dancer / Bed Of Pain / Hands On The White / Desolate Heart / Miss Another Meaning

DR. SIN (BRAZIL)
Line-Up: Michael Vescara (vocals), Eduardo Ardanuy (guitar), Andria Busic (bass), Ivan Busic (drums)

A renowned Brazilian Hard Rock outfit centred upon the dextrous talents of guitarist Eduardo Ardanuy. DR. SIN was created by a union of Ardanuy, a veteran of A CHAVE and SUPLA, along with the Busic siblings bassist Andria and drummer Ivan. Both brothers had journeyed through acts such as PLATINHA in 1985, CHEROKEE in 1987 and WANDER TAFFO in 1988. The pair would also feature on the 1991 TAFFO album 'Rosa Branca'.
DR. SIN's eponymous debut, recorded for Warner Music in America with the noted producer Stefan Galfas at the helm, would arrive in 1993 followed by 'Brutal', again laid down in the USA - this time with producer Johnny Montagnese, in 1995. DR. SIN would support a whole stream of visiting acts including L7, NIRVANA, BLACK SABBATH, AC/DC, GILLAN and KISS.

The act was quick to carve out a reputation as one of the most accomplished Brazilian acts and as such would open shows for visiting artists like DREAM THEATER, SCORPIONS and DIO in 1997. The band would also boost their numbers to a quartet with the introduction of ex-OBSESSION, LOUDNESS and YNGWIE MALMSTEEN singer Mike Vescara. Not only did the American produce their third album 'Insinity' but he would follow up the union by appearing in a live capacity as guest vocalist.

The following year would not only have DR. SIN guesting for YNGWIE MALMSTEEN but also landing the almost unique honour of having their live set 'Alive' included as a double package with the Swedish star's own 'Live In Brazil' opus. Other gigs included dates with QUIET RIOT. The previous studio outing 'Insinity' would also be granted a Japanese release through the Pony Canyon label, albeit with a completely revised track listing.

The 'Brutal' album would be re-issued in Japan during 1998 but re-titled 'Silent Scream'. Ardanuy would take time out to undertake the TRITONE project in collusion with Frank Solari and Sergio Buss. In 2000 Vescara renewed his relationship with the band being drafted as a full time member for the 'Dr. Sin II' album.

Andria Busic would join ANGRA then Progressive Metal band KARMA but would decamp in August 2001. Eduardo Ardanuy would add guest sessions to the 2002 BLEZQI ZATSAZ project album 'The Tide Turns' of SHAMAN keyboard player Fabio Riberio.

Albums:
DR. SIN, Warner Music (1993) (Brazilian release)
Emotional Catastrophe / Dirty Woman / Stone Cold Dead / Howlin' In The Shadows / The Fire Burns Cold / You Stole My Heart / Dr. Sin / Valley Of Dreams / Have You Ever Seen The Rain / Lonely World / Through My Window / Scream And Shout
BRUTAL, Warner Music (1995) (Brazilian release)
Silent Scream / Karma / Isolated / Down In The Trenches / Down In The Trenches (II) / Fire / Inner Voices / Child Of Sin / Hey You / Kizumba / Someone To Blame / Third World / Shed Your Skin / Years Gone / War
SILENT SCREAM, (1997)
Isolated / Silent Scream / Someone To Blame / Inner Voices / War / Years Gone / Down In The Trenches / Kizumba / Fire / Karma / Child Of Sin / Third World / Shed Your Skin / Hey You / Futebol, Muhler & Rock n' Roll
INSINITY, Pony Canyon PCCY-1311 (1997)

(Japanese release)
Free To Fly / Innocent Crime / Sometimes / Flying To Die (The Other Side) / Zero / Brother / S.O.B. / Living And Learning / Experimental Dog / Revolution / No Rules / Holy Man
INSINITY, Warner Music (1997) (Brazilian release)
Brother / Sometimes / Echoes Of Insanity / Revolution / Insomnia / Innocent Crime / Flying To Die (The Other Side) / No Rules / Wake Me Up / Living And Learning / Faces / Lost And Confused / Zero / S.O.B. / Futebol, Muhler & Rock n' Roll
ALIVE, Warner Music (1999)
Karma / Isolated / Down In The Trenches (Parts I & II) / Sometimes / Fire / Emotional Catastrophe / No Rules / Experimental Dog / Free To Fly
DR. SIN II, Warner Music (2000) (Brazilian release)
Time After Time / Danger / Gates Of Madness / Eternity / Fly Away / Miracles / Same Old Story / What Now / Pain / Devil Inside / Suffocation
SHADOWS OF LIGHT, Metal Mayhem Music (2001)
Time After Time / Miracles & Dreams / Shadows Of Light / Eternity / What Now / A Perfect Crime / Same Old Story (Get A Grip) / Fly Away / Inside The Pain / Gates Of Madness / Danger / Suffocation

DUNGEON (AUSTRALIA)
Line-Up: Tim Grose (vocals / guitar), Stuart Marshall (guitar), Brendan McDonald (bass), Steve Moore (drums)

Heavy Metal band with a turbulent history from the small outback town of Broken Hill. Founded in August of 1989 by "Lord" Tim Grose on guitars and vocals with bassist Eddie Tresize and drummer Ian De Bono. The band was brought up to strength with the addition of Carolyn Boon on keyboards and Justin Hansen on second guitar as Tresize was supplanted by Randall Hockling.

This line-up of DUNGEON lasted some six months prior to both Hockling and Hansen quitting. DUNGEON duly enrolled guitarist Dale Fletcher and bassist Jamie Baldwin but De Bono was to uproot himself shortly after, the drum stool then being filled briefly by Darryl Reiss.

By February of 1991 DUNGEON was in turmoil again as Dale Corney came in to oust Fletcher. By this stage DUNGEON operated simply as Lord Tim, Corney and a drum machine although numerous guitarists came and went. DUNGEON got back to strength with new recruits bassist George Smith, guitarist Steve Mikulic and ex-DR. ZEUS drummer Andrew Brody to record the band's first demo. These tapes were then released as the mini album 'Changing Moods' which also sees a guest contribution from SOUTHERN SONS drummer Virgil Donati. Brody then departed and DUNGEON pulled in ex-MAXIMUM CARNAGE drummer Wayne Harris.

A further member of MAXIMUM CARNAGE, bassist Justin Sayers, joined the fold just as Mikulic packed his bags.

DUNGEON were then signed to a new Australian label, Nu-Town, who managed to secure a Japanese deal for a further album. 'Demolition' was released in Japan containing new tracks alongside cuts from the 'Changing Moods' mini-album for which Sayers had reworked the bass lines.

Quite bizarrely to promote the album DUNGEON opted to enlist drummer Tyrone McMaster. Although he appeared on the album and in press photos McMaster could not drum! Sensibly the band roped in former ENTICER and ADDICTIVE drummer Steve Moore in his stead as recording got underway for the 'Resurrection' album. The line-up fractured once more when in July of 1999 Sayers bade farewell, going on to forge his own project KING OATH. This latest vacancy was filled by DR. ZEUS man Brendan McDonald.

During 2001 Dale Corney announced his departure. Stuart Marshall, a veteran of WISHING TREE, CORD and KARIZMA, was quickly inducted just up front of the 'Metal For The Brain XI' festival. DUNGEON would put in an extensive touring schedule that year, supporting YNGWIE MALMSTEEN, NEVERMORE and EDGUY as well as headlining the main stage at 'Metal For The Brain' and co-headlining the 'Screaming Symphony' and 'Metal Warriors' events in Melbourne as well as the 'Wintersun' festival in Canberra.

The band next set about self-financing the recording of a further studio album and in the interim issued a six track live promo cheekily dubbed 'Maiden Our Spare Time'. DUNGEON signed to the Melbourne based Metal Warriors label to release the August 2002 album 'A Rise To Power'.

Albums:
CHANGING MOODS, Dungeon DPI 001 (1995)
One Shot At Life / The Promise / Paradise / Slave Of Love / Changing Moods
DEMOLITION, TDK-CORE TDCN 5590 (1996)
Don't Leave Me / Call Me / Slave Of Love / Paradise / One Shot At Life / Changing Moods / This Time / Time To Die / I Am

Death / Lies / Vodka Frenzy / The Duel / Reflections
RESURRECTION, Warhead (1999)
Death From Above / Resurrection / Paradise / Judgement Day / Wake Up / Fight / Let It Go / Time To Die / I Am Death / No Way Out / The Legend Of Huma
A RISE TO POWER, Metal Warriors (2002)
The Prophecy / A Rise To Power / Netherlife (Black Roses Die) / Insanity's Fall / The Other Side / Stormchaser / Where Madness Hides / Lost In The Light / Life Is Black / The Birth: Trauma Begins / Traumatised / A Rise To Power (Reprise) / Wasted Years / Queen Of The Reich

DYNAMO (MEXICO)

Line-Up: Alfonso Romo (vocals), Jesus Durazo (guitar), Pablo Hoyo (guitar), Juan P. Navarro (bass), Raul Castillo (drums)

Power Metal unit conceived by former EXPIATORIO drummer Raul Castillo during 1996. Initially the band was made up of guitarists Ricardo Miller and Franco Soqui, bassist Ivan Valenzuela and vocalist Jorge, the latter a former member of FATHER FATE. Before long ex-SARCASMO six stringer Gustavo Figueroa had usurped Miller and Juan Pedro Navarro, previously with MENTAL, had occupied the bass position. Yet more changes witnessed the induction of a new frontman, former CUARENTENA singer Alfonso Romo.

December of 1999 saw the departure of Soqui but by early 2000 Jesus Durazo of EVANGELIUS had plugged the gap. With this line-up DYNAMO entered the recording studio to cut the self-financed album 'Raise The Power', released in December of that year. July of 2001 found DYNAMO welcoming into the fold another of Castillo's EXPIATORIO colleagues, guitarist Pablo Hoyo.

Albums:
RAISE THE POWER, (2000)
I Don't Remember The Time / Victory Is Ours / The Man Who Crossed / Under The Tree Of Sunset / Soldiers Of Sunlight / Silent In My Mind / Face Your Fear / Cosmic Palace / If Somebody…

DYSLESIA (FRANCE)

Line-Up: Thierry Lebourg (vocals), Fabrice Dutour (guitars), Francois Loprete (guitars), Jo Loprete (bass), Francois Brisk (drums)

Lyon based Symphonic Hard Rockers DYSLESIA opened proceedings with the self-financed 'My Own Revolution' album in 1999.

The band had their follow up on MTM Music 'Who Dares Wins' opus produced by Dennis Ward of PINK CREAM 69. A notable guest guitar slot comes courtesy of RHAPSODY's own LUCA TURILLI.

In their time DYSLESIA have opened for RHAPSODY, IRON SAVIOR, LABYRINTH and DEMONS & WIZARDS.

Albums:

WHO DARES WINS, MTM Metal 1704-4 (2001)
Beware Of Life Demons / Rest In Space / Unknown Fighter / Who Dares Wins / Fighting And Gone / Living In The Winter / Bring The Sunlight Back / Just About A Dream / The One You Are / Masquerade Of Life

EASY RIDER (SPAIN)
Line-Up: Ron Finn (vocals),
Javier Villanueva (guitar), Daniel
Castellanos (guitar), José
Villanueva (bass), Antonio
Chaves (drums)

Spanish Heavy Metal act EASY RIDER was
created in 1990 by guitarists Javier Villanueva
and Daniel Castellanos, bass player Jose A.
Villanueva and drummer Antonio M. Chaves.
Villanueva would handle lead vocal duties
when the band enrolled singer Eugenio
Garañeda, joined in 1996.
EASY RIDER issued their debut album,
´Perfecta Creación´, in 1997. A second
album, ´Lord Of The Storm´ released in 1998,
saw the band adopting English lyrics in an
attempt to break into the international market.
Touring found EASY RIDER picking up many
valuable guest slots to visiting international
artists such as YNGWIE MALMSTEEN,
BLIND GUARDIAN and MANOWAR. Their
burgeoning status would also be recognised
by 'Heavy Rock' magazine, whose readers
voted EASY RIDER the best newcomer of
1999.
Other high profile appearances included
showings at the 'Eurometal 99' festival
alongside STRATOVARIUS, GAMMA RAY,
HAMMERFALL and ANGRA.
EASY RIDER issued a third album, 'Evilution'
in 2000. The band appeared at the 'Rock
Machina 2000' festival with RUNNING WILD,
LABYRINTH, METALIUM, EDGUY, and
VIRGIN STEELE.
In September of 2001 the band brought in
new vocalist Ron Finn, previously a member
of American act MACE. Finn debuted with the
2002 offering 'Regeneration'.

Albums:
PERFECTA CREACION, Soho Music (1997)
Ojos De Fuego / El Mundo De Los Sueaos /
Vampire Prelude / Stranger / Perfecta
Creacion / Tiempo / Mundos Extraaos /
Desesperacion / No Face
LORD OF THE STORM, Soho Music (1998)
Lord Of The Storm / Changes / Death Of
Dreams / Seven / Eternal Sin / Serpents /
Savage Rage / See My Eyes / Different
Ways / Easy Riders
EVILUTION, Locomotive Music LM062
(2000)
Blessed / Wormwood / Babylon The Great /
Evilution / From The Tribes / Crowns Of Gold
/ Hiking Mars / Signs / The New Jerusalem /
Blazing Fire Victory / When The Thousand
Years Are Over 12 / So Shall Be
REGENERATION, Locomotive Music (2002)
Regeneration / Stranger / World Is Coming
Down / Nightmare / Where Angels Fly / No

Room In Hell / Spectre Of Sorrow / Freedom
Fighter / Eyes That Can't See / Goliath /
Chariots Of The Gods / Man Made Martyr

EDENBRIDGE (AUSTRIA)
Line-Up: Sabine Edelsbacher (vocals),
Lanvall (guitar / keyboards), Andreas Eibler
(guitar), Kurt Bednarsky (bass), Roland
Navratil (drums)

EDENBRIDGE are a Gothic Metal, or to use
the band's own terminology "Angelic
Bombastic Metal", act out of Linz created by
guitar and keyboard wizard and former solo
star LANVALL (real name Arne
Stockhammer) during 1998. EDENBRIDGE is
fronted by the vocal talents of Sabine
Edelsbacher. Drummer Roland Navratil is a
member of Metal band STORMWARNING.
EDENBRIDGE's debut album 'Sunrise In
Eden' would witness a guest contribution on
Sitar from the esteemed Austrian Progressive
Rock veteran GANDALF and a final mix
courtesy of PINK CREAM 69 bassist Dennis
Ward. The band's second album 'Arcana',
which found original guitarist Georg
Edelmann's place taken by another
STORMWARNING member Andreas Eibler,
would be licensed to Sensory Records in
America, King Records in Japan and the
Korean Dream On concern for a lavish double
vinyl set.
Sabine Edelsbacher would guest on the 2001
debut album from Argentinean Symphonic
Metal band BETO VASQUEZ INFINITY. She
would also lend her talents to the 2002 Rock
Opera project MISSA MERCURIA assembled
by a union of PINK CREAM 69, SILENT
FORCE and VANDEN PLAS personnel,
Edelsbacher portraying the character role of
the 'Water goddess'.

Albums:
SUNRISE IN EDEN, Massacre MAS CD248
(2000)
Cheyenne Spirit / Sunrise In Eden / Forever
Shine On / Holy Fire / Wings Of The Wind /
In The Rain / Midnight At Noon / Take Me
Back / My Last Step Beyond
ARCANA, Massacre MAS CD306 (2001)
Ascending / Starlight Reverie / The Palace /
A Moment Of Time / Fly On A Rainbow
Dream / Color My Sky / The Whisper Of The
Ages / Into The Light / Suspiria / Winter
Winds / Arcana

EDGUY (GERMANY)
Line-Up: Tobias Sammet (vocals / guitar),
Tobias Exxel (bass), Felix Bohnke (drums)

Melodic German Power Metal outfit. After the

127

EDGUY
Photo : Nico Wobben

debut album drummer Dominik Storch departed. Sessions for the 1998 album 'Vain Glory Opera' were fulfilled by Frank Lindenhall although a permanent drummer was found in Felix Bohnke, a former member of EXILED and - quite unbelievably - MERCILESS GNOME.

For 'Vain Glory Opera' STRATOVARIUS's Timo Tolkki guests on guitar whilst BLIND GUARDIAN's Hansi Kürsch also puts in an appearance.

EDGUY leader Tobias Sammet would guest on SQUEALER's 1998 album 'The Prophecy' and the same year would see SQUEALER bassist Tobias Exxel jump ship to join EDGUY.

Sammet assembled a mammoth cast for his AVANTASIA project of 2000. The eponymous album, which also featured EDGUY guitarist Jens Ludwig, saw guests from acts as diverse as GAMMA RAY, HELLOWEEN, RHAPSODY, STRATOVARIUS, AT VANCE, WITHIN TEMPTATION and VIRGIN STEELE.

Not to be outdone Tobias Exxel would also conceive a solo project entitled TARAXACUM. The resulting 'Spirit Of Freedom' album, released by MTM Metal records, would find Exxel's vision drawing in the talents of STEEL PROPHET vocalist Rick Mythiasin, ROUGH SILK keyboard player Ferdy Doernberg, his EDGUY colleague Felix Bohnke on drums and erstwhile SQUEALER man Frank Wolf also on drums. With EDGUY's progress accelerating a decision was made to re-issue the band's debut 'Savage Poetry' album. Remarkably the re-release would chart in several European territories.

A new album 'Mandrake' was launched in September, preceded by a taster CD single 'Painting On The Wall'. The release confirmed the still ascendant status of the band as it garnered valuable national chart placing in Germany, Sweden and France.

EDGUY got into the spirit of live action with an anonymous appearance at the Paris Dunois venue on October 7th. The band, cheekily billed as 'MANDRAKE', opened the show for HEAVENLY who were using the event as a release party for their 'Sign Of The Winner' album.

Singles/EPs:
Painting On The Wall (Edit version) / Golden Dawn / Wings Of A Dream 2001 / Painting On The Wall (Album version), AFM CD 050-5 (2001)

Albums:
SAVAGE POETRY, (1996) **72 FINLAND, 79 GERMANY, 60 SWEDEN**
Key To My Fate / Hallowed / Sands Of Time /

Secret Hell / Eyes Of The Tyrant / Frozen Candle / Roses To No One / Power And Majesty
KINGDOM OF MADNESS, AFM CD 37585-422 (1997)
Paradise / Wings Of A Dream / Heart Of Twilight / Dark Symphony / Deadmaker / Angel Rebellion / When A Hero Cries / Steel Church / The Kingdom
VAIN GLORY OPERA, AFM CD 38760-422 (1998)
Overture / Until We Rise Again / How Many Miles / Scarlet Rose / Out Of Control / Vain Glory Opera / Fairytale / Walk On Fighting / Tomorrow / No More Foolin' / Hymn
THEATRE OF SALVATION, AFM (1999) **50 SWEDEN**
The Healing Vision / Babylon / The Headless Game / Land Of The Miracle / Wake Up The King / Falling Down / Arrows Fly / Holy Shadows / Another Time / The Unbeliever / Theatre Of Salvation
MANDRAKE, AFM CD 050-2 (2001) **47 FRANCE, 19 GERMANY, 18 SWEDEN, 58 SWITZERLAND**
Tears Of A Mandrake / Golden Dawn / Jerusalem / All The Clowns / Nailed To The Wheel / Pharoah / Wash Away The Poison / Fallen Angels / Painting On The Wall / Save Us Now / The Devil And The Savant

EDWIN DARE (Toledo, OH, USA)
Line-Up: Bryce Barnes (vocals), Jeff Kollman (guitar), Kevin Chown (bass), Tom Kollman (drums)

Toledo, Ohio's EDWIN DARE originally emerged as an extremely Progressive Jazz Metal influenced outfit fronted by the operatic vocal style of Bryce Barnes. The band's second album, 'Can't Break Me', saw the group defining their own style to a degree.

The debut album was re-issued by the band in early 1997 following public demand after the cult success generated by 'Can't Break Me'.

Guitarist Jeff Kollman joined THE TRUTH then appeared with the UFO pairing of vocalist PHIL MOGG and bassist PETE WAY in their MOGG/WAY project for the 1999 'Chocolate Box' album.

JEFF KOLLMAN also sessioned on Phil Mogg's solo project, JOHN WEST's 'Permanent Marks' as well as finding time to cut his debut solo album 'Shedding Skin'.

Albums:
THE UNTHINKABLE DEED, Marmaduke CD (1992)
Do Me Right / It's Not For The World / The Killer / A Right And A Wrong Way / Oh

Darling / Don't Need No Money / Just A Heartbeat Away / Burning Feeling / Face The Truth / Love Poisons The Mind / Edwin Shreds / When We Had It All / Take Your Stand / Waiting For The Chance

CAN'T BREAK ME, Marmaduke CD (1994)
Feel The Power / Don't Listen To Your Head / The Backburner / Never Had Time / Lies / This Warrior / Gone & Run Away / End Of The Story / Test Of Will / Can't Break Me

MY TIME TO DIE, Marmaduke (1998)
I Feel It / Obsession Of Intense Desire / Take Away My Heart / Perfect Serenity / Weight Of The World / We Need To Hold On / Look To The Stars / My Time To Die / The Monster / Make Us Stronger

EIDOLON (CANADA)

Line-Up: Brian Soulard (vocals), Glen Drover (guitar), Adrian Robichaud (bass), Shawn Drover (drums)

Promising Toronto Power Metal band EIDOLON have made serious headway on mainland Europe where the genre commands high album sales and live audiences. EIDOLON, centred upon the sibling Drover duo of guitarist Glen and drummer Shawn, dates back to 1993.

Initially EIDOLON was a purely instrumental Metal studio endeavour but would evolve into a fully fledged band, adding singer Brian Soulard, second guitarist Slav Siminic and bassist Criss Bailey, for the recording of debut album 'Zero Hour'. Although the album was self-financed its undoubted quality assured distribution throughout the world.

With the departure of Siminic EIDOLON knuckled down to craft a follow up album, the conceptual 'Seven Spirits' released in 1997. Shortly after the album emerged Bailey decamped. He would soon be replaced by Adrian Robichaud. In the midst of recording the group's third effort 'Nightmare World' EIDOLON signed a deal with Metal Blade Records.

During 2001 EIDOLON returned to the studio embarking on a fourth album 'Hallowed Apparition'. Soulard would make way for new vocalist Pat Mulock.

EIDOLON gained some international recognition as guitarist, Glen Drover was handpicked by KING DIAMOND to play on his 'House Of God' album. The band's fifth CD 'Coma Nation' was released in April 2002.

Albums:
ZERO HOUR, (1996)
When Will It End / Zero Hour / Pain / The Golden Center / Hole in The Sky / Stranded /

EIDOLON

In Memory / Blood Rain / Eye Of The Storm / Fortress

SEVEN SPIRITS, (1997)
Confession / In Visions Past / Shattered Image: i) The Silent Denial / Shattered Image: ii) Soul Trap / Shattered Image: iii) Illusion / The Path / No Escape / Priest / Inner Demons / Set Me Free / The Seven Spirits / Diary of a Madman

NIGHTMARE WORLD, Metal Blade 14327 (2000)
Nightmare World / Noctern Aeternus (Eternal Night) / Lunar Mission / Eye Of Illusion / Repulsion / Fortress Of Red / Majestic Interlude (instrumental) / Glorified Suicide / Dreamscape

HALLOWED APPARITION, Metal Blade 3984-14371-2 (2001)
De-Evolution / Lords Of Desecration / Forever Be Free / Feed The Machine / Forgotten City / Prelude Into Fear / Mind Alterations / You Will Burn! / Hallowed Apparition / Atomic Rage

COMA NATION, Metal Blade (2002)
Nemesis / Coma Nation / Life In Agony / Scarred / Lost Voyage / A Day Of Infamy / Hunt You Down / The Pentacle Star / From Below / Within The Gates

EIDYLLION (ARGENTINA)

Line-Up: Pablo Balestri (vocals), Federico Fenizi (guitar), Fabricio Quiyotay (bass), Bruno Vitangeli (keyboards), Guillermo Bertinat (drums)

A Progressive Metal act out of Bahía Blanca. Founded in April of 1995, EIDYLLION's first visit to the studio produced a 1996 three track demo. The band at this stage incorporated lead vocalist Cristian Spigardi, guitarist Federico Fenizi, bass player Fernando Ferrari, keyboard player Walter Saleman and drummer Manuel Rivero. Fenizi already had a tradition with acts such as TRILOGIA, SIN PALABRAS and TRAGICO FIN DE SEMANA. EIDYLLION, now seeing Fernando Salvatori replacing Saleman, contributed the track 'El Séptimo Mandato' to a 1998 compilation.

The debut album 'Ilusiones' arrived in 2000. By 2002 EIDYLLION was being fronted by former EPSILON ZERO and CATARSIS singer Pablo Balestri. The rhythm section too would change hands to welcome in bassist Fabricio Quiyotay, a veteran of PAX, ASPEED, AVERNO and SAMADHI, and drummer Guillermo Bertinat of ASPEED and BLASFEMIA. Keyboards were in the hands of Bruno Vitangeli, previously with MITICA.

Albums:
ILUSIONES, (2000)

Adiós (Tormento Y Redención) / El Camino De La Fe / Portal De Dioses / Si Tu Alma Puede Ver / La Libertad Del Trovador / Siempre / Arde Tu Puñal / Pasión En Sangre / El Séptimo Mandato / Alza La Fé / Demasiado Tarde / Miradas Vacías

ELDRITCH (ITALY)

Line-Up: Terence Holler (vocals), Eugene Simone (guitar), Martin Keen (bass), Oleg Smirnoff (keyboards), Adriano Del Canto (drums)

Previously known as ZEUZ. ELDRITCH have propelled themselves to the forefront of Italian Progressive Metal. Featuring ex-NIGHTINGALE bassist Martin Keen, ELDRITCH debuted with the demo tape 'Eternal Mission' followed on by a further demo effort 'Reflections Of Sadness'. ELDRITCH also gained the honours of winning a "Battle of the Bands" competition and had their track 'Killing Dolls' on a subsequent compilation album. Four tracks from these tapes found their way alongside more recent material on their debut album 'Seeds Of Rage'.

During mid 2001 vocalist Terrence Holler and keyboard player Sean Henderson convened a Hard Rock side project with WHITE SKULL guitarist Nick Savio dubbed VICIOUS MARY.

Albums:
SEEDS OF RAGE, Inside Out Music IOMCD 002 (1995)
Incurably Ill / Under This Ground / Chains / Cage Of Sins / Colors / The Deaf And The Blind / Ultimate Solution / I Don't Know Why / Chalice Of Insanity / Blind Promise

HEADQUAKE, Inside Out Music IOMCD008 (1997)
Ghoulish Gift / The Last Embrace / Lord Of An Empty Place / Sometimes In Winter / At The Restless Sea / Salome's Dance / Erase / The Quest (Ion) / Clockwork Bed / Dawn Of The Dying

EL NINO, Inside Out Music (1998)
Fall From Grace / No Direction Home / Heretic Beholder / Scar / Bleed Mask Bleed / The Last Days Of The Year / From Dusk Till Dawn / To Be Or Not To Be (God) / El Nino

EL DRAGON (ARGENTINA)

Line-Up: Olaf Mangialavore (vocals / guitar), Cito Vitulli (bass), Frank Mangialavore (keyboards), Ganzo (drums)

Heavy Metal centred upon the famed figure of Juan Carlos 'Olaf' Mangialavore, a veteran of '70s Glam Rock act LULU, the '80s band RAYO X and also CHYCLE, releasing three albums with the latter. In 1990 Mangialavore, alongside his brother keyboard player Frank, founded the hard hitting Metal act EL DRAGON.

Following the 1991 debut 'La Mascara De Hierro' Frank Mangialavore departed, being replaced by erstwhile UZI man Hugo Morales. Bassist Cito Vitulli was the next to go so Morales switched instruments to cover that position. Morales himself decamped in 2001.

Albums:
LA MASCARA DE HIERRO, Megaton (1991)
VIKINGOS, Megaton (1994)
TESTIGO, Megaton (1998)

ELEGY (HOLLAND)
Line-Up: Ian Parry (vocals), Henk van der Laars (guitar), Patrick Rondat (guitar), Martin Helmantel (bass), Dirk Bruinenberg (drums)

Dutch outfit ELEGY debuted in 1986 with their 'Matricide' demo, which was then followed by a further tape in 1988 entitled 'Better Than Bells'. The same year ELEGY was able to tour Holland as support to KING DIAMOND and ANGELWITCH.

1990 the group released a further two track demo, 'The Elegant Solution', and toured supporting HELLION and BATTLEZONE. Vocalist Eduard Hovinga was drafted in following these shows and ELEGY released their fourth demo, 'Labyrinth Of Dreams'/ 'I'm No Fool' before the emergence of their debut album the following year.

ELEGY toured Japan, Holland, Germany and Belgium to promote the 'Labyrinth Of Dreams' release before undergoing a further line-up at the end of 1993 losing drummer Ed Warby to GOREFEST and was replaced by Dick Bruinenberg. The band also added guitarist Gilbert Pot superseding Arno van Brussel, who had also quit the ranks.

Front man Eduard Hovinga left the band to form Melodic Metal band PRIME TIME with ex-NARITA members guitarist Henrik Poulsen and bassist Chris D. Raikai debuting with 1998's 'The Unknown' album scoring a good deal of success in Japan.

1997's 'State Of Mind' album saw ELEGY fronted by Englishman IAN PARRY (a veteran of three solo albums as well as stints in VENGEANCE, HAMMERHEAD and AIRRACE) together with van de Laars, Bruinenberg and drummer Martin Helmantel. ELEGY promoted this effort by touring Germany sharing a bill with STRATOVARIUS. Added noted French guitarist PATRICK RONDAT for 2000's 'Forbidden Fruit' album. Early 2001 found Rondat on the road in Greece as live guitarist for Electronic Rock

legend JEAN MICHEL JARRE whilst Parry busied himself with a side concern CONSORTIUM PROJECT. This latter venture would also see contributions from Rondat and Bruinenberg. ELEGY's drummer would session on French guitarist Stephan Forte's ambitious ADAGIO concept outing 'Sanctus Ignis'.

ELEGY had their version of 'Rock & Roll' included on the Locomotive Music LED ZEPPELIN tribute album 'The Metal Zeppelin — The Music Remains The Same'.

Singles/EPs:
Take My Love / Labyrinth Of Dreams / Always With You / Spirits / Erase Me, T&T 0025-3 (1996) ('Primal Instinct' EP)

Albums:
LABYRINTH OF DREAMS, T&T 003-2 (1991)
The Grand Change / I'm No Fool / Take My Love / All Systems Go / Trouble In Paradise / Over And Out / Labyrinth Of Dreams / Mass Hysteria / Powergames / The Guiding Light
SUPREMACY, T&T 009-2 (1994)
Windows Of The World / Angels Grace / Poisoned Hearts / Just For Life / Anouk / Circles In The Sand / Darkest Night / Close Your Eyes / Supremacy / Erase Me
LOST, T&T 0017-2 (1995)
Lost / Everything / Clean Up Your Act / Always With You / Under Gods Naked Eye / 1998 (The Prophecy) / Spirits / Crossed The Line / Life It Again / Spanish Inquisition
STATE OF MIND, T&T TT0030-2 (1997)
Equinox / Visual Vortex / Trust / Beyond / Shadow Dancer / Aladdin's Cave / State Of Mind / Destiny Calling / Resurrection / Loser's Game / Suppression
MANIFESTATION OF FEAR, (1999)
Unorthodox Methods / Frenzy / Angel Without Wings / Savage Grace / Master Of Deception / Solitary Day (Living In An Ivory Tower) / Manifestation Of Fear / Victim Of Circumstances / The Forgotten / Redemption / Metamorphosis
FORBIDDEN FRUIT, (2000)
Icehouse / Force Majeure / Killing Time / Behind The Tears / The Great Charade / 'Til Eternity / Masquerade / Elegant Solution / I Believe / Forbidden Fruit / Sweet Revenge / Angel Without Wings / The Forgotten
PRINCIPLES OF PAIN, Avalon Marquee MICP-10295 (2002)
Under My Skin / The Inner Room / No Code No Honour / Walking Nightmare / Pilgrims Parade / Principles Of Pain / Creatures Of Habit / Silence In The Wind / Hypothesis / Missing Persons / A Child's Breath / Silence In The Wind (Acoustic version)

ELIXIR (UK)
Line-Up: Paul Taylor (vocals), Phil Denton (guitar), Norman Gordon (guitar), Kevin Dobbs (bass), Nigel Dobbs (drums)

A Traditional British Metal band hailing from Walthamstow, ELIXIR gained a reputation for dogged perseverance for both themselves and manager Seymour Mincer. ELIXIR personified the NWoBHM movement delivering back to basics, catchy Heavy Metal.
ELIXIR first got together in November 1983 with original female lead vocalist Sally Pike. The band, initially going under the titles of PURGATORY and HELLFIRE, was assembled by the Dobbs sibling rhythm section of bassist Kevin and drummer Nigel, along with erstwhile HGV and STRATUS guitarist Phil Denton. Within the space of just two gigs Pike had departed to join the short-lived All-Girl Rock troupe SWEET 16. She was replaced by former MIDAS man Paul Taylor, with Norman Gordon of HAZE also recruited prior to the band's three track 1984 demo 'Dead Man's Gold', 'Born Loser' and 'Deal With The Devil'. With Taylor ensconced ELIXIR debuted their new look line-up in January of 1985 at a gig supporting TOKYO BLADE.
In 1986 the group self-financed both, 'Treachery - Ride Like The Wind' single, and album 'The Son Of Odin' releases, although the band suffered the loss of bassist Kevin Dobbs who left in mid 1987 and was replaced by ex-SCHUTT and JOKER bassist Mark White.
ELIXIR briefly boasted among the ranks former IRON MAIDEN drummer Clive Burr, with whom they recorded the 'Lethal Potion' album, but he had departed by the time of its release and his place was taken by ex-SWEET SAVAGE drummer Stevie Hughes. However, ELIXIR folded during 1990.
After ELIXIR's demise singer Paul Taylor formed the 1990 act ENGLISH ELECTRIC and subsequently HAIR OF THE DOG with ex-TREASON guitarist Cullen Reavley in 1991. Taylor later reunited with Norman Gordon in BEGGARS, THIEVES AND MADMEN as well as operating the Blues act COLD TOWN. This latter act included another ELIXIR refugee guitarist Phil Denton. Gordon had been busying himself on the live circuit with Pop act VOX NOUVEAX, Rockers EMERALD DOGS and covers act SKYWALKER. Post ELIXIR the Dobbs brothers created SARATOGA with ex-MASTER vocalist Rob Angell and guitarists Brad Williams and Pete Lynskey.
Quite incredibly ELIXIR rose from the ashes in August of 2001 with plans set for recording of a new album 'The Idol'. Meantime 'The Son Of Odin' would be reissued by the Cult Metal Classics label complete with three extra tracks in 'Chariot Of The Gods', 'Winds Of Time' and a live version of 'Treachery'.

Singles/EPs:
Treachery - Ride Like The Wind, Elixir ELIXIR 1 (1986)

Albums:
THE SON OF ODIN, Elixir ELIXIR 2 (1986)
The Star Of Beshaan / Pandora's Box / Hold High The Flame / Children Of Tomorrow / Trial By Fire / Starflight / Dead Man's Gold / Treachery (Ride Like The Wind) / Son Of Odin
LETHAL POTION, Sonic CD9 (1990)
She's Got It / Sovereign Remedy / Llagaeran / Louise / Shadows Of The Night / All Together Again / Light In Your Heart / (Metal Trance Intro) Visions Of Darkness / Edge Of Eternity / Last Rays Of The Sun

ELVENKING (ITALY)
Line-Up: Damnagoras (vocals), Aydan (guitar), Jarpen (guitar), Gorlan (bass), Zender (drums)

ELVENKING blend Speed Metal with rustic Folk influence for a quite unique combination. The debut album, 'Heathenreel', produced by Fredrik Nordstrom and released by the German AFM label in July of 2001, included a cover version of SKYCLAD's 'Penny Dreadful'.
The band founded by guitarists Aydan and Jarpen, the latter then titled Dag'Or'Dil, during October 1997 along with bassist Sargon. Vocalist Damnagoras and drummer Zender (a.k.a. 'Stormgald') would finalise the line-up in 1998. Before recording of a promotional CD EP 'To Oak Woods Bestowed' Sargon made his exit. ELVENKING duly drafted five string bassist Gorlan as replacement.
The connection with SKYCLAD was strengthened when it was announced that erstwhile SKYCLAD and present day RETURN TO THE SABBAT vocalist Martin Walkyier would perform SKYCLAD songs live on stage with the band at the Italian 'Metal.It' festival in March of 2002. In August of that year ELVENKING would be confirmed to appear at the enormous 'Pepsi Sziget 2002' festival in Budapest, Hungary and also the Derby 'Bloodstock' event in the UK. The latter show would give fans a further chance to see ELVENKING delivering SKYCLAD songs with a guesting Martin Walkyier. As it transpired this collaboration with Walkyier would be extended as ELVENKING parted ways with

singer Damnagoras, due to ill health, a little over a week prior to the band's scheduled appearance 'Bloodstock'.

Singles/EPs:
To Oak Woods Bestowed / White Willow / Banquet Of Bards / Under The Tree Of Us'Dum, Elvenking (1999) ('To Oak Woods Bestowed' EP)

Albums:
HEATHENREEL, AFM (2001)
To Oak Woods Bestowed / Pagan Purity / The Dweller Of Rhymes / The Regality Dance / White Willow / Skywards / Oakenshield / Hobs An' Feathers / Conjuring Of The 14th / A Dreadful Strain / Seasonspeech

EMERALD (SWITZERLAND)

Line-Up: Jvo Julmy (vocals / guitar), Michael Vaucher (guitar), Stephan Kaufmann (bass), Thomas Vaucher (keyboards), Andy Bachler (drums)

EMERALD was borne in 1995, the product of a merger between erstwhile members of two recently fractured bands OPPRESS and DARK CRYSTAL. As such, EMERALD numbered vocalist Veronique Remy, guitarists Michael Vaucher and Jvo Julmy of DARK CRYSTAL and the former OPPRESS rhythm section comprising bassist Roger Winkler and drummer Stefan Neuhaus.

The band at first operated performing DARK CRYSTAL material but steadily built up a repertoire of originals. However, Remy departed necessitating Julmy taking on lead vocal responsibilities. Shortly after Winkler decamped. Pulling in bassist Adriano Troiano EMERALD debuted live in November of 1997, soon after taking on support gigs to M-FORCE.

In the Spring of 1998 Thomas Vaucher enrolled as keyboard player. With this line-up EMERALD cut the debut 1999 album 'Rebels Of Our Time'. This record drew favourable press reports across Europe.

Upfront of recording a second album 'Calling The Knights' Troiano was replaced by Stephan Kaufmann. 'Calling The Knights', which boasted a cover of the MEDIEVAL STEEL anthem, was delivered in June of 2001. The exposure to the new album would be greatly enhanced by track inclusions on compilations such as 'Metalcoven', 'Pounding Metal Vol IV' and 'Power Battle Vol. 2' in Germany and the Greek 'Holy Sword' collection.

The group, switching drummers to Andy Bachler, signed a contract with the German Shark label in late 2001. The first fruits of this liaison was a worldwide re-release of 'Calling The Knights' in February of 2002 adding new cover art plus bonus tracks.

Albums:
REBELS OF OUR TIME, (1999)
Intro / Forever Free / I Will Remember / Never Fall In Love / Let The Lightning Strike / Independence / You And I / Rebels Of Our Time
CALLING THE KNIGHTS, Emerald CD 01 0514 (2001)
Calling The Knights / Emerald Knights / Unreasonable Violence / Hard To Be True / Across The Sea / Victims Of Society / You Belong To Me / Shadowknight / Medieval Steel / Battlefield
CALLING THE KNIGHTS, Shark (2002)
Calling The Knights / Emerald Knights / Unreasonable Violence / Hard To Be True / Across The Sea / Victims Of Society / You Belong To Me / Shadowknight / Medieval Steel / Battlefield / I Will Remember / Independence

EMPIRE (GERMANY)

Line-Up: Lance King (vocals), Rolf Munkes (guitar), Neil Murray (bass), Gerald Kloos (drums)

Yet another in the long line of Hard Rock projects to use the well worn EMPIRE tag. This 2001 alliance was motivated by VANIZE guitarist and solo artist ROLF MUNKES. The six stringer could call on some heavyweight back for the debut album 'Hypnotica' including erstwhile WHITESNAKE, BLACK SABBATH and present day COMPANY OF SNAKES bassist Neil Murray, BALANCE OF POWER vocalist Lance King and erstwhile FALLACY drummer Gerald Kloos.

Both Munkes and Kloos had been members of earlier acts STATIC IMAGE and HOLEY WOOD. The drummer had also contributed to Munkes 1998 solo record 'No More Obscurity'.

Joining in on a session basis with EMPIRE were the esteemed ex-YNGWIE MALMSTEEN front man MARK BOALS, the veteran former OZZY OSBOURNE and RAINBOW keyboard maestro DON AIREY and YNGWIE MALMSTEEN and HAMMERFALL sticksman Anders Johansson.

Albums:
HYPNOTICA, Lion Music (2001)
Hypnotica / Fool In Love / Into The Light / You're All That I Am Looking For / Spread My Wings / Bad Bad Boy / Here I Am / I Will

Always Be There / A Different Sign / Shelter / Back To Me / Another Place Another Time

EMPTY TREMOR (ITALY)
Line-Up: Giovanni Di Luigi (vocals), Christian Tombetti (guitar), Marco Guerrini (guitar), Daniele Liverani (keyboards), Dennis Randi (bass), Stefano Ruzzi (drums)

Noted Progressive Metal act. EMPTY TREMOR, originally a covers band, went under the title of NOISE POLLUTIONE upon their formation in 1994. The following year heralded the name change to EMPTY TREMOR, the substitution of vocalist De Paoli Davide by Matteo Babbini and the recording of the demo 'Apocokyntosys'. The eight tracks delivered on this tape would mostly re-surface under differing titles on the debut album. However, in 1996 Babbini left the fold and a new frontman, Giovanni Di Luigi, was enrolled for recording of the debut album, reworking all the lyrics from the demos.
The band contributed a medley of DREAM THEATER songs plus an original composition 'The Message Keeper' to a tribute album 'Voices' in 1999. Keyboard player DANIELE LIVERANI, also an accomplished guitarist, also bowed in with his first solo outing 'Viewpoint'.
Just as Liverani issued his second solo album 'Daily Trauma' vocalist Giovanni Di Luigi decamped from EMPTY TREMOR in December of 2000.
Daniele Liverani, founded the hugely ambitious GENIUS concept album of 2002. A former EMPTY TREMOR vocalist, Titta Tani, would go on to join Progressive Metal band DGM and also front DAEMONIA

Albums:
APOCOLOKYNTOSYS, Rising Sun 35899 (1997)
The Eyes Of Universe / Rules Of Time / The Message Keeper / Running Rusty Nails / Apocolokyntosys / Middleman / Slice Of Life / Screaming Loud The Sins Of The World
EROS AND THANTOR, Elevate (2000)
Chapter I - The Future Needs Your Name / Chapter II - Always There / Chapter III - Lost In The Past / Chapter IV - Outside / Chapter V - Chinese Box / Chapter VI - Star / Chapter VII - Y2K / Chapter VIII - Just For Today / Chapter IX - The Timeless Night

EMPYRIA (CANADA)
Line-Up: Phillip Leite (vocals), Mike Kischnick (guitar), Ken Firomski (bass), Simon Adam (drums)

Formed in British Columbia in 1991, by guitarist Mike Kischnick and frontman Paul Falcon on lead vocals and bass. EMPYRIA followed a traditional path of gigs and demos, refining their craft until a pro-demo emerged in 1994 called 'Ornamental Ironworks'. Despite the musical climate of Metal in the mid '90s, the buzz about their brand of technical Progressive Power Metal, was strong enough that T&T, a subsidiary of Noise Records, signed the band for a one album deal in 1996. The result was their release 'Behind Closed Doors' which, despite some heavy weight critical acclaim, did little in terms of international sales. The band was back to being an indie act shortly there after. In 1997 Falcon left the band and Kischnick soon recruited Phillip Leite on vocals and Ken Firomski on bass.
A second CD the aptly titled 'Changing Currents' was released on their own label in 1998. What did not kill the band made them stronger as the next two years saw the band growing in popularity, appearing, on three compilation CDs and they continuing to write material.
The result of this hard work was that in 2000 the band was signed to the small label Nightmare Records, run by Lance King of GEMINI and BALANCE OF POWER. In November, Nightmare released 'The Legacy' in North America. 'The Legacy' was in a sense an EP that pulled together three or four part thread of songs from previous releases into one 25-minute epic called 'The Lighter Side of Darkness'. The EP also saw an ambitious and unique cover tune in the form of 'Synchronicity II' by THE POLICE. 2001 saw the band appear on another compilation, The 'West Coast Metal Fest', produced by the internationally famous, Vancouver metal speciality store, Scrape Records.
The band is still very much active and continues their unbroken pattern of a new CD every two years as their latest, 'Sense Of Mind', will be released in early 2002.

Albums:
BEHIND CLOSED DOORS, T&T TT023-2 (1995)
Test Of Time / Uncertain Reality / World's Apart / Lost In The Shadows / To Live Again / Solace / The Lighter Side Of Darkness / Secret Visions / Seasons Of Change / Behind Closed Doors / The Calling
CHANGING CURRENTS, Empyia EMP 002 (1999)
Changing Currents / Desperate Lives / Will Of A Heart / The Grand Illusion / Silent Rage / Reflections / Secrets Of The Damned / A Part Of Life
THE LEGACY, Nightmare NMR 0012 (2000)

The Lighter Side of Darkness / The Grand Illusion / Silent Rage / The Legacy / Synchronicity II / Years Behind
SENSE OF MIND, (2002)
Ties That Bind / No More Lies / In God's Hands / Heaven's Cry / Sense Of Mind / Where Prejudice Reigns / Long Road Home / Blackened Heart / A New Beginning / Forever

ENCHANT (CA, USA)
Line-Up: Ted Leonard (vocals), Douglas A. Ott (guitar / keyboards), Ed Platt (bass), Paul Craddick (drums/keyboards)

San Francisco based Progressive Rock outfit ENCHANT has gained a solid foothold on the European market garnered from a string of strong releases and high profile tours. The group was convened during 1989 by drummer Paul Craddick, guitarist Douglas Ott and keyboard player Michael Geimer. A series of demos ensued with Ott taking the lead vocal role before the band was brought up to strength in 1992 with the enlistment of bassist Ed Platt and former REVELATION and SPOONS vocalist Ted Leonard.
A deal was struck with the Dream Circle label for debut record 'A Blueprint Of Our World'. Material for this album would be laid down both in San Francisco and Liverpool, the British sessions produced by MARILLION guitarist Steve Rothery. Road work to promote the debut would see ENCHANT paired with touring partners JADIS for a string of European shows.
In 1995 the band switched labels to the Inside Out Music concern. ENCHANT contributed a cover of 'Changes' to the Mike Varney and Peter Morticelli compiled YES tribute album 'Tales From Yesterday', on Magna Carta Records, the same year and unveiled their sophomore record 'Wounded' in 1996.
ENCHANT supported DREAM THEATER then THRESHOLD in Europe during 1997. These dates would coincide with the release of the 'Time Lost...' album, a collection of outtakes and unreleased material. 1998's 'Break' would further the band's momentum with another round of European shows aligned with SPOCK'S BEARD and MARILLION.

Albums:
A BLUEPRINT OF THE WORLD, Dream Circle (1993)
The Thirst / Catharsis / Oasis / Acquaintance / Mae Dae / At Death's Door / East Of Eden / Nighttime Sky / Enchanted
WOUNDED, Inside Out Music (1996)
Below Zero / Fade 2 Grey / Pure / Broken /

Hostile World / Look Away / Armour / Distractions / Missing
TIME LOST..., Inside Out Music SPV 085-28362 (1997)
Blind Sided / New Moon / Under The Sun / Foundations / Interact / Standing Ground / Mettle Man
BREAK, Inside Out Music IOMCD028 (1998)
Break / King / My Enemy / Defenseless / The Lizard / Surrounded / Silence / In The Dark / My Gavel Hand / The Cross / Once A Week
JUGGLING 9 OR DROPPING 10, Inside Out Music IOMCD 064 (2000)
Paint The Picture / Rough Draft / What To Say / Bite My Tongue / Colors Fade / Juggling Knives / Black Eyes & Broken Glass / Elyse / Shell Of A Man / Broken Wave / Traces / Know That
BLINK OF AN EYE, Inside Out Music (2002) **92 GERMANY**
Under Fire / Monday / Seeds Of Hate / Flatline / Follow The Sun / Ultimate Gift / My Everafter / Invisible / Despicable / Prognosis

ENCRYPTION (GERMANY)
Line-Up: Norbert Hartmann (vocals), Christian Klein (guitar), Stefan Muller (guitar), Oliver Goss (bass), Johannes Klein (drums)

Franconian Progressive Thrashers ENCRYPTION was founded as CRYPTIC during 1995, issuing 'The Cryptogram' demo the following year and a 1997 debut album 'Shrouded In Mystery'.
During the final recording stages of the second album CRYPTIC would be delivered two blows. Not only did founder member and guitarist Manfred Herzog depart but also a Munich based band claimed legal right to the CRYPTIC band title. With artwork already completed for the record stickers were hastily made up bearing the new title of ENCRYPTION.
Second guitarist Stefan Muller was added to the ranks in August of 2001.

Albums:
SHROUDED IN MYSTERY, (1997)
Shrouded In Mystery / Lack Of Animosity / Brainchild / Oblivious Vapours / Predator One / My Messiah / Fog's Kiss / Throne Of Chaos
PERISHING BLACK LIGHT, (2000)
Perishing Black Light / Lambda Core / All Philistines / The Inmost Dance / Conquering The Night / Autumn Harvest

ENDLESS (BRAZIL)
Line-Up: Vitor Veiga (vocals), Cris Moura

(guitar), Leandro Monteiro (guitar), Rey Araujo (bass) Marcio Brito (keyboards), Serigio Sanchez (drums)

Albums:
ETERNAL WINDS, Megahard (2000)
Visions Of Tomorrow / Wasting My Time / Holy Ground / Guiding Light / Eagle's Top / Mind Of Indecision / Intro / Minstrels Of Dawn / Eternal Winds / I'm Alone / Good Bye
CELESTIAL DREAMS – THE REAL ILLUSION, Megahard (2001)

ENERTIA (Albany, NY, USA)
Line-Up: Scott Featherstone (vocals), Dave Stafford (guitar), Roman Singleton (guitar), Joe Paciolla (bass), Jeff Daily (drums)

Albany based Power inclined Thrash act ENERTIA came together during February of 1996 and have industriously embarked upon a programme of self-releases ever since commencing with July 1996's 'Law Of Three' mini-album. ENERTIA reaped valuable exposure as part of the independent movie 'These Days', performing 'Real' from the 1999 'Flashpoint' album.
ENERTIA would also act as the backing band for a METALLICA tribute released by Perris Records. Amongst the songs covered would be 'Ride The Lightning' featuring WATCHTOWER vocalist Jason McMaster, 'For Whom The Bell Tolls' and 'Master Of Puppets' fronted by erstwhile IRON MAIDEN singer PAUL DIANNO and 'Creeping Death' with vocals from Stevie Blaze. Also cut would be 'Welcome Home (Sanatorium)' and 'Sad But True', both with ENERTIA vocalist Scott Featherstone taking the lead. During 2002 ENERTIA set to work on recording a new album with famed Metal producer Neil Kernon.

Albums:
LAW OF THREE, Enertia (1996)
The Mirror / Child Now Lost / I Know Your Demons / Same Old Story / If I Were You
MOMENTUM, Enertia (1998)
Ripped Out / Dear God / And So You Fall / Six Weeks / Weight Of The World / You Know / Sever The Wicked / Walls
FLASHPOINT, Enertia (1999)
Victim Of Thought / Leave Me In Peace / Glitch / Crawling / Real / D.O.M. / Voices / Without End / What Hurts Me… / Right To Die

ENOLA GAY (GERMANY)
Line-Up: Peter Diersmann (vocals), Rainer Rage (guitar), Cagge (guitar), Christian Meyer (bass), Marc Könneke (drums)

ENOLA GAY came together in 1987 with an original line-up featuring vocalist Peter Diersmann and guitarists Rainer Rage, ex-SDI, and Carsten Duhme. In 1992 Duhme was superseded by Michael Hildebrandt and the band were brought up to strength by a rhythm section comprising bassist Christian Meyer and drummer Marc Könneke. This line-up released the third demo titled 'Spectrum Of Colours' in 1992.
After the release of the debut album the group toured Europe with STRATOVARIUS, although Rainer Rage would soon leave in 1996 and, now trimmed to a quartet, ENOLA GAY entered the studio to record second album 'Pressure' and later toured supporting ICED EARTH and NEVERMORE. Nico Luttenberg was added as second guitarist in 1997.
ENOLA GAY signed to the Century Media label for 1999's 'Strange Encounter' album. The band did manage to donate their version of BLACK SABBATH's 'Heaven And Hell' to the DIO tribute 'Holy Dio' but after the third release, their most Metal orientated, the band folded.

Albums:
FLY OFF THE HANDLE, Shark 104 (1995)
Fly Off The Handle / Close Cropped Head / Bad News / Last Generation / Spectrum Of Colours / Welcome / Never Be Without A Friend / Doomwatch / The Sign / Now Or Never
PRESSURE, Cream 008 (1996)
Back To Prison / Near The End / Who's My God? / Into The Void / Anxious Thoughts / Intrusions / Where The Mountain Meets The Sky / Pain / Eleanor Rigby / One Way Trip / Disappointed
STRANGE ENCOUNTER, Century Media CMCD77286 (1999)
Enola Gay / Sick Society / Browsing / Strange Encounter / Psycho Lover / Awakening / Rapacious Attack / Desire / Different I's / Escape From Reality / Thrill Of It All

ETERNA (BRAZIL)
Line-Up: Leandro Cacoilo (vocals), Paulo Frade (guitar), Jason Freitas (bass), Douglas Codonho (keyboards), Danilo Lopes (drums)

Brazilian Christian Power Metal act ETERNA debuted with the 1997 'Shema Israel' album. The band was originally a trio comprising vocalist bassist Alexandre Emanuel, guitarist Paulo Frade and drummer Danilo Lopes. A sophomore outing, 1999's 'Papyrus', was issued the following year in Europe with different artwork on the Italian Scarlet label. Two new members, vocalist Leandro Cacoilo and bass player Jason Freitas were added, for recording of the 2001 album 'The Gate'.

Albums:
SHEMA ISRAEL, (1997)
Shema Israel / Fiat Voluntas Tua / Lembra-Te! / Stay / I Have The Key / Piedade / Agony / Holy Shadow / The Word / Resgate / Deserto Da Alma
PAPYRUS, (1999)
Working Man / Longevity / Mary´s Son / Da Pacem Domine / The War Is Over! / Euthanasia / Social Sacrifice / Corruption / Resurrection / Papyrus (Part I + II) / Fight Recorder
THE GATE, Encore (2001)
Open The Gate / Entrance / Fly Away / Forgive Me / Fight / The Winter / Living Word / The Gate / Shine / A Matter Of Time / Amazing Shepherd / Sea Of Lights

ETERNAL DARKNESS (GERMANY)
Line-Up: Dietmar Bundschuh (vocals), Tom Haumann (guitar), Roberto D'Amico (bass), Thorsten Herrmann (keyboards), Norman Weiner (drums)

ETERNAL DARKNESS, from Swabia in Southern Germany, feature former X RAY vocalist Dietmar Bundschuh and erstwhile SYRACON guitarist Tom Haumann. Drummer Norman Weiner had been involved with covers band AFTER THE RAIN.
ETERNAL DARKNESS would employ the services of former SCREAMING and current DEFENDING THE FAITH bassist Roberto D'Amico for the 'Out Of Control' album. However, D'Amico had returned to the ranks of DEFENDING THE FAITH that same September.
The band was projecting to release a fresh album 'Valley Of The Kings' during 2002.

Albums:
STORIES, (1999)
OUT OF CONTROL, (2000)
Intro / Out Of Control / Borderline / Hear The Voices / Run For Your Life / Angel Fly / Pain / Like A Story / Destiny / One Step Closer

ETERNAL NIGHT (SPAIN)

Singles/EPs:
A Tail Of Mist & Moonlight / Under A Veil Of Darkness / Beyond The Grave / Master Of Illusion, (1999) ('Illusions Of Darkness' EP)

Albums:
HEAVEN'S KINGDOM WILL BE YOURS,
Donosti Rock (1998)

ETERNIA (SWEDEN)
Line-Up: Mats Dahlberg (vocals), Daniel Niemann (guitar), Ronny Blylod (guitar), Patrik Nordendahl (bass), Magnus Larsson (drums)

Albums:
THE GUARDIAN OF THE TREASURE, Eternia (1999)
Soldiers Of The Night / The Eye Of The Storm / The Guardian Of The Treasure / As I Fall / Goodbye
TALES OF POWER, Hans Edler Music (2002)
Taste Of Victory / To The Battlefields / Divine Immortality / Stories From The Past / Sailing Home / When The Legend Rides / Forever Unleashed / Shadoria / Shadoria Part II (Shadows Of Steel)

ETERNITY X (Cliffwood, NJ, USA)
Line-Up: Keith Sudano (vocals), Jeff Shernov (guitar), Jamie Mazur (keyboards), Zeek (bass), Jimmy Peruta (drums)

ETERNITY X offered Progressive Metal. The 'Zodiac' album, released in 1994, originally only came in cassette form until its CD re-release some four years later.
Guitarist Jeff Shernov, keyboard player Jamie Mazur and drummer Jimmy Peruta created a new project with ex-SEVEN WITCHES singer Bobby Lucas in 2000.

Albums:
THE NEVER ENDING DREAM, (1991)
AFTER THE SILENCE, (1993)
ZODIAC, (1994) (Cassette only)
MIND GAMES, Angular SKAN 8215.AR (1995)
Zodiac Prologue / Aries / Taurus / Gemini / Cancer / Leo / Virgo / Libra / Scorpio / Sagittarius / Capricorn / Aquarius / Pisces / Zodiac Epilogue / Fast Forward
THE EDGE, Angular SKAN 8206.AR (1997)
The Edge... (Introduction) / Fly Away / The Confession / The Edge Part 2... (The Looking Glass) / A Day In Verse / Imaginarium / The Edge Part 3... (Existence Chapter 1,000,009) / The Edge Of Madness / Rejection / Baptised By Fire / The Edge... Legacy / Reprise
ZODIAC, Angular SKAN 8209.AR (1998)
Firestorm / Mind Games / The Chase / The Savior And The Disease / Despair: Crawl Before You Walk / Despair: Viper II / Despair: Faith / Endless Journey / Eulogy / Eternity / Switchblade

ETHEREA (ITALY)
Line-Up: Sergio Casadei (vocals), Massimiliano Fabrizi (guitars), Alexandru Dafinei (bass), Francesco Guerra (keyboards), Claudio Crucianelli (drums)

Progressive Metal band. ETHEREA are fronted by Sergio Casadei, former singer with KINGCROW, EARTH SHAKER and SEAL OF FIRE. Guitarist Massimiliano Fabrizi is also an ex-EARTH SHAKER member whilst the rhythm, section of bassist Alexandru Dafinei and drummer Claudio Crucianelli have a tradition with BLACKWIND.
Initially a twin guitar band, founder member Francesco Saltelli decamped in 2000 leaving Fabrizi as sole guitarist.

EVASSION (SPAIN)
Line-Up: Boca (vocals), Alfonso Fernández (guitar), Oscar Bendala (guitar), Daniel Romero (bass), Laure Alvea (drums)

Seville classic Metal outfit EVASSION came into being during 1995, put together by former ARKANOS members guitarist Oscar Bendala and drummer Laure Alvea with singer J.C. 'Boca' Bocanegro, second guitarist Alfonso Fernández and erstwhile DOOMED TO FAILURE bassist Lelin. The demo 'Tax To Caronte' surfaced before the close of their first year of operation. A second effort, 'True Nature', was delivered in 1997 but the following year witnessed the departure of bassist Lelin.
EVASSION signed to the Avispa label, their debut being a collection of new and archive demo material. In late December of 2001 Lelin would act as substitute for Romero for a batch of gigs. In early 2002 Romero suffered a bad car accident which, although not putting him out of action, did force the four stringer to remain seated for the band's live gigs.

Albums:
EVASSION, Avispa (1999)
Desde El Otro Lado / Nemesis / Desterrados / Ya Es Hora / Medieval / That´s Not The Way / So Easy / Why Don't You Look At Me? / Tax To Caronte

EVERGREY (SWEDEN)
Line-Up: Tom S. Englund (vocals / guitar), Dan Bronelli (guitar), Daniel Nojd (bass), Will Chandra (keyboards), Patrick Carlsson (drums)

Highly regarded Swedish Progressive Metal band. EVERGREY's 1998 album 'The Dark Discovery', released on the GNW (Gothenburg Noise Works) label, witnessed guest performances from KING DIAMOND's Andy LaRocque, also acting as producer, and FREAK KITCHEN's Mattias La Eklundh.
EVERGREY switched to the Hall Of Sermon Gothic Rock specialists for 2000's 'Solitude, Dominance, Tragedy' outing. The album release party was held in Bochum, Germany at a gig sharing billing with RAGE.
However, bass player Daniel Nojd decamped and EVERGREY enlisted two new recruits, bassist Michael Hakansson and SOILWORK keyboard player Sven Karlsson, both erstwhile members of Black Metal band EMBRACED. Hakansson also divides his duties with THE FORSAKEN.
European dates saw the band opening proceedings at the German 'Bang Your Head' festival and touring alongside CRIMSON GLORY and KAMELOT.
The band would also find studio time the same year to donate their rendition of 'Rising Force' to a YNGWIE MALMSTEEN tribute album.
Later in the year guitarist Dan Bronelli made his exit too. The band endured by drafting Henric Danhage. EVERGREY signed to the Inside Out Music label for release of a third album, the September 2001 conceptual piece 'In Search For Truth'.
Keyboard player Sven Karlsson would be let go later in the year, his replacement being Chris Rehn. By 2002 EVERGREY had installed Rikard Zande in the keyboard role for recording of a new album with producer Andy LaRocque.

Albums:
THE DARK DISCOVERY, GNW GNW002 (1998)
Blackened Dawn / December 26th / Dark Discovery / As Light Is Our Darkness / Beyond Salvation / Closed Eyes / Trust And Betrayal / Shadowed / When The River Calls / For Every Tear That Falls / To Hope Is To Fear
SOLITUDE, DOMINANCE, TRAGEDY, Hall Of Sermon HOS 7111 (2000)
Solitude Within / Nosferatu / The Shocking Truth / A Scattered Me / She Speaks To The Dead / When Darkness Falls / Words Mean Nothing / Damnation / The Corey Curse
IN SEARCH OF THE TRUTH, Inside Out Music IOMA 2025-2 (2001) **59 SWEDEN**
The Masterplan / Rulers Of The Mind / Watching The Skies / State Of Paralysis / The Encounter / Mark Of The Triangle / Dark Waters / Different Worlds / Misled

EVIL WINGS (ITALY)
Line-Up: Franco Giaffreda (vocals / guitar), Giovanni Bellosi (bass), Rock Ostidich

(keyboards), Walter Rivolta (drums)

Formed in 1989, albeit with a different line-up to that listed above, EVIL WINGS released their debut demo, 'Shadeless Mountain', the same year before a further demo (1992's 'Behind The Sky') was made more commercially available.

In 1994 the band, heavily influenced by the likes of American Metal outfits, finally recorded their debut album for the Underground Symphony label. The sophomore 'Brightleaf' album followed in 1997.

Albums:
EVIL WINGS, Underground Symphony US CD-003 (1994)
Evil Wings / Rise To The Sunlight / Chrysalis / Fairies / Behind The Sky / Treasure Island / Mistress Of The Silent Sea / Enigma / In The Dream
BRIGHTLEAF, Underground Symphony USCD015 (1997)
The Rope Walkers / I Went Across The Time / Tales From Nowhere / The Script / Rain And Mist / Ben Rowi / Waiting For… / The Dragon Knight
COLORS OF THE NEW WORLD,
Adrenaline (2000)
Colors Of The New World / Flowers / Away / Searchin' / Starship / Big Old Roundabout / The Secret / The Stageline / Sell My Soul (Damnation) / 20th Of May / Colors Of The New World (Revisited)

EXCELSIS (SWITZERLAND)
Line-Up: Münggu Beyerler (vocals / bass), Rölu Schwab (guitar), Samson (guitar), Daniela Beyerler (keyboards), Küsu Herrmann (drums)

Albums:
ANDUIN THE RIVER, (1997)
Intro / Houses Of Healing / Beneath The Hills / Princess Of The Trees / Anduin The River / Maiden In Forbidden Garden / Mordor Speaks / In The Highlands / Gwaihir - The Name Of Bird / Back Into The Deepest Night - Outro / S'Annebäbeli
KURT OF KOPPIGEN, Shark (1999)
Intro / Before The Storm / Kurt Of Koppigen / Grimhilde / The Dragonslayer / The Lord Of Halten / Ambush Of Langenthal / Song Of Agnes / Distant Sky Or The Wild Hunt / The Lost Chapter / Baphomet's Oath / Lamm Am Hang / Lämmer Am Hänger
TALES OF TELL, (2001)
Intro / The Tombstone / Gfauni Ängle / Tell / The Tomorrow Song / Dragongroundalp / Forgotten Hymn / Täu Grosse Kämpfer /

Don't Destroy / Out Of Rain / Hillflames On High / Last Episode / Outro / Fritzebach

EXCITER (CANADA)
Line-Up: Dan Beehler (vocals / drums), John Ricci (guitar), Allan Johnson (bass)

Canadian Metal trio EXCITER, founded in Ontario in 1979 and almost certainly named after the infamous show opening JUDAS PRIEST track, made their presence known with some gut crunching Metal blessed by the raucous vocals of drummer Dan Beehler. EXCITER first got noticed courtesy of 'Heavy Metal Maniac' demo which quickly led to a deal with Mike Varney's Shrapnel label.

EXCITER's 1984 'Violence And Force' album was produced by THE RODS drummer Carl Canedy and soon shifted a healthy 75,000 copies. Its follow up 'Long Live The Loud' saw production from Guy Bidmead. The band backed up this release by touring Europe as support to ACCEPT in early 1985.

1986's Guy Bidmead produced 'Unveiling The Wicked' found long term member guitarist John Ricci departing to found BLACKSTAR. His replacement was Brian McPhee. EXCITER pulled in former SILENT PARTNER / SIMMONDS vocalist Jimmy Kunes but this liaison did not gell. After dates in Brazil the band added vocalist Rob Malnati for 1989's 'OTT' record.

Beehler decided to put EXCITER on ice during 1990 forming a new act KILJOY. Joining him on demos were former CRYPT bassist David Ledden and guitarist Joe Desmond.

Ricci and Beehler decided to re-energise EXCITER, once more bringing in bassist Ledden for the 'Kill After Kill' album produced by former AVALON musician Manfred Leidecker. The latter, along with ex-AVALON guitarist Brian Sim, would also handle their follow up 'Better Live Than Dead'. For live work EXCITER utilised the talents of bassist Jeff McDonald.

Recently the band returned with 'The Dark Command' issued on French Black Metal label Osmose Productions. The album was internationally given the thumbs up as a powerful return to form. Ricci had give new life to the band which now comprised an all new crew of vocalist Jacque Belanger, bassist Marc Charron and drummer Rick Charron. This unit solidified EXCITER's return with the 2000 'Blood Of Tyrants' opus. However, during September of 2001 it was learned that Belanger had bailed out.

Meantime Toronto Black Metal band MEGIDDO would pay homage by including a cover version of 'Violence And Force' on their 'The Devil And The Whore' album.

Further exposure would be garnered when up and coming American Metal band SEVEN WITCHES covered 'Pounding Metal' for their second album 'City Of Lost Souls'. The band has sustained enough interest to warrant a slew of live bootlegs including 'Devil's Soul', 'Live Beasts' and Night Of The Creeps'.

During early 2002 famed Virginian Heavy Metal band DECEASED would cover 'Violence And Force' on their 'Zombie Hymns' album.

Vocalist Jacque Belanger apparently left the band in May.

Singles/EPs:
Feel The Knife / Violence And Force, Music For Nations 12 KUT 113 (1985)

Albums:
HEAVY METAL MANIAC, Shrapnel (1983)
Holocaust / Heavy Metal Maniac / Mistress Of Evil / Rising Of The Dead / Cry Of The Banshee / Stand Up And Fight / Iron Dogs / Under Attack / Blackwitch
VIOLENCE AND FORCE, Music For Nations MFN 17 (1984)
Oblivion / Violence And Force / Scream In The Night / Pounding Metal / Evil Sinner / Destructor / Swords Of Darkness / Delivering To The Master / Saxons Of The Fire / War Is Hell
LONG LIVE THE LOUD, Music For Nations MFN 47 (1985)
Fall Out / Long Live The Loud / I Am The Beast / Victims Of Sacrifice / Beyond The Gates Of Doom / Sudden Impact / Born To Die / Wake Up Screaming
UNVEILING THE WICKED, Music For Nations MFN 61 (1989)
Break Down The Walls / Brainstorm / Die In The Night / (I Hate) School Rules / Shout It Out / Invasion - Waiting In The Dark / Living Evil / Live Fast, Die Young / Mission Destroy
O.T.T., Maze 854603 (1989)
Scream Bloody Murder / Back In The Night / Ready To Rock / O.T.T. / I Wanna Be King / Enemy Lines / Dying To Live / Playin' With Fire / Eyes In The Sky / Termination
KILL AFTER KILL, Noise N 0192-2 (1992)
Rain Of Terror / No Life, No Future / Cold Blooded Murder / Smashin' Em Down / Shadow Of The Cross / Dog Eat Dog / Anger, Hate And Destruction / Second Coming / Born To Kill (Live)
BETTER LIVE THAN DEAD - LIVE, Bleeding Hearts CDBLEED 5 (1993)
Stand Up And Fight / Heavy Metal Maniac / Victims Of Sacrifice / Under Attack / Sudden Impacts / Delivering To The Master / I Am The Beast / Blackwitch / Long Live The Loud / Rising Of The Dead / Cry Of The Banshee /

Pounding Metal / Violence And Force
THE DARK COMMAND, Osmose Productions OPCD 059 (1997)
The Dark Command / Burn At The Stake / Aggressor / Assassins In Rage / Ritual Death / Sacred War / Let Us Prey / Executioner / Suicide Overdose / Screams From The Gallows
BLOOD OF TYRANTS, Osmose Productions OPCD 089 (2000)
Metal Crusaders / Rule With An Iron Fist / Intruders / Predator / Martial Law / War Cry / Brutal Warning / Weapons Of Mass Destruction / Blood Of Tyrants / Violator

EXCITER (HOLLAND)
Line-Up: Gert Admiraal (vocals / bass), Marcel Admiraal (guitar), Marc Karsten (guitar), Walter Admiraal (drums)

A short-lived Dutch Metal band comprising the three Admiraal brothers, including a then 14 year old Marcel on guitar. The quartet gained some degree of infamy with an appearance in an early edition of 'Kerrang!' magazine in a short piece commenting on the band's two track demo, which was eventually followed a year later by the release of their debut single, 'All Night In Red Light', through WEA.

Singles/EPs:
All Night In Red Light / See The Diamond, WEA 18 986 (1982)

EXILE (ITALY)
Line-Up: Marco Salafia (vocals), Stefano Fabbri (guitar), Vincenzo Mandarano (guitar), Luciano Campione (bass), Giuseppe Portaro (drums)

Albums:
NIGHTMARE, Exile (2002)
Incoming / Thunder In The Soul / Danger Rock Zone / Dreams Know Me / Nightmare / Unreal

EXISES (HOLLAND)
Line-Up: Co Timmer (vocals), Michel Sietoff (guitar), Adri Sleyster (bass), Rene Schapp (keyboards), Berend Houter (drums)

A Progressive Metal act formed in 1984, EXISES released a self-produced, eponymous debut through Dutch independent Megaton in 1986. The record, featuring lead vocalist Frank Leurs, quickly gained the band a cult following in Holland, not least because it was actually available as the very first Hard Rock CD!

The album was later issued in the United

States although by the time the Sci-Fi concept album 'Reternity' was recorded the group had added new vocalist Co Timmer and keyboard player Rene Schapp to the ranks.

Albums:
EXISES, Megaton Boudisque (1986)
Fear For The Night / Misunderstood / Some Sort Of Freedom / Behind The Wall / Burn The Lights // Stay With Me / Brainstorm / Carry On
RETERNITY, Cymbeline CYMPLY 5079-2 (1996)
Point Of No Return / Meltdown Sector 6 / Sole Survivor / S.P.Y. / Realm Of Darkness / The Transformation / Fatal Miscount / Action Reset / Coming Man / Space Odyssey (The Voyage, Point Of No Return, Part II)

THE EXPERIENCE (GERMANY)
Line-Up: Roman Biewer (vocals / guitar), Sascha Willmes (guitar), Joe Reitz (bass), Christian Jost (keyboards), Renate Iffland (flute), Thomas Merschmann (drums)

Stuttgart based Progressive Metal act THE EXPERIENCE bowed in with the 1996 demo tape 'Mental Solitude', the impact of which garnered valuable support shows to artists such as NEVERMORE, ICED EARTH, SENTENCED and BOLT-THROWER. The band had been created earlier in 1994 and by 1996 cited a roster of Roman Biewer on vocals and guitar, guitarist Sascha Willmes, bassist Dirk Engelbert, keyboard player Christian Jost, flautist Renate Iffland and drummer Thomas Merschmann.
The AFM label soon snapped up the band for the opening January 1997 album 'Realusion', the band being rewarded by the influential 'Rock Hard' magazine as 'German newcomer of the year'.
Prior to recording the follow up 'Insight' THE EXPERIENCE made some significant line-up changes, bringing in fresh personnel-guitarist Oliver Schwinn, bass player Joe Reitz and drummer Tom Diener. Touring to promote the album witnessed support gigs to SUBWAY TO SALLY.
THE EXPERIENCE would then embark on an almost year long marathon in the recording studio assembling the conceptual 'Cid... A Reflection Of A Blue Mind'. During this process Carsten Grasmück supplanted Reitz and AFM Records let the band go. THE EXPERIENCE's third album was delivered as a self-financed effort in 2001.

Albums:
REALUSION, AFM AFMCD010-2 (1997)
INSIGHT, AFM AFMCD036-2 (1999)
Inside / Journey's End / Voice Of Doubt / My Pyramid / Lost My Faith / Walls / From The End... / Sentiment Turn / Resign / The Appearance Of The Spoil-Sport / ...To The Beginning / Outside
CID... A REFLECTION OF A BLUE MIND, (2001)

EXPLORERS CLUB (USA)

An ambitious Metal-edged Progressive Rock project involving DREAM THEATER men John Petrucci, Derek Sherinian and James LaBrie, EXPLORERS CLUB also featured the elite talents of MR. BIG's Billy Sheehan, MISSING PERSONS drummer extraordinaire Terry Bozzio, ROYAL HUNT vocalist D.C. Cooper, MAGELLAN's Trent and Wayne Gardner, DEATH, TESTAMENT and KONKHRA guitarist JAMES MURPHY, the revered YES guitarist STEVE HOWE, DALI DILEMMA members Matt Bradley and Matt Guillory along with CAIRO's Bret Douglas.
The project was inspired by YES' 'Union' album and launched by Trent Gardner alongside Magna Carta Records' Peter Morticelli and Mike Varney. Across the Progressive Rock world the EXPLORERS CLUB debut had a massive impact.
The success of the first album soon led to confirmation of a sophomore EXPLORERS CLUB venture, finally realised in August of 2002 with the issue of 'Raising The Mammoth'. The cast would comprise familiar notables such as Trent Gardner, James LaBrie and Terry Bozzio, as well as DREAM THEATER bassist John Myung, erstwhile MEGADETH guitarist MARTY FRIEDMAN, KANSAS men STEVE WALSH and KERRY LIVGREN, Gary Wehrkamp of SHADOW GALLERY.

Albums:
AGE OF IMPACT, Magna Carta MAX-9021-2 (1998)
1 - Fate Speaks / Impact 2 - Fading Fast / Impact 3 - No Returning / Impact 4 - Time Enough / Impact 5 - Last Call
RAISING THE MAMMOTH, Magna Carta MA-9046-2 (2002)

EXXPLORER (USA)
Line-Up: Lennie Rizzo (vocals), Kevin Kennedy (guitar), Ed LaVolpe (guitar), Jimmy G. (bass), Mike Moyer (drums)

Esteemed Heavy Metal band that made a lasting impression with their 1985 debut 'Symphonies Of Steel'. EXXPLORER split with vocalist Lennie Rizzo in early 1987 and replaced him with female singer Melissa Cahne. The band planned to begin work on a follow-up album to the debut tentatively titled 'Beg, Borrowed And Steel' for Black Dragon. However, the record was never released.

EXXPLORER rose from the grave in 1996 with a second album, 'Coldblackugly', on the German Massacre label, although guitarist Ed LaVolpe and drummer Mike Moyer were the only remaining members of the band that had recorded 'Symphonies Of Steel' eleven years earlier. The new EXXPLORER line-up featured vocalist B.W. Hocking Jr., LaVolpe's new guitar partner Fred Gorhau and bassist J. McCaffrey.

A third EXXPLORER album was released in Japan on the Brunette label, hinting at a FATES WARNING style with original vocalist Lennie Rizzo back in the band and still delivering the goods. The 'Symphonies of Steel' album would be reissued during 2002 adding an additional four brand new studio tracks 'The Magic Hills', 'Man From Nowhere', 'The Cycle' and 'You Made Me Live'.

Albums:
SYMPHONIES OF STEEL, Black Dragon 003 (1985)
City Streets / Prelusion / Run For Tomorrow / Exxplorer / World War III / Going To Hell / Objection Overruled: a) Guilty As Charged, b) Phantasmagoria / Metal Detectors / X-Termination
COLDBLACKUGLY, Massacre MASS CD 089 (1996)
Disfigured / Erotopathic / Fixed And Dilated / Seething In Oblivion / Acrostic I / Van Gogh's Ear / Snake And Scorpion / Acrostic 2 / Billion Dollar Babies / Acrostic 3 / Bloodletting / Poor Man / My Noose / That One Hopeful Song
A RECIPE FOR POWER, Brunette ALCB-3075 (1996)
Rockin' Bound / Life's Seduction / One / Bible Black / Smelling The Roses / Rock The Nation / Beg, Borrow And Steel / Just A Dream / Ride The Storm

EYEFEAR (AUSTRALIA)
Line-Up: Danny Cecati (vocals), Con Papazoglou (guitar), Rob Gorham (bass), Ryan Garrett (keyboards), Zain Kimmie

Melbourne Prog Power Metal dating to 1994. The independent 1996 album 'Edge Of Existence' saw EYEFEAR as a quintet comprising singer Jason Smart, guitarists Con Papazoglou and Ken Taylor, bassist Rob Gorham and drummer Zain Kimmie. Despite this release being at the receiving end of glowing reviews globally Jason Smart made a decision to leave in April of 1997. Earlier guitarist Ken Taylor had also made the break.

Anthony Porchia filled the six string vacancy and after some time EYEFEAR also drew in former HYPERION singer Jim Georgopoulos. The group also bolstered their sound with the addition of keyboard player Shiran Manan. This line-up cut the 'Dawn... A New Beginning' opus but then Georgopoulos, Porchia and Manan all departed.

In September of 2000 the former PEGAZUS singer Danny Cecati enrolled as did keyboard player Garrett Ryan.

Albums:
EDGE OF EXISTENCE, Eyefear DOA666 (1996)
DAWN... A NEW BEGINNING, Fotia (1999)
Dawn / Illumination Fades / Evermore

143

FACT (GERMANY)
Line-Up: Reent Froelich (vocals), Michael Otto (guitar), Patricia Huth (guitar), Thortsten Kath (bass), Peer Würfel (drums)

FACT figured amongst a large number of enthusiastic new German Heavy Metal bands to emerge in the Teutonic Rock boom of the early '80s, inspired by the New Wave of British Heavy Metal movement that had gone before.

Featuring female guitarist Patricia Huth amongst their number, FACT were signed to German independent label Earthshaker Records and quickly earned a reputation for some hard driving music and electrifying live performances.

Having released two albums through Earthshaker, and vocalist Reent Froelich having contributed to the X-MAS PROJECT in 1986 the band was to split in the late '80s, the singer later teaming up with drummer Peer Würfel in CROSSROADS.

Albums:
AS A MATTER OF... FACT, Earthshaker (1984)
Marauder / Sound Attack / Make It Real / Nightmare / Heavy Metal Powerplay / Prisoner / Run (Out Of The Night) / Suspected Quiet / Hard Times
WITHOUT WARNING, Earthshaker ES 4014 (1985)
Intro / Burning For Action / Without Warning / Hotter Than Hell / Mysterious King / Rock You To The Ground / Intro / 2001 / Get Ready To Win / Hear The Devil Crying / Dressed To Kill / Fight For The Metal

FACTORY OF ART (GERMANY)
Line-Up: Gunter (vocals), Flecke (guitar), Joe F. Winter (guitar / keyboards), Ron (bass), Wolf (drums)

FACTORY OF ART's debut album, 'Grasp', features guest appearances by Alex Krull of ATROCITY and Chris Boltendahl of GRAVEDIGGER.
The band became known for their Progressive Power Metal style which they mixed with Speed Metal and Thrash.

Singles/EPs:
Wings Of Destiny / Twilight Zone / Touch Of Cold Rain / No Better World, Factory Of Art (1993) ('No Better World' EP)
The Point Of No Return / Crown Of Creation / Silent Crying, AFM Records 014 (1997)
Story Of Pain / The Mass / Twilight Zone, Factory Of Art (1999)

Albums:
GRASP!!!, AFM Records CD 34325-422 (1996)
Never Dying Hero (N.D.H.) / No Fixed Address / Until The End Of Time / Live Fast / Wings Of Destiny / Character Of Society / The Other Side / Queen Of Seduction / Solitary Soldier / Long Way To The Height

FAITHFUL BREATH (GERMANY)
Line-Up: Heinz Milkuz (vocals / guitar), Horst Stabenow (bass), Uwe Otto (drums)

Dating back to the late '60s with a nucleus of bassist Horst Stabenow and vocalist / guitarist Heinrich Mikus. FAITHFUL BREATH's first album - a self-financed effort titled 'Fading Beauty' - was, amazingly, not released until 1974. It was a four year wait before the band recorded their second album, 'Back On My Hill', for Sky Records. However, the album was shelved and it took a legal battle before the album eventually surfaced in 1980.

The band actually split shortly after the second album's release but they were soon to reform as a three piece (drummer Uwe Otto rounding the band out) and pursued a far heavier direction with a Viking image to match!

Uwe Otto departed in 1982 to be replaced by Jurgen Dusterloh and by fourth album 'Hard Breath' FAITHFUL BREATH had established a healthy European following and switched labels to Mausoleum. Second guitarist Andy Honig and bassist Peter Dell were added at this juncture to augment the increasingly heavier sound.

The band's first album for Mausoleum, 'Gold N Glory', was an instant success and garnered the band much favourable response from media and fans alike. An immensely hard hitting Heavy Metal album produced by the team of noted German knob twiddler Michael Wagener and ACCEPT vocalist Udo Dirkschneider at Dieter Dierks' studios, 'Gold N Glory' established the band as a leading light in the German Metal scene however briefly.

After a bout of successful touring Andy Honig was replaced by Thilo Herrmann to record another fine effort 'Skol', an album that gained further mileage from the beer drinking and hell raising Viking image the group had given itself. Recorded at Dierks Studios once more 'Skol' benefited from a skilful production by producer Gerd Rautenbach.

In the wake of the album's release FAITHFUL BREATH actually performed a short East Coast tour of America before concentrating once more on Europe, with the 'Live' album emerging in 1986, although by 1987 the band had opted to change names to RISK.

Singles/EPs:
Back On My Hill, Sky 45003 (1980)
Die Morderbiene, Sky 106 (1981)
Hurricane, Sky 1055 (1983)
A Million Hearts, Mausoleum GUTS 8401
(1984)

Albums:
FADING BEAUTY, FB AA 6963233 (1974)
Autumn Fantasia: 1st Movement: Fading
Beauty, 2nd Movement: Lingering Cold /
Tharsis
BACK ON MY HILL, Sky 038 (1980)
Back On My Hill / Keep Me Away / This Is
My Love Song / Stick In Your Eyes /
Judgement Day
ROCK LIONS, Sky 055 (1981)
Hurricane / Better Times / Rock City / Rollin'
Into Our Life / Down, Down / Never Be Like
You / No Time / Rock n" Roll Woman
HARD BREATH, Sky 079 (1983)
Killers On The Loose / Give Me What I Need
/ Already Too Late / Dark Angel / Under My
Wheels / Kids, We Want The World / Illusions
/ Like An Eagle In The Sky / Warriors /
Riding To Mongolis / Fly To Another Star /
Night Comes Again
GOLD N' GLORY, Mausoleum SKULL 8335

(1984)
Don't Feel Hate / King Of The Rock /
Jailbreaker / A Million Hearts / Gold n' Glory
/ Play The Game / Princess In Disguise /
Don't Drive Me Mad
SKOL, Ambush HI 401001 (1986)
Start It Up / Double Dealer / Lady M. / Rock
Rebels / We Want You / Inside Out / Crazy In
Metal / Backstreet Heroes / Skol
LIVE, Noise N0051 08-4409 (1986)
Bacchu Beer / Gold n' Glory / Warriors / Like
An Eagle In The Sky / Princess In Disguise /
A Million Hearts / Jailbreaker / Play The
Game / King Of The Rock

FALCONER (SWEDEN)
Line-Up: Matthias Blad (vocals), Stefan
Weinerhall (guitar / bass), Karsten Larsson
(drums)

FALCONER is the brainchild of erstwhile
MITHOTYN guitarist Stefan Weinerhall.
Demos were cut during 2000 with vocalist
Matthias Blad that scored a deal with the
Metal Blade label. Blad's reputation had been
made not in other bands but as a theatre
singer. At the time of joining FALCONER he
was also rehearsing his upcoming lead role in
a production of 'Jesus Christ Superstar'!
Weinerhall's MITHOTYN colleague and ex-

FALCONER

DAWN drummer Karsten Larsson joined the fold in time for recording of the eponymous album.

The resulting record, produced by KING DIAMOND guitarist Andy LaRocque and issued in March 2001 in Europe and May in America, received glowing reviews for its traditional styling. European additions included the bonus track 'Per Tyrssons Dottar I Vange'.

FALCONER entered the studio with LaRocque in November 2001 to lay down the follow up album 'Chapters For A Vale Forlorn'. Weinerhall also operates the side project ATRYXION. Larsson has a Black Metal endeavour entitled CHOIR OF VENGEANCE.

Albums:
FALCONER, Metal Blade 14355 (2001)
Up On The Grave Of Guilt / Heresy In Disguise / Wings Of Serenity / A Quest For The Crown / Mindtraveller / Entering Eternity / Royal Galley / Substitutional World / Lord Of The Blacksmiths / The Past Still Live On / Per Tyrssons Döttar I Vänge
CHAPTERS FROM A VALE FORLORN, Metal Blade (2002)
Decadence Of Dignity / Enter The Glade / Lament Of A Minstrel / For Life And Liberty / We Sold Our Homesteads / The Clarion Call / Portals Of Light / Stand In Veneration / Busted To The Floor

THE FALLEN (Orange County, CA, USA)
Line-Up: Mike Granat (vocals / guitar), Mark Venier (guitar), Bryan Klinger (bass), Henry Higgs (drums)

Stoic Metal campaigners THE FALLEN, founded as THE CRESTFALLEN during 1992, endured nearly a decade of struggle and successive demo releases before finally landing a record deal in 2001. The group was convened as a trio of vocalist / guitarist Mike Granat, guitarist Mark Venier and drummer Max Wolff mixing traditional Metal with newer Death and retro Thrash influences. With the addition of bass player Bryan Klinger the band became known as THE FALLEN.

A demo cassette, 'The Perfect Darkness Of Death', arrived in 1993 which found the group fronted by lead vocalist Wagner Pierera. However, THE FALLEN was back to a quartet for 1994's 'Eventually Nothing Remained' session with Granet taking the lead vocal mantle. Wolff would be out of the picture by the band's third and fourth attempts, 1995's 'Turning Hollow' and the following year's 'Bloodletting: Victims Of The Order', drums being simply credited to 'Greg'. Keith Gordon took the drum stool for the 1997 session

'Bloodrush'.

THE FALLEN, now with Henry Higgs placed on drums, committed to CD for the first time with their 1999 three track EP 'Sector- 7G'. A self-financed full-length album 'The Tones In Which We Speak' emerged in 2000 leading to a deal with the Metal Blade label and the subsequent Bill Metoyer produced 'Front Toward Enemy'.

Albums:
FRONT TOWARDS ENEMY, Metal Blade 3984-14398-2 (2002)
Short Fuse / Blessings / What I Have Become / Keep Suffering / The Hopeless & The Frail / Front Toward Enemy / Shifting Our Vision / Killswitch / In Loathing / From Fragile To Strength / Eleven Years

FATAL OPERA (Orange City, FL, USA)
Line-Up: Andy Freeman (vocals), Billy Brehme (guitar), Stewart Samuelson (guitar), Travis Karcher (bass), Gar Samuelson (drums)

Drummer Gar Samuelson lays claim to prior membership of the volatile yet highly successful Thrash act MEGADETH. The debut FATAL OPERA album includes a cover of the BEATLES classic 'Lucy In The Sky With Diamonds'.

Albums:
THE ELEVENTH HOUR, Massacre MAS PC0120 (1997)
Would You? / Nothing Is Everything / Once I Was A Fly / Indiscretion / Inside-Outside / Lucy In The Sky / Wrist Twister / Mindfuck / Dredges (The Truth) / Three Steps / The End Of Me / My Psychiatrist / Devil's Monkey / Calling Of Lotar

FATES PROPHECY (BRAZIL)
Line-Up: Sergio Faga (vocals), Paulo De Almeida (guitar), Conrad Michelucci (guitar), Alexandre Ferreira (bass), Sandro Muniz (drums)

Founded in 1991, FATES PROPHECY was originally inspired into life by an appreciation of the NWOBHM movement. The first line-up of the band counted vocalist André Boragina, guitarists Paulo De Almeida and Cláudio Nogueira, bass player Júnior Mascaro and Paulo Maximiliano on drums. Shortly after formation Nogueira opted out and Ricardo Tokiwa became second guitarist in May of 1992.

FATES PROPHECY decided to cut a demo but these recordings matured into a 7" single release, 'Time To Live', issued by the WLM

Corporation. Unfortunately over the next few years the band was wrought by line-up changes and by 1994 only De Almeida and Boragina remained. The band was stabilised with the inauguration of guitarist Conrad Michelucci, bassist Alexandre Ferreira and drummer Sandro Muniz in August of that year. The new unit soon got down to recording and produced the 'Pay For Your Sins' demo.

Their debut album, 1998's 'Into The Mind', garnered exceptional praise among the Metal community. Reaction to the album prompted the Meteor City label to include FATES PROPHECY on their the 2001 IRON MAIDEN tribute album 'Slaves To The Power', the Brazilians donating their rendition of 'Wasted Years'. FATES PROPHECY would be the only South American act selected for the collection.

The 'Eyes Of Truth' album followed for the HTR label but the group would then be struck a heavy blow. Sadly vocalist Andre Boragina died in October 2001. Aged only 31 he had been battling against cancer. Persevering FATES PROPHECY enrolled singer Sergio Faga, a man who had already made his mark on the Die Hard HAMLET project album.

Singles/EPs:
Time To Live, WLM Corporation (1992)

Albums:
INTO THE MIND, (1998)
Time To Live / Land Of Proud / Pay For Your Sins / Back To Madness / The Preacher / Predictions / Never Too Young To Die / Dream Maker / Sands Of Time / To The Father, Son… / Walking Alone 12. Fates Prophecy
EYES OF TRUTH, HTR (2002)
Beast Within / Wings Of Fire / Seven Deadly Sins / Baptism Of Fire / Last Prayer / Eye Of Truth / Evil Ways / Childhood's Fear / The Last Revelation

FATES WARNING (Cincinnati, OH, USA)
Line-Up: Ray Alder (vocals), Jim Matheos (guitar), Joey Vera (bass), Mark Zonder (drums)

Stoic Progressive Metal band FATES WARNING has weathered nearly two decades of shifting musical trends with a steadfast fan base. Initially titled MISFIT in their original formation in 1982 with a line-up of vocalist John Arch, guitarists Victor Arduini and JIM MATHEOS, bassist Joe DiBase and drummer Steve Zimmerman. Renaming themselves FATES WARNING a series of demo recordings enabled the band to include a track on the 'Metal Massacre V' compilation

album in 1984. The resulting appreciation resulted in a long term deal with Metal Blade records which carries on to the present day.
The 1984 debut album 'Night On Brocken' established the band very firmly in the traditional Metal mould. Shortly after its release Arduini departed and in came ex-DEMONAX guitarist Frank Aresti.
The band got more complex with successive albums and the 1986 album 'Awaken The Guardian' broke this success Arch quit, unable to reconcile himself with the band's musical direction, and was to be superseded by Ray Alder.
This new line-up recorded the 'No Exit' album, released in March of 1988 and produced by the much in demand Max Norman, which included the twenty two minute epic 'The Ivory Gates Of Dreams'. FATES WARNING scored valuable airplay with the track 'Silent Cries' and the album gave the band increased sales. However, the band's stability suffered a further knock when Zimmerman opted out.
FATES WARNING added erstwhile WARLORD drummer Mark Zonder (a.k.a. 'Thunderchild') for touring in Europe prior to recording the Terry Brown produced 'Perfect Symmetry' album. DREAM THEATER's keyboard player Kevin Moore guested.
'Parallels' was another fine effort and saw FATES WARNING comfortably delving into more technical territory. 1997's 'A Pleasant Shade Of Grey' found bassist JOEY VERA, known for his lengthy tenure with Heavy Metal band ARMORED SAINT, joining the ranks, with Kevin Moore becoming a full-time band member as the band travelled a more Progressive direction than previously.
Both Ray Alder and Joey Vera involved themselves in the project band ENGINE with AGENT STEEL's guitarist Bernie Versailles for a highly rated eponymous 1999 album. JIM MATHEOS took a left turn for an almost soft Jazz solo album the same year 'Away With Words'.
FATES WARNING toured America in 2000 sharing a bill with NEVERMORE and PLANET X. The double live set 'Still Life' would see Japanese editions coming with a bonus exclusive rendition of the SCORPIONS 'In Trance'.
Touring commencing in April of 2001 would witness FATES WARNING on a strong package billing across America in alliance with Power Metal veterans SAVATAGE. The same year both Alder and Zonder would session on guitarist Nick Van Dyk's REDEMPTION project album. In March of 2002 Joey Vera, still maintaining his posts in both ARMORED SAINT and FATES WARNING, would team up with SAVATAGE guitarist Jack Frost's side endeavour SEVEN

WITCHES for European touring.

Matheos would remain active too; participating in an all new Prog Rock 'Supergroup' mentored by DREAM THEATER drummer Mike Portnoy. The impressive cast list for this venture also numbered PAIN OF SALVATION singer Daniel Gildenlöw, erstwhile DREAM THEATER and presently CHROMA KEY keyboard player Kevin Moore and ex-CYNIC and current GORDIAN KNOT bassist Sean Malone. Before long Gildenlöw was out of the frame and the band project was being billed as set OSI (Orchestra Of Strategic Influence). Former member Frank Aresti would be back in the news too, resurfacing with an eclectic solo Rock project billed as DRAGONSPOON.

Metal Blade Records would reissue the 'Night On Brocken' and 'The Spectre Within' albums for September. 'Night On Brocken' was clad in its original cover art, the first time on CD, and added four bonus rarities. Included would be an original 1984 MISFIT demo of 'Last Call', 1983 rehearsal tapes of 'The Calling' and 'Flight Of Icarus' and a live take of 'Kiss Of Death' recorded at the legendary L'Amour club. 'The Spectre Within' re-issue boasted a 1985 live version of 'Radio Underground', a rehearsal session of 'The Apparition' and two tracks from the DICKIE demos 'Kyrie Eleison' and 'Epitaph'.

Singles/EPs:
Silent Cries, Metal Blade (1988) (USA promotion)
Anarchy Divine, Metal Blade (1988) (Free 7" with 'Powerline' magazine)
Quietus, Metal Blade (1988) (USA promotion)
Through Different Eyes, Metal Blade (1989) (USA promotion)

Albums:
NIGHT ON BROCKEN, Metal Blade 71102 (1984)
Buried Alive / The Calling / Kiss Of Death / Night On Brocken / S.E.K. / Misfit / Shadowfax / Damnation / Soldier Boy
THE SPECTRE WITHIN, Metal Blade 72088 (1985)
Traveller In Time / Orphan Gypsy / Without A Trace / Pirates Of The Underground / The Apparition / Kyrie Eleison / Epitaph
AWAKEN THE GUARDIAN, Metal Blade 73231 (1986)
The Sorceress / Valley Of The Dolls / Fata Morgana / Guardian / Prelude To Ruin / Giant's Lore / Time Long Past / Exodus
NO EXIT, Metal Blade 73330 (1988)
No Exit / Anarchy Divine / Silent Cries / In A Word / Shades Of Heavenly Death / The

Ivory Gates Of Dreams, i) Innocence, ii) Cold Daze, iii) Daylight Dreamers, iv) Quietus, v) Ivory Tower, vi) Whispers In The Wind, vii) Acquiescence, viii Retrospect
PERFECT SYMMETRY, Metal Blade CDMZORRO 73 (1989)
Part Of The Machine / Through Different Eyes / Static Acts / A World Apart / At Fates Hands / The Arena / Chasing Time / Nothing Left To Say
PARALELLS, Metal Blade CDZORRO 31 (1991)
Leave The Past Behind / Life In Still Water / Eye To Eye / The Eleventh Hour / Point Of View / We Only Say Goodbye / Don't Follow Me / The Road Goes On Forever
INSIDE OUT, Massacre MASSCD 037 (1994)
Outside Looking In / Pale Fire / The Strand / Shelter Me / Island In The Stream / Down To The Wire / Face The Fear / Inward Band / Monument / Afterglow
CHASING TIME, Metal Blade 3984-14085-2 (1995)
Monument / The Apparition / Through Different Eyes / Point Of View / Prelude To Ruin / Quietus / Eye To Eye / Guardian / At Fates Fingers / Silent Cries / We Only Say Goodbye (Remix) / Damnation / Circles / The Eleventh Hour
A PLEASANT SHADE OF GREY, Metal Blade (1997)
Part I / Part II / Part III / Part IV / Part V / Part VI / Part VII / Part VIII / Part IX / Part X / Part XI / Part XII
STILL LIFE, Metal Blade 14188 (1998)
A Pleasant Shade Of Grey I-XII / The Ivory Gates Of Dreams / The Eleventh Hour / Point Of View / Monument / At Fates Hands / Prelude To Ruin / We Only Say Goodbye
DISCONNECTED, Metal Blade 14324 (2000)
Disconnected Part I / One / So / Pieces Of Me / Something From Nothing / Still Remains / Disconnected Part II

FIFTH ANGEL (Seattle, WA, USA)
Line-Up: Ted Pilot (vocals), James Byrd (guitar), Ed Archer (guitar), Kenny Kay (bass), Ken Mary (drums)

Power Metal band FIFTH ANGEL debuted with an awesome Terry Date produced album. Drummer Ken Mary had previous experience in the ranks of the RANDY HANSEN band, STRIKE, TKO before he was involved in getting FIFTH ANGEL off the ground and alongside Seattle buddies vocalist Ted Pilot, guitarists JAMES BYRD and Ed Archer and bassist Kenny Kay. Previous to founding FIFTH ANGEL Byrd had been operating in a UFO / SCORPIONS covers band.

FIFTH ANGEL first recorded an EP then a four track demo that was shopped to a variety of labels. Mike Varney's Shrapnel label would be the company keen enough to sign the group, utilising the original demo tracks allied to newly recorded material. RANDY HANSEN would guest as session bassist on four of the album tracks. Whilst helping to mix the album in San Francisco, Mary was tapped by Varney to play drums on CHASTAIN's 'Rulers Of The Wasteland' whilst there.

FIFTH ANGEL's first record garnered such laudatory reviews it was soon picked up by major label Epic Records who remixed it and reissued it in new sleeve artwork. The band also scored a management deal with the major Concrete Marketing group. Prior to its re-release however bassist Kenny Kay departed in favour of John Macko. In the transitory period Ken Mary also used the break to gain valuable experience by enrolling in ALICE COOPER's live act for his 'Constrictor' world tour of late 1987. Oddly, with a stack of laudatory reviews and major label backing FIFTH ANGEL splintered. Mary joined HOUSE OF LORDS in 1988. He later formed the vaguely Christian Alternative Metal group SOUL SHOCK REMEDY, eschewing the drums in favour of a singing position and adjusting his surname to Mari.

With the departure of James Byrd in 1988, FIFTH ANGEL recruited Kendall Bechtel in his stead. The 1989 album 'Time Will Tell', produced by Terry Brown, featured LISA DALBELLO on backing vocals.

James Byrd formed the grandly titled JAMES BYRD'S ATLANTIS RISING and released a self-titled album through Roadrunner in 1991. The band included ex-TKO and Q5 bassist Evan Sheely alongside the lesser known drummer Scott Hunt and vocalist Freddy Krumins. A JAMES BYRD solo album 'Octoglomerate' surfaced in 1993. The follow up, 1995's 'Son Of Man', would bear the rarest of endorsements from the guitar genius YNGWIE MALMSTEEN who penned sleeve notes highly praising the guitarist. Byrd would work with erstwhile LYNCH MOB singer Robert Mason for the 1996 effort 'The Apocalypse Chime'. That same year the guitarist founded his own Byrd Guitar Company.

Mary was back in a reformed HOUSE OF LORDS during 2000. JAMES BYRD continues to issue solo albums, the July 2002 'Anthems' album simply credited to BYRD.

Albums:
FIFTH ANGEL, Shrapnel / Roadrunner RR9688 (1986)
The Night / Shout It Out / Call Out The Warning / Fifth Angel / Wings Of Destiny / In The Fallout / Cry Out The Fools / Only The Strong Survive / Fade To Flames

FIFTH ANGEL, Epic 44201-1 (1986)
In The Fallout / Shout It Out / Call Out The Warning / Fifth Angel / Wings Of Destiny / The Night / Only The Strong Survive / Cry Out The Fools / Fade To Flames
TIME WILL TELL, Epic (1989)
Cathedral / Midnight Love / Seven Hours / Broken Dreams / Time Will Tell / Lights Out / Wait For Me / Angel Of Mercy / We Rule / So Long / Feel The Heat

FIFTH REASON (SWEDEN)
Line-Up: Kristian Andren (vocals), Marco A. Nicosia (guitar), Simon Johansson (guitar), Oscar Tillman (bass), Martin Larsson (drums)

FIFTH REASON can boast former members of such highly respected Metal acts as ABSTRAKT ALGEBRA, HEXENHAUS and MEMENTO MORI. The band came together in 1992, created by guitarist Simon Johansson and Niklas Oreland, offering a demo tape titled 'Stranded'.

Progress was halted when Johansson was enticed away to ABSTRAKT ALGEBRA to record their self-titled debut, although after leaving ABSTRAKT ALGEBRA in late 1996 Johansson joined up with MEMORY GARDEN prior to resurrecting FIFTH REASON, pulling in former TAD MOROSE and MEMONTO MORI vocalist Kristian Andren.

With the addition of bassist Oscar Tillman and drummer Martin Larsson FIFTH REASON were soon up and running, securing a deal with Heathendoom Records. Second guitarist Marco A. Nocosia, previously with HEXENHAUS, joined in time for recording.

MERCYFUL FATE and MEMENTO MORI guitarist Mike Wead produced the debut album, entitled 'Psychotic'.

Albums:
PSYCHOTIC, Heathendoom HDMCD004 (1997)
Psychotic / My Friend / This Journey Of Mine / Above, Below And Beyond / A Shadow Remains / Strange Intimation / In Between / A Final Wish
WITHIN OR WITHOUT, Scarlet (2002)
Nighttime Wishes / Within / River Of Lust / Day's Undone / Whore / Only Angels Know / Mourning Glory / Neverland

FIFTH SEASON (UK)
Line-Up: John Knight (vocals), David Ray (guitar), Kevin Jackson (bass), Jim Moore (keyboards), Jed Hawkins (drums)

Albums:
JOURNEY THROUGH AN OPEN MIND,
Fifth Season FSCD001 (1997)
Shadows Of Hope / A Little Rain (Must Fall) / Tomorrow's Conscience / Voice Of Insecurity / Of Profit To The Wise / Again / Age Of Light / Birth Of Acquisition / Enemy Unseen

FIGHT (UK / USA)
Line-Up: Rob Halford (vocals), Russ Parrish (guitar), Brian Tilse (guitar), Jay Jay (bass), Scott Travis (drums)

A joint Anglo / American, stripped down in-your-face Metal act. FIGHT was created by JUDAS PRIEST vocalist Rob Halford, a man whose vocal prowess is almost legendary. Wishing to pursue a radical change of direction from the more classic, technical style of JUDAS PRIEST, Halford bowed out after 1991's hugely successful 'Painkiller' world tour. Longstanding JUDAS PRIEST fans were somewhat bemused by a shift in his traditional leather and studs image to one that mimicked PANTERA's vocalist Phil Anselmo. It came as no surprise then that Halford began guesting at PANTERA shows and cut a

single, 'Light Out Of Black', with the band for a movie score.

Although the vocalist had the blessing of JUDAS PRIEST for this out of the blue project, a bitter verbal conflict ensued. As the accusations and counter-accusations flew Halford's twenty year tenure abruptly came to and end as he formed FIGHT, taking JUDAS PRIEST drummer Scott Travis with him.

The eagerly awaited debut album was light years removed from JUDAS PRIEST, Halford toning down his vocal range and opting for much simpler songs. Many critics panned the release as a lame PANTERA copy but in the main Halford managed to take many former fans with him.

Live dates in England were marred by paltry attendance figures with many JUDAS PRIEST fans feeling almost betrayed by Halford's endeavours. The vocalist reacted by issuing vitriolic statements about the British media. In the States Halford enjoyed better response and FIGHT toured there opening for the mighty METALLICA.

The interim 'Mutations' mini-album included a raucous live rendition of JUDAS PRIEST's 'Freewheel Burning'. 1994's 'A Small Deadly Space' found Mark Chaussee in the group in

FIGHT
Photo : Sean Denomey

150

place of WAR & PEACE guitarist Russ Parrish.

Halford was also busying himself outside of FIGHT with his E.M.A.S. Management organisation. Taking on Australian Thrashers ALLEGIANCE Halford secured a deal for the young act with major label Polygram.

FIGHT's days, however, were numbered. After a brief flirtation working with BLACK SABBATH guitarist TONY IOMMI (indeed, Halford had guested for BLACK SABBATH at the legendary Costa Mesa shows in late 1992 subbing for an absent Ronnie James Dio) the singer formed a new band under the title of HALFORD.

This later act re-titled itself GIMP then TWO, emerging with a Trent Reznor of NINE INCH NAILS produced Industrial Rock album 'Voyeurs' that, it is true to say, left many of Halford's fans scratching their heads in bemusement. Even more so when the man, now sporting a stage image that alternated between Nosferatu and blue rubber romper suits, seemingly denounced Metal as dead and buried.

Chaussee joined DANZIG in 1996 but bailed out just prior to their world tour. By 2000 Parrish was a member of the acclaimed spoof covers band METAL SHOP along with former L.A. GUNS man Ralph Saenz. Parrish would also double duties with Alternative Rockers THE DUCKS.

Much to the relief of his long suffering fans, now simply billed as HALFORD, resurrected his career in spectacular style during 2000 with the suitably titled 'Resurrection' album, a quite remarkable statement of Metal intent that charted internationally. HALFORD, signing up to IRON MAIDEN manager Rod Smallwood's firm for management and label, saw his profile rise sharply with a subsequent special guest slot to IRON MAIDEN's American dates.

<u>Albums:</u>
WAR OF WORDS, Epic 4745472 (1992)
Into The Pit / Nailed To The Gun / Life In Black / Immortal Sin / War Of Words / Laid To Rest / For All Eternity / Little Crazy / Contortion / Kill It / Vicious / Reality, A New Beginning
MUTATIONS, Epic 477243 2 (1993)
Into The Pit (Live) / Nailed To The Gun (Live) / Freewheel Burning (Live) / Little Crazy (Live) / War Of Words (Bloody Tongue Mix) / Kill It (Dutch Death Mix) / Immortal Sin (Tolerance Mix) / Little Crazy (Straight Jacket Mix)
A SMALL DEADLY SPACE, Epic 478400 2 (1994)
I Am Alive / Mouthpiece / Legacy Of Hate / Blowout In The Radio Room / Never Again /

Small Deadly Space / Gretna Greene / Beneath The Violence / Human Crate

FLYING SKULL (GERMANY)
Line-Up: Achim Nohl (vocals), Roland Saager (guitar), Stefan Uschwa (guitar), Elmar Birlo (bass), Ralph Blankart (drums)

<u>Albums:</u>
DARKNESS, Flying Skull 1st R. (1991)
Tommyknockers / Nightwalk / Lonesome Child / Darkness / Hawkeye / Child Of Icka / Annie / The Unknown Day
REVELATION, Flying Skull 2nd R. (1993)
Forgotten World (Genesis) / Red Death / 1912 / They / Take My Hand / Thumbs Down / Keep On Running

FORGOTTEN TALES (CANADA)
Line-Up: Sonia Pineault (vocals), Martin Desharnais (guitar), Pat Vir, (Bass), Frederick Desroches (keyboards) Cedric Prevost (drums)

FORGOTTEN TALES has the distinction of being one of Canada's only melodic European styled Metal bands. In a country known mostly for its Death and Thrash FORGOTTEN TALES are quite unique.

The band manager Rene Pineault wanted to develop a scene in Canada where melodic European style power Metal could flourish. Unfortunately that dream was difficult to accomplish so he set out and founded a band instead, trying to bring the music to the people. What started as a casual project has become an active viable entity driven by the power vocals of Sonia Pineault.

Since unleashing their debut the band have received favourable reviews in the underground press around the world for their professional production, excellent packaging and great songs.

<u>Albums:</u>
THE PROMISE, Forgotten Tales FTCD012001 (2001)
Intro / Word Of Truth / Cold Heart / Far Away / Gates Beyond Reality / Sanctuary / The Tale Of Neeris: Part I: She's Falling / The Tale Of Neeris: Part II: Deadly Grasp / The Tale Of Neeris: Part III: Endless Dreams / The Tale Of Neeris: Part IV: The Promise

FORTE (USA)
Line-Up: Kevin Valliquette (vocals), Jeff Scott (guitar), Greg Nicholson (bass), Greg Scott (drums)

Oklahoma Thrash Metal act FORTE arrived

with the 1990 demo tape 'Dementia By Design'. The band signed to Germany's Massacre Records for the debut album 'Stranger Than Fiction'. The line-up included former OLIVER MAGNUM singer James Randell, guitarist Jeff Scott, ex-LEGIONED MARCHER bassist Ghames 'Reverend' Jones and drummer Greg Scott. Touring would find FORTE reaping valuable high profile supports to acts such as DREAM THEATER, PANTERA, OVERKILL, SEPULTURA, SAVATAGE, WATCHTOWER and FLOTSAM & JETSAM.

The 1994 album 'Division' witnessed a radical change in the band format with vocals now in the hands of Bill Dollins, another erstwhile LEGIONED MARCHER man. The album included a cover version of ACCEPT's 'Fast As A Shark'. Yet again the band scored stronger and more diverse guest slots to the likes of FEAR FACTORY, LIFE OF AGONY and YNGWIE MALMSTEEN. Jones would also find time to deputise for GAMMACIDE.

The 1997 'Destructive' record saw another crop of new faces in vocalist David Thompson and bassist Richard Sharpe. Another extensive road jaunt found the new look FORTE opening for TESTAMENT, KING DIAMOND, EXODUS, MACHINE HEAD, SAXON and SKINLAB among others. The band stabilised their line-up and cut a further album, 'Rise Above' in 1999. This record would be promoted on the live circuit with an appearance at the 'Powermad' festival and tour work alongside DEATH, TESTAMENT, HAMMERFALL and MANOWAR. Despite the band's obvious progress on the live front and a string of consistent albums FORTE severed then severed ties with Massacre Records. Original singer James Randell made a return in November 1999, committing to tape the QUEENSRYCHE cover 'Prophecy' for a Frontiers Records tribute album released during 2000.

During January of 2002 the band announced its new line-up which now included DREAM KINGS vocalist Kevin Valliquette and bass player Greg Nicholson joining the mainstay inner circle of the Scott siblings. Under their new guise FORTE set to work on a fresh studio album projected for an early 2003 release.

Former member Reverend Jones travelled on to BLACK SYMPHONY during 1997 and was ensconced in the MICHAEL SCHENKER GROUP for the German guitar guru's 2001 opus 'Be Aware Of Scorpions'.

Albums:
STRANGER THAN FICTION, Massacre (1992)
Coming Of The Storm / The Inner Circle /
Stranger Than Fiction / G-13 (Devoid Of Thought) / Mein Madness / Time And Time Again / Digitator / Between The Lies / The Last Word / The Promise
DIVISION, Massacre (1994)
Dischord / Inhuman / Thirteen Steps / Last Machine / E 2 M.N. / In This Life / One Flesh / Division / Legacy Of Silence / Ultimatum / Back To Zero / Fast As A Shark
DESTRUCTIVE, Massacre (1997)
Barcode / Deviate / Hammer / Destructive / October / Heal Me / Strength / Never Sleep / The Hard Way / Art Of War / Eternal / Far Away
RISE ABOVE, Massacre (1999)
Man Against Machine / Fading Away / Ninety Nine / Forgiven / Rise Above / Destroyer / Poison Tongue / Burn / Over My Head / Until The End Of Time

FORTRESS UNDER SIEGE (GREECE)
Line-Up: Michael Smeros (vocals), Fotis Sotiropoulos (guitar), Nigel Foxxe (keyboards), Nick Redes (drums)

Previously known as GLADIATORS. FORTRESS UNDER SIEGE's line-up boasted former FLAMES and THANATOS front man Nigel Foxxe on keyboards and session bass from Aris Matheakakis.

Albums:
FORTRESS UNDER SIEGE, Metal Mad Music MMM 001 (1996)
Prison Cells (Within My Soul) / Soldier Boy / Robin Hood (Prince Of Thieves) / A Legacy In Stone

FOUR SEASONS (GREECE)

An underground, epic Heavy Metal band out of Thessaloniki mentored by one Chris Cagioglidis. Prior to forming FOUR SEASONS Cagioglidis had been a member of NORTHERN HORDE in 1990. This act was forced to disband when vocalist C. Giovanopoulos was called for military service. The remaining personnel created Power Metal band WIND, issuing the demos 'Tales Of Nordic Sea' in 1994 and 'Knights Of The Temple' in 1997. Cagioglidis bailed out of WIND in 1996 in order to prioritise FOUR SEASONS and thus go on to release a string of self-financed albums. The band has industriously managed to maintain a pace of one album a year commencing with 1997's 'The Gargoyles' right up to the alien themed 2001 effort 'Invaders'. Initially the band included Cagioglidis' NORTHERN HORDE and WIND colleague Lefteris Barboutis but he was to depart after 1998's 'The Battle'. This

left Cagioglidis to record 1999's 'Heavy Metal Force' entirely as a solo venture.

For 2000's 'New Era' lead singer Costas Bililis of DIMENSION Z, BRAINSTORM and HIGHER GROUND was enrolled. Reportedly FOUR SEASONS was structuring a full band unit during 2002.

Albums:

THE GARGOYLES, Four Seasons (1997)
The Gargoyles / Strengthening Of Morality / Merlin The Magician / The Vision / Time Machine / Gods Of Wrath / Northern Winds / One For All (All For One) / Though Shall Kill / Queen Of Seas / A Pray To The God Of Sea / Taste Revenge / Lord Of Wars
THE BATTLE, Four Seasons (1998)
Far Away… In Dreamland / Goodbye To A Friend / Supervisor / The Invitation / Magic Spells / Demons / Preparation For Battle / The Battle / Now The Story Ends / Farewell
HEAVY METAL FORCE, Four Seasons (1999)
Magical Lamp / Heavy Metal Force / 1821 / Northern Horde / Eternity / Just For The Fun / March Of Light / Bouree
NEW ERA, Four Seasons (2000)
Magical Lamp / Lord Of War (Parts I & II) / The Vision / Time Machine / The Battle / Spirits Of The Dead / The Gargoyles / One For All (All For One) / Goodbye To A Friend / 1821
INVADERS, Four Seasons (2001)

Arrival / Brain Machine / Mutiny (With Blood, Fire, Death) / Alien Spacecraft / Attack / Destruction Command / Kataklysm / Eyes Of The Dead

FREEDOM CALL (GERMANY)
Line-Up: Chris Bay (vocals / guitar), Sascha Gerstner (guitar), Ilker Ersin (bass), Dan Zimmermann (drums)

FREEDOM CALL arrived brandishing a refined Euro Melodic Speed Metal style with the 1999 opening shot 'Stairway To Fairyland' that soon propelled the band into German charts. The band numbered in their ranks the well known figure of drummer Dan Zimmermann, known for his Pop days with HEINZ and more importantly Metal bands LANZER, GAMMA RAY and IRON SAVIOR.

Both Zimmermann and vocalist Chris Bay had in their formative years been active with covers band CHINA WHITE and then LANZER. Bay would keep in touch with Zimmermann throughout the years, the singer working with MOON'DOC. This last act of Bay's would also feature FREEDOM CALL bassist Ilker Ersin. The band debuted live in Grenoble, France during May of 1999 supporting ANGRA and EDGUY. Later gigs across Europe in November found the band as special guests to Brit vets SAXON.

In Japan the JVC Victor label also released a mini-album, 'Taragon', the same year. Quite

153

surreally this disc included FREEDOM CALL's take on the ULTRAVOX hit 'Dancing With Tears In My Eyes'. SAXON's Biff Byford would lend his tonsils to the narrative on 'Tears Of Taragon'.

The 'Crystal Empire' album, recorded in Hamburg, Nuremberg, and Erlangen under the aegises of producers Chris Bay, Dan Zimmermann and Charlie Bauerfeind, saw ROUGH SILK and AXEL RUDI PELL keyboard player Ferdy Doernberg guesting on keyboards. Touring throughout the early part of 2001 had FREEDOM CALL backing the album on the road in Germany as part of a package billing with HAMMERFALL and VIRGIN STEELE. 'Crystal Empire' would peak at no. 94 in the national German album charts.

In September of 2001 guitarist Sascha Gerstner, having joined premier league act HELLOWEEN, was supplanted by Cedric Dupont of SYMPHORCE. FREEDOM CALL toured Scandinavia during October of 2002 supported by FULL STRIKE.

Albums:
STAIRWAY TO HEAVEN, SPV 085-21182 CD (1999)
Over The Rainbow / Tears Falling / Fairyland / Shine On / We LAre One / Hymn To The Brave / Tears Of Taragon / Graceland / Holy Knight / Another Day
CRYSTAL EMPIRE, SPV (2001)
35 FINLAND, 94 GERMANY, 67 SWEDEN
The King Of The Crystal Empire / Freedom Call / Rise Up / Farewell / Pharao / Call Of Fame / Heart Of The Rainbow / The Quest / Ocean / Palace Of Fantasy / The Wanderer
ETERNITY, SPV (2002) 55 GERMANY
Metal Invasion / The Eyes Of The World / Flying High / Land Of Light / Warriors / Ages Of Power / Turn Back Time / Island Of Dreams / The Spell / Bleeding Heart / Flame In The Night

FREEWILL (USA)
Line-Up: Tom Clark (vocals / drums), Chad Heyvoth (guitar), Paul Bakalars (guitar), Jason Peck (bass)

Albums:
PROGRESSIVE REGRESSION, Freewill E9801-2 (1998)
Indifference / Escape To Daylight / The Storm / Unmasked / Erase LThe Memory / Sheltered Life / Progressive Regression

FRETERNIA (SWEDEN)
Line-Up: Pasi Humppi (vocals), Tomas Wäppling (guitar), Peter Wiberg (bass), Tommie Johansson (keyboards), Martin

Tilander (drums)

Power-Speed Metal band FRETERNIA's first line-up comprised lead vocalist Tomas Wäppling, guitarists Patrik Lund and Bo Pettersson, bass player Peter Wiberg and drummer Stefan Svantesson. This unit cut the opening demo 'The Blood Of Mortals' in October of 1998 after which teenage keyboard player Tommie Johansson was drafted to fill out their sound. Ructions triggered the departure of both Pettersson and Wiberg the following year.

FRETERNIA soldiered on, shifting Wäppling over to bass and pulling in guitarist Mikael Bakajev and in this incarnation the group laid down tracks for a second demo 'Somewhere In Nowhere'. There are also reports of a split single shared with PERSUADER.

These sessions attracted the interest of the Loud n' Proud label and FRETERNIA were duly signed to produce the 'Warchants And Fairytales' debut. However, Wäppling felt his presence was not strong enough to complete lead vocal duties and the band brought in IRONWARE singer Pasi Humppi for recording. With the tapes completed another member was shed, Lund opting out for personal reasons. Upfront of the album release in July of 2000 Andreas Heleander was recruited on bass.

Unfortunately for the band their label went out of business before a second album could be commenced. FRETERNIA issued a three track promotion CD to plug the gap but, disillusioned, Wäppling bailed out with Johansson following shortly after. Losing their key members FRETERNIA announced they were to fold in April of 2001. At this stage Humppi was still active in his other act IRONWARE, having recruited former FRETERNIA bassist Peter Wiberg too.

However, after an abortive attempt to found another band FRETERNIA was resurrected as the main original cast settled their differences. During June of 2002 FRETERNIA drummer Stefan Svantesson departed to concentrate his efforts on his other act CRYSTAL EYES. Martin Tilander, coincidentally an erstwhile CRYSTAL EYES member, duly replaced him.

In 2002 the band donated their version of HELLOWEEN's 'Murderer', produced by KING DIAMOND guitarist Andy LaRocque, for the tribute album 'Keepers Of Jericho volume 2' for the Spanish Arise label. Arise would also handle the band's second album 'A Nightmare Story', produced by Pelle Saether and delivered in October.

Albums:
WARCHANTS AND FAIRYTALES, Loud n'

Proud (2000)
The Worst Of Enemies / Ride With The Wind / The War Of The Crown / Mistress Of The Deep Black Sea / Guardians Of The Night / The Woods Of The Elvenking / Dragonsong / Friends In Enemyland / The Flame
A NIGHTMARE STORY, Arise (2002)
Grimbor The Great / Arrival / The Dark Side / Shadowdancers / The Saviour / The Unexpected / New Hope / Battle Of Minds / Requiem

FRONTIER (UK)
Line-Up: Mick Witham (vocals), Rick Gilliat (guitar), Scott Bash (guitar), Conrad Walker (bass), Paul Gilliat (drums)

Mansfield based Metal band formed in 1990. FRONTIER released a self-financed album five years later.
In 2000 guitarist Rick Gilliat joined the LUTHER BELTZ BAND, later re-titled WYTCHFYNDE.

Albums:
DON'T JUST DO SOMETHING, STAND THERE, Frontiers FRN001 (1995)
Killing Fields / Who Are You / Last Sounding Count / Fire In Your Eyes / Only Waiting / Day By Day / Send Me Down (An Angel) / Dreaming

FROSTBITE (Matawan, NJ, USA)
Line-Up: Tommy Glick (vocals), Jack Frost (guitar), Patrick Moloney (bass), Joe Cattano (drums)

FROSTBITE's debut, 'Icy Hell', reportedly sold around 10,000 copies and was rather big in Belgium. The record was co-produced by Phil De Carlo, CINDERELLA guitarist Jeff Le Bar and Frost.
The second album eschewed melodic Hard Rock for a heavier grind direction.
For the 1997 release, produced by Steve Deacutis, FROSTBITE pulled in guest musicians such as PROPHET / SURGIN man Russell Arcara and SHOTGUN SYMPHONY's Charlie Calv.
In 1998 Frost helped form the side project THE BRONX CASKET CO alongside MISFITS vocalist Myke Hideous, OVERKILL drummer Tim Mallare and SHOTGUN SYMPHONY keyboard player Charlie Calv.
Jack Frost created a new act SEVEN WITCHES, duly signing them to Germany's Massacre Records in late 1998. A further union on the Massacre label found Frost as a member of SPEEED with ex-ANNIHILATOR vocalist Aaron Randell for the 'Powertrip Pigs' album.

2000 found Frost as part of the high profile METALIUM collective, featuring SAVATAGE guitarist Chris Caffrey. Frost played on the 'State Of Triumph' METALIUM album and through this connection his next port of call took him to SAVATAGE, replacing Al Pitrelli in 2001. Having toured Europe with SAVATAGE Frost was ousted by his predecessor in April of 2002.

Albums:
ICY HELL, Iron Glory (1994)
Money / Your Luv / Black Widow / Wish / Setting Sun / Spotlight / Do You Remember / Stand Tall / 2nd Time Around / Devil's Dandruff
SECRET ADMIRER, Underground Symphony USCD-011 (1996)
False Façade / Upside Down / Secret Admirer / Ended / So Much Of Nothing / Fragile Clowns / What's It Matter / She Fell In Love / Hold On
CAROUSEL, Neat Metal NM022 (1997)
Hypertermia / Monster / Different World / More Visible In Red / It's All Been Said / Someday / Safe Forever / Dictator / Mistakes / Leaving So Soon? / Leaving (Reprise) / Carousel

FULL STRIKE (SWEDEN)
Line-Up: Niclas Jonsson (vocals), Stefan Elmgren (guitar), Fredrik Olsson (guitar), Chris Savage Goldsmith (bass), Patrik Räfling (drums)

A high profile Melodic Metal side project convened by HAMMERFALL guitarist Stefan Elmgren during down time in the high flying Swedish Metal band's schedule in the latter half of 2001. Joining Elmgren on the FULL STRIKE venture would be erstwhile LOST HORIZON singer Niclas Jonsson, ex-CRAWLEY bassist Chris Savage Goldsmith and FREAK KITCHEN drummer Björn Fryklund.
Upon announcement of the May 2002 debut album 'We Will Rise' through the Spitfire label, Elmgren also revealed that Fryklund's position had been taken by a former HAMMERFALL compatriot Patrik Räfling and LOST HORIZON's Fredrik Olsson would augment the band for live work. FULL STRIKE debuted live in Gothenburg on April 19th and the album debuted on the Swedish national charts at a highly respectable no. 6 position. FULL STRIKE lent support to FREEDOM CALL's October Scandinavian tour dates.

Albums:
WE WILL RISE, Eagle Rock (2002)

155

STEFAN ELMGREN of FULL STRIKE
Photo : Nico Wobben

6 SWEDEN
End Of Time / Enlighten Me / We Will Rise /
Metal Minds / Silent Screams / Master Of My
Soul / Mandrake's Dream / When Will I Know
/ First Strike / Created Fantasy / Force Of
The World

FURIA ANIMAL (SPAIN)
Line-Up: Dani Milan (vocals), Pedro Lluch
(guitar), Tomas Gozalves (guitar), Miguel A.
Portillo (bass), Ricardo G. Celada
(keyboards), Fernando Espi Gonzales
(drums)

Heavy Metal act FURIA ANIMAL began life as
UNDERDOG in 1998 comprising ex-
SINESTESIA vocalist Dani Milan, guitarists
Pedro Lluch and Rubén Pacheco, bass player
Miguel A. Portillo, keyboard player Ricardo
García and drummer Fernando Espi
Gonzales of DEMENZIA and ARKANGEL.
During 2000 the band undertook their first
recording schedule, overseen by erstwhile
OVERLIFE bassist Leandro Martinez. Shortly
after the new title of FURIA ANIMAL was
adopted.
By 2002 the band had ex-WOLFGANG
guitarist Tomas Gozalves replacing Pacheco.
Keyboards were now in the hands of Marina
Llorca Esquerdo, previously with REKHEIM.
Ruben Sala Blasco, previously with SALEM,
was in command of bass duties.

Albums:
FURIA ANIMAL, Pies (2001)
Rebelion / Desvalido / Noches Amargas /
Paraiso / Furia Animal / Pide Perdon / Una
Vez Mas / Profecia / Marcado
AZOTANDO EL DESTINO, Pies (2002)
Retorno / En La Oscuridad / Azotando El
Destino / Entre Tu Y Yo / Otra Vida /
Enseñando A Matar / Tan Solo Tu / Mi Lugar
/ Dama Blanca / Hotel California / Antes De
Nacer

GALLOWS POLE
(GERMANY)
Line-Up: John ABC Smith
(vocals / bass), Zokk Milosh
(guitar), Adnan Davidoff (guitar),
Hakan Topcu (drums)

JOHN ABC SMITH had been operational in GALLOWS POLE, founded in Germany by three expatriated Yugoslavians, prior to joining the high profile German Sci-Fi Metal act SCANNER in 1993. Upon quitting SCANNER following the 'Mental Reservation' album and after a four year stint, Smith committed to recording a 1995 solo album 'The Revelation Of John'. He would also reactivate his former act GALLOWS POLE by re-enlisting guitarist Zokk Milosh and drummer Hakan Topcu. Initial gigs saw Amir Jesenkovic on second guitar before Adnan Davidoff took over.

The group's first commercially available product was the 1999 sampler EP 'Over The Rainbow' given away free with 'Rock Hard' magazine. The debut eponymous album arrived in March of 2000. Former ANGEL DUST and SCANNER vocalist S.L. Coe would act as producer.

Singles/EPs:
East Of Eden / Over The Rainbow / Strawberry Fields (If Ever…), (1999) ('Over The Rainbow' EP)

Albums:
GALLOWS POLE, Shark SHARK 2002 (2000)
Calling All Nations / Healer Of The World / Strawberry Fields / Tonight, Tonight / East Of Eden / Revelation Of John / Vision Of The Future / Messiah Supreme / Balkan Rhapsody / God Bless America / Gallows Pole / Outro
EXORCISM, Shark SHARK 2013 (2001)
Enemy Maker / Turn Of The Fortune / Astronomy Domine / Politicians / The Man That Was Used Up / Outta Here / Soul Survivor / Freedom To Fly / Waiting For Godot / Exorcism

GAMMA RAY (GERMANY)
Line-Up: Kai Hansen (vocals / guitar), Henjo Richter (guitar), Dirk Schlächter (bass), Dan Zimmermann (drums)

One of Germany's premier league Metal bands. Amazing as it might sound, GAMMA RAY 's roots lay in the surprising decision by guitarist Kai Hansen to split from HELLOWEEN just as the German group had begun to reach the peak of their success,

Hansen citing disillusionment with constant touring as the main reason for his departure. Teaming himself up with former TYRAN PACE vocalist Ralph Scheepers, Hansen quickly found almost instantaneous success again in a group that boasted bassist Uwe Wessels and drummer Matthias Burchardt in the initial line-up.

Having swiftly added ex-HOLY MOSES drummer Uli Kusch in place of Burchardt, GAMMA RAY's 1989 debut album, 'Heading For Tomorrow', reached number 2 in the Japanese charts and sold in excess of 180,000 copies throughout Europe. The following year Hansen would find time to produce the 'This Is The News' demo session for MEGACE.

1991's 'Sigh No More', which was produced by VICTORY's Tommy Newton and continued the success, selling over 150,000 copies worldwide. However, in mid 1992 Kusch and Wessel had quit. The drummer would eventually wind up in HELLOWEEN.

By early 1993 the band had recruited new members bassist Jan Rubach and drummer Thomas Nack. GAMMA RAY's third album, 'Insanity And Genius', appeared the same year and, interestingly, the 1993 single 'Future Madhouse' features on the B side a version of the BIRTH CONTROL track aptly titled 'Gamma Ray'.

Stunningly, Ralf Scheepers departed the group in 1994 after the rest of the band discovered he had applied for the job as vocalist for JUDAS PRIEST. This left Hansen to handle lead vocal duties in addition to supplying guitar and Kai made his front man debut on 1995's 'Land Of The Free' album, which also featured guest vocal parts from Hansen's prior HELLOWEEN colleague MICHAEL KISKE. Scheepers turned up fronting PRIMAL FEAR, a band including SINNER mainman Mat Sinner and with more than a few similarities to Birmingham's finest! Meantime Thomas Nack was operating a side project band oddly billed as TWORK in allegiance with former KINGDOM COME guitarist Heiko Radke.

GAMMA RAY played Germany in early 1995 on a touring festival billing including GRAVE DIGGER, GLENMORE, RUNNING WILD and RAGE, with the aptly titled 'Alive '95' record appearing the following year and featuring a cover version of NWoBHM act HOLOCAUST's 'Heavy Metal Mania'. The group would later record further cover songs, both JUDAS PRIEST numbers ('Victim Of Changes' and a Ralf Scheepers fronted version of 'Exciter') to two JUDAS PRIEST tribute albums.

In the Fall of 1996 GAMMA RAY split with both Rubach and Nack, the duo joined

KAI HANSEN of GAMMA RAY

ANESTHESIA, and brought in new blood in the form of bassist Dirk Schlächter and drummer Dan Zimmermann.

GAMMA RAY hit back in 1997 with a brand new studio album, the highly rated 'Somewhere Out In Space', also featuring Henjo Richter on guitars and keyboards, and excitedly toured in support of the 'meisterwerk'. The album included a cover version of URIAH HEEP's 'Return To Fantasy'. German dates included a headlining appearance at 'Heavy Oder Was?' magazine's 'Bang Your Head' festival in Tübingen, southern Germany before the group headed over to Japan during October for a particularly lengthy tour, certainly by Japanese standards. The 'Valley Of The Kings' EP, released the same year, included a cover version of JUDAS PRIEST's 'Victim Of Changes'.

Hansen also preoccupied himself outside of his main act by resurrecting one of his earliest bands IRON SAVIOR enlisting Zimmermann. As well as issuing an album IRON SAVIOR also hit the road in Europe. Zimmermann joined FREEDOM CALL. Despite being recognised as a 'fun' project IRON SAVIOR's career rocketed and a succession of albums and tours ensued. Coincidentally IRON SAVIOR would later enrol erstwhile GAMMA RAY drummer Thomas Nack into the fold for the 'Interlude' album.

The 'Powerplant' album saw cover artwork from Derek Riggs, renowned for his IRON MAIDEN album cover. More surprising was the cover of 'It's A Sin', originally by THE PET SHOP BOYS.

GAMMA RAY then released a 'best of' album with a twist. All the songs, voted for inclusion by the band's fans, were re-recorded. Both Hansen and Richter contributed to EDGUY's Tobias Sammet's mammoth AVANTASIA project album of 2000. In keeping with the EDGUY connection both Hansen and Schlächter would be on hand in the studio to mix TARAXACUM's conceptual 'Spirit Of Freedom's opus, conceived by EDGUY man Tobias Exxel.

GAMMA RAY returned in 2001 touting an album of freshly recorded material entitled 'No World Order'. Hansen had earlier in the year relinquished his post in side act IRON SAVIOR due to constantly conflicting timings between the two bands. Touring would see Mexican dates with MEGACE's Jorg Schror filling in temporarily for an injured Dirk Schlächter.

Ardent fans would be enticed by Japanese versions of the 'Heaven Or Hell' single which featured an exclusive cover version of THIN LIZZY's 'Angel Of Death'. Headline dates in Germany during October, topping a billing featuring SONATA ARTICA and VANISHING POINT, saw HELLOWEEN's Martin Großkopf assisting his erstwhile band mate Kai Hansen by filling in for an injured Dirk Schlächter.

GAMMA RAY would announce their first ever American show, billed as special guests to countrymen BLIND GUARDIAN, at the annual Atlanta 'ProgPower' festival. In the meantime Sanctuary Records would weigh in with a heavyweight re-release schedule of the first six GAMMA RAY albums all including extra tracks. 1989's debut 'Heading For Tomorrow' added 'Mr. Outlaw', 'Lonesome Stranger' and 'Sail On', sophomore effort 'Sigh No More's bonus tracks would be 'Heroes', a pre-production version of 'Dream Healer' and 'Who Do You Think You Are? Whilst 1993's 'Insanity And Genius' came complete with an extended take on 'Gamma Ray' a cover of JUDAS PRIEST's 'Exciter' and a live version of 'Save Us'. As for more recent outings 1995's 'Land Of The Free' boasted the inclusion of HOLOCAUST's 'Heavy Metal Mania', a pre-production rendition of 'As Time Goes By' and 'The Silence'. The 1997 album 'Somewhere Out In Space' added 'Return To Fantasy', 'Miracle' and another JUDAS PRIEST cover in 'Victim Of Changes' and lastly 1999's 'Powerplant's bonuses numbered 'A While In Dreamland', 'Rich And Famous' (2000 version) and RAINBOW's 'Long Live Rock n' Roll'.

GAMMA RAY would schedule tour dates in June as support to MOTÖRHEAD, the Moscow 'Long Live Rock n' Roll' festival upfront of headline shows across Eastern Europe. August found the band at the 'Soyorock 2002' festival in Kyung Gi Do, Korea, the 'Bloodfest' UK festival, and the 'Spodek Mystic' event in Katowice, Poland. GAMMA RAY's headline European dates, commencing in October, would be dubbed the 'Skeletons In The Closet' tour with a set list compiled from fan requests. Support act for these dates would be PARAGON. Whilst in North America for the Atlanta, Georgia 'ProgPower' festival the band announced a solitary Canadian show at Montreal, Quebec's Le Medley in mid November with strong support from EIDOLON and FORGOTTEN TALES.

Singles/EPs:
Space Eater / The Silence, Noise N0151-3 (1990) (Promotion release)
Heaven Can Wait / Who Do You Think You Are? / Sail On / Mr. Outlaw / Lonesome Stranger, Noise NO151-3 (1990)
Heaven Can Wait / Mr. Outlaw, Noise N0151-7 (1980) (7" single - Promotion release)
Heading For Tomorrow (Edit) / Heading

For Tomorrow, Noise (1990) (USA promotion)
Future Madhouse / Gamma Ray / Dream Healer, Noise NO203-3 (1993)
Rebellion In Dreamland / Land Of The Free / H.M. Mania / As Time Goes By, Noise N0227-3 (1995)
Miracle / Farewell / The Silence / While In Dreamland, Noise N0262-3 (1996) ('Silent Miracle' EP)
Valley Of The Kings / Somewhere Out In Space / Watcher In The Sky / Victim Of Changes, Noise N 0283-3 (1997)
Valley Of The Kings / The Winged Horse / Watcher In The Sky / Victim Of Changes, Victor VICP 60042 (1997) (Japanese release)
Heaven Or Hell / Solid / Angel Of Death, JVC Victor VICP-61450 (2001) (Japanese release)

Albums:
HEADING FOR TOMORROW, Noise N 0151-2 (1989)
Welcome / Lust For Life / Heaven Can Wait / Space Eater / Money / The Silence / Hold Your Ground / Free Time / Heading For Tomorrow / Look At Yourself / Sail On / Mr. Outlaw / Lonesome Stranger
SIGH NO MORE, Noise N 0178-2 (1991)
Changes / Rich And Famous / As Time Goes By / (We Won't) Stop The War / Father And Son / One With The World / Start Running / Countdown / Dream Healer / The Spirit
INSANITY AND GENIUS, Noise N 0203-2 (1993)
Tribute To The Past / No Return / Last Before The Storm / The Cave Principle / Future Madhouse / Gamma Ray / Insanity And Genius / 18 Years / Your Torn Is Over / Heal Me / Brothers
LAND OF THE FREE, Noise N0227-2 (1995)
Rebellion In Dreamland / Man On A Mission / Fairytale / All Of The Damned / Rising Of The Damned / Gods Of Deliverance / Farewell / Salvation's Calling / Land Of The Free / The Saviour / Abyss Of The Void / Time To Break Free / Afterlife / Heavy Metal Mania
ALIVE '95, Noise NO265-2 (1996)
Land Of The Free / Man On A Mission / Rebellion In Dreamland / Space Eater / Fairytale / Tribute To The Past / Heal Me / The Saviour / Abyss Of The Void / Ride The Sky / Heavy Metal Mania / Future World
SOMEWHERE OUT IN SPACE, Noise N 0283-2 (1997) **18 FINLAND, 39 GERMANY, 20 ITALY, 27 JAPAN, 59 SWEDEN**
Beyond The Black Hole / Men, Martians And Machines / No Stranger (Another Day In Life) / Somewhere Out In Space / The Guardians Of Mankind / The Landing / Valley Of The Kings / Pray / The Winged Horse /

Cosmic Chaos / Lost In The Future / Watcher In The Sky / Rising Star / Shine On / Return To Fantasy
THE KARAOKE ALBUM, JVC Victor VICP-60135 (1997) (Japanese release)
Beyond The Black Hole / Men, Martians And Machines / Valley Of The Kings / Somewhere Out In Space / Shine On / Space Eater / Abyss Of The Void / Man On A Mission / Time To Break Free / Heading For Tomorrow
POWERPLANT, Noise (1999) **51 SWEDEN**
Anywhere In The Galaxy / Razorblade Sigh / Send Me A Sign / Strangers In The Night / Gardens Of The Sinner / Short As Hell / It's A Sin / Heavy Metal Universe / Wings Of Destiny / Hand Of Fate / Armageddon
BLAST FROM THE PAST, Noise (2000)
Welcome / Lust For Life / Heaven Can Wait / Heading For Tomorrow / Changes / One With The World / Dream Healer / Tribute To The Past / Last Before The Storm / Heal Me / Rebellion In Dreamland / Man On A Mission / Land Of The Free / The Silence ('95 Version) / Beyond The Black Hole / Somewhere Out In Space / Valley Of The Kings / Anywhere In The Galaxy / Send Me A Sign / Armageddon
NO WORLD ORDER, Noise (2001) **19 FINLAND, 23 GERMANY**
Induction / Dethrone Tyranny / The Heart Of The Unicorn / Heaven Or Hell / New World Order / Damn The Machine / Solid. / Fire Below / Follow Me / Eagle / Lake Of Tears

GB ARTS (GERMANY)
Line-Up: Achim Reichert (vocals), Andre Rasfeld (guitar), Thomas Senff (bass), Andreas Beckmann (keyboards), Jörg Nazarow (drums)

Progressive Metal band GB ARTS' albums 'Return To Forever' and 'The Lake' were both produced by Russian guitar virtuoso VICTOR SMOLSKI.
2001's 'The Lake', released in Europe on the B-Mind label and in America courtesy of Pavement Music, saw Smolski also adding guest guitar solos. Other notable session appearances came from RAGE's Peavey Wagner, ANGEL DUST's Dirk Thurisch and RAGE, ARTENSION and METALIUM drummer Mike Terrana.
GB ARTS would act as support to SILENT FORCE's November 2002 European dates.

Albums:
RETURN TO FOREVER, B. Mind 27001 (1998)
City Of Light / Prophecy / Return To Forever / The Storm / Falling Rain / Behind The Mirror / Strange World / Through The Centuries / Time To Go / Parade Of The Innocence

161

THE LAKE, B. Mind 270010 (2000)
A Voice / The Surface / Silver Rain / Break
Free / My New World / The Chosen One / I
Can't Remember / Shadows Of Faces / Old
Warriors / The Darkest Is Over

GENIUS (ITALY)

A hugely ambitious 'Rock Opera' conceived
and mentored by EMPTY TREMOR guitar
player Daniele Liverani. A massive wealth of
global Rock talent was on hand to perform the
parts of individual characters to tell the tale of
the 'Genius' character's journey. Participating
were RING OF FIRE and YNGWIE
MALMSTEEN man MARK BOALS cast as
'Genius', LANA LANE as the 'Doorkeeper',
PAIN OF SALVATION's Daniel Gildenlow
portraying "Twin Spirit n. 32". GRAVE
DIGGER front man Chris Boltendahl donated
his services as the 'Stationmaster', Joe Vana
of MECCA as "King McChaos Consultant",
STEVE WALSH of KANSAS fame as "Wild
Tribe King". The veteran JOHN WETTON
would take on the part of "McChaos King",
Oliver Hartmann from German Metal band AT
VANCE as "Wild Tribe Consultant" and ex-
CRIMSON GLORY vocalist Midnight as
"Maindream". Other inclusions saw Philip
Bynoe of the STEVE VAI band and RING OF
FIRE playing "The Storyteller", and
DREAMTIDE's Olaf Senkbeil. Drums were in
the capable hands of Dario Ciccioni.

Albums:
GENIUS, Frontiers (2002)
Without Me Today / The Right Place /
Paradox / Twin Spirits Land / All Your Acts /
Dreams / My Pride / There's A Human /
Father / Terminate / I'm Afraid

GLADIATORS (GERMANY)
Line-Up: Alexander Thomä (vocals), Jens
Meinl (guitar), Jens Thomä (guitar), Maik
Metzner (bass), Sven Pöhland (drums)

Markneukirchen Metal act formulated during
the early '90s and, due to vocalist Alexander
Thomä's uncanny resemblance to a certain
Herr Dirkschneider of the Metal parish,
likened by many to ACCEPT. The act built up
a solid live reputation and was brought under
the management wing of UNREST singer
Sonke Lau. The debut album, 'Steel
Vengeance' produced by Lau, arrived in 1998
and GLADIATORS put in support slots to
GRAVE DIGGER, JAG PANZER and ANGEL
DUST.

Albums:
STEEL VENGEANCE, Black Arrow 20261

(1998)
Black Sun / Blind God / Back In The Arena /
We Are What We Are (Free Hearts) / Bloody
Rights / The Eyes Of The Children /
Saturday Night / Thousand Candles / All For
One / Future Dream / False Idols
BOUND TO STEEL, Black Arrow (1999)
Bound To Steel / Like An Eagle / Under The
Cross / Glory Or Die / Aces Up High / Street
Rockin´ Men / Redlight Zone / Child Of The
Dark / Fire Storm / Dreams Will Never Die

GLENMORE (GERMANY)
Line-Up: Jürgen Volk (vocals), Wolfgang
Heuchert (guitar), Olaf Adami (guitar),
Markus Ratheiser (bass), Dietrich Vogt
(drums)

Named after the famous whiskey,
GLENMORE were formed in 1982 as a
school band with an initial line-up of Jürgen
Volk on vocals and bass, guitarist Wolfgang
Heuchart and drummer Dietrich Vogt. The
group added bassist Markus Ratheiser in
1987 and ex-MASCOT guitarist Olaf Adami in
1990. GLENMORE's first demo in 1991 was
produced by ELOY mainman Frank
Bornemann. A further demo secured a deal
with Polydor Records. The group then busied
themselves before signing to label by playing
support gigs to VENGEANCE, HELLOWEEN,
SINNER and URIAH HEEP.
GLENMORE's debut album once more
employed the services of producer
Bornemann and associated promotion dates
included a German support to SAGA and
MANFRED MANN.
However, Dietrich Vogt was forced to quit due
to tinnitus weeks before recording the second
album 'For The Sake Of Truth'. For these
sessions GLENMORE used session
drummer Jorg Michael whose previous
credits included GRAVE DIGGER, RAGE,
HEADHUNTER and RUNNING WILD.
A permanent drummer was later found in
Michael Kasper as GLENMORE once more
toured Germany supporting ACCEPT,
SAXON, RUNNING WILD and RAGE.
In early 1996 GLENMORE appeared at the
'Bang Your Head' festival in Germany
headlined by BLIND GUARDIAN and, with no
new product forthcoming, Jürgen Volk kept
himself busy by forming a side project using
the RAW moniker.
Still, GLENMORE also recorded a new demo,
'Sacred Mission', which featured four brand
new tracks. However, Wolfgang Heuchert
opted to leave the group at the end of 1996
and was replaced by HOLY MOSES, RISK
and RUNNING WILD man Thilo Herrmann
before Olaf Adami and Michael Kasper also
quit with ex-LETTER X guitarist Rudiger Fleck

and new skinsman Dany Löble being drafted in their wake.

As the band began to demo material for a projected new album due in 1998 they managed to put in a showing at a German festival gig with PINK CREAM 69 and AXXIS in September 1997. Hermann returned to RUNNING WILD exacerbating the band's ongoing line-up problems.

By 1999 the band had evolved into RAWHEAD REX.

Albums:

MATERIALIZED, Polydor 519 098-2 (1993)
Hungry / Speak To Me / Riding On The Winds Of Change / The Voice / Take On A Shining Star / I Feel The Fire / Tell Me / Miracles / Don't Live The Life Of A Stranger / The End Of The Line

FOR THE SAKE OF TRUTH, Polydor 523 587-2 (1994)
Political Games / For The Sake Of Truth / Lost In A Daydream / TV War / King Of Almighty / Crime Of This Time / Broken Eyes / Soldier Of Fortune / Not Enough Song / My Way / Take A Look (Inside Your Heart) / Neverending

GORGON (JAPAN)

Line-Up: Shigeyuki Koide (vocals / bass), Naoki Kudo (guitar), Mutsuaki Suzuki (guitar), Kenji Naruse (drums)

Based in the city of Chiba and founded in 1995, Heavy Metal band GORGON have made it their life mission to honour the British Metal scene of the early '80s known as the New Wave of British Heavy Metal, or NWoBHM. Although the band composes original material all of their releases and their live shows are laced with obscure songs from the aforementioned era.

GORGON arrived on the scene brandishing a joint effort with MAGNESIUM in the form of the 1996 7" 'Heavy Metal Fever' EP. At this juncture the group comprised Shigeyuki Koide on vocals and bass, guitarists Naoki Kudo and Mutsuaki Suzuki with Kenji Naruse on the drums. That same year the 'Gorgon' EP arrived, the flip side of which featured a cover version of 'Ice Angels' originally by BITCHES SIN. Confusingly the band's next release in 1997 would be a further EP also called 'Gorgon', this time boasting another NWoBHM tribute with a version of BASHFUL ALLEY's 'Running Blind'.

GORGON would be unable to resist a further homage to the NWoBHM on their fourth release. The 1998 'Shadows Of The Night' carried their interpretation of the AXIS song 'Flame Burns On'. The 1999 'Force' EP, naturally hosting another cover in HOLOCAUST's 'Heavy Metal Mania', witnessed a change in the band line-up with Satoru Kawai being inducted as lead vocalist but GORGON losing the services on Kudo. 2000's 'Back Street Killer' effort, with a B side of SOLDIER's 'Sheralee', found GORGON now as a trio of Koide, Suzuki and Naruse. However, Naoki Kudo did lay down a guest lead guitar solo on 'Sheralee'.

GORGON's next product, released by the Czech View Beyond label, proved to be a 100% NWoBHM fuelled effort even down to the name of the EP 'The Official Bootleg - One Take No Dubs'. The four tracks given due deference would be BASHFUL ALLEY's 'Running Blind', BADGE's 'Silver Woman', SATAN's 'Heads Will Roll' and 'Baphomet' by ANGELWITCH. These tracks were all live in the studio recordings dating back to 1996. That same year a 1997 vintage live recording of 'Cold Hearted Woman' surfaced on a compilation cassette entitled 'The Bells Of The Mystical Empire'. The band also shared a split EP 'A Fool In Love' with the notorious SABBAT as well as having their cover version of SABBAT's 'Mion's Hill' contributed to a tribute album 'A Homage To Sabbat'.

In April of 2002 GORGON welcomed onboard second guitarist Noboru "Jero" Sakuma, the new member making his first impressions at live concerts held in Germany during June.

Singles/EPs:

Cold Hearted Woman, Street Lights Records LIGHTS 01 (1996) ('Heavy Metal Fever' split EP with MAGNESIUM)

Cold Hearted Woman (New mix version) / Ice Angels, Street Lights Records LIGHTS 02 (1996) ('Gorgon' EP)

Drifting Away / Running Blind / Midnight Highway Rider / Ride Like The Wind, Street Lights Records LIGHTS 03 (1997) ('Gorgon' EP)

Shadow Of The Night / Flame Burns On / A Lonely Man, Street Lights Records LIGHT 04 (1998) ('Shadow Of The Night' EP)

(Heavy Metal) Force / Heavy Metal Mania, Street Lights Records LIGHTS 05 (1999) ('The Force' EP)

Back Street Killer / Sheralee, Street Lights Records LIGHTS 06 (2000)

A Fool In Love, View Beyond (2001) (Split single with SABBAT)

Running Blind / Silver Woman / Heads Will Roll / Baphomet, Heavy Metal Super Stat HMSS 007 (2001) ('The Official Bootleg - One Take No Dubs' EP)

GOTHIC KNIGHTS (Brooklyn, NY, USA)

Line-Up: Rick Sanchez (vocals), John Tsantakis (guitar), Mario Consetino (bass),

Tony Cianciotto (drums)

An unadulterated Heavy Metal band out of Brooklyn. GOTHIC KNIGHTS came into being during 1990. An early member of the band, vocalist George Tsalikis, would bow out and later forge Speed Metal band ZANDELLE. Commercially GOTHIC KNIGHTS debuted with an eponymous effort in 1996, the band at this stage consisting of singer Rick Sanchez, guitarist John Tsantakis, bass player Mario Consetino and drummer Brian Dispot. Operating in Power Metal territory as an independent American act GOTHIC KNIGHTS stood out from the crowd. The band subsequently signed to the specialist Sentinel Steel label for a 1999 follow up 'Kingdom Of The Knights', notable for its inclusion of a version of JUDAS PRIEST's classic 'The Ripper'. By this juncture having shed both Sanchez and Dispot, their substitutes being lead vocalist Bryan 'Avatar' Waldman and drummer Kevin Myers.

The 2002 line-up comprised Consetino, Tsantakis, a returned vocalist Rick Sanchez and drummer Tony Cianciotto. This quartet would ready a new album 'Up From The Ashes'.

Albums:
GOTHIC KNIGHTS, (1996)
Creature Of The Dark / Bridge Keeper / Nightmare Of The Witch / Heart Of Sorrow / The Magi / War In The Sky / Darkest Knight
KINGDOM OF THE KNIGHTS, Sentinel Steel (1999)
At Dawn You Die / War In The Sky / Ring Of Souls / Song Of Roland / Demons Buried Within / That Evil Wizard / Keeper Of The Gate / The Ripper

GRACEPOINT (Minneapolis, MN, USA)
Line-Up: Matt Tennessen (vocals), Lon Kunze (guitar), Stefan Radzilowski (guitar), Sam van Moer (bass), Lance Reed (drums)

Albums:
SCIENCE OF DISCONTENT, Candlewax (1999)
Overwhelm / Attrition / The Gallery / Inside Track / Science Of Discontent / Shapechanger / Behind The Glass / The Following / Your World

ROLAND GRAPOW (GERMANY)

'The Four Seasons Of Life' album, released in 1997, proved to be the debut solo outing by HELLOWEEN guitarist Roland Grapow, who had begun his recording career in the early

'80s with RAMPAGE. Guests included PRIMAL FEAR's Ralph Scheepers, HELLOWEEN's rhythm section of bassist Marcus Großkopf and drummer Uli Kusch, ROUGH SILK keyboard player FERDY DOERNBERG and German guitar hero AXEL RUDI PELL.

Initial copies of the album had to be withdrawn because the cover artwork was deemed to be too close to that of famed Classical label Deutsche Gramaphon.

The 1999 album 'Kaleidoscope' has vocals from LOUDNESS and OBSESSION singer Michael Vescara, bass from YNGWIE MALMSTEEN man Barry Sparks and drums courtesy of ARTENSION and METALIUM's Mike Terrana.

Grapow would break away from HELLOWEEN in August of 2002 founding MASTERPLAN with ex-HELLOWEEN colleague drummer Uli Kusch and the esteemed Norwegian vocalist JORN LANDE. The guitarist would also donate a session to the 2002 album 'Heavy Machinery' from Swedish Metal band LOCOMOTIVE BREATH and to STRATOVARIUS front man TIMO KOTIPELTO's solo debut 'Waiting For The Dawn'.

Albums:
THE FOUR SEASONS OF LIFE, Reef Recordings SRE CD 702P (1997)
Prelude No. I (Presto) / The Winner / No More Disguise / Show Me The Way / I Remember / Dedicated To / Searching For Solutions / Strange Friend / Bread Of Charity / The 4 Seasons Of Life / Finale De Souvenir
KALEIDOSCOPE, JVC Victor VICP-60679 (1999)
Walk On Fire / Under The Same Sun / The Hunger / A Heartbeat Away / Hidden Answer / Till The End / Kaleidoscope / Angel Face / Listen To The Lyrics / Reaching Higher / Lord I'm Dying

GRAVE DIGGER (GERMANY)
Line-Up: Chris Boltondahl (vocals), Peter Masson (guitar), Willi Lackman (bass), Albert Eckardt (drums)

GRAVE DIGGER formed in 1980 in Gladbeck and their debut album, 'Heavy Metal Breakdown', with keyboard contributions from Dietmar Dillhardt, sold more than 40,000 copies in Europe, although the band had initially made their recording debut supplying two tracks to the 'Rock From Hell' compilation album.

The original line-up of the band incorporated vocalist / guitarist Peter Masson, bassist Chris Boltendahl and drummer Lutz

164

Schmelzer, a trio that remained stable until 1982 when Schmelzer left and was replaced by Philipp Seibel. The following year a decision was taken for Masson to concentrate on guitar duties and allowing Boltendahl to take over the microphone. A new bassist, Willi Lackmann was promptly recruited.

By the time the band came to record the 'Heavy Metal Breakdown' debut album Siebel had been replaced on drums by Albert Eckhart, although Willi Lackmann soon departed and Boltendahl filled the vacancy in order to record the 'Shoot Her Down' EP released after the album.

Although one Rene T. Bone (real name Rene Teichmann) is credited for playing bass on GRAVE DIGGER's second album, 1985's 'Witch Hunter', a brand new bassist, C.F. Brank had joined the band by the time Noise released the record. Indeed, bass duties were actually undertaken by both Boltendahl and Masson on the record as they had fired Teichmann during recording in March 1985.

GRAVE DIGGER's third album, 'Wargames', appeared in 1986 it was something of a disappointment to all concerned in terms of sales and led to the departure of Masson from the ranks.

Opting to go in a more commercial direction with new guitarist Uwe Lulis in tow the German outfit adopted the new title of DIGGER and recorded an album titled, rather misleadingly in hindsight, 'Stronger Than Ever'. Needless to say, the record flopped and the group split.

In the wake of the DIGGER disaster bassist Brank hooked up with S.A.D.O. whilst Lulis and Boltendahl opted to stay together and formed HAWAII with drummer Jochen Börner and bassist Rainer Bandzus, although the project never got beyond the demo stage.

In 1993 Boltendahl decided to reform GRAVE DIGGER, the new line-up featuring Boltendahl, Uwe Lulis, the experienced former ASGARD and IRON ANGEL bassist Tomi Gottlich and drummer Peter Breitenbach. This group released a four-track promo CD and 1993's 'The Reaper'. However, by 1994 Breitenbach was out, joining WARHEAD, in favour of the well travelled Jörg Michael, a man boasting a tradition with AVENGER, MEKONG DELTA, RAGE and HEADHUNTER amongst a string of others.

GRAVEDIGGER recorded the album 'Symphony Of Death' before Michael joined RUNNING WILD and new drummer Frank Ulrich teamed up with the Gladbeck crew.

Ulrich's tenure with the band was to be relatively brief. Although he played on 1995's 'Heart Of Darkness' album he encountered personal differences with his band mates and

GRAVE DIGGER

departed, being succeeded by former CAPRICORN and WALLOP drummer Stefan Arnold. Ulrich joined X WILD for their third album 'Savage Land'.

Returning to action with the conceptual 'Tunes Of War' record in 1996 the band toured Germany in 1997 with support from SINNER, the record having enjoyed several weeks in the loftier regions of the German national charts. GRAVE DIGGER's return to form came courtesy of 'Tunes Of War's ambitious concept. A conceptual piece based upon Scottish history and liberal in its use of that tried and trusted Heavy Metal instrument the bagpipes. The band also novelly invited the German Rock media on a trip through the ancient battlefields of Scotland.

GRAVE DIGGER stuck to the historical theme for 1998's 'Knights Of The Cross', an album based on the exploits of the Knights Templar, this album providing further momentum to their revival. Japanese variants of the album saw bonus tracks in covers of BLACK SABBATH's 'Children Of The Grave' and RAINBOW's 'Kill The King'. Despite this welcome reversal of fortunes the man behind the revival Tomi Göttlich decamped and was superseded by ex-RUNNING WILD, X WILD and CROSSROADS man Jens Becker.

Touring found the band on the road in Europe with IRON SAVIOUR and American act IMAGIKA. Both Boltendahl and Lulis would both guest on IMAGIKA's '… And So It Burns' album.

GRAVE DIGGER toured Germany in January of 2000 supported by Italians WHITE SKULL. Lulis departed toward the end of the year being swiftly replaced by Manni Schmidt, previously with RAGE. GRAVE DIGGER's tenth studio album, the mediaeval themed 'Excalibur', would once again find the band with a strong presence in the national album charts. The band this time taking journalists by bus from Germany to Stonehenge and Tintagel castle for the pre-launch listening party. A limited digi-pack run of this outing would include an exclusive track 'Black Cat' whilst the Japanese release, in keeping with tradition, held one more bonus cut namely a cover of IRON MAIDEN's 'Running Free'.

GRAVE DIGGER would delve into cover territory once more in late 2001 cutting a version of LED ZEPPELIN's 'No Quarter'. The band's set at the annual 'Wacken Open Air' in Germany would see the light of day as the 2002 live album 'Tunes Of Wacken'.

GRAVE DIGGER, together with support from BRAINSTORM, undertook European touring to kick off 2002. However, following January dates in Germany and shows in Southern Europe the band's projected Belgian and Dutch gigs for March would be cancelled as Schmidt was incapacitated with a virus the guitarist had caught whilst on the Iberian continent.

Also in March of 2002 former members guitarist Uwe Lulis and bassist Tommi Göttlich returned to the fore with the adventurous conceptually based REBELLION, taking on no less than the Bard's 'Macbeth' as the theme for their opening shot 'A Tragedy In Steele'. Joining the ex-GRAVE DIGGER personnel for REBELLION would be WARHEAD front man Bjorn Eilen on second guitar, drummer Randy Black from Canadian Thrashers ANNIHILATOR and vocalist Michael Seifert from Osnabruck acts BLACK DESTINY and XIRON. GRAVE DIGGER would set to work on yet another conceptual album for 2002 release as well as an autobiography of the band. A first for the act came in November, GRAVE DIGGER's first gig in Moscow at the 4,500 capacity Luzhniki Small Sport Hall co-headlining with BLAZE.

Singles/EPs:

Shoot Her Down / Storming The Brain / We Wanna Rock You, Noise N0016 50-1672 (1984)

Ride On / Spy Of Mason / Shadows Of A Moonless Night / Fight The Fight, Grave Digger (1993) (Promotion release)

Rebellion (The Clans Are Marching) / Truth / Dark Of The Sun / The Ballad Of Mary (Queen Of Scots), G.U.N. GUN 103 BMG (1996) (Promotion release)

Rebellion (Live) / The Dark Of The Sun / Heavy Metal Breakdown / Witchhunter / Headbanging Man, G.U.N. GUN 74321 48738 2 (1997) ('The Dark Of The Sun' EP)

Albums:

HEAVY METAL BREAKDOWN, Noise N007 08-1670 (1984)
Headbanging Man / Heavy Metal Breakdown / Back From The War / Yesterday / We Wanna Rock You / Legion Of The Lost / Tyrant / 2000 Lightyears From Home / Heart Attack

WITCHHUNTER, Noise N0020 (1985)
Witch Hunter / Nightdrifter / Get Ready For Power / Love Is A Game / Get Away / Fight For Freedom / School's Out / Friends Of Mine / Here I Stand

WARGAMES, Noise N0034 (1986)
Keep On Rockin' / Heaven Can Wait / Fire In Your Eyes / Let Your Heads Roll / Love Is Breaking My Heart / Paradise / (Enola Gay) Drop The Bomb / Fallout / Playin Fools / The End

BEST OF THE EIGHTIES, Noise NO234-2 (1992)
Heavy Metal Breakdown / Shoot Her Down / Get Away / Paradise / (Enola Gay) Drop The

Bomb / Fallout / Back From The War / Witch Hunter / Keep On Rockin' / 2000 Lightyears From Home / Heaven Can Wait / Headbanging Man / Night Drifter / We Wanna Rock You / Yesterday / Don't Kill The Children / Tears Of Blood / Girls Of Rock n' Roll

THE REAPER, G.U.N. GUN 032 BMG 74321 17142-2 (1993)
Tribute To Death / The Reaper / Ride On / Shadows Of A Moonless Night / Play Your Game (And Kill) / Wedding Day / Spy Of Mas'On / Under My Flag / Fight The Fight / Legion Of The Lost (Part II) / And The Devil Plays Piano / Ruler Mr. H. / The Madness Continues

SYMPHONY OF DEATH, G.U.N. GUN 039 BMG 74321 19908-2 (1994)
Intro / Symphony Of Death / Back To The Roots / House Of Horror / Shout It Out / World Of Fools / Wild And Dangerous

HEART OF DARKNESS, G.U.N. GUN 060 BMG 74321 24746-2 (1995)
Tears Of Madness / Shadowmaker / The Grave Dancer / Demon's Day / Warchild / Heart Of Darkness / Hate / Circle Of Witches / Black Death

HEART OF DARKNESS, G.U.N. GUN 060 BMG 74321 24746-2 (1995) (Digi pack version)
Tears Of Madness / Shadowmaker / The Grave Dancer / Demon's Day / Warchild / Heart Of Darkness / Hate / Circle Of Witches / Black Death / My Life / Dolphin's Cry

TUNES OF WAR, G.U.N. GUN 74321 39035-2 (1996)
The Brave / Scotland United / The Dark Of The Sun / William Wallace (Braveheart) / The Bruce / The Battle Of Flodden / The Ballad Of Mary (Queen Of Scots) / The Truth / Cry For Freedom (James VI) / Killing Time / Rebellion (The Clans Are Marching) / Culloden Muir / The Fall Of The Brave

KNIGHTS OF THE CROSS, G.U.N. (1998)
Deus Io Vult / Knights Of The Cross / Monks Of War / Heroes Of This Time / Fanatic Assassins / Lionheart / The Keeper Of The Holy Grail / Inquisition / Baphomet / Over The Sea / The Curse Of Jacques / The Battle Of Bannockburn

EXCALIBER, G.U.N. (1999)
The Secrets Of Merlin / Pendragon / Excalibur / The Round Table (Forever) / Morgana Le Fay / The Spell / Tristan's Fate / Lancelot / Mordred's Song / The Final War / Emerald Eyes / Avalon

THE GRAVE DIGGER, Nuclear Blast (2001)
47 GERMANY
Son Of Evil / The Grave Digger / Raven / Scythe Of Time / Spirits Of The Dead / The House / King Pest / Sacred Fire / Funeral Procession / Haunted Palace / Silence /

Black Cat
TUNES OF WACKEN, (2002)
Scotland United / Dark Of The Sun / The Reaper / The Round Table (Forever) / Excalibur / Circle Of Witches / Ballad Of Mary / Lionheart / Morgana Le Fay / Knights Of The Cross / Rebellion / HM Breakdown

GRAVEN IMAGE (MS, USA)
Line-Up: Maxx Christopher (vocals / guitar), James Houptmann (guitar), Brian Keith (bass), Olly Oliver (drums)

GRAVEN IMAGE was originally conceived as BLITZKRIEG. During the early '90s. Quite incredibly the band took some time to learn of the British NWoBHM stalwarts and duly adopted the title GRAVEN IMAGE in 1994. The 1995 mini-album 'Game Of Iron' found Paul Brown handling lead vocals with Matt Nutt on bass.
Nutt opted out in early 1996, being replaced by six string bassist Cory Shartier. With Paul Brown stepping down too guitarist Maxx Christopher took on lead vocal responsibilities. The band embarked upon their second release 'Emperor Of Eternity' in 1997 but found themselves struggling. The initial tapes were scrapped and the album completely re-recorded, finally arriving in 2000. Prior to the album seeing the light of day Brian Keith took the bass role.
Charles Allen joined the band in mid 2000.

Albums:
GAME OF IRON, (1995)
The Voyage / Game Of Iron / Crusader / Dancing With The Devil / Lost In A Dream
EMPEROR OF ETERNITY, Graven Music (2000)
Emperor Of Eternity / Skies Of Hail / Leif's Saga / Avalon / The Search / Walking Dead / Given / Take You / Graven Image

GRIFFIN (NORWAY)
Line-Up: Tommy Sebastian (vocals), Kai Nergaard (guitar), Marcus Silver (guitar), Johnny Wangberg (bass), Marius Karlsen (drums)

A 1998 formation GRIFFIN, led by BLOODTHORN guitarist Kai Nergaard and who deal in retro style traditional Thrash style Metal, was originally founded as a sideline to the members priority acts BLOODTHORN, DARK AGES and ATROX. A demo was duly cut, which uniquely featured the sounds of double bass and saxophone, and would remain unreleased. A second attempt, 'the 'Conquers The World' session, scored the band a deal with French label Season Of Mist for the October 2000 debut album 'Wasteland Serenades'.

GRIFFIN gained the valuable support slot to MAYHEM's European tour, bringing onboard new guitarist Marcus Silver shortly after. This revised line-up would cut a second GRIFFIN album, the more Metal inclined April 2002's 'The Sideshow'.

Albums:
WASTELAND SERENADES, Season Of Mist SOM034 (2000)
Mechanised Reality / The Usurper / Spice Keeps Me Silent / Obsession / New Business Capitalised / Hunger Strikes / Always Closing / Punishment Macabre / Exit 2000 / Wasteland Serenade / Dream Of The Dreamers (Bliss 2)
THE SIDESHOW, Season Of Mist SOM063 (2002)
Prologue / Shadows Of Deception / Horrific / Freakshow / The Last Rays Of A Dying Sun / Death Row League / What If / A Distant Shore / Vengeance Is Mine / Today's Castaway / Cosmic Revelation / Epilogue

GRIFFIN (San Rafael, CA, USA)
Line-Up: Billy McKay (vocals), Mike 'Yaz' Jastremski (guitar), Rick Cooper (guitar), Tom Spraybery (bass), Rick Wagner (drums)

GRIFFIN came together when ex-METAL CHURCH drummer Rick Wagner joined forces with vocalist William Rodrick 'Billy' McKay and guitarist Rick Cooper in 1980. After their first demo in 1982 the band quickly progressed into one brought up on a staple diet of British Heavy Metal and, at one time, featured guitarist Henry Hewitt, formerly 'U.S. Metal' compilation participants EXXE.

The band's ten song deep second demo initially proved difficult to obtain directly from the band, GRIFFIN oddly reluctant to let potential fans in on the fun, but soon emerged on the thriving tape trading circuit.

1983 GRIFFIN relocated to San Francisco's Bay Area supplementing their line-up with guitarist Mike 'Yaz' Jastremski and bassist Thomas Spraybery.

The material was quick to impress Shrapnel head Mike Varney who signed the group with 'Flight Of The Griffin' arriving in 1984. The album was a powerful statement of intent and second album 'Protectors Of The Lair' followed suit although minus Jastreemski and Sprayberry as GRIFFIN trimmed down to a trio.

Albums:
FLIGHT OF THE GRIFFIN, Shrapnel (1984)
Hawk The Slayer / Heavy Metal Attack /
Submission / Creeper / Flight Of The Griffin / Fire In The Sky / Hell Runneth Over / Judgement Day / Travelling In Time
PROTECTORS OF THE LAIR, Griffin (1986)
Eulogy Of Sorrow: Awakening / Hunger / Infinite Voyage / Cursed Be The Deceiver / Entity: Watching From The Sky / Sanctuary / Truth To The Cross / Poseidon Society / Eulogy Of Sorrow (Reprise)

GRIM REAPER (UK)
Line-Up: Steve Grimmett (vocals), Nick Bowcott (guitar), Dave Wanklin (bass), Lee Hams (drums)

Droitwich act GRIM REAPER secured a deal with Heavy Metal Records in 1981 following their inclusion on the compilation album 'HM Heroes'. At this time the line-up was vocalist Paul DeMercado, bassist Phil Matthews and drummer Angel Jacques alongside founder member guitarist Nick Bowcott. Their 'Bleed 'Em Dry' demo sold out of it's 500 copies. Many NWoBHM collectors believe the band released a 7" single, 'Can't Take Anymore', on Heavy Metal Records, but this was only a proposal and never saw the light of day.

Steve Grimmett was drafted in to replace DeMercado in 1982 from local act MEDUSA (which also featured guitarist Lance Perkins and bassist Eddie Smith - later to adopt the respective Nom de plumes of "Lance Rocket" and "Eddie Starr" in WRATHCHILD). Another early member was ex-ROUGH JUSTICE drummer Brian 'Thunderburst' Parry, later to join WRATHCHILD and ORIGINAL SIN. GRIM REAPER enrolled bassist Dave Wanklin and drummer Lee Harris, both of whom had been part of GRIM REAPER in the past, to create the most familiar line-up of the act.

Later that year the band signed to Ebony for their first full length album and Grimmett also found time to perform lead vocal duties for CHATEAUX's debut album (also on Ebony) as they found themselves in the studio minus a vocalist.

The debut GRIM REAPER album, although hideously under produced, actually fared exceptionally well in the U.S. Billboard top 100 through a licensing deal with RCA, where it eventually surpassed the 200,000 sales mark, peaking at number 53.

'See You In Hell' proved an apt title for the record as the band explored dark themes within tracks such as 'Dead On Arrival' wrapped around some classic British Metal riffs and Grimmett's extraordinary vocals. GRIM REAPER seemed able to successfully mesh melody with true aggression.

Oddly, for a period in early 1983 the band experimented with keyboard player Andy

Thomas but soon reverted to the tried and tested four piece formula and GRIM REAPER played an American club tour to promote the album alongside acts such as EXCITER and SANTERS.

The second album, 'Fear No Evil', again suffered from poor production but still bolstered success in the States where the band had been active with extensive touring including dates with URIAH HEEP, headliners with support act VICTORY then a show with DEEP PURPLE at the huge Texas Jam festival.

The third album saw GRIM REAPER emerge after a lengthy legal battle with Ebony to place their signatures directly with RCA in America and Lee Harris' drum stool position being taken over by Mark Simon . The band had originally recorded the album at Ebony studios but when tapes were sent to RCA they were judged to be of such poor sound quality as to be unusable. The album was completely re-recorded in America. The end result was the awesome album 'Rock You To Hell', produced by Max Norman, which really showed the band in its true light. An absolutely essential British Metal purchase. A cover version of BLUE OYSTER CULT's '(Don't Fear) The Reaper' was cut although not included.

GRIM REAPER teamed up with ARMORED SAINT and HELLOWEEN for the 'Hell On Wheels' American tour to promote the album. At this juncture Wanklin was replaced with ex-IDOL RICH bassist Geoff Curtis.

At this point RCA were keen to build on GRIM REAPER's profile and the proposed fourth album saw Bowcott writing new more mainstream material with the likes of SURGIN man Jack Ponti, a former associate of JON BON JOVI.

The band performed a few low key British gigs with a new rhythm section of bassist Benje Brittan, previously a member of HEALTH WARNING, and drummer Mark Simon, previously a member of local Glam act IPANEMA KATZ. Sadly, and inexplicably, it all went hideously wrong and the band split. Ironically, the classic 'Rock You To Hell' was never released in Britain.

In the wake of GRIM REAPER former members Wanklin and Hams left the music business altogether, while Steve Grimmett went on to front the ill fated ONSLAUGHT in a total mis-match of styles. Nick Bowcott fared little better with a new act BARFLY recording an album which never saw a release. The guitarist pursued a career in music journalism, writing for the US based 'Circus' amongst others, and made a guest appearance on the EYEWITNESS album of 1995.

STEVE GRIMMETT of GRIM REAPER
Photo : Flea

DAVE WANKLIN of GRIM REAPER
Photo : Flea

NICK BOWCOTT of GRIM REAPER
Photo : Flea

Steve Grimmett then pursued his own project LIONSHEART signed to Music For Nations and enjoying considerable success in Japan. Following three LIONSHEART albums Grimmett founded PRIDE with ex-KILLERS personnel and began work on a projected solo album. In early 1999 the man contributed backing vocals to the MARSHALL LAW album 'Warning From History'.

By rights GRIM REAPER should have been huge. The third album remains a tragic reminder of what could have been. Grimmett and Bowcott have plans though to re-record early material for a new GRIM REAPER release in the future.

2000 found Grimmett back in action forging a new act titled SEVEN DEADLY SINS. The band was billed as GRIM REAPER for the German Wacken festival the same year as the Spitfire label in America reissued all three albums.

During February of 2002 American Metal band SEVEN WITCHES, led by SAVATAGE guitarist Jack Frost, issued their 'Xiled To Infinity And One' album, complete with a cover version of GRIM REAPER's 'See You In Hell'.

Singles/EPs:
The Show Must Go On / Dead On Arrival, Ebony PB 13932 (1984)
The Show Must Go On / The Show Must Go On, RCA (1984) (USA promotion)
Fear No Evil / Fear No Evil, RCA (1985) (USA promotion release)

Lust For Freedom / Lust For Freedom, RCA (1987) (USA promotion)

Albums:
SEE YOU IN HELL, Ebony EBON 16 (1983) **53 USA**
Dead On Arrival / Liar / Wrath Of The Ripper / All Hell Let Loose / Now Or Never / Run For Your Life / The Show Must Go On / See You In Hell

FEAR NO EVIL, Ebony EBON 32 (1985)
Fear No Evil / A Matter Of Time / The Final Scream / Rock n' Roll Tonite / He Remembers, Do You? / Lay It On The Line / Never Comin' Back / (She's A) Ladykiller

ROCK YOU TO HELL, RCA 6250 1 (1987) **93 USA**
Rock You To Hell / Night Of The Vampire / Lust For Freedom / When Heaven Comes Down / Suck It And See / Rock Me 'Till I Die / You'll Wish That You Were Never Born / Waysted Love / I Want More

BEST OF GRIM REAPER, RCA 67813 (1999)
See You In Hell / Fear No Evil / Rock You To Hell / Wrath Of The Reaper / Lust For Freedom / Never Coming Back / All Hell Let Loose / The Show Must Go On / Let The Thunder Roar / Run For Your Life / Waysted Love / Now Or Never / Fight For The Last / Dead On Arrival / Lay It On The Line / Suck It And See / Final Scream

GRINDER (GERMANY)

Line-Up: Adrian (vocals / bass), Andy (guitar), Lario (guitar), Stefan Arnold (drums)

Metal band GRINDER debuted with the 'Sacred To Death' demo and included WALLOP drummer Stefan Arnold. GRINDER's debut album 'Dawn For The Living' was produced by Kalle Trapp, whilst the third release, 'Nothing Is Sacred', is noted for production by Harris Johns and Tom Stiehler. GRINDER later evolved into CAPRICORN. Guitarist Andy joined RAWBONE.
Arnold joined GRAVE DIGGER for their 'Tunes Of War' album.

Singles/EPs:
Reeling On The Edge / Incarnation Off / Truth In The Hands Of Judas / Just Another Scar (Live) / Dawn For The Living (Live) / F.O.A.D. (Live), No Remorse NRR1011 (1990)

Albums:
DAWN FOR THE LIVING, No Remorse NRR 1003 (1988)
Obsession / Dawn For The Living / Sinners Exile / Magician / Frenzied Hatred / Dying Flesh / Delirium / Traitor / F.O.A.D.
DEAD END, No Remorse NRR 1007 (1989)
Agent Orange / Dead End / The Blade Is Back / Inside / Just Another Scar / Total Control / Why / Train Raid / Unlock The Morgue
NOTHING IS SACRED, Noise (1991)
Drifting For 99 Seconds / Hymn For The Isolated / The Spirit Of Violence / Nothing Is Sacred / None Of The Brighter Days / Superior Being / Dear Mr. Sinister / Pavement Tango / The Nothing Song / NME

GUARDIAN ANGEL (GREECE)

Line-Up: Nikos Roussakis (vocals), Panayiotis Diakoyiannis (guitar), Alexandros Stavrakas (bass), Manos Matsos (drums)

Heavy Metal band GUARDIAN ANGEL first made an impression with the 19990 demo tape 'Travelling On The Wings Of Eternity'.

Singles/EPs:
Beyond The Twilight / Give Way To The Rush, Cygnus (1994)

Albums:
OBLIVION SEAS, Rising Sun (1997)

GUARDIAN'S NAIL (JAPAN)

Line-Up: Noriyuki Shinagawa (vocals), Tohuru Myanohara (guitar), Yasumoto Ohtani (guitar), Kiyoshi Seki (bass), Tai Shoda (drums)

"Melodious and powerful" Heavy Metal band GUARDIAN'S NAIL gained heavy exposure in Japan for their initial 1993 demo 'Guardian's Nail' when the track 'Call Of The Nightingale' received radio airplay courtesy of famed DJ and writer Captain Wada. The band followed it up in 1994 with a further cassette 'Second Wind' before self-financing the 'Believe' mini album. However, the band broke up and in March of 1998 bass player Kiyoshi Seki teamed up with MAELSTROM.

Albums:
BELIEVE, (1996)
Passion Red / The Past Love / Crossing Over The Valley / Riding On The Wind / Keep Believing Forever

GUARDIANS OF TIME (NORWAY)

Line-Up: Bernt Fjellstad (vocals), Rune Schellingerhout (guitar), Paul Olsen (guitar), Dag-Ove Johnsen (bass), Vidar Uleberg (drums)

Power Metal band GUARDIANS OF TIME feature erstwhile TRAIL OF TEARS drummer Vidar Uleberg and former SCARIOT vocalist Bernt Fjellstad in the ranks. The group was established during 1997 under the name A.T.A.W. comprising of Fjellestad on vocals, guitarists Rune Schellingerhout and Paul Olsen on guitar, bassist Tommy Viik and Thomas Færøvig on drums. In 1998 the rhythm section witnessed a complete change around with Uleberg taking the drum position and Dag-Ove Johnsen of DEMENTED and OLD WORDS NEW becoming the band's new bass player. With this revised roster the group evolved into GUARDIANS OF TIME.
In January of 2000 GUARDIANS OF TIME committed themselves to an inaugural three song demo entitled 'Soul Reaper'. Shortly afterward, Olsen took leave in order to study at the Hollywood Musicians Institute. Upon gaining a deal with the German label Shark Records the band, waiting for Olsen's re-recruitment, recorded the debut album 'Edge Of Tomorrow'. The album cover was noted for having been executed by Derek Riggs, famed for his prominent work with IRON MAIDEN.
Promoting the record GUARDIANS OF TIME put in festival performances at the Norwegian 'Total Festivalen' and the 'Quart' festival.

Albums:
EDGE OF TOMORROW, Shark (2001)
Prologue / Guardians Of Time / Payback / High Octane / Edge Of Tomorrow / Midnight Crime / Sail Away / Soul Reaper / As The Morning Rise / Tearless / Torn Apart / Gladiator

171

H HADES (NJ, USA)
Line-Up: Paul Smith (vocals),
Joe Casilli (guitar), Dan
Lorenzo (guitar), Anthony Vitti
(bass), Tom Coombs (drums)

A renowned name in Metal
circles. New Jersey's HADES have weathered
the storms of line-up changes and break ups
to consistently deliver ever improving slabs of
technical Heavy Metal. Having attained a
worthy cult following on American soil,
despite a sometimes overtly socio-political
lyrical stance, HADES has maintained a
sturdy fan base in Germany.
HADES underwent turbulent times in the
early '80s Vocalist Paul Smith left to join the
army and for a brief tenure was replaced with
John Callura. However, Callura was out within
weeks. Bassist Lou Ciarlo also quit leaving
HADES as just a duo of guitarist Dan Lorenzo
and drummer Tom Coombs.
Things stabilised somewhat with the addition
of bassist Sandy Handsel and guitarist Scott
LePage. As HADES found a new front man in
Alan Tecchio the band also pulled in ex-
ATTACKER bassist Jimmy Schulman. This
line-up recorded the 1985 'The Cross' single.
A further live demo 'Live At The Fox' (one of a
set of live tapes HADES released in 1986
others being 'Live At The China Club' and
'Live At Manhattans') secured HADES a deal
with Torrid Records. HADES objectives were
again hindered though, when Schulman
suffered a near fatal car crash putting live
work on ice for a lengthy period.
LePage joined Hardcore Rappers MUCKY
PUP on an amicable basis and HADES was
soon up to strength again by including
guitarist Ed Fuhrman.
Vocalist Allan Tecchio, opting to join Texan
Progressive   techno-metallers
WATCHTOWER for their 'Control And
Resistance' album, was supplanted by a
returning Paul Smith.
Lorenzo founded NON FICTION, along with a
returning Tecchio, releasing three albums
although HADES reunited for the 'Exist To
Resist' album. Tecchio later fronted POWER
in a guest capacity. All was running far from
smoothly however as soon after recording
various band members announced their
intention never to record with HADES again.
During April of 1988 HADES, back with
Tecchio and patching up their differences
once more, once more began rehearsing and
writing for a new album. LePage was reunited
with the act to put down bass and in came
new drummer Dave Lescindky.
Originally intended as a final farewell in 1995
the band issued 'Exist To Resist'. There are at
least three versions of this compilation with

the US, Black Pumpkin version adding four
bonus tracks. The CD had some material
recorded in 1989, at the very end of their first
run.   The US version also has alternate
artwork as well.
Fan demand to reissue the old demos
resulted in the band releasing 'The Lost Fox
Studio Sessions' during 1998.   The band
themselves admit the sound quality is terrible
and recommends it only for die-hard fans!
The time was right and the band, spurred by
the demand for classic Thrash, inked a deal
with Metal Blade Records
HADES added drummer Ron Lipinski in
August of 2000 and re-drafted Jimmy
Schulman on bass. The band put in a valuable
performance at the annual 'Wacken Open Air'
festival in Germany. Their 2000 album 'The
Downside' would see M.O.D. and S.O.D.'s
larger than life spokesman Billy Milano adding
backing vocals and D.D. Verni of OVERKILL
putting down session bass on the track 'Bitter
Suite No. 1'.
HADES released their latest musical chapter
'DamNation' in June of 2001. 2002 saw an
independent, 20th anniversary compilation
release 'Hades1982-2002' featuring tracks
from their entire career.

Singles/EPs:
Girls Will Be Girls / Social Disease, Hades
(1982) ('Deliver Us From Evil' EP)
The Cross / Widow's Mite, Hades (1985)

Albums:
RESISTING SUCCESS, Torrid (1987)
On To Illiad / Legal Tender / Sweet Revenge
/ Nightstalker / Resist Success / Widows
Mite / Cross / Masque Of The Red Death
IF AT FIRST YOU DON'T SUCCEED, Torrid
(1988)
Opinionate / Process Of Elimination / King In
Exile / In The Meantime / Rebel Without A
Brain / Aftermath Of Rebellion / I Too Eye /
Face The Fat Reality / Technical Difficulties
LIVE: ON LOCATION, Grand Slamm
38(1991)
The Leaders? / King In Exile / On To Illiad /
In The Meantime / Opinionate! / Rebel With
out A Brain / "A" / Rape Of Persephone / The
Cross / Face The Fat Reality / I Too Eye /
Aftermath Of Betrayal / Nightstalker / MES
(Technical Difficulties) / Diplomatic Immunity
EXIST TO RESIST, Art Of Music 51002
(1995)
Exist To Resist / Rape Of Persephone /
Doubt / Colorblind / Deter-My-Nation /
Throughout Me, Threw Out You / Second
Degree Sleepwalking/ A(G) / The Other /
The Leaders '95
THE LOST FOX STUDIO SESSIONS, Black

Pumpkin (1998)
The Leaders? / Sweet Revenge /
Nightstalker / Resist Success / Gamblin' With
Your Life / Deter My Nation / Rape Of
Persephone / Not A Part Of Your Life / Bete
Noir / Throughout Me, Threw Out You /
Amerasian Reparation / King In Exile /
Opinionate / A / Easy Way Out
SAVIOUR SELF, Metal Blade 3984- 14194-2
(1999)
Saviour Self / Decline And Fall Of The
American Empire / Our Father / Active
Contrition / To Know One / In The Words Of
The Profit / The Agnostic / Y2K / End Of The
Bargain / Fall / The Atheist
THE DOWN SIDE, Metal Blade 14283 (2000)
Ground Zero N.Y.C. / Align The Planets /
Bitter Suite #1 / Hoax / Pay The Price / Hail
To The Thief / Shove It / It's A Wonderful Lie
/ Become Dust / Responsible / The Me That
Might Have Been / Ground Zero (Reprise)
DAMNATION, Metal Blade 14372 (2001)
Bloast / Out The Window / DamNation /
Absorbed Force / Quit / Stressfest / Biocaust
/ This I Know / Momentary Clarity / California
Song / Stop And Go / Bad Vibrations

HALFORD (UK)
Line-Up: Rob Halford (vocals), Patrick
Lachman (guitar), Mike Chlasiak (guitar), Ray

Riendeau (bass), Bobby Jarzombek (drums)

For some twenty years as front man for
Birmingham metal legends JUDAS PRIEST
vocalist Rob Halford came to epitomise the
term Heavy Metal, not only in his onstage
regalia of extravagantly studded leather but
for a vocal range and expression that many
aspired to but few could match.
Halford's activity outside of JUDAS PRIEST
whilst he was still a member was minimal. He
contributed vocals to Ronnie James Dio's
HEAR N' AID 'Stars' Band Aid project and had
produced a demo for Phoenix act SURGICAL
STEEL. Other activity found the vocalist
adding his deft touch to the track 'Ready To
Burn' on KROKUS's 1983 album 'Headhunter'
and guesting with SKID ROW on their live
version of 'Delivering The Goods'.
Upon splitting from JUDAS PRIEST Halford
first cut the 'Light Out Of Black' track
borrowing the musicians from PANTERA. The
song was used on the 'Buffy The Vampire
Slayer' movie soundtrack. The vocalist then
created FIGHT with American musicians, a
tough act musically but sorely lacking the
finesse of JUDAS PRIEST. Many viewed the
act as highly derivative of PANTERA. After
three albums and high profile touring,
including supports to METALLICA and
ANTHRAX, Halford eventually folded FIGHT.

HALFORD

HALFORD

The singer was not of the news for long though as he performed with BLACK SABBATH at two shows in America when Ronnie James Dio pulled out. Halford learnt the entire set list in just two days and put in a creditable performance. Rumours abounded in 1997 that BLACK SABBATH guitarist TONY IOMMI and Halford were colluding on an projected album but this did not develop.

Halford (now sporting skin-tight blue rubber wear on stage!) signed his Industrial Metal act, then titled HALFORD, to NINE INCH NAILS guru Trent Reznor's record label for a further project album. HALFORD became GIMP and then TWO. By now adopting the Nosferatu look and proclaiming Metal to be dead, surprised nobody when, in January 1998 on MTV, he officially declared himself to be gay.

It came as no great shock that the TWO project proved disastrous and by late 1999 Halford had got back to his Metal roots announcing his return with an internet available download track 'Silent Screams'. This heralded a new management deal with Sanctuary (responsible for IRON MAIDEN) and a new album 'Resurrection' which many thought to be Halford's finest career effort yet. Whilst quelling JUDAS PRIEST re-formation rumours the album, which included a duet with IRON MAIDEN vocalist BRUCE DICKINSON, included a track co-written with JUDAS PRIEST song-writing collaborator BOB HALLIGAN JR. Halford's pre-production had involved discussions with Attie Bauw and Tom Allom, both with obvious JUDAS PRIEST connections.

The singer's live band included ex-SAN ANTONIO SLAYER, RIOT and SPASTIC INK drummer Rob Jarzombek, guitarists Patrick Lachmann (also a member of DIESEL MACHINE) and MIKE CHLASIACK and ex-TWO bass player Ray Riendeau.

Lachman's pre-HALFORD history had seen the guitarist, alongside his brother ex-GARGOYLE vocalist Tim Lachman, being involved with STATE OF THE ART in league with future RAISED BY ALIENS bassist Alex Sarabia and drummer Dennis Kelly. The Lachman siblings would later be found in both ERROR 7 and ELEVENTH HOUR with both of these acts donating tracks to an IRON MAIDEN tribute album before Pat hooked up with HALFORD.

Rob Halford toured as support to IRON MAIDEN in the UK during November and included numerous JUDAS PRIEST numbers in his live set including 'Electric Eye', 'Riding On The Wind', 'Tyrant' and 'Running Wild'. Halford would solidify the tie to IRON MAIDEN by acting as guests on their American dates as well as shows in South America including Mexico, Chile, Argentina and the gargantuan 'Rock In Rio' festival. A European headline tour in November saw American Thrashers OVERKILL as support. American headline dates were also squeezed in as well as a headline spurt in Japan where 'Resurrection' made a huge impact reaching number 4 in the album charts. Fans at these gigs were treated to rare live versions of JUDAS PRIEST tracks such as 'Stained Class' and 'Genocide'.

When the dust settled 'Resurrection' was deemed to have been an undisputed success story putting Halford back into the charts with a vengeance.

Rumours surfaced in late 2000 of a joint ROB HALFORD, BRUCE DICKINSON and Geoff Tate (of QUEENSRYCHE) future project suitably titled 'The Three Tremors'.

Early 2001 witnessed the surge of support captured on a double live album 'Live Insurrection'. Once again produced by Roy Z, not only did the record include the full live set but also reworked studio versions of JUDAS PRIEST out takes 'Heart Of A Lion' and 'Prisoner Of Your Eyes'. Japanese versions of the album on JVC Victor Records would also include a bonus track, a version of the SCORPIONS 'Blackout' with a guesting Rudolf Schenker.

In March of 2001 MIKE CHLASIAK issued his third solo album 'The Spilling'. Jarzombek and Riendeau would also get back to work on a new 2001 SPASTIK INK record. Lachman would forge a new project with erstwhile PRONG mainman Tommy Victor and drummer Dan Laudo.

Chlasiak would make the best of his HALFORD down time after recording his parts for the second studio album. The guitarist contributed guitar to a take on LED ZEPPELIN's 'Immigrant Song' by IAN PARRY for a tribute album and also on two cuts, 'Controlled' and 'Fear' on the 2002 PRIMAL FEAR opus 'Black Sun'. A whole triumvirate of HALFORD players would donate their services to the 2002 'Earthmaker' endeavour of ROYAL HUNT vocalist JOHN WEST, the album seeing sessions from Mike Chlasciak on guitar, Ray Riendeau on bass and Bobby Jarzombek on drums.

HALFORD readied a second studio album, 'Crucible', ready for release in mid 2002. A batch of European summer festivals throughout June and July would be announced including the 'Sweden Rock Festival', the Italian 'Gods Of Metal', the Greek 'Rockwave' event, Belgium's long established 'Graspop' show and both 'Bang Your Head' and 'With Full Force' in Germany. As it transpired HALFORD put on live sets in Sweden and Italy dominated by JUDAS

PRIEST classics. HALFORD would also be confirmed as the headline act at the 'Soyorock' festival in Kyung Gi Do, Korea during August but then made a public announcement stating that he was to withdraw from forthcoming gigs due to exhaustion. The singer had also taken the unusual step of apologising in print for recent lack lustre stage performances.

Reports also surfaced suggesting the singer was to make a cameo appearance, as a sex shop employee, in the Mickey Rourke movie 'Spun'. More tellingly Halford publicly expressed a desire to re-unite with former band mates JUDAS PRIEST. Guitarist Mike Chlasiak launched a side venture PAIN MUSEUM in August.

Albums:
RESURRECTION, Sanctuary (2000)
12 GERMANY, 7 GREECE, 21 SWEDEN, 140 USA
Resurrection / Made In Hell / Locked And Loaded / Night Fall / Silent Scream / The One You Love To Hate / Cyberworld / Slow Down / Twist / Temptation / Drive / Saviour
LIVE INSURRECTION, Metal Is MISDD007 (2001) **52 GERMANY, 57 SWEDEN**
Resurrection / Made In Hell / Into The Pit / Nailed To The Gun / Light Comes Out Of Black / Stained Class / Jawbreaker / Running Wild / Slow Down / The One You Love To Hate / Life In Black / Hell's Last Survivor / Sad Wings / Saviour / Silent Screams / Intro / Cyberworld / Hellion / Electric Eye / Riding On The Wind / Genocide / Beyond The Realms Of Death / Metal Gods / Breaking The Law 26. Tyrant / Screaming In The Dark / Heart Of A Lion / Prisoner Of Your Eyes
CRUCIBLE, Metal Is MISCD020 (2002)
104 CANADA, 31 FINLAND, 100 FRANCE, 33 GERMANY, 144 USA
Park Manor / Crucible / One Will / Betrayal / Handing Out Bullets / Hearts Of Darkness / Fugitive / Hearts Of Darkness / Crystal / Heretic / Golgotha / Wrath Of God / Weaving Sorrow / Sun / Trail Of Tears / Park Manor

HALLOWS EVE (Atlanta, GA, USA)
Line-Up: Stacy Anderson (vocals), David Stuart (guitar), Tommy Stewart (bass), Tym Helton (drums)

Atlanta Thrash Metal act HALLOWS EVE date back to 1984 with an initial line-up of vocalist Stacy Anderson, guitarists David Stuart and Skellator, bassist Tommy Stewart and drummer Tym Helton. The band's debut appearance came with the inclusion of the track 'Metal Merchants' on the Metal Blade

'Metal Massacre IV' compilation.

Drummer Ronny Appoldt appeared on the debut album although Tym Helton handled the drums on the tracks 'Metal Merchants' and 'Hallows Eve'.

Drums for 'Monument', which included a cover version of QUEEN's 'Sheer Heart Attack', are by Rob Clayton although for live work Paul Kopchinski occupied the drum stool. By the third album Tym Helton was back in the fold.

The track 'D.I.E.' was a featured track on the Metal Blade issued soundtrack album for the 1988 movie 'Black Roses'.

The group appeared to have split in late 1988 as Anderson departed to Los Angeles although Tommy Stewart and David Stuart carried on into the following year looking for new members and writing material.

The duo eventually found new guitarist JAMES MURPHY, previously having made his mark with AGENT STEEL, and drummer Tom Knight but the pair lasted barely a few months, Murphy joining DEATH and later played with OBITUARY, CANCER, TESTAMENT, KONKHRA, DISINCARNATE as well as issuing solo product.

Tommy Stewart later turned up as a member of FRAGILE X.

Albums:
TALES OF TERROR, Roadrunner RR 9772 (1985)
Plunging To Megadeath / Outer Limits / Horrorshow / The Mansion / There Are No Rules / Valley Of The Dolls / Metal Merchants / Hallows Eve
DEATH AND INSANITY, Roadrunner RR 9676-1 (1989)
Death And Insanity / Goblet Of Gore / Lethal Tendencies / Obituary / Plea Of The Aged / Suicide / D.I.E. (Death In Effect) / Attack Of The Iguana / Nefarious / Nobody Lives Forever / Death And Insanity (Reprise)
MONUMENT, Metal Blade 73290 (1988)
Speedfreak / Sheer Heart Attack / Rot Gut / Monument To Nothing / Pain Killer / The Mighty Decibel / Righteous Ones / No Sanctuary

HAMMER (UK)
Line-Up: The Dog (vocals), Kenny Nicholson (guitar), Bob Henman (guitar), Graeme Hutchinson (bass), Marty Day (drums)

Antecedent to HAMMER the trio of vocalist The Dog (real name Marty Wilkinson), guitarists Kenny Nicholson and Bob Henman had all operated with HOLLAND. Combining with a rhythm section of bass player Graeme Hutchinson and drummer Marty Day a new, harder edged union of HAMMER was formulated. Marty Day had also pre-HOLLAND been involved with AXIS whilst Kenny Nicholson had also served time with BLACK ROSE.

The HAMMER album 'Contract With Hell' was intended as a second HOLLAND record but legal moves from the American HOLLAND forced a name switch and gave the band an opportunity to considerably beef up their sound in the process. With the break up of HAMMER Nicholson founded FAST KUTZ releasing his third album by his third band for the Ebony label.

Albums:
CONTRACT WITH HELL, Ebony EBON 29 (1985)
Caution To The Wind / Try It / Hey You / Contract With Hell / Hard Hittin' Woman / Satellite / Prayer Of A Soldier / Across The Line

HAMMERFALL (SWEDEN)

Line-Up: Joacim Cans (vocals), Oscar Dronjac (guitar), Stefan Elmgren (guitar), Frederik Larsson (bass), Patrik Räfling (drums)

Founded in 1993 Sweden's HAMMERFALL made a truly startling impact with their 1997 debut album 'Glory To The Brave'. Unashamedly harking back to prime time traditional Metal and including a rousing cover of WARLORD's 'Child Of The Damned', the Scandinavian's astute notion of what the European Metal scene was waiting for was amply rewarded. The debut album crashed straight into the German national charts selling over 50,000 copies in the process, surprising even their record company.

The band began purely as an extracurricular activity by various members of Swedish Death Metal bands. Ex-CEREMONIAL OATH drummer Jesper Strömblad and guitarist Oscar Dronjac created HAMMERFALL as a leisure pursuit away from their then fulltime acts, Dronjac in CRYSTAL AGE and Strömblad with IN FLAMES. The line-up was completed by DARK TRANQUILITY vocalist Mikael Stanne and guitarist Nicke Sundin.

HAMMERFALL made an auspicious debut covering PRETTY MAIDS' 'Red Hot And Heavy' at 'Rockslaget', a local band competition in 1994. With HAMMERFALL drawing themselves up to the semi-finals by 1996 the band became more of a solid unit as Stanne bowed out of the show due to tour commitments with DARK TRANQUILITY and LUCIFERION / HIGHLANDER vocalist singer Joacim Cans was drafted.

HAMMERFALL now found themselves the subject of recording contract offers and various band members were now forced into making the decision to stay or concentrate on their other bands. Guitarist Glenn Ljungström was superseded by Stefan Elmgren and bassist Fredrik Larsson returned to NONE. His position was taken by BILLIONAIRE BOYS CLUB / KEEGAN man Magnus Rosen. Although a quintet HAMMERFALL were not shy in admitting that a sixth member, in the form of Jesper Strömblad, also assisted in the writing process and the Swedes eventually signed to German label Nuclear Blast.

The Rock media was quick to take the band to their hearts and the group's debut album, 'Glory To The Brave', gained 'Album of the month' awards in both 'Heavy Oder Was' and 'Rock Hard', capping it all by receiving an endorsement of maximum marks in 'Metal Hammer'. Nuclear Blast also released a limited edition vinyl version of the album in razorsaw shape, restricted to a mere 500 copies. However, not all went well on the release front as a single of 'Glory To The Brave' mistakenly included a rough mix live version of 'The Metal Age' instead of the planned 'I Believe'. The band were furious and duly vented their anger in the press. The original single is now a sought after rarity as from the second pressing the necessary correction was made.

To support the record HAMMERFALL toured in Germany mid position on a bill including veterans TANK and RAVEN consistently stealing the headliner's crowds. Further touring ensued as guests to GAMMA RAY and JAGPANZER in September 1997. HAMMERFALL kept up their tradition of traditional Metal on these dates by including the STORMWITCH song 'Ravenlord' in their set, and were honoured to be joined by former STORMWITCH vocalist Andy Muck during their set at the 'Bang Your Head II' festival in southern Germany in the fall of '97. The Swedes paid homage to German Metal legends ACCEPT by donating their version of 'Head Over Heels', with guest vocals from ACCEPT man Udo Dirkschneider, to the 'Tribute To Accept' album.

The sophomore 'Legacy Of Kings', once more utilising the writing services of Jesper Strömblad, also fared well. In Europe HAMMERFALL took to the festival scene with gusto appearing at the Dutch 'Dynamo' event, Germanys 'Rock Hard' and 'With Full Force' festivals, Italy's 'Monsters Of Rock' and Austria's 'Mind Over Matter' as well as the 'Karlshamm' outdoor gig in their homeland. HAMMERFALL recorded their third album with producer Michael Wagener in America. The launch party, held in Gothenburg during

MAGNUS of HAMMERFALL
Photo : Nico Wobben

JOACIN CANS of HAMMERFALL
Photo : Nico Wobben

OSCAR DRONJAC of HAMMERFALL
Photo : Nico Wobben

September, saw the band joined onstage at various intervals by RUNNING WILD drummer A.C., MOTÖRHEAD drummer Mikkey Dee and erstwhile ACCEPT frontman Udo Dirkschneider. The evening rounded off with a rendition of JUDAS PRIEST's seminal 'Breaking The Law' with the band members swapping instruments.

Later that year HAMMERFALL would pay homage to their predecessors by cutting tracks for various tribute albums. Shown the honours were 'Man On The Silver Mountain' for the SPV Records DIO tribute as well as ACCEPT's 'Head Over Heels' (featuring Udo Dirkschneider) and HELLOWEEN's 'I Want Out'. The latter would be issued as the lead track on a single further impacting on the Swedish and German charts.

The would tour took HAMMERFALL on a global expedition which included their debut American, Japanese and South American shows.

The band suffered a major tragedy in 1999 when tour manager Lelle Hildebrandt disappeared and was presumed murdered.

In 2000 HAMMERFALL bounced back in spectacular fashion debuting at number 1 in Sweden with 'Renegade' and also charting higher than previously in Germany. The accompanying 'Renegade' single would also crack the charts open and offer fans a cover version of HEAVY LOAD's 'Run With The Devil'. Touring in Europe saw HAMMERFALL headlining with guests VIRGIN STEELE and FREEDOM CALL.

During the summer of 2001 HAMMERFALL offered up their rendition of New York '80s Glamsters TWISTED SISTER's 'We're Gonna Make It' to the tribute album 'Twisted And Strange'. News also emerged that Cans was forming a pivotal part of the WARLORD resurrection project acting as frontman alongside original members Thunderchild and Destroyer.

Elmgren would partake in outside activities too forging the melodic Metal band FULL STRIKE in the latter half of 2001. Joining Elmgren on the FULL STRIKE venture would be erstwhile LOST HORIZON singer Niclas Jonsson, ex-CRAWLEY bassist Chris Savage Goldsmith and FREAK KITCHEN drummer Björn Fryklund. HAMMERFALL bassist Magnus Rosén would not be idle either, forging an "all star" Metal project by the name of EXECUTION fronted by Renato Tribuzy of Brazilian Power Metal band THOTEN.

Another act of interest to HAMMERFALL fans would be DREAM EVIL - debuting with the 2002 'Dragonslayer' album. Fronted by Niklas Isfeldt the group witnessed a union of guitarist Fredrik Nordstrom, MYSTIC PROPHECY and FIREWIND guitarist Gus G., bassist Peter Stalfors and drummer Snowy Shaw. The latter of course a veteran of the Scandinavian Metal scene noted for his work with MERCYFUL FATE, KING DIAMOND, MEMENTO MORI and NOTRE DAME. Isfeldt, Nordstrom and Stalfors would all boast strong HAMMERFALL connections. Isfeldt having acted as studio backing vocalist, Nordstrom

179

as HAMMERFALL's producer and Stalfors as song writer.

Upon announcement of Stefan Elmgren's May 2002 FULL STRIKE debut album 'We Will Rise' through the Spitfire label it also revealed that the drum position had been taken by a former HAMMERFALL compatriot Patrik Räfling and that LOST HORIZON's Fredrik Olsson would augment the band for live work. FULL STRIKE debuted live in Gothenburg on April 19th.

HAMMERFALL themselves would progress on their new album throughout the Spring and early summer. Recorded entirely digitally at HELLOWEEN vocalist ANDI DERIS's studio in Tenerife, the record would be produced by Charlie Bauerfiend. A cover version of CHASTAIN's 'Angel Of Mercy' would be laid down during this time. With the sessions finalised Johansson made time to session on Christian Metal band NARNIA's 2002 album 'The Great Fall'.

The band's momentum would be halted though with a vicious attack on HAMMERFALL frontman Joacim Cans just days before a scheduled video shoot for the single 'Hearts On Fire'. Cans was assaulted by a Black Metal fan with a beer glass at a bar in the group's hometown of Gotheburg on August 10th sustaining an injury around his right eye which required 25 stitches to close.

HAMMERFALL would be revealed to be acting as support act to DIO on the Rock veteran's November North American dates. A sustained bout of touring throughout Europe in January and February found MASTERPLAN as support act.

Singles/EPs:
Glory To The Brave (Radio Edit) / Hammerfall / I Believe / The Dragon Lies Bleeding, Nuclear Blast NB274 (1997) (German Promotion. 'Stone Cold' is mis-credited on the sleeve instead of 'The Dragon Lies Bleeding')
Glory To The Brave (Edit) / Hammerfall (Live) / Ravenlord / Glory To The Brave, Nuclear Blast (1997)
Heeding The Call / Eternal Dark / The Metal Age (Live) / Steel Meets Steel (Live) / Stone Cold (Live), Nuclear Blast (1999) **45 GERMANY**
I Want Out / At The End Of The Rainbow / Man On The Silver Mountain / Glory To The Brave (video), Nuclear Blast (1999) **75 GERMANY, 55 SWEDEN**
Renegade / Run With The Devil / Head Over Heels / Hammerfall In Wire World (Multimedia), Nuclear Blast NB 530-2 (2000) **45 AUSTRIA, 34 FINLAND, 89 GERMANY, 17 SWEDEN, 72 SWITZERLAND**
Always Will Be / The Fallen One / Always

Will Be (Acoustic) / Breaking The Law, Nuclear Blast (2001)
Hearts On Fire / We're Gonna Make It / Heeding The Call (Live) / Heeding The Call (Video), Nuclear Blast (2002)

Albums:
GLORY TO THE BRAVE, Nuclear Blast 27361 62652 (1997) **34 GERMANY**
The Dragon Lies Bleeding / The Metal Age / Hammerfall / I Believe / Child Of The Damned / Steel Meets Steel / Stone Cold / Unchained / Glory To The Brave
LEGACY OF KINGS, Nuclear Blast (1999) **15 SWEDEN**
Heeding The Call / Legacy Of Kings / Let The Hammer Fall / Dreamland / Remember Yesterday / At The End Of The Rainbow / Back To Back / Stronger Than All / Warriors Of Faith / The Fallen One
RENEGADE, Nuclear Blast (2000) **17 GERMANY, 1 SWEDEN**
Templars Of Steel / Keep The Flame Burning / Renegade / Living In Victory / Always Will Be / The Way Of The Warrior / Destined For Glory / The Champion / Raise The Hammer / A Legend Reborn
CRIMSON THUNDER, Nuclear Blast (2002)

HAMMERHEART (SLOVALKIA)
Line-Up: Denis Belá_ik (vocals / guitar), Mark Esto_in (guitar), Shisho (bass), Mario Zvara (drums)

Although based in Slovakia HAMMERHEART are proud purveyors of NWoBHM styled Heavy Metal. The band came together in 1994 with a line-up of Denis Belá_ik, Mark Esto_in, bass player Jan _intaj and drummer Martin Bartánus. However, in February 1996 Shisho took over on bass, featuring on the demo 'When Dark Dreams...' the following year.

Bartánus stepped down in early 1998 and Mario Zvara, an ex-member of WALKYRIE took his post. HAMMERHEART would then gain exposure with a track inclusion on the Metal Age compilation 'The Grimoire Of Exalted Deeds'. Support gigs included notable successes with ALICE COOPER, SAXON and SODOM.

In October of 2001 HAMMERHEART was hit a significant blow with the exiting of both Esto_in and Zvara. The band was soon patched up with the induction of guitarist Ian Glorian and drummer Adrian Ciel, both former GLORIAN members.

Singles/EPs:
Strange Feeling / When Dark Dreams Become Reality / The Last Twilight /

Wandering In Flames (1997) ('When Dark Dreams Become Reality' EP)

HAMMERSCHMITT (GERMANY)
Line-Up: Edu Keller (vocals), Diethard Schmitt (guitar), Andreas Püschel (guitar), Hans-Dieter Wolf (bass), Ralf Deutscher (drums)

A mid '80s German Metal band. Former HAMMERSCHMITT guitarist Andreas Püschel joined ASGARD in the early '90s.

Albums:
HAMMERSCHMITT, Rockport (1985)
Line Of Meridion (Intro) / Race To Hell / The Devil's Cry / Big City Action / I Go My Way / Tears In My Eyes / Air Born / Victims / Bringers Of War

HAMMERS RULE (Denver, CO, USA)
Line-Up: Blade Duncan (vocals), Spunki Mechlinski (guitar), Shaun Henley (bass), Chuck Hohn (drums)

Denver Thrash Metal act founded in 1984 and including former BLITZKRIEG drummer Chuck Hohn. HAMMERS RULE boasted quite a stageshow - smashing skulls with a huge sledgehammer. The 'Show No Mercy' debut album was delivered in white vinyl format.
Hohn quit in 1986, turning up as a bassist in a Lounge band. He would later join PAXTON'S EMPIRE and NC-17.

Albums:
SHOW NO MERCY, Tangents (1984)
Prelude / The Calm / Before The Storm / After The Bomb / Pool Of Piranhas / Castle Walls / Hammer's Rule / If Only You Knew / Set Me Free / She's A Rocker / Little Girls / Sex, Drugs And Rock n' Roll
AFTER THE BOMB, W.E.B Pentagram HRT-2 21983 D5 (1985)
Prelude / The Calm / Before The Storm / After The Bomb / Kamikaze / Mission of Death / Stop The World / If Only You Knew
SPONTANEOUS HUMAN COMBUSTION, Metal Enterprises (1991)
Marilyn Monroe / Spontaneous Human Combustion / Madman On The Loose / Shattered Glass / Icepick / Buried Alive / White Widow

HANGAR (BRAZIL)
Line-Up: Michael Polchowicz (vocals), Cristiano Wortmann (guitar), Luis Fernando Melo (bass), Aquiles Priester (drums)

A highly respected Progressive Metal band lent pedigree by the renowned Aquiles Priester on drums and tenor vocalist Michael Polchowicz, the latter's credentials reinforced by his membership of the Symphonic Orchestra of Porto Alegre. Priester's talents were utilised on PAUL DIANNO's 'Nomad' album and as an integral part of the TRITONE collective.
Cristiano Wortmann contributed lead guitar to the 1999 debut 'Last Time'. Eduardo Martinez Filho, previously with PANIC and POSTHUMOUS, joined the band on guitar in January of 2000 and featured on HANGAR's second album 'Inside Your Soul'.

Albums:
LAST TIME, (1999)
The Secrets Of The Sea / Like A Wind In The Sky / Voices / Absinth / Last Time / Angel Of The Stereo / Speed Limit 55 / Lost Dream
INSIDE YOUR SOUL, (2001)
The Soul Collector / Inside Your Soul / The Massacre Trilogy: Part 1 - Sailing The Seas Of Sorrow, Part 2 - To Tame A Land, Part 3 - Five Hundred's Enough / Saviour / The Vision / Legions Of Fate / Living In Trouble Part 1 / Living In Trouble Part 2 / No Command / Falling In Disgrace

HANKER (CANADA)
Line-Up: Pascal Cliché (vocals / guitar), Patrick Gravel (guitar), Denis Cossette (bass), Luc Gray (drums)

An industrious Quebec based Power styled Metal band created during 1985 with a line-up of vocalist / guitarist Pascal Cliché, guitarist Patrick Gravel and a rhythm section of Martin Jones and Jean-Francois Fillion. Drummer Luc Gray would enrol in 1990 as the band prepared for a 1991 demo.
HANKER issued the debut 1994 album 'In Our World' under their own steam, following it with the revised 'In Our World Revisited' in 1996 and fresh recordings 'The Dead Ringer' in 1997. HANKER signed to the Metal Disk label for the 2000 effort 'Snakes And Ladders'.
The band appeared at the ANVIL headlined Montreal 'Powerpack' festival on November 8th 2002.

Albums:
IN OUR WORLD, Hanker (1994)
I'd Like To Know / Bloodbath In Heaven / In Our World / Gardeners Of Pain / Cradle Of The Night / Disturbing The Brain / Fight The Light / Staring At The Rain / Pay No More / Lethal Liar / This Could Be Heaven
THE DEAD RINGER, Hanker (1997)
Unsung Hero / Holy Screen / You Won't Live

Eternally / The Clown / They Are Gone / Dead As The Night / The Age Of The Quick Fix / F.A.T.E. / No More War / United We Stand, Divided We Fall
SNAKES AND LADDERS, Metal Disk (2000)
Ad Patres / The Pardoner / Hail To You / Seven / Save Your Life / Confidence Man / Far From The Cradle / On The Verge Of Tears / Fool's Paradise / The Eternal Struggle / Behind The Curtain

HANOVER FIST (CANADA)
Line-Up: Frank Zirone (vocals), George Bernhardt (guitar), David Aplin (guitar), Chris Brockway (bass), David Applin (bass), Kim Hunt (drums)

Superb slice of crunching Canadian Heavy Metal with a confused history. HANOVER FIST were founded by WRABIT colleagues guitarist David Aplin and bassist Chris Brockway with erstwhile ZON and MOXY drummer Kim Hunt. The band fell apart in the studio with only vocalist Frank Zirone remaining.
Session guitar on the album came from ex-DAVID BOWIE man Stacy Heydon. Ex-MOXY drummer Danny Bilan also contributed.
MCA Records issued the debut album twice with revised track listing and different titles as HANOVER FIST became HANOVER. The 1985 re-release saw the addition of the BRYAN ADAMS track 'Fits Ya Good' but omitted 'Don't Let It Stop' and 'Should Be Rockin'.
Brockway joined LEE AARON for her 1986 album 'Call Of The Wild'. Bernhardt later worked with GREGG BISSONETTE on his eponymous solo album and appears on JEFF SCOTT SOTO's 1995 solo effort 'Love Parade'.
Not to be confused with the two American HANOVER FIST's from Indiana and North Carolina.

Singles/EPs:
Fits Ya Good / Hungry Eyes / Looking For Love, MCA (1985)

Albums:
HANOVER FIST, MCA (1983)
The Maze / Metal Of The Night / Hungry Eyes / Don't Let It Stop / Standing Six / Fear No Evil / Rock Bottom / High Speed Roller / Looking For Love / Should Be Rockin'
HUNGRY EYES, MCA (1985)
Fits Ya Good / Hungry Eyes / The Maze / Looking For Love / Standing Six / Fear No Evil / Metal Of The Night / Rock Bottom / High Speed Roller

HARD DAY (RUSSIA)
Line-Up: Vladimir Bazhin (vocals), Sergej Chesnokow (guitar), Mikhail Shakhijanov (bass), Alexei Nikanorov (drums)

Moscow based Power Metal band. HARD DAY's second 1989 album is in fact culled mainly from their debut 'Flight' with only three new songs. HARD DAY shared space with French acts ABSYNTHE and PASCAL MULOT for a split album 'Im Narrenland' in 1992.

Albums:
FLIGHT, (1988)
II, (1989)

HARPPIA (BRAZIL)
Line-Up: Percy Weiss (vocals), Flavio Goto (guitar), Claudio Cruz (bass), Tibério Correa (drums)

A Sao Paulo Metal band founded during 1982. HARPPIA released two cult albums in the 1985 debut 'Ferro E Fogo' and a 1987 follow up '7', both of which are highly sought after on the European collector's market.
The band was centred upon drummer Tibério Correa and included ex-AEROPLANO bassist Ricardo Ravache alongside guitarists Helcio Aguirra and Marcos Patriota for the first album issued by the Barato Afins label. However, the band suffered severe line-up ructions with both Patriota and Ravache leaving for CENTURIAS and Aguirra also bailing out to join GOLPE DE ESTADOS.
HARPPIA switched to the Rock Brigade label for sophomore outing '7', seeing Correa joined by vocalist Percy Weiss, guitarist Flavio Goto and bassist Claudio Cruz. This line-up too would crumple when Goto made his departure for LYNX. An all new look HARPPIA surfaced in 1996 touting a fresh album 'Harppia's Flight' and predictably a totally revised line-up. Correa had managed to retain the services of Cruz but also enrolled new faces vocalist Conrado Ledesma and guitarist Marcos Rizzato.

Albums:
FERRO E FEGO, Barato Afins BA 017 (1985)
7, Rock Brigade RBR170 (1987)
HARPPIA'S FLIGHT, Megahard MHR003 (1997)
Harppia's Flight / Hidden Wisdom / Army Of Strangers / Don't Ask For Death / Last Chance / Without Return / This Is My History / Hidden Wisdom / Army Of Strangers / Don't Ask For Death / Last Chance / Without Return / This Is My History

HARROW (HOLLAND)
Line-Up: Frank van Gerwen (vocals), Erik de Boer (guitar), Harry Wijering (guitar), Johnny Fraterman (bass), Ferry Bult (drums)

Power Metal act HARROW was formed in 1982 by former VANDENBERG guitar technician Harry Wijering. The band put out their first demo 'Fearful Awakening' in 1991. Signed to Noise Records in 1993 HARROW unfortunately lost the services of bassist Johnny Fratermann due to serious illness. His replacement was ex-WICKED MYSTIC bassist Freddy Meyer and the group later toured as support to KILLERS in addition to releasing three albums.

Albums:
THE RISING PHOENIX, RHR 7580 AB (1993)
Welcome To... / The Rising Phoenix / Blue Lightning / Moneymaker / Storm Of Difference / Stone Cold
THE PYLON OF INSANITY, Noise N00245-2 (1994)
The Isle Of Reality / The Pylon / Catstrike / Road To Nowhere / Wake Up And See / Eternal Chase / Monks / Timeless World / Lost Souls / Reverse Tales / The Last Sign
CALL OF THE UNBORN, Milecrest Music A2Z 85014 (1996)
Phantoms Of Despise / Call Of The Unborn / Trains Of Death / The Guardian / Disgrace Of The Giant / Both Sides / The Claw Of Destiny / Demolition / Terminal Attack / Friends / Punishment Day / Second Sight
EMBRACE THE WORLD, Power PR 0555 (1999)
Illusion Or Reality / The Sun / Nature's Cry / The Strength Of The Word / Masquerade Of War / Life Dies Down / The Maker / The Blueprint Of Life / Mother Of Disasters / Embrace The World / Illusion Or Reality / Trains Of Death (Live) / Don't Wait For Me (Live) / Catstrike (Live)

HAWAII (USA)
Line-Up: Gary St. Pierre (vocals), Marty Friedman (guitar), Tom Azcredo (guitar), Joe Galisha (bass), Jeff Graves (drums)

HAWAII were initially known as VIXEN in 1981 comprising vocalist Kim LaChance, erstwhile DEUCE guitarist MARTY FRIEDMAN, bassist Gary St. Pierre and drummer Jeff Graves. Shortly after their formation the band scored inclusion of their track 'Angels From The Dust' on the 'US Metal II' compilation album.
Further demos followed and a mini-album 'Made In Hawaii'. Strangely, the band's next

compilation cut 'Heavy Metal Virgin' on the Metal Blade Records 'Metal Massacre II' was credited to a pseudonym of ALOHA.
Shrapnel Records Mike Varney signed the band for the poorly produced but frenetic 'One Nation Underground'. St. Pierre departed for pastures new to front VICIOUS RUMOURS.
Further releases followed as the band got steadily more commercial. The mini-album 'Loud, Wild & Heavy' saw Friedman and Graves alongside fresh recruits vocalist Eddie Day and Joey Galisa on bass. HAWAII expanded by bringing in second guitarist Tom Azevedo for 'The Natives Are Restless'.
Friedman eventually dissolved the band and would turn up as founder member of CACOPHONY as well as releasing solo instrumental albums and more significantly joining MEGADETH.

Albums:
ONE NATION UNDERGROUND, Shrapnel 1009 (1983)
Living In Sin / Silent Nightmare / Escape The Night / You're Gonna Burn / One Nation Underground / Nitro Power / The Pit And The Pendulum / Secret Of The Stars / Overture Volcanica
LOUD, WILD AND HEAVY, Hawaii (1985)
Bad Boys Of Metal / Loud, Wild And Heavy / Escape The Night / Rhapsody In Black
THE NATIVES ARE RESTLESS, SPV Steamhammer (1985)
Call Of The Wild / Turn It Louder / V.P.H.B. / Beg For Mercy / Unfinished Business / Proud To Be Loud / Lies / Dynamite

H-BOMB (FRANCE)
Line-Up: Didier Izard (vocals), Armando Ferreira (guitar), Christian Martin (guitar), Phillipe Garcia (bass), Gerard Michel (drums)

Based in Levry in their three year history H-BOMB proved to be a vital force in French Heavy Metal. Created in November 1981 by Phillipe Garcia and Armando Ferreira, the group was snapped up by Dutch label Rave On and the mini-album recorded for the company was notable for its aggressive stance and French lyrics.
H-BOMB supported DEF LEPPARD, ACCEPT, ACID, TRUST and ANVIL in France and, for the second, full blown album, Ferreira drafted in his guitarist brother Paul to take the place of Christian Martin. The resulting 'Attaque' was a far superior release to the 'Coup De Metal' debut and featured rather graphic cover artwork depicting the band as victims of a nuclear attack, gruesome skin blistering and all...

The 1986 single 'Stop The Lights' featured a version of the ,MONTROSE classic 'Space Station No. 5' on the B side.

Singles/EPs:
Stop The Lights / Space Station No. 5, Axe Killer (1986)
To Feel Pain / Can't Stop Lovin' / Stop The Lights, Axe Killer (1986)

Albums:
COUP DE METAL, Rave On RLP 005 (1983)
H-Bomb / Dans Le Griffes D'Attila / Chasseur De Frime / Le Loup / Condamne A Mort / Coup De Metal
ATTAQUE, Rave On RLP 008 (1984)
Attaque / Exterminateurs / Dresse A Tuer / Gwendoline / Reve Du Puissance / Double Rang / Le Glaive / Crache Et Creve / Fou Sanguinaire / La Horde

HEADHUNTER (GERMANY)
Line-Up: Marcel 'Schmier' Schirmer (vocals / bass), Uwe 'Schmuddel' Hoffmann (guitar), Jörg Michael (drums)

Initially titled CURSE forming in 1990. Schmier had been the prime mover behind successful German thrashers DESTRUCTION. Guitarist Uwe 'Schmuddel' Hoffmann was ex-TALON whilst drummer Jörg Michael had plied his trade with AVENGER, LAOS, MEKONG DELTA, RAGE and RUNNING WILD. Michael continued to record and tour with STEELER guitarist AXEL RUDI PELL in addition to his work with HEADHUNTER.

The band toured Japan in 1990 and supported SAXON in Europe the same year before entering the studio to record the debut album 'Parody Of Life', a record on which GAMMA RAY's Kai Hansen guests on the track 'Cursed'.

Headline dates in 1993 saw ACCUSER and ANTIDOTE supporting. The band had released the follow up record 'A Bizarre Gardening Accident' and 1995's 'Rebirth', after a very real, very bad and less bizarre car crash involving 'Schmuddel' Hoffmann it remained unclear as to whether the group would ever record again.

Michael's talents post HEADHUNTER have seen his services retained by AXEL RUDI PELL as well as racking up credits with GRAVE DIGGER and STRATOVARIUS.

In 1998 Schmier re-forged DESTRUCTION for a second wind of success.

Albums:
PARODY OF LIFE, CBH Virgin 261 151 (1991)
Parody Of Life / Ease My Pain / Plead Guilty / Kick Over Your Traces / Force Of Habit / Caught In A Spider's Web / Cursed / Crack Brained / Trapped In Reality
A BIZARRE GARDENING ACCIDENT, Major 018/043-2 (1993)
Oh What A Pleasure / Signs Of Insanity / Hit Machine / Born In The Woods / Two Faced Promises / Ramalama / Boozer / Domo / Pangs Of Remorse / Character Assassination / Rude Philosophy / Deadly Instinct / Sex And Drugs And Rock n' Roll
REBIRTH, Major CC024 (1995)
Auf Geht's / Army's Of The Blind / Warhead / Unhuman World / Mistreated / Mindless / Change / Disco / Scares / Adrenalin / Strucked / Don't Bogart

HEATHEN (USA)
Line-Up: Dave Godfrey (vocals), Lee Altus (guitar), Doug Piercy (guitar), Mike Jazstrempski (bass), Carl Sacco (drums)

Noted Tech-Thrash mob HEATHEN were already veterans of the notorious Bay Area Thrash scene by the time of their formation in the early '80s. Drummer Carl Sacco was previously with THE LEWD, METAL CHURCH and MURDER whilst vocalist Sam Kress ran the Metal fanzine 'Whiplash'. Completing the line-up was guitarist Lee Altus. Lacking a bassist HEATHEN soldiered on, undertaking their first gigs without one. However, by April 1985 ex-SCEPTRE man Eric Wong had been enlisted. HEATHEN also drafted the scene veteran guitarist Doug Piercy, then a member of CONTROL but having previous credits with COBRA, DELTA and the highly influential ANVIL CHORUS.

After HEATHEN's first demo of 1986 Wong was ousted in favour of ex-GRIFFIN man Mike 'Yaz' Jastremski. Realising Kress was a better writer than a singer he bowed out in favour of former BLIND ILLUSION man Dave Godfrey.

Besides working with HEATHEN Piercy got his name around in 1986 by producing demos for such acts as MORDRED, LEGACY and ATTITUDE ADJUSTMENT.

Their debut album was produced by none other than veteran MONTROSE guitarist RONNIE MONTROSE and included a version of SWEET's 'Set Me Free'. Sacco departed shortly after recording of 'Breaking The Silence' and in his stead came Darren Minter. Jazstrempski was next to go and HEATHEN, minus a permanent bassist, utilised the talents of BLIND ILLUSION guitarist Mark Biedermann to record the bass parts on the 'Victims Of Deception' album. Guest guitar parts came courtesy of ANVIL CHORUS man

Thaen Rasmussen.

Breaking away from their American label Combat Records in 1987 HEATHEN purged Godfrey from the band after numerous interested labels expressed concerns over the band's frontman. Godfrey reacted by creating his own act LAUGHING DEAD. For a brief tenure in 1988 HEATHEN worked with erstwhile EXODUS and PIRANHA man Paul Ballof. HEATHEN also worked with David Wayne of METAL CHURCH but this liaison was even shorter. However, before long HEATHEN had re-enlisted Godfrey after Ballof had lasted less than a month. Swallowing their pride HEATHEN invited Godfrey back into the ranks and also recruited bass player Manny Bravo.

HEATHEN's line-up following the 'Victims Of Deception' album comprised Godfrey, Altus, Minter, Piercy and bassist Randy Laire. The album includes a cover of RAINBOW's 'Kill The King'.

In 1989 Altus auditioned for MEGADETH but shied off this possible union, being concerned the lifestyle of Mustaine's crew at the time.

Piercy opted out joining ANGELWITCH in January 1991. HEATHEN, back with Piercy, then toured Europe as support to Brazilians SEPULTURA. Tragedy struck though when Laire was killed in a car crash. Piercy later relocating to Germany to create THE COMPANY.

In 1992 Altus and Rasmussen united with VICIOUS RUMOURS drummer Larry Howe and MY VICTIM singer Jay to create BOMB THREAT touring the California clubs with a nostalgic set of NWOBHM covers.

Thaen Rasmussen took Piercy's place and Jason Vie Brooks took the bass role. Former REXXEN guitarist Ira Black was also inducted during 1992 but the band folded when Altus and Minter joined German Industrial Metal act DIE KRUPPS.

Godfrey joined INNER THRESHOLD, a band formed by ex-DEFIANCE members.

In 1995 Vie Brooks turned up as part of GRIP INC., the band created by former SLAYER drummer DAVE LOMBARDO and would later join HATE SQUAD. Black journeyed through EXODUS veteran Steve Souza's DOG FACE and the post TESLA formation of guitarist Tommy Skeoch UTERIS before joining VICIOUS RUMOURS in 2000.

HEATHEN reformed in 2000 with a line-up of Godfrey, Altus, Rasmussen, Vie Brooks and Minter.

Singles/EPs:
Set Me Free / Goblin's Blade, Combat 88561 8182-1 (1987)

Albums:
BREAKING THE SILENCE, Music For Nations MFN 75 (1987)
Death By Hanging / Goblin's Blade / Open The Grave / Pray For Death / Set Me Free / Breaking The Silence / World's End / Save The Skull
VICTIMS OF DECEPTION, Roadrunner RO 93312 (1989)
Hypnotised / Opiate Of The Masses / Heathen's Song / Kill The King / Fear Of The Unknown / Prisoners Of Fate / Morbid Curiosity / Guitarony / Mercy Is No Virtue

HEAVENBLAST (ITALY)

Line-Up: Marco La Corte (vocals), Alessandro Saponaro (guitar), Donatello Menna (guitar), Fabrizio Carota (bass), Diego Regina (keyboards), Diego Chiacchierini (drums)

Power Metal act HEAVENBLAST started life, founded by vocalist Marco La Morte and guitarist Alessandro Saponaro in late 1995, as a melodic Rock outfit but would evolve in time into a fully fledged Metal band. Second guitarist Donatello Menna was added in September of 1996 with drummer Diego Chiacchierini in June of 1997 and keyboard player Diego Regina in 1998.

HEAVENBLAST debuted with the demo 'The Crown Of The Light' in 1998. HEAVENBLAST signed to the Underground Symphony label for the inaugural eponymous 2001 album.

Albums:
HEAVENBLAST, Underground Symphony (2001)
Intro: We Don't Believe In Sorrow / Inside The Universe / Ready To Fly / Tomorrow King / The Hero Of The Eternal Flame / Statues In The Shade / Power Induction / Heavenblast / The Crown Of The Light / Last Smile

HEAVEN'S CRY (CANADA)

Line-Up: Sylvain Auclair (vocals / bass), Sebastian Boisvert (guitar), Pierre St. Jean (guitar), Luc D'Aoust (drums)

The band appeared at the ANVIL headlined Montreal 'Powerpack' festival on November 8th 2002.

Albums:
FOOD FOR THOUGHT SUBSTITUTE, Hypnotic HYPSD 1054 (1997)
Your God's Crime / Out Of Me / March / Alchemist / Gaia's Judgement / Face / Cruel Disguise / The Horde / Passage / Wings
PRIMAL POWER ADDICTION, DVS

DVS007 (2002)
2K Awe Tick / Masterdom's Profit / A New Paradigm / Divisions / A Higher Moral Ground / Komma / Remembrance / One Of Twentyfour / Waves / The Inner Stream Remains

HEAVENLY (FRANCE)
Line-Up: Ben Sotto (vocals), Frederic Leclercq (guitar), Pierre Emmanuel Pelisson (bass), Maxence Pilo (drums)

Paris based HEAVENLY was founded during 1994 by vocalist Ben Sotto and drummer Maxence Pilo, originally as a covers band dubiously entitled SATAN'S LAWYER! With the evolution into HEAVENLY came guitarist Anthony Parker and the ensuing three track demo session. These recordings were soon snapped up by the German Noise label but not before Parker made his exit. HEAVENLY soldiered on drafting two new members in guitarist CHRIS SAVOURNEY, who had three prior solo albums to his credit, and bassist Laurent Jean.
HEAVENLY's debut album 'Coming From The Sky', cut in Hannover and Hamburg during February 2000 and produced by Piet Sielck of IRON SAVIOR, would see both Sielck and GAMMA RAY mainman Kai Hansen guesting. Digipack versions added two exclusive tracks in 'Defender' and 'Promised Land'.
HEAVENLY's debut sold in quantity and the group would land the prestigious tour support slot to STRATOVARIUS in Europe. Just prior to these dates Pierre-Emmanuel Péllison supplanted Jean on bass and Frédéric Leclercq joined to bolster their live sound on keyboards.
The line-up shuffles were far from over though as Savourney decamped and Leclerq took over the lead guitar mantle. Savourney would create NORTHWIND, bowing in with the 2002 album 'Seasons'.
A second album, 'Sign Of The Winner' produced by Tommy Hansen, emerged in September of 2001.

Albums:
COMING FROM THE SKY, Noise (2000)
Coming From The Sky / Carry Your Heart / Riding Through Hell / Time Machine / Number One / Our Only Chance / Fairy Tale / My Turn Will Come / Until I Die / Million Ways
SIGN OF THE WINNER, Noise (2001)
132 FRANCE
Break The Silence / Destiny / Sign Of The Winner / The World Will Be Better / Condemned To Die / The Angel / Still Believe / The Sandman / Words Of Change / Until

The End

HEAVEN'S GATE (GERMANY)
Line-Up: Thomas Rettke (vocals), Bonny Bilske (guitar), Sascha Paeth (guitar), Manni Jordan (bass), Thorsten Müller (drums)

Wolfsburg based Metal band with inspiring Halfordesque vocals courtesy of ex-STEELTOWER man Thomas Retke. HEAVEN'S GATE were previously known as CARRION prior to adding lead guitarist Sascha Paeth.
Having released their debut album 'In Control' in 1988 the group supported W.A.S.P. on their 1989 tour of Germany, whilst road work promoting the 1990 mini-album 'Open The Gate...', produced by Ralf Krause, saw the band on the road in Germany with support act LAWDY.
Following the tour the band's label went bankrupt necessitating a label change to SPV Steamhammer, with whom the group released 'Livin' In Hysteria', an album produced by Charly Bauerfeind.
Having been associated with SPV ever since, 1996's 'Planet E' album found the group covering DALBELLO's 'Animal' and SPARKS' 'This Town Ain't Big Enough For The Both Of Us'. The record heralded a line-up change, with long time bassist Manni Jordan being replaced by a former drummer in the form of SARGENT FURY's Robert Hunecke-Rizzo. The revised band promptly toured Germany opening for AXXIS at the beginning of 1997.
It is worth noting that guitarist Sascha Paeth is also building a reputation as a producer, having worked with SIEGES EVEN, GAMMA RAY, RHAPSODY and ANGRA. In 1999 Paeth took on both production and bass duties for RHAPSODY guitarist LUCA TURILLI's 'King Of The Nordic Twilight' album. This outing also saw Robert Hunecke-Rizzo on drums.

Singles/EPs:
Livin' In Hysteria / Can't Stop Rockin' / Best Days Of My Life / Rock On, Steamhammer SPV 084-76312 (1991) (German promotional release)
Thin, Fake & Bold / Metal Hymn / Sidewalk Sinner / Best Days Of My Life (Acoustic version), SPV (1992) ('More Hysteria' EP)

Albums:
IN CONTROL, No Remorse NRR 1005 (1988)
The Gate / In Control / Turn It Down / Surrender / Hot Fever / Tyrants / Path Of Glory / Shadows / This Flight Tonight
OPEN THE GATE... AND WATCH!, No

Remorse NRR1012 (1990)
Open The Gate And Watch! / Touch The Light / Dancin' On A Rope / Rock On / Pictures In The Mirror / Cry It Out
LIVIN' IN HYSTERIA, SPV 008-76311 (1991)
Livin' In Hysteria / We Got The Time / The Neverending Fire / Empty Way To Nowhere / Fredless / Can't Stop Rockin' / Flashes / Best Days Of My Life / We Want It All / Gate Of Heaven
HELL FOR SALE!, SPV Steamhammer 084 76592 CD (1992)
Under Fire / Hell For Sale! / He's The Man / America / Atomic / Rising Sun / No Matter / Up An' Down / Don't Bring Me Down / White Evil / Always Look On The Bright Side Of Life
LIVE FOR SALE - LIVE IN JAPAN, SPV Steamhammer SPV (1993)
Overture / Metal Hymn / Under Fire / Hell For Sale! / We Got The Time / Path Of Glory / The Neverending Fire / Best Days Of My Life / Livin' In Hysteria / Tyrants / He's The Man / White Evil / Gate Of Heaven / In Control
PLANET E, SPV 085-18312 (1996)
Terminated World / Planet Earth / Back From The Dawn / On The Edge / The Children Play / Rebel Yell / Black Religion / Animal / Noah's Dream / This Town Ain't Big Enough For Both Of Us
MENERGY, SPV (1999)
Worldmachine / Mastermind / Menergy / Enter: Eternity / Breakin' Loose / Dreamland / Looking Back / Evolution / On My Knees / Dreamer-Believer / Glass People
BOXED, SPV (1999)
The Gate / In Control / Turn It Down / Surrender / Hot Fever / Tyrants / Paths Of Glory / Shadows / This Flight Tonight / Open The Gate And Watch! / Touch The Light / Dancin' On A Rope / Rock On / Pictures In The Mirror / Cry It Out / Thin, Fake & Bold / Metal Hymn / Sidewalk Sinner / Best Days Of My Life / Rising Sun / Noah's Dream / Planet Earth / The Children Play / In The Mood / Medley / Don't Bring Me Down

HEAVENWARD (GERMANY)
Line-Up: Stefan Keßel (vocals), Bernd Gröters (guitar), Achim Schneider (guitar), Oliver Müller (bass), Thomas Kelleners (drums)

HEAVENWARD vocalist Stefan Keßel would later join CENTAUR.

Albums:
WITHIN THESE DREAMS, D&S DSR-CD10004 (1991)

The Sky / Dreams In Disguise / Cold Embrace / Their Eyes / At First Nature / Raging Waters / Within These Walls / Holding The Key
A FUTURE WORTH TALKING ABOUT?, Inline Music 55G 8787 004 8 (1992)
Sign Of Things To Come / Poor Little Child / The Final Curtain / Dissolute Aura / Not Forgotten / Watch Out, Cry Out / Obvious End / Sane Madness

HEAVY LOAD (SWEDEN)
Line-Up: Ragne Wahlquist (vocals / guitar), Eddy Malm (guitar), Torbjorn Rogesjo (bass), Styrbjorn Wahlquist (drums)

A Highly influential and successful Swedish Metal outfit, HEAVY LOAD saw regular chart placing in their home country with a series of strong self-financed albums.
The band date to 1976 when brothers Ragne and Styrbjörn Wahlquist teamed up with bassist Michael Bachler. Heavy gigging ensued and the following year Bachler departed to be replaced by Dan Molen.
HEAVY LOAD scored their first album release in 1978 when Stockholm Record store Heavy Sound released 'Full Speed At High Level' and the trio undertook a headline tour of Sweden to promote its release.
By 1979 the touring schedule had taken its toll on Molen who quit. HEAVY LOAD added bassist Eero Koivisto and rhythm guitarist Leif 'Lillen' Liljegren to become a quartet. However, within months both new members had left (and later formed RED BARON in 1985, Liljegren also turned up as a member of TREAT at one point).
During the summer of 1979 the band found replacements in bassist Torbjörn Ragnesjö and ex-HIGH BROW guitarist Eddy Malm. HEAVY LOAD's next release was the 1981 mini-album 'Metal Conquest' which gained the band many honours, beating many international acts to grab the number one airplay position on the H.M.H. Metal radio station play list and charting in the national Swedish charts.
This success was capitalised on by an extensive headline tour, which included two live radio broadcasts from Malmo and Stockholm. A further album, 'Death And Glory', rounded off the year with another national chart placing.
1983 started with HEAVY LOAD releasing a concert video and recording the 'Stronger Than Evil' album. THIN LIZZY's enigmatic frontman PHIL LYNNOT, who was in Sweden promoting his solo album at the time appeared on the track 'Free'.
At this point HEAVY LOAD extended their

touring into Europe as album sales got stronger, although gigs were curtailed in mid 1984 when Ragnesjö departed. It was 1985 by the time HEAVY LOAD added new bassist Andreas Fritz to the ranks.

Having been self-financed since inception the band now sought a major record deal and soon signed with WEA. A single, 'Monsters Of The Night', was released backed up by further Swedish dates, but a projected album never materialised and Malm left to pursue a solo project. As a result HEAVY LOAD was put on ice as the Wahlquist brothers concentrated on building a recording studio that would be used later by CANDLEMASS amongst others.

In 1986 HEAVY LOAD recruited guitarist Patrik Karlsson to work on a new album, although further delays were caused when Fritz left to work with prior member Malm.

Still intent on recording a new album, former DAMNED and UFO bassist Paul Gray joined up, but business considerations at the recording studio has always forestalled any release, although a new HEAVY LOAD album still remains a possibility.

Still, the Wahlquist brothers have resurrected their Thunderload label to release the VENI DOMINE album 'Material Sanctuary' in 1995.

Singles/EPs:
Take Me Away / Tresspasser, Thunderload TSP 823(1982)
Free / Run With The Devil, Thunderload TSP 835 (1983)
Monsters Of The Night / I'm Alive, WEA 248 983 7 (1985)

Albums:
FULL SPEED AT HIGH LEVEL, Heavy Sound (1978)
Full Speed At High Level / Midnight Crawler / Moonlight Spell / Storm / In Two Minds / Rock n" Roll Freak / Caroline / Sons Of The Northern Light
METAL CONQUEST, Thunderload TMP 811 (1981)
You've Got The Power / Dark Nights / Heavy Metal Heaven / Hey / Heathens From The North
DEATH OR GLORY, Thunderload TLP 822) (1982) **47 SWEDEN**
Heavy Metal Angels (In Metal And Leather) / Might For Right / Something New / Bleeding Streets / The Guitar Is My Sword / Still There Is Time / Traveller / Little Lies / Daybreak Ecstasy
STRONGER THAN EVIL, Thunderload TLP834 (1984)
Run With The Devil / The King / Singing Swords / Dreaming / Stronger Than Evil / Free / Saturday Night / Roar Of The North

HEIMDALL (ITALY)
Line-Up: Claudio Gallo (vocals), Fabio Callouri (guitar), Carmelo Claps (guitar), Gianni Canu (bass), Sergio Duccillo (keyboards), Nicola Calluori (drums)

Italian epic Power Metallers HEIMDALL debuted with the 1998 album 'Lord Of The Sky' for Elevate Records, later issued in Japan during January of 1999 by Dream Chaser. Following the sophomore outing 'The Temple Of Theil', of which the Japanese variant included two extra tracks - an acoustic take on 'The Challenge' plus a cover version of JUDAS PRIEST's 'Breaking The Law', vocalist Claudio Gallo decamped.

HEIMDALL signed to the Scarlet Records label in 2002 for 'The Almighty' album. For this record they would be fronted by new singer Giacomo Mercaldo and re-joined by original drummer Nicola Calluori.

Albums:
THE TEMPLE OF THEIL, 99th Floor ERO3010 (1999)
Prelude: The Messenger / Follow The Signs / Secrets Of Time / The Oath / Fall In Tears / The Temple Of Theil / Symphony Of Twilight / Spirits Of Skyward / Scream Of Revenge / Then Night Will Fall / The Song Of Sidgar And Iselin / Finale
LORD OF THE SKY, Elevate ERO2005 (1999)
Galvor / Canticle Of Heimdall / Lord Of The Sky / Bifrost / The Island Of Ancient Stone / Under The Silent Moon / Fall Of The Bridge / Warriors Of Many Ages Past / The Challenge / Sunset / Epilogue
THE ALMIGHTY, Scarlet (2002)
The Calling / The Search / Eternal Race / Godhall / Wanderer / Return To The Fatherland / Last Journey / Beyond / Symit

HEIR APPARENT (Seattle, WA, USA)
Line-Up: Steve Benito (vocals), Terry Gorle (guitar), Derek Peace (bass), Michael Jackson (keyboards), Ray Black (drums)

Seattle Techno-Metal outfit HEIR APPARENT are rated highly by the esteemed German Rock magazine 'Rock Hard' who¯ cite the band's debut album as an all time classic of the genre. HEIR APPARENT was formed during 1983 originally fronted by former RENEGADE, REALMS and WARLOCK singer Paul Davidson. Completing the line up was guitarist Terry Gorle, ex-SABBATAR, HELMS DEEP and PERRENIAL bassist Derek Peace and drummer Jim Kovach. By late 1984 Kovach was supplanted by HELMS DEEP drummer Ray Black.

A 1985 demo secured the band a deal with French label Black Dragon Records. After the release of debut album 'Graceful Inheritance' a tour of Europe followed but proved disastrous attendance wise mainly due to the clash of schedules with the World Cup TV coverage. Peace then shocked the band by announcing he was moving to Los Angeles to undertake live work with SAVAGE GRACE. However, he was to return to the fold.

Keyboard player Michael Jackson augmented the line up in 1987 and later the same year Davidson departed for Pop act THE TREND and in came vocalist Steve Benito, previously a member of FRENCH KISS.

Although Gorle appears on the second album by its release he had been replaced on guitar by ex-HOUSE OF LORDS (not the Greg Giuffria founded band of the same name!) man Klaus Derendorf. HEIR APPARENT got back into action opening dates for CRIMSON GLORY on the West Coast of America. Black left and in his stead came Gary McCormick.

HEIR APPARENT resumed action for an appearance at the annual Wacken festival with singer Michael Flatters, their new frontman having made his mark fronting JAMES BYRD's album 'Flying Beyond The 9'. After this show Paul Davidson made a return whilst Peace and Schartz were shown their leaving cards. Flatters later hooked up with

TAKARA, PLASTIC BASTARD (under the pseudonym 'Peter Torque') and operated on the live circuit with VAN HALEN covers band JUNIORS GRADES.

The band, vowing to record a new studio album, debuted a new line-up of vocalist Bryan Hagan, guitarist Terry Gorle, bassist Bobby Ferkovich and drummer Clint Clark during July of 2002.

Albums:

GRACEFUL INHERITANCE, Black Dragon BD006 (1986)
Entrance / Another Candle / The Servant / Tear Down The Walls / Running From The Thunder / The Cloak / RIP / Hands Of Destiny / Keeper Of The Reign / Dragon's Lair / Masters Of Invasion / Nightmare / A.N.D....Dogro Lived On

ONE SMALL VOICE, Roadrunner RO 94722 (1989)
Just Imagine / Crossing The Border / Screaming / Alone Again / Cacophony Of Anger / The Sound Of Silence / We The People / Young Forever / One Small Voice / Decorated / The Fifth Season

HELICON (GERMANY)

Line-Up: Uwe Heepen (vocals), Tom Kusters (guitar), Christian Guth (guitar), Silvester

HEIR APPARENT
Photo : Nico Wobben

Walevski (bass), Andre Ostopezzo (drums)

Formed in 1986 and debuting with demo 'The Heimbach Tapes', HELICON released the 'Black And White' demo in 1989 and pressed this up as a self-financed single later in the year.

The band hit line-up problems which were unresolved until mid 1992 when HELICON signed with Noise Records. In 1994 HELICON shared space with GAMMA RAY, RAGE and CONCEPTION on the live compilation album 'Power Of Metal Live'.

The band settled on a group comprising Heepen, Kusters, Ostapeschen and new guitarist Andy Geisler by 1995, although HELICON would eventually split in frustration when they lost their record deal.

Singles/EPs:
Black And White / Woman, Helicon (1989)

Albums:
HELICON, Noise N0213-2 (1993)
The Story About Helicon / Helicon Part II / It's Rock n' Roll / Junk / Victim Of Love / Freedom / Black Andite / Come On Rock / Woman / There Is No Rose Without Thorns
MYSTERIOUS SKIPJACK, Noise N0243-2 (1995)
American Fever / Streetgang / Power Magic / Wild Vice Woman / Mysterious Skipjack / Giant Heart / Darkness Of Love / Versatile / Fly In The Sky / Shuffle

HELLION (Los Angeles, CA, USA)
Line-Up: Anne Boleyn (vocals), Alan Barlam (guitar), Ray Schenk (guitar), Bill Sweet (bass), Sean Kelly (drums)

HELLION, fronted by vocalist Ann Boleyn (who actually claimed some distant lineage to the decapitated former royal) made their mark on the Los Angeles circuit with a series of demos. One of these tapes was to emerge as the 'Hellion' mini-album and the band, now managed by Wendy Dio, were soon the focus of attention when the record was picked up in Europe by Music For Nations. However, disagreements between management and band were to break the band apart.

Barlam, Schenk and Kelly departed to form BURN after being convinced that a female lead singer was deterring major label attention. Retaining the HELLION name Boleyn soon regrouped to record a new album 'Screams In The Night' with a fresh line-up comprising guitarist Chet Thompson, former LION bassist Alex Campbell and formative era DOKKEN drummer Greg Pekka.

Boleyn contributed the track 'Monster Mash' to the 1987 movie 'Return Of The Living Dead - Part II' soundtrack.

The 1988 mini-album 'Postcards From The Asylum', with new bassist Dave Dutton, saw the reunion of original HELLION members Barlam and Kelly and features a cover of the JUDAS PRIEST classic 'Exciter'. Thompson meanwhile had a short spell with BRITTON.

The band put in a British club tour during early 1988 supported by MARSHALL LAW which saw the addition of former ALLEGANCE bassist Rex Tennyson, who would later join ex-CATS IN BOOTS vocalist Joel Ellis in HEAVY BONES.

'The Black Book' proved to HELLION's last outing to date. Boleyn published a novel to coincide with the release.

HELLION was resurrected in 1998 by Boleyn, Schenk and Kelly cutting a album the following year which awaits release. Fans were still waiting developments when it was learned in mid 2001 that Boleyn had recorded an album, produced by Mikey Davis, and was auditioning for an entire new band. This new unit, simply billed as ANN BOLEYN and comprising of guitarists Mike Guererro and Chris Kessler, former RHINO BUCKET man Eric Becica on bass and drummer Vince Rage, toured Japan in October.

Archive recordings, from a live show at the Country Club in Reseda in 1984, were slated for 2002 release billed as 'Cold Night In Hell'. A new Mikey Davis produced studio album 'Will Not Go Quietly' was also set for 2002. However, in August HELLION were back in the news for all the wrong reasons when manager James Howard Paul Jr. was accused of soliciting the murder of his wife. A few days later Paul Jr. was caught by Police attempting to break into Boleyn's house.

Singles/EPs:
Don't Take No (For An Answer) / Backstabber / Lookin' For A Good Time / Driving Hard, Bongos Lodus (1983) ('Hellion' EP)
Driving Hard / Black Night, Mystic (1983)
The Evil One / Exciter / Never More / Run For **Your Life**, Music For Nations MFN 82 (1987) ('Postcards From The Asylum' EP)

Albums:
HELLION, Music For Nations MFN 15 (1983)
Break The Spell / Don't Take No / Backstabber / Lookin' For A Good Time / Driving Hard / Up From The Depths
SCREAMS IN THE NIGHT, Music For Nations MFN 73 (1987)
Screams In The Night / Bad Attitude / Better Off Dead / Upside Down Guitar Solo / The

Hand / Explode / Easy Action / Put The Hammer Down / Stick 'Em / Children Of The Night / The Tower Of Air
THE BLACK BOOK, Music For Nations CDMFN 108 (1990)
Breakdown / The Black Book / Stormrider / Living In Hell / The Discovery / Losing Control / Arrest... Jail... Bail / Daemon Attack / Conspiracy / Amnesia / The Warning / The Room Behind The Door / The Atonement / Immigrant Song

HELLOWEEN (GERMANY)
Line-Up: Andy Deris (vocals), Michael Weikath (guitar), Roland Grapow (guitar), Marcus Großkopf (bass), Uli Kusch (drums)

German Power Metal band HELLOWEEN quickly developed a large and loyal fan base built upon a series of strong album releases that culminated in the twin album project 'Keeper Of The Seven Keys'. Stylistically HELLOWEEN have trod a path from Speed Metal through an ill fated dalliance with injecting oddball humour through to career revival delivering consistent melodic Metal. However, in spite of two decades of maturity HELLOWEEN are still known to show their Speed Metal teeth on occasion.
Kai Hansen, Marcus Großkopf and Ingo Schwichtenberg had been playing together since 1980 in SECOND HELL then IRON FIST. Vocalist Peter Sielck departed IRON FIST in 1982 effectively putting the band on ice, so during this period of inactivity Hansen received an offer to join POWERFOOL, featuring guitarist Michael Weikath. As things turned out Hansen lured Michael to his own band and then changed the name to HELLOWEEN.
The group came to prominence upon their signing to leading German Metal label Noise Records and three tracks on the notorious 'Death Metal' compilation album in 1984. Their debut mini-album, 'Helloween', and first, full-length album 'Walls of Jericho' provided HELLOWEEN with plenty of media attention and critical favour. The mid '80s saw a massive resurgence of interest in German Rock bands and HELLOWEEN quickly established themselves at the top of the heap with successive strong releases.
Following the release of the 'Judas' EP HELLOWEEN set about changing their musical direction, intending to add more scope to their music with the recruitment of PROPHECY's frontman MICHAEL KISKE, who took over vocal duties from Hansen. The band peaked with an elaborate brace of concept albums centred upon the 'The Keeper Of The Seven Keys' tale.
The first 'Keeper...' album, produced by

VICTORY's Tommy Newton, was a useful vehicle in gaining popularity for the band outside Europe. Worldwide it went on to sell over half a million copies, shifting over 125,000 in Germany alone. Released in America on the RCA label it peaked at no. 102 in the Billboard charts and its success enabled the band to appear as part of the 'Hell On Wheels' U.S. tour along with GRIM REAPER and ARMORED SAINT. RCA did not curry favour with the band though when they released the 13 minute track 'Halloween' as a 4 minute edited single!
These American dates were followed by the quintet's first tour of Japan prior to recording 'Keeper... Part 2' and, in 1988, HELLOWEEN appeared at the Castle Donington 'Monsters Of Rock' festival and toured as support to IRON MAIDEN throughout Europe before their own German headlining dates. In 1989 HELLOWEEN again toured America on the same bill as ANTHRAX and EXODUS. A live mini-album 'Live In The UK' charted in Great Britain but would provide ardent fans two more reasons to shell out for product as the record was issued in Japan as 'Keepers Live' with different artwork and in America as 'I Want Out - Live', again with completely different artwork.
However, stardom, and in particular touring, became anathema to the driving force behind HELLOWEEN, guitarist Kai Hansen. He left to form the studio project GAMMA RAY with former TYRAN PACE vocalist Ralph Scheepers with whom he had worked earlier in PROPHECY (and had previously offered the HELLOWEEN vocalist job to). Ironically, GAMMA RAY overtook HELLOWEEN in the popularity stakes shortly after. Hansen was replaced by ex-RAMPAGE guitarist Roland Grapow. Another shift in personnel saw the induction of drummer Riad 'Ritchie' Abdel-Nabi in November of 1992.
HELLOWEEN signed to IRON MAIDEN's management Sanctuary Music and, convinced that signing to a major label would further their career began efforts to extricate themselves from their Noise deal. The band signed to EMI and promptly landed themselves in a lengthy legal wrangle with Noise, who claimed that they were still under contract. During this period of inactivity the press speculated that Kiske was to join IRON MAIDEN.
Following all the delays, HELLOWEEN seemingly committed commercial suicide by releasing the ludicrously titled 'Pink Bubbles Go Ape' album. Supposed to show that the band had a sense of humour, the Chris Tsangarides produced album with song titles such as 'Heavy Metal Hamsters' only served to alienate their former fans. Indeed, worse

HELLOWEEN
Photo : Nico Wobben

HELLOWEEN
Photo : Nico Wobben

HELLOWEEN
Photo : Nico Wobben

was to come when Noise placed an injunction on the album, effectively stopping its release and any live work in Germany.

In 1993, EMI released the band's new album 'Chameleon', a record that was certainly not up to the standards of the past and found HELLOWEEN seriously lacking in direction.

HELLOWEEN, minus Abdel-Nabi who went on to create BABYLON 27 with erstwhile KINGDOM COME guitarist Heiko Radke-Siab, returned in the summer of 1994 signed to Rawpower, an offshoot of Castle Communications. As well as a new label the band had used their period away from the spotlight for a drastic rethink in both musical and personnel terms. Ingo Schwichtenberg and Michael Kiske both departed and in came former HOLY MOSES / GAMMA RAY member Uli Kusch and Andy Deris respectively, the latter being nabbed from the successful German outfit PINK CREAM 69.

Whilst MICHAEL KISKE released a solo album 'Instant Clarity' featuring Kai Hansen in 1996, fate was not as kind to ex-member Ingo Schwichtenberg who, suffering from depression and fighting a drug problem, committed suicide in 1995.

A new HELLOWEEN album, 'Keeper Of The Rings', ploughed a much more traditional path harking back to their Noise days. The album charted strongly in their home country and even reached the number 1 position in Japan. The group was forced to take a break in early 1995 when Deris suffered a throat infection forestalling any live work.

Still, the group returned in 1996 with the single, 'The Time Of The Oath', (which included covers of JEAN MICHEL JARRE's 'Magnetic Fields' and JUDAS PRIEST's 'Electric Eye') and an album of the same name, which found Tommy Hansen once more behind the desk. Touring with BRUCE DICKINSON and SKIN, HELLOWEEN were also to release 'High Live' during 1996.

HELLOWEEN made a triumphant return in 1998 with the 'Better Than Raw' album sounding heavier than ever. The album quickly racked up Japanese sales of quarter of a million plus. HELLOWEEN played selective European dates as guests to IRON MAIDEN.

Großkopf made space to execute a side endeavour SHOCKMACHINE during 1999. Joining in the proceedings for the eponymous album would be, vocalist Olly Lugosi, X-13 guitarist Rolly Feldman, HELLOWEEN members drummer Uli Kusch and guitarist ROLAND GRAPOW and ROUGH SILK keyboard player Ferdy Doernberg.

Kusch too would get in on the action pursuing his project CATCH THE RAINBOW, a conglomeration of name German Rockers dedicated to paying homage to RAINBOW. An album, 'A Tribute To Rainbow', arrived in 1999 which featured the entire HELLOWEEN cast, alongside GAMMA RAY, PRIMAL FEAR and BRAINSTORM personnel, as guests.

HELLOWEEN would shift labels to the ever expanding Nuclear Blast concern for their next effort 'The Dark Ride' issued in 2000.

Although charting well across Europe the making of the album would apparently put the band members under a strain which would publicly surface with great ramifications some time later. Although issued in Europe and Japan in 2000 'The Dark Ride' would have to wait a full two years for an American release. Großkopf contributed to EDGUY mainman Tobias Sammet's ambitious AVANTASIA eponymous project album of 2000.The same year saw the issue of a worthy HELLOWEEN tribute album 'The Keepers Of Jericho'. The album benefited from cover artwork by Uwe Karczewski, the man responsible for the sleeve artwork on HELLOWEEN classic albums 'Walls Of Jericho' and 'Keeper Of The Seven Keys'. The album included many of the European Metal scene's rising stars and saw reworkings by acts such as METALIUM, HEAVEN'S GATE, SONATA ARTICA and Italian acts RHAPSODY, DARK MOOR, LUCA TURILLI and LABYRINTH.

In August of 2001 the band suffered a major blow when both guitarist ROLAND GRAPOW and drummer Uli Kusch quit. The pair would soon be announced as having forged a fresh project with SYMPHONY X vocalist Russell Allen. However, news also leaked out that the duo had also assembled a project with the strange title of MR. TORTURE (later scrapped), cutting demos produced by ex-SABBAT guitarist Andy Sneap and confirming their intention to work with ex-HELLOWEEN vocalist MICHAEL KISKE. Later still it would transpire the Grapow / Kusch venture had been renamed MASTERPLAN and the pair were in cahoots with the highly rated erstwhile YNGWIE MALMSTEEN vocalist JORN LANDE. Grapow would find the time during this period to guest session on Swedish act LOCOMOTIVE BREATH's 'Heavy Machinery' album.

By mid September it was announced that British drummer Mark Cross had joined the HELLOWEEN fold. Cross had a cosmopolitan range of credits across the Rock field with Greek acts SCRAPTOWN, MAGNA CARTA and SPITFIRE, occult Metal band NIGHTFALL and more recently KINGDOM COME and METALIUM.

GAMMA RAY guitarist Henjo Richter would also be in the running although apparently his services were offered purely on a temporary basis. By July media attention was focused upon FREEDOM CALL guitarist Sascha Gerstner as being Grapow's successor, his recruitment being confirmed by mid August.

ANDI DERIS would donate his services to the GERMAN ROCK STARS October 2001 song 'Wings Of Freedom' in honour of the September 11th World Trade Center victims. Großkopf would assist his erstwhile HELLOWEEN colleague Kai Hansen by filling in for an injured Dirk Schlachter of GAMMA RAY for October German gigs. A lavish retrospective set, 'Treasure Chest', would be released in March of 2002 through the Metal Is label. The limited edition box set would come complete with a full bonus disc of rarities.

The undoubted international success of 'The Keepers Of Jericho' tribute album in 2000 spawned a further collection for 2002. 'The Keepers Of Jericho Part. II - A Tribute To Helloween' issued by the Spanish Arise label comprised respectful homage from artists such as IRON SAVIOR, POWERGOD, AXENSTAR, DRAGONLORD, HIGHLORD and FRETERNIA amongst many others.

Singles/EPs:
Judas / Ride The Sky (Live) / Guardians (Live), Noise N0048-6 (1986)
Halloween / Halloween, Noise (1986) (USA promotion)
Judas / Ride The Sky / Guardians / Victim Of Fate (Live) / Cry For Freedom (Live), Noise (1987) ('Judas' EP)
Future World / Starlight / A Little Time, Noise (1987)
Dr. Stein / Savage / Livin' Ain't No Crime, Noise HELLO 1 (1988) **57 UK**
Dr. Stein / Savage / Livin' Ain't No Crime / **Victim Of Fate**, Noise NO116-5 (1988) (3" CD single)
Dr. Stein / Savage, Noise NO116-6 (7" single)
I Want Out / Don't Run For Cover / Save Us, Noise NO126-3 (1988) **69 UK**
I Want Out / Don't Run For Cover, Noise NO126-6 (1988) (7" single)
I Want Out / Save Us / Don't Run For Cover, Noise NO126-5 (1988) (12" single)
Intro: Happy Halloween / I Want Out, Noise (1988) (USA promotion)
Kids Of The Century / Blue Suede Shoes / Shit And Lobster, EMI (1991) **56 UK**
Helloween / Keeper Of The Seven Keys, Noise (1991) (Free 12" with 'The Best, The Rest, The Rare' album)
Kids Of The Century / Blue Suede Shoes / Interview, Victor VICP 15005 (1992) (Japanese release)
Number One / Les Hambourgeois Walkways / You Run With The Pack, EMI 72348 80146 25 (1992)
Windmill / Cut In The Middle / Introduction / Get Me Out Of Here, EMI 7243 8 81065 2 8 (1993)
When The Sinner (Edit) / When The Sinner (Album version) / I Don't Care, You Don't Care, EMI 72438 805862 9 (1993)
When The Sinner (Edit) / I Don't Care, You Don't Care / Oriental Journey, Victor VICP

15025 (1993) (Japanese release)
I Don't Wanna Cry No More / Red Socks And The Smell Of Trees / Ain't Got Nothing Better, Victor VICP 15029 (1993) (Japanese release)
Step Out Of Hell / Cut In The Middle / Introduction / Get Me Out Of Here, Victor VICP 15030 (1993) (Japanese release)
Mr. Ego (Take Me Down) / Where The Rain Grows / Star Invasion / Can't Fight Your Desire, Rawpower CMS 6516-5 (1994)
Where The Rain Grows / Mr. Ego (Take Me Down) / Can't Fight Your Desire / Invasion, Victor VICP 15035 (1994) (Japanese release)
Perfect Gentleman / Cold Sweat, Rawpower RAWX 1002 (1994)
Perfect Gentleman / Cold Sweat / Silicon Dreams / Grapowski's Malmsuit, Victor VICP 15037 (1994) (Japanese release)
Cold Sweat plus Interview, Rawpower SPC 9526 (1994) (Free with limited edition version of 'Master Of The Rings' album)
Sole Survivor / In The Middle Of A Heartbeat / I Stole Your Love / Closer To Home, Victor VICP 15044 (1995) (Japanese release)
Steel Tormentor / A Million To One, Rawpower RAWP 1017 (1996) (Promotion release)
Power / We Burn / Rain/ Walk Your Way, Rawpower RAWX1014 (1996)
The Time Of The Oath / Magnetic Fields / Electric Eye, Rawpower RAWX 1018 (1996)
Forever And One (Neverland) / In The Middle Of A Heartbeat (Live) / Light In The Sky / Time Goes By, Rawpower RAWX 1033 (1996)
I Can / A Handful Of Pain / A Game We Shouldn't Play, Victor VICP 60193 (1998) (Japanese release)
If I Could Fly (Edit) / Deliver Us From Evil / If I Could Fly (Album version), Nuclear Blast NB 532-2 (2000)
Mr. Torture, (2000) (Japanese release)

Albums:
HELLOWEEN, Noise NO0021 (1985)
Victim Of Fate / Cry For Freedom / Starlight / Murderer / Warrior
WALLS OF JERICHO, Noise N0032 (1986)
Walls Of Jericho / Ride The Sky / Reptile / Guardians / Phantoms Of Death / Metal Invaders / Gorgar / Heavy Metal Is The Law / How Many Tears
KEEPER OF THE SEVEN KEYS – PART I, Noise NO061 (1987) **42 SWEDEN**
I'm Alive / Future World / Helloween / Twilight Of The Gods
KEEPER OF THE SEVEN KEYS – PART II, Noise NUK 117 (1988) **7 SWEDEN, 24 UK**
Invitation / Eagle Fly Free / You Always Walk Alone / March Of Time / Dr. Stein / Rise And Fall / We Got The Right / I Want Out / Keeper Of The Seven Keys
HELLOWEEN, Noise NO0088 (1988) (combines 'Helloween' mini-album, 'Walls Of Jericho' album and the 'Judas' EP in one package)
Starlight / Murderer / Warrior / Victim Of Fate / Cry For Freedom / Walls Of Jericho / Ride The Sky / Reptile / Guardians / Phantoms Of Death / Metal Invaders / Gorgar / Heavy Metal (Is The Law) / How Many Tears / Judas
PUMPKIN TRACKS, Noise (1989)
30 SWEDEN
Savage / Save Us / Victim Of Fate / Livin' Ain't No Crime / Don't Run For Cover / Judas / Future World / Murderer / Starlight / Phantoms Of Death / A Tale That Wasn't Right / I Want Out / March Of Time / I'm Alive
LIVE IN THE UK, EMI EMC 3558(1989)
25 SWEDEN, 26 UK
A Little Time / Dr. Stein / Future World / Rise And Fall / We Got The Right / I Want Out / How Many Tears
THE BEST, THE REST, THE RARE, Noise NO176 (1991)
I Want Out / Dr. Stein / Future World / Judas / Walls Of Jericho / Ride The Sky / Helloween / Livin' Ain't No Crime / Save Us / Victim Of Fate / Savage / Don't Run For Cover / Keeper Of The Seven Keys
PINK BUBBLES GO APE, EMI EMC 3588 (1991) **14 SWEDEN, 41 UK**
Pink Bubbles Go Ape / Kids Of The Century / Back On The Streets / Number One / Heavy Metal Hamsters / Goin' Home / Someone's Crying / Mankind / I'm Doing Fine Crazy Man / The Chance / Your Turn
CHAMELEON, EMI 7 89368 2 (1993)
35 SWEDEN
First Time / When The Sinner / I Don't Wanna Cry No More / Crazy Cat / Giants / Windmill / Revolution Now / San Francisco (Be Sure To Wear Flowers In Your Hair) / In The Night / Music / Step Out Of Hell / I Believe / Longing
KEEPER OF THE SEVEN KEYS - PART II, Noise NO240-2 (1994) (Re-issue, featuring bonus tracks)
Invitation / Eagle Fly Free / You Always Walk Alone / March Of Time / Dr. Stein / Rise And Fall / We Got The Right / I Want Out / Keeper Of The Seven Keys / Save Us / Don't Run For Cover / Livin' Ain't No Crime / Savage
MASTER OF THE RINGS, Rawpower RAW CSC 7150-2 (1994)
Irritation / Sole Survivor / Where The Rain Grows / Why? / Mr Ego (Take Me Down) / Perfect Gentleman / The Game Is On /

Secret Alibi / Take Me Home / In The Middle Of A Heartbeat / Still We Go

THE TIME OF THE OATH, Rawpower PD109 (1996)
We Burn / Steel Tormentor / Wake Up The Mountain / Power / Forever And One (Neverland) / Before The War / A Million To One / Anything My Mama Don't Like / Kings Will Be Kings / Mission Motherland / If I Knew / The Time Of The Oath

HIGH LIVE, Rawpower RAW DF116 (1996)
We Burn / Wake Up The Mountain / Sole Survivor / The Chance / Why / Eagle Fly Free / The Time Of The Oath / Future World / Dr. Stein / Before The War / Mr. Ego (Take Me Down) / Power / Where The Rain Grows / In The Middle Of A Heartbeat / Perfect Gentleman / Steel Tormentor

PUMPKIN BOX, Victor VICP 60 84-7 (1998) (Japanese release)
Starlight / Victim Of Hate / Cry For Freedom / Walls Of Jericho / Ride The Sky / Guardians / How Many Tears / Judas / Savage / Livin' Ain't No Crime / Save Us / Don't Run For Cover / Starlight (Michael Kiske version) / A Little Time (Version) / Victim Of Fate (Michael Kiske version) / Initiation / I'm Alive / Future World / Invitation / Eagle Fly Free / Rise And Fall / Dr. Stein / I Want Out / Halloween / Follow The Sign / Keeper Of The Seven Keys / Kids Of The Century / Mankind / The Chance / Don't Wanna Cry No More / First Time / When The Sinner / Windmill / Step Out Of Hell / A Little Time (Live) / Dr. Stein (Live) / Future World (Live) / How Many Tears (Live) / Interview with Kai Hansen / Halloween (Edit) / Interview with Michael Kiske, Michael Weikath and Roland Grapow / Eagle Fly Free (Edit) / Interview with Markus Großkopf, Uli Kusch, Harrie Smits, Jorn Ellerbrock and Andy Deris / Power (Outro)

BETTER THAN RAW, (1998) **8 FINLAND, 35 SWEDEN**
Deliberately Limited Preliminary Prelude Period In Z / Push / Falling Higher / Hey Lord / Don't Spit On My Mind / Revelation / Time / I Can / A Handful Of Pain / Laudate Dominium / Back On The Ground / Midnight Sun

METAL JUKEBOX, (1999) **49 GERMANY, 51 SWEDEN**
He's a Woman - She's a Man / Locomotive Breath / Lay All Your Love On Me / Space Oddity / From Out of Nowhere / All My Loving / Hocus Pocus / Faith Healer / Juggernaut / White Room / Mexican

THE DARK RIDE, Nuclear Blast (2000) **32 FINLAND, 26 GERMANY, 38 SWEDEN, 68 SWITZERLAND**
Behind The Portal / Mr. Torture / All Over The Nations / Escalation 666 / Mirror Mirror / If I Could Fly / Salvation / The Departed / The Sun Is Going Down / I Live For Your Pain / We Damn The Night / Immortal / The Dark Ride

TREASURE CHEST, Metal Is MISDD015 (2002)
Mr. Torture / I Can / Power / Where The Rain Grows / Eagle Fly Free / Future World / Metal Invaders / Murderer (Remix) / Starlight (Remix) / How Many Tears / Ride The Sky (Remix) / Halloween / A Little Time / A Tale That Wasn't Right / I Want Out / Keeper Of The Seven Keys (Remix) / Dr. Stein (Remix) / The Chance / Windmill / Sole Survivor / Perfect Gentleman / In The Middle Of A Heartbeat / Kings Will Be Kings / Time Of The Oath / Forever & One / Midnight Sun / Mr. Ego / Immortal / Mirror Mirror

HELREIDH (ITALY)
Line-Up: Franco Violo (vocals), Yorick (guitar), Alessandro Arcuri (bass), Daniele Soravia (keyboards), Luca Roggi (drums)

HELREIDH's 2002 album 'Fingerprints Of The Gods' was a double CD conceptual work. The second disc comprised covers of ADRAMELECH's 'Zephirious', WARLORD's 'Mrs. Victoria' and closed with a rendition of IRON MAIDEN's 'Stranger In A Strange Land'. The band's line-up for this outing incorporated vocalist Franco Violo, guitarists Aldo Pellegrini and Yorick, bassist and narrator Alex Arcuri, keyboard player Ivano Massa and drummer Salvatore Bonaccorso. HELREIDH keyboard player Daniele Soravia would later figure in MOONLIGHT CIRCUS, an alliance with BLACK JESTER guitarist Paolo Viani. Both Soravia and Viani would join the recently reformed cult American Power Metal band WARLORD in the summer of 2002.

Albums:
MEMORIES, Underground Symphony USCD-021 (1997)
Exordium / Mark The Wizard / Tale Of The Crypt / Endless Wars / Interludium / Suite De F. / The Departing Muse / Congedum

FINGERPRINTS OF THE GODS, Underground Symphony USCD-045 (2001)
Fingerprints Of The Gods / Migrations (Towards The Promise Land) / The Departing Muse (Orchestral Version) / Zephirus / Mrs. Victoria / Stranger In A Strange Land

HELSTAR (USA)
Line-Up: James Rivera (vocals), Larry Barragan (guitar), Andre Corbin (guitar), Jerry Abaraca (bass), Frank Ferreira (drums)

High octane Power based metallers HELSTAR, created in Houston during 1982, came to the fore on the underground tape trading scene with their debut 1983 demo. The band's original line-up comprised ex-DEATHWISH and SCORCHER vocalist James Rivera, guitarists Larry Barragan and Robert Trevin, bassist Jerry Abarca and drummer Rene Lima.

The impact made by the demo soon landed HELSTAR a deal with Combat Records in 1984 and the resulting debut album, 'Burning Star', was produced by drummer Carl Canedy of THE RODS. Ructions hit the band soon afterwards though and Trevin and Lima opted out to make way for guitarist Andre Corbin and drummer Frank Ferriera, whilst Barragan quit after a row with both the band's management and his colleagues. He intended forming a new band, BETRAYER, but was to quickly rejoin HELSTAR.

Following 'Remnants Of War' HELSTAR split from Combat and after relocating to Los Angeles signed a fresh deal with Metal Blade Records. 'A Distant Thunder' captured worthy reviews and HELSTAR proceeded to tour both America and then Europe opening for TANKARD and YNGWIE MALMSTEEN. Upon their return the band migrated back to their native Houston.

The 'Distant Thunder' album sees HELSTAR covering the SCORPIONS classic 'He's A Woman, She's A Man'.

A line up change saw HELSTAR split asunder with only Rivera and Barragan remaining. Fresh blood was soon drafted in the form of guitarist Tom Rogers, bassist Paul Medina and drummer Hector Pavan.

Following the 'Nosferatu' release HELSTAR cut a further demo tape consisting of 'Social Circles', 'Scalpel In The Skin', 'Sirens Of The Sun' and 'Change With Seasons'. The recording line-up was Rivera, Abaraca, Barragan and drummer Russell Deleon. Soon after Barragan withdrew from the metal scene finding a totally new calling with a Tex-Mex bar band. HELSTAR struggled on playing gigs on the local circuit but under a new title of VIGILANTE.

As VIGILANTE the band members began negotiation with MEGADETH bassist Dave Eleffson with the intention of recording a four track demo. However, circumstances forced their hand as, with the return of Abaraca and under pressure the band reverted back to their HELSTAR moniker. Also forcing the pace was MEGADETH's dumping from the support slot they had at the time with rock giants AEROSMITH. MEGADETH opted out of the tour at a Houston date when main man Dave Mustaine was unable to continue and Eleffson found himself with more time to work with HELSTAR, the planned demo then evolving into the 'Multiples Of Black' album.

By 1998 Rivera was fronting DESTINYS END for their 'Breathe Deep The Dark' album. The singer founded a new act in 2000 titled PROJECT RIVERA which now boasted Z-LOT-Z guitarist Eric Halpern, MYSTIC CROSS guitarist Don LaFon, OUTWORLD bassist Brent Marches, VICTIM keyboard player Adam Rawlings and drummer Rick Ward from MIDNIGHT CIRCUS.

It would be reported in August of 2001 that Rivera had joined FLOTSAM & JETSAM after their longstanding vocalist Eric A.K. departed. Rivera would then team up with SEVEN WITCHES, debuting with the band at their July appearance at the 'Classic Metal Fest II' in Cleveland, Ohio.

Albums:

BURNING STAR, Combat MX007 (1984)
Burning Star / Towards The Unknown / Witch's Eye / Run With The Pack / Leather And Lust / Possession / The Shadows Of Iga / Dracula's Castle
REMNANTS OF WAR, Noise N 0043 (1986)
Unidos Por Trjsteza / Remnants Of War / Conquest Of War / Evil Reign / Destroyer / Suicidal Nightmare / Dark Queen / Face The Wicked One / Angel Of Death
A DISTANT THUNDER, Roadrunner RR 95242 (1988)
King Is Dead / Bitter End / Abandon Ship / Tyrannicide / Scorcher / Genius Of Insanity / Whore Of Babylon / Winds Of Love / He's A Woman, She's A Man
NOSFERATU, Roadrunner RO 94382 (1989)
Rhapsody In Black / Baptised In Blood / To Sleep / Perchance To Scream / Harker's Tale (Mass Of Death) / Perseverance And Desperation / Curse Has Passed Away / Benediction / Harsh Reality / Swirling Madness / Von Am Lebem Destro Sturm / Aieliaria And Everon
MULTIPLES OF BLACK, Massacre MASSCD 053 (1995)
No Second Chance / Will It Catch Again / Lost To Be Found / When We Only Bleed / Reality / Good Day To Die / Beyond The Real Of Death / Save Time / Black Silhouette Skies / Last Serenade
T'WAS THE NIGHT OF A HELLISH XMAS, Metal Blade (2000)
Swirling Madness / The King Is Dead / Evil Reign / Abandon Ship / Baptised In Blood / To Sleep, Perchance To Scream / Harker's Tale / The Cursed Has Passed Away / Scorcher / Angel Of Death
THE JAMES RIVERA LEGACY, Iron Glory (2001)
Sirens Of The Sun / Changeless Season / Social Circle / Scalpel And The Skin /

Sinister Deity / Rage In The Wind / Black Silhouette Skies / Nightmare Extraordinaire / Changeless Season / Lost To Be Found, Found To Be Lost

HERETIC (Los Angeles, CA, USA)
Line-Up: Mike Howe (vocals), Brian Korban (guitar), Bobby Marquez (guitar), Dennis O'Hara (bass), Rick Merrick (drums)

HERETIC were amongst the fray when California's Thrash scene erupted but made their mark with some precise Speed Metal. The band's original vocalist Mike Torres departed prior to recording to team up with ABBATOIR for their 'Only Safe Place' album. The debut mini-album 'Torture Knows No Boundaries' features singer Julian Mendez who lost his position to Mike Howe in late 1987.

Howe appears on the 'Breaking Point' album but joined METAL CHURCH the same year. Two members of HERETIC, guitarist Brian Korban and bassist Dennis O'Hara would team up with noted METAL CHURCH vocalist David Wayne's REVEREND. Korban recently forged Christian Metal act MONTH OF SUNDAYS in league with erstwhile DELIVERANCE guitarist Glenn Rogers.

Albums:
TORTURE KNOWS NO BOUNDARY, Roadrunner RR 9640 (1987)
Riding With The Angels / Blood Will Tell / Portrait Of Faith / Whitechapel / Torture Knows No Boundary
BREAKING POINT, Roadrunner RR 95341 (1988)
Intro / The Heretic / And Kingdom Fall / The Circle / The Enemy Within / Time Runs Short / Pale Shelter / Shifting Fire / Let 'Em Bleed / Evil For Evil / The Search

HEXENHAUS (SWEDEN)
Line-Up: Tommie Agrippa (vocals), Mike Wead (guitar), Rick Meister (guitar), Jan Blomqvist (bass), Ralph Raideen (drums)

HEXENHAUS were originally titled MANNINYA BLADE, under which name they released one album.
Having adopted the new name in 1987, the band's line-up for the debut album ('A Tribute To Insanity') comprised vocalist Nicklas Johansson, ex-CANDLEMASS guitarist Mike Wead (real name Mikael Vikström), second guitarist DAMIEN man Rick Meister (real name Andreas Palm), bassist Jan Blomqvist and drummer Ralph 'Raideeen' Ryden.
In early 1989 Niclas Johansson left, to be superseded by former DAMIEN vocalist

Tommie Agrippa (real name Thomas Lundin). 1990's 'The Edge Of Eternity' album also features a fresh bassist in former NAGASAKI, DAMIEN and MANNYINA BLADE man Mårten Marteen (real name Mårten Sandberg).
MANNINYA BLADE re-formed in 1990 with Rutström, Leif Eriksson, Blomqvist and drummer Johan Eriksson, although Leif was to leave after the band cut a new demo tape in 1995.
For the third HEXENHAUS album, 'Awakening', only Wead and Lundlin remained with the band's new members being guitarist Marco A. Nicosia, ex-MEZZROW bassist Conny Welen and ex-PARASITE drummer John Billerhag.
After the album emerged Mike Wead created MEMENTO MORI then formed ABSTRAKT ALGEBRA with his old buddy, ex-CANDLEMASS bassist Lief Edling.
Marco Nicosia appeared on the 1997 album by FIFTH REASON 'Psychotic', a band founded by refugees from TAD MOROSE, ABSTRAKT ALGEBRA and MEMORY GARDEN.
Marteen joined MEMENTO MORI.

Albums:
A TRIBUTE TO INSANITY, Active ACTLP 6 (1988)
It / Eaten Alive / Delirious / As Darkness Falls: 1st Movement - a) Shades Of An Obscure Dream - b) A Fatal Attraction - c) In The Spiders Web. 2nd Movement - a) The Possession - b) The Damnation, 3rd Movement - a) On The Threshold Of Insanity, b) Behind Closed Doors, c) The Fall From Grace / Incubus / Death Walks Among Us / Memento Morie - The Dead Are Restless / Requiem
THE EDGE OF ETERNITY, Active ATVLP13 (1990)
Prelude / Toxic Threat / Prime Evil / Home Sweet Home / The House Of Lies / A Temple For The Soul / The Eternal Nightmare / At The Edge Of Eternity
AWAKENING, Active ATV19 (1991)
Shadows Of Sleep / Awakening / Betrayed (By Justice) / Necromonicon Ex Mortis / Code 29 / The Forthcoming Fall / Sea Of Blood / Paradise Of Pain / The Eternal Nightmare Act III / Incubus
DEJA VOODOO, Black Mark BMCD 98 (1997)
Dies Irae - Vreden's Dag / Reborn (At The Back Of Beyond) / Phobia / Nocturnal Rites / Dejavoodoo / From The Cradle To The Grave / Rise Babylon Rise

HIGHLORD (ITALY)
Line-Up: Vascé (vocals), Stefano Droetto (guitar), Diego De Vita (bass), Allessandro Muscio (keyboards), Luca Pellegrino (drums)

Power Metal band with strong Symphonic leanings. HIGHLORD, centred upon key players guitarist Stefano Droetto and keyboard player Alessandro Muscio, began life as AVATAR during 1997. Later inductees to the cause would be drummer Fabio Savello, bassist Enrico Grande and vocalist Roberto Messina, the latter also doubling frontman duties with SECRET SPHERE. However, within months Grande had bailed out and Diego De Vita took the position for the inaugural 'Avatar' demo.
The tape prompted a deal with the Underground Symphony label and set to work on a debut album in 1998. Changes were afoot though and not only would the band switch titles from AVATAR to HIGHLORD but also substitute Messina for a fresh frontman Vascé. In the midst of these tribulations the label and group also severed ties.
The Northwind Records label took the band in and switching studios to Torino's Musical Box facility the debut album 'Heir Of Power' was eventually laid down. Although the band readily acknowledged a below par production this initial Symphonic Speed Metal outing fared well and provided the catalyst for a string of gigs across Italy alongside acts such as DOMINE, SKYLARK and SECRET SPHERE. After this round of live activity Savella decamped in May of 2000. He would be replaced by Luca Pellegrino.
Japanese versions of HIGHLORD's July 2001 opus 'When The Aurora Falls...' would see the addition of two bonus tracks namely 'The Eclipse' and 'Will Of A King'. Extra exposure to the album would be garnered when tracks were set for inclusion on the soundtrack to two horror movies 'The Werewolf Chronicles' and 'Blood Of The Werewolf'.
Vascé decamped in 2001, HIGHLORD drafting DESDEMONA vocalist Andrea Marchisio for recording of a third album.

Albums:
HEIR OF POWER, Northwind (2000)
Ouverture in B min. / Through The Wind / Will Of A King / Stone Shaped Minds / The Eclipse / Burning Desire / Bloodwar In Heaven / Land Of Eternal Ice / Sand In The Wind
WHEN THE AURORA FALLS, Northwind (2001)
When The Aurora Falls... / Don't Kill Me Again / Frozen Heaven / We Are Gods / All I Want / Again / Perpetual Fury / Le Rouge Et Le Noir / Tears Of Darkness / You'll Never Be

Lonely

HITTMAN (New York, NY, USA)
Line-Up: Dirk Kennedy (vocals), Jim Bachi (guitar), Michael Buccell (bass), Chuck Kory (drums)

HITTMAN were founded in 1984 by erstwhile ATTILLA members guitarist Jim Bachi and bassist Michael Buccell together with former TAKASHI drummer Chuck Kory. The band soon added singer Dirk Kennedy, who had previously been involved in the formative stages of ANTHRAX and took on a name influenced by the comic book character He-Man.
The band added to their line-up with second guitarist Brian Fair, previously a member of ALIEN. In mid 1985 this line-up issued HITTMAN's first demo which gained the outfit their inaugural live appearance opening for STRYPER at Nassau Community College on Long Island. Further shows followed including guest slots to POISON, KIX, BLACK N'BLUE and SAXON.
The four track demo - containing 'Metal Sport', 'Sleepless Nights', 'Winds Of Warning' and 'Live For Tomorrow'- quickly began to elicit rave reviews, especially in Europe, although record companies were slow in picking up on the buzz.
In 1986 HITTMAN suffered from line-up ructions as Fair departed, reportedly due to a lack of commitment, to be supplanted by guitarist Greg Walls. Before too long Walls was out in favour of John Kristen.
Passed over by many labels purely because they were playing a more traditional brand of Metal than the in vogue Thrash of the day, it wasn't until 1988 when the New York quintet finally issued their debut product through German label SPV. HITTMAN had previously abandoned plans for a self-financed EP in order to hold out for a deal. Whilst the album features a metallic cover of the theme tune to the old American TV series 'Secret Agent Man' it did not feature demo favourite 'Live For Tomorrow', considered by most observers at the time to be one of the band's classic songs. The 'Vivas Machina' album featured new drummer Mark Jenkins and found HITTMAN moving ever further into Technical Metal waters.

Albums:
HITTMAN, SPV Steamhammer 857568 (1988)
Metal Sport / Dead On Arrival / Back Street Rebels / Behind The Lines / Test Of Time / Secret Agent Man / Will You Be There / Caught In The Crossfire / Breakout

VIVAS MACHINA, Steamhammer (1992)
Radio Waves / Listen / Say A Prayer For Me / Words / If You Can't Dance To It / Answer My Prayer / Partners In Crime / Renegade Man / Ballad Of Jackson Heights / Walk That Walk / Mercy

HOCCULTA (ITALY)
Line-Up: Massimo Lodini (vocals), Marco Bona (guitar), Luca Trabanelli (guitar), Tony Chiarito (bass), Floriano Buratti (drums)

Albums:
WARNING GAMES, Discotto (1984)
We'll Play Again / Owner Of The Earth / Total Confusion / Dream Of Death / Warning Games / Entity / We Give The Power / Witches' Chant
BACK IN THE DARK, Metal Master (1989)

HÖLLENHUNDE (GERMANY)
Line-Up: Hans Bergt (vocals), Thilo Herrmann (guitar), Markus Franck (bass), Dany Löble (drums)

A side project from RUNNING WILD guitarist Thilo Herrmann. When HÖLLENHUNDE dissolved the same year as the album release Herrmann resumed activities with RUNNING WILD. Drummer Dany Löble joined GLENMORE.

Albums:
ALPTRAUM, Höllenhunde (1997)
Niemannsland / Alptraum / Achterbahn / Vollmond / Lüge Nicht / Schau Dich Besser Zweimal Um

HOLOCROSS (USA)
Line-Up: Char R.G. (vocals), P.J. Macin (guitar), Max Uzax (bass), Ray Molinari (drums)

Albums:
HOLOCROSS, New Renaissance (1988)
Wolf Pack / Bombardment / Warpath / B. Hive / Seizure / Manslaughter / Murder Cycle / Drill / Ptomaine / Battle Stations

HOLLOW (SWEDEN)
Line-Up: Andreas Stoltz (vocals), Marcus Bigren (guitar), Thomas Nilsson (bass), Urban Wikström (drums)

The highly technical Metal act HOLLOW, noted for the extreme guitar talents of Marcus Bigren, was assembled in 1990 initially titled VALKYRIAN. Bigren was also dividing his loyalties with MESHUGGAH at the time. Committing himself totally to VALKYRIAN the guitarist opted for a name change to HOLLOW for the 1995 EP.
HOLLOW were soon snapped by the aggressive German label Nuclear Blast for the debut full length effort 'Modern Cathedral'. Stolz guested on the 1998 album from AUBERON 'The Tale Of Black'.

Singles/EPs:
Stand Or Fall / My Vision Fails / Break The Chains / When The Night Is Over, Zakana ZRCD005 (1995)

Albums:
MODERN CATHEDRAL, Nuclear Blast NB 291-2 (1997)
Trademark / Can You Hear Me / Speak To Me / Bagatell 3 / Crusaders / Lies / Wounds / In Your Arms / Whispers / Hold Your Banners High / What I Can Be / Waiting
ARCHITECT OF THE MIND, Nuclear Blast NB 358-2 (1999)
Transcending Sorrow / Cogito / Rain / Shadow God / Secluded Dreams / Walls Of Confusion / Binary Creed / Deified / Alone In Darkness / Shutdown / Father

HOLOSADE (UK)
Line-Up: Phillip De Sade (vocals), Jack Hammer (guitar), Gary Thomson (guitar), Mac (bass), Damien Lee (drums)

Darlington quintet HOLOSADE debuted in 1985 formed by former DARK HEART and REBEL vocalist Phillip De Sade. The band's first product was the cassette 'Vendetta', followed by a two track demo featuring 'Set Me Free' and 'Only In Love'. HOLOSADE also had the track 'Cries In The Night' featured on the Ebony Records compilation album 'The Metal Collection'.
Original bassist Kevin Hole was to depart in favour of DARK HEART and ROULETTE man Colin Bell in early 1986, as the band also added ex-PHANTOM guitarist Jack Hammer. This revised line-up recorded another two track cassette featuring 'Love It To Death' and 'Vicious'.
A further demo, 'Psycho'/'Eternal life', produced by Evo of WARFARE, was recorded at Neat Record's Impulse studios during 1987. Drummer Michael Lee (a.k.a. Damien Lee) opted to jump ship to major signing LITTLE ANGELS later that year and was later to join THE CULT and ROBERT PLANT. Interestingly enough he was later to deny any involvement with HOLOSADE whatsoever!
Colin Bell also departed and was replaced by EXXPLODER and PHANTOM bassist Mac in late 1987.
Following the release of the 'Hellhouse' debut on Powerstation Records, HOLOSADE

toured with DEMON and SKELETON CREW among others. Although a second album was planned, the band split from the label and HOLOSADE suffered a major blow when guitarist Jack Hammer (real name Simon Jones) went on to join SABBAT in early 1989. Bassist Mac teamed up with ACID REIGN. Substitutes were Paul Trotter and Chris Bently respectively. The band also added drummer Andy Barker.

Following the split from Powerstation and line-up reshuffling, HOLOSADE released a three track demo, 'The Return', but soon split and various members of later turned up during 1993 in new act DOMINION.

However, HOLOSADE re-formed in 1994 with Simon Jones reverting back to his stage persona of Jack Hammer. A second album was recorded but never released.

By 1998 Barker was running Metal magazine 'Sound Barrier' and playing drums once more, this time for INTENSE.

Singles/EPs:
Battleaxe, Other (1987)

Albums:
HELLHOUSE, Powerstation AMP16 (1988)
Look In The Mirror / Welcome To The Hellhouse / Love It To Death / Madame Guillotine / Psycho / Eternal Life / Bitter Sweet / Nightmare Reality

HOLY DRAGONS (KAZAKHSTAN)
Line-Up: Daniel Throne (vocals), Chris Caine (guitar), Jurgen Thunderson (guitar / drums), Steven Dreiko (bass)

HOLY DRAGONS claim to be Kazakhstan's first Heavy Metal band. The group, although wrought by an ever ebbing and flowing line-up of musicians with anglicised stage names, has nevertheless managed to issue a string of NWoBHM influenced releases. The band was formulated in May of 1997 by guitarist Jurgen Thunderstorm, a veteran of KINGSPEED, AXCESS and Black Metal act IZVERG, together with female guitarist Chris Caine, previously with GB-5 and LAMIA.

Initial cassette versions of 1998's 'Dragon Steel' released by Centre Records found the band being led by Andreas Kraft but for the CD format his vocals were replaced by those of new lead vocalist Daniel Throne. This new recruit brought his former band mate in VOOCK bass player Steven Dreiko with him. 1999's 'Knights Of The Camelot' album was recorded with a band line-up of Jurgen Thunderson on vocals and guitar, guitarist Chris Caine, bass guitarist Gil Sheffield and drummer Simon Sam.

The second 1999 'Rock Ballads' album was recorded for a local label on the promise of delivering, as the title suggests, a selection of soft Rock balladry. Instead HOLY DRAGONS delivered just over 40 minutes of Heavy Metal! This album would see Steven Dreiko installed on bass and Seva Sabbath on drums, although Jurgen Thunderson took over the drumming role from this point on.

2001 began with HOLY DRAGONS ousting their drummer citing "natural laziness" as a prime factor for his dismissal. The 'House Of The Winds' and 'Thunder In The Night' albums would be combined together with two Russian language tracks for cassette release in Kazakhstan in October of 2001. Despite the departure of both Daniel Throne and Steven Dreiko in December of due to "strong contradictions in creative and ideological views" HOLY DRAGONS would be in preparation for a new album billed as 'Judgement Day' slated for 2002. In March of that year new four string operative Muha Fly was drafted.

Albums:
DRAGON STEEL, (1998)
Holy Dragons / King Of Speed / Goblins & Knights / Wild Cat / Challenge Of Life / Sorry, Mama / Pharaoh / Enjoy The Storm / Mr. Fat Rat / Elven Holiday / Dragon Attack / Time Eats Silently
KNIGHTS OF THE CAMELOT, (1999)
Introduction / Legend Of Gold Moon, Princess Of The Valley / Don't Stop Rocking / Robin Hood / Land Of Dreams / Nobody's Fool / Knights Of Camelot / Mystery
ROCK BALLADS, (1999)
Rainbow's Gold / Mighty Warriors / Midnight Sky / Silver Mountain / Dragon Eyes / L.L.L. / Christmas Song / Living On The Edge
HOUSE OF THE WINDS, (2000)
Steel For The Steel / Prophecy Of Gods / You Hate It / Rage Of The Dragon Lords / Metal Vikings / Go & Fly (In The Middle Between Yesterday & Tomorrow) / House Of The Winds
THUNDER IN THE NIGHT, Dragonight Productions (2001)
In The Search Of Unicorn / Starlight Race / Fury Under Control / Turbo (911) / Mr. Drunkenstein / X-Files / Legend Of The Warriors / Glory War / Thunder In The Night

HOLY KNIGHTS (ITALY)
Line-Up: Mark Raven (vocals / keyboards), Federico Madonia (guitar), Danny Merthon (guitar), Syl Raven (bass), Claus Jorgen (drums)

Albums:
GATE THROUGH THE PAST, Underground

Symphony USCD-054 (2001)
March Of The Brave / Sir Percival (Immortal Knight) / Lord Of Nightmares / The Revival Of The Black Demon / Gate Through The Past / Love Against The Power Of Evil / Rondeau In A Minor / Quest Of Heroes - Part I / Quest Of Heroes - Part II / The Promise / Under The Light Of The Moon / When The Rest Let Down

HOLY MOTHER (New York, NY, USA)
Line-Up: Mike Tirelli (vocals), Spike Francis (guitar), Randy Coven (bass), Jim Harris (drums)

Heavy Metal band with obvious traditional British leanings and boasting a set of highly regarded musicians. HOLY MOTHER's influences from one particular Birmingham based band were so strong that they even had their advertising directly punning JUDAS PRIEST's 'Jugulator' opus.

Vocalist Mike Tirelli was previously with LAST LIX and also has appeared on numerous BURNING STARR albums. Bassist RANDY COVEN started his career with the late '70s band MORNING THUNDER which featured guitarist STEVE VAI and RAINBOW keyboard player David Rosentahl. The bassist issued a solo album in 1989 'Funk Me Tender' which has STEVE VAI and Al Pitrelli as guests. Coven also appears on the 1991 BURNING STARR album 'A Minor Disturbance'. Coven also forged one third of the band C.P.R. which also comprised ex-WIDOWMAKER, TALAS and ASIA hotshot guitarist Al Pitrelli and RAINBOW and BLUE OYSTER CULT drummer John O'Reilly for an eponymous album in 1993. Drummer Jim Harris has also sessioned for BURNING STARR.

The band put in an appearance at the 1998 Wacken festival in Germany alongside RIOT and VIRGIN STEELE.

RANDY COVEN had an industrious 2000. As well as working on fresh HOLY MOTHER material the four stringer began recording a solo album titled 'Witchway'. The bass player also joined two other bands to fill his spare time forming part of YNGWIE MALMSTEEN's new live band and uniting with the Swedish guitar God's band mates keyboard player Mats Olausson and drummer John Macaluso in A.R.K.

HOLY MOTHER donated their take on IRON MAIDEN's 'The Trooper' to the 'Slave To The Power' tribute record. During mid 2002 it would be revealed that Mike Tirelli had assembled a German / American project band billed as MESSIAH'S KISS, recording a debut album 'Reign Of Fire' for the SPV label.

Albums:
HOLY MOTHER, JVC Victor VICP 5639 (1996)
Call Me By My Real Name / Eden / The Train / In Our Minds / Say Goodbye / The Innocent Only / Your Song / Indian Summer / Dealin' With Me / Rage / Kayla
TOXIC RAIN, ABS 209 (1998)
Wars / Electric / Toxic Rain / The Rats Keep Running / My Destination / Live To Die / The River / You´ve Got Another Thing Comin´ / Symptom Of Withdrawal / Melting Pot / Losing My Bet
CRIMINAL AFTERLIFE, Crazy Life Music (1999)
Rage / Criminal Afterlife / Holy Diver / Cycle Of The Sun / Call The Ghost / Memory Never Dies / Armageddon's Call (Part One) / Armageddon's Call (Part Two) / Turned In The Gun / What If Tomorrow Never Comes / Lies / Life In Stone
MY WORLD WAR, Shark (2000)
Livin On Luck / Freakshow / The Itch / My World War / Where Their Children Play / Yesterday / Rebel Hell / High / Hunting / Save Me / Mr. Right / In The Gutter

HORIZON'S END (GREECE)
Line-Up: Vassilios Topalides (vocals), Emmanuel Pilidis (guitar), Kostas Scandalis (bass), Sakis Bandis (keyboards), Stergios Kourou (drums)

Albums:
SCULPTURE ON ICE, Music Is Intelligence (1998)
To Count The Stars / The New Jerusalem / Extropian / Traveller / Adorned With Flowers / Colours / Of Fire And Utterance
CONCRETE SURREAL, Steel Gallery SGR CD007 (2001)
Dividing Vanity / Sacred Lover / Two Steps And An Acknowledgement / The Road To Grovelling / Under The Face Of Regret / Taken In / Sandfalls / A Soul / Sleep

HOUSE OF SPIRITS (GERMANY)
Line-Up: Olaf Bilic (vocals), Uwe Baltrusch (guitar), Martin Hirsch (bass), Jörg Michael (drums)

HOUSE OF SPIRITS men Olaf Bilic and Martin Hirsch had both been members of JESTERS MARCH, whilst Uwe Baltrusch is ex-MEKONG DELTA and drummer Jörg Michael was formally with MEKONG DELTA, RUNNING WILD, GRAVE DIGGER and RAGE.

Baltrusch departed after the debut album making way for Benjamin Schippritt. HOUSE OF SPIRITS collapsed though with bassist

Martin Hirsch joining HILTON then Deathsters MORGOTH. Bilic put in vocal sessions with both FAITH HEALER and FALCON.

A four track demo secured a new deal with the Century Media label and once more drums were supplied by Jörg Michael. However, Michael's commitments as full time member of STRATOVARIUS and AXEL RUDI PELL meant the recruitment of new drummer Michael Strichen for live work.

Singles/EPs:
In My Heart (Single Version) / The Eye Of The Storm (Single Version) / In My Heart / The Eye Of The Storm, G.U.N. Gun 043 BMG (1994) ('Get The Spirit' EP promotion release)

Albums:
TURN OF THE TIDE, G.U.N. Gun 044 BMG 74321 (1994)
Dawn / Turn Of The Tide / Wasteland / Keep Me From Dreaming / Close To The Edge / He Waited / In My Heart / The Eye Of The Storm / In A Daze / Final Mistake / Time Has Come
PSYCHOSPHERE, Century Media CD 77228-2 (1999)
Take Me To The Other Side / Back On My Own / History Is Repeating / World Full Of Pain / Voices / Voice Of My Heart / Save The Secret / Time Is Drawing / Oblivion Night's / Dark & Light / Back At The Double /

Psychosphere

HUMAN FORTRESS
Line-Up: Jioti Parcharidis (vocals), Torsten Wolf (guitar), Volker Trost (guitar), Pablo J. Tammen (bass), Dirk Marquardt (keyboards), Laki Zaios (drums)

A Hannover Power Metal band HUMAN FORTRESS evolved from the Progressive Rock act TIMEZONE fronted by Michaela Senger. With Senger's departure, and after drafting ex-HYDROTOXIN man Pablo Tammen, the group evolved into HUMAN FORTRESS during 1999 debuting with a promotional mini album.

A second HUMAN FORTRESS outing entitled 'Lord Of Earth And Heavens Heir', produced by ex-VICTORY guitarist Tommy Newton, would follow on. Released in September 2001 by Limb Music the sophomore effort saw guest backing vocals from Michael Bormann of JADED HEART and RAIN.

Singles/EPs:
Amberdawn / Light Beyond Horizon / Stroke Of Fate / Little Flame, (1996) ('Human Fortress' EP)

Albums:
LORD OF EARTH AND HEAVEN'S HEIR, Limb Music Productions (2001)

HUMAN FORTRESS

The Dragon's Lair / Under Black Age Toil /
Lord Of Earth And Heaven's Heir / Divine
Astronomy / Stroke Of Fate / The Fortress /
Amber / Dawn / Forgive And Forget /
Damned To Bedlam / Light Beyond Horizon /
Little Flame

HYKSOS (USA)
Line-Up: Mark Bradley (vocals), Tony
Gonzales (guitar), Art Gonzalez (guitar),
Barry Benjamin (bass), Clay Guinaldo
(drums)

Heavily influenced by British Metal bands and
medieval imagery in all its glory. The band
also appeared on the 'Metal Massacre
Volume II' compilation with 'The Kings' in 1982
before disappearing.

Albums:
HYKSOS, Hyksos (1982)

HYPERION (AUSTRALIA)
Line-Up: Jim Georgopoulis (vocals), Corey
Romeo (guitar), Tony Brereton (guitar),
Cruze (bass), Lara Jorgavecic (keyboards),
Mark Wylie (drums)

Following the break up of HYPERION singer
Jim Georgopoulis would join up with
EYEFEAR, although his tenure would be
brief.

Singles/EPs:
Primal Storm / The Shroud / Runaway /
Animal Light / Inundation (Acoustic version),
Def DEF0027 (1995)

Albums:
INUNDATION, Def DEF0007 (1994)
Twilight Runner / The Kill / Stay Gold / Power
/ Autumn / Heartland / Soul Cry / Sundance /
Inundation

HYPERION (ITALY)
Line-Up: Matt McHantin (vocals), Alexander
Blake (guitar), Fabian Dale (bass), Mark
Katen (keyboards), Paul Raymonds (drums)

Bergamo based, guitar driven Symphonic
Power Metal with trademark Italian style
Operatic vocals.

Albums:
WHERE STONE IS UNSCARRED,
Massacre MAS CD0174 (1999)
Ardebeit Ad Aeturnum / Perpetual Burn /
Shades Of Sin / Eyes Full Of Fire / The
Mirror Of Soul / Chains Around The Time /
Neverending Wind / Till The End Of Time /
Labyrinth / Beyond The Sky / The Legion Of
Thunder

ICE AGE (USA)

Line-Up: Josh Pincus (vocals / keyboards), Jimmy Pappas (guitar), Arron DiCesare (bass), Hal Aponte (drums)

A guitar driven Progressive Rock act with a sense of the grandiose. ICE AGE was founded in 1992 by Greek born guitarist Jimmy Pappas and vocalist / keyboard player Josh Pincus. In 1993 the duo added former STAGES, THE LOST SOULS and COLD STEEL drummer Hal Aponte to the rankings. ICE AGE signed to Progressive Rock specialists Magna Carta for their debut 1999 album 'The Great Divide'.

The sophomore release 'Liberation' would follow in March 2001. However, ICE AGE would lose bassist Arron DiCesare shortly before the record hit the stores substituting him with Doug Odell. During 2001 Pincus would undertake extracurricular activities acting as live keyboard player for WESTWORLD.

Albums:

THE GREAT DIVIDE, Magna Carta MAX 9028-2 (1999)
Perpetual Child / Sleepwalker / Join / Spare Chicken Parts / Because Of You / Because Of You / The Bottom Line / Ice Age / One Look Away / Miles To Go / To Say Goodbye: Part 1 - Worthless Words / To Say Goodbye: Part 2 - On Our Way

LIBERATION, Magna Carta MA-9051-2 (2001)
Lhasa Road (No Surrender) / March Of The Red Dragon / The Blood Of Ages / A Thousand Years / When You're Ready / Musical Cages / Monolith / The Guardian Of Forever / Howl / The Wolf / To Say Goodbye: Part 3 - Still Here / Tong-Len

ICED EARTH (USA)

Line-Up: Matt Barlow (vocals), John Schaffer (guitar), Randy Shawver (guitar), Steve DiGeorgio (bass), Richard Christy (drums)

The traditional intense no compromise style of overblown Metal purveyed by ICED EARTH has seen the band rise from an obscure mid '80s indie band to legend status in Germany and mainland Europe. Musically the band have developed from formative years delivering Power Thrash to more refined, yet still none the less heavy, melodically charged Heavy Metal.

The band began life in 1985 titled PURGATORY with a teenage garage band line-up of vocalist Gene Adam, guitarists Jon

ICED EARTH
Photo : Nico Wobben

MATT BARLOW of ICED EARTH
Photo : Nico Wobben

Schaffer and Bill Owen, bassist Dave Abell and drummer Greg Seymour. Another ex-PURGATORY man bassist Richard Bateman also made a fleeting appearance and he was later to find prominence in AGENT STEEL and NASTY SAVAGE. As PURGATORY a demo entitled 'Psychotic Dreams' was released.

As the transition from PURGATORY to ICED EARTH began the band were still very much a horror shock outfit wearing cassocks onstage and dousing their audience in liver and blood as part of the theatrics. Thankfully these tactics were soon resigned to the pasty as ICED EARTH concentrated more on the music.

The first ICED EARTH recordings proper came in the form of the 'Horror Show' demo featuring one new composition 'Dracula' allied with two reworkings of PURGATORY tracks 'Jack' and 'In Jason's Mind', both from the 'Psychotic Dreams' demo.

ICED EARTH's next effort was the tape that secured their career and landed them a deal with Germany's Century Media Records. The 'Enter The Realm' demo comprising the tracks 'Colors', 'Enter The Realm', 'Nightmares', 'To Curse The Sky', 'Solitude' and 'Iced Earth'. ICED EARTH also made an appearance on the 'Metal Mercenaries' compilation album with a song produced by ex SAVATAGE bassist Keith Collins.

Seymour was briefly replaced by Mike McGill for a European tour after which both McGill was unceremoniously fired and the band also brought in drummer Richie Secharri as ICED EARTH struggled to keep a tight rein on their drummers.

The second release 'Night Of The Stormrider', for which Schaffer took over the lead vocal role, also saw John Greeley on the drum stool although predictably his tenure was short.

1995's 'Burnt Offerings' sees Rodney Beasley on drums. For the groundbreaking 'Dark Saga' album ICED EARTH recorded minus a permanent drummer employing the services of studio engineer Mark Prator. Abell quit soon after this release.

1997 release 'Days Of Purgatory' is a collection of re-worked tracks from the band's 'Enter The Realm' demo and cuts from the first two albums.

1998 had ICED EARTH putting in an almost triumphant performance at the German 'Wacken Open Air' festival as the 'Something Wicked This Way Comes' album cracked the German charts at number 19. The follow up, the ambitious treble live album 'Live In Athens', recorded in front of 120,000 fans, gave ICED EARTH a Greek number one.

Quite spectacularly Schaffer's side project DEMONS & WIZARDS, a union with BLIND GUARDIAN's Hansi Kirsch blew the European charts wide open, even scoring the guitarist a further number one in Greece. DEMONS & WIZARDS toured on the festival circuit with CONTROL DENIED / DEATH drummer Richard Christy.

By mid 2000, still without a permanent drummer, ICED EARTH pulled in Christy for live commitments. Ever industrious Christy also found time to commit to his side project band BURNING INSIDE with ACHERON's Michael Estes and BLACK WITCHERY's Steve Childers.

ICED EARTH's 'Horror Show' album found Christy being inducted into the ranks officially along with former DEATH / SADUS bassist Steve DiGeorgio. The interim 'Melancholy' mini-album included cover versions of BAD COMPANY's 'Shooting Star', BLACK SABBATH's 'Electric Funeral' and JUDAS PRIEST's 'The Ripper'.

Jimmy MacDonough joined the ICED EARTH clan as touring bassist for mid 2001. 'Horror Show' saw the band topping the Greek national charts yet again and with stronger than previous European chart positions in most territories.

Touring in America was to have stepped up significantly for the band when they were announced as openers to the JUDAS PRIEST and ANTHRAX tour. However, the terrorist attacks on the United States on September 11th resulted in the cancellation of this entire tour.

Century Media weighed in with the gargantuan 'Dark Genesis' box set to close 2001. The lavish package comprised remastered versions of early albums, the 'Enter The Realm' demo plus a bonus tribute disc 'Tribute To The Gods'.

This latter disc would be released separately during 2002 and saw ICED EARTH taking on 'Creatures Of The Night' and 'God Of Thunder' by KISS, 'Number Of The Beast' and 'Hallowed Be Thy Name' by IRON MAIDEN, 'Highway To Hell' and 'It's A Long Way To The Top' by AC/DC, 'Burnin' For You' and 'Cities On Flame With Rock n' Roll' from BLUE OYSTER CULT, 'Screaming For Vengeance' by JUDAS PRIEST, 'Dead Babies' by ALICE COOPER and BLACK SABBATH's 'Black Sabbath'.

The band's headline 'Feel The Horror' European tour would commence in Hardenberg, Holland on the 17th January 2002. It would then be back to their homeland for a run of headline dates kicking off on April 8th at the Everson Theater in Indianapolis. Strong support on these shows would come from Colorado label mates JAG PANZER and Swedish Deathsters IN FLAMES.

Albums:

ICED EARTH, Century Media CM 7714-2 (1990)
Iced Earth / Written On The Walls / Colors / Curse The Sky / Life And Death / Solitude / Funeral / When The Night Falls

NIGHT OF THE STORMRIDER, Century Media 9727-2 (1994)
Angels Holocaust / Stormrider / The Oath I Choose / Before The Vision / Mystical End / Desert Rain / Pure Evil / Reaching The End / Travel In Stygian

BURNT OFFERINGS, Century Media 77093-2 (1995)
Burnt Offerings / Last December / Diary / Brainwashed / Burning Oasis / Creator Failure / The Pierced Spirit / Dante's Inferno: i) Denial, Lust, Greed, ii) The Prodigal, The Wrathful, Medusa, iii) The False Witness, Angel Of Light

THE DARK SAGA, Century Media CM 77131-2 (1996)
Dark Saga / I Died For You / Violate / The Hunter / The Last Laugh / Depths Of Hell / Vengeance Is Mine / The Suffering: Scarred / Slave To The Dark / A Question Of Heaven

DAYS OF PURGATORY, Century Media 77165-2 (1997)
Enter The Realm / Colors / Angels Holocaust / Stormrider / Winter Nights / Nightmares / Before The Vision / Pure Evil / Solitude / The Funeral / When The Night Falls / Burnt Offerings / Cast In Stone / Desert Rain / Brainwashed / Life And Death / Creator Failure / Reaching The End / Travel In Stygian / Dante's Inferno / Iced Earth

SOMETHING WICKED THIS WAY COMES, Century Media CD77214-2 (1998)
19 GERMANY
Burning Times / Melancholy (Holy Martyr) / Disciples Of The Lie / Watching Over Me / Stand Alone / Consequences / My Own Savior / Reaping Stone / 1776 (Instrumental) / Blessed Are You Something Wicked (Trilogy) / Prophecy / Birth Of The Wicked / The Coming Curse

ALIVE IN ATHENS, Century Media (1999)
1 GREECE
Burning Times / Vengeance Is Mine / Pure Evil / My Own Savior / Melancholy (Holy Martyr) / Dante's Inferno / The Hunter / Travel In Stygian / Slave To The Dark / A Question Of Heaven / Dark Saga / Last Laugh / Last December / Watching Over Me / Angels Holocaust / Stormrider / Path I Choose / I Died For You / Prophecy / Birth Of The Wicked / The Coming Curse / Iced Earth / Stand Alone / Cast In Stone / Desert Rain / Brainwashed / Disciples Of The Lie / When The Night Falls / Diary / Blessed Are You / Violate

MELANCHOLY, Century Media (2000)

Melancholy / Shooting Star / Watching Over Me / Electric Funeral / I Died For You / The Ripper / Colors (Live)
HORROR SHOW, Century Media (2001)
32 AUSTRIA, 90 FRANCE, 30 GERMANY, 1 GREECE, 6 HOLLAND, 71 SWEDEN, 86 SWITZERLAND
Wolf / Damien / Jack / Ghost Of Freedom / Im-Ho-Tep (Pharaoh's Curse) / Jekyll & Hyde / Dragon's Child / Frankenstein / Dracula / The Phantom Opera Ghost
TRIBUTE TO THE GODS, Century Media (2002)
Creatures Of The Night / Number Of The Beast / Highway To Hell / Screaming For Vengeance / Hallowed Be Thy Name / God Of Thunder / Burnin' For You / Black Sabbath / It's A Long Way To The Top (If You Wanna Rock 'n' Roll) / Dead Babies / Cities On Flame With Rock & Roll

ILIUM (AUSTRALIA)

Newcastle based Metal band ILIUM included a cover version of JUDAS PRIEST" classic 'Green Manalishi (With The Two Pronged Crown)' on their debut EP.

Singles/EPs:
Half Life / Semblance / Antigone / The Green Manalishi (With The Two Pronged Crown), (2002) ('Ilium' EP)

ILLWILL (SWEDEN)
Line-Up: Yonas Af Dahlstrom (vocals), Andy LaRoque (guitar), Sharlee D'Angelo (bass), Snowy Shaw (drums)

ILLWILL are something of a Scandinavian Metal supergroup created by KING DIAMOND guitarist Andy LaRoque, MERCYFUL FATE bassist Sharlee D'Angelo and MEMENTO MORI / KING DIAMOND drummer Snowy Shaw.
Rounding off the team is DESERT PLAINS / TON OF BRICKS vocalist Yonas Af Dahlstrom.

Albums:
EVILUTION, Diamond DR 002 (1998)
Singh Hai / V For Vulgarians / Cult / Il Organizatione / Six Sec Sex / Whether With Or Without / Eternal Sleep / K.A.O.S. / Bid Farewell To Welfare / Who To Trust? / This Barren Life / 365 Reasons To Commit Suicide

INFERNO (FL, USA)
Line-Up: Jay Peele (vocals / guitar), Scott Brandle (guitar / keyboards), Paul Lapinski (bass), Kenny Philips (drums)

INFERNO date back to 1988, originally touting a standard Heavy Metal delivery. During the early '90s the group drifted into a more Progressive Metal direction. Guitarist Scott Brandle decamped in June of 1994, his place being taken by Keir Whitacre. A demo session, 'Architect', followed.

Albums:
PSYCHIC DISTANCE, Massacre (1994)
On The Threshold Of Depression / Psychic Distance / Sacrosanct Delusions / Cloaks / Public Eye / A.C.R.E. / Infinite Regress / Malice Domestic / Psychic Distance (Part 2)
PANELS, (1995)

INFINITE HORIZON (GERMANY)
Line-Up: Marc Lemler (vocals), Thomas Backer (guitar), Jens Hahn (guitar), Armin Schmidt (bass), Bastian Fuchs (keyboards), Christian Schmidt (drums)

Albums:
BEYOND INFINITY, (2001)
Spider's Web / You Break Down / Dark Side Of The Sun / Nowhereland / Like A Labyrinth / Alone In The Streets / Free Is My Soul / Questions

INGERMANLAND (NORWAY)

Albums:
SURFACE AS CEILING, (1999)
BEYOND EQUATOR, (2001)
Networked Vibrations / Mindware Lost / The First Moment / Delusion Of Madness / Sleeping With Worms / Art Dewy Prime

INISHMORE (SWITZERLAND)
Line-Up: Ramin Dänzer (vocals), Fabian Niggemeier (guitar), Zoltan Daraban (guitar), Daniel Novosel (bass), Pascal Gysi (keyboards), Jonas Dänzer (drums)

Albums:
THE FINAL DANCE, Inishmore (2000)
The Journey / Moonchildren / Riding The Winds / Memories / The Beginning / Unite / The Final Dance
THEATRE OF MY LIFE, Inishmore (2001)
Welcome To The Theatre / The Ravens Eye / Burn It Down / Revolution / I Can't Cry / Lost / When Heaven's Calling You / Gone / Farewell / The Theatre Of My Life: Act 1 - The Sign, Act 2 - Theatre Of My Life, Act 3 - Falling Down

INQUISICION (CHILE)
Line-Up: Paulo Domic (vocals), Manolo Schäfler (guitar), Christian Maturana (bass),

Carlos Hernández (drums)

Santiago Heavy Metal band INQUISICION was formulated in June of 1993 by TORTURER guitarist Manolo Schäfler, initially billed as SANTA INQUISICION. Carlos Hernández on drums and ex-PANZER man Freddy Alexis on lead vocals rounded the new band out. By 1994 Schäfler had thrown in the towel with TORTURER to concentrate on his new venture.

A demo tape was laid down after which Christian Maturana of Progressive act PSYKIS joined the band on bass. With this line-up INQUISICION recorded the debut album 'Steel Vengeance'. Released by the Argentinean label Dreamland Music 'Steel Vengeance' was ably promoted by a video for the track 'Innocent Sinner'. Shortly after the Toxic label married the 'Steel Vengeance' tracks with the group's original demo recordings and re-packaged this collection for a release entitled 'In Nomine'.

With Alexis decamping to WITCHBLADE the band inducted Pedro Galán as their new singer in September of 2000. Paulo Domic took over the mantle of lead vocalist during 2001.

Albums:
STEEL VENGEANCE, Dreamland Music (1996)
Prelude / Innocent Sinner / Sed Diabolus / Pagan Rites / Steel Vengeance / Fate Was Sealed / Message In Black / Torturer / The Ancient Light / Into The Labyrinth
IN NOMINE, Toxic (1997)
Intro / Innocent Sinner / Sed Diabolus / Pagan Rites / Steel Vengeance / Fate Was Sealed / Torturer / The Ancient Light / Into The Labyrinth / Mayday's Eve / Bats In The Bellfry / Holy Fire / The Dreamquest Of The Unknown Avalon
BLACK LEATHER FROM HELL, Miskatonic Music (1998)
Dragonslayer / Black Leather From Hell / Army Of Darkness / Midnight Avenger / The Axis Of The Mist / Witchcraft / Extermination / Devil Mistress / Mensaje Oculto
LIVE POSTHUMOUS, Miskatonic Music (2001)
Dragonslayer / Pagan Rites / Mayday's Eve / Into The Labyrinth / Army Of Darkness / Innocent Sinner / Unholy Rime / Hellracer

INSANIA (STOCKHOLM) (SWEDEN)
Line-Up: David Henriksson (vocals), Henrik Juhano (guitar), Niklas Dahlin (guitar), Tomas Stolt (bass), Patrik Västilä (keyboards), Mikko Olavi Kovsbäck (drums)

Stockholm Power Metal unit created in 1992 by erstwhile AVANCIA and JUVENILES guitarist Henrik Juhano, bass player Tomas Stolt along with drummer cum lead vocalist Mikko Olavi Korsbäck. Although the band added second guitarist Niklas Dahlin during early 1994 the line-up fractured when Stolt decamped just prior to the band's first gig in Järfälla . INSANIA persevered by pulling in a stand in but within months Stolt had made a return to the ranks.

Vocalist David Henriksson would enter the fold and INSANIA cut their inaugural demo in 1996 which secured a deal with No Fashion Records.

INSANIA debuted with the 1999 Tomas Skogsberg produced 'World Of Ice' record. Club dates in Sweden followed and INSANIA would also be granted the honour of an appearance at an outdoor festival headlined by MANOWAR.

The summer of 2000 found the band back in the recording studio for the follow up effort 'Sunrise In Riverland' produced by Mikko Karmila.

INSANIA would re-brand themselves INSANIA (STOCKHOLM) in latter years in order to avoid confusion with the already existing German and Czech INSANIA's.

Just upfront of recording a new album 'Fantasy' in May of 2002 INSANIA (STOCKHOLM) drafted a new vocalist in Ola Halén.

Albums:
WORLD OF ICE, No Fashion NFR035 (1999)
Insaniation / Fighting My Tears / Fire / With Courage And Pride / Forever Alone / Private 6-Machine / Paradisia / World Of Ice / Forever Is a Long Time / Furious Seas / Carried By Wings
SUNRISE IN RIVERLAND, No Fashion (2001)
Finlandia / The Land Of Wintersun / Heaven Or Hell / Beware Of The Dragons / Angels In The Sky / Lost In Time / Heading For Tomorrow / Sunrise In Riverland / Dangerous Mind / Seasons Of Life / Tears Of The Nature / Time Of The Prophecies / The Right To Be Free
FANTASY, No Fashion (2002)
Introduction / Life After Life / Illusions / Carry On / Master Of My Mind / Universe / Face The King / Fantasy / Vengeance / Mankind / Reflections Of Mine

INTENSE (UK)
Line-Up: Sean Hetherington (vocals), Ade Carloss (guitar), Dave Peake (guitar), Eddie Marsh (bass), Andy Wright (drums)

Traditional Power Metal band out of Basingstoke. INTENSE emerged with the 1996 'Blinded' demo and a line-up of vocalist Sean Hetherington, guitarists Dave Peake and Ade Carloss, bassist Eddie Marsh and drummer Andy Wright. Another member of the formative band, guitarist Chris Allen, would go on to found SHADOWKEEP.

The INTENSE debut album 'Dark Season' would be issued by Full Volume Records in August of 1999 as INTENSE became a regular on the UK club circuit. A further demo outing 'Defiant Till Death' also arrived but the bands line-up would collapse. Sole surviving member Sean Hetherington regrouped for another demo session 'The Chosen Ones' enlisting guitarist Nick Palmer, actually an earlier INTENSE member, and erstwhile HOLOSADE drummer Andy Barker. The latter would disembark in October 2000.

INTENSE recruited drummer Neil Ablard but would remain without a bassist for much of 2001. Former guitarist Dave Peake returned to the fold in April of 2002. Although INTENSE would announce their first live gig in two years, supporting SHADOWKEEP in Guildford during early June, the band still remained without a bassist.

Albums:
DARK SEASON, Intense INT DS 1 (1997)
Against The Grain / Deny / Greed / Dark Season / Crystal Mind / This Is Your Fate

INTRINSIC (San Luis Obispo, CA, USA)
Line-Up: Garret Graupner (vocals), Mike Mellinger (guitar), Ron Crawford (guitar), Joel Stern (bass), Chris Binns (drums)

Founded in 1983 by guitarists Ron Crawford and Mike Millinger, INTRINISIC opened for MEGADETH and ARMORED SAINT before parting company with vocalist Garret Graupner shortly after the debut album release.

The Californians worked for a period with ex-METAL CHURCH vocalist David Wayne during 1988 but his tenure with the group was by no means lengthy and he was already dabbling with HEATHEN before he quit the INTRINSIC camp.

The second album, 'Distortion Of Perspective', found INTRINSIC fronted by a new vocalist Lee Dehmer and guitarist Ron Crawford out of the fold in favour of Garrett Craddock.

INTRINSIC made an unexpected return in 1997 with the 'Closure' album. The line-up incorporated Dehmer, Mellinger, Craddock, Binns, and bassist Mike McClaughlin.

Albums:
INTRINSIC, No Wimp 007 (1987)
Ahead Of The Game / Hit The Streets / Condo / Rip!! / Possessor / No Return / Leaving Insane / Wasted Life
DISTORTION OF PERSPECTIVE, Cheese Flag (1990)
Distortion Of Perspective / Sail Into The Sun / Piracy / Maximator / Fear And Loathing
CLOSURE, Rokarola 728085004 (1997)
The Wheel / Up For The Slam / BKB / 3X0 / Falling In / End Times / Nothing Special / I Still Feel Ya / Bystander / Someone's Gotta Pay / Try My Luck / Visceral / Brutally Frank / The Reasons Why / Who Goes There?

INTRUDER (Nashville, TN, USA)

Singles/EPs:
Cover Up, Iron Works (1987)
Escape From Pain / 25 Or 6 To 4 / Cold Blooded Killer / Kiss Of Death / T.M. (You Paid The Price), Metal Blade (1990)

Albums:
LIVE TO DIE, Iron Works IW 1023 (1987)
Cover Up / Turn Back / Victory In Disguise / Live To Die / Kiss Of Death / Cold Blooded Killer / Blind Rage / T.M. (You Paid The Price)
A HIGHER FORM OF KILLING, Roadracer (1989)
Time Of Trouble / Martyr / Genetic Genocide / Second Chance / (I'm Not Your) Stepping Stone / Killing Winds / Sentence Is Death / Agents Of The Dark (MIB) / Antipathy
PSYCHO SAVANT, Metal Blade CDZORRO 25 (1991)
Face Of Hate / Gerl's Lament (When) / The Enemy Within / It's A Good Life / Invisible / Traitor To The Living / Final Word / N.G.R.I.

INVADER (GERMANY)
Line-Up: Peter Bekusch (vocals), Frank Hoffmeyer (guitar), Jürgen Keller (guitar), Uwe Theilbar (bass), Thomas Grabisch (drums)

Albums:
CHILDREN OF WAR, Bone Breaker (1986)
The Thing / Victory / March For Victory / Twilight Of The Gods / Black Sex / State Penitentiary For Mental Disorder / Land Of The North / Children Of War / Flying High / Days Of Sorrow

ION VEIN (Chicago, IL, USA)
Line-Up: Russ Klimczak (vocals), Chris Lotesto (guitar), John Maultha (guitar), Brian Gordon (bass), Scott Lang (drums)

Guitarist Chris Lotesto founded ION VEIN in 1989 as LATENT FURY. Adopted the name ION VEIN in 1994 with the addition of ex-COUNTER ATTAK vocalist Russ Klimczak. By March of 1996 the band had added former PROFILE drummer Scott Lang followed shortly by ex-DISSIDENT AGRESSOR bassist Brian Gordon and second guitarist John Malutha.

ION VEIN appeared at the 1998 'Powermad' Festival and contributed their version of 'Killers' to the IRON MAIDEN tribute album 'Call To Irons II'. Bass player Jonathon Quigley made his exit in February of 2002 for FINAL NATION. Erstwhile ION VEIN bassist Brian Gordon duly retook his position in the band. Gordon would also land session credits with famed Chicago Doom band NOVEMBER'S DOOM, appearing on their ''To Welcome The Fade' opus.

Albums:
BEYOND TOMORROW, (1999)
Horizons / Reflections Unclear / Fading Shadows / Heart Of The Matter / Static Vision / The Bridge Of Dawn / Here Today Gone Tomorrow / Beyond Tomorrow

IRON ANGEL (GERMANY)
Line-Up: Dirk Schroder (vocals), Sven Struven (guitar), Peter Wittke (guitar), Thorsten Lohmann (bass), Mike Matthes (drums)

Formed in 1983 by the former METAL GODS triumvirate of drummer Mike Matthes, bassist Thortsen Lohmann and guitarist Sven Struven. IRON ANGEL issued their second demo in 1984 'Legions Of Evil'. Jürgen Blackmore, son of DEEP PURPLE and RAINBOW guitarist RITCHIE BLACKMORE, joined the band in mid 1986.

In 1987 IRON ANGEL parted company with bassist Thorsten Lohmann, manoeuvring guitarist Peter Witthe over to bass and recruiting a new guitarist Stefan Kleinow. The Portuguese Black Thrash act ALASTOR would cover IRON ANGEL's 'Sinner' for their December 2001 album 'Hellward'.

Albums:
HELLISH CROSSFIRE, Steamhammer SPV 08-1853 (1985)
The Metallion / Sinner / Black Mass / The Church Of Lost Souls / Hunter In Chains / Rush Of Power / Legions Of Evil / Wife Of The Devil / Nightmare / Heavy Metal Soldiers
WINDS OF WAR, Steamhammer SPV 08-1880 (1986)
Winds Of War / Metalstorm / Son Of A Bitch / Vicious / Born To Rock / Fight For Your Life / Stronger Than Steel / Sea Of Flames / Creatures Of Destruction / Back To The Silence

IRON CLAD (BELGIUM)
Line-Up: Gunther Theys (vocals), Sammy (guitar / keyboards), Luc (bass), Rony (drums)

Employing plentiful heraldic imagery and a website that gives the user a guided tour of European castles as well as band info, IRON CLAD are a 'Medieval' Metal band fronted by none other than the renowned figure of ANCIENT RITES vocalist Gunther Theys. The band is centred upon guitarist / keyboard player Sammy who, along with drummer Rony and bassist Luc, previously operated in the 1987 Metal band DEMONIAH.

Sammy and Rony regrouped in 1999 to forge IRON CLAD. Sammy would relocate to California but distance did not curtail the project, guitars and keyboards recorded in the USA were then flown over to Belgium for the 'Lost In A Dream' album to be completed. Released in April of 2002 by the Good Life Recordings group, 'Lost In A Dream' saw guest guitar contributions from They's ANCIENT RITES comrade Erik Sprooten as well as Bart from Black Metal band SUHRIM. Besides IRON CLAD and ANCIENT RITES Theys also holds down membership of DANSE MACABRE and LION'S PRIDE. Rony also joins Theys in LION'S PRIDE whilst bassist Luc is a member of VOICE OF GLORY. Sammy pursues a solo venture billed as CLAD IN SHADOWS.

Albums:
LOST IN A DREAM, Good Life Recordings (2002)
The Conqueror (Intro) / Last Crusade / Medieval Times / Middle Ages / Ruins (Memories Of The Past) / Travel Through The Night / On The Wings Of The Wind / Flemish Victory / Land Of Nod / Melancholy / Deadly Force / The Loss (Outro)

IRON FIRE (DENMARK)
Line-Up: Martin Steene (vocals), Martin Slott (guitar), Jakob Lykkebo (bass), Gunnar Olsen (drums)

Danish Power Metal band that evolved through covers acts MISERY and DECADES OF DARKNESS during 1995. The band led by vocalist Martin Steene first arrived with a line-up including guitarist Kristian H. Martinsen, bassist Steve Mason and drummer Thomas Mogensen. A 1998 demo secured a deal with the established German Heavy Metal haven Noise Records although IRON FIRE had undergone a radical line-up overhaul. The debut 'Thunderstorm' record found Steene in alliance with rhythm guitarist Kristian Iversen, bassist Jakob Lykkebo and drummer Gunnar Olsen.

Turbulent times witnessed the exit of Iversen in May 2000 and Olsen in the July of the same year. By the time of the Tommy Hansen produced sophomore outing 'On The Edge' both positions had been filled by PUSH's Martin Slott and PUSH / SATURNUS man Morten Plenge respectively. This line-up debuted at the Swedish Motola Metal Festival in November 2000.

However, Plenge was forced to bow out after recording having suffering a damaged arm. At first Lars Oestergard took the drum stool before Tommy Olsen of PANGEA stepped in. By August of 2001 Olsen too had decamped. Early 2002 witnessed the exit of bassist Jakob Lykkebo. Nevertheless the band recorded a full album length demo entitled 'The Underworld' in order to procure a new record deal. Ex-CORPUS MORTALE guitarist Soren Jensen would be welcomed into the ranks during July.

Albums:
THUNDERSTORM, Noise (2000)
The Final Crusade / When Heroes Fall / Rise Of The Rainbow / Metal Victory / Thunderstorm / Behind The Mirror / Warriors Of Steel / Battle Of Freedom / Glory To The King / Angel Of Light / Until The End / Riding Free
ON THE EDGE, Noise (2001)
Eternal Damnation / The End Of It All / Prince Of Agony / On The Edge / Into The Abyss / Thunderspirit / Wanted Man / Lost n' Alone / Forever Evil / Here And Alive / Miracle / The Price Of Blood

IRON MAIDEN (UK)
Line-Up: Bruce Dickinson (vocals), Adrian Smith (guitar), Dave Murray (guitar), Janick Gers (guitar), Steve Harris (bass), Nicko McBrain (drums)

Emanating from the mid '70s Punk ridden East End of London, IRON MAIDEN challenged the New Wave by delivering highly charged, no compromise Heavy Metal. Within a few short years IRON MAIDEN had eclipsed all others to gain the undisputed title of the biggest British Heavy Metal band, not only laying waste to the British charts on a regular basis but conquering North America too. IRON MAIDEN would reign unchallenged until an unwelcome change of front man in

the mid '90s but in recent years have bounced back in quite spectacular style.

Formed by bassist Steve Harris and taking their name from a spiked coffin torture device IRON MAIDEN underwent many personnel changes from their initial 1975 line-up. Harris started out as part of INFLUENCE, a band that soon adopted the title of GYPSY'S KISS in time for their debut gig in 1972 performed by the band line-up comprising vocalist Bob Verschoyle, guitarist Dave Smith, bassist Harris and drummer Paul Sears.

In the main, GYPSY'S KISS gigs were centred around the London pub circuit and the band featured many covers in their set from the likes of DEEP PURPLE and FREE.

After a handful of gigs Harris joined Boogie merchants SMILER - vocalist Dennis Wilcock, guitarists Mick and Tony Clee and drummer Doug Sampson. Harris departed in 1975 to form IRON MAIDEN roping in vocalist Paul Mario Day, guitarists Terry Rance and Dave Sullivan and drummer Ron 'Rebel' Matthews. Paul Mario Day was soon ousted in favour of ex-SMILER and WARLOCK vocalist Dennis Wilcock who added lurid stage theatrics, such as garish make-up and blood spurting to the act. Rance and Sullivan also lost their positions to guitarists Dave Murray (previously with EVIL WAY) and Bob 'Angelo' Sawyer. Mario Day later fronted MORE and the SWEET.

A matter of months passed before Sawyer was out. Murray's initial tenure was also short-lived as within six months he had joined URCHIN and IRON MAIDEN became a single guitar band, recruiting ex-HOOKER musician Terry Wapram and also keyboardist Tony Moor. However, Ron Matthews left, later turning up in TORMÉ for a live album in 1994 and much later in 1999 as part of ATOMIC ROOSTER.

In his stead came Barry Purkis. IRON MAIDEN's new drummer had a heritage with numerous acts dating back to INOMINE PATRIS in 1972 but this revised line-up only completed one gig.

With both Moore and Wapram leaving for pastures new, Dave Murray was enticed back from URCHIN, although the line-up ructions were far from over as Wilcock quit followed by Purkis. The latter adopted the stage name of THUNDERSTICK and joined Blues Rock orientated competitors SAMSON, whilst Wilcock united with ex-IRON MAIDEN guitarist Terry Wapram to form VI.

IRON MAIDEN was re-assembled during 1978 bringing in ex-SMILER drummer Doug Sampson and adding former BIRD OF PREY vocalist PAUL DIANNO for a stable group that throughout 1979 employed a variety of second guitarists. Included were Paul Cairns,

IRON MAIDEN
Photo : Dimo Safari

Paul Todd and Tony Parsons, although the main quartet were the men who cut the legendary 'Soundhouse Tapes' EP which sold well through mail order and at live gigs.

Live shows at this point included a debut headliner at London's Marquee club plus a valuable support to MOTÖRHEAD. Interest was such that IRON MAIDEN began what was to be a lengthy relationship with EMI Records when the band, with Parsons at this point, scored two tracks on the 1979 NWoBHM compilation album 'Metal For Muthas'.

EMI signed the band in December of 1979 following a further batch of sold out Marquee headliners, having by now enjoyed being

214

championed by 'Sounds' and London based Rock Club DJ Neil Kay. However, in early 1980 Parsons was asked to leave and in came Dennis Stratton. A further change came when Sampson left to be replaced by ex-SAMSON drummer Clive Burr.

Stratton pre-IRON MAIDEN had been involved with UNITED. This 1978 act, fronted by Stratton, featured the veteran Andy Pyle on bass, of THE KINKS, SAVOY BROWN, ALVIN LEE and JUICY LUCY, John Gosling on keyboards from THE KINKS and drummer Ron Berg of SAVOY BROWN. When Stratton quit to join IRON MAIDEN Pyle, Berg and Gosling stuck together to create NETWORK. Previous to UNITED Stratton was also playing the London clubs with REMUS DOWN BOULEVARD. The band included two live tracks on the 1978 album 'Live - A Week At The Bridge E16'.

IRON MAIDEN began their live action for the year by headlining the 'Metal For Muthas' tour, which comprised a bill featuring PRAYING MANTIS among others. Their 'Running Free' debut single charted and IRON MAIDEN entered the history books by becoming the first band to perform live on 'Top Of The Pops' since THE WHO in 1973.

In March 1980 IRON MAIDEN opened for JUDAS PRIEST's 'British Steel' UK tour. Opinion was divided as to whether IRON MAIDEN were merely JUDAS PRIEST copyists or bona fide contenders, both Dianno and Murray in particular seemingly emulating their counterparts (Rob Halford and KK Downing) in the headline band in their choice of stage gear. Dianno did not help matters by suggesting to the press they would blow the headliners off the stage with ease. However, enough fans were impressed to launch the debut IRON MAIDEN album, released in April, to number 4 in the British charts. American editions of the album came with an extra track 'Sanctuary'.

Flushed with success the band undertook a well attended 42 date headline British tour and IRON MAIDEN also put in a scorching performance at the annual 'Reading Rock Festival' headlined by UFO, before setting off on a tour of Europe opening for KISS.

With little knowledge of IRON MAIDEN's turbulent past, it came as something of a surprise to many fans when the announcement came that Dennis Stratton had quit upon the KISS tour's completion. He was replaced by ex-URCHIN and BROADWAY BRATS guitarist Adrian Smith, but it didn't stop the crowds from filling out a British headline tour and sending another single. In a rare excursion for the band they had covered 'Women In Uniform', a track from the legendary Australian band SKYHOOKS.

'Women In Uniform' was also the sole studio track on the Japanese import 'Live!! + One' EP, the three live tracks ('Sanctuary', 'Phantom Of The Opera' and 'Drifter') having been recorded at a London Marquee show in July 1980.

With second album 'Killers', issued in February 1981, IRON MAIDEN succeeded in grinding through a mammoth world tour, kicking off with a British headline tour supported by French veterans TRUST. Further dates that took most of the year included headline dates in Japan and an American tour supporting JUDAS PRIEST once more. Yet again, American editions came complete with an extra track in 'Twilight Zone'.

MAIDEN finished off their American tour by playing dates with WHITESNAKE, HUMBLE PIE and UFO and returned to Europe to perform festival dates alongside KANSAS, BLUE OYSTER CULT and MOTÖRHEAD. Needless to say, such incessant touring had made 'Killers' a gold album in Britain, France and Japan.

On the peak of success fans were rightly stunned when PAUL DIANNO announced he was quitting, apparently due to the strains of touring and rumours quickly began circulating as to the identity of his replacement. Indeed, word alleged that IRON MAIDEN had secretly been auditioning singers whilst on tour in the America!

Still, the smart money was on SAMSON vocalist Bruce 'Bruce' Dickinson and, indeed, the man was announced as IRON MAIDEN's new vocalist shortly after SAMSON appeared at the 'Reading Rock Festival'. BRUCE DICKINSON promptly made his live debut with IRON MAIDEN in Bologna during early 1982.

Dianno meantime created LONEWOLF then in quick succession DIANNO for a far mellower outing than fans really desired. The man would later toughen up considerably over the years with BATTLEZONE and KILLERS but would always remain reliant on IRON MAIDEN material.

IRON MAIDEN's third album, 'Number Of The Beast', released in March 1982 proved a milestone, breaking the band internationally and giving the band numerous hit singles, including their first top ten smash with 'Run To The Hills', in Britain. Due to contractual obligations with his previous management Dickinson was unable to officially assist in the song-writing.

Another British tour proved enormously successful, as did European dates with openers BLACKFOOT and, yet again, the band supported JUDAS PRIEST in America. Other supports included stints with the

SCORPIONS, .38 SPECIAL and RAINBOW. The world tour was rounded off by Australian and Japanese dates.

Prior to the recording of the group's fourth album, 1983's 'Piece Of Mind', drummer Clive Burr was replaced by former PAT TRAVERS and TRUST man Nicko McBrain. Ironically, after a brief spell with ALCATRAZ, Burr joined TRUST for a short-lived stay before forming the more melodically inclined STRATUS and PRAYING MANTIS. McBrain had earlier in his career been a member of AXE, an outfit that included now noted producer and CHARLIE guitarist Terry Thomas, and also appears on albums by STREETWALKER and STRETCH. Just prior to joining up with MAIDEN McBrain had been involved with INFORMER, a band comprising of erstwhile STALLION vocalist John Elstar, ex-SIDEWINDER / STALLION guitarist STUART SMITH and WHITESNAKE bassist Neil Murray.

Following the album's release IRON MAIDEN launched into the by now obligatory, mammoth world tour preceded by 'Piece Of Mind' entering the American Billboard charts at number 127. The American tour started off with support acts FASTWAY and SAXON with Canadians CONEY HATCH (a particular favourite of Steve Harris) later replacing SAXON. Later guests were QUIET RIOT.

In the latter part of 1983 the quintet travelled to Europe, where MICHAEL SCHENKER GROUP opened, before appearing at one of the biggest Heavy Metal festivals ever. A TV special in Dortmund as part of the 'Rock Pop' televised concert series, the awesome bill also included SCORPIONS, JUDAS PRIEST, KROKUS, DEF LEPPARD, OZZY OSBOURNE, QUIET RIOT and MICHAEL SCHENKER GROUP over two days.

IRON MAIDEN launched their brand new album, the Ancient Egyptian flavoured 'Powerslave' in 1984 and the ensuing world tour saw the quintet performing their first dates in Poland during the autumn of 1984. In 1985, the band performed a set of seven sold out shows at the prestigious New York Radio City Music Hall venue with support act QUEENSRYCHE. Further American supports were handled by W.A.S.P., TWISTED SISTER and Germans ACCEPT.

The 'World Slavery' tour caught IRON MAIDEN delivering the decibels to 26 countries over 200 shows and spawned a hit live video and album 'Live After Death'.

During 1986 the band were ready to try a

IRON MAIDEN
Photo : Ross Haflin

more creative approach and, after recording in the Bahamas, Amsterdam and New York, released the Sci-Fi inspired 'Somewhere In Time' album heavily tinged with keyboard guitar workouts. Although the album was an undoubted success the band have leaned towards the starker, stripped down Metal sounds of yore on successive albums, often recording at Harris's home studio.

IRON MAIDEN's 1988 album 'Seventh Son Of A Seventh Son' came the closest the band ever came to producing a full blown concept album. The band was well known for overblown epics, but this time the theme held together an entire album.

The inevitable world tour shied away from the systematic city by city tour schedule and IRON MAIDEN blitzed their way through America and Europe by hopping from one major festival to another. The schedule's highlight was IRON MAIDEN headlining the "Monsters Of Rock" festival above KISS (IRON MAIDEN being the only band KISS has ever agreed to play beneath since 1974!), DAVID LEE ROTH, MEGADETH, GUNS N' ROSES and HELLOWEEN to a record breaking crowd of over 100,000. Further dates in Europe led to an arena tour of Britain.

1989 proved a quiet year for the band but an extremely busy time for its individual members. Both Smith and Dickinson released solo albums. Predictably, BRUCE DICKINSON scored major chart success' with both his album, 'Tattooed Millionaire', and a batch of hit singles. Smith meanwhile found the going tough with his more AOR influenced project A.S.A.P.

IRON MAIDEN reassembled early in 1990 to record 'No Prayer For The Dying'. For the first time in seven years the band line-up changed, with Smith departing to concentrate on solo work. Ex-GILLAN and WHITE SPIRIT guitarist Janick Gers, who had toured with Dickinson as part of his solo band, soon landed the job.

Yet again the new album, debuting at number 2 in the British charts, paved the way for a mammoth global tour. Opening with a low key club gig at Milton Keynes the tour, a more stripped down back to basics affair, sped through America before it was brought to an unforeseen close by the eruption of the Gulf war making planned dates in Australia and Japan unfeasible.

During 1990 Murray toyed with the idea of creating a solo project with American guitarist Nancy Chandler. Songs credited to Murray would turn up on Chandler's 1993 album by the band CHEYENNE.

During 1990 Steve Harris paid homage to two of his influences by covering the STRAY track 'All In Your Mind' and GOLDEN EARRING's 'Kill Me Ce Soir' as the B side to the 'Holy Smoke' single. Christmas of that year saw IRON MAIDEN leap into the record books when their latest single, 'Bring Your Daughter To The Slaughter' became the first Heavy Metal song to go straight into the British singles charts at number 1. Unbelievably, Radio One refused to play list the single, much to the band's indignation!

The 'Fear Of The Dark' album heralded another change for the band as, for the first time, sleeve artist Derek Riggs was not used. In came noted sci-fi artist Melvyn Grant who lent the album cover a more up to date feel. Once more IRON MAIDEN reached the British number 1 position in the album charts. In mid 1991 IRON MAIDEN performed headlining dates in America with support act ANTHRAX and also headlined the Roskilde festival in Denmark appearing on a bill with WINGER, PRIMUS and THE ALMIGHTY.

Throughout the tour rumours flew of BRUCE DICKINSON's discontent within the band. The vocalist had been strenuously pursuing his solo career as well as his new found additional career as a novelist.

IRON MAIDEN performed their final gig with Dickinson at Pinewood Studios. This swan song performance was staged in front of an audience of lucky members of the band's fan club. This turned out to be no ordinary gig either, as magician Simon Drake, noted for his gory stunts, put paid to members of the band prior to the finale of Dickinson being ritually slain by Drake at the end of the televised show.

With BRUCE DICKINSON having embarked on the solo trail IRON MAIDEN fans faced uncertain times. Many rumours followed that HELLOWEEN vocalist MICHAEL KISKE had got the job and it was known that erstwhile LA PAZ, MIDNIGHT BLUE and PRAYING MANTIS singer Doogie White had been asked back to audition twice. In the end though, and much to fans amazement, IRON MAIDEN recruited ex-WOLFSBANE vocalist Blaze Bayley in 1994. However, recording for the band's tenth studio album was slightly delayed when Bayley seriously injured his knee in a motorbike accident. During this enforced lay-off Nicko McBrain took time out to gig with pub rockers the PHIL HILBORNE BAND during 1994.

Although IRON MAIDEN lost their deal with EMI in America during 1995 (although they remained signed to the London office) the new record, the first to feature Bayley, entitled 'The X Factor' was widely acknowledged as being a too radical step for many IRON MAIDEN fans to follow. Bayley's vocals came in for some vicious criticism and swathes of hardcore fans lost faith. Amidst the commotion, rather interestingly the 'Lord Of The Flies' single featured a cover of UFO's 'Doctor Doctor' as a B-side.

Still, IRON MAIDEN toured heavily throughout the end of 1995 including dates in such far flung places as Israel and South Africa, although a planned Beirut show was cancelled by the authorities who insisted the show was likely to incite riots.

IRON MAIDEN's British and European shows saw Doom Metal act MY DYING BRIDE supporting as Steve Harris and Co were also able to perform a full blown tour of the former Eastern Bloc territories, embracing Bulgaria, Slovenia, Hungary, Poland, Czech Republic and Rumania.

In early 1996 the group opted to play a one-off club show at Nottingham's Rock City venue, a date that saw PSYCHO MOTEL, the latest band featuring Adrian Smith, supporting.

A mammoth 'Best Of The Beast' compilation arrived in September of 1996, the most impressive variant being a gargantuan quadruple vinyl set complete with lavish gatefold artwork and a limited edition book. A single, 'Virus', would accompany the album, various B sides of which offered fans a chance to hear archive IRON MAIDEN recordings of 'Sanctuary' and 'Wrathchild' from the 'Metal For Muthas' compilation and 'Prowler' and 'Invasion' lifted from 'The Soundhouse Tapes'.

Throughout 1997 IRON MAIDEN kept a low profile as they worked on a brand new album for release in 1998, although Harris did announce plans for his own record label, Beast Records. Steve's first signings were DIRTY DEEDS, the London based group fronted by ex-CHARIOT main man Pete Franklin.

IRON MAIDEN set out on tour once again during 1998 although attendance-wise their star was definitely waning, the band's loyal audience drifting away in obvious dissatisfaction at Bayley's abilities. South American shows had the band playing to capacity arena crowds though but with the political situation between Chile and Britain aggravated by the General Pinochet affair IRON MAIDEN wisely pulled out of shows there, ANTHRAX taking their stead. Meanwhile BRUCE DICKINSON's album 'Chemical Wedding' and tour was going great guns.

By early 1999 press speculation and the wish of the band's fans to see the band back in the top league finally won the day as Bayley was ousted by a returning BRUCE DICKINSON. Adrian Smith also rejoined making IRON MAIDEN an unexpected if welcome three guitar assault!

Bayley would later make a return with his new Metal act BLAZE and the resulting 'Silicon Messiah' album still retaining management links with the Sanctuary stable.

The rejuvenated IRON MAIDEN wowed America with a sold out 17 date tour before taking on European venues. Meantime a whole slew of tribute albums arrived in the stores such as Swedish efforts 'Made In Tribute' and 'Maiden Scandinavia', the American Meteor City 'Slave To The Power' release as well as PAUL DIANNO cropping up on '666 The Number One Beast'.

The subsequent 'Brave New World' album (internet reports of an album title of 'Majesty Of Gaia' would be proved false) vindicated the return of Dickinson with a vengeance. IRON MAIDEN scored a number 3 album in Germany with the 'Wicker Man' single going top ten in Britain. The album would blaze a trail across the international charts landing at number 7 in their homeland, 39 in the USA and even scoring a number one in the Heavy Metal strongholds both Sweden and Greece. Generally, the European continent's national charts found 'Brave New World' inhabiting the upper reaches, a definitive renewal of fortunes.

A batch of European festival performances was cancelled when Gers sustained injuries after falling offstage in Mannheim. IRON MAIDEN were back in action touring America in the latter half of the year with strong support from Sanctuary label mates HALFORD and QUEENSRYCHE. Although back in demand and pulling strong crowds IRON MAIDEN's resurgence was marred by the stabbing of four fans at their Los Angeles Verizon wireless Amphitheatre gig.

Quite bizarrely news emerged in 2000 that one of IRON MAIDEN's earliest guitarists Tony Parsons had created an IRON MAIDEN tribute band named METALWORKS 2000 including ex-ALICE COOPER and THE ALMIGHTY guitarist Pete Friezin and ex-JUDAS PRIEST drummer Lez Binks! Another ex-MAIDEN man erstwhile, singer PAUL DIANNO, billed as PAUL DIANNO AND THE BEAST, would also fan the flames in early 2001 issuing a live album comprising entirely of IRON MAIDEN songs.

A more surreal addition to the family came with the emergence of Californian act IRON MAIDENS, a quite unique tribute band being the first all female homage to IRON MAIDEN. The act includes some highly respected players in their own right featuring the PHANTOM BLUE duo of guitarist Josephine and drummer Linda McDonald, PROZACT

PRINCESS singer Jenny, ex-BANDIT guitarist Sara and NEW EDEN bassist Melanie Sisneros (a.k.a. "Stephanie Harris"). IRON MAIDEN themselves would bounce back in the expected spectacular style with the mammoth 'Live At The Rock In Rio' album in March of 2002. The same month the band would announce two benefit shows at the Brixton Academy in London in aid of former drummer Clive Burr who had been diagnosed with multiple sclerosis. Demand was such the run was extended to three sold out nights and in a further move the band informed fans that all proceeds from the next single, 'Run To The Hills', would be devoted to the MS fund. The single proved to be eminently collectable in three formats boasting exclusive tracks on each including archive 1982 live tracks featuring Burr on drums. The DVD version of 'Rock In Rio' would top the UK music video charts on its first week of release. Later in the year IRON MAIDEN would pitch in further to aid the Clive Burr Trust auctioning off a mammoth selection of band rarities including a full Nicko McBrain drum kit, autographed guitars and even an Eddie stage prop from the 'No Prayer For The Dying' tour.

As BRUCE DICKINSON unveiled plans for a further solo album and his intention to master the art of flying large passenger aircraft rumours also surfaced that NICKO McBRAIN had recently united with erstwhile ANTHRAX guitarist Dan Spitz for an undisclosed band project. This revelation would come as unexpectedly as Spitz had been out of the Rock n' Roll limelight for many years, becoming a vocal Christian since his departure from the band and devoting himself to gaining qualifications in the art of watch making.

On September 7th a trio of IRON MAIDEN players - drummer Nicko McBrain, guitarist Janick Gers, and vocalist Bruce Dickinson - surprised DEEP PURPLE fans by joining the Rock veterans on stage during their London Hammersmith Apollo gig for a rendition of the classic 'Smoke On The Water'.

November proved of great importance to fans as the band launched the leviathan 3 CD box set 'Eddies Archives', a collection of rare live material issued through Columbia Records dating from 1979 tracks right through until the band's headline show at Castle Donington in 1988. Incorporated would be 'Friday Rock Show' sessions from 1979, material pulled from the Reading Festival in 1980 and 1982 plus a compilation of B sides. In keeping with tradition the whole affair was lavishly packaged coming clad in a limited edition silver Eddie embossed casket. Besides the music the collection added an Eddie head shot glass and a family tree on parchment scroll. A further album, 'Edward The Great', would be released in North America the same day as 'Eddie's Archives' on 4th November.

Singles/EPs:
Invasion / Iron Maiden / Prowler, Rock Hard ROK 1 (1978) ('The Soundhouse Tapes' EP)
Running Free / Burning Ambition, EMI 5032(1980) **34 UK**
Sanctuary / Drifter / I've Got The Fire (Live), EMI 5065 (1980) **29 UK**
Women In Uniform / Invasion / Phantom Of The Opera (Live), EMI 5105 (1980) **35 UK**
Sanctuary (Live) / Phantom Of The Opera (Live) / Drifter (Live) / Women In Uniform, EMI EMS-41001 (1980) ('Live!! + One' EP, Japanese release)
Twilight Zone / Wrathchild, EMI 5145 (1981) **31 UK**
Purgatory / Ghenghis Khan, EMI 5184 (1981) **52 UK**
Remember Tomorrow (Live) / Killers (Live) / Running Free (Live) / Innocent Exile (Live), EMI 5219 (1981) **43 UK** ('Maiden Japan EP')
Run To The Hills / Total Eclipse, EMI 5263 (1982) **7 UK**
The Number Of The Beast / Remember Tomorrow, EMI 5287 (1982) **18 UK**
Flight Of Icarus / I've Got The Fire, EMI 5378 (1983) **11 UK**
The Trooper / Crosseyed Mary, EMI 5397 (1983) **12 UK**
Two Minutes To Midnight / Rainbow's Gold / Mission From 'Arry, EMI 5849 (1984) **11 UK**
Aces High / King Of Twilight / The Number Of The Beast (Live), EMI 5502 (1984) **20 UK**
Running Free (Live) / Sanctuary (Live), EMI 5532 (1985) **19 UK**
Run To The Hills (Live) / Phantom Of The Opera (Live) / Losfer Words (The Big' Orra) (Live), EMI 5542 (1985) **26 UK**
Wasted Years / Reach Out / The Sheriff Of Huddersfield, EMI 5583(1986) **18 UK**
Stranger In A Strange Land / That Girl / Juanita, EMI 5589 (1986) **22 UK**
Can I Play With Madness / Black Bart Blues / Massacre, EMI EM 49 (1988) **3 UK**
The Evil That Men Do / Prowler '88 / Charlotte The Harlot '88, EMI EM64 (1988) **5 UK**
The Clairvoyant (Live) / The Prisoner (Live) / Heaven Can Wait (Live), EMI EM 79 (1988) **6 UK**
Infinite Dreams (Live) / Killers (Live) / Still Life (Live), EMI EM 117(1989) **6 UK**
Running Free / Burning Ambition / Sanctuary / Drifter (Live) / I've Got The Fire (Live) / Listen With Nicko (Part One), EMI (1990) **10 UK**
Women in Uniform/ Invasion/ Phantom Of

The Opera / Twilight Zone / Wrathchild / Listen With Nicko (Part Two), EMI (1990) **10 UK**
Purgatory / Genghis Khan / Running Free / Remember Tomorrow / Killers / Innocent Exile / Listen With Nicko (Part Three), EMI (1990) **5 UK**
Run To The Hills / Total Eclipse / The Number Of The Beast / Remember Tomorrow (Live) Listen With Nicko (Part Four), EMI (1990) **3 UK**
Flight Of Icarus / I've Got The Fire / The Trooper / Cross Eyed Mary / Listen With Nicko (Part Five), EMI (1990) **7 UK**
Two Minutes To Midnight / Rainbow's Gold / Mission From 'Arry / Aces High / Kings Of Twilight / The Number Of The Beast (Live) / Listen With Nicko (Part Six), EMI (1990) **11 UK**
Running Free / Murders In The Rue Morgue / Run To The Hills / Phantom Of The Opera / Losfer Words (The Big' Orra) / Listen With Nicko (Part Seven), EMI (1990) **9 UK** Wasted Years / Reach Out/ The Sheriff Of Huddersfield / Stranger In A Strange Land / That Girl / Juanita / Listen With Nicko (Part Eight), EMI (1990) **9 UK**
Can I Play With Madness / Black Bart Blues / Massacre / The Evil That Men Do / Prowler '88 / Charlotte The Harlot '88 / Listen With Nicko (Part Nine), EMI (1990) **12 SWEDEN, 10 UK**
The Clairvoyant (Live) / The Prisoner (Live) / Heaven Can Wait (Live) / Infinite Dreams (Live) / Killers (Live) / Still Life (Live) / Listen With Nicko (Part Ten), EMI (1990) **11 UK**
Holy Smoke / All In Your Mind / Kill Me Ce Soir, EMI EM 153 (1990) **3 UK**
Bring your Daughter To The Slaughter / I'm A Mover / Communication Breakdown, EMI (1991) **1 UK**
Be Quick Or Be Dead / Nodding Donkey Blues / Space Station No 5, EMI (1992) **15 SWEDEN, 2 UK**
From Here To Eternity / Roll Over Vic Vella / No Prayer For The Dying, EMI 8 80132 2 (1992) **21 UK**
Fear Of The Dark (Live) / Hooks In You (Live), EMI EMPD 263 (1993) (7" picture disc)
Fear Of The Dark (Live) / Hooks In You (Live) / Bring Your Daughter To The Slaughter (Live), EMI CD EMS 263 (1993) (CD single)
Fear Of The Dark (Live) / Be Quick Or Be Dead (Live) / Hooks In You (Live), EMI 7243 8 80501 2 8 (1993) (CD single)
Hallowed Be Thy Name (Live) / Wrathchild (Live) EMI EMP 288 (1993) **9 UK**
Hallowed Be Thy Name (Live) / Wrathchild (Live) / The Trooper (Live) / Wasted Years (Live), EMI EMI 12 EMP 288 (1993) (12"

single)
Man On The Edge / The Edge Of Darkness / I Live My Way, EMI (1995) **10 UK**
Man On The Edge / The Edge Of Forever / Judgement Day / Blaze Bailey Interview Part I, EMI (1995)
Man On The Edge / The Edge Of Darkness / Justice Of The Peace / Blaze Bailey Interview Part II, EMI CDEM398 (1995)
Man On The Edge / The Edge Of Darkness / Justice Of The Peace / Judgement Day, EMI 7243 8 82425 2 3 (1995)
Lord Of The Flies / My Generation / Doctor, Doctor, EMI (1996)
Virus / My Generation / Doctor, Doctor, EMI 7243 8 83222 2 5 (1996) **16 UK**
Virus / Sanctuary / Wrathchild, EMI 7243 8 8 3172 2 1 (1996) (German release)
The Angel And The Gambler / The Aftermath (Live) / Man On The Edge (Video), EMI (1998) **18 UK**
The Angel And The Gambler / Blood On The World's Hands (Live) / Afraid To Shoot Strangers (Video), EMI (UK)
The Wicker Man, EMI (2000) **38 GERMANY, 9 UK**
Futureal / The Evil That Men Do (Live) / Man On The Edge (Live) / The Angel & The Gambler (Video), EMI (1998)
Out Of The Silent Planet / Aces High (Live), EMI (2000) (7" single) **66 GERMANY**
Out Of The Silent Planet / Wasted Years (Live) / Aces High (Live), EMI (2000) (12" picture disc)
Out Of The Silent Planet / Wasted Years (Live) / Aces High (Live) / Out Of The Silent Planet (Video), EMI (2000) (CD single)
Iron Maiden / The Number Of The Beast / Hallowed Be Thy Name / Sanctuary / Run To The Hills, EMI IMRIODJ01 (2001) ('Rock In Rio' promotion release)
Run To The Hills (Live 2001) / Children Of The Damned (Live 1982) / Total Eclipse (Live 1982) / Run To The Hills (Live 2001 video), EMI (2002) (CD single) **86 GERMANY**
Run To The Hills (Studio version) / 22 Acacia Avenue (Live 1982) / The Prisoner (Live 1982) / Run To The Hills (Video: Camp Chaos version), EMI (2002) (CD single)
Run To The Hills (Original single version) / Total Eclipse (Album version), EMI (2002) (7" red vinyl)

Albums:
IRON MAIDEN, EMI EMC 3330 (1980) **36 SWEDEN, 4 UK**
Prowler / Remember Tomorrow / Running Free / Phantom Of The Opera / Transylvania / Strange World / Charlotte The Harlot / Iron Maiden
KILLERS, EMI EMC 3357 (1981) **11 SWEDEN, 12 UK, 78 USA**

The Ides Of March / Wrathchild / Murders In The Rue Morgue / Another Life / Genghis Khan / Innocent Exile / Killers / Prodigal Son / Purgatory / Drifter

NUMBER OF THE BEAST, EMI EMC 3400 (1982) **7 SWEDEN, 1 UK, 33 USA**
Invaders / Children Of The Damned / The Prisoner / 22 Acacia Avenue / The Number Of The Beast / Run To The Hills / Gangland / Hallowed Be Thy Name

PIECE OF MIND, EMI EMA 800 (1983) **6 SWEDEN, 3 UK, 14 USA**
Where Eagles Dare / Revelations / Flight Of Icarus / Die With Your Boots On / The Trooper / Still Life / Quest For Fire / Sun And Steel / To Tame A Land

POWERSLAVE, EMI POWER 1 (1984) **5 SWEDEN, 2 UK, 21 USA**
Losfer Words / Aces High / Powerslave / Back In The Village / Rime Of The Ancient Mariner / Two Minutes To Midnight / Flash Of The Blade / The Duellists

LIVE AFTER DEATH (LIVE), EMI RIP 1 (1985) **8 SWEDEN, 2 UK, 19 USA**
Aces High / 2 Minutes To Midnight / The Trooper / Revelations / Flight Of Icarus / Rime Of The Ancient Mariner / Powerslave / The Number Of The Beast / Hallowed Be Thy Name / Iron Maiden / Run To The Hills / Running Free

SOMEWHERE IN TIME, EMI EMC 3512 (1986) **6 SWEDEN, 3 UK, 11 USA**
Caught Somewhere In Time / Wasted Years / Sea Of Madness / Heaven Can Wait / The Loneliness Of The Long Distance Runner / Stranger In A Strange Land / Deja-Vu / Alexander The Great

SEVENTH SON OF A SEVENTH SON, EMI EMD 1006 (1988) **3 SWEDEN, 1 UK, 12 USA**
Moonchild / Infinite Dreams / Can I Play With Madness / The Evil That Men Do / Seventh Son Of A Seventh Son / The Prophecy / The Clairvoyant / Only The Good Die Young

NO PRAYER FOR THE DYING, EMI EMD 1017 (1990) **17 NEW ZEALAND, 6 SWEDEN, 2 UK, 17 USA**
Tail Gunner / Holy Smoke / No Prayer For The Dying / Public Enemy Number One / Fates Warning / The Assassin / Run Silent Run Deep / Hooks In You / Bring Your Daughter... To The Slaughter / Mother Russia

FEAR OF THE DARK, EMI EMD1032 (1992) **44 NEW ZEALAND, 8 SWEDEN, 1 UK, 12 USA**
Be Quick Or Be Dead / From Here To Eternity / Afraid To Shoot Strangers / Fear Is The Key / Childhood's End / Wasting Love / The Fugitive / Chains Of Misery / The Apparition / Judas Be My Guide / Weekend Warrior / Fear Of The Dark

A REAL LIVE ONE (LIVE), EMI (1993)

30 SWEDEN, 3 UK
Be Quick Or Be Dead / From Here To Eternity / Can I Play With Madness / Wasting Love / Tailgunner / The Evil That Men Do / Afraid To Shoot Strangers / Bring Your Daughter To The Slaughter / Heaven Can Wait / The Clairvoyant / Fear Of The Dark

A REAL DEAD ONE (LIVE), EMI EMD 1048 (1993) **12 UK**
The Number Of The Beast / The Trooper / Prowler / Transylvania / Remember Tomorrow / Where Eagles Dare / Sanctuary / Running Free / Two Minutes To Midnight / Iron Maiden / Hallowed Be Thy Name

LIVE AT DONINGTON 1992, EMI CD DON 1 (1993) **23 UK**
Be Quick Or Be Dead / The Number Of The Beast / Wrathchild / From Here To Eternity / Can I Play With Madness / Wasting Love / Tailgunner / The Evil That Men Do / Afraid To Shoot Strangers

THE X FACTOR, EMI 7243 8 35819 2 4 (1995) **9 UK**
Sign Of The Cross / Lord Of The Flies / Man On The Edge / Fortunes Of War / Look For The Truth / The Aftermath / Judgement Of Heaven / Blood On The World's Hands / The Edge Of Darkness / 2 A.M. / The Unbeliever

BEST OF THE BEAST, EMI 7243 8 53184 2 9 (1996) **37 NEW ZEALAND, 16 UK**
The Number Of The Beast / Can I Play With Madness / Fear Of The Dark (Live) / Run To The Hills / Bring Your Daughter To The Slaughter / The Evil That Men Do / Aces High / Be Quick Or Be Dead / Two Minutes To Midnight / Man On The Edge / Virus / Running Free (Live) / Wasted Years / The Clairvoyant / The Trooper / Hallowed Be Thy Name

BEST OF THE BEAST, EMI 7243 8 53185 1 1 (1996) (Vinyl edition)
Virus / Sign Of The Cross / Afraid To Shoot Strangers (Live) / Man On The Edge / Be Quick Or Be Dead / Fear Of The Dark (Live) / Holy Smoke / Bring Your Daughter To The Slaughter / Seventh Son Of A Seventh Son / Can I Play With Madness / The Evil That Men Do / The Clairvoyant / Heaven Can Wait / Wasted Years / Two Minutes To Midnight / Running Free (Live) / Rime Of The Ancient Mariner (Live) / Aces High / Where Eagles Dare / The Trooper / The Number Of The Beast / Revelations (Live) / The Prisoner / Run To The Hills / Hallowed Be Thy Name / Wrathchild / Killers / Remember Tomorrow / Phantom Of The Opera / Sanctuary / Prowler / Invasion / Strange World / Iron Maiden

VIRTUAL XI, EMI 7243 4 93915 2 9 (1998) **12 FRANCE, 16 SWEDEN, 16 UK**
Futureal / The Angel And The Gambler / Lightning Strikes Twice / The Clansman /

When Two Worlds Collide / The Educated Fool / Don't Look To The Eyes Of A Stranger / Como Estais Amigos
BRAVE NEW WORLD, EMI 7243 5 26605 2 0 (2000) **10 AUSTRIA, 13 CANADA, 2 FINLAND, 3 FRANCE, 3 GERMANY, 1 GREECE, 16 HOLLAND, 5 ITALY, 5 JAPAN, 4 NORWAY, 6 SPAIN, 1 SWEDEN, 9 SWITZERLAND, 7 UK, 39 USA**
The Wicker Man / Ghost Of The Navigator / Brave New World / Blood Brothers / The Mercenary / Dream Of Mirrors / The Fallen Angel / The Nomad / Out Of The Silent Planet / The Thin Line Between Love And Hate
LIVE AT DONINGTON AUGUST 22ND 1992, Sanctuary C2K86048 (2002) (USA release)
Be Quick Or Be Dead / The Number Of The Beast / Wrathchild / From Here To Eternity / Can I Play With Madness / Wasting Love / Tailgunner / The Evil That Men Do / Afraid To Shoot Strangers / Fear Of The Dark / Bring Your Daughter To The Slaughter / The Clairvoyant / Heaven Can Wait / Run To The Hills / 2 Minutes To Midnight / Iron Maiden / Hallowed Be Thy Name / The Trooper / Sanctuary / Running Free
ROCK IN RIO, EMI (2002) **28 BELGIUM, 56 CANADA, 8 FINLAND, 25 FRANCE, 14 SWEDEN, 186 USA**
The Wicker Man / Ghost Of The Navigator / Brave New World / Wrathchild / 2 Minutes To Midnight / Blood Brothers / Sign Of The Cross / The Mercenary / The Trooper / Dream Of Mirrors / The Clansman / The Evil That Men Do / Fear Of The Dark / Iron Maiden / Number Of The Beast / Hallowed Be Thy Name / Sanctuary / Run To The Hills
EDDIE'S ARCHIVES, Columbia (2002)
Iron Maiden (Friday Rock Show session) / Running Free (Friday Rock Show session) / Transylvania (Friday Rock Show session) / Sanctuary (Friday Rock Show session) / Wrathchild (Live) / Run To The Hills (Live) / Children Of The Damned (Live) / The Number of The Beast (Live) / 22 Acacia Avenue (Live) / Transylvania (Live) / The Prisoner (Live) / Hallowed Be Thy Name (Live) / Phantom Of The Opera (Live) / Iron Maiden (Live) / Prowler (Live) / Remember Tomorrow (live) / Killers (Live) / Running Free (Live) / Transylvania (Live) / Iron Maiden (Live) / Moonchild (Live) / Wrathchild (Live) / Infinite Dreams (Live) / The Trooper (Live) / Seventh Son Of A Seventh Son (Live) / The Number Of The Beast (Live) / Hallowed Be Thy Name (Live) / Iron Maiden (Live) / Murders In The Rue Morgue (Live) / Wrathchild (Live) / Run To The Hills (Live) / Children Of The Damned (Live) / The

Number Of The Beast (Live) / Another Life (Live) / Killers (Live) / 22 Acacia Avenue (Live) / Total Eclipse (Live) / Transylvania (Live) / The Prisoner (Live) / Hallowed Be Thy Name (Live) / Phantom Of The Opera (Live) / Iron Maiden (Live) / Sanctuary (Live) / Drifter (Live) / Running Free (Live) / Prowler (Live) / Burning Ambition / Drifter (Live) / Invasion / Remember Tomorrow (Live) / I've Got The Fire / Cross-Eyed Mary / Rainbow's Gold / King Of Twilight / Reach Out / That Girl / Juanita / The Sheriff Of Huddersfield / Black Bart Blues / Prowler '88 / Charlotte The Harlot '88 / All In Your Mind / Kill Me Ce Soir / I'm A Mover / Communication Breakdown / Nodding Donkey Blues / Space Station No.5 / I Can't See My Feelings / Roll Over Vic Vella / Justice of The Peace / Judgement Day / My Generation / Doctor Doctor / Blood On The Worlds Hands (Live) / The Aftermath (Live) / Futureal (Live) / Wasted Years '99 (Live)
EDWARD THE GREAT, Columbia (2002)
Run To The Hills / The Number Of The Beast / Flight Of Icarus / The Trooper / 2 Minutes To Midnight / Wasted Years / Can I Play With Madness / The Evil That Men Do / The Clairvoyant / Infinite Dreams / Holy Smoke / Bring Your Daughter… To The Slaughter / Man On The Edge / Futureal / The Wicker Man / Fear Of The Dark (Live)

IRON SAVIOR (GERMANY)
Line-Up: Piet Sielck (vocals / guitar), Kai Hansen (guitar), Jan S. Eckert (bass), Thomen Stauch (drums)

IRON SAVIOR was a throwback to one of guitarist and German national Heavy Metal hero Kai Hansen's pre-HELLOWEEN / GAMMA RAY acts. Hansen resurrected IRON SAVIOR as his project band in the late '90s. The band can be traced back as far as vocalist Piet Sielck and guitarist Kai Hansen's school act GENTRY. This act was to win a school competition with a combination of original songs and covers from URIAH HEEP, LED ZEPPELIN and BLACK SABBATH. A demo was recorded before the addition of drummer Ingo Schwichtenberg and guitarist Markus Großkopf as a name change ensued to SECOND HELL. Tracks written during this period such as 'Gorgon', 'Phantoms Of Death', 'Murder' and 'Victim Of Fate' would later come to attention on the debut HELLOWEEN album. This period also saw the birth of the latter day GAMMA RAY track 'Heading For Tomorrow'.
Sielck left the band a year before SECOND HELL morphed into HELLOWEEN. Sielck's path would cross Hansen's some three years later and the former front man would end up

engineering the debut GAMMA RAY album. Sielck would also earn production credits with BLIND GUARDIAN, DOMAIN, SAXON, URIAH HEEP and GRAVE DIGGER. Having also written songs during this hectic schedule Sielck reunited with Hansen to forge IRON SAVIOR in January of 1997. The project was widely regarded in Germany as Hansen's more light-hearted method of letting off steam. A curious appraisal bearing in mind the popular guitarist's irrepressible grin during most GAMMA RAY performances. The debut eponymous album sees a cover of 'This Flight Tonight', a track made popular by NAZARETH.

IRON SAVIOR's 1998 German tour, with GAMMA RAY's Dan Zimmermann on drums, saw EDGUY as support act. In spite of being kick-started as a fun project IRON SAVIOR soon found themselves not only in possession of increasing album sales but a loyal fan base to boot. The 1999 'Interlude' mini album, which saw erstwhile GAMMA RAY and ANESTHESIA man Thomas Nack handling drum duties, sees a collection of live tracks including a cover of JUDAS PRIEST's 'Desert Plains'.

IRON SAVIOR supported RUNNING WILD on their 2000 tour of Germany. The late 2000 single release 'I've Been To Hell' included cover versions of JUDAS PRIEST's 'Hellion-Electric Eye' and the KROKUS track 'Headhunter'.

In 2001 the band announced that Hansen was to leave the ranks due to constant timing clashes with GAMMA RAY. The two parties separated as friends after a headline European tour supported by LABYRINTH and NOCTURNAL RITES. Bassist Jan S. Eckert would join the MASTERPLAN post HELLOWEEN endeavour of guitarist ROLAND GRAPOW and drummer Uli Kusch during 2002. Meantime Piet Sielck found space to produce the 'Against The World' debut from Italian Power Metal act AIRBORN. The band's 2002 album 'Condition Red' would once more bear witness to IRON SAVIOR's reverence of JUDAS PRIEST, Japanese editions featuring the bonus cover version 'Living After Midnight'. Drummer Thomas Nack injured his hand just upfront of the group's appearance at the 'Wacken Open Air' festival. IRON SAVIOR persevered, pulling in former HELLOWEEN and current MASTERPLAN drummer Uli Kusch as substitute for the show. Projected German dates would be pushed back in order to accommodate Nack's recuperation.

Singles/EPs:
I've Been To Hell / Never Say Die / Hellion-Electric Eye / Headhunter, Noise N0339-3 (2000)

Albums:
IRON SAVIOR, Noise N0286-2 (1997)
The Arrival / Atlantis Rising / Brave New World / Iron Savior / Riding On Fire / Break It Up / Assailant / Children Of The Wasteland

/ Protect The Law / Watcher In The Sky / For The World / This Flight Tonight
UNIFICATION, Noise (1998)
Coming Home / Starborn / Deadly Sleep / Forces Of Rage / Captain's Log / Brothers (Of The Past) / Eye To Eye / Mind Over Matter / Prisoner Of The Void / The Battle / Unchained / Forevermore 13. Gorgar ('98 version) / Neon Knights / Dragonslayer
INTERLUDE, Noise N0316-2 (1999)
Iron Savior / Brave New World / Watcher In The Sky / Riding On Fire / For The World / Contortions Of Time / Touching The Rainbow / Stonecold / The Hatchet Of War / Desert Plains
DARK ASSAULT, JVC Victor VICP-61248 (2001)
Never Say Die / Seek And Destroy / Solar Wings / I've Been To Hell / Dragons Rising / Predators / Made Of Metal / Firing The Guns / Eye Of The World / Back Into The Light / After The War / Delivering The Goods / Headhunter / The Hellion / Electric Eye
CONDITION RED, Noise (2002)
Titans Of Our Time / Protector / Ironbound / Condition Red / Warrior / Mindfeeder / Walls Of Fire / Tales Of The Bold / I Will Be There / No Heroes / Paradise / Thunderbird / Crazy

ISENGARD (SWEDEN)

Line-Up: Tony Ulvan (vocals), Ronnie Andréson (guitar), Janne Tillman (bass), Uffe Tillmann (drums)

Linköping Heavy Metal act created by the Tillman brothers rhythm section of bassist Janne (a.k.a. 'The Goat') and drummer Uffe. Janne Tillman had previous experience with DESIRE and ETERNITY'S END. The siblings created ISENGARD in the November of 1988 with vocalist / guitarist Ronnie Andréson joining during October 1991. The trio added lead vocalist Anders Gustavsson in May of 1992 for recording of a four track demo. However, Gustavsson bowed out before long and Andréson duly took over lead vocal chores.
The following year ISENGARD signed to the Danish Bums label, recording an album 'Feel No Fear'. This momentum was lost though as Bums went out of business before the record could be launched. 'Feel No Fear' finally surfaced in August of 1994.
ISENGARD pulled in singer Tony 'Odin' Ulvan for further demos and the recording of a track 'The Losing Of A Lost Paradise' for a compilation album. Unfortunately Uffe Tillman was suffering from an injury at the time so the song was laid down with the aid of a drum machine. The band's next move was to self-finance a sophomore full length album 'Enter The Dragon Empire'. The Japanese Super

Stop label issued this effort in the Far East in August of 1996.
A further contribution to a compilation found ISENGARD enlisting the services of vocalist Tommy Adolfsson from AC/DC covers band SLEAZY DC for the track 'The Tale Of The Dying Mermaid'. This song was delivered for the 1997 collection dubbed 'Environmental'.
ISENGARD's line-up for the September 2001 album 'Crownless Majesty', produced by Ragne Wahlquist of HEAVY LOAD fame, stood at Linus Melchoirsen on vocals, Ronnie Andréson on guitar, Janne Tillman on bass and drummer Uffe Tillman. Melchoirsen had joined the act in February of 1998, debuting with two tracks 'Praise The Lord' and a remake of 'Guardians (The King Will Return)' for a Loud n' Proud records compilation.

Singles/EPs:
Under The Dragons Wing / Mirror Of Sadness / The Cold Dream / Final Journey, Isengard ISENCD001 (1994) ('Under The Dragons Wing' EP)

Albums:
FEEL NO FEAR, Eurisko Music Production 49123 (1994)
Never Feel No Fear / Fire Of Isengard / ConvoStrings / Atomic Winter / Monastery / Prophecies Foretold / Darkages / Winds Of Odin / They Here / Human Race / Methylmist / Forest Of Illusion / Syrensong / Guardians (The King Will Return) / X-Factor / Caught By Fire
ENTER THE DRAGON EMPIRE, Soundshills (1996)
Mirror Of Sadness / Under The Dragons Wing / Within Her Heart / Perish In Flames / Forest Of Illusion / The Cold Dream / Never Feel No Fear / Final Journey
CROWNLESS MAJESTY, Hemisphere Entertainment (2001)
Dreamland / Coming Home / The Winds Of War / Stormcrow / Dragon Empire / Shadows Of Light / The Crownless Majesty / Armour Of Gods / Poltava / Eye Of The Storm

ISHTAR (SPAIN)

Line-Up: Vicente Amores (vocals), Juan Parreno (guitar), Laure Garijo (guitar), Susana Baixauli (bass), Iván Usen Ruiz López (keyboards), Juan Antonio Aroca (drums)

Singles/EPs:
Resurgir / La Profecía / Mago O Diós / El Túnel / Fantasias Y Leyendas, Ole (2001) ('Al Final Del Camino' EP)

IS PAIN (SPAIN)

Line-Up: Daniel Garcia (vocals), Paco Agra (guitar), Eduardo Martin (bass), Ismael Luengo (keyboards), Eduardo (drums)

Melodic Metal act IS PAIN's profile on the international market would benefit from having Timo Tolkki of STRATOVARIUS handling the final mix of their debut '1999' album.

Albums:
1999, Goldtrack (1999)
The Shadow / Space Happiness / Two Days In Paradise / Moving Over / Mind Escape / An Angel For Me / Blowing Down (Your Beggar Mind) / Realise / Not From God / The Pain Is Killing Me

IVANHOE (GERMANY)

Line-Up: Andreas B. Franck (vocals), Chuck Schuler (guitar), Giovanni Soulas (bass), Markus Britsch (keyboards), Lars Hörnig (drums)

Stuttgart based Progressive Metal act IVANHOE were formed by the triumvirate of Giovanni Soulas, Markus Britsch and Lars Hörnig. The band first came to prominence with their 1989 demo 'Written In Stone', although they had debuted with the earlier tape 'Behind The Walls' (with original guitarist Achim Welsch replaced later by Thomas Kovac).

For a short period of time the female vocalist Conny Ernst, ex-BATTLEFIELD, fronted the band, but 'Written In Stone' debuted American vocalist Scott Anderson. However, the front man opted to return to America, despite the good reviews the demo elicited from the Metal press, so Ralf Küchle was recruited to record a CD single entitled 'Play Express'.

Almost comically, Küchle was also to defect to America, forming MATRIX in Los Angeles, thus ex-WHISPER singer Andy B. Franck was enlisted.

Further line-up changes occurred when, in 1993, Kovac departed and in came Chuck Schuler. The band promptly recorded 'Rebellion And Indecision' for the 'Peace Eater' compilation and, in 1994, finally cut their debut album on WMMS.

IVANHOE would tour throughout Europe opening for ENCHANT and JADIS before recording the second album and touring with VANDEN PLAS.

In December 1995 Schuler quit and the following March Achim Welsch was welcomed back into the ranks to tour with NEVERMORE and ICED EARTH.

IVANHOE went on to record a third album,

'Polarised', and toured with SKYCLAD and VANDEN PLAS. However, by the late '90s disputes arose as to the ownership of the band name and Franck struck out on his own to issue the SYMPHORCE album 'Truth To Promises' in 1999. Continuing this association Franck would also enrol as front man for noted Metal act BRAINSTORM, managing to conduct both acts in parallel.

Soulas and Welsch created CHARISMA to issue the 1999 album 'Karma'.

Albums:
VISIONS AND REALITY, Music Is Intelligence WMMS 050 (1994)
Visions... / Deeper Ground / Left Alone / Fallen Reasons / Miracles Of A Master's Child / Eternal Light / Written In Stone / Wait / Into The Realm Of The Unknown / Rebellion And Indecision / ... And Reality
SYMBOLS OF TIME, Music Is Intelligence WMMS 100 (1995)
Symbols Of Time / Wide Open / By A Feeling / Raining Tears / Vibrations / Irrigate Poisoning / Through The Lies / Silent Ceremony
POLARISED, Music Is Intelligence WMMS 150 (1997)
Loneliest / Souls Of Fire / Hollow / Sunlight / Wasted Time / Glass On Skin / Suppression Of A Different Kind / Whipping The Flies / When I'm Old

IVORY KNIGHT (CANADA)

Line-Up: John Devadsan Perinbam (vocals / keyboards), Rob Gravelle (guitar), Steve Mercier (bass), George Nesrallah (drums)

Ottawa's IVORY KNIGHT, established by vocalist John Devadsan Perinbam, guitarist Joe Nesrallah and erstwhile ANNIHILATOR drummer Paul Malek, can trace their history back to the late '80s. Besides his activities with IVORY KNIGHT Perinbam had been involved with TROJAN HAMMER and THE JEFF WATERS PROJECT, both of course featuring ANNIHILATOR» guitarist Jeff Waters. The original version of IVORY KNIGHT issued a well received demo session 'Voices In Your Nightmare'.

A second tape, 'Breaking The Ice', would feature new man on bass Ian Halman, although Perinbam felt dissatisfied with the recordings and the demo remained shelved. IVORY KNIGHT splintered but would regroup under the handle SUDDEN THUNDER. In this incarnation the band, now with Sandor de Bretan on guitar, pursued a less Metallic direction. SUDDEN THUNDER issued a CD but Melek then made his exit to be replaced by Dushan Horvat. Nasrallah too had made a break, Rob Gravelle taking his place. Besides SUDDEN THUNDER, Perinbam also found time to operate other acts TALESPYN and THE BROKE BROTHERS and, as singer and later bassist, the eclectic DR. SQUISH.

In 1999 Perinbam resurrected the IVORY KNIGHT name along with a fresh line-up of SUDDEN THUNDER and DR. SQUISH guitarist Rob Gravelle, bass player Steve Mercier and drummer George Nesrallah. The latter cited credits with diverse acts such as KOMODO, NIHILITY, BIO_ENCRYPT, FOETUS AFTERMATH and VIZIGOTH. This unit recorded the self-financed album 'Up From The Ashes', released in May of 2001.

Albums:

UP FROM THE ASHES, Ivory Knight (2001)
Initiation / Into The Black / Yesman / Perfect 10 / Roads To Glory / Picture Of Innocence / Last Dance / Shattered Glass / True Signs Of Life

IVORY TOWER (GERMANY)

Line-Up: Andre Fischer (vocals), Sven Böge (guitar), Stephan Laschetzki (bass), Stephan Machon (keyboards), Thorsten Thrunke (drums)

IVORY TOWER

Progressive Power Metal band borne out of a former act AX N' SEX, having released the 'Victim Of Time' album during 1996. Erstwhile AX N' SEX personnel vocalist Andre Fischer, guitarist Sven Böge and drummer Thorsten Thrunke decided on a more technical Metal approach thus founding IVORY TOWER. New recruits into the fold for the debut 1998 album 'Ivory Tower', issued by Limb Music Productions, would be bassist Stephan Laschetzki and keyboard player Stephan Machon.

Peter Werner was inducted on keyboards following April 2000's 'Beyond The Stars' opus.

Albums:

IVORY TOWER, Limb Music Productions (1998)
One Life In Asia / A Distant Light / Alive / Spring / She / Music / Blinded
BEYOND THE STARS, (2000)
Silence / Secret In Me / Foreboding / Game Of Life / Peeping Tom / Beyond The Stars / When Thoughts Are Running Wild / Flight Into The Self / Treehouse Theme / Treehouse

JACOB'S DREAM
(Columbus, OH, USA)
Line-Up: David Taylor (vocals),
Jon Noble (guitar), Gary
Holtzman (guitar), James
Evans (bass), Steve Vaughn
(drums)

A Columbus, Ohio technical Power Metal
band known in a previous incarnation as
IRON ANGEL. The band formed in 1994
switching titles to JACOB'S DREAM in 1996
for a well received eponymous demo. The
band at this juncture comprised vocalist David
Taylor, guitarists Jon Noble and John Berry,
bass player Patrik Depappe, keyboard player
Paul Whitt and drummer Gary Holtzman.
These sessions soon secured a deal with
Metal Blade Records.

JACOB'S DREAM's first commercial outing
would witness a revised line-up with
Holtzman switching from drums to guitar,
flanking Berry alongside a fresh rhythm
section of bassist James Evans and drummer
Rick May. The album would see MAGNITUDE
9's Rob Johnson as studio guest on lead
guitar. Promotion for the album included
appearances at two prestigious German
Metal festivals, 'Bang Your Head' and 'Wacken
Open Air', as well as a showing at the

Baltimore 'Powermad' festival all in August.
The band returned to Europe for a full blown
tour third on the billing to ARMORED SAINT
and BRAINSTORM.

As 2001 broke both guitarists Jon Noble and
Gary Holtzman announced their departure. In
March JACOB'S DREAM filled the gap with
Derek 'D-Rock' Eddleblute, a veteran of
ROUGH CUT, DRIVING FORCE, FRENZY
and GROUND ZERO.

Following the release of the Metal Blade
'Theater Of War' album JACOB'S DREAM hit
a further period of ongoing line-up turbulence.
Drummer Billy Queen would make his exit
teaming up with GOLIATH during August of
2001.

A matter of months later the band was in a
state of flux yet again as, losing Eddleblute, it
re-enlisted both guitarists Jon Noble and
Gary Holtzman. The drum stool also saw swift
changes as Steve Vaughan, a former member
from early days known as IRON ANGEL,
resumed his place.

David Taylor departed in 2002 upfront of
recording a new album. Steve Vaughn would
relinquish the drum seat too and Gary
Holtzman resumed his position.

Albums:
JACOB'S DREAM, Metal Blade 3984-

JACOB'S DREAM

JACOB'S DREAM
Photo : Nico Wobben

14282-2 (2000)
Kinescope / Funambulism / Scape Goat /
Mad House Of Cain / Tale Of Fears /
Crusade / Black Watch / Love & Sorrow /
The Gathering / Never Surrender / The
Bleeding Tree / Violent Truth
THEATER OF WAR, Metal Blade 3984-
14363-2 (2001)
Sanctuary / Theater Of War / Traces Of Grace
/ Wisdom / The Warning / Sarah Williams / De
Machina Est Deo / Black Souls / Critical Mass

JAG PANZER (CO, USA)
Line-Up: Harry 'The Tyrant' Conklin '(vocals),
Mark Briody (guitar), Chris Broderick (guitar),
John Tetley (bass), Rikard Sternquist (drums)

Originally a covers band, JAG PANZER rose
to enjoy true cult status on the American
Metal scene and amplified this into major
appreciation on the European mainland later
in their career. The band have delved into
many styles and have been assailed by line
up tribulations but have won through, finally
stabilising their line-up and reaping the
rewards during the '90s.
The band had been playing the local club
circuit in their native Colorado for around two
years before, legend has it, Briody heard a
copy of the 'Monsters Of Rock' compilation
album commemorating the first ever festival at
Donington in 1980. The singer was blown
away by the likes of a participating SAXON
and RIOT. Promptly discovering NWoBHM
bands such as ANGELWITCH, the fledgling
band - then entitled TYRANT, set about
recording a demo of their first song 'Tower Of
Darkness'. Enthused by the results a further
demo demos contained the tracks
'Battlezones' and 'The Crucifix' which,
courtesy of a friend's persuasive efforts got
into the hands of both Metal Blade and Azra
in Los Angeles.
However, news also arrived of the already
established Los Angeles Metal band
TYRANT. With a name change in order the
band decided they liked the sound of the
Jagdpanzer WWII German tank destroyer but
subtly reworked the name for an American
audience as JAG PANZER. The band opted to
sign with Azra - on the strength of a higher
royalty offer and a colour cover for the debut
offering, the 'Tyrants' EP was issued in 1983.
The EP subsequently bore witness to a
myriad of collectable versions, including
various picture discs featuring a monster, a
lady with chainsaw, a torture rack and a
promotional release with a gas mask disc.
Just prior to the release JAG PANZER had
relocated to Los Angeles in an effort to crack
the big time. Initially, before the release of the
EP, gigs were hard to come by but as soon as

'Tyrants' was issued the group pulled over 400
people to their first gig.
In 1984 Azra released JAG PANZER's first
fully fledged album and 'Ample Destruction'
marked the recording debut of the newly
recruited JOEY TAFFOLA, who teamed up
with JAG PANZER's existing guitarist Mark
Briody in a formidable frontline. The band put
in support slots to acts as diverse as GRIM
REAPER and SLADE. In an effort to establish
a new recording deal JAG PANZER
committed two new songs to tape, 'Shadow
Thief' and 'Viper'.
Taffola, taking Carlson with him, quit for a solo
career, eventually debuting with the 1987
album 'Out Of The Sun' on Shrapnel Records
before teaming up with ALICE COOPER. In
1986 vocalist 'The Tyrant' (real name Harry
Conklin) appeared fronting a black metal
band SATAN'S HOST under the even
stranger pseudonym of 'Leviathan Thesiren'
releasing the album 'Metal from Hell'. Conklin
reverted back to his real name to enjoy a
fleeting tenure with New York cult rockers
RIOT. At his first RIOT live performance
Conklin unfortunately lost his voice and was
dumped. Conklin would also assemble TITAN
FORCE, issuing two albums - 1989's 'Titan
Force' on the U.S. Metal label and 1991's
'Winner / Loser' for the German Shark
Concern.
JAG PANZER regrouped drawing in guitarist
Christian Lesegue and drummer Rikard
Sternquist. A succession of vocalists then
flowed through the ranks including Chris
Cronk of KARIAN, Steve Montez and Bob
Parduba of Denver Metal band ALLOY CZAR.
With this line-up JAG PANZER self-financed
the recording of a fresh album's worth of
material 'Chain Of Command' which included
a re-make of IRON BUTTERFLY's
groundbreaking '60s hit 'In A Gadda Da Vida'.
On the live front the group guested for
HELLOWEEN and MEGADETH. A contract
with a major label was offered for 'Chain Of
Command' but the band deemed it too
restrictive and declined. Both Parduba and
Lesegue left soon after.
Meantime the 'Ample Destruction' album was
the subject of varying release formats with the
Canadian release on Banzai Records being
retitled 'License To Kill' and coming with an
extra track 'Black Sunday'. The British release
on Metalcore Records also added 'Black
Sunday' but in addition squeezed in 'Eyes Of
The Night' and 'Fallen Angel', the two latter
tracks recorded at a different session and
featuring new drummer Reynold 'Butch'
Carlson, who replaced original skinsman Rick
Hilyard.
With little activity officially, interest in the band
was sustained with the emergence in 1991 of

JAG PANZER
Photo : Nico Wobben

an unofficial split album with MAJESTY and of the 'Shadow Thief' bootleg in 1992.

The band cut a 1994 album 'Dissident Alliance' with new singer Daniel Conca and guitarist Chris Kostka but unfortunately, despite having the extra promotional push of a single 'Jeffrey Behind The Gate', this record, released by Rising Sun in Europe and Pavement Music in America, was universally panned by critics. Nevertheless, the band did manage to tour Europe for the first time as openers to OVERKILL before their two newest recruits made their exit. Conca made his mark with GOTHIC SLAM.

JAG PANZER made a return to the scene in 1996 tempted no doubt by the burgeoning interest in retro-trad metal in Europe and Japan. The band, re-enlisting Harry Conklin, demoed the more traditionally aligned tunes 'Future Shock', 'Ready To Strike' and 'Shadow Thief', promptly landing a deal with the German Century Media label. The resulting album, 'The Fourth Judgement' issued in August of 1997, was hailed as a renaissance for the band and the European Rock media in particular enthused over JAG PANZER's return to form. Notably JOEY TAFFOLA contributed lead guitar solos to the record but would be unable to tour. Chris Broderick took the vacant guitar slot for European dates billed alongside HAMMERFALL and GAMMA RAY.

'The Age Of Mastery' album, a collection of re-recorded archive tracks as requested by a poll of fans, confirmed the validity of the band's comeback. A nationwide American tour found JAG PANZER sharing stages with ICED EARTH. The band undertook a headlining tour of Germany to close off 1998 supported by ANGEL DUST, GLADIATORS and GB ARTS. Collectors would also be tempted by JAG PANZER's inclusion of a live version of 'Tyranny' on an 'Ungebrochen Metal' compilation.

Although 1999 would not deliver a new album, JAG PANZER did offer up their rendition of 'Children Of The Sea' to the DIO 'Holy Dio' Century Media tribute album and put in a sterling set at the 'Wacken Open Air' festival. As the year drew to a close Century Media surprised fans by offering a download of Mark Briody and Harry Conklin's Christmas song 'Do You See What I See'.

JAG PANZER would make a return with the May 2000 'Macbeth' inspired 'Thane To The Throne' opus. The ambitious album track 'The Prophecies (Fugue In D Minor)' would see the veritable inclusion of the Moscow string quartet. With 'Thane To The Throne' the band managed to elevate itself above cult status making serious headway on the sales front. The following year a diversion saw hockey

fans JAG PANZER reworking JUDAS PRIEST's 'You've Got Another Thing Comin'' into 'You've Got Another Cup Comin'', donated as a theme song to the Colorado Avalanches team. JAG PANZER's continued revival was bolstered by the arrival of the Jim Morris produced 'Mechanised Warfare' album in 2001.

JAG PANZER, alongside Swedish Deathsters IN FLAMES, would lend strong support to ICED EARTH's April 2002 American tour. The band would make available for these shows an exclusive DVD package dubbed 'The Era Of Kings And Conflict' hosting feature videos and a bootleg live film of a show in Switzerland.

Conklin would also be in action fronting the IRON MAIDEN tribute band POWERSLAVE 2000 in union with ex-LESE MAJESTY bassist Paul Stickney. In September of 2002 drummer Rikard Stjernquist announced that he had also joined up with BALLISTIC, the new band of former DEUCE, TENSION and WARDOG veteran Tom Gattis.

Singles/EPs:
Death Row / Battle Zones / Metal Melts The **Ice** / Iron Shadows, Azra DTR 007 (1983)
Jeffrey Behind The Gate / Spirit Suicide / Jeffrey Behind The Gate (Remix), Rising Sun 050-62303CDS (1994)

Albums:
AMPLE DESTRUCTION, Iron Works IW 1001 (1984)
Licensed To Kill / Warfare / Symphony Of Terror / Harder Than Steel / Generally Hostile / The Watching / Reign Of Tyrants / Cardiac Arrest / Crucifix: i) The Possession, ii) Suffer Unto Me, iii) Apostles Of The Damned, iv) The Beast, v) Armageddon
CHAIN OF COMMAND, Auburn (1987)
Prelude / Chain Of Command / Shadow Thief / She Waits / Ride Through The Storm / In A Gadda Da Vida / Never Surrender / Burning Heart / Sworn To Silence / Dream Theme / Gavotte In D
DISSIDENT ALLIANCE, Rising Sun (1994)
Jeffrey Behind The Gate / The Clown / Forsaken Child / Edge Of Blindness / Eve Of Penance / Last Dying Breath / Psycho Next Door / Spirit Suicide / GMV-407 / The Church / Whisper God
THE FOURTH JUDGEMENT, Century Media 771722 (1997)
Black / Call Of The Wild / Despair / Future Shock / Recompense / Ready To Strike / Tyranny / Shadow Thief / Sonet Of Sorrow / Judgement Day
THE AGE OF MASTERY, Century Media 77225-2 (1998)

Iron Eagle / Lustful And Free / Twilight Years / Sworn To Silence / False Messiah / The Age Of Mastery / Viper / Displacement / Chain Of Command / Take This Pain Away / Burning Heart / The Moors

THANE TO THE THRONE, Century Media (2000)

Thane Of Cawdor / King At A Price / Bloody Crime / The Premonitions / Treachery's Stain / Spectres Of The Past / Banquo's Final Rest / Three Voices Of Fate / Hell To Pay / The Prophecies (Fugue In D minor) / Insanity's Mind / Requiem For Lady MacBeth / Face Of Fear / Fall Of Dunsinane / Fate's Triumph / The Downward Fall / Tragedy Of MacBeth

MECHANIZED WARFARE, Century Media (2001)

Take To The Sky / Forever In Fear / Unworthy / The Silent / The Scarlet Letter / Choir Of Tears / Cold Is The Blade (And The Heart That Wields It) / Hidden In My Eyes / Power Surge / All Things Renewed

JAGUAR (UK)

Line-Up: Rob Reiss (vocals), Garry Peppard (guitar), Jeff Cox (bass), Chris Lovell (drums)

Bristol based JAGUAR elevated themselves to NWoBHM notoriety with their 'Axe Crazy' in 1982, although the band was actually formed in December 1979. Oddly, JAGUAR did not record until vocalist Bob Reiss, previously with STORMTROOPER, was found in April 1980. With front man in tow the group demoed and entered a 'Battle Of The Bands' contest coming fourth and a further demo followed at the end of 1980.

It was from the second demo that JAGUAR secured the track 'Stormchild' on the 1981 Heavy Metal Records compilation album 'Heavy Metal Heroes' and Heavy Metal followed this up with the 'Back Street Woman' single, which went on to sell over 4000 copies. However, JAGUAR fell out with Heavy Metal over re-pressing the single and, as well as losing their record company, JAGUAR lost their vocalist when Reiss left the band in early 1982.

Former HELLRAIZER singer Paul Merrill was recruited (after a temporary liaison with Bristol singer Andy Fox, now in-house promoter at the Bierkeller) and JAGUAR set off for Holland to headline a Dutch Rock festival. Neat Records mentor Dave Wood was in attendance and offered the band a deal, which they promptly took. The resulting debut Neat single, 'Axe Crazy', was a huge underground hit, being Neat's best selling single to date, and was much in demand on the American Heavy Metal circuit. JAGUAR promptly toured in Britain supporting the likes of STAMPEDE, THE RODS and THE STARFIGHTERS before going in to record their debut album, 'Power Games', in November 1982. By this time they had lost drummer Les Foster to TOK-IO ROSE. Career prospects looked promising for the band as the album garnered enthusiastic praise from the media and the band hooked up with Greybray Management, handling MOTORHEAD and GIRLSCHOOL at the time, in 1984.

Although featured on the second album 'This Time', drummer Chris Lovell was replaced shortly after its recording by Gary Davies. Many critics believed the band had mellowed out their characteristic sound too much with 'This Time' and the introduction of keyboard player Gareth Johnson for live work as support to GIRLSCHOOL seemed to bear this out. Having lost momentum with the album the band entered turbulent times. Davies decamped and Will Ng joined for recording of demos and subsequently Les Foster was re-recruited but by the close of 1985 JAGUAR called it a day.

JAGUAR was then effectively put on ice for over ten years. Peppard busied himself with AOR act THE ARENA whilst Jeff Cox teamed up with TARGA and THE LOST BOYS. This latter act issued the 'Diamond Dust' album through Communiqué Records. Davies joined melodic Rockers MULTI STOREY.

The ongoing fascination with NWoBHM in Japan and mainland Europe would prompt a re-release of the debut album in 1998. Reaction was such that JAGUAR duly regrouped. Emerging from the shadows JAGUAR performed their first gig at a low key club show in Wolverhampton on July 23rd 1999 as a warm up to a high profile appearance at the noted German 'Wacken Open Air' festival. The band line-up now consisted of Peppard, Jeff Cox, brother Nathan Cox on drums, whose previous acts include MOTHERLOVE, SMILER and SMOKIN', and ex-EXCLUSION and MURMUR vocalist Jamie Marten. The same line-up cut the comeback album 'Wake Me', issued in March of 2000 by Neat Metal Records.

Shortly after the issue of 'Wake Me' Jeff Cox made his exit, being replaced by Darren Furze. As Sanctuary Records issued the 'Power Games Anthology' album JAGUAR prepared a new studio album for 2002.

Singles/EPs:

Back Street Woman / Chasing The Dragon, Heavy Metal HEAVY 10 (1981)

Axe Crazy / War Machine, Neat NEAT 16 (1982)

Albums:

POWERGAMES, Neat NEAT 1007(1983)
Dutch Connection / Out Of Luck / Fox /
Master Game / No Lies / Run For Your Life /
Prisoner / Ain't No Fantasy / Raw Deal /
Cold Heart
THIS TIME, Roadrunner RR 9851 (1984)
This Time / Last Flight / A Taste Of Freedom
/ Another Lost Weekend / Stand Up (Tumble
Down) / Sleepwalker / Tear The Shackles
Down / Stranger / Driftwood / (Night Of)
Long Shadows
WAKE ME, Neat Metal NM041 (2000)
Mouth & Trousers / Junk / Sucker / Wake Me
/ Occasional Hell / Polish / Scrap Metal /
Power Games / Dawn Chorus / Pigeon
Access Point
POWER GAMES - ANTHOLOGY,
Sanctuary CMDDD413 (2002)
Back Street Woman / Chasing The Dragon /
Stormchild / Axe Crazy / War Machine /
Dutch Connection / Out Of Luck / The Fox /
Master Game / No Lies / Run For Your Life /
Prisoner / Ain't No Fantasy / Raw Deal /
Cold Heart / Dirty Tricks / Long Shadows /
Last Flight / This Time / Stand Up / A Taste
Of Freedom / Another Lost Weekend /
Sleepwalker / Tear Down The Shackles /
Driftwood / Mouth And Trousers / Junk /
Sucker / Wake Up / Occasional Hell / Polish /
Scrap Metal / Power Games / Dawn Chorus
/ Pigeon Access Point

JESTERS MARCH (GERMANY)
Line-Up: Olaf Bilic (vocals), Pierre Danielzyk
(guitar), Michael Bilic (guitar), Martin Hirsch
(bass), Oliver Schutrumpf (drums)

A Progressive Metal act. Olaf Bilic and bassist
Hirsch formed HOUSE OF SPIRITS in 1994
and promptly released a record through
G.U.N. Records. Hirsch would post HOUSE
OF SPIRITS join HILTON and Death Metal
act MORGOTH.

Albums:
BEYOND, Steamhammer SPV 084 76272
(1991)
Beyond / Middle Of Madness / Believe /
Jester's Rise / Rain Falls / False Religion /
Rhapsody In Lies / To Wicked Leaders / Into
The Void
ACTS, Steamhammer SPV 084 76452 (1992)
News / Paralysed / Run / Take The Pain /
Innocence / No Mans Land / Agony / Start
Fighting / Don't Turn / Spellbound / Leaving

JUDAS PRIEST (UK)
Line-Up: Ripper Owns (vocals), K.K.
Downing (guitar), Glenn Tipton (guitar), Ian
Hill (bass), Scott Travis (drums)

JUDAS PRIEST

JUDAS PRIEST rate as one of the most
successful of the pure Metal acts to emerge
from Great Britain. More than any other act
JUDAS PRIEST have steadfastly stuck to
their guns, preaching the cause of Heavy
Metal even in some of the toughest of times
for the genre. Their uncompromising ethos
has seen the band sell over 25 million albums
globally.
Characterised by a superb interplay between
guitarists K.K. Downing and GLENN TIPTON,
both of equal technical ability and each with
an immediately identifiable trademark
signature, JUDAS PRIEST have also
benefited enormously from some of the most
extreme vocal styles, courtesy of Rob
Halford.
Incredibly, since the singer's departure in
1992, after more than two decades with the
band JUDAS PRIEST have returned with an
even stronger, harder uncompromising sound
with new vocalist Tim 'Ripper' Owens, a man
whose vocal range matches that of even
Halford.
The present day line-up of this premier Metal
act features none of the original line-up which
first formed in early 1969 on the outskirts of
Birmingham. However, it should be noted that
in this early incarnation JUDAS PRIEST were
firmly based in the Blues.
The roots of the band trace back to 1967 and
a Birmingham act titled BLUE CONDITION
comprising ex-BITTERSWEET members
vocalist AL ATKINS (vocals) and bassist
Bruno Stapenhill together with drummer Pete

233

Boot. By 1968 BLUE CONDITION had split, with Boot later joining EXTREEM and Atkins and Stapenhill forming HALFBREED; a band also featuring guitarists Barry Civil and John Perry and former JUG drummer Jim Perry. Civil left to join FROOT and with Jim Perry departing too for Blues band F.B.I. (later of STALLION, LION and BODIE & JINX) the group opted for a re-think. HALFBREED changed titles to THE CHAPTER OF LIFE then THE JUG BLUES BAND but ultimately folded.

Atkins and Stapenhill regrouped titled SUGARSTACK with guitarists Michael Reeves and Jeff Furnival and drummer John Partridge. SUGARSTACK split with Reeves joining high profile Midlands act POSSESSED (reuniting with Boot) but he was to be killed in a road accident. Furnival joined EXTREEM.

Stapenhill and Partridge remained together and the name JUDAS PRIEST (A pun on the BOB DYLAN track 'The Ballad Of Frankie Lee And Judas Priest', was suggested. Pulling in guitarist John Perry to form the first line-up and concentrating on a hard edged Blues Rock direction JUDAS PRIEST set about gigging. Tragic circumstances intervened as within days Perry was killed in a suicide related car crash.

Still reeling from the shock the band set about auditioning guitarists and one of those to attend the sessions was a youthful K.K. Downing. Despite JUDAS PRIEST recognising that K.K. looked the part they passed in favour of the 17 year old Ernie Chataway. Downing had been passed on simply because the members of the band at the time were unable to imagine their act with such a heavy guitar sound, the blond guitarist having auditioned with an extreme variant on CREAM riffs and screaming solos.

In 1970, after prolonged gigging - their set often including covers by SPIRIT and QUICKSILVER MESSENGER SERVICE, the band signed a management deal with Alan Eade and cut two songs in the studio 'We'll Stay Together' and 'Good Time Woman'.

The tape led to interest from Immediate Records, the label owned by ROLLING STONES manager Andrew Loog Oldham. JUDAS PRIEST showcased for the label at a hotel in Walsall (among the audience was LED ZEPPELIN's singer ROBERT PLANT) and were duly signed up to a three year deal. Work progressed toward an album with the band recording the 'Holy Is The Man' / 'Mind Conception' acetate. However, early hopes were dashed as before any product could be released the company went bust.

Undaunted, the band played the Midlands club circuit for many years, steadily building up an enviable live reputation. However, JUDAS PRIEST split in the summer of 1970. Stapenhill formed RAM before joining a Soul act THE RYEGEE EXPLOSION. The bassist was subsequently to reunite with erstwhile BLUE CONDITION drummer Pete Boot and ex-JUDAS PRIEST guitarist Ernie Chataway in BULLION then SUICIDE.

Following the break up of JUDAS PRIEST Atkins joined forces with an as yet unnamed trio comprising of guitarist K.K. Downing, bassist Ian 'Skull' Hill and drummer John Ellis. The name FREIGHT had been suggested but at Atkins prompting once more the name JUDAS PRIEST was resurrected. With Downing now in control, the group moved swiftly away from the Blues and into new territory, which would later be defined as Heavy Metal.

The band's set now included covers by QUATERMASS and JIMI HENDRIX alongside new original material such as 'Mind Conception', 'Holy Is The Man' and 'Whiskey Woman'.

By 1971 former GLAD STALLION and TENDENCY JONES drummer Alan Moore had joined JUDAS PRIEST, Ellis having quit after a gig supporting SLADE. Moore stuck with the band until 1972 when he left to join PENDULUM and SUNDANCE. Moore was replaced by black drummer Chris 'Congo' Campbell. JUDAS PRIEST were by now regulars on the support circuit opening for STATUS QUO, FAMILY and THIN LIZZY.

The band had now signed a management deal with IMA, a Birmingham company run by Jim Simpson and BLACK SABBATH guitarist TONY IOMMI. Also on their books was THE FLYING HAT BAND (including in its ranks guitarist GLENN TIPTON), BULLION (Stapenhill's new act) and fellow Progressive heavyweights NECROMANDUS.

Following the departure of Atkins and Campbell in May 1973, erstwhile LORD LUCIFER and HIROSHIMA vocalist extraordinaire Rob John Halford enrolled along with ex-BAKERLOO and HIROSHIMA drummer John Hinch.

ROB HALFORD had, just previous to enrolling in JUDAS PRIEST, auditioned for the post of lead vocalist with London act the HEAVY METAL KIDS. Hinch meanwhile had missed out on BAKERLOO's success, leaving them just before their debut album.

AL ATKINS meanwhile teamed up with ex-JUDAS PRIEST bassist Bruno Stapenhill and former BUDGIE drummer Pete Boot to form LION, an act that gigged solidly until its demise in 1978. Stapenhill formed SUICIDE in the late '70s with Boot once more then WARHEAD.

The Downing / Halford / Hill / Hinch JUDAS

PRIEST line-up cut their first proper demo recording of 'Ladies' and 'Run Of The Mill', 'Caviar And Meths' in 1974, landing them a deal with Gull Records; a new Rock label set up by MCA Records A&R man David Howells. The song 'Whiskey Woman' had by now evolved into 'Victim Of Changes' after Halford had made a marriage of the Atkins penned song and his own 'Red Light Lady'.

The band, now managed by Midlands entrepreneur Dave Corke (although often using the pseudonym Eric Smith and whose office was a public telephone box!), toured heavily, even playing dates in Norway and Germany. One of Corke's more outlandish publicity plans was to exploit the fact that Halford was gay by issuing press photos billing the singer as 'Rob 'The Queen' Halford'. These photographs were printed but scrapped upon Halford's insistence.

A second guitarist in the form of GLENN TIPTON was recruited just before recording of the band's debut 'Rocka Rolla' album. David Howells felt that in order to set the band apart from other Rock acts they needed a unique angle and a heavier version of WISHBONE ASH was to be the model.

Tipton had made his name with fellow Birmingham outfit THE FLYING HAT BAND, an trio that featured Tipton on vocals / guitar, ex-GNIDROLOG bassist Mars Cowling (later to join PAT TRAVERS) and drummer Steve Palmer (brother of EMERSON LAKE & PALMER's Carl Palmer). THE FLYING HAT BAND had recorded an unreleased album for Vertigo. These sessions were consigned to be shelved because the label deemed them "Too heavy!!"

THE FLYING HAT BAND had been regular competitors of JUDAS PRIEST's on the Midlands club circuit and had actually just come off a European tour supporting DEEP PURPLE when Tipton opted to join JUDAS PRIEST.

This union of two guitarists with distinct sounds was to provide metal fans in the not too distant future with a twin guitar attack sound pushed to new levels of unparalleled ferocity beyond any WISHBONE ASH comparisons.

Producer Rodger Bain, who had made his name with BLACK SABBATH's early albums, apparently had a large say in the 'Rocka Rolla' album's production. Bain cut stage classic 'Cavier And Meths' from 8 minutes to a short instrumental and decided to leave off established tracks such as 'Victim Of Changes', 'Genocide', 'Tyrant' and 'The Ripper'. Although unrepresentative, the debut album provided the band with a useful launch platform and despite lukewarm reviews the album sleeve landed a graphic design award

lending more valuable publicity.

The band toured constantly, building up an impressive club following. Their British tour, supported by JAILBAIT, culminated in spectacular success at the 1975 Reading Festival. Incidentally, the bootleg of the Reading performance features the live favourite 'Mother Sun', which has never seen the light of day on vinyl. JUDAS PRIEST only recorded this song in an unfinished acoustic state for Gull.

JUDAS PRIEST were by now carving out a niche as the most aggressive Metal act on the circuit. Their next album, 'Sad Wings Of Destiny', was recorded with re-enlisted drummer Alan Moore. During his tenure with SUNDANCE he had recorded two albums for Decca 1973's 'Rain Steam Speed' and 1974's 'Chuffer'.

'Sad Wings Of Destiny', clad in an evocative Patrick Woodruffe artwork sleeve, would prove to be a groundbreaking album and songs such as 'Genocide', 'Tyrant' and 'Island Of Domination' proved JUDAS PRIEST were on their way. Also included was 'Victim Of Changes', a seven minute epic destined to be recognised as the band's all time classic and still performed in concert some 25 years later. The song had originated in the earlier track 'Red Light Lady' written by original band vocalist AL ATKINS. Combined with the newer 'Whiskey Woman' the songs fused together to create 'Victim Of Changes'.

Overall the quality of material captured on 'Sad Wings Of Destiny' without doubt portrayed an enormous creative leap from the 'Rocka Rolla' opus. Oddly the bulk of the songs were available for the debut, the band having been performing them live for many years previous.

The tour and general response to the album led to a worldwide deal with CBS Records, unfortunately whilst the band were still under contract to Gull Records, a £60,000 advance and the landmark 'Sin After Sin' album, produced by DEEP PURPLE bassist ROGER GLOVER.

'Sin After Sin', laid down with drums by renowned session man Simon Phillips, provided the momentum CBS were looking for and with major label backing JUDAS PRIEST were ready to take on the world. Interestingly JUDAS PRIEST reworked a much heavier cover of the JOAN BAEZ track 'Diamonds And Rust' originally laid down for Gull Records.

Although Phillips's services were requested on a full time basis the band eventually settled on ex-FANCY drummer Lez 'Feathertouch' Binks. 'Sin After Sin's producer, ROGER GLOVER, had previously used Binks on his 1974 concept album 'Butterfly Ball'.

235

JUDAS PRIEST's first American shows in 1977 climaxed with support slots to the mighty LED ZEPPELIN at the San Francisco 'Day On The Green' festival. Following their British tour, with fellow Brummies MAGNUM opening, ended with fans destroying the London Victoria Theatre venue as trouble flared between audience and heavy handed bouncers.

By this time it was apparent that JUDAS PRIEST had trouble with drummers, as each album had a different sticksman. This situation continued to the '90s with JUDAS PRIEST only employing drummers as needed until finally settling on their present line-up.

During 1978 JUDAS PRIEST saw 'Stained Class' add to their success with their first (heavily bootlegged) tour of Japan. The album, although thinly produced by Dennis Mackay, included a version of SPOOKY TOOTH's 'Better By You, Better Than Me' alongside the rip roaring acceleration of 'Exciter' and the majestic stage classic 'Beyond The Realms Of Death'. 'Stained Class' would be JUDAS PRIEST's first album to break into the Billboard top 200.

As America beckoned, a rapid change in image occurred from the gothic and medieval to menacing black leather that was to become their trademark. The vocalist switched from flowing silks to a leather peaked cap and bullwhip and Halford would even take to the stage riding on a Harley Davidson motorcycle. Halford's prescient sense of theatrics at this juncture in their career would not only brand the group with a globally identifiable stamp but also influence the entire Metal genre as a whole for many years to come.

The next album 'Killing Machine' provided their first hit singles in the shape of the anthemic drum driven 'Take On The World' and also 'Evening Star'. The album as a whole saw JUDAS PRIEST's shift to more Sci-Fi lyrical themes. Two successive sell-out British tours, the latter with LEA HART as guest, bolstered their support.

However, in America JUDAS PRIEST had to rename the album 'Hell Bent For Leather' as the record company felt the British title too violent. The band used this opportunity to add an extra track to the U.S. version, a cover of FLEETWOOD MAC's melancholy 'Green Manalishi' before JUDAS PRIEST undertook another lengthy American theatre tour alongside fellow Brits UFO.

JUDAS PRIEST's next album proved to be the band's undoubted classic 'Unleashed In The East', the first of many to be produced by 'Colonel' Tom Allom. The band's new producer had made his mark as engineer on the first two BLACK SABBATH albums then producing HUDSON-FORD and PAT TRAVERS. Allom captured the band's live ferocity on stage in Japan as JUDAS PRIEST truly became a world class act. The Japanese version of the album featured an extra four tracks which would filter through to the UK market in the form of single B sides.

As if to seal the stamp of approval from their increasing fan following, the first JUDAS PRIEST bootleg album 'The Ripper' appeared at this point. Taken from a recording from the sound desk at an American show in 1979, unfortunately for fans GLENN TIPTON's guitar is almost totally inaudible throughout.

Another incident the band may want to forget from that tour was when Rob Halford rode his Harley Davidson onstage at St. Pauls in Minneapolis and promptly drove straight into the orchestra pit! Fortunately for the singer, this nasty incident only resulted in cuts and bruises!

'British Steel' saw the arrival of ex-TRAPEZE drummer Dave Holland in favour of Binks (who went onto to work with TYTAN and LIONHEART before entering the world of session work) and caught JUDAS PRIEST favouring lengthy American tours. Nevertheless, a sell out British tour maintained their following at home, with support coming from rising Metal gods IRON MAIDEN.

With the New Wave of British Heavy Metal explosion at its peak, many fans attending the shows were more than mystified when it transpired that the support band looked remarkably similar to the headline act. IRON MAIDEN's guitarist Dave Murray was an almost copycat of Downing in dress and blond mane whilst vocalist PAUL DIANNO matched Halford for studded belts and wristbands.

Still, 'British Steel' - which peaked at no. 4 on the British charts, gave the band three British hit singles and TV appearances promoting 'Living After Midnight', 'Breaking The Law' and the anthem 'United' and America was beckoning ever brighter. (The album would be given a second wind in 2001 when a TV special prompted Scandinavian Rock fans to put the album back into the Swedish charts at no. 17 - higher than its original 1980 chart achievement!)

A lengthy bout of American touring would push 'British Steel' into Gold sales status and steady sales from then on eventually broke the Platinum marker. JUDAS PRIEST rammed the point home with what many regarded as a show stealing performance at the first ever Castle Donington 'Monsters Of Rock' festival headlined by RAINBOW.

Although 1981's 'Point Of Entry' album saw JUDAS PRIEST mellow considerably, much to the disfavour of British fans, the ensuing

American tour, again supported by IRON MAIDEN and also WHITESNAKE, saw the band rise in stature with increasingly lavish stage shows featuring huge banks of lights and hydraulic risers. However, JUDAS PRIEST returned for a successful British tour during 1981 with the hard hitting ACCEPT as support act. Some of the album's tougher tracks such as the majestic 'Desert Plains' and riff driven 'Hot Rockin' gave evidence that JUDAS PRIEST were still more than capable of delivering the goods.

It was to be the release of the 'Screaming For Vengeance' album that really cracked the States wide open for PRIEST, providing the band with their first platinum album and hit single in the catchy 'You've Got Another Thing Comin'. Such was the impact of this song on the American public it was being used for Burger King adverts in 1999!

During the tour, which following the lavish 'Point Of Entry' stage set had the band stripped down to the basic Marshall cab walls, JUDAS PRIEST broke off from their long term management Arnakatra and handled business affairs for themselves. Whilst still on the road lengthy negotiations took place and JUDAS PRIEST finally teamed up with Bill Curbishly, manager of ROBERT PLANT and THE WHO.

JUDAS PRIEST rounded off their 'Screaming...' dates with a showing at the prestigious US festival in San Bernadino were the band played to an awesome audience of over a quarter of a million people.

It is true to say that with the next album, the chest thumping 'Defenders Of The Faith', JUDAS PRIEST gave the public more of the same winning formula with another outrageous stage set for their American tour. These dates found the band in more ambitious mode recreating the album cover in the stage set with a central huge head and mouth flanked by rising claws which plucked Tipton and Downing from the stage. By the close of this latest extensive run of dates JUDAS PRIEST had chalked up yet another million seller. JUDAS PRIEST's status was further acknowledged by their billing on the Philadelphia stage of the global 'Live Aid' event in 1985.

The subsequent 'Turbo' heralded a new age of Metal for the band. Once again they had pushed the parameters of Hard Rock into controversial territory. Whilst some believed that the ZZ TOP inspired synth guitars heralded back to the poppier tunes of 'Point Of Entry' days, the album actually draw in many new fans.

Initially intended as a double set, apparently from which only the more commercial recordings were finally chosen, 'Turbo'

JUDAS PRIEST

actually enjoyed considerable success, gaining another Platinum album accolade bolstered by lavish videos for 'Turbo Lover' and 'Locked in'. The 'Turbo' tour was recorded for the excellent 'Priest Live' album and also spawned a superb Wayne Isham directed live concert video. Somewhat strangely for such a landmark album, the record company promotion seemed apathetic to say the least. In 1988 JUDAS PRIEST took time out to record some experimental tracks, including a DIANA ROSS cover version of 'You Are Everything' together with band originals 'I Will Return' and 'Runaround', with famed pop producers Stock, Aitken and Waterman. These sessions were never released as the band deemed the eventual results inappropriate and instead fell back on their instincts as successive albums would testify.

'Ram It Down', featuring a cover of CHUCK BERRY's 'Johnny B Goode', had JUDAS PRIEST back to basics with American shows including contemporary name acts such as SLAYER, who had recently covered 'Dissident Aggressor' from the 'Stained Class' album.

For the hugely successful 'Painkiller' album, which saw the band at their most ferocious, JUDAS PRIEST pulled in ex-HAWK and RACER X drummer Scott Travis, Holland having left due to touring pressures. The former drummer was later to attempt a series of TRAPEZE reformations. JUDAS PRIEST also ceased their liaison with long term producer Tom Allom in favour of Chris Tsangarides.

The 'Painkiller' world tour proved hugely successful, with a long stint in America with support acts TESTAMENT and MEGADETH before playing the 'Rock in Rio' festival in Brazil then hopping over to Europe with support act ANNIHILATOR prior to shows in Japan and Hawaii. However, one show that JUDAS PRIEST did not do well attendance wise was Reno, Nevada, scene of the 'subliminal messages' court case. JUDAS PRIEST only pulled in 4,000 fans despite donating profits from the show to local charities.

Previously, the band had been cited in a $3 million law suit by the parents of James Vance and Raymond Belknap, who alleged that hidden messages involved in JUDAS PRIEST songs directly incited a suicide attempt by the teenagers. The allegation was that the two had tried to kill themselves with a shotgun after listening to the track 'Better By You, Better Than Me' from the 'Stained Class' album, probably one of the band's most innocuous songs recorded and a cover version of a SPOOKY TOOTH track at that. Belknap succeeded in killing himself whilst

Vance survived, though horrifically mutilated. Bizarrely, the assertions centred around Halford's breathing techniques during recording, the victim's families claiming this audible noise on the track was a barely hidden message of "Do it". The families lost the legal issue and sadly Vance died a few months before the court case.

All in all though the 'Painkiller' album put JUDAS PRIEST back at the top of the Heavy Metal pile. In a shock move, and to the utter dismay of fans worldwide Rob Halford left the band in 1992 as inter-band arguments raged focusing on his PANTERA style solo project FIGHT and the subsequent 1993 album 'War Of Words'.

Rob Halford busied himself with further FIGHT releases 'Mutations' (1994) and 'A Small Deadly Space' (1995) subsequently touring as guest to ANTHRAX and METALLICA. In general, the expected media response was unforthcoming and sometimes even hostile, leading to ultimately poor sales. In 1996 he formed a new act HALFORD and later the same year began work on a short lived project with BLACK SABBATH guitarist TONY IOMMI before going off in an Industrial direction for a project in conjunction with NINE INCH NAILS supremo Trent Reznor titled TWO.

During the lengthy lull GLENN TIPTON released his first solo album, 'Baptism Of Fire', on Atlantic Records. The album found the guitarist working with old and new guns such as MR. BIG bassist Billy Sheehan, SUICIDAL TENDENCIES man Robert Trujillo, UGLY KID JOE's Shannon Larkin, prior BAD 4 GOOD member Brooks Wackerman, C.J. De Villar and even THE WHO's John Entwistle.

Also in the ranks was former BLACK SABBATH, RAINBOW and WHITESNAKE drummer COZY POWELL, a link up that prompted many rumours. However, JUDAS PRIEST got back into gear with Scott Travis. Although Travis had been working with Halford's FIGHT he had remained loyal to the JUDAS PRIEST camp.

Meantime JUDAS PRIEST were honoured by not one but two tribute albums. Titled 'Legends Of Metal - A Tribute To JUDAS PRIEST' the Century Media two volume set featured JUDAS PRIEST classics covered by the likes of HELLOWEEN, SAXON, U.D.O., TESTAMENT, RAGE, MERCYFUL FATE, ICED EARTH, BLIND GUARDIAN, NEVERMORE, KREATOR, ANGRA and STRATOVARIUS among others. Although a commercial success it was readily pointed out by critics that none of the alternate versions matched the originals.

Rumours were by now in full force as to who

was to occupy the still vacant vocal position, with former GAMMA RAY singer Ralf Scheepers being constantly put in the frame. The German did not exactly help matters by touring in a tribute band titled JUST PRIEST! Former ACCEPT vocalist David Reece would also audition. Another acknowledged close contender was Pennsylvania born D.C. COOPER, later to join Danish Rockers ROYAL HUNT.

May 1996 JUDAS PRIEST finally announced their new vocalist to be American born, 28 year old Ohio native 'Ripper' Owens; previously with WINTER'S BANE, TWIST OF FATE and Grunge tribute act SEATTLE. The singer had also been employed fronting a JUDAS PRIEST tribute band BRITISH STEEL, a video tape of which had secured the audition.

1997's 'Jugulator' heralded the return of undiluted Heavy Metal from JUDAS PRIEST in spectacular fashion as not only, and quite incredibly, had Downing and Tipton surpassed themselves with their most extreme music to date. 'Ripper' easily outstripped the recent accomplishments made by Halford, a feat many longstanding JUDAS PRIEST fans had thought impossible. Owens inaugural live shows threw the newcomer straight in at the deep end with an ambitious tour of America where healthy audience attendance verified the fact that JUDAS PRIEST fans had not drifted away in the 7 year hiatus. Later shows on this tour saw British perennials MOTÖRHEAD as openers. After a string of very successful dates in the United States JUDAS PRIEST hit continental Europe again, this time with Dutch label mates GOREFEST as openers. The band were set to return to the stage in early 1998, although only two shows were arranged for the United Kingdom, in London and Wolverhampton.

The latter half of 1998 had the band basking in the glory of their quite awesome double live CD 'Live Meltdown' and resuming live dates in America and Mexico, including dates with MEGADETH. Meantime the Ranch Life label pulled off a coup with the issue of the 'Concert Classics' live album culled from a vintage 1980 show. Although PRIEST fans were quick to snap copies up its release was swiftly cancelled thereafter due to objections from the band's management.

The return of JUDAS PRIEST had done much to reinvigorate the European Metal scene, the impact creating a number of bizarre releases. Not only has Ralf Scheepers released the JUDAS PRIEST sound-a-like PRIMAL FEAR album (including an album cover that more than evokes memories of 'Screaming For Vengeance') but ex-JUDAS PRIEST men AL ATKINS and Dave Holland have resurfaced with the 'Victim Of Changes' album. a record made up of reworkings of ancient JUDAS PRIEST numbers.

With interest high the band found themselves nominated for a prestigious Grammy award for the track 'Bullettrain'. JUDAS PRIEST seemingly were to get back into the thick of it in mid 1999 when they were confirmed as special guests on the touring 'Ozzfest' extravaganza in America. Hopes for further dates were dashed however as JUDAS PRIEST announced the suspension of these dates, the band being in the throes of negotiating a new record contract, this time with Atlantic Records in America.

A further tribute album emerged in 1999 titled 'Hell Bent For Metal' comprising more extreme acts such as AGENT STEEL, ANGEL CORPSE, STEEL PROPHET, VITAL REMAINS and paradoxically WINTER'S BANE.

Although out of the limelight themselves JUDAS PRIEST remained in the public eye due to the movie 'Metal God'. The film, based on a New York Times article in 1997 by journalist Andrew Revkin titled 'Metal Head Becomes a Metal God' based on Ripper's ascendancy to stardom. The movie project, slated to star Brad Pitt and 'Friends' actress Jennifer Anniston, and was to portray the rapid rise to fame of Ripper Owens from warehouse clerk to front man for his all time favourite band.

Fans were kept in anticipation with a projected new JUDAS PRIEST album scheduled for late 2000. An American summer tour was announced with an arena billing combining forces with NAZARETH and the SCORPIONS but by April these proposed gigs would be pulled as the band maintained they needed further studio time. Meantime the embers were kept stoked by the release on Century Media Records of a repackaged WINTER'S BANE album 'Heart Of A Killer' featuring Ripper. Travis has also kept busy having reformed RACER X as a side project for a fresh album.

By late 2000, with no new JUDAS PRIEST album on the horizon, the rumour machine was in full flight suggesting in-fighting between Ripper and the rest of the band about the new material. Wilder allegations had Ripper ready to take the vocal position in PANTERA paving the way for Halford's return. HALFORD meanwhile was on the road in America guesting for IRON MAIDEN and including numerous JUDAS PRIEST songs in his repertoire including 'Running Wild', 'Electric Eye', 'Tyrant', and 'Genocide', a welcome rarity in 'Stained Class' and 'Riding On The Wind'.

JUDAS PRIEST

Quite bizarrely news emerged in 2000 that one of IRON MAIDEN's earliest guitarists Tony Parsons had created an IRON MAIDEN tribute band named METALWORKS 2000 including ex-ALICE COOPER and THE ALMIGHTY guitarist Pete Friezin and ex-JUDAS PRIEST drummer Lez Binks!

The band name was kept in the headlines throughout November 2000 when German Metal band IRON SAVIOUR gave a high tech overhaul to 'Hellion / Electric Eye' and premier American band ICED EARTH issued their take on 'The Ripper'.

JUDAS PRIEST were honoured once more on the 'Punk Goes Metal' tribute compilation when DIVIT covered 'Breaking The Law'. U.S. Girl band THE DONNAS would also spruce up 'Living After Midnight' on their 'Turn 21' album. Another leftfield tribute witnessed an all star cast of Los Angeles Rockers participating on the Cleopatra tribute album 'Breakin' The Law', a record made up of industrial and electronic reworks of PRIEST staples. Featured were WARRANT's Jani Lane, BANG TANGO's Joe Leste, FASTER PUSSYCAT's Taime Downe, LOVE / HATE's Jizzy Pearl, QUIREBOYS Spike, CIRCUS OF POWERS Alex Mitchell, UNION's John Corabi, WARRIOR SOUL's Kory Clarke, BULLETBOYS Marq Torien and L.A. GUNS Phil Lewis. Perhaps the most enlightening track on the album was ELECTRIC HELLFIRE CLUB's radical interpretation of 'Green Manalishi'.

In spite of all this related activity though one singular fact remained that frustratingly JUDAS PRIEST themselves appeared publicly to be on hiatus throughout 2000.

Travis would manage to squeeze in a solitary RACER X gig in support of their 'Superheroes' album at the Hollywood Whiskey in May of 2001 as PRIEST fans limbered themselves up for release of the 'Demolition' album. Touring in Europe would see a run of dates in Spain supported by SAVATAGE as well as European festival headlining slots such as the German 'With Full Force' and 'Bang Your Head' events.

Meantime in America the band's name was being kept in the spotlight by Boston Pop Rockers AMERICAN HI FI whose video for their hit single 'Flavour Of The Weak' had the band members reverting to their teenage years waiting in the parking lot for a 1981 JUDAS PRIEST gig!

'Demolition' finally arrived in July 2001 backed up by the single 'Machine Man'. Japanese fans would be treated to an extra track entitled 'What's My Name'. For such an important release the omens for 'Demolition' did not look good as many critics savaged the album. However, as the dust settled the Rock media

in general began an about turn with many journalists claiming 'Demolition' to be one of the band's finest works. The band put in a sell out London gig upfront of American tour dates due to commence on the 14th September at the Los Angeles Universal Amphitheatre. Running mates for the first two month leg were slated as ANTHRAX and ICED EARTH. Also arriving was the movie 'Rock Star'. The film had seen many changes from its inception and JUDAS PRIEST fans were now in the quite surreal position of seeing a movie on public release about Owens but officially nothing to do with the band. The lead role had switched from Brad Pitt to Mark Wahlberg, who had previously made his name in the music world as teen rapper MARKY MARK. The 'group' also boasted the talents of OZZY OSBOURNE, BLACK LABEL SOCIETY guitarist ZAKK WYLDE, DOKKEN and WAR AND PEACE bassist Jeff Pilson and BONHAM, VIRGINIA WOLF and AIRRACE drummer Jason Bonham.

In the movie, echoing Ripper's tenure with BRITISH STEEL, Wahlberg heads a STEEL DRAGON tribute act BLOOD POLLUTION. The real life drummer for BLOOD POLLUTION is played by another bona fide genuine Rocker Blas Elias of SLAUGHTER. The movie was mooted in its original form to have the members of JUDAS PRIEST contributing music and acting as advisors but strong disagreements as the direction of the story lines led to the formation of an all new band and revised film title. Promoting their 'Demolition' album JUDAS PRIEST would state for the record that 'Rock Star' was not the Owens story and if the film made any implications or statements to that effect they would be sued. A quite bizarre situation for fans of the band and Rock fans in general who all knew the behind the scenes story.

In light of the World Trade Centre terrorist attacks on the USA on September 11th JUDAS PRIEST, then performing in Mexico, cancelled their entire American tour, re-scheduling the dates for 2002. In the meantime the band put in a December 19th gig at the London Brixton Academy supported by SAXON.

The classic 1980 'British Steel' album would be given a second wind in 2001 when a TV special prompted Scandinavian Rock fans to put the album back into the Swedish charts at no. 17 - higher than its original 1980 chart achievement!

JUDAS PRIEST, together with ANTHRAX, resumed their American tour in January 2002. In light of recent tribulations the tour was deemed a huge success performing to capacity crowds. As well as including new 'Demolition' material the band would resurrect some rarely performed vintage tracks such as 'Desert Plains' and the 'United' anthem. The Columbia Records re-issue campaign concluded in March with the last clutch of four albums, all with extra tracks. 'Painkiller' added an unreleased studio take 'Living Bad Dreams' plus a live version of 'Leather Rebel'. 'Ram It Down' offered live tracks 'Bloodstone' and 'Night Comes Down'. 'Live' added three further live cuts 'Screaming For Vengeance', 'Rock Hard, Ride Free' and 'Hell Bent For Leather' whilst 'Turbo' came with the unreleased 'All Fired Up' and live 'Locked In'.

JUDAS PRIEST would announce another exhaustive set of U.S. tour dates throughout the Summer and Fall of 2002 commencing in Toledo, Ohio in early July. Longstanding fans would be pleased at the inclusion in the set of the rarely performed classic 'Exciter' as well as 'Devil's Child'. Included in the tour would be an August date at the Sunken Garden Theater in San Antonio, Texas supported by BUDGIE and REVEREND.

A further heavyweight JUDAS PRIEST tribute album was delivered by the Nuclear Blast label in September. Amongst the track inclusions would be ANNIHILATOR's 'Hell Bent For Leather', PRIMAL FEAR's 'Metal Gods', WITCHERY's Riding On The Wind' and ICED EARTH's 'Screaming For Vengeance'. SIEBENBURGEN contributed 'Jawbreaker' with HAMMERFALL donating 'Breaking The Law', BENEDICTION's 'Electric Eye', DEATH's 'Painkiller', SILENT FORCE's 'All Guns Blazing' STEEL PROPHET's 'Dreamer, Deceiver', ARMORED SAINT's 'Never Satisfied', THERION's 'Green Manalishi' and THUNDERSTONE's 'Diamonds And Rust'.

The band's long established leather clad image came under fire in August when P.E.T.A. (People for the Ethical Treatment of Animals) sent an open letter to the band requesting the lyrics to 'Hell Bent For Leather' be changed to 'Hell Bent For Pleather', pleather being a hide substitute. On a more concrete note the DVD 'Live In London' topped the German national charts in its first week of release.

Singles/EPs:
Rocka Rolla / Never Satisfied, Gull GULS 6 (1974)
Deceiver / The Ripper, Gull (1976)
The Ripper / Island Of Domination, Gull GULS 31 (1976)
Diamonds And Rust / Dissident Aggressor, CBS 5222 (1977)
Better By You Better Than Me / Invader, CBS 6077 (1978)
Exciter / Dissident Aggressor, Epic 06 5P 22 (1978) (Japanese release)

Evening Star / Star Breaker (Live), CBS 6719 (1978)
Before The Dawn / Rock Forever, CBS (1978)
The Green Manalishi (With The Two Pronged Crown) / Rock Forever, Columbia 3-1100 (1978) (USA release)
Take On The World / Starbreaker, CBS 6915(1979) **14 UK**
Diamonds And Rust (Live) / Starbreaker (Live), Columbia 1 11135 (1979) (USA release)
Evening Star / Beyond The Realms Of Death / The Green Manalishi (With The Two-Pronged Crown), CBS 7312 (1979) (7" single) **53 UK**
Evening Star / Beyond The Realms Of Death (Live In Cleveland) / The Green Manalishi (With The Two Pronged Crown) (Studio Version), CBS 7312 (1979) (12" single)
The Ripper / Victim Of Changes / Never Satisfied, Gull GULS 7112 (1979)
Living After Midnight / Delivering The Goods (Live), CBS 8379 (1980) **12 UK**
Living After Midnight / Delivering The Goods (Live) / Evil Fantasies (Live In Tokyo), CBS 12 8379 (1980) (12" single)
Living After Midnight / Metal Gods, Columbia 1-11308 (1980) (USA release)
Breaking The Law / Metal Gods, CBS 8644 (1980) **12 UK**
United / United, CBS 11 11396 (1980) (USA promotion)
United / Grinder, CBS 8897 (1980) **26 UK**
Heading Out To The Highway / All The Way, CBS A 1091 (1981) (USA release)
Heading Out To The Highway / Rock Forever / Hell Bent For Leather, Columbia 11-02083 (1981) (USA release)
Don't Go / Solar Angels, CBS 9520(1981) **51 UK**
Hot Rockin' / Breaking The Law (Live) / Living After Midnight (Live), CBS 1153 (1981) **60 UK**
Rock Forever / Hell Bent For Leather (Live) / Beyond The Realms Of Death (Live), CBS A12 1864 (1981) (12" single)
Hot Rockin' (Live) / Troubleshooter (Live), Columbia AS 900 (1981) (USA promotion)
You've Got Another Thing Comin' / Exciter, CBS A 2611 (1982) **66 UK, 67 USA**
Take These Chains / Judas Priest Audio File, CBS A 2822(1982)
The Green Manalishi (With The Two Pronged Crown) / Breaking The Law / You've Got Another Thing Comin', Epic 123P537 (1982) (12" single)
Tyrant / Rocka Rolla / Genocide, Gull GULS 7612 (1983)
You've Got Another Thing Comin' / Diamonds And Rust (Live), CBS (1982)

Tyrant / Rocka Rolla / Genocide, Gull GULS 7612 (1983)
The Hellion (Live) / Electric Eye (Live) / Riding On The Wind (Live), Columbia 1603 AS (1983) (USA promotion release)
Sinner / Exciter / Hell Bent For Leather / The Ripper / Hot Rockin' / Green Manalishi (With The Two Pronged Crown), Pickwick SCOOP 33 (1983)
Heavy Duty, CBS (1983) (USA promotion release)
Freewheel Burning / Breaking The Law / You've Got Another Thing Coming, CBS A 4054 (1984) **42 UK**
Freewheel Burning / Breaking The Law (Live) / You've Got Another Thing Comin' (Live), CBS A124054 (1984) (12" single) Freewheel Burning, CBS (1984) (Spanish promotion)
Some Heads Are Gonna Roll / The Green Manalishi (With The Two Pronged Crown) (Live) / Jawbreaker, CBS A 4289(1984)
Love Bites / Jawbreaker, CBS (1984)
Love Bites / Love Bites, CBS XSM 171 683 (1984) (USA promotion)
Turbo Lover / Hot For Love, Columbia A 7048(1986)
Turbo Lover (Extended Version) / Hot For Love, Columbia A12 7048 (1986) (12" single) Locked In (Single Version) / Locked In (LP Version), Columbia (1986) (12" single USA promotion)
Locked In (Extended Version) / Reckless / Desert Plains (Live) / Freewheel Burning (Live), Columbia A12 7144(1986) (12" single)
Locked In / Reckless / Desert Plains (Live) / Freewheel Burning (Live), Columbia QTA 7144 (1986)
Parental Guidance / Parental Guidance, Columbia (1986) (USA promotion release)
Parental Guidance / Turbo Lover (Hi-Octane Mix) / Private Property (Live), Columbia 650 1066 (1987) (12" single)
Johnny B Goode / Rock You All Around The World / Turbo Lover, Atlantic A 9114 (1988) **64 UK**
Ram It Down / Heavy Metal / Freewheel Burning (Live), Columbia 651689 3 (1988)
Blood Red Skies, Columbia (1988) (USA promotion)
I'm A Rocker, Columbia (1988) (USA promotion)
Living After Midnight / Breaking The Law, Old Gold OG9864 (1989)
Painkiller / United / Better By You, Better Than Me, Columbia 656273 7(1991) **74 UK**
Painkiller / United / Hell Patrol, Columbia (1991)
A Touch Of Evil / Between The Hammer And The Anvil / You've Got Another Thing Comin', Columbia 656589 0(1991) **58 UK**

A Touch Of Evil / Between The Hammer And The Anvil / You've Got Another Thing Comin' (Live), Columbia (1991) (12" single)
A Touch Of Evil (Edit Version) / A Touch Of Evil (LP Version), Columbia (1991) (USA promotion)
Night Crawler (Edit Version) / Breaking The Law (Live) / Living After Midnight (Live), Columbia 659097-2 (1993) **63 UK**
Nightcrawler (Edit Version) / Night Crawler (LP Version), Columbia (1993) (USA promotion)
Bullet Train, SPV 80000128(1997) (Promotion release)
Bullet Train / Rapid Fire (Re-recorded version) / The Green Manalishi (With The Two Pronged Crown) (Re-recorded version), Zero Corporation (1997) (Japanese release)
Machine Man / Subterfuge / Burn In Hell (Video), SPV 056-72453 (2001)
90 GERMANY

Albums:
ROCKA ROLLA, Gull GULP 1005 (1974)
One For The Road / Rocka Rolla / Winter / Deep Freeze / Winter Retreat / Cheater / Never Satisfied / Run Of The Mill / Dying To Meet You / Caviar And Meths
SAD WINGS OF DESTINY, Gull GULP 1015 (1976)
Prelude / Tyrant / Genocide / Epitaph / Island Of Domination / Victim Of Changes / Ripper / Dreamer Deceiver / Deceiver
GULL ROCK, King (1976) (Japanese compilation release)
The Ripper / Dreamer Deceiver / Deceiver / Rocka Rolla
SIN AFTER SIN, CBS 82008 (1977)
49 SWEDEN, 23 UK
Sinner / Diamonds And Rust / Starbreaker / Let Us Prey / Here Come The Tears / Call For The Priest / Dissident Aggressor / Last Rose Of Summer / Raw Deal
STAINED CLASS, CBS 82430 (1978)
27 UK, 178 USA
Exciter / White Heat, Red Hot / Better By You, Better Than Me / Stained Class / Invader / Saints In Hell / Savage / Beyond The Realms Of Death / Heroes End
BEST OF JUDAS PRIEST, Gull GULP 1026 (1978)
Dying To Meet You / Never Satisfied / Rocka Rolla / Diamonds And Rust / Victim Of Changes / Island Of Domination / The Ripper / Deceiver
KILLING MACHINE, CBS 83135 (1978)
32 UK
Delivering The Goods / Evening Star / Hell Bent For Leather / Take On The World / Killing Machine / Running Wild / Rock Forever / Before The Dawn / Evil Fantasies
HELL BENT FOR LEATHER, Columbia

(1978) (USA release) **128 USA**
Delivering The Goods / Evening Star / Hell
Bent For Leather / Take On The World /
Killing Machine / Running Wild / Rock
Forever / Before The Dawn / Evil Fantasies /
The Green Manalishi (With The Two Pronged
Crown) (Studio Version)
UNLEASHED IN THE EAST (LIVE), CBS
83852 (1979) **10 UK, 70 USA**
Exciter / Running Wild / Sinner / The Ripper /
Green Manalishi / Diamonds And Rust /
Victim Of Changes / Genocide / Tyrant
PRIEST IN THE EAST (LIVE), Epic (1979)
(Japanese release)
Exciter / Running Wild / Sinner / The Ripper /
The Green Manalishi (With The Two Pronged
Crown) / Diamonds And Rust / Victim Of
Changes / Genocide / Tyrant / Rock Forever
/ Delivering The Goods / Hell Bent For
Leather / Starbreaker
BRITISH STEEL, CBS 84160 (1980)
20 SWEDEN, 4 UK, 34 USA
Metal Gods / Breaking The Law / Grinder /
United / Rapid Fire / You Don't Have To Be
Old To Be Wise / Living After Midnight / The
Rage / Steeler
HERO, HERO, Gull (1980)
Prelude / Tyrant / Rocka Rolla / One For The
Road / Victim Of Changes / Dying To Meet
You / Never Satisfied / Dreamer Deceiver /
Deceiver / Winter / Deep Freeze / Winter
Retreat / Cheater / Diamonds And Rust /
Run Of The Mill / Genocide / Caviar And
Meths
POINT OF ENTRY, CBS 84834(1981)
14 SWEDEN, 14 UK, 39 USA
Don't Go / Turning Circles / Heading Out To
The Highway / Desert Plains / Solar Angels /
Troubleshooter / Hot Rockin' / All The Way /
You Say Yes
SCREAMING FOR VENGEANCE, CBS
85941 (1982) **14 SWEDEN, 11 UK, 17 USA**
Hellion / Electric Eye / Riding On The Wind /
Take These Chains / You've Got Another
Thing Coming / Screaming For Vengeance /
Pain And Pleasure / Fever / Devil's Child
DEFENDERS OF THE FAITH, CBS 25713
(1984) **2 SWEDEN, 19 UK, 18 USA**
Freewheel Burning / Jawbreaker / Rock
Hard, Ride Free / The Sentinel / Love Bites /
Eat Me Alive / Some Heads Are Gonna Roll
/ Night Comes Down / Heavy Duty /
Defenders Of The Faith
TURBO, Columbia 26641 (1986)
10 SWEDEN, 33 UK, 17 USA
Turbo Lover / Locked In / Private Property /
Parental Guidance / Rock You All Around
The World / Out In The Cold / Wild Nights,
Hot And Crazy Days / Hot For Love /
Reckless
PRIEST LIVE, Columbia 450 639-1 (1987)
19 SWEDEN, 47 UK, 38 USA

Out In The Cold / Heading Out To The
Highway / Metal Gods / Breaking The Law /
Love Bites / Some Heads Are Gonna Roll /
The Sentinel / Private Property / Rock You
All Around The World / Electric Eye / Turbo
Lover / Freewheel Burning / Parental
Guidance / Living After Midnight / You've Got
Another Thing Coming
RAM IT DOWN, Columbia 461108 1 (1988)
5 SWEDEN, 24 UK, 31 USA
Ram It Down / Heavy Metal / Love Zone /
Come And Get It / Hard As Iron / Blood Red
Skies / I'm A Rocker / Johnny B Goode /
Love You To Death / Monsters Of Rock
THE COLLECTION, Castle CCSMC 213
(1989)
PAINKILLER, Columbia 4672901 (1990)
19 SWEDEN, 24 UK, 26 USA
Painkiller / Hell Patrol / All Guns Blazing /
Leather Rebel / Metal Meltdown /
Nightcrawler / Between The Hammer And
The Anvil / A Touch Of Evil / Battle Hymn /
One Shot At Glory
PURE CLASSIC GOLD!, Columbia XPCD
261 (1993) (USA Promotion release)
Electric Eye / Victim Of Changes / Painkiller /
Turbo Lover / Exciter / You've Got Another
Thing Comin' / Heading Out To The Highway
/ Sinner / Screaming For Vengeance /
Nightcrawler
METALWORKS, Columbia (1993) 37 UK
Hellion / Electric Eye / Victim Of Changes /
Painkiller / Eat Me Alive / Devil's Child /
Dissident Aggressor / Delivering The Goods
/ Exciter / Breaking The Law / Hell Bent For
Leather / Blood Red Skies / Metal Gods /
Before The Dawn / Turbo Lover / Ram It
Down / Metal Meltdown / Screaming For
Vengeance / You've Got Another Thing
Comin' / Beyond The Realms Of Death /
Solar Angels / Bloodstone / Desert Plains /
Wild Nights, Hot And Crazy Days / Heading
Out To The Highway / Living After Midnight /
A Touch Of Evil / The Rage / Night Comes
Down / Sinner / Freewheel Burning /
Nightcrawler
STAR BOX, Epic ESCA 5858 (1993)
(Japanese release)
Exciter / The Sentinel / Breaking The Law /
Some Heads Are Gonna Roll / Green
Manalishi (With The Two Pronged Crown) /
Beyond The Realms Of Death / Hot Rockin' /
Sinner / Living After Midnight / Rock You All
Around The World / Dissident Aggressor /
You've Got Another Thing Comin' / All Guns
Blazing / Heavy Metal
ANTHOLOGY, Gull TECX-25883 (1995)
The Ripper / Tyrant / Victim Of Changes /
Rocka Rolla / One For The Road / Dreamer
Deceiver / Deceiver / Cheater / Winter /
Deep Freeze / Winter Retreat / Genocide /
Dying To Meet You / Diamonds And Rust /

JUDAS PRIEST

245

Epitaph / Island Of Domination / Never Satisfied / Cavier And Meths
PRISONERS OF PAIN, Sony A 28064 (1996)
Breaking The Law / Screaming For Vengeance / Metal Gods / Hell Bent For Leather / Let Us Prey / Burnin' Up / Some Heads Are Gonna Roll / The Green Manalishi (With The Two Pronged Crown) / Love Bites / Living After Midnight
THE BEAST OF JUDAS PRIEST, Deluxe (1996)
Dying To Meet You / Never Satisfied / Rocka Rolla / Diamonds And Rust / Victim Of Changes / Island Of Domination / The Ripper / Deceiver / One For The Road / Dreamer Deceiver / Prelude / Cavier And Meths / Epitaph / Tyrant / Genocide
JUGULATOR, SPV 085-18782 (1997)
9 GERMANY, 33 SWEDEN, 82 USA
Jugulator / Blood Stained / Dead Meat / Death Row / Decapitate / Burn In Hell / Brain Dead / Abductors / Bullet Train / Cathedral Spires
LIVING AFTER MIDNIGHT, Sony 4872422 (1997)
Better By You, Better Than Me / Take On The World / The Green Manalishi (With The Two Pronged Crown) / Living After Midnight / Breaking The Law / United / Hot Rockin' / You've Got Another Thing Comin' / The Hellion / Electric Eye / Freewheel Burning / Some Heads Are Gonna Roll / Turbo Lover / Locked In / Johnny B. Goode / Ram It Down / Painkiller / Touch Of Evil
PRIEST, LIVE & RARE, Sony 493008-2 (1998)
Beyond The Reams Of Death / White Heat, Red Hot / Starbreaker / Breaking The Law / Living After Midnight / The Green Manalishi (With The Two Pronged Crown) / Breaking The Law / You've Got Another Thing Comin' / Private Property / Turbo Lover (High Octane mix)
LIVE METAL MELTDOWN, CMC International 86261 (1998)
The Hellion / Electric Eye / Metal Gods / Grinder / Rapid Fire / Blood Stained / The Sentinel / Touch Of Evil / Burn In Hell / The Ripper / Bullet Train / Beyond The Realms Of Death / Death Row / Metal Meltdown / Night Crawler / Abductors / Victim Of Changes / Diamonds And Rust / Breaking The Law / The Green Manalishi (With The Two Pronged Crown) / Painkiller / You've Got Another Thing Coming / Hell Bent For Leather / Living After Midnight
CONCERT CLASSICS, Ranch Life (1998)
Hell Bent For Leather / Ripper / Running Wild / Living After Midnight / Sinner / Beyond The Realms Of Death / You Don't Have To Be Old To Be Wise / Grinder / Victim Of

Changes / Steeler / Genocide / Tyrant / Green Manalishi (With The Two Pronged Crown)
SIMPLY THE BEST, Sony (1999)
Living After Midnight / Breaking The Law / Painkiller / Don't Go / All Guns Blazing / Parental Guidance / Rock Forever / Night Crawler / Evening Star / Before The Dawn / Diamonds And Rust / Jawbreaker / Freewheel Burning
GENOCIDE, Recall 273 (2000)
One For The Road / Rocka Rolla / Winter / Deep Freeze / Winter Retreat / Cheater / Never Satisfied / Run Of The Mill / Dying To Meet You / Caviar And Meths / Diamonds And Rust / Victim Of Changes / The Ripper / Dreamer Deceiver / Deceiver / Prelude / Tyrant / Genocide / Epitaph / Island of Domination
DYING TO MEET YOU, Sonotec (2001)
One For The Road / Rocka Rolla / Winter / Deep Freeze / Winter Retreat / Cheater / Never Satisfied / Run Of The Mill / Dying To Meet You / Cavier And Meths
BREAKING THE LAW, Sony (2001)
Solar Angels / Heading Out To The Highway / Diamonds And Rust / Troubleshooter / Breaking The Law / Sinner / Beyond The Realms Of Death / Grinder / Hot Rockin' / You Don't Have To Be Old To Be Wise / Victim Of Changes / Green Manalishi (With The Two Pronged Crown) / Hell Bent For Leather / Living After Midnight
DEMOLITION, Atlantic 83480 (2001)
50 AUSTRIA, 72 FRANCE, 16 GERMANY, 55 SWEDEN, 89 SWITZERLAND
Machine Man / One On One / Hell Is Home / Jekyll & Hyde / Close To You / Devil Digger / Bloodsuckers / In Between / Feed On Me / Subterfuge / Lost & Found / Cyberface / Metal Messiah
LIMITED EDITION COLLECTOR'S SAMPLER, Sony SAMPCD11067 (2002) (Promotion release)
You've Got Another Thing Comin' / Metal Gods / The Green Manalishi (With The Two Pronged Crown) / Diamonds And Rust / Parental Guidance / Between The Hammer And The Anvil / Beyond The Realms Of Death (Live) / Private Property (Live) / Turbo Lover (Video) / You've Got Another Thing Comin' (Video)

KALEDON (ITALY)
Line-Up: Claudio Conti (vocals), Alex Mele (guitar), Tommy Nemesio (guitar), Paolo Lezziroli (bass), David Folchitto (drums)

The inception of KALEDON lay in the departure from RIVER OF CHANGE of guitarist Alex Mele during 1998. Bringing together vocalist Anthony Drago, rhythm guitarist Tommaso Nemesio, bass player Paolo Lezziroli and drummer Dario Sacco KALEDON was borne, soon recording the 1999 demo 'Spirit Of The Dragon'. The band would then introduce RIVER OF CHANGE keyboard player Fabio Bernadi, re-recording 'Spirit Of The Dragon' with additional keyboard textures and laying down a further demo 'God Says Yes'. The band's labours paid off, KALEDON being invited to open for DIO in June of 2000.

With significant line-up changes taking place, the drafting of new singer Claudio Conti, another RIVER OF CHANGE veteran, and drummer David 'War Machine' Folchitto, KALEDON opted to re-record 'God Says Yes' to highlight these new personnel. The group would also bring in a new keyboard player, former GHOST RIDER man Daniele Fuligni. Signing to the Steelborn label KALEDON cut their debut album 'Legend Of The Forgotten Reign'. The band would also donate renditions of MANOWAR and DEEP PURPLE tracks for tribute albums.

Albums:
LEGEND OF THE FORGOTTEN REIGN, Steelborn (2002)
The Calling / In Search Of Kaledon / Army Of The Undead King / Thunder In The Sky / Streets Of The Kingdom / Spirit Of The Dragon / Hero Of The Land / God Says Yes / Deep Forest / Desert Land Of Warriors / The Jackal's Fall

KALMAH (FINLAND)
Line-Up: Pekka Kokko (vocals), Antti Kokko (guitar), Altti Vetelinen (bass), Pasi Hiltula (keyboards), Petri Sankala (drums)

KALMAH was borne out of a musical union in 1993 by vocalist Pekka Kokko and ETERNAL TEARS OF SORROW drummer Petri Sankala entitled ANCESTOR. In this incarnation the duo cut a series of demos, later enlisting guitarist Antti Kokko and keyboard player Antti Matti Talala. ANCESTOR would bow out with their fifth session 'Under The Burbot's Nest' and evolve into KALMAH during August of 1998. This transition not only saw a name change but a shift in musical direction from Death Metal to a more melodically inclined path. KALMAH heralded their arrival with the 'Svieri Obraza' promotional tape in late 1999.

Bassist Altti Vetelinen, another ETERNAL TEARS OF SORROW man, was inducted during Spring of 2000. Shortly after Talala would be usurped by Pasi Hiltula as the band signed to the Spikefarm label for the debut record 'Swamplord'. The album would see releases in Japan, through King Records, and America on Century Media.

Prior to recording of the sophomore 'They Will Return' album both Altti Vetelinen and Petri Sankala bowed out. KALMAH was brought back up to strength with the addition of two CATAMENIA personnel, bassist Timo Lehtinen and drummer Janne Kusmin. 'They Will Return' was notable for the inclusion of a cover of MEGADETH's 'Skin O' My Teeth'.

Albums:
SWAMPLORD, Spikefarm NAULA 012 (2000)
Evil In You / Withering Away / Heritance Of Berija / Black Roija / Dance Of The Water / Hades / Alteration / Using The Word
THEY WILL RETURN, Spikefarm (2002)
Hollow Heart / Swamphell / Principle Hero / Human Fates / They Will Return / Kill The Idealist / The Blind Leader / My Nation / Skin O' My Teeth

KAMELOT (USA)
Line-Up: Mark Vanderbilt (vocals), Thomas Youngblood (guitar), Glenn Barry (bass), Dave Pavlicko (keyboards), Richard Warner (drums)

Noted Progressive Metal band. Prior to the recording of third album 'Siege Perilous' KAMELOT recruited Roy Khan on vocals, previously with the highly rated defunct Norwegian Progressive Metal band CONCEPTION. Youngblood founded a side project MONARQUE in 1999 fronted buy none other than former KAMELOT vocalist Mark Vanderbilt.

The band's 2001 album was put in jeopardy by Khan becoming the victim of a car crash. The singer emerged relatively unscathed though and sessions for the 'Karma' album continued apace.

KAMELOT would put in a series of European festival performances in the summer of 2001 appearing at Italy's 'Gods Of Metal', Germany's 'Bang Your Head' and Spain's 'Rock Machine' events. 'Karma' became the band's debut chart showing in Germany reaching no. 85 in the national charts.

KAMELOT
Photo : Nico Wobben

Youngblood would also contribute to the adventurous 2001 CONSORTIUM PROJECT debut album.

KAMELOT forged an alliance with AXXIS for a lengthy run of European tour dates commencing on the 16th of January 2002 at the Planet B in Korbach, Germany. AXXIS headlined on German dates before switching to the role of opening act for shows in the rest of Europe. These shows would see KAMELOT employing the services of RHAPSODY drummer Alex Holzwarth as a stand in for the first nine shows. Regular drummer Casey Grillo took back the reins for the Offenbach gig.

Albums:
ETERNITY, Noise N 0226-2 (1995)
Eternity / Black Tower / Call Of The Sea / Proud Nomad / Red Sands / One Of The Hunted / Fire Within / Warbird / What About Me / Etude Jongcleur / The Gleeman
DOMINION, Noise N 0272-2 (1996)
Ascension / Heaven / Rise Again / One Day I'll Win / We Are Not Separate / Birth Of A Hero / Creation / Sin / Song Of Roland / Crossing Two Rivers / Troubled Mind
SIEGE PERILOUS, Noise N 0297-2 (1998)
Providence / Millennium / King's Eyes / Expedition / Where I Reign / Parting Visions / Once A Dream / Rhydin / Irea / Siege
THE FOURTH LEGACY, Noise (2000)
New Allegiance / The Fourth Legacy / Silent Goddess / Desert Reign / Nights Of Arabia / The Shadow Of Uther / A Sailorman's Hymn / Alexandria / The Inquisitor / Glory / Until Kingdom Come / Lunar Sanctum
EXPEDITION, Noise (2000)
Intro / Until Kingdom Come / Expedition / The Shadow Of Uther / Millennium / A Sailorman's Hymn / The Fourth Legacy / Call Of The Sea / Desert Reign / Nights Of Arabia / We Three Kings / One Day / We Are Not Separate…
KARMA, Noise (2001) 85 GERMANY
Regalis Apertura / Forever / Wings Of Despair / The Spell / Don't You Cry / Karma / The Light I Shine On You / Temples Of Gold / Across The Highlands / Elizabeth I: Mirror, Mirror / Elizabeth II: Requiem For The Innocent / Fall From Grace

KARMA (BRAZIL)
Line-Up: Thiago Bianchi (vocals), Chico Dehira (guitar), Felipe Andreolli (bass), Fabrizio Di Sarno (keyboards), Marcell Cardoso (drums)

Technically accomplished Power Metal. KARMA musicians keyboard player Fabrizio Di Sarno and guitarist Chico Dehira would session on PAUL DIANNO's 'Nomad' album.

Extracurricular activities for other KARMA members included vocalist Thiago Bianchi and drummer Marcell Cardoso appearing on the FIRESIGN debut album.

In August of 2001 bassist Andria Busic, an erstwhile member of DR. SIN, would be replaced by former ANGRA man Felipe Andreolli.

KARMA have donated a track to the QUEENSRYCHE tribute album 'Warning Of Raging Empires'.

KENZINER (FINLAND / USA)
Line-Up: Stephen Fredrick (vocals), Jarno Keskinen (guitar / bass), Dennis Lesh (drums)

Centred upon the talents of Finnish guitar guru Jarno Keskinen. Recorded in Atlanta, Georgia Symphonic Metal act KENZINER's 1998 album 'Timescape' is produced by noted American guitarist DAVID T. CHASTAIN. Session bass and keyboards were courtesy of David Shew. Drums come from TROUBLE, CHASTAIN and STYGIAN man Dennis Lesh. Vocalist Stephen Fredrick is ex-BILLY THE KID.

KENZINER made a successful return with 'The Prophecies' album.

Fredrick and another former member Brian Harris would, in collusion with guitarist Gus G. and bassist Konstantine, create FIREWIND for the 2001 album 'Between Heaven And Hell'.

Albums:
TIMESCAPE, Inside Out Music LMP 9806-004 CD (1998)
Future Signs / Into The Light / Images Of The Past / Dreamer / Thru The End / Timescape / Walking In The Rain/ Seasons / In The Silence / Land Of Shadows
THE PROPHECIES, Limb Music Productions (1999)
Live Forever / The Razor's Edge / Carry On Tomorrow / Race With Time / Trail Of Tears / Eternity / Dimensions / Like A Paradise / Through The Fire / Prophecies

KILLERS (UK)
Line-Up: Paul Dianno (vocals), Nick Burr (guitar), Cliff Evans (guitar), Gavin Cooper (bass), Steve Hopgood (drums)

Fronted by IRON MAIDEN and BATTLEZONE former vocalist PAUL DIANNO. KILLERS, named after IRON MAIDEN's classic second album, struck a blow for meat n' potatoes traditional Metal with their release of 'Murder One' in 1992. The band formed in America with an initial line-up of Dianno, ex-CHICKENSHACK, HEAD

249

FIRST and TANK guitarist Cliff Evans, ex-DRIVE SHE SAID guitarist Ray Ditone, RAVEN bassist John Gallagher and former CHINATOWN, PERSIAN RISK, JAGGED EDGE and PASSION drummer Steve Hopgood.

With this line-up in place KILLERS undertook a tour of South America having previously laid down a studio session recorded in New York for a 'live' album intended solely for South American release. These tapes comprised IRON MAIDEN and BATTLEZONE songs.

Scoring a deal with RCA Records in America (by auditioning with a set made up entirely of IRON MAIDEN songs!) KILLERS changed the band around by adding former IDOL RICH and PASSION guitarist Nick Burr and ex-PASSION bassist Gavin Cooper, with Gallagher having left to reform RAVEN. The subsequent album featured a reworking of IRON MAIDEN's 'Remember Tomorrow' and a cover of T-REX's 'Children Of The Revolution' which was lifted as a single.

KILLERS toured heavily first in Britain on a club level before departing for America then a series of shows at large venues in Japan. Upon their return to Britain more club dates were slotted in, but by now it had become apparent that success in their homeland was a forlorn hope.

At this juncture the previously recorded New York session was released unofficially world-wide much to the band's chagrin.

KILLERS signed to Newcastle's Bleeding Hearts Records in 1994 and released the menacingly heavy 'Menace To Society' album. The band were still dogged with problems though as Dianno found himself incarcerated in L.A.'s County Jail on drugs and firearms charges! After three months in the slammer the vocalist was eventually bailed to return to Britain to finish the album.

This interlude behind bars was to interrupt the band's progress further though as an attempt to capitalise on a live showing at the Los Angeles Foundation Forum event was scuppered when upon setting foot on American soil Dianno was handcuffed and put onto the next plane home.

A live album (aptly titled 'Killers Live') was later recorded for a 1996 release. Dianno himself launched further solo albums in a more melodic vein before resurrecting his old unit BATTLEZONE for a sell out Brazilian tour in January of 1998. Erstwhile KILLERS colleagues Cooper and Burr joined him on this South American jaunt. Burr then teamed up with ex-GRIM REAPER front man Steve Grimmett for his LIONSHEART band and a later project titled PRIDE. Another KILLERS man, drummer Peter Newdect, would join Grimmett on venture entitled SEVEN DEADLY SINS.

Although Evans has busied himself with TANK on tour and in the studio KILLERS was, minus Dianno, still a going concern in 2000 with rumours that PRAYING MANTIS singer Tony O'Hora may well be the new front man. Dianno meantime had resurrected DIANNO for the successful 'Nomad' album, recorded entirely with Brazilian musicians.

Both Dianno and Evans would act as session guests on the 2001 'Longevity' album issued by German Gothic Metal band RE VISION. During 2002 Dianno was back in the limelight, performing live with a band unit entitled PAUL DIANNO & KILLERS and promoting a no holds barred autobiography 'The Beast'.

Albums:
MURDER ONE, RCA Zoo PD 90643 (1992)
Impaler / The Beast Arises / Children Of The Revolution / S&M / Takin' No Prisoners / Marshall Lokjaw / Protector / Dreamkeeper / Awakening / Remember Tomorrow
MENACE TO SOCIETY, Bleeding Hearts BLEED 11 (1994)
Advance And Be Recognised / Die By The Gun / Menace To Society / ? / Think Brutal / Past Due / Faith Healer / IChemical Imbalance / A Song For You / Three Words / Conscience / City Of Fools
SOUTH AMERICAN ASSAULT LIVE, Magnetic Air 4701-4 (1994)
Overloaded / Wrathchild / Murders In The Rue Morgue / Phantom Of The Opera / Children Of Madness / Sanctuary / Strange World / Smoke On The Water
KILLERS LIVE, Hardware HR001 (1996)
Advance And Be Recognised / Marshall Lokjaw / The Beast / Wrathchild / A Song For You / Three Words / Impaler / Murders In The Rue Morgue / Children Of The Revolution / Chemical Imbalance / Remember Tomorrow / Protector / Die By The Gun / Faith Healer / Sanctuary / Phantom Of The Opera
NEW, LIVE & RARE, Bleeding Hearts CDBLEED 28 (1998)
Advance And Be Recognised / Die By The Gun / Marshall Lokjaw / Wrathchild / Three Words / Faith Healer / Murders In The Rue Morgue / Children Of The Revolution / Sanctuary / Phantom Of The Opera / City Of Fools / Chemical Imbalance / Past Due / Impaler / Protector / Menace To Society / Remember Tomorrow / Think Brutal / The Beast / A Song For You
LIVE AT THE WHISKEY, Spitfire 5173-2 (2001)
Impaler / Wrathchild / A Song For You / Marshall Lokjaw / Children Of The Revolution / Three Words / Protector / Die By The Gun / Remember Tomorrow / Phantom

Of The Opera / Sanctuary

KINETIC DISSENT (Atlanta, GA, USA)
Line-Up: Dwight Bales (vocals), Stephan Danyo (guitar), Rick McConnell (guitar), Troy Stephens (bass), Ed Reimer (drums)

Albums:
I WILL FIGHT NO MORE FOREVER,
Roadracer RRD 9327 (1991)
Cults Of Unreason / Banished / Melanin / 12 Angry Men / Social Syndrome / I Will Fight No More Forever / Novocaine Response / Testing Ground / Reworked

KING (SLOVALKIA)

A solo Heavy Metal venture from keyboard player Ivan Kral, a.k.a. 'King', previously of Death Metal band LUNATIC GODS. Kral employed vocalist / bassist Dodo and guitarist Hirax for recording of the 'Royal Metal' record.

Albums:
ROYAL METAL, Impact (2000)
Metal Anthem / Prince Mojmir I / A Maiden From The Castle / Killing Fields / Face Behind The Glass (Sophia Bosniak) / Wizard / Snivanie O Sne

KING DIAMOND (DENMARK)
Line-Up: King Diamond (vocals), Pete Blakk (guitar), Andy LaRocque (guitar), Hal Patino (bass), Mickey Dee (drums)

KING DIAMOND
Photo : Nico Wobben

In April 1985 cult Satanic Metal band MERCYFUL FATE finally split and enigmatic vocalist King Diamond regrouped with MERCYFUL FATE guitarist Michael Denner and bassist Timi G. Hansen (formerly known as Timi Grabber), forming a new band centred around his own stage personality KING DIAMOND. The other original band members were ex-NADIR and GEISHA drummer Mickey Dee (real name Delaoglou) and guitarist Floyd Konstandin, the latter being superseded by former TRAFALGER guitarist Andy LaRocque.

King opted to concentrate his efforts mainly on America, where MERCYFUL FATE had built a strong and loyal following. The debut album, 'Fatal Portrait' echoed heavily his former band but with more emphasis on overblown horror theatrics. The lyrical shift was a wise one as King had been previously been exposed for his completely naive lack of understanding of Satanism and the occult themes that peppered the lyrics of MERCYFUL FATE.

King had fallen into the trap of getting involved in a conversation with 'Kerrang!' magazine journalist Dave Dickson on the subject of Aleister Crowley and Magick for which, according to the interview that saw print, he had few answers. Allegedly an ardent follower of Crowley's philosophies and supposed Satanic practices (he was quick to claim responsibility for the 'demon' that electrocuted GIRLSCHOOL's Kim McAullife), King fell victim to someone who had recently taken a few widely available quotes inviting King to comment. King's credibility never really recovered in the eyes of the European media. The second album, 'Abigail', was the first in a series of concept affairs that KING DIAMOND were to turn into highly elaborate stage-shows. Following recording of 'Abigail' Michael Denner left due to feeling the pressure of being constantly on the road and was swiftly replaced with ex-MADISON guitarist Michael 'Moon' Myllynen.

'Abigail' was toured around America with Chicago Christian Doom Metal band TROUBLE, then KING DIAMOND undertook 15 shows in Germany opening for MOTÖRHEAD as well as headline shows. The hard graft of touring paid off and in America 'Abigail' reached number 123 in the Billboard charts selling over 150,000 copies. Prior to recording next album 'Them', KING DIAMOND relocated to Los Angeles in order to have a realistic crack at the American market. The band also replaced Myllynen and Timi Hansen with ex-GEISHA guitarist Pete Blakk and bassist Hal Patino.

'Them' (another conceptual affair) bolstered the continuing success of KING DIAMOND in

KING DIAMOND
Photo : Nico Wobben

America by charting in the Billboard top 100, but touring plans were initially shelved to allow the band to contribute soundtrack music to the horror movie 'Boggs'. Following the recording of 'Them' drummer Mickey Dee quit, later to work with DON DOKKEN and WWIII before landing a permanent stay in MOTÖRHEAD. He was replaced with San Franciscan Chris Whitemyer, previously drum tech for WHITESNAKE's Tommy Aldridge, although the next record, 'Conspiracy' (which continued the plot of 'Them') beckoned in another drummer in Swedish native Snowy Shaw.

Shaw (real name Tommy Helgesson) would later record with MEMENTO MORI and WHIPPED CREAM in addition to joining King in a reformation of MERCYFUL FATE.

More line-up changes befell the group shortly after recording1990's 'The Eye' when long-time guitarist Pete Blakk quit to form his own band TOTEM.

Around the turn of the decade King chose to reform MERCYFUL FATE, although he also carried on his solo career and was to add a new complement of band members for the KING DIAMOND comeback affair entitled 'The Spider's Lullaby' in 1995. The new band included recently added bassist Mike Webb and guitarist Charlie D'Angelo. The album proved a solid success, gaining chart places in Sweden, Denmark and Finland and was the first for new label Massacre, King having ended his long term association with Roadrunner Records with the 'Live In Europe '87 - Abigail' album back in 1991.

A further record appeared in 1996 entitled 'The Graveyard' before, in late 1997, Roadrunner Records reissued the KING DIAMOND back catalogue in remastered form, with some albums featuring additional bonus tracks. Both 'The Eye' and 'Live In Europe '87' were also remastered but do not have any additional material added. Shaw, D'Angelo and La Rocque ventured into outside activity by founding ILLWILL releasing a 1998 album.

1998's 'Voodoo' album, another horror conceptual effort, saw King and LaRocque (who, in the interim, had produced the debut album by Sweden's MIDVINTER during 1997) joined by second guitarist Herb Simonson, bassist Chrise Estes and drummer John Luke Herbert. The band added Canadian guitarist Glen Drover from the highly rated EIDOLON for tour work. Drover would subsequently appear on the 2000 KING DIAMOND album 'House Of God'. Former bassist Hal Patino also returned to the ranks in 2000 ousting David Harbour.

With KING DIAMOND signing to the Metal Blade label for European releases former label Massacre Records were quick to issue a compilation entitled 'Nightmare In The Nineties'. The King would contribute guest vocals to FOO FIGHTERS man Dave Grohl's Metal elite PROBOT project album of 2001.

2002 proved an eventful year for KING DIAMOND with a rare admission from an artist that album sales were on a downturn. The band landed the blame squarely on downloading and advised fans they would be recording a new album entitled 'The Puppet Master' at King's home studio to save on recording costs.

Singles/EPs:
No Presents For Christmas / Charon, Roadrunner RR12485 (1987)
The Family Ghost / Shrine, Roadrunner (1987)
Halloween / Them / No Presents / Shrine / Lake / Phone Call, Roadrunner RR 2455 1 (1988)
Welcome Home, Roadrunner (1988) (USA promotion)

Albums:
FATAL PORTRAIT, Roadrunner RR9721 (1986) 33 SWEDEN
The Candle / The Jonah / The Portrait / Dressed In White / Charon / Lurking In The Dark / Halloween / Voices From The Past / Haunted
ABIGAIL, Roadrunner RR 9622 (1987) **39 SWEDEN, 123 USA**
Funeral / Arrival / A Mansion In The Darkness / Family Ghost / The 7th Day Of July 1777 / Possession / Abigail / Black Horsemen
THEM, Roadrunner RR 9550 (1988) **38 SWEDEN**
Out From The Asylum / Welcome Home / The Invisible Guests / Tea / Mother's Getting Weaker / Bye, Bye, Missy / A Broken Spell / The Accusation Chair / Them / Twilight Symphony / Coming Home
CONSPIRACY, Roadrunner RR 9461 2 (1989) **41 SWEDEN**
At The Graves / Sleepless Nights / Lies / A Visit From The Dead / The Wedding Dream / Amon Belongs To Them / Something Weird / Victimised / Let It Be Done / Cremation
THE EYE, Roadrunner RR 9346 (1990)
Eye Of The Witch / The Trial (Chambre Ardente) / Burn / Two Little Girls / Into The Convent / Father Picard / Behind These Walls / The Meetings / Insanity / 1642 Imprisonment / The Curse
LIVE IN EUROPE '87 - ABIGAIL (LIVE), Roadrunner RR 9287 (1991)
Funeral / Arrival / Come To The Sabbath / The Family Ghost / The 7th Day Of July 1777 / Portrait / The Possession / Abigail /

253

The Candle / No Presents For Christmas
A DANGEROUS MEETING, Roadrunner RR
9117-2 (1992) (Best of compilation CD with
MERCYFUL FATE)
The Candle / Charon / Halloween / No
Presents For Christmas / Arrival / Abigail /
Welcome Home / Sleepless Nights / Eye Of
The Witch
THE SPIDER'S LULLABY, Massacre
MASSCD 062 (1995)
From The Other Side / Killer / The Poltergeist
/ Dreams / Moonlight / Six Feet Under / The
Spider's Lullabye / Eastmann's Cure / Room
17 / To The Morgue
THE GRAVEYARD, Massacre MASS CD
103 (1996)
The Graveyard / Black Hill Sanatorium /
Waiting / Heads On The Wall / Whispers /
I'm Not A Stranger / Digging Graves / Meet
Me At Midnight / Sleep Tight Little Baby /
Daddy / Trick Or Treat / Up From The Grave /
I Am / Lucy Forever
FATAL PORTRAIT, Roadrunner RR 8789-2
(1997) (Remastered, reissue featuring bonus
tracks)
The Cradle / The Jonah / The Portrait /
Dressed In White / Charon / Lurking In The
Dark / Halloween / Voices From The Past /
Haunted / No Presents For Christmas / The
Lake
ABIGAIL, Roadrunner RR 8788-2 (1997)
(Re-mastered, reissue featuring bonus
tracks)
Funeral / Arrival / A Mansion In Darkness /
The Family Ghost / The 7th Day Of July
1777 / Omens / The Possession / Abigail /
Black Horsemen / Shrine / A Mansion In
Darkness (Rough Mix) / The Family Ghost
(Rough Mix) / The Possession (Rough Mix)
THEM, Roadrunner RR 8785-2 (1997) (Re-
mastered reissue featuring bonus tracks)
Out From The Asylum / Welcome Home /
The Invisible Guests / Tea / Mother's Getting
Weaker / Bye, Bye Missy / A Broken Spell /
The Accusation Chair / "Them" / Twilight
Symphony / Coming Home / Phone Call /
The Invisible Guests (Rehearsal) / Bye, Bye
Missy (Rehearsal)
CONSPIRACY, Roadrunner RR 8787-2
(1997) (Remastered reissue featuring bonus
tracks)
At The Graves / Sleepless Nights / Lies / A
Visit From The Dead / The Wedding Dream /
"Amon" Belongs To "Them" / Something
Weird / Victimised / Let It Be Done /
Cremation / At The Graves (Alternate Mix) /
Cremation (Live Show Mix)
VOODOO, Massacre MAS CD0155 (1998)
55 SWEDEN
Louisiana Darkness / 'L.O.A.' House / Life
After Death / Voodoo / A Secret / Salem /
One Down, Two To Go/ Sending Of Dead /

Sarah's Night / The Exorcist / Unclean Spirits
/ Cross Of Baron Samedi / If Only They
Knew / Aftermath
HOUSE OF GOD, Massacre (2000)
60 SWEDEN
Upon The Cross / The Trees Have Eyes /
Follow The Wolf / House Of God / Black
Devil / The Pact / Goodbye / Just A Shadow
/ Help!!! / Passenger To Hell / Catacombs /
This Place Is Terrible / Peace Of Mind
**20 YEARS AGO – A NIGHT OF
REHEARSAL**, Metal Blade 14359 (2001)
Locked Up In The Snow / Holy Mountain
Lights / Crazy Tonight / Virgin / Kill For Fun /
The End / Road Life / Soul Overture / Doctor
Cranium / Disgrace / I Need Blood / Radar
Love
ABIGAIL II - THE REVENGE, Metal Blade
(2002) **24 FINLAND, 42 SWEDEN**
Spare This Life (Intro) / The Storm / A
Mansion In Sorrow / Miriam / Little One /
Slippery Stairs / The Crypt / Broken Glass /
More Than Pain / The Wheelchair / Spirits /
Mommy / Sorry Dear (Outro)

TIMO KOTIPELTI (FINLAND)

STRATOVARIUS singer TIMO KOTIPELTO
would release his debut solo album 'Waiting
For The Dawn' through the German Century
Media label. The record, a conceptual piece
based on Egyptian mythology and clad in
artwork by the famed IRON MAIDEN artist
Derek Riggs proved to be much harder edged
affair than the Symphonic inclinations of
STRATOVARIUS, and boasted a major haul
of guest sessioneers.
Included were STRATOVARIUS colleague
Jari Kainulainen, Mike Romeo of
SYMPHONY X, ROLAND GRAPOW of
HELLOWEEN and MASTERPLAN,
WARMEN's Sami Virtanen, Janne Warmen of
WARMEN and CHILDREN OF BODOM,
Mikko Harkin of SONATA ARCTICA, drummer
Mirka Rantanen of WARMEN,
THUNDERSTONE and TUNNELVISION and
Gas from H.I.M.
Japanese versions of the album on the
Avalon Marquee label added an exclusive
track 'Secret Name'.

Albums:
WAITING FOR THE DAWN, Century Media
(2002)
Intro / Travel Through Time / Beginning /
Lord Of Eternity / Knowledge And Wisdom /
Battle Of The Gods / Beauty Has Come /
Vizier / Chosen By Re / Waiting For The
Dawn / Arise / Movement Of The Nile

KRLES (CZECH REPUBLIC)

Albums:
DEJTE PLAMENIUM CO HORI, (2000)
_elezo Zlato A Hn_j / Bastard / Kráv n' Roll /
Notorhead / Dejte Plamen_m Co Ho_í /
Hymna Politik_ / No_ní M_ra / Harley
Chrchleyson / Esmeralda / Geronimo
TO, SIA Production (2001)
_erti Jdou / O Cem Vítr Zpívá / Posledního
Kousne Pes / Je_t_ Jednou !? / Ostrov
Doklad_ / Carrie / Kletba / TO (Kruh Se
Uzavírá)

LÄÄZ ROCKIT
(San Francisco, CA, USA)
Line-Up: Michael Coons
(vocals), Aaron Jellum (guitar),
Phil Kettner (guitar), Willy Lange
(bass), Victor Agnello (drums)

LÄÄZ ROCKIT was formed by vocalist Michael Coons and guitarist Aaron Jellum who stole second guitarist Phil Kettner from a rival local outfit. The inaugural bass player Dave Starr actually named the band (after a Sci-Fi weapon in a Clint Eastwood movie) as in their formative days they were called DEPTH CHARGE.

Having added drummer Victor Agnello to the ranks LÄÄZ ROCKIT replaced Starr in 1983 with Willy Lange following a support slot to RATT. Starr created power trio BLACK LEATHER before joining VICIOUS RUMOURS.

LÄÄZ ROCKIT were originally signed to RATT manager Marshall Berle's Timecoast label, but Berle disbanded the company once his charges had been picked up by Atlantic, leaving the door open for Mark Leonard's Target concern to sign the group, releasing the debut 'City's Gonna Burn' album in September 1984.

LÄÄZ ROCKIT began a tour of America in support of their debut album as opening act to GRIM REAPER and EXCITER, but were unceremoniously removed after three shows. Lange would audition for the position of bassist for METALLICA in 1986.

With 'Know Your Enemy' gaining the band more media attention LÄÄZ ROCKIT managed some European shows opening for MOTÖRHEAD and a slot on the prestigious Aardschok Festival in Holland. Agnello departed, but returned in time for American dates. Further British shows saw the band opening for EXODUS.

The band toured Europe with support from Dutchmen OSIRIS in 1989. The 1991 album 'Nothing Sacred' saw Coons and Jellum joined by bassist Scott Dominguez, guitarist Scott Sargeant and drummer Dave Chavarri. Erstwhile LÄÄZ ROCKIT guitarist Ken Savitch joined Illinois's SINDROME during 1991.

Sargeant joined KILLING CULTURE before teaming up with SKINLAB in 1998. Chavarri joined PRO-PAIN.

Singles/EPs:
Holiday In Cambodia / Mirror To Madness / Prelude To Death (Live) / Forced To Fight (Live), Roadracer RO 24361 (1990)

Albums:
CITY'S GONNA BURN, Target (1984)

City's Gonna Burn / Caught In The Act / Take No Prisoners / Dead Man's Eyes / Forced To Fight / Silent Scream / Prelude / Something More
NO STRANGER TO DANGER, Steamhammer 081866 (1985)
Dreams Die Hard / I've Got Time / Town To Town / Backbreaker / Stand Alone / Spared From The Fire / Off The Deep End / Tonight Alive / Wrecking Machine
KNOW YOUR ENEMY, Music For Nations MFN 81 (1987)
Demolition/ Last Breath / Euroshima / Most Dangerous Game / Shot To Hell / Say Goodbye M.F. / Self Destruct / Means To An End / I'm Electric / Mad Axe Attack / Shit's Ugly
ANNIHILATION PRINCIPLE, Enigma CDENV 521 (1989)
Mirror Into Madness / Chasin' Charlie / Fire In The Hole / Shadow Company / Holiday In Cambodia / Mob Justice / Bad Blood
NOTHING SACRED, Roadracer (1991)
In The Name Of The Father And The Gun / Into The Asylum / Greed Machine / Too Far Gone / Curiosity Kills / Suicide City / The Enemy Within / Nobody's Child / Silence Is A Lie / Necropolis
TASTE OF REBELLION (LIVE), (1991)
In The Name Of The Father And The Gun... / Greed Machine / Fire In The Hole / City's Gonna Burn / Leatherface / The Omen / Suicide City / The Enemy Within / Prelude To Death / Into The Asylum / Holiday In Cambodia / Curiosity Kills

LABYRINTH (ITALY)
Line-Up: Joe Terry (vocals), Olaf Thörsen (guitar), Anders Rain (guitar), Chriz Breeze (bass), Frank Andiver (drums / keyboards)

Progressive Power Metal. LABYRINTH issued the 'Midnight Resistance' six track demo tape to secure a deal with Underground Symphony Records for the 'No Limits' record. During 1997 LABYRINTH would replace vocalist Fabio Leone with Dan Keying for live work. The latter would be invited to join the band full time but opted to create his own Power Metal act CYDONIA.

Vocalist Joe Terry, under his real name of Fabio Leone, joined two acts ATHENA and RHAPSODY, the latter being highly successful.

LABYRINTH at this juncture comprised guitarists Olaf Thörsen (Carlo Magnani) and Anders Rain (Andrea Cantarelli) on guitars, Andrew McPauls (Andrea De Paoli) on keyboards, Rob Tyrant (Roberto Tiranti) on vocals, Chris Breeze (Cristiano Bertocco) on bass, and VISION DIVINE man Matt Stancioiu on drums.

As a side venture Andrew McPauls issued the 1998 SHADOWS OF STEEL eponymous album, also bringing in his LABYRINTH colleagues Olaf Thörsen, Chris Breeze and Frank Andivers as guests. Matt Stancioiu would aid ALICE IN DARKLAND for their opening demo and hook up with Keying's CYDONIA during 1999.

The 1999 mini-album 'Timeless Crime' would give fans an added extra in the form of an unaccredited 'hidden' track, a version of SANCTUARY's 'Die For My Sins'.

Leone and Thörsen would reunite in 2000 for the VISION DIVINE project and eponymous album. Thörsen would guest on the 2000 SKYLARK album 'Divine Gates'. Ex-LABYRINTH drummer Frank Andiver would later turn up as a member of the WONDERLAND project band.

Singles/EPs:
Piece Of Time / In The Shade / Call Me / Miles Away, Underground Symphony USCD-005 (1995)

Albums:
NO LIMITS, Underground Symphony USCD007 (1996)
Mortal Sin / Midnight Resistance / Dreamland / Piece Of Time / Vertigo / In The Shade / No Limits / The Right Sign / Red Zone / Time Has Come / Looking For
RETURN TO HEAVEN DENIED, Metal Blade (1998)
Moonlight / New Horizons / The Night Of Dreams / Lady Lost In Time / State Of Grace / Heaven Denied / Thunder / Feel (Legend B. remix) / Time After Time / Falling Rain / Die For Freedom
TIMELESS CRIME, Metal Blade 14259 (1999)
Save Me / Out Of Memory / In The Shade / Falling Rain / Die For My Sins
SONS OF THUNDER, Metal Blade 14325 (2000)
Chapter 1 / Kathryn / Sons Of Thunder / Elegy / Behind The Mask / Touch The Rainbow / Rage Of The King / Save Me / Love / I Feel You

LANA LANE (USA)

Concord, California native LANA LANE, highly popular in Japan, deals in Symphonic melodic Rock. Indeed, Lane has made such an impression on the genre she is known as "The Queen of Symphonic Rock". The debut album, which featured BLUE MURDER and THE FIRM bassist TONY FRANKLIN, guitarist Neil Citron, drummer Tommy Amato and keyboard player ERIK NORLANDER,

was widely acknowledged to contain some superior music blighted by a horrendous mix and production. The debut was entirely remixed and new music added for a 1998 re-release.

Her 2000 record 'Queen Of The Ocean' would see Citron, Norlander and Amato all involved yet again along with guitarist Mark McCrite and stick bassist Don Schiff.

Lane would guest on the 2001 album 'Fata Morgana' for Dutch veterans HELLOISE. The lady would add to ever rapidly growing catalogue in January of 2002 with the 'Project Shangri La' opus. Guests included RING OF FIRE leader MARK BOALS and Henge Engelke of DREAMTIDE. Lane would also figure prominently on the STAR ONE 'Space Metal' Sci-Fi concept album assembled by ARYEON's Arjen Anthony Lucassen, gracing the Japanese variant's exclusive extra track, a cover of LED ZEPPELIN's 'No Quarter'.

LANA LANE would put in an American show at the Troubadour venue in West Hollywood on April 22nd to mark the commencement of a world tour. The band for this occasion would prove a cast list of notables including ERIK NORLANDER, AYREON guitarist Arjen Anthony Lucassen, stick bassist Don Schiff and BLACK SABBATH and DIO drummer Vinnie Appice.

LANA LANE

Albums:
LOVE IS AN ILLUSION, Avalon Marquee (1995)

Love Is An Illusion Prelude / Love Is An Illusion / Coloured Life / Cold Outside / Through The Fire / Through The Rain / Faerie Tale State Of Mind / Dream Burnin' Down / Can't Find My Way Home / Love Is An Illusion Postlude
CURIOUS GOODS, Belle Antique (1996)
Curious Goods Part One / Emerald City / Escher's Staircase / Heart Of Dawn / Take A Breath / Reverie / Satyr's Moon / Symphony Of Angels (Arias And Fables) / Two Can Play That Game / Voices / Do It Again / Curious Goods Part Two / Clouds
BALLAD COLLECTION, Avalon Marquee (1998)
Avalon / Athena's Shadow / Stardust / Through The Fire (Acoustic version) / When Time Stood Still / Clouds (1998 version) / Heart Of Dawn (1998 version) / Take A Breath (1998 version) / Across The Universe / Avalon Reprise
LIVE IN JAPAN, Avalon Marquee (1998)
Garden Of The Moon / Coloured Life / Destination Roswell / Seasons / Love Is An Illusion / Under The Olive Tree / Moongarden / Through The Fire / Escher's Staircase / Faerie Tale State Of Mind / Symphony Of Angels
LOVE IS AN ILLUSION, Avalon Marquee (1998)
Love Is An Illusion Prelude / Love Is An Illusion / Coloured Life / Cold Outside / Into The Ether / Through The Fire / Love Is An Illusion Interlude / Through The Rain / Faerie Tale State Of Mind / Dream Burnin' Down / Can't Find My Way Home / A Night In The Garden / Love Is An Illusion Postlude
GARDEN OF THE MOON, Avalon Marquee (1998)
River Of The Stars / Destination Roswell / Seasons / Moongarden / Evolution Revolution / Under The Olive Tree / Eternal Waters / Dream Of The Dragonfly / Garden Of The Moon / Symphony Of Angels (Live With Rocket Scientists)
QUEEN OF THE OCEAN, Limb Music Productions LMP 993 009CD (1999)
In The Hall Of The Ocean Queen / Night Falls / Queen Of The Ocean / Let Heaven In / Frankenstein Unbound / Souls Of The Mermaids / Rainbows End / Without You / Through The Rain / Escher's Staircase (Live) / Symphony Of Angels (Live)
SECRETS OF ASTROLOGY, Avalon Marquee MICP-10176 (2000)
Astrology Prelude / Secrets Of Astrology / Alexandria / Raining / The Bell / Speed Of Sound / Under The Sun / Tarot / Asherah / Guardian Angel / Long Winter Dreams / Astrology Postlude / Romeo & Juliet
PROJECT SHANGRI LA, Avalon Marquee MICP-10280 (2002)

Redemption Part I / Project Shangri La / Encore / Before You Go / The Nightingale / The Beast Within You / Tears Of Babylon / Ebbtide / (Life Is) Only A Dream / Time To Say Goodbye / Redemption Part II / I Believe In You

LANDGUARD (ITALY)
Line-Up: Michelle Sorrentino (vocals), Marco Ruggeriero (guitar), Armando Scala (guitar), Stefan Quitadamo (bass), Raffaele Acarpa (keyboards), Walter Montane (drums)

A Naples based Power Metal band that included erstwhile STORMWIND guitarist Marco Ruggeriero in the ranks. LANDGUARD would bow in with the 1998 demo 'The Land Of The Nymphs'. Apparently the band cut a 1999 album for the Underground Symphony label dubbed 'The Manuscript Of Helgwar' but information on this release is conflicting.
Both Ruggeriero and vocalist Michele Sorrentino would join fellow Metal band NAMELESS CRIME in 1999.

LANFEAR (GERMANY)
Line-Up: Stefan Zörner (vocals / keyboards), Markus Ullrich (guitar), Alexander Palma (bass), Jürgen Schrenk (drums)

Highly experimental Metal act.

Albums:
TOWERS, Lanfear LFCD 21120001 (1989)
Full Pride / Precious Time / Ancient Skies / She's Never Left The Day / Vale Auditu / Time's Dark Laughter / Galtron's Tale / Unseen / The Towers Of February: I) Shore Leaves, II) Axiom-Moixa, III) Inter Menses Februarium Et, IV) Soliloquy
ZERO POEMS, Horn Music FK 5991 CD (1999)
Zero Poems / Turn The Tide / Eight Silent Chambers / Epilogue June, 2054 A.D. / How Come / My Karma Told Me / To Sear The Flood / Enlin – Genesis / Naked / Twilight / Electric Storm, 2053 A.D.

LANZER (GERMANY)
Line-Up: Andi Mersch (vocals), Eric Kern (guitar), Rainer Kern (guitar), Matthias Böhm (bass), Ralf Kern (keyboards), Daniel Zimmermann (drums)

LANZER formed in 1987 putting in a heavy touring schedule from then on. In 1989 LANZER had put in over 120 gigs promoting the 'Use It Or Lose It' album. The band would later enrol former TYRAN PACE vocalist Andi Mersch.
GAMMA RAY's Dirk Schlächter produces the

'Under A Different Sun' album. Guests included Kai Hansen of GAMMA RAY on guitar and Sascha Paeth of HEAVEN'S GATE on keyboards.

Drummer Daniel Zimmermann joined GAMMA RAY in time for their 'Somewhere Out In Space' album.

Albums:
USE IT OR LOSE IT, Perfect Beat (1987)
Ocean Of Tears / We Are The Kids / Black Crusader / Use It Or Lose It / All The Night / Take Your Love / Make It Loud / Red, Bad, Leather / Stevie
UNDER A DIFFERENT SUN, A2Z Records 000030.2 (1995)
Vapouriser / Blood City / One Night... / Gods Of War / Bury War / Strike Back / Twist The Knife / We Are The Law / All You Ever Wanted / Children Of The Revolution / The Song And The Wind

LAOS (GERMANY)

Line-Up: Gudrun Laos (vocals), Ralf Hansmeyer (guitar), Frank Fricke (guitar), Thomas Röben (bass), Wolfgang Schindler (keyboards), Jörg Michael (drums)

Female fronted Metal band founded by former LIVING DEATH guitarist Frank Fricke. LAOS drummer Jörg Michael is ex-AVENGER, RAGE and MEKONG DELTA. The much in demand sticksman would later journey through HEADHUNTER, GLENMORE, GRAVE DIGGER and RUNNING WILD.
LAOS bassist Thomas Röben would later join CROSSROADS.

Singles/EPs:
Now That It's Over, Teldec (1990)
I Want It / **Badlands**, Teldec (1990)

Albums:
WE WANT IT, Teldec 9031-70802-1 (1990)
I Want It / Why Is A Good Love / Now That It's Over / Straight To The Top / Jericho / Heartbreak Road / We Called It Love / Long Shot / Badlands / Higher Ground / One More Night

LAST WARNING (ITALY)

Line-Up: Campanotti Diego (vocals), Pin Antonio (guitar), Ferrara Andrea (guitar), Venuto Stefano (bass), Venier Gianluca (keyboards), Agnoluzzi Emanuele (drums)

Progressive Metal act LAST WARNING has been in existence since 1987 but have undergone many line-up changes. The band has over the years supported such visiting artists as DREAM THEATER, QUEENSRYCHE and CRIMSON GLORY. LAST WARNING issued the 1988 'Bloody Dreams' demo.

Albums:
FROM THE FLOOR OF THE WELL, Music Is Intelligence WMMS 054 (1994)
From The Floor Of The Well / Without Power / Mistery / On The Wire / Scream To The Mirror / Killing Dust / Rain On The Flame / Faith And Mistery

LEATHERWOLF (Los Angeles, CA, USA)

Line-Up: Michael Oliverei (vocals / guitar), Carey Howe (guitar), Geoffrey Gayer (guitar), Paul Carmens (bass), Dean Roberts (drums)

Based in Los Angeles, Power Metal act LEATHERWOLF were founded in 1981 and in their rise to signing with a major label supported POISON, MÖTLEY CRÜE, GREAT WHITE and W.A.S.P. along the way. The band had two factors that would set LEATHERWOLF apart from the majority of Metal bands. One being an unashamed L.A. 'look', rare for a trad Metal act, and the other being an onstage three guitar pronged attack. The group had originally released product on the Tropical label (a subsidiary of Enigma) and this record was issued a year later (with the addition of extra tracks) in Britain as 'Endangered Species' by the Heavy Metal label.

LEATHERWOLF's Matt Hurich deputised for STRYPER bassist Tim Gaines when he mysteriously disappeared. However Hurich soon lost his position in STRYPER when Gaines returned and would later relinquish his post in LEATHERWOLF too.

The 1987 self-titled album, produced by Kevin Beamish noted for his softer AOR work, featured new bassist Paul Carmen. 'Street Ready', produced by Beamish once more, was recorded at Compass Point in the Bahamas and mixed by Michael Wagener and was released in Britain to coincide with a support tour during March 1989 to Japanese outfit VOW WOW. LEATHERWOLF also opened for ZED YAGO in Germany.

In 1992 members of LEATHERWOLF turned up in the melodic Rock act HAIL MARY.

A new shorn haired version of LEATHERWOLF returned in 1999 with a self-financed album 'Wide Open' although by this stage Carey Howe was also operating with another band venture entitled 420KOMA. The reception afforded 'Wide Open' showed LEATHERWOLF's fan base had remained resilient during the hiatus. However, long-term vocalist Oliverei quit in August of 2000.

LEATHERWOLF announced a new front man in Chris Adams during March of 2002.

Singles/EPs:
Hideaway / **Too Much**, Island IS 416 (1989)
Hideaway / **Too Much** / Rule The Night, Island 12IS 416 (1989) (12" single)

Albums:
LEATHERWOLF, Tropical Enigma E-1116 (1984)
Spiter / Endangered Species / Tonight's The Night / The Hook / Season Of The Witch / Off The Track / Kill And Kill Again / Vagrant / Leatherwolf
ENDANGERED SPECIES, Heavy Metal America HM USA39 (1985)
Spiter / Endangered Species / Tonight's The Night / The Hook / Season Of The Witch / Off The Track / Kill And Kill Again / Vagrant / Leatherwolf
LEATHERWOLF, Island ILPS 9889 (1987)
Rise Or Fall / The Calling / Share A Dream / Cry Out / Gypsies And Thieves / Bad Moon Rising / Princess Of Love / Magical Eyes / Rule The Night
STREET READY, Island ILPS 9927 (1989)
Wicked Ways / Street Ready / Hideaway / Take A Chance / Black Knight / Thunder / The Way I Feel / Too Much / Lonely Road / Spirits In The Wind
WIDE OPEN, Leatherwolf Music (1999)
Kill And Kill Again / Endangered Species / Gypsies & Thieves / Street Ready / Spirits In The Wind / Tools Of Discipline / Season Of The Witch / Tonight Is The Night / Hideaway / Wicked Ways / Thunder / The Calling / Break On Through / Spiter

LEFAY (SWEDEN)
Line-Up: Charles Rytkönen (vocals), Tony Eriksson (guitars), Peter Grehn (guitar), Jonas Sonderling (drums)

Essentially MORGANA LEFAY with a name change. However, confusion reigned when other members of MORGANA LEFAY resurrected themselves under the original title and both acts subsequently started to operate in parallel.
LEFAY front man Charles Rytkönen and drummer Jonas Sonderling are founder members of MORGANA LEFAY whilst guitarist Peter Grehn is also a member of FANTASMAGORIA. The band also added drummer Robin Engström from FANTASMAGORIA.
Just as MORGANA LEFAY had seemingly set on track for greater things, a split in the ranks occurred when members Jonas Soederlind, Joakim Heder and Daniel Persson all

vacated. MORGANA LEFAY regrouped by enlisting a triumvirate of former FANTASMAGORIA personnel in Peter Grehn, Robin Engström and Micke Åsentorp.
With Black Mark Records contractually owners of the MORGANA LEFAY brand the revised act adopted the title LEFAY and signed to Noise Records. This new unit issued 'The Seventh Seal' album in 1999 as well as a reworked version of the debut 'Symphony Of The Damned'.
LEFAY issued a statement that they were to cease operations in 2000. However, late 2001 brought news that a re-formation was on the cards and, indeed, LEFAY duly resurfaced for a new album and live work.
Charles Rytkönen would contribute session lead vocals to the 2002 TAD MOROSE album 'Matters Of The Dark'. The man would also be singled out for media speculation regarding the vacancy for vocalist with American Metal band SEVEN WITCHES but this hypothesised union would not transpire.

Albums:
THE SEVENTH SEAL, Noise N 0312-2 (1999)
End Of Living / The Seventh Seal / I Am / The Boon He Gives / Moonlight Night / Child Of Time / Harga / So Strange / As Far As I Can Go / Shadow Empire
SYMPHONY FOR THE DAMNED, Noise (1999)
The Whore Of Babylon / Symphony Of The Damned / Fatal Illusions / Last Rites / Lullaby / The Secret Doctrine / Tequila / Catacombs / War Without End / Crazy / Captain Howdy / Strange Way 13. Cocaine
SAVE OUR SOULS, Noise (2000)
Save Our Souls / Cimmerian Dream / Sleepwalker / Epicedium / When Gargoyles Fly / What Dreams Forbode / Bloodred Sky / Help Me Out Of Her / The Quest For Reality / The Choice

LEGEND MAKER (COLOMBIA)
Line-Up: Diego Gomez (vocals), Mauricio Ochoa (guitar), Fabian Alicastro (guitar), Julian Gonzales (bass), Luis Fernando (keyboards), Juan Felipe (drums)

Technical Metal act from the unlikely South American state of Columbia. Created in the city of Cali by guitarist Mauricio Ochoa and keyboard player Luis Fernando as the Spanish language MESTER DE JUGLARIA. A 1997 demo session submitted to the American label Defiled Records would be passed on to renaissance Metal specialist Dennis Gulbey who was intrigued. Together, Gulbey and the band hatched the idea for

LEFAY
Photo : Nico Wobben

LEGEND MAKER pulling in American singer Mike Grant.

Grant had experience behind him with MORPHEUS, COLD OCTOBER, OBSCURE and OCEAN SEVEN as well as briefly fronting NEW EDEN. Four tracks would be cut for a projected EP with instrumental tracks laid down in Columbia and Grant adding vocals in Los Angeles. However, the EP idea was scrapped and further sessions would be arranged to boost the venture up to full album status.

LEGEND MAKER would endure a constantly shifting line-up throughout 1999. In October bassist Luis K departed to be substituted by Julian Gonzales. By December drummer Jorge Paz too decamped, in his stead coming Juan Felipe. The group would also add to the roster guitarist Fabian Alicastro.

As Grant concentrated full time on his US project ONWARD the group would enlist Diego Gomez as their new front man.

Albums:
THE PATH TO GLORY, (1999)
Leonelda / Sands Of Time / To Hell Or To Heaven / Story / Moon Seasons / Last Chapter

LETTER X (GERMANY)
Line-Up: Michael Bormann (vocals), Rüdiger Fleck (guitar), Michael Faisst (guitar), Frank Hildenbrandt (bass), Jürgen Stahl (keyboards), Marco Ieva (drums)

An early '90s German melodic Metal band, LETTER X supported AXXIS, PRETTY MAIDS and STORMWITCH in their time whilst leaving a musical legacy three albums deep. The band debuted with 1991's 'Time Of The Gathering', LETTER X underwent a drastic line-up change for the second album. Prior to the recording of 1992's 'Born Into Darkness' the group parted company with vocalist Martin Obermeier, guitarist Joachim Gassman and drummer Frank Kraus, the latter to end up as drummer for DEMON DRIVE.

New recruits were found in Michael Bomann on vocals, Michael Faisst on guitar and drummer Marco Leva. The departed Obermeier, who had played with bassist Frank Hildenbrandt in MASCOT in pre-LETTER X days, involved himself in a variety of Rock and Pop projects before fronting CHINCHILLA. Gassmann, on the other hand, recorded the 'War Of The Wizard' album with STORMWITCH in 1992.

'Born Into Darkness' was produced by ELOY mentor Frank Bornemann, but a third album (the Japanese only released 'Reflections')

would not appear until 1996. By this time LETTER X had found a new singer as Bomann, now going under his real name of MICHAEL BORMANN, had long since formed the rival Melodic Rock outfit JADED HEART. LETTER X guitarist Rüdiger Fleck wound up joining GLENMORE in July 1997. He would subsequently found the hard edged Metal band RAWHEAD REXX with GLENMORE singer Jurgen Volk. MICHAEL BORMANN, besides his activities with JADED HEART and SILENT FORCE, would issue a debut solo album in February of 2002.

Albums:
TIME OF THE GATHERING, Steamhammer 084-7692 (1991)
Time Of The Gathering / Break Of Dawn / Verdict / Strong Believer / Leather On Leather / Unknown Heroes / Lost And Lonely / Deep In The Night / Into The Future / Princess Of The Dark
BORN INTO DARKNESS, Steamhammer 084-76502 (1992)
Train Of Fools / Wall Of Confusion / Visions / Born Into Darkness / Illusions / We Live In Fear / Nowhere / Neverending Love / The Sign / We're Alive
REFLECTIONS, Zero Corporation XRCN 1269 (1996)
Snowman / No Way Out / Falling / No Solution / Final Destination / The Warning / More Than I Can Say / Reflections (Of Madness) / Crucified

LEVIATHAN (ARGENTINA)
Line-Up: Javier C. Pereyra (vocals / guitar), Elvago (bass), Ariel Perdu-K (drums)

Buenos Aires Metal trio forged in 1994 with an initial line-up of vocalist / guitarist Javier C. Pereyra, bass player Elvago and drummer Gyver. LEVIATHAN staked their claim with the 1995 demo cassette 'El Primer Paso De La Bestia'. All 666 copies soon sold encouraging the band to self-finance an eponymous debut album, which arrived in May of 1996. Following recording Ariel Perdu-K took the place of Gyver.

LEVIATHAN's next move, via their own now established Leviathan Records, was to compile a collection of various Argentinean bands for the collection 'Las Mejores Voces De Metal'. LEVIATHAN themselves contributed two brand new songs to this 1997 effort. Back on track with their own release schedule the group recorded an ambitious double album set 'Rito Bicefalo' for 1999 issue. The following year LEVIATHAN toured Spain.

The band's third album, 'Del Lado Del Rock',

proved to be composed entirely of cover songs, LEVIATHAN honouring the likes of BARON ROJO, ANGELS OF HELL and KAMIKAZE amongst others.

Albums:
RITO BICEFALO, Leviathan (1999)
Intro / It Holds Rock (1,000 Years) / Wrist Of TV / Gritalo / Poisonous Line / Ironico To Be / First World / In The Streets / I Complete Cigarette / Under Control / Nonceven / Leviathan II / Antiheroes / God Of My Heroes / Numca Mas / Engendros Power / Abrepuertas / Aim Of The Work / They Robbed My Memories / Behemoth / Street Duende / The Blues Of Camila
DEL LADO DEL ROCK, Leviathan (2001)
Marginalized / Destroying Agonias / The Train Goes Away / God Hears That You Have Given / It Watches Towards The Stop / Postcrucificcion / To The Other Side Of Silence / Monday At The Dawn / They Do Not Bomb Buenos Aires / Wherever These All / Desconfio / Single I Want Rock n' Roll / To My Way / Dirty Lady

LEVIATHAN (CO, USA)
Line-Up: Jeff Ward (vocals), Ronnie Skeen (guitar), John Lutzow (guitar), Derek Blake (bass), Trevor Heffer (drums)

Progressive Thrash out of Colorado and named after JAG PANZER vocalist Harry Conklin's pseudonym 'Leviathan', adopted whilst fronting his side act SATAN'S HOST. Musically LEVIATHAN's early works are somewhat akin to technical Euro Thrash but as the act's career moved forward they would tone down considerably.
Former SONIC FURY guitar players Steve Fugate and Ronnie Skeen forged LEVIATHAN during 1989. Fugate would decamp in 1991, making way for John Lutzow.
The debut 1992 album sees a line-up of mainstay guitarists Ronnie Skeen and John Lutzow, vocalist Tom Braden and a rhythm section of bassist James Escobedo and drummer Ty Tammeus. For the sophomore 1994 record 'Deepest Secrets Beneath' Braden was usurped by Jack Aragon.
LEVIATHAN switched to the German Century Media concern for 1996's 'Riddles, Secrets, Poetry And Outrage'. The band had changed radically both musically and in the personnel department veering into a straight Progressive Rock direction fronted by new singer Jeff Ward. LEVIATHAN had also summoned up a fresh team of bass player Derek Blake and drummer Trevor Heffer.
Although LEVIATHAN would stabilise its line-up for 1997's 'Scoring The Chapter' little has been heard since.
Ronnie Skeen did venture outside of LEVIATHAN for a Prog Power Metal concept IRON FORTRESS in league with vocalist Tim Lawrence. This outfit released an eponymous album through Germany's Hellion label.

Albums:
LEVIATHAN, (1992)
Fear Of Change / Degenerating Paradise / Two Roads To Nowhere / Beast Of Burden / Leviathan
DEEPEST SECRETS BENEATH, RTN RTN 41201 (1994)
Confidence Not Arrogance / Sanctuary / The Calling / Painful Pursuit Of Passion And Purpose / Not Always Lost / The Falling Snow / Run Forever / Disenchanted Dreams (Of Conformity) / Speed Kills
RIDDLES, SECRETS, POETRY AND OUTRAGE, Century Media (1996)
Census Of Stars / Mindless Game Control / Madness Endeavor / Pages Of Time / Are First Loves Forgotten? / So Where Is God? / Confusion / Don't Look To Me / Passion Above All Else
SCORING THE CHAPTERS, Corrosive CRD 77362 (1997)
Salvation / Friends Imaginary / Paying The Toll / The Door / J. Christopher's Haunting / If These Walls Could Talk / All Sins Returned / Scar Barrow's Fare / The Last King Of The Highlands / Born Unto (But Don't Belong To Me) / Leftist Out / Turning Up Broken / Failing Avalon / Apologies Wanting To Make Good / Legacy Departing

LEVITICUS (SWEDEN)
Line-Up: Terry H. (vocals), Björn Stiggson (guitar), Ez Gomer (bass), Kjell Andersson (drums)

A Swedish Christian Metal act of some repute, LEVITICUS' first album, 'Jag Skall Segra', was re-recorded in English and issued on the American Shadow label as 'I Shall Conquer' and featured the initial band line-up of bassist / vocalist Håkan Andersson, guitarist Björn Stigsson and drummer Kjell Andersson.
By the time of the 'Setting Fire To The Earth' album Håkan Andersson had left in favour of former QUINZY singer Terry H (real name Terje Hjortander) and LEVITICUS also added bassist Sven Ez Gomer.
Shortly after the album release both Hjortander and Gomer quit to form JET CIRCUS. Ex-MOTHERLODE vocalist Sonny Larsson was to take over the mike stand, but left within months. However, Larsson did

appear on Stigsson's solo album, 'Together With Friends', released in 1987.

For the 'Knights Of Heaven' record the group worked with new members Nicklas Franklin (bass) and erstwhile AXIA vocalist Peo Petttersson, but the group split in the mid '90s and Stigsson was reunited with Larsson when the duo formed the rougher sounding White Metal band XT.

Singles/EPs:
Stå Och Titta På / Följ Mej / Leva Som Man Lär / Min Mastare, Stanley & Andre SAMLP 52 00003 (1982)
Let Me Fight / Day By Day, Stanley & Andre SAM5213 (1984)
Love Is Love / Flames Of Fire, Royal Music RMS023 (1987)
Isn't It Love / Born Again, Royal Music RMS033 (1989)

Albums:
JAGSKALLSEGRA, Stanley & Andre SAMLP 5209 (1983)
I SHALL CONQUER, Shadow LS 5899 (1984)
I Shall Conquer / Let Me Fight / He's My Life / Doubt / Action More Than Words / All Is Calm / Day By Day / Strive Forwards / Psalm 23 / Folj Mig / Leva Som Han Lar / Min Mastare
THE STRONGEST POWER, Pure Metal (1985)
The Winner / Deborah And Barek / On The Rock / King Of Kings / Stay With Us / I Got Power / Look Around / I Love You / A New Day / Light For The World.
SETTING FIRE TO THE EARTH, Royal Music RMLP 027 (1987)
Flames Of Fire / Saved / The First And The Last / I'm A Believer / Don't Go Out / Elijah On Carmel / The Suffering Servant / Get Up / Love Is Love
KNIGHTS OF HEAVEN, Royal Music RMCD040 (1990)
Born Again / The World Goes Round / Isn't It Love / Oh Lord / Feel So Good / Strong Love / Messiah / Over The Hills / For Once In My Life / Live On Fire
THE BEST OF LEVITICUS, Viva VIVAD 132 (1994)
The Winner / Over The Hills / Lovin' My Woman / The Suffering Servant / I Got Power / Look Around / Oh Lord / Stand Up / Flames Of Fire / All Is Calm / Born Again / I Love You / A New Day / Deborah & Barak / On The Rock / Psalm 23

LIAR SYMPHONY (BRAZIL)
Line-Up: Villa Nolasco (vocals), Pedro Esteves (guitar), Marcos Brandao (bass), Vinicius Moure (keyboards), Miro Rocha (drums)

Power Metal band LIAR SYMPHONY formed in 1993, issuing two demo tapes, 'First Moves' and 'Power', upfront of the 2000 album 'Affair Of Honour'.

Albums:
AFFAIR OF HONOUR, Megahard (2001)
Soldier's Dream / The Final Combat / The Crowning Of The Night / Warning / Negative Foreseeing / Lonely Track / Doomsday / Humanquina / Die But Don't Lose / The Winner / Victory

LIEGE LORD (USA)
Line-Up: Joe Comeau (vocals), Paul Nelson (guitar), Tony Truglio (guitar), Matt Vinci (bass), Frank Cortese (drums)

PAUL NELSON of LIEGE LORD
Photo : Nico Wobben

Highly rated Connecticut Metal outfit heavily influenced by classic British Metal. Formed by the core of bassist Matt Vinci, guitarist Tony Truglio, drummer Frank Cortese and singer Andy Michaud in late '82. The five piece gained a deal with the French Black Dragon label following major press interest in Europe for their demo tapes and shaped picture disc EP issued by the Ironworks label. The band was created in 1983 originally billed DECIEVER, as the name suggests a JUDAS PRIEST cover band, adopting the title LIEGE LORD the following year.

264

LIEGE LORD
Photo : Nico Wobben

Plans for a self-financed, four track EP turned into a full blown album with the aid of Black Dragon after the company was recommended to LIEGE LORD by SAVAGE GRACE's Christian Logue

LIEGE LORD's debut album, 'Freedom's Rise' was released in 1985. The album was actually issued in America on the Ironworks label although its release there was not advertised, distribution was non-existent at best and the album came dressed in shabby black and white packaging. The Black Dragon variant though, clad in a high class fantasy artwork sleeve, would score the band acclaim amongst the European Metal press.

According to reports at the time Black Dragon terminated their relationship with the band prior to the release of the proposed second album claiming that the record was "too Thrash oriented" and thus rejecting it.

However the LIEGE LORD saga with Ironworks did not end there and a whole slew of collectibles surfaced during this relationship. The 'Freedom's Rise' album would be released as a limited gatefold issue, 'Farewell' would see the light of day as a single in a series of cut to shape picture discs such as a heart shape, Viking shape as well as 6 and 8 edged variants. In 1987 a collection of demo tracks would also leak out

on picture disc restricted to a mere 150 copies.

Metal Blade stepped in to snap LIEGE LORD up, although at this point McCarthy quit the group and was swiftly replaced by Paul Nelson, a man who could claim to have been instructed by no less a player than the esteemed STEVE VAI. The band got back into action with the 1987 effort 'Burn To My Touch', produced by Joe Bouchard of BLUE OYSTER CULT fame. Although the 1988 album 'Master Control', including a cover version of RAINBOW's 'Kill The King', engineered by Terry Date and featuring new lead vocalist Joe Comeau, would be widely recognised as an underground Power Metal classic the band found themselves in the midst of the '90s Metal backlash. LIEGE LORD toured America co-headlining with Canadians ANVIL before a run of East Coast shows with Swedish Doom lords CANDLEMASS but would ultimately fold.

Guitarist Paul Nelson would join the Def Jam artists the B-STOOLS. Ex-LIEGE LORD singer Joe Comeau would be fronting Canadian Speed Metal band ANNIHILATOR by 2000. He would also rack up credits with New Jersey Thrashers OVERKILL. However, Comeau and Nelson would reunite for a one off project in late 2000 cutting their version of

'Too Scared To Run' for a URIAH HEEP tribute album as well as 'Dungeons Are Calling' for a similar SAVATAGE effort, both released by the German Century Media label. PAUL NELSON would also issue the solo album 'Look'. The guitarist put in a spate of sessions including appearances on the JASON BECKER tribute 'Warmth In The Wilderness' and on a rendition of QUEENSRYCHE's 'Speak' included on the New York City benefit album 'United - We All Stand Together' assembled by the Italian Frontiers label.

Recently LIEGE LORD reunited for a one-off performance at the annual 'Wacken Open Air' festival in Germany. The line up comprised Nelson, Comeau, OVERKILL and ANVIL man Sebastian Marino on guitar and the rhythm section of Marino's side project RAMROD.

Singles/EPs:
Prodigy / Wielding Iron Fists / Dark Tale / Amnesty / Vials Of Wrath / Legionnaire, (1985) ('Prodigy' EP)
Black Lit Knights / Legend, Metal Blade 8148 (1987) (USA promotion release)

Albums:
FREEDOMS RISE, Black Dragon BD004 (1985)
Prodigy / Wielding Iron Fists / Dark Tale / Amnesty / Rage Of Angels / Vials Of Wrath / Warriors Farewell / For The King / Legionnaire
WARRIORS FAREWELL, Ironworks IW1013 (1987)
BURN TO MY TOUCH, Metal Blade 8148 (1987)
Transgressor / Birds Of Prey / Cast Out / Portrait Of Despair / Black Lit Knights / Maniac's Mask / Legend / Walking Fire / Speed Of Sound
MASTER CONTROL, Metal Blade 72268 (1988)
Fear Itself / Eye Of The Storm / Master Control / Kill The King / Soldier's Fortune / Feel The Blade / Broken Wasteland / Rapture / Suspicion / Fallout

LIFE AFTER DEATH (USA)
Line-Up: Jack Emerick (vocals), Giovanni Santos (guitar), Terry Williams (guitar), Ray Burke (bass), Gonzo Sandoval (drums)

Following the demise of ARMOURED SAINT as vocalist John Bush departed to join ANTHRAX, founder members and brothers guitarist Phil Sandoval and drummer Gonzo Sandoval founded LIFE AFTER DEATH.
The band's initial line-up incorporated the two Sandovals, vocalist Jack Emerick, ex-

FOREVER, FOREPLAY and WARRIOR bassist Ray Burke and second guitarist John Goodwin. After a debut demo and heavy touring schedule both Phil Sandoval and Goodwin departed.

New recruits were Terry Williams and Giovanni Santos. This revised line-up gigged harder still but within a year had opted to tone down their previously over the top metallic sound to a more traditional Hard Rock feel.

In late 1994 LIFE AFTER DEATH recorded a five track demo featuring the songs 'Hard times', 'Red Light', 'My Life', 'Mother' and 'Don't Believe A Word' after which the band undertook further live dates but under the assumed name of STIKMAN.

LIFE AFTER DEATH's debut album featured cover versions of THIN LIZZY's 'Don't Believe A Word' and CREAM's 'Sunshine Of Your Love'.

ARMORED SAINT reformed in 1999. Burke turned up as guest on former IMPELLITERRI vocalist BOB ROCK's solo album 'Rage Of Creation'.

Albums:
LIFE AFTER DEATH, Rising Sun 352813 (1996)
Tagger / Hard Time / Red Light / My Life / Borrowed Time / Life After Death / Mother / Homegrown / Love And Destruction / Don't Believe A Word / Sunshine Of Your Love

LIGEIA (GERMANY)
Line-Up: Daniela Unglert (vocals), Jorg Mayer (guitar), Michael Sommer (bass), Sascha Shilling (drums)

A female fronted Metal band created by the erstwhile REST IN PAIN triumvirate of vocalist Daniela Unglert, guitarist Jorg Mayer and bassist Wolfgang Fetzer. With the addition of drummer Michael Urthaler the new band unit took the title ANGEL DUSK. Just prior to recording the 'Made Of Stone' debut a revised title of LIGEIA, after the Edgar Allan Poe story, was chosen.

Albums:
MADE OF STONE, (2000)
Dragonheart / Children Of The Lost / Mephista / Angel Dusk / Suicidal Dreams / Flying Dragon / Fist Of Steel / The Story Of Guy Fawkes / It's Time
BEYOND THE SKY, (2002)
Mistress Of The Night / Wings Of Fire / Beyond The Sky / Gloria / Here We Are / Angelwitch / Noise Of Silence / Walpurgis Night / Last Desire / Night Of The Cross

266

LIONS BREED (GERMANY)

Line-Up: Ulrich Rohmann (vocals), Axel Julius (guitar), Thomas Sopha (guitar), Martin Bork (bass), Michael Ecker (drums)

Formed in 1982 as a quartet with bassist Martin Bork singing lead vocal, LIONS BREED added ex-CHALLENGER vocalist Ulrich Rohmann in 1983. Drummer Michael Ecker quit only to return and by 1988 LIONS BREED had transformed themselves into Sci-Fi Metal act SCANNER.

Albums:
DAMN THE NIGHT, Earthshaker ES4008 (1985)
Mental Domination / Heavy Current / Scarover / All Right Be Damned / Live And Let Die / Neon City / Lady Of The Night / Mystery Game / Valve Of Hell

LIONS PRIDE (BELGIUM)

Line-Up: Willy Becker (vocals), Benito Boccasile (guitar), Clarence Akkermans (guitar), Johan Westhoven (bass), Pino Morciano (drums)

One of a number of Belgian Metal bands that sprang up with the emergence of the Mausoleum label in the early '80s.

Albums:
BREAKING OUT, Mausoleum SKULL8336 (1984)
The Nighthunter / Working Class / A Real Friend / The Eyes Of A Lion / Breaking Out / Sixty Nine / Struggle For Live / Let Music Rule The World

LIONS SHARE (SWEDEN)

Line-Up: Andy Engberg (vocals), Lars Criss (guitar), Andy Loos (bass), Kay Backlund (keyboards), Johan Koleberg (drums)

A highly recommended, powerful yet exceptionally melodic Metal band that has released a string of very classy albums. LIONS SHARE were created in 1987 around guitarist Lars Criss. Other members included keyboard player Kay Backlund, vocalist Marcus Nordenberg and bassist Mikael Hansson. This line-up recorded the 'Ghost Town Queen' single in 1988 before parting company.

However, the band re-formed (ostensibly as a solo project from Criss), in order to fulfil a commitment for a track inclusion on a Belgian compilation album in 1992. The vocalist put together a studio band for the recording of 'Nothing's Free' that featured many of Sweden's better known musician's. Included were CANDLEMASS vocalist Thomas Vikström, ex-GREAT KING RAT vocalist Conny Lind, TALISMAN bassist Marcel Jacob, VENI DOMINE's keyboard player P.A. Danielsson and ex-TALK OF THE TOWN drummer Johan Koleberg.

A temporary line-up for the band was forged in 1993 that included ex-SORCEROR vocalist Andy Engberg and former GLORY bassist Andy Loos. LIONS SHARE promptly recorded their debut album, having signed to Japan's Zero label, in 1994. The record was reissued in Europe through Local Hero (and later Long Island) in 1995. Following the release of the album, Loos made way for ex-STEAMROLLER bassist Pontus Egberg.

LIONS SHARE contributed a fine version of JUDAS PRIEST's 'Touch Of Evil' to the 1996 Century Media tribute album before 1997 saw the release of LIONS SHARE's second album, aptly titled 'Two'.

As an aside, during inactive periods LIONS SHARE have been known to keep their hand in under the guise of a KISS tribute act titled KYSS.

The 1999 album 'Fall From Grace' includes an ambitious cover of CITY BOY's 'The Day The Earth Caught Fire'.

The 2000 'Perspective' album is a compilation of the first two records remastered with extra material.

LIONS SHARE added former SWEDISH EROTICA vocalist Tony Niva for their fourth studio album 'Entrance'. Guests included TOMMY DENANDER and former YNGWIE MALMSTEEN band members vocalist Göran Edman and keyboard player Mats Olausson. Former CANDLEMASS singer Thomas Vikström also sessions.

In April of 2002 it was revealed that LIONS SHARE guitarist Lars Criss had assembled a side venture billed as COSMIC SPHERE. Other participants included Antti Wirman of WARMEN and CRAYDAWN, Tapio Oksanen of CRAYDAWN and erstwhile RISING FAITH drummer Kristian Enqvist. Meantime former LIONS SHARE singer Andy Engberg busied himself with Norwegian guitarist TORBEN ENVOLDSEN's new project band entitled SECTION A. The project also featured ex-DREAM THEATER keyboard player DEREK SHERINEN and VANDEN PLAS drummer Andreas Lill.

During the summer Criss revealed plans to assemble a further band endeavour billed as TYKOON. Included alumni would be RAINMAKER, PRISONER and RADIOACTIVE mentor TOMMY DENANDER, vocalist Leif Sundin of MICHAEL SCHENKER GROUP, GREAT KING RAT and JOHN NORUM band and GLORY's bass player Andy Loos. Yet another LIONS SHARE spin off, C.R.A.N.K., would witness a union of Pontus Egberg and Johan Koleberg with CANDLEMASS guitarist Mats "Mappe" Björkman as well as singer Alex Swerdh and guitarist Ulf Larsson of the KISS cover band KYSS.

Singles/EPs:
Ghost Town Queen / I'm On A Roll, Cufs Skivclubb CUF008 (1988)
Sins Of The Father / Scarecrow / Just In Time To Be Late, Local Hero LHM 0365 (1995)

Albums:
LIONS SHARE, Local Hero LHM 0407 (1995)
Sins Of A Father / Arabia / Scarecrow / Play By The Rules / Judgement Day / Nothing's Free / Haunted / Just In Time To Be Late / Taking On The World / Searchin' For Answers
TWO, Century Media CD77154-2 (1997)
Wild At Heart / Lord Of The Pain / Transient / Don't Come Easy / Shadows / Baptism Of Fire / Flash In The Night / World Gone Wrong / Rat-Race
FALL FROM GRACE, Bareknuckle Avex AVCD 11707 (1999)
The Edge Of Sanity / Unholy Rites / Fall From Grace / Drowning / Remembrance / The Day The Earth Caught Fire / A Hole Of Black / A Touch Of Evil
PERSPECTIVE, Massacre MAS CD0268 (2000)
Sins Of A Father / Scarecrow / Arabia / Play By The Rules / I Don't Believe In Love / Judgement Day / Haunted / Just In Time To Be Late / Lion's Share / Searchin' For Answers / Shadows / Baptism Of Fire / Wild At Heart / Flash In The Night / Transient / Don't Come Easy / World Gone Wrong / Rat Race / Lord Of The Pain / Nothing's Free
ENTRANCE, Massacre (2001)
Entrance / Shotgun Messiah / Waiting / Through The Clouds / Lost / Mystery / Believe / War Machine / On And On / Losing My Head / Free Your Mind

LOGAR'S DIARY (GERMANY)
Line-Up: Hagen Hirschmann (vocals), Steven Schubert (guitar), Christoph Uhl (guitar), Felix Gretzer (bass), Michael Kwandt (keyboards), Stefan Renner (drums)

A highly rated Berlin based fantasy infused Power Metal band that takes their entire concept from the role-playing game 'Earthdawn'. The band's debut album, a completely self-financed affair, sold out of two pressing of 1000 copies within a matter of months of release.

The group would have two cover tracks included on tribute albums, LOGAR'S DIARY appearing on an Italian MANOWAR collection with 'Blood Of My Enemies' and also delivering the RUNNING WILD track 'Riding The Storm' for another. The band first performed live in April of 2002.

Albums:
BOOK 1, IOSTROS, Logar's Diary (2001)
Earthdawn (Intro) / Lonely On The Serpent River / Travelling To The Blood Woods / Ti´An - A Troubadour´s Ballad / Demon In The Kaer / Travar - The Golden City / Home Of The Traders - Barterstown / King´s Hall / Iostros / My Love Still Exists / Déjà Vu (Outro)

LONEWOLF (FRANCE)
Line-Up: Jens Borner (vocals / guitar), Dams (guitar), Dryss (bass), Felix Borner (drums)

LONEWOLF was formed in 1993, issuing the six track demo 'The Calling' the following year. Although a 7" EP 'Holy Evil' arrived in 1995 the band split up shortly after. A re-formation took place during 2001.

Singles/EPs:
The Dark Ages / Holy Evil / Buried Alive, (1995) ('Holy Evil' EP)

Albums:
MARCH INTO THE ARENA, (2001)
Morbid Beauty / March Into The Arena / Pagan Glory / Curse Of The 7 Seas / Forgotten Shadows / Towards The Light / Buried Alive / Holy Evil

LOOKING GLASS SELF (GERMANY)
Line-Up: Andre Matos (vocals), Marcus Steffan (guitar), Oliver Holzwarth (bass), Alex Holzwarth (drums)

A Prog Metal boasting high pedigree. The core of LOOKING GLASS SELF was assembled in 2000 by the former SIEGES EVEN trio of guitarist Marcys Steffan, bassist Oliver Holzwarth and brother Alex Holzwarth on drums. Joining them would be none other than erstwhile ANGRA singer Andre Matos. The rhythm section was in high demand, Alex performing on ANGRA's 'Angel's Cry' release and Oliver a member of BLIND GUARDIAN and DEMONS & WIZARDS.

The group recorded a four track demo 'Equinox' in 2000, drawing in the services of STRATOVARIUS keyboard player Jens Johansson for the occasion. The Holzwarths both sessioned on the PARADOX album 'Collision Course'.

However, although still very much operational

as of 2002 Matos had made his exit to concentrate on SHAMAN and the remaining players were prioritising other ventures, Alex with RHAPSODY and Oliver with BLIND GUARDIAN.

LORDIAN GUARD (USA)
Line-Up: Bidonne Jayre-Riemenschnieder (vocals), William J. Tsamis (guitar / keyboards), Michael Cerularius (drums)

LORDIAN GUARD was essentially an extension of epic metal outfit WARLORD and masterminded by guitarist William J. Tsamis, previously known in his WARLORD incarnation as 'Destroyer'. LORDIAN GUARD displayed both the power and pomposity of WARLORD even reworking much of their predecessors material.

The band were created in 1995 by Tsamis following his first post-WARLORD project with a solo cassette 'Sea Of Tranquillity' in 1992 under the name of LORDIAN WINDS.

The debut from LORDIAN GUARD sees a continuation from an unreleased WARLORD project 'My Name Is Man' based on the Milton poem 'Paradise Lost'. This came with the inclusion of two works 'Lost Archangel' and 'My Name Is Man'.

Albums:
WOE TO THE INHABITANTS OF THE EARTH, Hellion HE 020196 (1996)
War In Heaven / Winds Of Thor / Lost Archangel / My Name Is Man / Revelation XIX / In Peace He Comes Again

THE LORD WEIRD SLOUGH FEG
(San Francisco, CA, USA)
Line-Up: Mike Scalzi (vocals / guitar), John Cobbett (guitar), Adrian Maestas (bass), Greg Haa (drums)

A strange monicker for an equally bizarre band. THE LORD WEIRD SLOUGH FEG, the name being taken from a Celtic mythological figure as chronicled in the Ta'in Bo Cuailgne stories, are an out and out Doom / Psych flavoured Heavy Metal band but with added avant-garde twists. The Irish historical theme permeates through all the band's releases. Oddly, the band's label Dragonheart claims the act is influenced by MANOWAR, MANILLA ROAD and CIRITH UNGOL, an assertion the band themselves officially deny! The San Francisco based group, founded by Pennsylvania native Mike Scalzi and drummer Greg Haa originally from Maryland, was founded in 1990 with the intention of offering 'honour Metal', inspired by the singer's interest in Celtic myth. This fascination crossed over into early live shows, the war painted band adorning their stages with torches and bones. The 1990 incarnation of the band saw Scalzi and Haa joined by guitarist Chris Haa and bassist Justin Phelps. A succession of line-up changes, including bass player Stu Kane in 1994, witnessed the group in a constant state of flux until recording of the debut album.

The second album 'Twilight Of The Idols' was initially issued by the Doomed Planet label in North America as a vinyl release in 1998. An exclusive track entitled 'The Room' surfaced on the Bad Posture 'Metal Injection' album the same year. The Italian Dragonheart concern picked the 'Twilight Of The Idols' album up for international CD release the following year adding two extra tracks 'We'll Meet Again' and 'Warpspasm'.

In 1999 THE LORD WEIRD SLOUGH FEG line up was credited as front man Mike Scalzi, guitarist John Cobbett, bass player Jim Mack and drummer Greg Haa.

Although the 2000 'Down Among The Deadman' album would see the inclusion of John Torres, erstwhile member of ANGELWITCH and LÄÄZ ROCKIT, on bass, guitarist John Cobbett's brother Dan took over four string responsibilities upon the recording sessions' conclusion.

THE LORD WEIRD SLOUGH FEG toured Europe with SOLSTICE and TWISTED TOWER DIRE during July 2000. This relationship with SOLSTICE would be cemented further as both bands contributed tracks to a MANOWAR cover versions single issued by Doomed Planet in 2001. THE LORD WEIRD SLOUGH FEG donated 'Fast Taker', marking the inauguration of new bassist Adrian Maestas.

John Cobbett and Mike Scalzi busied themselves with the extreme Metal side venture HAMMERS OF MISFORTUNE (previously heralded as UNHOLY CADAVER), releasing the album 'The Bastard'.

The British Miskatonic Foundations label would reissue the debut album clad in new artwork and with extra tracks during 2002. Germany's Metal Supremacy label would release the same album in vinyl format. In June the band paired up with TWISTED TOWER DIRE for a run of shows in Germany. A fresh studio album, provisionally billed as 'The Traveller', was scheduled for 2002 release.

Singles/EPs:
Fast Taker, Doomed Planet (2001) (Split single with SOLSTICE)

THE LORD WEIRD SLOUGH FEG, (1997)
Shadows Of The Unborn / 20th Century
Wretch / Blarney Stone / The Red Branch /
Why Not / High Season III / High Season IV
/ Highway Corsair
TWILIGHT OF THE IDOLS, Dragonheart
CHAOS 005CD (1999)
Funeral March / Highlander / High Season II
/ The Pangs Of Ulster / Brave Connor Mac /
The Wickerman / Slough Feg / The Great Ice
Wars / Life In The Dark Age / Warpspasm /
Bi-Polar Disorder / The Wizard's Vengeance /
We'll Meet Again
DOWN AMONG THE DEADMEN,
Dragonheart (2000)
Sky Chariots / Walls Of Shame / Warriors
Dawn / Beast In The Broch / Heavy Metal
Monk / Fergus Mac Roich / Cauldron Of
Blood / Troll Pack / Traders And Gunboats /
Psionic Illuminations / Marauder / High
Season / Death Machine
THE LORD WEIRD SLOUGH FEG,
Miskatonic Foundation (2002)
Shadows Of The Unborn / 20th Century
Wretch / Blarney Stone / The Red Branch /
Why Not / Highway Corsair / High Season
III / High Season IV / Intro / The Mask /
High Season I / High Season II / The Red
Branch (Demo version) / The Room /
Headhunter

LOST FOREVER (BRAZIL)
Line-Up: Hugo Navia (vocals), Fabbio Nunes
(guitar), Nelson Magalhães (guitars), André
de Lemos (bass), Kiko Lealki (keyboards),
Renê Shulte (drums)

Progressive Metal act of Rio de Janeiro
created in 1997 as a trio of Fabio Nunes
handling lead vocals and guitar, bassist César
Severus and drummer Mauro Fogaça. Later
Will Vallante was inducted as second guitarist
and Nunes relinquished the lead vocal role
over to former VELVET GREEN man Hugo
Navia. Shortly after these additions though
Severus decamped, forging the Gothic Metal
act POETICUS SEVERUS.
LOST FOREVER was bolstered with the
addition of two personnel from another local
act ALIBI SUSPEITO in bassist Henrique
Camarão and keyboard player Kiko Lealki.
Finally in 1998 LOST FOREVER began to
appear on the local live circuit and set about
recording demos. However, internal disputes
would split the band in two.
Regrouping, LOST FOREVER drew in fresh
blood in the form of ex-NO FATE guitarist
Nelson Magalhães, former INFLUENCE bass
player André de Lemos and erstwhile
GRIMOIRE and ADVENA drummer Renê
Shulte.

LOST FOREVER's line-up problems would
be far from over though. Both Shulte and
Lealki decamped. Jefferson Spinassé took on
the keyboard position but was in turn soon
substituted by Felipe Oliveira and in quick
succession Daniel Melo. Latterly LOST
FOREVER employed Yahn Wagner on the
keys.
The band would be preparing a full-blown
album for 2002.

Singles/EPs:
Between The Shadows (Intro) / The Lies
Behind The Mirror / Damned Train / The
Shadow By Your Side / Fetters Of The
Destiny, (2000) ('Lost Forever' EP)

LOST HORIZON (SWEDEN)
Line-Up: Daniel Heiman (vocals), Wojtek
Lisicki (guitar), Martin Furangen (bass),
Christian Nyqvist (drums)

Albums:
AWAKENING THE WORLD, Music For
Nations (2001)
The Quickening / Heart Of Storm / Sworn In
the Metal Wind / The Song Of Air / World
Through My Fateless Eyes / Perfect Warrior /
Denial Of Fate / Welcome Back / The
Kingdom Of My Will / The Redintegration

MAD AXEMAN
(GERMANY)
Line-Up: Ulli Dreyer (vocals), Pete Esser (guitar), Norbert Kribus (guitar), Ulli Grzeschik (bass), Stefan Schneider (drums)

Albums:
MAD AXEMAN, Mausoleum (1985)
Mad Axeman (Comin' Home) / Hell Raiser / Magic Lips / Pearl Harbour / Double Cheatin' Girl / Bastard / Come On And Feel It / Mad At Me / Sometimes / Too Late To Run

MAD BUTCHER (GERMANY)
Line-Up: Harry Elbrecht (vocals / bass), Sidney Keller (guitar), Rolli Borchert (guitar), Rainer Gullan (drums)

Albums:
METAL LIGHTNING ATTACK, Earthshaker (1985)
Rock Shock / Mad Butcher / Right Or Wrong / Night Of The Wolf / Zero Talk / Bad Chile' Runnin' / Burn It Down / Livin' In Sin / Speed Of Light / Fearless, Heartless
METAL MEAT, Metal Enterprise (1990)
Remember / Drivin' Drivin' / U Can't Stand It / Looser / Flesh In The Night / Freewind / Machine / Hypnotised / Silhouette In Red / Children Of Tomorrow

MADSWORD (ITALY)
Line-Up: Axel Becker (vocals / guitar), Jens-Uwe Schnorr (guitar), Kai Saß (bass), Olli Gerds (drums)

An Italian Progressive Rock band, MADSWORD covered DREAM THEATER's 'The Ytse Jam' on the 'Evolution' debut. By the time of the 2000 'Global Village' album MADSWORD had despatched front man Dante Zanelli and brought in singer Andrea Bedin with guitarist Gianni Guerra and keyboard player Lorenzo Castellarin.

Albums:
EVOLUTION, Underground Symphony USCD 006 (1995)
Tsushima / Evolution / Through The Sky / Digital Trick / The Ytse Jam
GLOBAL VILLAGE, Underground Symphony USCD 044 (2000)
Connect / Time In The Ice / How Much Progress / Darknened Rooms / Living Hexadecimal / Mind's Bug / Travelling Through A Wire / Behind The Consciousness Of Memory / A New Beginning?

MAEVE OF CONNACHT (ITALY)
Line-Up: Hubi Miesel (vocals), Paolo Viani (guitar), Mani Pallinger (bass), Eve Sonderberg (keyboards), Mike Sarembe (drums)

Melodic, Progressive Metal acted forged by former members of ASGARD and BLACK JESTER. Lead vocals were assumed by erstwhile DREAMSCAPE singer HUBI MIESEL, later to release a solo album entitled 'Cut'. MAEVE OF CONNACHT guitarist Paolo Viani, an ex-BLACK JESTER member, was announced as having joined the recently re-formed cult American Power Metal band WARLORD during mid 2002.

Albums:
IMAGINARY TALES, Dragon's Music (2001)
The Gift Of Life / Broken Memory / Forever / What Does It Mean? / The Sun / Enchanted Skies / Princess Of Connacht / Another Chapter / Clouds Of Connacht

MAGNALUCIUS (CHILE)
Line-Up: Eliab Gómez (vocals), Luis Astudillo (guitar), Sergio Rubilar (guitar), Javier Grandón (bass), César Astudillo (keyboards), Manuel Valenzuela (drums)

MAGNALUCIUS are a Concepción Symphonic Metal outfit. The group's origins can be traced back to when HYDRA vocalist Manuel Valenzuela and guitarist Cesar Astudillo decided to found a trad Heavy Metal covers act dubbed BIOSOLVES. Playing in clubs and universities BIOSOLVES, with Valenzuela switching roles to become a drummer, also numbered Cesar and Eduardo Troncoso on guitar, bassist Sebastian with lead vocalist Victor Campos. Shuffles in the line-up saw the departure of Sebastian, Astudillo manoeuvring to keyboards and the introduction of ENIGMA guitarist Eduardo and EXCELSIOR bass player Javier Grandón. Eventually former MACROFOBIA singer Eliab 'Javi' Gómez became the new lead singer. This new formation titled themselves MAGNALUCIUS, taking the name after a character in a fantasy book.

The new group debuted live with a support gig to Death Metal band UNDERCROFT after which second guitarist Sergio Rubilar, having left the band BELFEGOR, was enrolled into the ranks of MAGNALUCIUS. Parallel to their priority endeavour MAGNALUCIUS members were also active in a band entitled MEDULA in league with members of THUMAN and fronted by their old BIOSELVES comrade Victor Campos.

With guitarist Eduardo making his exit the

271

band took the opportunity presented by the demise of THUMAN to induct their guitarist Luis Astudillo as swift replacement. This line-up then recorded the first demo, which featured English lyrics. MAGNALUCIUS entered the studios once more in February of 2002 to lay down their debut album.

Albums:
MAGNALUCIUS, THE QUEST..., (2002)
Overture / Hordes Under The Moon / Never Dying / Divine Melody / The Quest For The Dragontooth / God Breath / Manziker's Tears / Fight For Power / Twilight Mysteries / Flame Of Hope / Prometheus / Claws

MAGNITUDE 9 (USA)
Line-Up: Corey Brown (vocals), Rob Johnson (guitar), Kevin Chown (bass), Joseph Anastacio Glean (keyboards), John Homan (drums)

Technical Metal act. Corey Brown is ex-vocalist with PSYCODRAMA whilst bassist Kevin Chown is ex-TILES and ARTENSION. The 1999 album 'Chaos To Control' was mixed by DC TALK drummer Rick May. MAGNITUDE 9 guitarist Rob Johnson issued a solo album 'Guitarchetecture' in 1999 which saw contributions from drummers May and John Homan.
MAGNITUDE 9's January 2001 record 'Reality In Focus' would be issued in Japan with an additional track, a version of RAINBOW's seminal 'Man On The Silver Mountain'.
Chown also records with EDWIN DARE and has toured recently with TONY MACALPINE. The four stringer is never less than industrious. The summer of 2001 had him on the road with LIFE, DEATH & GIANTS, THE LOUNGE LIZARDS and THE BLUES ROCKERS.

Albums:
CHAOS TO CONTROL, Inside Out Music IOMCD 027 (1998)
End Of Time / Voices / Into The Sun / Keeper Of Your Soul / Secrets Within / Another World / Don't Say / After Tomorrow / Y2K / Writings
REALITY IN FOCUS, Inside Out Music IOMCD 065 (2001)
No Turning Back / What My Eyes Have Seen / Far Beyond Illusion / Afterlife / The End Of Days / Lost Along The Way / Flight Of Icarus / Temples Of Gold / Quiet Desperation / Mind Over Fear

MAJESTIC (SWEDEN)
Line-Up: Jonas Blum (vocals), Peter Espinoza (guitar), Martin Wezowski (bass), Richard Andersson (keyboards), Joel Linder (drums)

Previously operating under the name of LAB RAT and founded by ex-NASTY IDOLS and SAD WINGS guitarist Peter Espinoza alongside keyboard player Richard Andersson. Later recruits to bring the band into force would be former POLE POSITION singer Jonas Blum, bassist Martin Wezowski of THE DRUGS and ORIGINAL SIN and TENEBRE drummer Joel Linder.
After promoting the debut album 'Abstract Symphony' on tour in Europe with PRETTY MAIDS the band splintered with only Andersson remaining. Rebuilding MAJESTIC he inducted a whole new roster of players comprising FAITH TABBOO vocalist Apollo Papathanasio, guitarist Magnus Nordh, bass player Dick Lovgren with AGREGATOR, DARKANE, ARCH ENEMY and ARMAGEDDON drummer Peter Wildoer. This line-up cut the 2000 album 'Trinity Overture' and put in a headline tour of Japan.
Members of MAJESTIC guest on the 2000 album 'Skeleton Scales' from REPTILIAN.
Andersson would figure in the band line-up for French guitarist Stephan Forte's epic ADAGIO Progressive Power Metal concept album 'Sanctus Ignis'.
By September of 2002 it seemed as though MAJESTIC had run its course.

Albums:
ABSTRACT SYMPHONY, Massacre (1999)
Golden Sea / Losers Shades Of Hell / Standing Alone / Silence / Crimson Sun / Ceasefire / Black Moon Rising / Blood Of The Tail / Shadows From Beyond / Nitro Pitbull / Seekers Battlefield / Abstract Symphony
TRINITY OVERTURE, Massacre (2000)
Entering The Arena / Voodoo Treasure / The Rapture Of Canaan / I'll Shoot The Moon / Resurrection / Curtain Of Fire / The Breath Of Horus / Approaching The Storm / Confucius / Trinity Overture

MAJESTY (GERMANY)
Line-Up: Tarek Maghary (vocals / guitar), Udo Keppner (guitar), Martin Hehn (bass), Andreas Moll (Keyboards), Ingo Zadravec (drums)

MAJESTY are a Power Metal band out of Germany fronted by half Arabian singer Tarek "Metal Son" Maghary. MAJESTY, initially a trio of Maghary, guitarist Udo Keppner and the then sixteen year old drummer Ingo Zadravec, arrived during 1997. Soon after the band's formation Markus Pruszydlo was added on keyboards. Enlisting former GATECRASH bassist Martin Hehn, MAJESTY emerged touting an eponymous 1998 demo tape, followed by a second effort 'Metal Monarchs'. The departure of Pruszydlo during 1999 saw the vacancy swiftly filled by Andreas Moll of WILD MAGICS. The band's debut album 'Keep It True', completely self-financed by the band, would be released by the Russian Irond label. Drummer Ingo Zadravec later made way for Michael Gräter.

MAJESTY signed to the domestic Massacre label for the 'Sword & Sorcery' album. Undoubtedly inspired by MANOWAR the band wore their influences proud, laying down a version of 'Battle Hymn' for a tribute album. The album would not only included cover art from long term MANOWAR collaborator Ken Kelly but even had Ross the Boss guesting a guitar solo on the track 'Heavy Metal'. Vinyl versions of the album added an extra exclusive track 'Ride And Fight'.

Singles/EPs:
Keep It True / Son Of Metal, (2001)

Albums:
KEEP IT TRUE, Irond (2002)
Keep It True / Strong As Steel / Hail To Majesty / Son Of Metal / Into The Night / Metal Force / We Will Ride / Last Revolution
SWORD & SORCERY, Massacre (2002)
Sword & Sorcery / Fields Of War / Heavy Metal / Epic War / Ride Silent! / Fist Of Steel / Aria Of Bravery / Metal To The Metalheads

MALICE (Los Angeles, CA, USA)
Line-Up: James Neal (vocals), Jay Reynolds (guitar), Mick Zane (guitar), Mark Behn (bass),

MALICE were a highly impressive Los Angeles based Metal band noted for strenuous live work and founded firmly in the JUDAS PRIEST camp. Not only did MALICE sound like JUDAS PRIEST by warrant of their heavy European guitar riffing but vocalist James Neal, a practising Buddhist, sounded uncannily like JUDAS PRIEST front man Rob Halford and guitarist Jay Reynolds was a deadringer for JUDAS PRIEST guitarist K.K. Downing. MALICE's insistence on wearing studded black leather only compounded the comparisons.

Formed by Portland émigrés, bassist Mark Behn had previously played in FIRE EYE and had also played in another local outfit, KHARMA, who also included Pete Holmes, better known in later years for his role in BLACK N' BLUE.

Guitarist Mick Zane had started out with the 1978 act RUDE AWAKENING, fronted by Matt McCourt, later of WILD DOGS infamy. Zane and McCourt, alongside WILD DOGS guitarist Jeff Horton and BLACK N' BLUE man Pete Holmes, would share a later band, DMZ, in 1981. Jay Reynolds was part of the same club scene, coincidentally appearing in the Matt McCourt fronted acts 1979's Punk band the VIOLATORS and THE RAVERS.

Making their initial vinyl appearance on the first 'Metal Massacre' compilation album - the only band to contribute two tracks - with 'Captive Of Light' and 'Kick You Down', MALICE were in fact at that stage not yet a band, the five members only deciding on a permanent union following the sessions. The buzz on MALICE was now on a rollercoaster, with the respected Dutch magazine Aardschock giving the band a cover story a mere two months after their formation.

The band's first gig came in November 1982 appearing at Los Angeles Troubadour Club sharing a bill with METALLICA and PANDEMONIUM.

The band's ensuing Michael Wagener produced demo proved an immense tour de force and MALICE soon found themselves at the centre of a record company bidding war. Atlantic Records snapped up the band and the demo comprised half of MALICE's first album 'In The Beginning', the remaining tracks being produced by Ashley Howe.

Second album 'License To Kill', found MALICE with new drummer Cliff Carothers. Produced by Max Norman the record was another strong contender. Guests in the studio included MEGADETH men Dave Mustaine and Dave Ellefson and BLACK N' BLUE's Tommy Thayer and Jaime St. James. MALICE toured with W.A.S.P. on the West Coast and despite making headway with a strong record, a European tour supporting Thrashers SLAYER proved to be a disastrous mismatch with the headliner's fans hostility showing itself openly with spitting and verbal abuse.

MALICE folded in late 1987. Reynolds was very briefly to flirt with MEGADETH, although the friend he entrusted this confidential information to and tutored Reynolds on MEGADETH riffs, Jeff Young, put his own name forward and landed the coveted position.

A third MALICE release, 'Crazy In The Night' was issued in 1988, although none of the tracks featured Neal, his place having been taken in the studio by PAUL SABU. A strange union bearing in mind Sabu's AOR history. Neal did, however, appear in a concert sequence in the movie 'Vice Versa'.

Zane, Behn and Carothers attempted to sustain MALICE but with no product forthcoming they split the band. In 1995 Zane and Behn returned to the fray with the Los Angeles based MONSTER, releasing the 'Through The Eyes Of The World' album on Long Island Records. MONSTER featured Behn's old KHARMA band mate Pete Holmes and previously unknown vocalist Mark Isham.

Singles/EPs:
Captive Of Light / Vice Versa / Crazy In The Night / Death Or Glory, Metal Blade 734414 (1989)

Albums:
IN THE BEGINNING..., Atlantic 781 250-1 (1985)
Rockin' With You / Into The Ground / Air Attack / Stellar Masters / Tarot Dealer / Squeeze It Dry / Hellrider / No Haven For The Raven / The Unwanted / Godz Of Thunder
LICENSE TO KILL, Atlantic 81714-1 (1986)
Sinister Double / License To Kill / Against The Empire / Vigilante / Chain Gang Woman / Christine / Murder / Breathin' Down Your Neck / Circle Of Fire

MALISHA (USA)
Line-Up: Kim La Chance (vocals), Randy Hano (guitar), Darry Shihado (bass), Joe Silva (drums)

Formed by ex-VIXEN and HAWAII front woman Kim La Chance in November of 1982. MALISHA served up straightforward no frills aggressive Metal on their debut 1983 demo. MALISHA formed with a line up of La Chance, guitarist Randy Hano, bass player Darry Shihado and drummer Ivar. The latter would be superseded first by Craig Brooks, then Rick Dingman.
The track 'Valkyrie' on the 'Serve Your Savage Beast' album would be dedicated to Janne Stark, guitarist with Swedish outfit OVERDRIVE.
Post MALISHA, La Chance created the 1992 act DRIVEN STEEL, comprising guitarist Julia Roberts (presumably not the actress!), bassist Kelly Heckart and drummer Franco Geneta.

Singles/EPs:
Give It All You've Got, Malisha (1983)

Albums:
SERVE YOUR SAVAGE BEAST, Shardan Kane (1986)
Valkyrie / Love For The Day / Step Through Eternity / Serve Your Savage Beast / What I Believe / Power Flight / Metal Wars / Burning Rage / Hands Of The Ripper

YNGWIE MALMSTEEN (SWEDEN)

Swedish born Yngwie Malmsteen is an incredibly talented guitarist whose reputation was founded upon some blistering demos (including back up from SILVER MOUNTAIN musicians) doing the rounds of ardent tape traders in the early '80s. Malmsteen plays with lightning speed and awesome accuracy that draws on everything from Baroque to such major Rock influences as DEEP PURPLE / RAINBOW man RITCHIE BLACKMORE, ULI JON ROTH and beyond.
Malmsteen's first band was POWERHOUSE, put together when the fledgling guitar guru was merely thirteen years old. Elevating himself through various cover outfits, most notably a DEEP PURPLE inspired band entitled BURN, Yngwie formed RISING FORCE with EUROPE bassist John Levén and drummer Peter Udd in 1978.
Malmsteen was briefly a member of HIGHBROW in 1981 but the band folded shortly after. In 1982 CBS Records in Sweden paid for a recording session, but eventually passed on the band and the proposed single, 'You're Going To Break Them All' / 'Horizons', was never released. RISING FORCE split with Levén eventually teaming up with EUROPE and Udd joining the GLORY BELLS BAND, although recordings from this era were released as the bootleg 'Rising Force' album issued in 1986. Allegedly, these tapes were put out by an previous member of Yngwie's band as he felt money was due to him!
It was at this juncture in his career, and following a multitude of varying line-ups, that Malmsteen joined forces with SILVER MOUNTAIN, finding himself alongside the brotherly duo of drummer Anders Johansson and keyboard player Jens Johanssson. Both musicians were heavily steeped in the classical influences that so intrigued Yngwie. The resulting demos were passed by Yngwie to Guitar Player magazine journalist Mike Varney who immediately set wheels in motion to bring Malmsteen to America and his Shrapnel label. Meanwhile, Malmsteen's tapes had been heavily traded and such was the rabid appreciation of these mainly instrumental demos (much influenced by ULI JON ROTH) that in the Metal hotbed of San Francisco, led by the influential 'Metal Mania' fanzine, Yngwie was proclaimed as a 'God'.
The initial plan was for Malmsteen to record a solo album. In Los Angeles STEELER (fronted by original vocalist Ron Keel together with bassist Rik Fox and drummer Mark Edwards, who had both joined the group after Keel moved the band to Los Angeles), had just signed to Shrapnel Records. Seeing an opportunity they convinced Malmsteen and

Varney that their band was a far more commercially accessible vehicle in which to spread the word. Malmsteen relocated from Sweden and joined STEELER in early 1983. The resulting debut album on Varney's own Shrapnel label proved to be an out-and-out Metal work and was, naturally, highlighted by some blistering guitar work. Yngwie was soon splashed all over the guitar magazines and heralded a revolution of superspeed guitarists. However, even at this early stage the media became suspicious and were always eager to knock Yngwie at every opportunity.

Following the demise of STEELER (who evolved into KEEL), Malmsteen's name was linked to numerous heavyweight Hard Rock bands such as UFO, OZZY OSBOURNE and DIO but opted to join another new act. This duly arrived in the shape of ALCATRAZZ with veteran vocalist GRAHAM BONNET (RAINBOW, MICHAEL SCHENKER GROUP) and ex-NEW ENGLAND men, keyboardist Jimmy Waldo and bassist Gary Shea. Drums were handled by erstwhile PIPEDREAM man Jan Uvena. The group signed to Andy Trueman management and Rocshire Records.

With ALCATRAZZ, Malmsteen cut one studio album, 'No Parole From Rock n' Roll' and the live album 'Live Sentence', the latter recorded in Japan. The first ALCATRAZZ album, albeit heavily marred by a very tepid Dennis McKay production, furthered the Malmsteen cause; whilst the live album received idol-like adulation in Japan, where Bonnet was already a household name.

Keen to pursue a solo career Malmsteen moved on to form his own vehicle, RISING FORCE, signing to Polydor in 1983, retaining the guiding managerial hand of Andy Trueman. Personnel enlisted for the recording included Jens Johansson, former JETHRO TULL drummer Barriemore Barlow and new found vocalist JEFF SCOTT SOTO.

The debut album is a breathtaking display of guitar wizardry, with Malmsteen proudly displaying his talents to the full on such tracks as the eight minute instrumental '''Icarus Dream Suite Opus 4' and 'Black Star'. Yngwie's growing legion of fans hailed the release as a true revelation of genius. Guitar magazines lapped it up with equal reverence whilst the mainstream Rock press savaged the album as a short sighted exercise in self aggrandisement.

Undeterred, Malmsteen released 'Marching Out' in 1985, which seemed to polarise views on his position in the Rock world even further. For this album Yngwie once again used Jens Johansson and Soto, but also enlisted Anders Johansson and bassist Marcel Jacob,

previously with HIGHBROW and POWER. This was the line-up that Yngwie took on the road supporting AC/DC in America and headlining with TALAS as support.

By his third album, 'Trilogy', the long drawn out guitar showcases were giving way to cleaner cut songs and a new vocalist Marc Boals - who had formerly plied his trade as bassist with TED NUGENT - was recruited to lend a smoother edge to the proceedings. However, Boals was quickly ejected, later forming STEELHOUSE LANE and also fronting BILLIONAIRE BOYS CLUB, and Soto was back in the saddle for Yngwie's next American tour opening for Canadians TRIUMPH. Jacob meantime would go onto BILLIONAIRE BOYS CLUB and TALISMAN.

Malmsteen's career has been dogged by media insinuations that he cannot write a 'good song' which unfortunately has resulted in the guitarist trying to defend himself much too often. This constant criticism led to the 'Odyssey' album wherein, as well as the addition of bassist Bob Daisley, former RAINBOW vocalist JOE LYNN TURNER was recruited for an ill fated and tempestuous relationship. The album strangely gave Yngwie probably his greatest success worldwide, with both the album and single 'Heaven Tonight' doing well. Needless to say, another line-up change saw former PAT TRAVERS bassist Barry Dunaway coming in to fill Daisley's shoes for the tour.

The world tour also provided a valuable first for Malmsteen as he played 20 sold out shows in the Soviet Union to over 240,000 people after continually being voted best guitarist in Russian polls. These gigs were recorded and eventually surfaced as 'Trial By Fire - Live In Leningrad'. Turner eventually jumped ship to front probably the least successful line-up yet of DEEP PURPLE but not before igniting a bitter war of words between the two. Dunaway would later join SARAYA.

It was all change again as Yngwie brought in an entirely new, all Swedish band comprising bassist Svante Henryson, keyboard player Mats Olausson, ex-NORDEN LIGHT drummer Michael van Knorring and ex-MADISON and JOHN NORUM vocalist Goran Edman for his next album. Typically, a line-up change occurred shortly after with van Knorring making way for former MOGG and STEAMROLLER drummer Bo Sundberg.

Despite a strong performance on record, Goran Edman proved embarrassingly naive onstage during the first tour, to the point of Malmsteen himself joining in with audience jeers!

Disgruntled with his view of lack of record company support, Malmsteen shrugged off

Polydor to sign to Elektra for his next album. However, the momentum was maintained as 1992's 'Fire And Ice' debuted in the Japanese charts at the coveted number 1 position.

With Edman off for pastures new (including latterly STREET TALK) Malmsteen's 1994 vocalist was former OBSESSION and LOUDNESS front man Mike Vescara. Other new additions were ZILLION, BEAU NASTY and ARTENSION drummer Mike Terrana, keyboardist Mats Olausson and bassist Barry Sparks. Malmsteen completed a successful American club tour with former DRIVER drummer B.J. Zampa to round up 1994.

Terrana later joined METALIUM and RAGE. Zampa would work with THUNDERHEAD and DAVID WAYNE'S METAL CHURCH.

The guitarist's 1995 album, 'Magnum Opus' co-produced by Chris Tsangarides, once more topped the Japanese charts upon its release before the guitarist teamed up with Jeff Scott Soto in 1996, making a guest appearance on the debut album by HUMAN CLAY.

Clearly keen to do just what the hell he wanted, Malmsteen's 1996 album, aptly titled 'Inspiration', was made up of cover versions of classics by bands such as KANSAS, DEEP PURPLE, SCORPIONS and RUSH. It saw a return for vocalist Marc Boals together with bassist Barry Dunaway and veteran drummer Tommy Aldridge, a man who boasts credits with BLACK OAK ARKANSAS, OZZY OSBOURNE and WHITESNAKE. Other featured artists include vocalists JEFF SCOTT SOTO and JOE LYNN TURNER.

Predictably touring soon had the band fracturing with Malmsteen quite incredibly declaring Aldridge to be "useless" and Boals onstage presence like that of "a strange combination of a man and a woman"!!

However, Malmsteen, after admitting a long battle against a reliance on alcohol, returned in 1997 in partnership with ex-RAINBOW, BLACK SABBATH and WHITESNAKE drummer COZY POWELL. With a 1997 album entitled 'Facing The Animal', produced by Chris Tsangarides (THIN LIZZY / JUDAS PRIEST), the guitarist was to issue what many determined to be his finest work to date.

The album featured a new vocalist in former TREAT, SWEDISH EROTICA and ABSTRAKT ALGEBRA man Mats Leven (recommended to Malmsteen by CANDLEMASS and ABSTRAKT ALGEBRA bassist Leif Edling), bassist Barry Dunaway and keyboard player Mats Olausson.

As well as ploughing his Rock furrow, Malmsteen also indulged himself the same year by recording a classical album together with ex-RAINBOW keyboard player David Rosenthal and the Prague Philharmonic Orchestra.

1999's 'Alchemy' album, engineered by Chris Tsangarides but produced by Malmsteen himself, saw a return of vocalist Mark Boals, Dunaway and Olauson. Drums were courtesy of POWERMAD, TNT and RIOT man John Macaluso.

Malmsteen lent a guest session to his former vocalist Mike Vescara's MVP project 'Windows' in 1999. The album also included bassist Barry Sparks and drummer B.J. Zampa.

Meantime Macaluso and Olasson busied themselves on side project ARK fronted by vocalist JORN LANDE of THE SNAKES.

The ever industrious guitarist was back in 2000 with a fresh album 'War To End All Wars'. The European version of the album included a bonus track, a version of the QUATERMASS cut 'Black Sheep Of The Family' with guest vocalist Anders Kahn. Ironically this was the song that led to the dispute which originally fractured RITCHIE BLACKMORE away from DEEP PURPLE and into RAINBOW.

Boals and Olasson were retained for the album but bass was now in the hands of HOLY MOTHER and C.P.R. four stringer Randy Coven. Breaking with tradition the album cover was a Frank Frazetta original 'Deathdealer 5'.

Malmsteen's other band mates formed a tighter bond the same year when Coven joined ARK. Coven was also working on his solo project 'Witchway'.

MARK BOALS was not to be left out and released his debut solo effort 'Ring Of Fire' the same day as Yngwie's record. Boals utilised the prodigious talents of guitarist TONY McALPINE, ARTENSION keyboard player Vitalij Kuprij and PLANET X drummer Virgil Donati. His live band included former YNGWIE MALMSTEEN bassist Barry Dunaway.

YNGWIE MALMSTEEN toured America in November on a package bill with DIO and DORO. Boals quit on the eve of these dates and the band duly went on the road as an instrumental act with Malmsteen lending vocals to a version of JIMI HENDRIX's 'Red House'. The most well known Malmsteen credited singer JEFF SCOTT SOTO turned up at the Los Angeles gig to guest. The front man's position was eventually taken by VAGABOND, THE SNAKES, MILLENIUM and ARK vocalist JORN LANDE.

Typically the band line-up did not stay the course. During an American tour rumours leaked out that both Lande and Macaluso were denied access to Canada, the pair being without the necessary visas. Matters appeared to come to a head when Lande was involved in a backstage 'dispute' in Cleveland and walked out. Macaluso, who had been performing with a broken finger, followed his friend.

Meantime Malmsteen, Olaussen and Coven, swiftly revising the set to include more instrumental work outs and JIMI HENDRIX covers, performed as a power trio in Canada then cancelled the remaining dates and attempted to lure former members JEFF SCOTT SOTO and Barriemore Barlow back into the fold. Soto was swiftly announced as Lande's replacement although discussions had also taken place with the familiar MARK BOALS (now fronting the all star EMPIRE with another ex-Malmsteen man drummer Anders Johansson) and also ex-RAINBOW man Doogie White. Within days Cleveland Rock band M.S.O.D. had announced that their drummer, the suitably named Ed Rock, had joined Yngwie to complete the tour but this idea was soon scotched.

On a more positive note Malmsteen was invited by the Chinese government to undertake a full-blown nationwide tour of the country. Plans were laid for Yngwie to combine shows and concertos with the Chinese National Orchestra in Beijing, Xian, Shanghai and other cities.

Malmsteen would finally announce a revised line up for a string of September Central and South American dates commencing in Mexico. The new look group was fronted by erstwhile RAINBOW and MIDNIGHT BLUE singer Doogie White with BLACKMORE'S NIGHT bassist Mike Cervino, the esteemed DEREK SHERINAN of PLANET X, PLATYPUS, ALICE COOPER and DREAM THEATER on keyboards and, keeping up the Swedish quota, STORMWIND and WITHOUT GRIEF drummer Patrik Johansson.

Quite predictably the tour ran into trouble although not from any by now expected internal ructions. In the wake of the September 11th World Trade Center disaster the band performed a Brazilian gig in Porte Allegre. According to reports Malmsteen closed off his guitar solo section with the customary 'Star Spangled Banner' anthem to which the crowd started to jeer. Band members believed the audience were chanting "Osama! Osama!" and reacted accordingly. At the close of the set Malmsteen alone walked out for an encore blasting through another rendition of 'Star Spangled Banner' and retorting "God Bless America - Fuck you all".

Yngwie's next move would be to record a brand new classical Baroque style piece recorded with the New Japan Philharmonic Orchestra. Fans would also delight at the release of archive RISING FORCE material issued by the Swedish Powerline label in the form of the 'Birth Of The Sun' album. It would be revealed that Malmsteen's new album, provisionally entitled 'Attack', would be recorded with a line-up of Yngwie Malmsteen on both guitars and bass; Doogie White on vocals, Derek Sherinian on keyboards and Patrik Johansson on drums. The guitarist also took a left turn out of the Rock field to contribute a guitar solo to Swedish Folk singer AASA JINDER's album 'Faith, Hope And Love'.

Other activities found White forging yet another band endeavour, VISUAL SURVEILLANCE OF EXTREMITIES in league with guitarist BILLY LIESEGANG, and guesting on the British spoof Rockers SACK TRICK 2002 opus 'Sheep In KISS Make Up', an album entirely composed of KISS cover versions. The singer also became a familiar sound in Spain and France when his vocals, on the QUEEN track 'Friends Will Be Friends', were used on an Amstel Beer commercial.

Meantime DEREK SHERINAN cut another solo album, on which Yngwie duly guested, and found the time to join up with BILLY IDOL's band for his North American summer 'Kiss The Skull' tour. Limbering up to promote his 'Attack' album Yngwie uncharacteristically scheduled a TV showing as guest on the hugely popular Swedish STV children's comedy show 'Alram Est'.

Pony Canyon would follow up the success of 'Attack' with a collection of early recordings dubbed 'Genesis' in December. This album compiled recordings dating from 1980, a twelve minute rendition of JIMI HENDRIX's 'Voodoo Chile' plus other rarities.

Singles/EPs:
I Am A Viking / Don't Let It End, Polydor 7DM 0130 (1985) (Japanese release)
I'll See The Light Tonight / Far Beyond The Sun / I Am A Viking, Polydor 883073-7 (1985)
You Don't Remember, I'll Never Forget, Polydor (1986) (Promotion release)
Fire / Cryin', Polydor (1986) (Promotional release)
Save Your Love / Motherless Child, Polydor 877 598-7 (1986)
Heaven Tonight / Riot In The Dungeons / Rising Force / Trilogy Opus Suite 5, Polydor YJMX1 (1988)
Making Love, Polydor PO 79 (1990)
Bedroom Eyes, Polygram (1990) (USA Promotion)
Dragonfly, Elektra (1992) (USA Promotion)
Teaser / Perpetual / Broken Glass, Elektra 66439-2 (1992)
I Can't Wait / Aftermath / Rising Force (Live)

/ Far Beyond The Sun (Live) / Power And Glory, Pony Canyon PCCY 00629 (1994) (Japanese release)

Albums:
RISING FORCE, Polydor 825 324-1 (1984) **14 SWEDEN, 60 USA**
Black Star / Far Beyond The Sun / Now Your Ships Are Burned / Evil Eye / Icarus Dream Suite / As Above, So Below / Little Savage / Farewell
MARCHING OUT, Polydor POLD 5183 (1985) **9 SWEDEN, 52 USA**
Prelude / I'll See The Light Tonight / Don't Let It End / Disciples Of Hell / I Am A Viking / Overture 1383 / Anguish And Fear / On The Run Again / Soldier Without Faith / Caught In The Middle / Marching Out
TRILOGY, Polydor POLD 5204 (1986) **18 SWEDEN, 44 USA**
You Don't Remember, I'll Never Forget / Liar / Queen In Love / Crying / Fury / Fire / Magic Mirror / Dark ages / Trilogy Opus Suite 5
ODYSSEY, Polydor POLD 5224 (1988) **7 SWEDEN, 27 UK, 40 USA**
Rising Force / Hold On / Heaven Tonight / Dreaming / Bite The Bullet / Riot In The Dungeons / Deja Vu / Crystal Ball / Now Is The Time / Faster Than The Speed Of Light / Krakatau / Memories
TRIAL BY FIRE – LIVE IN LENINGRAD, Polydor 839726 1 (1989) **31 SWEDEN, 65 UK**
Liar / Queen In Love / Deja Vu / Far Beyond The Sun / Heaven Tonight / Dreaming / You Don't Remember, I'll Never Forget / Trilogy Suite Opus 5 / Spasebo Blues / Crystal Ball / Black Star / Spanish Castle Magic
ECLIPSE, Polydor 843 361-2 (1990) **12 UK, 43 UK**
Making Love / Bedroom Eyes / Save Our Love / Motherless Child / Devil In Disguise / Judas / What Do You Want / Demon Driver / Faultline / See You In Hell (Don't Be Late) / Eclipse
THE YNGWIE MALMSTEEN COLLECTION, Polydor 849271 (1992)
Black Star / Far Beyond The Sun / I'll See The Light Tonight / You Don't Remember, I'll Never Forget / Liar / Queen In Love / Hold On / Heaven Tonight / Deja Vu / Guitar Solo / Spanish Castle Magic / Judas / Making Love / Eclipse
FIRE AND ICE, Elektra 7559611371 (1992) **1 JAPAN, 11 SWEDEN, 57 UK**
Perpetual / Dragonfly / Teaser / How Many Miles To Babylon / Cry No More / No Mercy / C'est La Vie / Leviathan / Fire And Ice / Forever Is A Long Time / I'm My Own Enemy / All I Want Is Everything / Golden Dawn / Final Curtain
SEVENTH SIGN, Music For Nations MFN 158 (1994)
Never Die / I Don't Know / Meant To Be / Forever One / Hairtrigger / Brothers / Seventh Sign / Bad Blood / Prisoner Of Your Love / Pyramid Of Cheops / Crash And Burn / Sorrow
MAGNUM OPUS, Music For Nations MFN 188 (1995) **1 JAPAN**
Vengeance / No Love Lost / Tomorrow's Gone / The Only One / I'd Die Without You / Overture 1622 / Voodoo / Cross The Line / Time Will Tell / Fire In The Sky / Amberdawn
INSPIRATION, Music For Nations MFN200 (1996)
Carry On My Wayward Son / Pictures Of Home / Gates Of Babylon / Manic Depression / In The Dead Of The Night / Mistreated / The Sails Of Charon / Demon's Eye / Anthem / Child In Time
FACING THE ANIMAL, Mercury (1997) **39 SWEDEN**
Braveheart / Facing The Animal / Enemy / Sacrifice / Like An Angel / My Resurrection / Another Time / Heathens From The North / Alone In Paradise / End Of My Rope / Only The Strong / Poison In Your Veins / Air On A Theme
LIVE!!, Pony Canyon PCCY-01278 (1998)
Resurrection / Facing The Animal / Rising Force / Bedroom Eyes / Far Beyond The Sun / Like An Angel / Brave Heart / Seventh Sign / Trilogy Suite (including Red House & Badfinger) / Gates Of Babylon / Alone In Paradise / Pictures Of Home / Never Die / Black Star / I'll See The Light
MILLENNIUM SUITE FOR ELECTRIC GUITAR AND ORCHESTRA, Pony Canyon PMDI 01211 (1998)
Icarus Dream Fanfare / Cavallino Rampante / Fugue / Prelude To April / Toccata / Andante / Sarabande / Allegro / Adagio / Vivace / Presto Vivace / Finale
CONCERTO SUITE FOR ELECTRIC GUITAR AND ORCHESTRA IN E FLAT MINOR OPUS 1 (MILLENNIUM CLASSIC VERSION), Pony Canyon (1998)
Icarus Dream Fanfare / Cavalino Rampante / Fugue / Prelude To April / Toccata / Andante / Sarabande / Allegro / Adagio / Vivace / Presto Vivace / Finale
ALCHEMY, Dreamcatcher CRIDE 20 (1999)
Blitzkrieg / Leonardo / Playing With Fire / Stand (The) / Wield My Sword / Blue / Legion Of The Damned / Daemon Dance (7,405.926) / Hanger 18, Area 51 / Voodoo Nights / Asylum: a) Asylum, b) Sky Euphoria, c) Quantum Leap
THE BEST OF 1990-1999, Dreamcatcher (2000)
Gimme, Gimme, Gimme / Never Die / Brothers / Seventh Sign / Vengeance / Voodoo / Facing The Animal / Like An Angel

/ Another Time / Rising Force (Live) / Gates Of Babylon (Live) / Blue / Hanger 18, Area 51 / Cavalino Rampante
ANTHOLOGY 1994-1999, Pony Canyon PCCY-01446 (2000)
Gimme! Gimme! Gimme! (A Man After Midnight) / Never Die / Brothers / Seventh Sign / Crash And Burn / Vengeance / Fire In The Sky / Like An Angel - For April / My Resurrection / Another Time / Rising Force (Live) / I'll See The Light, Tonight (Live) / Wield My Sword / Hangar 18, Area 51 / Flamenco Diablo / Amadeus Quattro Valvole
WAR TO END ALL WARS, Pony Canyon PCCY-01423 (2000)
Prophet Of Doom / Crucify / Bad Reputation / Catch 22 / Masquerade / Arpeggios From Hell / Miracle Of Life / Wizard / Prelude / Wild One / Tarot / Instrumental Institution / War To End All Wars / Black Sheep Of The Family
CONCERT SUITE LIVE WITH THE NEW JAPAN PHILHARMONIC, Pony Canyon PCCY-01551 (2001)
Black Star (Orchestra) / Trilogy Suite: First movement / Brothers / Icarus Dream Fanfare / Cavallino Rampante / Fugue / Prelude To April / Toccata / Andante / Sarabande / Allegro / Vivace / Presto Vivace / Finale / Blitzkrieg / Far Beyond The Sun
ATTACK, Pony Canyon PCCY-01582 (2002)
11 JAPAN
Razor Eater / Rise Up / Valley Of The Kings / Ship Of Fools / Attack / Baroque & Roll / Stronghold / Mad Dog / In The Name Of God / Freedom Isn't Free / Majestic Blue / Valhalla / Touch The Sky / Ironclad / Nobody's Fool

MANIA (GERMANY)
Line-Up: Chris Klauke (vocals), Frank Nottelmann (guitar), Thies Bendixen (guitar), Didy Mackel (bass), Rainer Heubel (drums)

Hamburg Heavy Metal band. Featuring ex-PROPHECY vocalist Chris Klauke, for a short period of time guitarist Holger Wendt was a member of MANIA. Wendt wound up nine years later playing in R.A.W. with GLENMORE vocalist Jürgen Volk and the former JEALOUS HEART rhythm section of bassist Werner Hauser and drummer Chris Grenzer. MANIA's Chris Klauke later formed ABRAXAS.

Singles/EPs:
Message / Deliverance, Mania (1988)

Albums:
WIZARD OF THE LOST KINGDOM, Noise NUK 127 (1988)

Mufty's Arrival / Wizard Of The Lost Kingdom / Night Of The Blade / Gods Of Fire / Under The Sign Of The Cross / Break Out / Mufty's Departure
CHANGING TIMES, Noise NUK 139 (1989)
Prelude / The Expulsion / Turn Towards The Light / No Way Back / Be Strong / To The End Of The World / The Vision / Gambler / We Don't Need War / Violent Time

MANILLA ROAD (USA)
Line-Up: Mark Shelton (vocals / guitar), Scott Park (bass), Rick Fisher (drums)

Cult underground Metal band with a lengthy history. Mike Metz contributes keyboards to the 'Crystal Logic' album. Fisher lost his place to Randy Foxe upfront of the 'Open The Gates' album.
More recently, a 'Best Of' collection appeared through Black Dragon in association with the Greek version of 'Metal Hammer' magazine. A 14 track affair, the album clocked in at approximately 72 minutes in length.
Quite incredibly MANILLA ROAD returned in 2001 with a new album 'Atlantis Rising' on the German Iron Glory label and a performance at the German 'Bang Your Head' festival. The band line-up stood at vocalist / guitarist Mark Shelton, bassist Mark Anderson and drummer Scott Peters. STAMPING GROUND's Darby Pentecoast would also lend backing vocals.

Singles/EPs:
The Ninth Wave / Witches Brew, Black Dragon (1985) (Free 12" with 'Open The Gates' LP)

Albums:
INVASION, Roadster (1981)
The Dream Goes On / Cat And Mouse / Far Side Of The Sun / Street Jammer / The Empire
METAL, Roadster (1982)
Enter The Warrior / Defender / Queen Of The Black Coast / Metal / Out Of Control With Rock n' Roll / Cage Of Mirrors / Far Side Of The Sun
CRYSTAL LOGIC, Black Dragon (1983)
Prologue / Necropolis / Crystal Logic / Feeling Free Again / The Riddle Master / The Ram / The Veils Of Negative Existence / Dreams Of Eschaton / Epilogue
OPEN THE GATES, Black Dragon BD002 (1985)
Metalsorm / Open The Gates / Astronomica / Weavers Of The Web / Heavy Metal To The World / The Fires Of Mars / Road Of Kings /

MANILLA ROAD
Photo : Nico Wobben

Hour Of The Dragon
THE DELUGE, Black Dragon (1986)
Dementia / Shadow In The Black / Divine
Victim / Hammer Of The Witches / Morbid
Tabernacle / Taken By Storm / The Deluge: i)
Eye Of The Sea, ii) The Drowned Lands, iii)
Engulfed Cathedral / Friction In Mass / Rest
In Pieces
MYSTIFICATION, Black Dragon BD024
(1987)
Masque Of The Red Death / Valley Of
Unrest / Spirits Of The Dead / Haunted
Palace / Mystification / Up From The Crypt /
Children Of The Night / Dragon Star / Death
By The Hammer
LIVE ROADKILL, Black Dragon BD033
(1988)
Dementia / Open The Gates / Mystification /
The Deluge /Masque Of The Red Death /
Witches Brew / Spirits Of The Dead / Far
Side Of The Sun
OUT OF THE ABYSS, Black Dragon BD037
(1989)
Whitechapel / Rites Of Blood / Out Of The
Abyss / Return Of The Old Ones / Black
Cauldron / Midnight Meat Train / War In
Heaven / Slaughterhouse / Helicon
THE COURTS OF CHAOS, Black Dragon
(1990)
Road To Chaos / Dig Me No Grave / DOA /
Into The Courts Of Chaos / From Beyond / A
Touch Of Madness / Vlad The Impaler / The
Prophecy / The Books Of Skelos: i) The
Book Of Ancients, ii) The Book Of Shadows,
iii) The Book Of Skulls
CIRCUS MAXIMUS, Black Dragon BDCD 53
(1992)
**LIVE BY THE SWORD – THE VERY BEST
OF MANILLA ROAD**, Black Dragon BD
MH002 (1998)
Riddle Master / The Veils Of Negative
Existence / Dreams Of Eschaton / Metal
Storm / Weavers Of The Web / Hour Of The
Dragon / Witch's Brew / Divine Victim /
Shadow In The Black / Friction In Mass / The
Deluge / Masque Of The Red Death / Valley
Of Unrest / Up From The Crypt
ATLANTIS RISING, Iron Glory (2001)
Atlantis Rising / Lemuria / Sea Witch /
Resurrection / Decimation / Flight Of The
Ravens / March Of The Gods / Siege Of
Atland / War Of The Gods

MANITOU (NORWAY)
Line-Up: Øyvind Hægeland (vocals), Ole P.
Fredriksen (guitar), Jan Schulze (guitar), Tom
Erikson (bass), Per B Aanonsen (drums)

MANITOU released a solitary acclaimed
Progressive Metal album before folding.
MANITOU singer Øyvind Hægeland would

later front another technically based Prog
Metal act of high repute SPIRAL
ARCHITECT.

Albums:
ENTRANCE, Mind The Gap MTG CD 2666
(1995)
Servants Of The Greed / Ache Falls Dead
Calm / Coven (Autumn Arrives) / Ship Of
Dreams / The Forlorne / Entrance /
Shadowhunt / Into Plumbless Oceans /
Prophecy Of The Sleeper / The Prediction /
When Silence Descends

MANNINYA BLADE (SWEDEN)
Line-Up: Leif Eriksson (vocals), Nicke
Johansson (guitar), Adde Pahim (guitar),
Blomman Blomqvist (bass), Ingemar
Lundeberg (drums)

Boden band MANNINYA BLADE date as far
back as 1980. At that early stage the band
comprised vocalist Leif Eriksson, guitarist
Nicklas Johansson, bassist Jan Blomqvist
and drummer Ingemar Lundeberg.
A second guitarist, Michael Vikström (a.k.a.
Mike Wead), was added to the group in order
to record demo tapes, but the axe slinger
chose to move to Stockholm to create the
Metal leviathan CANDLEMASS. He was
immediately replaced by Jerry Rutström
before quitting to be succeeded by ex-
DAMIEN guitarist Andreas Palm.
Shortly after the release of the debut album
Lundeberg left the band, whilst Leif Eriksson
departed following the recording of the
'Incubus' demo (a four track affair) in 1988. As
a result, Johansson took over vocal duties
and the group shortened their name to
MANNINYA in the process.
Lundeberg was eventually replaced by Martin
Eriksson, until he was asked to leave and the
group subsequently re-enlisted Michael
Vikström and adopted the new monicker of
HEXENHAUS in mid 1988. Under this new
title (with Palm renamed 'Rick Moister') the
Swedes recorded the 'Tribute To Insanity'
album.
MANNINYA BLADE reformed in 1990 with
Rutström, Leif Eriksson, Blomqvist and
drummer Johan Eriksson, although Leif was
to leave after the band cut a new demo tape
in 1995.
Martin Eriksson was to later enjoy stardom as
Techno artist E-TYPE on a world-wide scale
in the mid '90s!
Another MANNINYA BLADE bass player
Marre Martini (also known as Mårten
Marteen) would journey through DAMIEN,
LOST SOULS and MISERY LOVES
COMPANY.

Singles/EPs:
The Barbarian / Ripper Attack, Platina
PLO2 (1984)

Albums:
MERCHANTS IN METAL, Killerwatt KILP
54005 (1986)
Live Life At Speed / Fireborn / Bearer Of The
Ring / Attila The Hun / Raiders / Dance To
Evil / No Pax Romana / Nosferatu / A
Voyage To Hades / Metal Pride

MANOWAR (USA)
Line-Up: Eric Adams (vocals), Ross The
Boss (guitar), Joey De Maio (bass), Scott
Columbus (drums)

Barbarian bedecked MANOWAR are noted
for being amongst the pinnacle of true
unwavering out-and-out Heavy Metal bands.
Over a lengthy career MANOWAR have
steadfastly refused to compromise and as
such have built up a staunch fan base. Bassist
and band leader Joey De Maio first had a stab
at creating a Metal band when he formed a
power trio with ex-ELF vocalist / guitarist
David Feinstein and drummer Carl Canedy. In
spite of achieving a heavy sound the
triumvirate could not gel and Feinstein and
Canedy quickly assembled THE RODS.
MANOWAR were founded when De Maio,
previously with Ronnie James Dio's ELF and
THUNDER, was working as a stagehand to
BLACK SABBATH. French act SHAKIN'
STREET were the support band and De Maio
soon struck up a strong alliance with their
American guitarist Ross 'The Boss' Funicello,
a fellow New Yorker whose other credentials
included noted Punk Metal act THE
DICTATORS and New Yorkers LYRE. With so
much in common, upon their return to the
States the pair jammed together and
immediately set the wheels in motion to piece
together the ideal Metal band, an idea that
had originally been formulated backstage at
the BLACK SABBATH show at Newcastle City
Hall! Adding ex-KIDZ vocalist Eric Adams and
finally drummer Kirk Kennedy, MANOWAR
was born.
After recording a crude demo tape for a mere
$250, produced by THE RODS drummer Carl
Canedy, MANOWAR were, nevertheless, able
to attract label attention from EMI America.
The company gave the quartet the
opportunity to record a better quality demo
and soon signed the group.
Whilst recording their debut album 'Battle
Hymns' with new drummer Donnie Hamzik,
MANOWAR also gained backing from Bill
Aucoin at Aucoin Management. Aucoin had

been greatly instrumental in putting KISS on
the map back in the '70s.
Recorded in Florida, 'Battle Hymns' featured
none other than the legendary Orson Welles
appearing in a narrator's role on the track
'Dark Avenger'. The album's release
prompted a wave of hype surrounding the
group, their 'mannish' image and belief in 'true
Heavy Metal', a form of music the group
passionately described as being the most
glorious form of music in the world. It wasn't
enough to save them from being
unceremoniously dropped from EMI
America's roster and also parting company
with Aucoin when a new deal wasn't
immediately forthcoming. The loss of the EMI
America deal prevented MANOWAR from
making a planned appearance at the Reading
Festival in Britain during August '82.
Drummer Hamzik was dispensed with in early
1983 and MANOWAR unveiled the new man
behind the skins, Scott Columbus, at two gigs
in New York opened by VIRGIN STEELE. The
shows marked the band's first live
appearances in their home city, although the
quartet had previously played headlining gigs
in Chicago and a short tour in the South East
opening for TED NUGENT.
Taking monies owed to them by EMI America
for breach of contract, MANOWAR retreated
upstate and recorded a brand new album 'Into
Glory Ride', their first with Scott Columbus.
The drummer had reportedly been
discovered by a female fan of the band,
beating aluminium in a local foundry!
By the Summer of 1983 MANOWAR had
inked a new deal (in blood!) with Johnny
Zazula's Megaforce label. The 'Into Glory
Ride' album appeared around the same time
as a second recording with Orson Welles,
'Defender', materialised on a 12" single
release backed with 'Gloves Of Metal'. Welles
had recorded this piece at the same time as
'Dark Avenger', but the song had not made
the 'Battle Hymns' album.
During early 1984 MANOWAR issued the
'Hail To England' album, a record titled as a
tribute to their British fan base. Recorded in
12 days and costing an estimated $20,000 in
Toronto's Phase One Studios, the Jack
Richardson produced album included Joey
DeMaio's legendary 'Black Arrows' Piccolo
bass solo and the St. Mary's Cathedral choir
gracing the title track.
The group finally debuted in Britain during
March 1984 with a brace of shows and by
June the quartet announced that they had
signed to Virgin's Ten Records and intended
to record with Jack Richardson again to
create an album tentatively titled 'Sign Of The
Hammer'.

The album was released in September and preceded with the apt 'All Men Play On 10' single as the New York outfit announced further British and European dates for October the same year.

However, 1986 had the band maintaining a low profile as MANOWAR split away from their record label. Following a jaunt to Europe during Easter opening for MOTÖRHEAD as part of the 'Easter Metal Blast' festivals it was announced that MANOWAR had inked a deal with major label Atlantic Records.

Pre-production was handled by Eddie Kramer but come final recording the band were to produce themselves. The resulting album 'Fighting The World', released in March 1987, gave MANOWAR access to the necessary studio time and budget in which to truly capture their awesome sound.

On the eve of the release of the 'Kings Of Metal' album in 1988, MANOWAR were hit with the inconceivable as Ross the Boss quit, the guitarist quickly announcing a liaison with his ex-DICTATORS colleague Dick Manitoba in his new act WILD KINGDOM. He would then put THE PACK together in 1989 with vocalist Frank Vestry, bassist Ronnie G., keyboard player Larry Soc and drummer Rich Fazio before recording an album with HEYDAY.

MANOWAR added Chicago-ite Dave 'The Death Dealer' Shankle to the group almost immediately, having met the guitarist whilst recording the new album at Universal Recording Studios.

September 1989 brought with it the announcement that Scott Columbus had been forced to quit the group due to personal business away from the group, but he was back at the tubs for a European trek in December.

However, MANOWAR would ultimately replace Scott with the enigmatic Rhino, whose first act as a member of the band would be to torch his own drum kit after the outgoing Columbus presented him with a new set!

Karl Logan was drafted into the ranks during the summer of 1994 as Shankle opted out to create his own DAVE SHANKLE GROUP.

MANOWAR visited Brazil in November 1996 before touring Europe once more during April 1997, culminating in a massive show at the Forest National in Brussels, a 7,000 or so capacity venue. The shows were being filmed and recorded for a live album and video scheduled for release in late 1997 / early 1998.

'Hell On Stage' exceeded all expectations in Germany when it went on to sell in excess of 40,000 copies on the first day of release. The DVD format would later break into the national

MANOWAR
Photo : Olaf Heine

top ten.

During 2001 German Metal band POWERGOD would cover 'Kill With Power' on their 'Bleed For The Gods' album. MANOWAR themselves would break their silence in April of 2002 with a new single 'Warriors Of The World United'. This single would not only enter the German national charts high but would rise over the next two weeks to number 15 - the highest chart placing ever for a Nuclear Blast act, selling over 80,000 copies in the process.

The band also pleased their fan base by announcing a North American 'Gods Of War' tour. Initial dates saw HAVOCHATE and USURPER as support with Norwegian Black Metal act IMMORTAL and American Death Metal unit CATASTROPHIC added for a second leg. Select supports also came from Chicago's BLUDGEON, a Thrash Metal act signed to MANOWAR's own newly founded Magic Circle Music label.

'Warriors Of The World' would prove to be the most bombastic MANOWAR release to date. Included would be a grandiose interpretation of the Puccini Opera standard 'Nessun Dorma' alongside a patriotic 'An American Trilogy', an amalgam of U.S. Civil War anthems and the band's 25th anniversary homage to none other than ELVIS PRESLEY. Japanese versions of the 'Warriors Of The World' album came complete with an extra track, a live version of 'Kill With Power'.

The advent of the album would prompt near hysteria in Germany, with 'Warriors Of The World' at one stage outselling EMINEM's latest release and being tipped for no. 1 album status. The record eventually bowed in at a highly respectable no. 2 position. The band put in an in store performance with a difference at the Saturn record branch in Hamburg, foregoing the usual acoustic or playback norm and blasting the audience with a full P.A. powered live set. Another first for the band, and one which amply displayed their determination to deliver only true Metal, was an appearance on the British Pop TV show 'Top Of The Pops'. MANOWAR naturally insisted on playing live! The resurgence of interest in MANOWAR would be confirmed when the band's 1992 album 'The Triumph Of Steel' was certified gold in Germany for sales in excess of 250,000 copies.

The band would capitalise on their recent success by releasing a double A side single of 'An American Trilogy' / 'The Fight For Freedom' in August 19th, the 25th anniversary of ELVIS PRESLEY's death. The single not only put the band back into the national charts in Germany but reinvigorated album sales, pushing 'Warriors Of The World' back into the upper reaches of the album chart. An extensive tour of major German venues would be scheduled for December.

Singles/EPs:
Defender / Gloves Of Metal, Music For Nations KUT102 (1982)
All Men Play On 10 / Mountains, Ten TEN 30-12 (1984)
Blow Your Speakers / Violence And Bloodshed, Atlantic B 9463 T (1987)
Kings Of Metal / Herz Aus Stahl / Pleasure Slave, Atlantic (1988) (German release)
Courage / Today Is A Good Day To Die, (1994)
Courage (Live) / Courage (24 Bit remastered album version) / Metal Warriors (Live), (1994)
Defender (Original version) / Hatred, Music For Nations (1994)
Metal Warriors / Herz Aus Stahl / Fighting The World (Live) / Metal Warriors (Live), Atlantic AMCY 534 (1995) (Japanese release)
Metal Warriors / Herz Aus Stahl / Fighting The World (Live), Atlantic (1995)
Return Of The Warlord / Warlord (Live), MCA (1996)
Number 1 (LP version) / Blood Of My Enemies (Live) / Kill With Power (Live), MCA (1996)
Manowar / Kill With Power / Hail And Kill, (1999) ('Live In Spain' EP)
Carry On / Kill With Power / Kings Of Metal, (1999) ('Live In Portugal' EP)
Kings Of Metal / Herz Aus Stahl / Metal Warriors, (1999) ('Live In Germany' EP)
Lady Marmalade / Metal Warriors / Kill With Power / Courage (French studio version), Wargram CNR 3048905 (1999) ('Live In France' EP)
Metal Daze (Live) / Master Of The Wind (Live) / Heart Of Steel (Live), Nuclear Blast NB 379-2 (1999) (Promotion release)
Warriors Of The World United / March For Revenge (By The Soldiers Of Death) (Video) / Carry On (Video), Nuclear Blast 118461 (2002) **15 GERMANY**
An American Trilogy / The Fight For Freedom / Nessun Dorma, Nuclear Blast (2002) 71 GERMANY

Albums:
BATTLE HYMNS, Liberty LT 51125 (1982)
Death Tone / Metal Daze / Fast Taker / Shell Shock / Battle Hymns / Dark Avenger / William's Tale
INTO GLORY RIDE, Music For Nations MFN 6 (1983)
Warlord / Secret Of Steel / Gloves Of Metal / Gates Of Valhalla / Hatred / Revelation (Death's Angel) / March For Revenge (By

The Soldiers Of Death)
HAIL TO ENGLAND, Music For Nations MFN 19 (1984) **83 UK**
Blood Of My Enemies / Each Dawn I Die / Kill With Power / Hail To England / Army Of The Immortals / Black Arrows / Bridge Of Death
SIGN OF THE HAMMER, Ten DIX10 (1984) **34 SWEDEN, 73 UK**
All Men Play On 10 / Animals / Thor / Mountains / Sign Of The Hammer / Oath / Thunderpick / Guyana (Cult Of The Damned)
FIGHTING THE WORLD, Atco 790 563-1 (1987) **27 SWEDEN**
Fighting The World / Blow Your Speakers / Carry On / Violence And Bloodshed / Defender / Drums Of Doom / Holy War / Blackwind, Fire And Steel
KINGS OF METAL, Atlantic K 781 930 2 (1988) **45 SWEDEN**
Wheels Of Fire / Kings Of Metal / Heart Of Steel / Sting Of The Bumblebee / Crown And The Ring / Kingdom Come / Hail And Kill / Warrior's Prayer / Blood Of The Kings
TRIUMPH OF STEEL, Atlantic 7567824231 (1992)
Achilles, Agony And Ecstasy In Eight Parts / Metal Warriors / Ride The Dragon / Spirit Of The Cherokee / Burning / Power Of The Sword / Demon's Whip / Master Of The Wind
THE HELL OF STEEL, Atlantic 7567-80579-2 (1994)
Fighting The World / Kings Of Metal / The Demon's Whip / The Warriors Prayer / Defender / The Crown And The Ring / Blow Your Speakers / Metal Warriors / Black Wind, Fire And Steel / Hail And Kill / The Power Of Thy Sword / Hers Aus Stahl / Kingdom Come / Master Of The Wind
LOUDER THAN HELL, MCA (1996)
Return Of The Warlord / Brothers Of Metal (Part One) / The Gods Made Heavy Metal / Courage / Number One / Outlaw / King / Today Is A Good Day To Die / My Spirit Lives On / The Power
HELL ON WHEELS - LIVE, Universal UMD 70062 (1997)
Manowar / Kings Of Metal / Kill With Power / Sign Of The Hammer / My Spirit Lives On / Piano Interlude / Courage / Spirit Horse Of The Cherokee / Blood Of My Enemies / Hail And Kill / Warriors Of The World / Wheels Of Fire / Metal Warriors / Army Of The Immortals / Black Arrows / Fighting The World / Thor The Power Head / King / The Gods Made Heavy Metal / Black Wind, Fire And Steel / Return Of The Warlord / Carry On / Battle hymn
ANTHOLOGY, Connoisseur VSOP CD 235 (1997)
Manowar / Metal Daze / Fast Taker / Battle Hymns / All Men Play On 10 / Sign Of The Hammer / Fighting The World / Blow Your

Speakers / Heart Of Steel / Blood Of The Kings / Violence And Bloodshed / Wheels Of Fire / Metal Warriors / The Demon's Whip
STEEL WARRIORS, BMG (1998)
Secret Of Steel / Black Arrows / Each Dawn I Die / Hatred / Warlord / Gloves Of Metal / Bridge Of Death / Hail To England / Kill With Power / March For Revenge (By The Soldiers Of Death) / Gates Of Valhalla / Army Of The Immortals
THE KINGDOM OF STEEL, Universal (1998)
Manowar / Blood Of My Enemies / Kill With Power / Sign Of The Hammer / Courage / Fighting The World / Kings Of Metal / Metal Warriors / Heart Of Steel / Number One / The Gods Made Heavy Metal / Hail And Kill / Warlord / The Power / Battle Hymn / The Crown And The Ring
SECRETS OF STEEL, MCA 70058 (1998)
Warlord / Secret Of Steel / Gloves Of Metal / Gates Of Valhalla / Hatred / Revelation (Death's Angel) / March For Revenge (By The Soldiers Of Death) / Blood Of My Enemies / Each Dawn I Die / Kill With Power / Hail To England / Army Of The Immortals / Black Arrows / Bridge Of Death
HELL ON STAGE LIVE, Nuclear Blast 27361 63792 (1999) **50 AUSTRIA, 18 GERMANY, 48 PORTUGAL**
Metal Daze / Dark Avenger / March For Revenge / Hatred / Gates Of Valhalla / Bridge Of Death / William's Tale / Guyana (Cult Of The Damned) / The Warrior's Prayer / Blood Of The Kings / Sting Of The Bumblebee / Heart Of Steel / Master Of The Wind / Outlaw / The Power / The Crown And The Ring
WARRIORS OF THE WORLD, Metal Blade 3984-14414-2 (2002) **6 AUSTRIA, 26 FINLAND, 40 FRANCE, 2 GERMANY, 31 ITALY, 15 NORWAY, 25 SPAIN, 13 SWEDEN, 35 SWITZERLAND**
Call To Arms / The Fight For Freedom / Nessun Dorma / Valhalla / Swords In The Wind / An American Trilogy / The March / Warriors Of The World United / Hand Of Doom / House Of Death / Fight Until We Die

MANTICORA (DENMARK)
Line-Up: Lars F. Larsen (vocals), Kristian H. Larsen (guitar), Flemming Schultz (guitar), Rene S. Nielsen (bass), Mads Volf (drums)

Power Metal act MANTICORA's roots lay in the dissolution of FEAR ITSELF in 1996. Erstwhile FEAR ITSELF members vocalist Lars F. Larsen and guitarist Kristian H. Larsen teamed up with former RIP N' TEAR and HUMAN FACTOR drummer Mads Volf and ex-SCARECROWS bassist Rene S. Nielsen. MANTICORA added keyboard player Jeppe Eg for the April 2001 album 'Darkness With

MANTICORA
Photo : Nico Wobben

Tales To Tell', released by the Italian Scarlet label. The man had earlier performed live with BLAZING ETERNITY. Upon the album release the band integrated bass player Kasper Gram as well as a new lead guitarist, Martin Arendal. The band would return in 2002, touting a Jacob Hansen produced album 'Hyperion', a concept outing inspired by the science fiction novel by Dan Simmons.

Singles/EPs:
Dead End Solution / How? / In Silence / The Pain You Offer / In Your Face, (1997)

Albums:
ROOTS OF ETERNITY, Black Lotus BLRCD012 (1999)
From The Beyond / The Vision / Beyond The Walls Of Sleep / The Horde / Private Hell / When Forever Ends / Intoxicated / Nowhere Land / Pale Faces / Roars Of Eternity
DARKNESS WITH TALES TO TELL, Scarlet SC031-2 (2001)
From Beyond / The Chance Of Dying In A Dream / Dynasty Of Fear / Dragon's Mist / Felice / The Nightfall War / The Puzzle / Critical Mass / Lost Souls / The Twilight Shadow / Shadows With Tales To Tell
HYPERION, Scarlet (2002)

MARSHALL LAW (UK)
Line-Up: Andy Pyke (vocals), Dave Martin (guitar), Andy Southwell (guitar), Andy Faulkner (bass), Paul Brookes (drums)

ANDY PYKE of MARSHALL LAW

MARSHALL LAW- very heavy and proud of it. Birmingham's MARSHALL LAW offer twin guitar Power Metal powered by the exceptional talents of twin guitarists Andy Southwell and Dave Martin, a duo that displayed on their seminal 'Warning From History' opus they could outstrip any Schenker / Jabs or Tipton / Downing comparisons with ease.

MARSHALL LAW benefited in their early days from the enthusiastic management of Birmingham DJ Dave Juste and the seemingly tireless ability to undertake enormous club tours, including supports to GYPSY QUEEN and HELLION; building up a loyal fan base along the way.

Formed by former DETROIT, DAMIEN and VIVA vocalist Andy Pyke, the original line-up featured Pyke on vocals and drums together with ex-CHINAWHITE and SHADOWLANDS guitarist Dave Martin, bassist Nigel and guitarist Darren Horton. Antecedent to MARSHALL LAW Martin had also been involved with ELECTRIC WARRIOR, an act that featured latter day ASYLUM vocalist Stan and his sister drummer Yola, as well as STARFIGHTERS and (briefly) UFO guitarist Rik Sandford.

MARSHALL LAW added drummer Alan Kelly, who ultimately left to join SHY. Horton also left to later form SIAM and was replaced by ex-REALM and IVORY guitarist Andy Southwell. Bassist Nigel also departed, later to join Progressive Rock outfit ARK, and was superseded by Malcolm Gould. This line-up recorded the demo 'Future Shock' in 1988.

Despite their efforts the media and major record companies remained unmoved, with the British Rock press refusing to see the band as anything more than pretenders to the throne of JUDAS PRIEST.

Undeterred, MARSHALL LAW recorded their first album for local label FM Revolver, but in doing so, lost most of their finest songs to what many regarded as a lacklustre production by REDBEARDS members Ian Allen and Dave Keates.

It was decided at this point to sack their bassist - the official excuse being that he was too short! The allegedly diminutive Malcolm Gould promptly formed LOVE AND WAR. The somewhat taller benefactor of the vacant bass position was Roger Davis, previously with ROULETTE, and the band still continued to gig hard.

Another record for FM Revolver followed, the mini-album 'Power Crazy', which debuted new drummer Lee Morris. Pyke meantime was to contribute guest vocals to CEREBRAL FIX's version of JUDAS PRIEST's hit 'Living After Midnight'.

A change of management to the same

organisation that handled MAGNUM saw a period of inactivity whilst a major deal was searched for, but in vain. MARSHALL LAW recorded a third album, 'Powergame', with production by former MAGNUM guitarist ROBIN GEORGE, but this only saw sporadic releases in Japan, where it reached number 6 in the national Rock chart proving a huge seller, and Spain. A thousand copies were also pressed up on the band's own System X Records for sale at gigs.

A live album was recorded, but was to remain unreleased for some time, and the group would choose to disband, playing their last gig at Nottingham Rock City in September 1992 and subsequently folding around December. Martin reunited with original drummer Mick Donovan in a new project. Southwell formed an acoustic act with his girlfriend. Davies found employment with ex-LITTLE ANGELS vocalist TOBY JEPSON. Morris joined high profile Gothic Rock act PARADISE LOST in 1995.

However, due to fan pressure MARSHALL LAW duly reformed in late 1995 to issue the well received live album 'Law In The Raw' on Neat Metal Records. Strangely Neat Metal Records issued press statements that this recording was culled from a JUDAS PRIEST support gig although in reality it was taken from a band headline performance.

Still essentially a studio project at this stage, the band did manage a brace of local gigs utilising the rhythm section from NOISEGATE, although the 1997 studio album 'Metal Detector' actually finds credited drummer Glen Viner being in reality a drum machine! Oddly this jest passed many reviewers by who subsequently included the mysterious Mr. Viner into band biographies.

'Metal Detector' once more pulled in worthy reviews with increased sales in Germany and Japan. The band recorded the follow up 'Warning From History' in early 1999. The album included guest contributors Steve Grimmett of GRIM REAPER and LIONSHEART and MAGNUM's Tony Clarkin. The Neat Metal press statement for this album too makes another glaring mistake erroneously claiming drums were performed by NOISEGATE's Chris Green.

The 'Warning From History' outing saw the band's first release in South America with Rock Brigade Records in Brazil, Chile and Argentina. Shortly after recording the band dispensed with their existing rhythm section pulling in ex-SIAM bassist Andy Faulkner and former BENEDICTION and WHITE TRASH drummer Paul Brookes.

To promote the album MARSHALL LAW put in local supports to BATTLEZONE and a show at the 'Bang Your Head' Festival in

MARSHALL LAW

southern Germany sharing a bill with DEEP PURPLE, W.A.S.P. and MOTÖRHEAD, as well as a performance at the Wacken festival playing to over 30,000 people.

During 2000 the band recorded a version of SLADE's 'We'll Bring The House Down' with a guesting Bev Bevan of BLACK SABBATH on drums. Although the track was produced by the esteemed Terry Thomas this has still yet to surface.

MARSHALL LAW members Roy Davis and Andy Faulkner would gain production credits on the 2000 RICOCHET album 'The Singles'. Davis would also be found to be active with TOBY JEPSON once again, appearing on the 2002 'Refresh' EP. Some of Pyke's earlier recordings also surfaced with the release of a vintage live DAMIEN album.

Singles/EPs:
WORLD OF MADNESS / Cry Out From The Dark / All For Rock / The Heat Is Rising, Heavy Metal 12 HM 172 (1991)

Albums:
MARSHALL LAW, Heavy Metal HMR 138 (1990)
Armageddon / Under The Hammer / Rock The Nation / Marshall Law / Hearts And Thunder / Screaming / We're Hot / Feel It / System X / Future Shock / When Will It End
POWERGAME, System X (1993)
Chain Of Youth / Another Generation / Searching For Paradise / Naked Aggression / No Justice / Powergame / Edge Of The World / Psychodrama / Dead Zone / Leviathan
LAW IN THE RAW (LIVE), Neat Metal NM008 (1996)
Chain Of Youth / Another Generation / Screaming / Psychodrama / Searching For Paradise / Naked Aggression / Under The Hammer / System X / Powergame / Hearts And Thunder / Marshall Law / Electric Eye / Leviathan
METAL DETECTOR, Neat Metal NM023 (1997)
Osmium / Twisted This / War / Seek And You Shall Find / Swarm / Feed The Need / Devices / Addicted To The Pain / Empowerment / The Sands Of Time / Meganoid / The Seeds Of Change / Iridium
WARNING FROM HISTORY, Neat Metal NM035 (1999)
Foregathering / Victory At Last / Locked And Loaded / Remembered Forever / Harbinger Of Doom / Blood On Blood / Crucified / March Of History / Pray For Deliverance / Godking / Retreat / Storming To Power

MASTERPLAN (GERMANY)

Line-Up: Jorn Lande (vocals), Roland Grapow (guitar), Jan S. Eckert (bass), Janne Warmen (keyboards), Uli Kusch (drums)

MASTERPLAN

MASTERPLAN is the high profile post HELLOWEEN endeavour of guitarist ROLAND GRAPOW and drummer Uli Kusch. The pair severed ties with HELLOWEEN in late 2001, at first titling their new venture MR. TORTURE. The highly rated Norwegian singer JORN LANDE, a veteran of YNGWIE MALMSTEEN, ARK, MILLENNIUM and MUNDANUS IMPERIUM amongst many others, filled the vocalist position. With IRON SAVIOR man Jan S. Eckert on the bass the Finnish CHILDREN OF BODOM and WARMEN keyboard player Janne Warmen made up the ranks. The album, produced by FOZZY and former SABBAT guitarist Andy Sneap, included a cover version of LED ZEPPELIN's 'Black Dog' and a duet between Lande and erstwhile HELLOWEEN vocalist MICHAEL KISKE on the track 'Heroes'.

Kusch would loan himself out to IRON SAVIOR for a one-off gig in August when their regular drummer Thomas Nack injured his hand just upfront of the group's appearance at the 'Wacken Open Air' festival. MASTERPLAN had their version of 'Black Dog' included on the Locomotive Music LED ZEPPELIN tribute album 'The Metal Zeppelin — The Music Remains The Same'.

The band debuted commercially with an EP

entitled 'Enlighten Me' issued through the AFM label in November. A sustained bout of European touring had MASTERPLAN confirmed as support for HAMMERFALL's January and February European trek. However, the band would see its first casualty when Janne Wirman pulled out, unable to commit due to commitments with CHILDREN OF BODOM. A replacement was found swiftly in Axel Mackenrott from CATCH THE RAINBOW and PUNCH TV.

Singles/EPs:
Enlighten Me EP, AFM (2002)

MEDIEVAL STEEL (USA)
Line-Up: Bobby Franklin (vocals), John Roth (guitar), Chuck Jones (guitar), Jeff Boydstun (bass), Bill Jones (drums)

Almost ten years after MEDIEVEL STEEL's eponymous album release guitarist John Roth would be hired to replace Paul Taylor in WINGER for their 'Pull' tour.

Albums:
MEDIEVEL STEEL, SUR (1984)
Medieval Steel / Warlords / Battle Beyond The Stars / Echoes

MEDUZA (SWEDEN)
Line-Up: Apollo Papathanasios (vocals), Stefan Berg (guitar), John Edstrom (bass), Jan Larsson (keyboards), Ola Grönlund (drums)

MEDUZA was borne out of guitarist Stefan Berg's previous act AUTUMN LORDS. With his former band Berg had traded in '70s style retro Trad Rock but would opt for Symphonic Metal with MEDUZA to better highlight Berg's undoubted guitar skills. Berg had initially made his presence felt upon the Rock world with membership of the mid '90s Christian Rock act LAUDAMUS.
The last line-up of AUTUMN LORDS in 2000 had included drummer Ola Grönlund and bassist John Edstrom and this rhythm section would join Berg in MEDUZA. For the opening demo session the new group would be joined by keyboard player Jan Larsson and the esteemed Kristian Andren on session vocals - a veteran campaigner of FIFTH REASON, MEMENTO MORI, TAD MOROSE and WUTHERING HEIGHTS.
The inaugural album 'Now And Forever' would find MEDUZA utilising the talents of Greek born Apollo Papathanasios of MAJESTIC as lead vocalist.

Albums:
NOW AND FOREVER, (2002)
Now And Forever / Holy Ground / Hounds Of Hell / Sleep / Touch The Sky / I Will Rise / Twilight Of My Mind / Shed No Tears / Curse Of Pharao / Land Of Forgotten Dreams / Burn In Hell

MEGACE (GERMANY)
Line-Up: Melanie Bock (vocals), Jörg Schror (guitar), Klaus Florian 'Dirty' Möller (guitar), Christian Wulff (bass), Andreas Düwel (drums)

A progressively inclined Thrash act founded back in February of 1988 by the trio of vocalist Melanie Bock, guitarist Jörg Schror and bassist Michael Muller. A month later MEGACE was completed by the enrolment of guitarist Robin Kortt and drummer Thorsten Jungermann. The latter's tenure would be brief though and soon Kai Alex Spiekermann was manning the drum kit. Further changes in personnel occurred when ex-ANESTHESIA man Klaus Florian 'Dirty' Möller supplanted Kortt in September. With this line-up MEGACE cut their opening demo session 'The Sign Of The Ape'.
Spiekermann left in the summer of 1989 to hook up with fellow Thrash act DESERT STORM, his place duly being taken by KILGORE's Rainer Behn as MEGACE demoed tracks for Aarrrggg Records dubbed the 'Human Errors' sessions.
In December of the same year Muller made his exit, eventually being substituted by DROWNING IN REAL's Christian Wulff in February of 1990. Further ructions that same year found Behn out of the picture, although he did hang around to complete the 'This Is The News' demo. Engineered by GAMMA RAY's Kai Hansen 'This Is The News' garnered valuable press and saw track inclusions on the 'Brown Bottles Go Ape' compilation album. Following recording Carsten Schubert took over the drummer's role.
MEGACE's debut album 'Human Errors' emerged in July of 1991. The band hit yet more line-up problems in August of 1992 when both Schubert and Möller exited. Stefan Spiedel, another DROWNING IN REAL member, took over guitar whilst the group had to wait until April of 1993 before the drummer's vacancy was filled by ex-NURNBERGER PROZESS man Stephan Gora.
MEGACE then completed the 'Pseudo Identity' promotional tape, strengthening the GAMMA RAY connection with Dirk Schlachter acting as engineer. In May of 1994 Gora bade farewell and Andreas Düwel took up

residency behind the kit.

The band's second album, 'Inner War', hit the stores during May of 1999. Ambitiously it included a cover version of 'Synchronicity' by THE POLICE.

In 2000 the band donated their take on 'The Dogs Of War' to a PINK FLOYD compilation 'Signs Of Life'. MEGACE would also feature on the 'Unbroken Metal' magazine split 7" EP with another cover, this time MOTORHEAD's 'Iron Fist' with lead vocals from Schror. Another MOTORHEAD cover 'Sacrifice', once more with Schror handling vocals, appeared on the 'Motormorphosis' tribute album.

In 2001 Schror took time out to aid GAMMA RAY on their Mexican dates substituting on bass for an injured Dirk Schlachter.

Albums:
HUMAN ERRORS, Magic 3770022 (1991)
Something Incomprehensible / Law Enforcement Agency / Repetitions Of Human Errors / Let Me Explain / Save Your Dignity / No Brain / No Pain / Discord / Monofaces / Better To Forget
INNER WAR, Angular SKAN 8217.AR (1999)
Cry / Schweissnaht / Two / Inner War / Ciphers / Synchronicity / Conclusion (Reprise) / Industrial Dictatorship / Guilty / First-Take-Ponka-Song / Instinct, Science, Faith / Affengesicht / ...Which Have Been Predicted / Rain

MEGORA (SWITZERLAND)
Line-Up: Piotr Sommer (vocals / guitar), Toni Scherrer (guitar), Dominik Schieweck (bass), Tommy Braselmann (drums)

A melodic, Power Metal act, MEGORA supported METAL CHURCH in their time and followed the 'Waiting' album with a new demo that, it would appear, failed to procure the group a new deal.

Albums:
WAITING, Megora (1993)
All Blood Runs The Same / Moonstill Waters / Ship Of Monotony / Waiting For Salvation / A Matter Of Course / Invisible Darkness / Neither Fish Nor Fowl

MEKONG DELTA (GERMANY)
Line-Up: Wolfgang Borgmann (vocals), Uwe Baltrusch (guitar), Ralph Hubert (bass), Jörg Michael (drums)

MEKONG DELTA originally went under pseudonyms to protect their true identities; bassist Ralph Hubert being known as Bjorn Eklund for example. Drummer Jörg Michael was a member of RAGE at the time.

LIVING DEATH guitarists Frank Fricke and Reiner Kelch performed on the debut album under the guises of Vincent St. John and Rolf Stein. Former SODOM and U.D.O. guitarist Uwe Baltrusch played on the 'Principle Of Doubt' album.

Unable to attend the recording of 'The Gnome' EP Jörg Michael's place was taken by HOLY MOSES and GAMMA RAY drummer Uli Kusch. Michael's highly rated skills would find the stickman journeying through LAOS, HEADHUNTER, GLENMORE, GRAVE DIGGER and RUNNING WILD.

Vocalist Wolfgang Borgmann left in 1990 to be replaced by ex-SIREN singer Douglas Lee. Michael joined HEADHUNTER.

Another ex-MEKONG DELTA drummer Peter Haas of AIN'T DEAD YET and CALHOUN CONQUER later joined BABYLON SAD and KROKUS.

Singles/EPs:
The Gnome / The Hut Of Baba Yaga / Without Honour / The Cure, Aaarrg AAARRG 8 (1987)
Toccata / Black Betty / Interludium, Aaarrg AAARRG 17 (1989)

Albums:
MEKONG DELTA, Aaarrg AAARRG 4 (1987)
Without Honour / The Cure / The Hut Of Baba Yaga / Heroes Grief / Kill The Enemy / Black Sabbath
THE MUSIC OF ERICH ZANN, Aaarrg AAARRG 11 (1988)
Age Of Agony / True Lies / Confession Of Madness / Hatred / Interludium (Begging For Mercy) / Prophecy / Memories Of Tomorrow / I, King, Will Come / The Final Deluge / Epilogue
PRINCIPLE OF DOUBT, Aaarrg AAARRG 19 (1989)
A Question Of Trust (Cyberpunk) / The Principle Of Doubt / Once I Believed / Ever Since Time Began / Curse Of Reality / Twilight Zone (Lord Fouls Hort) / Shades Of Doom (Cyberpunk 2) / The Jester / El Colibri / No Friend Of Mine
DANCES OF DEATH (AND OTHER WALKING SHADOWS), Aaarrg ARG 23034-2 (1990)
Dances Of Death: I) Introduction, II) Eruption, III) Beyond The Gates, IV) Outburst, V) Days Of Betrayal, VI) Restless, VII) Sanctuary, VIII) Finale / Transgressor / True Believers / Night On A Bare Mountain
KALEIDOSCOPE, IRS 986963 (1991)
I.N.N.O.C.E.N.T.? / Sphere Eclipse / Dance On A Volcano / Dreaming / Heartbeat / Heartbeat / Shadow Walker / Sabre Dance / Misunderstanding / About Science
CLASSICS, Aaarrg ARG 27045-2 (1993)

Interludium (Begging For Mercy) (Part I) / Toccata / Twilight Zone / The Gnome / The Hut Of Baba Yaga / Night On A Bare Mountain / Interluduim (Part II) / El Colibri
LIVE AT AN EXHIBITION, Metal Machine RTD 3120042238 (1993)
The Cure / Transgression / True Believers / Night On A Bare Mountain / Memories Of Tomorrow / Hut Of Baba Yaga / Hero's Grief / True Lies / Toccata
VISIONS FUGITIVES, Bullet Proof CDVEST 19 (1994)
Them / Imagination / Suite For Group And Orchestra: a) Introduction (The Danger In Dreams / The Chronicle Of Doubts - Book 3 / Chapter 1) / b) Preludium (Lord Kevin's Lament / The Chronicle Of Doubts - Book 2 / Chapter 8) / c) Allegro (Mhorams Victory / The Chronicle Of Doubts - Book 3 / Chapter 15) / d) Dance (The Corrupt / The Chronicle Of Doubts - Book 3 / Chapter 18) / e) Fugue (Knowledge / The Chronicle Of Doubts - Book 2 / Chapter 23 / f) Postludium (Lena's Daughter / The Chronicle Of Doubts - Book 2 / Chapter 21) / The Healer / Days Of Sorrow
PICTURES AT AN EXIBITION, Bullet Proof IRSCD993 626 (1996)
Promenade / Gnomus / Interludium / II Vecchio Castello / Interludium / Tuileries (Dispute D'Enfants Apres Jeux) / Bydtlo / Interludium / Ballet Of The Unhatched Chicks / "Samule" Goldenberg And "Schmuyle" / Promenade / Lomoges: Le Marché (La Grande Nouvelle) / Catacombae (Sepulcrum Romancum) / Lingua Mortis / The Hut On Chicken's Legs / The Heroic Gate (In The Old Capital Of Kiev)

MEPHISTO (GERMANY)
Line-Up: Uwe Suerick (vocals / guitar), Andreas Hladik (guitar), Andreas Rippelmeier (guitar), Marc Schulz (bass), Wolfgang Mann (drums)

A German Speed Metal act, MEPHISTO's 'Megalomania' EP consisted of two demos originally recorded in 1986. Guitarist Andreas Rippelmeier and bassist Marc Schulz would later join HEAVENWARD.

Singles/EPs:
Megalomania EP, Wrong Again WAR (1996)

Albums:
MEPHISTO, Miracle (1988)
Prologue / Mephisto / X-Rays / In Dubio Contra Reum / Save Your Rights / Battle Of Kerovnia / Holy Child
IN SEARCH OF LOST REFUGE, Rockport SPV 08 96 421 (1991)

Intro - Nature / Aliens / Valley Of The Dolls / Unexpected Changes / Senseless Marching / A Fatal Development / The Final Chapter / Refugium (N.B.)

MERCURY RISING (Rosedale, MD, USA)
Line-Up: Clarence Osbourne (vocals), Hal Dolliver (guitar), Gary Goldsmith (guitar), Chris Brush (bass), Jeff Moos (drums)

Albums:
UPON DEAF EARS, Noise N0278-2 (1996)
Upon Deaf Ears / Light To Grow / Halfway To Forever / Minute Man / Zeros And Ones / It's War / Prayer / Where Fear Ends
BUILDING ROME, Noise N 0292-2 (1998)
Cathedrals / Building Rome / The Occurrence Of Tomorrow / A Narrow Door / Moment Of Truth / Of Lesser Men / Renaissance / Think

MERCYFUL FATE (DENMARK)
Line-Up: King Diamond (vocals), Hank Shermann (guitar), Michael Denner (guitar) Timi Grabber (bass), Kim Ruzz (drums)

MERCYFUL FATE were borne out of the ashes of Danish Punk Heavy Rock outfit THE BRATS, a group formed in the late '70s by guitarists Hank Shermann and Michael Denner alongside vocalist Yenz (later to turn up fronting GEISHA and Y) and drummer Monroe.
THE BRATS recorded one track for a 1979 Punk/Metal crossover compilation album called 'Pair Punk' and released one full album on CBS Records '1980 Brats' which made quite an impact in Europe, selling particularly well in France. It even led to the track 'Zombie People' picking up British airplay courtesy of Capital Radio's Alan Freeman.
'1980 Brats' was basically a Metal album with Punk overtones with THE BRATS' although the album also included a quirky Russian Folk song sung in Russian by Denner! However, the group disbanded and Hank Shermann soon linked up again with Michael Denner (who had formed DANGERZONE), BLACK ROSE front man KING DIAMOND (real name Kim Peterson) and DANGERZONE bassist Timi Grabber along with drummer Kim Ruzz, subsequently recording a four track demo. The tape featured the tracks 'Some Day', 'Death Kiss', 'Love Criminals' and 'Combat Zone', once more under THE BRATS name.
Former footballer King Diamond had already made a name for himself in Europe with the BLACK ROSE stage-show, which thrived on blood n' gore theatrics. This was a trait that was to spill over heavily into his new band. Diamond immediately stamped his distinctive

seal on the proceedings with his uniquely high range vocals. Shortly after the demo, the band switched monickers to MERCYFUL FATE and 'Love Criminals' began to pick up heavy airplay on Dutch radio thanks to the healthy state of the underground tape trading scene at the time.

MERCYFUL FATE demoed twice more and on the strength of the second tape were invited to England by Darryl Johnston at Ebony Records to add a track ('Black Funeral') to the 'Metallic Storm' compilation. MERCYFUL FATE also recorded 'Walkin' Back To Hell' during the Ebony session but this was never released.

With interest in Holland almost outpacing the rest of Europe, MERCYFUL FATE signed to Dutch record company Rave On in September 1982 and released the four track mini-album 'Corpse Without A Soul'. Its impact on the underground metal scene was huge and Ron Quintana's San Francisco magazine 'Metal Mania' voted it EP of the year

Whilst in England on a short tour in March 1983 (including a memorable show at the Clarendon Hotel in London's Hammersmith district) the band recorded a cult session for BBC Radio One's 'Friday Rock Show' featuring the tracks 'Evil', 'Satan's Fall' and 'Curse Of The Pharoahs'.

As momentum gathered MERCYFUL FATE soon split with Rave On and signed to Roadrunner in Europe and Music For Nations for Britain in early 1983. They recorded their debut full length album 'Melissa', so titled in honour of a notorious Danish medieval witch whose skull Diamond claimed to own. A single 'Black Masses'/'Black Funeral' was also issued.

As a live act MERCYFUL FATE were an extremely heavy proposition, with the twin guitar work of Shermann and Denner added to the distinctive, wailing histrionics of King Diamond's style and his penchant for microphone stands made of human thigh bones and pseudo satanic overtones. It is fair to say that the band certainly made an impression!

MERCYFUL FATE promoted the 'Melissa' album heavily, opening for the likes of URIAH HEEP, GILLAN and GIRLSCHOOL. Regrettably with the latter King claimed responsibility for invoking the 'evil presence' which electrocuted GIRLSCHOOL vocalist Kim McAullife at a show in Copenhagen.

The band also courted controversy when they pulled out of a British tour supporting MANOWAR after just one date at St Albans City Hall. MERCYFUL FATE claimed that as they had contributed financially to the costs of the tour they were being treated unfairly by the headliners as regards set up times and sound-checking. MANOWAR refuted the allegations and MERCYFUL FATE were promptly ditched in favour of Birmingham support band CRAZY ANGEL.

In May of 1984 MERCYFUL FATE recorded their second album, 'Don't Break The Oath', with producer Henrik Lund and embarked on their first American dates as headliners and as openers for MOTÖRHEAD. The album was another success, scoring many European chart positions.

The Danes were hit with the departure of Hank Shermann in 1985. The guitarist opted to form the much more commercial FATE. This group achieved critical acclaim but little else before Shermann reunited with Michael Denner to forge ZOSER MEZ in a more traditional Metal mould at the start of the new decade.

With Shermann out of the group it wouldn't be long before King opted to break the band up in order to pursue a different course with KING DIAMOND. Taking Denner and Timi Grabber (now using the monicker Timi G. Hansen) with him King would tend to eschew the satanic overtones of MERCYFUL FATE in order to pursue more conceptual, horror themes.

Having achieved a great deal of success with KING DIAMOND it would be after hearing some of the material the reunited duo of Shermann and Denner in ZOSER MEZ that King felt the time was right to reform MERCYFUL FATE with Shermann, Denner, and Hansen. Original drummer Kim Ruzz could not be torn away from his day job as a postman, so Morten Neilson laid down the drums for the comeback album. MERCYFUL FATE's reunion show was at the legendary Dynamo festival in Eindhoven, Holland during June 1993.

The 'In The Shadows' album from the reborn MERCYFUL FATE had the added interest of featuring guest drummer Lars Ulrich of METALLICA on a revamped version of the 1982 demo track 'Return Of The Vampire'.

The subsequent 'The Bellwitch' release turned out to be a mini-album comprising three live numbers and two new songs ('The Bellwitch' and 'Is That You Melissa?', although the ensuing 'Time' release would witness the group on full throttle once more and touring America in early 1995 supported by Doom act SOLITUDE AETUNUS.

MERCYFUL FATE added drummer Bjorn T. Holm to the line-up in early 1996. The 'Into The Unknown' album featured new bassist Sharlee D'Angelo.

In late 1997 Roadrunner Records reissued the early titles in remastered form and featuring the odd bonus track to boot, whilst

Shermann and Holm have also busied themselves working on a band project under the name of GUTRIX and have so far released the album 'Mushroom Songs'. D'Angelo and Wead also created side project HEMISFEAR.

Shermann released a side project album 'Sick In The Head' under the title VIRUS 7 in 2000. During mid 2001 it was announced that Mike Wead had joined THE HAUNTED supplanting the outgoing Anders Björler. However, a subsequent American tour witnessed not Wead but THE CROWN guitarist Marcus Sunesson taking the vacancy.

January of 2002 would witness the departure of MERCYFUL FATE from long term label Metal Blade. Meantime, guitarist MICHAEL DENNER taking the solo route, founded a band comprising KING DIAMOND bassist Hal Patino, former MERCYFUL FATE drummer Morten Nielsen, vocalist Jesper Harrits and second guitarist Carsten Volsing - a man with an apparent 'early' MERCYFUL FATE history.

Singles/EPs:
A Corpse Without A Soul / Nuns Have No Fun / Doomed By The Living Dead / Devil Eyes, Rave On RMLP002 (1982)
Black Masses / Black Funeral, Music For Nations MFNKUT 106 (1983)

Albums:
MELISSA, Music For Nations MFN 28 (1983)
Evil / Curse Of The Pharoahs / Into The Coven / At The Sound Of The Demon Bell / Black Funeral / Satan's Fall / Melissa
DON'T BREAK THE OATH, Roadrunner RR 9835(1984) **33 SWEDEN**
The Oath / Gypsy / Desecration Of Souls / Nightmare / Come To The Sabbath / To One Far Away / Dangerous Meeting / Welcome, Prince Of Hell / Night Of The Unborn
THE BEGINNING, Roadrunner RR 9603 (1987)
Doomed By The Living Dead / A Corpse Without A Soul / Nuns Have No Fun / Devil Eyes / Curse Of The Pharoahs / Evil / Satan's Fall / Black Masses
RETURN OF THE VAMPIRE, Roadrunner RR 9184 (1992)
Burning The Cross / Curse Of The Pharoahs / Return Of The Vampire / On A Night Of Full Moon / A Corpse Without A Soul / Death Kiss / Leave My Soul Alone / MDA / You Asked For It
IN THE SHADOWS, Metal Blade ZORRO 61 (1993)
Egypt / The Bell Witch / The Old Oak / Shadows / A Gruesome Time / Thirteen Invitations / Room Of Golden Air / Legend Of The Headless Rider / Is That You Melissa? /

Return Of The Vampire
THE BELL WITCH, Metal Blade ZORRO 78 (1994)
The Bell Witch / Is That You, Melissa? / Curse Of The Pharoahs / Egypt / Come To The Sabbath / Black Funeral
TIME, Metal Blade ZORRO 80 (1994)
Nightmare Be Thy Name / Angel Of Light / Witches Dance / The Mad Arab / My Demon / Time / The Preacher / Lady In Black / Mirror / The Afterlife / Castillo Des Mortes
INTO THE UNKNOWN, Metal Blade 3984-17026-2 (1996)
Lucifer / The Uninvited Guest / Ghost Of Change / Listen To The Bell / Fifteen Men (And A Bottle Of Rum) / Into The Unknown / Under The Spell / Deadtime / Holy Water / Kutulu (The Mad Arab - Part Two)
DEAD AGAIN, Metal Blade 3984 14159-2 (1998)
Torture (1629) / The Night / Since Forever / The Lady Who Cries / Banshee / Mandrake / Sucking Your Blood / Dead Again / Fear / Crossroads
9, Metal Blade (1999)
Last Rites / Church Of Saint Anne / Sold My Soul / House On The Hill / Burn In Hell / The Grave / Insane / Kiss The Demon / Buried Alive / 9

MESMERIZE (ITALY)
Line-Up: Folco Orlandini (vocals), Piero Paravidino (guitar), Paulo Chiodini (guitar), Andrea Tito (bass), Andrea Garavaglia (drums)

MESMERIZE are an unashamedly traditionally based Heavy Metal band noted not only for their own legend, myth and Sci-Fi themed albums but for vocalist Folco Orlandini's numerous sessions on works by other high profile artists such as KHALI, TIME MACHINE, WHITE SKULL and SKYLARK.

The band was created as THE MESMERIZERS during 1988 with an inaugural line-up of Orlandini, guitarists Piero Paravidino and Paulo Chiodini, bass player Luca Valisi and drummer Andrea Garavaglia. In 1990 Valisi was ousted by Paulo Fiori and the band would put in their first live gigs in November the following year. A debut demo session 'R.I.P. Mesmerised' also arrived that year with a second effort, 'Tregenda', in September 1993 and THE MESMERIZERS added new bassist Andrea Tito in December of 1994.

TIME MACHINE would be the first act to borrow the services of Orlandini, drafting the singer for their 'Act II: Galileo' album. In 1997 it would be the turn of WHITE SKULL, Orlandini gracing their 'Embittered' opus. 1997 would also witness the band name change to simply MESMERIZE. Orlandino would aid SKYLARK vocalist EDDY ANTONONI on his solo album 'When Waters Become Ice'. MESMERISE themselves would get to bow in with the July 1998 album 'Tales Of Wonder' issued by the Underground Symphony label.

1999 proved eventful for the band, committing a cover version of IRON MAIDEN's 'The Prisoner' to the 'Children Of The Damned' tribute album and Orlandini's talents once more being on hand for an outside artist - this time their vocalist loaned out to SKYLARK for their conceptual 'Divine Gates Part I: Gate Of Hell' record, playing the role of 'Guardian Angel'. Orlandini's next port of call would be vocalising for KHALI on their debut, an outfit created by erstwhile TIME MACHINE members. MESMERIZE would be invited to perform on a TRUST tribute album conceived by the French Axe Killer label offering up their take on 'Préfabrique'.

A whole glut of tribute performances duly ensued. MESMERIZE would add their version of 'The Needle Lies' to the Dwell Records QUEENSRYCHE tribute 'Rebellion and SAVATAGE's 'Sirens' to another Dwell collection 'Return Of The Mountain King'. For the American Midwest label the band conjured up 'Die Young', with a guesting Dario Beretta of Power Metal band DRAKKER, for a Dio era BLACK SABBATH collection. A more obscure outing would be their contribution of a live session of 'Manowar' for 'The Religion Of Steel' MANOWAR homage put together by the fanzine 'Knights Of Sunrise'. Orlandini would revisit his 'Guardian angel' role with SKYLARK for a second term on their sequel 'Divine Gates Part II: Gate Of Heaven'.

In early 2002 no less than two MESMERIZE albums would be issued within weeks of each other. The hugely delayed 'Vulture's Paradise' surfaced in January from Underground Symphony whilst new label Dragonheart issued new recording 'Off The Beaten Path' in February.

Albums:
TALES OF WONDER, Underground Symphony USCD 028 (1998)
The Werewolf / Hell On Wheels / Logan's Run / Children Of Reality / Sea Of Lies / Ragnarök / Danse Macabre / The Catalyst / Forging The Darksword / War Journal / Flatliners / Chorus Of The Rain
VULTURE'S PARADISE, Underground Symphony USCD 052 (2002)
Vultures Paradise / The Cube / Screams Of A Dying World / Chains Of Life / D'Ailleurs / Winter Tears / Tierra Santa / Die Young / Tierra Santa (English version)
OFF THE BEATEN PATH, Dragonheart

(2002)
Argos Died Twice / King Of Terror / Off The Beaten Path / Jail TV / Warriors (When The Battle Calls) / Pit Of Charming Snakes / Where Skye Meets The Sea / Doom Of The Darksword / The Ancient Prophecy / Overdoze / Gates Of Mercy

METAL CHURCH (Seattle, WA, USA)
Line-Up: David Wayne (vocals), Craig Wells (guitar), Kurdt Vanderhoof (guitar), Duke Erikson (bass), Kirk Arrington (drums)

METAL CHURCH rank as one of the true founders of the early '80s American Thrash Metal scene. Guitarist Kurdt Vanderhoof created the band upon his departure from Punk act THE LEWD in 1981. As THE LEWD evolved into more of a Hardcore Thrash act Vanderhoof found himself more and more interested in the Metal scene. During a 1980 gig LEVIATHAN members guitarist Rick Condran and Aaron Zimpel got into a conversation with Vanderhoof and discussed the idea of an 'ultimate' Metal band. As Vanderhoof, Condran, bassist Steve Haat and drummer Aron Winer created ANVIL CHORUS - THE CHURCH OF METAL, the remnants of LEVIATHAN, Zimpel, bassist Bill Skinner and drummer Kenny Feragen became Progressive Rock trio VIENNA.

The first Vanderhoof all instrumental demo comprised the LEVIATHAN track 'Red Skies', 'Heads Will Roll' and 'Merciless Onslaught'. The formative band went through numerous drummers (they even invited a pre-METALLICA Lars Ulrich to join).

A pair of other local musicians, guitarists Thaen Rasmussen (ex-VY-KING) and Doug Piercy (ex-COBRA / DELTA) liked the name ANVIL CHORUS so much they took it for themselves. They did however offer acknowledgement with the homage to their inspiration with the track 'Bow To The Church Of Metal'. Vanderhoof trimmed the name of his act down to simply METAL CHURCH.

SINISTER SAVAGE man Billy McKay fronted METAL CHURCH for a brief spell prior to founding GRIFFIN. Singer Ed Bull was invited to join the band but Condran objected. When the guitarist quit METAL CHURCH Bull was on the mike stand the very next day. With the abandonment of VIENNA Zimpel also joined forgoing his normal front man position to become METAL CHURCH's drummer. With this line-up METAL CHURCH cut their second demo. This four track affair included a reworking of 'Heads Will Roll' titled 'Put The Chains On', an ANVIL CHORUS number 'Arab Nations', 'Wake Up And Die' and 'The Trap Is Set'. The latter track displayed the enmity between Bull and Condran as the singer's chorus of "Die Ricky, Die!" amply illustrates!

However, despite intensive tape trading, this early incarnation of METAL CHURCH folded, with Haat going on to a temporary stint with GRIFFIN then Glamsters JETBOY. Bull founded CONTROL with guitarists Dino Scarposi and Bill Tuder. A later version of CONTROL featured another ANVIL CHORUS man guitarist Doug Piercy, later of HEATHEN. Zimpel meantime joined the ranks of ANVIL CHORUS. Vanderhoof journeyed back to Seattle to create SCHRAPNEL. In 1983 this act had evolved into METAL CHURCH with a line-up of Vanderhoof, vocalist David Wayne, guitarist Craig Wells, bassist Duke Erikson and drummer Kirk Arrington. An earlier SCHRAPNEL vocalist Mike Murphy opened up the vacancy for Wayne by bailing out to join ROGUES GALLERY.

In 1984, METAL CHURCH signed to the Seattle based Ground Zero label and released the critically acclaimed, self-titled debut the same year. The band had previously contributed the track 'Deathwish' to the label's 'Northwest Metalfest' compilation album.

The debut album was to be reissued by Elektra in 1985 following the signing of a major deal that would propel the group to the forefront of the mid '80s Thrash Metal boom.

In 1986, METAL CHURCH released their second album, 'The Dark', an album that quickly warranted its status as one of the premier Metal release of the '80s and probably the band's finest moment to date. However, in a band bust up Wayne was ejected, the singer working with former LIZZY BORDEN guitarist Gene Allen, then REVEREND and later joining INTRINSIC. Wayne also had a brief union with HEATHEN. 1988's 'Deadly Blessing' album saw METAL CHURCH now fronted by erstwhile HERETIC singer Mike Howe and with former BLIND ILLUSION man James Marshall augmenting Wells on guitar.

Vanderhoof's dislike of touring prompted his opting out. However, Vanderhoof was to remain a central character within METAL CHURCH as a songwriter and conspirator and regained his taste for playing by forming HALL AFLAME and releasing an album through IRS.

Initially the band drafted in guitarist Mark Baker to fulfil Vanderhoof's role for touring in America but added Marshall on a full time basis.

Howe had been suggested to the band by Vanderhoof, the guitarist having produced the debut HERETIC album.

In 1992 Howe got his name onto the second BOOTSAUCE album 'Bull', guesting on the track 'Touching Cloth'. Marshall meantime boosted the band's profile in an unusual manner when he was drafted into METALLICA on a temporary basis. Hetfield had burnt his hand and deputised his guitar duties to Marshall for much of their American tour. This was the second time Marshall had depped for Hetfield, the first was in 1987 when the front man had broken his wrist skateboarding.

Following 1994's 'Hanging In The Balance', released on JOAN JETT's Blackheart label, METAL CHURCH fizzled out.

During 1997, Vanderhoof made his recording comeback in the modestly titled VANDERHOOF, a band that also comprised old METAL CHURCH colleague Kirk Arrington. Although the VANDERHOOF album surprised many with its undoubted quality, under pressure from their German record label the classic 'The Dark' era METAL CHURCH reunited in mid 1998. The band heralded their return with probably their most over the top release to date with a live album culled from tapes recorded in the mid eighties.

The band bounced back with a fresh studio album 'Masterpeace' (somewhat confusingly released with the track titles in completely the wrong order) touring Europe on a double package with THUNDERHEAD.

By 2000 METAL CHURCH had a new rhythm section of bassist Brian Lake and drummer Jeff Wade, both members of VANDERHOOF. The story took a further twist when it emerged that Wayne had set up a fresh act titled DAVID WAYNE'S METAL CHURCH! Joining him were ex-WARRIOR guitarist Joe Floyd, former JOINT FORCES, GEEZER and THUNDERHEAD guitarist Jimi Bell and drummer B.J. Zampa, a veteran of YNGWIE MALMSTEEN, MVP, TONY MACALPINE and THUNDERHEAD. Bell also operates the covers band TATTERED TRAMPS.

Singles/EPs:
Fake Healer, Elektra PRO CD 8051 (1989) (USA promotion)
Watch The Children Pray, Elektra (1989) (USA promotion)
Badlands, Elektra (1989) (USA promotion)

Albums:
METAL CHURCH, Ground Zero (1984)
Beyond The Black / Metal Church / Merciless Onslaught / Gods Of Wrath / Hitman / In The Blood / (My Favorite) Nightmare / Battalions / Highway Star
THE DARK, Elektra 9 60493-2 (1986)
92 USA
Ton Of Bricks / Start The Fire / Method To

Your Madness / Watch The Children Pray /
The Dark / Psycho / Line Of Death / Burial
At Sea / Western Alliance
BLESSING IN DISGUISE, Elektra K 96087-
2 (1989) **75 USA**
Fake Healer / Rest In Pieces / Of Unsound
Mind / Anthem To The Estranged / Badlands
/ Spell Can't Be Broken / It's A Secret /
Cannot Tell A Lie / Powers That Be
THE HUMAN FACTOR, Epic 4678162 (1991)
Human Factor / Date With Poverty / Final
Word / In Mourning / In Harm's Way / In Due
Time / Agent Green / Flee From Reality /
Betrayed / Fight Song
HANGING IN THE BALANCE, Blackheart
BH1001 (1994)
Gods Of Second Chance / Losers In The
Game / Hypnotised / No Friend Of Mine /
Waiting For A Saviour / Conductor / Little
Boy / Down By The river / End Of The Age /
Lovers And Madmen / A Subtle War
LIVE, SPV 085-18562 CD (1998)
Ton Of Bricks / Hitman / Start The Fire /
Gods Of Wrath / The Dark / Psycho / Watch
The Children Pray / Beyond The Black /
Metal Church / Highway Star
MASTERPEACE, SPV 085-18702 CD (1999)
Sleeps With Thunder / Falldown / Into Dust /
Kiss For The Dead / Lb Of Cure / Faster
Than Life / Masterpeace / All Your Sorrows /
They Signed In Blood / Toys In The Attic /
Sand Kings

METALIUM (GERMANY / USA)
Line-Up: Henning Basse (vocals), Matthias
Lange (guitar), Lars Ratz (bass), Michael
Ehre (drums)

A highly successful project band initiated by
former VELVET VIPER and VIVA bassist Lars
Ratz, SAVATAGE guitarist Chris Caffrey,
second guitarist Matthias Lange and BEAU
GESTE, ARTENSION and YNGWIE
MALMSTEEN drummer Mike Terrana.
METALIUM's debut 1999 album 'Millennium
Metal Chapter One' made a major impact on
the international scene. Recorded for
Armageddon Products the record's global
reach was aided by licenses with Massacre
Records in Europe, Pavement for North
America, Avalon Marquee in Japan and in
South American territories via Hellion
Records.
METALIUM toured as support to PRIMAL
FEAR & SINERGY in Europe during 1999 but
not before Terrana had opted out to join
RAGE.
Lange would also put in a guest appearance
on the SHOCKMACHINE 1999 debut,
performing on the Japanese edition bonus cut
cover version of OZZY OSBOURNE's 'Steal
Away The Night'.

METALIUM
Photo : Nico Wobben

The band pulled in British born Mark Cross
whose credits stretched across Greek acts
such as SCRAPTOWN, MAGNA CARTA and
SPITFIRE as well as occult Metal band
NIGHTFALL. Whilst in the employ of
METALIUM Cross would also session on
KINGDOM COME's 'Too' album. METALIUM
would make inroads into the DVD market too
with the issue of 'Metallian Attack - Part One'.
Both Cross and Lange would also operate on
the German club circuit with JUDAS PRIEST
tribute band ELECTRIC EYE, an all star
collective including X-13 and
SHOCKMACHINE guitarist Rolly Feldman,
PARAGON bass player Big M and X-13 singer
Jorg Wesenberg.
By August of 2001 Cross decamped joining
premier German Metal act HELLOWEEN.
METALIUM appointed Michael Ehre of
MURDER ONE as substitute for Cross on the
third album 'Hero Nation - Chapter Three'.
Featured guests included the esteemed
personages of keyboard players DON AIREY,
a veteran of OZZY OSBOURNE, RAINBOW
and WHITESNAKE amongst many others,
and erstwhile URIAH HEEP man KEN
HENSLEY.
Live promotion throughout the summer saw
headline shows with support from
EDENBRIDGE. September found the band
performing at an all star Metal benefit festival
in aid of victims of the Elbe flooding. Joining
the band onstage for this show would be
guest Jutta Weinhold of ZED YAGO as well as
KEN HENSLEY with his distinctive Hammond

METALIUM
Photo : Nico Wobben

organ sound. The band would then journey to Brazil in October for a run of dates supported by EDENBRIDGE.

Albums:
MILLENIUM METAL CHAPTER ONE,
Massacre MASCD0191 (1999)
Circle Of Fate / Fight / Dream Of Doom / Break The Spell / Revelation / Metalium / Metamorphosis / Void Of Fire / Free Forever / Strike Down The Heathen / Pilgrimage / Metalians / Smoke On The Water
STATE OF TRIUMPH - CHAPTER TWO,
Massacre (2000)
The Elements (Prelude) / Steel Avenger / Years Of Darion / Break Out / Erania / Stygian Flames / Prophecy / Eye Of The Storm / Inner Sight / Metalians Triumph / Music
HERO NATION – CHAPTER THREE,
Massacre (2002)
Source of Souls / Revenge Of Tizona / In The Name Of Blood / Rasputin / Odin's Spell / Accused To Be A Witch / Throne In The Sky / Odyssey / Fate Conquered The Power / Infinite Love / Hero-Nation

METALSWORD (GERMANY)
Line-Up: Jay Jay 'The Fist' (vocals), Rick (guitar), Steve Tomaszerro (guitar), Rank Frank (bass), TA (drums)

Albums:
HARDER THAN STEEL, Wishbone (1985)
Take Off / Stormriders / The Exorcist / Dying For The Sword / March For The Damned / Disco Is Fuck

METALUCIFER (JAPAN)
Line-Up: Gezolucifer (vocals / bass), Blumi (guitar), Tormentor (drums)

A notorious Japanese Metal band that has cultured legendary status despite being a side venture of SABBAT's Gezol. METALUCIFER, titled after the SABBAT track 'Metalucifer And Evilucifer', came into being during 1995. A string of limited edition releases have been aimed squarely at the die hard Metal collectors market, many of them being graced by photos of the illustrious old school Metal aficionado Neal 'Metal Master' Tanaka.
METALUCIFER's debut, the 1996 'Heavy Metal Hunter' EP, found the band comprising front man Gezolucifer handling lead vocals and bass, Elizabagore of SABBAT on guitar and Elizaveat from GORE on both guitar and drums.
Appeasing their cult following in Europe METALUCIFER toured Germany during 2000

as a trio of Gezolucifer, METAL INQUISITOR guitarist Blumi and DESASTER drummer Tormentor. A limited edition 7" single emerging that year, 'Warriors Again', would see Bill Andrews of MASSACRE and DEATH repute on the drum stool. Two editions of 'Warriors Again' would be pressed with 500 available in regular black vinyl and a further pressing manufactured in red vinyl.
Recording the 2001 album 'Heavy Metal Chainsaw', issued by Iron Pegasus in Germany and R.I.P. in America with differing cover art, would be a METALUCIFER line up of Gezolucifer on vocals and bass, guitarists Blumi, Elizabagore and Elizaveat with drummer Tormentor.

Singles/EPs:
Heavy Metal Hunter (Part I) / Monster Of The Earth / Fallen Angel / Wolf Man (Japanese version) / Bloody Countess (Japanese version) / Headbanging (Japanese version), Metal Proof (1996) ('Heavy Metal Hunter' EP. 1,000 copies)
Warriors Again / Soul Of Warriors, Iron Pegasus (2000) (7" single)
Warriors Ride On The Chariots / Heavy Metal Revolution / Dracula, Iron Pegasus (2001) (12" single)

Albums:
HEAVY METAL DRILL, Metal Proof (1996)
Heavy Metal Is My Way / Heavy Metal Drill / Heavy Metal Hunter (Part II) / Wolf Man / Bloody Countess / Soul Of Warriors / Headbanging / Metalucifer / Iron n' Steel n' Metal
HEAVY METAL CHAINSAW, R.I.P. (2001)
Heavy Metal Chainsaw / Flight Of Iron Pegasus / Warriors Ride On The Chariots / My Way Is Heavy Metal / Heavy Metal Samurai / Dracula / Metalucifer (Part II) / Lost Sanctuary

METROPOLIS (GERMANY)
Line-Up: Marco Verfürth (vocals), Armin Prokein (guitar), Frank Hüsken (bass), Holger Selig (keyboards), Martin Baumann (drums)

A German Progressive Metal band. The group recorded and released the self-financed 'Behind Mysterious Walls' debut album in 1995.

Albums:
BEHIND MYSTERIOUS WALLS, Metropolis MET001 (1995)
Impossible Dream / Back / Streetchild / Rooms Of Desolation / Walls Of Mystery / Good Bye

SHADOW OF THE PAST, Metropolis MET002 (1998)
Tell Me / Deformed / Lies / Shadows Of The Past / Back / Living A Lie / Rooms Of Desolation / Remember / Walls Of Mystery

MIDIAN (ITALY)
Line-Up: Francesco Foggi (vocals), Lorenzo Bellacci (guitar), Christiano Bonci (bass / keyboards), Simone Baldini Tosi (keyboards / violin), Lorenzo Travaglini (drums)

Progressive edged Metal with the added novelty of violin.

Albums:
SOUL INSIDE, Pick Up PKPROG 1900 (1994)
In My Winter / No God (For Me) / Inside / Poem / Wind / The Road (Inside Of Me, It's Shouting Out To You) / One To Another

MINDCAGE (USA)
Line-Up: Mike Gray (vocals), Dietrick Hardwick (guitar / keyboards), Brian Howell (bass), Jon Crowther (drums)

Albums:
ENCAPSULATION, Perpetual Motion Media 60355-52752 (2000)

MINDFEED (UK)
Line-Up: Glynn Morgan (vocals / guitar), Jase Birnie (bass), Jay Micciche (drums)

MINDFEED was the culmination of the talents of two ex-THRESHOLD members, vocalist Glynn Morgan and drummer Jay Micciche. The 'Perfect Life?' album was produced by former SABBAT guitarist Andy Sneap. Additional bass tracks were laid down by JADIS, ARK and IQ man John Jowitt.
In 1999 ex-STORMWATCH guitarist John Slater would join the band for a European tour supporting SYMPHONY X before he joined ex-IRON MAIDEN vocalist Blaze Bayley in his 2000 act BLAZE. Meantime Micciche teamed up with Kent Nu-Metallers VACANT STARE in 2000 and would also deputise for KILL II THIS on the road.
With vacancies in both drummer and guitarist departments MINDFEED enrolled erstwhile SAXON man Dave Brougham on drums in May of 1999 and, on a temporary basis, Steve Ramsey of SKYCLAD on guitar.
MINDFEED debuted this line-up at the annual 'Wacken Open Air' festival although their performance was severely affected due to Ramsey having been beaten up by over zealous backstage security. The guitarist completed the gig with a bloody head injury.

Albums:
PERFECT LIFE?, Inside Out Music IOMCD 010 (1997)
Unreal World / Perfect Life? / Fear / Mother / Change / Always Never / My Heart Bleeds / Live Forever / If Like Me / The Beckoning / Open Your Eyes
TEN MILES HIGH, Inside Out Music IOMCD 022 (1998)
Waiting / Words / Cold Smile / Ten Miles High / Bleed / InnLocent / We Stand - We Fall / Look Like You? / Mother (Acoustic)

MINDSCAPE (HOLLAND)
Line-Up: Robert van Haren (vocals), Pat Glass (guitar), Rob van Lingen (guitar), Wilfried Broekmann (drums)

A Dutch Heavy Metal act, MINDSCAPE released a self-financed album in 1991 that featured some very Geoff Tate style vocal work from frontman Robert van Haren. Bass parts on the record were supplied by Guus Riteco.

Albums:
MINDSCAPE, Mindscape MS001 (1993)
Million Miles / Tripping In Dimension / Jamie's Clearing Up The Sky / Back From The Light / The Price Too High / When Daylight Comes

MOB RULES (GERMANY)
Line-Up: Klaus Dirks (vocals), Matthias Mineur (guitar), Oliver Fuhlhage (guitar), Torsten Plorin (bass), Arved Mannott (drums)

Wilhelmshaven melodic Metal band MOB RULES was created during 1994 by erstwhile VAN BLANC musicians guitarist Matthias Mineur and bassist Torsten Plorin. Pulling in vocalist Klaus Dirks and drummer Arved Mannott the quartet began to gig. Opening slots included shows with PINK CREAM 69, C.I.T.A. and CROSSROADS.
During the Spring of 1996 MOB RULES added second guitarist Oliver Fuhlhage and a self-financed mini-album prompted a deal with Limb Music Productions for the March 1999 'Savage Land' album. Media reaction in Europe was encouraging and the band toured Germany on a co-headline jaunt with IVORY TOWER. Other shows witnessed valuable support slots to OVERKILL and the SCORPIONS as well as an appearance at the 'Wacken Open Air' festival in 2000.
A sophomore Sascha Paeth produced opus 'Temple Of Two Suns' arrived in 2000. Thomas Rettke of HEAVEN'S GATE and Susanne Möhle of HEAVEN'S GATE and HYPERCHILD supply backing vocals. Live

work had the band crossing Europe in 2001 packaged with COMPANY OF SNAKES.

MOB RULES, promoting a single 'Lord Of Madness', returned to live action during July of 2002 acting as support to SAVATAGE, topping this activity off with an appearance at the 'Wacken Open Air' festival. The band's third album arrived in September of 2002 'Hollowed Be Thy Name'. Guests include Peavey Wagner of RAGE on the track 'How The Gypsy Was Born' and ex-HELLOWEEN guitarist ROLAND GRAPOW on both 'All Above The Atmosphere' and 'Way Of The World'.

Albums:

SAVAGE LAND, Limb Music Productions LMP 9903-008 (1999)
Prologue / Insurgia / Rain Song / Hold Back The Light / Secret Signs / Savage Land Part I (Strangers In Time) / Savage Land Part II (Pianista) / Savage Land Part III (No Reason Why) / Coast To Coast / Blaze Of First Warning / Pray For Sunlight / Down In Nowhere Land / End Of All Days
TEMPLE OF TWO SUNS, Limb Music Productions LMP 0011- 025CD (2000)
The Temple Fanfare / Pilot Of Earth / Outer Space / Celebration Day (Sun Serenade, Opus I) / Flag Of Life (Sun Serenade, Opus II) / Unknown Man / Hold On / Evolution's Falling / Inside The Fire / Eyes Of All Young / Hold On (Reprise)
HOLLOWED BE THY NAME, SPV 085-7444-2 (2002)
Hollowed Be Thy Name / Speed Of Life / (In The Land Of) Wind And Rain / House On Fire / Ghost Town / How The Gypsy Was Born / All Above The Atmosphere / Lord Of Madness / A.D.C.O.E. / Way Of The World

DARIO MOLLO / TONY MARTIN
(ITALY / UK)

Originally titled THE CAGE, this union of ex-ALLIANCE and BLACK SABBATH vocalist TONY MARTIN and Italian CROSSBONES guitarist Dario Mollo resulted in a classy debut album of hard, melodic Metal. To avoid confusion with another act of the same name the band switched titles to DARIO MOLLO / TONY MARTIN.

Veteran ex-RAINBOW keyboard player DON AIREY joins them for this record which was produced by Kit Woolven. The rhythm section is courtesy of CROSSBONES members Fulvio Gaslini on bass and Ezio Secomandi on drums with keyboards courtesy of Elio Maugeri. 'Stormbringer' is a cover of the DEEP PURPLE track.

MOB RULES

To close out 2001 Mollo joined forces once more with DON AIREY and ex-RAINBOW vocalist GRAHAM BONNET for a series of British club gigs. A second DARIO MOLLO / TONY MARTIN album 'Cage II' was set to arrive in May of 2002. Confusingly though this album was still being credited to THE CAGE. By mid 2001 Martin, alongside his former BLACK SABBATH colleague bassist Neil Murray, had joined American act RONDINELLI, led incidentally by another erstwhile BLACK SABBATH man drummer Bobby Rondinelli. Martin would also involve himself with BAILEY'S COMET, acting as front man for a batch of 2002 British club dates.

Albums:
THE CAGE, Dreamcatcher CRIDE17 (1999)
Cry Myself To Death / Time To Kill / The Cage - If You Believe / Relax / Smoke And Mirrors / Infinity / Dead Man Dancing / This Kind Of Love / Stormbringer / Soul Searching
THE CAGE 2, Frontiers (2002)
Terra Toria / Overload / Life Love And Everything / Balance Of Power / Amore Silenzioso / II / Wind Of Change / Theater Of Dreams / What A Strange Thing Love Is / Dazed And Confused / Guardian Angel / Poison Roses

MONSTER (USA)

Line-Up: Mark Isham (vocals), Mick Zane (guitar), Mark Behn (bass), Pete Holmes (drums)

Both MONSTER men bassist Mark Behn and guitarist Mick Zane were previously band mates in MALICE. Drummer Pete Holmes bashed the skins for BLACK N' BLUE and all three had known each other back in Portland, Oregon where both groups were originally from. In fact, Behn and Holmes had played together previously in KHARMA.
MALICE and BLACK N' BLUE split up at around the same time, Behn and Zane deciding to snare the highly rated Holmes before another band offered him a gig. They worked as a trio for around two and a half years before finally recruiting a vocalist in the form of Mark Isham from New York, having auditioned around 100 other front men with no success.
Prior to the release of the Max Norman produced MONSTER debut album both Behn and Holmes had been moonlighting, recording demos with DEEP PURPLE vocalist IAN GILLAN during 1995.
The album includes backing vocals from YNGWIE MALMSTEEN and TALISMAN vocalist JEFF SCOTT SOTO.

Albums:
THROUGH THE EYES OF THE WORLD, Long Island LIR 00073 (1995)
Spirit Of The Night / Fire In Your Eyes / All Guns Loaded / One Night / Say You Care / South Side Billy / All She Wants / Get Over It / Don't Get Your Heart Set / Over Now / She's Got It

MOONLIGHT CIRCUS (ITALY)

Line-Up: Massimo Zanatt (vocals), Paulo Viani (guitar), Gianluca Tassi (bass), Daniele Soravia (keyboards), Alberto Masiero (drums)

MOONLIGHT CIRCUS feature BLACK JESTER members guitarist Paulo Viani and drummer Alberto Masiero alongside HELREIDH keyboard player Daniele Soravia and EPICA and DARK LORD vocalist Allessandro Zecchi. In November of 2001 MOONLIGHT CIRCUS parted ways with Zecchi. A new vocalist would swiftly be inducted in the form of Massimo Zannata.
Both Viani and Soravia would be hastily enrolled into the live ranks of the famed U.S. Power Metal act WARLORD for a one-off performance at the German 'Wacken Open Air' festival in August of 2002. The guitarist also figured in the Progressive Metal band MAEVE OF CONNACHT.

Albums:
OUTSKIRTS OF REALITY, Elevate (2000)
Nightfall / Silver Surfer / Two Shadows (The Prophecy) / Whirls Of The Past / Ballad For A Falling Star / July Days / Outskirts Of Reality

MOON OF STEEL (ITALY)

Line-Up: Dennis A. Ruggeri (vocals), Vic de Lamare (guitar), J.J. Angel (guitar), Mark 'Moon' Vaccaro (bass), Ray 'Skip' Northiend (drums)

A 'True Metal' act in the manner of MANOWAR, Lucretia Records reissued MOON OF STEEL's amusingly titled 'Spaghetti Rock' album under the new name of 'Passions' in 1995.
Vocalist Dennis Andrea Ruggeri fronted TIME MACHINE for their debut album in 1993.
The 2000 MOON OF STEEL album 'Beyond The Edges' features a cover version of DREAM THEATER's 'You Not Me'.

Albums:
SPAGHETTI ROCK, Imtratimt 100.146 (1990)
Spanish Flame / Shy Girl / When The Clouds

Fall / It Won't Be The Reason / Medley: the Moon (instrumental) / Time's Marching Fast / Tonight / Flying High
PASSIONS, Lucretia LUCD 95005 (1995)
Spanish Flame / It Won't Be The Reason / Shy Girl / When The Clouds Fall / The Moon / Time's Marching Fast / Tonight / Flying High
BEYOND THE EDGES, Rising Sun (2000)

MORBID JESTER (GERMANY)
Line-up: Matthias Georg (vocals), Thomas Strömmer (guitar), Mario Bäcker (guitar), Udo Krause (bass), Markus Hain (drums)

MORBID JESTER was created in 1988 by erstwhile members of Punk band MILZBRAND. The band toured Germany with GLENMORE and SAXON.
MORBID JESTER's second album, 'Until The Battle Is Won', was produced by ex-SCANNER vocalist S.L. Coe.
The MORBID JESTER line-up for the 'Gates To Valhalla' album featured vocalist Stefan Scholl, guitarists Thomas Strömmer and Mario Bäcker, bass player Udo Krause and drummer Markus Hain.

Albums:
FIRST AUDIENCE, (1992)
UNTIL THE BATTLE IS WON, 1MF Records 377.0040-2-42 (1995)
In Co-operation / Revenge / Go Away / Souldoctor / In The Night / No Name City / Another Life / Warriors / Until The Battle Is Won
IRONY OF FATE, Morbid Jester (1996)
Destroyed / So Tired / The Defendant / Nervous Breakdown / Desert In The Rain / Irony Of Fate / Tattered Drunken Knight / Judgement Day / Why Him? / The Fair Sex / Why Him? (Shortcut)
GATES TO VALHALLA, Iron Glory 5 1005 20 561 (1999)
Gates To Valhalla / Stallion Of Steel / Nuclear Contamination / Armageddon / Godzilla / Cardinal Syn / Fallen Angel / Lost Son / From Dusk Till Dawn / Dancin' On Fire / Warriors Gloryride (Intro) / In The Sign Of Evil

MORGANA LEFAY (SWEDEN)
Line-Up: Charles Rytkönen (vocals), Tony Eriksson (guitar), Daniel Persson (guitar), Joakim Heder (bass), Jonas Söderlind (drums)

Previously titled DAMAGE, this Swedish group, drafting SEPHER JEZIRAH singer Charles Rytkönen, changed their name to MORGANA LE FAY during 1989. Original guitarist Stefan Jonsson bowed out at this juncture allowing another SEPHER JEZIRAH member, guitarist Tommi Karppanen, to join the fold. The 1992 debut, self-financed album, featuring original bassist Joakim Lundberg, is extremely scarce, only 537 copies being pressed. The same year keyboard player Ulf Petersson joined GALLEON.
MORGANA LEFAY cut a demo entitled 'Rumours Of Rain' which prompted the interest of Black Mark Records, the label taking the band on for the 1993 'Knowing Just As I' album. Touring in Germany found the band on the road with CEMETERY and INVOCATOR.
For the group's third album, December 1993's 'The Secret Doctrine', MORGANA LE FAY's line-up incorporated vocalist Charles Rytkönen, guitarists Tommi Karppanen and Tony Eriksson, bassist Joakim Heder and drummer Jonas Söderlind. However, in June of 1994, just after shooting a video for the track 'Rooms Of Sleep', Karppanen decamped. To fulfil live obligations the band drafted FANTASMAGORIA and SHOTGUN ALLEY guitarist Peter Grehn. A permanent replacement would be found in Daniel Persson, first making his presence felt on the February 1995 'Sanctified' album.
The 1995 compilation album 'Past, Present, Future' includes cover versions of CRIMSON GLORY's 'Lost Reflection' and, strangely, ABBA's 'Voulez Vous'! The group toured Germany in late 1995 as support to GAMMA RAY before issuing a brand new album in 1996.
The 'Maleficium' record scored highly with the European Rock media and the band undertook a headline European tour to promote it, supported by German Power Metal act BRAINSTORM and Texan Doomsters SOLITUDE AETURNUS.
Black Mark issued the compilation 'Fata Morgana' during 1998 in order to highlight the faster paced material of the band. Just as MORGANA LEFAY seemed set on track for greater things though a split in the ranks occurred when Jonas Soederlind, Joakim Heder and Daniel Persson all vacated.
MORGANA LEFAY regrouped by enlisting a triumvirate of former FANTASMAGORIA personnel in Peter Grehn, Robin Engström and Micke Åsentorp.
With Black Mark Records contractually owners of the MORGANA LEFAY brand the revised act adopted the title LEFAY and signed to Noise Records. This new unit issued 'The Seventh Seal' album in 1999 as well as a re-worked version of the debut 'Symphony Of The Damned'.
LEFAY issued a statement that they were to cease operations in 2000. However, late 2001 brought news that a re-formation was on the

cards and, indeed, LEFAY duly resurfaced for a new album and live work.

Albums:
SYMPHONY FOR THE DAMNED, Fata Morgana Music JOMES BAND 007 (1992)
Whore Of Babylon / Symphony Of The Damned / Fatal Illusions / Last Rites / Lullaby / The Secret Doctrine / Tequila / Catacombs / War Without End
KNOWING JUST AS I, Black Mark BMCD 28 (1993)
Enter The Oblivion / Red Moon / Salute The Sage / Rumours Of Pain / Excalibur / Modern Devil / Wonderland / Razamanaz / Battle Of Evermore / Knowing Just As I
THE SECRET DOCTRINE, Black Mark BMCD 42 (1993)
Rooms Of Sleep / What I Am / Alley Of Oaks / Soldiers Of The Holy Empire / Paradise Lost / Nowhere Island / The Mirror / State Of Intoxication / Cold World / Lord Of The Rings / Last Rites / Dying Evolution / The Secret Doctrine
SANCTIFIED, Black Mark BMCD 63 (1995)
Out Of The Silence / Time Is God / To Isengard / Why? / Mad Messiah / Another Dawn / In The Court Of The Crimson King / Sorrow Calls / Where Insanity Rules / Shadows Of God / Gil Gad (The Sanctified)
PAST, PRESENT, FUTURE, Black Mark BMCD 84 (1995)
Sculptures Of Pain / Lost Reflections / Rumours Of Rain / Alley Of Oaks / Battle Of Evermore / Voulez Vous / The Mirror / Last Rites / Sorrow Calls / Why? / Symphony Of The Damned
MALEFICIUM, Black Mark BMCD 86 (1996)
The Chamber Of Confession / The Source Of Pain / Victim Of The Inquisition / Madness / A Final Farewell / Maleficium / It / Master Of The Masquerade / Witches Garden / Dragons Lair / The Devil In Me / Where Fallen Angels Rule / Creatures Of The Hierarchy / Nemesis
FATA MORGANA, Black Mark (1998)
Master Of The Masquerade / Time Is God / Nowhere Island / Maleficium / Red Moon / To Isengard / Lord Of The Rings / Madness / What Am I / Excalibur / Mad Messiah / Paradise Lost / Wonderland / The Source Of Pain

MORIFADE (SWEDEN)
Line-Up: Stefan Petersson (vocals), Robin Arnell (guitar), Jesper Johansson (guitar), Henrik Weimedal (bass), Fredrik Eriksson (keyboards), Kim Arnell (drums)

Symphonic Metal act dating back to 1992. In their original incarnation of GOTHIC the band, based in the town of Vikingstad,

comprised in early 1992 guitarists Jesper Johansson and Fredrik Johansson together with NEPHENZY drummer Kim Arnell. Shortly after THALION bassist Henrik Weimedal rounded off the line-up with Fredrik Johansson taking care of lead vocals. After recording of a 1995 demo 'The Hourglass' the band was joined by front man Christian Stinga-Borg. At this juncture Jesper Johansson would also be moonlighting with HYPNOS KINGDOM.

MORIFADE signed to the Loud n' Proud label for the 'Across The Starlit Sky' EP. However, following this release Stinga-Borg was let go. A new vocalist, Stefan Petersson of SAVAGE SKULLS and MINDS EYE, was inducted and appeared on MORIFADE's contribution of two tracks to the Loud n Proud compilation album 'Born To Walk Against The Wind Vol.1'. Whilst preparations were in place for recording of a full length album founder member Fredrik Johansson made his exit. Nevertheless, 'Possession Of Power' was duly laid down and released in August of 1999.

During 2000 MORIFADE introduced two new personnel, ex-NEPHENZY guitarist Adrian Kanebäck and former TAD MOROSE keyboard player Fredrik Eriksson. The revised MORIFADE entered the Los Angered Studios of KING DIAMOND guitarist Andy LaRocque in May to execute a second EP with the title of 'Cast A Spell'. This four track affair included a cover of the PHENOMENA track 'Dance With The Devil'.

Splitting away from Loud n' Proud MORIFADE signed to the Dutch Hammerheart label. The line-up suffered a further casualty though when Kanebäck backed out. Drummer Kim Arnell's younger brother Robin of FATAL GLORY promptly filled the vacancy. MORIFADE once again resumed recording with Andy LaRocque in mid 2001, their next outing 'Imaginarium' being issued in April of 2002.

Singles/EPs:
Enter The Past / Tomorrow Knows / Starlit Sky / Distant World, Loud n' Proud LNP 001 (1998) ('Across The Starlit Sky' EP)
Cast A Spell / As Time Decide / Tomorrow Knows / Dance With The Devil, (2000)

Albums:
POSSESSION OF POWER, Loud n' Proud LNP010 (1999)
Possession Of Power / Dragonlord / Cast A Spell / Ending Of Time / The Signs / My Own Majesty / To Live Forever / The Vision And The Temple / World Of Steel / A Northern Rhyme / Ancient Prophecy
IMAGINARIUM, Hammerheart (2002)

Lost Within A Shade / Escape / Rising Higher / Nevermore / The Enemy Within / Dark Images / In Martyria / Revive For Awhile / The Secrecy / Reborn / Whispering Voices

MUNDANUS IMPERIUM (NORWAY)

Line-Up: Jorn Lande (vocals), Peter Thuve (guitar), Bent E. Holm (keyboards), Lars Wiik (bass / drums)

Aggressive, extreme edged Progressive Metal. MUNDANUS IMPERIUM are fronted by the highly respected figure of VAGABOND and THE SNAKES man JORN LANDE. The 1999 album features a version of RAINBOW's classic track 'Stargazer'. Lande also worked on a side project A.R.K. in 1999 with ex-CONCEPTION men Tore Ostby and Ingar Amlien together with TNT and YNGWIE MALMSTEEN drummer John Macaluso.

During 2000 Lande issued his debut solo album and also performed guest lead vocals for MILLENIUM. He joined YNGWIE MALMSTEEN's band in November of that year. Proving ever the journeyman Lande would be ensconced in the MASTERPLAN project band of ex-HELLOWEEN members guitarist ROLAND GRAPOW and drummer Uli Kusch by late 2001.

Albums:

THE SPECTRAL SPHERES CORONATION, Nuclear Blast NB 27361 63222 (1999)

Distant Conglomeration / The Life Of What You Seek / Beyond The Earthly / Starwars / Predominate / Stargazer / The Unborn Breathes In Silence / If The Universe Transformed

MUTINY (GREECE)

Line-Up: Alexis Zervanos (vocals), George Frantzis (guitar), Agis Krimpenis (guitar), Michael Feidakis (bass), George Zaxos (drums)

Metal act forged in 1993 by the rhythm section of bassist Michael Feidakis and drummer George Zaxos. MUTINY, then operating in Speed Metal territory, would enrol guitar player George Frantzis in 1995 and second guitar player Agis Krimpenis in March of 1996. This latter recruit would steer the band into more melodic waters.

The band opted to cut a demo session in 1998 billed as 'Faded Pages'. Still minus a lead vocalist at this juncture the group enlisted the services of SWAN CHRISTY man Kostas Makris to perform the roles. Also aiding in the studio would be keyboard player Iraklis Gialantzidis of SWAN CHRISTY and SEPTIC FLESH. However, Makris would only contribute to three songs before the parties fell out. SPITFIRE veteran Alexis Balakakis took the reins for the fourth and final song.

The band pulled in erstwhile OUTCAST man Oustikas Nikos to assume lead vocal duties but his tenure lasted a mere three months. Alexis Zervanos finally filled the front man vacancy and MUTINY delivered the 1999 EP 'Guilty As Charged'.

MUTINY signed to the newly established Steel Gallery label for the 2000 full length album 'Muted'.

Albums:

MUTED, Steel Gallery SGR-CD002 (2000)

Horror Unveiled / Silenced / The Place Called Earth / Changing Seasons / People's Heads / Traces / Hopeless / Guilty As Charged / The Cross-Bone Flag

MYRMIDION CREED (GERMANY)

Line-Up: Volker Riedel (vocals), Jan Toporski (guitar), Michael Schäfer (guitar), Walter Schlay (bass), Gerd Müller (drums)

A German Progressive Rock band, MYRMIDION CREED released their very complex debut through Inline Music. 'Through Painful Eyes', whilst receiving glowing reviews, would be the first and last album Volker Riedel would record as he would quit the music business in 1996.

Albums:

THROUGH PAINFUL EYES, Gorgon 8263-2 (1994)

Floating / Ice On The Water / Broken Rainbow / Suffer In Silence / Outside The Mirror / Losu Savjest / Dreamstory / Thoughts Of Hope

MYSTIC PROPHECY (GERMANY)

Line-Up: R.D. Liapakis (vocals), Gus G. (guitar), Martin Albrecht (bass), Dennis Ekdahl (drums)

MYSTIC PROPHECY boast a pedigree line up with two VALLEY'S EVE members in vocalist R.D. Liapakis and bassist Martin Albrecht, DREAM EVIL and NIGHTRAGE guitarist Gus G. and RAISE HELL drummer Dennis Ekdahl. Albrecht was also a member of cult Metal veterans STORMWITCH.

The Greek born Gus G., besides holding down membership of the Swedish based DREAM EVIL and having his own solo venture FIREWIND, would contribute guest lead guitar solos to the 2002 OLD MAN'S CHILD album.

Albums:
VENGEANCE, B. Mind (2001)
1545 The Beginning / Sky's Burning /
Damnation & Darkness / Welcome In The
Damned Circle / Dark Side Of The Moon /
River Of Hate / In The Mirror / In The
Distance / When Shadow´s Fall / Fallen
Angel

NAMELESS CRIME (ITALY)
Line-Up: Fabio Manda (vocals), Alessandro Tuccillo (guitar), Marco Ruggiero (guitar), Raffaele Lanzuise (bass), Dario Graziano (drums)

A deliberately retro '80s styled Heavy Metal band, NAMELESS CRIME was forged during 1998 by the erstwhile ATOMIC CHILD triumvirate of guitarist Alessandro Tuccillo, bassist Raffaele Lanzuise and drummer Dario Graziano. The following year the band was solidified with the addition of two ex-LANDGUARD members, guitarist Marco Ruggiero - a man also citing credits with STORMWIND, and singer Michele Sorrentino. With this line-up NAMELESS CRIME committed to CD a demo session in November of 2000.

However, in February of 2001 Sorrentino made his exit. The band duly made up the numbers by enlisting CAPITIVUS DIABOLI front man Fabio Manda. NAMELESS CRIME secured a deal with the Nocturnal Music label during February of 2002.

NARNIA (SWEDEN)

Line-Up: Christian Liljegren (vocals), Carl Johan Grimmark (guitar), Jakob Persson (bass), Martin Claesson (keyboards), Andreas Johansson (drums)

A Jönköping based Christian outfit with a fondness for Speed guitar influenced Hard Rock. Vocalist Christian Liljegren is ex-BORDERLINE whilst guitarist Carl Johann Grimmark was previously with SENTINEL. Both musicians were also active members of MODEST ATTRACTION, only severing ties officially upon the NARNIA album release. In 1996 MODEST ATTRACTION guitarist Stephan Mohlin bowed just upfront of a German tour and Grimmark was quickly drafted as replacement to fulfil these dates. When Mohlin signalled his departure was permanent Grimmark joined up as a full member. However, during this period the Liljegren / Grimmark axis would be plotting the future of NARNIA.

Although primarily recorded as a duo of Liljegren and Grimmark, NARNIA pulled in further musicians to provide a full band compliment after the album release. Enrolled were former SENTINEL bassist Jakob Persson, keyboard player Martin Claesson and drummer Andreas Johansson. NARNIA's debut album also featured a guest appearance from LOCOMOTIVE BREATH guitarist Janne Stark. The lyrical content of the 'Awakening' debut is sourced heavily from the works of C.J. Lewis.

With the tapes completed NARNIA became the subject of a global bidding war for the band signature. Eventually the group contracted 'Awakening' to the Japanese Pony Canyon label. At this stage MODEST ATTRACTION commitments still kept Liljegren and Grimmark busy on the road in Europe for a further bout of touring. NARNIA meantime, citing a line-up comprising Liljegren and Grimmark with bassist Jakob Persson, keyboard player Martin Claésson and drummer Fredrik Junhammar debuted on the live stage at the Swedish 'Ungkraft' festival in March of 1997. After this show Junhammar made his exit.

'Awakening' was released in the Far East in mid July and Andreas Johansson became the band's new drummer the following month. Shortly after the band took up another label offer from Nuclear Blast to license the album across Europe. The European version of 'Awakening' was delivered in February of 1998. NARNIA geared up for a lengthy bout of touring with support shows to STRATOVARIUS in Finland. NARNIA got to grips with recording a second album 'Long Live The King' that summer and once wrapped the group headed out on a package European tour in alliance with BLACK SYMPHONY and DIO throughout Germany and Switzerland.

1999 proved a reflective year for the band with 'Long Live The King' falling short of the healthy sales achieved by its predecessor. Christian Liljegren and Andreas Johansson took time out to unite with the STORMWIND duo of guitarist Andreas Olsson and keyboard player Per Hallman to forge the WISDOM CALL project for an eponymous album. Grimmark too embarked on a side venture, laying down a version of YNGWIE MALMSTEEN's 'Dark Ages' with singer Pär Hagström for a tribute album and put in a guest appearance on the debut LOCOMOTIVE BREATH album

During 2000 NARNIA regrouped to forge third album 'Desert Land'. The group also made space to cut a rendition of URIAH HEEP's 'Sunrise' for a tribute album. On the live circuit NARNIA criss crossed Europe and performed in England for the first time at the world famous Christian 'Greenbelt' festival. For Dutch gigs MODEST ATTRACTION's Mick Norström acted as temporary stand in. 'Desert Land' was issued just prior to Christmas in Japan and in February 2001 for Europe. The same year Grimmark unveiled plans for a side act billed as SYSTEM BREAKDOWN.

NARNIA would spend much of 2002 in preparation for their fourth album 'The Great

Fall'. Guest artists contributing in the studio would be Eric Clayton of SAVIOUR MACHINE and HAMMERFALL drummer Anders Johansson.

Albums:
AWAKENING, Nuclear Blast NB303-2 (1997)
Break The Chains / No More Shadows From The Past / The Return Of Aslan / Heavenly Love / Time Of Changes / The Awakening / Touch From You / Sign Of The Time
LONG LIVE THE KING, Nuclear Blast NB 359-2 (1999)
Gates Of Cair Paravel / Living Water / Shelter Through The Pain / The Mission / What You Give Is What You Get / The Lost Son / Long Live The King / Dangerous Game / Star Over Bethlehem / Shadowlands
DESERT LAND, Nuclear Blast (2001)
Inner Sanctum / The Witch & The Lion / Falling From The Throne / Revolution Of Mother Earth / The Light At The End Of The Tunnel / Angels Are Crying / Walking The Wire / Misty Morning / Trapped In This Age

NASTY SAVAGE (Brandon, FL, USA)
Line-Up: Nasty Ronnie (vocals), Ben Meyer (guitar), David Austin (guitar), Fred Dregischan (bass), Curtis Beeson (drums)

Fronted by professional wrestler Nasty Ronnie (real name Ronnie Galletti), NASTY SAVAGE were first formed in 1982 by guitarist Ben Mayer and bassist Fred Dregischan. They first appeared with a debut four track demo entitled 'Wages Of Mayhem' in early 1984 consisting of the songs 'Unchained Angel', 'Savage Desire', 'Witches Sabbath' and 'XXX'

However, NASTY SAVAGE had trouble retaining bassists. Whilst the first album saw co-founder Fred Dregischan very much involved he was replaced by Dezso Istvan Bartha for 'Indulgence', Chris Moorhouse was subsequently recruited for the 'Abstract Reality' EP and ex-PURGATORY, ICED EARTH and AGENT STEEL bassist Richard Bateman joined the band for 'Penetration Point'.

Drummer Curtis Beeson quit in the Spring of 1989 as NASTY SAVAGE ultimately folded. Both Beeson and Meyer would forge a union with erstwhile LAST RITES members to create HAVOC MASS for the 1993 album 'Killing The Future'.

By the mid '90s Galletti had founded INFERNAL, their 1995 demo being released commercially in 2000.

Bateman founded AFTER DEATH in 1999 together with erstwhile MORBID ANGEL and NOCTURNUS man Mike Browning. Beyer was to be found on SKULLVIEW's 1999 album 'Kings Of The Universe'.

Both Meyer and Beeson are members of LOWBROW with ex-OBITUARY and SIX FEET UNDER vocalist Allen West and DEATH's Scott Carino. LOWBROW debuted with the 2000 album 'Victims At Play'.

In August of 2002 NASTY SAVAGE, citing the line-up which recorded the group's final full length release, 1989's 'Penetration Point', of Ronnie Galletti, Ben Meyer, David Austin, Richard Bateman and Curtis Beeson, reunited to record two brand new tracks 'Sardonic Mosaic' and 'Wage of Mayhem' with engineer Mark Praeter.

Singles/EPS:
Abstract Reality / Unchained Angel / Eromantic Vertigo / You Snooze, You Lose, Roadrunner RR 9566 (1988)

Albums:
NASTY SAVAGE, Metal Blade (1985)
No Sympathy / Gladiator / Fear Beyond The Vision / Metal Knights / Asmodeus / Dungeon Of Pleasure / The Morgue / Instigator / Psycho Path / End Of Time
INDULGENCE, Metal Blade 72186-4 (1987)
Stabbed In The Back / Divination / XXX / Indulgence / Inferno / Hypnotic Trance / Incursion Dementia / Distorted Fanatic? ?
PENTRATION POINT, Roadracer RO 94181 (1989)
Welcome Wagon / Irrational / Ritual Submission / Powerslam / Sin Eater / Penetration Point / Puzzled / Horizertical / Family Circus

NEMESIS (GERMANY)
Line-Up: Adrian Ergün (vocals / bass), Axel Katzmann (guitar), Arnulf Tunn (drums)

Metal band with pedigree. Frontman Adrian Ergün was previously with GRINDER and CAPRICORN whilst guitarist Axel Katzmann and Arnulf Tunn are both members of TANKARD.

Albums:
NEMESIS, RTD 397 0021 2 (1997)
All About Art / The Godfather / Brothers In Death / Ants That Bleed / Slave To The Land Of The Free / G.H.A.D. / Witness / A Trance Of Masses

NEVERMORE (Seattle, WA, USA)
Line-Up: Warrel Dane (vocals), Pat O'Brien (guitar), Jeff Loomis (guitar), Jim Sheppard (bass), Van Williams (drums)

NEVERMORE
Photo : Nico Wobben

NEVERMORE
Photo : Nico Wobben

Technical Speed Metal outfit NEVERMORE was created in 1995 by ex-SANCTUARY men vocalist Warrel Dane, guitarist Jeff Loomis, bassist Bill Sheppard and drummer Mark Arrington. Loomis had also been with EXPERIMENT FEAR. Initial demos kindled the interest of renowned producer Neil Kernon who offered his services promptly for further recordings. The resulting tapes landed NEVERMORE a deal with Germany's Century Media Records.

Kernon continued his relationship with the band producing extra tracks to make up NEVERMORE's eponymous February 1995 debut. Rave reviews followed and NEVERMORE, now augmenting their line up with second guitarist Pat O' Brien, set out touring America alongside DEATH. It was during this tour that Dane's infamously long hair nearly proved to be his undoing. Falling drunkenly asleep next to the wheel of the band truck a roadie drove off not realising the singer was there. Dane's mane caught in the axle of the vehicle as it dragged him 30 yards down the road. For the rest of the dates the vocalist had to walk with the aid of sticks.

Tour dates, with Dane recovered, had the band supporting BLIND GUARDIAN in Germany winding up a world tour by appearing before 100,000 people at the prestigious 'Dynamo' festival in Holland.

An interim limited edition EP followed in July of the same year titled 'In Memory' that included radical reworkings of BAUHAUS tracks 'Silent Hedges' segued with 'Double

Dare'.

In late 1997, following a European tour alongside fellow Americans ICED EARTH, O'Brien joined gore mongers CANNIBAL CORPSE. His position was taken by former FORBIDDEN axeman Tim Calvert.

During 1998 NEVERMORE toured America with FLOTSAM & JETSAM prior to further European shows with OVERKILL.

NEVERMORE trimmed to a quartet for 2000's 'Dead Heart In A Dead World' with the loss of Calvert. The band, now with secondary guitars supplied by AGGRESSION CORE man Curran Murphy, toured America the same year sharing a package bill with FATES WARNING and PLANET X. A September 2001 run of dates in America would find NEVERMORE as guests to SAVATAGE. The band put in a further burst of dates as headliners kicking off at the L'Amour venue in Brooklyn on November 23rd. Guests for these dates would be OVERKILL and SCAR CULTURE.

During November guitarist Curran Murphy bailed out to join Canadians ANNIHILATOR. In early 2002 drummer Van Williams unveiled details of his PURE SWEET HELL side endeavour. A six track demo would see Williams joined by Christ Eichhorn on guitar, bass and keyboards. The pair would strengthen the NEVERMORE connection by enlisting guitarist Jeff Loomis to lay down a guest solo on the song 'Faded' whilst former NEVERMORE and current ANNIHILATOR guitarist Curran Murphy appears in the track

311

WARRELL DANE of NEVERMORE
Photo : Nico Wobben

'Shadow'.

For European dates and an announcement that the band had been invited to appear at selected gigs on the US 'Vans Warped' tour, a first for a Metal act, NEVERMORE drafted ex-VICIOUS RUMORS, TESTAMENT and present day DRAGONLORD guitarist Steve Smyth to fill the vacancy left by Murphy. However, the prestigious 'Vans Warped' dates would subsequently be cancelled. Meantime the band would feature two live tracks, 'Engines Of Hate' and 'Beyond Within' recorded at the Hollywood Roxy in September of 2001, as part of the Century Media tenth anniversary DVD release. The band also cut a rendition of 'Ride The Lightning' for a Nuclear Blast METALLICA tribute collection.

Singles/EPs:

Optimist Or Pessimist / Matricide / In Memory / Silent Hedges - Double Dare / The Sorrowed Man, Century Media DIGICD 77121-2 (1995) ('In Memory' EP)

Albums:

NEVERMORE, Century Media 77091-2 (1995)
What Tomorrow Knows / CBF / The Sanity Assassin / Garden Of Gray / Sea Of Possibilities / The Hurting Words / Timothy Leary / Godmoney
THE POLITICS OF ECSTASY, Century Media 77132-2 (1996)
Seven Tongues Of God / This Sacrament / Next In Line / Passenger / The Politics Of Ecstasy / Lost / The Tienanmen Man / Precognition / 42147 / The Learning
DREAMING NEON BLACK, Century Media 7891-2 (1999)
Ophidian / Beyond Within / The Death Of Passion / I Am The Dog / Dreaming Neon Black / Deconstruction / The Fault Of The Flesh / The Lotus Eaters / Poison Godmachine / All Play Dead / Cenotaph / No More Will / Forever
DEAD HEART IN A COLD WORLD, Century Media (2000) **57 GERMANY**
Narcosynthesis / We Disintegrate / Inside Four Walls / Evolution 169 / The River Dragon Has Come / The Heart Collector / Engines Of Hate / The Sound Of Silence / Insignificant / Believe In Nothing / Dead Heart In A Dead World

NEW EDEN (CA, USA)

Line-Up: Victor Vaca (vocals), Horacio Colmenares (guitar), Dan Delucie (guitar), Nardo Andi (bass), Brian Craig (drums)

A heavyweight Progressive Metal band founded in 1998 and centred on guitarist Horacio Colmenares, an erstwhile member of STEEL PROPHET. The band, fronted by singer Victor Vaca, opened proceedings with the 'Savage Garden' demo which swiftly led to a deal with Dennis Gulbey's Sentinel Steel label for the 'Through The Make Believe' inaugural album. NEW EDEN at this juncture boasted a roll call of Colmenares, Vaca, guitarist Dan Delucie and the erstwhile SHADOW INSANE rhythm section of bassist Nardo Andi and drummer Brian Craig.

Problems with the cover artwork led to the release of the NEW EDEN debut album to be delayed from its original late '96 release date, by which time both Vaca and Craig had quit to form a new band in a similar musical vein.

OBSCURE vocalist Mike Grant quickly filled Vaca's place although his tenure would be brief. Grant would go on to LEGEND MAKER and ex-HELSTAR front man James Rivera recorded their next four track demo although still remaining a member of CHAOTIC ORDER. The inclusion of Rivera ignited a bidding war between various European labels to secure the band for their next record. When the dust settled NEW EDEN had signed up to the German Nuclear Blast concern. However, with Rivera unable to make up his mind whether he should leave CHAOTIC ORDER for NEW EDEN in a permanent move NEW EDEN decided to draft in another vocalist.

Meantime Rivera, Delucie, Andi and Craig had created DESTINY'S END, signing to the Metal Blade label for the 'Breathe Deep The Dark' opus.

The new voice at the NEW EDEN microphone would be New Yorker Tony De Vita. Their new front man's credits numbered stints with INVASION, a brief spell with ODIN, WIRED, MISBEHAVIN' and appearing on the CARFAX ABBEY album 'Danse Macabre'. NEW EDEN would also welcome in further fresh recruits in the form of guitarist Tim Thomas and drummer Ozzy Echavarra for the 'Obscure Master Plan' album issued in 1998.

During 2001 the band enrolled bassist Melanie Sisneros on loan from Californian Metal act RAVEN MAD and the uniquely all female IRON MAIDEN tribute band the IRON MAIDENS in which the Sisneros ("Stephanie Harris"!) stars alongside PHANTOM BLUE members. Before long she would be inducted into the ranks as a full time member performing at the 'Classic Metal' festival in Kalamazoo and the 'Bang Your Head' event in Houston. The band would also find time to record two cover tracks for tribute albums, namely AC/DC's 'You Ain't Got Ahold On Me' and BLACK SABBATH's 'Wheels Of Confusion'.

NEW EDEN drummer Dave Chedrick would

temporarily act as substitute in PROTOTYPE during May of 2002. In July of 2002 Melanie Sisneros would be announced as new bassist for the Finnish based Power Metal band SINERGY. In September NEW EDEN revealed that none other than former STEEL PROPHET vocalist Rick Mythiasin was to front the band for their next album provisionally billed as 'Stagnant Progression'. This move came despite Mythiasin breaking his leg in three places whilst trying to perform a handstand (!)

Albums:
THROUGH THE MAKE BELIEVE, Sentinel Steel SSTEEL002 (1997)
Through The Make Believe / Nightmare / Captive Soul / Sepuku / Bullet Head / Now That You Have Gone / Unlock The Door / Symptoms Of Time / Piracy / Sunshine / Empty Man
OBSCURE MASTERPLAN, Nuclear Blast NB 341-2 (1998)
The Promise / Evil Logic / I Am / Dance Of The Dead / Demons Of Earth / Epitaph / Flicker Of Faith / Shades Of You / Sorrows / Land Of Filth And Money

NIGHTMARE (FRANCE)
Line-Up: Jo Amore (vocals), Nicolas De Dominicus (guitar), Jean Stripploi (guitar), Yves Campion (bass), David Amore (drums)

A veteran French Metal act making their presence felt with early album releases on the British Ebony label. NIGHTMARE replaced vocalist Christopher Houpert with erstwhile BRONX man Jean-Marie Boix for the 'Power Of The Universe' album, the group's second release.
NIGHTMARE reformed for 1999 mini-album 'Astral Deliverance' issued by the Adipocere label. The record was dedicated to the band's late front man Boix who had died tragically young in April of the same year. NIGHTMARE, now fronted by Jo Amore, solidified their return by putting in a 2000 appearance at the famous German Wacken festival. The band backed it up with the double 'Live Deliverance' album which boasted cover versions of ACCEPT's 'Metal Heart' and SORTILEGE's theme tune, complete with a guesting Patrick Liotard of PRESENCE.
NIGHTMARE switched to Napalm Records for October 2001's studio effort 'Cosmovision'. Famed French guitarist PATRICK RONDAT of ELEGY would guest on the track 'Spirit Of The Sunset'.

Albums:
WAITING FOR THE TWILIGHT, Ebony

EBON 22 (1984)
Trust A Crowd / Waiting For The Twilight / Too Late / Royal Death / Drive Down To Hell / Lord Of The Sky / The Legend / Fool In The Scene
POWER OF THE UNIVERSE, Ebony EBON30 (1985)
Running For The Deal / Diamond Crown / Prowler In The Night / Power Of The Universe / Let's Go / Judgement Day / Princess Of The Rising Sun / Invisible World
ASTRAL DELIVERANCE, Adipocere CDAR 048 (1999)
Astral Deliverance / The Legend / Heart Of Fire / Princess Of The Rising Sun / Howlers Of Insanity
LIVE DELIVERANCE, Adipocere (2000)
Astral Deliverance / The Legend / Trust A Crowd / Princess Of The Rising Sun / Let's Go / Waiting For The Twilight - Le Jour Du Châtiment / Diamond Crown / Heart Of Fire / Power Of The Universe / Too Late / Judgement Day / Invisible World / Howlers Of Insanity / Fool On The Scene / Prowler In The Night / Drive Down To Hell / Sortilège / Lord Of The Sky / Metal Heart
COSMOVISION, Napalm (2001)
Roads To Nazca (Intro) / Cosmovision / Corridors Of Knowledge / Spirits Of The Sunset / The Church / Behold The Nighttime / Necropolis / The Cemetery Road / Kill For The New Messiah / The Spiral Of Madness / Last Flight To Sirius / Riddle In The Ocean

NOCTURNAL RITES (SWEDEN)
Line-Up: Jonny Lindqvist (vocals), Fredrik Mannberg (guitar), Nils Norberg (guitar), Nils Erikssen (bass), Owe Lingvall (drums)

Founded in 1990 by guitarist / vocalist Frederik Mannberg as NECROMONIC in a more extreme Death Metal vein, NOCTURNAL RITES, from Umeå in northern Sweden, shifted the emphasis to a more streamlined traditional Metal approach with the recruitment of ex-GOTHAM CITY vocalist Anders Zackarisson. The band cut their only demo to date, 'The Obscure' with Mannberg on lead vocals, in early 1991.
Although 'The Obscure' attracted label interest the band opted to play the waiting game, not least because of the rapid shift in their music to more melodic pastures. Around this time drummer Tommy Eriksson, also involved with SHADOWSEEDS, decamped and was duly substituted by Ulf Andersson, a former member of NAGLFAR. NOCTURNAL RITES also added a second guitarist, Mikael Söderström. Their new direction also called for a new style of singing too resulting in the recruitment of ex-GOTHAM CITY vocalist

NOCTURNAL RIGHTS
Photo : Volker Beushausen

Anders Zackrisson. A further series of songs were put down on tape and prompted interest from the Dark Age label which signed the band in 1994. Dark Age in turn licensed the album to Dave Constable's Megarock concern. 'In A Time Of Blood And Fire' garnered international praise, setting the band up for bigger and better things to come. Despite this positive step Söderström decided to leave, his vacancy soon filled by former AUBERON man Nils Norberg.

NOCTURNAL RITES second album 'Tales Of Mystery And Imagination' was issued in Japan in late 1997 and was picked up by the German Century Media label for Europe the following year. The band benefited hugely from the renewed focus on traditional Metal as spotlighted by fellow Swedes HAMMERFALL and 1998's 'Tales Of Mystery And Imagination' sold well. The band put in extensive touring in Europe opening for OVERKILL and playing alongside NEVERMORE and ANGELDUST.

'The Sacred Talisman' capitalised on progress and introduced a new drummer in Owe Lingvall. Once more they set out onto European soil for a lengthy run of shows allied with NEVERMORE and LEFAY. However, Zackrisson decided he want out at this critical juncture. Inaugurating Jonny Lindqvist the

group got straight back into the studio to commit 'The Afterlife' to tape, this record witnessing the introduction of Mattias Bernhardsson on keyboards.

NOCTURNAL RITES would tour Europe with LABYRINTH and IRON SAVIOR during April 2001. A new album 'Shadowland' arrived in September proving the band were still as aggressive and as unashamedly heavy as ever.

Albums:
IN A TIME OF BLOOD AND FIRE,
Megarock MRCD032 (1995)
Sword Of Steel / Skyline / Flame / Black Death / In A Time Of Blood And Fire / Dawnspell / Lay Of Ennai / Winds Of Death / Rest In Peace / Dragonisle
TALES OF MYSTERY AND IMAGINATION,
Century Media 77208-2 (1998)
Ring Of Steel / Dark Secret / Test Of Time / Lost In Time / The Vision / Warrior's Return / Change The World / Pentagram / Eye Of The Demon / End Of The World / The Curse / Burn In Hell
THE SACRED TALISMAN, Century Media CD 7932-2 (1999)
Destiny Calls / The Iron Force / Ride On / Free At Last / Hold On To The Flame / Eternity Holds / Fire Comes To Ice / The

315

Legend Lives On / The King's Command / Unholy Powers (Night Of The Witch) / Glorious
AFTERLIFE, Century Media (2000)
Afterlife / Wake Up Dead / The Sinners Cross / Hell And Back / The Sign / The Devil´s Child / Genetic Distortion Sequence / Sacrifice / Temple Of The Dead / Hellenium
SHADOWLAND, Century Media 8132-2 (2002)
Eyes Of The Dead / Shadowland / Invincible / Revelation / Never Die / Underworld / Vengeance / Faceless God / Birth Of Chaos / The Watcher

NOISEHUNTER (GERMANY)

Line-Up: Hanny Vasiliadis (vocals / guitar), Erwin Perle (guitar), Reiner Hormel (bass), Ronny Lewandowski (drums)

NOISEHUNTER can date their inception as a band as far back as 1977, although they wouldn't record their debut album until 1986 after being picked up by Gama Records. Bassist Reiner Hormel was superseded by Matthias Nicklas following the debut album. Their biggest success unarguably came when appearing at a festival in Essen in front of 6,000 people.

Albums:
TIME TO FIGHT, Scratch LP SL 7023 (1986)
Love Screen / Made Out Of Metal / Necromancer / Rock n' Roll Outlaws / Time To Fight / Federal Republic Of Metal / Hellbound Fever / Back To The Roots / Stormbringer
SPELL OF NOISE, Scratch LP 805270 938 (1987)
On The Run / Fever / The City's Gonna Burn / Hot For Livin' / I Would Die For You / Back To Rock / Metal Lover / Straight Shooter / I'm On Fire
TOO YOUNG TO DIE, ZYX Records (1989)
Bad Boys Done Dirty / In The City / Too Young To Die / Looking Out For No One / Ruler Of The Dark / Worlds Attack / I Want Your Body / Restless / Girl Don't Mind / Dancing Fingers

NORTHERN LIGHTS (TURKEY)

Line-Up: Cihan (vocals), Serhat (guitar), Alen (guitar), Ilker (bass), Tancan (drums)

Singles/EPs:
Lightro / Land Of Light / Into The Winds / The Siege / Rising Hate, (2001) ('Northern Lights' EP)

NORTHWIND (FRANCE)

Line-Up: Franck Midoux (vocals), Chris

Savourney (guitar), Gilles Thiebaut (bass), Nicolas Ory (keyboards), Yannick Pierre (drums)

A melodic Metal act founded by highly rated guitarist CHRIS SAVOURNEY following his departure from HEAVENLY in March of 2001. As a solo artist Savourney has issued three albums. Vocalist Franck Midoux and keyboard player Nicolas Ory were recruited from the ranks of CENTAURE. Bass player Gilles Thiebaut was previously with STARGAZER and CHRYSALID.

Albums:
SEASONS, Z Records ZR 1997072 (2002)
Seasons / Forever And A Day / Dreaming / It's A Warning / Masquerade / Out From Fire / Wasted In Paradise / Winter

NORTHWIND (SPAIN)

Line-Up: Txema Trinidad (vocals), Daniel González Suárez (guitar), Constantino Hevia Toraño (guitar), Miguel Fernández (bass), Helena Pinto Póo (keyboards), Fernando Argüelles Osorio (drums)

Power Metal band. NORTHWIND was formulated during 1998 by guitarists Constantino Hevia Toraño and Luis Fernández of ANTANO, bass player José Gálvez and former SANTERIA drummer Rubén González. Before long González was substituted by erstwhile HEIMDALL man Fernando Argüelles Osorio. The bass role changed hands first to Eladio Martínez then in quick succession Miguel Fernández, another SANTERIA veteran. The ex-SANTERIA contingent was further boosted with the inauguration of singer Jose María 'Txema' Trinidad and Emilio Gutiérrez was enrolled on keyboards.
NORTHWIND began recording in July of 2000 for the 'Viento Del Norte' album. However, Luis Fernandez bailed out, being replaced by Daniel González Suárez from CLAN DE LOS MCLEOD. The band retired to the Bunker Studios owned by AVALANCH guitarist Alberto Rionda to complete the record, which surfaced on the Goimusic label during 2001.
NORTHWIND drafted keyboard player Helena Pinto Póo, also a member of RELATIVE SILENCE for recording of the second album 'El Retorno Del Rey - Crónicas De Áravan Part 1'. This effort was recorded in Germany and produced by SILENT FORCE guitarist Alex Beyrodt.

Albums:
VIENTO DEL MORTE, Goimusic (2001)

Viento Del Norte / Paraíso De Sombras / Retroceder Mañana / Lágrimas De Hielo / Santos Guerreros En Los Mares / Canto De Los Infieles / Hijos De La Fe / Dioses Muertos / El Sueño / La Ultima Lucha
EL RETORNO DEL REY (CRONICAS DE ARAVON PARTE I), (2002)
Profecía / Cuando Salga El Sol / El Oráculo / Imohën / El Susurro Del Viento / La Morada De Celler / Maestro De La Nada / Senderos Divinos / A Las Puertas Del Edén / El Lago Y El Dragón / Bajo El Altar / El Retorno Del Rey / Cielo Gris / Epílogo / Ensis Diva

NOSTRADAMEUS (SWEDEN)
Line-Up: Freddy Persson (vocals), Jake Freden (guitar), Michael Aberg (guitar), Thomas Antonsson (bass), Esko Salow (drums)

NOSTRADAMEUS operate in melodic Speed Metal territory. The band was conceived in 1998, a GAMMA RAY and IRON SAVIOUR gig inspiring the VAPID Death Metal pairing of guitarist Jake Freden and vocalist Freddy Persson to embark upon a new venture. Initially VAPID drummer Gustav and second guitarist Erik sat in for rehearsals with Persson handling both vocals and bass guitar. This unit recorded a demo in December of 1998 funded by Magnus Lundbäck of Gain Records. The tape caught the attention of several German labels and in early 1999 NOSTRADAMEUS signed to the AFM label.
After recording of the debut album 'Words Of Nostradameus' the stand in members were substituted by guitarist Michael Åberg, bassist Thomas Antonsson and drummer Jesse. A second album 'The Prophet Of Evil' arrived in August of 2001. For touring as support to EDGUY in Europe during November and December NOSTRADAMEUS drafted a new drummer Esko Salow.

Albums:
WORDS OF NOSTRADAMEUS, AFM AFM039 (2000)
Words Of Nostradameus / The Vision / Out Of This World / Nightmare Prophecy / Without Your Love / Master Of The Night / Black Fate / The Crown's Inn / Resurrection / Brothers In Chains / One For All, All For One
THE PROPHET OF EVIL, AFM 0046792AFM (2001)
The Prophet Of Evil / Hymn To These Lands / Evil Prophecies / Murder / Requiem (I Will Honour Thy…) / In Prison / The Escape / The Power's In Your Hands / Gathering Resistance / The Final Battle / Scream Of Anger

THE THIRD PROPHECY, AFM (2003)

NOT FRAGILE (GERMANY)
Line-Up: Torsten Buczko (vocals / guitar), Raico Ebel (guitar / keyboards), Matthias Belter (bass), Markus Köhn (drums)

Singles/EPs:
Lost In A Dream / Break Down The Walls / One Way To Glory, Hellion 001 (1989)
Fire In The Night, Hellion (1989)

Albums:
WHO DARES WINS, Metalother OTH13 (1988)
Rael / With All My Might / High Into Heaven / Opus 7-3 / Down In The Streets / Out Of Law / Craze And Hunger / Bbbrrräää
THE RETURN, Not Fragile NF001 (1995)
Intro / Flight Of The Intruder / Who Dares Wins / Undertaker / Hungry For Love / Kiss Of Fire / Homeless / Don't Give Up / W.I.R. (Unplugged)

OBSESSION (CT, USA)
Line-Up: Mike Vescara
(vocals), Bruce Vitale (guitar),
Art Maco (guitar), Matt
Keragus (bass), Jay Mezias
(drums)

Metal band from Connecticut
founded in 1983. OBSESSION debuted with a
cut on the Metal Blade 'Metal Massacre'
compilation series prompting their signature
to the label for a full length outing 'Marshall
Law'.

Vocalist Michael Vescara's post OBSESSION
career includes a recording stint with
Japanese metallers LOUDNESS. Following
LOUDNESS' decision to recruit a Japanese
front man back into the band, Vescara was
hired by Swedish speed guitar guru YNGWIE
MALMSTEEN with whom he recorded and
toured. His global reach would be extended
with terms on Brazilian Metal band DR. SIN.
In 1997 he issued a Japanese release solo
album. Vescara also guests on HELLOWEEN
guitarist ROLAND GRAPOW's 'Kaleidoscope'
record and issued his own MVP album in
1999. By 2001 Vescara was fronting JOE
STUMP'S REIGN OF TERROR for the
'Sacred Ground' album.

An erstwhile OBSESSION guitarist, Robert
Marcello, would later come to the fore with the
band IRON HORSE, fronted by ex-KEEL
singer Ron Keel. Coincidentally the album
would be produced by Vescara. In mid 2002
Marcello united with the RATT duo of guitarist
John Corabi, also probably better known for
his role as front man in MÖTLEY CRÜE, and
drummer Bobby Blotzer for an album project
under the band name TWENTY 4 SEVEN.

Singles/EPs:
Only The Strong Will Survive / Hatred Unto
Death / The Execution / Marshall Law, Metal
Blade 71028 (1984) ('Marshall Law' EP)

Albums:
SCARRED FOR LIFE, Enigma ST 3212
(1986)
Scarred For Life / Winner Take All / Losing
My Mind / In The End / Bang 'Em Till They
Bleed / Hy Lai 31568 - Take No Prisoners /
Taking Your Chances / Run Into The Night /
Tomorrow Hides No Lies
METHODS OF MADNESS, Enigma ST-
73262 (1987)
Four Play / Hard To The Core / High Treason
/ For The Love Of Money / Killer Elite /
Desperate To Survive / Method Of Madness
/ Too Wild To Tame / Always On The Run /
Panic In The Streets

OCTOBER 31 (USA)
Line-Up: King Fowley (vocals), Brian
Williams (guitar), Jason Tedder (guitar), Jim
Hunter (bass), Dave Castillo (drums)

Project band of DECEASED's King Fowley
and guitarist Brian 'Hellstorm' Williams.
Forged in 1995 the Fowley / Williams axis laid
down the demo tape 'Voyage To Infinity'
before inducting bassist Jim Hunter. Still as a
trio with Fowley responsible for both lead
vocals and drums OCTOBER 31 recorded the
debut 'Fire Still Awaits You' album for R.I.P.
Records, issued in 1997. This effort caught
the ear of hardened Metal collectors axis with its
cover version of WITCHKILLER's 'Day Of The
Saxons'. The band also contributed a new
track 'The Chosen One' to a compilation
'Metal Injection' for the Bad Posture label.

For the follow up EP 'Visions Of The End',
which saw a version of LIZZY BORDEN's
'Give 'Em The Axe', the group added second
guitar player Kevin Lewis. Another outing was
the IRON MAIDEN cover of 'Public Enema
Number One' donated to the Dwell Records
tribute 'A Call To Irons'.

The line-up remained stable for the next
album 'Meet Thy Maker'. As was now
becoming tradition an old Metal staple was
dusted off, OCTOBER 31 lending new life to
SAXON's 'Power And The Glory' on this
occasion. The group recruited Chuck Parsons
to fulfil live lead vocal duties. A restricted gold
vinyl reissue of 'Fire Still Awaits You'
predictably sold out immediately. Fowley's
own Old Metal label had re-released 'Vision
Of The End' adding the original demo tracks
plus a take on JAG PANZER's 'Harder Than
Steel'. The group also made an impression on
the Dwell OZZY OSBOURNE tribute
collection 'Land Of The Wizard' with 'I Don't
Know'.

With the underground word on the band
spreading globally Metal Blade Records
picked up 'Meet Thy Maker' for European
distribution in April of 2000, coupling it with
the 'Visions Of The End' material. To promote
this release OCTOBER 31 announced the
inauguration of new lead singer Shaun Pelata
but within weeks this latest member was out
of the picture. Pulling in David Castillo of
Death Metal band HATRED as drummer,
travelled to Germany for an appearance at
the world renowned 'Wacken Open Air'
festival. After this gig Lewis stepped down.

During February of 2001 TWISTED TOWER
DIRE guitarist Scott Waldrop and vocalist
Tony Taylor seconded themselves to
OCTOBER 31 for recording of the 'Salem's
Curse' single, the flip side of which covered
JUDAS PRIEST's 'Electric Eye'. By February
of the following year Taylor opted out in order

to concentrate on his priority act.

As 2002 drew in OCTOBER 31 evolved yet again. With King Fowley as front man, the guitar team now comprised Brian Williams and Jason Tedder with Jim Hunter on bass and David Castillo re-ensconced on drums.

OCTOBER 31's Brian Williams also operates a side project dubbed K-OCTAVE in alliance with vocalist Shawn Pelata, guitarist Jason Tedder, bassist Cliff Paul and drummer Tom Berry. K-OCTAVE issued the 2001 album 'Outer Limits' through Germany's Hellion Records.

Singles/EPs:

Visions Of The End / The Chosen One / Servants And Slaves / Give 'Em The Axe / The Legend Of The Haunted Sea, Old Metal (1998) ('Visions Of The End' EP)

Salem's Curse '01 / Electric Eye, Maniacal (2001)

Albums:

THE FIRE AWAITS YOU, R.I.P. (1997)
The Warlock / Salem's Curse / The Fire Awaits You / Lost City / Voyage To Infinity / Day Of The Saxons / Vindication / A Million Goodbyes

VISIONS OF THE END, Old Metal (1999)
Visions Of The End / The Chosen One /

Servants And Slaves / Give 'Em The Axe / The Legend Of The Haunted Sea / Voyage To Infinity / The Fire Awaits You / Child Of The Damned / When Darkness Covers The Sun / Harder Than Steel

MEET THY MAKER, R.I.P. (2000)
Meet Thy Maker / Just An Illusion / For There Is War! / Far From Danger Now / Power And The Glory / The Verdict / Behind The Castle Walls

VISIONS OF THE END, R.I.P. (2000)
The Chosen One / Visions Of The End / Servants And Slaves / Give 'Em The Axe / The Legend Of The Haunted Sea / Child Of The Damned / When Darkness Covers The Sun

ODIN (Los Angeles, CA, USA)
Line-Up: Randy O (vocals), Jeff Duncan (guitar), Aaron Samson (bass), Shawn Duncan (drums)

Unfortunately ODIN are more famous in the mass market for their appearance in the Rockumentary 'The Decline And Fall Of Western Civilisation Part II: The Metal Years' than any recorded product. In the Metal world ODIN's name has long ranked as one of the most hallowed cult acts to bless the American scene. Guitarist Brad Parker appears on the

1983 EP. Under the pseudonym of Damien C. Phillips Parker had actually been a member of the fledgling METALLICA. His stay lasted just one gig.

Vocalist Randy O Roberg would depart to secure a solo deal with Atlantic Records. After an abortive spell working with ex-HOLLAND guitarist Mike Batio in MICHAEL ANGELO during 1988 Roberg formed the LOST BOYS with Jeff Duncan and bassist Jimmy Tavis, a late recruit into ODIN, releasing the 1990 album 'Lost And Found'.

Another attempt to re-assemble the band would include guitarist Tim Kelly and New Yorker Tony De Vita, a former member of INVASION, on vocals. This unit would soon dissolve with De Vita journeying through WIRED, MISBEHAVIN and CARFAX ABBEY prior to winding up in Progressive Metal act NEW EDEN. Kelly would change tack to find platinum fame with SLAUGHTER before his untimely demise.

Shawn Duncan played with MADAM X prior to that group's eventual end in early 1989. Duncan later joined ARMORED SAINT before founding BIRD OF PREY. In 2000 the Duncan siblings assembled side project band DC4 together with yet another Duncan family member bassist Matt.

Jeff Duncan is presently a member of the resurrected ARMORED SAINT. Renewed interest in '80s US Metal and cult acts such as ODIN in particular would put the focus back on the band as Japanese label JVC Victor issued the 'Fight For Your Life' album in June of 2001.

Singles/EPs:
Caution / The Blade / Midnight Flight / Judgement Day, Duff (1983)

Albums:
DON'T TAKE NO FOR AN ANSWER, Half Wet GWD 1290509 (1985)
The Writer / One Day To Live / Shining Love / Solar Eye / Don't Take No For An Answer / Judgement Day
THE GODS MUST BE CRAZY, JVC Victor (1987)
FIGHT FOR YOUR LIFE, (1988)
12 O' Clock High / Love Action / She Was The One / I Get What I Want / Serenade To The Court / Modern Day King / Stranger Tonight / Time And Time Again / I'm Gonna Get You / Push / Fight For Your Life
BY THE GODS, Perris 2004 (2001)
The Writer / One Day To Live / Shining Love / Solar Eye / Don't Take No For An Answer / Judgement Day / Little Gypsy / She Needs My Love / No Reason To Run / Over Your Head / She Was The One / Play The Fool /

Matter Of Time / Judgement Day / Midnight Flight / The Blade

OLIVER / DAWSON SAXON (UK)
Line-Up: John Ward (vocals), Graham Oliver (guitar), Hadyn Conway (guitar), Steve Dawson (bass), Nigel Durham (drums)

During the '90s the future of Northern British Metal band SAXON became clouded with doubt as the band effectively split into two. Founder members guitarist Graham Oliver and bass player Steve Dawson reunited to forge SON OF A BITCH and an album 'Victim You' fronted by THUNDERHEAD's Ted Bullett. Vocalist Biff Byford forged ahead with SAXON but for a while both parties operated live simply as SAXON prompting the inevitable court case. The Oliver/Dawson incarnation of the band strengthened their case by recruiting Pete Gill, a veteran of MOTÖRHEAD and, of course, SAXON.

To further confuse matters SAXON's 'Destiny' era drummer Nigel Durham had replaced Pete Gill in SON OF A BITCH but not before being asked to by Byford to replace Glockler in SAXON!

Even as late as early 1999 SAXON were being billed as performing in British clubs but this was in reality SON OF A BITCH. The dates were subsequently cancelled due to illness. Oliver disbanded SON OF A BITCH later that year to form a JIMI HENDRIX tribute band with his son on drums. However, by June the pair had teamed up with members of STORMWATCH and WITCHFYNDE to create the LUTHAR BELTZ BAND for live gigs.

Oliver and Dawson came back to the fore in early 2000 announcing an operating title of OLIVER/ DAWSON SAXON. Joining them were drummer Durham, former SARACEN guitarist Hadyn Conway and ex-HURRICANE, MADAM X, SHAME and SHY vocalist John Ward. The band was invited to open shows on DIO's October 2002 UK dates.

Albums:
RE: LANDED, Phoenix Music PHMUKCD001 (2001)

OLIVER MAGNUM (USA)
Line-Up: James Randel (vocals), Monte Humphrey (guitar), Dan Kurtz (bass), Curt Daugherty (drums)

Underground, technically minded Power Metal band out of Oklahoma. OLIVER MAGNUM made an initial impression with the '01986' demo tape. Original vocalist Mark Mueller would opt out prior to recording of the debut album. OLIVER MAGNUM actually conducted live gigs as a purely instrumental show before inducting new singer James Randel.

When OLIVER MAGNUM dissolved Randel teamed up with FORTE.

Singles/EPs:
Invertigo / Soon To Be Sane / Words Of Peace / Lies / Artificial Incineration, (1992) ('Drive By' EP)

Albums:
OLIVER MAGNUM, New Renaissance 08-9809 (1989)
Sister Cybele / The Last Prophet / Old World Nites / Evilution / Trapped / Mendes Prey / Tongue Tied / Silent Scream (Prelude To Death)
THE COLLECTION, (1990)
Trapped / Silent Scream / Old World Nights 2' 10" / Fahrenheit 451 / Metal Cruelty / Invertigo / Soon To Be Sane / Words Of Peace / Lies / Artificial Incineration / Troubled Life / Sick Of It All / American Queen / Necessary Evil / Time To Tell

OMEN (Los Angeles, CA, USA)
Line-Up: Kevin Goocher (vocals), Kenny Powell (guitar), Andy Haas (bass), Rick Murray (drums)

Traditional Heavy Metal band formed by ex-SACRED BLADE guitarist Kenny Powell. The band had been created during 1983 by Oklahoma natives guitarists Kenny Powell and Jody Henry along with drummer Steve Wittig. Unable to assemble a full band unit Powell took time out to work with SAVAGE GRACE. This tenure would be short-lived though and, brandishing a cassette of tapes originally scored for SAVAGE GRACE, Powell duly scored a deal with Brian Slagel and Metal Blade Records for OMEN.

The band line-up was completed with vocalist J.D. Kimball as OMEN debuted with the 'Battle Cry' album. Although blighted by an amateurish album cover OMEN's brand of Power Thrash style Metal won many converts worldwide.

A succession of albums ensued but OMEN were unable to extract themselves from a cult following into the mainstream.

The 1988 'Nightmares' mini-album contains a live version of the AC/DC classic 'Whole Lotta Rosie'. Kimball departed before this release and OMEN pulled in vocalist Coburn Pharr for the 'Escape To Nowhere' album which featured a version of GOLDEN EARRING's 'Radar Love'. Originally the album, produced by the esteemed Paul O'Neill, was to have

been entitled 'Era Of Crisis' but many of the original tracks slated for the album would be rejected by O'Neill. Despite the tribulations OMEN scored valuable radio play with the track 'Thorn In Your Flesh'. Upon completion of a ten week run of live shows across America a disillusioned Powell decamped.

After the release of 1989's compilation 'Teeth Of The Hydra' Pharr opted out to join high profile Canadians ANNIHILATOR. Powell joined forces with vocalist Steve Kelley, bassist Andy Haas and drummer Doug Stevens to create STEP CHILD issuing a demo in 1991.

With a renaissance of '80s American Metal in Europe during the mid '90s OMEN was forced out of retirement due to fan pressure. Powell emerged with a new look OMEN that included his son Greg Powell on lead vocals and guitar, bassist Andy Haas and drummer Rick Murray.

This unit cut the comeback 'Reopening The Gates' album for Germany's Massacre Records and undertook a successful bout of European touring backing up FATES WARNING. After these dates Greg Powell embarked on his own career with STOMPING GROUND.

OMEN enlisted the services of Kevin Goocher and set to task on a new album projected for 2002 release titled 'Eternal Black Dawn'. Earlier in the year OMEN, with support band BATTLEROAR, had toured Greece to enthusiastic response.

Original OMEN bassist Jody Henry was touting a fresh act in 2002 billed as CELEBRITY CRUSH. OMEN busied themselves in recording a brand new studio album 'Eternal Black Dawn'.

Albums:
BATTLE CRY, Roadrunner RR 9818 (1984)
Death Rider / The Axeman / Last Rites / Dragon's Breath / Be My Wench / Battle Cry / Die By The Blade / Prince Of Darkness / Bring Out The Beast / In The Arena
WARNING OF DANGER, Roadrunner RR 9738 (1985)
Warning Of Danger / March On / Ruby Eyes (Of The Serpent) / Don't Fear The Night / VBP / Premonition / Termination / Make Me Your King / Red Horizon / Hell's Gates
THE CURSE, Roadrunner RR 9661 (1986)
The Curse / Kill On Sight / Holy Martyr / Eye Of The Storm / S.R.B. / Teeth Of The Hydra / At All Cost / Destiny / Bounty Hunter / The Larch
NIGHTMARES, Metal Blade SQ-73266 (1987)
Nightmares / Shock Treatment / Dragon's Breath / Termination / Bounty Hunter / Whole Lotta Rosie (Live)

ESCAPE TO NOWHERE, Roadrunner RR 9544-2 (1988)

It's Not Easy / Radar Love / Escape To Nowhere / Cry For The Morning / Thorn In Your Flesh / Poisoned / Nomads / King Of The Hill / No Way Out

TEETH OF THE HYDRA, Metal Blade 3948 14206CD (1989)

Holy Martyr / Termination / Dragon's Breath / Teeth Of The Hydra / Battle Cry / The Curse / Nightmares / Bounty Hunter / Thorn In Your Flesh / Die By The Blade / Hell's Gates

REOPENING THE GATES, Massacre MAS PCO124 (1997)

Dead March / Uneven Plow / Chained / Rain Down / Reopening The Gates / Everything / Well Fed / Crushing Day / Saturday Into The Ground

ONWARD (USA)

Line-Up: Michael Grant (vocals), Toby Knapp (guitar), Randy LaFrance (bass), Jon Pereau (drums)

Heavy Metal band ONWARD came to prominence with the media attention focussed on the super speed shredding abilities of guitarist TOBY KNAPP. The Montana raised Knapp had previously issued a solo album 'Guitar Distortion' for the Shrapnel label and prior to forging ONWARD had even been inducted into the realms of Black Metal with his outfit DARKEN.

Knapp would form an alliance with bass player Randy LaFrance and drummer Jon Pereau, both members of covers act BIG TROUBLE, to create ONWARD and initial demos would spark the interest of Sentinel Steel Records owner Dennis Gulbey who, in turn, suggested singer Mike Grant.

Grant had credits already with MORPHEUS, OCEAN SEVEN, OBSCURE, COLD OCTOBER and briefly held down a tenure with NEW EDEN. The vocalist had also cut an album for Gulbey with Colombian Metal band LEGEND MAKER 'A Path To Glory'. Now an up to strength quartet ONWARD would record their inaugural outing 'Evermoving'. Originally slated as a Sentinel Steel release the finished product impressed Germany's Century Media label enough to sign the act.

Touring would find ONWARD putting in shows at the Lansburg, Illinois 'ProgPower' festival, the Kalamazoo 'Classic Rock' festival and the Los Angeles 'November To Dismember' event. The band's second album 'Reawaken' included a cover version of 'Clockwork Toy' by LOUDNESS. The first pressing of the album provided a huge bonus to fans as it included an extra free CD compilation 'Prepare For Battle' comprising Power Metal acts of such repute as JAG PANZER, BLIND GUARDIAN,

ICED EARTH, NEVERMORE and ANGEL DUST. The band would also donate their versions of URIAH HEEP's 'Bird Of Prey' and SAVATAGE's 'Strange Wings' to tribute albums.

Latterly Chris Payette has supplanted LaFrance's position. ONWARD would be announced as support act for REVEREND's August 2002 West Coast tour of America.

Albums:

EVERMOVING, Century Media (2000)

The Kindness Of Strangers / Onward / The Waterfall Enchantress / The Last Sunset / Absolution Mine / Witches Winter Eternal / Storm Coming Soon / The Lost Side Of The World

REAWAKEN, Metal Blade 8105-2 (2002)

Reawaken / Night / The Seven Tides Of Labyrinthine / Where Evil Follows / Eye Of The Nightmare / My Darkest Room / In Due Time / Clockwork Toy / Who Saw The Last Star Fall? / The Next Triumph: Remembrance / The Next Triumph: Reawakening

ORACLE (Jacksonville, FL, USA)

Line-Up: William Wren (vocals), Kent Smedley (guitar), Kevin Reid (bass), Brent Smedley (drums)

The 'As Darkness Reigns' album is regarded as an obscure classic of the genre. ORACLE singer William Wren would later be found fronting MYSTIC FORCE.

Albums:

AS DARKNESS REIGNS, Massacre MASS CD 012 (1993)

Prisoner (Of Your Own Soul) / Nightmares / No Faith For The Liar / As Darkness Reigns / Paradise (On The Edge Of The World) / Knights Of The Round Table / The Watcher / Prodigy / In The End

ORACLE (Greensboro, NC, USA)

Line-Up: Shawn Pelata (vocals), Robert Kerns (guitar), Thomas Mitchell (bass), Jay Denny (drums)

North Carolina's Christian Metal act ORACLE was founded in 1990. Original guitar player Jimmy Weaver would make his exit just prior to recording of the 'Selah' album, originally issued in 1992.

'Selah' would see a re-release courtesy of the M8 label packaged as a split CD with another Christian Metal band EMERALD and their 1987 album 'Armed For Battle'. Oddly the M8 re-issue misnames bassist Thomas Mitchell as 'Thomas Hughes' and claims ORACLE emanate from California.

322

ORATORY

Albums:
SELAH, (1992)
Passage Denied / Harlots Destiny / Witches
And Warlocks / The Purging Fire / Desolate
Kings / Legion / Rebecca

ORATORY (PORTUGAL)
Line-Up: Marco Alves (vocals), Ana Lana
(vocals), Miguel Gomez (guitar), Rui Santos
(bass), Antonio Silva (keyboards), Joao
Rodriguez (drums)

A Portuguese Metal band with a novelty of
shared male and female lead vocals courtesy
of Marco Alves and Ana Lana. ORATORY
debuted with the 1996 'Enchantation' demo. A
further demo 'Sarcastic Soul' issued in 1997
preceded the 'Last Prophecy' mini-album for
the Recital label. Reaction to this recording
prompted a deal with German Melodic Rock
specialists Limb Music Productions.
The Luis Barros produced 2000 album
'Illusion Dimensions' would see TARANTULA
guitarist Paulo Barros as session guest. Uwe
Lulis of GRAVE DIGGER and REBELLION
would produce ORATORY's 2002 album
'Beyond Earth'. The Portuguese Recital
version of the album came with a bonus track,
a live version of 'Metal Messenger', whilst the
German Limb Music Productions variant
added a cover version of THE BANGLES
'Eternal Flame'.

Albums:
LAST PROPHECY, Recital (1999)
The Other Side Of The Sea / Last Prophecy
/ Life In Another Star / Oratory
ILLUSION DIMENSIONS, Limb Music
Productions 0009-020CD (2000)
Illusion Dimensions / With Glory And Melody
/ Fight For The Light / Kingdom's Legacy /
Metal Messenger / In The Sky / Last
Prophecy / Life In Another Star / Rising Land
/ Choose Your Future / World Of Illusion /
Galaxy
BEYOND EARTH, Recital (2002)
Old Man's Prophecy / Living Wisdom /
Concilium / Song Of Lust / Eternal / Your
Glory Won't Last Forever / Victory Of Light /
Story Of All Times / Heroes From The Past /
Beyond Earth / A New Quest

OSIRIS (HOLLAND)
Line-Up: Bram Oever (vocals), Geert
Kerrsies (guitar), Maurice Oudhof (guitar),
Rene Bronwasser (bass), Marc Fien (drums)

A very technical Power Metal band. OSIRIS
came together in 1985 with Robbie Woning of
DEADHEAD, but this incarnation would soon
split.
The only remaining original member of the
band, drummer Marc Fein, reassembled
OSIRIS with the above line-up in 1987. The
group recorded two demos - 'Inextricable
Reversal' in 1989 and 'Equivocal Quiescence'
in 1991 - before getting the chance to put an
album together.

1992's 'Futurity And Human Depressions' turned out to be a highly complex Speed Metal outing with histrionic vocals.

OSIRIS went on to support Americans LÄÄZ ROCKITT on their 1992 European tour.

Albums:
FUTURITY AND HUMAN DEPRESSIONS, Shark (1992)
Futurity (Something To Think About) / Mass Termination / Inextricable / Out Of Inspiration / Inner Recession / Fallacy (The Asylum) / Frozen Memory

OSTROGOTH (BELGIUM)
Line-Up: Peter De Windt (vocals), June Martins (guitar), Rudy Vercruysse (guitar), Sylvian Charotti (bass), Chris Taerwe (keyboards), Mario Pauwels (drums)

Debuting on the Mausoleum compilation 'If It's Loud, We're Proud', Belgian outfit OSTROGOTH originally went under the pseudonyms of Red Star, Sphinx, White Shark, Bronco and Grizzly before revealing their true names on the 'Ecstasy And Danger' debut album in 1984. The band had formed sometime during the late '70s, being initially fronted by singer Luc Minne. With the introduction of THE RAG man Rudy Vercruysse joining Hans Van de Kerkhove to form up the twin guitar team in 1981 OSTROGOTH also switched singers to Marc De Brouwer.

OSTROGOTH debuted with the 1983 EP 'Full Moon's Eyes' in 1983. For this outing the band members adopted the pseudonyms of De Brouwer as 'Red Star', Van de Kerkhove as 'Sphinx', Vercruysse 'White Shark', drummer Marco Pauwels 'Grizzly' and bassist Marnix Van De Kauter as 'Bronco'. The EP had originally been intended as a self-financed effort but after an airing of two tracks on a local radio station Mausoleum Records offered the band a deal. Their first album, 'Ecstasy And Danger' also released by Mausoleum in 1984' and kicking off unconventionally with a huge guitar solo, pulled in favourable reviews across Europe.

The group released a sophomore effort, 'Too Hot', in 1985 before undergoing something of a change for the third album in 1987. A drastic reshuffling of the group saw ex-CROSSFIRE vocalist Peter De Windt replacing original singer Marc De Brouwer. De Windt had actually already recorded with OSTROGOTH, contributing backing vocals on 'Too Hot'. New Brazilian guitarist June Martins came in for Hans Van de Kerckhove and bassist Marnix Van De Kauter was succeeded by Sylvian Charotti. However, this line-up soon faltered and folded.

Van De Kauter, Martins and Charotti were soon back in action with a new band entitled HERMETIC BORTHERHOOD. De Windt later joined the Belgian group MYSTERY in the mid '90s and by 1998 was vocalist for AFFAIR. Drummer Mario Pauwels joined SHELLSHOCK. Guitarist Rudy Vercruysse created a covers band RUN 4 H with erstwhile BAD LIZARD singer Eddy Termote.

OSTROGOTH re-formed for a concert in Athens during September 2002.

Singles/EPs:
Full Moon Eyes / Heroes Museum / Paris By Night / Rock Fever, Mausoleum 504112-2 (1983) ('Full Moon Eyes' EP)

Albums:
ECSTASY AND DANGER, Mausoleum 7041117-2 (1984)
Queen Of Desire / Ecstasy And Danger / A Bitch Again / Stormbringer / Scream Out / Lords Of Thunder / The New Generation / Do It Right
TOO HOT, Mausoleum 704139-2 (1985)
Too Hot / Shoot Back / Sign Of Life / The Gardens Of Marrakech / Love In The Street / Night Women (Don't Like Me) / Endless Winter Days / Catch The Sound Of Peace / Halloween
FEELINGS OF FURY, Mausoleum 704151-2 (1987)
Conquest / The Introduction / Samurai / Love Can Wait / We Are The Ace / The Hunter / Get Out Of My Life / What The Hell Is Going On / Vlad Strigol

OUTSIDE (GERMANY)
Line-Up: Karlheinz Scherthan (vocals / bass), Peter Weber (guitar), Volker Gutting (guitar / keyboards), Rudi Herzenstiel (drums)

A German Heavy Metal group formed in 1983, OUTSIDE's first demo ('Metal Killer') received positive reviews when released in 1984 and the vibe on the band enabled them to produce the single 'Action' / 'Heavy Metal' a year later.

In the mid '80s the group was chosen to play at the 'Monster Nachwuchs Festival' in Ludwigsburg's Rockfabrik club - beating off competition from over 1,200 other bands vying for a slice of the action - and would later support the likes of TOKYO BLADE, TRANCE, TRYAN' PACE and GRAVE DIGGER.

Having released two albums in their time, the second one is noted for featuring new guitarist Andy Zeckra in place of Peter Weber.

Singles/EPs:
Action / Heavy Metal, (1985)

Albums:
MAGIC SACRAFICE, Rockport (1986)
Hot n' Ready / Home To You / Magic
Sacrifice / 300 Days
NEVER IN SECURITY, Powerline (1988)
Wild Scud To Hell / Dangerous Games /
Heavy Metal / Can't Stand Lonely Nights / Is
It Love

OVERDRIVE (SWEDEN)

Line-Up: Pelle Thuresson (vocals), Janne
Stark (guitar), Kjell Jacobson (guitar), Kenth
Eriksson (bass), Kenta Svensson (drums)

OVERDRIVE was formed in August 1980
from the union of the two Swedish bands
OCEAN and PARADIZE. Drummer Kenta
Svensson and guitarist Kjell Jacobson had
released two previous singles and the album
entitled 'The But' with OCEAN, whilst
PARADIZE had a single release in 1979.
OVERDRIVE began primarily as a covers
band, playing songs by the like of DEF
LEPPARD and RIOT. However, in 1981 they
released a self-financed 12" titled 'Reflexions',
which gained the band a deal with Planet
Records.
During 1982 OVERDRIVE contributed two
tracks, 'Damnation Angel' and 'Tonight', to the
S.O.S. Records compilation album
'Rockslaget' and in April 1983 their debut
album 'Metal Attack' was released to excellent
reviews. OVERDRIVE would play as support
to E.F. BAND, MERCYFUL FATE and
PRETTY MAIDS following the record's
release.
After the sophomore effort 'Swords And
Axes', bassist Kenth Eriksson left to join
INTERACTION, making way for another
erstwhile OCEAN member in Zoltan Djember.
However, this union would be short-lived as
OVERDRIVE split the same year.
Guitarist Janne Stark and vocalist Pelle
Thuresson formed a new outfit titled
OVERHEAT as Thuresson made the move to
bass guitar and the duo completed their new
band with former HIGH VOLTAGE vocalist
Gernot Iverson and drumming colleague Paul
Gustavsson, a veteran of HIGH VOLTAGE,
MERCY and TURBO. However, this group
only ever recorded demos.
Whilst their former band mates attempted to
move forward with OVERHEAT, Svensson
and Jacobson formed PRIDE prior to the
latter joining E TYPE and recording a track for
a compilation album. Janne Stark maintained
his presence on the scene by contributing
solo pieces to the 'Guitar Heroes Of Sweden'

collection released by the B.O.R.G. label
during 1990 and on the 'Guitar Heroes Of
Sweden Vol 2' issued the following year on the
Ghost imprint.
OVERDRIVE briefly re-formed in 1992 with
Stark, Thuresson, Svensson and ex-E TYPE
vocalist Jørgen Aspring joining together for a
demo, although things would pretty much
dissolve afterwards. OVERDRIVE have been
known to play the odd re-formation gig from
time to time since, especially after both
albums were re-issued on CD by Megarock
Records in late 1995 through the Rock
Treasures imprint.
Janne Stark has since put together a brand
new group - LOCOMOTIVE BREATH (named
in honour of the JETHRO TULL song of the
same moniker) - and signed a deal with the
German Bluestone label for the release of the
band's debut album in late 1997. His erstwhile
OVERDRIVE colleague Kjell Jacobsson also
contributes.
Janne also published his excellent 'The
Encyclopaedia Of Swedish Hard Rock And
Heavy Metal' in 1996, the definitive work on
the subject. He also continues to contribute to
a number of Rock publications around the
world. Stark also made his presence felt on
the 1997 debut album from acclaimed
Christian Metal act NARNIA, 'The Awakening'
featuring a guest solo from the man.
Incidentally, 1998 also saw further evidence
of the OVERDRIVE old guard making
themselves known with a new project,
CROSSEYED MARY, featuring Svensson
and Thuresson.
Two tracks from OVERDRIVE's 1980 demo
'Overdrive' and '20th Century' would be
pressed up as a 7" picture disc during 2000.
This revival of interest in the band was further
fostered by the 2001 album 'Mission Of
Destruction' released by the American
Crook'D concern comprising live material
from 1982, the band's farewell gig at Gräsvik
in 1985 and their 1997 'Karlshamn Rock'
reunion gig. The Rock Treasures label
weighed in with re-issues of the original
albums adding bonus cuts in the form of five
demo tracks to 'Metal Attack ' and the
'Reflexions' EP material to 'Swords And
Axes'.
Stark issued his second volume of 'The
Encyclopaedia Of Swedish Hard Rock And
Heavy Metal' in September of 2002.

Singles/EPs:
Lady Luck / Girls Will Be Girls / High
Infidelity / You Give Me Hell / Reflexions,
Overdrive ODEP 1001 (1981)
Overdrive / 20th Century, Stormbringer
SKULL 9086P (2000)

Albums:

METAL ATTACK, Planet MOP 3025 (1983)
Back On The Hunt / Heart Of Stone /
Breakin' Out / Confused / Metal Attack / The
Battle / Doomwatch / Sweet Fear / Freelance
/ Time Will Tell
SWORDS AND AXES, Planet MOP 3029
(1984)
Away / Black Revenge / Fightin' Man / Burn
In Hell / Swords And Axes / Living In Sin /
Mission Of Destruction / Ode To Juliet /
Broken Hearted
MISSION OF DESTRUCTION, Crook'D
(2002)
Battle Of Rock / Doomwatch / Tonight / High
Infidelity / Out Of The Mist / Confused /
Midnight Cruiser / Lady Luck / Swords And
Axes / The Battle / Breaking Out / Burn In
Hell / Black Revenge / Mission Of
Destruction / Damnation Angel / Tonight

OVERLORDE (NJ, USA)

Line-Up: Pat O'Donnell (vocals), Mark
Edwards (guitar), John M. Bunucci (bass),
David L. Wrenn (drums)

New Jersey Metal band OVERLORDE was
created in 1985 comprising John 'Kong'
Bunucci of FINAL PLEA on vocals and bass,
PARTHENON guitarist Mark 'M.E.' Edwards
and drummer Dave Wrenn. This trio would put
in their inaugural live shows in December of
that year. In early 1986 Pat O'Donnell of
TROX took the lead vocal mantle for a five
track, self-financed EP. This outing combined
three studio tracks with live recordings of 'The
Longest Day' and 'Time Machine'.

OVERLORDE made a switch in singers to
Rod Tyler Loiza in 1988 but this revised act
only managed a handful of shows before
breaking up. Bunucci re-formed his previous
act FINAL PLEA whilst Edwards created
BREAKER M.E. Wrenn was to be found as
part of PERSIA.

OVERLORDE would reunite delivering not
only a well received demo but also Bavarian
beer tankards and even an official teddy bear!
This new version of the band would be fronted
by Bobby Lucas, known for his work with acts
such as SEVEN WITCHES, EXHIBITION and
MORBID SIN. The regrouped band made
their official live debut at the 2001 'Powermad'
festival. However, the band actually had
earlier put in an unannounced gig at Mel's
Tavern in Pennsylvania as a warm up.

Singles/EPs:

Snow Giant / The Masque Of The Red
Death / Overlorde / The Longest Day (Live) /
Time Machine (Live), Strike Zone SZR 101
(1987)

OZ (FINLAND)

Line-Up: Eero 'Ape De Martini' Hämäläinen
(vocals), Kari 'Spookie Wolf' Elo (guitar),
Tauno 'Jay C. Blade' Vajavaara (bass), Pekka
'Mark Ruffneck' Mark (drums)

Amongst the first Finnish Metal bands to
really make an impression, OZ were
responsible for recording the unintentionally
hilarious 'Turn The Cross Upside Down' single
in 1984.

Although OZ started life in Finland they would
eventually drift over to Sweden (a fact that
has often caused some confusion over the
nationality of the group), obviously recruiting
the odd Swedish musician along the way.
Whilst drummer Pekka Mark wound up being
the mainstay in the band, the only member of
OZ to appear on all five albums, vocalist Eero
Hämäläinen was eventually replaced by
Tapani Anshelm; Kari Elo by Swedish born
Michael Lundholm and Tauno Vajavaara by
Fredrik Thörnblorm (another Swede). The
enigmatic Speedy Fox was listed as guitarist
from the 'Fire In The Brain' album to 1986's
'Decibel Storm' release.

Bass player Tobbe Moen, later to join RED
FUN, has also been a member of OZ.

Singles/EPs:

Turn The Cross Upside Down / Gambler /
Search Lights, Tyfon Wave 12-8401 (1984)

Albums:

HEAVY METAL HEROES - HEY YOU, Wave
8005 (1982)
Hey You / Call From Your Eyes / Runnin' The
Line / Rather Knight / Saturday Knight /
Second-Hand Lady / In The Chains /
Capricorn Man
FIRE IN THE BRAIN, Wave 8006 (1983)
Search Lights / Fortune / Megalomaniac /
Black Candles / Gambler / Stop Believin' /
Free Me, Leave Me / Fire In The Brain
III WARNING, RCA PL 70564 (1984)
Third Warning / Crucified / Runner / Rock n'
Roll Widow / Samurai / Born Out Of Time /
To Bad To Be True / Total Metal
DECIBEL STORM, RCA PL 71024 (1986)
Eyes Of The Stranger / Starrider / Teenage
Rampage / Disaster Dreamer / Firestarter /
Exterminator / Black Tattoo / Sound Of
Speed / The Show Must Go On
ROLL THE DICE, Black Mark BMCD 11
(1991)
Roll The Dice / Last Generation / Rock On /
Midnight Lady / Runaway / Out Of Touch /
Thousand Miles / Alive / Not Enough / Night
Crime

PAGAN (SWEDEN)
Line-Up: Daniel Björnarås (vocals), Rolf Penoson (guitars), Ken Olsson (bass), Björn Öhrfeldt (drums)

PAGAN's music is overblown thunderous Metal. PAGAN started out in 1987 as a solo project by ex-SOLID bassist Ken Olsson and colleague Daniel Björnarås before recruiting a band to record the1989, Per Edwardsson produced demo.

The band's debut album, 'Pagan', secured a release with the U.S. Metal label and features a cover version of LED ZEPPELIN's 'Immigrant Song'.

For the second album, 'The Weight' in 1993, guitarists Mattias Eklundh of FATE, FREAK KITCHEN and BISCAYA's Martin Hedström also contributed. Björnarås also made way for former RAMPAGE vocalist Olof Lindgren. PAGAN now have a new guitarist in ex-ACHERON man Anders Fagerstrand.

Drummer Björn Öhrfeldt would become a temporary member of DESTINY during 1998. Anders Fagerstrand would also team up with DESTINY during 1999, featuring on recordings for DEMON and YNGWIE MALMSTEEN tracks for tribute albums.

Albums:
PAGAN, US Metal USCD18 (1990)
Deep Cutting Steel / Odin / Immigrant Song / Anyway But Backwards / Greg's Song / Dead Heroes / Call Of The Wolf / Northwind / Exordial Enlightenment / Damned
THE WEIGHT, Brave 93001 (1993)
Beyond Reach Of Tomorrow / Moral Poison / Strange Desire / The Key To Eternity / Weight Of The World / Lightbringer / Life Into Light / Puppet Show / In The Eyes Of The World

PAIN (GERMANY)
Line-Up: Stanley Falk (vocals / guitar), Peter Arrow (guitar), Andrew Sommer (bass), Andy Lee (drums)

Albums:
INSANITY, Noise (1986)
On My Knees / I'm Gonna Love / Spending The Night Alone / Call Of The Wild / (Intro) The Groove Of Love / Out For Tonight / It's Raining Blood / Insanity / Heavy Metal Warrior

PAIN OF SALVATION (SWEDEN)
Line-Up: Daniel Gildenlöw (vocals / guitar), Johan Hallgren (guitar), Kristoffer Gildenlöw (bass), Fredrik Hermansson (keyboards), Johan Langell (drums)

PAIN OF SALVATION, based out of Eskilstuna in Sweden, rank as one of the frontrunners of the mid '90s Progressive Rock boom in Europe. The group has released a commanding series of albums that has rapidly elevated the band to headline status. PAIN OF SALVATION's roots lay in the 1984 pre-teen act of vocalist / guitarist Daniel Gildenlöw REALITY. A bassist with this band, Magnus Johansson, would later join the renowned MESHUGGAH. By 1991 REALITY had switched titles to PAIN OF SALVATION.

In December of 1994 bassist Gustaf Hielm would be supplanted by the 16 year old Kristoffer Gildenlöw. A keyboard player, Fredrik Hermansson, was added to the ranks in the Autumn of 1996 and a subsequent demo secured a deal with the Swedish Roasting House label. The 'Entropia' record emerged in Japan on the Marquee label in August 1997 but would take a full two years to achieve a European release. As 1998 drew in guitarist Daniel Magdic decamped necessitating the recruitment of Johan Hallgren for the album 'One Hour By The Concrete Lake'.

This latest album was released in Asia late 1998, in Europe in early 1999 and in USA late 1999. Reaction to the record saw PAIN OF SALVATION jumping labels to the Inside Out concern. Touring would see the group in alliance with Britain's THRESHOLD and Italians ELDRITCH throughout Europe in March of 1999.

PAIN OF SALVATION, promoting the lavish concept album 'Perfect Element', headlined the Dutch 'Progpower' festival in 2000 and put in co-headline European dates with ARENA during September. Daniel Gildenlöw broke two fingers in an onstage fall on this trek and would perform many gigs with his arm in a plaster cast.

2001 would find PAIN OF SALVATION hitting the international festival circuit with gusto, headlining the February 'Progpower' event and even the European DREAM THEATER Fan Club Convention in Paris during May. At this latter event DREAM THEATER's Mike Portnoy deigned to jam with the band. Other festival appearances included the American 'Powermad' event as well as the Dutch 'Progpower' show.

Daniel Gildenlöw would join the Progressive "supergroup" TRANSATLANTIC for their November European tour dates. The Portnoy connection would be solidified in May of 2002 when it was revealed that Gildenlöw was to front the DREAM THEATER drummer's new side venture. Besides the PAIN OF SALVATION front man and Portnoy the group also cited an impressive cast list of erstwhile

DREAM THEATER and presently CHROMA KEY keyboard player Kevin Moore, FATES WARNING guitarist Jim Matheos, ex-CYNIC and current GORDIAN KNOT bassist Sean Malone. However, the following month Gildenlöw's involvement with the project would come to an end.

Singles/EPs:
Ashes (Radio edit) / Used (Album version) / The Big Machine / Ashes (Album version), Inside Out Music IOMCD070 (2000)

Albums:
ENTROPIA, Inside Out Music IOMCD040 (1997)
! (Foreward) / Welcome To Entropia / Winning A War / People Passing By / Oblivion Ocean / Stress / Revival / Void Of Her / To The End / Circles / Nightmist / Plains Of Dawn / Leaving Entropia (Epilogue)
ONE HOUR BY THE CONCRETE LAKE, Inside Out Music IOMCD030 (1998)
Spirit Of The Land / Inside / The Big Machine / New Years Eve / Handful Of Nothing / Water / Home / Black Hills / Pilgrim / Shore Serenity / Inside Out
THE PERFECT ELEMENT - PART 1, Inside Out Music IOMA2019-2 (2000)
Used / In ThLe Flesh / Ashes / Morning On Earth / Idioglossia / Her Voices / Dedication / King Of Loss / Reconciliation / Song For The Innocent / Falling / The Perfect Element
THE PERFECT ELEMENT - LIMITED EDITION, Inside Out Music IOMCD067 (2000)
Used / In The Flesh / Ashes / Morning On Earth / Idioglossia / Her Voices / Dedication / King Of Loss / Reconciliation / Song For The Innocent / Falling / The Perfect Element / Beyond The Mirror / Never Learn To Fly / Time Weaver's Tale / Ashes (Video) / The Making Of Ashes (Video) / Interview / ! (Video) / Pilgrim (Video) / The Big Machine (Video) / Time Weaver's Tale (Demo) / Repent (Demo) / Unknowing (Demo)
REMEDY LANE, Inside Out Music IOMCD092 (2002)
Of Two Beginnings / Ending Theme / Fandango / A Trace Of Blood / This Heart Of Mine / Undertow / Rope Ends / Chain Sling / Dryad Of The Woods / Remedy Lane / Waking Every God / Second Love / Beyond The Pale

PANDÆMONIUM (ITALY)
Line-Up: Daniel Reda (vocals), Alex Niall (guitar), Ragman (guitar), Lorenzo Zirilli (bass), Giulio Capone (keyboards), Simone Barbieri (drums)

During January of 2001 guitarist Ragman and drummer Simone Barbieri made their exit to found a new act BOD. In March PANDÆMONIUM's line-up was struck again when second guitarist Alex Niall disembarked too.

Albums:
...AND THE RUNES BEGIN TO PRAY, Underground Symphony USCD035 (1999)
The Alchemist / Birth Of The Fallen Angel / Sabbath Day / Wings Of The Wind / The Dark Before… / The War Of Races / ...The Light / Lone Warrior / Pandæmonium / The Alchemist (Piano version)

PARADOX (GERMANY)
Line-Up: Charly Steinhauer (vocals / guitar), Markus Spyth (guitar), Roland Stahl (bass), Axel Blaha (drums)

A late '80s Speed Metal band from Würzburg founded in February of 1986. Founder members frontman Charly Steinhauer and drummer Axel Blaha are both ex-WARHEAD with other original members being guitarist Markus Spyth and bass player Roland Stahl. A July 1986 demo scored a deal with the Roadrunner label that November. The band cut a further demo 'Mystery' in 1987 and had the track 'Pray To The Godz Of Wrath' featured as the lead track on the compilation 'Teutonic Invasion', before their Roadrunner deal resulted in a Kalle Trapp produced debut 'Product Of Imagination' in 1988.
'Product Of Imagination' brought the band enormous rewards in their homeland, PARADOX being voted by both 'Rock Hard' and 'Metal Hammer' magazines as best newcomer act and coming only behind established veterans SCORPIONS and ACCEPT as highest regarded German band. Touring in December of 1987 had the band on the road with Swiss act DRIFTER. The group also chalked up important festival appearances at the infamous Dutch 'Dynamo' event and the 'Festa Avante' in Portugal.
A new look PARADOX recorded the Harris Johns produced second album, 'Heresy', the band having drafted new guitarist Dieter Roth and bassist Matthias Schmitt. Erstwhile CRONOS TITAN guitarist Kai Paseman was recruited in November of 1989 but shortly after PARADOX would then go into a period of hibernation. Paseman founded the KRAUTS, an act which evolved into DECLARATION OF DEPENDENCE issuing two albums.
PARADOX were reunited for a 'Wacken Open Air' show in August of 1999. Joining Steinhauer and Paseman would be the

esteemed SIEGES EVEN sibling rhythm section of bass player Oliver and drummer Alex Holzwarth. Besides making their mark with Progressive Metal act SIEGES EVEN the brothers have contributed to many other high profile acts - Oliver to BLIND GUARDIAN and Alex to Italian Symphonic Metal band RHAPSODY and Brazilians ANGRA.

The 'Collision Course' album arrived in Germany during August of 2000 and issued later in North America through Century Media and in Japan through King Records. The album closed with a notable cover version of the SCORPIONS 'Dynamite'. Japanese versions of the album came with no less than three extra tracks: 'Pray To The Godz Of Wrath', 'Paradox' and 'Execution'. The band also contributed to a Nuclear Blast ABBA tribute album.

Oliver Holzwarth later teamed up with DEMONS & WIZARDS.

The band was dealt a double blow in early 2002 as Steinhauer, due to a medical condition, was ordered by doctors not to sing again and guitarist Kai Pasemann opted out to pursue a career in law.

Albums:
PRODUCT OF IMAGINATION, Roadrunner RR9563 (1988)
Opening Theme / Paradox / Death, Screaming And Pain / Product Of Imagination / Continuation Of Invasion / Mystery / Kill That Beast / Pray To The Gods Of Wrath / Beyond Space / Wotan II
HERESY, Roadracer RO 9506-1 (1989)
Heresy / Search For Perfection / Killtime / Crusaders Revenge / The Burning / Massacre Of The Cathars / Serenity / 700 Years On / Castle In The Wind
COLLISION COURSE, AFM CD 042 (2000)
Decade Of Sorrow / Collision Course / Rearrange The Past / Path of Denial / Saviour / Blamed For Nothing / Prostitution Of Society / Shattered Illusions / Sadness / Over-Shadowed / Dynamite

PARAGON (GERMANY)

Line-Up: Andreas Babuschkin (vocals), Claudius Cremer (guitar), Martin Christian (guitar), Jan Bünning (bass), Markus Corby (drums)

A respected Hamburg based Power Metal act formed in 1990 by guitarist Martin Christian, PARAGON released their first demo in 1992 titled 'Enter The Crypt' and a further tape a year later 'Maelstrom Of Decline'. Having also contributed one song on the 'Peace Eater Vol. 3' compilation the group released their debut self-financed album, 'Into The Black', in 1994

on which new vocalist Kay Carstens - previously with the AC/DC cover band BON SCOTT for six years - appeared for the first time.

The group supported WARPATH, GOREFEST, POLTERGEIST, INCUBATOR and RUMBLE MILITIA and at the end of '94 PARAGON began work on what would become second album 'World Of Sin'. The band at this stage numbered Carstens, Christian, second guitarist Daniel Görner - previously a member of BAD INFLUENCE, bass player Dirk Sturzbecher and drummer Kay Noise. However, in 1996 Christian would put the band on ice for a period. Eventually PARAGON regrouped with Christian convening an all new line-up comprising new faces vocalist Andreas Babuschkin and erstwhile ENTIRE DEFEAT bass player Jan Bünning alongside former personnel drummer Markus Corby and guitarist Claudius Cremer.

In the Autumn of 1997 the band entered the Spiderhouse studios to cut the Harris Johns produced comeback album 'The Final Command'. Signing to the Bossy Ogress label the album, which featured a take on WARRIOR's 'Fighting For The Earth', emerged in August of 1998. Although reviews were laudatory PARAGON could not hook up with any decent tours and so opted for a quick return to the studio in January of 1999. Working with Harris Johns again the band duly delivered the 'Chalice Of Steel' album that year. A bonus track on this album proved to be a rendition of EXCITER's 'Violence And Force'.

The band severed connections with Bossy Ogress and crafted a three track demo comprising 'Thunderstorm', 'Deathsquad' and 'New Dark Age' in order to locate another label, soon receiving an offer from Hamburg based Remedy Records. 'Steelbound' would be produced by Piet Sielck of IRON SAVIOR. Recording of the drums for this album would be in the capable hands of HELLOWEEN's Markus Großkopf and SHOCK MACHINE's Karsten Kreppert.

Upon release 'Steelbound' became the subject of exemplary reviews from the top German Metal press such as 'Rock Hard' and 'Metal Hammer' magazines. Road work saw the band acting as openers for IRON SAVIOR throughout April and May of 2001 as well as a valuable showing at the 'Wacken Open Air' festival.

PARAGON would retain the successful partnership with Piet Sielck for the May 2002 opus 'Law Of The Blade'. As well as a limited edition vinyl picture disc format Remedy also issued a digipack version with a bonus track, a cover of SAXON's 'To Hell And Back Again'.

329

Live dates had PARAGON as support to both SAXON and VIRGIN STEELE in the summer of 2002. The band donated their version of 'Metal Invader' to an Arise Records HELLOWEEN tribute offering.

Albums:
INTO THE BLACK, Paragon LC 5448 (1994)
Into The Black / Bring The Hammer Down / Sinister Rising / Crossed Out / Torn And Frayed
WORLD OF SIN, Blue Merle Edel 0086222 (1995)
Intro / Needful Things / Maelstrom Of Decline / World Of Sin / Beyond The Void / Thrill Of The Kill / No Hope For Life / Into The Black / Drug Fiend / Bring The Hammer Down
THE FINAL COMMAND, Bossy Ogress (1998)
Feel The Knife / Under The Gun / Eternal Life / Ashes / Warriors Of Ice / Fighting For The Earth / War Inside My Head / The Final Command / Eye For An Eye
CHALICE OF STEEL, Bossy Ogress (1999)
Intro - Awakening Of The Beast / Dragon's Flight / Legions Of Metal / Chalice Of Steel / Wheels Of Eternity / Desecrate / Dark Tale / Casting Shadows / Burn At The Stake / Journey Home / A.D. 2000 / Violence And Force
STEELBOUND, Remedy (2001)
Thunderstorm / Steelbound / Deathsquad / New Dark Age / Don't Wake The Dead / Reign Of Fear / Burning Bridges / Tears Of The Damned / Face II Face / Immortal / World Of Sin
LAW OF THE BLADE, Remedy (2002)
Abducted / Palace Of Sin / Armies Of The Tyrant / Law Of The Blade / Across The Wastelands / Shadow World / Allied Forces / Empire's Fall / The Journey's End / Back To Globy / To Hell And Back Again

PARALYSIS (HOLLAND)
Line-Up: Nick Davies (vocals / guitar), Fausto Dhanis (guitar), Roger de Rijke (bass), Stephen van Haestregt (drums)

An aggressive Power Metal act, PARALYSIS emerged during 1987, soon cutting the 'State Of Shock' demo. The following year the band weathered its first line-up changes as drummer Andre Nijssen was replaced by SACRAMENT man Stephen van Haestregt. Subsequently singer Mark de Smit opted out, being substituted by Stephen's brother Jean-Paul. A new demo recording 'Trivial Round Of Life' in 1989 afforded PARALYSIS some valuable live action supporting the likes of DONOR, WHIPLASH and SADUS amongst others. The band then set about laying down tracks for a third tape but in the midst of these sessions Jean-Paul Haestregt broke ranks. The tracks were completed with the aid of Lex Vogelaar, known on the scene for his contributions to TARGET, ORPHANAGE and LYCANTHROPE.

Drafting Englishman Nick Davies PARALYSIS embarked upon crafting a fresh demo 'Arctic Sleep'. However, the band judged the results so highly this would in fact emerge as the group's first commercial product in 1992. The band self-produced their 'Visions' album, later re-recording two songs from the record for the mini-album released by the Defrosting label a year later.

Guitarist Fausto Dhanis quit the group after the 1995 release, the band bringing in twin guitarists Eric Bos and a returning Jean-Paul van Haestregt.

Signing to the German AFM label PARALYSIS recorded the 'Architecture Of The Imagination' album, released in May of 2000. Drummer Stephen van Haestregt would loan himself out to WITHIN TEMPTATION in June of 2002.

Albums:
ARCTIC SLEEP, (1992)
Intifadah / Special Operations Executive / Powers Of Olo / Inhuman (E) / Arctic Sleep
VISIONS, Paralysis (1994)
Altered States / Passages I / Experimental Factor Genocide / Lost In The Darkness / The Waters Cry / Point Of No return / Twisted / Tardis / Without Shadow Of A Doubt / Passages II / In Memoriam / Enemies Within / Escape From Yesterday / Sunitpar
WONDERLAND, Defrosting 2-K (1995)
Wonderland / In Memoriam (Remix) / My Room / Escape From Yesterday / Inhumane (Re-Edit)
ARCHITECTURE OF THE IMAGINATION, AFM (2000)
No One / Picture Picture / Visions / Broken / Fly / The Truth / Architecture Of The Imagination / Shallow / Footsteps / Trip / Empty Head

PARAZITE (SWEDEN)
Line-Up: Larsa Bengtsson (vocals), Ola Renske (guitar), Linkan Andersson (guitar), Martin Karlsson (bass), Geron Fritofsson (drums)

A Swedish band with a liking for Speed Metal.

Singles/EPs:
Live In Pain / A Different Kind Of Livin' / Bastard / Cry Baby, Parazite PZCD001 (1994)

330

PARIAH (UK)
Line-Up: Mick Jackson (vocals), Steve Ramsey (guitar), Russ Tippins (guitar), Graeme English (bass), Sean Taylor (drums).

Formed from SATAN, a band that achieved great success in Europe on the German Steamhammer label, PARIAH was basically the same band, but a name change was thought in order due to the connotations of the old monicker.

The first album was recorded with producer Roy Rowland. Unfortunately, 'The Kindred' was never given a British release as PARIAH concentrated on the lucrative European market.

The second album, recorded at Horus Studios and produced by the band, built upon the success of the debut and proved that the name change had been the correct move as PARIAH albums sold in greater numbers than previous SATAN records. However, PARIAH folded amidst financial wranglings with their record company, even though a third album was recorded at Links Studios in Newcastle during 1993. It remained unreleased, but the band that recorded it featured guitarists Steve Ramsey and Russ Tippins, bassist Graeme English, ex-SATAN and BATTLEAXE drummer Ian McCormack and former TYSONDOG vocalist Alan Hunter.

As Ramsey and English went on to form the excellent Folk Metal band SKYCLAD erstwhile drummer Sean Taylor joined BLITZKRIEG.

The 1993 recordings were finally issued by the band members themselves as 'Unity' in 1997.

Albums:
THE KINDRED, Steamhammer 08-7526 (1988)
Gerrymander / The Rope / Scapegoat / Foreign Bodies / La Guerra / Inhumane / Killing For Company / Icons Of Hypocrisy / Promise Of Remembrance
BLAZE OF OBSCURITY, Steamhammer SPV 85-7595 (1989)
Missionary Of Mercy / Puppet Regime / Canary / Blaze Of Obscurity / Retaliate! / Hypochondriac / Enemy Within / The Brotherhood
UNITY, (1997)
Unity / Reactionary / Walking Wounded / No Exit / Snakes & Ladders / One Of Us / Saboteurs / Mutual Street / The Jonah / Learning To Crawl

PATRIARCH (BELGIUM)
Line-Up: Herman Cambre (vocals), Jan Geerts (guitar), Freddy Mylemans (guitar), Paul Verboven (bass), Herman Cambre (drums)

Originally known as PARIAH and formed by guitarist Freddy Mylemans in March 1983. The band issued a self-titled demo the same year followed in 1984 by a second four track tape 'Evil Wings'. The band had to be put on ice in 1988 when bassist Jan T'Seyen was killed in a road accident. However, before the end of the year the band had re-formed (confusingly with a vocalist and drummer that share the same name!), but due to press coverage of the British version of PARIAH opted to change titles to PATRIARCH. A new demo secured a deal with German label Shark Records.

Following two albums PATRIARCH split with their label and underwent a massive line-up change. Only guitarist Freddy Mylemans remained from the original line-up as he was joined by new members in vocalist Erik Rinkes, guitarist Jan Van Bulck, bassist Paul Verboven and drummer Frank Dresselaers.

This line-up released a demo in 1995 featuring 'Parade Of Fools', 'The End Of The Day', 'I Machine' and 'Changing Matter'.

Albums:
PROPHECY, Shark 016 (1991)
At The Warlord's Command / Dance / Children Of The Moon / Shadowland / Father Kreator / Castle Of Darkness / Kmar-Q-Luque / Island Of Insanity / Prophecy / Pilgrims Of The Dark Age
WORLD WITHIN WORLDS, Rock Power R.P. 003 (1993)
Leviathans / The Watching Eve / Lady Of The Lines / Steleas Of Ghorfa (instrumental) / World Within Worlds / Decadence Within / Burning Grounds / Forsaken Wisdom / Strange Reality

PAYNE'S GREY (GERMANY)
Line-Up: Hagen Schmidt (vocals), Huluk Balikei (vocals), Jan Schröeder (guitar / flute), Martin Mannhardt (bass), Tomek Turek (keyboards), Axel Baudendistel (drums)

PAYNE'S GREY formed in 1989 and were quick to release two demos, the second of which (1992's 'Infinity') receiving a great deal of critical acclaim.

Having been spurred on by the father of vocalist Hagen Schmidt, PAYNE'S GREY promptly wrote the music to the 'Kadath Decoded' album based upon one of H.P. Lovecraft novels.

This self-financed CD, with a running time of some 70 minutes, debuted in December 1995 although the group would subsequently endure problems in trying to keep a permanent keyboard player in the ranks.

PAYNE'S GREY's original choice, Tomek Turek, also played in an orchestra and was forced to leave the group due to his commitments in that area. His replacement, Michael Ehninger, became too busy with his own band SYNERGETIC DIVERSITY and thus a tour with PSYCHOTIC WALTZ in Europe was undertaken with TALIESYN man Rüdiger Blank.

In addition to PAYNE'S GREY, Haluk Balikei also performs with his NARCISS side project.

Albums:
KADATH DECODED, Grau GRAU001 (1996)
Dream Sequence / Sunset City / The Cavern Of Flame / Moonlight Waters / Procession / A Hymn To The Cats / The Way To Ngranek / Within The Vault / Reaching Kadeth / Nyarlathoteps Reception / Riding The Shantak / Finale: Sunset City (Part Two)

PEGAZUS (AUSTRALIA)
Line-Up: Rob Thompson (vocals), Johnny Stoj (guitar), Hanny Mohamed (bass), Robbie Stoj (drums)

ROB THOMPSON of PEGAZUS

A no frills Victoria based band on a mission to resurrect unpretentious Heavy Metal complete with studs and leather to match. PEGAZUS scored notable exposure by landing a deal with the German Nuclear Blast label for their second album 'Wings Of Destiny'. PEGAZUS was created in 1993 by the Stojcevski brothers, guitarist Johnny and drummer Robbie, first performing live, and breaking a club attendance record to boot, in August of 1994. The Stojcevskis, better known simply as 'Stoj', had previously plied their trade with THE BOYS IN BLACK and THIN LIZZY cover band LIVE N' DANGEROUS. The band's debut album, an eponymous effort recorded in under a week and delivered in 1995 on the band's own Pegazus Music label, featured lead vocalist Justin Flemming and bassist Dave King.

Flemming would make his exit and for a short term PEGAZUS operated as a trio with Johnny Stoj taking on the lead vocal role. In May of 1996 Danny Cecati was brought onboard for recording of demo which comprised two new originals, 'Mothers Earth' and 'Witches Hex', alongside covers of JUDAS PRIEST's 'Victim Of Changes' and BLACK SABBATH's 'Symptom Of The Universe'. A second self-financed album then followed in 'Wings Of Destiny'. This opus would duly be picked up by the German Nuclear Blast label, repackaged with all new artwork and reissued for the European market.

PEGAZUS put in an appearance at the 1998 'Wacken Open Air' and 'Rock Hard' Metal festivals in Germany during August of 1998 and also toured Europe later in the year as support to HAMMERFALL, PRIMAL FEAR and LABYRINTH. For these shows PEGAZUS drafted bassist Eric Martin.

The Australians would lend their no compromise version of ACCEPT's 'Restless And Wild' classic to a Nuclear Blast 1999 tribute album. For their third effort 'Breaking The Chains' PEGAZUS pulled in former AMETHYST, SPARTACUS and STARCHAMBER bassist Corey Betts. The band would also figure on the Nuclear Blast compilation 'Death Is Just The Beginning Volume 6", donating a rendition of BLACK SABBATH's 'Time Machine'.

Vocalist Danny Cecati left the band in 1999 for ANARION. He would be superseded by Rob Thompson, a veteran of SWEET CYANIDE, HEADRUSH and POWERSURGE. With this line-up PEGAZUS bowed in with their fourth offering 'The Headless Horseman'. However, an interim THIN LIZZY tribute EP, with Johnny Stoj on lead vocals, had been in the works, the band cutting an original composition 'Ballad Of A Thin Man' in honour of PHIL LYNNOT and two THIN LIZZY covers in 'Warriors' and 'Jailbreak'. As it transpired 'Ballad Of A Thin Man' would turn up on the 'Headless

Horseman' album.

Bassist Corey Betts would announce his departure but stayed on for the recording sessions. Betts had been for some time involved with ARKAYA, an act that evolved from KYMERA. Featuring vocalist John Gio, CYCLONE TRACY guitarist Steve Janevski and AMETHYST drummer Vestra ARKAYA, for a brief spell, also had erstwhile PEGAZUS frontman Danny Cecati as their lead vocalist. The ties between PEGAZUS and ARKAYA were strengthened when it was learned that ARKAYA guitarist Hanny Mohamed had taken the bass position vacancy in PEGAZUS, coincidentally just as Betts short lived tenure with ARKAYA had come to an end. Mohamed would maintain a foot in both camps.

Albums:
PEGAZUS, Pegazus Music (1995)
Apache Warriors / Bastards Of War / Speed Demon / Cry For The Angel / Pain Is My Friend / Pegasus / Our Father And The Holy Ghost / King Of The Jungle / Free As A Bird / Past Life / I'm On Fire
WINGS OF DESTINY, Metal Warriors MFM 767 (1997)
Wings Of Steel / Cry Out / Braveheart / Mother Earth / Enchanted World / Life On Mars (Instrumental) / The Werewolf / Witches Hex / Destiny
BREAKING THE CHAINS, Nuclear Blast NB 420-2 (1999)
Metal Forever / The Crusade / Queen Evil / Breaking The Chains / Tears Of The Angels / Chariot Of The Gods / Emerald Eyes / Bastards Of War / Apache Warrior / A Little Time
THE HEADLESS HORSEMAN, Nuclear Blast NB 716-2 (2002)
The Headless Horseman / Nightstalker / A Call To Arms / The Patriot / Look To The Stars / Dragon Slayer / Spread Your Wings / Forever Chasing Rainbows / Victim / Neon Angel / Ballad Of A Thin Man

AXEL RUDI PELL (GERMANY)

German guitar hero Axel Rudi Pell learnt his chops in the Bochum based outfit he originally founded as SINNER in 1980, namely STEELER. Having quit the group in November 1988 due to his frustration with the band's direction, SPV took up their option on him as a solo artist.

The label boss, Manfred Schultz had been so impressed with a three track demo recorded by Pell (featuring the tracks 'Broken Heart', 'Cold As Ice' and 'Promised Dreams', recorded with one-time STEELER vocalist Karl Holthaus), that he had no hesitation in offering the guitarist a deal.

In recording his first solo foray, 'Wild Obsession', Axel chose to work with ex-VICTORY vocalist Charlie Huhn alongside bassists Bodo Smuszinsky, BONFIRE's Jörg Deisinger and Pell's erstwhile STEELER colleague Volker Krawczak, with former AVENGER, RAGE and MEKONG DELTA drummer Jörg Michael rounding things out.

'Nasty Reputation' features former JOSHUA, M.A.R.S. and DRIVER vocalist ROB ROCK and features a reputable cover of the DEEP PURPLE ballad 'When A Blind Man Cries'. Jörg Michael once again handled drum duties whilst bass parts were supplied by Volker Krawczak.

With dates lined up in Europe as part of a 'Metal Hammer' sponsored tour Rock dropped a bombshell when he announced he had prior commitments to IMPELLITERRI. Pell sought 'Aardschok' magazine editor Metal Mike regarding a replacement and JEFF SCOTT SOTO was duly suggested. The former YNGWIE MALMSTEEN man stepped into the breach to fulfil the tour dates.

'Eternal Prisoner' debuted Soto and included keyboard contributions from Kai Raglewski of THE DUNE. 'The Ballads' album followed, the record being a compilation of Pell's lighter career moments to date including a Karl Holterhaus version of 'Broken Heart'. This album, the first of a series, sold well and highlighted Pell's appeal to the female market. 1994's 'Between The Walls' found Pell's band line-up of Krawczak, Michael and Soto stable with new keyboard player Julie Greaux, previously a member of BILLY IDOL's band. Pell's debut live effort 'Live In Germany' continued the upward sales trend.

Soto also sang on the subsequent releases 'Black Moon Pyramid' and 'Magic' despite his other commitments to numerous band projects including TAKARA and TALISMAN. Soto was also earning a crust fronting Las Vegas '70s covers act BOOGIE NIGHTS! 'Black Moon Pyramid' caught RAGE's Peavey Wagner sessioning on bass.

1998's 'Oceans Of Time' found Pell, Krawczak and Michael joined be former KILLERHIT, BRUNETTE and HARDLINE vocalist Johnny Gioeli and ROUGH SILK keyboard player Ferdy Doernberg.

The 2000 "best of" album 'The Wizard's Chosen Few' included two new numbers 'Ghosthunter' and 'Broken Dreams'. Between bouts of working with Pell drummer Jörg Michael has also racked up credits with HEADHUNTER, LAOS, GLENMORE, GRAVE DIGGER, STRATOVARIUS and RUNNING WILD.

Pell made a 2002 return to action with the April 'Shadow Zone' album. His band for this

AXEL RUDI PELL
Photo : Nico Wobben

outing numbered vocalist Johnny Gioeli, bassist Volker Krawczak, keyboard player Ferdy Doernberg and drummer Mike Terrana. The latter, a permanent member of RAGE, also boasts terms with YNGWIE MALMSTEEN, METALIUM and ARTENSION. Promoting 'Shadow Zone' Pell geared up for headline European dates taking out on the road female backing singers as part of his band and support act SOUL DOCTOR. A live album culled from these dates, billed as 'Knights Live', would be scheduled for later the same year. This release would be accompanied by a DVD release 'Knight Treasures (Live & More)' which included backstage footage, the promotional video for 'The Cry Of The Gypsy' plus the archive STEELER video 'The Deeper The Night'.

Singles/EPs:

(Hear You) Calling Me / (Don't Trust The) Promised Dreams, Steamhammer (1989)
Broken Heart / Wild Cat, Steamhammer 001 76156 (1990)
Forever Young / Your Life (Not Close Enough To Paradise), Steamhammer 855-76663 (1993)

Albums:

WILD OBSESSION, Steamhammer (1989)
Wild Cat / Call Of The Wild Dogs / Slave Of Love / Cold As Ice / Broken Heart / Call Her Princess / Snake Eyes / Hear You Calling Me / Return Of The Calyph From The Apocalypse Of Babylon / (Don't Trust The) Promised Dreams
NASTY REPUTATION, Steamhammer SPV 084 67342 (1991)
I Will Survive / Nasty Reputation / Fighting The Law / Wanted Man / When A Blind Man Cries / Land Of The Giants / Firewall / Unchain The Thunder / Open Doors:- Part One - Experience, Part Two - The Journey , Part Three - Sugar Big Daddy
ETERNAL PRISONER, Steamhammer SPV 084-76602 (1992)
Streets Of Fire / Long Time / Eternal Prisoner / Your Life (Not Close Enough To Paradise) / Wheels Rolling On / Sweet Lil' Suzie / Dreams Of Passion / Shoot Her To The Moon / Ride The Bullet
THE BALLADS, Steamhammer SPV 084-76642 (1993)
You Want Love / Forever Young / Dreams Of Passion / Your Life (Not Close Enough To Paradise) / Tearin' Out My Heart / When A Blind Man Cries / Broken Heart (Demo Version) / Open Doors (Part Two: The Journey) / Falling Tears / Broken Heart (Guitar Version)
BETWEEN THE WALLS, Steamhammer

SPV 084-76822 (1994)
The Curse / Talk Of The Guns / Warrior / Cry Of The Gypsy / Casbah / Outlaw / Wishing Well / Innocent Child / Between The Walls / Desert Fire
MADE IN GERMANY (LIVE), Steamhammer SPV 085-76972 (1995)
Talk Of The Guns / Nasty Reputation / Mistreated / Warrior / Snake Eyes / Casbah (Inc. Eternal Prisoner) / Call Her Princess / Fire On The Mountain
BLACK MOON PYRAMID, Steamhammer SPV 085-18282 (1996)
Return Of The Pharoah / Gettin' Dangerous / Fool Fool / Hole In The Sky / Touch The Rainbow / Sphinx's Revenge / You And I / Silent Angel / Black Moon Pyramid / Serenade Of Darkness (Opus 1 Adagio Con Agresso) / Visions In The Night / Aqua Solution / Aquarius Dance / Silent Angel (Guitar Version)
MAGIC, Steamhammer SPV 085-18362 CD (1997)
Swamp Castle Overture (Intro) / Nightmare / Playing With Fire / Magic / Turned To Stone / The Clown Is Dead / Prisoners Of The Sea / Light In The Sky / The Eyes Of The Lost
OCEANS OF TIME, Steamhammer SPV (1998) **58 GERMANY**
Slaves Of The Twilight (Intro) / Pay The price / Carousel / Ashes From The Oath / Ride The Rainbow / The Gates Of The Seven Seals / Oceans Of Time / Prelude To The Moon / Living On The Wildside / Holy Creatures
THE BALLADS II, Steamhammer SPV (1999)
Come Back To Me / Broken Heart / The Clown Is Dead / Oceans Of Time / I Believe In You / Ashes From The Oath / Silent Angel (Guitar version) / The Eyes Of The Lost / Innocent Child / Silent Angel / Hey Joe
MASQUERADE BALL, SPV (2000) **37 GERMANY**
Carousel / The Masquerade Ball / Ghosthunter / Oceans Of Time / Still I'm Sad / Come Back To Me / Burn - Purple Haze - Call Her Princess / Total Eclipse Opus 2 Allegro E Andantté / Eternal Prisoner / Fool Fool / Casbah / Snake Eyes (Live) / Mistreated (Live) / Magic / The Clown Is Dead / Nasty Reputation / Land Of The Giants / Hear You Calling Me
THE WIZARD'S CHOSEN FEW, SPV (2000)
Broken Dreams / Carousel / The Masquerade Ball / Ghosthunter / Oceans Of Time / Still I'm Sad / Come Back To Me / Burn - Purple Haze - Call Her Princess / Total Eclipse Opus 2 Allegro E Andantté / Eternal Prisoner / Fool Fool / Casbah / Snake Eyes (Live) / Mistreated (Live) / Magic / The Clown Is Dead / Nasty Reputation /

335

Land Of The Giants / Hear You Calling Me
SHADOWZONE, SPV (2002) **22 GERMANY**
The Curse Of The Chains (Intro) / Edge Of
The World / Coming Home / Live For The
King / Follow The Sign / Heartbreaker / Saint
Of Fools / Time Of The Truth / All The Rest
Of My Life / Under The Gun
KNIGHTS LIVE, SPV (2002)
Edge Of The World / Nasty Reputation / Tear
Down The Walls / Medley: Masquerade Ball -
Casbah - Drum Solo - Stargazer - Casbah /
Follow The Sign / Fool Fool / Carousel / The
Clown Is Dead / Call Her Princess / Snake
Eyes / Warrior

PHANTOM LORD (BELGIUM)
Line-Up: Simon Berger (vocals / guitar),
Gunther Wassel (guitar), Klaus Schwartzen
(bass), Wolfgang Gundermann (drums)

Albums:
PHANTOM LORD, Pentagram (1985)
Live Fast, Rock Hard / Mad Bash / Hang
Tough / I'm In H.E.A.T. / Mach Ten / Speed
Kills / Fight The Thunder / Phantom Lord /
White Fire
EVIL NEVER SLEEPS, LSR (1986)
Speed Demons / Highway Of Death / Call Of
The Wild / Battle Zone (Guitar Solo) / Evil
Never Sleeps / Mercy Killer / Wicked World /
Avenging Angels

PHOENIX RIZING (NORWAY)
Line-Up: Tom R. Piippo (vocals), Jack R.
Olsen (guitar), Yngve Olsen (guitar), Knut
Egil Tøftum (bass), Morten Pettersen
(drums)

Norwegian Symphonic Metal band PHOENIX
RIZING rose from a previous 1994 act entitled
TWILIGHT CENTURY. With this group Tom
Piippo handled both lead vocals and drums.
TWILIGHT CENTURY dissolved in 1995 but
would shortly after reconvene re-billed as
PHOENIX RIZING. New recruits would be
bass player Knut Egil Tøftum and Morten
Pettersen.
The 'Rise From The Ashes' debut surfaced in
1998 on Facefront Records, a division of the
Voices Of Wonder label.

Albums:
RISE FROM THE ASHES, Facefront FF004
(1998)
Rise From The Ashes / Enclosed By Your
Destiny / Without Warning / Released /
Under A Crimson Sky / The Challenge /
Army Of The Lost Souls / Messengers Of
War / Dark Clouds Gathering / Roses Are
Red

POISON ASP (GERMANY)
Line-Up: Tosse (vocals / guitar), Michel
(guitar), Robby (bass), Crisse (drums)

Singles/EPs:
Intro - Hellfire At The Airbase / Euthanasia
/ Beyond The Walls Of Sleep / I Am The
Grass / Traitor, Semaphore (1990) ('Beyond
The Walls Of Sleep' EP)

POWERGOD (GERMANY)
Line-Up: Leo L. Sing (vocals), Riff Randall
(guitar / bass), Hama Hart (drums)

The anonymous Metal band POWERGOD
debuted in 1999 on the Massacre label with
their 'Evilution Part I' opus. The line-up
purported to be vocalist Leo. L. Sing, guitarist
Riff Randall, actually former SODOM six
stringer Andy Brings, and drummer Haan
'Hama Hart' Hartmann. For the sophomore
release of 2000 'President Evil' (Alex Koch) of
SPIRAL TOWER took the vocal position.
A third album, 'Bleed For The Gods', arrived in
October 2001 and proved to comprise solely
of cover versions of '80s Metal classics.
Honoured artists included SAVAGE GRACE,
AGENT STEEL, METAL CHURCH,
CHASTAIN, MANOWAR, HEAR N' AID,
WARLOCK, NASTY SAVAGE, YNGWIE
MALMSTEEN, Q5, TNT, ANTHRAX,
STRYPER, DRIVER, HALLOWS EVE and
LIZZY BORDEN. Guest session players
included ROUGH SILK keyboard player
FERDY DOERNBERG, vocalist ROB ROCK
as well as members of WARLOCK, AGENT
STEEL, STORMWIND, HOLY MOSES and
even 'Rock Hard' magazine head supremo
Gotz Kuhnemund (a.k.a. 'Sir Pommes').
POWERGOD would head up a European set
of dates during October of 2002 billed with
CHINCHILLA, and VALLEY'S EVE. The band
also cut a version of HELLOWEEN's
'Starlight' for a tribute album and also a take
on BLACK SABBATH's 'Neon Knights' for the
WW3 collection 'Back To The Stonehenge
Gods - A Tribute To Black Sabbath'.
Bass player Jörg Andraczek would be
appointed for live work.

Albums:
EVILUTION PART I, Massacre MAS
CD0187 (1999)
Children Of Lost Horizons / No Brain, No
Pain / Mean, Clean, Fighting Machine / Gods
Of War / Into The Battle / Salvation / I'm On
Fire / Evilution Part 1: Overture In Black
Minor / Evilution Part 1: The Gates Of Hades
/ Evilution Part 1: Hero's Tears / Evilution
Part 1: Rising
EVILUTION PART II: BACK TO ATTACK,

Massacre (2000)
Back To Attack / Lost Illusions / The Eagle &
The Rainbow / Anybody Home / Temple Of
The Forbidden Eye / Observator / Powergod
/ Prisoner / Esper / Evilution Part II
BLEED FOR THE GODS, Massacre (2001)
Lion's Roar - Bound To Be Free / Bleed For
The Godz / Metal Church / Ruler Of The
Wasteland / Kill With Power / Stars / Burning
The Witches / I´m A Viking / X X X / Steel
The Light / Tor With The Hammer /
Madhouse / Metal Merchants / Red Rum /
Soldiers Under Command / You And I
EVILUTION III - NEMESIS, Massacre (2002)
Dead Serious / Call Of Freedom / Courtroom
Of Traitors / Massacre Machinery / Got Milk?
/ Parting Gift / Reduced To The Maximum /
Monsterman / 6-4-5 / Evilution Part III

POWER OF OMENS

(San Antonio, TX, USA)
Line-Up: Chris Salinas (vocals), Dave
Gallegos (guitar), Henry Sanchez (bass),
Andrew Sanchez (keyboards), Alex Arelano
(drums)

Albums:
EYES OF THE ORACLE, Elevate ER02004
(1998)
Inner Voices / Alone I Stand / Word On A
Line / The Fall / The Quest / The Naked Mind
/ Time / Test Of Wills / Tears Of The Wind

POWER QUEST

(UK / NEW ZEALAND / ITALY)
Line-Up: Alessio Garavello (vocals), Adam
Bickers (guitar), Sam Totman (guitar),
Andrea Martongelli (guitar), Steve Scott
(bass), Steve Williams (keyboards)

POWER QUEST, a Symphonic inclined Metal
act in the Euro tradition, was borne out of
keyboard player Steve Williams departure
from London Power Metal act
DRAGONHEART (later DRAGONFORCE) in
March of 2001. Williams also had prior
experience with DOG DAY SUNRISE. Joining
him would be former DRAGONHEART and
SHADOWKEEP New Zealand born bassist
Steve Scott and D.R.S. guitarist Adam
Bickers. Also joining the new unit would be
Sam Totman, also operational as a current
member of DRAGONFORCE and Black
Metal act DEMONIAC, and in April 2002
POWER QUEST pulled in Italian singer
Alessio Garavello of ARTHEMIS.
The band increased their Italian contingent
with the recruitment of a third guitarist,
another ARTHEMIS member Andrea
Martongelli, in July. Martongelli was drawn in
just in time to contribute guitar solos to the

debut album 'Wings Of Forever'.

Albums:
WINGS OF FOREVER, Underground
Symphony USCD 068 (2002)

POWERS COURT (St. Louis, MO, USA)

Line-Up: Danie Powers (vocals / guitar /
mandolins / keyboards), Steve Murray
(bass), Mike Evans (drums)

St. Louis melancholic Power Metal trio
POWERS COURT, arrived on the scene with
a 1992 demo under the band name
EQUINOX. Led by the multi talented Danie
Powers, a woman who not only masters
guitar, mandolin and keyboards, but is in
possession of a four and a half octave range,
the act secured the interest of Italian Metal
revivalist label Dragonheart Records.
Powers had previously been involved with
Metal covers act MEANSTREAK before
forging CRUCIBLE with bassist B.J. Blair and
drummer BLZ Bob. This unit, with Monty York
taking over on bass, evolved into EQUINOX.
A further change in the four string role
witnessed erstwhile EXODUST and RAZOR
BLAZE man Steve Murray being drafted as in
1994 the group morphed once again into
POWERS COURT for a debut self-financed
1996 album.
A name switch to POWERS COURT saw the
band taking on their 2001 album 'Nine Kinds
Of Hell'. Session drums came courtesy of
Rick Kramer.

Albums:
POWER'S COURT, Power's Court PC1066-
2099 (1996)
Lord Of Winds And Breezes / Spellbinder /
Suffer in Silence / Dying Embers / High
Priestess / Master Plan / Deceiver / Season
Of The Witch
NINE KINDS OF HELL, Dragonheart (2001)
Emptiness / Conquistador / House Of
Sorrow / Darkened Paradise / Agnostica /
Tanzania / Tragedy Of Faust / Devil's Triangle
/ Echoes Of Silence

POWER SYMPHONY (ITALY)

Line-Up: Michela D'Orlando (vocals), Marco
Cecconi (guitar), Daniele Viola (bass),
Sergio Giovenzana (drums)

Female fronted Pavia, Lombardy based Metal
act POWER SYMPHONY was founded by
vocalist Michela D'Orlando and guitarist
Marco Cecconi during September of 1991.
The band toured the clubs and entered
numerous competitions until they landed the
tour support to LABYRINTH's national set of

dates in 1996.
The band signed to North Wind Records for the 1999 album 'Evillot'. Following its release keyboard player Claudio Berra made his exit, the position being taken by former DOMINIUM man Marco Volpe. Other changes would witness the enlistment of bass player Fabio Iannone and erstwhile BURIED SOULS, ABNEGATE, NODE and ALICE IN DARKLAND drummer Lino Sistu.
POWER SYMPHONY cut their second album 'Lightbringer' in 2000. Joey Vera of ARMORED SAINT and FATES WARNING took on production responsibilities.

Albums:
EVILLOT, North Winds NW CD001 (1999)
Battles In The Twilight / Shores Of My Land / Evillot / The Curse Of Every Man / Inferno Suite - Into The Shadowed Forest / Inferno Suite - Inferno / Inferno Suite - Confutatis / I Am The Bard
LIGHTBRINGER, (2000)
The Way Of The Sword / Lucifer / Gethsemane / Never Dream Of Goodness / Song Of Men / Quest For Knowledge / The Necromancer

PRETTY MAIDS (DENMARK)
Line-Up: Ronnie Atkins (vocals), Ken Hammer (guitar), Pete Collins (guitar), Allan Delong (bass), Phil Moorheed (drums)

A very heavy, yet melodic, band from Horsen in Denmark, PRETTY MAIDS was formed in 1981 by guitarist Ken Hammer and originally started off as a THIN LIZZY and RAINBOW covers band, but soon progressed to their own material.
PRETTY MAIDS' first demo - recorded in late '82 - featured 'Shelley The Maid' and 'City Lights'. A few months later a second demo was cut, with the tracks 'Children Of Tomorrow', 'Fantasy' and 'Warchild'. These demo tracks (with the addition of 'Bad Boy') were released by the Stoke-On-Trent based Bullet Records in Britain and P.A.R. Records in America.
Not long after the 'Pretty Maids' mini-album appeared, PRETTY MAIDS secured initial dates in Britain supporting fellow Bullett act LE GRIFFE on a club tour in 1983. Much championed by 'Metal Forces' magazine supremo Bernard Doe, the act quickly gained a major deal with Epic in Denmark.
Prior to recording 'Red Hot And Heavy', original guitarist Pete Collins was replaced by Rick Hansen and bassist John Darrow by erstwhile SHYLOCK member Allan Delong. However, Hansen left on completion of the album necessitating the re-recruitment of Collins.

The band opened for BLACK SABBATH in Denmark in 1983 as promotion for the debut album. PRETTY MAIDS also performed at Metal festivals in Belgium and Poland alongside HANOI ROCKS before embarking on a British support slot with SAXON in 1985.
Returning to action in 1987 with the 'Future World' album, PRETTY MAIDS had spent the recording period holed up in New York and the album featured guest backing vocals from veteran RAINBOW and MICHAEL SCHENKER GROUP vocalist GRAHAM BONNET.
In late 1988 guitarist Angel Schleifer left to join German act BONFIRE and would be replaced by Ricky Marx.
'Jump The Gun' was produced by DEEP PURPLE bassist ROGER GLOVER and features Glover and DEEP PURPLE drummer Ian Paice as guest musicians.
The 1990 Christmas EP featured DEEP PURPLE vocalist on the track 'A Merry Jingle', itself a cover of the SEX PISTOLS / THIN LIZZY track.
At the beginning of 1991 PRETTY MAIDS parted company with bassist Delong, drummer Moorhead and guitarist Ricky Marx. The group celebrated their 10th anniversary with 1991's 'Sin-Decade' album as PRETTY MAIDS settled on a group consisting of Atkins, Hammer, bassist Ken Jackson and drummer Michael Fast
1992 witnessed the acoustical offering 'Offside' and a new studio affair, 'Stripped', appeared the following year.
In 1995 the band had left the confines of Sony Music and signed a new deal with German label Massacre. The first fruits of the new alliance were the Flemming Rasmussen produced 'Scream' and PRETTY MAIDS appearance at a number of European festivals that year, including Pinkpop on the same bill as VAN HALEN and PAGE/PLANT.
At the end of 1995 the group issued a long awaited live album, 'Screamin' Live', which found the group delivering the highlights from their 13 year history on one package.
In March 1997 the Tommy Hansen produced 'Spooked' emerged featuring a timely cover of KISS' 'Hard Luck Woman' amongst a welter of new material that surely ranks as some of the heaviest ever recorded by the Danes.
The 1999 album 'First Cuts... And Then Some' packages all the band's EP's together for the first time. Also included is a cover version of SLADE's 'Far Far Away', originally intended for the 'Stripped' album.

Singles/EPs:
Red Hot And Heavy / Children Of Tomorrow / Waitin' For The Time, CBS A12 6237 (1985)

Future World, Epic (1987) (USA Promotion flexidisc)
Love Games / Needles In The Dark / Yellow Rain, CBS 650-4376 (1987)
In Santa's Claws / A Merry Jingle / Eye Of The Storm (Live) / Red Hot And Heavy (Live) / Rock The House (Live), CBS 46774-2 (1990)
Savage Heart / Over And Out, CBS 655-884-3 (1990)

Albums:
PRETTY MAIDS, Bullet CULP 1 (1983)
City Light / Fantasy / Shelly The Maid / Bad Boys / Children Of Tomorrow / Nowhere To Run
RED HOT AND HEAVY, CBS 26207 (1984)
Fortune / Back To Back / Red Hot And Heavy / Waitin' For The Time / Cold Killer / Battle Of Pride / Night Danger / A Place In The Night / Queen Of Dreams / Little Darling
FUTURE WORLD, CBS BFE 40713(1987) 22 SWEDEN
Future World / Rodeo / We Came To Rock / Yellow Rain / Loud n' Proud / Love Games / Needles In The Dark / Eye Of The Storm / Long Way To Go / Rock Zone / Bring On The Bad News
JUMP THE GUN, CBS 4663651 (1990) **39 SWEDEN**
Lethal Heroes / Don't Settle For Less / Rock The House / Savage Heart / Young Blood / Headlines / Jump The Gun / Partners In Crime / Attention / Hang Tough / Over And Out / Dream On
SIN - DECADE, CBS 471275 2 (1991) **50 SWEDEN**
Running Out / Who Said Money / Nightmare In The Neighbourhood / Sin-Decade / Come On Tough, Come On Nasty / Raise Your Flag / Credit Card Lover / Know It Ain't Easy / Healing Touch / In The Flesh / Please Don't Leave Me
OFFSIDE, Sony 472266 (1992)
Heartbeat From Heaven / Please Don't Leave Me / In The Minds Of The Young / "39" / Fly Away
STRIPPED, Columbia 473964-2 (1993)
If It Ain't Gonna Change / Please Don't Leave Me / In The Minds Of The Young / Too Late, Too Loud / Say The Word / 6.39 / Heartbeat From Heaven / How Does It Feel / I'll Be There / Savage Heart
SCREAM, Massacre CD047 (1995)
Rise / Scream / Psycho Time Bomb Planet Earth / This Love / Walk Away / No Messiah / In A World Of Your Own / Don't Turn Your Sex On Me / Adrenalin Junkie / Anytime Anywhere
SCREAMIN' LIVE, Massacre MASS CD081 (1995)
Psycho Time Bomb Planet Earth / Rock The

House / Rise / Walk Away / Scream / Yellow Rain / Sin Decade / Savage Heart / No Messiah / Please Don't Leave Me / Lovegames / Future World / Back To Back / Red Hot And Heavy
SPOOKED, Massacre MAS PC0119 (1997)
Resurrection / Freakshow / Dead Or Alive / Die With Your Dreams / Fly Me Out / Live Until It Hurts / Spooked / Twitch / If It Can't Be Love / Never Too Late / Your Mind Is Where The Money Is / Hard Luck Woman / The One That Should Not Be
THE BEST OF: BACK TO BACK, Massacre (1998)
Fortuna / Back To Back / Attention / Dead Or Alive / When It All Comes Down / Forever And eternal / Savage Heart / Love Games / Walk Away / Sin Decade / Waitin' For The Time / Yellow Rain / Twisted / Future World / Please Don't Leave Me / Red, Hot And Heavy / Det Bedste Til Mig Og Mine Venner
ANYTHING WORTH DOING IS WORTH OVERDOING, Massacre MAS CD0170 (1999)
Snakes In Eden / Destination Paradise / Hell On High Heels / When The Angels Cry / Back Off / Only In America / With These Eyes / Anything Worth Doing Is Worth Overdoing / Scent Of My Prey / Face Me / Loveshine
FIRST CUTS... AND THEN SOME, Massacre MASCD0227 (1999)
City Light / Fantasy / Shelly The Maid / Bad Boys / Children Of Tomorrow / Nowhere To Run / In Santa's Claws / A Merry Jingle / Eye Of The Storm (Live) / Red, Hot And Heavy (Live) / Rock The House (Live) / Far Far Away
CARPE DIEM, Massacre (2000)
Until It Dies / Carpe Diem / Wouldn't Miss You / Clay / Tortured Spirit / Violent Tribe / Unwritten Pages / For Once In Your Life / Poisoned Pleasures / Time Awaits For No One / They Are All Alike / Invisible Chains
PLANET PANIC, JVC Victor VICP-61795 (2002)
Virtual Brutality / Playing God / He Who Never Lived / Face Of My Enemy / Not What You Think / Natural High / Who's Gonna Change / Worthless / One Way To Rock / Enter Forevermore

PREYER (UK)
Line-Up: Pete McIntosh (vocals), James Rees (guitar), Craig Thomas (guitar), Phil Scourfield (bass), Phil John (drums)

Welsh Metal band forged in the traditional Heavy Metal mould with studs and leathers to match. PREYER were quite an interesting act, especially live, where vocalist Pete McIntosh had a penchant for whirling an executioner's axe above his head during shows!

Formed as a quartet in the early '80s by former PAGEANT vocalist Pete McIntosh, former SHANGHAI bassist Phil Scourfield, guitarist Craig Thomas and drummer Phil John. The group's first offering was the 'Fear Of The Dark' demo before second guitarist James Rees joined in July 1985 shortly after a second demo, 'On The Prowl', having split from his previous act MAMMATH.

PREYER signed to Ebony Records to release the 'Terminator' album in 1987. Unfortunately, PREYER were a rare sight on the gig circuit only getting in a few club gigs, including supporting GRIM REAPER, before their demise.

Drummer Phil John left in 1987 to team up with ex-SAMURAI guitarist Craig Riggsdale to form TALON. John's replacement was Lloyd Coates. Coates would later form GUN HILL with former URIAH HEEP and LUCIFERS FRIEND vocalist John Lawton.

Albums:

TERMINATOR, Ebony EBON 40 (1987)
The Right / Terminator / Leather And Chains / Over The Top / Beware The Night / Shout It Out / Rock Crusader / Rifferama

PRIMAL FEAR (GERMANY)
Line-Up: Ralph Scheepers (vocals), Stefan Leibling (guitar), Henry Wolter (guitar), Matt Sinner (bass), Klaus Sperling (drums)

Despite featuring a version of DEEP PURPLE's 'Speed King' the first offering fronted by ex-GAMMA RAY vocalist Ralph Scheeper's act PRIMAL FEAR is in the main heavily rooted in traditional Heavy Metal territory. From a standing start PRIMAL FEAR, conceived by MATT SINNER, the leading force behind his own popular namesake act SINNER, have quickly rose to become one of Germany's leading Metal outfits with considerable sales and a loyal fan base. The band has also made a significant impact on the global Metal market delivering a series of albums blessed with tight song-writing honed with characteristic muscular riffs.

Previous to the formation of PRIMAL FEAR Sinner had carved his reputation with a consistent string of SINNER albums dating back to the mid '80s as well as embellishing his record with a solo album and repute as an in demand producer. Sinner had signed the PRIMAL FEAR project to the Japanese JVC Victor label upfront of negotiating a deal with Nuclear Blast in Germany. Meantime Ralph Scheepers had come close to the landing the

job as vocalist for JUDAS PRIEST and was in fact gigging with a cover band titled JUST PRIEST. The vocalist already had a contract secured with Japanese label JVC and PRIMAL FEAR was borne when Sinner pulled in Scheepers and SINNER colleague Tom Neumann for recording. The debut album saw drums from PROLOPOWER's Klaus Sperling. Scheeper's former GAMMA RAY guitar partner Kai Hansen also contributed to three tracks.

Germany's late '90s appetite for traditional Metal and Scheepers standing in the Metal community, it was not such a great surprise that the debut album charted in its homeland. In 1998 PRIMAL FEAR toured Europe sharing billing with RUNNING WILD. The band also put in numerous festival appearances including the infamous Dutch 'Dynamo' festival where the band hit the stage at 3 O' Clock in the morning.

The second album 'Jaws Of Death' saw the inclusion of a cover of RAINBOW's 'Kill The King'. At this time the band also cut a take on ACCEPT's 'Breaker' for a Nuclear Blast ACCEPT tribute album. PRIMAL FEAR, now with Klaus Sperling back on the drum kit, toured Germany in 1999 supported by METALIUM and SINERGY. The band also extended their reach into a further ten European countries as well as gigs in Brazil and double headliners in Japan with SINNER. Supporting the third album 'Nuclear Fire' the band, now with Scheepers sporting a shaved head, toured Germany in February 2001 with support from CHILDREN OF BODOM and SACRED STEEL. In Europe the band gigged across a total of twelve nations. The album gave the band another chart success reaching no. 37 in the German national charts. Another showing at the annual Wacken festival ensued and the band would also put in their debut showing on British soil with an appearance at the Derby 'Bloodstock' festival. Two US festival appearances, their North American debut, would also figure on the band's itinerary.

PRIMAL FEAR would donate a rendition of GARY MOORE's 'Out In The Fields' to the PHIL LYNOTT tribute album 'The Spirit Of The Black Rose'. In September the band issued a new single comprising their version of 'Out In The Fields', ACCEPT's 'Breaker' and RAINBOW's 'Kill The King'.

Both Scheepers and Sinner would donate their services to the GERMAN ROCK STARS October 2001 song 'Wings Of Freedom' in honour of the September 11th World Trade Center victims. Meantime drummer Klaus Sperling could be found as a member of Death Metal band MY DARKEST FEAR on their 'Massive Brutality' album. This side act of

PRIMAL FEAR
Photo : Roland Guth

Sperling's also numbered AZMODAN vocalist René Pfeiffer and SACRED STEEL personnel Jörg M. Knittel and Oliver Großhans.

HALFORD guitarist MIKE CHLASCIAK would contribute guest guitar solos to two tracks on the 2002 PRIMAL FEAR album 'Black Sun' namely 'Controlled' and 'Fear'. The record gave PRIMAL FEAR their fourth consecutive German chart entry, landing at no. 55. An extensive live schedule would be announced commencing with Russian shows in August upfront of a lengthy European trek and South American action in Colombia, Mexico and Brazil. An extensive run of European dates had the band paired up with RAGE.

Mat Sinner would add guest session lead vocals on U.S. guitarist RICK RENSTROM's solo album 'Until The Bitter End', featuring on the track 'Calling on Vengeance'. Meantime PRIMAL FEAR had their version of 'The Rover' included on the Locomotive Music LED ZEPPELIN tribute album 'The Metal Zeppelin — The Music Remains The Same' and would record 'Seek And Destroy' for a Nuclear Blast METALLICA collection.

Albums:
PRIMAL FEAR, Nuclear Blast NB 302-2 (1998) **48 GERMANY**
Primal Fear / Chainbreaker / Silver And Gold

/ Promised Land / Formula One / Dollars / Nine Lives / Tears Of Rage / Speedking / Battalions Of Hate / Running In The Dust / Thunderdome
JAWS OF DEATH, Nuclear Blast NB 391-2 (1999)
Jaws Of Death / Final Embrace / Save A Prayer / Church Of Blood / Into The Future / Under Your Spell / Play To Kill / Nation In Fear / When The Night Comes / Fight To Survive / Hatred In My Soul / Kill The King
NUCLEAR FIRE, Nuclear Blast (2001)
37 GERMANY, 71 ITALY, 77 SWITZERLAND
Angel In Black / Kiss Of Death / Back From Hell / Now Or Never / Fight The Fire / Eye Of An Angel / Bleed For Me / Nuclear Fire / Red Rain / Iron Fist In A Velvet Glove / Fire On The Horizon / Living For Metal
BLACK SUN, Nuclear Blast NB 500-2 (2002)
55 GERMANY, 72 ITALY
Countdown To Insanity / Black Sun / Armageddon / Lightyears From Home / Revolution / Fear / Mind Control / Magic Eye / Mind Machine / Silence / We Go Down / Cold Day In Hell / Controlled

PROJECTO (ITALY)
Line-Up: Robert Bruccoleri (vocals), Vic Mazzoni (guitar), Fabio Zunino (bass), P.J. Abba (keyboards), Luca Grosso (drums)

As the name implies PROJECTO is an assemblage of Italian Metal talent. Convened by SHADOWS OF STEEL and SKYLARK guitarist Vic Mazzoni the group cut its teeth with an April 1994 demo 'The Playing Room'. Vocals for these formative tapes were contributed by Wild Steel of SHADOWS OF STEEL. After adding ARMALITE keyboard player P.J. Abba a second tape 'Points Of View' was delivered the following year and in 1996 singer Robert Bruccoleri and drummer Luca Grosso completed the line-up.

LABYRINTH man Frank Andiver produced PROJECTO's eponymous 1998 debut, recorded for the Underground Symphony label.

During 2000 PROJECTO recorded a version of WARLORD's 'Deliver Us From Evil' and SAVATAGE's 'Follow Me' for tribute albums.

Albums:
PROJECTO, Underground Symphony USCD029 (1998)
Death In Dreamland / Freedom / Alone In The Mirror / Fade Away / Alchemy / Childhood Dreams / Pantomime / Battletime / Projecto / Doomsday Fight / Evilness / Believe In Love
CROWN OF AGES, Underground Symphony USCD046 (2001)
Heart And Steel / Guardian Soldiers / Warrior Soul / Innocent Eyes / Black Sorcerer / Thunder Of Love / Fight In The Sky / The Samain Tournament / Blood And Faith / Crown Of Ages / Final Alliance

PSYCHODRAMA (Denver, CO, USA)
Line-Up: Corey Brown (vocals), Hercules J. Castro (guitar), Bart Barlettano (guitar), Brian Dail (bass), Mackenzie Kerr (drums)

Dating from the early nineties Denver Power Metal act PSYCODRAMA first came to attention with the 'Illusion' demo. This cassette saw extensive sales and realised a deal with David T. Chastain's label Leviathan Records to record the debut 'The Illusion' album.

Ex-RATT bassist Juan Croucier produced the 1997 PSYCODRAMA album. It includes a version of THE BEATLES 'Come Together'.

Corey Brown, teaming up with ex-TILES bassist Kevin Chown, was later to be seen fronting MAGNETUDE 9 for their 1998 album 'Chaos To Control'.

Albums:
THE ILLUSION, Massacre (1995)
BENT, Massacre MAS PC0135 (1997)
Blind / Stuck / No Return / Know / Change / Quiet Sky / Bent / Fear / Come Together

PYRAMID (SPAIN)
Line-Up: Javier Cespedes (vocals), Tony Vallés (guitar), Manu González (bass), Javier Camps (keyboards), Roger Guardia (drums)

Barcelona Progressive Metal band PYRAMID was created in 1998 by erstwhile HANGER 18, LOS SUAVES and MANZANO guitarist Tony Vallés. An eponymous debut album emerged in 1998 and touring ensued nationally alongside the likes of veteran domestic acts OBUS and BARON ROJO. The following year PYRAMID donated their version of 'Powerslave' to the IRON MAIDEN tribute album 'Transylvania 666'.

PYRAMID's second album 'The Immaculate Lie' was released in November 2000 by Locomotive Music.

Albums:
PYRAMID, Arise (1999)
Living Free / Ghost / Troya Horse / The Prodigal Son / Before The Rain / Out Of This World
THE IMMACULATE LIE, Locomotive Music (2000)
Epilogue / Hell Freezes Over / Utopia City / Merciful Lies / One Of A Kind / The Mastery Of Flight / Show Me / Armageddon / Virtual Superhuman / The Prodigal Son

Q5 (Seattle, WA, USA)
Line-Up: Jonathan K. (vocals), Rick Pierce (guitar), Floyd Rose (guitar), Evan Sheeley (bass), Gary Thompson (drums)

Seattle's Q5 followed the decision by guitarist Floyd Rose, inventor of the Floyd Rose Tremelo system, and vocalist Jonathan Scott Palmerton to put a new band together after leaving their previous group C.O.R.E. Rick Pierce, Evan Sheeley and Gary Thompson formed a mass exodus from the ranks of TKO to join the pair to round out the Q5 line-up. Q5's legacy is generally regarded as the track 'Steel The Light', a superb piece of melodic Metal that the band were unfortunately unable to match. Entering the studio in early 1983, Q5 recorded a seven track, album quality demo featuring the tracks 'Teenage Runaway', 'Nothing Ventured, Nothing Gained', 'She's A Dancer', 'No Way To Treat A Lady', 'Waiting For Your Love', 'In The Night' and 'Lovin' You Too Long'.

Managed by HEART's then management team, once the decision to shoot for a full-blown album was made the resulting product was first released in limited numbers on the Albatross label, but was issued in a different sleeve for European consumption when Q5 signed to Music For Nations.

Produced by Floyd Rose and Mike Flicker, only three of the songs from the original Q5 demo made it onto the 'Steel The Light' album.

With the demise of Q5 Pierce and singer Jonathon K. built up a fresh act entitled NIGHTSHADE and issued the 'Dead Of Night' album in 1992. Pierce surprisingly teamed up with his former TKO employer, front man Brad Sinsel, in a one-off project dubbed SUICIDE SQUAD.

During 2001 German Metal band POWERGOD would cover 'Steel The Light' on their 'Bleed For The Gods' album.

Singles/EPs:
Steel The Light / Steel The Light (Album version) / That's Alright With You, Music For Nations 12 KUT 115 (1985)

Albums:
STEEL THE LIGHT, Music For Nations MFN 39 (1985)
Missing In Action / Lonely Lady / Steel The Light / Pull The Trigger / Ain't No Way To Treat A Lady / In The Night / Come And Gone / Rock On / Teenage Runaway
WHEN THE MIRROR CRACKS, Music For Nations MFN 64 (1986)

Livin' On The Borderline / Your Tears (Will Follow Me) / Never Gonna Love Again / Stand By Me / When The Mirror Cracks / Runaway / In The Rain / I Can't Wait / Cold Heart / Let Go

QUEENSRYCHE (Bellevue, WA, USA)
Line-Up: Geoff Tate (vocals), Kelly Gray (guitar), Michael Wilton (guitar), Eddie Jackson (bass), Scott Rockenfield (drums)

Cited by many as the catalyst of the '80s Power Metal movement QUEENSRYCHE delivered a majestic form of Heavy Metal laden with a unique melodic bent and topped by the quite awesome vocal abilities of Geoff Tate. After a run of 'trial and error' albums which hinted at great promise the band broke the floodgates with the seminal 'Operation Mindcrime' concept album. This single work would break the band internationally and set the standard for a legion of imitators. Although the band sustained this dynamic with the subsequent 'Empire' opus they have struggled since, oddly seeming to eschew the grandiose style that so typified the band in favour of simpler themes.

Beginning life as Bellevue's THE MOB in 1981. The band found their singer when GEOFF TATE, vocalist with MYTH a Seattle metal band that supported the likes of CULPRIT and WILD DOGS, split away from his act in late 1982 as THE MOB became QUEENSRYCH (without the now more familiar 'E' ending).

The individual members had all trod the boards with fledgling Seattle Metal bands. Tate had debuted with TYRANT then BABYLON before MYTH. Guitarists Chris DeGarmo and Michael Wilton had stuck together through JOKER and CROSSFIRE, the latter act including drummer Scott Rockenfield. DeGarmo had also had a stint with TEMPEST.

QUEENSRYCHE's June 1982 four track demo recorded in drummer Scott Rockenfield's parent's basement that featured 'The Lady Wore Black', 'Queen Of The Reich', 'Blinded' and 'Nightrider'. The band soon created waves on the underground tape trading circuit with many comparing the band to prime time British Metal with comparisons being drawn with Geoff Tate's operatic style and the precise riffing of guitarists Michael Wilton and Chris DeGarmo.

A local record store owned by the husband and wife team of Kim And Diana Harris were impressed enough to press up the demo on their 206 record label. The subsequent EP released in May 1983 being known as 'Queen of the Reich'. With a commercial release QUEENSRYCHE (now having added the 'E'

343

QUEENSRYCHE Photo : Sean Denomey

to their title) garnering ecstatic worldwide press were soon snapped up by EMI America Records.

The debut album 'The Warning', produced by James Guthrie and recorded at the world famous Abbey Road Studios proved to be an over ambitious effort marred by spreading good ideas too thinly.

QUEENSRYCHE toured Britain as support to DIO before returning to America for a series of dates with IRON MAIDEN and BON JOVI.

Second attempt 'Rage For Order', produced by Neil Kernon, was a major statement of intent justifying their early promise. The first single from 'Rage For Order', 'Gonna Get Close To You', was a spirited cover of the song penned by Canadian artist DALBELLO. The original had appeared on her 'Whomanfoursays' album. The singer played the female interest in QUEENSRYCHE's video of the track.

Despite 'Rage For Order' seeing an obvious maturing of lyrical and musical content the band were universally vilified for their decision to wear garish eye-liner and lipstick on the sleeve photographs. Learning their lesson quickly the band got back to basics with haste and set out on a mammoth American tour. However, there were rumours that behind the scenes their financial affairs were on shaky ground. Following the tour dates QUEENSRYCHE ditched their previous management team, signing a new deal with the Q Prime organisation, responsible for careers of DEF LEPPARD and METALLICA.

Q Prime's declared first duty was to bankrupt the band due to an alleged $700,000 of touring debts. Nevertheless, from this nadir the band were to rise, phoenix like, with their next effort 'Operation Mindcrime', a ground breaking Peter Collins produced album of such magnitude it was to set the band's career straight for good.

'Operation Mindcrime' was a brave move for a band at the crossroads between success and failure. Undaunted the band pulled out all the stops crafting a superb weave of metal, theatrics and sinister plot line. Orchestration was aided by the recruitment of Michael Kamen, noted for his movie scores.

The band toured America in mid 1989 opening for Q Prime colleagues DEF LEPPARD before British shows as headliners then back to the states supporting METALLICA. The later shows utilised more of the theatrics to build the album scenario in the live situation, in particular bringing in the talents of Seattle born Pamela Moore to play the singing part of Sister Mary onstage.

'Operation Mindcrime', in spite of massive global media adulation upon its release had been a relatively slow seller, at first finding it

tough going to even equal sales of 'Rage For Order'. The relentless grind of taking the music to the people via the live format had paid off though and the record was to be set on a path of steady sales that would last for many years. This creeping enthusiasm for the band would see their next album 'Empire' benefit from a huge underground fan base that would see it break the multi-platinum sales barrier with consummate ease.

'Empire' held no less than three hit singles with the ballad 'Silent Lucidity' hitting the American top ten and being nominated for a Grammy award.

The 'Building Empires' American tour would see QUEENSRYCHE on the road for nearly a year and a half. Opening shows in America had SUICIDAL TENDENCIES as support and after Canadian dates WARRIOR SOUL picked up the guest slot for further American gigs. QUEENSRYCHE also slotted in dates in Japan and the Brazilian 'Rock in Rio' festival prior to an appearance at the Castle Donington 'Monsters of Rock' festival headlined by AC/DC.

The band's previous album 'Operation Mindcrime' was being pulled along by the success of 'Empire' and, still featuring heavily in the live set, was fast becoming the band's all time classic. To keep the fire burning on the concept album QUEENSRYCHE recorded and videoed two shows at Madison, Milwaukee and La Crosse, Wisconsin that featured 'Operation Mindcrime' in its entirety and subsequently released as 'Operation Livecrime'.

The lull in QUEENSRYCHE activity was broken by the release of the 1993 'Real World' single, a track recorded for the soundtrack to the Arnold Schwarzenegger movie 'Last Action Hero'.

For a band for which line-up problems had been non-existent throughout their career to date it came as somewhat of a shock to fans in late 1997 when DeGarmo announced he was to quit. The guitarist soon busied himself recording with INFLATABLE SOULE front man Peter Cornell, brother of SOUNDGARDEN's Chris Cornell yet surprisingly was unveiled in June 1998 as a member of ALICE IN CHAINS guitarist Jerry Cantrell's solo touring band. De Garmo would later demo material with other ex-ALICE IN CHAINS men bassist Mike Inez and drummer Sean Kinney. This union, together with SPONGE / CRUD singer Vinnie Dombroski, would transpire as SPYS 4 DARWIN and eventually resulted in an album 'Microfish'.

QUEENSRYCHE, with Kelly Gray bowing in as new guitarist, toured America in 2000 as support to IRON MAIDEN. Solo shows would witness the band including the unexpected cover of U2's 'Bullet The Blue Sky'. Two tribute albums to QUEENSRYCHE would be released the same year. It would also be learned that Geoff Tate had convened a solo project.

2001 found QUEENSRYCHE signing up to Sanctuary Records. The band recorded two shows on the 27th and 28th July 2001 at Seattle's Moore Theater for their first release with the new partnership, a lavishly packaged double live CD 'Live Evolution'. Although the album would rekindle the media and fan enthusiasm afforded to early works there would be a minor hiccup when it was revealed the first 75,000 pressings came with incorrectly labelled track orders and other mis-prints.

Drummer Scott Rockenfield revealed his outside venture with partner Paul Speer. Suitably titled ROCKENFIELD / SPEER the duo would release the album 'Hell's Canyon'. Yet another QUEENSRYCHE offshoot would be SLAVES TO THE SYSTEM which found both Rockenfield and Gray in league with Damon Johnson and Roman Glick of BROTHER CANE along with Scotty Heard of SWEATY NIPPLES. Michael Wilton was not to be left out, emerging with his SOULBLENDER project in league with MY SISTERS MACHINE vocalist and former ALICE IN CHAINS member Nick Pollock, guitarist Dave Groves and drummer Wes Hallam. SOULBENDER would lay down a seven track EP exclusively for industry promotion purposes.

GEOFF TATE too would hit the solo trail, announcing an album project originally billed as 'Old World Order' for June 2002. Tate's recording band for this venture comprised guitarists Jeff Carrell and Scott Moughton, bassist Cris Fox, keyboard player Howard Chillcott and SADHAPPY drummer Evan Schiller.

During mid May QUEENSRYCHE announced that guitarist Kelly Gray was no longer with the band, fuelling immediate speculation that Chris DeGarmo was set to make a return. This latest conjecture was soon denied officially by the band as wishful thinking. GEOFF TATE meantime announced details of his debut solo tour, commencing June 22nd at the Sky Church venue in Seattle. In promotion for his solo venture Tate stunned long standing fans when he reportedly admitted that he had never been a "Metalhead" and cited Electronic Pop acts as his main inspiration. SCOTT ROCKENFIELD also took the opportunity to strike out solo, debuting with his album 'The X Chapters'.

Singles/EPs:
Take Hold Of The Flame / Nightrider, EMI

America EA 183 (1984) (7" single)
Gonna Get Close To You / Prophecy, EMI America EA 22 (1986) (7" single)
Gonna Get Close To You / Prophecy / Queen Of The Reich (Live In Tokyo) / Deliverance (Live In Tokyo), EMI America EAD 22 (1986) (12" single)
Suite Sister Mary / Overseeing The Operation - Excerpts From 'Operation Mindcrime': I Remember Now / Revolution Calling / Operation Mindcrime / Breaking The Silence / Eyes Of A Stranger, EMI Manhattan 10 QR1 (1988)
Eyes Of A Stranger / Queen Of The Reich, EMI Manhattan MT 65 (1989) (7" single) **59 UK**
Eyes Of A Stranger / Queen Of The Reich / Walk In The Shadows / Take Hold Of The Flame, EMI Manhattan 12MT 65 (1989) (12" single)
Eyes Of A Stranger / Queen Of The Reich / Take Hold Of The Flame / Prophecy, EMI Manhattan CDMT 65 (1989) (CD single)
Empire / Scarborough Fair - Canticle, EMI Manhattan MT 90 (1990) (7" single) **61 UK**
Empire / Scarborough Fair - Canticle / Prophecy, EMI Manhattan CDMT 90 (1990) (CD single)
Silent Lucidity / The Mission (Live), EMI Manhattan MT 94 (1991) (7" single) **34 UK, 9 USA**
Silent Lucidity / The Mission (Live) / Eyes Of A Stranger, EMI Manhattan 12MT 94 (1991) (12" single)
Silent Lucidity / The Mission (Live) / Della Brown, EMI Manhattan CDMT 94 (1991) (CD single)
Best I Can / I Dream In Infared (Acoustic), EMI Manhattan MT 97 (1991) (7" single) **36 UK**
Best I Can / I Dream In Infared (Acoustic) / Prophecy, EMI Manhattan 10MT 97 (1991) (10" single)
Best I Can / I Dream In Infared (Acoustic) / Prophecy / Best I Can (Radio edit), EMI Manhattan CDMT 97 (1991) (CD single)
Jet City Woman / Empire (Live), EMI America MT 98 (1991) (7" single) **39 UK**
Jet City Woman / Empire (Live) / Walk In The Shadows (Live), EMI America 10MT 98 (1991) (10" single)
Jet City Woman / Empire (Live) / Queen Of The Reich / Walk In The Shadows (Live), EMI America CDMT 98 (1991) (CD single)
Silent Lucidity / I Don't Believe In Love (Live), EMI Manhattan MT 104 (1992) (7" single) **18 UK**
Silent Lucidity / Last Time In Paris / Take Hold Of The Flame, EMI Manhattan 12MT 104 (1992) (12" single)
Silent Lucidity / Suite Sister Mary (Live) / Last Time In Paris, EMI Manhattan CDMT

104 (1992) (CD single)

Silent Lucidity / Eyes Of A Stranger (Live) /Operation: Mindcrime, EMI Manhattan CDMTS 104 (1992) (CD single)

I Am I / Real World / Someone Else?, EMI 12 MT 109 (1995) (12" gold vinyl single) **45 UK**

I Am I / Real World / Someone Else? / Dirty L'il Secret, EMI CDMT 109 (1995) (CD single)

Bridge / The Killing Words (Live), EMI MTPD 111 (1995) (7" picture disc single) **40 UK**

Bridge / The Killing Words (Live) / The Lady Wore Black (Live) / Damaged (Live), EMI CDMTS 111 (1995) (CD single)

Bridge / Silent Lucidity (Live) / My Empty Room (Live) / Real World (Live), EMI CDMTSX 111 (1995) (CD single)

Albums:

QUEEN OF THE REICH, 206 R 101 (1983) **81 USA**

Queen Of The Reich / Nightrider / Blinded / The Lady Wore Black

THE WARNING, EMI America TCATAK 108 (1984) **61 USA**

The Warning / En Force / Deliverance / No Sanctuary / NM 156 / Take Hold Of The Flame / Before The Storm / Child Of Fire / Roads To Madness

RAGE FOR ORDER, EMI AML 3105 (1986) **66 UK, 47 USA**

Walk In The Shadows / I Dream In Infared / The Whisper / Gonna Get Close To You / The Killing Words / Surgical Strike / Neue Regal / Chemical Youth (We Are Rebellion) / London / Screaming In Digital / I Will Remember

OPERATION MINDCRIME, EMI CDMTL 1023 (1988) **58 UK, 50 USA**

I Remember Now / Anarchy X / Revolution Calling / Operation: Mindcrime / Speak / Spreading The Disease / Mission / Suite Sister Mary / Needle Lies / Electric Requiem / Breaking The Silence / I Don't Believe In Love / Waiting For 22 / My Empty Room / Eyes Of A Stranger

OPERATION LIVECRIME, EMI DPRO 4811 (1991) **38 USA** (available in boxed set with Live video)

I Remember Now / Anarchy-X / Revolution Calling / Operation: Mindcrime / Speak / Spreading The Disease / The Mission / Suite Sister Mary / The Needle Lies / Electric Requiem / Breaking The Silence / I Don't Believe In Love / Waiting For 22 / My Empty Room / Eyes Of A Stranger

EMPIRE, EMI Manhattan CDMTL 1058 (1990) **50 NEW ZEALAND, 13 UK, 7 USA**

Best I Can / The Thin Line / Jet City Woman / Della Brown / Another Rainy Night (Without You) / Empire / Resistance / Silent Lucidity /

Hand On Heart / One And Only / Anybody Listening?

PROMISED LAND, EMI CD 1081 (1994) **13 UK, 3 USA**

9.28 am / I Am I / Damaged / Out Of Mind / Bridge / Promised Land / Disconnected / Lady Jane / My Global Mind / One More Time / Someone Else?

HEAR IN THE NOW FRONTIER, EMI 56141 (1997) **13 SWEDEN, 19 GERMANY, 46 UK, 19 USA**

Sign Of The Times / Cuckoo's Nest / Get A Life / The Voice Inside / Some People Fly / Saved / You / Hero / Miles Away / Reach / All I Want / Hit The Black / Anytime-Anywhere / Spool

Q2K, Atlantic 83225 (1999) **60 SWEDEN**

Falling Down / Sacred Ground / One Life / When The Rain Comes / How Could I? / Beside You / Liquid Sky / Breakdown / Burning Man / Wot Kinda Man / The Right Side Of My Mind

GREATEST HITS, EMI (2000)

Queen Of The Reich / The Lady Wore Black / Warning / Take Hold Of The Flame / Walk In The Shadows / I Dream In Infrared / I Don't Believe In Love / Eyes Of A Stranger / Jet City Woman / Empire / Silent Lucidity / I Am I / Bridge / Sign Of The Times / Chasing Blue Sky / Someone Else?

LIVE EVOLUTION, Sanctuary 84523 (2001)

NM 156 Reich / Walk In The Shadows / Roads To Madness / The Lady Wore Black / London / Screaming In Digital / Take Hold Of The Flame / Queen Of The Reich / I Remember Now / Anarchy X / Revolution Calling / Spreading The Disease / Electric Requiem / Mission / Suite Sister Mary / I Don't Believe In Love / My Empty Room / Eyes Of A Stranger / I Am I / Damaged / Empire / Silent Lucidity / Another Rainy Night (Without You) / Jet City Woman / Liquid Sky / Sacred Ground / Breakdown / Falling Down / The Right Side Of My Mind / Hit The Black

THE QUIET ROOM (Denver, CO, USA)

Line-Up: Pete Jewell (vocals), George Glasco (guitar), Jason Boudreau (guitar), Rob Franklin Munshower (bass), Jeff Janeczko (keyboards), Graeme Wood (drums)

Denver based Progressive Rock unit. THE QUIET ROOM, so titled after an Edgar Allen Poe short story theme, heralded their arrival with the 'Introspect' album. The act had been founded in 1992 by guitarist Jason Boudreau. Later enlistees would be second guitarist George Glasco followed by drummer Mike Rice and vocalist Chadd Castor during 1993. In this incarnation THE QUIET ROOM cut a

347

three song demo. Keyboard player Jeff
Janecczko would be added in late 1994 and
bass player Josh Luebbers in mid 1995.
The band would be picked up by the Metal
Blade label who would reissue 'Introspect'
and release the sophomore outing
'Reconceive' by which time Pete Jewell,
adding a distinct harder edge, had supplanted
Castor. Other new faces would be bass player
Robert Franklin Munshower and drummer
Graeme Wood.
By 2001 THE QUIET ROOM were yet again
on the search for a vocalist.

Albums:
INTROSPECT, Underground Symphony
USCD-019 (1997)
A Different Scene / Grudge / Second Time
Around / Altered Past / Drowning / Laughing
At Your Expense / Holding On / Extramental /
Suspended Seconds / Undetermined
RECONCEIVE, Metal Blade 14295 (2000)
Suffercation / Choke On Me / Your Hate /
Reason For Change / Realms Of Deceit /
Controlling Nation / Room 15 / Less Than
Zero / Face Your Judgment / This Pain / Two
Minutes Hate

RACER X (USA)

Line-Up: Jeff Martin (vocals), Paul Gilbert (guitar), Bruce Bouillet (guitar), John Alderete (bass), Scott Travis (drums)

A group assembled by former BLACK SHEEP guitarist PAUL GILBERT, a discovery of Shrapnel Records' Mike Varney. RACER X amounted to a band of 'musician's musicians', but still made Rock fans sit up and take notice proving to be a suitable springboard to launch the career of the whiz kid guitarist. Musically RACER X dealt in technically enhanced Metal and quickly built up a cult following which grew in stature with the various high profile exploits of the individual band members after the band's demise.

Varney, who raved over the youngster's talents in his regular column in 'Guitar Player' magazine, discovered Gilbert as a 15 year old budding guitar hero. Gilbert was encouraged to move to Los Angeles from his home in Greensburg, Pennsylvania to attend the renowned Guitar Institute of Technology (later renamed the Musician's Institute) school where Paul soon turned from pupil into tutor by the time he was 21!

It was here that Paul discovered fellow axe slinger Bruce Bouillet and quickly invited his pupil to join the fledgling RACER X, a band that would eventually boast ex-SURGICAL STEEL front man vocalist Jeff Martin, bassist John Alderete and former NO BROS drummer Harry Gnoschosser. Ex-HAWK man Scott Travis soon replaced the latter.

Naturally, RACER X would gain a deal with Varney's Shrapnel label and unleashed the 'Street Lethal' album in 1986. The band's second album included the track 'Heart Of A Lion', written by JUDAS PRIEST and given to RACER X by vocalist Rob Halford unbeknownst to the rest of the band or their management.

Scott Travis would be enticed away into the ranks of British Metal legends JUDAS PRIEST revitalising that band in many people's eyes for their 1990 'Painkiller' album. Gilbert would join MR. BIG and Martin hooked up with ex-OZZY OSBOURNE guitarist JAKE E. LEE to play drums in BADLANDS.

RACER X added one Chris Arvin in place of Gilbert and soldiered on, although the last line-up of RACER X saw Bouillet and Alderete joined by ex-ANGORA vocalist / guitarist John Corabi and former SHARK ISLAND and AMERICADE drummer Walt Woodward III. Before long RACER X evolved into THE SCREAM, via SAINTS AND SINNERS, and scored a new deal with Hollywood Records. Following one album release Corabi was

lured away to the big time replacing VINCE NEIL in MÖTLEY CRÜE and THE SCREAM became DC10.

Gilbert emerged as part of the successful 'supergroup' MR. BIG scoring numerous hit albums and a Number 1 American single. Travis landed the key position as drummer for arch metal veterans JUDAS PRIEST on their 1990 'Painkiller' album. He also made an appearance in JUDAS PRIEST singer Rob Halford's solo FIGHT project before rejoining JUDAS PRIEST.

Both Gilbert and Bouillet were to lend their tuition skills to PHANTOM BLUE guitarists Michelle Meldrum and Nicole Couch. Conversely, Aldrete was to tutor Kim Nielsen from the same band.

Jeff Martin turned to the drums, joining BADLANDS in the drummer's role and teamed up with erstwhile SURGICAL STEEL colleague Greg Chaisson to form a solid rhythm section as Martin took the place of Eric Singer.

Martin and Chaisson continued to work together post BADLANDS in the Christian outfit RED SEA, recording the 'Blood' album in 1995.

Martin, Gilbert, Bouillet and Alderete would be reunited on Gilbert's first solo album, 'King Of Clubs', recorded during 1997 and released later that year through Atlantic. The record would be reissued upon it being licensed to Mayhem Records some six months into the following year.

As Gilbert departed from MR. BIG Martin became part of the guitarist's touring band for the 1998 album 'Flying Dog' and resulting live album 'Beehive Live'.

RACER X emerged once more with the full classic line-up (now as a side project - Travis still very much a member of JUDAS PRIEST after their reunion in 1997) for the 'Technical Difficulties' album.

Martin joined UFO on drums for their ill-fated European tour in 2000. A further new album emerged in 2000 with 'Superheroes' ploughing a Sci-Fi theme throughout. The American release of the album, released by Shrapnel Records, differed from other territories in that profanities used in the tracks 'Evil Joe' and 'O.H.B.' were deleted.

RACER X, now with Gilbert a resident of Japan, would reconvene to squeeze in a solitary gig at the Hollywood Whiskey to promote the 'Superheroes' album upfront of Travis's JUDAS PRIEST commitments.

By 2001 Martin was ensconced in the MICHAEL SCHENKER GROUP as drummer for the German guitar legend's 'Be Aware Of Scorpions' opus. Martin's vocal abilities would also be on hand as he features as lead on the Japanese release bonus cut 'Ride The

Lightning'.

Albums:

STREET LETHAL, Shrapnel (1986)
Frenzy / Street Lethal / Into The Night /
Blowin' Up The Radio / Hotter Than Fire / On
The Loose / Loud And Clear / Y.R.O. /
Dangerous Love / Getaway / Rock It
SECOND HEAT, Roadrunner RR 34 9601
(1986)
Sacrifice / Gone Too Far / Scarified / Sunlit
Nights / Hammer Away / Heart Of A Lion /
Motor Man / Moonage Daydream / Living
The Hard Way / Lady Killer
EXTREME VOLUME (LIVE), Roadrunner
RR 9530-2 (1988)
Loud And Clear / Dangerous Love / Bruce's
Solo / Gone Too Far / John's Solo / She
Wants Control / Scit Scat Wah / Into The
Night / Paul's Solo / Motor Man / Scott's Solo
/ Set The World On Fire
LIVE EXTREME VOLUME 2, Roadrunner
RR 91422 (1994)
Hammer Away / Poison Eyes / Heart Of A
Lion / Moonage Daydream / Sunlit Nights /
Give It To Me / On The Loose / Rock It /
Detroit Rock City
TECHNICAL DIFFICULTIES, (2000)
Phallic Tractor / Fire Of Rock / Snakebite /
17th Moon / Technical Difficulties / Bolts In
My Heart / Poison Eyes / Give It To Me /
Miss Mistreated / Waiting / B.R.O. / The
Executioner's Song
**SUPER HEROES - ADVENTURES OF
RACER X MEN**, (2000)
Super Heroes / Let The Spirit Fly / King Of
Monsters / Dead Man's Shoes / Godzilla
2000 / Time Before The Sun / Mad At The
World / Evil Show / O.H.B. / Viking Son
SNOWBALL OF DOOM, Mascot (2002)
17th Moon / Into The Night / Let The Spirit
Fly / Street Lethal / Dead Man's Shoes /
Scarified / Get Away / Snakebite / Hammer
Away / Evil Joe / Phallic Tractor / Fire Of
Rock / O.H.B. / Godzilla

RACES (GERMANY)
Line-Up: Richard Meier (vocals), Frank Heed
(guitar), Peer Schleutner (bass), Andreas
Schnitt (drums)

Mainz based Power Metal band RACES
debuted in 1987 releasing the 'Beginning Of A
Nightmare' demo in 1989. Further demos
followed in the form of 1990's 'Welcome To
Amityville', 1991's 'Last Great Act Of
Defiance' and 1992's 'Seeds Of Aggression'.
RACES issued a yet further demo 'Total
Violence' before frontman Richard Meier
decamped to SHARKRAGE for a 1996 album.

RADAGHAST (CHILE)
Line-Up: Rodrigo Gil (Vocals), Gustavo
Toledo (guitar), Pablo Garcia Pfingsten
(guitar), Daniel Toledo (bass), Domenico
Zunino (keyboards), Alvaro Ignacio Miranda
Parra (drums)

Albums:
ARKAN, (2001)
God Of Thunder / Fly To Live / Live In The
Eternity / Freedom For All / Fire And Pain /
Arkan

RAGE (GERMANY)
Line-Up: Peter 'Peavey' Wagner (vocals /
bass), Victor Smolski (guitar), Mike Terrana
(drums)

RAGE was formed from the rampant Heavy
Metal band AVENGER with a line-up of Peter
Wagner, guitarists Jochen Schroeder and
Thomas Gruning and drummer Jörg Michael.
AVENGER released the 'Prayer Of Steel'
album and 'Depraved To Black' EP on
Wishbone Records before adopting the title of
RAGE in 1986, due to confusion with the
English AVENGER.
Signing to Noise Records to release 'Reign Of
Fear', RAGE toured Germany on a bill with
KREATOR and DESTRUCTION in 1986.
Shortly after the tour, Gruning left and his
position was filled by the high profile figure of
ex-WARLOCK guitarist Rudy Graf. Michael
also operated in the 'anonymous' avant-garde
side project MEKONG DELTA during 1987.
By 1988 both Graf and Michael were out,
superseded by guitarist Manni Schmidt and
drummer Chris Efthimiades. Michael would
become the permanent drummer for German
guitar hero AXEL RUDI PELL and rack up
impressive credits with fellow Teutonic Metal
bands HEADHUNTER, GRAVE DIGGER,
GLENMORE and RUNNING WILD. 1988's
'Perfect Man' album enjoyed considerable
critical success with the media and went on to
sell over 30,000 copies in Europe alone. In
1990 RAGE toured Germany as support to
RUNNING WILD.
Having released 'Reflections Of A Shadow' in
1991 RAGE's 1992 album, 'Trapped', featured
a cover of the renowned ACCEPT classic
'Fast As A Shark' and Japanese issues also
added two bonus cuts in 'Innocent Guilty' and
'Marching Heroes - The Wooden Cross'. The
group would subsequently fulfil the ambition
of touring in Japan and later joined SAXON
and MOTÖRHEAD in Europe on the 'Eagles
And Bombers' tour in Europe.
RAGE undertook further touring in 1993 on a
bill alongside GAMMA RAY and Norwegians
CONCEPTION as they were surely about to

unleash the album of their career in 'A Missing Link'. In 1994 guitarist Schmidt left the band. His position was filled by Spiros Efthimiades and ex-PYRACANDA man Sven Fischer and the ensuing 'Ten Years In Rage' album featured new cuts alongside old favourites.

RAGE split from Noise Records in 1994 following many other German acts to G.U.N. Records, an arm of major label BMG. The band undertook a short burst of seven dates during June 1995 in their homeland supported by GLENMORE.

After their debut for G.U.N. Records RAGE played a series of 'Summer Metal Meetings' together with RUNNING WILD, GRAVEDIGGER, GAMMA RAY, GLENMORE and ICED EARTH and, in 1996, released the 'Lingua Mortis' album. The record found the band joined by the Symphony Orchestra of Prague playing some of their best cuts.

RAGE suffered a mass walkout in 1999 when both the Efthimiades brothers and second guitarist Sven Fischer decamped leaving Peavey Wagner flying solo. Undaunted Wagner pulled in former BEAU NASTY, YNGWIE MALMSTEEN, ARTENSION, METALIUM drummer American Mike Terrana and Russian guitar virtuoso VICTOR SMOLSKI, quickly bowing back in with the 'Ghosts' album. In Germany this new incarnation of RAGE would debut at the Wacken festival then set off on an extensive tour of Russia.

2000 found Wagner guesting on the GB ARTS album 'The Lake'. Smolski too would session outside of RAGE contributing lead solos to the PERSONAL WAR 'Newtimechaos' outing. Ex-RAGE man Manni Schmidt joined GRAVE DIGGER in December of 2000.

RAGE's 2001 album 'Welcome To The Other Side' would land the group an unexpected bonus when the track 'Straight To Hell' would be chosen for the soundtrack to the movie 'Der Schuh Des Manitu'. This film would fortuitously turn out to be one of the most commercially successful German language films ever.

Terrana would also be found sessioning, in his case on the DRIVEN project album put together by ex-DIO guitarist Tracy G. The drummer also regrouped with ARTENSION for a 2002 comeback album 'Sacred Pathway' as well as perform on the 'Shadow Zone' album from German guitar hero AXEL RUDI PELL. A further collaboration had the sticksman forging the VOODOO TABOO band project in collaboration with French guitarist CYRIL ARCHARD.

The RAGE April 2002 album 'Unity' would see the Japanese release boasting the traditional extra track in the form of 'Darkness Turns To Light'. The band embarked on a full scale world tour commencing in Seol at the 'World Rock Festival' before continuing on for dates in Japan. RAGE would also schedule a date in August at the 'Soyorock 2002' festival in Kyung Gi Do, Korea. An extensive September run of European concerts found RAGE paired up with PRIMAL FEAR. The band made space to cut a rendition of 'Motorbreath' for a Nuclear Blast METALLICA tribute collection.

Singles/EPs:
Invisible Horizons / Lost Side Of The World / Law And Order, Noise NO136-6 (1989) ('Invisible Horizons' EP)
Woman / Ashes / Battlefield / Waiting For The Moon / What's Up, Noise NO169-3 (1991) ('Extended Power' EP)
Beyond The Wall / Bury All Life/ On The Edge / I Want You / (Those Who Got) Nothing To Lose / Last Goodbye / Light Into The Darkness / Dust, Noise NO202-3 (1992) ('Beyond The Wall' EP)
The Crawling Chaos / Black In Mind / Alive But Dead / Shadow Out Of Time, G.U.N. GUN 061 BMG (1995) (Promotional release)

Albums:
REIGN OF FEAR, Noise NO038 (1986)
Scared To Death / Deceiver / Reign Of Fear / Hand Of Glory / Raw Energy / Echoes Of Evil / Chaste Flesh / Suicide / Machinery / Scaffold
EXECUTION GUARANTEED, Noise NO073 (1987)
Down By Law / Execution Guaranteed / Before The Storm / Street Wolf / Deadly Error / Hatred / Grapes Of Wrath / Mental Decay / When You're Dead
PERFECT MAN, Noise N0112 (1988)
Wasteland / In The Darkest Hour / Animal Instinct / Perfect Man / Sinister Thinking / Supersonic Hydromatic / Don't Fear The Winter / Death In The Afternoon / A Pilgrim's Path / Time And Place / Round Trip / Between The Lines
SECRETS IN A WEIRD WORLD, Noise NO0137 (1989)
Intro (Opus 32 No. 3) / Time Waits For No One / Make My Day / The Inner Search / Invisible Horizons / She / Light Into The Darkness / Distant Voices / Without A Trace
REFLECTIONS OF A SHADOW, Noise N0160 (1991)
Introduction (A Bit More Of Green) / That's Human Bondage / True Face In Everyone / Flowers That Fade In My Hand / Reflections Of A Shadow / Can't Get Out / Waiting For The Moon / Saddle The Wind / Dust Nobody Knows

TRAPPED, Noise N0189 (1992)
Shame On You / Solitary Man / Enough Is
Enough / Medicine / Questions / Take Me To
The Water / Power And Greed / The Body
Talks / Not Forever / Beyond The Wall Of
Sleep / Baby, I'm Your Nightmare / Fast As A
Shark / Difference / Innocent Guilty /
Marching Heroes - The Wooden Cross
THE MISSING LINK, Noise NO217 (1994)
The Firestorm / Nevermore / Refuge / The
Pit And The Pendulum / From The
Underworld / Certain Days / Who Dares? /
Wake Me When I'm Dead / Lost In The Ice /
Her Diary's Black Pages / The Missing Link /
Raw Caress
TEN YEARS IN RAGE, Noise N0219-2
(1994)
Vertigo / She Killed And Smiled / Destination
Day / Take My Blood / No Sign Of Life /
Submission / The Unknown / Dangerous
Heritage / Prayers Of Steel / The Blow In A
Row.
BLACK IN MIND, G.U.N. GUN 062 BMG
74321 27743-2 (1995)
Black In Mind / The Crawling Chaos / Alive
But Dead / Sent By The Devil / Shadow Out
Of Time / Spider's Web / In A Nameless
Time / The Icecold Hand Of Destiny /
Forever Until I Die / The Rage / The Price Of
War / Start / All This Time
**PRAYERS OF STEEL / DEPRAVED TO
BLACK**, G.U.N. GUN 062 BMG 74321
24484-2 (1995) (3,000 only Limited edition
free with the 'Black In Mind' Album.
Previously released under as AVENGER)
Battlefield / Southcross Union / Prayers Of
Steel / Halloween / Faster Than Hell /
Adoration / Rise Of The Creature / Sword
Made Of Steel / Bloodlust / Assorted By
Satan / Depraved To Black / Down To The
Bone / Prayers Of Steel (Live) / Faster Than
Hell (Live)
LINGUA MORTIS, G.U.N. GUN 090 BMG
74321 36667-2 (1996)
In A Nameless Time / Alive But Dead /
Medley a) Don't Fear The Winter, b) Black In
Mind, c) Firestorm, d) Sent By The Devil, e)
Lost In The Ice / All This Time / Alive But
Dead
END OF ALL DAYS, G.U.N. GUN 101 BMG
74321 39036-2 (1996)
Under Control / Higher Than The Sky / Deep
In The Blackest Hole / End Of All Days /
Visions / Desperation / Voice From The Vault
/ Let The Night Begin / Fortress / Frozen Fire
/ Talking To The Dead / Face Behind The
Mask / Silent Victory / Fading Hours / The
Sleep / The Trooper
THIRTEEN, G.U.N. GUN 74321 56314-2
(1998)
Overture / From The Cradle To The Grave /
Days Of December / Sign Of Heaven /

Incomplete / Turn The Page / Heartblood /
Over And Over / In Vain (I Won't Go Down) /
Immortal Sin / Paint It Black / Just Alone
GHOSTS, G.U.N. (1999) 31 GERMANY
Beginning of the End / Back In Time /
Ghosts / Wash My Sins Away / Fear / Love
And Fear Unite / Vanished In Haze / Spiritual
Awakening / Love After Death / More Than A
Lifetime / Tomorrow's Yesterday / End Of
Eternity
WELCOME TO THE OTHER SIDE, G.U.N.
(2001)
Trauma / Paint The Devil On The Wall / The
Mirror In Your Eyes / R.I.P. (Tribute To
Dishonour Part 1) / One More Time (Tribute
To Dishonour Part 2) / Requiem (Tribute To
Dishonour Part 3) / I'm Crucified (Tribute To
Dishonour Part 4) / No Lies / Point Of No
Return / Leave It All Behind / Deep In The
Night / Welcome To The Other Side / Lunatic
/ Riders On The Moonlight / Straight To Hell /
After The End / Sister Demon
BEST OF ALL G.U.N. YEARS, G.U.N.
(2001)
Straight To Hell / Days Of December / Back
In Time / Alive But Dead / Deep In The
Blackest Hole / The Mirror In Your Eyes /
Black In Mind / Higher Than The Sky /
Spiritual Awakening / The Crawling Chaos /
Six Feet Under Ground / Just Another
Wasted Day / From The Cradle To The Grave
/ Medley: Don't Fear The Winter-Black In
Mind - Firestorm - Send By The Devil - Lost
In The Ice
UNITY, G.U.N. (2002)
All I Want / Insanity / Down / Set This World
On Fire / Dies Irae / World Of Pain /
Shadows / Living My Dream / Seven Deadly
Sins / You Want It, You'll Get It / Unity

RAGING STORM (GREECE)
Line-Up: George Drimilis (vocals), Chris
Mossalos (guitar), Dimitris Delis (guitar),
Harry Boudamour (bass), George Vassaras
(drums)

Epic Metal band RAGING STORM are
attempt to resurrect an '80s Metal sound. The
group was pieced together in 1997 by
guitarist Chris Mossalos and bass player
Harry Boudamour. A succession of other
players came and went until the line-up
stabilised with the addition of singer George
Drimilis, guitarist Dimitris Delis and drummer
George Vassaras. The group's debut live
showing came in October of 2000, sharing
the stage with AIRGED LAMH and INNER
WISH. Since then RAGING STORM has
supported visiting artists such as ANVIL,
BROCAS HELM and PRIMAL FEAR.

353

Kingdom Of Hades / Holy War / Minotaur / Heavy Metal Faith, (2001) ('Sailing For Glory Under The Raging Storm' EP)

Albums:
RAGING STORM, Metalfighters (2002)
Intro / Raging Storm / Sons Of Valhalla / The Devil Speaks / The Warrior / Holy War / Heavy Metal Faith / Kingdom Of Hades / Minotaur / The Last Stand

RAILWAY (GERMANY)
Line-Up: Walter Wicha (vocals), Robert Haslinger (guitar), Hermann Janowitz (guitar), Werner Thaller (bass), Hasi Haslinger (drums)

RAILWAY can track their inception back to 1978 when the Haslinger brothers, guitarist Robert and drummer Hasi, assembled the first form.

The band debuted with two tracks on the Noise Records compilation album 'Rock From Hell' before signing to Roadrunner Records. They then toured Europe as support to TOKYO BLADE, BONFIRE and MOTÖRHEAD. Guitarist Florian Allgayer had superseded Kanowitz by the 'Climax' album. RAILWAY also substituted Wicha for vocalist Armin Schuler. RAILWAY split in April 1987 but re-formed much later.

The comeback album 'Welcome Tonite' saw RAILWAY handling business affairs themselves. With distribution through SPV the album outsold its predecessors in a matter of weeks.

1993's line-up incorporated guitarist / vocalist Robert Haslinger, guitarist Mike Sperner, bassist Harry Enzian and drummer Erhard Haslinger.

Singles/EPs:
Tomorrow / Nighttime / Never The Sun, Railway (198-) ('Backstage All Areas' EP)
I'm A Looser / Lick It, Stick It (Live) / Heavy And Loud (Live), Highwire (Live) / Never The Sun (Radio Edit), Point Music POI 101 (1994) ('I'm A Looser' EP)

Albums:
RAILWAY, Roadrunner RR 9821 (1984)
Heavy Metal Fever / Out To Kill / Screaming After Midnight / Take It Away / Night Rider / Dirty Boys / Crazy / Stone In My Bed / Hell Soldiers
RAILWAY II, Roadrunner RR 976 (1986)
Lick It, Stick It / Go Down / D.O.A. / Lady Life / Dreamin' / Fight With The Killer / All Night Long / Dying In The Dust / I Wanna Run / I'm A Looser / Stronger Than Rock

CLIMAX, Roadrunner RR9667 (1987)
Breakout / Heavy And Loud / Take The Chance / Rockets / First Shot / Boys Get Drunk / Ready To Rock / Miss Lilly / I'm On Fire / Don't Try To Mess... / High Wire / Come On
TO BE CONTINUED, Intercord IRS 986.949 (1991)
Weekend In Rock / No Mercy / Hit Down The Highway / Real Love / Black Billy / Shake All Night / 'Til You Be Back / Dreams / Stand By Me / Love Just For Money / If You Wanna / All Night / To Be Continued
WELCOME TONITE, SPV 084-76622 (1993)
Welcome Tonite / Steelhorse Riding / Red Light - Green Light / Let It Be / Turn Me Up n' Down / Living B Side U / Drums Of Freedom (Indian Rap) / Story Of Love / Rock n' Roll / Ride On
PERSECUTION MANIA, Point Music 8248 (1995)
Persecution Mania / Darkness Mistery / Foreign Supplies / Hero / U.N.O. / Everybody Needs Somebody / Get Up - Get Down / Face The Truth / Queeny / The World Is Outta Control

RATA BLANCA (ARGENTINA)
Line-Up: Adrian Barilari (vocals), Walter Giardino (guitar), Sergio Berdichevsky (guitar), Guillermo Sanchez (bass), Hugo Bistolfi (keyboards), Gustavo Rowek (drums)

A revered name on the South American Metal circuit. RATA BLANCA, led by former V8 guitarist Walter Giardino, established a reputation that inspired countless other bands in their wake. RATA BLANCA was borne out of a 1985 demo commissioned by Giardino in 1985, originally intended as a vehicle to establish ties with the UK market. The tape was recorded utilising vocalist Rodolfo Cava, bass player Yulie Ruth and drummer Gustavo Rowek. However, Giardino was so inspired by the final result the planned relocation to Great Britain was put on hold.

RATA BLANCA was convened as a full band unit for an eponymous debut album in 1988. Joining Giardino would be lead vocalist Saul Blanch, second guitarist Sergio Berdichevsky, bassist Guillermo Sanchez and drummer Gustavo Rowek. The album, which included spin off singles 'El Sueño De La Gitana' and 'Chico Callejero', proved a huge success. Despite this huge leap forward Blanch bowed out and RATA BLANCA entered its second stage with the induction of singer Adrian Barilari and keyboard player Hugo Bistolfi. Support slots to IAN GILLAN promoted RATA BLANCA's second album 'Magos, Espadas Y Rosas'. The album generated huge praise, surpassing the million sales mark globally.

The band's third album 'Guerrero del Arco Iris', titled in honour of the Greenpeace 'Rainbow Warrior' ship, was debuted live in front of over 30,000 fans at a single concert in Velez Sarsfield Stadium, still holding the record today as the biggest ever gig for a local band.

The group would undertake live work across all of South America and into Mexico and even Los Angeles, performing at the famous Whiskey A Go Go club. Back in Buenos Aires RATA BLANCA cut a groundbreaking live album recorded over three nights at the Opera Theatre with a full chamber orchestra. Live dates further afield had the band trekking across Portugal and Spain, recording their fourth album 'El Libro Oculto' there.

With the close of the world tour both Bistolfi and Barilari decided to leave. The erstwhile RATA BLANCA duo duly founded ALIANZA issuing three albums, 'Sueños Del Mundo' in 1993, 'Alianza' in 1994 and 'Huellas' in 1999. RATA BLANCA meantime pulled in Mario Ian on vocals with Javier Retamozo on keyboards and persevered.

A fifth album, the exceptionally heavy 'Entre El Cielo Y El Infierno' ('Between Heaven And Hell'), was recorded in the midst of a 1994 world tour. RATA BLANCA performed at the Brazilian 'Monsters Of Rock' festival in Sao Paolo sharing the stage with international heavyweights OZZY OSBOURNE, ALICE COOPER and MEGADETH before an audience of 100,000. In Argentina the live album recorded earlier in 1992 'En Vivo En Buenos Aires' was finally issued.

With popularity waning in their homeland Mario Ian made his exit in 1996. RATA BLANCA appointed Gabriel Marian to the frontman position for the 'Rata Blanca VII' album. The band was in a fractious state, it becoming public knowledge that other band members were keen to decamp but had been persuaded to stay on for the sessions. The album received little promotion and in April of 1998 Giardino signalled the end of the band.

Gustavo Rowek and Sergio Berdichevsky assembled a fresh Heavy Metal act NATIVO, going on to publish two albums 'Consumo' in 1999 and 'Futuro' in 2001. Giardino too founded a new endeavour billed as TEMPLE. He would tour Argentina during 1999 then put together a new band which found former RATA BLANCA singer Adrian Barilari as guest singer. Eventually Guillermo Sanchez came in on bass and re-titling the band RATA BLANCA gigs were held in Bolivia. Returning to Argentina Hugo Bistolfi returned to the fold too.

In 2001 a gathering of South American Metal talent paid homage with the tribute album 'La Leyenda Continúa'. Included would be artists such as AZEROTH, BETO VASQUEZ INFINITY, HUMANIMAL and ROSACRUZ. Both Adrián Barilari and Walter Giardino made a special appearance uniting with members of premier league Finnish bands NIGHTWISH and STRATOVARIUS, guitarist Emppu Vuorinen, bassist Sami Vänskä, keyboard player Jens Johansson and drummer Jukka Nevalainen on the track 'La Leyenda Del Hada Y El Mago'.

The new RATA BLANCA, with Fernando Scacella on drums, toured South America and Mexico to enthusiastic response. A compilation 'Grandes Canciones' was backed by further gigs including shows in Spain. A new studio album 'El Camino del Fuego' was delivered in June of 2002.

Albums:

RATA BLANCA, PolyGram Discos S.A. (1988)
La Misma Mujer / Sólo Para Amarte / Gente Del Sur / Rompe El Hechizo / El Sueño De La Gitana / Chico Callejero / Preludio Obsesivo / El Ultimo Ataque / Otoño Medieval

MAGOS, ESPADAS & ROSAS, PolyGram Discos S.A. (1990)
La Leyenda Del Hada Y El Mago / Mujer Amante / El Beso De La Bruja / Haz Tu Jugada / El Camino Del Sol / Dias Duros / Porque Es Tan Dificil Amar

GUERRERO DEL ARCO IRIS, PolyGram Discos S.A. (1991)
Hombre De Hielo / Angeles De Acero / Noche Sin Sueños / La LBoca Del Lobo / Quizá Empieces Otra Vez / Guerrero Del Arco Iris / Abrazando Al Rock And Roll / Los Ojos Del Dragon / Nada Es Fácil Sin Tu Amor

EL LIBRO OCULTO, Ariola (1993)
Basura / Asesinos / Cuarto Poder / Lejos De Casa / Agord, La Bruja

ENTRE EL CIELO Y EL INFIERNO, Ariola (1994)
En El Bajo Flores / Bajo Control / Jerusalén / Sombra Inerte Del Amor / Obsesión / Patria / Herederos De La Fe / Sin Tu Amor Nada Existe / Máquina / Fantasma Azul / Banda Viajera

EN VIVO EN BUENOS AIRES, PolyGram Discos S.A. (1996)
Quiza Empieces Otra Vez / Solo Para Amarte / Hombre De Hielo / Angeles De Acero / Aria En Sol, De La Suite #13 / 3 Movimiento De La Primavera / Capricho Arabe - Preludio Obsesivo / Dias Duros / Nada Es Facil Sin Tu Amor / La Leyenda Del Hada Y El Mago

RATA BLANCA VII, Ariola (1997)
Madame X / Rey De La Revolucion / Pastel De Rocas / La Historia De Un Muchacho /

La Cancion Del Sol / Héroes / Vuelo Nocturno / La Caja / Ella / Mr. Cósmico / Vieja Lucy / Viejo Amigo / Anarquía / Libranos Del Mal

LOS CLASICOS DEL ROCK EN ESPANOL: RATA BLANCA, (1999)
GRANDES CANCIONES, Tocka Discos (2000)
El Sueño De La Gitana / Solo Para Amarte / Dias Duros /Porque Es Tan Dificil Amar / Chico Callejero / Preludio Obsesivo / Mujer Amante / Guerrero Del Arco Iris / Noche Sin Sueños / Abrazando Al Rock And Roll / La Leyenda Del Hada Y El Mago / Mujer Amante (Acoustic)

EL CAMINO DEL FUEGO, Rata (2002)
El Amo Del Camino / Volviendo A Casa / La Cancion Del Guerrero / Abeja Reina / Lluvia Púrpura / Señora Furia / Sinfonía Fantástica / Cuando La Luz Oscurece / En Nombre De Dios? / Caballo Salvaje

RAVEN (UK)

Line-Up: John Gallagher (vocals / bass), Mark Gallagher (guitar), Rob 'Wacko' Hunter (drums)

Newcastle "Athletic Rock" outfit that made a huge impact on the NWoBHM but sadly failed to live up to initial promise in their home country despite recognition abroad. Their early efforts are manic Metal sprints through excellent riffs and high-pitched distinctive vocals. Despite waning popularity in Britain RAVEN command respect and a healthy fan base across the world witnessed by sizeable followings in Germany and Japan as well as cult status in America.

RAVEN date back to 1974 with an initial line-up of brothers John and Mark Gallagher and Paul Bowden. However, at this fledgling stage RAVEN had only one classical guitar between them! Santa Claus came to the rescue and in December of that year the band got electric guitars for Christmas.

RAVEN's first live date in December 1975 was memorable if not only for the fact that both Gallagher brothers managed to fall offstage. By this point the band had added drummer Paul Sherrif. Within months Sherrif was out in favour of Mick Kenworthy. In this incarnation RAVEN opened for THE STRANGLERS and THE MOTORS locally. One of RAVEN's early headlining gigs included a Hells Angels convention where the band were ordered to play 'Born To Be Wild' no less than ten times in the pouring rain. The band only stalled the show by Mark faking an electric shock!

Kenworthy drifted away in late 1977 to be replaced by Sean Taylor. Bowden also departed in 1979 having his position filled by Pete Shore. RAVEN suffered another blow when Taylor quit, eventually to join SATAN.

Augmenting the band line-up once more with the addition of drummer Rob Hunter whose previous act FASTBREEDER also included future DURAN DURAN guitarist ANDY TAYLOR. RAVEN cut their first two track demo featuring "She Don't Need Your Money' and 'Wiped Out'. Courtesy of TYGERS OF PAN TANG manager Tom Noble this tape secured the band a deal with local Newcastle label Neat Records.

RAVEN's debut single 'Don't Need Your Money' created a huge swell of interest in the band and helped the first album reach the British album charts. During 1980 RAVEN also had a track 'Let It Rip' on the 'Brute Force' compilation album. At the time RAVEN were certainly originators of the fast and powerful approach.

Album number two 'Wiped Out' saw the songs getting faster and the band honing their direction. Regrettably the intended mixes for the album were not used and substituted for a mix unapproved by the band. However, the band's fans were still impressed. RAVEN's first American shows in 1982, alongside RIOT and ANVIL, were promoted by Johnny Zazula of the 'Rock n Roll Heaven' record store in New Jersey.

Producer Michael Wagner was drafted in for 'All For One' as RAVEN sought a more mature sound. It was also their first American release for Zazula's Megaforce label. This Affiliation led to RAVEN's first 36 date American tour with opening act METALLICA; further tours had EXODUS and ANTHRAX supporting.

At RAVEN's 1984 New York show the band headlined above METALLICA and ANTHRAX. Rumour has it that an A&R representative for Elektra Records was suitably impressed by RAVEN but upon inquiring to the band's name was informed it was METALLICA. Once signed the same person was confused to find the band he had signed were now a quartet and not a trio. Allegedly...

With Megaforce's connection to Atlantic Records 1984 saw RAVEN ink a major deal. Atlantic, however, maneuvered the band away from their speed attack towards a more mainstream approach even getting the band to wear bizarre spacesuit stage gear. RAVEN's audience were by now finding it hard to equate the killer live act with a succession of records that were ever more experimental, even drafting in horn sections at one point. RAVEN undertook a 1985 American tour utilizing JUDAS PRIEST's 'Screaming For Vengeance' stage set. The show included a pyro rocket firing guitar that set fire to the venue roof in San Diego.

RAVEN also contributed two tracks to the movie soundtrack of 'Hot Moves'. Songs cut were 'Hot Moves' and 'Ladykiller'.

'The Pack Is Back' was produced by Eddie Kramer but did little to stop the rot. RAVEN toured once more with support from fellow Brits TANK. Further shows supporting TWISTED SISTER where to follow but the headliner pulled out at the last minute. 1986 saw RAVEN opening for JUDAS PRIEST in America before headline dates. The tour ended with support shows to YNGWIE MALMSTEEN.

To promote 'Life's A Bitch' RAVEN made up a three band touring package including SLAYER and W.A.S.P. RAVEN fared well in front of rabid SLAYER fans intent on demoralising W.A.S.P.

Hunter departed without warning in 1987 following Atlantic severing all ties with the band and RAVEN found an able replacement in former SIMMONDS, BURNING STARR and PENTAGRAM drummer Joe Hasselvander prior to signing a new deal with Combat Records.

RAVEN were back out on the road in America for headlining dates promoting 'Nothing Exceeds Like Excess' before another batch of gigs with TESTAMENT through into 1989. The band's first European tour for many years was offered with KREATOR, a German act that had recently covered a RAVEN track. Impressed by KREATOR's organization RAVEN soon signed to their management and record label.

In 1990 John Gallagher assembled an extracurricular project titled SLIDER comprising of former BLUE CHEER, SIMMONDS and SHAKIN' STREET guitarist Duck McDonald, ex-RODS and SIMMONDS bassist Gary Bordonaro and session player Bob Fortunato. The band issued one album 'The Slider Project' on Feedback Records in 1990.

The 'Architect Of Fear' album was a welcome return to previous heaviness. RAVEN set out on European dates with RUNNING WILD. However, RAVEN was to go on ice shortly after.

John Gallagher formed KILLERS with former IRON MAIDEN vocalist PAUL DIANNO, ex-TANK guitarist Cliff Evans, DRIVE SHE SAID guitarist Ray Ditone and former PERSIAN RISK drummer Steve Hopgood for a proposed tour of South America. A rehearsal tape, recorded in an empty venue in New York, featuring Gallagher later surfaced as the 'South American Assault' album.

The 1992 EP 'Heads up' prompted yet more European dates with support act RISK. 1993 proved a disastrous year for the band as John's house burned down as well as having all his guitars stolen.

In 1994 RAVEN performed at the Los Angeles Foundations Forum in an effort to secure a new deal. Before long RAVEN had signed to Japanese label Zero recording 'Glow' the same year. Hungry for the road the band performed American dates in early 1995 with WIDOWMAKER and ANVIL before headline shows of Japan. One of these shows became the 'Destroy All Monsters - Live In Japan' album.

The band toured Germany alongside TANK and newcomers HAMMERFALL during 1997. The band returned with renewed vigour during 1999 with a fresh studio album 'One For All' produced by Michael Wagener. The album would be issued in Europe by Massacre Records and the following year licensed into America via Metal Blade. A retrospective box set, provisionally entitled 'Stark Raven Mad', would also be announced but fell by the wayside. The band therefore took matters into their own hands issuing a collection of demos and rarities billed 'Raw Tracks'. Various territories saw differing track listings with the American version closing on a take of QUEEN's 'Tie Your Mother Down'. Japanese variants ended with 'All For One' and 'Young Blood' whilst the European imprint's last tracks would be 'Architect Of Fear' and 'Enemy'.

RAVEN toured Germany in early 2000 as guests to U.D.O. The two acts would unite once again for a series of American mid summer 2001 dates.

Singles/EPs:
Don't Need Your Money / Wiped Out, Neat NEAT 06 (1980)
Hard Ride / Crazy World, Neat NEAT 11 (1980)
Crash, Bang, Wallop / Firepower / Run Them Down / Rock Hard, Neat NEAT 15 (1981)
Break The Chain / Ballad Of Marshall Stack, Neat NEAT 28 (1983) (with UDO DIRKSCHNEIDER)
Born To Be Wild / Inquisitor, Neat NEAT 29 (1983) (with UDO DIRKSCHNEIDER)
Born To Be Wild / Inquisitor / Break The Chain, Neat NEAT 29-12 (1983) (12" single) (with UDO DIRKSCHNEIDER)
On And On / On And On, Atlantic PR702 (1984) (USA Promotion)
Pray For The Sun / On And On / The Bottom Line, Atlantic 786901 (1985)
Speed Of The Reflex / Do Or Die / How Did Ya Get So Crazy / Seen It On The TV / Gimme Just A Little, Atlantic 81670 (1986) ('Mad' EP)
Gimme Some Lovin', / One On, Atlantic

357

A9453 (1986)

Albums:
ROCK UNTIL YOU DROP, Neat NEAT 1001 (1981) 63 UK
Hard Ride / Hell Patrol / Don't Need Your Money / Over The Top / 39/40 / For The Future / Rock Until You Drop / Nobody's Hero / Hell Raiser / Action / Lambs To The Slaughter / Tyrant Of The Airways
WIPED OUT, Neat NEAT 1004 (1982)
Faster Than The Speed Of Light / Bring The Hammer Down / Firepower / Read All About It / To The Limit - To The Top / Battlezone / Live At The Inferno / Star War / U.X.B. / 20-21 / Hold Back The Fire / Chainsaw
ALL FOR ONE, Neat NEAT 1011 (1983)
Take Control / Mind Over Metal / Sledgehammer Rock / All For One / Run Silent, Run Deep / Hung, Drawn And Quartered / Break The Chain / Take It Away / Seek And Destroy / Athletic Rock
LIVE AT THE INFERNO, Megaforce MRI 969 (1984)
Live At The Inferno / Take Control / Mind Over Metal / Crash Bang Wallop / Rock Until You Drop / Faster Than The Speed Of Light / All For One / Forbidden Planet / Star War / Tyrant Of The Airways / Run Silent, Run Deep / Crazy World / Let It Rip / G.A.R.B.O. / Wiped Out / Firepower / Don't Need Your Money / Break The Chain / Hell Patrol / Live At The Inferno
STAY HARD, Atlantic 81241-1 (1985)
Stay Hard / When The Going Gets Tough / On And On / Get It Right / Restless Child / The Power And The Glory / Pray For The Sun / Hard Ride / Extract The Action / The Bottom Line
THE DEVIL'S CARRION, Rawpower LP003 (1985)
Hard Ride / Bring The Hammer Down / Inquisitor / All For One / Hellraiser / Action / Live At The Inferno / Crash Bang Wallop / The Ballad Of Marshall Stack / Crazy World / Rock Until You Drop / Don't Need Your Money / Hell Patrol / Rock Hard / Faster Than The Speed Of Light / Wiped Out / Break The Chains / Read All About It / Firepower / Athletic Rock / Run Silent, Run Deep
THE PACK IS BACK, Atlantic 81629 (1986)
The Pack Is Back / Gimme Some Lovin' / Screaming Down The House / Young Blood / Hyperactive / Rock Dogs / Don't Let It Die / Get Into Your Car And Drive / All I Need / Nightmare Ride
LIFE'S A BITCH, Atlantic 81734 (1987)
The Savage And The Hungry / Pick Your Window / Life's A Bitch / Never Forgive / Iron League / On The Wings Of An Eagle / Overload / You're A Liar / Fuel To The Fire /

Only The Strong Survive / Juggernaut / Playing With The Razor / Finger On The Trigger
NOTHING EXCEEDS LIKE EXCESS, Under One Flag FLAG 28 (1988)
Behemoth / Die For Allah / Gimme A Break / Into The Jaws Of Death / In The Name Of Death / Stick It / Lay Down The Law / You Got A Screw Loose / Thunderlord / The King / Hard As Nails / Kick Your Ass
UNRELEASED TRACKS, Teichiku TECP 25450 (1990) (Japanese release)
Crash, Bang, Wallop / Rock Hard / Run Them Down / Don't Need Your Money / wiped Out / Crazy World / Born To Be Wild / Inquisitor / ...Plus Surprising Message
ARCHITECT OF FEAR, Steamhammer SPV 008 76281 (1991)
Intro / Architect Of Fear / Disciple / Got The Devil / Part Of The Machine / Under The Skin / White Hot Anger / Can't Run And Hide / Blind Leading The Blind / Relentless / Just Let Me Go / Heart Attack / Sold Down The River
RADIO HELL, Raw Fruit FRSCD009 (1992) (including VENOM & WARFARE tracks)
Lambs To The Slaughter / Hold Back The Fire / Hard Ride / Chainsaw
HEAD'S UP, Steamhammer 76-76392 (1992)
Hell On Earth / World Comes Tumbling / Stay Human / All For One / Into The Jaws Of Death / Can't Run And Hide
MIND OVER METAL, Success 16088 (1994)
GLOW, Steamhammer SPV 084-12092 (1995)
Watch You Drown / Spite / True Believer / So Close / Altar / The Dark Side / The Rocker / Turn You On / Far And Wide / Victim / Gimme A Reason / Slip Away
DESTROY ALL MONSTERS - LIVE IN JAPAN, SPV 085-12132 (1995)
Victim / Live At The Inferno / Crash, Bang, Wallop / True Believer / Into The Jaws Of Death / Hard As Nails / Die For Allah / Guitar Solo / Speed Of The Reflex / Run Silent, Run Deep / Mind Over Metal / Gimme A Reason / Inquisitor / For The Future / Bass Solo / Architect Of Fear / White Hot Anger / Drum Solo / Break The Chain
EVERYTHING LOUDER, Fresh Fruit SPV CD 085-12162 (1997)
Blind Eye / No Pain, No Gain / Sweet Jane / Holy Grail / Hungry / Insane / Everything Louder / ??? / Between The Wheels / Losing My Mind / Get Your Finger Out / Wilderness Of Broken Glass / !!! / Fingers Do The Walking / Bonus
ONE FOR ALL, Massacre MASCD0206 (1999)
Seven Shades / Double Talk / Roll With The Punches / Get Your Motor Running / To Be Broken / Derailed / The Hunger Inside / Top

Of The World / In The Line Of Fire / Kangaroo / New Religion / Last Ride
RAW TRACKS, Metal Blade 14729 (1999)
Firepower / Don't Need Your Money / Savage & The Hungry / Nightmare Ride / Get It Right / On & On / Extract The Action / Barbarian / Thunderlord / Gimme A Break / Move Over / White Hot Anger / Altar / Tie Your Mother Down

RAVENLOFT (BRAZIL)
Line-Up: Sérgio Mazul (vocals), Marcio Miranda (guitar), Andrey Romaniuk (bass), Thiago Mussi (drums)

Heavy Metal act RAVENLOFT have undergone turbulent times in their short history, actually breaking up in March of 2001. Prior to dissolving the band, held together by bassist Andrey Romaniuk, lost personnel such as Fábio Macuco and keyboard player Sergio Imanichi in September of 2000, added Thiago C. Cordeiro the following month but finally ground to a halt.
Romaniuk and singer Sérgio Mazul resurrected RAVENLOFT in September of 2001 although they would lose half of their twin guitar team - Jorge A. Miera - just before their debut recordings. Both Marco Carporasso and Mauricio Taborda of DRAGONHEART lent their backing vocals to the 'Crowning Battle' EP of 2002. Osmar Adriano came in on second guitar once these sessions had been completed.

Singles/EPs:
Intro / The Last Warrior / Never Surrender / Crowning Battle, (2002) ('Crowning Battle' EP)

RAWHEAD REXX (GERMANY)
Line-Up: Jürgen Volk (vocals), Rüdiger Fleck (guitar), Face (bass), Dany Loble (drums)

Power Metal band RAWHEAD REXX, fronted by the vocal talents of Jürgen Volk was founded from the ashes of Hard Rockers GLENMORE. Other members boast credits with HOLLENHUNDE, LETTER X and EROTIC JESUS. Prior to creating RAWHEAD REXX Volk had operated as frontman for R.A.W.
Issuing the Charlie Bauerfeind produced eponymous debut in early 2001 the band toured Germany as support to ANNIHILATOR and NEVERMORE. 'Rawhead Rexx', which came complete with a gory PC game to match the bloodthirsty cover art, saw release in Europe through AFM Records and via Rock Brigade in Brazil.
The band put in an appearance at the

Spanish 'Rock Machina' festival in July of 2002 prior to commencing work on a second album, once again produced by Bauerfeind.

Albums:
RAWHEAD REXX, AFM (2001)
The Curse / Town Of Skulls / Opposing Force / Mr. Hyde / Holy War / Sons Of Mayhem / Rawhead Rexx / Request / Blood On My Hands / The Wolf / Pain / Don't Tear Me Down / The Scream

REACTOR (GERMANY)
Line-Up: S.L. Coe (vocals), Thorsten Schwalm (guitar), Markus Baier (guitar), Robert Käfferlein (bass), Markus Sturz (drums)

REACTOR trade in Teutonic melodic metal. Based in Augsburg, Southern Germany, REACTOR was formulated during 1988 by CHEYENNE guitarist Markus Baier and VETO drummer Muck Langmair. Later additions to the ranks saw a full band being rounded out by erstwhile MONTEREY personnel guitarist Thorsten Schwalm and bass player Robert Käfferlein alongside singer Jerry Bryant. This unit gigged heavily and issued an eight track demo.
The band started out commercially with the May 1991 'Rather Dead Than Dishonoured' album. This outing secured strong interest in Japan and garnered a contract with the Zero Corporation for a further record, 'Revelation', issued in 1993. However, all was not well internally and after an appearance at the Dortmund 'Horror Infernal' concert a split in the ranks resulted in Bryant and Langmair opting out.
For their third album, 1995's 'Farewell To Reality' the band inducted vocalist S.L. Coe, a veteran of both ANGELDUST and SCANNER, and Markus Sturz of TRACE FAIR on the drums.
The frontman would decamp shortly after, later entering the world of production and releasing a solo album credited to C.O.E.
REACTOR persevered as a trio with Käfferlein taking on lead vocal responsibilities backed by Baier and Sturz for a 1997 tour of Germany paired with ARMISTICE. The new look REACTOR displayed their mettle for the first time with a 1998 EP 'Raw Meat'. The album 'A Short Fairy Tale' capitalised on this and in 1999 a demo was realised, 'The South Strikes Back'. That same year the REACTOR membership was boosted with the addition of TRACE FAIR guitarist Hand Riechelt and bass player Daniel Unzner from Death Metal act PROFANITY.
REACTOR recorded the track 'Augschburg'

RAWHEAD REXX
Photo : Nico Wobben

for an EP to raise funds for the local Augsburg Panthers junior jockey team.

Singles/EPs:
Raw Meat / Fly / The Hero Of The Day / Speed I Need (Live), React (1998)
Augschburg / Beerkilla, (2002)

Albums:
RATHER DEAD THAN DISHONOURED, DMP 012-91 (1991)
Reactor / Help Me... / Fight For Rock / Set Us Free / Look For Mercy / Speed I Need / Red Baron / Listen To Me / Witches On Fire
REVELATION, React 3770033.2.38 (1993)
MTI's / Their Curse / Jack The Ripper / Leave Me Alone / Hell Ain't Half Full Yet / Dog / Preacher's Vice / Women Stick At Nothing
FAREWELL TO REALITY, 1MF React 377.0038-2-42 (1995)
Living In A Trance / Farewell To Past / In The Line Of Fire / When Bosnia Falls / U.T.O.P.I.A. / House Of Pain / Blood And Fire / Conquer The Past / High Price Of Passion / Roadracin'
A SHORT FAIRY TALE, React BMP 98002 (1998)
Enter The Light / Raw Meat / Holy Sinner / A Short Fairy Tale / Testator / Pleasure Slave / Mindkiller / Fly / The Hero Of The Day / Geronimo / Speed I Need (Live studio session)

REQUIEM (FINLAND)
Line-Up: Jouni Nikula (vocals / guitar), Arto Räisälä (guitar), Pasi Kauppinen (bass), Henrik Klingenberg (keyboards), Jari Huttunen (drums)

Haapajärvi based neo Symphonic Power Metal band REQUIEM was founded in during the autumn of 1999, with an initial line-up of guitarist Arto Räisälä, bass player Matti Auvinen and drummer Rami Repola. This trio issued a three track debut promotional CD entitled 'Gods Of War' the same autumn.
As 2000 drew in Repola departed, being replaced by Jari Huttunen. REQUIEM were at this stage growing apart from prior Death Metal influences and leaning toward more orchestrated Metal territory, so they duly enlisted the services of keyboard player Ahti Komu and second guitarist Teemu Hänninen. With this line-up REQUIEM cut a self-financed mini-album 'Into The Night'.
2000 also saw the REQUIEM roster further strengthened with the induction of erstwhile MYSTERIUM vocalist/guitarist Jouni Nikula to the fold. With their new frontman REQUIEM re-recorded vocal parts for the 'Into The Night'

opus reissuing the record in a limited edition with Nikula's newly implanted vocal lines.
2001 was set to see a third self-financed release but REQUIEM would score a record deal with the Portuguese Sound Riot label. Komu would make his exit and REQUIEM undertook live gigs with stand in keyboard players on a temporary basis. Henrik Klingenberg joined the band in the keyboard role but further ructions occurred in the bass department, Matti Auvinen making way for new man Pasi Kauppinen. The new album, 'The Arrival', arrived in March of 2002. REQUIEM stepped up a gear with this release delivering full blown neo-Classical Progressive Metal clad in an elaborate Jason Juta designed fantasy album sleeve.
Both bass player Pasi Kauppinen and keyboard player Henrik Klingenberg also play in a band called SILENT VOICES.

Singles/EPs:
Gods Of War / Whispering Wind / Power And Glory, (1999)

Albums:
INTO THE NIGHT, (2000)
Into The Night / Morning Star / Kiss Of The Vampire / Fire Dragon / Roadkill / Flaming Vengeance
THE ARRIVAL, Sound Riot SRP.14 (2002)
Arrival / Revival / Broken Alliance / Whispers / The Invisible Touch / Forgotten Path / Halls Of Eternity / Liquid Hours / Masquerade

RENACER (ARGENTINA)
Line-Up: Christian Bertoncelli (vocals), Juan Pablo Kilberg (guitar), Fernando Ullua (bass), Jorge Perini (drums)

Buenos Aires Power Metal band founded in 1996 as IMPERIO by vocalist Christian Bertoncelli, previously with HORCAS, and guitar player Gustavo Gorosito. With the name switch to RENANCER during 2001 former ALEGORY guitarist Juan Pablo Kilberg took the place of Gorosito. Jorge Perini, drummer with JERIKO and having worked with PAUL DIANNO, was also enrolled alongside bassist Fernando Ullua and SINERGIA keyboard player Hernán Vasallo.
Included as bonus tracks on the 'Hoy Como Ayer' EP would be cover versions of ANGELES DEL INFIERNO's ' El Principio Del Fin' and RATA BLANCA's 'Chico Callejero'. A full album of demo material entitled 'Canciones Inmortales' from the IMPERIO days accompanied the release.
During 2002 RENACER contributed a batch of cover tracks to tribute albums, recording

DEEP PURPLE's 'A Gypsy's Kiss' for the Spanish release 'Sueños Púrpura: Homenaje a Deep Purple', METALLICA's 'Wherever I May Roam' for the 'Reyes Del Metal' collection, HERMETICA's 'Sepulcro Civil' and 'No Esperen Por Mi' by BLOKE.

Singles/EPs:
Hoy Como Ayer / Falsidad / Preguntandome Por Que / Sueños Perdidos / Chico Callejero / Tierra De Nadie / El Principio Del Fin, Star 3 004 (2001) ('Hoy Como Ayer' EP)

RICK RENSTROM (USA)

Guitarist Rick Renstrom made his name under the employ of respected Metal singer ROB ROCK and with his act WICKED WAYS. Striking out solo he would draw in a wealth on international Heavy Metal talent to guest on his debut 2002 'Until The Bitter End' album.

Featured on vocals would be former CRIMSON GLORY and SEVEN WITCHES frontman Wade Black on the track 'Towers Of Babylon', SINNER's Matt Sinner, ROB ROCK himself and EDGUY and AVANTASIA mainman Tobias Sammet. Other contributors included ROUGH SILK and AXEL RUDI PELL keyboard player FERDY DOERNBERG and ICED EARTH and DEATH drummer Richard Christy.

Albums:
UNTIL THE BITTER END, (2003)

REVEREND (CA, USA)

Line-Up: David Wayne (vocals), Stuart Fujinama (guitar), Brian Korban (guitar), Dennis O'Hara (bass), Rick Basha (drums)

The history of REVEREND, HERETIC and METAL CHURCH are truly intertwined in a "holy trinity" (pun fully intended) of Thrash Metal. In an odd twist of fate after the dissolution of HERETIC which saw singer Mike Howe leave to join METAL CHURCH, the band evolved into REVEREND and recruited ex-METAL CHURCH vocalist David Wayne. Guitarists Stuart Fujinami and Brian Korban along with bassist Dennis O'Hara were all members of HERETIC. Joining them would be drummer Stuart Vogel. By the 1990 album Vogel had made way for drummer Rick Basha.

After the success of the debut EP on Caroline Records and capitalising on Wayne's history with METAL CHURCH the band signed with Charisma, a small but stable record label. The Charisma full- length debut, 'World Won't Miss You', was a rampaging affair, cranking the brutality up just a notch above and beyond either of the previous acts. The album was dedicated to Dave Pritchard of ARMOURED SAINT and featured Rocky George of SUICIDAL TENDENCIES as a guest as well as Chris Goss of MASTERS OF REALITY.

Late 1990, early 1991 saw some big changes in the line-up with Fujinama, O'Hara and Basha all departing with Angelo Espino joining to play bass and Jason Ian appearing on drums. The album, 'Play God', was another punishing opus, and the band had utilised a second guitarist in the studio by the name of Tommy "V" Verdonck. The release also featured a ripping cover of the CREEDENCE CLEARWATER REVIVAL tune 'Fortunate Son' and also had Juan Garcia of EVIL DEAD providing some backing vocals.

Unfortunately, with the onset of grunge and alternative music, Thrash started to loose momentum and the band capped the first stage of their career with a six-song Live EP simply called 'Live'. 1992 saw the addition of Ernesto F. Martinez on guitar for the live recording. The short punchy live EP was considered to be a nice cap on the career of REVEREND as the band entered a period of inactivity.

With Wayne's departure from METAL CHURCH post their comeback 'Masterpeace' opus the singer reactivated REVEREND. A limited edition four track EP, 'A Gathering Of Demons', was made available solely through the band's website.

Wayne would then found a further act simply titled WAYNE. Cutting an album billed as 'Metal Church', complete with the characteristic guitar-cross icon and the WAYNE logo rendered in METAL CHURCH's own familiar font left no doubting to which audience the frontman was pitching.

During 2000 Wayne and WARRIOR guitarist Joe Floyd would produce the BYFIST 'Adrenalin' EP.

After several years of inactivity and spurred perhaps by the global resurgence in Metal, REVEREND re-emerged in 2001 with an independent 4 song EP called 'A Gathering Of Demons'. The EP was notable for the song 'Legion' which was a reworking, both musically and lyrically, of the METAL CHURCH song 'Fake Healer'. The line-up now consisted of Wayne and newcomers guitarist Chris Nelson, bassist John Stalman and Todd Stolz on drums. It was the heaviest recording by the band to date.

During 2000 Wayne and WARRIOR guitarist Joe Floyd would produce the BYFIST 'Adrenalin' EP. This connection was strengthened when BYFIST guitarists Davey Lee and Notch Vara duly joined Wayne's REVEREND supplanting guitarist Chris

Nelson and bassist John Stahlman.

Singles/EPs:
Massacre The Innocent / Down / Stealing
My Mind / Legion, Neck Damage (2001) ('A
Gathering Of Demons' EP)

Albums:
REVERAND, Caroline (1989)
Power Of Persuasion / Dimensional
Confusion / Wretched Excess / Ritual
WORLD WON'T MISS YOU, Charisma
(1990)
Remission / Another Form Of Greed /
Scattered Wits / Desperate / Leader Of Fools
/ World Won't Miss You / Rude Awakening /
Gunpoint / Killing Time / 11th Hour / Hand Of
Doom
PLAY GOD, Charisma (1991)
Butcher Of Baghdad / Heaven On Earth /
Fortunate Son / Blessings / Promised Land /
Play God / Warp The Mind / What You're
Looking For / Blackened Thrive / Death Of
Me / Far Away
LIVE, Charisma 92149-2 (1992)
Gunpoint / World Won't Miss You / Scattered
Witts / B.O.B / Promised Land / The Power
Of Persuasion

RHAPSODY (ITALY)

Line-Up: Fabio Leone (vocals), Luca Turilli
(guitar), Alessandro Lotta (bass), Alex
Staropoli (keyboards), Daniele Carbonera
(drums)

Trieste based epic Metal act RHAPSODY
started life in 1993 under the name of
THUNDERCROSS. Galvanising guitarist
Luca Turilli's classical heritage, his father
being a famous concert cellist, with
symphonic Metal made the
THUNDERCROSS demo stand out from the
crowd attracting the attention of noted
German melodic Rock guru Limb Schnoor.
Signing to Schnoor's LMP production
company the band soon changed titles to
RHAPSODY.
As RHAPSODY, fronted by ex-LABYRINTH
and present day ATHENA vocalist Fabio
Leone, the act debuted with the seven track
'Eternal Glory' demo tape in 1995.
RHAPSODY's debut album 'Legendary Tales'
scored the band massive plaudits across the
European Metal community. Bass player
Andrea Furlan departed prior to its release.
Despite RHAPSODY's rising profile Leone
still stuck out his vocal position with ATHENA.
RHAPSODY's second album, which found ex-
SINESTHESIA bassist Alessandro Lotta
joining, really put the band on the map selling
in excess of 100,000 copies in Europe alone.

The band was also joined by ex-SIEGES
EVEN drummer Alex Holzwarth and former
DREAM CHILD guitarist Dominique Leuquin.
Turilli issued a highly successful solo album in
1999. Leone busied himself with an outside
project too forming VISION DIVINE for a self-
titled album in alliance with LABYRINTH
guitarist Olaf Thörsen in 2000.
RHAPSODY committed their version of
'Guardians' to the 2000 HELLOWEEN tribute
album 'Keepers Of Jericho'.
Holzwarth united some of his ex-SIEGES
EVEN colleagues to found project act
LOOKING GLASS SELF in 2000. The
drummer was also found sessioning on
EDGUY's Tobias Sammet's mammoth
AVANTASIA project album the same year.
Meantime Fabio Leone would guest on the
2001 debut album from Argentinean
Symphonic Metal band BETO VASQUEZ
INFINITY, a band that often performed
RHAPSODY's 'Land Of Immortals' as a cover
version at gigs.
RHAPSODY re-emerged in November 2001
with the grandiose 'Rain Of A Thousand
Flames' opus. The following month it would be
announced that bassist Alessandro Lotta had
been replaced by Patrice Guers, a man
boasting credits with PATRICK RONDAT and
CONSORTIUM PROJECT. RHAPSODY
drummer Alex Holzwarth acted as a stand in
for the first nine shows of KAMELOT's
January 2002 European dates. Regular
KAMELOT drummer Casey Grillo took back
the reins for their Offenbach gig. RHAPSODY
would continue with touring in Europe with an
April schedule packaged alongside ANGEL
DUST and AT VANCE.
The band would reveal plans for two working
project, one entitled 'Rhapsody In Black' and
the other a J.R.R. Tolkein inspired 'Lord Of
The Rings' piece. However by June
RHAPSODY had scotched both ideas,
apparently deeming 'Rhapsody In Black' as
not in keeping with the band's 'positive' image.
During August BLIND GUARDIAN pulled in
the services of RHAPSODY drummer Alex
Holzwarth for Brazilian dates, as regular
drummer Thomas Stauch was suffering from
a tendon infection.

Singles/EPs:
Emerald Sword / Where Dragons Fly / Land
Of Immortals, Limb Music Productions
(1998)
Holy Thunderforce, Inside Out Music SPV
CDS 055-41333 (2000)

Albums:
LEGENDARY TALES, Inside Out Music
(1997)

RHAPSODY
Photo : Nico Wobben

Ira Tenax / Warrior Of Ice Rage Of The Winter / Forest Of Unicorns / Flames Of Revenge / Virgin Skies / Land Of Immortals / Echoes Of Tragedy / Lord Of The Thunder / Legendary Tales

SYMPHONY OF ENCHANTED LANDS, Inside Out Music (1998)

Epicus Foror / Emerald Sword / Wisdom Of The Kings / Heroes Of The Lost Valley / Eternal Glory / Beyond The Gates Of Infinity / Wings Of Destiny / The Dark Tower Of Abyss / Riding The Wings Of Eternity / Symphony Of Enchanted Lands

DAWN OF VICTORY, Inside Out Music (2000) **32 GERMANY, 54 SWEDEN**

Lux Triumphans / Dawn Of Victory / Triumph For My Magic Steel / The Village Of Dwarves / Dargor, Shadowlord Of The Black Mountain / The Bloody Rage / Holy Thunderforce / Trolls In The Dark / The Last Winged Unicorn / The Mighty Ride Of The Firelord

RAIN OF A THOUSAND FLAMES, Limb Music Productions LMP 0110-36 (2001) **117 FRANCE**

Rain Of A Thousand Flames / Deadly Omen / Queen Of The Dark Horizons / Rhymes Of A Tragic Poem - The Gothic Saga: Tears Of A Dying Angel / Rhymes Of A Tragic Poem - The Gothic Saga: Elnor's Magic Valley / Rhymes Of A Tragic Poem - The Gothic Saga: The Poem's Evil Page / Rhymes Of A Tragic Poem - The Gothic Saga: The Wizard's Last Rhymes

POWER OF THE DRAGONFLAME, Limb Music Productions LMP 0203-040 CD (2002) **31 FINLAND, 34 FRANCE, 29 SWEDEN**

In Tenebris / Knightrider Of Doom / The Power Of The Dragonflame / The March Of The Swordmaster / When Demons Awake / Agony Is My Name / Steelgods Of The Last Apocalypse / The Pride Of The Tyrant / Lamento Eroico / Rise From The Sea Of Flames / Gargoyles, Angels Of Darkness: i) Angeli Di Pietra Mistica / Gargoyles, Angels Of Darkness: ii) Warlord's Last Challenge / Gargoyles, Angels Of Darkness: iii) ...And The Legend Ends...

RIOT (USA)

Line-Up: Rhett Forrester (vocals), Mark Reale (guitar), Rick Ventura (guitar), Kip Leming (bass), Sandy Slavin (drums)

RIOT could well lay claim to being the cult Rock outfit of America. The band, although dogged by unrelenting external business problems have released a succession of well honed albums of impeccable quality. Somewhat strangely for, a full bore Hard Rock outfit, RIOT's trademark became a cuddly baby seal that adorned many of their album covers. As the years progressed RIOT's

sound developed from quality Hard Rock to a more technical Metal direction which served the band well on the European market. The band were founded in 1975 by former THE PEOPLE / KON TIKI guitarist Mark Reale, bassist Phil Fiet, ex-KON TIKI drummer Peter Bitelli, soon after adding vocalist Guy Speranza.

The band's first recordings came with a four track tape laid down for inclusion on a proposed New York Anthology compilation album. With the backers of this projected album journeying to the French Midem music festival in order to get a deal for the album. Meantime, the band had decided on a tamer approach bringing in keyboard player Steve Costello.

The band were stunned to learn upon the production company's return that there was an enthusiasm only for the RIOT tracks and that the compilation idea was now shelved in favour of a full blown RIOT release. With this in mind the band, ditching the keyboards and pulling in second guitarist Louie 'L.A.' Kouvaris, set about recording their debut album for local company Fire Sign Records, two tracks from the initial sessions, 'Angel With A Broken Wing' and 'Desperation' making it onto the album intact.

RIOT's 'Rock City' album featured a line-up of guitarists Reale and Kouvaris, Bitelli, Speranza, and new bass player Jimmy Iommi.

RIOT set about a succession of local New York gigs before venturing further afield, appearing at a festival in Florida headlined by NEAL YOUNG and undertaking a run of Ohio gigs opening for THE GODZ. Further dates in 1978 were brought about by an invite to guest for SAMMY HAGAR on dates in Texas. For the first time RIOT were made aware of a growing fan base. Often called back for encores the band soon learned that local rock D.J. Joe Anthony had been plugging 'Rock City' with a vengeance.

Returning to New York the rot set in as RIOT effectively stagnated. Disillusioned by the then current music scene RIOT even contemplated adopting a New Wave approach after a producer insisted this was the way to go. In this climate of despair RIOT almost fragmented for good. The situation got so bad that Reale and Speranza teamed up with Fiet once more and a drummer named Freddie to create another band. After a handful of gigs a call came from a promoter that RIOT were required to open the show for AC/DC's 'Highway to Hell' Texan leg of the tour alongside MOLLY HATCHET. Reale and Speranza were quick to resurrect the band pulling in Fiet again and former REX drummer Sandy Slavin for this fortnight's worth of high

RIOT

profile shows.

This highpoint was duly dashed by another lengthy period in the doldrums at home in New York and, seeing the craze for disco and punk seemingly taking over, RIOT once more were on the verge of breaking up. The telephone call that pulled them back from the brink came from further than Texas, this time as it was from England that the band's saviour appeared as they were told that tracks from the debut album were appearing in the British 'Sounds' magazine Heavy Metal charts.

Kouvaris, disillusioned by the fact that his mellow styled song-writing contributions were all being rejected, departed during recording of 1979's 'Narita', his place being taken by former RIOT roadie Rick Ventura. The album, named after the controversial new international airport built on the site of ancient burial grounds near Tokyo, garnered RIOT much praise in Europe.

RIOT was offered a support stint in England opening for SAMMY HAGAR which they naturally accepted. The British arm of Ariola Records jumped in with an offer to provide the necessary funding but just prior to departure Capitol Records offered the band a worldwide deal which RIOT took up. The SAMMY HAGAR shows proved a huge success and RIOT threw in some club headliners in Britain to round things off.

The band kept busy by gaining the third on the bill position on the American 'Black n' Blue' tour featuring rock legends BLUE OYSTER CULT and BLACK SABBATH this live work culminating in an appearance at the inaugural 'Monsters Of Rock' festival in Britain during 1980. RIOT shared a bill alongside TOUCH, SAXON, SCORPIONS, JUDAS PRIEST and RAINBOW.

Prime guru Cliff Bernstein, convinced of the band's global potential and a long time fan of RIOT, began negotiations with the band's New York production company in order to manage the act but a deal was unable to be sealed.

Fiet by now had had enough and left. His musical path in later years was to include a tenure with JOAN JETT and playing on the BILLY IDOL hit 'White Wedding'.

Capitol Records meanwhile had persuaded the band to pursue a more radio friendly AOR direction, even motioning that make up and a glitzier image was a distinct possibility and recordings along these lines commenced. With feedback from the British and Europe indicating a preference for more harder edged material RIOT, now with bassist Cliff 'Kip' Leming, scrapped all these initial tracks with the exception of the song 'Swords And Tequila' and laid down a brash untamed hard rock album. The band were pleased with the outcome but Capitol, in the words of Reale, "Freaked!".

The band and Capitol agreed to sever ties and at a Brooklyn showcase Elektra Records signed the band after witnessing just three numbers. The new label bought the 'Fire Down Under' tapes and RIOT got back to work on the road. In America they supported MAHOGANY RUSH, TRIUMPH, SAXON and GRAND FUNK RAILROAD before returning to England in 1981 opening for SAXON on the Big Teasers From Barnsley's 'Denim And Leather' tour. RIOT visited Britain earlier in the year and participated in the legendary 'Heavy Metal Holocaust' festival at Port Vale Football Club's stadium in Burslem, Staffordshire on the same bill as MOTÖRHEAD, OZZY OSBOURNE, TRIUMPH and VARDIS. Subsequent proposed dates across Europe with OZZY OSBOURNE and SAXON on the so-called 'Heavy Metal Battles' tour were curtailed though when 'Fire Down Under' entered the American Billboard album charts and RIOT were recalled to support RUSH on their mighty 'Moving pictures' nationwide tour.

With a chart album and being part of the most successful tour of the year RIOT were crushed when Speranza, battling with his religious convictions and the rock n' roll lifestyle, announced his intention to leave the band mid way through the dates.

The singer agreed to finish the tour and after much persuasion offered to record the next album. When the band's management realised that Speranza would only record with RIOT on condition the managers were not allowed to enter the recording studio the band were immediately pulled off the RUSH tour in North Carolina with no notice.

With negotiations now frantic RIOT returned home to New York on the tour bus only to be told they had to jump back on the RUSH shows again. RIOT missed one show in Atlanta but resumed their position for the next day's gig in Tennessee. An elaborate though wholly see through cover story had been concocted by the band's management that Speranza had been taken suddenly ill with food poisoning from a 7-11 burrito!

The RUSH tour ended with two sold out New Jersey shows and Speranza finally left the band. RIOT held auditions and drafted in RHETT FORRESTER, previously an New York club covers band RACHEL, in time for the recording of 'Restless Breed' album of 1982 and touring with the SCORPIONS and WHITESNAKE in America.

Forrester proved to be more of an energetic front man live and gave RIOT a new edge. His lifestyle though was lived almost too near the edge and a batch of shows opening for RAINBOW on their American 'Straight Between The Eyes' tour were cancelled when the singer simply vanished, turning up a week later in hospital with a mysterious illness.

The band got back into the swing supporting KISS on their American 'Lick It Up' extravaganza, which also featured VANDENBERG, and threw in a bunch of headliners on the West Coast. One bizarre date actually saw RIOT opening for RATT and STEELER. The toll was beginning to tell though. The band had left Elektra and signed with the Canadian independent label Quality for the release of new album, the patriotic 'Born In America' (later reissued by Grand Slamm in the United States). Coming off the road in 1983, both Reale and Slavin agreed they were flogging a dead horse. Forrester opted out in 1984 to pursue a solo career opening with the 'Out Of The Darkness' in the same year.

Rick Ventura had left RIOT around the same time as Forrester, being replaced by 19 year old Gerard T. Trevino. The band then parted company with both label and management and Reale quickly decided to terminate the group in order to pursue a different musical avenue. Sandy Slavin joined forces once more with Fiet and ex-TKO guitarist Adam Brenner in ADAM BOMB.

Mark Reale formed NARITA (originally the MARK REALE PROJECT), releasing a three track demo in 1985 featuring the tracks 'The Feeling Is Gone', 'Liar' and 'Thundersteel'. NARITA featured members of SAN ANTONIO SLAYER bassist Don van Stavern and drummer Dave McClain. A series of auditions in Los Angeles endeavouring to locate a vocalist followed but with no luck so SAN ANTONIO SLAYER front man Steve Cooper was enrolled.

NARITA played live throughout the mid west of America until Slavin convinced Reale that RIOT still retained a sizeable fan base and a reunion tour would work in their favour. In 1983 RIOT regrouped, now comprising of Reale, Slavin and van Satavern. Approaches were made to both Speranza and Forrester but the former was uninterested and the latter involved with his solo work.

RIOT finally emerged fronted by ex-JAGPANZER / SATAN'S HOST vocalist Harry 'The Tyrant' Conklin and a three month touring schedule was set up. Disaster struck almost immediately though when four songs into the band's debut show, the first of two sold out nights at Los Angeles Troubadour, Conklin lost his voice. Conklin bailed out to create TITAN FORCE. Cancelling the tour hasty auditions were held and a vocalist named Steffan travelled into the desert with RIOT for a test gig at an obscure club. It was a dismal failure prompting Reale to re-contact Forrester. This time Rhett took the bait and a Reale / Forrester / van Stavern / Slavin RIOT line-up commenced touring.

Coming off the road the old malaise was quick to set in. Effectively RIOT, now located in Los Angeles, were destitute. Although they were the subject of healthy record company interest Mark Reale was actually living in his car at this juncture and the band was dealt a huge blow when Forrester was soon to depart once again. (Sadly, in early 1994, Forrester was murdered, gunned down trying to prevent an armed robbery in Atlanta.)

A major rethink was required and subsequently Reale journeyed back to New York to renew the acquaintance with his old management team. A new band was quickly assembled as Slavin, opting out, undertook studio work at this point including a guest appearance on TED NUGENT's 1986 'Little Miss Dangerous' album. He would later appear in ACE FREHLEY's live band.

Reale and van Stavern were joined by STEELER, LION and BURNING STARR drummer MARK EDWARDS and vocalist Tony Moore (real name Morvido). The new band cut four demo tracks which led to a deal with major label CBS Records.

1988's comeback album 'Thundersteel', recorded over a lengthy period in downtime at the management's recording studio, was issued on CBS in America, Epic in Europe. A video was shot for the song 'Bloodstreets' and once more RIOT got back on the road in America.

Former RAINBOW and DEEP PURPLE singer JOE LYNN TURNER makes a guest appearance on 'The Privilege Of Power' album. Indeed the record also includes a contribution from the TOWER POWER HORNS and a whole slew of well known New York session musicians.

The return of RIOT led to increased interest in Japan, with the 'Rock City' and 'Narita' albums being released on CD. Alongside these were a brand new live album, culled from RIOT's British performances at the Donington 1980 'Monsters Of Rock' festival and a 1981 London Hammersmith Odeon show being issued in the far East.

New bassist Pete Perez, previously with CARRION, replaced van Stavern in 1990 and line-up changes struck the band once more in the mid '90s with former STUTTERING JOHN vocalist Michael Dimeo and guitarist Mike Flyntz being drafted. RIOT now specifically began to concentrate on the European and Japanese markets.

RIOT's stature is now such in Japan that in recent times the band have toured there on a consistent basis in 1989, 1990, '94 and '96. A 1995 Japanese issue live album was compiled without the band's knowledge, the recordings being given to Sony Japan taken from a camcorder microphone and a single DAT tape.

In 1993 the band were due to play in continental Europe as part of a Power Metal package deal with TITAN FORCE but this was cancelled. A further set of shows with METAL CHURCH was pulled too leaving the band frustrated at being unable to perform in Europe.

1994's 'Nightbreaker' featured a brand new version of 'Outlaw' and covers of the MOODY BLUES' 'Whiter Shade Of Pale' and DEEP PURPLE's 'Burn'. 'Nightbreaker' would be released by various labels globally and at least three different sleeve designs were employed, the European license through Rising Sun Records being one of the more effective with a shark cover. The Japanese version of the album featured the bonus cut of 'Black Mountain Woman'. Its conceptual follow up was 'The Brethren Of The Long House' (based around a story line of the plight of the native Americans and which featured a cover version of GARY MOORE / PHIL LYNNOT's 'Out In The Fields'). RIOT finally got to tour in Europe in 1996 on a bill alongside WHIPLASH and SKYCLAD.

Needless to say RIOT's latest album sees a new member, drummer John Macaluso (ex-POWERMAD and TNT), replacing Bobby Jarzombek who had opted for a solo career with his project SPASTIC INK, an outfit that coincidentally features Pete Perez. By 2000 Jarzombek was a member of ex-JUDAS PRIEST vocalist Rob Halberd's HALFORD band.

In 1998 Don Van Stavern re-emerged with the Industrial outfit PITBULL DAYCARE. Macaluso also found time to perform drumming duties for YNGWIE MALMSTEEN and A.R.K. It was to be Mark Reale though that launched the highest profile side venture with the Melodic Rock outfit WESTWORLD. Debuting for Roadrunner Records the band, fronted by TNT vocalist Tony Harnell, also comprised DANGER DANGER bass player Bruno Ravel and former BLUE OYSTER CULT and RAINBOW drummer John O'Reilly. August of the same year saw RIOT putting in a performance at the German 'Wacken Open Air' festival. Early 2000 found RIOT headlining in Germany once again for a tour which saw strong support from Canada's ANVIL plus AGENT STEEL and DOMINE.

In 2002 bassist Pete Perez was announced as the latest recruit into David Wayne's REVEREND. RIOT would make a return in August touting a brand new studio album for Metal Blade entitled 'Through The Storm'. This new outing included two cover versions with UFO's 'Only You Can Rock Me' and an instrumental variation on THE BEATLES 'Here Comes The Sun'. The recording line-up for this effort stood at guitarists Mark Reale and Mike Flyntz vocalist Mike Dimeo bass player Pete Perez and former BLACK SABBATH and RAINBOW man Bobby Rondinelli on drums.

Singles/EPs:
Outlaw / Rock City (Live), Elektra K 12565 (1981)
Angel Eyes / 15 Rivers / Red Reign / Turning The Hands Of Time, Zero Corporation (1997) (Japanese release)

Albums:
ROCK CITY, Ariola ARL 5007 (1977)
Desperation / Warrior / Rock City / Overdrive / Angel / Tokyo Rose / Heart Of Fire / Gypsy Queen / This Is What I Get
NARITA, Capitol E-ST 12081 (1979)
Waiting For The Taking / 49er / Kick Down The Wall / Born To Be Wild / Narita / Here We Come Again / Do It Up / Hot For Love / White Rock / Road Racin'
FIRE DOWN UNDER, Elektra K 52315 (1981) **90 USA**
Swords And Tequila / Fire Down Under / Feel The Same / Outlaw / Don't Bring Me Down / Don't Hold Back / Altar Of The King / No Lies / Run For Your Life / Flashbacks
RESTLESS BREED, Elektra K 52398 (1982)
Hard Lovin' Man / C.I.A. / Restless Breed / When I Was Young / Loanshark / Loved By You / Showdown / Dream Away / Violent Crimes
RIOT LIVE, Elektra (1982)
Hard Lovin' Man / Showdown / Loved By You / Loanshark / Restless Breed / Swords And Tequila
BORN IN AMERICA, Grand Slam SLAM 6 (1983)
Born In America / You Burn In Me / Wings Of Fire / Running From The Law / Devil Woman / Vigilante Killer / Heavy Metal Machine / Where Soldiers Rule / Gunfighter / Promised Land
THUNDERSTEEL, Epic 4609762 (1988)
Thundersteel / Fight Or Fall / Sign Of The Crimson Storm / Flight Of The Warrior / On Wings Of Eagles / Johnny's Back / Bloodstreets / Run For Your Life / Buried Alive (Tell Tale Heart)
RIOT LIVE, CBS (1989) (Japanese release)
Intro/ Angel / Do It Up / Road Racin' / White Rock / Warrior / Narita / Tokyo Rose / Overdrive / Rock City / Back On The Non Stop / Kick Down The Wall / Train Kept A Rollin' / Road Racin'
THE PRIVILEGE OF POWER, CBS Associated ZK45132 (1990)
On Your Knees / Metal Soldiers / Runaway / Killer / Dance Of Death / Storming The Gates Of Hell / Maryanne / Little Miss Death / Black Leather And Glittering Steel / Racing With The Devil On A Spanish Highway (Revisited)
GREATEST HITS '78-'90, Sony (1993) (Japanese release)
Warrior / 49er / Overdrive / Kick Down The

Wall / Tokyo Rose / Road Racin' / Narita / Flight Of The Warrior / Metal Soldiers / Runaway / Johnny's Back / Sign Of The Crimson Storm / Killer / Storming The Gates Of Hell / Bloodstreets / Thundersteel
NIGHTBREAKER, Rising Sun 084 62222 (1994)
Soldier / Destiny / Burn / In Your Eyes / Nightbreaker / Medicine Man / Silent Scream / Magic Maker / I'm On The Run / Babylon / Outlaw
RIOT LIVE II, Sony (1995) (Japanese release)
THE BRETHREN OF THE LONGHOUSE, Rising Sun SRCS 7852 (1996)
The Last Of The Mohicans (Intro) / Glory Calling / Rolling Thunder / Rain / Wounded Heart / The Brethren Of The Long House / Out In The Fields / Santa Maria / Blood Of The English / Ghost Dance / Shenandoah / Holy Land / The Last Of The Mohicans
FIRE DOWN UNDER, High Vaultage HV-1021 (1997) (CD re-issue with bonus tracks)
Swords And Tequila / Fire Down Under / Feel The Same / Outlaw / Don't Bring Me Down / Don't Hold Back / Altar Of The King / No Lies / Run For Your Life / Flashbacks / Struck By Lightning / Misty Morning Rain / You're All I Needed Tonight / One Step Closer / Hot Life
INISHMORE, Metal Blade 3984-14150-2 (1998)
Black Water / Kings Are Falling / Should I Run / Gypsy / Angel Eyes / The Man / Cry For The Dying / Inishmore (Forsaken Heart) / Liberty / Watching The Signs / Turning The Hands Of Time
SHINE ON - LIVE, Metal Blade 14182 (1998)
Black Water / Angel Eyes / Soldier / The Man / Kings Are Falling / Bloodstreets / Watching The Signs / Cry For The Dying / Irish Trilogy: Inishmore (Forsaken Heart) / Irish Trilogy: Inishmore / Irish Trilogy: Danny Boy / Liberty / Gypsy / The Last of Mohicans (Intro) / Glory Calling / Thundersteel / Nightbreaker
RIOT IN JAPAN - LIVE!!, Metal Blade 14241 (1999)
Minutes To Showtime / On Your Knees...In Tokyo! / Metal Soldiers / Runaway / Tokyo Rose...In Osaka! / Rock City / Outlaw / Killer / Skins & Bones part 1 / Skins & Bones part 2 / Johnny's Back... In Tokyo! / Flight Of The Warrior / Ladies And Gentleman... Mark Reale / Japan Cakes / Narita / Warrior / The Dressing Room - The Encore Begins... In Tokyo! - The Encore Continues / Smoke On The Water... In New York!
SONS OF SOCIETY, Metal Blade 14249 (1999)
Snake Charmer / On the Wings Of Life / Sons Of Society / Twist Of Fate / Bad

369

Machine / Cover Me / Dragonfire / The Law /
Time to Bleed / Somewhere / Promises
THROUGH THE STORM, Metal Blade (2002)
Turn The Tables / Lost Inside This World /
Chains Revolving / Through The Storm / Let
It Show / Burn The Sun / To My Head /
Essential Enemies / Only You Can Rock Me /
Isle Of Shadows

RISING FAITH (SWEDEN)
Line-Up: Kristian Wallin (vocals / guitar),
Jimmie Bergqvist (guitar), Stefan Englund
(bass), Kristian Engqvist (drums)

A melodic Heavy Metal act founded in 1999.
Frontman Kristian Wallin had previously been
a member of MEDOW whilst the rhythm
section of bass player Stefan Englund and
drummer Kristian Engqvist are both veterans
of Death Metal band SICKNESS. Guitar
player Jimmie Bergqvist has formerly
operated in a HELLOWEEN covers band.
The year of their inception would witness the
issuing of a debut demo swiftly followed by
the self-financed mini-album 'Imagination'.
These latter recordings saw production
credits given to KING DIAMOND's Andy
LaRocque.
RISING FAITH also feature on the French
'Metallion' magazine compilation 'Rising
Forces' and the 2000 'Witchcraft & Folklore'
collection.
During November of 2001 Wallin opted to
concentrate solely on lead vocals thus
RISING FAITH duly enrolled Fredrik
Jordanius of CONVICTION into the vacant
guitar role.
In April of 2002 it was revealed that erstwhile
RISING FAITH man Kristian Enqvist had
assembled a side venture billed as COSMIC
SPHERE. Other participants included Antti
Wirman of WARMEN and CRAYDAWN, Tapio
Oksanen of CRAYDAWN and LIONS SHARE
guitarist Lars Criss.

Albums:
IMAGINATION, (1999)
Marching On / Road To Eternity / Where
Sanity Grows / The Other Side / Imagination
THE INNER TRUTH, (2001)
Final Day / Aeons Of Silence / Imagination /
The Inner Truth / Cryptic Wisdom / Road To
Eternity / A Different View / Ancient
Memories / Sacred Oath / Marching On /
The Scenery

RISK (GERMANY)
Line-Up: Heinrich Mikus (vocals / guitar),
Roman Keymer (guitar), Peter Dell (bass),
Jürgen Düsterloh (drums)

Mikus, Dell and Dusterloh are all former
FAITHFUL BREATH personnel. To the
international market it remains a mystery as
to why FAITHFUL BREATH opted the change
to RISK as the Viking helmeted Germans
were making solid progress with a series of
well received albums.
RISK drafted former guitarist Thilo Herrmann,
previously a member of the early '70s
Progressive Rock band MAMMUT.
Herrmann was to join HOLY MOSES in July
1988. Herrmann would return to RISK shortly
after. Herrmann later joined RUNNING WILD
and GLENMORE during the mid '90s.
The 'Turpitude' album saw the addition of
guitarist Christian Sumser with Mikus
handling bass as well as lead vocals.

Singles/EPs:
Ratman / Germans / Violent Science / Skid
Row Kid, Steamhammer CD 76-7608 (1989)
('Ratman' EP)

Albums:
THE DAILY HORROR NEWS,
Steamhammer 087572 (1988)
Living In Chaos / Roadwar / D.N.S. Madness
/ Revolution Now / Alien Terror / Speed Kills /
Rommes Fritz / Strike
HELL'S ANIMALS, Steamhammer CD 85-
7593 (1989)
Monkey Business / Perfect Kill / Dead Or
Alive / The Secret Of Our Destiny / Siciliam
Showdown / Torture And Pain / Mindshock /
Meglomania / Russian Nights / Epilogue
DIRTY SURFACES, Steamhammer SPV
0876231 (1990)
Beach Panic / Pyromaniac Man / Legend Of
The Kings / Warchild / Paralysed / Like A
Rollercoaster / Blood Is Red / Letter From
Beyond / Bury My Heart
THE REBORN, Steamhammer SPV
0876231 (1992)
Arise / Last Warning / Be No More / Lullaby /
Awakening / Turn Back To Ecstasy / Eclipse /
The Night Will Fall / Phantasmagoria /
Armageddon (Fight Back) / No One Will
Remember
TURPITUDE, Steamhammer (1993)
Cry / Show No Mercy / So Weird / Hopeless
Ground / Materialised / Serious Mysterious /
The Day Will Come / And We Don't Care /
Squeeze My Skull And Brains / Not True

ROB ROCK (USA)

Vocalist Rob Rock cut his first solo album in
2000. Rock had made his name with a series
of guitar virtuoso themed acts such as VICE,
JOSHUA, IMPELLITERRI, M.A.R.S.,
DRIVER and for German guitar hero AXEL

RUDI PELL on his 'Nasty Reputation' outing. Produced by Roy Z the 'Rage Of Creation' album featured ex-FOREVER and present day WARRIOR bassist Ray Burke, SAHARA and DRIVER drummer Reynold 'Butch' Carlson and a guest appearance on the tracks 'Media Machine' and 'All I Need' from ex-BADLANDS and OZZY OSBOURNE guitarist JAKE E. LEE. The record would hold a further surprise with an adventurous and downright heavy cover version of the ABBA track 'Eagle'.

Rock also spent time in 2000 recording with WARRIOR and contributed the same year to EDGUY mainman Tobias Sammet's ambitious AVANTASIA eponymous album project.

Rock planned on live dates to promote the album assembling a live band comprising of guitarists Angelo Janotti and RICK RENSTROM of WICKED WAYS, bass player Stephen Elder of WICKED WAYS and GEMINI drummer Tracy Shell. Rock toured Europe throughout March of 2001 as guest to AXEL RUDI PELL.

A new album, slated for release during 2002, would once again be produced by Roy Z. Bob Rossi would be added to Rock's band for live work. Guitarist RICK RENSTROM Struck out solo drawing in a wealth on international Heavy Metal talent to guest on his debut 2002 ROB ROCK produced 'Until The Bitter End' album.

Albums:
RAGE OF CREATION, Rob Rock Music RRM 9394 (2000)
In The Beginning / The Sun Will Rise Again / One Way Out / Judgement Day / Streets Of Madness / Eagle / Beautiful Lady / All I Need / Media Machine / In The Night / Never Too Late / Forever

ROUGH SILK (GERMANY)

Line-Up: Jan Barnett (vocals), Hilmer Staacke (guitar), Ralf Schwertner (bass), Ferdy Doernberg (keyboards), Herbert Hartmann (drums)

Groomed for success by the ACCEPT management stable, following valuable German supports to SAXON and DEEP PURPLE, Hannover's ROUGH SILK not too surprisingly had their debut album produced by ACCEPT drummer Stefan Kaufmann.

They were supported HELLOWEEN on their 1994 British tour promoting the 1994 'Walls Of Never' album.

Switching to Massacre Records ROUGH SILK once more proved their hunger for the road by jumping on tours by DIO, MANOWAR

and AXXIS. Meantime keyboard player FERDY DOERNBERG issued his first solo album. The keyboard maestro is also an active member of AXEL RUDI PELL's band appearing on many albums by the guitar wizard.

Guitarist Hilmer Staacke lost his position prior to recording the 1996 album. His position was filled by Andreas Laszewski.

The 'Mephisto' album saw the band pulling in new recruits guitarist Nils Wunderlich and drummer Curt Doernberg.

The 1999 compilation album 'Wheels Of Time' includes numerous remixes of tracks plus four brand new songs.

Ferdy Doernberg issued a further solo album in 2000 although this time the project went under the STORYTELLER'S RAIN handle. Drummer Herbert Hartmann returned to the fold for recording of 'Symphony Of Life' issued on U.D.O. vocalist Udo Dirkschneider's Breaker label. The album was co-produced by the esteemed figure of Jon Oliva of SAVATAGE, the man himself donating session vocals too.

In 2001 Doernberg would guest on the ambitious TARAXACUM project album 'Spirit Of Freedom' conceived by EDGUY man Tobias Exxel. Prior to recording of a new album 'End Of Infinity' for Breaker Records in 2002 singer Thomas Ludolphy parted company with the band. No moves were made to fill the vacancy, the remaining members opting to share lead vocal responsibilities.

Albums:
ROOTS OF HATE, RCA 74321 12796 2 (1993)
The Grapes Of Wrath / Roots Of Hate / The Deep Of The Night / Calls To The World / When Thunder Roars / Candle In The Rain / Cemetery Dawn / Sentimental Trust / Wasteland Serenader / Through The Fire / Ups And Downs / Why? / Eyes Of A Stranger / Forever
WALLS OF NEVER, Mausoleum 904 103-2 (1994)
Walls Of Never / H8 What You Want / Somebody's Out There / Toxical Roses / One More For The Ride / Gloria In Destiny / Never Loose Again / Missing You / Lust Is A Killer / Never Say Never / Don't Leave Me Now / The Clown
CIRCLE OF PAIN... OR: THE SECRET LIES OF TIMEKEEPING, Massacre MASSCD0115 (1996)
The End / Insania / Circle Of Pain / Les Chiens De La Guerre / Life Goes On / When The Skunk's Got You Down / ...And The Wind Screams In Anger / For Once In My Life / On The Wrong Side Of The Moon / The

Mysterious Boot Hill Grave Inscription / The Angel And The Raven / The Beginning (Instrumental)

MEPHISTO, Massacre MAS CD0144 (1997)
Mystery Bay / Recall / Mephisto / Subway Angels Caravan / My Last Farewell / Dust To Sand / Glissando / Stay Gold / Far From Home / The Day Of The Loner / Wheels Of Time

BEYOND THE SUNDOWN, Massacre MAS CD0172 (1998)
From Here To Eternity / Nosferatu / Beyond The Sundown / Gods Of Darkness / A Matter Of Size / Neutrophobia / Face To Faith / Something To Believe In / When Life And Pain Unite / Friends / Where The Red Waters Flow / Never Lose Again '98

WHEELS OF TIME, Massacre MAD CD0219 (1999)
Plane You Down / Beyond The Sundown / Insania / In The Deep Of The Night / Subway Angel's Caravan / Pianoman / Somebody's Out There / My Last Farewell / Gods Of Darkness / Roots Of Hate / The Clown / Nosferatu / Walls Of Never / A Matter Of Size / Wisdom Of Steel / Circle Of Pain / Never Say Never / Just A Mouldrin' Body / Desert Wind / Friends / Mephisto / Something To Believe In / Wheels Of Time / Never Lose Again / The Angel And The Raven / The End

SYMPHONY OF LIFE, Breaker (2001)
Symphony Of Life (Overture Of Death, Symphony Of Life) / Suicide King & Chaos Queen / Savannah / Lucifer / The Truth / Nice Day For A Funeral / Opposite Of Yes / Silicone / Under The Guillotine / Stories To Tell / Savannah (Radio edit) / Nice Day For Funeral (Radio edit)

END OF INFINITY, SPV (2002)
Isolation / The Fiddler On The Skeleton Horse / Carry On / Ambrosia / End Of Infinity / By Your Side / Trans-Destination/ Set Me Free / Restless Heart / Hang Over City (Lucifer's Hotel) / Dolly The Sheep Meets Frank The Stein / My Little Friend

ROYAL HUNT (SWEDEN / DENMARK)
Line-Up: D.C. Cooper (vocals), Jakob Kjaer (guitar), Andre Anderson (keyboards), Steen Morgensen (bass), Kenneth Olsen (drums)

Heavily keyboard orientated, Danish Rockers ROYAL HUNT, have made quite an impact on the mainland European Rock scene. The idea for the band was forged in 1992 by keyboard player Andre Anderson. Anderson, actually a native of Moscow, emigrated to Denmark to find further suitable musicians where he located bassist Steen Morgensen. Vocalist Henrik Brockman brought guitarist Jacob Kjaer with him and with this line-up ROYAL

HUNT laid down their initial demos. The band's first tapes featured the cuts 'Age Gone Wild', 'Give It Up', 'One By One' and 'Heart Of The City'.

ROYAL HUNT's debut album 'Land Of Broken Hearts' was initially only to see a Scandinavian release. The album found its way into the hands of the respected Japanese "Rock guru" Captain Wada. His reaction instigated two Japanese tours and huge album sales.

Brockman quit the band in December of 1994, ROYAL HUNT filling the gap with American D.C. COOPER. The new vocalist just had two weeks to learn ROYAL HUNT's set before the band set out on a world tour.

ROYAL HUNT ventured to America for the first time where they supported WARRANT prior to recording the 'Moving Target' record. Once more the resulting product received glowing reviews in Europe and Japan, even being nominated for a Grammy award in Denmark for best rock album.

ROYAL HUNT's popularity in Japan has now reached the level whereby the Japanese national wrestling federation put in a request to the band to record some music especially for their sporting events. ROYAL HUNT obliged with the tracks 'Champions Of Wrestling', 'Wake Up' and 'Chono Masahiro'.

The last leg of the 'Moving Target' tour had ROYAL HUNT sharing a bill in Europe with GOTTHARD. Keeping up the momentum between studio releases a live album and video was issued, both recorded at the Gotada U-Port Theatre in Tokyo.

Allan Sørensen contributed drums for the 1997 'Paradox' album. ROYAL HUNT supported SAXON throughout their German tour of the same year prior to headline shows with guests HOUSE OF SHAKIRA.

In 1998 Sørensen, together with ex-NARITA guitarist Henrik Poulsen and former ELEGY singer Eduard Hovinga created PRIME TIME. Andersen guested on keyboards for their debut 'The Unknown' album. By the time of PRIME TIME's sophomore effort 'The Miracle' Olsen had joined the band on drums.

ROYAL HUNT switched labels to SPV who promptly reissued 'Paradox' with a bonus live CD recorded on the band's 1997 Japanese tour.

The 1999 ROYAL HUNT album 'Fear' saw the departure of D.C. Cooper and beckoned in new vocalist JOHN WEST, previously with ARTENSION and BADLANDS.

In 2000 Morgensen formed an alliance with ex-MIDNIGHT BLUE and RAINBOW singer Doogie White to create the band CORNERSTONE debuting with the 'Arrival' album.

The bands August 2001 album 'The Mission',

released by Now And Then / Frontiers in Europe and Century Media in the USA, would transpire to be an ambitious concept affair based on the famous Sci-Fi novel 'The Martian Chronicles' by Ray Bradbury. ROYAL HUNT's quartet at this juncture comprised Andre Andersen, Steen Morgensen, John West, and Jacob Kjaer.

During early 2002 ANDRE ANDERSON would weigh in with his second solo album 'Black On Black'. JOHN WEST would also pursue a high profile endeavour outside of the ROYAL HUNT by forging the 'Earthmaker' album. This a liaison hooked West up with the SAVATAGE duo of guitarist Chris Caffrey and Jeff Plate, HALFORD personnel MIKE CHLASIAK on guitar, Ray Riendau on bass and Bobby Jarzombek on drums and on keyboards Lonnie Park. ANDRE ANDERSON and VITALIJ KUPRIJ also donated their efforts.

Meantime ROYAL HUNT would be announced as special guests to Denmark's PRETTY MAIDS for European touring in April.

Singles/EPs:
Clown In The Mirror / Stranded (Acoustic Version) / Land Of Broken Hearts (Acoustic Version) / Age Gone Wild (Acoustic Version) / Kingdom Dark (Acoustic Version) / Bad Luck, Royal Hunt (1994) ('The Maxi Single' EP)
Far Away / Double Conversion (Instrumental) / Intro Wasted Time (Live Version) / Flight (Live Version) / Stranded (Live Version) / Epilogue (Live Version), Rondel TECW-20002 (1995) ('Far Away' EP)
Last Goodbye, Seagull (1996) (Promotional release)
Message To God (Radio edit) / The Final Lullaby / Far Away (Acoustic Version), Teichiku TECW 12486 (1997) (Japanese release)
Message To God / The Final Lullaby, Semaphore 50582 (1997)

Albums:
LAND OF BROKEN HEARTS, Royal RR CD7001 (1994)
Running Wild / Easy Rider / Flight / Age Gone Wild / Martial Arts / One By One / Heart Of The City / Land Of Broken Hearts / Freeway Jam / Kingdom Dark
CLOWN IN THE MIRROR, Royal RR CD9009-2 (1995)
Intro / Wasted Time / Ten To Life / On The Run / Clown In The Mirror / Third Stage / Bodyguard / Legion Of The Damned / Here Today, Gone Tomorrow / Bad Blood / Epilogue

MOVING TARGET, Seagull SICD 9601 (1996)
Last Goodbye / 1348 / Makin' A Mess / Far Away / Step By Step / Autograph / Stay Down / Give It Up / Time
ROYAL HUNT 1996 (LIVE), Semaphore 37432-427 (1997)
Flight / 1348 / Wasted Time / Stay Down / On The Run / Stranded / Keyboard Solo / Martial Arts / Far Away / Last Goodbye / Land Of Broken Hearts / Makin' A Mess / Clown In The Mirror / Guitar Solo / Step By Step / Drums And Bass Solo / Running Wild / Epilogue / Age Gone Wild (Acoustic Version) / Ten To Life (Acoustic Version) / Legion Of The Damned (Acoustic Version) / Kingdom Dark / Time
PARADOX, Semaphore 50610-422 (1997)
The Awakening / River Of Pain / Tearing Down The World / Message To God / Long Way Home / Time Will Tell / Silent Scream / It's Over / Tearing Down The World (Radio Edit) / Message To God (radio edit) / Time Will Tell (Radio Edit) / Silent Scream (Radio Edit) / Martial Arts / Restless
PARADOX: CLOSING THE CHAPTER (LIVE), Steamhammer SPV (1999) (free CD with 'Paradox' reissue)
Ava Maria Guarani / The Awakening / River Of Pain / Tearing The World / Message To God / Long Way Home / Time Will Tell / Silent Scream / It's Over
FEAR, Steamhammer SPV (1999)
Fear / Faces Of War / Cold City Lights / Lies / Follow Me / Voices / Sea Of Time
THE WATCHERS, (2001)
Intervention (Full version) / Lies (Live) / Flight (Live) / Message To God (Live) / Epilogue (Live) / One By One / Clown In The Mirror / Day In Day Out / Legion Of The Damned / Intervention (Radio edit)
THE MISSION, Century Media (2001)
Take Off (August 2001 - The Settlers) / The Mission (January 1999 - Rocket Summer) / Exit Gravity (October 2002 - The Shore) / Surrender (April 2000 - The Third Expedition) / Clean Sweep (April 2005 - Usher II) / Judgement Day (June 2001 - And The Moon Be Still As Bright) / Metamorphosis (February 2002 - The Locusts) / World Wide War (August 2026 - There Will Come Soft Rains) / Dreamline (February 2003 - Interim) / Out Of Reach (August 2002 - Night Meeting) / Fourth Dimension (November 2005 - The Watchers) / Days Of No Trust (April 2026 - The Long Years) / Total Recall (November 2005 - The Off Season)
ON THE MISSION 2002 - THE VERY BEST OF ROYAL HUNT, Teichiku TECI-24124 (2002) (Japanese release)
Flight / Land Of Broken Hearts / Martial Arts

/ Clown In The Mirror / Epilogue / Time / Far Away / Message To God / Lies / Cold City Lights / World Wide War / Surrender / U-Turn (Instrumental version)

RUNNING WILD (GERMANY)

Line-Up: Rock n' Rolf (vocals / guitar), Majk Moti (guitar), Jens Becker (bass), Iain Finlay (drums)

Hamburg's RUNNING WILD debuted with the album 'Gates To Purgatory', a record laden with nonsensical occultism but soon developed a unique, if bizarre, image based around pirates which they have fostered to the present day. Led by Rock n' Rolf (real name Rolf Kasparek) RUNNING WILD have proved to be a mainstay of the German Metal scene with consistently high profile albums and tours.

The band started out in the early '80s billed as GRANITE HEART switching to RUNNING WILD for their first demo in 1982. The band's first line-up consisted of Rock n' Rolf, guitarist Uwe Bendig, bassist Michael Hoffmann and drummer Jörg Schwarz. By the band's second tape the following year only Rock n' Rolf remained. Fresh blood was provided by guitarist Preacher, bassist Stephan Borisso and drummer Hasche Haggemann. RUNNING WILD's third demo 'Heavy Metal Like A Hammerblow' secured a deal with Noise Records.

The release of the 'Branded And Exiled' album, with new guitarist Majik Moti, in 1985 saw RUNNING WILD receive an invitation to open for American Glam Rockers MÖTLEY CRÜE's German 'Theatre Of Pain' tour dates. One of the first German Thrash bands to tour America RUNNING WILD undertook a lengthy club tour with CELTIC FROST and VOIVOD, although following the release of the popular 'Under Jolly Roger' album drummer Hasche quit (and now works for the Rockfabrik club in Ludwigsburg), being substituted by Stefan Scwarzmann. The band yielded to another blow shortly after when bassist Stephan Borisso departed to join U.D.O. Before long Schwarzmann followed for the same destination.

The rhythm section was re-established with the recruitment of bassist Jens Becker and English drummer Iain Finlay for the 'Death Or Glory' album. German dates in 1990 found RAGE supporting.

The line-up would remain less than stable as guitarist Majk Moti departed in early 1991 and was replaced by Axel Morgan.

The 'Pile Of Skulls' album in 1992 saw the addition of former U.D.O. rhythm section bassist Thomas Smuszynski and the return of drummer Stefan Schwarzmann and was

recorded in Studio M in Hildesheim. Becker deputised for touring partners CROSSROADS the same year.

RUNNING WILD would effectively split down the middle with Becker, Schwarzmann and Morgan creating X WILD, an outfit that lasted for three albums. Becker was later to join GRAVE DIGGER.

Two years later the group released their eighth album, 'Black Hand Inn', the record featuring the fifteen minute epic 'Genesis', RUNNING WILD's alternative view on the theory of evolution.

1995 yielded 'Masquerade' - recorded with Gerhard 'Anyway' Wölfe at Horus Sound in Hannover. The group immediately played the 'Summer Metal Meetings' with the likes of RAGE and GRAVE DIGGER.

With the band inoperative for a period new guitarist Thilo Hermann, previously with HOLY MOSES and RISK, joined GLENMORE for live work but would return to RUNNING WILD the following year. Schwarzmann continued his musical chairs by emerging once again as the man behind the kit for U.D.O. in 1997.

The same year Herrmann put together the side project HÖLLENHUNDE for the 'Alptraum' album with GLENMORE drummer Dany Löble. When HÖLLENHUNDE dissolved the same year as the album release Herrmann resumed activities with RUNNING WILD.

For the 1997 release, which saw RUNNING WILD switching to the G.U.N. label, Rock n' Rolf was joined by Smuszynski, Hermann and drummer Jörg Michael. The latter boasted credits with AVENGER, RAGE, MEKONG DELTA, LAOS, HEADHUNTER, GRAVE DIGGER and AXEL RUDI PELL.

1998 found the band returning with a brand new studio affair. The 'Victory' album had Rolf, Herrmann and Smuszynski joined by Angelo Sasso. The latter being a pseudonym for a non-Metal drummer not wishing to be associated with the genre!

For touring RUNNING WILD pulled in erstwhile RAGE drummer Chris Efthimiades as Michael had committed himself fully to STRATOVARIUS.

The band, now including new bass player Peter Pichel, would spend the latter half of 2001 recording new album 'The Brotherhood'. Rock n' Rolf put in a cameo appearance in the video for famous German spoof act the DONUTS cover version of TWISTED SISTER's 'We're Not Gonna Take It' in September of 2002.

Singles/EPs:

Victim Of States Power / Walpurgis Night (The Sign Of Women's Fight) / Satan, Noise N0010 (1984) ('Walpurgis Night' EP)

Bad To The Bone / Battle Of Waterloo / March On, Noise EM 116 (1989) ('Bad To The Bone' EP)
Wild Animal / Chains And Leather / Tear Down The Walls / Störtebeker, Noise NO173-3 (1990) ('Wild Animal' EP)
Little Big Horn / Billy The Kid / Genocide, Noise (1991) ('Little Big Horn' EP)
Lead Or Gold / Hanged, Drawn And Quartered / Win Or Be Drowned, EMI 8 80248-2 (1992)
The Privateer EP, EMI (1994)

Albums:
GATES TO PURGATORY, Noise N0012 08-167 (1984)
Victim Of States Power / Adrian (Son Of Satan) / Preacher / Black Demon / Soldiers Of Hell / Genghis Khan / Prisoner Of Our Time / Diabolical Force
BRANDED AND EXILED, Noise NO0030 (1985)
Branded And Exiled / Gods Of Iron / Realm Of Shades / Mordor / Fight The Oppression / Evil Spirit / Marching To Die / Chains And Leather
UNDER JOLLY ROGER, Noise NO064 (1987)
Under Jolly Roger / War In The Gutter / Raw Ride / Beggar's Night / Raise Your Fist / Land Of Ice / Diamonds In The Black Chest / Mercyless Game
READY FOR BOARDING (LIVE), Noise NO0108 (1988)
Hymn Of Long John Silver / Under Jolly Roger / Genghis Khan / Raise Your Fist / Purgatory / Mordor / Diabolic Force / Raw Ride / Adrian (S.O.S.) / Prisoner Of Our Time
PORT ROYAL, Noise NO122-2 (1988)
Port Royal / Raging Fire / Into The Arena / Uaschitschun / Final Gates / Conquistadores / Blown To Kingdom Come / Warchild / Mutiny / Calico Jack
DEATH OR GLORY, Noise NO172-2 (1990)
Riding The Storm / Renegade / Evilution / Running Blood / Highland Glory (The Eternal Fight) / Marooned / Bad To The Bone / Tortuga Bay / Death Or Glory / Battle At Waterloo / March On
BLAZON STONE, Noise NO171 (1990)
Blazon Stone / Lone Wolf / Slavery / Fire And Ice / Little Big Horn / Over The Rainbow / White Masque / Rolling Wheels / Bloody Red Rose / Straight To Hell / Head Or Tails / Billy The Kid / Genocide
THE FIRST YEARS OF PIRACY, Noise N184-1 (1991)
Under Jolly Roger / Branded And Exiled / Soldiers Of Hell / Raise Your Fist / Walpurgis Night / Fight The Oppression / Marching To Die / Raw Ride / Diamonds Of The Black

Chest / Prisoner Of Our Time
PILE OF SKULLS, Electrola EMI 7 80651-2 (1992)
Chamber Of Lies / Whirlwind / Sinister Eyes / Black Wings Of Death / Fistful Of Dynamite / Roaring Thunder / Pile Of Skulls / Lead Or Gold / White Buffalo / Jenning's Revenge / Treasure Island
BLACK HAND INN, EMI 7 80651-2 (1994)
The Curse / Black Hand Inn / Mr. Deadhead / Soulless / The Privateer / Fight The Fire Of Hate / The Phantom Of The Black Hand Hill / Freewind Rider / Powder And Iron / Dragonmen / Genesis (The Making And Fall Of Man)
MASQUERADE, Noise NO261-2 (1995)
The Contract / The Crypts Of Hades / Masquerade / Demonized / Black Soul / Lions Of The Sea / Rebel At Heart / Wheel Of Doom / Metalhead / Soleil Royale / Men In Black / Underworld
THE RIVALRY, G.U.N. GUN 155 (1997)
March Of The Final Battle (The End Of All Evil) / The Rivalry / Kiss Of Death / Firebreather / Return Of The Dragon / Resurrection / Ballad Of William Kidd / Agents Of Black / Fire And Thunder / The Poison. Adventure Galley / Man On The Moon / War And Peace
VICTORY, G.U.N. GUN CD 74321 71502-2 (2000)
Fall Of Dorkas / When Time Runs Out / Timeriders / Into The Fire / Revolution / The Final Waltz / Tsar / The Hussar / The Guardian / Return Of The Gods / Silent Killer / Victory
SINGLES COLLECTION, (2000)
Walpurgis Night (Demo) / Satan (Demo) / March On / Hanged, Drawn And Quartered / Win Or Be Drowned / Wild Animal / Tear Down The Walls / Störtebeker / Billy The Kid / Genocide / Chamber Of Lies - White Buffalo / Poisoned Blood / Dancing On The Minefield / Genesis (The Making And The Fall Of Man)
THE BROTHERHOOD, G.U.N. (2002)
Welcome To Hell / Soulstripper / The Brotherhood / Powerride / Siberian Winter / Detonator / Pirate Song / U-Nation / Dr. Horror / The Ghost / Crossfire / Faceless

SABATAN (SPAIN)
Line-Up: Miguel A. Pulido (vocals), David Ballester (guitar), Ricardo Ruiz (guitar), Marco Morouco (bass), Eduardo Olmo (drums)

A traditional Heavy Metal band from Madrid. SABATAN was created in 1995 with an initial quartet of vocalist Elisa Candelas, guitarist David Ballester, second guitarist Jorg Dimitrov and drummer Juan Carlos Alegria. A demo arrived the same year entitled 'Not Of This Earth' and in 1997 the band got the opportunity to open for OBUS.

During 1998 both Dimitrov and Alegria left the band. SABATAN pulled in replacements Antonio Herrero on drums and guitar player Jaime Aldea. The next to leave would be Candelas, bailing out to team up with DARK MOOR. This loss would put SABATAN on hold for a period.

One year later Ballester regrouped enlisting new singer Javier Blanco, Ricardo Ruiz on guitar, Octavio Ortega on bass and Rafael Diaz of KNELL ODISSEY and later EASY RIDER on the drums. However, this line-up managed just the one gig and SABATAN morphed again incorporating singer Antonio Cerezuela and drummer Eduardo Olmos. This unit issued the 'Sabatan' demo before Olmos too made his exit, his substitute being Marco Marouco in time for support gigs to SAXON.

In 2001 further changes occurred with Cerezuela's position being taken by Miguel A. Pulido. In their new guise SABATAN cut another promotional EP 'Metal Louder'.

Singles/EPs:
Unborn Son / Faithful Legions / Shake Your Head / Hunting In The Dark / Knight Of The Night, (1999) ('Sabatan' EP)

SACRED STEEL (GERMANY)
Line-Up: Gerrit P. Metz (vocals), Jörg M. Knittel (guitar), Oliver Großhans (guitar), Jens Sonnenberg (bass), Mathias Straub (drums)

Intent on using the words 'Metal' or 'Steel' at least once in every song delivered on their debut album, German outfit SACRED STEEL have taken on the mantle of Metal crusaders with an impressive dedication. The Ludwigsburg band was rooted in the 1990 Progressive Metal acts VARIETY OF ARTS. This band in turn became TRAGEDY DIVINE in 1994 releasing the 1996 album 'Visions Of Power'. However, vocalist Gerrit P. Metz and guitarist Jörg M. Knittel wished to forego the

Progressive pretensions and found an earthier back to basics Heavy Metal band and as such SACRED STEEL was conceived.

The band's inaugural line-up saw Metz and Knittel joined by ex-REBIRTH rhythm guitarist Oliver Großhans, bassist Patrick Schmidt and drummer Mathias Straub. Before long Jens Sonnenberg had usurped Schmidt. Live shows, including a supports to SCANNER and BLITZKRIEG, and a demo secured a deal in April 1997 with - naturally - Metal Blade Records, SACRED STEEL becoming the first ever German band to sign to the label.

Having recorded their debut album, 'Reborn In Steel', during August and September the same year the Stuttgart based quintet appeared at the 'Bang Your Head II' festival whilst in the midst of recording. This show had the band performing TENSION's 'Downfall Of Evil', complete with a guesting ex-DEUCE, TENSION and latter WARDOG mainman Tom Gattis.

The 1998 album, 'Wargods Of Metal' produced by Bill Metoyer, included a rousing version of OMEN's 'Battle Cry'. Its arrival was preceded by a live performance of the new material at the 'Wacken Open Air' festival, SACRED STEEL of course appearing on the 'True Metal' stage.

SACRED STEEL's 1999 started with an appearance on the 'Unbroken Metal' Metal TV show tie in compilation CD. Featured track was a demo version of 'Crusaders Of The Metal Blade'. Metz also gained recording credits by sessioning on Dutch theatric Black Metal band GODDESS OF DESIRE's take on the MERCYFUL FATE classic 'Nuns Have No Fun'. February and March of 1999 saw the band SACRED STEEL participating, as support to NEVERMORE's 'Dreaming Neon Black' European dates, also sharing the stage with Swedish acts MORGANA LEFAY and NOCTURNAL RITES.

SACRED STEEL would also put in a valuable showing at the 'Wacken Open Air' Metal festival in August although their appearance had not been scheduled. Black Metal act MARDUK had pulled out and therefore the organisers, finding SACRED STEEL band members relaxing backstage, coaxed them into a fill in performance. Fortunately the band were fully rehearsed in anticipation of their next European tour, the 'Crusaders Of Metal' dates in alliance with WARDOG and DESTINY'S END. To round the year off SACRED STEEL contributed to the Nuclear Blast ACCEPT tribute album with their interpretation of 'Fight It Back'.

Vinyl versions of the May 2000 release 'Bloodlust' included an exclusive track 'Journey To The City Of The Dreaming Dead'.

376

The part conceptual album, which if anything found the band mellowing slightly, was engineered and mixed by Achim Köhler. SACRED STEEL supported CHILDREN OF BODOM and PRIMAL FEAR for a German tour in February 2001. SACRED STEEL would also donate their rendition of URIAH HEEP's 'Return To Fantasy' to a Century Media tribute compilation. In April SACRED STEEL personnel Jörg M. Knittel and Oliver Großhans would be found as part of the Death Metal project MY DARKEST HATE delivering the 'Massive Brutality' album through Knittel's own Iron Glory label. The band, founded by Knittel back in 1998, also involved AZMODAN vocalist René Pfeiffer and PRIMAL FEAR drummer Klaus Sperling. SACRED STEEL signed a new contract with the Massacre Records label for their fourth album 'Slaughter Prophecy' for February 2002 release. Initially plans were afoot to cover GRIM REAPER's 'See You In Hell' but the track did not make the final running order. The record would transpire to be a much darker themed album than previous efforts. A vinyl version, suitably limited to just 666 copies, added an exclusive bonus track 'Crush The Holy, Save The Damned'. Another rarity surfaced with SACRED STEEL's cover version of the DEATH track 'Zombie Ritual'. Originally recorded during the 'Bloodlust' sessions the song was donated to a Christmas compilation album put out by the famed German Metal venue the Rockfabrik in Ludwigsburg and limited to 3800 copies.

SACRED STEEL
Photo : Jimmy Reek

Albums:
REBORN IN STEEL, Metal Blade 3984-14146-2 (1997)
Metal Reigns Supreme / Battle Angel / Trapped In Hell / True Force Of Iron Glory / Reborn In Steel / Purified By Pain / Sword Of The King / In The Mouth Of Madness / Kill The Deceiver / Sacred Steel
WARGODS OF METAL, Metal Blade 3891-14196-2 (1998)
Blessed By The Gods / Wargods Of Metal / Tonight The Witches Ride / Iron Legions / Carnage Rules The Fields Of Death / Army Of Metalheads / Battle Cry / Dethrone The Tyrant King / By Steel We Rule / Crusaders Of The Metal Blade / Empire Of Steel / Declaration Of War / Heavy Metal To The End
BLOODLUST, Metal Blade (2000)
Stormhammer / The Oath Of Blood / By The Wrath Of The Unborn / Blood On My Steel / Metal Is War / Sacred Warriors Of Steel / Dark Forces Lead Me To The Brimstone Gate / Master Of Thy Fate / Lust For Blood / Throne Of Metal
SLAUGHTER PROPHECY, Massacre MASCD 0307 (2002)
The Immortal Curse / Slaughter Prophecy (Vengeance For The Dead) / Sacred Bloody Steel / The Rites Of Sacrifice / Raise The Metal Fist / Pagan Heart / Faces Of The Antichrist / Lay Me To My Grave / Crush The Holy, Save The Damned / Let The Witches Burn / Invocation Of The Nameless Ones

SAD IRON (HOLLAND)
Line-Up: Herke van der Poel (vocals), Bernard Rive (guitar), Leo Ockeleon (bass), Jacques Van Develen (drums)

A fairly accomplished Heavy Metal band blighted by having 'Total Damnation' graced with one of the most amateurish album covers ever, nevertheless SAD IRON's inaugural vinyl effort was a split live album with SEDUCER.

Albums:
HOLLAND HEAVY METAL VOLUME ONE, Universe (1982) (Split LP with SEDUCER).
Thunder And Lightning / Sad Iron / Get Out, Get Off / Racing Down The Highway / Schoolgirls
TOTAL DAMNATION, Universe (1984)
Demon's Night / Prisoners / We All Praise The Devil / Rock n' Roll Rendezvous / Hellfighter / Total Damnation / Three Crown Saws
THE ANTICHRIST, Universe (1985)
Living Like A Rat / S.M. / Day Of Doom / You're Obsessed / We Play To Kill / Where Warwinds Blow / Posers / Powerthrash

SAGITTARIUS (NORWAY)
Line-Up: Nicko (vocals), Kurt E. (guitar), Mosen (bass), Per Williams (keyboards), Roy

A.L. (drums)

A Norwegian Progressive Metal act, the first two SAGITTARIUS albums were actually released on one CD package.
For the 1997 EP 'Jole's Joke' SAGITTARIUS were down to a quartet with bassist Mosen out and guitarist Kurt E. being supplanted by Jørgen Von Krogh.

Singles/EPs:
Jole's Joke / Saivo / Rahkisvuoda Mearrihisvuohta / Vision, Voices Of Wonder VOW060CD (1997)

Albums:
VOICE OF DOOM, Sagittarius Music SACD931 (1993)
The Gathering / Too Much Hell - Part I / Escape / Blessed By God / The Law / Crusader / We Don't Want / Filled With Life / Do It With A Kiss / Too Much Hell - Part II / Voice Of Doom / Never An End / Let Your Spirit See
LOAHPA JIENAT, Sagittarius Music SACD931 (1993)
Coahkkanan / Stuimmit Algu / Báhtarit / Buressivdnadusain / Lahka / Eat Hálit / Soadi / Ealliman / 54 / Oaivamususfaide / Stuimmit / Lahpa Jienat / Li Goasse Loahppa
SANITY OF MADNESS, Voices Of Wonder 3340-2 (1994)
Explorer / Elements / Child Molester / Believe Me / Sanity Of Madness / Nameless Man / Silvertear

SAINTS ANGER (GERMANY)
Line-Up: Harald Piller (vocals / guitar), Jürgen Kief (guitar), Joachim Walter (bass), Harald Reiter (drums)

Originally starting out as a trio in 1981 with Harald Piller, Joachim Walter and Harald Reiter SAINTS ANGER added second guitarist Jürgen Keif in 1983 in time to record two demo tapes in the same year.
SAINTS ANGER was very much inspired by classic German Metal and this fact came through on the 1985 album 'Danger Metal'.

Albums:
DANGER METAL, Mausoleum SKULL 8363 (1985)
The Bullet / Wrong Or Right / Danger Metal / Highway / The Ghost's Tale / Liberation / Crashing On Steel / Hero / Megalomania

SALAMANDRA (CZECH REPUBLIC)
Line-Up: Dalibor Halamicek (vocals), Pavel Silva (guitar), Karel Repecky (guitar), Jarda Dufek (bass), Marek Lankoci (keyboards), Daniel Jurecek (drums)

SALAMANDRA describe themselves as Gothic Power Metal. Guitarist Pavel Silva of REA SYLVIA and ARKUS notoriety conceived the group. For the January 1999 'Twilight Of Legends' album SALAMANDRA featured GROG vocalist Dalibor 'Panther' Halamicek, guitarists Pavel Silva and Karel Repecky, PUNISHMENT bassist Ales Klimsa and EUTHANASIA keyboard player Marek Lankoci. One "Blackcount Baalberith", a.k.a. Daniel Jurecek, would deliver session drums. Jarda Dufek replaced Klimsa on bass for the December 2000 conceptual follow up 'Skarremar'.
SALAMANDRA would commit their version of 'Judas' to the HELLOWEEN tribute album 'The Eastern Pumpkin'.

Albums:
TWILIGHT OF LEGENDS, Leviathan (1999)
Prelude / With Gods On Their Side / Misty Riders / The Mourning / Rise / Royal Hearing / Obstinavi Animo / Warriors / Silent Memory / War Is Over / Twilight Of Legends
SKARREMAR, Leviathan (2000)
The Time - Go Back Through Ages / The Legend - Reign Of The Wicked / The Silence (Comes Before A Storm) / The Toady - All Hope Abandon / The Lover - A Kiss Goodbye / The King - Skarremar's Pride / The Army - Dead End Battles / The Singer - Remember The Legend / The Traitor - Roads To Hell / The Coward - Hail The King / The Dead - Cantata Oscura / The Coming - Midnight Creatures / The Revenge - Legends Come True / The End - Freedom's Won Back / The Beginning

SALEM'S WYCH (USA)
Line-Up: Ron Johnson (vocals), Mark Gast (guitar), Tom Bronicki (guitar), Keith Jann (bass), Bill Neff (drums)

The cult Metal band SALEM'S WYCH, having last delivered product in 1986 with their highly collectable 'Betrayer Of Kings' album, would surprise many by making a comeback some fifteen years later with the 2002 album 'Through All Eternity'.

Albums:
BETRAYER OF KINGS, Metal War MWR001 (1986)
Betrayer Of Kings / Never Ending Battle / Attack / All Hail To The Queen / Time Is No More / Run From The Devil / Furor's Reign / Sweet Revenge / Fight Till The End
THROUGH ALL ETERNITY, (2002)

Through All Eternity / Blasphemy / No Better Than / Show No Mercy / Dust To Dust / Feel My Pain / What Should I Believe / Slave To The Master / Fallen From Grace / All I'll Ever Be / Hate / Beyond Forgiven / Crucified For Life

SAMHAIN (RUSSIA)
Line-Up: Sergey 'Immortal' Bendrikov (vocals), Lyudmila Abramova (vocals), Nick Simonov (keyboards)

Epic Russian Symphonic Metal that employed two vocalists in Sergey 'Immortal' Bendrikov and Lyudmila Abramova. SAMHAIN had debuted in 2000 with the 'Herimos' sessions. Included on the 2002 'Revival' album would be session players guitarist Roman Guriev and drummer Anton Smoliyanin. The Tibetan Monastic Choir was utilised for massed vocals on the track 'The Monster That Cries', surely a first in the world of Metal.

Albums:
REVIVAL, Irond 02-309 (2002)
Requiem Aeternam / Fallen Crusade / The Matrix / The Monster That Cries / Louisa's Black Roses / The Last Lullaby / Universal Mirror / Illusion Rain /
O Sole Mio

SAMURAI (UK)
Line-Up: Len Williams (vocals), Huw Lewis (guitar), Craig Riggsdale (guitar), Neil Rogers (bass), Michael Davies (drums)

South Wales derived Heavy Metal band SAMURAI released two strong albums, marred only by lacklustre production. The group's last recordings figured on a two track demo in 1987, featuring 'Show Me Your Love' and 'Stay With Me Tonight' which showed SAMURAI veering more towards American territory. The group garnered interest in America before the band strangely split.
Guitarist Craig Riggsdale formed TALAN with ex-PREYER drummer Phil Johns for the 'Spellbinder' single.

Singles/EPs:
Fires Of Hell / Dreams Of The World, Ebony (1984)

Albums:
SACRED BLADE, Ebony EBON24 (1984)
Fires Of Hell / I've Got What You Need / Rock Steady / Dreams Of The World / Fire In Your Eyes / Survivor / Gonna Rock Tonight / Hold On
WEAPON MASTER, Ebony EBON37 (1986)

HUW LEWIS of SAMURAI
Photo : Flea

We Rock All Night / Fighter / Hold On / Too Hot To Hold / You Better Be Ready / Into The Night / Aiming For You / Weapon Master

SAN ANTONIO SLAYER
(San Antonio, TX, USA)
Line-Up: Steve Cooper (vocals), Ron Jarzombek (guitar), Art Villarreal (guitar), Don van Stavern (bass), Dave McClain (drums)

SAN ANTONIO SLAYER, previously known simply as SLAYER, this Texan based band prefixed their title with the name of their home city when confusion arose with the more prominent Los Angeles thrashers of the same name.
Between albums, bassist Don van Stavern forged the MARK REALE PROJECT with RIOT guitarist Mark Reale. This project then became known as NARITA, as vocalist Steve Cooper and drummer Dave McClain also became involved. von Stavern would join RIOT once Reale had resurrected his cult outfit.
Guitarist Art Villarreal was supplanted by Bob Catlin for the 'Go For The Throat' album.
Guitarist Ron Jarzombek reared his head again in 1997 with the SPASTIC INK album 'Ink Complete' and would later join RIOT and ex-JUDAS PRIEST vocalist Rob Halford for his 2000 touring band..
Don van Stavern turned up in 1998 as one of the instigators behind the Industrial Techno outfit PITBULL DAYCARE.

379

Albums:
PREPARE TO DIE, Rainforrest (1983)
The Door / Warrior / Prepare To Die / The
Final Holocaust / Unholy Book / To Ride The
Demon Out
GO FOR THE THROAT, Under Den Linden
D.D.L.-1 (1988)
Go For The Throat / Upon Us, The End / If
You Want Evil / Off With Their Heads / Ride
Of The Horsemen / Ancient Swords / T.L.O.
22 / The Witch Must Burn / Hell Will Be Thy
Name / Power To Burn

SANCTUARY (Seattle, WA, USA)
Line-Up: Warrel Dane (vocals), Lenny
Rutledge (guitar), Sean Blosl (guitar), Jim
Sheppard (bass), Dave Budbill (drums)

SANCTUARY, dating back to 1985, may just
hold the record for the band with the longest
hair in the world. The speed Metal group
came to prominence with the inclusion of a
brace of demo cuts on the 'Northwest
Metalfest' compilation album. Immediately
apparent was that vocalist Warrell Dane was
in possession of one of the most powerful
throats on the Metal scene.
The debut album, produced by MEGADETH
mainman Dave Mustaine, features a rather
weighty cover of JEFFERSON AIRPLANE's
acid daze classic 'White Rabbit'.
SANCTUARY proceeded to tour Europe as
support to MEGADETH before recording the
impressive 'Into The Mirror Black'.
SANCTUARY broke up with Dane forging
NEVERMORE finding cult success in Europe.
Dane's name was tenuously linked with the
then vacant vocal position in JUDAS PRIEST
during 1996.

Albums:
REFUGE DENIED, Epic 460 811-2 (1987)
Battle Angels / Termination Force / Die For
My Sins / Soldiers Of Steel / Sanctuary /
White Rabbit / Ascension To Destiny / The
Third War / Veil Of Disguise
INTO THE MIRROR BLACK, Epic 465 876-2
(1990)
Future Tense / Taste Revenge / Long Since
Dark / Epitaph / Eden Lies Obscured / The
Mirror Black / Seasons Of Destruction / One
More Murder / Communion

SANVOISEN (GERMANY)
Line-Up: Vagelis Maranis (vocals), Hendrik
Boettcher (guitar), Angel Schönbrunn
(guitar), Horst-Christian Andree (bass), Ulf
S. Gokeler (drums)

SANVOISEN are a Progressive Metal outfit
fronted by Greek vocalist Vagelis Maranis.

Drummer Ulf Gokeler had previously played
in a band together with former IVANHOE
singer Andy B. Franck for a short period.
SANVOISEN recorded its first demo in 1993
(three years after the group's inception)
before a more professional, four track tape
was cut with erstwhile SCORPIONS
keyboard player Luke Herzog. This was sent
to all the major labels before Noise Records
moved in to sign the outfit and placed them in
a studio with VICTORY's Tommy Newton and
the aforementioned Herzog to concoct the
debut album 'Exotic Ways'.
The second album, 'Soul seasons', was also
produced by Newton and first released in
Japan before Noise offered it for European
consumption and the band toured with
URIAH HEEP, DEEP PURPLE and SAXON.
In 1997 Gokeler bailed out. Former LETTER
X man Marco Ieva took his position.

Albums:
EXOTIC WAYS, Noise NO2212 (1995)
Colours Around / The Law / It's Over / Tears
For No One / Under Permission / The Blind /
What I Mean / No Place For Me / Believe /
Time Is Not / I'm Alive
SOUL SEASONS, Noise NO2792 (1996)
Spirits / Mindwars / Behind My Dreams / The
Difference / Soul Seasons / Against The
Fears / Broken Silence / Waiting For The
Rain / Somebody's Stolen My Name

SARATOGA (SPAIN)
Line-Up: Leo Jimenez (vocals), Jerónimo
Ramiro (guitar), Niko del Hierro (bass),
Daniel Perez (drums)

Respected Spanish Metal band forged by two
veterans of the Rock scene, guitarist
Jerónimo 'Jero' Ramiro of ÑU and erstwhile
BARON ROJO bass player Niko del Hierro.
This pair conjured up the concept of
SARATOGA in late 1992, soon inducting
drummer Marcos Parra. However, following
initial rehearsals Parra opted out. Joaquin
Arellano, previously with MURO, occupied the
drum stool and the group was also rounded
out with the inauguration of former MASSADA
singer Antonio Dominguez. It would be this
quartet that debuted live as SARATOGA,
opening shows for RATA BLANCA among
others.
Once tested live the group decided on a
change of singer, deeming Dominguez too
Rock n' Roll and not Metal enough for their
tastes. Subsequently in May of 1993 Fortu
Sanchez, another scene veteran of OBUS,
joined the clan.
SARATOGA signed to the Avispa label in late
1994, launching their eponymous debut the

following year. Extensive tour work throughout Spain then ensued.

SARATOGA's 1996 album 'Tributo' was comprised entirely of cover versions, paying homage to Spanish Rock institutions all the members had been previously engaged with such as BARON ROJO, PANZER, OBUS, SANTA, BANZAI and MURO. The album's release would not be a complete call for celebration though as Sanchez decided to quit on the day of its release. SARATOGA quickly filled the vacancy with Gabriel Boente. A further album, October 1997's 'Mi Ciudad', was delivered but in 1998 the departure of both Boente and Arellano took many by surprise. Auditions yielded drummer Daniel Perez of ECZEMA and singer Leo Jimenez. This new unit cut the 1999 album 'Vientos De Guerra' ('Winds Of War') with the double live 'Tiempos De Directo' emerging in 2000. The group also committed a cover version of JUDAS PRIEST's 'Painkiller' to the tribute album 'Metal Gods'. Jimenez would also add guest vocals to the track 'Las Ruinas Del Edén' on the AVALANCH album 'El Ángel Caido'.

Retaining a stable line-up SARATOGA issued the 'Agotara' album in March of 2002. An English language version was also in the pipeline.

Albums:
SARATOGA, Avispa (1995)
Grita / Ningun Precio Por La Paz / Tortura / Loco / 20 Anos / Eres Tu / Ojos De Mujer / Prisonero / Ojo Por Ojo / Cunas De Ortigas
TRIBUTO, Avispa (1996)
Resistire / Mas Duro Que Nunca / No Dudaria / Fuera De La Rey / Voy A Tu Ciudad / Vallecas 1996 / Reencarnacion / Autopista / Junto A Ti / Mirada Asesina / Que Tire La Toalla
MI CIUDAD, Avispa (1997)
Intro / Mi Ciudad / Basta / Luz De Neón / El Espejo / Por La Puerta De Atrás / Rojo Fuego / El Viejo Vagón / Sueños / Balas De Odio / Lejos De Ti / Salvaje / Uno Del Montón / Perro Traidor
VIENTOS DE GUERRA, Avispa ACD 042 CDA (1999)
La Iguana / Vientos De Guerra / Más De Mi Años / Sólo Un Motivo / Aprendiendo A Ser Yunque (Para Llegar A Ser Martillo) / Heavy Metal / Charlie Se Fue / Extraño Silencio / Hielo Líquido / El Ministro / Estrellas Las Del Cielo / Manos Unidas / A Sangre Y Fuego / Si Te Vas / Ruge El Motor
TIEMPOS DE DIRECTO, (2000)
Presentación / Vientos De Guerra / Más De Mil Años / Aprendiendo A Ser Yunque (Para Llegar A Ser Martillo) / Perro Traidor / Solo Un Motivo / Ningún Precio Por La Paz /

Heavy Metal / A Sangre Y Fuego / Manos Unidas / Lejos De Ti / Loco / Se Olvidó / Ruge El Motor / Charlie Se Fue / Lagrimas De Dolor / Rojo Fuego / Estrellas Las Del Cielo / Grita / Basta / Mi Ciudad
AGOTARAS, (2002)
11901 / Con Mano Izquierda / Tras Las Rejas / A Morir / Las Puertas Del Cielo / El Gran Cazador / Oscura La Luz / Rompehuesos / Parte De Mi / Viaje Por La Mente / Mercenario / Doblan Las Campanas / Resurrección / Ratas

SARISSA (GREECE)
Line-Up: Jimmy Selalmazidis (guitar / bass), Fotis Kanistras (drums)

A Thessaloniki Power Metal act, Greek duo SARISSA were supported by vocalist / keyboardist Sotos Noukas and guitarists Drosos 'Sakis' Drivas and Stelios Petronella.

Albums:
SARISSA, Cactus CACCD002 (1994)
Intro - Immortal Souls / Survival / Macedonian Army / Marathon / Sarissa / Athiest / King Of All Kings / Intro-Strong Wings / Winner

SATAN (UK)
Line-Up: Lou Taylor (vocals), Russ Tippins (guitar), Steve Ramsey (guitar), Graham English (bass), Sean Taylor (drums),

Newcastle Heavy Metal act SATAN began life in 1979 and would create a huge cult interest for themselves in Europe and the West coast of America with their first album, 1983's 'Court In The Act'.

The original SATAN line up included guitarist Russ Tippins and Steve Ramsey, vocalist Andrew Frepp, bassist Steven Bee and drummer Andy Read. Paul Smith, however, soon replaced Frepp.

At this stage SATAN was still a school act. Bee was superseded on bass by Graham English and Steve Allsop took over on vocals. Read's position behind the drum stool was relinquished to Ian McCormack who was to be usurped in favour of RAVEN man Sean Taylor and would later turn up in BATTLEAXE. Read, meantime, still served the band as a roadie.

The group's first demo, "Into The Fire', featured vocalist Trevor Robinson, but following the debut single 'Kiss Of Death' in 1979 Robinson departed in favour of Lou Taylor.

Lou Taylor would stick with the group until just prior to the recording of 'Caught In The Act'. Taylor's position was taken by Ian Swift before he too was replaced by the well known figure of BLITZKREIG and AVENGER vocalist Brian Ross for recording as Swift filled Ross' boots in the AVENGER ranks.

Curiously, Brian Ross was replaced by the returning Lou Taylor following 'Court In The Act', the band claiming that a lack of image onstage to be the main reason that Ross was asked to leave. Incidentally, during this period drummer Sean Taylor was also drumming for WARRIOR as a sideline.

Shortly after this latest change of vocalists in 1985, SATAN renamed themselves after Lou's previous band BLIND FURY and recorded the far more commercial 'Out Of Reach' which saw sales slide.

Meanwhile the 'Court In The Act' album was, as mentioned, fast becoming a cult classic on the West coast of America. The band promptly kicked out Lou and renamed themselves SATAN, citing American interest in 'Court In The Act' for this change back to a more Metallic approach. SATAN recruiting ex-ROUGH EDGE vocalist Mick Jackson in the process.

Following his final departure Lou Taylor went on to front TOUR DE FORCE and PERSIAN RISK and later became a known figure on the London club scene as a Rock DJ. English and Ramsey later found European success with the innovative SKYCLAD, whilst Tippins is now a member of Folk Rock act McALLUM and is also in an ABBA cover band!

A Ross / Tippins / Ramsey / English / Taylor SATAN reunion album was on the cards at one point, but this project was allegedly shelved by one of the musician's wives!! A further stab at a re-formation came when Brian Ross attempted to resurrect the band for a one-off appearance at the German 'Wacken Open Air' festival but it was to no avail.

Singles/EPs:
Kiss Of Death / Heads Will Roll, Guardian GRC 145 (1979)
Key To Oblivion / Hear Evil, See Evil, Speak Evil / Fuck You / The Ice Man, Steamhammer SPV 60-1898 (1986) ('Into The Future' EP)

Albums:
COURT IN THE ACT, Roadrunner RR 9894 (1983)
Into The Fire / Trial By Fire / Blades Of Steel / No Turning Back / Broken Treaties / Break Free / Hunt You Down / Dark side Of Innocence
SUSPENDED SENTENCE, Steamhammer 08-1837 (1987)
92nd Symphony / Who Dies Wins / 11th

Commandment / Suicidal Justice / Vandal (Hostile Youth) / SCUM (Socially Condemned Undesirable Misfits) / Avalanche Of A Million Hearts / Calculated Execution (Driller Killer)

SAVAGE GRACE (Los Angeles, CA, USA)
Line-Up: Mike Smith (vocals), Chris Logue (guitar), Mike Marshall (guitar), Brian East (bass), Dan Finch III (drums)

SAVAGE GRACE evolved from the band MARQUIS DE SADE, created in 1981. With the addition of guitarist Kenny Powell in February of 1983 the band decided on a name switch to SAVAGE GRACE, the first line-up being guitarists Powell and Christian Logue, bassist Brian East and drummer Don Finch.

Brian East had relocated to Los Angeles from Seattle where he had recorded a couple of singles with the semi-Glam troupe ALLEYBRAT.

SAVAGE GRACE debuted with a cut 'Sceptors Of Deceit' on the Metal Blade Records compilation album 'Metal Massacre II'. An EP, 'The Dominatress' quickly followed. Wishing to augment their sound SAVAGE GRACE pulled in lead vocalist John Birke in time for recording of 'The Dominatress' EP.

Birke departed to pursue mellower music. Birke, whose last shows with the band included gigs in San Francisco with SLAYER and EXODUS, actually found out about his dismissal second hand, the band announcing it on air during a radio interview. SAVAGE GRACE also lost guitarist Kenny Powell shortly after. Powell went on to create power metallers OMEN.

SAVAGE GRACE were soon back up to full strength bringing in vocalist Mike Smith and former AGENT STEEL guitarist Mike Marshall. However, the guitar parts on the 'Master Of Disguise' album were performed by Logue as Marshall was added some two months after recording.

The 'After The Fall From Grace' album sees the supplanting of drummer Dan Finch III by Mark Marcum.

The 1987 single sees East replaced with bassist Brian Peace.

Singles/EPs:
The Dominatress / Live To Burn / Too Young To Die / Fight For Your Life / Curse The Night, Metal Blade (1983)
Ride Into The Night / We March On / The Healing Hand / Burn, Semaphore 1012 (1987)
Albums:
MASTER OF DISGUISE, Black Dragon 001

(1985)
Lion's Roar / Bound To Be Free / Fear My
Way / Sins Of The Damned / Into The Fire /
Master Of Disguise / Sons Of Iniquity / No
One Left To Blame / Guitar Solo
AFTER THE FALL FROM GRACE, Black
Dragon (1986)
A Call To Arms / We Came, We Saw, We
Conquered / After The Fall From Grace /
Trial By Fire / Palestinia / Age Of Innocence /
Flesh And Blood / Destination Unknown /
Tales Of Mystery

SAVAGE STEEL (CANADA)
Line-Up: Paul Gleneicki (vocals), Marshall
Birch (guitar), Mark Taluitie (bass), Brian
Vella (drums)

SAVAGE STEEL's debut album, on the
California based New Renaissance label
owned by HELLION vocalist Ann Boleyn,
came in blue vinyl. Bassist Mark Taluitie was
substituted by Stephan Turrer for the 'Do Or
Die' album, produced by SAGA man Steve
Negus.

Albums:
BEGINS WITH A NIGHTMARE, New
Renaissance (1987)
Hit From The Rear / The Betrayal /
Chambers Of Darkness / On The Attack /
Nightprowler / Streets Of Indecision / A Night
On The Horizon / Switchblade Man
DO OR DIE, Maze Music (1988)
Mind Over Matter / It's Do Or Die / Enough
Is Enough / Time After Time / Better Late
Than Never / Men Of War / Evil Eye / Get
Me Out Of Here

SAVALLION DAWN (GERMANY)
Line-Up: Ernesto Monteiro (vocals), Philipp
Roeske (guitar), Thomas Klein (guitar), Lars
Tiede (bass), Nikolas Fritz (drums)

Melodic Power Metal unit dating to 1999. The
SAVALLION DAWN line-up that put together
the 'Black Skies' demo that same year
comprised vocalist Michael Beckers,
guitarists Phillip Roeske and Dirk Schramme,
bassist Lars Tiede and drummer Nikolas Fritz.
The demo succeeded in garnering healthy
praise throughout the Metal media but live
action was curtailed when Beckers withdrew.
Eventually the band located a new singer in
Carl Delius of DEADLY SIN.
During 2001 SAVALLION DAWN was wrought
by significant line-up ructions as Delius
decamped in March and Schramme the
following June. Thomas Klein filled the guitar
vacancy and Ernesto Monteiro, of Uruguayan
descent, became SAVALLION DAWN's new

lead vocalist. The band issued the self-
financed album 'The Charge' during 2002.

Albums:
THE CHARGE, (2002)
Set Me Free / Price To Escape / Down In
Silence / Destiny / Seven Signs / Onward /
Nightmares Of Past

SAVATAGE (USA)
Line-Up: Damond Jiniya (vocals), Jon Oliva
(vocals / keyboards), Criss Caffrey (guitar),
Al Pitrelli (guitar), Johnny Lee Middleton
(bass), Jeff Plate (drums)

JOHNNY LEE MIDDLETON of SAVATAGE
Photo : Nico Wobben

SAVATAGE, one of the most individualistic of
acts to have broken out of the '80s metal
boom, began life as a school trio titled
METROPOLIS. With the Oliva brothers Jon
on vocals and bass, with Chris on guitar
teaming up with drummer Steve Wacholz the
teenagers paid their dues in the Florida clubs
performing cover sets by such artists as
DEEP PURPLE and BLACK SABBATH. From
these humble origins SAVATAGE would grow
into an act that set itself apart from the pack,
possessing two unique talents in Jon Oliva's
thundering vocals and Chris Oliva's supreme
guitar talents. Despite gaining a major label
deal SAVATAGE would swim against the tide
releasing a succession of commendable but

JON OLIVA of SAVATAGE
Photo : Nico Wobben

overlooked albums. Eventually their tenacity paid off with the introduction of producer Paul O'Neill's more progressive themes drew in a loyal international audience.

As the desire for original material grew the founding threesome forged AVATAR, having two tracks included on a local compilation album and then releasing the now extremely rare 'City Beneath The Surface' EP in 1983. By the Summer the group had become SAVATAGE and one of the earliest shows performed was opening for SHOOTING STAR as work progressed on a debut album entitled 'Sirens'. For 'Sirens', the Oliva brothers and Wacholz were joined by new bassist Keith Collins were credited with "Shrieks Of Terror", "Metalaxe", "Barbaric Cannons" and "The Bottom End" respectively.

The band were subsequently snapped up by major label Atlantic and delivered a titanic tour de force in the Max Norman produced 'Power Of The Night'. This album proved beyond all doubt that SAVATAGE were a major force to be reckoned with a set of class songs bolstered by uncompromising and unadulterated heaviness.

However, SAVATAGE then strangely stalled, hitting their creative nadir with 1986's 'Fight For The Rock'. The previous power and commitment was tempered by blatant commercialism, including an uninspired rendition of FREE's 'Wishing Well', and the record was soundly panned by critics and fans alike. Jon Oliva took the strain so badly he reportedly resorted to drink and drugs. The

band endeavoured to tour but their singer's downhill spiral forced the cancellation of many dates with the band being put on hold whilst Oliva cleaned up. In this period of turmoil Chris Oliva was approached by OZZY OSBOURNE and MEGADETH amongst others but loyally chose to remain steadfast to SAVATAGE.

'Hall Of The Mountain King', which without doubt sparked a renaissance for the band, was the first album that captured SAVATAGE spreading their musical wings further including as it does a radical reworking of the Grieg classic 'Hall Of The Mountain King'. Former BLACK SABBATH vocalist RAY GILLEN guests on the track 'Strange Wings'. The band added former HEAVEN guitarist Chris Caffrey for live work guesting for DIO and MEGADETH in America and a European date at the legendary 'Aardschock' festival in Holland. With the completion of these dates Caffrey would join DIRTY LOOKS but would make a return to SAVATAGE and by recording of the 'Gutter Ballet' album Caffrey had earned his stripes becoming a full time member.

The 1991 release 'Streets - A Rock Opera', which featured the Metropolitan Opera Children's Choir and now minus Caffrey, was an ambitious affair conceptually based upon the fortunes of A New York musician embroiled in the world of street drugs. Although a fine release and one that surpassed the sales of previous efforts 'Streets' was often overlooked suffering from unfortunate timing, coming as it did soon after the massive impact of QUEENSRYCHE's 'Operation Mindcrime' concept album.

In 1993 SAVATAGE, bereft of the core membership of Jon Oliva and Steve Wacholz, issued the 'Edge Of Thorns' opus. The year would be overshadowed though by the death of Criss Oliva. Travelling home from a Rock concert on the night of October 17th Oliva's car was hit head on by a truck that strayed into his lane. The guitarist's wife Dawn would eventually recover but the 30 year old guitarist was killed outright.

Jon Oliva resolved to pursue SAVATAGE with renewed vigour following the death of his brother. 'Handful Of Rain', with keyboard and song-writing back in the hands of Jon Oliva, saw a SAVATAGE line-up of Middleton, Wacholz, vocalist Zachary Stevens, previously with Boston band WICKED WITCH, and former TESTAMENT guitarist Alex Skolnick. The latter was merely on loan from his own project, the Funk Rock flavoured EXHIBIT A, but did fulfil tour dates appearing twice a night as EXHIBIT A were the support band! These shows would witness the induction of new drummer Jeff Plate.

CHRIS CAFFREY of SAVATAGE
Photo : Nico Wobben

As a diversion from their priority act Oliva and Caffrey would issue an album from their side project DOCTOR BUTCHER, a record that surprised many with its unbridled heaviness.

Skolnick upon his departure from the band joined OZZY OSBOURNE's band although his stay was fleeting - one secret gig at Nottingham's Rock City venue. SAVATAGE meanwhile pulled in ex-C.P.R., TALAS, ALICE COOPER, ASIA and WIDOWMAKER guitarist Al Pitrelli, a man whose past credits were both an indicator of his versatility and his demand.

The SAVATAGE live release 'Ghost In The Ruins', although initially only a Japanese release, was issued in Europe after it flooded into the European market by import. The recordings, dating from between 1987 and 1990, amply displayed Criss Oliva's undoubted talents.

Metal Blade Records re-release of 'The Dungeons Are Calling' in 1997 adds an extra "lost" track 'Fighting For Your Love' as well as a live version of 'Sirens'. The same year's re-issue of 'Sirens' is rounded off with two further archive cuts 'Lady In Disguise' and 'The Message'.

In late 1996 O'Neill and SAVATAGE members Oliva, Pitrelli and Middleton were involved in the Christmas rock album 'Christmas Eve And Other Stories' under the name of TRANS-SIBERIAN ORCHESTRA. The album includes 'Christmas Eve - Sarajevo' lifted directly from the 'Dead Winter Dead' sessions. Pitrelli made time during 1997 to contribute to the FLESH AND BLOOD Blues project band assembled by former DRIVE, SHE SAID mainman Mark Mangold and TYKETTO vocalist Danny Vaughn.

SAVATAGE undertook a mammoth European tour during late 1997 supported by fellow Americans VANDERHOOF. Caffrey found downtime in SAVATAGE's schedule to record the METALIUM project band's first album 'Millennium Metal'.

By early 1999 Pitrelli was performing live work with BLUE OYSTER CULT. 2000 found Pitrelli leaving for fresh pastures in MEGADETH.

SAVATAGE, newly signed to SPV in Europe and Nuclear Blast in America, spent the bulk of 2000 recording a new concept album 'Poets And Madmen', its proposed release date being put back many times due to work on the third TRANS SIBERIAN ORCHESTRA album. Meantime a tribute album 'Return Of The Mountain King' surfaced.

In November it was announced that Zachary Stevens had departed the band. The holiday period was taken up with TRANS SIBERIAN ORCHESTRA dates novelly splitting the project into two to satisfy demand. Johnny Lee Middleton anchored the 'East' version of the act whilst the 'West' variant had Caffrey alongside SAVATAGE drummer Jeff Plate and erstwhile six string colleague Alex Skolnick.

An announcement in early March 2001 saw the inclusion of Florida native and ex-DIET OF WORMS man Damond Jiniya as the bands new lead vocalist with second guitar in the hands of Jack Frost. The latter had been a member of Caffrey's METALIUM project as well as spreading his talents over such acts as SEVEN WITCHES, SPEEED and BRONX CASKET CO.

'Poets And Madmen' would finally arrive in April, its debut at number 7 in the national German album charts providing ample proof of SAVATAGE fans patience. Touring in America had FATES WARNING as support act.

SAVATAGE toured Europe putting in festival appearances at the Italian 'Gods Of Metal' event, Germany's 'Bang Your Head' show and the infamous Dutch 'Dynamo' gig prior to supporting JUDAS PRIEST on their Spanish dates. These Iberian shows proved more memorable for guitarist Chris Caffrey than he would have liked though as the musician was struck with severe food poisoning. Soldiering on with the tour Caffrey was eventually hospitalised in Holland.

Headlining gigs in Brazil found native act HANGER as support. A run of American headlining shows beginning in San Francisco on September 5th would roll out with NEVERMORE as opening act. However, in light of the terrorist strikes on New York and Washington SAVATAGE pulled their projected European return dates. They would later be rescheduled for early 2002 announced with VICIOUS RUMOURS and BLAZE as opening acts.

Caffrey would take time out to act as session guitarist for erstwhile 24-7 SPYZ bassist Rick Skatore's new BLOCK 16 project debut. Along with Jeff Plate the guitarist also weighed in with ROYAL HUNT vocalist JOHN WEST's 'Earthmaker' project album. Frost dived straight back into action with both SEVEN WITCHES and BRONX CASKET CO. Meantime it would be learned that erstwhile singer Zachary Stevens had re-emerged touting a fresh venture entitled CIRCLE II CIRCLE. This project, which saw Stevens collaborating with Chris Caffrey, soon scored a label deal with AFM Records in Germany.

In early April fans would be surprised to say the least at an official announcement that Jack Frost had been fired with SAVATAGE re-recruiting Al Pitrelli from the recently disintegrated MEGADETH. However, before taking up this post Pitrelli would undertake live work with former SKID ROW vocalist SEBASTIAN BACH. In an odd twist of events Jeff Waters of Canadian Thrash veterans ANNIHILATOR would end up joining SAVATAGE for their summer European 2002 dates. The only recently re-inducted Al Pitrelli was unable to make the tour due to "prior commitments". Within 24 hours it would be announced that Pitrelli and forged a fresh band union with former MEGADETH alumni guitarist MARTY FRIEDMAN, bassist David Ellefson and drummer Jimmy DeGrasso.

Singles/EPs:
City Beneath The Surface (Live) / 24 Hours (Live), Edel Concrete 0086252RAD (1995) (Free CD single with 'Dead Winter Dead' album)
DT Jesus (Live) / Believe (Live) / Gutter Ballet (Live) / This Is Where You Should Be (Live), Edel 0089505CTR (1996) (Promotional release)
Commissar / Drive / Voyage, SPV (2001) 88 GERMANY

Albums:
SIRENS, Music For Nations CDMFN 48 (1985)
Sirens / Holocaust / I Believe / Rage / On The Run / Twisted Little Sister / Living For The Night / Scream Murder / Out On The Streets
THE DUNGEONS ARE CALLING, Music For Nations CDMFN42 (1985)
The Dungeons Are Calling / By The Grace Of The Witch / Visions / Midas Knight / City Beneath The Surface / The Whip
POWER OF THE NIGHT, Atlantic 781 247-1 (1985)
Power Of The Night / Unusual / Warriors / Necrophilia / Washed Out / Hard For Love / Fountain Of Youth / Skull Session / Stuck On You / In The Dream
FIGHT FOR THE ROCK, Atlantic 781 634-1 (1986)
Fight For The Rock / Out On The Streets / Crying For Love / Day After Day / The Edge Of Midnight / Hyde / Lady In Disguise / She's Only Rock n' Roll / Wishing Well / Red Light Paradise
HALL OF THE MOUNTAIN KING, Atlantic 781775-2 (1987)
24 Hours Ago / Beyond The Doors Of The Dark / Legions / Strange Wings / Prelude To Madness / Hall Of The Mountain King / The Price You Pay / White Witch / Last Dawn / Devastation
GUTTER BALLET, Atlantic 782008-2 (1990)
Of Rage And War / Gutter Ballet / Temptation Revelation / When The Crowds Are Gone / Silk And Steel / She's In Love /

Hounds / The Unholy / Mentally Yours / Summer's Rain / Thorazine Shuffle
STREETS - A ROCK OPERA, Atlantic 7567-82320-2 (1991)
Streets / Jesus Saves / Tonight He Grins Again- Strange Reality / A Little Too Far / You're Alive - Sammy And Tex / St. Patrick's / Can You Hear Me Now / New York City Don't Mean Nothing / Ghost In The Ruins / If I Go Away / Agony And Ecstasy - Heal My Soul / Somewhere In Time- Believe
EDGE OF THORNS, Atlantic 756782488-2 (1993)
Edge Of Thorns / He Carves His Stone / Lights Out / Skraggy's Tomb / Labyrinths / Follow Me / Exit Music / Degrees Of Sanity / Conversation Piece / All That I Bleed / Damien / Miles Away / Sleep
HANDFUL OF RAIN, Bulletproof CDVEST 32 (1994)
Taunting Cobras / Handful Of Rain / Chance / Stare Into The Sun / Castles Burning / Visions / Watching You Fall / Nothing's Going On / Symmetry / Alone You Breathe (Criss's Song)
SIRENS - DUNGEONS ARE CALLING, Metal Blade CDZORRO 83 (1994)
Sirens / Holocaust / I Believe / Rage / On The Run / Twisted Little Sister / Living For The Night / Scream Murder / Out On The Streets / Lady In Disguise / The Message / The Dungeons Are Calling / By The Grace Of The Witch / Visions / Midas Knight / City Beneath The Surface / The Whip / Fighting For Your Love / Sirens (Live)
DEAD WINTER DEAD, Edel Concrete 0086252RAD (1996)
Overture / Sarajevo / This Is The Time (1990) / I Am / Starlight / Doesn't Matter Anyway / This Isn't What We Meant / Mozart And Madness / Memory (Dead Winter Dead Intro) / Dead Winter Dead / One Child / Christmas Eve (Sarajevo 12/24) / Not What You See
JAPAN LIVE '94, Zero XRCN 1257 (1996) (Japanese release)
Taunting Cobras / Edge Of Thorns / Chance / Nothin' Going On / He Carves His Stone / Jesus Saves / Watching You Fall / Castles Burning / All That I Bleed / Handful Of Rain / Sirens / Gutter Ballet
GHOST IN THE RUINS - LIVE: A TRIBUTE TO CRISS OLIVA, Fresh Fruit SPV 085-12142 (1996)
City Beneath The Surface / 24 Hours Ago / Legions / Strange Wings / Gutter Ballet / When The Crowds Are Gone / Of Rage And War / The Dungeons Are Calling / Sirens / Hounds / Criss Intro / Hall Of The Mountain King / Post Script
FROM THE GUTTER TO THE STAGE - THE BEST OF SAVATAGE 1981-1995, Edel

0089412CTR (1996)
Sirens (Live) / Power Of The Night / Prelude
To Madness / Hall Of The Mountain King /
24 Hours Ago / Gutter Ballet / When The
Crowds Are Gone / Silk And Steel / New
York City Don't Mean Nothing / Agony And
Ecstasy / Believe / Edge Of Thorns / Chance
/ Mozart And Madness / One Child /
Shotgun Innocence / Forever After / This Is
Where You Should Be / D.T. Jesus (Jesus
Saves)
THE WAKE OF MAGELLAN, Edel Concrete
0089832CTRP (1998) **11 GERMANY**
The Ocean / Welcome / Turns To Me /
Morning Sun / Another Way / Blackjack
Guillotine / Paragons Of Innocence /
Complaint In The System / Underture / The
Wake Of Magellan / Anymore / The Storm /
The Hourglass
BELIEVE, Zero Corporation (1998)
(Japanese release)
Believe / Visions / Taunting Cobras / Handful
Of Rain / Chance / Sarajevo / This Is The
Time / This Isn't What We Meant / Christmas
Eve (Sarajevo 12-24) / Edge Of Thorns
(Live) / Gutter Ballet (Live) / The Dungeons
Are Calling / Sirens / Criss Oliva Guitar Solo
/ Hall Of The Mountain King / Alone You
Breathe
POETS AND MADMEN, Nuclear Blast 6618
(2001) **7 GERMANY**
There In The Silence / Commissar / I Seek
Power / Drive / Morphine Child / The Rumor
/ Man In The Mirror / Surrender / Awaken /
Back To Reason / Stay

SAXON (UK)
Line-Up: Biff Byford (vocals), Doug Scarrett
(guitars), Paul Quinn (guitars), Nibs Carter
(bass), Fritz Randow (drums)

A veritable British Rock institution, SAXON
have for over twenty years experienced the
exalted heights of chart success as well as
battling through more lean years. The band
found favour at first in their homeland, made
serious headway into the American market
before concentrating on mainland Europe
where the act still maintain a sizeable
following. Musically SAXON are instantly
characterised by Biff Byford's distinctive and
quite enormous vocal holler and an ability to
craft some of the most memorable riffs in
Metal. During their major label period the
band suffered from a serious miscalculation in
terms of direction, mellowing out significantly,
but have more than made up for it in recent
times with superb albums such as 'Unleash
The Beast'.
Although coming to prominence in 1980 with
the groundbreaking 'Wheels Of Steel' album
the origins of the band can be traced back a

BIFF BYFORD of SAXON

full decade earlier with the formation in 1970
of BLUE CONDITION by guitarist GRAHAM
OLIVER and bassist Steve 'Dobby' Dawson. A
blues orientated Hard Rock outfit BLUE
CONDITION would evolve into S.O.B. by
1974 (named after the FREE album 'Tons Of
Sobs') retaining the same line-up of Oliver,
Dawson, vocalist / guitarist Steve Furth and
drummer John Walker.
The following year Furth was to depart to
concentrate on a Blues career as S.O.B.
began pursuing a steadily heavier direction.
Another local act COAST (named after the
TRAPEZE track 'Coast To Coast) were in the
midst of disintegration and the suggestion
was made that bassist Peter 'Biff' Byford
assume the mantle of S.O.B. vocalist. A deal
was reached whereby COAST guitarist Paul
Quinn was also enrolled. During this early
period S.O.B. gigged hard, the pressure
telling as Walker quit. His position was taken
briefly by Dave Cowell. After a matter of
weeks former GLITTER BAND drummer Pete
Gill had made the position permanent as
S.O.B. became SON OF A BITCH.
During this period Byford and Quinn joined
the JOHN VERITY BAND with the former on
bass. When Verity became a member of
ARGENT Byford & Quinn kept gigging under
the JOHN VERITY BAND handle for a short
time. Eventually they diverted their efforts
back to SON OF A BITCH.
With their new name SON OF A BITCH
debuted at Bradford's Talk Of The Town venue
where an EMI Records executive, Pete
Hinton, became convinced of their potential.

The band was in turn referred to French label Carrere Records and a contract was signed in Paris.

As recording for the debut album ensued the record company judged that there would be strong opposition in America from distributors for the tag SON OF A BITCH and the band were persuaded to adopt the fresh title of SAXON.

The band's debut album was produced by John Verity.

Following their workmanlike eponymous debut album for the French Carrere label in 1979 SAXON found themselves opportunely amidst the full force of the NWoBHM movement as they released the classic 'Wheels Of Steel' album the following year. This album, actually far more representative of SON OF A BITCH's live set than its predecessor, provided the band with biker anthems and hard hitting Metal SAXON became renowned for. Many believe that SAXON have never bettered tracks such as 'Wheels Of Steel', 'Motorcycle Man' and '747 (Strangers In The Night)'. In Britain the band toured heavily supporting MOTÖRHEAD and NAZARETH as 'Wheels Of Steel' gave the band a high chart placing and two hit singles. The band would also appear at the inaugural 'Monsters Of Rock' event at Castle Donington in August 1980 alongside the likes of a headlining RAINBOW, the SCORPIONS and JUDAS PRIEST amongst others.

Later the same year they capitalised on their popularity with the 'Strong Arm Of The Law' album, touring Europe as support to JUDAS PRIEST before headlining Britain with support act LIMELIGHT. Better was to follow as the world tour continued with American dates providing support to RUSH in many 20,000 capacity sold out arenas, the stakes getting higher as SAXON landed the guest position to AC/DC's gigantic 'Back In Black' American tour. SAXON rounded off their American foray opening shows for BLACK SABBATH and BLUE OYSTER CULT.

'Denim And Leather' bolstered SAXON's fan base in 1981 with both 'And The Bands Played On' (written about their Castle Donington festival showing) and 'Never Surrender' keeping the band in the singles charts, but by 1982 Pete Gill was out. The official band explanation was that their former drummer had damaged his hand but other sources suggest he was fired. The former drummer would eventually join MOTÖRHEAD in 1984 for the 'Orgasmatron' album. SAXON's replacement was TOYAH drummer Nigel Glockler who debuted on the live 'Eagle Has Landed' album.

As SAXON performed a ground breaking tour of America in 1984 on the back of 'The Power

And The Glory' and 'Crusader' albums during a period that saw the band exploring more melodic areas of Metal.

SAXON's 1984 American shows first saw a bout of co-headline shows with MÖTLEY CRÜE prior to support dates with IRON MAIDEN. The band returned to Europe for another lengthy tour with guests ACCEPT.

For the 'Crusader' tour the band employed a huge stage set, based on castle battlements although the band also became embroiled in a lengthy legal dispute with former label Carrere for alleged non-payment of royalties. This situation finally resolved itself in late 1985 when Parlophone gained rights to the band's back catalogue.

SAXON's first album for new label Parlophone - 'Innocence Is No Excuse', produced by Simon Hanhart, was released whilst former label Carrere were still in court, claiming the band were still signed to them, the band touring Britain in 1985 supported by Danes PRETTY MAIDS.

SAXON's second EMI album, the Gary Lyons produced 'Rock The Nations' saw the departure of a disillusioned STEVE DAWSON. He was replaced by former HERITAGE and STATETROOPER man Paul 'Fasker' Johnson, although Byford had actually recorded all the bass parts for the album.

SAXON toured Britain again in 1986, with guests in the form of Japanese act LOUDNESS and American shows found the band on a co-headliner with YNGWIE MALMSTEEN. However, many felt that the EMI affiliated Parlophone did not regard SAXON as a priority act and the subsequent album 'Destiny', with new drummer Nigel Durham, did little to revive the band's career or dispute the theory. However, the band's spirited cover of the CHRISTOPHER CROSS hit 'Ride Like The Wind' did revive their fortunes temporarily. Ultimately, in 1988 EMI dropped the band and both Glockler and Dawson quit.

The end of the '80s and their loss of major label EMI found SAXON support faltering. Glockler found a new home with GTR in America whilst Dawson briefly formed USI with drummer Nigel Durham and vocalist / guitarist Steve Johnson before bailing out. In 1993 Dawson formed WANTED, again uniting with Durham, new members guitarist Hayden Conway and vocalist Adrian Davidson.

However, Nigel Glockler returned to SAXON in 1989 as and the group set about an enormous British tour to reawaken interest based on the live album 'Rock n' Roll Gypsies', released on Roadrunner Records. But Johnson left to join USI and was replaced by Tim 'Nibbs' Carter as another lengthy tour

389

of Germany was undertaken sharing the billing with MANOWAR. The same year Byford would find time to guest session on the 'Kaizoku' album by Japanese act AIR PAVILION.

SAXON started 1991 by releasing the Kalle Trapp produced 'Solid Ball Of Rock' album. SAXON's world tour to promote the album took them to such far flung territories as Argentina, Brazil, Paraguay, Uruguay and even New Zealand. The follow up 'Forever Free' was released in Germany with different sleeve artwork to that of the British version. Interest in their homeland had waned and the gaming company Games Workshop issued 'Forever Free' with suitably lavish Sci-Fi artwork.

SAXON remained a strong draw in Germany and would put in another highly successful German tour co-headlining with MOTÖRHEAD, dubbed the 'Bombers And Eagles' tour. The pairing also put in one show at London's Hammersmith Odeon. SAXON later toured Britain as headliners with support act FRANKENSTEIN, but fared badly attendance wise.

In 1995 Paul Quinn contributed guest guitar parts to German act SARGENT FURY's 'Turn The Page' album, but earlier in the year his longstanding guitar partner GRAHAM OLIVER surprisingly quit in shortly after the release of the new 'Dogs Of War' album. His position was filled by Doug Scarrett on SAXON's subsequent British tour supported by CHINA BEACH.

'Dogs Of War', although a fine album giving ample evidence of SAXON's prolonged return to form, found the band at their nadir of popularity in Britain. Released on Virgin Records in Germany the small independent HTD issued the record in Britain.

The group also toured in Germany with GLENMORE and played further dates in Texas. The band also appeared at the Christmas Metal Meeting dates in Germany with BLIND GUARDIAN. Some shows were recorded for what would become the 'The Eagle Has Landed Part II' live album.

SAXON cut a rare tribute in 1996 offering their version of 'You've Got Another Thing Comin'' to the JUDAS PRIEST tribute 'Legends Of Metal'.

The departed GRAHAM OLIVER reunited with erstwhile SAXON cohorts Pete Gill and STEVE DAWSON to form a new act and in the process issued legal proceedings to claim the name SAXON for themselves!

Eventually, after much public bickering, Oliver's new band titled themselves SON OF A BITCH, a throwback to pre-SAXON days. Further members were added in ex-THUNDERHEAD vocalist Ted Bullet and guitarist Aidan Conway.

The band meanwhile regrouped, pulling out all the stops for their next effort The resulting album, 'Unleash The Beast', took many by surprise as SAXON delivered an album that was to rank alongside 'Wheels Of Steel' as being one of their finest efforts. The album pushed SAXON back to the very forefront of the Metal scene again and included a touching tribute to their long term highly respected tour manager J.J. who had passed away the year before.

Naturally, the band set out on the road in Europe with support act ROYAL HUNT and ex-VICTORY and ELOY man Fritz Randow on the drum stool, but some of the dates sadly were marred by poor attendance, not to due the band's status, but to confusion over concert dates. Nevertheless, the strength of the 'Unleash The Beast' album proved beyond doubt that SAXON still had a point to prove, the band putting in a batch of British concert dates in 1998.

1998 also saw SAXON returning to America for a string of shows before an appearance at the Brazilian 'Monsters Of Rock' festival. The world tour ended in Holland as support to DEEP PURPLE. Quinn put some outside activity in by laying down guitars on the IRON MAIDEN tribute '666 The Number Of The Beast'.

SAXON's future seemed unclear as SON OF A BITCH frequently performed billed as SAXON as, they ded at a Dutch Festival alongside KINGDOME COME, Spanish dates with THUNDER and even British shows. To further confuse matters 'Destiny' era drummer Nigel Durham replaced Gill in SON OF A BITCH but not before being asked to by Byford to replace Glockler in SAXON!

Even as late as early 1999 SAXON were billed as performing in British clubs but this was in reality SON OF A BITCH. The dates were subsequently cancelled due to illness. Oliver disbanded SON OF A BITCH later that year to form a JIMI HENDRIX tribute band with his son on drums. However, by June the pair had teamed up with members of STORMWATCH and WITCHFYNDE to create the LUTHAR BELTZ BAND.

Oliver and Dawson came back to the fore in early 2000 announcing an operating title of OLIVER/DAWSON SAXON. Joining them were drummer Durham, guitarist Haydn Conway and ex-HURRICANE, MADAM X and SHY vocalist John Ward.

The welcome archive 'Live At Donnington 1980' release strangely, for a British label, mis-spells the venue of this world famous event. The release 'Diamonds And Nuggets' featured early unreleased material dating as far back as pre SAXON 1971.

Randow joined MOON'DOC in 2000. Quinn used downtime in 2000 to aid THRESHOLD vocalist ANDY McDERMOTT on his debut solo album 'In The Meantime'.

Late 2000 saw the debut OLIVER/DAWSON SAXON release, a live album recorded in the Czech Republic titled 'Re: Landed'. In other SAXON associated activity mid 2001 had Nigel Glockler and Doug Scarrett debuting their side project MAD MEN AND ENGLISH DOGS.

The 2001 SAXON album 'Killing Ground', produced by NIKOLO KOTZEV of BRAZEN ABBOTT and NOSTRODAMUS and mixed by erstwhile ACCEPT guitarist Hermann Frank, would see the band embarking on a rare foray into the world of cover versions. This time cutting their rendition of KING CRIMSON's epic 'Court Of The Crimson King'. Initial copies of the album would come with a bonus disc entitled 'Classics Re-recorded' comprising eight staples re-cut by the 2001 line-up.

Another traditionally lengthy bout of touring would follow commencing with a headline slot at the Ibiza 'Bike Week' festival in September before October UK gigs. SAXON's European trek would finally wind down in Germany during late November. The band would then support JUDAS PRIEST at their London Brixton Academy gig in December. During 2002 SAXON returned to the American touring circuit, opening proceedings with an appearance at the Asbury Park, New Jersey 'Metal Meltdown' festival in early April. Later shows had SAXON at the Belgian 'Grasspop' Metal Meeting festival in July as well as Moscow during August.

Ex-SAXON bassist STEVE DAWSON would issue a solo album 'Pandemonium Circus' in February of 2002. Drummer Fritz Randow would contribute his services to SINNER's 2002 album 'Let There Be Execution'.

Elaborating on the successful 'Classics Re-recorded' project of the previous year SAXON's 2002 album 'Heavy Metal Thunder' would turn out to be a set of reworked classics. Initial copies of the album also included a bonus disc, which added a live video of 'Killing Ground' from the Wacken festival, and five tracks recorded live in San Antonio during April of 2002. A European tour set for January of 2003 would see WOLF and EAGLE as support.

Singles/EPs:

Big Teaser / Rainbow Theme / Frozen Rainbow, Carrere (1979)
Big Teaser / Stallions Of The Highway, Carrere CAR 118 (1979)
Backs To The Wall / Militia Guard, Carrere CAR 129 (1979)

Wheels Of Steel / Stand Up And Be Counted, Carrere CAR 143 (1980) **20 UK**
747 (Strangers In The Night) / See The Light Shining, Carrere CAR 151 (1980) **13 UK**
Backs To The Wall, Carrere HM 6 (1980) **64 UK**
Big Teaser, Carrere HM 5 (1980) **66 UK**
Suzie Hold On / Judgement Day (Live), Carrere CAR 170 (1980)
Strong Arm Of The Law / Taking Your Chances, Carrere CAR 170 (1980) **63 UK**
Motorcycle Man, Carrere (1980) (Japanese release)
Wheels Of Steel / 747 (Strangers In The Night), WEA APC 8 (1981)
And The Bands Played On / Hungry Years / Heavy Metal Thunder, Carrere CAR 180 (1981) **12 UK**
Never Surrender / 20, 000 Feet, Carrere CAR 204 (1981) **18 UK**
Never Surrender / 20,000 Feet / Bap - Shoo - Ap (Live) / Street Fighting Gang, Carrere CAR 204 (1981) (12" single)
Princess Of The Night / Fire In The Sky, Carrere CAR 208 (1981) **57 UK**
Heavy Metal Thunder, Carrere CAR 242 (1982)
Power And The Glory / See The Light Shining, RCA SAXON 1 (1983) (7" single) **32 UK**
Power And The Glory / See The Light Shining (Live) / Denim And Leather (Live), RCA SAXON 1 (1983) (12" single)
This Town Rocks, Carrere (1983) (12" USA Promotion release)
Nightmare / Midas Touch, Carrere 284 (1983) (7" single) **50 UK**
Nightmare / Midas Touch / 747 (Strangers In The Night) (Live), Carrere 284 (1983) (12" single)
Sailing To America / A Little Bit Of What You Fancy, Carrere CART 301 (1983)
Do It All For You / Just Let Me Rock, Carrere (1984)
Back On The Streets / Live Fast Die Young, Parlophone R 6103 (1985) (7" single) **75 UK**
Back On The Streets / Live Fast Die Young / Back On The Streets (Edited Version), Parlophone R 6103 (1985) (12" single)
Rockin' Again / Krakatoa / Gonna Shout (Live), EMI (1985)
Rock n' Roll Gypsy / Krakatoa, Parlophone R 6122 (1986) (7" single) **71 UK**
Rock n' Roll Gypsy / Krakatoa / The Melody: Heavy Metal Thunder / Taking Your Chances / Stand Up And Be Counted / Warrior, Parlophone 12 RA 6122 (1986) (12" single)
Waiting For The Night / Chase The Fade, EMI 5575 (1986) (7" single) **66 UK**
Waiting For The Night / Chase The Fade /

Waiting For The Night (Edited Version), Parlophone K 060 2014096 (1986) (12" single)
Rock The Nations /747 (Strangers In The Night) / And The Bands Played On, EMI (1986)
Northern Lady / Everybody Up (Live) / Dallas 1PM, EMI (1987)
Ride Like The Wind / Red Alert / Back On The Streets (Live) / Rock The Nations (Live), EMI EM 43 (1988) **52 UK**
I Can't Wait Anymore / Broken Heroes, EMI EM 54 (1988) (7" single) **71 UK**
I Can't Wait Anymore / Broken Heroes / Gonna Shout, EMI EM 54 (1988) (12" single)
Requiem (We Will Remember) (Single Version) / Altar Of The Gods / Requiem (We Will Remember) / Reeperbahn Stomp, Virgin 664 023 (1990)
And The Bands Played On / 747 (Strangers In The Night) / Never Surrender, Old Gold (1992)
Forever Free / Iron Wheels, Warhammer (1993)

Albums:
SAXON, Carrere CAL 110 (1979)
Still Fit To Boogie / Militia Guard / Rainbow Theme / Frozen Rainbow / Big Teaser / Judgement Day / Stallions Of The Highway / Backs To The Wall
WHEELS OF STEEL, Carrere CAL 115 (1980) **36 SWEDEN, 5 UK**
Wheels Of Steel / Motorcycle Man / Stand Up And Be Counted / 747 (Strangers In The Night) / Freeway Man / See The Light Shining / Fighting Gang / Suzi Hold On / Machine Gun
STRONG ARM OF THE LAW, Carrere CAL 120 (1980) **37 SWEDEN, 11 UK**
Strong Arm Of The Law / Heavy Metal Thunder / To Hell And Back Again / Taking Your Chances / 20,000 Feet / Sixth Form Girls / Hungry Years / Dallas 1 PM
DENIM AND LEATHER, Carrere CAL 128 (1982) **21 SWEDEN, 9 UK**
Princess Of The Night / Denim And Leather / Out Of Control / Never Surrender / Rough And Ready / And The Bands Played On / Midnight Rider / Fire In The Sky / Play It Loud
EAGLE HAS LANDED (LIVE), Carrere CAL 157 (1982) **30 SWEDEN, 5 UK**
Motorcycle Man / 747 (Strangers In The Night) / Princess Of The Night / Strong Arm Of The Law / Heavy Metal Thunder / See The Light Shining / 20,000 Feet / Wheels Of Steel / Freeway Man / Fighting Gang / Suzi Hold On / Machine Gun
POWER AND THE GLORY, Carrere CAL 147 (1983) **9 SWEDEN, 15 UK**
Redline / Warrior / Power And The Glory /

Nightmare / Midas Touch / This Town Rocks / Watching The Sky / The Eagle Has Landed
CRUSADER, Carrere CAL 200 (1984)
15 SWEDEN, 18 UK
Sailing To America / A Little Bit Of What You Fancy / Just Let Me Rock / Set Me Free / Do It All For You / Bad Boys / Rock City / Run For Your Lives
STRONG ARM METAL, Carrere (1984)
747 (Strangers In The Night) / Wheels Of Steel / Strong Arm Of The Law / Never Surrender / Dallas 1PM / And The Bands Played On / Denim And Leather / Motorcycle Man
INNOCENCE IS NO EXCUSE, Parlophone SAXON 2 (1985) **18 SWEDEN, 36 UK**
Rockin' Again / Call Of The Wild / Back On The Streets / Everything You've Got / The Devil Rides Out / Rock n' Roll Gypsy / Broken Heroes / Gonna Shout / Everybody Up
ROCK THE NATIONS, EMI EMC 3515 (1986) **26 SWEDEN, 34 UK**
Rock The Nation / Battle Cry / Waiting For The Night / We Came Here To Rock / You Ain't No Angel / Running Hot / Party 'Til You Puke / Empty Promises / Motorcycle Man / Northern Lady
DESTINY, EMI EMC 3543 (1988)
30 SWEDEN, 49 UK
Ride Like The Wind / Where The Lightning Strikes / I Can't Wait Anymore / Calm Before The Storm / S.O.S. (Too Bad) / Song For Emma / For Whom The Bell Tolls / We Are Strong / Jericho Siren / Red Alert
ANTHOLOGY, Rawpower (1988)
Rockin' Again / Rock n' Roll Gypsy / Stallions Of The Highway / Battle Cry / Party 'Til You Puke / Backs To The Wall / Sixth Form Girls / Heavy Metal Thunder / Midnight Rider / Out Of Control / Power And The Glory / Warrior / Just Let Me Rock / Rock City / Machine Gun / Freeway Mad / Wheels Of Steel / Midas Touch / Suzi Hold On / Still Fit To Boogie
ROCK N' ROLL GYPSIES (LIVE), Roadrunner RR9416 (1990)
Power And The Glory / And The Bands Played On / Rock The Nations / Dallas 1PM / Broken Heroes / Battle Cry / Rock n' Roll Gypsy / Northern Lady / I Can't Wait Anymore / This Town Rocks / The Eagle Has Landed / Just Let Me Rock
BACK ON THE STREETS, Connoisseur (1990)
Power And The Glory / Backs To The Wall / Watching The Sky / Never Surrender / Princess Of The Night / Motorcycle Man / 747 (Strangers In The Night) / Wheels Of Steel / Nightmare / Back On The Streets / Rock n' Roll Gypsy / Broken Heroes / Devil Rides Out / Party 'Til You Puke / Rock The Nations / Waiting For The Night / I Can't Wait

Anymore / We Are Strong / Midnight Rider / Ride Like The Wind

GREATEST HITS LIVE, Castle Communications (1990)
Opening Theme / Heavy Metal Thunder / Rock And Roll Gypsy / And The Bands Played On / 20,000 Feet / Ride Like The Wind / Motorcycle Man / 747 (Strangers In The Night) / See The Light Shinin' / Frozen Rainbow / Princess Of The Night / Wheels Of Steel / Denim And Leather / Crusader / Rockin' again / Back On The Streets

SOLID BALL OF ROCK, Virgin AVL (1991)
Solid Ball Of Rock / Altar Of The Gods / Requiem (We Will Remember) / Lights In The Sky / I Just Can't Get Enough / Baptism Of Fire / Ain't Gonna Take It / I'm On Fire / Overture In B Minor / Refugee / Bavarian Beaver / Crash Dive

THE BEST OF SAXON, EMI CDP 7 96065-2 (1991)
The Eagle Has Landed / Ride Like The Wind / Crusader / Rainbow Theme / Frozen Rainbow / Midas Touch / Denim And Leather / Broken Heroes / Dallas 1PM / 747 (Strangers In The Night) (Live) / Princess Of The Night (Live)

FOREVER FREE, Warhammer WARCD 10 (1993)
Forever Free / Hole In The Sky / Just Wanna Make Love To You / Get Down And Dirty / Iron Wheels / One Step Away / Can't Stop Rockin' / Nighthunter / Grind / Cloud Nine

DOGS OF WAR, Virgin 7243 839983 2 6 (1995)
Dogs Of War / Burning Wheels / Don't Worry / Big Twin Rolling (Coming Home) / Hold On / The Great White Buffalo / Demolition Alley / Walking Through Tokyo / Give It All Away / Yesterday's Gone

CHAMPIONS OF ROCK, Disky (1996)
Big Teaser / Judgement Day / Stallions Of The Highway / Backs To The Wall / Still Fit To Boogie / Power And The Glory / Warrior / To Hell And Back Again / Hungry Years / Sixth Form Girls / Where The Lightning Strikes / Calm Before The Storm / For Whom The Bell Tolls / Red Alert / Back On The Streets / Rock n' Roll Gypsy

A COLLECTION OF METAL, EMI (1996)
747 (Strangers In The Night) (Edit) / Rock n' Roll Gypsy / And The Bands Played On / Back On The Streets / Ride Like The Wind / Big Teaser / I Can't Wait Anymore (Remix) / Broken Heroes (Live) / Raise Some Hell / Denim And Leather / Rock The Nations / Motorcycle Man / Everybody Up / Rock City / Set Me Free / Play It Loud

THE EAGLE HAS LANDED - PART II, CBH Virgin 841 630-2 (1996)
Intro - Warlord / Dogs Of War / Forever Free / Requiem / Crusader / Light In The Sky /

Iron Wheels / Ain't Gonna Take It - Nibbs' Bavarian Bass / Crash Dive / Refugee / Solid Ball Of Rock / Great White Buffalo / The Eagle Has Landed - Paul Quinn Guitar Feature / Princess Of The Night / Can't Stop Rockin / Denim And Leather - Doug Scarrett Guitar Feature / Wheels Of Steel / Demolition Alley

UNLEASH THE BEAST, Virgin VGP 000 132 (1997)
Gothic Dreams / Unleash The Beast / Terminal Velocity / Circle Of Lights / Thin Red Line / Ministry Of Fools / The Preacher / Bloodletter / Cut Out The Disease / Absent Friends / All Breaking Loose

BURRN PRESENTS THE BEST OF SAXON, Toshiba EMI TOCP 50497 (1998) (Japanese release)
Heavy Metal Thunder / Never Surrender / Wheels Of Steel / Strong Arm Of The Law / And The Bands Played On / Power And The Glory / Battle Cry / Motorcycle Man / I Can't Wait Anymore / S.O.S. / Song For Emma / Rock The Nations / Broken Heroes / 747 (Strangers In The Night) (Live) / Princess Of The Night (Live) / Denim And Leather

BBC SESSIONS, EMI 97772 (1998)
Backs To The Wall / Stallions Of The Highway / Motorcycle Man / Still Fit To Boogie / 747 (Strangers In The Night) / 20,000 Feet / Dallas 1PM / The Eagle Has Landed / Power And The Glory / Never Surrender / Rock The Nations / Wheels Of Steel / Waiting For The Night / Strong Arm Of The Law

METALHEAD, CBH SPV 085-21502 (1999)
Intro / Metalhead / Travellers In Time / Conquistador / What Goes Around, Comes Around / Song Of Evil / All Guns Blazing / Prisoner / Piss Off Bomb / Watching You / Sea Of Life

LIVE AT DONNINGTON 1980, Angel Air SJPCD045 (2000)
Motorcycle Man / Still Fit To Boogie / Freeway Mad / Backs To The Wall / Wheels Of Steel / Bap Shoo Ap / 747 (Strangers In The Night) / Stallions Of The Highway / Machine Gun

DIAMONDS AND NUGGETS, Angel Air SJPCD070 (2000)
Stallions Of The Highway (Live) / Midnight Rider (Live) / Frozen Rainbow (Live) / Turn Out The Lights / Coming To The Rescue / See The Light Shining / Stand Up And Be Counted / freeway Mad (Part II) / Ann Marie / Lift Up Your Eyes / Street Fighting Man / Still Fit To Rock n' Roll / Big Teaser / Frozen Rainbow / Walking / Make 'Em Rock / Stone Room Jam / Ain't You Glad To Be Alive / Freeway Mad (Part I)

STRONG ARM OF THE LAW - DENIM & LEATHER - THE BACK TO BACK

COLLECTION, Axekiller (2001)
Heavy Metal Thunder / To Hell And Back Again / Strong Arm Of The Law / Taking Our Chances / 20,000 Feet / Hungry Years / Sixth Form Girls / Dallas 1 PM / Motorcycle Man (Live) / 747 (Strangers In The Night) (Live) / Princess Of The Night / Never Surrender / Out Of Control / Rough And Ready / Play It Loud / And The Bands Played On / Midnight Rider / Fire In The Sky / Denim And Leather / See The Light Shining (Live) / Wheels Of Steel (Live)

BEAST OF ROCK, CAS Records (2001)
Turn Out The Lights / Coming To The Rescue / See The Light Shining / Stand Up And Be Counted / Freeway Mad / Ann Marie / Lift Up Your Eyes / Street Fighting Man / Still Fit To Rock n' Roll / Big Teaser (Original) / Frozen Rainbow / Walking / Make 'Em Rock / Stone Room Jam / Ain't You Glad To Be Alive

KILLING GROUND, SPV (2001)
141 FRANCE, 26 GERMANY
Prelude To War / Killing Ground / In The Court Of The Crimson King / Coming Home / Till Hell Freezes Over / Dragon's Lair / You Don't Know What You've Got / Deeds Of Glory / Running For The Border / Rock Is Our Life

HEAVY METAL THUNDER, SPV (2002)
Power & The Glory / Strong Arm Of The Law / Heavy Metal Thunder / And The Bands Played On / Crusader / Dallas 1pm / Princess Of The Night / Wheels Of Steel / 747 (Strangers In The Night) / Motorcycle Man / Never Surrender / Denim & Leather / Backs To The Wall / Broken Heroes (Live) / Dragon's Lair (Live) / The Eagle Has Landed (Live) / 20,000 Ft. (Live) / Crusader (Live) / Killing Ground (Video)

SCANNER (GERMANY)
Line-Up: Michael Knoblich (vocals), Axel Julius (guitar), Thomas Sopha (guitar), Martin Bork (bass), Wolfgang Kolorz (drums)

Previously known as LIONS BREED, a Metal act that released a 1985 album on the Earthshaker label entitled 'Damn The Night', the group underwent line-up changes and became SCANNER in 1986, adopting an on stage Sci-Fi image. The group's debut album, 'Hypertrace', was produced by ELOY vocalist Frank Bornemann. Backing vocals for this outing were contributed by TYRAN PACE man Ralph Scheepers. Japanese versions of this album added the exclusive track 'Galactos'.

By the time the second album, 'Terminal Earth', had been released the group had parted company with Knoblich, the singer briefly joining JESTER'S MARCH recording a demo with that band, and replaced him with the Yugoslavian born ex-ANGEL DUST front man S.L. Coe. This was not their first choice though, SCANNER just having missed out by a matter of days to GAMMA RAY in securing the services of Ralph Scheepers. Soon personality clashes soon erupted between Coe and his band mates and the vocalist was forced out. The band would split for a period with Coe going on to found REACTOR for a series of albums. In later years S.L. Coe would prove industrious as a producer as well as touting his own Metal band C.O.E.

Guitarist Axel Julius reformed SCANNER to release the 'Mental Reservation' album in 1995 for the Massacre label. The band comprised Polish vocalist Haridon Lee, real name Leszek Szpigiel and previously having fronted CROW, bassist John A.B.C. Smith of GALLOW'S POLE and drummer D.D. Bucco for this album, although Smith was succeeded by Marc Simon after the record was released.

1997's 'Ball Of The Damned' would prove an ambitious affair as the band took on a cover version of QUEEN's epic 'Innuendo'. Ralph Scheepers, by now in PRIMAL FEAR, also appeared once more lending vocals to 'Puppet On A String'. Touring to promote the album saw headline European dates with support act UNREST before a further round of shows on a package billing with FATES WARNING and OMEN.

With SCANNER once more entering a lengthy period of hiatus JOHN A.B.C. SMITH reactivated GALLOW'S POLE. As a solo artist he would also release the 1995 album 'The Revelation Of John'. Szpigiel also made a return, now billing himself as 'Naked Duke' and fronting his band DUKE for a 2001 EP 'Escape From Reality'.

SCANNER would be back in 2002 brandishing a new studio album 'Scantropolis'. At this stage the new look band comprised vocalist Lisa Croft, guitarists Axel Julius and Thilo Zaun, bass player Marc Simon, keyboard player Johannes Brunn and drummer Jan Zimmer. The album would close with an unaccredited version of 'Till The Ferryman Dies' recorded live in Stockholm.

Albums:
HYPERTRACE, Noise NO111-1 (1988)
Warp 7 / Terrion / Locked Out / Across The Universe / R.M.U. / Grapes Of Fear / Retaliation Positive / Killing Fields / Wizard Force

TERMINAL EARTH, Noise NO141-1 (1990)
The Law / Not Alone / Wonder / Buy Or Die / Touch The Light / Terminal Earth / From The Dust Of Ages / The Challenge

MENTAL RESERVATION, Massacre CD058

(1995)
Break The Seal / Upright Liar / After The Storm / Your Infallible Smile / Conception Of A Cure / Into A Brave Man's Mind / Out Of Nowhere / Nightmare / Rubberman / Wrong Lane Society / 20th Century Crusade
BALL OF THE DAMNED, Massacre MASS PC0118 (1997)
Puppet On A String / Frozen Under The Sun / We Start It Tomorrow / True Stories Teller / Tollshocked / Lord Barker's Theme / Ball Of The Damned / Judge On The Run / Innuendo
SCANTROPOLIS, Massacre (2002)
Till The Ferryman Dies / Hallowed Be My Name / Flight Of The Eagle / Turn Of The Tide / Always Alien / Engel Brecht's / Sister Mary / The Gambler / R.I.P. - Rest In Pain / Till The Ferryman Dies (Live)

SEA OF DREAMS (NORWAY)

Line-Up: Jim Lynwood Foss (vocals), Tond Are (guitar), John Martin Haarr (bass), Svein Magne Kleven (keyboards), Svein Harald Kleppe (drums)

Progressive Euro style Metal. Keyboard player Jørgen Manke supplanted previous incumbent Svein Magne Kleven for the second album 'Land Of Flames'.

Albums:
DAWN OF TIME, Sea Of Dreams 196 (1996)
Enter The Sea Of Dreams / First Step / Pain / Dimensions Of Time / Point Of No Return / Preach Of Fire / Under The Rainbow / Legends / Wait For The Day / Black Roses / Sheila / Dawn Of Time
LAND OF FLAMES, Sea Of Dreams (1998)
Eagle / Temple Of Dreams / Vanishing Son / Last Trooper / Illusions: Part 1 - Awake, Part 2 - The Journey, Part 3 - Phantasm, Part 4 - Dissilusion, Part 5 - Independence Day / Morning Rain / Strong Winds / Land Of Flames

SECRET SPHERE (ITALY)

Line-Up: Roberto Messina (vocals), Aldo Lonobile (guitar), Paulo Giantotti (guitar), Andrea Buratto (bass), Antonio Agate (keyboards), Luca Cartasegna (drums)

Bombastic Symphonic Metal band forged by guitarist Aldo Lonobile in July of 1997. Lonobile gathered around him an initial line-up roster of vocalist Roberto Messina (also a member at that time of Symphonic Speed Metal act AVATAR - later HIGHLORD), guitarist Gianmaria Saggi, bassist Andrea Buratto and drummer Cristiano Scagliotti. A constant flux in the membership tally finally

settled down by the close of the year with new faces keyboard player Antonio Agate and guitarist Paolo Gianotti being inducted.
September 1998 found SECRET SPHERE in the studio for their debut promotional tape 'Between Story And Legend'. Scagliotti left shortly after these sessions to be replaced by Luca Cartasegna. The demo secured a deal with Elevate Records for the inaugural conceptual album 'Mistress Of The Shadowlight'. Backing vocals were lent by members of both WHITE SKULL and BLACK JESTER.
Italian headline dates were put in to promote the album which led in quick succession to recording of HELLOWEEN track, 'How Many Tears', for the tribute album 'Keepers Of Jericho' issued on Arise Records.
The band's second album, 'A Time Never Come' released in March of 2001, proved to be a heavier beast than its predecessor. Backing vocals this time were on hand from Roberto Bruccoleri of PROJECTO and Terence Holler of ELDRITCH.
SECRET SPHERE vocalist Roberto Messina would also contribute guest vocals to the HEMISPHERE album of December 2000 and worked with French Progressive Metal act ALKEMYST during 2001. Lonobile would also perform extracurricular activities laying down session guitar for the debut BEHOLDER album 'The Legend Begins'.
SECRET SPHERE got back to touring with dates in France during November in alliance with FREEDOM CALL and SONATA ARTICA.

Albums:
MISTRESS OF THE SHADOW LIGHT, Elevate (1997)
Dawn Of Time / Age Of Wizard / Recall Of The Valkyrie / On The Wings Of Sun / Twilight Of Fairy Tale / White Lion / Labyrinth Of Glass / Siren / Secret Sphere / Last Moment Of Eternity
A TIME NEVER COME, Elevate (2001)
Gate Of Wisdom / Legend / Under The Flag Of Mary Read / Only The Brave / Emotions / Oblivion / Lady Of Silence / The Misery Of Love / Paganini's Nightmare (Theme From Caprice No. 5) / Lost Land Of Lyonesse / Ascension / Chameleon / Dr. Faustus

SECTOR 9 (USA)

Line-Up: Wade Black (vocals), Ben Jackson (guitar), Jimmy Delisi (guitar), Jesse Martillo (drums)

SECTOR 9 was a 2001 formation based upon the talents of former CRIMSON GLORY members vocalist Wade Black and guitarist Ben Jackson. Joining the duo were drummer

Jesse Martillo and erstwhile NAKED SCHOOLGIRLS and JULIETT guitarist Jimmy Delisi. By August NOCTURNUS bassist Emo Mowery had also been drafted. Black would also session for SAVATAGE guitarist JACK FROST in November on his SEVEN WITCHES side project album.

Jackson also operated a side band simply known as THE BEN JACKSON GROUP involving Jackson on vocals and guitar, guitarist Mark Borgmeyer, bass player Danny Binz and drummer Rich Tabor. Band mate Wade Black would session on the debut record 'Here I Come'.

SERAPHIM (TAIWAN)
Line-Up: Pay (vocals), Kessier (guitar), Dan (guitar), Jax (bass), Simon (drums)

Female fronted Power Metal band out of Taiwan founded by the former FIREDANCE duo of guitarist Kessier and bassist Jax along with ex-JACKHAMMER guitarist Dan and erstwhile ASSASSIN drummer Simon. SERAPHIM, who employ the operatic lead vocal of Pay, issued their debut 'The Soul That Never Dies' in 2001, originally sung in Chinese. An English language version was released in March of 2002 by the Spanish Arise label.

SERAPHIM began recording a second album 'The Equal Spirit' in Sweden with producer Fredrik Nordstrom.

Albums:
THE SOUL THAT NEVER DIES, Arise (2002)
Prelude / Love Hate / Emptiness / Immortal Silence / The Soul That Never Dies / Samsara / Mind's Sky / Forever / Canticle / Light Of The Setting Sun / Majestic Farewell

SERPENT MOVES (GERMANY)
Line-Up: Carsten Frank (vocals / guitar), Sebastian Schmidt (vocals / guitar), Dirk Zelmer (vocals / bass), Arnd Riebe (drums)

Founded in Hannover as ATMOSFEAR during 1996 this act blend both Power and Death Metal. The rhythm section of bassist Dirk Zelmer and drummer Arnd Riebe had been prior members of INFERNAL ROW whilst front man Carsten Frank had held down terms with both OBLIVIAN and SCAVANGER.

Evolving into SERPENT MOVES in 1999 the group inducted former WINTERDOME keyboard player Sebastian Schmidt toward the close of that year.

Albums:
CURSE OF TIME, (1999)

Eternal Reign / Bloodfall / Dance Of The Bonedragon / Ivory Tower / Curse Of Time / Never Prologue
ORGANIC MACHINE, (2001)

SEVEN GATES (ITALY)
Line-Up: Federico Puleri (vocals), Marco Moroni (guitar), Tommaso Vitali (guitar), Simone Vermigli (bass), Fabrizio Marnica (keyboards), Paolo Baroni (drums)

Florence based, Symphonic inclined Power Metal act SEVEN GATES are rooted in the most unlikely of sources as many of the founding members were involved with an "official" BON JOVI tribute band. These musicians, adding drummer Paolo Baroni and vocalist Max Carrai put together SEVEN GATES in March of 1999 as another cover outfit, this time concentrating on Power Metal renditions. Slowly but surely original compositions crept into the live set. Carrai bade his farewell in August of 2000 and the band filled the vacancy with Federico Puleri. Adding keyboard player Fabrizio Marnica an EP 'Demo 2000' was recorded.

A deal was struck with the Brazilian Megahard label and the debut 'Unreality' arrived in October of 2002.

SEVEN GATES would donate a track 'Until Death Do Us Part' to the Underground Symphony SWORD tribute album in early 2002.

Singles/EPs:
Forever With Me / Dream Or Nightmare / Download / Lords Of The Night, (2000)
('Demo 2000' EP)

Albums:
UNREALITY, Megahard (2002)
Beyond the Gates / Forever With Me / Shadows / Prisoner In Your Mind / Mysterious Gods / Battle Of Britain / On The Moon / Lords Of The Night / Lament Of The Sins / Unreality / Download

SEVENTH AVENUE (GERMANY)
Line-Up: Herbie Langhans (vocals / guitar), William Hieb (bass), Louis Schock (drums)

A Christian Melodic traditional Metal act dating back to 1989. A 1993 demo 'First Strike' surfaced prior to the debut 'Rainbowland' album. Andi Gutjahr of TREASURE SEEKER and LIGHTMARE contributed guitar to the 1998 outing 'Southgate'. For the 2002 album SEVENTH AVENUE comprised a quartet of front man Herbie Langhans, guitarist Florian Gottsleben, bassist Geronimo Staens and drummer Mike Pfluger.

Goodbye (Acoustic Version) / Where You Belong / Gone With The Summer / Southgate / Boat On The River / Goodbye (Radio Version) / Goodbye (Piano Version), (1999)

Albums:
RAINBOWLAND, Treasureland (1995)
Theme From Rainbowland / Rainbowland / Way To Paradise ('95 Version) / Pray / Loving You / On The Road Again / Funeral Speech (Rest In Peace Intro) / Rest In Peace / Die / Just Believe / Love Goes / Children / Prince Of Peace / Loving You (Metal Version)
TALES OF TALES, D&S Records DSR CD033 (1997)
Prolog / Tales Of Tales / Heaven Tears / Time / Temptation / Where Are You? / Grave Of Heart / Iron Man / Pink Elephant / This Night / Sailing
SOUTHGATE, (1998)
Introduce / Southgate / Protection Of Fools / Carol / Father / May The Best One Win / Puppet Of The Mighty / Storm / Heart In Your Hand / Nameless Child / Big City Sharks / Goodbye
BETWEEN THE WORLDS, (2002)

SEVENTH ONE (SWEDEN)

Line-Up: Rino Fredh (vocals), Christoffer Hermansson (guitar), Johannes Losbäck (guitar), Jörgen Olsson (bass), Tobas Kjellgren (drums)

A Power Metal act that issued three demos to date, 1999's 'Seventh One', the 2000 effort 'Through Burning Skies' and 'The Celestial Prophecy' during 2001 on their way to securing a record contract. The group, based out of Hunnebostrand, was conceived in late 1997 by guitarists Christoffer Hermansson of SOUL REAPER and TEARS OF SAHARA and Johannes Losbäck of DECAMERON repute. The fledgling band would be brought up to strength with the addition of former ANGUISH and TEARS OF SAHARAH vocalist Rino Fredh, ex-LOST bassist Jörgen Olsson and drummer Jonny Edvardsson. The band won a series of awards at the Swedish West coast contest 'Rock Of Bohuslän', the prize for which was a demo recording. After numerous delays these sessions surfaced in 1999.
Exposure in mainland Europe was increased with the inclusion of the demo track 'The Seventh Eye' on a cover mount CD of unsigned acts 'Unerhört' on the esteemed German Rock magazine 'Rock Hard'.

For the demo 'The Celestial Prophecy' SEVENTH ONE drafted new drummer Mats Karlsson. Interest in Germany was high and SEVENTH ONE duly signed a development deal with METALIUM's Lars Ratz for recording. At this stage Tobias Kjellgren, a veteran of extreme Metal bands DISSECTION, DECAMERON, SWORDMASTER, SACRAMENTUM and SOUL REAPER, was pulled in on the drum stool for debut album 'Sacrifice', released through the Massacre label in October 2002.

Albums:
SACRIFICE, Massacre (2002)

SEVENTH SEAL (BRAZIL)

Line-Up: Ricardo Peres (vocals), Tiago Claro (guitar), Ricardo Busato (guitar), Guilherme Busato (bass), Roberto Moratti (drums)

Albums:
PREMONITION, Megahard (2002)

SHADOW GALLERY (USA)

Line-Up: Mike Baker (vocals), Gary Wehrkamp (guitar), Brendt Allman (guitar), Carl Cadden James (bass), Joe Nevolo (drums)

SHADOW GALLERY were previously known as SORCEROR, an '80s cover band specialising in the more intricate traditional Rock sounds of artists such as RUSH and YNGWIE MALMSTEEN on the club circuit. SORCEROR comprised vocalist Mike Baker, guitarist Ron Evans, bass player Carl Cadden-James and drummer John Coonie. In 1985 the band inducted Chris Ingles on second guitar, manoeuvring him to the role of keyboard player when guitarist Brendt Allman enrolled later that same year. The group adopted an increasing repertoire of original material but were to lose Ingles along the way. A band demo reached Mike Varney, head of Shrapnel Records and at that time in the process of establishing a new Progressive Rock label Magna Carta. SORCEROR shed Ron Evans and took on the new title of SHADOW GALLERY. A further demo session secured contracts with Magna Carta in August of 1991.
The debut album, that featured session drummer Ben Timely, was released to a lukewarm response and only saw distribution in Europe and Japan, but by second attempt 1995's 'Carved In Stone', with the addition of second guitarist Gary Wehrkamp of THE BOXTOPS, the band was beginning to make headway. However, drummer Kevin Soffera quit just after the record's release. The band

devoted time to recording material for a slew of tribute albums. SHADOW GALLERY committed their version of 'Time' to the PINK FLOYD offering 'The Moon Revisited' as well as contributions to the GENESIS tribute 'Supper's Ready' and the YES homage 'Tales Of Yesterday'. The group would also forge links with DREAM THEATER's Mike Portnoy and MR. BIG's Billy Sheehan to cut tracks for a RUSH tribute 'Working Man'.

September 1998's 'Tyranny' concept album, which saw the introduction of drummer Joe Nevolo, sees a guest appearance by ROYAL HUNT's D.C. Cooper. Drums were in the hands of Joe Nevolo. Toward the close of that year SHADOW GALLERY became involved in piecing together a brand new outfit in union with James LaBrie of DREAM THEATER fame entitled MULLMUZZLER. These sessions, titled 'Keep It To Yourself' surfaced through the Magna Carta label during mid 1999. Baker's talents would also be on hand for the 'Leonardo Da Vinci - The Absolute Man' concept album.

In 2000 Gary Wehrkamp would session on the 'Flight of the Universal Migrator' album by the leading Dutch concept band AYREON, featuring on the track 'Through the Worm Hole'. Whilst working on material for a new record entitled 'Legacy' the band members would divide their time to afford space for a second MULLMUZZLER project.

Wehrkamp also donated his skills to the Progressive Rock tour de force EXPLORERS CLUB album 'Raising The Mammoth' in 2002.

Albums:
SHADOW GALLERY, Magna Carta (1992)
The Dance Of Fools / Darktown / Mystified / Questions At Hand / The Final Hour / Say Goodbye To The Morning / The Queen Of The City Of Ice
CARVED IN STONE, Magna Carta MA-9001-2 (1995)
Cliffhanger / Crystyalline Dream / Don't Ever Cry, Just Remember / Warcry / Celtic Princess / Deeper Than Life / Alaska / Ghostship
TYRANNY, Roadrunner RR 8695-2 (1998)
Stiletto In Hand / War For Sale / Out Of Nowhere / Mystery / Hope For Us? / Victims / Broken / I Believe / Roads Of Thunder / Spoken Words / New World Order / Chased / Ghost Of A Chance / Christmas Day
LEGACY, Roadrunner (2001)
Cliffhanger / Destination Unknown / Colors / Society Of The Mind / Legacy / First Light

SHADOWKEEP (UK)
Line-Up: Rogue M. (vocals), Chris Allen (guitar), Nicki Robson (guitar), Steve Scott (bass), Scott Higham (drums)

SHADOWKEEP are a Surrey based Power Progressive Metal band led by Belgian vocalist Rogue M. and guitarists Chris Allen and Nicki Robson. Created during the late '90s SHADOWKEEP were one of a handful of British traditional Metal bands and as such came to prominence rapidly.

Allen, a former member of Basingstoke's

SHADOW KEEP

INTENSE, and Robson were previously in a band project entitled SIRE with drummer Russell King. When King split away to join COMPLICITY in December 1998 SIRE folded. Allen and Robson resolved to forge ahead with a new group and pulled in ex-HALYCON man Rogue M. on vocals, ex-PATRICIA MORRISON BAND bassist Jim Daley and their SIRE colleague Russell King on drums.

SHADOWKEEP was groomed in its formative stages by Karl Groom and Clive Nolan of THRESHOLD, the band recording at their Thin Ice studios for what would turn out to be the debut 6 track 'Shadowkeep' mini-album. This release soon drew attention from mainland Europe and a deal was secured with German label Limb Music Productions.

The band's first full length album, 'Corruption Within', emerged in September 2000. The group's influences were amply demonstrated with a close out unaccredited version of QUEENSRYCHE's 'Queen Of The Reich'. This track was also donated to the Dwell Records QUEENSRYCHE tribute album 'Rebellion'.

The band landed a number of high profile support slots including opening for DIO in Belgium, HALFORD in France and ANGELWITCH in London. Following these dates SHADOWKEEP discharged their rhythm section and grafted on a fresh team of the New Zealand born ex-DRAGONHEART bassist Steve Scott and former ANGELWITCH drummer Scott Higham. By March of 2002 Scott, prioritising his other act POWER QUEST, had been replaced by Steve Kightley.

Albums:
SHADOWKEEP, (1999)
Dark Tower / Inner Sanctum / Altar Of Madness / Cast Out / The Silver Sword / Murder
CORRUPTION WITHIN, Limb Music Productions (2000)
Dark Tower / The Trial Of Your Betrayal / Mark Of The Usurper / Altar Of Madness / Corruption Within / Cast Out / Meta-Morale / The Silver Sword / Death: A New Horizon / Murder / Inner Sanctum / Queen Of The Reich

SHADOWS OF IGA (GERMANY)
Line-Up: Oliver Weinsheimer (vocals), Thomas Hübner (guitar), Markus Müssig (guitar), Jürgen Zadra (bass), Matthias Höfling (drums)

A German Power Metal act SHADOWS OF IGA were influenced by American trad Metal bands. In fact, the group named itself after a HELSTAR track.

SHADOWS OF IGA toured with PHANTOMS OF FUTURE in 1997.

Albums:
...THE DARKSIDE, Iga 001 (1995)
Fight For Honour / The Silent Assassin / Cries From The Darkside / Sea Of Tears / Fallen Hero / Shadows Of The Past / False Pride / Changes

SHADOWS OF STEEL (ITALY)
Line-Up: Wild Steel (vocals), Andrè La Fisic (guitar), Steve Wavamas (bass), Andrew McPauls (keyboards), Gianca (drums)

Genoese theatrical Power Metal act assembled in October of 1996. The SHADOWS OF STEEL project was credited to a band line-up of masked vocalist Wild Steel, guitarist Andrè La Fisic, former BLOODY EYES and THE FAGS bass player Steve Wavamas, keyboardist Andrew McPauls (a.k.a. Andrea De Paoli) and drummer Gianca. They would, besides McPauls membership of premier Metal band LABYRINTH, boast other strong LABYRINTH connections. The November 1997 'Shadows Of Steel' album saw the inclusion of such LABYRINTH luminaries as guitarists Olaf Thörsen, bass player Chris Breeze and drummer Frank Andiver. Vic Mazzoni, guitarist with SKYLARK, PROJECTO and WONDERLAND also features.

The second album 'Twilight' was issued as a double CD set. The second CD comprised entirely of cover versions such as CRIMSON GLORY's 'Painted Skies' and AGENT STEEL's 'The Calling' and 'Agent Of Steel' and saw Andrea Tower Torricini performing bass duties. The 2000 four track 'Heroes' EP found the SHADOWS OF STEEL line-up fluxing, now comprising Wild Steel, Wavamas, Frank Andiver and new faces guitarists Yackson and Ice Reaven, both of SEEDBACK, along with keyboard player Francis Scarlet. Yackson had also spent terms with both SIN and DESECRATE. That same year the band would have their version of 'Strange Wings' included on the SAVATAGE tribute album 'Return Of The Mountain King'. However, by mid 2001 Scarlet was no longer in the picture. It would be revealed in February of 2002 that Wild Steel and Steve Wavamas, in league with Rob Tyrant, had convened a further band project billed as ATHLANTIS. Meantime SHADOWS OF STEEL cut a cover version of SWORD's 'State Of Shock' for an Underground Symphony tribute album. The 'Second Floor' album was issued in Japan by the Soundholic label but would have to wait until September for a European release.

Singles/EPs:
Heroes / Welcome To Heaven / Wings Of Glory / The Hawk, Underground Symphony USCD-042 (2000) ('Heroes' EP)

Albums:
SHADOWS OF STEEL, Underground Symphony USCD-024 (1997)
Countdown / Shadows Of Steel / The Playing Room IV / Journey / Out Of The Darkness / The Island / Storied Windows / Winterland / Day As Lions / Fly Away / Kingdom / Gone With The Wind
TWILIGHT, Underground Symphony USCD-030 (1998)
Hawk And Lion / Twilight / Goodbye / Fly Away / Destination Unknown / Prelusion / Run For Tomorrow / Painted Skies / The Calling / Agent Of Steel
SECOND FLOOR, Underground Symphony USCD-049 (2002)
Prelude / Second Floor / Somewhere High Above / Heroes / King Of The Island / Dame And Lord / December / Crying / Distant Voices / Talk To The Wind / Playing Room V

SHAMAN (BRAZIL)
Line-Up: Andre Matos (vocals), Hugo Mariutti (guitar), Luis Mariutti (bass), Fabio Ribeiro (keyboards), Ricardo Confessori (drums)

SHAMAN is the high profile spin off from the hugely successful Brazilian Prog Metal band ANGRA. A major split in the ranks saw vocalist Andre Matos and the rhythm section of bassist Luis Mariutti and drummer Ricardo Confessori all decamping in 2000. Matos began work on a solo project billed as VIRGO in Germany. Whilst in Europe Matos would also front the Prog Metal union LOOKING GLASS SELF conceived by the erstwhile SIEGES EVEN trio of guitarist Marcus Steffan, bass player Oliver Holzwarth and drummer Alex Holzwarth. The singer contributed to a 2000 demo 'Equinox' before bowing out and turning his attention to SHAMAN.

In May of 2002 SHAMAN keyboard player Fabio Ribeiro issued the second album from his BLEZQI ZATSAZ solo project entitled 'The Tide Turns'. The album included guests such as SHAMAN guitar player Hugo Mariutti, ANGRA guitarist Kiko Loureiro, and DR. SIN guitarist Edu Ardanuy. It would not be the only such endeavour on the agenda, as Andre Matos participated in ABYDOS, a Progressive Rock assembly put together by producer Stefan Glas also including vocalist Andy Kuntz and drummer Andreas Lill of VANDEN PLAS and ELEGY singer IAN PARRY. The singer would also put in a guest showing on fellow Brazilian act SAGGA's 'Planetude' album.

SHAMAN's debut would be scheduled at the close of July through the Italian Lucretia label for European territories whilst major label Universal took the band on for South America. Brazilian headline dates commenced on August 21st in Porto Alegre.

Albums:
RITUAL, JVC Victor VICP-61893 (2002)
Ancient Winds / Here I Am / Distant Thunder / For Tomorrow / Time Will Come / Over Your Head / Fairy Tale / Blind Spell / Ritual / Pride

SHARKRAGE (GERMANY)
Line-Up: Richard Meier (vocals), René Tornier (guitar), Gerrit Staps (guitar), Thomas Junk (bass), Kai Bergbolt (drums)

SHARKRAGE of Mainz tread the boundaries between Thrash and Power Metal. The band, founded during 1995, is centred upon former RACES lead vocalist Richie Meier and guitarist Rene Tornier. SHARKRAGE made their entrance with the December 1995 promotional cassette 'Surgeon Of Sorcery' which found Meier and Tornier joined by guitarist Klaus Erpenbach, bassist Jens Wagner and drummer Peter Roth.

SHARKRAGE would switch drummers to Martin Angres in 1996 upfront of undertaking their debut gig in Offenbach alongside FRACTURE. Before the year was out the group had issued the first album 'Moonlandscape' but had lost the services of Erpenbach. In 1997 keyboard player Christine Schulte augmented the SHARKRAGE sound for the sophomore 'Dreamland Area 51' mini-album. Schulte would then decamp to Black Metal band AGATHODAIMON. A further shuffle would see Angres making way in favour of Andreas Schmitt.

The third album 'Bloody Vengeance' saw release in 2000. In 2001 SHARKRAGE's longstanding bassist Jens Wagner bowed out. His place would find Thomas Junk. The drum position would find Marian Kovacik holding down the position for a brief spell before he was usurped by Kai Bergbolt.

Singles/EPs:
Moonlandscape / Secret Of Silence / Lucifer / Atheist / The Jaws / Jaws Part II, (1996) ('Moonlandscape' EP)
Who Are You / Magic Word / Dreamland Area 51 / Cold As Ice / In My Dreams,

Sharkrage BAZE SR 1197 (1997)
('Dreamland Area 51' EP)

Albums:
BLOODY VENGEANCE, (2000)
Seventh Sign / Devil's Son / Bloody
Vengeance / Seed Of Aggression / Welcome
To Death / Atheist / Under The Blade / In
The Name Of JC / Forgotten Time /
Moonlandscape

SIDEREAL (COLOMBIA)
Line-Up: Felipe Machado (vocals / bass),
Yesid Corredor (guitar), Germán Guerra
(guitar), César Suarez (drums)

Sci-Fi influenced Metal band SIDEREAL
bowed in with a self-financed 2001 album
'Vortex Of Oblivion', the band comprising
vocalist / bassist Felipe Machado and
guitarists Germán Guerra and Yesid Corredor.
After recording the band introduced drummer
Richard Sabogal who put in a showing on a
2001 demo session. However, Sabogal made
his exit in April of 2001 and subsequently
Jose Valenzuela joined up in June for live
work but was soon to depart.
In January of 2002 drummer César Suarez
enrolled.

Albums:
VORTEX OF OBLIVION, (2000)
Vortex Of Oblivion / Final Frontier / Sharp On
The Edge / Onward Facing / Collision Of The
Force / The Chosen One / Saga I: Into The
Will Of Fate / Saga II: The Battle / Saga III:
The Triumph Of Dark / Fearless Twilight
Sons

SIEGES EVEN (GERMANY)
Line-Up: Greg Keller (vocals), Wolfgang
Zenk (guitar), Oli Holzwarth (bass), Börk
Keller (keyboards), Alexendar Holzwarth
(drums)

A Progressive, Thrash inclined Metal band
from Munich, SIEGES EVEN's first trio of
albums were recorded with Marcus Steffen on
guitar. However, having left the group in 1992
he was replaced by Wolfgang Zenk. The first
two albums ('Life Cycle' and 'Steps') also
featured the vocal work of Franz Herde, but
'Sense Of Change' witnessed the recruitment
of Jogie Kaiser.
Oddly, Kaiser opted to pursue a career in
musicals and left the group after recording the
album, SIEGES EVEN eventually replacing
him with Greg Keller. This was a man who had
previously recorded with METRICAL CHARM,
a quite well known band on the German
underground Metal scene at the time.

Following Greg's relocation from Cologne to
Munich SIEGES EVEN set to work on the
new album 'Sophisticated', produced by noted
Metal knob twiddler Charlie Bauerfeind (the
man having also produced the two previous
band efforts).
During 1996 SIEGES EVEN were augmented
with the arrival of Greg's brother Börk Keller
on keyboards. Börk had also been a member
of METRICAL CHARM.
Drummer Alex Holzwarth joined Italian
Symphonic Metal act RHAPSODY. Bassist
Oliver Holzwarth joined BLIND GUARDIAN
and toured with the DEMONS AND
WIZARDS project band.
The Holzwarth brothers united in 2000 with
guitarist Markus Steffan to found LOOKING
GLASS SELF. Initially this venture employed
Jens Johansson of STRATOVARIUS on
keyboards and ANGRA singer Andre Matos
for a demo 'Equinox' although the Brazilian
later bowed out. The brothers would also
session on the re-formation album by
PARADOX 'Collision Course' the same year.

Albums:
LIFE CYCLE, Steamhammer 08 7558 (1988)
Las Palabras Secreto De Libertad
(Repression And Resistance) / Life Cycle /
Apocalyptic Disposition / The Roads To Illiad
/ David / Straggler From Atlantis / Arcane
STEPS, Steamhammer 084 76212 (1991)
Tangerine Windows Of Solace: I) Alba, II)
Epitome, III) Apotheosis, IV) Seasons Of
Seclusion (The Prison), V) An Essay Of
Relief (A Tangerine Dream), VI)
Disintegration Of Lasting Hope, VII) Elegy
(Window Of Perception) / Steps / Corridors /
The Vacuum Tube Processor / An Act Of
Acquiescence / Anthem Chapter I / Anthem
Chapter II
A SENSE OF CHANGE, Steamhammer 084
76212 (1995)
Prelude: Ode To Sisyphus / The Waking
Hours / Behind Closed Doors / Change Of
Seasons / Dimensions / Prime / Epigram For
The Last Straw / These Empty Places
SOPHISTICATED, Under Siege Semaphore
CD 32683 (1995)
Reporter / Trouble Talker / Middle Course /
Sophisticated / Dreamer / As The World
Moves On / Wintertime / Water The Barren
Tree / War / Fatal / / The More The Less
UNEVEN, Semaphore 37746-422 (1997)
Disrespectfully Yours / What If? / Trainsong /
Rise And Shine / Scratches In The Rind /
Different Pace / What's Up God? / Love Is As
Warm As Tears

SIGMA (ITALY)
Line-Up: Anthony Pecere (vocals), Frank

Rider (guitar), Max Adams (guitar), Pasko (bass), A.J. (keyboards), Andrew Dal Zio (drums)

Milan Power Metal band SIGMA, although heralding their arrival in 1998, had actually been operational as LOVE MACHINE for some ten years previous, having released three albums under their former title. Throughout January and February of 2001 SIGMA toured Italy as support act to LABYRINTH. However, once this live work was completed vocalist Val Shieldon bowed out. The new front man would be Anthony Pecere, his investiture announced in June.

Albums:
SIGMA; Atrheia ATR CD 0004 (2001)
Four Directions / End Of Time / Guardians / King Of The Nightmares / Minded Walls / Legacy / Follow The Sign / Fading Memories / Mighty Sword / Until Tomorrow / Land Of Freedom / Maniac

SIGMA SENTINEL (URUGUAY)
Line-Up: Charly Sifcola (vocals), Gianfranco Giudici (guitar), Pierino Cerruti (keyboards), Natalia Arocena (bass), Gino (drums)

Uruguayan "neo-Classical" Power Metal band SIGMA SENTINEL were preparing a debut album for 2002 release. For many years the band, created in March of 1998, operated as SIGMA. They adopted the name switch in 2002.

The first formation of the band, known as ARKHAM ASYLUM and steering into a Thrash Metal direction, comprised vocalist Leonardo Turianski, guitarists Gianfranco Giudici and Mario Chicho Stocco, bassist Natalia Arocena and drummer Gino. Previous to ARKHAM ASYLUM Stocco had been enrolled with CYGNUS X whilst both Gino and Turianski had been members of ASPA.

After more than a year of rehearsals but no live action Turianski bailed and the subsequent cleaner sounds of new singer Richard Fernandez helped draw the band toward more melodic pastures. However, this latest recruit was himself usurped by Ernesto Monteiro with Stocco being substituted by ex-MORBID BLOOD man Carlos Garrido. The latter's tenure would last a matter of months before keyboard player Pierino Cerruti took the position as the band, then known as SIGMA, drifted into melodic Power Metal territory.

With the group once again switching singers, this time to incorporate Charly Sifcola, the group adopted the fresh title SIGMA SENTINEL.

SILENCER (Denver, CO, USA)
Line-Up: Keith Spargo (vocals / guitar), Ritchie Wilkison (guitar), Jeff Alexis (bass), Nick Seelinger (drums)

Denver Power Thrash act SILENCER, founded in 1998 by ex-PARAGON front man Keith Spargo, have made a major impact in a relatively short span of time. The group's rhythm section incorporates ex-PSYCHOTIC INSIGHT bassist Jeff Alexis and former DRUDGERY and BLYND JUSTICE drummer Nick Seelinger. During the band's formative months SILENCER operated with stand in bassists in the form of Chris Marye of the SLEWHOUNDS and Dale Storm from BLEEDING FAITH. The group delivered their opening shot, the 'Kozmos' mini-album, upfront of a split live affair shared with SERBERUS. These recordings would include a version of IRON MAIDEN's 'Wrathchild' with a guesting Harry Conklin of JAG PANZER on vocals.

The band would contribute a version of BLACK SABBATH's 'Into The Void' to the WWIII tribute album 'Hail To The Stonehenge Gods'.

In December of 2001 guitarist Mat Bollen decamped. Latterly the band has added second guitarist Ritchie Wilkison, a veteran of DROP DEAD and international acts ANGEL DUST and DEMONS & WIZARDS.

Upon completion of SILENCER's Spring 2002 dates both Wilkison and Seelinger would journey to Europe for tour work with ANGEL DUST. SILENCER returned in late October with a five track EP entitled 'Structures'.

Singles/EPs:
Black Hole Engine [Markarian 573] / The Bruising Feast / Structures / This Mythic Image / Megalith, (2002) ('Structures' EP)

Albums:
KOZMOS, (2001)
Mourning Star / Kozmos / Easter Island / Missing Hope / Industrial Command
BLACK FLAMES AND BURNING WORLDS, Crash Inc. (2001) (Split album with SERBERUS)
Intro: Easter Island / The Error Of Your Ways / Industrial Command / Missing Hope / Descending The Ziggurat / Cold War / Wrathchild

SILENT FORCE (GERMANY / SWEDEN)
Line-Up: D.C. Cooper (vocals) Alex Beyroth (guitar), Jurgen Steinmetz (bass), Thorsten Rohre (keyboards), Andre Hilgers (drums)

SILENT FORCE was the union of former

ROYAL HUNT vocalist D.C. COOPER and guitarist Alex Beyroth. Beyroth (sometimes known as 'Beyrodt') is credited with past endeavours such as WILD AXIS, SHORTINO, SINNER and THE SYGNET. When initially announced the band went under the title ALLIED FORCES. The line-up on the debut 2000 album 'The Empire Of The Future' also included bassist Fleisch, keyboard player Thorsten Rohre and drummer Andre Hilgers, the latter a former member of THE SYGNET. To promote the album Cooper and Beyroth undertook a short series of acoustic shows in Japan. Fleisch would lose his place to ex-HEADSTONE EPITAPH bassist Jurgen Steinmetz upfront of December gigs in Europe sharing billing with HEAVENLY and STRATOVARIUS.

The 2001 album 'Infatuator' would include a cover version of JUDAS PRIEST's 'All Guns Blazing'.

2002 would also bring about an adventurous 'Rock Opera' project as a result of an alliance between SILENT FORCE members vocalist D.C. COOPER and guitarist Alex Beyrodt together with personnel from PINK CREAM 69 and VANDEN PLAS. The Dennis Ward produced endeavour, entitled MISSA MERCURIA, had lyrics penned by Cooper with music contributed by Beyrodt, PINK CREAM 69's Alfred Koffler and the VANDEN PLAS duo of Günter Werno and Stephan Lill. Musicians sessioning numbered Beyrodt on guitar, VANDEN PLAS men Stephan Lill on guitar and Günter Werno on keyboards as well as PINK CREAM 69ers Alfred Koffler, Andreas Lill, and Dennis Ward. D.C. COOPER would aid on lead vocals portraying the character of 'Firegod' whilst 'Airgod' was handled by Andy Kuntz of VANDEN PLAS, Sabine Edelsbacher of EDENBRIDGE as the 'Water goddess', Lori Williams playing the 'Earth goddess', Isolde Groß as 'Mercuria' and PINK CREAM 69's David Readman provided narration.

Upfront of SILENT FORCE's appearance at the Atlanta, Georgia 'ProgPower' festival the band undertook a short spate of European headliners in November supported by GB ARTS.

Albums:
THE EMPIRE OF FUTURE, Massacre MAS CD0249 (2000)
The Beginning / Live For the Day / Empire Of Future / Saints And Sinners / Tell Me Why / New Experiment / Six Past The Hour / Broken Wings / We Must Remain / I'll Be There
INFATUATOR, Massacre (2001)
Overture / Fall Into Oblivion / Hear Me Calling / Promised Land / Infatuator / We

Must Use The Power / Last Time Trilogy / Cena Libera / Gladiator / The Blade / Pain / All Guns Blazing / World Aflame / In Your Arms / Northern Lights

SILVER MOUNTAIN (SWEDEN)
Line-Up: Christer Mentzer (vocals), Jonas Hansson (guitar), Per Stadin (bass), Martin Hedener (drums)

Initially an instrumental group SILVER MOUNTAIN, formed in 1978, were based around the duo of bassist Per Stadin and vocalist/guitarist Jonas Hansson. Amongst the band's earliest members were keyboard player Jens Johansson and his drummer brother Anders Johansson, both of whom joined YNGWIE MALMSTEEN.

The debut 1979 single featured a line-up of guitarist Morgan Alm, bassist Ingmar Stenqvist and drummer Mårtin Hedener. SILVER MOUNTAIN added the Johansson brothers in 1982 from Jazz-fusion band SLEM.

SILVER MOUNTAIN's debut commercial release with the Johansson brothers came in the form of the track 'She Needs' on the 1982 GS Music compilation 'Skånsk Rock'. Both brothers quit to join YNGWIE MALMSTEEN after the 'Shakin Brains' album. There are bootlegs culled from jam sessions circulating that feature the Johansson brothers, Yngwie Malmsteen and Per Stadin from this period.

For the 'Universe' album SILVER MOUNTAIN added ex-NORDEN LIGHT singer Christer Mentzer and re-recruited Hedener on drums. In mid 1986 SILVER MOUNTAIN changed vocalists from Mentzer to Johan Dahlström. Hedener also lost his place for the second time to new recruit Kjell Gustavsson.

Hansson pursued a solo project the JONAS HANSSON BAND but by 1998 a full-blown SILVER MOUNTAIN reformation was rumoured. 1999 found Anders Johansson performing on ACES HIGH's second album 'Pull No Punches'. SILVER MOUNTAIN - Jonas Hansson, Anders Johansson, Per Stadin and Jens Johansson - finally released their re-formation album 'Breakin' Chains', issued by the Japanese Marquee label, in the summer of 2001.

Singles/EPs:
Man Of No Present Existence / Axeman And The Virgin, Eutone EUSM 227 (1979)

Albums:
SHAKIN' BRAINS, Roadrunner RR 9884 (1983)
1789 / Aftermath / Always / Necrosexual Killer / Destruction Song / Vikings / Looking

403

For You / Spring Maiden / King Of The Sea / Keep On Keepin' On
UNIVERSE, Roadrunner RR 9800 (1985)
Shakin' Brains / Universe / Call Of The Rose / Handled Roughly / Why / Help Me / Walking To The Shadow / Too Late / Niagara
LIVE IN JAPAN, SMS SP25-5281 (1986)
Shakin' Brains / Universe / Always / Why / Handled Roughly / Meaningless / Walking In The Shadow
ROSES AND CHAMPAGNE, Hex HRLP 881 (1988)
Romeo And Juliet / Light The Light / Where Are You / Forest Of Cries / Coming Home / Paris / Paradise Smile / Not You Baby / Downtown Junkie
BREAKIN' CHAINS, (2001)
Prophet Of Doom / Before The Storm / Felo De Se / Man Of No Present Existence / Scarlet Pimpernel / Maniac / Axeman & The Virgin / Breakin' Chains / Rider Of The Night / A.S.W.A.S.T. / The Butterfly / Dance Around The Fire / Milattack / Resurrection

SINERGY (USA / FINLAND)

Line-Up: Kimberley Goss (vocals), Alexi Laiho (guitar), Roope Latvala (guitar), Janne Parviainen (drums)

SINERGY

Metal band founded by lead vocalist Kimberly Goss, having previously carved a reputation as a keyboard player and backing vocalist with acts such as DIMMU BORGIR, THERION and ANCIENT. Bass was in the hands of Sharlee D'Angelo, a veteran of

MERCYFUL FATE, WITCHERY and ARCH ENEMY. The band's original drummer was Ronny Milianowicz of SATURNINE and FALCON repute whilst guitars came courtesy of THY SERPENT, IMPALED NAZARENE and CHILDREN OF BODOM man Alex Laiho. SINERGY debuted live supporting METALIUM and PRIMAL FEAR in Europe during 1999. Session keyboards on the band's early dates came courtesy of Erna Siikavarta. However, following an Autumn tour of Japan in union with CHILDREN OF BODOM and IN FLAMES Milianowicz opted out, duly creating the Symphonic Metal act DIONYSUS.

SINERGY adopted a fresh line-up for the second album 'To Hell And Back'. Joining Goss were TAROT bassist Marco Hietala, TO DIE FOR drummer Tommi Lillmann and WALTARI guitarist Roope Latvala. The album included a twisted cover of the BLONDIE hit 'Hanging On The Telephone'.

Both Goss and Latvala would session on the 2000 debut 'Unknown Soldier' album by WARMEN.

As Laiho's commitments to the increasingly successful CHILDREN OF BODOM for live work SINERGY pulled in second guitarist Peter Huss.

Milianowicz created DIONYSUS in 2000 with LORD BYRON and LUCA TURILLI vocalist Olaf Hayer and NATION members Johnny Öhlin and bassist Magnus Norberg.

Drummer Tommi Lillman, after recording the third album 'Suicide By My Side' sessions, parted ways with the band in August 2001. He would be replaced by Mats Karlsson. However, this latest recruit would decamp shortly after these recording sessions. New man on the drum stool would be Janne Parviainen, a veteran of WALTARI, JIMSONWEED and BARATHRUM.

Hietala would team up with NIGHTWISH, replacing the departed bassist Sami Vänskä, during October of 2001. Along with TAROT colleague and keyboard player Janne Tolsa would also convene a 2001 endeavour dubbed VIRTUOCITY. Other players in this project included Jaska Raatikainen of CHILDREN OF BODOM, Jaron Sebastian Raven and Peter James Goodman.

SINERGY's line-up tribulations continued into 2002 as in May bassist Marco Hietala was let go, temporarily being replaced by session musician Lauri Porra. Japanese dates in June with Brazilians ANGRA would be preceded by SINERGY guitarists Alexi Laiho and Roope Latvala conducting three ESP guitar clinics in Japan. The following month Melanie Sisneros, previously with NEW EDEN and RAVEN MAD, would be added to the line-up. Sisneros is also famed for her role as 'Stephanie Harris' in the renowned tribute band IRON MAIDENS.

SINERGY announced an extensive run of European tour dates throughout November and December co-headlining with DARK TRANQUILITY.

Albums:

BEWARE THE HEAVENS, Nuclear Blast (1999)
Venomous Vixens / The Fourth World / Born Unto Fire and Passion / The Warrior Princess / Beware The Heavens / Razor Blade Salvation / Swarmed / Pulsation / Virtual Future

TO HELL AND BACK, Nuclear Blast NB 503-2 (2000) **27 FINLAND**
The Bitch Is Back / Midnight Madness / Lead Us To War / Laid To Rest / Gallowmere / Return To The Fourth World / Last Escape / Wake Up In Hell / Hanging On The Telephone

SUICIDE BY MY SIDE, Nuclear Blast NB697-2 (2002) **11 FINLAND**
I Spit On Your Grave / The Sin Trade / Violated / Me, Myself, My Enemy / Written In Stone / Nowhere For No One / Passage To The Fourth World / Shadow Island / Suicide By My Side / Remembrance

SINNER (GERMANY)

Line-Up: Mat Sinner (vocals / bass), Tom Naumann (guitar), Henny Wolter (guitar), Frank Rössler (keyboards), Fritz Randow (drums)

A resilient and unrelentingly heavy, hard hitting yet melodic act led by namesake vocalist / bassist Matt Sinner. Always based around the mainstay Matt Sinner, this hard hitting Rock act are regrettably better known outside of Germany for their former members works than SINNER material. A shame, because SINNER have laid down some impressive material over the years and have proven consistently popular in their native country. SINNER debuted with a line-up of ex-SHIVA bassist / vocalist Mattias Sinner (real name Lasch), ex-ELECTRIC PAIN guitarist Frank Mittelbach and ex-STUTTGART axe slinger Calo Rapallo alongside erstwhile TYRAN PACE drummer Edgar Patrik.

1984's 'Danger Zone' album found the group touting a line-up comprising Sinner, guitarist S.G. Stoner, bassist Mick Shirley and drummer Ralf Schulz (Patrick having left for a position in BONFIRE). The next album, 'Touch Of Sin' saw the addition of ex-ACCEPT guitarist Herman Frank and ex-VICTORY drummer Bernie Van Der Graaf. However, Frank's stay was short-lived as he left to join

Van Der Graaf's erstwhile band VICTORY!

SINNER added a new guitar duo featuring erstwhile GRAVESTONE man Mathias Dieth (later to join U.D.O.) and former MAD MAX member Chris Gerhard for the 'Comin' Out Fighting' album in 1986, Gerhard becoming better known as Angel Schliefer. In fact, in 1987 Schliefer left to join Denmark's PRETTY MAIDS (later BONFIRE & DEMON DRIVE) his position being filled by Andy Susemihl.

1987 saw 'Dangerous Charm' being unleashed. An extremely melodic album, guitars were handled by Susemihl and Armin Mücke, although the latter quit after the album was recorded. He would soon be joined by Susemihl quitting to join U.D.O. Susemihl would also go forward to form LAZY with ZAR singer Tommy Bloch, a project that would record a number of impressive demos, before putting a solo album together.

During 1990 MAT SINNER issued the solo album 'Back To The Bullet' with a completely new band. Musicians included guitarists Alex Beyrodt (ex-WILD AXIS / SHORTINO) and Tom Naumann (ex-FREEZE FRAME / PRIVACY), keyboard player Frank Rössler, together with drummer Tommy Resch. The same line-up reformed SINNER to issue the 1992 album 'No More Alibis' on Mausoleum.

Intent on keeping the name very much to the fore SINNER undertook a headline tour of Germany in January 1994 with new drummer ex-VICTORY, ELOY and EPITAPH man Fritz Randow and in April of the same year the band guested for MR. BIG on their European tour. This renewed bout of touring coincided with the arrival of a "best of" package from Noise that featured a rousing cover of BILLY IDOL's 'Rebel Yell', which remains a live favourite to this day. The 'Respect' album would see the inclusion of former SEVEN CRIMES guitarist Volker Dorfler - later of Southern Rockers LIZARD.

The group's stock seriously improved after signing to Koch International as SINNER achieved success with the 1995 album 'Bottom Line', a record that remained in the Japanese national charts for over five weeks. A live album was made available to cash in on SINNER's renewed standing. Entitled 'In The Line Of Fire', the album was recorded and mixed by Achim Köhler.

SINNER performed dates with SAVATAGE in early 1996 and, the following year, the new SINNER masterpiece, 'Judgement Day', arrived through High Gain Records. To promote the album SINNER hit the road with GRAVEDIGGER and, in September, the group were to be found on the bill of the 'Bang Your Head' festival in Tübingen, Germany, Mat Sinner and Tom Naumann forged PRIMAL FEAR, the Heavy Metal outfit led by

ex-GAMMA RAY vocalist Ralf Scheepers in 1998. Since its inception PRIMAL FEAR has outranked SINNER in terms of sales and German chart positions although Mat Sinner has kept a foot in both camps throughout. SINNER would peak with the 1998 album 'The Nature Of Evil' which reached no. 63 on the national German album charts promoted by a support tour in Europe to DEEP PURPLE.

The JVC Victor label in Japan would issue a lavish double CD compilation entitled 'Emerald' backing up doubled up re-releases of 'Danger Zone / Touch Of Sin' and 'Comin Out Fightin / Dangerous Charm'. The European market would be delivered the silver box packaged 'Second Decade' collection. SINNER guitarist Alex Beyrodt evolved his THE SYGNET project into an album release in 1999 and also founded SILENT FORCE with ROYAL HUNT vocalist D.C. Cooper in 2000 for a self-titled album. In 2001 Beyrodt would be found guesting on the sophomore HEAVENLY album.

Sinner would donate his services to the GERMAN ROCK STARS October 2001 song 'Wings Of Freedom' in honour of the September 11th World Trade Center victims. Although Matt Sinner would be preoccupied with PRIMAL FEAR's fourth album 'Black Sun' in early 2002 SINNER would still feature on the agenda, a new album with the projected title of 'There Will be Execution' slated for January 2003 issue. The record, recorded by a band resurrecting the 'Bottom Line' era roster comprising of Sinner, guitarists Tom Naumann and Henny Wolter, keyboard player Frank Rössler with SAXON drummer Fritz Randow, was slated to include a cover version of MONTROSE's classic 'Rock The Nation'. The band also cut a rendition of Wherever I May Roam' for a Nuclear Blast METALLICA tribute collection.

Mat Sinner would add guest session lead vocals on U.S. guitarist RICK RENSTROM's solo album 'Until The Bitter End', featuring on the track 'Calling on Vengeance'.

Singles/EPs:
Bad Girl / The Storm Broke Loose, Noise NOO28 (1985)
Out Of Control / Bad Girl / The Shiver, Noise NOO29 (1985)
Born To Rock / Masquerade, Noise NOO36 (1986)
Hypnotised / Don't Tell Me (That The Love Is Gone), Noise N0053 (1986)
Fight The Fight / Tomorrow Doesn't Matter, Noise NO104 (1987)
Knife In My Heart / Concrete Jungle, Noise

N0107 (1987)
Rebel Yell / Germany Rocks, Noise N0059 (1989)
Where Were You / Rebel At Heart, (Previously Unreleased Rough Mix) / I'm Not Over Yet, Mausoleum 904008.3 (1992)
Fire In The Dark / Respect, GSE 0235-2 (1994)
Say Goodbye / Fire In The Dark, Koch International 34329-2 (1995)

Albums:
WILD N' EVIL, SL Records (1982)
Loser Of Love / No Speed Limit / Murder / Ridin' The White Horse / Lost In A Dream / Heat Of The Nite / F.T.A. / Silly Thing / Shakin' The Devil's Hand / The Sin / Trouble
FAST DECISION, Scratch (1983)
Runnin' Wild / Crazy / Prelude No. 7 / Magic / One Last Look / Fast Decision / Trouble Boys / In The City / Chains / Rockin'
DANGERZONE, Noise N0013 08-1661 (1984)
Danger Zone / No Place In Heaven / Scene Of A Crime / Lupo Manaro / Fast, Hard And Loud / The Shiver / Razor Blade / Shadow In The Night / Wild Winds / Rattlesnake
TOUCH OF SIN, Noise N0026 (1985)
Born To Rock / Emerald / Bad Girl / Shout! / The Storm Broke Loose / Out Of Control / Too Late To Runaway / Hand Of Fate / Masquerade / Open Arms / Fast Decision / Knife In My Heart
COMIN' OUT FIGHTING, Noise N0049 08-4405 (1986)
Hypnotised / Faster Than Light / Comin' Out Fighting / Age Of Rock / Rebel Yell / Lost In A Minute / Don't Tell Me (That The Love Is Gone) / Germany Rocks / Playin' With Fire / Madhouse
DANGEROUS CHARM, Noise N08-4458 (1987)
Back In My Arms / Concrete Jungle / Dangerous Charm / Everybody / Fight The Fight / Gipsy / Knife In My Heart / Last Dance / Nobody Rocks Like You / Tomorrow Doesn't Matter Tonight
NO MORE ALIBIS, Mausoleum 904008.2 (1992)
When A Heart Breaks / Good Times / Burning Heart / Where Were You / Save Me / Boys In Trouble / Thrill Of A Lifetime / Don't Wanna Lose You / Chasing My Dreams / So Excitable / I'm Not Over You Yet
GERMANY ROCKS-THE BEST OF, Noise NO235-2 (1994)
Born To Rock / Lost In A Minute / Knife In My Heart / Rebel Yell / Everybody / Respect / Germany Rocks / Bad Girl / Back To The Bullet / Back In My Arms / Hypnotised / Masquerade / Danger Zone / Faster Than Light / The Concrete Jungle / Out Of Control

RESPECT, GSE 5211-2 (1994)
Respect / Things Get Started / Fire In The Dark / Don't Let This Dream Die Young / Modern World / Beds Are Burning / Little Victory / Every Little Step / Believer / Valley Of Tears / Shattered Dreams / Knife In My Heart / What's So Bad About Feeling Good
BOTTOM LINE, Koch International 34261-2 (1995)
The Biggest Lie / Roses Of Yesterday / When Silence Falls / All Men Are Heroes / I Can't Stop The Fire / We'll Make It All Right / Rage Of A Hurricane / Mercy Killer / Dead End Street / In The Heart Of The Young / Hearts Of Steel / Say Goodbye
IN THE LINE OF FIRE (LIVE), Zero Corporation (1995) (Japanese release)
When Silence Falls / Comin' Out Fighting / All Men Are Heroes / Back In My Arms / Respect / The Biggest Lie / Born To Rock / Knife In My Heart / Rebel Yell / Rage Of A Hurricane / Everybody / Modern World / There's Only One Way To Rock
JUDGEMENT DAY, High Gain 4 014548 006161 (1997)
Used To The Truth / Troublemaker / Jump The Gun / Judgement Day / Pray For Mercy / White Lightning / Blue Tattoo / School Of Hard Knocks / The Fugitive / Deathwalker / Streets Of Sin
THE NATURE OF EVIL, Nuclear Blast NB 324-2 (1998) **63 GERMANY**
Devil's River / A Question Of Honour / Justice From Hell / The Nature Of Evil / Some Truth / Darksoul / Faith And Conviction / Rising / Walk The Darkside / Trust No One / The Sun Goes Down
THE SECOND DECADE, Nuclear Blast (1999)
The Second Decade / Jump The Gun / When Silence Falls / Devil's River / Used To The Truth / A Question Of Honour / The Truth Is Out There / Balls To The Wall / Judgement Day / The Biggest Lie / Streets Of Sin / Rage Of A Hurricane / The Nature Of Evil / Born To Rock / Respect
EMERALD, JVC Victor VICP-60942 (1999) (Japanese release)
Danger Zone / The Shiver / Shadow In The Night / Wild Winds / Emerald / Bad Girl / Shout! / The Storm Broke Loose / Too Late To Runaway / Hypnotised / Faster Than Light / Rebel Yell / Lost In A Minute / Don't Tell Me / Playing With Fire / Concrete Jungle / Knife In My Heart / Everybody / Back In My Arms / Gipsy / Chasing My Dreams / Burning Heart / Respect / Fire In The Dark / Modern World / When Silence Falls / The Biggest Lie / We'll Make It Alright / Rage Of A Hurricane / Dead End Street / White Lightning / Used To The Truth / Judgement Day / A Question Of Honour / The Nature Of Evil / Calm Before

The Storm
THE END OF SANCTUARY, Nuclear Blast
NB 471-2 (2000) **87 GERMANY**
Signed, Sealed & Delivered / Blood
Relations / The End Of Sanctuary / Pain In
Your Neck / Edge Of The Blade / The
Prophecy / Destiny / Congress Of Deceit /
Heavy Duty / Night Of The Wolf / Broken
World / Hand Of The Saint
THERE WILL BE EXECUTION, Nuclear
Blast (2003)
Higher Level Of Violence / There Will Be
Execution / Requiem For A Sinner / Locked
& Loaded / Finalizer / The River / God
Raises The Dead / Die On Command /
Liberty Of Death / Black Monday / Crown Of
Thorns

MAT SINNER (GERMANY)
Line-Up: Mat Sinner (vocals), Alex Beyrodt
(guitar), Tom Naumann (guitar), Tommy
Geiger (bass), Tommy Resch (drums)

In 1990 SINNER mainman Mat Sinner
released his first solo album. It also spawned
two single releases.
Musicians included guitarists Alex Beyrodt
(ex-WILD AXIS / SHORTINO) and Tom
Naumann (ex-FREEZE FRAME / PRIVACY),
keyboard player Frank Rössler, together with
drummer Tommy Resch. The same line-up
reformed SINNER to issue the 1992 album
'No More Alibis' on Mausoleum.
Beyrodt later created THE SYGNET and
SILENT FORCE.

Singles/EPs:
Every Second Counts / Back To The
Bullet, BMG Ariola 663466 (1990)
Call My Name / She's Got The Look, BMG
Ariola 663799 (1990)

Albums:
BACK TO THE BULLET, BMG Ariola CD
260949 (1990)
Back To The Bullet / Tear Down The Wall /
Every Second Counts / Call My Name /
Crazy Horses / In The Name Of Rock n' Roll
/ Wildest Dreams / Down Undercover / Face
To Face / Crying In The Wires

SIRENS (GERMANY)
Line-Up: Dragon Power (vocals / bass),
Danny Wizard (guitar), Tommy Thunder
(drums)

A deliberately retro, '80s style 'True' Heavy
Metal act out of Nuremberg. SIRENS, so titled
after the SAVATAGE album, came into being
during 1995 as a trio led by vocalist / bassist
'Dragon Power', a veteran guitarist of IVORY

and DEATHMASS. Onstage with SIREN
Dragon Power wields medieval two handed
swords whilst leading semi-naked women on
chains!
The 'Approaching The Island' demo of 1995
and the subsequent 1996 sessions 'Power
Kid' and 'Empire Of Clouds' led in turn to the
extremely limited 'Empire Of Clouds' EP,
restricted to just 66 copies. Further demo
sessions ensued prior to recording of debut
album 'Nameless World' released in 1997.
Drums for this album, which included cover
versions of IRON MAIDEN's 'Phantom Of The
Opera' and BLACK SABBATH's 'Paranoid',
were credited to 'Rock Earthquake'.
During this period Dragon Power was also
operational on the German club circuit with
his IRON MAIDEN covers band ACES HIGH.
When SIRENS regrouped for the second
album 'The Battle Dragon' Dragon Power,
responsible for all vocals, guitars and bass,
would be joined by former comrade in arms
Rock Earthquake. With recording complete
new personnel guitarist Danny Wizard and
drummer Tommy Thunder enrolled.
Dragon Power is also front man for ARISE.

Singles/EPs:
Empire Of Clouds EP, (1996)

Albums:
NAMELESS WORLD, (1997)
THE BATTLE DRAGON, (1999)
**SPARK, TORCH & DRAGONFIRE -
DRAGON BLOOD 1996-2000**, (2000)
GLOBAL KILLERS, (2001)
The Dragon Spirit Of Sirens / Renegade /
Mindfood / Celestial Kingdom / Children Of
The Damned / Dragonless World / A Dream /
Hunger´s Burning / Very Last Breath / San
Francisco / Free Your Mind / Outro / Free
Your Mind (Edit) / Very Last Breath (Live) /
Celestial Kingdom (Live) / R.W.D. (Live) /
Take On Me / B-Head Your Move / Paranoid /
Political Tyranny / Touch Too Much / Empire
Of Clouds / Bride Of Steel / Dirty Streets /
Free Your Mind / Sadistic Soldiers

SIX MAGICS (CHILE)
Line-Up: Sergio Dominguez (vocals), Erick
Avila (guitar), Gabriel Hildago (guitar),
Mauricio Nader (bass), Sebastian Carrasco
(keyboards), Pablo Stragnaro (drums)

Santiago Heavy Metal band created in 1996
by school friends vocalist Sergio Villarroel,
guitarists Erick Avila and Nicolás Espinoza,
bassist J.Pablo Pizarro and drummer Pablo
Stagnaro. Within a year SIX MAGICS had
recorded the EP 'Trilogía De Un Guerrero'.
The following year Pizarro relocated to

France and Rodolfo Sánchez de Lozada duly stepped into the vacancy. Further changes found Sergio Domínguez becoming their new lead vocalist in 1999 and Sebastián Carrasco added as keyboard player. With this incarnation of the band SIX MAGICS laid down the Classically influenced Metal album 'Dead Kings of the Unholy Valley' in August of 2001.

In 2002 there were two more changes to the band with Mauricio Nader supplanting Rodolfo Sanchez de Lozada and Gabriel Hidalgo substituting for Espinoza.

Albums:
DEAD KINGS OF THE UNHOLY VALLEY, (2001)
Storm / Infinite Keeper / Guardian Of Fire / Talisman / Agony Of A Hero / Metal Century / La Trilogia: I) Eternal Warrior, II) Prince Of Pure Light, III) Dead Kings Of The Unholy Valley

SKANNERS (ITALY)
Line-Up: Claudio Pisoni (vocals), Fabio Tenca (guitar), Dino Lucchi (guitar), Corrado Gasser (bass), Luigi Sandrini (drums)

An Italian Speed Metal mob, SKANNERS from Bolzano date back to 1982 and have been known to have supported DIO, TWISTED SISTER, HELLOWEEN, MOTÖRHEAD and MANOWAR on home turf. For their opening album 'Dirty Armada' the band stood at lead singer Claudio Pisoni, guitarists Fabio Tenca and Massimo 'Max' Quinzio, bass player Korrado Gasser and Luigi Sandrini on the drums. Having had the track 'Dirty Armada' featured on the 1984 compilation album 'Rock News Of Vienna'. Guitarist Massimo Quinzio departed in early 1987 to be replaced by Dino Lucchi, and SKANNERS scored a track, 'Turn It Louder Now', on the 1988 compilation album 'Metal Shock'.

Ex-SCRATCH bassist Roberto Vajente superseded Covado Gasser in 1990. The group made a comeback with a 1995 album 'The Magic Square', Pisoni and Tenca being joined by bassist Dino Lucchi and drummer Jack Alemanno. This same quartet cut a live album in 1998. SKANNERS comprised Pisoni, guitarists Fabio Tenca and Walter Unterhauser, bass player Renato Olivari and drummer Jack Alemanno for the 2002 'Flagellus Dei' opus.

Albums:
DIRTY ARMADA, (1986)
TV Shock / Rock Rock City / Skanners / Everybody's Crazy / Black Eagle / Walking On The Wall / Steel And Fire / Dirty Armada / Running Back / Starlight / Scorpion Rider / Rock Rock City (Reprise)
PICTURES OF WAR, CGD 20720 (1988)
Pictures Of War / Something Very Special / Drowning Down The Drain / She's Like A Boy / Fight Back / Turn It Louder Now / We Are Night / Wild / One Night
THE MAGIC SQUARE, Südton 95008-2 (1996)
Undertaker / Beyond Death / Trimurti / Magic Square / On My Way / Without You / You Feel The Power / Insane / Metal Party / Angel / Ciara Teobaldo / True Stories
SKANNERS LIVE, (1998)
Intro / TV Shock / Clara E Teobaldo / Metal Party / Undertaker / The Dark Side / Pictures Of War / She´s Like A Boy / Everybody´s Crazy / Rock Rock City / Drum solo / Phenomena / Oltrisarco In The Night / Black Eagle / Andromeda / Fight Back / Wild / The Magic Square
FLAGELLUS DEI, Underground Symphony (2002)
Flagellum Dei / Blood In My Eyes / Time Of War / Nightrider / Minister Of Fear / Beast Of Hell / Full Moon's Eyes / It's My Life / M.P.+

SKULLVIEW (USA)
Line-Up: Quimby Lewis (vocals), Dean Tavernier (guitar), Dave Hillegonds (guitar), Pete Clemens (bass), Joe Garavalia (drums)

SKULLVIEW include ex-POWER OPERA and TRAUMA front man Quimby 'Earthquake' Lewis. The group's original formation included guitarists Dean Tavernier of BLACK FUNERAL repute and Chris Lambersie but the latter was superseded by former CHRONIC BLACK man Dave Hillegonds in late 1996. Bassist Pete Clemens is an erstwhile member of SHADES OF GREY and SEA OF TRANQUILITY whilst drummer Joe Garavalia was previously bassist for RESURRECTION and UNDERTAKER.

In June of 2000 Lewis opted out and SKULLVIEW pulled in Joe Lawson as replacement. However, by August Lewis was back at the helm. In December of 2000 a previously unreleased version of 'Hand Of Zeus' was included on a split 7" single issued by Syren Records and shared with St. Louis act DRIZZIT.

The 'Consequences Of Failure' album would see a vinyl release through the German Bonehead label.

Singles/EPs:
Hand Of Zeus, Syren (2000) (Split single with DRIZZIT)

409

Albums:
LEGENDS OF VALOR, R.I.P. (1998)
The Night Of Metalkill / Blood On The Blade / Undesired Hateful Ways / Watching Below From My Moonlight Throne / Stone Of A Thousand Spells / Dreamworld Terror (In The Valley Of Metal) / Into The Walls Of Knowledge / Gleam Of The Skull Part I (The Power)
KINGS OF THE UNIVERSE, R.I.P. (1999)
Kings Of The Universe / Hand Of Zeus / In League With The Dragon / Cobwebs And Shadowed Images / Mourning Light / War Within The Sky / Blast Furnace / The Power Of The Gleam Of The Skull (Part 2)
CONSEQUENCES OF FAILURE, R.I.P. (2001)
Time For Violence / Skullview (Warrior) / Palace Of The Boundless Cold / Wrath Of The Sorcerer / Armed With An Axe / The Archmage / Seek The Old Man For Knowledge / Leviticus / Gleam Of The Skull (Part 3 - Back From Whence It Came) / Digital Bitch

SKYLARK (ITALY)
Line-Up: Fabio Dozzo (vocals), Max Faracci (guitar), Niko Tordini (guitar), Roby Brodo Potenti (bass), Eddy Antonini (keyboards), Francesco Tettix Meles (drums)

Italian Power / Progressive Metal band. SKYLARK have built quite a reputation in their homeland with successive releases. The album 'After The Storm' is in fact a re-release of the debut record remastered with extra tracks.
The 2000 two set album project pairing 'Divine Gates' sees guest showings from Folco Orlandini of MESMERIZE as the 'Guardian Angel' character, guitarist Vic Mazzoni of PROJECTO and LABYRINTH members guitarist Olaf Thorsen and vocalist Rob Tyrant. SKYLARK's reputation would burgeon throughout 2000 as mainland Europe and Japan took to the band. Evidence of this rising status came with their inclusion on the HELLOWEEN tribute album 'Keepers Of Jericho' donating their take on 'Twilight Of The Gods'. The group would also headline the Spanish 'Rock Machina 2000' festival and score a no. 1 album in the import charts for the highly respected Japanese Rock magazine 'Burrn'.
Keyboard player EDDY ANTONINI has released a 1998 solo album 'When Water Became Ice'. Japanese versions of SKYLARK's 2001 album 'The Princess Day' included an extra exclusive track 'Princess Of The Snow'.

Singles/EPs:
Tribute To W.A. Mozart: Eine Kleine Nachtmusik - K5255 - Allegro / Skylark (Edit) / Was Called Empire / Albatross On Sea, Underground Symphony USCD 013 (1999)
Belzebu (Edit) / Among The Clouds / A Star In The Universe ('99 version) / Twilight, Underground Symphony USCD 036 (1999)

Albums:
THE HORIZON AND THE STORM, EA 1 (1995)
The Horizon (Piano Intro) / Fear Of The Moon / Little Girl / Skylark / Crystal Lake / A Star In The Universe / Escape From The Dark / The Storm
DRAGON'S SECRETS, Underground Symphony US CD-017DP (1997)
The Temple / Creature Of The Devil / The Answers / Waiting For The Princess / Light / Princess Of The Snow / Dragon's Secrets
AFTER THE STORM, Underground Symphony USCD-014 (1998)
The Horizon (Piano Intro) / Fear Of The Moon / Little Girl / Skylark / Crystal Lake / A Star In The Universe / Escape From The Dark / The Storm / Tribute To W.A. Mozart / Skylark (Edit) / Was Called Empire / Albatros On Sea
DIVINE GATES PART I: GATE OF HELL, Underground Symphony USCD-040 (2000)
Intro / Welcome / The Triumph / Belzebu / The Last Question / Earthquake / I Can't Find Love Tonight / Satan Arise / Why Did You Tell The Princess? / Lift For The Sky / Dance Of Stars
DIVINE GATES PART II: GATE OF HEAVEN, Underground Symphony USCD-050 (2000)
Among The Clouds / Who Is God? / Lady Of The Sky / Monday 13 October / Insanity Is The Truth / The Guardian Angel / The Heaven Church / Last Christmas In Hell / Outro / A Star In The Universe ('99 version)
THE PRINCESS' DAY, Underground Symphony USCD-060 (2001)
The Princess' Day / I Will Cry Tonight / Journey Through The Fire / Another Life / Rufus (Intro) / Rufus / Rufus II: Symbol Of Freedom / The Tragedy / White Warrior

SONATA ARCTICA (FINLAND)
Line-Up: Tony Kakko (vocals / keyboards), Jani Liimatainen (guitar), Janne Kivilahti (bass), Mikko Harkin (keyboards), Tommy Portimo (drums)

Kemi based Symphonic Metal band SONATA ARCTICA have made a great impression on the European Metal scene not only with their grandiose sense of style but in that uniquely

the band employs two keyboard players live for an extra double dose of pomposity. The band was founded in 1995 playing much poppier music under the original band name of TRICKY BEANS! Although the band would issue demo recordings under that name the members soon got wise to a name change to SONATA ARCTICA and progress subsequently proved rapid from that point.

As TRICKY BEANS the band - pursuing an experimental Pop direction, would issue three demo sessions in 'Friend Till The End', 'Agre Pamppers' and 'Peacemaker'. Line-up shuffles during 1997 forced a subtle name re-arrangement to that of TRICKY MEANS and a further promotional recording entitled 'Full Moon'.

The Spinefarm label showed interest just as a title switch to SONATA ARCTICA was adopted and the band debuted with the 1999 'Unopened' single. However, the initial batch of CDs proved faulty - in actual fact featuring slowed down recordings, and were duly recalled. Revised variants would though succeed in gaining the band laudable press coverage across Europe.

With SONATA ARCTICA in ascendancy front man Tony Kakko opted to enrol another keyboard player in order to concentrate on his lead vocal role. KENZINER's Mikko Harkin

duly took the role on as SONATA ARCTICA gained a valuable support slot to the 2000 STRATOVARIUS and RHAPSODY European tour.

The band contributed their version of 'I Want Out' to the HELLOWEEN tribute album 'Keepers Of Jericho'. SONATA ARCTICA's 'Successor' mini-album included the HELLOWEEN cover plus a SCORPIONS cover version 'Still Loving You' and live tracks recorded at the Seinäjoki 'Provinssirock' festival. Various international versions would add extra live tracks, Japanese variants having 'Unopened' and 'Full Moon', French releases having '8th Commandment' and 'Letter To Dana' whilst South American issues had all these plus 'Kingdom For A Heart'.

In early 2001 bass player Janne Kivilahti would bow out and the band drafted Marko Paasikoski to the position, actually an earlier holder of the post. Further live work would find the band landing a prestigious slot at the Helsinki 'Monsters Of The Millennium' festival alongside RATT, DIO and ALICE COOPER.

Vocalist Tony Kakko would guest on the NIGHTWISH single 'Over The Hills And Far Away'.

Liimatainen would venture out with a side concern ALTARIA in 2001. Joining him on this project would be the erstwhile BLINDSIDE rhythm section of bassist Marko Pukkila and drummer Tony Smedjebacka along with singer Johan Mattjus. This quartet debuted in November with the three track 'Sleeping Visions' promotional EP.

SONATA ARCTICA's 'Last Drop Falls' single would include a version of IRON MAIDEN's 'Die With Your Boots On'. This track, alongside an adventurous rendition of BETTE MIDLER's 'Wind Beneath My Wings' also made an appearance on the Japanese 'Orientation' EP. The band also cut a rendition of 'Fade To Black' for a Nuclear Blast METALLICA tribute collection.

Keyboard player Mikko Harkin announced his departure in September of 2002.

Singles/EPs:
Unopened / Mary Lou, (1999)
Wolf And Raven / Peacemaker, Spinefarm SPI 110 CD (2001)
Last Drop Falls / Die With Your Boots On / Mary Lou (Acoustic version), Spinefarm SPI 135 CD (2001)
Black Sheep / Mary Lou (Acoustic version) / The Wind Beneath My Wings / Die With Your Boots On / Wolf And Raven (Video) / Interview, Avalon Marquee MICP-10256 (2001) ('Orientation' EP)

Albums:
SUCCESSOR, Spinefarm SPI 106CD (2000)
Full Moon (Edit) / Still Loving You / I Want Out / San Sebastian / Shy / Replica (Live) / My Land (Live)
SILENCE, Century Media (2000) **3 FINLAND**
...Of Silence / Weballergy / False News Travel Fast / The End Of This Chapter / Black Sheep / Land Of The Free / Last Drop Falls / San Sebastian (Revisited) / Sing In Silence / Revontulet / Tallulah / Wolf And Raven / The Power Of One
ECLIPTICA, Century Media (2000)
Blank File / My Land / 8th Commandment / Replica / Kingdom For A Heart / Full Moon / Letter To Dana / Unopened / Picturing The Past / Destruction Preventer
SONGS OF SILENCE - LIVE IN TOKYO,
Avalon Marquee MICP-10290 (2002) (Japanese release)
Intro / Weballergy / Kingdom For A Heart / Sing In Silence / False News Travel Fast / Last Drop Falls / Respect The Wilderness / Fullmoon / The End Of This Chapter / The Power Of One / Replica / My Land / Black Sheep / Wolf & Raven / Blank File / Land Of The Free / Peacemaker
SONGS OF SILENCE - LIVE IN TOKYO,
Spinefarm (2002) (European release)
Intro / Weballergy / Kingdom For A Heart / Sing In Silence / False News Travel Fast /

Last Drop Falls / Respect The Wilderness / Fullmoon / The End Of This Chapter / Replica / My Land / Black Sheep / Wolf & Raven

SOUL CAGES (GERMANY)
Line-Up: Thorsten Staroske (vocals / guitar), Knut Nitschke (guitar), Stephan Tigges (bass), Jörg Nitschke (drums)

A melodic, Progressive Metal band, SOUL CAGES toured Germany in 1996 on a bill including VENI DOMINE and SAVIOUR MACHINE. They are complemented live with female backing vocalist Beate Kuhbier.

Albums:
SOUL CAGES, Massacre CD032 (1994)
The Narrow Path Of Truth / New Horizons / Reflections / Mindtrip / Actors Of No Return / Incommunicado / Soul Cages / Rainbow
MOMENTS, Massacre CD085 (1996)
Freezing / The Naked World / Moments / Methode No. 23 / In Our Hands / Elegy / Impressions / My Spiritual Home
CRAFT, Massacre (1999)
Pressure / A Part Of Me / Falling / Piano / The Light Of Day / Imprisoned / Force Of A Dream / Result Of Convenience / Before (For Bert)

SPIRAL ARCHITECT (NORWAY)
Line-Up: Øyvind Hægeland (vocals), Steinar Gundersen (guitar), Andreas Jonsson (guitar), Lars K. Norberg (bass), Asgeir Mickelson (drums)

Oslo outfit forged in 1993, produced by a union of ANESTHESIA members guitarist Kaj Gornitzka, bass player Lars K. Norberg and drummer Asgeir Mickelson with erstwhile KING'S QUEST guitarist Steinar Gundersen. This new unit opted to pursue an offbeat Jazz / Fusion flavoured technical Metal direction. SPIRAL ARCHITECT personnel have strong affiliations with the extreme Metal scene in Norway.

The band debuted with a brace of tracks, 'Fountainhead' and 'Purpose', included on the 1995 compilation collection 'A Gathering...'. Session lead vocals for these recordings were provided by Leif Knashaug. When submited to a demo the tracks reaped heady praise from the Progressive Metal movement. The band found a permanent singer in ex-MANITOU man Øyvind Hægeland during 1996 and decided on retreating from the Progressive Metal scene and pursuing their own path of creativity.

In 1997 SPIRAL ARCHITECT signed to the American Sensory label for the album 'A

Sceptic's Universe'. The record, laid down in Texas, was produced by the Grammy award winning Neil Kernon. Japanese versions, originally scheduled for release in December of 1999 but held back until January 2000 by the Avalon Marquee label held an additional track in the FATES WARNING cover 'Prelude To Ruin', originally donated to the tribute album 'Through Different Eyes'. Regular versions of the album surfaced in January of 2000. With recording complete Andreas Jonsson took the place of Gornitzka.

With SPIRAL ARCHITECT's musical prowess now established globally the individual band members would find themselves the subject of intense demand. Whilst remaining loyal to SPIRAL ARCHITECT Mickelson was inducted into the ranks of BORKNAGAR for their 'Quintessence' album. Gundersen meantime also teamed up with another high profile Black Metal act, joining SATYRICON for European touring. During 2001 Mickelson would session for ENSLAVEMENT OF BEAUTY and on SPASTIK INK's 'Ink Compatible' album. Meantime Hægeland guested on MAYHEM's 'Grand Declaration Of War'.

2002 found both Gundersen and Norberg ensconsed in the ranks of SATYRICON whilst Mickelson remained rooted in BORKNAGAR as well as finding time to lay down drums on the VINTERSORG record 'Visions From The Spiral Generator'. Three SPIRAL ARCHITECT members, guitarist 'Azarek', bassist 'Maztema' and drummer Asgeir Mickelson would unite with ex-1349 singer Balfori for the side project LUNARIS, issuing the 2002 album 'The Infinite'.

Albums:
A SCEPTIC'S UNIVERSE, Sensory (2000)
Spinning / Excessit / Moving Spirit / Occam's Razor / Insect / Cloud Constructor / Conjuring Collapse / Adaptability / Fountainhead

SPIRAL TOWER (GERMANY)
Line-Up: Alex Koch (vocals), Sven Podgurski (guitar), Bernhard Altmann (bass), Frank Zubosch (drums)

SPIRAL TOWER were born out of the implosion of TRAGEDY DIVINE. Whilst TRAGEDY DIVINE leather and stud loaded singer Gerrit P. Mutz and guitarist Jörg Michael Knittel founded the chest beating SACRED STEEL the remaining trio of guitarist Sven Podgurski, bassist Bernhard Altmann and drummer Frank 'Zube' Zubosch created SPIRAL TOWER.

Albums:
MINDKILLER, Massacre (1999)
The Eyes Of The Blind / The Martyr Is Dead / Messenger From God / On The Wings Of An Eagle / Tired Faces / Lord Of The Shadows / Heartkiller / Looking Down On The Moon / Execute In Excuse / Feel The Tears

SPIRIT HEAVEN (BRAZIL)
Line-Up: Paulo Braz (vocals), Rodrigo Jota (guitar), Samuel Bacci (guitar), André Pozzobon (bass), Fábio Laguna (keyboards), Guilherme Gaspar (drums)

Singles/EPs:
Wake Up And Fight / Black Roses, (1999)

Albums:
ARIA'S KINGDOM, Megahard (2001)
Spirit Heaven / Wake Up And Fight / The Return / Aria (Legacy Of Heaven) / Bring Back My Crown / The Blessing Way / Black Roses / Your Nightmare Is Over / Venial Sins / Princess Of The Night

SPITFIRE (GREECE)
Line-Up: Dinos Costakis (vocals), Elias Loginidis (guitar), Thanon Kremides (bass), George Velentzas (keyboards), Costas Kirlakidis (drums)

A Greek Metal band named after the legendary British fighter plane of World War Two fame. Vocalist Dino Costakis was badly injured in a car crash curtailing the band's career.

The act returned re-titled SPEEDFIRE for legal reasons for a 1990 live album.

Albums:
FIRST ATTACK, EMI 062-1701221 (1986)
Street Fighter / Lead Me On / Whispers / Lady Of The Night / Explosion / Walk Alone / Evil Thoughts Around / Guilty Dreams

SQUEALER (GERMANY)
Line-Up: Andy Henner (vocals), Lars Doring (guitar), Michael Schiel (guitar), Michael Kasper (bass), Mike Terrana (drums)

Metal outfit SQUEALER's first product was the 1987 demo 'Ready To Fight' followed by a further demo in 'One Beer Too Much' in 1988. Initially a straight ahead Hard Rock act SQUEALER progressively developed into the accelerated Speed Metal of Thrash. Latter day releases found SQUEALER slowing the pace somewhat.

SQUEALER were in a position to offer an EP, 'Human Traces', in 1989 although it would be four years before a debut album arrived.

413

In early 1995 drummer Franky Wolf decamped. Tobias Exxel, previously a member of teen band HERESY, would be inducted as bassist but would in fact contribute both bass and guitar to the 1995 album 'Wrong Time, Wrong Place?'

1998 would witness Tobias Exxel's departure. The guitarist set to work on a project band entitled TARAXACUM, combining this endeavour with his enrolment as bass player into EDGUY.

The 1999 album 'The Prophecy' sees SQUEALER with guitarists Lars Doring and Michael Schiel, drummer Martin Winter and keyboard services donated by Tilo Rockstroh. EDGUY's Tobias Sammet guests on the track 'Friends For Life'. Quite bizarrely SQUEALER cover DEPECHE MODE's 'Enjoy The Silence' too. Released on AFM Records in Europe 'The Prophecy' would be licensed to Metal Blade for North America in July of 2000.

The 2000 album 'Made For Eternity' has guest appearances from drummer Mike Terrana, a veteran of ARTENSION, YNGWIE MALMSTEEN and fellow German act RAGE, alongside HELLOWEEN guitarist ROLAND GRAPOW. SQUEALER committed their version of 'Victim Of Fate' to the HELLOWEEN tribute album 'Keepers Of Jericho'.

Terrana would commit to the band for European touring alongside EDGUY.

In 2001 former drummer Frank Wolf would guest on the ambitious TARAXACUM project album 'Spirit Of Freedom' conceived by EDGUY and erstwhile SQUEALER man Tobias Exxel. SQUEALER would spend the latter half of 2001 recording a new album 'Under The Cross' under the guidance of producers ex-VICTORY guitarist Tommy Newton and ex-SABBAT guitarist Andy Sneap. An odd inclusion on this record would be a cover of the '70s Pop hit 'In Zaire'.

Singles/EPs:
The Casualty / Lose Of Independence / Bereft Of Senses / I Will Fight / Insanity, Squealer (1989) ('Human Traces' EP)

Albums:
MAKE YOUR DAY, AFM Records 21477 (1993)
A Little Piece Of Death / Behold The Lion / Make Your Day / Thoughts / The Wanderer / Tears Of Hate / RAP / Scaring The Winds / The Man Who Never Was
WRONG TIME, WRONG PLACE?, AFM Records 25702 (1995)
Intro / Liar / Wrong Time Wrong Place / Time Doesn't Wait / Hellcome In Heaven / Love To Hate You / Dying Forbidden! / Don't Wanna

Be Like You / Whose Afraid Of Yellow Snow?
THE PROPHECY, AFM Records CD026 (1999)
The Prophecy (The Final Sign) / Friends For Life /...But No One Cares / Live Everyday / Hold On Tight / To Die For (...Your Sins) / Nowhere To Hide / I See The World / The Meaning Of Life / Enjoy The Silence / The Prophecy (Follow Me)
MADE FOR ETERNITY, AFM Records (2000)
End Of The World / The Final Daylight / Nothing To Believe / Don't Fear Your Life / The Eternity Of A Day / Show Me The Way / No One To Blame / People Are People / Free Your Mind / Hellcome In Heaven
UNDER THE CROSS, AFM Records (2002)
Painful Lust / Facing The Death / My Last Goodbye / Thinking Allowed! / Under The Cross / Rules Of Life /'Down And Out / Fade Away / Out Of The Dark / In Zaire / Low Budget Heroes

STEEL ATTACK (SWEDEN)
Line-Up: Steve Steel (vocals), John Allan (guitar), Andreas De Vera, Dennis Vestman

With a name like STEEL ATTACK this Swedish outfit could only ever be a Power Metal band. The group began life as MAYER'S EVE during 1995 but an ever fluctuating line-up resulted in an eventual title switch to STEEL ATTACK during 1997. Guitarist John Allen joined the fold in May of 1998 and a demo session billed 'Mighty Sword Of Power' secured a deal with the AFM Records label.

STEEL ATTACK debuted with the P.O. Saether produced 'Where Mankind Fails' in 1999. Live work was limited but did include an appearance at the German 2000 'Wacken Open Air' festival. STEEL ATTACK returned in 2001 with sophomore release 'Fall Into Madness'. The band would draft a new singer, Dick Johnson, for their third album recorded during 2002.

Albums:
WHERE MANKIND FAILS, AFM (1999)
Dragon's Skull / Where Mankind Fails / Island Of Gods / Heading For The Lair / Village Of Agabha / The Furious Spirit Of Death / The Creation Of Be-Lou (The Tragic Kingdom Part I) / The Awakening (The Tragic Kingdom Part II) / Thunder Knight / Forgotten Land
FALL INTO MADNESS, AFM (2001)
Fall Into Madness / The Beast / Guardians / Holy Swordsmen / Judgement Day / Wings Of Faith / Clearing The Mind / Fireballs / Defender Of The Crown

STEEL CAGE (ITALY)

Line-Up: Bruno Guarascio (vocals), Gianluca Rungetti (guitar), Giuseppe Rungetti (guitar), Joshua Campana (bass), Genny Eneghes (drums)

STEEL CAGE was originally entitled APOCALYPSE now upon their formation in 1994 with the band members taking on stage names of Tyr, Sharko, Rage and Machine. Adopting the new title STEEL CAGE the band released the 'Abyss Of Steel' demo in 1996. Bruno Guarascio would supplant Valerio on vocals for the 1999 self-financed EP 'Visions Of Dark Millennium'.

Singles/EPs:
Quick Fire / Solitary Reaper / The Liar / Cage Of Sounds / Dreams Of Green, (1999) ('Visions Of Dark Millennium' EP)

STEELER (GERMANY)

Line-Up: Peter Burtz (vocals), Axel Rudi Pell (guitar), Thomas Eder (guitar), Volker Krawczak (bass), Jan Yildaral (drums)

STEELER emerged during a particularly golden period in the history of German Metal providing a worthy legacy of some finely crafted Metal albums and provide the launch pad for noted guitarist AXEL RUDI PELL. Formed in Bochum, STEELER had originally used the name SINNER, and the band was put together by guitarist Axel Rudi Pell and bassist Volker Krawczak.

Pell joined his first band at the age of 14 between 1974 and 1975 with whom he took his first tentative steps. The band, a school outfit called SILVER STONES, at least taught Pell the art of tuning a guitar, evolving into FIREBIRD. With the group splitting in 1976 Pell took a hiatus from music until joining a local act called MERCY and, subsequently, DEVIL'S DEATH, with whom he proceeded to play the regional school and club circuits.

Having formed STEELER with Krawczak, the duo recruited FALLEN ANGEL guitarist Thomas Eder and a drummer in Siggi Wiesemöller. The fledgling group recorded their first demo during 1982, utilising the services of vocalist Karl Holthaus, on loan from local act NEMO (although he had also been known to have fronted a group called GLADIATOR).

STEELER took the demos to SCORPIONS producer Dieter Dierks who chose not to pursue his original interest in the band, although the tape fell into the hands of ACCEPT who were having problems with Udo Dirkschneider at the time and were covertly auditioning possible replacements. ACCEPT auditioned Holthaus, but eventually settled their differences with Dirkschneider without the press getting wind of the original problem.

The band received a fair amount of interest from demo track 'Call Her Princess' being aired on Tony Jasper's Rock show on the British Forces Broadcasting Service (BFBS) radio station. STEELER then not only recruited a permanent singer in Thomas Eder's former FALLEN ANGEL band mate Peter Burtz, they also hooked up with the newly formed Earthshaker label for a two record deal, releasing the debut 'Steeler' album in 1984.

STEELER's first album, recorded in a mere eleven days and with new drummer Jan Yildiral, sold a respectable 9,000 copies, although a proposed tour with WARLOCK turned into a disaster, apparently due to problems with WARLOCK's manager and petty jealousy existing between the two groups.

The band's second album, 'Rulin' The Earth', took between 14 or 15 days and was laid down at Horus Sound in Hanover and would sell 18,000 copies as the group proceeded to play every "toilet" they could in a bid for greater recognition.

With the Earthshaker deal now over with STEELER signed to SPV, although legal problems with Earthshaker would persist for some time afterward especially concerning the payment of royalties. Having begun working on demo tapes of songs for the proposed third album STEELER parted company with Volker Krawczak. As the subject of the band's image had come up it had been decided that the unfortunate bassist, a portly chap, did not particularly fit into the scheme of things and the band felt it had no choice but to replace him. Krawczak would refuse to speak with his former colleagues for a good three years afterwards! Volker's place was taken by French bassist Herve Rossi, previously with ANTHRACITE and a friend of drummer Jan Yildiral. Whilst Rossi certainly fitted STEELER's concept on the image front, it was quickly discovered that he was rather lacking in any prowess as a musician. Rossi may have been hired for looking like the renowned bassist Nikki Sixx, but he didn't play a note on the third album, 1986's 'Strike Back', a guesting Tommy Newton from VICTORY doing the honours.

The album was produced by ELOY's Frank Bornemann, although Axel Rudi Pell claims the majority of the work was in effect carried out by Czech born engineer Jan Nimec. Ex-SCORPIONS guitarist ULI JON ROTH was in the same studio at the time and Pell took the opportunity of inviting him to play on a track that appeared on a 'Metal Hammer' compilation album at the time.

Having dispatched Rossi back to France, STEELER recruited ex-AXE VICTIMS rhythm guitarist Roland Hag as the band's new bass player and hit the road, managing to add some shows in Holland and Switzerland to the regular German commitments.

'Strike Back', benefiting from better material, improved musicianship and a polished production, picked up sales in the region of 33,000 and set the mood for the recording of fourth album 'Undercover Animal'.

Despite touring Germany with SAXON the 'Undercover Animal' only wound up selling 21,000 copies. It would be during the writing of songs for the planned fifth album that AXEL RUDI PELL decided to leave the group, disenchanted at the band's more pop chorus oriented direction, officially departing on November 11th 1988. The guitarist would go on to enjoy a considerable degree of commercial success in his own right.

STEELER opted to continue without Pell, hiring a guitarist from the Frankfurt area known as Vic and firing Jan Yildiral. The group recorded a three track demo and played a comeback show at Bochum's Zeche club, but split three or four months down the line.

Wheras Pell chose to pursue what turned out to be a very successful solo career (having teamed up with his old pal Volker Krawczak once more!), his former colleagues have engaged themselves in a variety of other careers. At one time Peter Burtz was the editor of German Metal magazine 'Metal Hammer' before taking the opportunity to work in the upper echelons of the EMI record label. Drummer Jan Yildiral now runs a travel agency, whilst Thomas Eder is working for a radio station reporting on events in the local courts.

Singles/EPs:
Night After Night / Waiting For A Star, Steamhammer 01-1884 (1986)
Undercover Animal, Steamhammer (1988)

Albums:
STEELER, Earthshaker ES 4001 (1984)
Chains Are Broken / Gonna Find Some Place In Hell / Heavy Metal Century / Sent From The Evil / Long Way / Call Her Princess / Love For Sale / Hydrophobia / Fallen Angel
RULIN' THE EARTH, Earthshaker ES 4009 (1985)
The Resolution / Ruling The Earth / Shellshock / Let The Blood Run Red / Heading For The End / Maniac / Run With The Pack / S.F.M. 1 / Turning Wheels
STRIKE BACK, Steamhammer SPV 08-1890 (1986)

Chain Gang / Money Doesn't Count / Danger Comeback / Icecold / Messing Around With Fire / Rockin' The City / Strike Back / Night After Night / Waiting For A Star
UNDERCOVER ANIMAL, Steamhammer SPV 08-7510 (1988)
(I'll Be) Hunter Or Hunted / Undercover Animal / Shadow In The Redlight / Hard Breaks / Criminal / Rely On Rock / Stand Tall / The Deeper The Night / Knock Me Out / Bad To The Bone

STEELER (USA)

Line-Up: Ron Keel (vocals), Yngwie Malmsteen (guitar), Rik Fox (bass), Mark Edwards (drums)

Originally hailing from Nashville, Tennessee, the Ron Keel fronted STEELER debuted with a self-financed single, 'Cold Day In Hell', and it was this track they contributed to the first pressing of Brian Slagel's first 'Metal Massacre' compilation (subsequent pressings found BLACK N' BLUE having replaced them). Keel had been born in Georgia but had moved to Phoenix, Arizona as a child before moving back to the East Coast to wind up in Nashville where he put STEELER together. The band that recorded the single comprised Keel, guitarist Michael Dunigan, bassist Tim Morrison and drummer Bobby Eva.

After moving to Los Angeles, STEELER signed to Shrapnel Records and label boss Mike Varney helped reshape the group by bringing in Swedish protege YNGWIE MALMSTEEN in place of original guitarist Dunigan; whilst the rhythm section was also replaced by bassist Rik Fox and drummer MARK EDWARDS. Fox had turned down an earlier offer from ANGEL to join the band.

Produced by Mike Varney, STEELER's debut album featured LE MANS vocalist Peter Marrino in a backing vocalist capacity. STEELER made significant waves on the international Rock scene with export copies in high demand. Although an unashamed showcase for Malmsteen the cohesive quality of the album would be one the Swede would struggle to attain in his future career.

The group would soon suffer the loss of Malmsteen to ALCATRAZZ and Rik Fox was to leave along with Edwards. MITCH PERRY, Greg Chaisson and Bobby Marks replaced them respectively before the group ultimately fragmented.

Following his departure from STEELER, Rik Fox helped to found W.A.S.P. with Blackie Lawless and later formed SIN before being ousted by his band mates who promptly renamed the group JAG WIRE. He then attempted to form a band with erstwhile ALIEN vocalist Frank Starr.

After the demise of STEELER, Ron Keel formed the Shrapnel backed KEEL, subsequently enjoying a sustained period in the limelight with that band as it moved onto major label success.

Bobby Marks was initially involved along with Greg Chaisson's bass playing brother Kenny and guitarists MARK FERRARI and David Michael-Phillips. Edwards skills would post STEELER be employed with RIOT, BURNING STARR and LION.

Chaisson was to find greater prominence in BADLANDS whilst Perry joined Australian Rockers HEAVEN before a stint with MICHAEL SCHENKER GROUP.

<u>Singles/EPs:</u>
Cold Day In Hell / Take Her Down, Ravage MAK011 (1982)

<u>Albums:</u>
STEELER, Shrapnel 1007 (1983)
Cold Day In Hell / Backseat Driver / No Way Out / Hot On Your Heels / Abduction / On The Rox / Down To The Wire / Born To Rock / Serenade

STEEL PROPHET (USA)
Line-Up: Rick Mythiasin (vocals), Steve Kachinsky-Blakmoor (guitar), John Pons (guitar), Vince Du Juan Dennis (bass), Pete Parada (drums)

The highly respected STEEL PROPHET deliver technically minded Progressive Heavy Metal. Previous to the release of the 1997 album STEEL PROPHET lost two members with guitarist Horacio Colmenares forging NEW EDEN. The album itself is assembled from numerous reworkings of earlier material including 'Passage Of Time (Amber Leaves)' from the band's 1987 demo and a cover of IRON MAIDEN's 'Purgatory'.

Guitarist Bernie Versye contributes to the song 'Hate'.

Recording bassist Vince Du Juan Dennis was loaned to PRONG for a nationwide tour. STEEL PROPHET were far from over however with vocalist Rick Mythiasin being admitted to drug rehabilitation centres twice during actual recording, the song 'Death Of Innocence' even missing a whole verse and chorus because Mythiasin was too sick to perform it. The bad luck continued as Du Juan Dennis was shot in the chest after the album's completion. The bassist survived.

During 1999 STEEL PROPHET cut their homage to JUDAS PRIEST with their take on 'Dream Deceiver' appearing on the 'Hell Bent For Metal' tribute album.

STEEL PROPHET's 2000 release 'Genesis'

brings together the band's 1989 'Inner Ascendance' demo together with various cover versions of tracks by JUDAS PRIEST, IRON MAIDEN, METALLICA, BLACK SABBATH and surprisingly SIMPLE MINDS!

STEEL PROPHET drafted new members Jim Williams on guitar and Karl Rosqvist on drums the same year replacing Kevin Cafferty and John Pons. Mythiasin would embark on a side project assembled by Tobias Exxel of German act EDGUY. This union, the 'Spirit Of Freedom' album, was released under the TARAXACUM banner in 2001. The singer would also session on the late 2001 REDEMPTION project assembled by guitarist Nick Van Dyk.

Rick Mythiasin made his exit from STEEL PROPHET to concentrate solely on TARAXACUM during July of 2002. However, by September, and despite Mythiasin breaking his leg in three places whilst trying to perform a handstand (!), Mythiasin had enrolled with NEW EDEN for their 'Stagnant Progression'.

<u>Albums:</u>
INTO THE VOID (HALLUCENIGENIC CONCEPTION), Art Of Music 70410 (1997)
The Revenant / Death Of Innocence / Trapped In The Trip / Your Failure Inscribed In Stone / Passage Of Time (Amber Leaves...) / Of The Dream / Ides Of March-Purgatory / What's Behind The Veils? / Idols / Hate
DARK HALLUCINATIONS, Nuclear Blast NB 350-2 (1999)
Montag / New Life / Strange Encounter / The Secret / We Are Not Alone / Betrayal / Look What You've Done / Scarred For Life / Spectres
MESSIAH, Nuclear Blast NB 436-2 (2000)
The Ides Of March / Messiah / Vengeance Attained / Mysteries Of Inequity / Dawn Of Man / Earth And Sky / Goddess Arise / Unseen / 07/03/47 / Rapture / Ghosts Once Past
GENESIS, Nuclear Blast NB 546-2 (2000)
Death / Sleep Of Despair / Inner Ascendance / Life / Nihilisms Spell / Technocricide / Fast As A Shark / Gangland / Ides Of March - Purgatory / Fade To Black / Dream Deceiver / Neon Knights / Don't You Forget About Me
BOOK OF THE DEAD, Nuclear Blast NB 558-2 (2001)
When Six Was Nine / Tragic Flaws / Escaped / Soleares / Church Of Mind / Burning Into Blackness / The Chamber / Locked Out / Ruby Dreams (Faith And Hope) / Phobia / Anger Seething / Oleander
UNSEEN, Nuclear Blast NB 1009-2 (2002)
Truth / Rainwalker / One Way Out /

Shattered Apart / Among The Damned / Bolero / Mirror, Mirror, Life After Life / Blackest Of Hearts / Martyred / Magenta / Killers Confession / Magenta Reprise

STEELTOWER (GERMANY)

Line-Up: Thomas Rettke (vocals), Ingo Millek (guitar), Bernd Kaufholz (guitar), Manfred Jordan (bass), Thorsten Müller (drums)

A powerful German Heavy Metal act. STEELTOWER would evolve into HEAVENS GATE.

<u>Albums:</u>
NIGHT OF THE DOG, Mausoleum ES 4005 (1985)
Intro / Night Of The Dog / Hell And Fire / Save My Life / Angel's Devil / Gotta Believe No Angel / Break The Law / Powerdrive / Bring Up The Night / Devil's Dreamer

STEEL VENGEANCE (MI, USA)

Line-Up: Scott Carlson (vocals), Bob
— Lindstrom (guitar), Michael Wickstrom (guitar / keyboards), Steve Cavalier (bass), Andy Anderson (drums)

This semi-legendary cult Metal band have undergone more than a few line-up changes over the years. By the time the group recorded their 'Call Off The Dogs' debut album for the French Black Dragon label original vocalist Rock Rothweiler, guitarist Jay Carr and bassist Jeff Way had all quit from the line-up that had recorded a three track EP in 1984. STEEL VENGEANCE issued a demo tape earlier the same year which included drummer Carl Elliot.

Carr's replacement, Bob Lindstrom, was replaced himself by Tracy Kerbuski for the 'Prisoners' album, which also saw the arrival of Tom Vileho on drums in place of Andy Anderson.

In early 1987 the group were reported to have recruited a 14 year old drummer in the form of Tim Gilderloos.

The fourth album, 1989's 'Never Lettin' Go', found new vocalist Scott Nocon fronting STEEL VENGEANCE who also boasted a new guitarist in Glenn Rogers and a brand new rhythm section comprising bassist Killer Cerogatti and drummer John Draper. Guitarist / keyboardist Michael Wickstrom was thus the only original member of the band.

However, 1991's 'Live: Among The Dead' found Jason Saige on vocals on a recording of performances captured at shows in Ventura and San Diego during 1990.

<u>Singles/EPs:</u>

Your Time Has Come / Back Street Girl / Black Leather, Kingdom (1984)

<u>Albums:</u>
CALL OFF THE DOGS, Black Dragon (1985)
Night Turns To Day / Dreams Come True / Time To Live, Time To Die / Devil's Lair / 3 O' Clock In The Morning / Victim Of Love / Midnight Machine / Queen Of The Night / Will Not Be Defeated / Our Love Was Yesterday
SECOND OFFENSE, Black Dragon BD 017 (1986)
Beware The Wizard / She Moves In The Night / Eyes That Cannot See / Useless Information / Breakin' Away / Open The Door / Don't Waste It On Me / Pleasure With Pain / Just One More Time / Dead Or Alive
PRISONERS, Black Dragon BD028 (1988)
Burned Out / Destroy / Streets Of Gold / She'll Never Tell / Under World / Prisoners / Run From The Law / Till Tomorrow / Vengeance Is Mine / Can't Stop The Rain
NEVER LETTIN' GO, Black Dragon (1989)
Epitaph / Beware The Wizard / Hard Man / She's Back / Never Lettin' Go / Victim Of Sin / Sing It Out / Your Time Has Come / I Surrender
LIVE: AMONG THE DEAD, Black Dragon (1991)
Pariah / Standing Alone / Nightfall / In For The Kill / Our Love Was Yesterday / Go To Hell From School / Scarred / No More / Mind Over Matter / Never Lettin' Go / Time To Live, Time To Die / Stalemate / I Bring You Lies / Right Side Of The Track

STEEL WARRIOR (BRAZIL)

Line-Up: André Fabian Mees Tulipano (vocals / guitar), Boon Yu (guitar), Anderson Agostinho (bass), Paulo Cesar Winter (keyboards), Culver Yu Sit Lim (drums)

Heavy Metal band STEEL WARRIOR is led by the former NOSFERATU and HERAGE singer André Fabian Mees Tulipano and includes the Hong Kong natives Boon You Sim on guitar and Culver Yu Sit Lim on drums. STEEL WARRIOR came into being during 1996, initially as a trio of André Fabian Mees Tulipano, Culver Yu Sit Lim and bassist Anderson Xavier. Robert Nietsche was added on second guitar but following recording of a two track demo Pedro Giovani took on this role.

STEEL WARRIOR gained a valuable support slot to GAMMA RAY just prior to recording of their Murillo da Rós produced debut album 'Visions From The Mistland'. However, shortly after completion Xavier bowed out and another erstwhile HERAGE man, Anderson Agostinho, became the band's new bassist.

Albums:
VISIONS FROM THE MISTLAND, (1999)
The First Vision / Son Of An Eagle / Revenge / Garden Of Souls / Crossing The Mist / Steel Warrior / Rasolam / Wind Of Sorrow / Blind Faith / Twilight Hills
ARMY OF THE TIME, (2002)
Beyond The Twilight Hills / Army Of The Time / Guardians Of The Desert Sea / Spell Of Witches World / Power Metal / Divine Wind Of Sho / The First Warrior / When We Were Kings / Your Majesty's Return / Farewell Ride

STONE (FINLAND)
Line-Up: Janne Joutsenniemi (vocals / bass), Roope Latvala (guitar), Nirri (guitar), Pekka Kasari (drums)

Highly successful in their native Finland STONE scored a number one hit with their 'Back To The Stoneage' EP in 1988 and were picked up by the MCA affiliated Mechanic Records for the release of a self-titled debut album in territories outside Finland. Indeed, with backing from the label STONE toured America as support to TESTAMENT before returning home and adding ex-AIRDASH guitarist Nirri in 1990.
1992 the MCA deal was history and the 'Emotional Playground' album found the Finns signed to Black Mark, with a live album released the following year.
Although nothing has appeared to have been heard from STONE since, drummer Pekka Kasari joined AMORPHIS for their 1996 album 'Elegy'. The rising stars of Finnish Metal CHILDREN OF BODOM covered the STONE track 'In Command' for inclusion on their no. 1 single 'Downfall' in 1999.

Singles/EPs:
Back To The Stone Age EP, (1988)

Albums:
STONE, Mechanic MCA 42175 (1988)
Get Stoned / No Commands / Eat Your Pride / The Day Of Death / Reached Out / Real Delusion / Brain Damage / Escape / Final Countdown / Overtake
NO ANASTHESIA, Megamania (1988)
Sweet Dreams / Empty Corner / Back To The Stone Age / Concrete Malformation / No Anaesthesia / Light Entertainment / Kill The Dead / Meat Mincing Machine
NO ANASTEHESIA, Megamania (1988) (Japanese release)
Sweet Dreams / Empty Corner / Back To The

Stone Age / Concrete Malformation / No Anaesthesia / Light Entertainment / Kill The Dead / Meat Mincing Machine / Get Stoned / No Commands / Eat Your Pride / The Day Of Death / Reached Out / Escape / Final Countdown
EMOTIONAL PLAYGROUND, Black Mark BMCD13 (1992)
Small Tales / Home Bass / Last Chance / Above The Grey Sky / Mad Hatter's Den / Dead End / Adrift / Haven / Years After / Time Dive / Missionary Of Charity / Emotional Playground
FREE-LIVE, Black Mark BMCD 38 (1993)
Get Around / Empty Corner / Small Tales / Mad Hatter's Den / Sweet Dreams / Above The Grey Sky / Real Delusion / The Day Of Death / Last Chance / White Worms / Haven / Emotional Playground / No Commands / Missionary Of Charity / Overtake / Vengeance Of The Ghostrider

STORMHAMMER (GERMANY)
Line-Up: Tommy Lion (vocals), Al (guitar), Maniac (guitar), Horst (bass), Markus (keyboards), Django (drums)

STORMHAMMER are fronted by Tommy Lion, former lead vocalist for Swiss act DRIFTER and featuring on both that act's 1987 'Reality Turns To Dust' and follow up 'Nowhere To Hide' albums.
The band started life billed as LIZARD, not to be confused with the other German Southern Rock flavoured act of the same name. The group subsequently shifted to STEAMHAMMER but once more encountered confusion with the '70s band. Finally, the more Metal STORMHAMMER was decided upon.
Following recording of the 2001 opus 'Cold Desert Moon' keyboard player Markus bowed out.
The band would spend much of 2002 working on a new album 'Cyber Mortis' although sessions were delayed as bad luck struck the band with bassist Horst breaking his hand.

Albums:
FIREBALL, (2000)
Seven Gates / Prisoner / High On Devotion / Guardians / Destiny / Holy War / Possibilities / Sacred Heart / Forever / FireBall / Shadow Dancer
COLD DESERT MOON, (2001)
Sinner's Soul / The Law / Breach Of Faith / Yells Of Rage / Misty Hills / Children Of The Dawn / Doomsday / Cold Desert Moon / A Dragon's Tear / Nobody's Child / Masquerade Of Life / The Strength Of Wisdom

STORMHUNTER (GERMANY)

Line-Up: Dietmar Bosler (vocals), Timo Sattler (guitar), Stefan Müller (guitar), Johannes Wehrmann (drums)

Newcomers on the Power Metal scene, STORMHUNTER have already undergone turbulent times in their short history. The band gathered their forces in January of 1998 brandishing an initial line-up of vocalist Dennis Helm, guitarists Achim Heinzelmann and Stefan Müller with drummer Ralf Ziegler. By the following year Helm had departed, being replaced by Detlef Förster. 'Evil Avenger' supplanted Heinzelmann in January of 2001, the new line-up debuting with the four track demo 'First Battle' in June.

Further ructions saw the departure of both Detlef Förster and Evil Avenger. As the band had their track 'Knights Of Metal' included on the compilation album 'The Reaper Comes' new personnel vocalist Dietmar Bosler and guitarist Timo Sattler made up the numbers once again in April of 2002. However, later that same month founder member drummer Ralf Ziegler packed his bags. He would be replaced by Johannes Wehrmann.

In September of 2002 Bosler also decamped.

STORMWARRIOR (GERMANY)

Line-Up: Thunder Axe (vocals / guitar), Scythewielder (guitar), Hammerlord (bass), Evil Steel (drums)

Northern German renaissance Heavy Metal band. Assembled by vocalist / guitar 'Thunder Axe' (Lars Ramcke) and drummer 'Evil Steel' (Andrè Schumann) the band was quickly brought up to strength with the addition of guitarist 'Scythewielder' (Scott Bölter) and bass player Tim Zienert. This formation conceived the 1999 demo tape 'Metal Victory'.

A second session 'Barbaric Steel' followed prompting live appearances at such events as the 'Headbangers Open Air' and 'Warriors Of Steel' festivals. In 2001 two STORMWARRIOR tracks were released as a limited edition EP 'Possessed By Metal' by the Italian Dream Evil label Shortly after though Zienery decamped, being substituted by 'Hammerlord' (Gabriel Palermo). Signing to Hamburg's Remedy label STORMWARRIOR issued a further 7" picture disc single 'Spikes & Leather' in 2002.

The eponymous debut album would benefit from production handled courtesy of GAMMA RAY's Kai Hansen and Dirk Schlächter. Besides their work behind the desk the pair would step up for guest spots too, Hansen featuring on both 'Chains Of Slavery' & 'Heavy Metal (Is The Law)' whilst Schlächter graced

'Deathe By The Blade' with a guitar solo. HELLOWEEN bassist Markus Großkopf got in on the action too, laying down distinctive chords on 'Heavy Metal (Is The Law)'.

STORMWARRIOR performed at the 'Wacken Open Air' event that same year.

Singles/EPs:
Heavy Metal Fire / Defenders Of Metal, Dream Evil (2001) ('Possessed By Metal' EP)
Spikes & Leather, Remedy (2002)

Albums:
STORMWARRIOR, Remedy (2002)
The Hammer Returneth (Intro) / Signe Of The Warlorde / Sons Of Steele / Bounde By The Oathe / Deceiver / The Axewielder / Deathe By The Blade / Thunderer / Iron Prayers / Defenders Of Metal / Chains Of Slavery / Heavy Metal (Is The Law)

STORMWIND (GERMANY)

Line-Up: Klaus Lemm (vocals), Niko Böhm (guitar), Wolla Böhm (guitar), Rudy Kay (bass), Olly Kliem (drums)

Singles/EPs:
Warbringer / Hot Love / Iron Rock, Wishbone WB1512 (1985)

Albums:
TAKEN BY STORM, Wishbone (1984)
Hard Sins / Chaos / The Next Could Be You / Striker / Thunder & Lightning / Evil's Child / She-Devil / Fairy Of Dreams / Breaker / Warlord

STORMWIND (SWEDEN)

Line-Up: Thomas Vikström (vocals), Thomas Wolf (guitar). Andreas Olsson (bass), Kasper Dahlberg (keyboards), Patrik Johansson (drums)

STORMWIND is the neo-Classical Symphonic Rock venture of guitarist Thomas Wolf. As well as having credits with earlier bands such as FIREBIRDS, DEMONS and BLACK VELVET Wolf was also the national Swedish Karate champion in 1993! STORMWIND debuted in April of 1995 with a demo.

Ex-EUROPE man Ian Haughland and vocalist Anna Norberg guest on the 1998 'Stargate' album. The same year Wolf would put in appearances on tribute albums to both YNGWIE MALMSTEEN and COZY POWELL.

The band's third album 'Heaven Can Wait' sees guitarist Thomas Wolf joined by CANDLEMASS, TALK OF THE TOWN and BRAZEN ABBOTT vocalist Thomas Vikström,

TREASURE LAND keyboard player Kaspar Dahlberg, bassist Andreas Olsson (from EUROPE cover band SEVENTH SIGN) and WITHOUT GRIEF drummer Patrik Johansson. The latter would join YNGWIE MALMSTEEN's band for South American dates in September 2001.

The STORMWIND duo of bass guitarist Andreas Olsson and keyboard player Per Hallman would unite with NARNIA members vocalist Christian Liljegren and drummer Andreas Johansson to forge the WISDOM CALL project band for a 2001 eponymous album released by Massacre Records.

Wolf would put in a showing on the 2001 JASON BECKER tribute with a rendition of DAVID LEE ROTH's 'A Little Ain't Enough'. This track would re-surface as a bonus cut on Japanese versions of STORMWIND's 'Reflections' album.

Albums:

STRAIGHT FROM YOUR HEART, (199-)
Love Bites / Gimme, Gimme, Gimme / Wings Of Tomorrow / A Lesson Of Love / Shadow Of The Past / Crusade Of Rock / Straight From Your Heart / Way Of Love / In Your Eyes / Nightfall

STARGATE, Dreamchaser (1998)
Pegasus / Hit By The Sun / Masquerade Of Love / Aliens / Time Won't Tell / Sakura Opus / Stargate / Cry For Your Love / Beyond Lies / Tears Of Confession / Drive My Way Home / Miramar

HEAVEN CAN WAIT, Dreamchaser (1999)
Shang Ri-La / Eye Of The Storm / She / Heaven Can Wait / Mountain Of Zion / Magic Night / Forever Free / Marco Polo / Ashes In Your Hands / Caelum Exspectare Potest

RESURRECTION, Massacre MAS CD0250 (2000)
Phoenix Rising / Ship Of Salvation / Soul Dance / Seven Seas / Passion / Blinded Eyes / Synphonia Millenialis / Samurai / Holy Land

REFLECTIONS, (2001)
Genesis / War Of Troy / The Man Behind The Iron Mask / Reflections / Illusion / Golden Tears / Queen For Nine Days / Dynasty / Assassin Of Honour / Ramses / Venezia / A Little Ain't Enough

STORMWITCH (GERMANY)

Line-Up: Andy Mück (vocals), Harold 'Lee Tarot' Spengler (guitar), Stefan 'Steve Merchant' Kauffmann (guitar), Ronny 'Ronny Pearson' Gleisberg (bass), Peter

Now considered to be something of a classic German Metal band, having influenced late '90s outfits like HAMMERFALL in their wake,

vocalist Andreas 'Aldrian' Mück, guitarist Harold Spengler and Stefan Kauffmann first played together in 1979 as the band LEMON SYLVAN.

Releasing a four track demo, 'The Cave Of Steenfall', in 1983 the group added drummer Peter Langer and bassist Thomas Gleisburg in 1984 as the transition was made to STORMWITCH. The group released their debut album, 'Walpurgis Night', through Scratch in 1984 and followed it up with the sophomore effort 'Tales Of Terror'. A third album, 'Stronger Than Heaven', arrived in 1986.

In order to push 1988's 'The Beauty And The Beast' album STORMWITCH hit the road supporting RISK and RUNNING WILD before adding guitarist Wolfgang Schuldi to the ranks in 1989.

Andy Hunter replaced Ronny Gleisberg for 1989's 'Eye Of The Storm' album before former ROUGH man Martin Albrecht took over on bass in 1990 and STORMWITCH played with BONFIRE in Czechoslovakia before a German tour with KROKUS.

In 1992 the group released the 'War Of The Wizards' album with two new guitarists; namely Damir Uzunovic and ex-LETTER X man Joe Gassmann, although only the former would play on the swan song 'Shogun' album in 1994. Another former guitarist, Robert Balci, would subsequently forge Power Metal band DEFENDING THE FAITH in January of 1998.

Although having split up in 1996, STORMWITCH, as mentioned, are still prominent due to the adulation afforded them by the all conquering Swedish trad Metal revivalists HAMMERFALL. The Scandinavians regularly cover STORMWITCH tracks live and included their version of 'Ravenlord' as the B side to their 'Glory To The Brave' single. Indeed. Mück made a guest appearance with the band when they played at the 'Heavy Oder Was?' organised 'Bang Your Head II' festival in September 1997.

A STORMWITCH compilation album, 'Priest Of Evil', was due to be released through B.O. Records in 1998.

Spengler co-produced the 1998 BRAINSTORM album 'Unholy'. Erstwhile STORMWITCH men drummer Peter Langer and guitarist Damir Uzunovic would unite with former AGENT ORANGE bassist Matthias Mailänder, keyboard player Mathias Nagl and RITUAL SPIRIT lead vocalist Dirk Schaeffner to forge THE ARMADA.

STORMWITCH would be back in 2002, releasing a brand new studio album 'Dance Of The Witches' on the Silverdust label. This outing boasted a completely overhauled line up. Featured guitarists would be Martin Winkler of NIGHTWOLF and Fabian Schwarz from TYRAN PACE and RITUAL SPIRIT. The rest of the band comprised FALLEN 2 PIECES bass player Dominik Schwarz, TYRAN PACE keyboard player Alex Schmidt and drummer Marc Oppold, the latter having credits with SATAN'S CRYPT, TYRANT and DEATH IN ACTION.

Albums:
WALPURGIS NIGHT, Scratch 95008 (1984)
Cave Of Steenfall / Priest Of Evil / Skull And Crossbones / Werewolves On The Hunt / Walpurgis Night / Flower In The Wind / Warlord / Excalibur / Thunderland
TALES OF TERROR, Scratch (1985)
Intro / Point Of No Return / Hell's Still Alive / Masque Of The Red Death / Arabian Nights / Intro / Sword Of Sagon / Trust In The Fire / Nightstalker / Lost Legions / When The Bat Bites
STRONGER THAN HEAVEN, Scratch 941312 (1986)
Intro / Rats In The Attic / Eternia / Jonathon's Diary / Slave To Moonlight / Stronger Than Heaven / Ravenlord / Allies Of The Dark / Dorian Grey
THE BEAUTY AND THE BEAST, Scratch 805 528-928 (1988)
Call Of The Wicked / Beauty And The Beast / Just For One Night / Emerald Eye / Tears By The Firelight / Tigers Of The Sea / Russia's On Fire / Cheyenne / Where The Eagles Retreat / Welcome To Bedlam
EYE OF THE STORM, Hot Blood (1989)
Paradise / Heart Of Ice / I Want You Around / King In The Ring / Tarred And Feathered / Eye Of The Storm / Another World Apart / Steel In The Red Light / Rondo Ain Turca / Take Me Home
MAGYAROR SZAGON (LIVE), T-34 (1989)
(Hungarian release)
Intro / Call Of The Wicked / Emerald Eye / Stronger Than Heaven / Tigers Of The Sea / Dorian Gray / Guitar solo / Russia's On Fire / Trust In The Fire / Cheyenne (Where The Eagles Retreat) / Walpurgis Night
THE BEST OF STORMWITCH, Scratch 54064 (1992)
The Beauty And The Beast / Welcome To Bedlam / Emerald Eye / Tears By The Firelight / Stronger Than Heaven / Point Of No Return / Walpurgis Night (Live) / Rats In The Attic / King In The Ring / Paradise / Eye Of The Storm
WAR OF THE WIZARDS, SPV Steamhammer SPV 084-76532 (1993)
Listen To The Stories / Theja / Magic Mirror / Wooden Drum / War Of The Wizards / Dragon's Day / Time / Fate's On The Rise / A Promise Of Old / The Way To Go / Wanderer

SHOGUN, Steamhammer SPV 084-76842 (1994)
Stranded / Liar / Garden Of Pain / Seven Fares (And Two Hearts) / Forbidden / Victory Is Mine / Let Lessons Begin / The King Of Minos / She's The Sun / Good Times - Bad Times / I'll Never Forget / Somewhere
PRIEST OF EVIL, Bossy Ogress BO 004 (1998)
Intro - Rats In The Attic / Hell's Still Alive / Stronger Than Heaven / Trust In The Fire / Priest Of Evil / Masque Of The Red Death / Jonathon's Diary / Intro- Sword Of Sagon / Ravenlord / Skull And Crossbones / Arabian Nights / Dorian Gray / Intro - No Point Of Return / Eternia / Walpurgis Night (Live)
DANCE WITH THE WITCHES, Silverdust (2002)
Intro - Men Of Miracles / Dance With The Witches / Jeanne D`Arc / The Knights Of Lights / The Devil`s Bride / Nothing More / The House Of Usher / The King Of Terrors / Proud And Honest / My World / The Altar Of Love / Together

THE STORYTELLER (SWEDEN)
Line-Up: L.G. Persson (vocals / bass), Erin Gornostajev (guitar), Fredrik Groth (guitars / keyboards), Martin Hjerpe (drums)

THE STORYTELLER started life as an acoustic liaison between vocalist L.G. Persson and guitarist Fredrik Groth in late 1995. This unit was augmented by vocalist Magnus Björk and guitarist Jocke Lundström for recording of a three track demo session. At this juncture the band was going under the title of STORYTELLER. (They became THE STORYTELLER) in 2000).

In mid 1996 Groth departed and was duly replaced by Per Nilsson. Internal manoeuvring would see Lundström switching to the drum role. This revised unit cut a fresh demo but dissatisfied with STORYTELLER's musical direction Persson put the band on ice for a term.

However, by December 1997 Persson and Groth re-forged links to have another stab at STORYTELLER. Enlisted on the drum stool would be Martin Hjerpe. A radical shift in direction also witnessed the acoustic bent of previous material ditched in favour of Germanic inspired Power Metal.

Anders Östlin enrolled as bassist and in April of 1998 a further demo CDR led to a strong interest from the established German Noise label. It was not to be plain sailing though. Although Noise liked the music they expressed the opinion that STORYTELLER required a new vocalist. The band stuck to their guns and recorded another two tracks retaining Persson on lead vocals. This effort saw a further rebuttal from Noise and the band was forced into a re-think on their strategy.

Persson took to the bass role and Anders Östlin became a keyboard player. A few months later he left the band.

STORYTELLER auditioned numerous potential lead vocalists and this search would find a new band member when Lasse Martinsen turned out to be a better guitarist than a vocalist. Unable to locate a front man STORYTELLER re-instated Persson into the role.

Mid 1999 brought forth a record deal with the No Fashion concern.

Shortly after recording the debut eponymous album at Studio Fredman in Gothenburg Martinsen was replaced by Erik Gornostajev. The record arrived on the racks in May of 2000. Japanese editions, as in keeping with tradition, boasted an extra exclusive track namely a demo version of 'Chant Of The Thieves' dating back to 1995.

Promoting the album with live work THE STORYTELLER was fortunate at one October gig to have both Oskar Dronjac and Joacim Cans of HAMMERFALL guest onstage with an impromptu jam of MANOWAR's 'Black Wind, Fire And Steel'!

Two weeks before commencement of recording for a second album Erik Gornostajev quit. Pärka Kankanranta came in for the album sessions but after a mere brace of gigs he too was gone.

During August of 2001 Jacob Wennerqvist took on guitar duties. The band's second album 'Crossroad' would be issued in Japan, complete with a bonus recording of IRON MAIDEN's 'Moonchild', during December.

Albums:
THE STORYTELLER, No Fashion NFR044 (2000)
And The Legend Begins / Guardians Of Kail / Always Be There / Sense Of Steel / Power Within / Book Of Mystery / Like A Wind / A Test Of Endurance And Strength / Chant Of The Thieves / The Storyteller
CROSSROAD, No Fashion NFR056 (2001)
And The Legend Continues / The Unknown / The Secret's Revealed / Eye Of The Storm / A Passage Through Mountain / Ambush / Loss Of A Friend / Crossroad / Kingdom Above / The Moment Of Truth

STRAMONIO (ITALY)
Line-Up: Federico De Vescovi (vocals), Nicola Balliana (guitar), Cristiano Zanvettor (bass), Luca De Lazzaro (keyboards), Roberto De Cesero (drums)

Initially known as TRILOGY SUITE upon their formation in 1992 and comprising vocalist Federico De Vescovi, guitarist Nicola Balliana, bass player Andrea Bellantoni, Luca De Lazzaro on the keyboards and Francesco Anselmi on drums.

Some appearances on local compilation albums led to the debut demo session 'When Body Dies Soul Lives'. After these recording TRILOGY SUITE parted ways with their rhythm section which put the band on hold for nearly a year. Finally the induction of drummer Roberto De Cesero and bassist Cristiano Zanvettor signalled a return to action and a name switch to STRAMONIO. The group would also draft Luca Arrighini on second guitar.

A demo, 'Awake The Jester' scored valuable positive media coverage and a contract with the Northwind label. In April of 1999 STRAMONIO set about recording debut album 'Season Of Imagination'. The follow up, 'Mother Invention', arrived via the Italian Frontiers label in July of 2002.

Albums:
SEASON OF IMAGINATION, Northwind (2000)
Awake The Jester / Ashes In The Wind / I Swim In The Air / Get Lost In Time / Without You / The Song Of The Harvest Fly / Vital Elation
MOTHER INVENTION, Frontiers (2002)
Desert Night / Appointment With Life / Snow Crystal / In My Eyes / Loose From A Dam / Antarctic Oasis / Here I Am / Time / Someone Like Me

STRATOVARIUS (FINLAND)
Line-Up: Timo Kotipelti (vocals), Timo Tolkki (guitar), Jaru Kainulainen (bass), Antti Ikonen (keyboards), Tuomo Lassila (drums)

Undeniably led by guitarist Timo Tolkki STRATOVARIUS, the undisputed kings of Finnish Hard Rock, originally formed as far back as 1979. Their grandiose style of elaborately polished Metal has not only brought enormous rewards internationally for the Finns but has inspired a whole new genre of Rock Music known as Symphonic Metal.

The first incarnation of the group included Staffan Strählmann on guitar and drummer Tuomo Lassila and the group, a four piece at first. Strählmann was replaced by Timo Tolkki, previously with ROADBLOCK, in 1983. STRATOVARIUS would sign to CBS Records in the late '80s and debut with 'Fright Night' during 1989.

The group found themselves dropped after 'Fright Night' flopped and also had to replace

STRATOVARIUS

bassist Jyrki Lentonen with Jari Behm. A new deal was negotiated with Shark Records for 1993's 'Twilight Time'. But Noise Records were quick to move in to sign the Finns for 1994's 'Dream Space', although the album marked the debut of yet another bassist - Jari Kainulainen having joined the group prior to recording.

At this point Timo Tolkki decided to concentrate solely on guitar playing, necessitating the recruitment of vocalist TIMO KOTIPELTI to the fold for 1995's 'The Fourth Dimension'.

Following a European tour with label mates ENOLA GAY keyboard player Antti Ikonen and drummer Tuomo Lassila both quit. In order to record the 'Episode' album ex-YNGWIE MALMSTEEN and DIO keyboardist Jens Johansson and drummer Jörg Michael were added. Michael's credits read like a who's who of German Metal having racked up credits with AVENGER, RAGE, MEKONG DELTA, HEADHUNTER, LAOS, GRAVE DIGGER, AXEL RUDI PELL and RUNNING WILD amongst others.

A proposed tour in 1996 with VIRGIN STEELE to coincide with the new album's release was cancelled after the American band's vocalist David DeFeis was injured in a car accident. In the autumn STRATOVARIUS

hit the road with RAGE before preparing to lay down the new 'Visions' record, again enlisting Jens Johansson and Jörg Michael.

A 1998 live album 'Visions Of Europe' followed.

1998's studio record 'Destiny' gave STRATOVARIUS a prestigious number one in their homeland and opened up a whole new international market to the band.

As STRATOVARIUS switched labels to Nuclear Blast previous label Noise issued an obligatory "best of" titled 'The Chosen Ones' that included tracks previously only available in Japan.

2000 found Michael sessioning for HOUSE OF SPIRITS on their 'Psychosphere' album. Jari Kainulainen too would be employed on outside activities, guesting on the WARMEN 'Unknown Soldier' opus.

Tolkki released a solo album ('Classical Variations And Themes') through Shark in 1994 and made a guest appearance on the 1998 EDGUY album 'Vain Glory Opera'. Tolkki also busies himself with production handling the 1997 album from fellow Finns THE 69 EYES amongst others.

The band announced a period of self-imposed exile during 2001 predicting a new studio album for 2003. In the interim Nuclear Blast would issue the 'Intermission' collection which combined foreign rarities with cover versions of JUDAS PRIEST's 'Bloodstone' and RAINBOW's 'I Surrender' and 'Kill The King', the latter with lead vocals by Timo Tolkki.

TIMO KOTIPELTI would record his debut solo album 'Waiting For The Dawn' for the Century Media label. A conceptual piece rooted in Egyptian mythology it would prove a much harder edged affair than expected.

Singles/EPs:

The Kiss Of Judas / Black Diamond / The Kiss Of Judas (demo) / Uncertainty (Live) / Fourth Reich (Live), T&T TT 0031-3 (1997) (German promotional release)

Black Diamond / The Kiss Of Judas / The Kiss Of Judas (demo) / We Hold The Key (Live) / Fourth Reich (Live), Victor 97 3 21 (1997) (Japanese release)

Hunting High And Low / Millennium / Neon Light Child / Hunting High And Low (Demo version) / Millennium (Demo version), Nuclear Blast (2000)

A Million Light Years Away / Celestial Dream / Phoenix / Infinity / A Million Light Years Away (Video), Nuclear Blast NB 569-2 (2000)

Albums:

FRIGHT NIGHT, CBS 4634161 (1989)
Future Shock / False Messiah / Black Night / Witch-Hunt / Fire Dance / Fright Night / Night Screamer / Darkness / Goodbye

TWILIGHT TIME, Shark 033 (1993)
Break The Ice / The Hands Of Time / Madness Strikes At Midnight / Metal Frenzy / Twilight Time / The Hills Have Eyes / Out Of The Shadows / Lead Us Into The Light

DREAMSPACE, Noise T&T 008-2 (1994)
Chasing Shadows / 4th Reich / Eyes Of The World/ Hold On To Your Dreams / Magic Carpet Ride / We Are The Future / Tears Of Ice / Dreamspace / Reign Of Terror / Thin Ice / Atlantis / Abyss / Shattered / Wings Of Tomorrow / Full Moon

THE FOURTH DIMENSION, Noise T&T 0014-2 (1995)
Against The Wind / Distant Skies / Galaxies / Winter / Stratovarius / Lord Of All Wasteland / 030366 / Nightfall / We Hold The Key / Twilight Symphony / Call Of The Wilderness

EPISODE, T&T TT0014-2 (1996)
Father Time / Will The Sun Rise? / Eternity / Episode / Speed Of Light / Uncertainty / Seasons Of Change / Strasphere / Babylon / Tomorrow / Night Time Eclipse / Forever

VISIONS, T&T TT 0031-2 (1997)
The Kiss Of Judas / Black Diamond /

STRATOVARIUS
Photo : Nico Wobben

Forever Free / Before The Winter / Legions /
The Abyss Of Your Eyes / Holy Light /
Paradise / Coming Home / Visions -
Southern Cross
VISIONS OF EUROPE: LIVE, T&T TT0038-
2 (1998)
Forever Free / Kiss Of Judas / Father Time /
Distant Skies / Season Of Change / Speed
Of Light / Twilight Symphony / Holy Solos /
Visions / Will The Sun Rise? / Forever /
Black Diamond / Against The Wind /
Paradise / Legions
DESTINY, T&T TT0040-2 (1998)
Destiny / S.O.S. / No Turning Back / 4000
Rainy Nights / Rebel / Years Go By / Playing
With Fire / Venus In The Morning / Anthem
Of The World / Cold Winter Nights
THE CHOSEN ONES, Noise (1999)
Black Diamond / Twilight Time / Father Time
/ The Hands Of Time / Dream With Me /
Paradise / Out Of The Shadows / Forever /
Full Moon / The Kiss Of Judas / S.O.S. /
Dreamspace / Against The Wind / Speed Of
Light / 4000 Rainy Nights / Will The Sun
Rise?
14 DIAMONDS, JVC Victor (2000)
(Japanese release)
The Hands Of Time / Distant Skies /
Tomorrow / Coming Home / Destiny / Future
Shock / Black Diamond / Why Are We Here?
/ We Are The Future / Forever / Hunting High
And Low / The Kiss Of Judas / Rebel /
Mother Gaia
INFINITE, Nuclear Blast 27361 64642
(2000) **1 FINLAND, 28 GERMANY,
34 ITALY, 71 POLAND, 63 SWEDEN**
Hunting High And Low / Millennium / Mother
Gaia / Phoenix / Glory Of The World / A
Million Light Years Away / Freedom / Infinity /
Celestial Dreams
INTERMISSION, Nuclear Blast (2001)
**9 FINLAND, 91 FRANCE, 73 GERMANY,
85 SWITZERLAND**
Will My Soul Ever Rest In Peace? / Falling
Into Fantasy / The Curtains Are Falling /
Requiem / Requiem / Kill The King / I
Surrender (Live) / Keep The Flame / Why
Are We Here? / What Can I Say / Dream
With Me / When The Night Meets The Day /
It's A Mystery / Cold Winter Nights / Hunting
High & Low (Live)

SUN CAGED (HOLLAND)
Line-Up: Andre Vuurboom (vocals), Marcel
Coenen (guitar), Rob van der Loo (bass),
Joest van der Broek (keyboards), Dennis
Leeflang (drums)

SUN CAGED is an adventurous Progressive
Metal band that features no less than four
current members of TIME MACHINE in
guitarist Marcel Coenen, bass player Rob van

der Loo, keyboard player Joest van der Broek
and drummer Dennis Leeflang. The latter also
cites previous membership with premier
Doom act WITHIN TEMPTATION as well as
NEMESIS and TREASON. Coenen was
previously a member of ProgRock act
LEMUR VOICE. Van der Loo's prior tenures
number AGONY, ANGUISH and
SOULCATCHER.
SUN CAGED came together in the Spring of
1999, issuing the 2000 'Scar Winter' demo
before enlisting van der Broek and vocalist
Sascha Burchardt. The 'Dominion' EP arrived
in October of 2001. SUN CAGED replaced
Burchardt with Andre Vuurboom of
IMPERIUM and VERA in May of 2002.

Singles/EPs:
Curiosity Kills / Four Guilders / Sides / The
Escape, (2001) ('Dominion' EP)

SUPERIOR (GERMANY)
Line-Up: Michael Tangermann (vocals),
Bernd Basmer (guitar), Michael Müller
(guitar / keyboards), Martin Reichhart (bass),
Jan-Marco Becker (keyboards), Thomas
Mayer (drums)

A Kaiserlautern based Progressive Metal act
that came onto the scene buoyed by the
impact of their first impressive demo;
SUPERIOR scored the distinction of playing
alongside BON JOVI, LITA FORD and
CRAAFT at a benefit concert during 1989.
Following the debut album release,
SUPERIOR toured Germany extensively as
guests of VIRGIN STEELE and ANGRA, after
the original openers KAMELOT were forced
to pull out. SUPERIOR's luck did not hold
however, as after a handful of shows
keyboard player Jan-Marco Becker broke his
hand.
Still, SUPERIOR have built up a sizeable
following in France on the strength of the
debut 'Behind' album.

Albums:
BEHIND, T&T TT0026-2 (1996)
The Truth Ain't Kind / Why / Dial 911 /
Tomorrow's Eve / Hades / Escape From
Reality / Dreamtime / Tainted Silence / Total
Void / Until The End

SUPREME MAJESTY (SWEDEN)
Line-Up: Joakim Olsson (vocals), Chrille
Andersson (guitars), Rille Svensson
(guitars), Daniel Andersson (bass), Jocke
Unger (drums)

SUPREME MAJESTY is a Gothenburg
melody based Power Metal act forged in

SUN CAGED
Photo : Nico Wobben

SUPERIOR
Photo : Nico Wobben

1999. The July 2001 debut 'Tales Of A Tragic Kingdom' arrived courtesy of Germany's Massacre Records.

The band membership initially sprang from the Black influenced Death Metal combo MORTUM with guitarists Chrille Andersson, Rille Svensson and drummer Bartek Nalezinski all involved. Andersson also had ties with NON SERVIAM (billed as 'Tyr') and HELLSPELL.

SUPREME MAJESTY's first vocalist, Rikard Larson, was a veteran of MAGICA and MERCY, the latter act where he went under the stage name 'Rick Wine'. The group bowed in with the mini-album 'Divine Empire' in June 1999.

Erstwhile DEEP QUEST singer Joakim Olsson would take the microphone for the 2001 album 'Tales Of A Tragic Kingdom'. The bands rhythm section also saw an about change with Daniel Andersson on bass - also performing as guitarist in NON SERVIAM (as 'Janos') - and IMMERSED IN BLOOD drummer Jocke Unger arriving.

Keyboard player Julius Chmielewsky was added to the ranks in the summer of 2001.

Albums:
DIVINE EMPIRE, Loud n' Proud (1999)
No Farewells / Die In A Dream / King Of Eternity's Realm / The Blood We Spilled
TALES OF A TRAGIC KINGDOM, Massacre MAS CD0279 (2001)
Strike Like Thunder / Not Of This World / Towards The Northern Star / Forever I'll Be / Let It Go / Tales Of A Tragic Kingdom / Queen Of Egypt / Keeper Of The Dead / Supreme Majesty / Eye Of The Storm

SWORD (CANADA)
Line-Up: Rick Hughes (vocals), Mike Plant (guitar), Mike Larock (bass), Dan Hughes (drums)

Montreal's SWORD made a heady impact with their crunching debut 'Metalized' backed up with a European support tour to MOTÖRHEAD.

The Italian Underground Symphony label assembled a tribute album to SWORD during 2002.

Albums:
METALIZED, Aquarius ARR 541 (1986)
F.T.W / Children Of Heaven / Stoned Again / Dare To Spit / Outta Control / The End Of The Night / Runaway / Where To Hide / Stuck In Rock / Evil Spell
SWEET DREAMS, Roadracer RO 9476-1 (1988)
Sweet Dreams / The Trouble Is / Land Of The

Brave / Back Off / Prepare To Die / Caught In The Act / Until Death Do Us Part / The Threat / Life On The Sharp Edge / State Of Shock

SYMBOLS (BRAZIL)
Line-Up: Demian Tiguez (vocals / guitar), Cezar Talarico (bass), Fabrizio di Sarno (keyboards), Rodrigo Mello (drums)

SYMBOLS are a Progressive Metal act known internationally for providing vocalist Eduardo Falaschi to the regrouped ANGRA following the departure of Andre Matos. Previous to this defection SYMBOLS had issued two highly regarded albums. Forming during 1997 the first SYMBOLS line-up appointed Falaschi, guitarists Demian Tiguez and Rodrigo Arjonas, bassist Tito Falaschi, keyboard player Marcelo Panzardi and drummer Rodrigo Mello. Their first album, simply entitled 'Symbols', arrived the following year.

After the issue of a second album 'Call To The End' in 1999 SYMBOLS contributed a track 'Stormy Nights' to the 2001 conceptual album 'William Shakespeare's Hamlet'. However, line-up problems would then strike for the first time, resulting in the departure of both first of all Arjonas and then Tito Falaschi. Only a few months later Eduardo Falaschi received the call from ANGRA.

With SYMBOLS now only comprising Demian Tiguez and Rodrigo Mello a new unit was built up. Tiguez took on lead vocals and new members Cezar 'The Frog' Talarico on bass and keyboard player Fabrizio di Sarno were inducted. The renewed SYMBOLS debuted live in São Paulo during December of 2001 and set about recording a third album the following month. Mello also records with Metal band WIZARDS.

Albums:
SYMBOLS, (1998)
Scream Of People / What Can I Do? / Hard Feelings / Save My Soul / Like Mars / Love Through The Night / Rest In Paradise / You / Eyes In Flames / The Traveller
CALL THE END, (1999)
Introduction / Eyes In Flames / Power Machine / Call To The End / The Traveller / Introspection / Save Africa / Stop The Wars / Sons Of Lord / Everything I Want

SYMPHONY X (South Amboy, NJ, USA)
Line-Up: Russell Allen (vocals), Michael Romeo (guitar), Thomas Miller (bass), Michael Pinnella (keyboards), Jason Rollo (drums)

Outrageously Progressive Metal band formed

429

by the ex-PHANTOM'S OPERA duo of guitarist Michael Romeo and bassist Thomas Miller, SYMPHONY X's main markets would appear to be in Japan and continental Europe, especially France. The group's self-titled first album was released in Japan in 1994. The vocalist, one-time PHANTOM'S OPERA man Rod Tyler, was replaced soon afterwards by Russell Allen.

'The Divine Wings Of Tragedy' album included the near twenty one minute long epic title track.

In addition to work on a brand new album for 1998 (entitled 'Twilight In Olympus' and the first album to feature new drummer Tom Walling), Michael Romeo also found time to release his first solo album. This was a package originally laid down as a demo in the early '90s that gained the guitarist a great deal of interest from the likes of Shrapnel Records' Mike Varney.

During 2001 drummer Jason Rollo would participate in guitarist Nick Van Dyk's REDEMPTION project. Michael Romeo would guest session on STRATOVARIUS front man TIMO KOTIPELTO's debut solo record 'Waiting For The Dawn'. A lavish double live album 'Live In Europe' arrived in 2001. The same set would see a re-release in Japan through the Toshiba EMI label re-titled 'Live On The Edge Of Forever'.

Although the band would be announced for the 2002 'Bang Your Head' festival in Germany SYMPHONY X pulled out when front man Russell Allen was found to be suffering from intestinal bleeding requiring emergency medical treatment. An extensive run of North American dates in November and December saw the band operating as support act to BLIND GUARDIAN.

Albums:
SYMPHONY X, (1994)
Into The Dementia / The Raging Season / Premonition / Masquerade / Absinthe And Rue / Shades Of Grey / Taunting The Notorious / Rapture Or Pain / Thorns Of Sorrow / A Lesson Before Dying
THE DAMNATION GAME, Inside Out Music IOMCD004 (1995)
The Damnation Game / Dressed To Kill / The Edge Of Forever / Savage Curtain / Whispers / The Haunting / Secrets / A Winter's Dream - Prelude (Part I) / A Winter's Dream - The Ascension (Part II)
THE DIVINE WINGS OF TRAGEDY, Inside Out Music IOMCD009 (1997)
Of Sins And Shadows / Sea Of Lies / Out Of The Ashes / The Accolade / Pharoah / The Eyes Of Medusa / The Witching Hour / The Divine Wings Of Tragedy / Candlelight Fantasia

TWILIGHT IN OLYMPUS, Inside Out Music IOMCD021 (1998)
Smoke And Mirrors / Church Of The Machine / Sonata / In The Dragon's Den / Through The Looking Glass (Part I, II, III) / The Relic / Orion - The Hunter / Lady Of The Snow
V – THE NEW MYTHOLOGY SUITE, Metal Blade 14344 (2000)
Prelude / Evolution (The Grand Design) / Fallen / Transcendence (Segue) / Communion And The Oracle / The Bird-Serpent War - Cataclysm / On The Breath Of Poseidon (Segue) / Egypt / The Death Of Balance - Lacrymosa / Absence Of Light / A Fool's Paradise / Rediscovery (Segue) / Rediscovery, Pt. 2: The New Mythology
LIVE IN EUROPE, (2001) 145 FRANCE
Intro / Evolution (The Grand Design) / Fallen / Transcendence / Communion And The Oracle / The Bird-Serpent War - Cataclysm / On The Breath Of Poseidon / Egypt / The Death Of Balance - Candlelight Fantasia / The Eyes Of Medusa / Smoke And Mirrors / Church Of The Machine / Through The Looking Glass / Of Sins And Shadows / Sea Of Lies / The Divine Wings Of Tragedy
THE ODYSSEY, Inside Out Music (2002)
The Odyssey / King Of Terrors / Awakenings / Incantations Of The Apprentice / Inferno (Unleash The Fire) / Wait With The Wicked / Accolade II / Frontiers / The Turning

SYMPHORCE (GERMANY)
Line-Up: Andreas B. Franck (vocals), Cedric Dupont (guitar), Dennis Wohlbold (bass), H.P. Walter (keyboards), Stefan Koellner (drums)

Power Metal act led by ex-IVANHOE and present day BRAINSTORM singer Andreas B. Franck. The group debuted for Noise Records in 1999 with the 'Truth To Promises', at this stage having a line-up of Franck, guitarist Stef Bertolla, bassist Mike Hammer, keyboard player H.P. Walter and drummer Stefan Koellner. Cedric Dupont had supplanted Bertolla by the time of the 2000 'Sinctuary' follow up, overall praised as a significant improvement on the opening effort. Guitarist Cedric Dupont of SYMPHORCE would supplant Sascha Gerstner in FREEDOM CALL during September 2001. The six stringer would maintain a foot in both camps. For their third album SYMPHORCE signed up to the Metal Blade album, releasing the Achim Köhler produced 'Phorcefulahead' during October of 2002.

TAD MOROSE (SWEDEN)

Line-Up: Kristian 'Krille' Andren (vocals), Christer 'Krunt' Andersson (guitar), Anders Modd (bass), Fredrik Eriksson (keyboards), Peter Moren (drums)

TAD MOROSE date to 1991 with an initial line-up of vocalist Anders 'Wispen' Westlund, guitarist Christer 'Krunt' Andersson, bassist Per-Ola 'Rossi' Olsson and drummer Dan Eriksson, although the association with Westlund didn't last very long. Even so, the man was to be heard on the group's first demo.

As a deal with Black Mark was signed on the back of the tape's promise Kristian 'Krille' Andren was added to the group, closely followed by keyboard player Fredrik Eriksson in late 1993.

The debut TAD MOROSE album, 'Leaving His Past Behind', was released in 1994. Unfortunately, drummer Dan Eriksson quit the same year, necessitating the recruitment of Peter Moren. This new line-up stuck together for the making of 1995's 'Sender Of Thoughts'.

Anders Modd was added on bass in place of the departed Olsson in '95 and TAD MOROSE subsequently premiered this new roster at the 'Black Mark Festival' on a bill with MORGANA LE FAY, CEMETARY and MEMENTO MORI.

Modd made his recording debut with the group on the 'Paradigma' EP, a release produced by Mike Wead of HEXENHAUS and ABSTRAKT ALGEBRA fame.

In 1996 the group was hit with the departure of Andren to MEMENTO MORI. He now titles himself 'Urban Breed'.

Keyboard player Fredrik Eriksson has also released a 7" single with a studio side project band called SOLITUDE. Urban Breed would make a return to the ranks for the 1997 effort 'A Mended Rhyme'.

The 1998 TAD MOROSE line-up stood at mainstay Christer Andersson on guitar, Urban Breed on vocals, second guitarist Daniel Olsson, bassist Anders Modd and drummer Peter Morén. This version of the band cut the 2000 'Undead' album.

The 2002 TAD MOROSE album 'Matters Of The Dark' would witness guest sessions courtesy of LEFAY vocalist Charles Rytkonen and backing vocal contributions by DIVINE SIN's Fredde Lundberg and WOLVERINE's Stefan Zell. The band put in tour work across Europe allied with DEMON and CHINCHILLA before putting in a showing at the 'Milwaukee Metalfest' event.

TAD MOROSE
Photo : Benny Backeby

Voices Are Calling / Leaving The Past
Behind / Eternal Lies, Black Mark BMCD39
(1993) (Promotion release)
Sender Of Thoughts / Lost In Time / Here
After, Black Mark BMCD 56 (1995)
Stories Around A Tale / Eyes So Tired /
Where Dreams Collide / Absent Illusion /
Another Paradigm, Black Mark BMCD85
(1995) ('Paradigma' EP)

Albums:
LEAVING THE PAST BEHIND, Black Mark
BMCD 43 (1994)
Eternal Lies / Miracle / Voices Are Calling /
Reach For The Sky / Eyes Of A Stranger /
Save Me / 1388 / Leaving The Past Behind /
Reflections / Way Of History
SENDER OF THOUGHTS, Black Mark
BMCD 62 (1995)
Fading Pictures / Sender Of Thoughts /
Morning Sun / Lost In Time / Different Eyes /
Time Of Silence / Forever Gone / Circle Of
Souls / Here After / Gates Of Babylon /
Netherworld
A MENDED RHYME, Black Mark BMCD 87
(1997)
Circuit Vision / But Angels Shine/ A Mended
Rhyme / The Trader Of Souls / Time Of No
Sun / Dragon Tide / Goddess Of Chaos /
The Vacant Lot / Guest Of The Inquisition
REFLECTIONS, Black Mark (2000)
But Angels Shine / A Mended Rhyme /
Trader Of Souls / Stories Around A Tale /
Where Dreams Collide / Fading Pictures /
Morning Sun / Narrow Minded / Power Of
The Night
UNDEAD, Century Media (2000)
Servant Of The Bones / Another Time
Around / Where The Sun Never Shines /
Order Of The Seven Poles / Undead / No
Tears In The Rain / Lord On High /
Corporate Masters / No Wings To Burn / The
Dead And His Son
MATTERS OF THE DARK, Century Media
(2001)
Sword Of Retribution / Matters Of The Dark /
Ethereal Soul / I Know Your Name / In The
Shadows / Another Way / New Clear Skies /
Riding The Beast / Reason Of The Ghost /
The Devil's Finger / Don't Pray For Me

TALAMASCA (Appleton, WI, USA)
Line-Up: Steve Gentz (vocals), Andy
Paredes (guitar), Brad Sculer (bass),
Matthew Lee Belanger (drums)

TALAMASCA, taking their name from Ann
Rice's 'Vampire Chronicles', are a technical
Progressive Metal outfit forged in 1994.
Vocalist Steve Gentz would join the fold in
1997 and fronted the band for the inaugural
1998 album 'Projections'. Reviews were
positive, particularly in Europe, and
TALAMASCA gained further recognition by
being included on the major German 'Rock
Hard' magazine's 'Unerhort' cover mount
compilation.
TALAMASCA covered QUEENSRYCHE's
'The Whisper' for the Siegen Records tribute
album 'Warning: Minds Of Raging Empires'.

Albums:
PROJECTIONS, (1998)
Consumed / In A Mind / Secret Life / Self
Aware / Faded / Vietnam Eternam /
Resistance / Lost Within
ASCENSION, (2001)
Cry For War / Twisted Strand / Unspoken
Word / Realisation / Fear / Collective /
Virtuous Man / Whisper

TALAN (UK)
Line-Up: Dave Hughes (vocals), Craig
Riggsdale (guitar), Steve Palmer (guitar),
Adam Bamford (keyboards), Phil Johns
(drums)

A hard hitting Welsh band with emphasis on
classic British Metal riffs, TALAN was formed
by ex-SAMURAI guitarist Craig Riggsdale
and ex-PREYER drummer Phil Johns. The
band released a 1989 demo, 'Invasion',
before the 'Spellbinder' single arrived in 1990.

Singles/EPs:
Spellbinder, (1990)

TARAMIS (AUSTRALIA)
Line-Up: Shane Southby (vocals), George
Larin (guitar), Evan Harris (bass), Dave
Browne (drums)

A Melbourne technical Metal band founded
during 1984 and originally billed as
PROWLER. The band's debut 'Queen Of
Thieves' was issued on the local Metal For
Melbourne label and also picked up by Metal
Blade for an American release.
Guitarist Craig Robertson and bassist Danny
Komorr had bade farewell before recording of
a second album, 1991's 'Stretch Of The
Imagination'. Domestically the record was put
out by Central Station and the Rising Sun
concern licensed it for European territories.
TARAMIS endeavoured throughout the '90s
contributing tracks to compilations such as
'Lonely Star' to the 1992 'Australian Metal'
collection and 'Dreaming' to a 1993 venture
'While My Guitar Gently Kills Your Mother'.
Reportedly TARAMIS were still a going
concern as recently as 1998.

Albums:
QUEEN OF THIEVES, Metal Blade 72287 (1988)
Lord Of The Blackflies / Doesn't Seem / The Chosen / Path To Aquilonia / Queen Of Thieves / Without A Warning / Wolves / My Life
STRETCH OF THE IMAGINATION, Central Station (1991)
Dreaming / Diceman / Maze Of Glory / Another Tomorrow / Behind These Eyes / Jigaboo Boogie / Lonely Star / Delayed Reaction

TARAXACUM (GERMANY)
Line-Up: Rick Mythiasin (vocals), Tobias Exxel (guitars / bass), Ferdy Doernberg (keyboards), Frank Wolf (drums), Felix Bohnke (drums)

Another in the long line of post millennium European project concept albums. TARAXACUM's 'Spirit Of Freedom's opus was conceived by EDGUY man Tobias Exxel. The album drew in the talents of STEEL PROPHET vocalist Rick Mythiasin, ROUGH SILK and AXEL RUDI PELL keyboard player FERDY DOERNBERG, his EDGUY colleague Felix Bohnke on drums and erstwhile SQUEALER man Frank Wolf also on drums. The whole affair was mixed in the studio by GAMMA RAY men Kai Hansen and Dirk Schlächter.
Rick Mythiasin made his exit from STEEL PROPHET to concentrate solely on TARAXACUM during July of 2002. However, by September, despite Mythiasin breaking his leg in three places whilst trying to perform a handstand (!), Mythiasin had enrolled with NEW EDEN for their 'Stagnant Progression'.

Albums:
SPIRIT OF FREEDOM, MTM Metal (2001)
Spirit Of Freedom / Blast Off / Alone / Circle Of Fools / Delirium / Life Goes On / Never Let You Go / Believe In You / Think!

TARGET (BELGIUM)
Line-Up: Guy De Graeve (vocals), Chris De Turch (guitar), Franky Van Aerde (guitar), Johan Susant (bass), Christ Brnems (drums)

Belgian Metal band TARGET released a four track demo in 1987 produced by Ralph Hubert. Original guitarist Detruck departed on the eve of recording the debut album 'Mission Executed' and was substituted by ex-LYCANTHROPE's Lex Vogelaar.
Bassist Johan Susant loaned his services temporarily to HOLY MOSES for a European tour with DIRTY ROTTEN IMBECILES.

TARGET's 1988 album 'Master Project Genesis' saw vocalist Steve Gray fronting the band.
Former TARGET guitarist Lex Vogelaar later formed ORPHANAGE. He would also session on demos for PARALYSIS.

Albums:
MISSION EXECUTED, Aaarrg AAARRG 7 (1987)
Mission To The Andes / Hordes Of Insanity / They Walk In Front / Warriors Of The Holy One / Nuclear Waste / The Gathering / Under Dominion (Of Death) / Deathblow
MASTER PROJECT GENESIS, Aaarrg AAARRG 16 (1988)
The Coming Of Chaos / Ultimate Unity / Digital Regency / Absolution By Termination / Dehumanisation / March Of The Machines / Secrets Of The Dome / Master Project Genesis

TAROT (FINLAND)
Line-Up: Marco Hietala (vocals / guitar / bass), Zachary Hietala (guitar), Janne Tolsa (keyboards), Pecu Cinnari (drums)

A highly rated Metal act. The TAROT debut 'The Spell Of Iron' arrived in late 1986. In a novel marketing ploy initial copies of the album came with a one-sided bonus 7" boasting a drum solo entitled 'Aaaargh! What's Goin' On Here?!' by Pecu Cinnari. After the 1988 album 'Follow Me Into Madness' TAROT faded.
TAROT frontman Marco Hietala would apparently be in line as one of the frontrunners to replace BRUCE DICKINSON in IRON MAIDEN. However, TAROT bounced back in 1993, finding renewed international success afforded by their 'To Live Forever' album. Of interest to fans was the 'As One' EP of 1995 which included a cover version of JETHRO TULL's 'Locomotive Breath'.
Hietala would later join the high profile Kimberly Goss led Power Metal band SINERGY. During October of 2001 Hietala would supplant bassist Sami Vänskä in NIGHTWISH.
Hietala, along with TAROT colleague keyboard player Janne Tolsa would also convene a 2001 act dubbed VIRTUOCITY. Other players involved included drummer Jaska Raatikainen of CHILDREN OF BODOM. Jaron Sebastian Raven and Peter James Goodman. Hietala and Raatikainen would also session on the EVEMASTER 'Wither' EP of the same year, guesting on a cover version of TAROT's very own 'Wings Of Darkness'.

434

Wings Of Darkness / Back In The Fire, Flamingo FGMX002 (1986) (12" single)
Aaaargh! What's Goin' On Here?!, Flamingo FGS117 (1986) (One sided free single)
Love's Not Made For My Kind / Things That Crawl At Night, Flamingo FGS124 (1986)
Angels Of Pain EP, Bluelight BLR 4539-2 (1995)
As One / Dancing On The Wire (Live) / Lady Deceiver (Live) / Locomotive Breath, Bluelight BLR 4539-2 (1995)
Warhead / Beyond Troy (Single version) / The Colour Of Your Blood (Live), Bluelight BLR 4544-2 (1997)
The Punishment / Tears Of Steel (Live) / Children Of The Grave (Live), Blastic Heaven BHR 4551-2 (1998)

Albums:
THE SPELL OF IRON, Flamingo FGL 4010 (1986)
Midwinter Nights / Dancing On The Wire / Back In The Fire / Love's Not For My Kind / Never Forever / The Spell Of Iron / De Mortui Nil Nisi Bene / Pharao / Wings Of Darkness / Things That Crawl In The Night
FOLLOW ME INTO MADNESS, Flamingo FGL 4026 (1988)
Descendants Of Power / Rose On The Grave / Lady Deceiver / Follow Me Into Madness / Blood Runs Cold - Happy End / No Return / I Don't Care Anymore / Breathing Fire / I Spit Venom / Shadow In My Heart
TO LIVE FOREVER, Bluelight BLR 3316CD (1993)
Do You Wanna Live Forever / The Colour Of Your Blood / The Invisible Hand / Live Hard Die Hard / Sunken Graves / The Chosen / Born Into The Flame / In My Blood / Tears Of Steel / My Enslaver / Shame / Iron Stars / Children Of The Grave / Guardian Angel
TO LIVE AGAIN, Zero XRCN 1199 (1995) (Japanese release)
Children Of The Grave / Live Hard, Die Hard / Iron Stars / No Return / Tears Of Steel / Breathing Fire / Midwinter Nights / Wings Of Darkness / Rose On The Grave / Things That Crawl At Night / Dancing On The Wire / Lady Deceiver / The Colour Of Your Blood / The Chosen / Kill The King / Do You Wanna Live Forever
STIGMATA, Bluelight BLR 3321-2 (1995)
Angel Of Pain / E.T.I. / Shades In Glass / As One / State Of Grace / Race The Light / Expected To Heal / Sleepless / The Teeth / Stigmata (I Feel For You)
FOR THE GLORY OF NOTHING, Blastic Heaven BHR 3347-2 (1998)
Crawlspace / Warhead / I'm Here / Shining Black / Beyond Troy / Dark Star Burning /

The Scourger / Ghosts Of Me / The Punishment / Ice

TAROT'S MYST (GERMANY)
Line-Up: Tommy Bloch (vocals), Uwe Hormann (guitars / keyboards), Jens Hormann (bass), Dieter Bernert (drums)

TAROT'S MYST allied former ZAR vocalist Tommy Bloch, ex-CHROMING ROSE guitarist Uwe Hormann and erstwhile BRAINSTORM drummer Dieter Bernert.

Albums:
ODYSSEY, Bossy Ogress BO14 (1999)
Blood On The Horizon / Troja / The Giant's Eye / Lord Of The Winds / The Creature Within / Kingdom Of The Shadow / Siren's Song / Jaws Of The Deep / Come Hell Or High Water / Flame In The Maze / The One To Bend The Bow / Flesh And Blood / Odyssey

TEUTONIC (GERMANY)
Line-Up: Mark Phantom (vocals), Ventor (guitar), Stef (bass), Lothar (drums)

German Heavy Metal delivered "the old way". The group came into being during 1991 under the original title of TEUTONIC CRUELTY with a band roll call of Holger on vocals and bass, guitarists Wolfgang 'Ventor' Pohl and Volker with Lothar on drums. The band became simply TEUTONIC during 1994 at the same juncture drawing in fresh blood Benny on lead vocals, Wersi on guitar supplanting Volker and new bassist Roland. However, the following year Roland exited and Benny added bass to his responsibilities. Sometime during 1996 TEUTONIC imploded due to internal friction. During this period Benny, Wersi, Ventor and Roland would all busy themselves with HIMMELFARTH. This act had actually been active since 1989. HIMMELFARTH too was to fold in 1998.
TEUTONIC would be resurrected in the August of 1999. This variant of the band saw Wersi on both lead vocals on guitar, Ventor on second guitar Stef as bass player and on the drums Lothar 'Effe' Pohl. It took a year before the band performed live, acting as openers to THE LORD WEIRD SLOUGH FEG and SOLSTICE. Mark Phantom took over the vocal reins in January of 2001. Shortly after Wersi decided to leave the band.

Singles/EPs:
Teutonic Invasion EP, (2001)

THOTEN (BRAZIL)
Line-Up: Renato Tribuzy (vocals), Frank

Schieber (guitar), Itho Cruz (bass), Sidney Sohn (keyboards), Marcos Barzo (drums)

Power Metal band out of Rio De Janeiro. Founded in 1997 THOTEN boast the talents of frontman Renato Tribuzy, regarded by the Brazilian Rock media as one of the country's best Metal vocalists. In their opening year THOTEN issued the self-financed 'Belief Of A New World' EP and would put in support shows to SAVATAGE.

The debut album, 'Beyond The Tomorrow' released by the Metal Gallery label, was produced by ANGRA guitarist Kiko Loureiro. European editions, licensed to the Italian Scarlet Records, came with an extra bonus track 'Scream'.

The band suffered a severe blow in February of 2002 when it was learned that drummer Marcos Barzo had been stabbed during an attempted robbery at his house. Fortunately the sticksman survived the attack. In May Renato Tribuzy announced a new 'all star' project in league with HAMMERFALL bassist Magnus Rosén going by the name of EXECUTION.

Albums:
BEYOND THE TOMORROW, (2001)
Ashes In The Abyss / Keeping Silence / Above The Law / Wicked Soul / Christened By Flame / Altar Of Freedom / Wild Life / Lady Of The Lake / Open Fire / Beyond The Tomorrow

THRESHOLD (UK)
Line-Up: Damian Wilson (vocals), Karl Groom (guitar), Nick Midson (guitar), Rich West (keyboards), Jon Jeary (bass), Tony Grinham (drums)

A hard edged Progressive Rock act. THRESHOLD was formed in 1988 by guitarists Nick Midson and Karl Groom together with drummer Tony Grinham. THRESHOLD added bassist Jon Jeary, vocalist DAMIAN WILSON and keyboard player Richard West in 1991. Guitarist Karl Groom also doubles as guitarist for SHADOWLANDS.

Wilson appeared as guest lead vocalist on LANDMARQ's 1992 'Solitary Witness' album, co-produced by Groom. Wilson later quit THRESHOLD following recording of the first album 'Wounded Land', his name being connected to the then vacant vocal position with IRON MAIDEN. Wilson then added vocals to another LANDMARQ album 'The Vision Pit' before he settled with American act LA SALLE. Wilson also issued a solo album 'Cosmas' in 1997.

Prior to the recording of the second album, THRESHOLD appeared at a prestigious Belgian open air festival on a bill including PARADISE LOST, TYKETTO, GOTTHARD and WHITESNAKE. 'Psychadelicatessen', featured vocalist Glynn Morgan and whilst SHADOWLAND drummer Nick Harradence had joined the group prior to recording his stay was a temporary one (one gig!) and for the album the drum stool had been filled by Jay Micciche. THRESHOLD then undertook dates supporting DREAM THEATER. During 1995 a five track live album, 'Livedelica', emerged before work on the 'Extinct Instinct' commenced.

Following his (unsuccessful) liaison with LA SALLE Damien Wilson returned alongside new drummer Mark Heaney as vocalist Geoff Morgan opted out to create MINDFEED, in collusion with Jay Miccichie on drums. The pair released the 'Perfect Life?' album in 1998. By 2000 Micciche had joined Kent Nu-Metallers VACANT STARE and also deputised for KILL II THIS.

By 1999 THRESHOLD were fronted by ex-SARGENT FURY vocalist Andy McDermott. On the drum stool was Janne James. An interim set of remixes and rare material surfaced entitled 'Decadent'. Following the commercial success of the 'Clone' album THRESHOLD moved to a larger record label Inside Out Music. McDermott also began work on his debut solo album 'In The Meantime' working with his ex-SARGENT FURY colleague bassist Carsten Rebentisch and SAXON guitarist Paul Quinn. Groom took time out to produce the new album for fellow British Progsters PENDRAGON. THRESHOLD would headline the first 'ProgPower Europe' festival in October 2002.

Albums:
WOUNDED LAND, Giant Electric Pea GEPCD 1005 (1994)
Consume To Live / Days Of Dearth / Sanity's End / Paradox / Surface To Air / Mother Earth / Siege Of Baghdad / Keep It With Mine
PSYCHEDELICATESSEN, Giant Electric Pea GEPCD1014 (1995)
Sunseeker / A Tension Of Souls / Into The Light / Will To Give / Under The Sun / Babylon Rising / He Is I am / Innocent / Devoted
LIVEDELICA, Giant Electric Pea GEPCD 1015 (1995)
A Tension Of Souls / Sanity's End / Innocent / Surface To Air / Paradox
EXTINCT INSTINCT, Giant Electric Pea GEPCD1019 (1996)
Exposed / Somatography / Eat The Unicorn / Forever / Virtual Isolation / The Whispering /

Lake Of Despond / Clear / Life Flow / Part Of The Chaos
CLONE, (1998)
Freaks / Angels / The Latent Gene / Lovelorn / Change / Life's Too Good / Goodbye Mother Earth / Voyager II / Sunrise On Mars
DECADENT, Nonstop Music NSCD001 (1999)
Virtual Isolation (Radio edit) / Intervention (1999 remix) / Sunseeker (Radio edit) / Voyager II (Urban version) / Devoted (Fan club remix) / Change (Unplugged) / Mother Earth (1999 remix) / Exposed (Radio edit) / Lost (Japanese release) / Into The Light (1999 remix) / Paradox (Club mix) / He Is I Am (Drum & Bass version)
HYPOTHETICAL, Inside Out Music IOMLTDCD 073 (2001)
Light And Space / Turn On Tune In / The Ravages Of Time / Sheltering Sky / Oceanbound / Long Way Home / Keep My Head / Narcissus / Life Flow
CRITICAL MASS, Inside Out Music (2002)
78 GERMANY
Phenomenon / Choices / Falling Away / Fragmentation / Echoes Of Life / Round And Round / Avalon / Critical Mass Part 1 / Critical Mass Part 2 / Critical Mass Part 3

THUNDERCRAFT (GERMANY)
Line-Up: Karl Heinz Zastrow (vocals), Martin Reinke (guitar), Michael Wölke (guitar), Rüdiger Wolf (bass), Uwe Okunick (drums)

Albums:
FIGHTING FOR SURVIVAL, Boom (1984)
Intro / Taste Of Hell / Virgin Killer / On The Ladder Of Madness / Face The Truth / L.A. / Sexual Virus / Life Is A Misery / Victim Of Rock n' Roll / Wicked Boy / Final

THUNDERSTEEL (GERMANY)
Line-Up: Nils Lange (vocals), Sven Semmerlrodt (guitar), Gerrit Schaefer (guitar), Ralf Drechsler (bass), Norman Schaefer (drums)

A Power Metal act. THUNDERSTEEL's first recording was the demo 'Thunder And Steel'. Previous to recording of the debut album THUNDERSTEEL had supported the likes of TANKARD, HEADHUNTER and EROSION before a second demo tape 'Heavy, Loud And Mean' secured a deal with the Black Mark label.
The group supported HELLOWEEN and MOTÖRHEAD in their time.

Singles/EPs:
Flash And Thunder / In The Night / Tears Of Pain, Black Mark BMCD 53P (1994)

Albums:
THUNDERSTEEL, Black Mark BMCD 53 (1994)
Burning In Hell / Flash And Thunder / I Want You / Face The Evil / Nightmare / In The Night / Cold As Ice / Tears Of Pain

THUNDERSTONE (FINLAND)
Line-Up: Pasi Rantanen (vocals), Nino Laurenne (guitar), Titus Hjelm (bass), Kari Tornack (keyboards), Mirka Rantanen (drums)

THUNDERSTONE, although founded as recently as early 2000, hold a membership of qualified pedigree. The group was conceived by guitar player Nino Laurenne, an erstwhile member of Thrash Metal act ANTIDOTE. Joining him on initial demos would be ex-HEAT and present day TUNNELVISION drummer Mirka Rantanen.
The pair would later recruit former INCREDIBLE BRAINSHELLS and ANTIDOTE bassist Titus Hjelm and TUNNELVISION vocalist Pasi Rantanen for a further batch of tapes. Janne Wirman, keyboard player with CHILDREN OF BODOM and WARMEN, would session. During the summer of 2001 Kari Tornack, another TUNNELVISION member, would fill in the keyboard role as THUNDERSTONE signed to the Nuclear Blast label. A debut album would be produced by Mikko Karmila. Japanese variants, issued by the Avalon Marquee label, included a bonus cover version of JUDAS PRIEST's 'Diamonds And Rust'.
The Rantanen brothers also operate with WARMEN.

Albums:
THUNDERSTONE, Nuclear Blast NB 1002-2 (2002)
Let The Demons Free / Virus / World's Cry / Me, My Enemy / Will To Power / Weak / Eyes Of A Stranger / Like Father, Like Son / Voice In A Dream / Spread My Wings

THYESTEAN FEAST (FINLAND)
Line-Up: M. Häkkinen (vocals), J. Savimäki (guitar), M. Saarinen (guitar), M. Saikkonen (bass), Matti Pirttimäki (keyboards), J. Raatikainen (drums)

Dark, Gothic fuelled symphonic Metal. THYESTEAN FEAST's first step into the commercial arena was with the 1999 demo 'Ophion's Messiah'. Unhappy with the recording quality of this effort a further session followed entitled 'The Fall Of Astraea'. Keyboard player Matti Pirttimäki was then inducted. Following the recording of the

'Cycles Of Worldburn' album drummer Toni Sotikoff was replaced by J. Raatikainen.

Albums:

CYCLES OF WORLDBURN, Trisol (2001)
Cindemonium / White Widow / Order Of The Elder Serpent / Oblivion's Bliss / The Fall Of Astraea / Unio Mystica / Cycles Of Worldburn / Prophecy Of The Last Days / Chimera Curse / Treason

THY MAJESTIE (ITALY)

Line-Up: Dario Grillo (vocals), Giovanni Santini (guitar), Maurizio Malta (guitar), Dario D'Alessandro (bass), Giusseppe Bondi (keyboards), Claudio Diprima (drums)

Symphonic Metal act THY MAJESTIE started life as THY MAJESTY but changed the spelling when it was discovered there was a German Black Metal band of the same name. The band had been created in 1998 and laid down their 'Perpetual Glory' demo in March of that year at the 'Circle of Power' studios – actually drummer Claudio Diprima's bedroom! Dario D'Allessandro, former guitarist with DRAGON'S BREATH, would take over the bass role from previous incumbent Michele Cristofalo just prior to these sessions.

These tapes duly secured a deal with the Scarlet label for the 2000 debut album 'The Lasting Power', an entirely conceptual affair based upon the Terry Brooks fantasy novel 'The Saga Of Shannara' and featuring full orchestration and guest female vocals from DAKURA's Eva Rondinelli. South American licensed variants of 'The Lasting Power' added two bonus cuts in 'Hywelbane' and 'Facing The Beast' taken from the 'Perpetual Glory' demo.

THY MAJESTIE would record a cover version of STRYPER's 'In God We Trust' for their 'Hastings 1066' 2002 album.

Albums:

THE LASTING POWER, Scarlet (2000)
Thy Majestie Theme / Wings Of Wind / March Of The Damned / Under Siege / Name Of Tragedy / Durnovaria / ...At The Village / Mystery Of Forest / Cruenta Pugna / The Green Lands / Sword Of Justice / Tears Of Sorrow / Treachery / Nymph's Recall / Time To Battle
HASTINGS 1066, (2002)
Rerun Memoria / The King And The Warrior /

TIERRA SANTA
Photo : Nico Wobben

Intro: Echoes / Echoes Of War / The Sight Of Telham / Incipit Bellum / Intro: Scream / The Scream Of Teillefer / Intro: Anger / Anger Of Fate / Intro: Pride / The Pride Of A Housecarl / Through The Bridge Of Spears / Demons Of The Crown / In God We Trust

TIERRA SANTA (SPAIN)
Line-Up: Angel (vocals / guitar), Arturo (guitar), Roberto (bass), Paco (keyboards), Iñaki (drums)

TIERRA SANTA, founded in 1997, deal in epic Power Metal. The group supported DIO in Spain during October of 1998. On the covers front TIERRA SANTA have had their version of IRON MAIDEN's 'Flight Of Icarus' donated to the 'Transylvania 666' collection and also 'Communication Breakdown' included on the Locomotive Music LED ZEPPELIN tribute album 'The Metal Zeppelin — The Music Remains The Same'.

Singles/EPs:
Pegaso / El Laberinto Del Minotauro, (2000) ('Cuando La Tierra Tola El Cielo' EP)

Albums:
MEDIEVAL, Locomotive Music (1999)
Medieval / Tierra Santa / Leyenda / Desterrado / Hijos Del Odio / Vikingos / Reino De Sueños / Nunca Mas
LEGENDARIO, (1999)
La Profecia / Séptima Estrella / La Cruzada / El Bastón Del Diablo / Reconquista / Legendario / La Mano De Dios / Atlántida / Drácula / Los Diez Mandamientos
TIERRAS DEL EYENDA, Iron Glory (2000)
La Tormenta / Tierras De Leyenda / Sodoma Y Gomorra / La Cancion Del Pirata I / La Cancion Del Pirata II / El Secreto Del Faraon / La Momia / La Torre De Babel / Una Juventud Perdida / La Caja De Pandora / El Caballo De Troya
SANGRE DE REYES, (2001)
David Y El Gigante / La Ciudad Secreta / Pegaso / Juana De Arco / La Sombra De La Bestia / Dos Vidas (Prologo "La Armada") / La Armada Invencible / El Laberinto Del Minotauro / El Amor De Mi Vida / Ml Tierra / Sangre De Reyes

TILES (Detroit, MI, USA)
Line-Up: Paul Rarick (vocals), Chris Herin (guitar), Jeff Whittle (bass), Pat Deleon (drums)

A thought provoking and technically challenging Progressive Rock act out of Detroit founded in February of 1993. Their debut, simply titled 'Tiles', created waves on the underground Metal scene prompting licensing offers from Dream Circle in Europe and Teichiku in Japan. 'Fence The Clear', released in the Spring of 1997 increased both the band's profile and sales. Japanese variants added extra material in the form of demo outtakes, one of which 'No Failure', would be revisited for TILES third album retitled as 'Facing Failure'.

To promote the Terry Brown produced 'Presents Of Mind' album TILES lent support to DREAM THEATER's November 1999 dates. 'Presents Of Mind's assorted international variations witnessed a whole slew of extra tracks. North American editions boasted live in the studio tracks whilst Japanese copies came with an outtake 'Ambition' from the debut album. The band would spend much of 2001 working on a projected album provisionally billed as 'Window Dressing'.

Albums:
TILES, Standing Pavement SPR94001 (1995)
Analysis Paralysis / Token Pledge / Retrospect / Trading Places / Bridges Of Grace / Dancing Dogs / Scattergram / Dress Rehearsal / Supply And Demand
FENCE THE CLEAR, Inside Out Music IOMCD014 (1997)
Patterns: I) The Balancing Lot, II) Patterns / Beneath The Surface / Cactus Valley / Another's Hand / The Wading Pool / Gameshow / Fallen Pieces / Changing The Guard / Gabby's Happy Song / Checkerboards
PRESENTS OF MIND, Inside Out Music SPV - 085-31382CD (1999)
Static / Modification / Crossing Swords / Facing Failure / The Learning Curve / Ballad Of The Sacred Cows / The Sandtrap Jig / Taking Control / Safe Procedures / Reasonable Doubt
PRESENCE IN EUROPE 1999, Standing Pavement (2000)
Introduction / Patterns / Token Pledge / Static / Modification / Ballad Of The Sacred Cows / Facing Failure / Another's Hand

TIME MACHINE (ITALY)
Line-Up: Folco Orlandini (vocals), Joe Tacconi (guitar), Ivan Oggioni (guitar), Lorenzo Dehó (bass,/keyboards), Antonio Rotta (drums)

A revered Italian Progressive Metal band, TIME MACHINE has, over a series of adventurous concept albums of great depth, generated a worthy cult following on the international market. Their 'Act II: Galileo' and

'Evil' outings are regarded as genuine classics of their ilk. TIME MACHINE was formed by bassist Lorenzo Dehó in 1992. A year later TIME MACHINE debuted with the 'Project: Time Scanning' album, although former MOON OF STEEL vocalist Andrea Ruggeri and the group's original guitarist quit the ranks at some point afterwards.

New singer Folco Orlandini and erstwhile MOON OF STEEL guitarist Joe Taccone joined for the 'Act II: Galileo', which was a concept work based upon the life of Galileo Galilei. The 1997 'Shades Of Time' release included a cover version of BLACK SABBATH's 'Heaven And Hell'.

Orlandini was forced into national service after the album was released and the Italian's recruited Morby in his place in time for gigs in their homeland opening for ANGRA. The following year Morby was out and in came new vocalist Nick Fortarezza for 1999's 'Eternity Ends' album. Although TIME MACHINE would then retire to work on fresh material fans of the band would be given some comfort by the KHALI side project release.

The 2001 TIME MACHINE album 'Evil', preceded by the 'Aliger Daemon' EP, would continue the conceptual sagas running through the band's body of work. An ambitious affair, 'Evil' was grounded in the novel 'Cherudek' by the famed Italian author Valerio Evangelisti who also contributed to the lyrics of the album. 'Evil' would be hailed by Prog Rock media globally as one of the finest albums of its genre that year. Lucretia Records matched the epic quality of the music by packaging 'Evil' in a lavish A5 digipack format.

During 2002 Lorenzo Dehó would aid Danish Symphonic Metal act WUTHERING HEIGHTS with session bass on their 'To Travel For Evermore' album.

Singles/EPs:
Dungeons Of The Vatican / 7533 a. C., Ab Urbe Condita / Medieval Lady, Lucretia LU 94003 (1994) ('Dungeons Of The Vatican' EP)

Albums:
PROJEKT: TIME SCANNING, LMTR 10 (1993)
Back Across The Centuries, I: Time Machine / 753 a. C., Ab Urbe Condita, I: Breaking Borders, II: Subtle Aggression, Mind Kill, III: Riots In The Colonies, IV: Divine Intervention, V: For The Glory Of The Nation, VI: Setting Borders / Holy Man, I: Religion, What Religion?, II: Industrial Crusaders, III: Religion, What Religion? (Reprise) / Lover's Night In Venice / Medieval Lady / Past And Future I: Memories, II: Present, III: Hope / History, I: Earth's Dawn, II: History, III: Life Again
ACT II: GALILLEO, Spell SLRCD001 (1996)
A New World / Guilt / Regrets / The Holy Office / The Old World / A Nightmare / Mighty Visions / The Trial / Pain
SHADES OF TIME, Lucretia LU 97015-2 (1997)
Silent Revolution / 1,000 Rainy Nights / New Religion / Heaven & Hell / Never Ending Love / Past & Future (1997 version)
ETERNITY ENDS, Lucretia (1999)
End Of Darkness / Falling Star / I, The Subversive Nazarene / Hidden Pain / Eternity Ends / I Believe Again / Desert Of Souls / Behind The Cross / Sphynx (The Witness) / When The Night Surrounds Me / Pilatus / Dark Again
HIDDEN SECRETS, Lucretia LU20001-2 (2000)
Riots In The Colonies / Stargazer / I Hold The Key / Eternity Ends / Silent Revolution / Behind The Cross / I Believe Again / 1,000 Rainy Nights / Falling Star / I, The Subversive Nazarene / Past And Future / Mother / Dungeons Of The Vatican / White Collars / Will You Remember / Burning In The Wind / Desert Of Souls / Sphynx (The Witness) / New Religion / I Hold The Key / Prisoner Of Dreams / Never-Ending Love / Virgin Of The Temple / Love Without Sin Part I / Obscure Medieval Lady / Earth's Dawn (History) / Hidden Pain
EVIL, Lucretia LU20015-2 (2001)
Gerona / Where's My Heaven? / Army Of The Dead / Kiss Of Fire / Ecclesia Spiritualis / Neghentropia / Evil Lies / Angel Of Death / Hailing Souls / Silent Bells

GLENN TIPTON (UK)

JUDAS PRIEST guitarist Glenn Tipton recorded his first ever solo album during the band's lengthy hiatus between 1992 and 1997. Fans would be pleasantly surprised to hear that Tipton had not attempted to relinquish his heritage with 'Baptism Of Fire' but conjured up a proud Heavy Metal album, one in which the guitarist also delivered his first lead vocal performance.

Titled 'Baptism Of Fire' the album features many guest contributors including veteran drummer COZY POWELL, MR. BIG bassist Billy Sheehan, OZZY OSBOURNE and SUICIDAL TENDENCIES bassist Rob Trujillo and the UGLY KID JOE pair of vocalist Whitfield Crane and drummer Shannon Larkin.

Ex-DEAR MR. PRESIDENT and STEVIE SALAS COLORCODE bassist CJ De Villar and erstwhile BAD 4 GOOD drummer Brooks

Wackerman also appear.

Amongst the Tipton penned tracks on the album the guitarist also chose to include a cover of the ROLLING STONES chestnut 'Paint It Black'. The guitarist returned to action with JUDAS PRIEST shortly after appearing on their comeback 'Jugulator' album.

Singles/EPs:
Paint It Black / Himalaya, Atlantic (1997) (USA promotion release)

Albums:
BAPTISM OF FIRE, Atlantic 7567 82974-2 (1997)
Hard Core / Paint It Black / Enter The Storm / Fuel Me Up / Extinct / Baptism Of Fire / The Healer / Cruise Control / Kill Or Be Killed / Voodoo Brother / Left For Dead

TITAN FORCE (Denver, CO, USA)

Line-Up: Harry Conklin (vocals), Mario Flores (guitar), Bill Richardson (guitar / keyboards), John Flores (bass), Stefan Flores (drums)

Band formed by ex-JAGPANZER, SATAN'S HOST and RIOT vocalist Harry Conklin. The singer returned to JAGPANZER upon their reformation and subsequent second wind of success. The Flores siblings created covers band HIP POCKET.

Albums:
TITAN FORCE, US Metal US017CD (1989)
Chase Your Dreams / Master Of Disguise / Lord Desire / Toll Of Pain / Will O' The Wisp / Blaze Of Glory / Wings Of Rage / New Age Rebels / Fool On The Run
WINNERS / **LOSER**, Shark SHARK 021CD (1991)
Fields Of Valor / Shadow Of A Promise / Winner/Loser / Face To Face / Eyes Of The Young / One And All / Small Price To Pay / Dreamscape

TORCH (SWEDEN)

Line-Up: Dan Dark (vocals), Chris J. First (guitar), Claus Wildt (guitar), Ian Greg (bass), Steve Streaker (drums)

TORCH were a powerful, traditional yet unrelentingly fast paced Metal act that garnered lots of praise in their time.

Guitarist Claus Wildt relocated to America to join MASI. Wildt's guitar partner Chris First and drummer Steve Streaker (real name Hakan Hedlund) are now ensconced in CRYSTAL PRIDE.

Vocalist Dan Dark (real name Östen Bidebo) later fronted a cover act titled BLÄÄSTERS.

Singles/EPs:
Bad Girls / The Serpent / Cut Throat Tactics, Record Pool MAXIPOOL001 (1983)

Albums:
FIRERAISER, Tandan TEP001 (1983)
Beyond / Fireraiser / Pain / Mercenary / Retribution
TORCH, Sword LP001 (1984)
Warlock / Beauty And The Beast / Watcher Of The Night / Rage Age / Beyond The Threshold Of Pain / Battle Axe / Hatchet Man / Sweet Desire / Sinister Eyes / Gladiator
ELEKTRIKISS, Sword LP004 (1985)
Thunderstruck / Elektrikiss / Hot On Your Heels / Runnin' Riot / Victims Love / Bad Girls / Cut Throat Tactics / When The Going Gets Tough... / Limelight

TORNADO (SERBIA)

Line-Up: Philip Zmaher (vocals), Neboysha Tasich (guitar / vocals), George Letich (guitar / keyboards / vocals), Steven Bukvich (guitars), Sinisha Tasich (bass)

A Serbian Power Metal act out of Novi Sad that pursues a wide ranging slew of influences including Byzantine Medieval, Renaissance and Baroque neo-Classical music. TORNADO also mark a difference by employing three lead vocalists. The 'Triumph Of The King' debut saw release in May of 2002 through the German Angular label.

Albums:
TRIUMPH OF THE KING, Angular (2002)
Coming Of The King / We Must Revenge / Fight To Win / Black Swan Rider / The Wall / I Love Japan / Alone In The Dark (Midnight Prayer) / Whisper of The Past / Heavy Metal Symphony: Eternal Mystery-Epitaph / Triumph of The King

TOTAL ECLIPSE (USA)

Line-Up: Andi Giardina (vocals), Erik Cameron (guitar), Chris Cameron (guitar), Owen Hart (bass), Ramon Ochoa (drums)

Albums:
ASHES OF EDEN, Limb Music Productions (2002)

TOXIK (New York, NY, USA)

Line-Up: Charles Sabin (vocals), Josh Christian (guitar), John Donnelly (guitar), Brian Bonini (bass), Tad Leger (drums)

TOXIK added second guitarist John Donnelly prior to beginning work on their second album, 'Think This', in Florida. A few months later vocalist Mike Sanders was replaced by Charlie Sabin.

Singles/EPs:
There Stood The Fence / Out On The Tiles, Roadracer (1989)

Albums:
WORLD CIRCUS, Roadrunner RR 349572 (1988)
Heart Attack / Social Overload / Pain And Misery / Voices / Door To Hell / World Circus / 47 Seconds Of Sanity / False Prophets / Haunted Earth / Victims
THINK THIS, Roadracer RO 94602 (1989)
Think This / Creed / Spontaneous / There Stood The Fence / Black And White / WIR NJN 8 (In God) / Machine Dream / Shotgun Logic / Time After Time / Technical Arrogance / Out On The Tiles

TRAGEDY (ARGENTINA)
Line-Up: Esteban Peréz (vocals / guitar), Pablo Belaunzarán (guitar), Emiliano Tambussi (bass), Maximiliano Peréz (drums)

Power Metal band TRAGEDY was convened during 1997 with a line-up of frontman Esteban Peréz, guitarist Cristian Abarca, bassist Emiliano Tambussi and drummer Maximiliano Peréz. The following year Abarca decamped in order to join HELKER. His replacement, Pablo Belaunzarán, would join the fold in October of 1999. The self-financed album 'Gates To Efinity' arrived in 2001 and included a live version of 'Searching An Answer'.

Albums:
GATES TO INFINITY, (2001)
Intro - Mission / Gates to Infinity / Knight Of Victory / Something´s Calling / Searching The Answer / Silence In Paradise / Warrior / Legend Of The Gods / Waiting For The Call / Searching The Answer (Live)

TRAGEDY DIVINE (GERMANY)
Line-Up: Gerrit Philip Mutz (vocals), Jörg Michael Knittel (guitar), Sven Podgursky (guitar), Bernard Altmann (bass), Frank Zube (drums)

Formed under the title of VALLEY OF ARTS in Ludwigsburg during 1990, this Progressive Metal band became TRAGEDY DIVINE in 1994 after releasing a demo entitled 'Dreams Of Perfection' and submitting the song 'Garden Of Mischief' to the 'Peace Eater Sampler Vol. III' compilation
With the adoption of the new band name the

German quintet opted to discontinue writing complex material and decided to go for a more Heavy Metal approach.
After the appearance of the 'Apostles Of Deceit' demo TRAGEDY DIVINE released the 'Visions Of Power' album in the spring of 1996 before encountering a number of problems. These ructions eventually resulting in a switch to the SACRED STEEL moniker, adopting a full on Metal image and signing a deal with Metal Blade in 1997.

Albums:
VISIONS OF POWER, T&T TT0021-2 (1996)
Die In My Dreams / I Married A Witch / Visions Of Power / Seize Control / Tyrant Shadows / Veils Of Solemn Black / Bleeding Crystal Tears / Ritual Damnation / Nightmare Reality / Tragedy Divine

TRAMPIRE (GERMANY)
Line-Up: Boris Cabal (vocals), 'Baby' Gerd Lücking (guitar), 'Mega' Mike Bargon (guitar), 'Kid' Karsten Lücking (bass), Jensi Foorhees (drums)

Albums:
TALKING TO FOOLS, Hellion Bald Head (1992)
The Beginning / Sinner / Voices Of Pain / Black Widow / Trampire / Can You Feel The Night / Moonlight / Talking To Fools / Journey / Civil War / Cry Out / Freibier

TREASURE LAND (SWEDEN)
Line-Up: Zenny Gram (vocals), Jonas Hörnqvist (guitar), Magnus Lind (bass), Kaspar Dahlqvist (keyboards), Magnus Hörnqvist (drums)

TREASURE LAND's original vocalist, Zenny Gram, was previously the frontman for DESTINY but following the release of the 'Questions' debut album he parted company with the group. TREASURE LAND have since announced a new vocalist in JEKYLL & HYDE frontman Jakob Samuelsson.

Albums:
QUESTIONS, T&T TT 0029-2 (1997)
The Gift / Misery/ Why / Demons / To Live Again / Miracle / Spirits / Kingdom / Eat The Rain
GATEWAY, T&T TT 0037-7 (1998)
King Of All Kings / Where Tomorrow Will Remain / Dreams Of Reality / Rendezvous / A Winter's Night / Heaven / Possessed / Voices / Liar

TREASURESEEKER (BRAZIL)
Line-Up: Olaf Hayer (vocals), Andy Gutjahr

(guitar), Marc Piras (guitar), Willi Heib (bass), Danilo Batdorf (drums)

A 2001 Christian White Metal project. TREASURE SEEKER's 'A Tribute To The Past' album was a collection of Rock cover versions beefed up into Power Metal workouts. The band project gelled together a cast of well respected South American players including vocalist Olaf Hayer from DIONYSUS and the LUCA TURILLI band, guitarists Andy Gutjahr of LIGHTMARE and Marc Piras of TOY BOX, bassist Willi Heib of SEVENTH AVENUE and drummer Danilo Batdorf from SERPENT KILLER.

Tracks covered included songs originally undertaken by acts such as STRYPER, BRIDE, SAINT, CREED, LEVITICUS, BLOODGOOD, REZ, JERUSALEM, FORCE 3 and German veterans HELLOWEEN.

<u>Albums:</u>
A TRIBUTE TO THE PAST, (2001)
A Tribute To The Past / Too Late For Living / To Hell With The Devil / Flames Of Fire / Out Of The Darkness / Silence Screams / Rebels Of Jesus Christ / Warrior Of Light / Heroes / Meet Again

TRIVIAL ACT (NORWAY)
Line-Up: Kim Isaksen (vocals), Björn Andreasson (guitar), Hakon Salveson (guitar), Svend Ole Heggedal (bass), Erik Wroldsen (drums)

Progressive Metal act TRIVIAL ACT originally demoed under the band title of CEMETERY GATES, but adopted TRIVIAL ACT so as not to be confused with the plethora of Norwegian Death Metal acts. As CEMETERY GATES the band issued the 1992 'Mirror Never Lies' demo. Previous to that the band had evolved through MALTRACTOR and EMPIRE.

<u>Albums:</u>
MINDSCAPE, Facefront FF0002 (1997)
Mindscape / Dream Dwell - Part I / Rainbow Valley / Forbidden Eye / E.P. / Vanish / Crossing Bridges / Dream Dwell - Part II

TROJAN (UK)
Line-Up: Graeme Wyatt (vocals), Pete Wadeson (guitar), Ted Twigg (bass), Sam Hall (drums)

TROJAN featured the track 'Premonition' on the Ebony Records compilation 'Metal Maniaxe' in 1982 before signing to Roadrunner and recording the Guy Bidmead produced 'Chasing The Storm' album in 1985. TROJAN later changed their name to TALION

and released the 'Killing The World' album on Peaceville. Bassist Ted Twigg and drummer Sam Hall were replaced by Phillip Gavin and Johnny Lee Jackson respectively.

<u>Albums:</u>
CHASING THE STORM, Roadrunner RR 9756 (1985)
Chasing The Storm / Tonight We've Got It Made / Only The Strong Survive / Hypnotised / Backstabber / Icehouse / Take No Prisoners / Hot n' Ready / Help Me / Aggressor

TSUNAMI (CA, USA)
Line-Up: Doug Denton (vocals), Tatsuya Miyazaki (guitar), Tomataka Yammoto (guitar), Max Load (bass), Scott Sherman (drums)

An intriguing San Jose Metal band that featured two Japanese guitarists. TSUNAMI certainly impressed with their debut album but seemed unable to capitalise on this initial momentum. Vocalist Doug Denton quit in 1986.

The second album, 'Tough Under Fire' recorded for the German Intercord label, found Max Load (going under the name of Salvador Max?) as the sole survivor from the debut, the band being rounded out by new musicians comprising vocalist / guitarist Koshi Shioya ('K.O.'), guitarist Jamie Francis and drummer Steven Tsutsumi. However, shortly after this release TSUNAMI folded.

TSUNAMI apparently reformed of late with a line up of Max Load (now billed as 'Maximus Load'), Shioya and Tsutsumi.

<u>Albums:</u>
TSUNAMI, Music For Nations MFN 9 (1983)
Firewater / Fade To Black / Runaround / You'll Never Lay A Finger On Me / Teaser / Face of Death / Revenge / Ninja / Call Off The Dogs / Masters Of The Night
TOUGH UNDER FIRE, Intercord (1990)
Lost In Motion / Same Old Thing / The Runaround / Tough Under Fire / Room Of Doom / Money / Love To Hurt You / Love & War / In The Rain / World Without Walls

TT QUICK (Osbornville, NJ, USA)
Line-Up: Mark Tornillo (vocals), David Dipietro (guitar), Walt Fortune (bass), Glenn Evans (drums)

A renowned force on the New York club scene TT QUICK impressed many and soon built up a sizeable cult following. Guitarist David Dipietro's skills were especially singled out, as a guitar tutor the man had taught both

ZAKK WYLDE of the OZZY OSBOURNE band and SKID ROW's Dave Sabo.

The opening 'TT Quick' mini-album featured a rendition of JOHN FOGERTY's 'Fortunate Son'.

As drummer Glen Evans joined NUCLEAR ASSAULT former HELLCATS man Erik Ferro replaced him for the 'Metal Of Honor' album, which surprisingly included a cover of the DAVE CLARK FIVE's 'Glad All Over'. Internationally, TT QUICK peaked with the crunching 'Metal Of Honor', the album landing many commendable reviews, wide ranging media coverage and healthy sales. Touring saw TT QUICK opening for such major acts as ACCEPT, METALLICA, MEGADETH, MOTORHEAD and IRON MAIDEN.

The band hit a major stumbling block when Ferro was forced out due to family illness. Unable to replace their drummer TT QUICK disbanded. Dipietro also later joined NUCLEAR ASSAULT.

TT QUICK would reform with the original line-up sporadically over the intervening years, these reunions resulting in the 1989 'Sloppy Seconds' album and the live 'Thrown Together Live' opus recorded in 1990.

The band, retaining the classic line-up, reformed on a permanent basis in 2000 for the tattoo themed 'Ink' album.

Albums:
TT QUICK, Avalanche MARZ 2002 (1984)
Go For The Throat / Fortunate Son / Child Of Sin / Metal Man / Victims
METAL OF HONOR, Megaforce / Island ILPS 9847 (1986)
Metal Of Honor / Front Burner / Hard As Rock / Child Of Sin / Asleep At The Wheel / Come Beat The Band / Hell To Pay / Queen Of The Scene / Glad All Over / Siren Song
SLOPPY SECONDS, Halycon 65431 (1989)
Eye Of The Storm / Deliver Me / Save Some For Me / Method Or Madness / Rock You Over / Isolation Booth / White Spots / Rule The World
THROWN TOGETHER LIVE, Halycon (1992)
Intro - Kickin' Ass & Talkin' Names / Metal Man / Eye Of The Storm / Asleep At The Wheel / Deliver Me / Front Burner / Isolation Booth / Child Of Sin / Beat The Band / Metal Of Honor / Go For The Throat
INK, Ocean (2000)
Ink / Subterrania / Whippin' Time / World On Display / Run / Age Of Treachery / Thick As Thieves / Stone Dirt Cowboy / Water Song / Back To The Bottom / Take A Lickin'

TUATHA DE DANAAN (BRAZIL)

Line-Up: Bruno Maia (vocals / guitar), Rodrigo Berne (guitar), Giovani Mendonca (bass), Leonardo Godstfriedt (violin), Rafael Costa (keyboards), Rodrigo Abreu (drums)

A Celtic inspired, medieval Metal band. TUATHA DE DANAAN released a brace of demos, 'The Last Pendragon' and 'Faeryage', prior to the eponymous debut album.

Albums:
TUATHA DE DANAAN, (2000)
Us / Tuatha De Danann / Beltane / The Bards Of The Infinity / Queen Of The Witches / Faeryage / Oisin / Imrahma
TINGARALANTINGA DUM, (2002)
The Dance Of The Little Ones / Battle Song / Behold The Horned King / Tan Pinga Ra Tan / Finganforn / Vercingetorix / Celtia / Some Tunes To Fly / Tingaralatinga Dum / Macdara

LUCA TURILLI (ITALY)

Solo outings from RHAPSODY guitarist LUCA TURILLI. As expected the 'King Of The Nordic Twilight' album, a huge seller in Europe, dealt in trademark Symphonic Fantasy Metal. The main vocals would be handled by Olaf Hayer with Sascha Paeth of HEAVEN'S GATE responsible for both overall production and bass with Robert Hunecke-Rizzo of HEAVEN'S GATE and SARGENT FURY on drums. Rannveig Sif Sigurdardottir would take on the lead vocal role for the track 'Princess Aurora'.

Olaf Hayer would later front DIONYSUS and the 2001 Christian "White Power Metal" TREASURE SEEKER project.

Singles/EPs:
The Ancient Forest Of Elves / Warrior's Pride (Duet version) / Knight Of Immortal Fire, Limb Music Productions LMP 9908-12CD (1999)

Albums:
KING OF THE NORDIC TWILIGHT, Limb Music Productions LMP 9909-13CD (1999)
To Magic Horizons / Black Dragon / Legend Of Steel / Lord Of The Winter Snow / Princess Aurora / The Ancient Forest Of Elves / Throne Of Ice / Where Heroes Lie / Warrior's Pride / Kings Of The Nordic Twilight
DEMONHEART, Inside Out Music (2002)

TWILIGHT (DENMARK)
Line-Up: Anders Engberg (vocals), Jan Strandh (guitar), Micke Därth (guitar), Kim Mikkelsen (bass), Finn Zierler (keyboards), Thomas Freden (drums)

A Danish Power Metal band fronted by former SORCEROR singer Anders Engberg.

TWILIGHT are produced by Tommy Hansen. The 2000 release 'The Edge' is in fact a pressing of the band's 1992 demo.

Guitarist Jan Strandh also operates a side project titled MASTER MASSIVE. Anders Engberg found a wider international audience fronting the highly rated LION'S SHARE. In 2001 keyboard player Finn Zierler conceived the conceptual BEYOND TWILIGHT album 'The Devil's Hall Of Fame'.

Albums:
EYE FOR AN EYE, Olafsongs OCD 029 (1994) (Danish release)
Come Night Come Evil / Eye For An Eye / Imperfection / Flashbacks / River Of Styx / Sol Et Luna / Trial By Fire / The Meeting / To The End / Sail Away
EYE FOR AN EYE, Seagull 35641 SICD 9610 (1996)
Salem / Struck By Destiny / Flashbacks / Helios / Trial By Fire / The Meeting / Eye For An Eye / River Of Styx / Sail Away / Ghost / Imperfection / To The End
THE EDGE, Zierler (2000)
Far Beyond The Edge Of Sanity / Blacklight / Salem / Twilight / Struck By Destiny / The Nightmare / The Black Manifest

TWILIGHT GUARDIANS (FINLAND)
Line-Up: Vesa Virtanen (vocals), Carl-Johan Gustafsson (guitar), Antti Valtamo (keyboards), Mikko Tång (bass), Henri Suominen (drums)

Albums:
LAND OF THE KINGS, (1998)
TALES OF THE BRAVE, Angular SKAN 8222.AR (2000)
Eternal Glory / Land Of The Kings / Wings Of The Gods / Angel Without Wings / Just Let Me / Running Wild / Snowfall / Last Of My Kind / Night Of The Black Swan / Forgotten Land / Gods Of Time / Twilight Guardians

TWISTED TOWER DIRE (VA, USA)
Line-Up: Tony Taylor (vocals), Scott Waldrop (guitar), Jim Murad (drums), Mark Stauffer (drums

Virginia based epic 'True' Metal act TWISTED TOWER DIRE have evolved out of a Black Metal background through an inception in Doom territory to a trad renaissance, and highly respected, Heavy Metal band. TWISTED TOWER DIRE first made themselves public with the issue of a 1995 two track demo proudly entitled 'Hail Northern Virginia'. The band upon its inception incorporated two members from arch Black

TWISTED TOWER DIRE

Metal act ARGHOSLENT in guitarist Nick Mertaugh, also of THOKK, and drummer Mark Stauffer, the latter also citing credits with ULTERIOR MOTIVES. TWISTED TOWER DIRE, so named after a lyric from one of Mertaugh's THOKK compositions, was rounded out by erstwhile GOLGOTHA members guitarist Scott Waldrop and bassist Jim Murad and singer Tom Phillips of PARASITIC INFESTATION.

A split 10" single 'Mourner In The Nethermists' in league with COLD MOURNING, issued by Bad Posture Records in 1996, would mark the band's inaugural commercial release. Before too long Phillips, leaving to join WHILE HEAVEN WEPT, made way for the classically trained Janet Rubin and Mertaugh departed. The group would revert back to the demo process for a 1997 tape 'Triumphing True Metal' before being featured the following year on a split double pack 7" EP on the Game Two imprint 'Fourteen Inches Of Fury' donating the track 'Fuck You (Consume 24 Beers Before Listening)'. Other acts featured on this release would be Doom merchants REVELATION, Germany's NAEVUS and Hungarian band MOOD. That same year the song 'Starflight Requiem' would be donated to the Bad posture compilation 'Metal Injection'. Rubin though had made her exit to pursue a career on the Opera stage in Germany and in mid 1998 TWISTED TOWER DIRE duly enrolled the imposing figure of the bald and heavily tattooed ex-GOLGOTHA singer Tony Taylor and second guitarist Dave Boyd.

In 1999 TWISTED TOWER DIRE made their presence felt on the IRON MAIDEN tribute album 'Maiden America' put out by Twilight Records. The track contributed, a medley of 'Powerslave' songs, would be found in unedited form as part of a batch of cover

445

versions. These numbering MANOWAR's 'Revelation' and VOIVOID's 'Forgotten In Space' with drummer Mark Stauffer taking the lead vocal mantle, included as bonus tracks to the vinyl version of TWISTED TOWER DIRE's debut full length album 'The Curse Of Twisted Tower'. Although criticised for its weak production the record nevertheless impressed many critics with the sheer integrity and strength of the material.

The band's second split 10" release came with a Near Dark Productions union with SOLSTICE, the band offering up the track 'Mourner In The Mist' as their contribution.

During February of 2001 guitarist Scott Waldrop and vocalist Tony Taylor seconded themselves to King Fowley's OCTOBER 31. TWISTED TOWER DIRE themselves would self-finance a 2001 European tour performing at the 'Wacken Open Air' festival and putting on shows in England. The October 2001 TWISTED TOWER DIRE album, originally projected as 'Passages' but finally emerging billed as 'The Isle Of Hydra', would see release through the Miskatonic Foundation label of SOLSTICE's Rich Walker plus licenses to Hellion Records in Germany and the Metal Supremacy imprint for a vinyl version. TWISTED TOWER DIRE cut a version of BLACK SABBATH's 'Turn Up The Night' for a 2002 tribute album.

Recently Murad has been supplanted by new bass player Mike 'Mushroom'.

Singles/EPs:
Fuck You (Must Consume 24 Beers Before Listening), Game Two (1998) ('Fourteen Inches Of Fury' EP. Split double pack single with NAEVUS, MOOD & REVELATION)

Albums:
CURSE OF THE TWISTED TOWER, (1999)
Land Of Illusions / Hail Dark Rider / The Curse Of Twisted Tower Dire / The Epic War Never Ends / Rue Of The Forsaken Sleepkeeper (Part 2) / Lament Nocturne / The Valkyrie Death Squadrons / The Witchs Eyes
ISLE OF THE HYDRA, Miskatonic Foundation (2001)
Battle Cry / The Isle Of Hydra / When The Daylight Fades / Daggers Blade / Ride The Night / The Longing / Sign Of The Storm / Final Stand / Dying Breath

TWYSTER (GERMANY)
Line-Up: Coco (vocals), Christian Gahmann (guitar), Ralf Jahnel (guitar), Oliver Emde (bass), Andrés Vergara-Ruiz (drums)

Female fronted Metal band founded during

1995 by former BLAZON personnel guitarist Ralf Jahnel and bassist Oliver Emde. TWYSTER's 2002 album 'Lunatic Siren' amply demonstrated the German nations bizarre sense of humour by oddly including a cover version of A-HA's Pop hit 'The Sun Always Shines On TV'.

Albums:
ZIPPER JARS, (1997)
LUNATIC SIREN, Massacre (2002)
May-Day / Mrs. Borden / Twyster / 50 Bloody Bucks / The Cloven Hoof / Valhalla / High Noon / Dark Destiny / Thunderland / Don't Break The Silence / The Sun Always Shines On TV / Two Wild Hearts

TYRAN PACE (GERMANY)
Line-Up: Ralf Scheepers (vocals), Oliver Kaufmann (guitar), Michael D. Young (guitar), Frank Mittelbach (guitar), Andy Ahues (bass), Edgar Patrick (drums)

German outfit TYRAN PACE are noted as a starting block for the careers of vocalist Ralph Scheepers and drummer Edgar Patrick. Scheepers pre-TYRAN PACE band was called BEAST OF PREY.

Whilst Scheepers went on to some degree of fame and fortune fronting GAMMA RAY and PRIMAL FEAR, Patrick (real name Edgar Witzemann) enjoyed stints with SINNER and BONFIRE and also played on PAUL SAMSON's 'Joint Forces' album. Patrick had been replaced by Andy Fallscheer by the time the 'Watching You' album was recorded.

TYRAN PACE had actually parted company with guitarists Michael D. Young and Frank Mittelbach fairly early on after the 'Eye To Eye' album was released in 1984, the remaining members choosing to merely add a single guitarist, Callo Rapallo, in place of the departed duo.

HELLOWEEN guitarist Kai Hansen took note of the band offering Scheepers the position of vocalist with HELLOWEEN. For the time being the frontman declined the offer.

Rapallo himself was replaced by Davor Sertic (later to turn up in KASHMYR) for the 'Watching You' album.

TYRAN PACE dissolved when Hansen once more tried to entice Scheepers away, this time to his post HELLOWEEN act GAMMA RAY. Scheepers departed and TYRAN PACE floundered. Another TYRAN PACE vocalist Andi Mersch would join Metal band LANZER in 1992.

TYRAN PACE returned in the late '90s with Michael Dees taking the role of frontman.

Albums:
EYE TO EYE, Blackboard & Chalk (1984)
Highway Knights / Knives And Bones / Black
Leather Beauty / Let It Rock / Fight Forever /
Eye To Eye / State Of Kind / Come Get It /
Leave Me Tonight
LONG LIVE METAL, Noise SPV 08-4413
(1985)
Shock Waves / Red Sweat / Play All Night /
Law And Order / Wheels Of Love / Hot To
Rock / Shakedown / Night Of The Wolves /
Raid The Victims / Killers On The Highway
WATCHING YOU, Noise SPV 08-4413 (1987)
Saints Of Rock / Cry Out / Hands In The Air
/ Criminal / Matter Of Time / Get Down /
Madness / Fire In Your Eyes / We Are Strong
TAKE A SEAT IN THE HIGH ROW, Bossy
Ogress 0073672 BO (1998)
The Day Before The Day After / Gone With
The Secret / Motor Of Society / Answers /
Follow Me / A Penny For Your Thoughts /
Your Second Me / This Story / Lake Of Shit /
Eternity / Feeling Vs Time

TYRANT (AUSTRALIA)
Line-Up: Neil Wilson (vocals), Andrew Zarins
(guitar), Grant Wallace (guitar), Dave
McDonnell (bass), Robert Zarins (drums)

Tasmanian Metal band founded in 1983.
Despite causing a commotion on their home
island and subsequently in mainland Australia
TYRANT would collapse leaving as their
legacy an infamous demo recording. TYRANT
was forged by vocalist Neil Wilson, the Zarins
siblings guitarist Andrew and drummer
Robert, second guitarist Grant Wallace and
bassist Tim Partridge, the latter an erstwhile
member of THE KEVIN BORICH
EXPERIENCE. The band cut a 1984 demo
'Never Too Loud' - its title taken from a ROSE
TATTOO concert poster - and soon made
headway on the live circuit. Leaving Tasmania
behind, after a farewell concert with a
capacity 2000 crowd in Hobart, TYRANT
relocated to Sydney. There the band's
growing stature dictated headline status at
the 'Metal Crusade' festival.
TYRANT, unable to secure a deal, would
ultimately fold. The band revived itself in 1998
re-drafting most of the original members. The
solitary new face was ex-PREACHER bassist
Dave McDonnell. TYRANT recorded their
debut album 'Freaks Of Nature' for issue in
2001. The album would include the early
notorious demo as bonus tracks. The band
announced a new bassist, former SLYDER
man Andy Hatton, in March of 2002.

Albums:
FREAKS OF NATURE, (2001)

Intro / Freaks Of Nature / Daddy's Little Girl /
Dressed To Kill / Better Off Dead / Money / I
Don't Need Religion / Feelings / Color My
World / Lovechild / Never Too Loud / Lamb
To The Slaughter / Thunder And Steel / War
Of The Roses

TYRANT (GERMANY)
Line-Up: Kerrmit (vocals), Carl Tomaschko
(guitar), Holgar Thiele (guitar), Andre Papack
(bass), Micky Budde (drums)

A German Metal band, TYRANT were fronted
by the hilariously named Kerrmit and issued a
number of independent albums through the
mid to late '80s.
For their fourth album, 1988's 'Ruling The
World', TYRANT underwent a major line-up
change by ditching a guitarist and their
rhythm section. Alongside Kerrmit and 'King'
Carl Tomaschko the band's new recruits were
guitarist Phil Zanella, keyboard player Robert
Kosch, bassist Chris Peterson and former
GRAVESTONE drummer Dieter Behle.

Singles/EPs:
Wanna Make Love / Look Out, Tyrant (1984)

Albums:
MEAN MACHINE, Corona (1985)
Free For All / We Stay Free / Making Noise
And Drinking Beer / I'm Ready / Wanna
Make Love / Tyrant / Invaders / Grapes Of
Wrath / Blondsuckin' Woman / Killer Cat
FIGHT FOR YOUR LIFE, Scratch 941308
(1986)
Dark Eyes Of London / Up The Hammer /
Fight For Your Life / Metal Rules /
Streetfighter / Two Down One To Go /
Goddess / Danger / Can't Stand Still / We
Will Rock
RUNNING HOT, Scratch (1986)
Rock Your Bottom / Breakout / Taste Of
Paradise / When The Raven Flies Again /
Running Hot / Fire At Sea / Take The Most
Dangerous Way / Get Ready / She's A Killer
/ Starlight
RULING THE WORLD, Scratch (1988)
Burn You / Blind Revolution / Set 'Em On
Fire / Killing The Peace We Fall / Wild Cats /
She Makes Me Hot (Hot) / Wild And Free /
Ruling The World / Beat It / On The Wings
Of Endless
LIVE & CRAZY, (1990)
I'm Crazy / Free For All / Making Noise And
Drinking Beer / Bloodsucking Woman / Get
Ready / Set 'em On Fire / Steamhammer /
Rock Your Bottom / Let's Dance / Wanna
Make Love

447

TYRANT (Temple City, CA, USA)
Glen May (vocals), Rocky Rockwell (guitar), Greg May (bass), G. Stanley Burtis (drums)

Californian Power Thrash Metal act TYRANT was formed by bassist Greg May and vocalist Doug Anderson in Pasadena, California during. Previous to TYRANT guitarist Rocky Rockwell had operated the act VISIONS which included a pre-STRYPER Tim Gaines. By 1982 Anderson's position had been taken by Glen May.

TYRANT would then be approached by Brian Slagel of Metal Blade Records with a proposition to appear on the 'Metal Massacre III' compilation album. TYRANT duly accepted, submitting the impressive Bill Metoyer produced 'Battle Of Armageddon'. Response was such Metal Blade signed the band up for a full album deal. Metoyer would handle production duties for the group's debut 'Legions Of The Dead' album released in August of 1985. Another Metoyer crafted record, 'Too Late To Pray' with G. Stanley Burtis taking Roy's place on the drum stool, arrived the following year.

Reportedly TYRANT was offered support slots to acts of such weight as SLAYER, SAVATAGE and MERCYFUL FATE but apparently declined these offers.

The band would be put on ice for many years until interest was rekindled by the 1994 CD re-issue of 'Metal Massacre III'. The German label Art Of Music snapped the band up and TYRANT duly delivered the 1996 comeback effort 'King Of Kings'. Both previous albums would also be reissued but on the eve of promotional touring Rockwell backed out. The vacancy was filled by Anthony Romero, an erstwhile member of BLOODLUST.

TYRANT would commit further tracks to tape in 1997 as well as contributing songs to Dwell Records tribute albums to MOTÖRHEAD and BLACK SABBATH.

Albums:
LEGIONS OF THE DEAD, Roadrunner RR 9765 (1985)
Warriors Of Metal / Fall Into The Hands Of Evil / The Battle Of Armageddon / Legions Of The Dead / Tyrant's Revelation / Listen To The Preacher / Knight Of Darkness / Thru The Night / Time Is Running Low / Sacrifice
TOO LATE TO PRAY, Roadrunner RR 9658 (1988)
Tyrants Revelation II / Too Late To Pray / Beyond The Grave / Valley Of Death / Nazarene / Bells Of Hades / Into The Flames / Babylon / Verdalack / Beginning Of The End / Eve Of Destruction
KING OF KINGS, Semaphore 60607 (1996)
Tyrant's Revelation III / King Of Kings / Fast

Lane / Dance With The Devil / Ancient Fire / Nowhere To Run / When Night Falls / Tighten The Vice / Coast To Coast / War

TYRANT EYES (GERMANY)
Line-Up: Alexander Reimund (vocals), Marcus Amend (guitar), Michael Apfel (bass), Jürgen Bormuth (keyboards), Sascha Tilger (drums)

Metal band that has supported SAXON, TOM ANGELRIPPER and SACRED STEEL.

Albums:
BOOK OF SOULS, Bossy Ogress BO018CD (1999)
Book Of Souls / Broken Wings / Dark Side Of The Moon / Timebomb / Shadows From Heaven / Land Of Death / When The Storm Comes Down / Fly To The Rainbow / Of Rage And Honor / The Gate

TYRANT'S REIGN (IL, USA)
Line-Up: Randy Barron (vocals), Karl Miller (guitar), Chris Nelken (guitar), Phil Fouch (bass), Gabriel Anthony (drums)

TYRANT'S REIGN issued a solitary self-financed and now extremely rare mini-album. Guitarist Jeff Baghepour would make his exit just prior to recording of the album.

Vocalist Randy Barron was later to found WINTERKILL releasing the 1997 album 'A Feast For A Beggar'. Drummer Gabriel Anthony was to join MOTHERFUNK whilst guitarist Karl Miller plies his trade with PSYCHOSIS.

Ex-TYRANT's REIGN men guitarist Jeff Baghepour and bassist Phil Fouch would unite with Russ Barron (Randy's sibling), keyboard player Michelle O'Day and drummer Donny Mizanira to found the Power Metal band PHOENIX RISING. This act, after a name change to CRYPTIC VISION, later recorded an album.

Albums:
YEAR OF THE TYRANT, Cynical (1987)
Tyrant's Reign / Jack The Ripper / Untamed / Deadly Eyes / Reign Of Terror / Fadeaway

TYSONDOG (UK)
Line-Up: Clutch Carruthers (vocals), Paul Burdis (guitar), Alan Hunter (guitar), Kevin Wynn (bass), Ged Wolf (drums).

Newcastle Heavy Metal band TYSONDOG amusingly took their name from the bassist's girlfriend's dog! The band was rooted in an earlier act billed as ORCHRIST which comprised vocalist Alan Hunter, guitarist Paul

Burdis, bass player Kev Wynn and drummer Kev Hunter. The latter, brother of RAVEN's Rob 'Wacko' Hunter, would make his exit to act as RAVEN roadie. Peter Reeve duly took over the drum stool position as TYSONDOG started to receive label interest from such now renowned indies as Ebony, Music For Nations, Roadrunner and Newcastle's own Neat Records.

Signing to Neat TYSONDOG cut the 1983 single track 'Eat The Rich', featuring Alan Hunter on lead vocals. However, shortly after recording this track a lead vocalist was deemed crucial to the band's line-up and 'Clutch' Carruthers was inducted. Carruthers laid down his vocals on the B side 'Dead Meat'. With the single just in the shops Reeves opted out. Nevertheless, progress was swift and 'Eat The Rich' even garnered valuable exposure being featured in 'The Chain' movie. The band set about recording their debut album 'Beware Of The Dog'. Ged 'Wolf' Cooke sat in on drums but would quit immediately after recording team up with ATOMKRAFT. He was replaced by Rob Walker. Although 'Beware Of The Dog' was produced by Cronos of VENOM, the man himself proclaimed afterwards that he thought the band were "shit" and nothing more than JUDAS PRIEST imitators, stating that he had done it purely as a favour because Wolf was the brother of VENOM manager Eric Cook!

Although acknowledged to be blighted by a particularly thin drum sound reception to the album though was, in the main, enthusiastic especially in mainland Europe. Gigs ensued including prestigious shows in Holland at the Dynamo club and at the 'Aardschok' festival. The 'Shoot To Kill' EP followed in 1985. TYSONDOG was slated to support American Shock Rockers MADAME X but this tour was pulled.

Signing to Eric Cooke of VENOM repute for management TYSONDOG set to work on a second, album 'Crimes Of Insanity', the single from which would be a cover version of ALICE COOPER's seminal 'School's Out' hit. Hunter backed out once these sessions were over and the band opted to persevere as a quartet. Oddly the 'School's Out' single would be promoted by a new look TYSONDOG, eschewing the familiar leather and studs for teased, hairsprayed hair and glammier apparel. The band did get to grace the stage with WARLOCK for a run through of JUDAS PRIEST's 'You've Got Another Thing Comin'' at Kerrang magazine's 100th edition celebrations but a more substantial support tour to VENOM in North America fell through due to visa problems. The bad luck continued as Carruthers was involved in a car crash on the way to a vital gig at London's Marquee club.

TYSONDOG had already started demoing material for a proposed third album when they learned Neat Records was no longer interested. The band announced it was to fold and a swansong gig in Newcastle saw Alan Hunter joining them onstage for a final time.

Wynn teamed up with ex-TYGERS OF PAN TANG vocalist Jess Cox in TYGER TYGER. Alan Hunter featured in ATOMKRAFT and also performed vocals on the third PARIAH album, recorded in 1993, which until recently remained unreleased.

The Brazilian Rock Brigade label would re-issue both albums complete with tracks from the 'Shoot To Kill' sessions. In 2002 the Sanctuary label compiled all the available band material for the 'Painted Heroes' collection.

Singles/EPs:
Eat The Rich / Dead Meat, Neat NEAT 33 (1984)
Shoot To Kill / Changeling / Hammerhead / Back To The Bullet, Neat NEAT 46 (1985)
School's Out / Don't Let The Bastards Grind Ya Down, Neat NEAT 56 (1986)
School's Out / Don't Let The Bastards Grind Ya Down / Back To The Bullet, Neat NEAT 56 (1986) (12" single)

Albums:
BEWARE OF THE DOG, Neat NEAT 1017 (1985)
Hammerhead / Dog Soldiers / Demon / The Inquisitor / Dead Meat / Painted Heroes / Voice From The Grave / The Butcher / In The End
CRIMES OF INSANITY, Neat NEAT 1031 (1986)
Taste The Hate / Don't Let The Bastards Grind Ya Down / Blood Money / The Machine / School's Out / Street Thunder / Hotter Than Hell / Judgement Day / Eat The Rich / Smack Attack
PAINTED HEROES, Castle Music CMDDD552 (2002)
Hammerhead / Dog Soldiers / Demon / The Inquisitor / Dead Meat / Painted Heroes / Voices From The Grave / Day Of The Butcher / In The End / Shoot To Kill / Changeling / Taste Of Hate / Don't Let The Bastards (Grind You Down) / Blood Money / Time Machine / School's Out / Street Thunder / Hotter Than Hell / Judgement Day / Eat The Rich / Smack Attack / Back To The Bullet

TYTAN (UK)
Line-Up: Kal Swann (vocals), Steve Mann (guitar), Steve Gibbs (guitar), Kevin Riddles

(bass), Dave Dufort (drums)

Ex-ANGEL WITCH men Dave Dufort and Kevin Riddles formed TYTAN in September 1981. The original incarnation of the band allied Dufort, Riddles, vocalist Kal Swann and guitarists Steve Gibbs and Stuart Adams. Dufort had pre-ANGELWITCH amassed quite a history in the Rock world with bands stretching back into the early '60s including THE VOICE, THE SCENERY, MIKE OLDFIELD and KEVIN AYERS. The drummer was also involved in NWoBHMers the E.F. BAND.

Despite a fanfare of press Adams left within months and later turned up fronting LYIN' RAMPANT. He was superseded by ex-A II Z man Gary Owens.

TYTAN received substantial major record company interest, but signed to Kamaflage Records and laid down plans to release the 'Blind Men And Fools' single during 1982 in advance of a proposed album. Unfortunately, despite the album being recorded, without Gary Owens who quit the group in the summer of 1982, Kamaflage Records went under before it could be released. It would not be before 1985 when the album, aptly titled 'Rough Justice', finally emerged through the Metal Masters label.

Dave Dufort also quit and following his departure from the group Dufort re-christened himself Richie D'For and formed NEVADDA FOXX (originally titled KAMIKAZE) with vocalist former DEEP MACHINE and ANGELWITCH Roger Marsden, guitarist Chris Mallia and bassist Richard Vernon.

Dufort went on to form TROY and the highly rated "Glam-Power" act PHANTASM, in league with BLADERUNNER guitarist Gary Jones, before changing his name to Herman Jerian and recording historical theme music based on the life of Richard the Lionheart!

TYTAN meanwhile were forced to rely on outside help to keep active as the long awaited 'Blind Men And Fools' was finally released during September 1982. The band roped in hired hands in the form of ex-LIAR, WILD HORSES and LIONHEART guitarist Steve Mann and ex-JUDAS PRIEST and LIONHEART drummer Les Binks. The band toured Britain opening for the TYGERS OF PAN TANG in October 1982 as TYTAN eventually recruited a permanent drummer in Tony Boden.

Boden's stay was short lived and he was eventually replaced by former TORA TORA and A II Z drummer Simon Wright, after reports had originally surfaced that another ex-A II Z drummer, Karl Reti, had been in the frame for the job.

However, TYTAN would eventually drift apart as, in July 1983, Simon Wright auditioned for AC/DC and got the job, later joining DIO then MR. RUDE and UFO, whilst Gibbs joined CHINATOWN.

Swann later relocated to Los Angeles to form LION with ex-STEELER drummer MARK EDWARDS, ex-LONE STAR guitarist Tony Smith and bassist Arthur Campbell. With LION Swann found considerable success in Japan and continued to enjoy the loyalty of a huge fan following with the subsequent BAD MOON RISING.

Mann would join the MICHAEL SCHENKER GROUP.

Singles/EPs:
Blind Men And Fools / The Ballad Of Edward Case / Sad Man, Kamaflage KAM 6 (1982)

Albums:
ROUGH JUSTICE, Metal Masters METALP 105 (1985)
Blind Men And Fools / Money For Love / Women On The Frontline / Cold Bitch / Ballad Of Edward Case / Rude Awakening / The Watcher / Far Cry / Sad Man / Forever Gone / Don't Play Their Way / Far Side Of Destiny

450

U.D.O. (GERMANY)

Line-Up: Udo Dirkschneider (vocals), Matthias Dieth (guitar), Andy Susemihl (guitar), Dieter Rubach (bass), Thomas Franke (drums)

The diminutive Udo Dirkschneider had been a founding member and lead vocalist of German Metal legends ACCEPT since their inception in 1972. With his uniquely coarse vocal style, skinhead haircut and baton wielding stage presence Dirkschneider would quickly become the focal point for the band on the world stage. He chose to sensationally quit the group at the height of their success in order to form U.D.O. Rumours of splits in the ACCEPT ranks had been filtering through for a number of years so Dirkschneider's break was hardly a surprise.

Viewed very much as Dirkschneider's solo project, despite constant protestations from the band that he had assembled, U.D.O. debuted in 1987 with the hard hitting and uncompromising Mark Dodson produced 'Animal House'. This was an album comprising of ex-ACCEPT tracks deemed "too heavy" for the act!

Although the initial U.D.O. line-up comprised of former WARLOCK men guitarist Peter Szigeti and bassist Frank Rittel and drummer Thomas Franke, ex-SINNER guitarists Matthias Dieth and ANDY SUSEMIHL were later recruited in favour of Szigeti who would found CORACKO and STONEWASHED. Pre-SINNER Dieth had played guitar for GRAVESTONE recording three albums. With U.D.O. his extreme guitar talents would come to the fore.

Touring showed Susemihl's preference for lighter material and he in turn was superseded by Wolfgang Bohm of DARXON. 1989's 'Mean Machine', once more produced by Dodson, and served up more of the same fare but was a record penned by the band themselves. The band also benefited from a complete new rhythm section of former RUNNING WILD members bassist Thomas Smuszynski and drummer Stefan Schwarzmann as U.D.O. went on to open for OZZY OSBOURNE on his British tour of that year.

However, in 1990 the chain smoking Dirkschneider suffered a massive heart attack, which came close to claiming his life. The man himself put it down to working too hard as during the making of a new album, 'Faceless World', the band were without management, increasing the singer's work load.

U.D.O.

U.D.O.
Photo : Nico Wobben

Both 'Faceless world' and the subsequent 'Timebomb' album were produced by ACCEPT drummer Stefan Kaufmann. Touring for 'Timebomb' saw Susemihl back in the ranks but sustained fan pressure on ACCEPT's members to reform was almost unrelenting.

Indeed, in 1993 Dirkschneider could resist the lure of an ACCEPT reformation no longer and teamed up once more with his old act as Smusynnski and Schwarzmann rejoined RUNNING WILD for the 'Pile Of Skulls' album in 1994. Bohm created UNIVERSE with erstwhile DARXON and AXE VICTIMS personnel. ANDY SUSEMIHL founded MR. PERFECT for a 1993 album and issued a solo album 'Life Among The Roaches'.

Despite the new link with ACCEPT, Dirkschneider still kept his group on the side and contributed a worthy cover of 'Metal Gods' to the Century Media Records JUDAS PRIEST tribute album in 1996. The line-up for this one-off track was Dirkschneider, Dieth, Schwarzmann, Michael Voss of CASANOVA and DEMON DRIVE on bass and Stefan Kaufmann on rhythm guitar. Media expectation was high and interest was rewarded with a new U.D.O. album titled 'Solid'.

With the record released through new label G.U.N. Records in 1997 a tour of Germany in the fall ensued finding Stefan Kaufmann and ex-SIN CITY and BULLET man Fitty Wienhold on bass, Jürgen Graf on guitar and a returning Stefan Schwarzmann on drums. Dirkschneider was then once more involved with ACCEPT as a further reunion occurred the same year on the back of a live album. October of 1997 found U.D.O. on the road in Europe supported by RANDOM, BLACKSHINE and M-FORCE.

The 1998 U.D.O. album 'No Limits', retaining the previous line-up, again saw strong sales and is of note for including a re-recording of the ACCEPT classic 'I'm A Rebel' and a version of the SUPERMAX track 'Lovemachine'. Adding Swiss former SLEEK and GOTTHARD guitarist Igor Gianola and fellow Swiss native drummer Lorenzo Milani U.D.O. toured America in late 2000 sharing a bill with SAXON.

A welcome live album 'Live From Russia' arrived in October of 2001. The U.D.O. band at this juncture comprised Dirkschneider, guitarists Stefan Kaufmann and Igor Gianola, bass player Fitty Wienhold and drummer Lorenzo Milani. Another addition to U.D.O. fans collections was the release of Nuclear Blast's second ACCEPT tribute album which novelly witnessed U.D.O. tackling 'X.T.C.', a track culled from the only Udo Dirkschneider-less ACCEPT album, 1989's 'Eat The Heat'.

U.D.O. returned in 2002 with the new studio album 'Man And Machine'. The record included a duet with German Metal queen DORO on the song 'Dancing With An Angel'. Japanese variants came with two extra tracks, namely live versions of 'Metal Eater' and 'Heart Of Gold'. Touring in Scandinavia during March found VANIZE and CYBERYRA as support. Earlier, Kaufmann had been responsible for producing the September 2001 CYBERYRA album 'Mindcontrol' released through Dirkschneider's own Breaker label. Later gigs in mainland Europe throughout October and November of 2002 saw CRYSTAL BALL as opening act.

Singles/EPs:
They Want War / Hot Tonight / Go Back To Hell, RCA PT 41678 (1988)
Heart Of Gold / Blitz Of Lightning / Living On The Frontline, RCA PD 43514 (1990)

Albums:
ANIMAL HOUSE, RCA PL71552 (1987)
41 SWEDEN
Animal House / Go Back To Hell / They Want War / Black Widow / In The Darkness / Lay Down The Law / We Want It Loud / Warrior / Coming Home / Run For Cover
MEAN MACHINE, RCA PL 71994 (1988)
Don't Look Back / Break The Rules / We're History / Painted Love / Mean Machine / Dirty Boys / Streets On Fire / Lost Passion / Sweet Little Child / Catch My Fall / Still In Love With You
FACELESS WORLD, RCA PL 74510(1990)
37 SWEDEN
Heart Of Gold / Blitz Of Lightning / System Of Life / Faceless World / Stranger / Living On A Frontline / Trip To Nowhere / Can't Get Enough / Unspoken Words / Future Land / Restricted Area / Born To Run
TIME BOMB, RCA PD74953 (1991)
The Gutter / Metal Eater / Thunderforce / Overloaded / Burning Heat / Back In Pain / Timebomb / Powersquad / Kick In The Face / Soldiers Of Darkness / Metal Maniac Mastermind
SOLID, G.U.N. GUN 122 BMG 74321 46249-2 (1997)
Independence Day / Two Faced Woman / Desperate Balls / The Punisher / Devil's Dice / Bad Luck / Preacher Of The Night / Hate Stinger / Braindead Gero / Pray For The Hunted / The Healer
NO LIMITS, G.U.N. GUN 158 (1998)
The Gate / Freelance Man / Way Of Life / No Limits / With A Vengeance / One Step To Fate / Backstreet Loner / Raise The Crown / Manhunt / Rated X / Lovemachine / I'm A Rebel / Azrael

HOLY, Nuclear Blast 27361 6435 (1999)
96 GERMANY
Holy / Raiders Of Beyond / Shout It Out /
Recall The Sin / Thunder In The Tower /
Back Off / Friends Will Be Friends / State
Run Operation / Danger / Ride The Storm /
Cut Me Out
BEST OF, G.U.N. (1999)
Animal House / Break The Rules / Heart Of
Gold / Two Faced Woman / Metal Eater /
Desperate Balls / Future Land /
Independence Day / They Want War / In The
Darkness / Freelance Man / No Limits 13.
Timebomb / Lovemachine / I'm A Rebel /
Faceless World / The Key
LIVE FROM RUSSIA, Breaker (2001)
Holy / Raiders Of Beyond / Midnight Mover /
Independence Day / Metal Eater / Protectors
Of Terror / Animal House / Turn Me On /
Drum Solo / T.V. War / No Limits / Run If You
Can / Winter Dreams / In The Darkness /
Like A Loaded Gun / Recall The Sin / Break
The Rules / Midnight Highway / Heaven Is
Hell / Monster Man / Living On A Frontline /
Heart Of Gold / Shout It Out / Cut Me Out
25. I'm A Rebel / They Want War
MAN AND MACHINE, Breaker SPV CD
085-57472 (2002)
Man And Machine / Private Eye / The Dawn
Of The Gods / Silent Cry / Like A Lion /
Black Heart / Network Nightmare / Animal
Instinct / Dancing With An Angel / Hard To
Be Honest / Unknown Traveller

UNDER SIEGE (GERMANY)
Line-Up: Peter Kulp (vocals), Uwe Becker
(guitar), Tobias Fischer (guitar), Andreas
Vogel (bass), Thorsten Vollhardt (drums)

A highly rated Power Metal band from
Germany.

Singles/EPs:
Mental Health / The Wall / Prophet Of Doom
/ The Garden / Wild Melody, Uniseg
02031996-0001 (1996) ('Wild Melodies' EP)

UNIVERSE (SWEDEN)
Line-Up: Kjell Wallen (vocals), Michael Kling
(guitar), Per Nilsson (guitar), Hasse Hagman
(bass), Mic Michaeli (keyboards), Anders
Wetterström (drums)

Örebo based Power Metal band UNIVERSE
supported NAZERETH on their 1984
Swedish tour before keyboard player Mic
Michaeli left to join EUROPE, prior to the
'Universe' album being recorded. His
replacement was Freddie Kriström.

Albums:

UNIVERSE, Sonet SMLP 3 (1985)
UNLEASHED POWER (DENMARK)
Line-Up: John Matthias (vocals), Ken
Jacobson (guitar), John Lievano (bass),
Edward Owen (drums)

A Danish / American Power Metal
collaboration, UNLEASHED POWER bassist
John Lievano and drummer Edward Owen
form the American rhythm section. Danes
John Matthias on vocals and guitarist Ken
'Jack' Jacobsen comprise the Danish
contingent and were both previously with
AVALON.
UNLEASHED POWER issued the
'Blindfolded' and 'Quintet Of Spheres' demos
in 1991 that eventually resulted in a self-
financed album release of the same title two
years later. The group relocated to the States
in order to work on a second effort that would
eventually see them going in a more Thrash
based direction.
Mysteriously, in the summer of 1994 Lievano
disappeared whilst embarking on a trip by
train and is believed to have fallen from one of
the carriages en route. After the event it was
determined Lievano had slipped on wet metal
plates between two trains, breaking his neck.
He was just 27. Disillusioned, drummer Ed
Owens made his exit.
The 1997 album sees a whole new band
including journeyman drummer Jörg Michael
of RUNNING WILD, GRAVE DIGGER and
STRATOVARIUS to name but a few, bass
player Tony Spagone and American vocalist
Brian T. Chaffee.
The band now appear to go under the title of
U.P.

Albums:
QUINTET OF SPHERES, Unleashed Power
(1993)
I.O.D. / Blindfolded / The Devour / Entombed
/ The Envoy Of Sophistry / Quintet Of
Spheres / It's About Hypocrites / Hibernate /
Dejected Spirits / Unleashed Power
DEADLY SINS, Unleashed Power (1996)
(Advance tape)
Gateway / Etude / What They Don't Know /
Mindfailure / Thou Shalt Live / Nefarious/
Cataclysm / ...At The Lowest Point /
Calendar/ Section Terminal / Perpetrator Of
Dreams / "23"
MIND FAILURE, Verdict VE 102 (1999)
Gateway To Deadly Sins / Etude / What They
Don't Know / Mindfailure / Thou Shalt Live /
Cataclysm / Nefarious / Section Terminal
ABSORBED, Verdict VE 103 (2000)
Absorbed / Calendar / Perpetrator Of Dreams
/ ...At The Lowest Point / Statis

VALHALLA (AUSTRIA)
Line-Up: Ralf Brandstätter
(vocals / guitar / keyboards),
Martin Kainbrecht (bass), Daniel
Konrad (drums)

A 'true' Heavy Metal band from the Trieben area of Austria. The band was created from a prior act MELOTA. The band first struck with the self-financed album 'Thoughts Of Glory' during July 1999. However, just prior to recording bass player Siegfried was supplanted by Martin Kainbrecht. Produced by Michael Kackl, a successful Austrian Pop artist, the record left the band feeling far from satisfied with the sound of the final result.
A second album 'By The Gods', again funded by the band, arrived in March of 2000. VALHALLA managed to release a further record 'Destination Day' in September of the same year. A track from this outing garnered increased exposure for the band by appearing on a German compilation album.
The band's fourth album 'Northman' saw the use of German language lyrics for the first time. Two tracks 'The Sword Of My Father' and
'In The Shadows' were subsequently included on the BHT label's compilation 'Sounds Of Hell To Come'. 'The Sword Of My Father' also surfaced on both the 'Pounding Metal Vol.4' and 'Atlantida Vol. 11' samplers too. VALHALLA donated two brand new tracks to a limited edition split album shared with ELIZABETHA. The band's spirit of self-industry won through finally as the Portuguese label Hallucination offered to pick up the 'Northman' album for distribution and commissioned a new album 'Power And Might'.

Singles/EPs:
Defenders Of Midgrad / Behind The Dark, (2002) (Split EP with ELIZABETHA)

Albums:
THOUGHTS OF GLORY, Valhalla (1999)
Ride The Storm (Intro) / Messiah / For Glory / Stronger Than Ever Before / Silver Halls / The Power Of Steel / Ancient Gods Calling (Outro)
BY THE GODS, Valhalla (2000)
Heroes Of Desolation / Eternal Night / The First Dominion / Arrows Of Chaos Part 1 / Die For The Gods / Mights Of All Storms / Sword Of Dawn / Bring Forth The King / Into My Destiny / Blacknight Warrior / Sacred Leather / Ragnarök
DESTINATION DAY, Valhalla (2000)
Destination Day / Stronger Than Ever Before / Die For The Gods / The Burning Force /

The Power Of Steel / For Glory / Banished In Hell / Sacred Leather / Mights Of All Storms / Ragnarök / Eternal Night
NORTHMAN, Valhalla (2001)
Phönix Aus Der Asche / Undead Life / In The Shadows / Northman / Of Mortals And Gods / The Legacy / Where The Soul Was Given / Runes Of Death / A.........r / Remember Your Ancestors / The Sword Of My Father / Die Heerscharen Meines Volkes / Der Weg Des Nordmannes / Thunderbay / Victory

VALHALLA (SPAIN)
Line-Up: Javi Navarro (vocals), Ignacio Garamendi (guitar), Mikel Martinez (guitar), Jose Felix (bass), Ivan Corcuera (drums)

Power Metal act VALHALLA was founded as a trio of vocalist and guitarist Ignacio 'Jevo' Garamendi, bassist Iván Valdemoros and second guitarist Xabier Coto in 1997. The line-up soon shifted shape with Mikel Martinez supplanting Coto, this unit issuing the 'Guardians Of Metal' demo. In the spring of 1999 vocalist Javi 'Paxta' Navarro was enrolled, taking the pressure off Garamendi. VALHALLA debuted with the 'Once Upon A Time' album through Zero Records although by this stage Valdemoros had decamped, being replaced by Jose 'Txeki' Felix.

Albums:
ONCE UPON A TIME, Zero (2001)
The Awakening / Ride Of Norsemen / Metalopolis / Resurrection / Egypt / The Outlaw / To The Other Side / Born By Metal / The Oak / Hymn Of Victory / Humans

VALIANCE (ITALY)
Line-Up: Carmine Gottardo (vocals), Marco De Angelis (guitar), Mario Esposito (guitar), Gian Paolo Costantini (bass), Ciro Esposito (keyboards), Alessandro Romano (drums)

VALIANCE grew out of the NWoBHM styled TIXOTOPIA band. Dating back to late 1993 this Naples based teenage endeavour comprised lead vocalist Mario Mosca, guitarists Marco De Angelis and Valerio Bontempo, bassist Gian Paolo Costantini and Alessandro Romano on drums. This roster remained stable until September of 1996. The strangely titled 'Killing The Pig Killer' demo was issued the same month but at the same juncture both Mosca and Bontempo broke away.
The band sealed the gap in their ranks with singer Alessandro de Simone and guitarist Mario Esposito in January the following year. Veering towards a more Germanic, Power Metal style the band laid down further

recordings from which 'King Of Toys' subsequently featured on the Whiplash Productions compilation 'Into The Underground Vol. II'.

VALIANCE then opted to broaden their sound with the introduction of keyboards on the demo 'Beyond The Line'. A further tape, 'Time Enchanter', marked the appointment of vocalist Carmine Gottardo and keyboard player Ciro Esposito.

The VALIANCE debut album 'The Unglorious Conspiracy' arrived during 2000. The band would spend much of 2002 working on a follow up provisionally billed as 'Wayfaring'.

Albums:
THE UNGLORIOUS CONSPIRACY, (2000)
Betrayal / Swords Made Of Me / Sleepers' Reign / Search For The Cross / Ocean Of Thoughts / Clouds Of Insanity / Sandful Eyes / Livin' Throughout Time / King Of Toys / Ancestral Quest / Towards Silence

VALKIRIA (CHILE)
Line-Up: Jaime Salva (vocals), Tracy Mackay (vocals), Daniel Román (guitar), Daniel Villalobos (guitar), Fran Muñoz (drums)

Incorporated in 1999 by guitarists Daniel Villalobos and Daniel Román VALKIRIA offer no frills Heavy Metal but with the added attraction of female harmony vocals courtesy of Tracy Mackay. The first version of VALKIRIA had Claudio Guerra as lead vocalist.

In March 2000 Fran Muñoz was inducted as the band's new drummer and Alvaro Aguirre came in on bass, this pair debuting on the 2001 'La espada de Fuego'. However, Rodrigo Matus took the role of bassist in August that year.

2002 brought about further changes with Javier Ugarte taking on four string responsibilities and Tracy Mackay joining as second vocalist. Later Jaime Salva would usurp Guerra.

VALLEY'S EVE (GERMANY)
Line-Up: Roberto Dimitri Liapkis (vocals), Frank Pane (guitar), Martin Albrecht (bass), Tony Mang (keyboards), Frank Huber (drums)

A Metal band dating back to 1993. With the introduction of Greek born singer MYSTIC PROPHECY's Roberto Dimitri Liapkis in 1995 the band took on a new musical direction into the realms of Progressive Metal, evident on their January 1996 debut 'Prodiga'. At this stage the band line-up comprised Liapkis, guitarist Mario Cavasin, bass player Dietmar Aumann, keyboard player Tony Mang and drummer Christian Vitek.

VALLEY'S EVE then signed to the B. Mind label for a follow up 'The Atmosphere Of Silence'. This progress would not be without a line-up shuffle though, Martin Albrecht of MYSTIC PROPHECY and STORMWITCH repute taking Aumman's place and Markus Krings enrolling as drummer. Tour dates had the band on the road throughout Germany and the low countries supporting RAGE and NIGHTWISH. However, with the completion of these gigs Mario Cavasin bowed out in August of 2000. Frank Pane, previously with BURN and RED TO GREY, filled the six string vacancy and the drum stool changed hands over to ex-TRACE and TRIPLE X man Frank Huber.

Promoting the 'Deception Of Pain' album VALLEY'S EVE would tour Europe packaged with CHINCHILLA and POWERGOD during October of 2002.

Albums:
PRODIGIA, (1997)
Escape / Stigmata / Self Proclaimed Messiah / Ulterior Quest / Amnesia / Dawn On Tears / Unconscious / Misconception / Trivial / Last Question / Eleftheria / Perishable / Beverage Of Life
THE ATMOSPHERE OF SILENCE, B. Mind (2000)
Religion-War / Room Of Answers / My Last Breath / When The Sun And Stars Refuse To Shine / A Raven Beside Me / Humans Load / Place Of Nightmares / Close To Your Eyes / Nostalgia / Power Of Soul / My Inner Vision
DECEPTION OF PAIN, Limb Music Productions (2002)
The Fire Burns / Point Of No Return / The Sun / In Your Head / Mirror In Your Eyes / Kingdom Of Pain / Dark Room / Creating Gods / Falling / Open The Gates / Dark Shadows On The Wall / Unholy Power 13. Shadows Of Misery

VAMPYR (GERMANY)
Line-Up: Wolfgang Schwarz (vocals), Ralf Hollmer (guitar), Ironhead Sterzik (guitar), Nil Conan Mayr (bass), Roman Sterzik (drums)

A German Heavy Metal act with plentiful Speed Metal influence.

Albums:
CRY OUT FOR METAL, Hot Blood (1985)
Oath / Sinner / Indianapolis / Hell Bent Angels / Scytherman / Mercy Killing / Metal Hymn '86 / Warrior / Breakin' Metal / Vampyr

VANADIUM (ITALY)
Line-Up: Pino Scotto (vocals), Claudio

Acquini (guitar), Domenico Pranters (bass), Ruggero Zanoli (keyboards), Lio Mascheroni (drums)

One of Italy's leading Metal bands of the day, VANADIUM debuted in 1982 with 'Metal Rock' before replacing guitarist Claudio Acquini with Stefano Tessario for 1983's 'Race With The Devil' album.

Not to be confused with the German Hard Rock act of the same title that also issued a number of albums. Frontman PINO SCOTTO later issued a solo album 'Segnali Di Fuoco'.

Albums:
METAL ROCK, Durium (1982)
We Want Live Rock n' Roll / I Never Lost Control / Heavy Metal / Make Me Feel Better / Looking For Love / On Fire / Running On The Road / Queen Of The Night
RACE WITH THE DEVIL, Durium (1983)
Get Up, Shake Up / I Gotta Clash With You / Don't Be Looking Back / A Race With The Devil / Running Wild / Fire Trails / Outside Of Society / Russian Roulette
GAME OVER, Durium (1984)
Streets Of Danger / I'm Leaving You / Wartrains / Too Young To Die / Pretty Heartbreaker / The Hunter / Don't Let Your Master Down / Game Over
ON STREETS OF DANGER - LIVE, Durium (1985)
You Can't Stop The Music / Streets Of Danger / Get Up, Shake Up / Wartrains / We Want Live Rock n' Roll / On Fire / Fire Trails / Pretty Heartbreaker / Don't Be Lookin' Back / A Race With The Devil / The Hunter
CORRUPTION OF INNOCENCE, ZYX Music (1987)
Backbone Of Society / Down n' Out (Broken Inside) / Gimme So Much / Corrupted Innocence / Winds Of Destruction / Talk Of The Town / Images / Dangerous Game / Over The Limit
BORN TO FIGHT, Durium DAI 30420 (1987)
Run Too Fast / Still Got Time / Before It's Too Late / Easy Way To Love / I Was Born To Rock / Never Before / Ridge Farm / Arms In The Air
SEVENTH HEAVEN, (1989)
Italian Girl / Natural Born Loner / Take My Blues Away / Seventh Heaven / Bad Attitude / One Way Ride / Kill The Killer / Step Ahead Of Time / To Be A Number One / Warriors
NEL CUORE DEL CAOS, (1995)
Nel Cuore Del Caos / Nero Sogno Grunge / Stivali Con Le Ali / Come Il Piombo (Game Over) / Il Mondo Di Lù / Sono Sotto Shock / Vodka E Luna / Piazza San Rock / Summer Of '69 / Ancore On The Roa

VANDEN PLAS (GERMANY)
Line-Up: Andy Kuntz (vocals), Stephen Lill (guitar), Torsten Reichert (bass), Gunther Werno (keyboards), Andreas Lill (drums)

Progressively charged Metal band of high repute. VANDEN PLAS first got together in 1985, releasing a single entitled 'Raining In My Heart' the following year. The current formation of the band came together in 1990, keyboard player Günther being previously with JULIET.

Before gaining a record deal the band's strength of musicianship led to an engagement performing the Rock opera 'Jesus Christ Superstar' in Saarbrucken from October 1992 to April 1994. The success of this venture prompted similar work on productions of 'The Little Shop Of Horrors' and 'The Rocky Horror Picture Show'.

Influenced heavily by the Progressive Rock scene alongside a mix of Metal and classical music, VANDEN PLAS won a host of admirers with the Roko Kohlmeyer of ROKO fame co-producing the debut album 'Colour Temple' in 1995. The band followed it up with a headlining club tour in Europe, picking up a huge following in France.

In 1996 the group chose to record a mini-album entitled 'AcCult', a record comprised acoustical versions of songs from 'Colour Temple' plus covers of MARILLION's 'Kayleigh' and SAIGON KICK's 'Spanish Rain'.

The group finally found time to release the second, full album 'The God Thing' during 1997 and made it over to Britain to support DREAM THEATER in London at the end of the year. 1998 opened with further DREAM THEATER dates in Europe and a follow up to the 'AcCult' concept, 'AcCult II', was scheduled for a November release date but never transpired.

VANDEN PLAS covered a version of DOKKEN's 'Kiss Of Death' in 1999 that featured guest vocals from DON DOKKEN himself. The band toured Germany in early 2000 with support from CHINCHILLA and DYSLESIA.

Plans for a 2001 album were put on hold when it was discovered guitarist Stephan Lill was suffering from Carpal Tunnel Syndrome. The record, 'Beyond Daylight', would finally arrive in January of 2002. Limited edition variants included a bonus track, a cover of «KANSAS» 'Point Of Know Return'.

VANDEN PLAS's own keyboard player Gunter Werno and guitarist Stephan Lill would both feature heavily on the CONSORTIUM PROJECT 2001 debut album. VANDEN PLAS plans for European touring throughout April would be curtailed

when Andy Kuntz's father died. The dates would be rescheduled for the summer.

During the interim drummer Andreas Lill busied himself with Norwegian guitarist TORBEN ENVOLDSEN's new project band entitled SECTION A. The project also featuring ex-KISS and DREAM THEATER keyboard player DEREK SHERINEN and former LION'S SHARE singer Andy Engberg. It would not be the only such endeavour on the agenda, as both Lill and Kuntz participated in ABYDOS, a Progressive Rock assembly put together by producer Stefan Glas also including IAN PARRY of ELEGY and SHAMAN singer Andre Matos.

2002 would also bring about an adventurous 'Rock Opera' project as a result of an alliance between VANDEN PLAS members, erstwhile ROYAL HUNT and current SILENT FORCE vocalist D.C. COOPER and personnel from PINK CREAM 69. The Dennis Ward produced endeavour, entitled, MISSA MERCURIA, had lyrics penned by Cooper with music contributed by PINK CREAM 69's Alfred Koffler, SILENT FORCE's Alex Beyrodt and the VANDEN PLAS duo of Günter Werno and Stephan Lill. Musicians sessioning numbered VANDEN PLAS men Stephan Lill on guitar and Günter Werno on keyboards, PINK CREAM 69ers Alfred Koffler, Andreas Lill,

and Dennis Ward with SILENT FORCE's Alex Beyrodt on guitar. Andy Kuntz would aid on lead vocals portraying the character of 'Airgod' whilst 'Firegod' was handled by D.C. COOPER, Sabine Edelsbacher of EDENBRIDGE as the 'Water goddess', Lori Williams playing the 'Earth goddess', Isolde Groß as 'Mercuria' and PINK CREAM 69's David Readman provided narration.

Singles/EPs:
Raining In My Heart, (1986)
Fire, (1991)
I Don't Miss You / Shape Of My Heart / Into The Sun / How Many Tears (French version), Inside Out Music IOMCD055 (2000)

Albums:
COLOUR TEMPLE, Dream Circle DCD 9517 (1995)
Father / Push / When The Wind Blows / My Crying / Soul Survives / Anytime / Judas / Back To Me / How Many Tears
ACCULT, Dream Circle DCD 9629 (1996)
My Crying / Theme From 'Pseudo Silk Kimono' / Kayleigh / Father / Georgia On My Mind / How Many Tears / Des Hauts, Des Bas / Spanish Rain / Days Of Thunder
THE GOD THING, CNR Music 3032212 (1997)

Fire Blossom / Rainmaker / Garden Of Stones / In You I Believe / Day I Die / Crown Of Thorns / We're Not God / Salt In Wounds / You Fly / Combien De Larmes
FAR OFF GRACE, Inside Out Music IOMCD043 (1999)
I Can See / Far Off Grace / Into The Sun / Where's The Man / Inside Of Your Head / Don't Miss You / Iodic Rain / Fields Of Hope / I'm With You
SPIRIT OF LIVE, Inside Out Music (2000)
I Can See / Into The Sun / Soul Survives / How Many Tears / Don't Miss You / Journey To Paris / Spirit Of Life / Iodic Rain / Far Off Grace / Kiss Of Death / Rainmaker
BEYOND DAYLIGHT, Inside Out Music IOMCD093 (2002)
Nightwalker / Cold Wind / Scarlet Flowerfields / Healing Tree / End Of All Days / Free The Fire / Can You Hear Me / Phoenix / Beyond Daylight

VANEXA (ITALY)
Line-Up: Marco Spinelli (vocals), Roberto Merlono (guitar), Sergio Pagnacco (bass), Silvano Bottari (drums)

VANEXA were at the forefront of the growing Italian Metal scene in the early '80s.

Albums:
VANEXA, Durium (1983)
Metal City Rockers / Lost War Sons / I Wanna See Fires / 1000 Nights / If You Fear The Pain / Across The Ruins / Rainbow In The Dark
BACK FROM THE RUINS, Minatauro (1988)
Midnight Wolves / Bloodmoney / Creation / It's Over / Hanged Man / Night Rain On The Ruins / We All Will Die / Hiroshima

VANISHING POINT (AUSTRALIA)
Line-Up: Silvio Massaro (vocals), Chris Porcianko (guitar), Tom Vucur (guitar), Joe Del Mastro (bass), Danny Olding (keyboards), Jack Lukic (drums)

VANISHING POINTS's second album 'Tangled In Dream', released in Europe by German label Limb Music Productions, would include a cover version of PINK FLOYD's 'On The Turning Away'.

Albums:
IN THOUGHT, Angular SKAN 8216.AR (1998)
The Only One / Vanishing Point / Wind / In Company Of Darkness / Dream Maker / Sunlit Windows / Blind / Forgotten Self / A Memory / Inner Peace

VANISHING POINT

TANGLED IN DREAM, Steel Warriors MWGOLD0100-2 (2002)
Surreal / Samsara / Closer Apart / Bring On The Rain / Never Walk Away / The Real You / Two Minds One Soul / I Will Awake / Dancing With The Devil / Father (7 Years) / Tangled In Dream / Inner Peace / On The Turning Away

VANIZE (GERMANY)
Line-Up: Peter Dirkschneider (vocals), Markus Becker (guitar), Marcus Bielenberg (bass), Andre Hilgers (drums)

Former DANTON vocalist Peter Dirkschneider is the brother of ACCEPT vocalist Udo Dirkschneider. Bassist Marcus Bielenberg is also ex-DANTON. Musically the Dirkschneider family breeding would be more than evident, VANIZE delivering quality hard Metal with their opening demo, the 1994 three track tape - featuring the songs 'Don't Go Down', 'Trouble Makers' and 'We're Back', which scored 'Demo of the month' in the influential 'Rock Hard' magazine.
VANIZE toured with RAVEN, CORACKO and RISK during 1991, although original guitarist Carsten Hensel departed in 1992 leaving VANIZE as a quartet. The group, replacing drummer Pierre Fienhold with Andre Hilgers, finally issued a full album during 1995 entitled 'Twins?'. Touring found the band out on the road in Germany with TANKARD and RUNNING WILD. 1997 found the band on the road in support of U.D.O. and AXXIS and the following year the siblings would unite again for a joint U.D.O. / VANIZE tour of Sweden before this billing made its way into Spain during 1999. In June of the same year the Stefan Kaufmann produced 'Bootlicker' album arrived, promoted by German dates as support to veteran American Thrashers TESTAMENT.
VANIZE would be back in action for a third stab with July 2000's 'High Proof' opus. Touring found the familiar U.D.O. / VANIZE package back on Swedish soil.
VANIZE added guitarist EMPIRE Ralf Munkes in late 2000 replacing Markus Becker.

Albums:
TWINS?, Cheerio CH10005 (1995)
Holy War / Heading For Tomorrow / They're Back / Nowhere To Hide / Evil Eyes / Roll The Dice / Baby's On Crack / Don't Go Down / We Stay Loud / Hell Is Back / Troublemakers
BOOTLICKER, Radiation NB 412-2 (1999)
Bootlicker / Train To Hell / Whips And Chains / Call Of The Hunter / One Law For Them / Night Hunter / No Time For Heroes / The Healer / R.I.P. / Tomorrow / In The Eye Of The Storm
HIGH PROOF, Nuclear Blast (2000)
The Final Breath / Minute Man / Double Dealing / Therapy / Rolling / Master And Servant / Break Down The Walls / Negative / What You Give Is What You Get / Loosing The Ground / You Cant Stop Us Now

VAUXDHIVL (AUSTRALIA)
Line-Up: Stacy Handchild (vocals), Frederic Leduc (guitar), Edward Katz (bass / keyboards), Chris Deloy (drums)

Albums:
GAZE INTO THE LIGHT, Advent 001 (1994)

VELVET VIPER (GERMANY)
Line-Up: Jutta Weinhold (vocals), Roy Last (guitar), Lars Ratz (bass), Bubi (drums)

VELVET VIPER was essentially ZED YAGO reformed by vocalist Jutta and drummer Bubi. The band were unable to use the previous title due to a legal injunction by former ZED YAGO members.
The original line-up of VELVET VIPER included ex WARLOCK guitarist Peter Szigeti together with guitarist David Moore and the first album featured a guest appearance by ZENO guitarist Joe Roth. VELVET VIPER reformed in 1992, signing to the TAOB label, with Weinhold, Bubi, guitarist Roy Last (ex-ROY LAST GROUP) and bassist Lars Ratz. A second album was released the same year.
Ratz worked with UDO LINDENBERG and VIVA and would found the successful METALIUM in 1999. Moore teamed up with British Folk Rockers SKYCLAD for tour work whilst Szigeti joined CORACKO, CROWN OF THORNS and STONEWASHED.

Albums:
VELVET VIPER, TAOB (1991)
Merlin / Brainsuckers Thommyknockers / Perceval / HM Rebels / Parsifal / Millstone Of Rage / Hammerhouse / World Beyond The World / Icebreaker / King Arthur / Lost Children / Ring Of Stone
THE 4TH QUEST FOR FORSAKEN, TAOB SPV 084-24792 (1992)
The Valkyrie / Savage Dreams / Highland Queen / Modern Knights / Mother Of All Voices / Forefather Stella / Ancient Warriors / Horsewoman / Valkyries / Trojan War

VENI DOMINE (SWEDEN)
Line-Up: Fredrik Ohlsson (vocals / guitar), Torbjörn Weinesjö (guitar), Magnus Thorman (bass), Thomas Weinesjö (drums)

High class Christian Metallers VENI DOMINE have established themselves with a brace of superb albums of orchestral Metal. Classical influences abound and the band are even unafraid to use chanting monks for effect! HEAVY LOAD's Wahlqvist brothers Ragne and Styrbjörn produced VENI DOMINE's first brace of albums. The band was rooted in an earlier act dubbed GLORIFY, a Sollentuna based union of ex-DISCIPLES guitarist Torbjörn Weinesjö, his sibling drummer Thomas, singer Fredrik Ohlsson and bass player Anders Olofsson. In 1988 Olofsson was supplanted by Magnus Thorman and the group adopted the revised title of SEVENTH SEAL, performing at the British Christian 'Greenbelt' festival under that name during 1990. This show resulted in a deal with the British based Kingsway label. However, due to a proliferation of acts titled SEVENTH SEAL the name VENI DOMINE was decided upon.

As VENI DOMINE the band debuted with the 'Fall Babylon Fall' album, oddly initially recorded in Eastbourne, England during the summer of the previous year. Unsatisfied with the result the band pulled in the Wahlqvist brothers to complete the job back in Sweden. Issued through the Christian R.E.X. label it would soon make an impression upon the regular Rock market. The cover artwork for 'Fall Babylon Fall' was executed by the highly rated fantasy artist Rodney Matthews.

VENI DOMINE toured Germany in 1996 on a bill with SAVIOUR MACHINE and SOUL CAGES to further promote the 'Material Sanctuary' album, once again clad in a superb Rodney Matthews sleeve design. Keyboards on the album were donated by Mats Lidbrandt. With renewed interest generated by the second record Massacre Records re-released debut 'Fall Babylon Fall' in 1997 complete with 'Visions' as a bonus track.

For the third album, 'Spiritual Wasteland', VENI DOMINE inducted new members bass player Gabriel Ingemarson and BISHOP GARDEN keyboard player Mattias Cederlund.

Vocalist Fredrik Ohlsson also fronts HOAX, an outfit featuring ex-CANDLEMASS guitarist Lasse Johansson. The singer was also involved with ZOIC with the guitarist and his CANDLEMASS colleagues guitarist Mats 'Mappe' Björkman and drummer Janne Lindh for a well received 1996 album 'Total Level Of Destruction'.

VENI DOMINE's 2002 line-up stood at vocalist Fredrik Sjöholm (having changed his name from Ohlsson), guitarist Torbjörn Weinesjö, bass player Gabriel Ingemarson and Thomas Weinesjö on drums. A fourth album was being readied for late 2002

release.

Albums:
FALL BABYLON FALL, REX 7901 420057 (1992)
Face Of The Prosecutor / King Of The Jews / In The Day Of The Sentinel / Wisdom Calls / Armageddon / O Great City / The Chronicle Of The Seven Seals, Part I: The Scroll And The Lamb, Part II: The Seals, Part III: The Golden Censer
MATERIAL SANCTUARY, Massacre MASS CD074 (1995)
The Meeting / Eccesinstes / Material Sanctuary / Ritual Of The Sinner / The Mass / Behold The Signs / Wrath Of The Lion / Beyond The Doom / Baroque Moderne
SPIRITUAL WASTELAND, Thunderload (1998)
Dawn Of Time / Last Letter From Earth / If I Fall Asleep / Hysterical History / Riddle Of Eternity / The Temple / Someone's Knocking / Silent Lamb / 1st Of Ten / The Letter

VEX (GERMANY)
Line-Up: Chris (vocals), Tom (guitar), Andy (bass), Engel (drums)

A Power Metal quartet created during 1992. VEX parted company with original guitarist Danny and replaced him with Tom in 1994.

Albums:
ACT OF REVENGE, D&S Records DSR 016 (1995)
Shattered Memories / Lost My Luck / Act Of Revenge / Fall / Becoming Harder Than Life / Won't Be Fooled Again / No Right To Life / Pulling My Own Strings / Schizophrenia / Killed By Life / B.M.

VICIOUS RUMORS (CA, USA)
Line-Up: Geoff Thorpe (vocals / guitar), Steve Smyth (guitar), Tommy Sisco (bass), Larry Howe (drums)

A Power / Thrash Metal band of great repute, VICIOUS RUMORS formed in San Francisco in the early '80s, co-founded by guitarist Geoff Thorpe. Finding a niche market on the European mainland during the '90s VICIOUS RUMORS would develop their sound into a more streamlined melodic Metal style.

The band would quickly be taken under the wing of guitar guru and Shrapnel Records boss Mike Varney, Thorpe meeting the man through Varney's ROCK JUSTICE project. At the time of their meeting Varney was in the process of putting the Shrapnel Records label together, a company that first made its name with the 'U.S. Metal' series of compilation

VICIOUS RUMORS
Photo : Nico Wobben

albums that pushed the playing of the guitarists in the individual bands concerned well to the fore.

VICIOUS RUMORS line-up of 1983 comprised vocalist Mark Tate, guitarists Geoff Thorpe and Jim Cassero, bass player Jim Barnacle and drummer Jim Lange. The latter had supplanted Walt Perkins. At this stage VICIOUS RUMORS were heavily reliant on image with coordinated black and blue stage costumes and with their singer entering the stage held aloft in a coffin borne by monks!

Bassist Dave Starr had been a member of fellow Metal band LÄÄZ ROCKIT, actually a founder member having renamed that act from their previous title of DEPTH CHARGE. Fired from LÄÄZ ROCKIT in 1983 Starr hooked created a power trio titled BLACK LEATHER with guitarist Rick Richards and drummer Jim Wells. The following year Starr formed part of the regrouped VICIOUS RUMORS completing a line-up of ex-HAWAII singer Gary St. Pierre, guitarist Geoff Thorpe and drummer Charles Emmil.

During this period VAIN guitarist Jamie Rowe (then titled 'Chuck Mooney') made some recordings with VICIOUS RUMORS. Drummer for this period was Don Selzer.

VICIOUS RUMORS made their first recorded appearance on 'U.S. Metal Volume III' with the track 'Ultimate Death'. At the time Thorpe had been looking for the perfect guitar partner and getting nowhere. Former BLACK LEATHER man Rick Richards filled in for one gig. Varney introduced him to a discovery of his from Delaware called VINNIE MOORE. In no time at all, Moore was in the group and the group were put in the studio by Varney to record a debut album for Shrapnel in 1985.

That first record 'Soldiers Of The Night', released in Europe through a licensing deal with Roadrunner, featured St. Pierre on vocals, Moore and Thorpe on guitar, bassist Dave Starr and drummer Larry Howe.

Moore, only ever a temporary member, would quit to pursue his goal of solo stardom and VICIOUS RUMORS promptly picked up former TYRANT man Terry Montana as a quick replacement. Montana lasted a year, recording demos and actually touring to promote the first album.

After Montana's services were dispensed with, Alameda, California raised Mark McGee came into the frame. Formerly a member of local act OVERDRIVE (in the dual role of vocalist and rhythm guitarist), McGee had also spent a period of time in the ranks of fading Pomp Rock outfit STARCASTLE.

McGee made his debut with VICIOUS RUMORS on 1988's 'Digital Dictator' album, a record that also premiered ex-RUFFIANS / VILLIAN vocalist Carl Albert in place of the departed Gary St. Pierre.

VICIOUS RUMORS hooked up with SAVATAGE manager Robert Zemsky and consequently major label Atlantic Records for the eponymous 1990 album. The record title was originally 'Immortal Battalion'.

VICIOUS RUMORS toured America on a headlining club jaunt prior to European dates with DEATH ANGEL and FORBIDDEN as well as a performance at the prestigious 'Dynamo' festival in Holland.

For 1991's 'Welcome To The Ball' the band toured Europe with SAVATAGE and put in further headline club gigs in America. Japanese dates resulted in the live 'Plug In And Hang On - Live In Tokyo' album.

The following year VICIOUS RUMORS were dealt two body blows. Not only were they dropped by Atlantic but also Thorpe was found to be suffering from Carpal Tunnel Syndrome and had to undergo surgery for his condition. For a short while the band operated as a quartet without him. Howe filled his downtime by creating side project BOMB THREAT with HEATHEN members Lee Altus and Thaen Rasmussen with singer Jay from MY VICTIM. BOMB THREAT toured the California clubs playing a nostalgic set of NWOBHM covers.

By mid 1993 Thorpe was recovered enough to get out on the road again but by November line-up problems beset the band with Starr being fired.

In April 1995 VICIOUS RUMORS took another hammer blow when Albert was killed in an accident. The singer hung on to life for a few days but was eventually pronounced brain dead. McGee also quit the band eventually uniting with GREGG ALLMAN.

Thorpe took over lead vocals for the 1996 album 'Something Burning' as guitarist Steve Smyth also bolstered the band. The following year VICIOUS RUMORS drafted vocalist Brian O'Connor. High profile European dates would see the group guesting for ACCEPT. Back in America further gigs were put in as openers to established artists such as THIN LIZZY, RAINBOW and BLUE OYSTER CULT. The band would play to their biggest audiences though during 1998, billed as special guests to Germany's BLIND GUARDIAN on their European tour.

In 1999 VICIOUS RUMORS announced their new vocalist to be ex-HIGH TREASON and MEGATON BLONDE man Morgan Thorn. Smyth joined TESTAMENT in the same year. The band bounced back in 2001 with the 'Sadistic Symphony' album. VICIOUS RUMORS new look incorporated Thorn, Thorpe, guitarist Ira Black, bassist Cornbread and drummer Atma Anur.

Black's history traces back through REXXEN,

the 1992 incarnation of HEATHEN, UTERIS (featuring ex-TESLA guitarist Tommy Skeoch) and DOGFACE with erstwhile EXODUS man Steve Souza.

Bassist Cornbread is ex-BIZARRO, the band founded by ex-FORBIDDEN and TESTAMENT guitarist Glen Alvelais whilst drummer Atma Anur boasts numerous studio appearances with diverse acts such as DAVID BOWIE, JOURNEY, TONY MACALPINE and MARTY FRIEDMAN.

It would leak out that both Thorn and Cornbread had actually split away from the band in early 2001 but had resolved whatever differences of opinion there were and rejoined the fold.

Former VICIOUS RUMORS personnel bassist Dave Starr and drummer Larry Howe would both join CHASTAIN in 2001. Meantime Ira Black delved into nostalgia by forming part of the reunion of '80s Thrash act MERCENARY.

With the release of the 'Sadistic Symphony' album VICIOUS RUMORS once again changed tack, re-employing Brian O'Connor on vocals. The band hooked up with SAVATAGE and BLAZE for European tour dates commencing in Sweden during January 2002 but would soon pull out citing friction with BLAZE.

Albums:
SOLDIERS OF THE NIGHT, Roadrunner RR 9734 (1986)
Premonition / Ride (Into The Sun) / Medusa / Soldiers Of The Night / Murder / March Or Die / Blitz The World / Invader / In Fire / Domestic Bliss / Blistering Winds
DIGITAL DICTATOR, Roadrunner RR 9571 (1988)
Replicant / Digital Dictator / Minute To Kill / Towns On Fire / Lady Took A Chance / Worlds And Machines / The Crest / R.L.H./ Condemned / Out Of The Shadows
VICIOUS RUMORS, Atlantic 7567820752 (1990)
Don't Wait For Me / World Church / On The Edge / Ship Of Fools / Can You Hear It / Down To The Temple / Hellraiser / Electric Twilight / Thrill Of The Hunt / Axe And Smash
WELCOME TO THE BALL, Atlantic 75682276121 (1991)
Abandoned / You Only Live Twice / Saviour From Anger / Children / Dust To Dust / Raise Your Hands / Strange Behaviour / Six Stepsisters / Mastermind / When Love Comes Down / Ends Of The Earth
PLUG IN AND HANG ON - LIVE IN TOKYO, Atlantic (1992)
Abandoned / Savior From Anger / Down To The Temple / Ship Of Fools / Lady Took A

Chance / When Love Comes Down / March Or Die / Don't Wait For Me
WORD OF MOUTH, SPV Steamhammer 084-62232 (1994)
Against The Grain / All Rights Reserved / The Voice / Thinking Of You / Thunder And Pain (Part 1) / Thunder And Pain (Part 2) / No Fate / Sense Of Security / Dreaming / Building no. 6 / Ministry Of Fear / Music Box
SOMETHING BURNING, Massacre MASSCD091 (1996)
Ball Hog / Mouth / Out Of My Misery / Something Burning / Concentration / Chopping Block / Perpetual / Strip Search / Make It Real / Free To Go
CYBERCHRIST, Massacre CD0142 (1998)
Cyberchrist / Buried Alive / Kill The Day / No Apologies / Fear Of God / Gigs Eviction / Barcelona / Downpour / Candles Burn / Fiend / Faith
SADISTIC SYMPHONY, (2001)
Break / Sadistic Symphony / March Of The Damned / Blacklight / Puritan Demons / Born Again Hard / Neodymium Man / Elevator To Hell / Cerebral Sea / Ascension / Liquify

VIGILANCE (GERMANY)
Line-Up: Frank-Otto Conrad (vocals), Uwe Fleischhauer (guitar), Dago Gerdes (bass), Günter Eiken (keyboards), Kai-Uwe Broek (drums)

A Progressive Metal band from northern Germany, VIGILANCE's 1997 album was also issued in a German language recording titled 'Irrlicht'.

Albums:
BEHIND THE MASK, Music Is Intelligence WMMS 089 (1996)
Intro / Calls Over Ashes / Time To Remember / Another Ordinary Day / Confide / Behind The Mask / Levitation / Dream (And You'll Believe) / Changes / River Of Eternal Screams / Suicide Boulevard
SECRECY, Music Is Intelligence WMMS CD 170 (1997)
Crimson / Heavenward / Now And Forevermore / Unfinished Life / Vivien / Grave Dancers / Watercolors / The Maze / Symbolic / Lost Babylon

VIGILANTE (JAPAN)
Line-Up: Hideaki Niwa (vocals), Hiroshi Omoto (guitar), Kazuaki Horie (guitar), Makoto Unno (bass), Kazuhisa Yoshimura (drums)

Albums:
CHAOS - PILGRIMIGE, Eternal Riddle ERVG 0001-2 (1998)

Chaos – Pilgrimage / Antisocial Maniacs / Holy Prose / Liars / Raise The Titanic / Fatal Superstition / A Nightprayer / Imprisoned / The Reviving World / Relapse Of Your Privacy
EDGE OF TIME, Massacre MAS CD0226 (1999)
Judgement Day / Tease Of Influence / Prisoner Of Fate / Blame & Praise / Kingdom Fall (Suicidal Wind) / Under The Strain / The Silent Majority / Burn In Agony / The Edge Of Time / The Wondering Traveller / Thumbnail At You

VIKING (Los Angeles, CA, USA)
Line-Up: Ron Eriksen (vocals), Brett Eriksen (guitar), James Lareau (bass), Matt Jordan (drums)

VIKING were a hard hitting Speed / Thrash Metal act out of Los Angeles. The band had a blistering rise over two highly praised albums before dropping out of the scene entirely when half of the band became born again Christians. VIKING was founded in the Spring of 1986 by guitarist Ron Daniels of the HAGS, drummer Matt Jordan of BARRIER and bass player James Lareau of Punk act LETHAL GENE.
This trio, along with singer Tony Spider, founded TRACER releasing one demo session. TRACER, now minus Spider, evolved into VIKING when Daniels discovered he could sing whilst jamming SLAYER songs at a rehearsal. Guitarist Brett completed the line-up.
As VIKING the band opted to promote the appropriate image and therefore both Daniels and Brett took the stage name 'Eriksen'. After just two gigs VIKING were signed to the Metal Blade label, committing the track 'Hellbound' to the 'Metal Massacre VIII' compilation then launching a full blown album 'Do Or Die'. Critics enthused over the sheer heaviness of the band and Ron Eriksen's vocals were singled out for particular praise.
Ron Eriksen would lend his vocal talents to the DARK ANGEL album 'Leave Scars', duetting with Ron Rinehart on the song 'Promise Of Agony'.
VIKING would go into the studio to cut a second album 'Man Of Straw' with engineer Bill Metoyer. However, Daniels had recently converted to Christianity and would re-write a large degree of the lyrics just prior to recording.
In May of 1990 both Daniels and Jordan would exit citing a conflict of interests between the Heavy Metal lifestyle and their faith. VIKING folded. These days Daniels is Pastor at Calvary Chapel, Cheyenne.

Albums:
DO OR DIE, Metal Blade 72225 (1988)
Warlord / Hellbound / Militia Of Death / Prelude - Scavenger / Valhalla / Burning From Within / Berserker / Killer Unleashed / Do Or Die
MAN OF STRAW, Caroline 1396 (1989)
White Death / They Raped The Land / Twilight Fate / The Trial / Case Of The Stubborns / Winter / Hell Is For Children / Creative Divorce / Man of Straw

VILLIAN (USA)
Line-Up: Carl Albert (vocals), Leon B. Smith (guitar), Greg E. Noll (guitar), Tommy Sisco (bass), Rob Quiellen (drums)

The late Carl Albert, an ex-member of RUFFIANS, joined VICIOUS RUMORS.

Albums:
ONLY TIME WILL TELL, Relentless (1986)
Kamikaze / Only Time Will Tell / Tie Your Mother Down / She'll Make You Fall (In Love) / Kids Of Crime / Just Close Your Eyes / Thrills In The Night

VIPER (BRAZIL)
Line-Up: Pit Passarell (vocals / bass), Yves Passarell (guitar), Felipe Machado (guitar), Renato Graccia (drums)

A heavily Euro influenced Speed Metal act created during 1985 by teenage brothers guitarist Yves and bassist Pit Passarell. Joining them would be the equally youthful vocalist Andre Matos, second guitar player Felipe Machado and drummer Casi Audi. VIPER announced their presence with the 'Killara Sword' demo which soon snagged a deal with the domestic Rock Brigade label. Promoting the debut 'Soldiers Of Sunrise' album VIPER would support MOTÖRHEAD.
For 1989's 'Theatre Of Fate' opus VIPER switched drummers, bringing in Sergio Facci. However, Guilherme Martin would be drafted on the drum stool for tour work and Renato Graccia finally settled then the position.
At this juncture Andre Matos split away from the band, apparently over a conflict of interest in stylistic direction. The erstwhile vocalist would found the immensely successful Progressive Metal act ANGRA. Pit Passarell took over the vocal mantle as VIPER trimmed down to a quartet.
By now VIPER's reputation had spread internationally with the 'Theatre Of Fate' album licensed to Japan in 1991 and Europe the following year. 1992 would also see VIPER scoring a huge Brazilian radio hit with the track 'Rebel Maniacs'.

The 1994 'Live - Maniacs In Japan' album would include the band's cover version of QUEEN's 'We Will Rock You' alongside a take of the RAMONES 'I Wanna Be Sedated'.

The 'Coma Rage' record, released in 1995, saw strong Hardcore elements being introduced into the band's sound.

Yves Passarel would unite onstage for a slice of nostalgia with former vocalist Andre Matos in 2001 as Matos debuted his post ANGRA outfit SHAMAN.

Albums:
SOLDIERS OF SUNRISE, Rock Brigade (1987)
Knights Of Destruction / Nightmares / The Whipper / Wings Of The Evil / H.R. / Soldiers Of Sunrise / Signs Of The Night / Killera (Princess Of Hell) / Law Of The Sword
THEATRE OF FATE, (1989)
Illusions / At Least A Chance / To Live Again / A Cry From The Edge / Living For The Night / Prelude To Oblivion / Theatre Of Fate / Moonlight
EVOLUTION, (1992)
Coming From The Inside / Evolution / Rebel Maniac / Dead Light / The Shelter / Still the Same / Wasted / Pictures Of Hate / Dance Of Madness / The Spreading Soul / We Will Rock You
VIPERA SAPIENS, (1993)
Acid Heart / Silent Enemy / Crime / Wasted Again / Killing World / The Spreading Soul (Acoustic version)
LIVE - MANIACS IN JAPAN, (1994)
Intro - Coming From The Inside / To Live Again / A Cry From The Edge / Dead Light / Knights Of Destruction / We Will Rock You / Acid Heart / Still The Same - Drum Solo / Evolution / Nao Quero Dinheiro / Living For The Night / Rebel Maniac / I Wanna Be Sedated
COMA RAGE, (1995)
Coma Rage / Straight Ahead / Somebody Told Me You're Dead / Makin Love / Blast! / God Machine / Far And Near / The Last Song / If I Die By Hate Day Before / 405 South / A Face In The Crowd / I Fought the Law / Keep The Words
TEM PRA TODO MUNDI, (1996)
Dinheiro / Crime Na Cidade / 8 De Abril / Sabado / Not Ready To Get Up / Quinze Anos / Na Cara Do Gol / The One You Need / Lucinha Bordon / Alvo / Um Dia / Mais Do Mesmo
THE VERY BEST OF VIPER - EVERYBODY, EVERYBODY, (1999)
Not Ready To Get Up / Dead Light / I Fought The Law / Rebel Maniac / 8 De Abril / Coma Rage / Não Quero Dinheiro (Live) / The One You Need / Killing World / Crime na Cidade / A Cry From The Edge (Live) / Evolution /

Living For The Night / The Shelter / Keep The Words / Soldiers Of Sunrise

VIRGIN STEELE (Long Island, NY, USA)
Line-Up: David D. DeFeis (vocals), Edward Pursino (guitar), Rob DeMartino (bass), Joey Ayvazian (drums)

VIRGIN STEELE were amongst a leading number of new American Hard Rock bands taking their cue from British groups from the '70s and pioneering a new form of Pomp Rock. The seeds of the band were laid when Starr, actually of French origin and living there until he was nine years old, relocated back to America after a further spell in France having held a position in leading French rock outfit TRUST early on in their career. Indeed, Starr claims to have played with the group for what amounted to their first ever gig at the Olympia Theatre in Paris.

Upon returning to the America, Starr had begun playing with drummer Joey Ayvazian in 1981 and the duo quickly recruited vocalist / keyboard player David DeFeis after being impressed with his rendition of DEEP PURPLE's 'Child In Time' at his audition. DeFeis had previously been with MOUNTAIN ASH.

The band's first bassist was Kelly Nichols although DeFeis drafted bassist Joe O'Reilly into the frame. Nichols would join ANGELS IN VAIN then relocate to Los Angeles later to join FASTER PUSSYCAT and L.A. GUNS.

Based in Long Island, VIRGIN STEELE became the first signings to former Secret Records boss Martin Hooker's new Metal label Music For Nations. The band's debut album, originally intended as a demo and costing a mere $1,000, was released in Europe with the landmark catalogue number MFN 1 in 1983. It had originally appeared on the group's own label, Starr claiming that it had sold 5000 copies in the first two and a half weeks.

Amongst VIRGIN STEELE's earliest, high profile shows were two dates in New York opening for MANOWAR and the group were quick to begin work on a second album, 'Guardians Of The Flame'.

During 1984 various members of VIRGIN STEELE appeared anonymously on two Thrash albums billed as EXORCIST and DEVIL CHILDE.

VIRGIN STEELE parted company with Jack Starr due to musical differences. As the guitarist went on to forge a reasonably successful career for himself as a solo artist with his BURNING STARR band projects, VIRGIN STEELE eventually replaced him with Edward Pursino, a high school friend of DeFeis.

DAVID DEFEIS of VIRGIN STEELE
Photo : Nico Wobben

After Starr had left the band, his former colleagues seemingly discovered that he had copyrighted the band name. Eventually, the situation was resolved and the group was able to continue with the moniker. The group eventually returned with the 'Noble Savage' album, a record released on their Canadian manager Zoran Busic's Cobra label. Busic had once been the manager of Canuck Prog Rock outfit SAGA.

In 1986 DeFeis produced the second BURNING STARR album 'No Turning Back' and added keyboards. DeFeis also put in time with another Cobra label act, female thrashers ORIGINAL SIN, producing their debut album 'Sin Will Find You Out' albeit under the pseudonym of "The Lion".

Both Pursino and DeFeis would also contribute anonymously to the second album 'Stay Ugly' from spoof Thrash Metal band PILEDRIVER.

With enthusiasm at a high VIRGIN STEELE undertook two tours of Europe in 1987 supporting MANOWAR then BLACK SABBATH before recording of 'Age Of Consent'. The album, released in late 1988, did not feature Joe O'Reilly and bass was supplied by DeFeis and Pursino.

In a lengthy period of downtime for VIRGIN STEELE Starr and DeFeis reunited briefly in 1990 with the act SMOKESTACK LIGHTNING in union with ex-FOGHAT bassist Craig McGregor. This Blues Rock act's life span was short with a later recruit being bassist Rob DiMartino, later of RONDINELLI.

VIRGIN STEELE pulled in former DIO, GREAT WHITE and RONDINELLI bassist Teddy Cook for the 'Life Among The Ruins' album. However, the bass sessions were finished by Rob DeMartino. VIRGIN STEELE promoted the album with a lengthy headlining jaunt in Europe.

DeFeis' next project was the epic and ambitious concept 'The Marriage Of Heaven And Hell'. During recording DiMartino left to join RAINBOW, albeit briefly. Pursino took over bass duties. In 1995 a projected tour of Europe was cancelled when headline act URIAH HEEP pulled out. The band regrouped with DiMartino for a headline European schedule later in the year as VIRGIN STEELE drafted a new drummer Frank Gilchrist.

The 1997 extensively reworked re-release of 'Age Of Consent' sees a revision of the original track order and additional newly recorded bonus tracks, amongst them a heavily keyboard orientated rework of JUDAS PRIEST's 'Desert Plains'.

The band appeared on the bill of the 'Heavy Oder Was?' magazine organised 'Bang Your Head' festival in Tübingen, Germany in September 1997.

The 1999 album 'The House Of Atreus' is an ambitious concept based on Greek mythology. DeFeis toured this in Europe as an equally ambitious stage play. With the release of the second part of the concept 'The House Of Atreus Act II' in 2000 VIRGIN STEELE took to the road in Europe as guests of HAMMERFALL to open the new year.

De Feis lent his talents to EDGUY mainman Tobias Sammet's adventurous AVANTASIA eponymous project album the same year.

To mark VIRGIN STEELE's 20th anniversary in 2002 the act planned a greatest hits package entitled 'Hymns To Victory' and a further affair billed as 'The Book Of Burning'. The latter would feature early material culled from both 'Virgin Steele I' and 'Guardians Of The Flame' re-recorded by the current VIRGIN STEELE line-up in addition to no less than eight unreleased bonus tracks.

Singles/EPs:
A Cry In The Night / I Am The One / Go Down Fighting / Virgin Steele, Music For Nations 12KUT 104 (1983)
Don't Say Goodbye (Tonight) / I Am The One / Go Down Fighting / Wait For The Night, Mongol Horde (1984)

Albums:
VIRGIN STEELE, VS CEP 0001 (1982)
Danger Zone / American Girl / Dead End Kids / Drive On Thru / Still In Love With You / Children Of The Storm / Pictures On You / Pulverizer / Living In Sin / Virgin Steele
GUARDIANS OF THE FLAME, Music For Nations MFN 5 (1983)
Don't Say Goodbye (Tonight) / Burn The Sun / Life Of Crime / The Redeemer / Birth Through Fire / Guardians Of The Flame / Metal City / Hell Or High water / Go All The Way / A Cry In The Night
BURN THE SUN, Maze (1983) (Canadian Release)
WAIT FOR THE NIGHT, Mongol Horde (1984) (Canadian release)
NOBLE SAVAGE, Steamhammer 08 1836 (1985)
We Rule The Night / I'm On Fire / Thy Kingdom Come / Image Of A Faun At Twilight / Noble Savage / Fight Tooth And Nail / The Evil In Her Eyes / Rock Me / Don't Close Your Eyes / The Angel Of Light
AGE OF CONSENT, Steamhammer SPV (1988)
On The Wings Of The Night / Seventeen / Tragedy / Stay On Top / Chains Of Fire / The Burning Of Rome / Let It Roar / Lion In Winter / Cry Forever / We Are Eternal
LIFE AMONG THE RUINS, T&T TT 0006-2

(1993)
Sex Religion Machine / Love Is Pain / Jet Black / Invitation / I Dress In Black (Woman With No Shadow) / Crown Of Thorns / Cage Of Angels / Never Believed In Good-Bye / Too Hot To Handle / Love's Gone / Snakeskin Voodoo Man / Wild Fire Woman / Cry Forever / Haunting The Last Hours / Last Rose Of Summer

THE MARRIAGE OF HEAVEN AND HELL PART ONE, T&T 0012-2 (1994)
I Will Come For You / Weeping Of The Spirits / Blood And Gasoline / Self Crucifixion / Last Supper / Warrior's Lament / Trail Of Tears / The Raven Song / Forever I Will Roam / I Wake Up Screaming / House Of Dust / Blood Of The Saints / Life Among The Ruins / The Marriage Of Heaven And Hell

THE MARRIAGE OF HEAVEN AND HELL PART TWO, T&T TT 0019-2 (1995)
A Symphony Of Steele / Crown Of Glory / From Chaos To Creation / Twilight Of The Gods / Rising Unchained / Transfiguration / Prometheus The Fallen One / Emalaith / Strawgirl / Devil - Angel / Unholy Water / Victory Is Mine / The Marriage Of Heaven And Hell Revisited

AGE OF CONSENT, T&T TT 0032-2 (1997)
The Burning Of Rome (Cry For Pompeii) / Let It Roar / Prelude To Evening / Lion In Winter / Stranger At The Gate / Perfect Mansions (Mountains Of The Sun) / Coils Of The Serpent / Serpent's Kiss / On The Wings Of The Night / Seventeen / Tragedy / Stay On Top / Chains Of Fire / Desert Plains / Cry Forever/ We Are Eternal

INVICTUS, T&T (1998)
The Blood Of Vengeance / Invictus / Mind, Body, Spirit / In The Arms Of The Death God / Through Blood And Fire / Sword Of The Gods / God Of Our Sorrows / Vow Of Honour / Defiance / Dust From The Burning (A Season In Purgatory) / Amaranth / A Whisper Of Death / Dominion Day / A Shadow Of Fear / Theme From 'The Marriage Of Heaven And Hell / Veni, Vidi, Vici

THE HOUSE OF ATREUS ACT I: KINGDOM OF THE FEARLESS, T&T TT 0042-2 (1999) **58 GERMANY, 24 GREECE**
Kingdom Of The Fearless (The Destruction Of Troy) / Blaze Of Victory (The Watchman's Song) / Through The Ring Of Fire / Prelude In A Minor (The Voyage Home) / Death Darkly Closed Their Eyes (The Messenger's Song) / In Triumph Or Tragedy / Return Of The King / Flames Of The Black Star (The Arrows Of Herakles) / Narcissus / And Hecate Smiled / A Song Of Prophecy / Child Of Desolation / G Minor Invention (Descent Into Death's Twilight Kingdom) / Day Of Wrath / Great Sword Of Flame / The Gift Of

Tantalos / Iphigenia In Hades / The Fire God / Garden Of Lamentation / Agony And Shame / Gate Of Kings / Via Sacra

MAGICK FIRE MUSIC, Noise (2000)
Wings Of Vengeance / Flames Of Thy Power (From Blood They Rise) / Prometheus The Fallen One (Savage Unbound mix) / Gate Of Kings (Acoustic version) / Agamemnon's Last Hour (Silver Sided Death) / Great Sword Of Flame (Psycho rough mix)

THE HOUSE OF ATREUS ACT II: WINGS OF VENGEANCE, T&T 0051-2 (2000) **93 GERMANY**
Wings Of Vengeance / Hymn To The Gods Of Night / Fire Of Ecstasy / The Oracle Of Apollo / The Voice As Weapon / Moira / Nemesis / The Wine Of Violence / A Token Of My Hatred / Summoning The Powers / Flames Of Thy Power (From Blood They Rise) / Arms Of Mercury / By The Gods Suite I - By The Gods / By The Gods Suite II - Areopagos / By The Gods Suite III - The Judgement Of The Son / By The Gods Suite IV - Hammer The Winds / By The Gods Suite V - Guilt Or Innocence / Legends Suite I - The Fields Of Asphodel / Legends Suite II - When The Legends Die / Legends Suite III - Anemone (Withered Hopes... Forsaken) / The Waters Of Acheron / Fantasy And Fugue In D Minor (The Death Of Orestes) / Resurrection Day (The Finale)

BOOK OF BURNING, Noise (2002)
Conjuration Of The Watcher / Don't Say Goodbye (Tonight) / Rain Of Fire / Annihilation / Hellfire Woman / Children Of The Storm / The Chosen Ones / The Succubus / Minuet In G Minor / The Redeemer / I Am The One / Hot And Wild / Birth Through Fire / Guardians Of The Flame / The Final Days / A Cry In The Night

HYMNS TO VICTORY, Noise (2002)
Flames Of Thy Power / Through The Ring Of Fire / Invictus / Crown Of Glory (Unscarred) / Kingdom Of The Fearless / The Spirit Of Steele / A Symphony Of Steele / The Burning Of Rome / I Will Come For You / Saturday Night / Noble Savage / The Mists Of Avalon / Emalaith

VIRGO (BRAZIL / GERMANY)
Line-Up: Andre Matos (vocals / piano), Sascha Paeth (guitar), Olaf Reitmeier (bass), Miro (keyboards), Robert Hunecke-Rizzo (drums)

VIRGO was the 2001 post ANGRA vehicle for vocalist Andre Matos. The eponymous debut album would also see heavy contributions from Sascha Paeth of Germany's HEAVEN'S GATE. Other contributors to the debut album, titled 'Virgo' but using the astrological symbol so often called 'M.P.' (Matos / Paeth), would

469

be bass player Olaf Reitmeier, keyboard player Miro and drummer Robert Hunecke-Rizzo.

Matos would pursue his SHAMAN project after completion of the album.

Albums:
VIRGO, JVC Victor VICP-61505 (2001)
To Be / Crazy Me? / Take Me Home / Baby Doll / No Need To Have An Answer / Discovery / Street Of Babylon / River / Blowing Away / I Want You To Know / Fiction

VISION DIVINE (ITALY)
Line-Up: Fabio Leone (vocals), Olaf Thörsen (guitar), Andrea Torricini (bass), Andrew McPauls (keyboards), Mat Stancioiu (drums)

VISION DIVINE were assembled by erstwhile LABYRINTH members vocalist Fabio Leone and guitarist Olaf Thörsen (a.k.a. Carlo Magnani), debuting with an eponymous album. The relationship between LABYRINTH and VISION DIVINE is complex as besides Leone and Thörsen's involvement keyboard player Andrew McPauls (Andrea De Paoli) on keyboards and drummer Matt Stancioiu also cite LABYRINTH credits.

VISION DIVINE bassist Andrea 'Tower' Torricini lists credits with TRINITY OF STEEL, METAL KINGS and as session performer for Speed Metal band SHADOWS OF STEEL. Besides VISION DIVINE Torricini also operates the Power Metal project band WONDERLAND in league with his ex-SHADOWS OF STEEL colleagues and former LABYRINTH drummer Frank Andiver. Thörsen would also guest on the 2000 SKYLARK album 'Divine Gates'.

Albums:
VISION DIVINE, Arthreia (2000)
New Eden / On The Wings Of The Storm / Black Mask Of Fear / Exodus / The Whisper / Forgotten Worlds / Vision Divine / The Final Countdown / The Miracle / Forever Young / Of Light And Darkness
SEND ME AN ANGEL, JVC Victor VICP-61733 (2002)
Incipit / Send Me An Angel / Pain / Away From You / Black & White / The Call / Taste Of A Goodbye / Apocalypse Coming / Nemesis / Flame Of Hate / Take On Me

VOICE (GERMANY)
Line-Up: Oliver Glas (vocals), Thommy Neuhierl (guitar), Rico Hendel (guitar), Soren Glas (bass), Matthias Loscher (keyboards), Stefan Schwarzmann (drums)

A Power Metal band created in 1996 and fronted by Oliver Glas. VOICE made their entrance with the 1998 'Prediction' album released by AFM Records. The VOICE line-up for this album comprised Glas on vocals, guitarists Thommy Neuhierl and Rico Hendel, bass player Soren Glas, keyboard player Matthias Loscher and drummer Arnd Otto.

VOICE's line-up would remain stable for the follow up 'Trapped In Anguish'. During 2001 the Stefan Schwarzmann, the renowned erstwhile ACCEPT, U.D.O. and RUNNING WILD drummer, would supplant Otto.

Albums:
PREDICTION, AFM 38665-422 (1998)
Victim Of The Glory / The Prediction / Sand Creek / Project Daydream / I'll Be There / Tears In The Darkness / Stonehenge
TRAPPED IN ANGUISH, AFM 0046632AFM (1999)
No Way Out / Twilight Dreams / Behind Your Reflections / The Silent Way / Colder Than Ice / The Gunslinger / Disappeared Heroes / In The Night / The Journey
GOLDEN SIGNS, AFM (2001)
Golden Signs / Days Of Trust / On My Way / Doubtful Times / Deadly Embrace / Without Compulsion / The Old Brightness / The Last Dance / The Prediction (2001) / The Visitor

WANING MOON
(CHILE)
Line-Up: Francisco Gomez (vocals), Marcelo Oehninger (guitar), José Tomás Montecinos (bass), Eduardo Schälichli (keyboards), Luciano Oehninger (drums)

Dating back to 1999, Talagante based WANING MOON was the creation of guitarist Marcelo Oehninger. Although the band's debut gig was in January of 1999, with Oehninger joined onstage by bassist Sasha Panjkovic and drummer Luciano Oehninger, it was not to be until the later introduction of lead singer Diego Noguera the band adopted the title WANING MOON.
Both Panjkovic and a briefly introduced keyboard player broke ranks during 2000 curtailing activity for much of the year. By 2001 Eduardo Schälchli had been introduced as the group's new keyboard player and subsequently former SINNER SOUL man Eduardo Luna took over bass duties. Bringing in a fresh lead vocalist, Francisco Gómez, WANING MOON cut the demo 'Silver Steed'. After these sessions Santiago Kegevic assumed the role of bass player.

WARCRY (SPAIN)
Line-Up: Víctor García (vocals), Pablo García (guitar), Fernando Mon (guitar), Alvaro Jardón (bass), Alberto Ardines (drums)

WARCRY members vocalist Víctor García, guitarist Fernando Mon and drummer Alberto Ardines are all veterans of premier Spanish Power Metal band AVALANCH. Guitarist Pablo García is from RELATIVE SILENCE whilst bass player Alvaro Jardón has credits with DARNA.

Albums:
WARCRY, Avispa (2002)
Intro / Luz Del Norte / Quiero / Nadie / Pueblo Maldito / Cada Vez / Senor / Al Salir El Sol / Trono Del Metal / Hoy Gano Yo / Nana / Amanecer

WARDOG (USA)
Line-Up: Tom Gattis (vocals / guitar), Chris Catero (vocals / bass), John Herrera (drums)

WARDOG front man Tom Gattis is ex-DEUCE and TENSION. The 'Scorched Earth' album sees drum duties shared between John Herrera and Ross Martinez. The band put in an appearance at the 1998 'Bang Your Head' Festival in Germany where they were joined onstage by a guesting IRON MAIDEN vocalist

BRUCE DICKINSON.
WARDOG duly donated their take on 'Purgatory' to a 2000 IRON MAIDEN tribute record 'Slaves To The Power'. Gattis announced the formation of a new band entitled AFTERBURN. This was a reunion with erstwhile TENSION colleague Tim O'Connor on bass, Bulgarian master guitarist Peter Petev and ex-VYPER and PRIZONER drummer Michael Scott. The title of this new venture would later be switched to BALLISTIC.

Albums:
SCORCHED EARTH, Metal Blade 3984-14112-2 (1997)
Scorched Earth / Sounds Of War / Broken But Not Dead / Seeing Is Believing / Nothing Left / Killing Speed / Bucket 'O Beer / Cuz / Tomb Of The Slain / Beast Of Damnation

WARHAG (CANADA)
Line-Up: Kyle Schkorche (vocals), Kurt Phillips (guitar), Joy Toyota-Phillips (bass), Kevin MacEachern (drums)

A Christian Power Metal band. WARHAG feature guitarist Kurt Phillips of WITCHKILLER repute and female bassist Joy Toyota-Phillips. The 'Sinister Grip' release of 2002 includes a reworking of WITCHKILLER's 'Day Of The Saxons'. The release was limited to just 500 copies.

Albums:
SINISTER GRIP, (2002)
First Nations / Rage Of Angels / Into The Castle / Sinister Grip / Mean Mouth / Brutal Orbit / Saxon's Return

WARHEAD (GERMANY)
Line-Up: Björn Eilen (vocals / guitar), Benjamin Zur Heide (bass), Peter Breitenbach (drums)

The Heavy Metal act WARHEAD duo of vocalist Björn Eilen and drummer Peter Breitenbach were members of mid '80s Rock act INVERNESS. Breitenbach would later journey through GRAVE DIGGER from 1991 to 1993, assembling WARHEAD later the same year. Bassist Benjamin Zur Heide had previously found experience with Punk act THE TOASTERS and Indie band DIE ZEUGEN.
The band would debut with the High Gain 1997 record 'Good Part For Each', capitalising on this by signing to the Noise label for a sophomore outing 'Perfect/Infect'. WARHEAD's third album, 'Beyond Recall' would be produced by GRAVE DIGGER

guitarist Uwe Lulis. In February of 2000 WARHEAD augmented their live sound for support dates with U.D.O. with the addition of second guitarist Florian Albers, a former member of the bizarrely titled PUDDINGTIME BASTARDS.

The 2001 official bootleg release, recorded on the band's 2000 support tour to U.D.O., included a cover of the SAVATAGE classic 'City Beneath The Surface'. By this stage WARHEAD were on the search for a vocalist, Eilen having departed in May of 2000.

Eilen turned up once again as a member of REBELLION, a union with ex-GRAVE DIGGER members guitarist Uwe Lulis and bassist Tommi Göttlich. The adventurous conceptually based REBELLION took on no less than the Bard's 'Macbeth' as the theme for their opening shot 'A Tragedy In Steele'. REBELLION would also include drummer Randy Black from Canadian Thrashers ANNIHILATOR and vocalist Michael Seifert from Osnabruck acts BLACK DESTINY and XIRON.

Albums:

GOOD PART FOR EACH, High Gain 8800954 (1997)
15th Century / Let Me Die / Good Christian / Hatred / Blindly / Good Part For Each / Going To The Center / Carrie White / The Healing / Inbetween / Warhead / Missiles
PERFECT / INFECT, Noise (1998)
Listen! / The Other Side / Celebrate Your Loot / Six Billion Reasons To Hate / Flashback Of A Poor Man / Shut Your Mouth / Perfect/Infect / Into The Light / Scream / K.Y.N. (Kill Your Neighbor) / Behind My Eyes
BEYOND RECALL, Noise (2000)
Senseless / Blackout / The Trial / Desert Trip / Hour Of Death / Memories / A Piece Of Your Flesh / Forced / The Last Butterfly / Lord / Electrocute! / I Swear / Beyond Recall
LIVE IN MUNCHEN - OFFICIAL BOOTLEG, (2001)
15th Century / Let Me Die / Good Part For Each / City Beneath The Surface / Carrie White / Blindly / Warhead / K.Y.N. (Kill Your Neighbor)

WARLOCK (GERMANY)
Line-Up: Dorothee Pesch (vocals), Rudy Graf (guitar), Peter Szigeti (guitar), Frank Rittel (bass), Michael Eurich (drums)

With German Metal being taken to the global masses by the likes of SCORPIONS and ACCEPT in the '80s it was to be the female fronted WARLOCK who had the next shot at commercial success worldwide. Despite major backing, their obvious talents and delectable lead vocalist WARLOCK fell apart just as they were poised to break big. WARLOCK first came together in 1982 in Dusseldorf, Pesch having paid her dues as solo singer in the Dusseldorf cathedral choir before joining Heavy Metal band SNAKEBITE.

The band started out with their Mausoleum Records debut with an uncompromising Heavy Metal sound courtesy of the twin guitars and with a truly gifted Metal vocalist in Pesch. Although opening Mausoleum album 'Burning The Witches' is laden down with too many stodgy Metal-by-numbers songs the underlying quality of the band shone through. By their signing with major label Vertigo WARLOCK had matured as songwriters and consequently 'Hellbound' is a far superior effort.

Not only blessed with a dynamic range Pesch also retained a unique and natural rasp to her vocal style that combined with her looks marked her as a valuable focal point for WARLOCK. 'Kerrang' magazine's normally highbrow Derek Oliver was a keen supporter, confessing in print for a desire to "dip his sausage in the Pesch shop"! At one point magazines raced to get pictures of Pesch when at a Dutch gig, and unbeknown to her for a few seconds, her studded leather bra came undone. Naturally the photographers had a field day with the image providing some Metal magazines with welcome posters.

The band supported W.A.S.P. on a British tour in 1986 promoting the 'True As Steel' album. Despite this progress on the international scale WARLOCK's internal politics were none too good and Graf was to join RAGE in 1986. Szigeti quit in 1987 for U.D.O. to be replaced by American Tommy Bolin. The line-up for the 'Triumph And Agony' album found Pesch and Bolin being joined by bassist Tommy Hendrickson and drummer Michael Eurich. As the '90s drew in it was clear that WARLOCK the band had been demoted. Any pretence at a band project was dropped in 1989 when the 'Force Majuere' album was issued under the title of simply DORO. The band at this point featured ex-RAINBOW drummer Bobby Rondinelli, guitarist John Devin and bassist Tommy Hendrikson. Keyboards were contributed by DIO's Claude Schnell. DORO, relocating to New York and teamed up with outside songwriters along with GENE SIMMONS of KISS in the production chair, was being groomed as a potential solo star.

In 1992 Rittel and Szigeti formed CORACKO (later titled STONEWASHED) with vocalist Dirk Wicke and drummer Marin Englar. Eurich joined CASANOVA. Hendrickson later journeyed through WAR AND PEACE and

DORO OF WARLOCK
Photo : Nico Wobben

JAILHOUSE. The man also supplied bass to GEORGE LYNCH's 1993 album 'Sacred Groove'.

During 2001 German Metal band POWERGOD would cover 'Burning The Witches' on their 'Bleed For The Gods' album. DORO is still a major Metal icon in her native land with a steady stream of solo releases behind her. Always popular in Germany, more recent albums have seen DORO's fan base widening globally.

PETER SZIGETI of WARLOCK
Photo : Matt Sampspon

Singles/EPs:
Without You / Burning The Witches, Mausoleum GUTS 8402 (1984)
You Hurt My Soul (On And On) / Turn It On / Evil, Vertigo 884 256-1Q (1985)
You Hurt My Soul (On And On) / Evil, Vertigo 884 902-1Q (1985) (7" single)
All Night / Hellbound, Vertigo 880 902-1 (1985)
Fight For Rock / Mr Gold / Midnite In China / You Hurt My Soul / Turn It On / Evil, Vertigo (1986)
Für Immer / Metal Tango / Kiss Of Death, Vertigo 870 398-2 (1987)
Für Immer / Metal Tango, Vertigo (1987) (7" single)
East Meets West / I Rule The Ruins, Vertigo (1987) (Promotion release)
All We Are, Mercury (1987) (USA Promotion)

Albums:
BURNING THE WITCHES, Mausoleum SKULL 8325 (1984)
Signs Of Satan / After The Bomb / Dark Fade / Homicide Rocker / Without You / Metal Racer / Burning The Witches / Hateful Guy / Holding Me
HELLBOUND, Vertigo 824 660-1 (1985)
Hellbound / All Night / Earthshaker Rock / Wrathchild / Down And Out / Out Of Control / Time To Die / Shout It Out / Catch My Heart
TRUE AS STEEL, Vertigo VERHCD 830 237-2 (1986)
Mr. Gold / Fight For Rock / Love In The Danger Zone / Speed Of Sound / Midnite In China / Vorwarts: All right! / True As Steel / Lady In A Rock n" Roll Hell / Love Song / Igloo On The Moon (Reckless) / T.O.B.
TRIUMPH AND AGONY, Vertigo VERH 50 (1987) **50 UK, 80 USA**
All We Are / Three Minute Warning / I Rule The Ruins / Kiss Of Death / Make Time For Love / East Meets West / Touch Of Evil / Metal Tango / Cold, Cold World / Fur Immer
RARE DIAMONDS, Vertigo 848 353 1 (1991)
All We Are / Unholy Love (DORO) / Für Immer / True As Steel / Beyond The Trees (DORO) / East Meets West (Live) / Rare Diamonds (Live) (DORO) / You Hurt My Soul / Hellbound / Burning The Witches / Out Of Control / A Whiter Shade Of Pale (DORO) / Without You / Love Song

WARLORD (CA, USA)
Line-Up: Damien King (vocals), Destroyer (guitar), The Raven (bass), Sentinel (keyboards), Thunderchild (drums)

Claiming to hail "from the North", WARLORD plied classical Hard Rock from the less mysterious climes of Los Angeles. Despite limited releases WARLORD, founded by erstwhile RUSSIAN ROULLETE drummer 'Thunderchild' (a.k.a. Mark Zonder) and guitarist 'Destroyer' (William J. Tsamis), soon garnered a cult following among dedicated Metal fans. With a theatrical stage show that embellished the grandiose musical approach, WARLORD were picked up by Brian Slagel's Metal Blade Records and debuted with a six track album entitled 'Deliver Us' in 1983, by which time they had become a trio with the addition of bassist 'Archangel' (Dave Waltry). With the recruitment of a new vocalist Rick Cunningham, dubbed 'Damien King II', WARLORD returned to action with the 'Lost And Lonely Days' 12" in 1984. This would be followed by the more ambitious 'And The Cannons Of Destruction Have Begun'. Cunningham would be replaced on lead vocals by Rick Anderson, or 'Damien King III'. With WARLORD's collapse Zonder teamed up with Progressive Metal band FATES WARNING.

A full decade later the track 'Child Of The Damned' would later be covered by Sweden's HAMMERFALL for their groundbreaking 1997 retroMetal revival album 'Glory To The Brave'. King reciprocated by guesting on HAMMERFALL's follow up 'Legacy Of Kings'. The HAMMERFALL connection would not end there as it was announced that WARLORD had been re-formed by guitarist William J. Tsamis and drummer Mark Zonder in mid 2001 with HAMMERFALL vocalist Joacim Cans fronting the entire affair.

The long awaited comeback album 'Rising Out Of The Ashes' was duly delivered in July of 2002. Taking onboard Italian management a fresh live band found Joacim Cans, Mark Zonder and William J. Tsamis joined by second guitarist Paolo Viani of BLACK JESTER and MOONLIGHT CIRCUS, keyboard player Daniele Soravia of MOONLIGHT CIRCUS and HELREIDH and SIGMA bassist Pasko. The band was signed to appear at the annual German 'Wacken Open Air' festival as a co-headline act.

Singles/EPs:
Lost And Lonely Days / Aliens, Metal Blade 71082 (1984)

Albums:
DELIVER US, Metal Blade MBR 1005 (1983)
Deliver Us From Evil / Winter Tears / Child Of The Damned / Penny For A Poor Man / Black Mass / Lucifer's Hammer
AND THE CANNONS OF DESTRUCTION HAVE BEGUN, Metal Blade 71112 (1984)
Lucifer's Hammer / Lost And Lonely Days / Black Mass / Soliloquy / Aliens / Child Of The Damned / Deliver Us From Evil
THY KINGDOM COME, Roadrunner RR 9637 (1987)
Mrs Victoria / Aliens / Child Of The Damned / Beginning / Lucifer's Hammer / Black Mass / Lost And Lonely Days / Soliloquy / Deliver Us From Evil / Hands And Feet
THE BEST OF WARLORD, Metal Blade CDZORRO 69 (1989)
Deliver Us From Evil / Winter Tears / Child Of The Damned / Penny For A Poor Man / Black Mass / Lucifer's Hammer / Mrs Victoria / Aliens / Lost And Lonely Days / Beginning / Lucifer's Hammer / Soliloquy / MCMLXXXIV / Child Of The Damned
RISING OUT OF THE ASHES, Athreia (2002)
Battle Of The Living Dead / Enemy Mind / Invaders / Winds Of Thor / War In Heaven / My Name Is Man / Lucifer's Hammer / Sons Of A Dream / Achilles Revenge

WAR MACHINE (UK)
Line-Up: Bernadette Mooney (vocals), Steve White (guitar), Lez Fry (bass), Brian Waugh (drums)

Outfit put together by former ATOMKRAFT guitarist Steve White in 1983 with original drummer Steve Smith who was superseded by Brian Waugh for the album. Waugh was then later to depart and drummer Chris Buggy took on the role.

In 1989 WAR MACHINE regrouped to record a three track demo after which Mooney departed. Buggy also left to be replaced by Mark Savage who in turn performed drum duties on VENOM guitarist MANTAS solo album. Savage now fronts for XLR8R as lead vocalist.

Albums:
UNKNOWN SOLDIER, Neat NEAT 1036 (1986)
Sacred Hold / On The Edge / Power / No Time / Dangerous / Can't Wait / No Place To Hide / Warrior

WARMEN (FINLAND)
Line-Up: Pasi Rantanen (vocals), Kimberley Goss (vocals), Sami Virtanen (guitar), Roope Latvala (guitar), Jari Kainulainen (bass), Janne Wirman (keyboards), Mirka Rantenen (drums)

WARMEN is a solo undertaking of the much esteemed CHILDREN OF BODOM keyboard player Janne Wirman. The man had also been employed on a session basis for demo work by THUNDERSTONE. For the debut 'Unknown Soldier' album Wirman employed TUNNELVISION members guitarist Sami Virtanen and drummer Mirka Rantenen, the latter also in the employ of THUNDERSTONE. Also involved in the project was STRATOVARIUS bassist Jari Kainulainen, WISARD's Antti Warmen and Pekka Palmo, SINERGY and WALTARI guitarist Roope Latvala and SINERGY vocalist Kimberley Goss.

The first album was issued by Spinefarm in their native Finland and by the Toys Factory label in Japan with an extra track 'Dead Reflection'.

The band released an ambitious cover version of HEART's 'Alone' as a single in Finland during October of 2001. WARMEN debuted live the following month fronted by former TUNNELVISION and present day THUNDERSTONE vocalist Pasi Rantanen.

A trio of WARMEN personnel, Sami Virtanen,

Janne Warmen and Mirka Rantanen, would session on the 2002 'Waiting For The Dawn' solo album by STRATOVARIUS front man TIMO KOTIPELTI. Janne Warmen would also figure as part of the MASTERPLAN band assembled by HELLOWEEN refugees guitarist ROLAND GRAPOW and drummer Uli Kusch.

Singles/EPs:
Alone / Dead Reflection, Spinefarm SPI 124CD (2001)

Albums:
UNKNOWN SOLDIER, Spinefarm SPI88CD (2000)
Introduction / The Evil That Warmen Do / Devil's Mistress / Hopeless Optimism / Unknown Soldier / Fire Within / Warcry Of Salieri / Into The Oblivion / Piano Intro / Treasure Within / Soldiers Of Fortune
BEYOND ABILITIES, Spinefarm SPI139CD (2001)
Beyond Abilities / Spark / Hidden / Trip To... / Dawn / Singer's Chance / Alone / Confessions / Salieri Strikes Back / War Of Worlds / Finale

WARRIOR (San Diego, CA, USA)

Line-Up: Parramore McCarty (vocals), Joe Floyd (guitar), Tommy Asakawa (guitar), Bruce Turgon (bass), Jimmy Volpe (drums)

Not to be confused with the Vinnie Vincent fronted band of the same name; this much tougher Los Angeles based outfit WARRIOR also came to the fore with a hugely impressive demo. Formed by the nucleus of guitarists Joe Floyd and Tommy Asakawa in San Diego, the pair hooked up with vocalist Parramore McCarty in Los Angeles in 1983, working with a number of rhythm sections and under different names (including RED) before agreeing to go for WARRIOR.

Upon signing to Virgin's 10 imprint, the quartet recorded the 'Fighting For The Earth' album in 1985, although some of the raw energy and "heaviosity" found on the demo tended to be lost on the actual record.

The bass and drum tracks on the album were actually played by original band members Rick Bennett and Liam Jason respectively. The pair had both been replaced by ex-BLACK SHEEP bassist Bruce Turgon and Los Angeles club veteran Jimmy Volpe (who had once been in a group called CHAMELEON with ex-BUX and JOE PERRY PROJECT vocalist Ralph Morman) on drums upon its release. Jason would go on to join RHINO BUCKET later surprising the Rock community by trans-gendering into Jackie Enx.

Despite a fair amount of hype, including a trip to Britain where WARRIOR played at the Marquee Club in London and appeared on Channel 4's 'ECT' Rock programme, the group would soon break up. Joe Floyd started an unnamed band project with ex-WARLORD drummer Mark Zonder. Volpe joined FOREPLAY.

After a very short term engagement with ROUGH CUTT in late 1987, vocalist Parramore McCarty later recorded an album with ex-BILLY IDOL guitarist STEVE STEVENS billed as the ATOMIC PLAYBOYS. Bruce Turgon, having recorded with old BLACK SHEEP mate LOU GRAMM on the FOREIGNER singer's solo works, teamed up with him again in the ranks of SHADOWKING before he was invited to replace Rick Wills in FOREIGNER when Gramm rejoined the group for the recording of the 'Mr. Moonlight' album.

WARRIOR were resurrected in 1998 with the recording of a brand new album ('Ancient Futures'), although only McCarty and Floyd remained from the original line-up.

The album, released through German label Dream Circle, was recorded in part with TRIBE OF GYPSIES guitarist Roy Z in a playing and writing capacity. Backing up its release the band appeased German fans by putting in a sterling performance at the 1998 Wacken Festival.

2000 found the band's line-up including ex-FOREVER bassist Ray Burke and the esteemed JOSHUA, DRIVER and IMPELLITERRI singer ROB ROCK on vocal duties. Floyd aided erstwhile METAL CHURCH vocalist David Wayne's WAYNE in September 2000 and would also act as producer for DESTINY'S END's 'Transition' album.

Singles/EPs:
Fighting For The Earth / Only The Strong Survive, 10 TENY 38 (1985)

Albums:
FIGHTING FOR THE EARTH, 10 XID 6 (1985)
Fighting For The Earth / Only The Strong Survive / Ruler / Mind Over Matter / Defenders Of Creation / Day Of Evil (Beware) / Cold Fire / P.T.M.I / Welcome Aboard
ANCIENT FUTURE, Dream Circle DCD 9839 (1998)
Fight Or Fall / Pray / Who Sane? / Learn To Love / Tonight We Ride / Power / White Mansions / The Rush / Tear It Down / Ancient Future
THE CODE OF LIFE, Nuclear Blast (2001)

Day Of Reckoning / Kill The Machine /
Standing / We Are One / Open Your Eyes /
Pantheon / Code Of Life / Soul Survivor /
The Endless Beginning / The Fools' Theme /
Insignificance / Retribution

W.A.S.P. (Los Angeles, CA, USA)
Line-Up: Blackie Lawless (vocals / guitar),
Darrell Roberts (guitar), Mike Duda (bass),
Frankie Banali (drums)

W.A.S.P. emerged from the early '80s hotbed
of Los Angeles Metal, taking the visual
theatrics of the genre over the edge, thus
guaranteeing attention. The band's potential
was heightened by outrageous stage shows
that had main protagonist vocalist / bassist
Blackie Lawless involved in the mock torture
of a woman bound to a rack onstage,
throwing raw meat into the audience - all this
whilst wearing a chainsaw codpiece with his
arse cheeks on display.
Lawless (real name Steve Duren), who had
first trod the boards with east coast outfit
BLACK RABBIT, had honed his craft with an
inclusion in the NEW YORK DOLLS during
their final post Johnny Thunders days.
Lawless at this time was operating under the
pseudonym of Blackie Goozeman. Lawless
then migrated through Los Angeles acts

KILLER CAIN, SISTER and LONDON, the
latter seeing Lawless alongside future
MÖTLEY CRÜE bassist Nikki Sixx for a short
period.
1975's SISTER, featuring Lawless, guitarist
Randy Piper and drummer Tony Richards
pulled in guitarist Chris Holmes the following
year. The guitarist's advert had been spotted
in the porn mag 'Hustler'. The band drafted
Rik Fox in on bass guitar in 1978 and shortly
after the band switched titles to W.A.S.P.
The band set about gigging on the Los
Angeles club scene stoking up a fearsome
reputation. W.A.S.P.'s first official line-up being
Lawless, Piper, Fox and Richards. Piper had
also been playing with L.A. ROCKS previous
to this incarnation.
The band's abbreviated nomenclature of
W.A.S.P. also helped fuel the controversy (in
the same manner that KISS was supposed to
be an abbreviation of Knights In Satan's
Service) as Lawless' publicity machine
dropped hints that the act's real name was
We Are Sexual Perverts. Bearing in mind the
KISS inspirations the growing myth was
further cemented by KISS guitarist ACE
FREHLEY pitching in to produce the band's
first set of demos.
Before long Fox was to leave (to create
STEELER and SIN) and Don Costa took over
the bass position. Costa's tenure was brief as

W.A.S.P.

the man joined DANTE FOX (a prototype of GREAT WHITE), DAMIEN and then OZZY OSBOURNE for a fleeting if eventful tenure. Drummer Gary Holland also figured in the band but he too left for DANTE FOX.

The version of W.A.S.P. that first came to attention comprised the towering figure of Lawless now on bass, wild eyed guitarist Chris Holmes, second guitarist Piper and drummer Richards.

W.A.S.P. were quickly pulled into the Capitol Records fold and gained the extra boost of signing to the heavyweight management team of Sanctuary Music (responsible for IRON MAIDEN) only to have their projected first single, the controversially titled Mike Varney produced, 'Animal (Fuck Like A Beast)' refused release. The track eventually emerged through the independent label Music For Nations in Britain.

The tough debut album provided ample evidence that W.A.S.P., and particularly Lawless, were accomplished songwriters behind the hype. By now the band were sporting Sci-Fi wasteland warrior stage garb with Piper having to haul various pipework on his back. At frenzied shows in America fans took audience participation to the extremes of throwing animal brains and pigs heads onstage.

W.A.S.P. hit Britain in September 1984 to great anticipation supported by English Shock Rockers WRATHCHILD prior to a solid six months touring America as support to KISS and BLACK SABBATH. The tour heralded the appearance of former ROADMASTER and THE B'ZZ drummer Stephen Riley in place of the ousted Tony Richards. Riley had not long joined KEEL when the job came up.

The Spencer Proffer produced 'The Last Command' album caught the band progressing into slightly more refined territory 'The Last Command' charted worldwide and extensive touring, including opening for KROKUS in America, bolstered by two radio hits 'Wild Child' and 'Blind In Texas'.

For the third album W.A.S.P. realigned themselves as Randy Piper departed, the guitarist seeking a liaison with ALICE COOPER which failed to materialise. Lawless took over rhythm guitar and ex-KING KOBRA bassist Johnny Rod joined the team.

The resulting album 'Inside The Electric Circus', including covers of URIAH HEEP's 'Easy Livin' and HUMBLE PIE's 'I Don't Need No Doctor' found W.A.S.P. struggling to maintain the momentum as regards song-writing quality. A fresh stage show, more Bill Barnum than blood n' bondage, had many wondering whether the glory gory days of yore were over - this despite an album cover featuring a naked Lawless. Nevertheless

W.A.S.P. still pulled in the crowds for the obligatory world tour, Germans WARLOCK supporting in Britain, and the lack of Blackie's notorious codpiece was more than made up for by a new flame-throwing version.

By now the American moral rights organisation, the P.M.R.C., (Parental Music Resource Center) an outfit led by the political evangelism of senator's wife Tipper Gore, were hounding heavy metal for its supposed anti-social machinations. W.A.S.P. were an easy target and constantly put under the spotlight, naturally only boosting their infamy. W.A.S.P. were featured as the main protagonists in Gore's book 'Raising PG (Parental Guidance) kids in an X rated society' in which Lawless' lyrics were printed without permission, and worse- altered.

The band were to win the day with the priceless value of publicity being topped by Lawless's lawsuit against the P.M.R.C. for abuse of copyright being won by the band.

Matters did not fare so well though with their support band for their early 1987 American tour as new bad boys SLAYER harangued the headliners in the press at every opportunity. SLAYER maintained it was in fact they and not Lawless' crew that were selling the majority of the tickets and further that W.A.S.P. were finding it difficult in the extreme to follow their act.

Regardless, a consolidated live album 'Live In The Raw' culled from the band's last three shows in San Bernadino, San Diego and Long Beach Arena on the 'Welcome To The Electric Circus' tour, kept up the pace but once again omitted 'Animal', the staple work of W.A.S.P.'s live set.

However, a studio track 'Scream Until You Like It' - recorded for the soundtrack to the movie 'Ghoulies II', was released and kept the band's profile in the charts. The promotional video even utilised the fiendish mini-monsters from the movie to effect.

A six week tour of America duly ensued although W.A.S.P. were finding that P.M.R.C. pressure was still able to deny them access to many cities.

W.A.S.P. were thrown into further controversy over the cover artwork for their 1988 single, a live version of the stage favourite 'Animal'. Depicting a dog about to molest a woman even Lawless was to pour scorn on it denying any involvement.

Blackie was to devote serious effort during this period to making his views on free speech well known with a series of lectures and seminars. This was the background for W.A.S.P.'s latest album 'The Headless Children', generally acknowledged as being one of the band's finest works to date.

Randy Piper reappeared with an outfit called

ANIMAL in June 1988 boasting band mates Rich Lewis on vocals, Shredder on guitar, Burn on bass and Steve Solon on drums. Steve Riley quit W.A.S.P. and went off to join L.A. GUNS, making way for former QUIET RIOT drummer Frankie Banali as W.A.S.P. launched their renaissance meisterwork. Reputedly coming in three times over budget at a whopping half a million dollars 'The Headless Children' gave ample evidence as to Lawless's views on censorship and politics, all backed by the finest Metal the band had crafted to date. Keyboard parts, strangely in keeping with the overall menace of the record, were added by former URIAH HEEP / BLACKFOOT veteran KEN HENSLEY. Only one cover was thrown in, a rousing version of THE WHO's 'The Real Me' although the band also cut JETHRO TULL's 'Locomotive Breath' which would appear as a single B side.

The resulting tour, complete with a stage set based on the all engulfing skull of the album cover and disturbing real life horror video footage, did well but a burnt out Holmes, who had incidentally recently married LITA FORD, quit in Europe curtailing the planned string of dates. Many who had seen his drunken appearance in the movie 'Decline And Fall Of Western Civilisation Part II: The Metal Years' saw a stark portrait of a man facing his self-made abyss. Holmes forged the short-lived PSYCHO SQUAD.

With W.A.S.P. effectively on hold Rod and Banali opted out to create a new act GERONIMO with ex-KEEL, ICON and KING KOBRA guitarist David Michael Phillips and singer Thomas Adam Kelly. It is alleged that Rod later ended up serving a prison term for some misdemeanour or another.

Lawless persevered now as BLACKIE LAWLESS AND W.A.S.P. pulling in session musicians, including Hensley once more and ex-BALANCE / MEAT LOAF guitarist Bob Kulick, for a further concept album 'The Crimson Idol'. Initial drum tracks were laid down by Banali but were re-recorded by one-time IMPELLITERRI drummer Stet Howland. Heralded as a rock opera by Lawless the album succeeded in drawing back many fans who had grown disillusioned with Holmes departure.

Rod made a return and, reverting back to simply W.A.S.P., the band now incorporated Lawless, Howland and guitarist Dan McCabe. Ex-DRIVER and IMPELLITERRI keyboard player Philip Wolfe was added for live work. Touring, including a return visit to the Castle Donington 'Monsters Of Rock' festival, had the W.A.S.P. figurehead alongside Rod, Howland and guitarist Doug Blair, the latter having supplanted McCabe.

Doubtless fired by the success of shocker MARILYN MANSON and the rejuvenated ALICE COOPER Lawless rolled W.A.S.P. out once more during 1997 with a show and album 'Kill, Fuck, Die' that out grossed all its predecessors. A much trumpeted reconciliation between Lawless and Holmes fired press enthusiasm. Completing the line-up was Stetland and bassist Mike Duda.

The 2000 'Best Of The Best' compilation includes two new cuts 'Unreal' and a take of ELTON JOHN's 'Saturday Night's Alright For Fighting'. A further 2000 album, the live 'The Sting Worldwide', was initially broadcast live over the internet.

W.A.S.P.'s rhythm section of Duda and Howland formed part of the project band KILLING MACHINE along with ex-LOUDNESS, DR. SIN and OBSESSION vocalist Mike Vescara for a self-titled 2000 album.

As the band launched the 2001 'Unholy Terror' album it was revealed that for a short period Holmes was out of the band and replaced by TUFF / ALCOHOLICA guitarist Darrell Roberts. The pair soon switched positions once more as Holmes apparently reconvened with W.A.S.P. and Roberts journeyed back to TUFF. Confusion would reign though when Roberts pulled out of a projected TUFF gig at the last minute apparently rejoining W.A.S.P. American touring to promote 'Unholy Terror', with Roberts installed as guitarist, ensued on August 22nd at the Boynton Beach Orbit, Florida. Support for the two month trek came from MUSHROOMHEAD and DOG FASHION DISCO.

W.A.S.P., with a rerecruited QUIET RIOT's Frankie Banali on drums, geared up for a new studio album for June of 2002 provisionally titled 'Dying For The World'. The album concept was apparently fired by Lawless, re-invigorated with patriotism following the 9-11 terrorist attacks, having received letters from tank commanders in the Gulf War who had gone into battle blaring 'Wild Child' and 'Fuck Like A Beast' over their sound systems. Japanese variants on the JVC Victor label added three exclusive tracks 'Stone Cold Killers, 'Rubberman' and an acoustic take of 'Hallowed Ground'. Lawless announced upfront of any touring that live promotion for 'Dying For The World' would not be extensive as W.A.S.P. were already engaged in formulating a brand new concept album. Nevertheless, live dates in North America throughout October and November would see support from a package billing of ALABAMA THUNDERPUSSY, ENGINE and STEPHEN PEARCY. These projected dates would hit difficulties though as first ALABAMA THUNDERPUSSY and STEPHEN PEARCY withdrew, DIRT was then added and finally in late September the whole tour was cancelled. W.A.S.P. drummer Stet Howland announced the formation of a side venture dubbed THE HOWLIN' DOGS joining forces with vocalist / bassist Bryce Barnes of BLACKFOOT and EDWIN DARE, ENGINE JOE guitarist Joe Monroe and guitarist Steve Lutke of TOBASCO KAT.

Singles/EPs:
Animal (Fuck Like A Beast) / Animal (Fuck Like A Beast) (Live), Capitol CL 331 (1984) (7" release - withdrawn)
Animal (Fuck Like A Beast) / Show No Mercy, Music For Nations MFN 12 KUT 109 (1984)
I Wanna Be Somebody / Tormentor, Capitol 12CL 336 (1984) (12" single) **15 SWEDEN**
Schooldaze / Paint It Black, Capitol CL 344 (1985)
Blind In Texas / Savage, Capitol CL 374 (1985)
Blind In Texas / Savage / I Wanna Be Somebody (Live), Capitol 12CL 374 (1985) (12" single)
Wild Child / Mississippi Queen, Capitol CL 388 (1986) **71 UK**
Wild Child / Mississippi Queen / On Your Knees / Hellion, Capitol CLD 388 (1986) (Double 7" single)
Wild Child / Mississippi Queen / Wild Child (Wild mix), Capitol 12CL 388 (1986) (12' single)
9.5 Nasty / Easy Livin', Capitol CL 432 (1986) (7" release) **70 UK**
9.5 Nasty / Easy Livin' / Flesh And Fire, Capitol 12CL 432 (1986) (12" single)
Scream Until You Like It / Shoot It From The Hip (Live), Capitol CL 458 (1987) **32 UK**
Scream Until You Like It / Shoot It From The Hip (Live) / Sleeping (In The Fire) (Live), Capitol 12CL 458 (1987) (12" single)
I Don't Need No Doctor (Live) / Widow Maker (Live), Capitol CL 469 (1987) **31 UK**
I Don't Need No Doctor (Live) / Widow Maker (Live) / Sex Drive (Live), Capitol 12CL 469 (1987) (12" single)
Live Animal (Fuck Like A Beast), D.B. Blues / Animal (Fuck Like A Beast), Music For Nations (1988) **61 UK**
Mean Mothafuckin' Man / Locomotive Breath, Capitol CL 521 (1989) **21 UK**
Mean Mothafuckin' Man / Locomotive Breath / For Whom The Bell Tolls, Capitol 12CL 521 (1989) (12" single)
The Real Me / The Lake Of Fools, Capitol CL 534 (1989) **23 UK**
The Real Me / The Lake Of Fools / War Cry, Capitol 12CL 534 (1989) (12" single)
Forever Free / L.O.V.E. Machine (Live), Capitol CL 546 (1989)

Forever Free / L.O.V.E. Machine (Live) / Blind In Texas (Live), Capitol 12CL 546 (1989) (12" single)
Chainsaw Charlie (Murders In The New Morgue) / Phantoms In The Mirror, Parlophone RS 6308 (1992) **17 UK**
Chainsaw Charlie (Murders In The New Morgue) / Phantoms In The Mirror / Story Of Jonathon (Prologue To The Crimson Idol), Capitol 12RG 6308 (1992) (12" single)
The Idol / The Story Of Jonathon (Prologue To The Crimson Idol Part II), Parlophone RS 6314 (1992) **41 UK**
The Idol / The Story Of Jonathon (Prologue To The Crimson Idol Part II) / The Eulogy, Parlophone CD RS 6314 (1992) (CD single)
I Am One / Wild Child, Parlophone R 6324 (1992) **56 UK**
I Am One / Wild Child / Charlie Chainsaw / I Wanna Be Somebody, Parlophone 10RG 6324 (1992) (10" single)
I Am One / The Invisible Boy / The Real Me / The Great Misconception of Me, Parlophone CDRS 6324 (1992) (CD single)
Sunset And Babylon / Animal (Fuck Like A Beast), Parlophone CL 698 (1993) **38 UK**
Sunset And Babylon / Animal (Fuck Like A Beast) / Sleeping (In The Fire) / I Wanna Be Somebody, Parlophone CDCL 698 (1993) (CD single)
Sunset And Babylon / Animal (Fuck Like A Beast) / Hellion / Show No Mercy, Parlophone 12CLP 698 (1993) (12" single)
Sunset And Babylon / Animal (Fuck Like A Beast) / School Daze / On Your Knees, Parlophone 12 CL 698 (1993) (12" single)
Black Forever / Goodbye America, Rawpower RAWT 1007 (1995)
Black Forever / Goodbye America / Skin Walker / One Tribe, Rawpower RAWX 1005 (1995) (CD single)
Black Forever / Goodbye America / Long Way To The Top / Whole Lotta Rosie, Rawpower RAWX 1006 (1995) (CD single)
Kill, Fuck, Die, Rawpower RAWX 1041 (1997) (Promotion)

Albums:
W.A.S.P., Capitol EJ 2401951 (1984) **51 UK, 74 USA**
I Wanna Be Somebody / L.O.V.E. Machine / Flame / B.A.D. / School Daze / Hellion / Sleeping (In The Fire) / On Your Knees / Tormentor / Torture Never Stops
THE LAST COMMAND, Capitol WASP2 (1985) **15 SWEDEN, 48 UK, 49 USA**
Wild Child / Ballcrusher / Fistful Of Diamonds / Cries In The Night / Blind In Texas / Widowmaker / Running Wild In The Streets / Sex Drive / Last Command / Jack Action
INSIDE THE ELECTRIC CIRCUS, Capitol

EST 2025 (1986)
35 SWEDEN, 53 UK, 60 USA
Big Welcome / I Don't Need No Doctor / 9.5
Nasty / Restless Gypsy / Shoot From The
Hip / I'm Alive / Easy Livin' / Sweet Cheetah
/ Manimal / King Of Sodom And Gomorrah /
Rock Rolls On
LIVE IN THE RAW, Capitol EST 2040 (1987)
23 UK, 77 USA
Inside The Electric Circus / I Don't Need No
Doctor / L.O.V.E. Machine / Wild Child / 9.5
Nasty / Sleeping (In The Fire) / Manimal / I
Wanna Be Somebody / Harder, Faster /
Blind In Texas / Scream Until You Like It
THE HEADLESS CHILDREN, Capitol
EST2087 (1989) **8 UK, 48 USA**
Heretic (The Lost Child) / The Headless
Children / Thunderhead / Mean Man /
Neutron Bomber / Mephisto Waltz / Forever
Free / Maneater / Rebel In The F.D.G.
THE CRIMSON IDOL, Capitol PCSD 118
(1992) **31 SWEDEN, 21 UK**
Titanic Overture / Invisible Boy / Arena Of
Pleasure / Chainsaw Charlie (Murders In
The New Morgue) / Gypsy Meets The Boy /
Dr. Rockter / I Am One / Hold On To My
Heart / Great Misconception Of Me
FIRST BLOOD... LAST CUTS, Capitol
CDESTG 2217 (1993) 69 UK
Animal (Fuck Like A Beast) / L.O.V.E.
Machine (remix) / I Wanna Be Somebody
(remix) / On Your Knees / Blind In Texas /
Wild Child (remix) / I Don't Need No Doctor
(remix) / Real Me / The Headless Children /
Mean Man / Forever Free / Chainsaw Charlie
/ Idol / Sunset And Babylon / Hold On To My
Heart / Rock And Roll To Death
STILL NOT BLACK ENOUGH, Rawpower
(1995) **52 UK**
Still Not Black Enough / Somebody To Love /
Black Forever / Scared To Death / Goodbye
America / Keep Holding On / Rock And Roll
To Death / Breathe / I Can't / No Way Out Of
Here
KILL, FUCK, DIE, Rawpower RAWCD114
(1997)
Kill, Fuck, Die / Take The Addiction / My
Tortured Eyes / Killahead / Kill Your Pretty
Face / Fetus / Little Death / U / Wicked Love
/ The Horror
DOUBLE LIVE ASSASSINS, Snapper
SMDCD275 (1998)
On Your Knees / I Don't Need No Doctor /
Hellion / Chainsaw Charlie (Murders In The
New Morgue) / Wild Child / Animal (Fuck
Like A Beast) / L.O.V.E. Machine / Killahead
/ I Wanna Be Somebody / U / The Real Me /
Kill Your Pretty Face / The Horror / Blind in
Texas / The Headless Children / The Idol /
Crimson Idol Medley / Little Death / Mean
Man - Rock n' Roll To Death
HELLDORADO, Snapper SMACD818 (1999)

49 SWEDEN
Drive By / Helldorado / Don't Cry (Just Suck)
/ Damnation Angels / Dirty Balls / High On
The Flames / Cocaine Cowboys / Can't Die
Tonight / Saturday Night Cockfight / Hot
Rods To Hell (Helldorado Reprise)
BEST OF THE BEST, Apocalypse
SMACD825 (2000)
Saturday Night's Alright For Fighting / Animal
(Fuck Like A Beast) / I Wanna Be Somebody
/ L.O.V.E. Machine / On Your Knees / Show
No Mercy / Blind In Texas / Sex Drive / 9-5
N.A.S.T.Y. / Mean Man / Chainsaw Charlie
(Murders In The Rue Morgue) / Unreal /
Helldorado / Dirty Balls
THE STING WORLDWIDE, Apocalypse
SMACD836 (2000)
Helldorado / Electric Circus / Chainsaw
Charlie / Wild Child / L.O.V.E. Machine /
Animal / Sleeping In The Fire / Damnation
Angels / Dirty Balls / The Real Me / I Wanna
Be Somebody / Blind In Texas
UNHOLY TERROR, Metal Is (2001)
88 GERMANY
Let It Roar / Hate To Love Me / Loco-Motive
Man / Unholy Terror / Charisma / Who
Slayed Baby Jane? / Euphoria / Raven Heart
/ Evermore / Wasted White Boys
DYING FOR THE WORLD, Metal Is
MISCD022 (2002) 72 GERMANY
Shadow Man / My Wicked Heart / Black
Bone Torso / Hell For Eternity / Hallowed
Ground / Revengeance / Trail Of Tears /
Stone Cold Killers / Rubber Man / Hallowed
Ground (Acoustic)

WATCHTOWER (TX, USA)
Line-Up: Alan Tecchio (vocals), Ron
Jarzombek (guitar), Doug Keyser (bass),
Rick Colaluca (drums)

Metal band renowned for their inventiveness
and complexity. Formed by drummer Rick
Colaluca and bassist Doug Keyser in 1981,
the original incarnation of WATCHTOWER
also included vocalist Jason McMaster and
guitarist BILLY WHITE. WATCHTOWER
debuted with an out of place track on a
hardcore compilation record 'A Texas
Hardcore Compilation: Cottage Cheese From
The Lips Of Death'. The band also recorded a
proposed debut album for Rainforest
Records. The label went bust and the tapes
subsequently became highly sought after on
the tape trading scene.
McMaster's talents were highly regarded and
in 1986 the man turned down an offer from
PANTERA. Whilst McMaster recorded with
WATCHTOWER on their debut album and
stuck with them for five months, one of his
side bands, DANGEROUS TOYS, eventually
got picked up by Columbia. Jason, naturally,

481

quit. Keyser meantime auditioned for METALLICA following the loss of Cliff Burton reportedly getting into the final placing.

McMaster was eventually replaced by ex-MILITIA and ASSAILANT singer Mike Soliz. The man's tenure was short though and after a 1987 demo 'Instruments Of Random Murder' former HADES vocalist Alan Tecchio took the position. Tecchio had actually been tipped off about the vacancy by McMaster, urging his fellow singer to put in a call to Keyser.

Billy White joined DON DOKKEN's solo group and would later form the BILLY WHITE TRIO in the mid '90s. WATCHTOWER recruited Ron Jarzombek, who previously played with SAN ANTONIO SLAYER and Mark Reale's NARITA, to the ranks three years before the recording of the second album took place in 1989. Amusingly, the band was known at one point for playing a live, Metallic rendition of MICHAEL JACKSON's 'Billie Jean'!

WATCHTOWER guested for CORONER on a 1990 European tour after which Tecchio bailed out to join NON FICTION in June. WATCHTOWER were for a short period fronted by Scott of CONFESSOR.

Tecchio would re-join his original act HADES for a re-formation whilst post DANGEROUS TOYS McMaster would appear on albums from BROKEN TEETH and GODZILLA MOTOR COMPANY. Doug Keyser and Rick Colaluca were to be found in the ranks of RETARDED ELF. During mid 2002 the Monster label issued a collection of archive WATCHTOWER demos, rehearsal tapes and live recordings entitled 'Demonstrations In Chaos'. Also included would be 'Meltdown' from the 1984 Texan Plan 9 compilation 'Cottage Cheese From The Lips Of Death'.

Albums:

ENERGETIC DISASSEMBLY, Zombo 44452 (1985)
Violent Charge / Asylum / Tyrants In Distress / Social Fears / Energetic Disassembly / Argonne Forest / Cimmerian Shadows / Meltdown

CONTROL AND RESISTANCE, Noise N 0140-2 (1990)
Instruments Of Random Murder / Eldritch / Mayday In Kiev / Fall Of Reason / Control And Resistance / Hidden Instincts / Life Cycles / Dangerous Toy

DEMONSTRATIONS IN CHAOS, Monster (2002)
Meltdown (Demo) / Asylum (Demo) / Argonne Forest (Demo) / Social Fears (Demo) / Tyrants In Distress (Demo) / Energetic Disassembly (Demo) / Cimmerian Shadows (Demo) / The Eldritch (Demo) / Instruments Of Random Murder (Demo) / Hidden Instincts (Demo) / The Fall Of Reason (Demo) / Control And Resistance (Live) / Cathode Ray Window (Live) / Ballad Assassin (Live) / Meltdown

WAYNE (USA)
Line-Up: David Wayne (vocals), Jimi Bell (guitar), Craig Wells (guitar), Mark Franco (bass), B.J. Zampa (drums)

A twist in the tale of renowned and highly respected Thrash veterans METAL CHURCH. Following the comeback studio album 'Masterpeace' METAL CHURCH, not for the first time in their career, parted ways with singer David Wayne. The man had originally fronted the band from 1983 onwards lending his distinctive bellow to what many regard as METAL CHURCH's finest moments the debut 'Metal Church' and the mammoth second effort 'The Dark'.

Wayne would decamp at the pinnacle make or break juncture of METAL CHURCH's success in what many analysts at the time perceived was a rash move. Years later it would be revealed the singer had bailed out in order to clean up from drug abuse. Wayne resurfaced with REVEREND issuing a further string of commendable, if not commercially successful, albums. METAL CHURCH persevered, turning in solid and even inspiring works with Wayne's replacement Mike Howe but would ultimately bite the dust. The band, complete with Wayne and much of the classic line-up, reunited for the 'Masterpeace' album but fractures began to show yet again. With the METAL CHURCH membership in disarray at the turn of the millennium it emerged that Wayne had set up a fresh act initially titled DAVID WAYNE'S METAL CHURCH! Joining him were METAL CHURCH colleague and guitarist Craig Wells, former JOINT FORCES, GEEZER and THUNDERHEAD guitarist Jimi Bell and drummer B.J. Zampa, a veteran of YNGWIE MALMSTEEN, MVP, TONY MACALPINE and THUNDERHEAD. Bell also operates the covers band TATTERED TRAMPS.

The resulting album, released by the German Nuclear Blast label and naturally called 'Metal Church', not only witnessed the reintroduction of METAL CHURCH's famous guitar-cross device on the cover art but sported a WAYNE icon in the exact logotype as METAL CHURCH. The record would also sport a cover version of MOUNTAIN's 'Mississippi Queen'.

Wayne would not neglect his REVEREND act though, inducting BYFIST guitarists Davey Lee and Notch Vara into the fold during March of 2002.

Albums:
METAL CHURCH, Nuclear Blast (2001)
The Choice / The Hammer Will Fall / Soos Creek Cemetery / Hannibal / Burning At The Stake / D.S.D. / Nightmare Part II / Vlad / Ballad For Marianne / Mississippi Queen

WEAPON (UK)
Line-Up: Danny Hynes (vocals), Jeff Summers (guitar), Barry Downes (bass), Bruce Bisland (drums)

WEAPON evolved from FAST RELIEF featuring guitarist Jeff Summers, bassist Pete Armitage and vocalist Danny Hynes. Ex-LIP SERVICE drummer Bruce Bisland and former INNER CITY UNIT bassist Barry Downes joined in early 1980 as the band adopted the new name of WEAPON and scored a deal with Virgin Publishing.
MOTÖRHEAD's guitarist Fast Eddie Clarke caught the band at a Virgin showcase gig and offered WEAPON the support to MOTÖRHEAD's UK tour of late 1980. The single, an excellent slice of NWoBHM, was released to coincide with these dates and garnered considerable media praise.
WEAPON undertook various headlining shows in early 1981 but soon ground to a halt. Bisland quit to form an act with ex-MORE personnel guitarist Laurie Mansworth and ex-IRON MAIDEN vocalist Paul Mario Day. This liaison was short-lived however and Summers and Bisland formed WILDFIRE.
WEAPON underwent a major line-up shuffle adding ex-IRON MAIDEN and PRAYING MANTIS guitarist Rob Angelo and former LAUTREC drummer John Phillips. This version of the band only lasted a few months before folding. Angelo opted for the pub circuit with an act titled NITRO BLUES.
Hynes had a stab at re-forming WEAPON in 1984 with a line-up comprising Hynes, Bisland (on loan from WILDFIRE), guitarists Ian Simmons and Malcolm McNulty and bassist Billy Kulke. The band recorded a few demos financed by SWEET's Andy Scott before calling it a day.
Bisland's career has moved through ex-MICHAEL SCHENKER GROUP vocalist Gary Barden's STATETROOPER to SWEET and PRAYING MANTIS. Kulke joined LISA DOMINIQUE's band, JAGGED EDGE and FIRST STRIKE.

Singles/EPs:
It's A Mad, Mad World / Set The Stage Alight, Weapon WEP 1 (1980)

WEAPON X (Meriden, CT, USA)
Line-Up: Martin O'Brien (vocals), Vinnie Guarniere (guitar), Max Lopez (bass), Eric Setreus (drums)

Metal act WEAPON X was contrived during September of 1997 by guitarist Vinnie Guarniere, bassist Max Lopez and drummer Eric Setreus. By August of 1998 the band was joined by vocalist Luca Petracca, this version of WEAPON X committing to the three track demo session 'Ready'. In February of 2000 Irishman Martin O'Brien took over the lead vocal mantle.
WEAPON X's debut album, the Buck Brundage produced 'Behind These Walls', was delivered in September of 2001. Tour work to promote the release witnessed support gigs to artists such as SAVATAGE, FATES WARNING, RATT, W.A.S.P. and DOKKEN amongst others.

Albums:
BEHIND THESE WALLS, Buzzhead (2001)
Behind These Walls / Falling Down / Give Me More / Hearts Get Broken / Love Doesn't Come This Way / Mr. Sinister / Superstitious / Run Through The Rain / Down / Sometimes Life / Thunderstorm / Hunter-Killer / That's Just You

JOHN WEST (Cortland, NY, USA)

Incredibly gifted vocalist from the hometown of another Rock legend Ronnie James Dio. West has been a member of BADLANDS, ARTENSION, MICHAEL LEE FIRKINS BAND and latterly Sweden's melodic Rock outfit ROYAL HUNT. The singer was also working on a proposed project with esteemed drummer COZY POWELL prior to his untimely death. These latter recordings surfaced as the Japanese release 'Especially For You'.
1996 West had fronted SAINTS AND SINNERS. Although the band never got off the ground the line-up included four former WHITESNAKE members drummer COZY POWELL, bassist Neil Murray and guitarists BERNIE MARSDEN and MICKY MOODY.
West's debut solo album features guitar from George Bellas, better known for his role in MOGG/WAY.
In down time between projects West toured America with a band including ARTENSION drummer Mike Terrana (now with RAGE) and SAVATAGE guitarist Chris Caffrey.
The 1998 solo album 'Permanent Mark' sees guitar from ex-EDWIN DARE man Jeff Kollman, coincidentally guitarist on the second MOGG/WAY album.
West also put in a showing with LYNCH MOB, stepping in to fulfil live dates when Robert

Mason pulled out. 2001 would find West fronting live shows in America for DAVID 'ROCK' FEINSTEIN. West would also reconvene the classic ARTENSION line-up for a comeback album 'Sacred Pathway'.

In early 2002 it would be announced that West had taken time out from ROYAL HUNT's schedule to assemble the 'Earth Maker' album project, a concept piece based on the journeys of the Native American mythical spirit Shenandoah. This heavyweight alliance saw West teamed up with the HALFORD triumvirate of guitarist MIKE CHLASIAK, bassist Ray Riendau and drummer Bobby Jarzombek, ARTENSION bassist Kevin Chown and the SAVATAGE duo of guitarist Chris Caffrey and Jeff Plate. Session guests in the studio included ROYAL HUNT's own ANDRE ANDERSEN and ARTENSION colleague VITALIJ KUPRIJ.

Albums:
MIND JOURNEYS, (1997)
Eastern Horizon / Lady Ice / Fair Trade / One Way / Mind Journey / The Castle Is Haunted / Veil Of The Blind / Dragon's Eye / Hands In The Fire / Lost In Time
PERMANENT MARK, Shrapnel SH11192 (1998)
Permanent Mark / Restless Heart / High Speed Life / The Burning Times / Pariah / Revolutionary / Destiny / History's The Future / Ship Of Dreams / Iron Horses
EARTHMAKER, Frontiers (2002)
Soul Of The Beast / When Worlds Collide / Sleep Of The Dead / Stand, Sentinel / Life / Warrior Spirit / Mystic Wings / Love Is Pain / Earth Maker / Soul To Soul

WHITE SKULL (ITALY)
Line-Up: Federica De Boni (vocals), Tony Fonto (guitar), Max (guitar), Fabio (bass), Alex (drums)

Deliberately retro female fronted Italian Metal act formed in 1991. WHITE SKULL, centred on founder member guitarist Tony Fonto, arrived with the debut demo tape 'Save The Planet'. These sessions led swiftly to a union with Underground Symphony Records.

Their first commercially available product, the 1995 'I Won't Burn Alone' album, heralded a series of Italian club gigs and set the scene for the 1997 sophomore outing 'Embittered'. Guest backing vocals on this release would be contributed by Folco Orlandini of MESMERIZE. By now WHITE SKULL's distinctive brand of classic Metal and in particular Federica De Boni's vocal capabilities were making waves further afield in Europe and Japan.

'Embittered' promotion dates included a run of gigs opening for New York Thrashers OVERKILL and a valuable appearance at the Milan 'Gods Of Metal' festival as well as Berlin's 'Harley Davidson Jamboree' in Berlin sharing the stage with DORO and U.D.O.

The interim February 1999 'Asgard' mini-album, which included guest vocals courtesy of an impressed Chris Boltendahl of GRAVE DIGGER, would fire the interest of the burgeoning Nuclear Blast label in Germany. 'Tales From The North', which once again featured Chris Boltendahl, witnessed WHITE SKULL's switch of labels. The union with Boltendahl was solidified when WHITE SKULL opened for GRAVE DIGGER's European dates.

The band would switch to Udo Dirkschneider's Breaker Record label (still administered by Nuclear Blast) for the 'Public Glory, Secret Agony' concept album.

In August of 2001 WHITE SKULL replaced female vocalist Federica De Boni with an Argentinean male counterpart named Gus Gabarro. WHITE SKULL had their version of 'Stairway To Heaven' included on the 2002 Locomotive Music LED ZEPPELIN tribute album 'The Metal Zeppelin — The Music Remains The Same'.

Albums:
I WON'T BURN ALONE, Underground Symphony US CD-004 (1996)
Because I / Living On The Highway / Pray / In The Page Of Unreason / Mama / Someone Call It Love / I Won't Burn Alone / Nasty / Hey Boy / White Lady / Save The Planet / The Train
EMBITTERED, Underground Symphony US CD-020 (1997)
Embittered / Revenge Is Sweet / It's My Life / Old Friends / Love Is / Mountain's End / What's Up / Flesh, Blood And Faith / She Won't Wait All The Night / I Don't Know About Sex / B.T.B.W. Italy
ASGARD, Underground Symphony USCD-034 (1999)
Asgard / Haegen The Cruel / Tears By The Firelight / Adramelch
TALES FROM THE NORTH, Underground Symphony USCD-038 (1999)
The Quest (Intro) / Tales From The North / Asgard / Gods Of The Sea / Viking's Tomb / Kriemhild Story / The Killing Queen / The Terrible Slaughter / Horant / Fighting And Feasting / Here We Are / Still Alive (Outro)
PUBLIC GLORY, SECRET AGONY, Nuclear Blast NB 548-2 (2000)
The Quest / Tales From The North / Asgard / Gods Of The Sea / Viking's Tomb / Kriemheld Story / The Killing Queen / The Terrible Slaughter / Horant / Sighting And

Easting / Here We Are / Still Alive
THE DARK AGE, Frontiers (2002)
Penitenziaqite (Intro) / The Dark Age / Grand Inquisitor / Maid Of Orleans / New Crusade / The Edict / Voice From Heaven / Devil's Woman / Torture / A New Handbook / Sentence Of Death / Theme For The Innocence

WILD DOGS (Portland, OR, USA)
Line-Up: Matthew T. McCourt (vocals), Jeff Mark Horton (guitar), Danny Kurth (bass), Deen Castronovo (drums)

WILD DOGS achieved local notoriety in America's North West as a ferocious live act and would regularly appear at the Crossroads Center in Bellevue, Washington (a suburb of Seattle) on bills that would usually also boast local heroes CULPRIT and OVERLORD. Interestingly, one of WILD DOGS' opening bands back in 1982 happened to be MYTH. This group would become QUEENSRYCHE.
WILD DOGS were fronted by vocalist Matthew McCourt, a man whose history spanned acts such as RUDE AWAKENING in 1978 with a pre-MALICE Mick Zane as well as THE VIOLATORS and THE RAVERS, both acts coincidentally featuring another future MALICE man guitarist Jay Reynolds. Just previous to WILD DOGS McCourt was singing for DMZ in 1981, reunited with Mick Zane, guitarist Jeff Horton and ranked alongside Pete Holmes - later of BLACK N' BLUE.
The group's first demo saw the band borrowing drummer Jaime St. James from fellow Portland outfit MOVIE STAR. St. James would become better known as a vocalist, fronting MOVIE STAR which subsequently transformed into BLACK N' BLUE. A permanent drummer would be found in Deen Castronovo just as WILD DOGS were signed by Mike Varney's Shrapnel label. However, McCourt would decamp to found EVIL GENIUS with a line-up of guitarists Kip Doran and Chris Jacobsen, bassist Ken Goldstein and drummer Ben Linton. EVIL GENIUS recorded an album although it would remain consigned to the vaults. McCourt's next move was to record a 1986 album with MAYHEM and later works with DR. MASTERMIND.
Managed by former JOURNEY and NIGHTRANGER lighting director Ken Mednick WILD DOGS, now comprising Michael Furlong, Jeff Marks, Deen Castronovo and new bassist Rick Bartel, recorded the 'Reign Of Terror' album. MICHAEL FURLONG went on to record two highly commendable AOR type solo albums. Castronovo later came to prominence playing with BAD ENGLISH and HARDLINE. During downtime in HARDLINE's schedule Castronovo and McCourt resurrected WILD DOGS but the union was brief. The drummer resumed his ever upward spiralling career with OZZY OSBOURNE and BLACK SABBATH bassist Geezer Butler's GEEZER venture. McCourt entered into various band ventures such as EASTSIDE STRANGLER with EVIL GENIUS guitarist Kip Doran and, for a fleeting spell, Deen Castronovo. By 1992 the singer was fronting up MEATHOOK in league with POISON IDEA's Kevin Sanders. McCourt auditioned for JUDAS PRIEST in 1993 but was unsuccessful.
It was not the end of the story though. Castronovo rekindled WILD DOGS once again in 1998. Although the drummer soon opted out of this latest reformation, to join the AOR mega-band JOURNEY, McCourt would keep the flame alive. During August of 1999 WILD DOGS acted as support to a DOKKEN and GREAT WHITE double billing, guested for DIO in March of 2000 and BLUE OYSTER CULT the following year. An album of demos and outtakes, 'Better Late Than Never', also emerged. Confusingly for a short period the new look WILD DOGS operated as EVIL GENIUS before reverting back to WILD DOGS.
Besides WILD DOGS McCourt plays out the role of Rob Halford in JUDAS PRIEST covers band BRITISH STEEL.

Albums:
WILD DOGS, Shrapnel 1003 (1983)
Life Is Just A Game / The Tonight Show / The Evil In Me / Born To Rock / Never Gonna Stop / Two Wrongs / Take Another Prisoner / I Need A Love / You Can't Escape Your Lies
MAN'S BEST FRIEND, Shrapnel 1012 (1984)
Livin' On The Streets / Not Stoppin' / Woman In Chains / Beauty And A Beast / Believe In Me / Rock's Not Dead / Endless Nights / Ready Or Not / Stick To Your Guns
REIGN OF TERROR, Music For Nations MFN80 (1987)
Metal Fuel (In The Blood) / Man Against Machine / Call Of The Dark / Siberian Vacation / Psychoradio / Streets Of Berlin / Spellshock / Reign Of Terror / We Rule The Night

WINDFALL (GREECE)
Line-Up: Tasos Karapapazoglou (vocals), Leonidas Deligiorgis (guitar), Iraklis Deligiorgis (bass), Kostas Giannikopoulos (keyboards), Vagelis Bouboutinis (drums)

Kavala based WINDFALL began during July

485

1997 as a side venture of the Deligiorgis brothers, guitarist Leonidas and bassist Iraklis. Both at the time were also members of HATRED. The pair united with NEMESIS personnel vocalist Tasos Karapapazoglou, guitarist Kostas Paraskeras and drummer Kostas Tsirpinakis for studio sessions, which resulted in the 'Crystallized' four track EP.

Upon its release in November of 1999 the Deligiorgis siblings quit the ranks of HATRED. WINDFALL would return to the studio for demo recordings, these tapes prompting a deal from the newly established Steel Gallery label. Shortly before the release of debut album 'Adamantia' Tsirpinakis was usurped by Vagelis Bouboutinis.

The band would boost its numbers in May of 2001 enlisting keyboard player Kostas Giannikopoulos.

Albums:
ADAMANTIA, Steel Gallery SGR CD-002 (2001)
Adamantia / Emerald Seas / Frozen Rose / Missing Pages / Sleeping Sounds / Obsession / Walk Of A Dreamer /

WINTERKILL (Calumet City, IL, USA)
Line-Up: Randy Barron (vocals), Jeff West (guitar), Brent Sullivan (bass), Tony Rios (drums)

WINTERKILL's rhythm section of bassist Brent Sullivan and drummer Tony Rios are both ex-SLAUGHTER XSTROYES. Vocalist Randy Barron is ex-TYRANT'S REIGN. The band opened with the 1995 release 'A Feast For A Beggar' following this up with 1998's 'Freedom'.

Rios and Sullivan joined SPIRIT WEB with former SYRIS members in 2000 to record an eponymous album.

WINTERKILL supported SAXON and U.D.O. in America during October 2000.

Chuck White, previously with MICHAEL ANGELO, would handle drums for new tracks on the 'Taming The Wolves' album, the band's debut European release through the MTM Metal label. The record featured new material alongside older cuts from the two predecessor albums.

Albums:
A FEAST FOR A BEGGAR, (1997)
Erotic Abode / Virus / A Feast For A Beggar / Resurrected / Eternity / Far And Beyond / Hellraiser / Solitary Man / Funeral March / When We Die
FREEDOM, Wildfire (1988)
Freedom / Tokyo's Burning / Carnevil / Thee Awakening / Green Eyed Lady / Heir To The

Throne / The Storm / Danielle / You Anger Me / Equilibrium / Time (Is Of The Essence) / Leavin' (Live)
TAMING THE WOLVES, MTM Metal 1704-6 (2000)
High On Life / New Attitude / Break You / Walk Away / Virus / Feast For A Beggar / Resurrected / Eternity / Hellraiser / Carnevil / Tokyo's Burning / The Awakening

WINTERLONG (SWEDEN)
Line-Up: Hussni Morsare (vocals / guitar), Thorbjorn Englund (guitar), Erik Tornberg (bass), Toni Erkkila (drums)

Swedish Metal band WINTERLONG had their debut album 'Valley Of The Lost' produced by renowned guitarist LARS ERIC MATTSON. During March of 2002 guitar player Thorbjörn Englund was reportedly replaced by Payre Kankanranta, a former colleague of vocalist Hussni Morsare's previous act JAVELIN and also citing membership of Belgian Progressive Metal band DRAGONFIRE. However, it would then be revealed that Englund was in fact assembling a new look WINTERLONG, minus singer Hussni Morsare, for a 2002 album. Session drums for this effort would be provided by Anders Johansson of YNGWIE MALMSTEEN and HAMMERFALL repute as well as Andreas Lill of VANDEN PLAS.

A further project, billed as STAR QUEEN, had both Thorbjorn Englund and Erik Tornberg working alongside LARS ERIC MATTSON, vocalist Stella Tormanoff, Bob Katsionis keyboard player and drummer Tony Eriksson for a 2002 album through the Finnish Lion Music label.

Albums:
VALLEY OF THE LOST, Lion Music LMC 2104-2 (2001)
From Heaven To Hell / Sky Travellers / Winterlong / Valley Of The Lost / The Water Spirit / Nosferatu / Mystery Of Life / Victory / Written In Blood / Driven By Insanity

WINTER'S BANE (Akron, OH, USA)
Line-Up: Lou St. Paul (vocals / guitar), Dave Hayes (guitar), Dennis Hayes (bass), Todd Bertolotte (drums)

This band are known for being JUDAS PRIEST vocalist Tim 'Ripper' Owens first commercial port of call. Owens features on WINTER'S BANE's debut 1993 album 'Heart Of A Killer', a concept outing exploring the gruesome exploits of Judge Cohagen. The WINTER'S BANE line-up at this juncture comprised Owens, guitarist Lou St. Paul, second guitarist David Hayes, bassist Dennis Hayes and drummer Terry Salem.

St. Paul doubled up on lead vocals for the 'Season Of Brutality' follow up after the departure of Owens, the singer opting out to concentrate his efforts on the club scene and his JUDAS PRIEST cover band BRITISH STEEL. 'Season Of Brutality' saw the introduction of new drummer Todd Bertolette. 'Girth', released in 1997, is generally regarded to be WINTER'S BANE's heaviest effort to date.

WINTER'S BANE cut 'Steeler' for the 1999 JUDAS PRIEST tribute album 'Hell Bent For Metal'.

The 2000 re-release of 'Heart Of A Killer' through the Century Media label includes a bonus CD of rare demo material. In 2001 St. Paul would found a side act dubbed SILHOUETTE in alliance with AVALON vocalist Chity Somapala. This union had dissolved by the following year.

Albums:
HEART OF THE KILLER, Massacre MASS CD013 (1993)
Wages Of Sin / Blink Of An Eye / Heart Of A Killer / Horror Glances / The Silhouette / Reflections Within / Haunted House / Night Shade / Winters Bane / Cleansing Mother
SEASON OF BRUTALITY, (199-)
GIRTH, DCA (1998)
C-4 / Kill Procedure / Away / Color / X-Iled / Alexandria / Porcelain God / Hunting Time / Download / Spells Death / Dark Paradise
HEART OF A KILLER, Century Media (2000)
Wages Of Sin / Blink Of An Eye / Heart Of A Killer / Horror Glances / Silhouette / Reflection Within / Haunted House / Nightshade / Winters Bane / Cleansing Mother / Wages Of Sin (Live) / Blink Of An Eye (Live) / Heart Of A Killer (Live) / Horror Glances (Live) / Silhouette (Live) / Reflections Within (Live) / Haunted House (Live) / Fear Of Death (Live) / Cleansing Mother (Live) / My Dagger's Revenge (Demo version) / Eyes Of The Deceiver (Demo version) / Seven Nations (Instrumental demo version)

WISARD (FINLAND)
Line-Up: Luis Herrero (vocals), Antti Wirman (guitar), Jaakko Teittinen (guitar), Fabio Oksanen (bass), Vili Ollila (keyboards), Mikko Sepponen (drums)

Heavy Metal project conjured up by PRIMUS MOTOR guitarist Antti Wirman and keyboardist Mikael Blomberg in 1997. Guitarist Pekka Palmu would enrol that same year and in 1998 bass player Janne

'Tukkapöyhy' Katalkin was added. A series of drummers was tried out before Mikko 'Basarit' Sepponen stabilised the position and lead vocalist Luis Herrero rounded WISARD off.

WISARD's first achievement was the recording of a 1999 three track demo but after these sessions Blomberg opted out. The group cut the album 'Open Skies' then saw Katalkin also leave. At the group's appearance at the 2002 'Nummirock' festival Markus Lindén filled in but soon after the bass role went to Fabio 'Jorma' Oksanen.

By June of 2001, with the addition of Vili Ollila on keyboards, the band had switched titles to CRAYDAWN, recording a three song demo. Palmu was subsequently substituted by Jaakko Teittinen.

Albums:
OPEN SKIES, (2001)
Open Skies / My Way / Breaking Through / Never Forgotten / Through The Mist / Ravaging The Souls / Warriors Of Lightning / Drowning

WISDOM CALL (SWEDEN)
Line-Up: Christian Liljegren (vocals), Stefan Olsson (guitars), Fredrik Aberg (guitars), Andreas Olsson (bass), Per Hallmann (keyboards), Andreas Johansson (drums)

WISDOM CALL is A Scandinavian fusion of NARNIA members vocalist Christian Liljegren and drummer Andreas Johansson with the STORMWIND duo of guitarist Andreas Olsson and keyboard player Per Hallman. Song-writing contributions for the 2001 eponymous debut record would be donated by LION'S SHARE guitarist Lars Chriss. The band also covers EUROPE's 'Wings Of Tomorrow'.

Albums:
WISDOM CALL, Massacre (2001)
Power From The Sky / The Last Generation / I Believe / Never Satisfied / Wings Of Tomorrow / Through Fire / One Way Out / Hold On To The Truth / 15 Years / Time

WITCHERY (SWEDEN)
Line-Up: Toxine (vocals), Patrick Jensen (guitar), Ricard Corpse (guitar), Sharlee D'Angelo (bass), Mique (drums)

Trad Metal merchants WITCHERY were created in 1997 from the ashes of SÉANCE and SATANIC SLAUGHTER. Both vocalist Toxine and drummer Mique had also been members of TOTAL DEATH whilst Mique had also been involved in MORGUE together with guitarist Ricard Corpse. Toxine would cut his teeth on the Rock scene with his debut Punk act PASSIVA MONGOLOIDER as far back as 1979.

The band has set itself apart from the crowd by blending elements of Black, Death and retro 'Thrashback' styled Metal, this amalgamation seeing WITCHERY rapidly attaining solid international sales. Musically WITCHERY are unafraid to show their influences as made evident by the frequent '80s Metal cover versions that litter their catalogue.

WITCHERY came together when SATANIC SLAUGHTER vocalist Ztephan Dark fired his entire band just days before a scheduled album recording. Undaunted the quartet stuck together to found WITCHERY enlisting MERCYFUL FATE and ILLWILL bassist Sharlee D'Angelo. The latter's priority commitments to MERCYFUL FATE meant that recording of the debut WITCHERY album was delayed until the Autumn of 1997.

The band put in their debut show in April 1998 in Copenhagen although minus Ricard who was too ill to perform.

The 1999 mini-album 'Restless And Dead' comprises originals plus various covers including ACCEPT's 'Restless And Wild', BLACK SABBATH's 'Neon Knights', W.A.S.P.'s 'I Wanna Be Somebody' and JUDAS PRIEST's 'Riding On The Wind'.

WITCHERY put in a showing at the renowned German Wacken Metal festival in 1999.

Guitarist Patrick Jensen, also operates with THE HAUNTED. Toxine and Corpse also busy themselves with INFERNAL. Mique has a side project entitled RHOCA GIL.

Latterly WITCHERY have cut versions of KING DIAMOND's 'The Shrine' and the SCORPIONS 'China White' for tribute albums.

Albums:
RESTLESS AND DEAD, Necropolis NR029 (1998)
The Reaper / Witchery / Midnight At The Graveyard / The Hangman / Awaiting The Exorcist / All Evil / House Of Raining Blood / Into Purgatory / Born In The Night / Restless And Dead
WITCHBURNER, Necropolis NR034 (1999)
Fast As A Shark / I Wanna Be Somebody / Riding On The Wind / Neon Knights / The Howling / The Executioner / Witchburner
DEAD, HOT AND READY, Necropolis (2000)
Demonication / A Paler Shade Of Death / The Guillotine / Resurrection / Full Moon / The Dead And The Dance Done / Dead, Hot And Ready / The Devil's Triangle / Call Of The Coven / On A Black Horse Thru Hell...
SYMPHONY FOR THE DEVIL, Necropolis (2001)
The Storm / Unholy Wars / Inquisition /

Omens / Bone Mill / None Buried Deeper / Wicked / Called For By Death / Hearse Of The Pharaohs / Shallow Grave / Enshrined / The One

WITCHHAMMER (NORWAY)
Line-Up: Per Stale Petersson (vocals), Tor E. Hakonsen (guitar), Finn C. Gjaerlangsen (bass), Jan E. Eide (drums)

Thrashers WITCHHAMMER, despite leaving a solitary legacy of one self-financed album, made quite an impression on the Scandinavian Metal scene. The band came into being during August of 1986 being boosted to a quintet with the enrolment of bassist Finn C. Gjaerlangsen just prior to their inaugural gig. Bass had originally been the domain of lead vocalist Per Ståle Pettersen, WITCHHAMMER being rounded out by guitarists Tor Erik Håkonsen and Peder Kjøs alongside drummer Jan Erik Eide. The band's singer had already carved out a considerable reputation for himself albeit not in the Metal world but as lead actor in productions such as 'Les Miserables' and 'Jesus Christ Superstar'. Projected demo recordings would in actual fact provide the catalyst for recording of a full length album, a project that was finalised in September of 1988. As WITCHHAMMER touted the tapes to labels in search of a deal, a tour with ARTCH was finalised. However, Kjøs decamped with little warning. WITCHHAMMER swiftly inducted Frank Wilhelmsen as replacement. With the culmination of the ARTCH dates WITCHHAMMER headlined an annual Thrash Metal festival in Bergen. Wilhelmsen would then depart in order to join METAL THUNDER and in a paradoxical turn of events METAL THUNDER six stringer Morten Skute duly teamed up with WITCHHAMMER. The '1497' album finally arrived in March of 1990 to positive reviews internationally. A headline Norwegian tour as well as Swedish gigs bolstered the band's reputation and once again WITCHHAMMER topped the bill at the Bergen Thrash festival. Valuable exposure would also be garnered when an Oslo show was broadcast on national television.

A follow up album was recorded later the same year but in September Skute made his exit. The album tapes would remain consigned to the vaults for a decade as WITCHHAMMER remained inactive, eventually resurfacing in 2000 billed as 'The Lost Tapes'. Recently WITCHHAMMER have re-formed for live work.

Albums:
1487, Semaphore W001 (1991)

Intro / Transylvania / Kill All In Sight / Burning Court / The Whore Of Babylon / Enola Gay / Hallow's Eve / My Execution / By This Axe I Rule / Curiosity About Death
THE LOST TAPES, Dazed (2000)
Human Rights / Confrontation / No Name / Deliver Us From Evil / Beware the Child / The Ultimate Constellation / Be All End All / On My Own / Touch Of An Angel

WITCHKILLER (CANADA)
Line-Up: Doug Adams (vocals), Kurt Phillips (guitar), Todd Pilon (bass), Steve Batky (drums)

The WITCHKILLER album saw a split CD release in Germany sharing space with OBSESSION. Both vocalist Doug Adams and bassist Todd Pilon joined RECKLESS for their 'Heart Of Steel' album.
Former WITCHKILLER drummer Steve Napoleon founded I NAPOLEON as a singer. Guitarist Kurt Phillips would later found Christian Power Metal band WARHAG in union with his bass playing wife Joy Toyota-Phillips. WARHAG's 2002 release 'Sinister Grip' included a reworking of WITCHKILLER's 'Day Of The Saxons'.

Albums:
DAY OF THE SAXONS, Metal Blade 71029 (1984)
Day Of The Saxons / Riders Of Doom / Cry Wolf / Beg For Mercy / Penance For Past Sins

WITHOUT WARNING (USA)
Line-Up: Jack Bielata (vocals), Ted Burger (guitar), Vinnie Fontanetta (keyboards), Graham Thomson (bass), Steve Michael (drums)

WITHOUT WARNING first appeared in 1993 with the Eddie Kramer produced 'Making Time' album that enjoyed considerable success in Japan.
Guitarist Ted Burger, from Rochester, New York, had previously worked as a sound engineer for the CHESTERFIELD KINGS and had first played in a band during his High School years alongside older brother Tim on drums and friend Graham Thomson as bassist.
Burger later played in the group LITTLE SISTER with keyboard player Vinnie Fontanetta and drummer Steve Michael that evolved into WITHOUT WARNING. The Alex Perialas produced second album, 'Believe', surfaced in May 1995.
1998's 'Step Beyond' was expected to be supported by a European tour in September

1998 opening for label mates SYMPHONY X.

Albums:
MAKING TIME, (1993)
BELIEVE, (1995)
Deepest Dreams / What / In My Name / Far From Eden / Who Can You Blame / Believe In Me / Envisioned / Eye On The World / Evil Needs / Believe
STEP BEYOND, Inside Out Music SPV 085-28702 CD (1998)
Step Beyond / More / Prophet / Gracefully / Who Am I / Turning Pages / To The End / The Embrace / Remember Me

WIZARD (GERMANY)
Line-Up: Sven D'Anna (vocals), Michael Maass (guitar), Volker Leson (bass), Snoppi Denn (drums)

WIZARD are a no pretensions Power Metal act formed in 1989 by drummer Snoppi Denn (a.k.a. Sören van Heek). After several line-up shuffles the act pulled in guitarist Michael Maass, bassist Volker Leson and vocalist Sven D'Anna during 1991, that same year issuing the 'Legion Of Doom' demo tape. The self-financed 1995 album 'Son Of Darkness' heralded the band's arrival. A further effort, 'Battle Of Metal' released on WIZARD's own Bow Records in 1997, would prompt tour supports to acts such as EDGUY, DIANNO and SACRED STEEL.
The quartet returned to the studio in December 1998 to craft a third studio release 'Bound By Metal'. However, the band was rocked when Maass was forced to opt out due to health problems. WIZARD did not enlist a replacement but weathered the storm until Maass' recovery saw the six stringer back in the fold.
WIZARD signed to Limb Music Productions for the 2001 album 'Head Of The Deceiver'. The record saw a production credit going to erstwhile GRAVE DIGGER guitarist Uwe Lullis.

Albums:
SON OF DARKNESS, (1995)
Sign Of The Wizard / Death Or Glory / Rain Of Death / Dawn Of Evil / Lovesong / Enemy Die / Son Of Darkness / Master Of The Sea Of Gods / Lonely Wolfe / Fuck Your Ass
BATTLE OF METAL, (1997)
In The Beginning / Thunder Warriors / The Call Of Evil / Named By The Devil / The War Of Demons / Lost Souls / Zorian Karcoon / Pain / The Kidnapping / The Liberation / An Angry God / You Prayed To God For Mercy / Bad Times / Thoughts / The Weapons Of The Gods / Heavy Metal Will Never Die / The

489

Second Oath / Our Hate Will Burn You / Army Of The Gods / Dragon Lords / Battle Of Metal
BOUND BY METAL, (1999)
Hammer Bow Axe And Sword / Brave Warriors / Dark Wings / Mighty Wizard / A Nice Day To Die / Gladiators Of Steel / Unicorn / Believe In Metal / Spill The Blood Of Our Enemies / Battlefield Of Death / Bound By Metal
HEAD OF THE DECEIVER, Limb Music Productions 106-030CD (2001)
Evitum Okol / Magic Potion / Head Of The Deceiver / Collective Mind / Defenders Of Metal / Calm Of The Storm / Demon Witches / Iron War / The First One / Revenge / True Metal

WIZARDS (BRAZIL)
Line-Up: Christian Passos (vocals), Cadu

'Kadu' Averbach (guitar), Filipe Guerra (bass), Charles Dalla (keyboards), Rodrigo Mello (drums)

Following recording of the fourth WIZARDS album 'The Kingdom' the band parted ways with longstanding rhythm section bass player Mendel Ben Waisberg and drummer Bezi Waisberg. New drummer Rodrigo Mello was previously a member of DRAGSTER and SYMBOLS whilst the four string replacement Filipe Guerra cites terms of duty with SKYSCRAPER and TWILIGHT.

Albums:
WIZARDS, (1995)
Magic Moon / Guardian Of Their Own Souls / New Life / Distant Voice / No More / Rock n' Roll Forever / Arabian Caravan / Some Friends / Freedom / Wizards

490

SOUND OF LIFE, (1996)
Madness / Psycho Maze / Dangerous Way /
A Promise Of Love / Pico / I'll Believe /
Reach Out / Black City / Sound Of Life /
Wizards II
BEYOND THE SIGHT, (1998)
W / Thunderbolt / Crack / Shine (Tribute To
Helloween) / The Play / Shadows And Light /
I Don't Give A Damn / Flight / Killing Blues /
Nest Of Words / Memories Of Avalon
THE KINGDOM, Teichiku TKCS-85039
(2002)
The Kingdom / King Without A Crown /
Fallen Angels / Riding The Twilight /
Daydreaming / Willing To Be Free / The Call
Of War / Sinners And Saints / Love And
Recall / Step Back / Bring Down The House

WOLFCRY (GREECE)
Line-Up: Costas Hatzigeorgiou (vocals),
Simos Kaggelaris (guitar), Spiros Triantafillou
(bass), Andreas Kourtidis (drums)

Founded as VANGUARD during 1992 the
group switched to WOLFCRY, recording a
track 'Angelsign' for a projected, but
cancelled, compilation album. The line-up of
the band at this juncture stood at drummer
Andreas Kourtidis, guitarist Vasilis, bassist
Antonis and DARK NOVA singer John acting
as a session member.
The band was inactive for a couple of years
but re-formed during August of 1996 for a
demo 'The Ivory Tower'. Founder member
Kourtidis assembled an all new unit, which
saw OBSECRATION members John and
Spiros Ruthven handling guitar and bass
duties respectively along with another
session vocalist, John Georgopoulos of
AIRGED LAMH. The band would gain
exposure, being featured on the 'War Zone 3'
compilation issued by the noted Greek Metal
magazine 'Metal Invader'.
WOLFCRY would morph again as erstwhile
SENTINEL man Costas Hatzigeorgiou took
the lead vocal mantle and MOONGLEAM
member Dreamwolf took over guitar, bass
and keyboards. A subsequent 1999 demo
session, with DARK NOVA's Elias Koskoris
aiding on lead guitar, led to the recording of
the album 'Power Within', originally slated for
release through the German Iron Glory label.
Ultimately 'Power Within', laid down utilising a
returning Ruthven on bass and new face
Eleni on keyboards, would emerge via the
Black Lotus concern in December of 2001.

Albums:
POWER WITHIN, Black Lotus (2001)
Power Within / The Journey / Lonewolf's
Destiny / The Fate Of A Lonely Bard /

Reflections / Part Of A Play / Nightriders /
Dawn Of Glory - Neverending War / Sons Of
Gods

WOLFEN (GERMANY)
Line-Up: Andreas von Lipinski (vocals),
Frank J. Noras (guitar), Björn Grüne (guitar),
Gernot Thiel (bass), Holger Bloempott
(drums)

Köln Power Metal act WOLFEN blazed a trail
with a string of demos to mark their arrival
including 1995's 'Mission Of Freedom', 1996's
'No Sleep 'Til Dawn', 1997's 'Blindfold In
Stone' and an untitled 1998 effort. The 1996
and 1997 sessions would be combined for
commercial release as the 'No Sleep 'Til
Blindfold' album.
WOLFEN's first proper commercial release
came in 1999 with the 'Apocalyptic Waltz'
album. The November 2000 Jörg Rainer
Friede produced 'Don't Trust The White'
record was released by TTS Media Music.

Albums:
NO SLEEP 'TIL BLINDFOLD, (1997)
No Sleep 'Til Dawn / Judgement Day /
Verschenkte Tage / King Of Kings / Falsche
Freunde / Hell Freezes Over / Wolfen /
Schwarz / Wolf 359 / Blindfold In Stone
APOCALYPTIC WALTZ, (1999)
Terror / The Great Day Of His Wrath / Devil's
Paradise / Alphraan / The Unexpected /
Sound Crucifiction / S.F.T. / McDeath /
Caught In The Trap
DON'T TRUST THE WHITE, TTS Media
Music (2000)
Beyond The Surface / Burn In Hell / Wolfen /
Terror / The Unexpected / Sound Crucifiction
/ Under The Blue Sky / The Great Day Of
His Wrath / 2006 / Caught In The Trap / The
Last Judgement

WONDERLAND (ITALY)
Line-Up: Alex Hall (vocals), Vic Mazzoni
(guitar), Giaime (guitar), Andrea Torricini
(bass), Frank Andiver (drums)

A Power Metal project outfit of VISION
DIVINE bassist Andrea 'Tower' Torricini. The
four stringer, who also listed credits with
TRINITY OF STEEL, METAL KINGS and as
session performer for Speed Metal band
SHADOWS OF STEEL, assembled the elite
of Italian Metal to aid him in the
WONDERLAND venture.
Vocals were on hand from former ATOMIC
HEART and PLEASURE DREAMS man Alex
Hall. Guitars came courtesy of PROJECTO's
Vic Mazzoni, also a veteran of SHADOWS
OF STEEL and SKYLARK, alongside

erstwhile METAL KINGS and TRINITY OF STEEL man Giaime. Drums would be delegated to Frank Andiver of ANGER, LABYRINTH and SHADOWS OF STEEL.

WONDERLAND committed two cover versions to Underground Symphony tribute albums during 2001, namely WARLORD's 'Lost And Lonely Days' to the 'Glory To The King' album and the SAVATAGE tune 'Tonight He Grins Again' for the 'Return Of The Mountain King' collection.

The eponymous debut album surfaced in September 2001.

Singles/EPs:
Somewhere In My Eyes (Radio version) / Nothing's Left To Say / Lost And Lonely Days / Goodbye, Underground Symphony US CD039 (1999) ('Somewhere In My Eyes' EP)

Albums:
WONDERLAND, Underground Symphony (2001)
The Fallen Angel / Moonchild / Freedom / Look Into The Sky (Somewhere In My Eyes) / Summer Waiting / Nothing Left To Say / Wonderland / Tower Of Wonders / Here I Am / Hello

WORLD OF SILENCE (SWEDEN)
Line-Up: Mathias Sandqvist (vocals), Mikael Dahlqvist (guitar), Fredric Danielsson (bass), Thomas Heder (keyboards), Bruno Andersen (drums)

WORLD OF SILENCE, operating in Progressive Metal territory, include no less than three erstwhile members of Black Metal act GODGORY- namely guitarist Mikael Dahlqvist, bassist Fredric Danielsson and keyboard player Thomas Heder. Despite not being active GODGORY members since that band's second album the trio has continued to session on recent GODGORY albums.

Albums:
WINDOW OF HEAVEN, Black Mark BMCD 100 (1996)
Point Of No Return / Window Of Heaven / Mirror Of Contempt / Dreamweaver / Another World / Enigma / Box Of A Thousand Choices / Eyes
MINDSCAPES, Black Mark BMCD 127 (1998)
Four Seasons / Times To Come / Alone / In Search / Still All Is Silent / Daze /

WRAITH (UK)
Line-Up: Jedd Clarc (vocals), Gregg Russell (guitar), Andy Gamble (guitar), Steve Clark (bass), Andy Reynolds (drums)

Formed in 1988 by Gregg Russell following the demise of Nottingham Glam act DEUCE the original line-up, formulated by former punk ex-ABDUCTERS rhythm guitarist Scott "Scarey" Carey, featured ex-DEUCE personnel drummer Emmy (Simon Hemstock) and bassist Rimmo (Steven Rimmington) alongside ex-LOVECHILD vocalist Jedd Clarc. WRAITH's career would see them go from Hard Rock to Heavy Metal through to Alternative Rock before dissolving. WRAITH released a self-financed single 'Lonely' / 'Rock They Stand For' on PBM Records distributed by FM Revolver bolstered by an impressive advertising campaign. The single received solid reviews prompting a six track mini-album 'Naked Aggression', again a self financed effort, produced by LIMELIGHT guitarist Glenn Scrimshaw. The track 'Under The Hammer' was co-written with UFO bassist PETE WAY. This recording firmly placed WRAITH in the British Metal camp and with a manufacturing run of just 500 and graced in a 'banned' cover 'Naked Aggression' is now a sought after collectors item. Founding member Scott Carey was replaced in the studio by former ESPRIT and DEUCE guitarist Ken Tilley but within weeks Tilley was out of the picture and bringing a court action against Russell for grievous bodily harm! This episode was followed by an extensive series of club gigs.

Rimmo and Hemstock were given their marching orders. Rimmo joined the FIREBYRDS in 1993 with ex-TATTOOED LOVE BOYS and PRAYING MANTIS drummer Mick Ransome and former RED DOGS guitarist Paul Guerin. Hemstock joined SLEEZEPATROL then another Nottingham band SIX GUN (re-titling themselves CRITICAL MASS in 1996). Although CRITICAL MASS recorded an album this was never released.

Amidst almost complete media apathy the band again stuck their hands in their pockets to finance a full length album following on from a tape for sale only at gigs entitled 'Desire'. During this period new members Andy Gamble, Andy Reynolds and Steve Clark joined the fold.

The band impressed producer Guy Bidmead enough to handle studio duties and cut the album in three weeks. However, the resultant tapes were not what the band expected from a known producer and the project was put on ice while the band gigged and searched for a label.

New label Warhammer Records picked them up and the album tapes were remixed by UFO bassist PETE WAY and guitarist Laurence Archer and released as 'Danger Calling'.

WRAITH toured constantly upon its outing including supporting UFO and LEGS DIAMOND on UK tours and shooting a video for the track 'Hungry'. The album would go on to sell over 5,000 copies in the UK alone.

With the first album selling well abroad the second album was recorded with engineer Mark Bruce at the famed Rich Bitch Studios in Birmingham. The album 'Riot' was a superb slab of British Heavy Metal showing great song writing potential and is highly recommended. The media however, had different ideas and slated WRAITH for ignoring the Grunge bandwagon and labelling them 'Trad Rock', in those fickle times almost a term of abuse.

The album still sold well, outselling its predecessor in the UK but after a series of successful French festivals the band called it a day in 1993. They regrouped in a far Poppier guise under the name FREE SPIRIT dispensing with bassist Clark. In this (short haired) incarnation the band released a self-financed 12" EP.

In 1995 Russell had resurrected WRAITH together with Reynolds and Gamble, the latter now on bass guitar. Clarc, opting for a career in Techno under the fresh pseudonym of 'Rix', was replaced by former PANIC IN DETROIT vocalist Mike Barker.

Gamble departed as recording for the fourth album 'Schizophrenia' began, his position being quickly filled by the notable figure of American ex-PHANTOM BLUE bassist Kim Neilsen. 'Schizophrenia' took onboard re-worked songs from the FREE SPIRIT sessions and displayed a much more modern Rock edge. The Japanese version of the album was to have featured a cover of JUDAS PRIEST's 'Starbreaker' but this recording remained consigned to the vaults.

Former MARS, GODSEND and SLEEZEPATROL man Mole deputised on drums during 1996. WRAITH, now complete with erstwhile members of PANIC IN DETROIT, were still a going concern during 1999 although Russell was known to be earning on the side as a tattoo artist and more exotically as a stripper under the stage name Ice!!

Singles/EPs:
Lonely / Rock They Stand For, PMP Records SSCT1 (1988)
Cursed / Get What I Want From You, Warhammer (1993) (12" promotion release)

Albums:
NAKED AGGRESSION, Aztec Communications AZT 001(1989)
Fall Into The Fire / Under The Hammer /

WRAITH
Photo : Ross Halfin

Born To Rock / Wraith / I Want More / Killer Instinct
DANGER CALLING, Warhammer WAR 0880 (1992)
Hungry / Crazy / One Foot In The Grave / Breakin' All The Rules / I Can't Control Myself / Close To The Edge / Danger Calling / You've Got The Right / Crawlin' / Second Best / Like A Hurricane
RIOT, Warhammer WAR 0853 (1993)
Russian Roulette / Human Zoo / Get What I Want / Shattered / Cursed / Riot / Pride Of Youth / You've Got It Coming / Downonme / Shove It
SCHIZOPHRENIA, Neat Metal NM013 (1996)
Get Out Of My Head / Gates Of Babylon / Take Me For A Lover / Inside Me / The Next Big Thing? / Seven / Tongue, Tied And Twisted / Schizophrenia / Resurrection / New Religion / Rain

WRAITH (USA)
Line-Up: James Alexander Wraith (vocals), Dean Allen (guitar), Tony Carducci (guitar), Phil Wix (bass), Richard Dahl Jr. (drums)

South Florida Progressive Power Metal outfit led by vocalist Joseph 'Brat Prince' Alexander 'Wraith', a.k.a. Joseph Hahn, an ex-member of Los Angeles act VICIOUS CIRCLE. WRAITH, who would portray an overtly Gothic image, signed to the Progressive Arts Music label for a projected album 'Dark Gifts' but it is unclear as to whether the album ever surfaced. WRAITH featured on a slew of tribute albums contributing a rendition of 'Atomic Punk' to the VAN HALEN salute 'Runnin' With The Devil', '24 Hours Ago' to a SAVATAGE collection and 'Let It Go' to a DEF LEPPARD tribute.
At one stage the group included former IMPULSE drummer Emil Stefanov and bassist 'Gorilla' but the recording line-up included a revised rhythm section of bassist Phil Wix and drummer Richard Dahl Jr. The latter was announced as leaving the group midway through the sessions.
Guitarist Tony Carducci also has credits with STEVIE NICKS.

WUTHERING HEIGHTS (DENMARK)
Line-Up: Kristian Andrén (vocals), Erik Ravn (guitar / bass), Henrik Flyman (guitar), Rune S. Brink (keyboards), Morten Sørensen (drums)

Copenhagen's Symphonic Metal band WUTHERING HEIGHTS are rooted in the early '90s act MINAS TIRITH, a unit comprising vocalist / guitarist Erik Ravn, guitarist Martin Røpcke, bass player Morten Birch and drummer Kenneth Saandvig. This band issued an eponymous 1992 demo cassette after which Ravn and Saandvig founded VERGELMIR. Under this guise the band, rounded out by lead vocalist Troels Liebgott, guitarist Jannik B. Larsen, bass guitarist Tim Mogensen and keyboard player Tim Christensen, issued a 1995 promotion tape. Ravn and Saandvig would then found WUTHERING HEIGHTS, reworking many of the VERGELMIR songs.
WUTHERING HEIGHTS 1997 album 'Within' saw a line-up comprising Swedish vocalist Kristian 'Krille', Andrén, guitarist Erik Ravn, bassist Kaspar Gram, keyboard player Rune S. Brink and drummer Kenneth Saandvig. Andrén had already made a sizeable impression on the Rock scene having fronted acts such as STREET TALK, FIFTH REASON, MEMENTO MORI and TAD MOROSE. Embellishing touches would be added by flautist Troels Liebgott and violinist Henriette Cordes. The same cast, only substituting Saandvig for Morten Nødgaard, would completely re-record the album with producer Jacob Hansen at the helm for a commercial reissue during October 1999.
For the 2002 record, the Tommy Hansen produced 'To Travel For Evermore', AURORA's Morten Sørensen took over on bass whilst Ravn took on bass duties. Guest bass sessions would come courtesy of Lorenzo Dehó from Italian acts KHALI and TIME MACHINE. Japanese versions of the 2002 album 'To Travel For Evermore', released by the Toshiba EMI label, added the exclusive bonus track 'When The Jester Cries'. Following recording the band added Henrik Flyman of ZOOL and MOAHNI MOAHNA on second guitar.

Albums:
WITHIN, Sensory SR3006 (1999)
Enter The Cave / Hunter In The Dark / Too Great Thy Gift / Sorrow In Memoriam / Dreamwalker / The Bird / The Wanderer´s Farewell
TO TRAVEL FOR EVERMORE, Sensory SR3013 (2002)
Behind Tearstained Ice / The Nevershining Stones / Dancer In The Light / Lost Realms / Battle Of The Seasons / A Sinner's Confession / See Tomorrow Shine / Through Within To Beyond / River Oblivion

WWIII (USA)
Line-Up: Mandy Lion (vocals), Tracy G. (guitar), Jimmy Bain (bass), Vinnie Appice (drums)

WWIII are heralded by some, most notably DEF LEPPARD's Joe Elliott, as having made "the heaviest album of all time!" The sole album is undoubtedly the heaviest venture any of the esteemed band members have ever been involved in but is marred by outrageously pre-pubescent lyrics. Although primarily an American project WWIII did include the hoary bass veteran Jimmy Bain, a man who had more than made his mark with WILD HORSES, RAINBOW and DIO.

Previous line-ups, centred upon Lion, included KINGDOM COME guitarist Danny Stag and bassist Johnny B. Frank and JOHNNY CRASH guitarist Chris Stewart. For the album former FINAL NOTICE man Tracy G was enrolled.

The rhythm section was completed by Vinnie Appice, a colleague of Bain's in DIO and also previously in BLACK SABBATH.

Following the album release WWIII toured harder than many expected on the club circuit and as support to IRON MAIDEN but ultimately found themselves with less than staggering record sales to show for their effort. Appice drifted away, turning up once more in BLACK SABBATH for their 'Dehumaniser' album, and the band struggled on with former KING DIAMOND drummer Mickey Dee.

WWIII floundered without a record deal and Dee forged a permanent relationship with MOTÖRHEAD. Lion created WICKED ALLIANCE with ex-OZZY OSBOURNE / BADLANDS guitarist JAKE E. LEE for a series of club gigs in 1994.

By 1997 both Tracy G and Appice were firmly ensconced in DIO although the pair did take time out to record as yet unreleased material with UFO's Phil Mogg and Pete Way.

1999 found Lion back with Lee for a forthcoming WICKED ALLIANCE album. Bain rejoined DIO the same year. WWIII would be resurrected in 2001 for live shows with Lion, Bain and Dee joined by WARRIOR guitarist Joe Floyd.

Albums:

WW III, Hollywood WWCD3 570004-2 (1990)
Time For Terror / Love You To Death / Over The Rainbow / Call Me Devil / Children Of The Revolution / Go Down / Love At First Bite / The Harder They Come / Atomic Sex Appeal / Drive You Crazy / The Cage

WYVERN (ITALY)
Line-Up: Fabio Bonaccorsi (vocals), Giorgio Comella (guitar), Sandro Belledi (guitar), Fausto Tinello (bass), Fabrizio Bernadi (drums)

Dating back to 1985 this Italian Speed Metal act would declare their intentions with the 'Wyvern' demo. This tape would be capitalised on with a further session 'Back To The Ancient Rage' and the album 'The Red Flame Of Pain'. In 1994 another promotional cassette 'Seasons Of Power' emerged.

The late '90s would witness a dispute over ownership of the name WYVERN with the Swedish act signed to Last Episode Records. The Italian WYVERN, replacing guitarist / keyboard player Simone Ferrari with erstwhile LISTERIA man Luciano Toscani in November of 2000, signed to the Underground Symphony label for a projected album 'Lords Of Winter'.

Albums:

THE RED FLAME OF PAIN, VLP 2710 (1990)
Fight For Your Life / Wyvern / Prophecy / Behind Bars / It's A Waste Of Time / …And The End / (Stop) Adolescent Sex

WYVERN (SWEDEN)
Line-Up: Toni Kocmut (vocals), Andreas Sjöström (guitar), Henrik Hedberg (guitar), Petter Broman (bass), Peter Nagy (drums)

For the second WYVERN album, 2001's 'No Defiance Of Fate', the band added new yet experienced members drummer Peter Nagy of MÖRK GRYNING, ETERNAL OATH and HYPOCRITE and lead vocalist Toni Kocmut from SINS OF OMISSION. Bassist Jonas Berndt decamped in early 2002, however, former member Petter Broman would soon be re-inducted into the fold.

Albums:

THE WILDFIRE, Bossy Ogress 007396-2 (1999)
Prelude / Metal Marauder / March Of Metal / At The End Of Time / Victory Or Death / Re-coronation / Glory In The Sky / Taste The Winter / Metallians Of Death / Iron In The Night / The Wildfire
NO DEFIANCE OF FATE, No Fashion (2001)
Horizon Of Glory / The Liquid And The Metal / Morningstar / Starborn / The Last Ordeal / Like Dogs Climbing Up The Moon / Defiance Of Fate / Northern Union / The Power Of Wyvern

XERXES (SWITZERLAND)
Line-Up: Adrian Moser (vocals / bass), Michael Cueni (guitar), Christian Moser (guitar), Jose Espasandin (keyboards), Martin Fringeli (drums)

Albums:
BEYOND MY IMAGINATION, General Inquisitor Torquemado's Witchunt GIT001 (1994)
Longing / The Thief From Darrenlow / Time For Revolution / Beyond My Imagination / To The Poets Of This World

X-RAY (GERMANY)
Line-Up: Tommy Ray (vocals), Modesto Vasquez (guitar), Tom Elba (guitar), Miguel Di Muzio (bass), Bernd Heining (drums)

German Power Metal band. X-RAY vocalist Tommy Ray quit to join CHINCHILLA in early 1998.

Albums:
DEHUMANIZED, Cream 007 (1996)
Let The Rain Begin / Congratulation / Wake Up / My Own War / Go Down / L.D. 50 / Sorrow And Pain / Born Into Darkness / Alive But Dead / Weltschmerz / Nailed To The Cross

X WILD (GERMANY)
Line-Up: Frank Knight (vocals), Axel Morgan (guitar), Jens Becker (bass), Stefan Schwarzmann (drums)

X WILD was formed by three ex-RUNNING WILD members together with former INSECTOCUTOR vocalist Frank Knight. Bassist Jens Becker had also had a stint with CROSSROADS. Whilst drummer Stefan Schwarzmann had enjoyed a stint with U.D.O. None too surprisingly the 1994 debut 'So What?' bears a marked resemblance to RUNNING WILD.
X WILD toured Germany as support to their sophomore outing 'Monster Effect' but following completion of the dates Schwarzmann departed to found Punk act DIE SUICIDE. The drummer was also to collaborate with ex-ACCEPT vocalist Udo Dirkschneider joining his U.D.O. band for a second time.
X WILD's last offering 'Savage Land', based upon a concept theme of Knight's, saw ex-GRAVE DIGGER drummer Frank Ulrich in the fold.
In 1997 Becker joined GRAVE DIGGER bringing with him the concept for their 'Knights Of The Cross' renaissance record.

Vocalist Frank Knight would by the turn of the millennium be fronting a rejuvenated NWoBHM legend BUFFALO.

Albums:
SO WHAT?, Edel 86032RAD (1994)
Can't Tame The Wild / Dealing With The Devil / Scarred To The Bone / Wild Frontier / Sky Bolter / Beastmaster / Kid Racer / Into The Light / Freeway Devil / Mystica Deamonica / Thousand Guns / Different (So What)
MONSTER EFFECT, Edel 86112RAD (1995)
Wild Knight / Souls Of Sin / Theatre Of Blood / Heads Held High / Dr Sardonicus / Sinners Are Winners / Monster Effects / Serpents Kiss / Sons Of Darkness / D.Y.T.W.A.C. / King Of Speed
SAVAGE LAND, Blue Merle 0086582 CTR (1996)
Savageland (Intro) / Braveheart / Savageland / Born For War / Murder In Thy Name / Children Of The Underground / Dragonslair / Die Like A Man / Field Of Blackbirds / Clash Of The Titans / Hunting The Damned / Chaos Ends

ZANDELLE

(Brooklyn, NY, USA)
Line-Up: George Tsalikis
(vocals / bass), T.W. Durfy
(guitar), Anthony Maglio
(guitar), Bob Delmini (drums)

A speed fuelled Power Metal act out of Brooklyn fronted by erstwhile GOTHIC KNIGHTS member George Tsalikis. ZANDELLE was created as a trio with Tsalikis on vocals and bass, guitarist Kirk Passomonti and drummer Amit Lahav during November of 1995. This unit recorded a self-financed album, issued in 1996. Healthy press reports soon found this record being picked up by the Sentinel Steel specialist label and as such, word of ZANDELLE's prowess spread rapidly. However, with Lahav embroiled in medical studies the band's drummer was forced to prioritise on his career and John Lasanta duly stepped in as ZANDELLE's new sticksman.

For ZANDELLE's second album 'Shadows Of Reality' the band would be joined by guitarist Anthony Maglio, a former member of SILENCE and GOD FORBID and the fifteen year old Joe Hartoularos. The initial introduction of Maglio, intended to be employed as part of a twin guitar team, forced Passomonti out of the picture and prompted the arrival of Hartoularos.

Drummer Bob Delmini, previously with LEGEND, was enrolled in 1999 as ZANDELLE began to receive offers of live dates nationwide. However, Hartoularos then bailed out putting the band in search of a lead guitarist yet again. T.W. Durfy, replying to a classified ad, would be recruited in August of 2000 in time for recording of the 'Twilight On Humanity' opus. Hartoularos would make a return for live action as stand in bassist.

Albums:
ZANDELLE, (1996)
Ecstasy / Medieval Ways / Nightmare / The Underdark / Evil Entity / Angel
SHADOWS OF REALITY, (1998)
Dusk / Darkness Of The Night / Flight Of The Dragon / The Warrior / Queen Witch / The Abyss / Bringer Of Doom / Soul Of Darkness / Crimson Rain / Megan's Song
TWILIGHT ON HUMANITY, Limb Music Productions LMP 0209-042 CD (2002)
Warlords Of Steel / The Champion / A Hero's Quest / Lord Of Thunder / Immortal Realms / Delusions / Eternal Love / Sunrise / The Cycle / Twilight On Humanity

ZANISTER (USA)

Line-Up: Brian Sarvela (vocals), David T. Chastain (guitar), Michael Harris (guitar), James Martin (bass), Brian Harris (drums)

ZANISTER is another in the long line of projects from the ever prolific guitarist DAVID T. CHASTAIN, best known for his acts CJSS and CHASTAIN. ZANISTER also include ARCH RIVAL's Michael Harris. ZANISTER, also comprising erstwhile REIGN OF TERROR singer Brian Sarvela, bassist James Martin and with drums supplied by Michael Harris' brother and MY OWN VICTIM member Brian Harris, debuted with 'Symphonica Mellennia' during 1999.

The 2000 record 'Fear No Man' includes drums from VICIOUS RUMOURS man Atma Anur. 'Fear No Man', released domestically Chastain's own Leviathan label saw a European issue through the German Shark concern.

Albums:
SYMPHONICA MELLENNIA, Shark 99902 (1999)
Fighters In The Sky / We Will Bring Glory Tonight / Save Me Now / Searching For Freedom / The Edge Of Sanity / Let Them Live / Born In Cold Blood / Downfall / Children Of The Gods / The Evil Will Survive
FEAR NO MAN, Leviathan 2011-2 (2000)
The Shades They Color Three / You Live For Greed / Generation Breakdown / The Fallen / Lost Control / Words Of Fate / Hell On Earth / Fear No Man / Grip Of The Groove / Got To Live My Life / Egyptian Nights

ZED YAGO (GERMANY)

Line-Up: Jutta Weinhold (vocals), Gunnar (guitar), Jimmy (guitar), Tatch (bass), Bubi (drums)

Conceptual outfit conceived in 1986 and based around the fictional daughter of the flying Dutchman named 'Zed Yago'. The band is characterised by ex-BRESLAU vocalist Jutta's distinctive operatic vocal style and musical leanings toward the Wagnerian epic. Toured Germany as support to DEEP PURPLE in 1988.

JUTTA WEINHOLD went solo. Drummer Bubi forged VELVET VIPER with Weinhold, guitarist Dave Moore (later of SKYCLAD), and ex-WARLOCK guitarist Peter Szigeti. ZENO's Jochen Roth guested on guitar. A later VELVET VIPER line-up retained Weinhold and Bubi but added ROY LAST GROUP guitarist Roy Last and a pre METALIUM Lars Ratz on bass.

The drummer also issued an album under the title BUBI THE SCHMEID.

Singles/EPs:

Black Bone Song / Zed Yago / Rockin' For The Nation, RCA PB 49389 (1989)
Pilgrim's Choir, RCA (1989)

Albums:
FROM OVER YONDER, Steamhammer SPV 08-7517 (1988)
The Spell From Over Yonder / The Flying Dutchman / Zed Yago / Queen And Priest / Revenge / United Pirate Kingdom / Stay The Course / Rebel Ladies / Rockin' For The Nation
PILGRIMAGE, RCA PL71949 (1989)
Pilgrim Choir / Pilgrimage / The Fear Of Death / Pioneer Of The Storm / Black Bone Song / Rose Of Martyrdom / The Man Who Stole The Holy Fire / Achilles Heel / The Pale Man / Omega Child / Fallen Angel

ZNOWHITE (Chicago, IL, USA)

Line-Up: Nicole Lee (vocals), Ian Tafoya (guitar), Scott Schafer (bass), Sparks Tafoya (drums)

For a relatively short period Chicago Metal band ZNOWHITE used the traditional method of spelling their moniker and performed as SNOWHITE, the irony being at the time that, apart from frontwoman Nicole Lee, the group consisted of black musicians.

ZNOWHITE was seen as a vehicle for the undoubted talents of guitarist Ian Tafoya. Nicole Lee had originally been engaged as the band's manager but was persuaded to front the group by Tafoya. They were joined in the ranks by his brother Sparks (drums) and cousin Nicky Tafoya (bass) all of whom had played together in a number of previous groups. After the recording of early demos Nicky departed to be briefly replaced by the mysteriously titled Amp Dawg.

After rave reviews, particularly in Europe, ZNOWHITE would sign to the (what appeared to be) German affiliated EMA label after a debut vinyl appearance on the 'Metal Massacre III' compilation with the track 'Hellbent'.

In truth, EMA Polydisc was ZNOWHITE's own label. Having self-financed the recording of an album under the belief that Megaforce would be signing the group, the band decided to release product themselves after the deal fell through. Obtaining manufacturing and distribution channels through Enigma in America, a three track, red vinyl flexi-disc was made available to fans through specialist record stores or via the band (the EP contained three tracks from ZNOWHITE's demo tape). ZNOWHITE's debut album, 'All Hail To Thee' was released in 1984 and boasted an unknown guest guitarist on the

opening 'Sledgehammer'.

A second album, 'Kick 'Em When They're Down', was released a year later followed by 1986's 'Live Suicide' album. This record was taken from a show in Cleveland, Ohio during December the previous year. By this time the band had been augmented on tour by bassist Scott Schafer.

1988's 'Act Of God' would be the Chicago group's one and only album with Roadrunner Records. At this point Schafer had replaced Sparks Tafoya on the drums and Alex Olivera took over on bass, as Ian Tafoya became the sole black musicians in the ranks.

Unfortunately, Nicole Lee split the ranks after 'Act Of God' hit the stores. ZNOWHITE, having hired new drummer, ex-TOOLS OF IGNORANCE man John Slattery for the tour after Olivera quit (and was briefly succeeded by Scott Schafer) replaced her with erstwhile SENTINAL BEAST vocalist Debbie Gunn.

A proposed ZNOWHITE album with Gunn, 'Land Of The Greed, Home Of The Depraved', was never recorded as the singer was out of the band by April 1989. Gunn later moved to Britain in the early '90s to join the Swedish all-girl outfit ICE AGE. She was replaced by Brian Troch as Ian Tafoya chose to work with a male vocalist for the first time.

The 'All Hail To Thee' album eventually made it to CD in 1998 in remastered form on Axe Killer. The 'Kick 'Em When They're Down' opus featured as bonus tracks.

Troch, Schafer and Slattery founded CYCLONE TEMPLE with guitarist Greg Fulton for the 1991 album 'I Hate Therefore I Am'.

Singles/EPs:
Live For The Weekend / Never Felt Like This / Vengeance, EMA Germany 1007ZW (1983) (Red vinyl flexi-disc)

Albums:
ALL HAIL TO THEE, EMA Polydisc / Enigma E-1077 (1984)
Sledgehammer / Saturday Night / Somethin' For Nothin' / Bringin' The Hammer Down / Do Or Die / Never Felt Like This / Rock City Destination
KICK 'EM WHEN THEY'RE DOWN, EMA Polydisc / Enigma 72024-1 (1985)
Live For The Weekend / All Hail To Thee / Run Like The Wind / Too Late / Turn Up The Pain
LIVE SUICIDE, EMA Polydisc / Erika ZER606 (1986)
Hell Bent / Bringin' The Hammer Down / There's No Tomorrow / Too Late / Rock City Destination / Night On Parole / Rest In Peace

ACT OF GOD, Roadrunner RR9587-1 (1988)
To The Last Breath / Baptised By Fire / Pure
Blood / War Machine / Thunderdome / Rest
In Peace / Disease Bigotry / A Soldier's
Creed / Something Wicked (This Way
Comes)

ZONATA (SWEDEN)

Line-Up: Johannes Nyberg (vocals /
keyboards), John Nyberg (guitar), Niclas
Karlsson (guitar), Mattias Asplund (bass),
Mikael Hörnqvist (drums)

A Boras based Power Metal band forged in
early 1998. ZONATA's demo recording 'The
Copenhagen Tapes' would swiftly land the
group a deal with Germany's Century Media
Records. The debut record 'Tunes Of Steel'
would be produced by HOLY MOSES guitarist
Andy Classen.
During September of 2000 ZONATA would
lose guitarist Henrik Carlsson. Opting to
persevere as a quartet the band cut their
second album 'Reality' with producer Sascha
Paethe. Touring to promote the release would
see support gigs to NOCTURNAL RITES.
By September of 2001 ZONATA were brought
back up to full strength with the addition of
erstwhile CRYSTAL EYES and FIERCE
CONVICTION guitarist Niclas Karlsson.
A new studio album 'Buried Alive' would be in
the pipeline for 2002 release.

Albums:
TUNES OF STEEL, JVC Victor VICP-60952
(2000)
Dream Child / Geronimo / Thor - The
Thundergod / Beyond The Rainbow /
Criticised / Welcome To This World Of Fun /
The Evil Shadow / Bring You Down To Hell /
Zonata / Viking
REALITY, Century Media (2001)
Reality / Divided We Stand / Illusion Of
Madness / Hollow Rain / Symphony Of The
Night / Forever / Wheel Of Life / Dimension
To Freedom / Evil Mind / Life? / Intro - Gate
Of Fear

Also available from

CHERRY RED BOOKS

ISBN 1-901447-30-8

Rockdetector
A-Z of BLACK METAL
Garry Sharpe-Young

Throughout the history of Rock no other genre has pushed the boundaries of aural extremity and social rebellion quite like Black Metal. Many of the bands in this book operate way beyond the parameters of the established Rock scene carving their own left hand path in the darkest depths of true underground music.

Over a decade Black Metal has spawned legions of bands making up a truly global rebellion. For the first time ever this ultimate authority documents detailed biographies, line-ups and full discographies with track listings of over 1,000 groups.

Included are in-depth treatises on the major artists such as CRADLE OF FILTH, DIMMU BORGIR, EMPEROR, MAYHEM, IMMORTAL and MARDUK as well as spanning out to include sub-genres such as Viking Metal, the Black Ambient scene and even the ultimate irony of Christian Black Metal. Also chronicled are the originators such as VENOM, WITCHFYNDE, BATHORY and MERCYFUL FATE.

Paper covers, 416 pages, £14.99 in UK

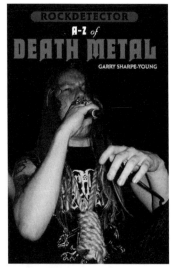

ISBN 1-901447-35-9

Rockdetector
A-Z of DEATH METAL
Garry Sharpe-Young

Reviled and revered in equal measure since its inception over a decade ago the phenomenon known as Death Metal has pushed Hard Rock music to the very edge of acceptability and way beyond. Born out of the Thrash Metal eruption, Death Metal took vocals to the realms of the unintelligibly insane, drove the blastbeats harder and pushed guitar riffs into a swarming blur. The familiar mythical subject matter of its parent Heavy Metal, and its bastard offspring Grindcore, has become the pariah of the music world as much as the depths of the underground scene has fostered and nurtured its steady growth to this day with each band striving to achieve renewed goals of sickness.

From the founding fathers such as NAPALM DEATH, CARCASS, DEATH, INCANTATION, IMPETIGO and MORBID ANGEL to the rise of Swedish Death Metal legends IN FLAMES, CARNAGE and AT THE GATES, the Death Metal of MARDUK, the Christian Death Metal of MORTIFICATION and the politically charged Noisecore of AGATHOCLES. All genres old and new are analyzed in depth with full career histories and detailed discographies.

No area of the globe has provided a safe haven and this book documents the burgeoning uprise of Death Metal bands in the Far East, Eastern Europe and South America.

Be warned - even though some of the band names are not for the faint-hearted the song titles will leave you reeling.

Paper covers, 416 pages, £14.99 in UK

www.cherryred.co.uk

Also available from

CHERRY RED BOOKS

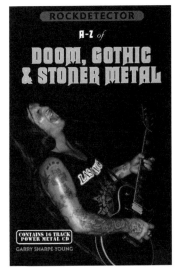

ISBN 1-901447-14-6

Rockdetector
A-Z of DOOM, GOTHIC & STONER METAL Garry Sharpe-Young

Laboured, mournful and crushingly heavy. The anaesthetising, sloth like riffs of Doom Metal, the bong fuelled lazy retro Rock that is Stoner and the melancholy strains of Gothic Metal- it's all here. Rooted in ancient instigators such as PENTAGRAM, ATOMIC ROOSTER and the mightiest of the mighty- BLACK SABBATH, Doom has defied all the odds to spawn a huge global fanbase.

The impact of Doom can be felt not only in the respect afforded to faithful cult acts such as THE OBSESSED and TROUBLE but in burgeoning enormity of both the BLACK SABBATH legend and sheer scale of album sales. The rude health of those that have been handed on the flame, the new breed such as MY DYING BRIDE, CATHEDRAL, PARADISE LOST, NOVEMBER'S DOOM and CANDLEMASS, has morphed the genre into one of their own making.

In recent years Doom has taken a left turn into the desert wastelands of America and returned as Stoner. Bands like KYUSS, FU MANCHU, ALABAMA THUNDERPUSSY, IRONBOSS and hundreds of others pulling in legions of fans. The Europeans meantime added Electronica into the blend to create Darkwave and hordes of Metal bands discovered that adding a female vocalist, a Gothic touch and the introduction of avant garde instrumentation lent a whole new lease of life. Numerous artists placed firmly in genres such as Death Metal and Black Metal readily experiment with Doom and Gothic whilst groundbreaking artists such as RAIN FELL WITHIN and AUTUMN'S TEARS lend the whole scene ongoing re-invigoration.

Each and every band is included with an enormous wealth of historical detail and full global discography. From the full, weighty and unedited account of BLACK SABBATH'S tortured history and spanning Stoner, Gothic and Darkwave this book is the first to chronicle the underground world wide phenomena that is Doom.

Paper covers, 455 pages £14.99 in UK

ISBN 1–901447–09–X

Rockdetector
A-Z of THRASH METAL
Garry Sharpe-Young

THRASH METAL. At first mocked by the Rock traditionalists Thrash would swamp the hard 'n' heavy world propelling one of it's own - METALLICA, to the very pinnacle of Rock's elite.

In the early 80s Thrash breathed new life into the Rock scene providing older acts with a much needed kick. This new force opened the floodgates to armies of teens armed with flying Vs, bullet belts and a sense of purpose that would fuel genres such as THRASHCORE, CROSSOVER and TECHNICAL SPEED METAL. Without Thrash there would be no DEATH METAL, no BLACK METAL. That explosion of aggression has seen subsequent afterblasts, most recently in Europe and South America where there has been a genuine renaissance of Thrash Metal.

Without doubt Thrash Metal continues to make its mark in the biggest possible way. The 'big four' METALLICA, MEGADETH, ANTHRAX and SLAYER are all documented here in the greatest possible detail with full, up to the minute histories, exclusive photographs and global discographies. No stone is left unturned in pursuit of knowledge of ex-members, rare recordings and career milestones. The author has interviewed all these major acts. Indeed, he was the last journalist to interview Metallica's late Cliff Burton. The early days of Megadeth are straight from the mouth of Dave Mustaine.

Also covered are the legion of groundbreaking Bay Area acts such as METAL CHURCH, TESTAMENT, EXODUS, DEATH ANGEL and HIRAX. The European Thrash explosion of KREATOR, RAGE, DESTRUCTION, SODOM, GRAVE DIGGER and HELLOWEEN is also covered in frightening detail. The PAGAN THRASH of SABBAT, the avant garde eccentricity of CELTIC FROST and the FUNK THRASH of MORDED - it's all here. The second wave of Thrash with major artists such as SEPULTURA, PANTERA and MACHINE HEAD takes the genre right up to the new breed of Thrashers, now a truly world-wide phenomenon. All examined in depth.

Thrash Metal is not only alive, it is thriving. If you thought this rawest form of Heavy Metal was consigned to the past, this book will deliver a rude awakening! Read the book, buy the records and bang that head!!

Paper covers, 460 pages £14.99 in UK

www.cherryred.co.uk

Also available from

CHERRY RED BOOKS

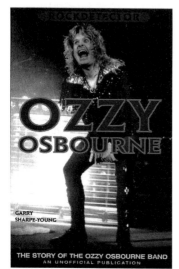

ISBN 1-901447-08-1
Paper covers 368 pages £14.99 in UK

Rockdetector
OZZY OSBOURNE
THE STORY OF THE OZZY OSBOURNE BAND
(AN UNOFFICIAL PUBLICATION)
Garry Sharpe-Young

Until 1978 THE original and definitive Heavy Metal band BLACK SABBATH was fronted by the irrepressible Ozzy Osbourne. With Osbourne at the helm BLACK SABBATH sold tens of millions of albums. When he finally broke away to fly solo Ozzy would achieve the unthinkable. Not only would he deliver one of the seminal Rock records ever crafted to mark his resurrection but he also used it as a career-making catalyst that would see him trounce his former band mates and evolve into a cult icon.

Along the way Ozzy displayed an enviable knack of choosing a series of groundbreaking guitarists such as Randy Rhoads, Jake E. Lee and Zakk Wylde. There would also be the unsung heroes such as songwriter extraordinaire Bob Daisley and a series of world renowned bassists, drummers and keyboard players.

This then is the story of the Ozzy Osbourne band - in their own words and detailed exclusively here for the first time.

Chronicled with first-hand interviews, this is the real story of the first prototype Blizzard of Ozz band, how Ozzy met Randy Rhoads, the painful saga of Rhoads' replacement Bernie Tormé and the torturous audition processes for successive guitarists and drummers told by both successful and unsuccessful candidates.

The Ozzy Osbourne story - as told by Bob Daisley, Lee Kerslake, Tommy Aldridge, Bernie Tormé, Brad Gillis, Steve Vai, Phil Soussan, Carmine Appice and many, many more.

Garry Sharpe-Young has interviewed more than twenty Ozzy band members and associates solely for this work thus making it the most detailed account of Ozzy's career so far.

"Ozzy Osbourne's solo career would prove spectacular, bizarre and extremely lucrative..." ROUGH GUIDE TO ROCK

Rockdetector
BLACK SABBATH
Garry Sharpe-Young
FORTHCOMING EARLY 2003
ISBN 1-901447-16-2

Over a full decade Black Sabbath had dominated Heavy Metal. As much as Led Zeppelin scorned the term, Black Sabbath embraced it. In an age of bona fide super-groups Sabbath were unquestionably the heaviest thing stalking the planet and quite remarkably had remained a solid unit where others around them suffered ongoing membership fall-outs and line-up re-incarnations. Tony Iommi, Geezer Butler, Ozzy Osbourne and Bill Ward had weathered internal storms just as ferocious as every other band out on the circuit but had remained resolute. They had conquered the globe, sold close to 50 million albums and without concession had not pulled back one iota from delivering absolute, pure Heavy Metal.

In 1977 the unthinkable happened. Ozzy Osbourne decamped. He would be lured back for one last album "Never Say Die", before flying solo, rapidly building a band unit that would equal the repute of the mothership. The Iommi / Butler / Ward triumvirate at first bounced back in quite spectacular fashion by re-inventing themselves courtesy of their new frontman, the highly gifted Ronnie James Dio. Two classic albums followed but then the picture shattered. For the next two decades Black Sabbath faltered on a rocky path between all too brief moments of genius and fallow desperation. Only Tony Iommi stuck to his guns, the lynchpin amidst a tangled web of chaos. A succession of vocalists took up the challenge- Ian Gillan, Jeff Fenholt, David Donato, Glenn Hughes, Ray Gillen, Tony Martin and Ronnie James Dio once again. Harried by the press at every turn, Tony Iommi nevertheless succeeded in breathing new life into Black Sabbath time and time again. With the band's back catalogue still in heavy demand, those albums crafted in these times of adversity are now recognised as some of Sabbath's finest moments and the huge array of players that travelled through the ranks is now a constant source of fascination and rumours for Sabbath fanatics. Here, for the very first time with exclusive interviews conducted for this book including ones with the late Ray Gillen and Cozy Powell as well as the highly controversial figure of Jeff Fenholt and mysterious Dave Donato, is the definitive account of those years. The auditioning, song writing and recording processes of albums such as "Born Again", "Eternal Idol" and "Seventh Star" are examined in depth making this the definitive account. Author Garry Sharpe-Young is editor in chief at www.rockdetector.com the world's biggest Rock devoted database.

Also available from **CHERRY RED BOOKS**

**Indie Hits
1980-1989**
The Complete UK
Independent Charts
(Singles & Albums)

**Compiled by
Barry Lazell**

Paper covers, 314 pages,
£14.99 in UK

**Songs In The
Key Of Z**
The Curious
Universe of
Outsider Music

Irwin Chusid

Paper covers, 311 pages,
fully illustrated,
£11.99 in UK

**Cor Baby, That's
Really Me!**
(New Millennium
Hardback Edition)

John Otway

Hardback, 192 pages and
16 pages of photographs,
£11.99 in UK

**The Legendary
Joe Meek**
The Telstar Man

John Repsch

Paper covers, 350 pages
plus photographs £14.99
in UK

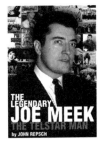

All the Young Dudes
Mott the Hoople and
Ian Hunter
The Biography

Campbell Devine

Paper covers, 448 pages
and 16 pages of photo-
graphs, £14.99 in UK

Random Precision
Recording The Music
Of Syd Barrett
1965 – 1974

David Parker

Paper covers, 320 pages,
photographs through-
out, £14.99n UK

Embryo
A Pink Floyd
Chronology
1966 – 1971

**Nick Hodges & Ian
Priston**

Paper covers, 302 pages
and photographs
throughout, £14.99 in UK

Those Were The Days
An Unofficial History
Of The Beatles Apple
Organization
1967-2002

Stefan Granados

Paper covers, 300 pages,
including photographs,
£14.99 in UK

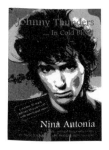

Johnny Thunders
In Cold Blood

Nina Antonia

Paper covers, 270 pages
and photographs
throughout,
£14.99 in UK

The Rolling Stones
Complete Recording
Sessions 1962-2002

Martin Elliott

Paper covers, 576 pages,
plus 16 pages
of photographs,
£14.99 in UK

www.cherryred.co.uk

CHERRY RED BOOKS

We are always looking for interesting books to publish.
They can be either new manuscripts or re-issues of deleted books.
If you have any good ideas then please
get in touch with us.

CHERRY RED BOOKS
a division of Cherry Red Records Ltd.
Unit 17, Elysium Gate West,
126-128 New King's Road
London SW6 4LZ

E-mail: iain@cherryred.co.uk
Web: www.cherryred.co.uk

ROCKDETECTOR: A TO Z OF POWER METAL – FREE CD

1. MARSHALL LAW - Leviathan (Live) (Pyke / Martin)
© 1996 Marshall Law / SGO Music.
From the album POWER GAME OR LAW IN THE RAW

2. METALIUM - Revenge Of Tizona (Metalium)
© 2002 Armageddon Products / Tornado International,
Warner Chappell.
From the album HERO NATION - CHAPTER THREE

3. NOCTURNAL RITES - Shadowland (Nocturnal Rites)
© 2002 Century Media Records / Magic Arts Publishing.
From the album SHADOWLAND

4. LIEGE LORD - Broken Wasteland (Comeau/Nelson) BMI
© 1989 Metal Blade Records www.liegelord.com
www.paulnelsonguitar.com
From the album MASTER CONTROL

5. PEGAZUS - The Headless Horseman (Johnny Stoj)
© 2002 Nuclear Blast Records / Prophecies Publishing
From the album THE HEADLESS HORSEMAN

6. SEVENTH ONE - Eternal Life Lies In (Seventh One)
© 2002 Armageddon Products / Tornado International,
Warner Chappell. From the album SACRIFICE

7. TWISTED TOWER DIRE - Dagger's Blade
(Scott Waldrop/Tony Taylor)
© 2002 Twisted Tower Dire.
From the The Miskatonic Foundation album THE ISLE OF HYDRA
Twisted Tower Dire appears courtesy of Remedy Records

8. NEVERMORE - Inside Four Walls (Loomis / Dane)
© 2002 Edgy Records Ltd. From the Edgy Records album
ABSOLUTE POWER

9. BLITZKREIG - Legion (Paul Nesbitt/Brian Ross)
© 2002 Edgy Records Ltd. From the Edgy Records album
ABSOLUTE POWER

10. CRYONIC TEMPLE - Rivers Of Pain
(Cryonic Temple / L. Ahonen / Johansson)
© 2002 Underground Symphony. From the album CHAPTER 1

11. CAGE - Final Solution (Garcia/Peck)
© 2001 Cage / Molten Metal USA. From the album ASTROLOGY

12. VYNDYKATOR - Tapping The Vain
(Vyndykator / Steve Ratchen / Bob Mitchell)
© 2002 Vyndykators / Vyntunes.
From the album HEAVEN SENT FROM HELL

13. ZANDELLE - Immortal Realms (Zandelle)
© 2002 Limp Music Products.
From the album TWILIGHT ON HUMANITY

14. JAG PANZER - The Scarlet Letter (Briody / Conklin)
© 2001 Century Media Records / Magic Arts Publishing.
From the album MECHANIZED WARFARE

15. SHADOWKEEP - Fear And Loathing (Shadowkeep)
© 2002 Limb Music Products. From the album A CHAOS THEORY

16. ICED EARTH - Jack (Iced Earth)
© 2000 Century Media Records / Magic Arts Publishing.
From the album HORROR SHOW